PRENTICE HALL
LITERATURE

False Start by painter, sculptor, and printmaker Jasper Johns (b. 1930) is a playful example of "art-as-object"— a combination of painting and sculpture that emerged during the 1950s. With random labels stenciled over thick patches of paint and painted objects, this artwork demonstrates a break from the usual abstract style of the 1940s and the 1950s. Johns's style has been called "art of assemblage" for its use of ordinary and familiar objects and its blend of three-dimensional objects.

PENGUIN **EDITION**

PEARSON

Prentice
Hall

Upper Saddle River, New Jersey

Boston, Massachusetts

ISBN 0-13-131716-4

10 V063 11

Cover: *False Start, 1959*, oil on canvas, Jasper Johns, (b.1930) / Private Collection, Lauros / Giraudon / www.bridgeman.co.uk. Cover art © Jasper Johns / Licensed by VAGA, New York, NY

ACKNOWLEDGMENTS

Grateful acknowledgment is made to the following for copyrighted material:

Arte Público Press "Baseball" by Lionel García is reproduced with the permission from the publisher of *I Can Hear the Cowbells Ring* (Houston: Arte Público Press - University of Houston, 1994). Reprinted by permission of Arte Público Press.

Brent Ashabranner "Always to Remember: The Vision of Maya Ying Lin" by Brent Ashabranner from *Always to Remember*. Reprinted by permission of the author.

The Bancroft Library "Tears of Autumn" from *The Forbidden Stitch* by Yoshiko Uchida. Copyright © 1989 by Yoshiko Uchida. Courtesy of the Bancroft Library, University of California, Berkeley. Reprinted by permission of The Bancroft Library.

Black Issues Book Review "Zora Neale Hurston: A Life in Letters, Book Review" by Zakia Carter from *Black Issues Book Review*, Nov-Dec 2002; www.bibookreview.com. Reprinted by permission of Black Issues Book Review.

Brandt & Hochman Literary Agents, Inc. "Western Wagons" by Rosemary Carr Benét from *A Book of Americans* by Rosemary and Stephen Vincent Benét. Henry Holt & Company. Copyright © 1933 by Rosemary and Stephen Vincent Benét. Copyright renewed © 1961 Rosemary Carr Benét. Reprinted by permission of Brandt and Hochman Literary Agents, Inc.

CBS News Archives. "Stephen King: His books, His Life, His Wife" from *60 Minutes Interview With Lesley Stahl* (August 2, 1998). Copyright © 1998 CBS News. Reprinted by permission of CBS News Archives.

Curtis Brown, Ltd. From My Own True Name by Pat Mora. Copyright © 2000 by Pat Mora. Published by Arte Público Press. Reprinted by permission of Curtis Brown, Ltd.

Curtis Brown London "Who Can Replace a Man?" by Brian W. Aldiss from *Masterpieces: The Best Science Fiction Of The Century*. Copyright © 2001 by Orson Scott Card and Tekno Books. All rights reserved. Reprinted by permission of Curtis Brown London.

Charlotte Observer "The Season's Curmudgeon Sees the Light" by Mary C. Curtis from www.charlotte.com. Copyright © 2004 Knight Ridder. All Rights Reserved. Reprinted by permission of Mary C. Curtis.

Child Heath Association of Sewickley Recipe for Thumbprint Cookies (p. 185) from *Three Rivers Cookbook*. Copyright © 1973 Child Health Association of Sewickley, Inc. Sewickley, PA.

The Christian Science Monitor "Lots in space: Orbiting junk, from old satellites to space gloves, has scientists worried for spacecraft & engineers working on ways to clean it up" by Peter N. Spotts

Acknowledgements continued on page R60, which constitutes an extension of this copyright page.

CONTRIBUTING AUTHORS

The contributing authors guided the direction and philosophy of *Prentice Hall Literature: Penguin Edition.* Working with the development team, they helped to build the pedagogical integrity of the program and to ensure its relevance for today's teachers and students.

Kevin Feldman

Kevin Feldman, Ed.D. is the Director of Reading and Intervention for the Sonoma County Office of Education and an independent educational consultant. He publishes and provides consultancy and training nationally, focusing upon improving school-wide literacy skills as well as targeted interventions for struggling readers, special needs students and second language learners. Dr. Feldman is the co-author of the California Special Education Reading Task Force report and the lead program author for the 2002 Prentice Hall secondary language arts program *Timeless Voices: Timeless Themes.* He serves as technical consultant to the California Reading and Literature Project and the CalSTAT State Special Education Improvement Project. Dr. Feldman has taught for nineteen years at the university level in Special Education and Master's level programs for University of California, Riverside and Sonoma State University.

Dr. Feldman earned his undergraduate degree in Psychology from Washington State University and has a Master's Degree from UC Riverside in Special Education, Learning Disabilities and Instructional Design. He has an Ed.D. from the University of San Francisco in Curriculum and Instruction.

Kate Kinsella

Kate Kinsella, Ed.D. is a teacher educator in the Department of Secondary Education at San Francisco State University. She teaches coursework addressing academic language and literacy development in linguistically and culturally diverse classrooms. She maintains secondary classroom involvement by teaching an academic literacy class for adolescent English learners through the University's Step to College Program. She publishes and provides consultancy and training nationally, focusing upon responsible instructional practices that provide second language learners and less proficient readers in grades 4-12 with the language and literacy skills vital to educational mobility.

Dr. Kinsella is the program author for *Reading in the Content Areas: Strategies for Reading Success,* published by Pearson Learning and the lead program author for the 2002 Prentice Hall secondary language arts program *Timeless Voices: Timeless Themes.* She is the co-editor of the CATESOL Journal (CA Assn. of Teachers of ESL) and serves on the editorial board for the *California Reader.* A former Fulbright scholar, Dr. Kinsella has received numerous awards, including the prestigious Marcus Foster Memorial Reading Award, offered by the California Reading Association in 2002 to a California educator who has made a significant statewide impact on both policy and pedagogy in the area of literacy.

Sharon Vaughn

Sharon Vaughn, Ph.D., is the H.E. Hartfelder/The Southland Corporation Regents Professor at the University of Texas and also director of the Vaughn Gross Center for Reading and Language Arts at the University of Texas (VGCRLA). As director of the VGCRLA, she leads more than five major initiatives, including The Central Regional Reading First Technical Assistance Center; the Three-Tier Reading Research Project; a bilingual-biliteracy (English/Spanish) intervention research study; the first through fourth grade Teacher Reading Academies that have been used for teacher education throughout Texas and the nation; and the creation of online professional development in reading for teachers and other interested professionals.

Dr. Vaughn has published more than ten books and over one hundred research articles. She is Editor in Chief of the *Journal of Learning Disabilities* and serves on the editorial board of more than ten research journals, including the *Journal of Educational Psychology,* the *American Educational Research Journal,* and the *Journal of Special Education.*

Differentiated Instruction Advisor
Don Deshler

Don Deshler, Ph.D, is the Director of the Center for Research on Learning (CRL) at the University of Kansas. Dr. Deshler's expertise centers on adolescent literacy, learning strategic instruction, and instructional strategies for teaching content area classes to academically diverse classes. He is the author of Teaching Content to *All: Evidence-Based Inclusive Practices in Middle and Secondary Schools,* a text which presents the instructional practices that have been tested and validated through his research at CRL.

UNIT AUTHORS

An award-winning contemporary author hosts each unit in each level of Prentice Hall Literature. *Serving as a guide for your students, these authors introduce literary concepts, answer questions about their work, and discuss their own writing processes, using their works as models. Following are the featured unit authors for Grade 8.*

Patricia C. **McKissack (b. 1944)**

Unit 1: Fiction and Nonfiction Patricia McKissack is a master of both fiction and nonfiction. She has collaborated with her husband, Fredrick McKissack, on many nonfiction books that illuminate African American history. Their book *Christmas in the Big House, Christmas in the Quarters* won the Coretta Scott King Award. Ms. McKissack has also written prize-winning works of fiction, such as *The Dark-Thirty: Southern Tales of the Supernatural.*

Judith **Ortiz Cofer (b. 1952)**

Unit 2: Short Stories Judith Ortiz Cofer is the ideal role model for the short-story unit. Her volume of short stories *An Island Like You* received the 1995 Reforma Pura Belpré Medal and the American Library Association's annual citation as one of the best books for young adults. In addition, her novel *The Line of the Sun* was nominated for a Pulitzer Prize. Cofer's varied works bridge the cultures of Puerto Rico and the U.S. mainland.

Andrew **Mishkin (b. 1958)**

Unit 3: Types of Nonfiction Andrew Mishkin is well suited to explain various types of nonfiction. A senior engineer at California's famous Jet Propulsion Laboratory, he has written *Sojourner*, a popular account of the 1997 Mars mission; maintained a Web log describing the 2004 Mars mission; and written technical papers for scientists. He is also the designer of the system used to operate the *Spirit* and *Opportunity* rovers on Mars.

Jacqueline **Woodson (b. 1963)**

Unit 4: Poetry Though known as a fiction writer for young adults with many awards to her credit, Jacqueline Woodson is the ideal guide for this unit on poetry. Recently, she staked out new ground by writing *Locomotion*, a book that tells a story through verse. The success of *Locomotion*, which was a National Book Award Finalist, indicates that her poetry is just as compelling as her prose.

Cherie **Bennett (b. 1960)**

Unit 5: Drama Cherie Bennett is well qualified as a guide to drama. A popular playwright, novelist, and columnist read by teens around the world, Cherie Bennett says that drama is her greatest love. With her husband, Jeff Gottesfeld, she has created many plays for both the stage and television. These plays include *Anne Frank & Me*, praised as "eloquent and poignant" by *The New York Times*, and episodes of the Warner Brothers television series *Smallville*.

Lan Samantha **Chang (b. 1965)**

Unit 6: Themes in American Stories Writer Lan Samantha Chang has a special interest in the oral tradition. She believes that her immigrant background inspired her to read and write fiction that incorporates the spoken voice. The author of *Hunger: A Novella and Stories* and the novel *Inheritance*, Chang won the California Book Awards Silver Medal and was nominated for the PEN/Hemingway Literature Prize.

PROGRAM ADVISORS

The program advisors provided ongoing input throughout the development of *Prentice Hall Literature: Penguin Edition.* Their valuable insights ensure that the perspectives of the teachers throughout the country are represented within this literature series.

Sherice Alford
Language Arts Instructor
Cape Fear Senior High School
Fayetteville, North Carolina

Leslie Ballard
State Director
North Central Association CASI
Indiana State University
Terre Haute, Indiana

Heather Barnes
Language Arts Instructor
Central Crossing High School
Grove City, Ohio

Kathryn Shelley-Barnes
District Support Specialist
Traverse City Central High School
Traverse City, Michigan

Karen C. Lilly-Bowyer
Instructional Services Assessment Team
Winston-Salem Forsyth County Schools
Winston-Salem, North Carolina

Lee Bromberger
English Department Chairperson
Mukwonago High School
Mukwonago, Wisconsin

Shawn L. Brumfield
Literacy Coach
Horace Mann Middle School
Los Angeles Unified School District
Local 3
Los Angeles, California

Susanne Buttrey
Librarian
Sycamore Middle School
Pleasant View, Tennessee

Denise Campbell
K-12 Literacy Content Coordinator
Cherry Creek School District
Centennial, Colorado

Patricia A. Cantrowitz
Language Arts Instructor (Retired)
Union-Endicott High School
Endicott, New York

Holly Carr
Language Arts Instructor
Central Crossing High School
Grove City, Ohio

Melody Renee Chalmers
Language Arts Instructor
E. E. Smith High School
Fayetteville, North Carolina

Susan Cisna
Language Arts Instructor
East Prairie Junior High School
Tuscola, Illinois

Barbra Evans-Thompson
English Department Chairperson
Westover High School
Fayetteville, North Carolina

Ebony Forte
Language Arts Instructor
Pine Forest Senior High School
Fayetteville, North Carolina

Linda Fund
Reading Specialist
Ezra L. Nolan Middle School #40
Jersey City, New Jersey

Karen Gibson, Ph.D.
Communication Arts Program Leader
Appleton Area School District
Appleton, Wisconsin

Gail Hacker
Language Arts Instructor, Retired
North Charleston High School
North Charleston, South Carolina

Kimberly Hartman
Language Arts Instructor
Franklin Heights High School
Columbus, Ohio

Doris Sue Hawkins
Language Arts Instructor
C. W. Otto Middle School
Lansing, Michigan

Darby Holley
Language Arts Instructor
Henry L. Sneed Middle School
Florence, South Carolina

Helen Hudson
Language Arts Instructor
Crawfordsville High School
Crawfordsville, Indiana

Kathleen Keane
English Department Chairperson
Foxborough High School
Foxborough, Massachusetts

John Kiser
English Curriculum Specialist (Retired)
Charlotte-Mecklenburg Schools
Charlotte, North Carolina

Cheryl W. Lee
Language Arts Instructor
Douglas Byrd High School
Fayetteville, North Carolina

Carrie Lichtenberg
Language Arts Instructor
Highlands High School
Ft. Thomas, Kentucky

Catherine Linn
Language Arts Instructor
Palm Springs High School
Palm Desert, California

Agathaniki Locklear
District Technology Resource Teacher
Kenton County Schools
Ft. Wright, Kentucky

John Ludy
Language Arts Instructor
Fremont High School
Fremont, Indiana

Leigh Lo Matthewson
Language Arts Instructor
Albuquerque Public Schools
Albuquerque, New Mexico

Sherrie McDowell
Language Arts Instructor
Central High School
Cheyenne, Wyoming

Suzanne Mitoraj
English/Language Arts Consultant
Berlin, Connecticut

Nancy Monroe
Language Arts Instructor
Bolton High School
Alexandria, Louisiana

Gail Phelps
Language Arts Instructor
Northwood Middle School
North Little Rock, Arkansas

Matthew Scanlon
K-12 Humanities Supervisor
Hackettstown Public Schools
Hackettstown, New Jersey

John Scott
Language Arts Instructor (Retired)
Hampton City Schools
Hampton City, Virginia

Jean Shope
Language Arts Instructor
Grant Middle School
Albuquerque, New Mexico

Margaret St. Sauver
Staff Development-English/Language Arts
St. Paul Public Schools
St. Paul, Minnesota

Steve Thalheimer
Language Arts Instructor
Lawrenceburg High School
Lawrenceburg, Indiana

Cathy Robbs Turner
Director of Academies
Chattanooga Central High School
Harrison, Tennessee

Sandra VanBelois
Language Arts Instructor
Jack Britt High School
Fayetteville, North Carolina

Martha Lee Wildman
Language Arts Instructor
Delsea Regional High School
Franklinville, New Jersey

Melissa Williams
Language Arts Instructor
Delsea Regional High School
Franklinville, New Jersey

Charles Youngs
HS Language Arts Curriculum Facilitator
Bethel Park High School
Bethel Park, Pennsylvania

CONTENTS IN BRIEF

Unit 1 Fiction and Nonfiction

How does fact relate to fiction?

How do we deal with conflict?

Unit 3

Types of Nonfiction
Narrative, Expository, and Persuasive

PART **1**

Strategies for Determining the Main Idea   435

How do we learn about the world?

Unit 4 Poetry

What inspires us?

Unit 5 Drama

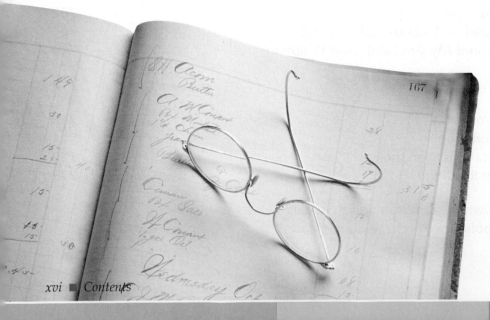

How do our experiences help shape us?

Unit 6

Themes in American Stories

PART **2** **Strategies for Setting a Purpose for Reading** **987**

SELECTIONS BY READING SKILL

▇ Unit 1

▇ Unit Two

Unit Three

Unit Four

SELECTIONS BY THEME

■ Coming of Age

■ Meeting Challenges

Quest for Freedom

From Sea to Shining Sea

Contents ■ *xxv*

INFORMATIONAL TEXTS AND OTHER NONFICTION

■ **Reading Informational Materials—Instructional Workshops**

■ **Additional Nonfiction—Selections by Type**

■ Literature in Context—Reading in the Content Areas

A wealth of expository nonfiction is found throughout this program.
Nonfiction texts are highlighted in red in the Index.

COMPARING LITERARY WORKS

SKILLS WORKSHOPS

■ Writing Workshops

■ Spelling Workshops

■ Communications Workshops

Fiction and Nonfiction

Unit 1 Overview

Introduction
Exploring Fiction and Nonfiction

Part 1: Make Predictions

Part 2: Author's Purpose

Introduction:
Fiction and Nonfiction

Patricia C.
McKissack

Patricia C. McKissack
Talks About the Forms

Nonfiction is a factual account of a person, place, or event, while a story with imaginary elements is **fiction.** Fiction is usually read for fun, but a lot of truth also can be found in its pages. Although nonfiction books are used to gather facts about a subject, they can be fun to read, too.

▲ Patricia C. McKissack has written numerous works of fiction and nonfiction about the history and experiences of African Americans.

Traveling in Worlds Real and Imaginary

When I was growing up, I read both fiction and nonfiction. The library was one of my favorite places, because it gave me access to books. And the books I read allowed me to leap over the racial barriers an African American child faced in the South during the 1950s and 60s.

I was able to travel in worlds both seen and unseen, real and imaginary. I rediscovered the ancient past with Artemis, Athena and Freya, and ventured into the tombs of the great Pharaohs of Egypt. I saw the future with Ray Bradbury and traveled to the center of the Earth with Jules Verne. I've cheered for the good guys, sneered at the villains, and cried real tears when my favorite literary character, Atticus Finch from *To Kill a Mockingbird*, stood his ground. I saw the face of death and heard the voice of despair, only to find hope on the very next page.

▼ **Critical Viewing** If you were the figure in this illustration would you be reading fiction or nonfiction? **[Respond]**

Nonfiction Moves From Facts to Truth

My curiosity and love of learning led me to become a teacher and later a writer. My first book was a biography I wrote to share with my students. I learned early in my writing career that facts alone are not enough in a work of nonfiction, as Frank Lloyd Wright suggests in the quotation shown here.

Once the research is completed, I have to sort and evaluate the many bits and pieces of information I've gathered. After that, I am still faced with the challenge of communicating the truth of an experience by presenting dry and uninteresting facts in a fair-minded and interesting way.

The truth is more important than the facts.

—Frank Lloyd Wright, American Architect

Fiction Combines Facts With Possibilities

As a reader, I savor fiction the way one eats a yummy hot-fudge sundae—slowly and joyfully. As a writer, I try to bring the same enthusiasm into my narratives. Fiction is not true, but fictional characters are sometimes more deliciously real than living people.

In order to create believable **characters, actions,** and **settings,** I explore how things operate within the realm of reality. Then, I search the thoughts and emotions of my fictional characters and decide how these characters function within the realm of possibility. Combining the real and the possible helps create a believable story.

More About the Author

Patricia C. **McKissack** (b. 1944)

As a writing team, Patricia C. McKissack and her husband, Fredrick (b. 1939), usually have four or five books in progress at any time. Their goal is to write the stories about African Americans that have been "left out, forgotten, misrepresented, or minimized by mainstream history texts."

Fast Facts

▶ Research for *Christmas in the Big House* took this writing team to a plantation in the Tidewater area in Virginia.
▶ Patricia C. McKissack has written fiction on her own.

Learning About Fiction and Nonfiction

Elements of Fiction

Fiction is prose writing that tells about characters and events from the author's imagination. All works of fiction share certain basic elements.

- **Setting** is the time and place where the story takes place.
- **Plot** is the sequence of events that takes you through a story. The plot of a story includes the **conflict**, or problem, and then at the end, the **resolution**, or conclusion.
- **Characters** are the people or animals that take part in the story's action. A **character's traits,** or qualities, can affect his or her thoughts, decisions, and actions.
- **Point of view** is the perspective from which a story is told.
- **First-person point of view** is the perspective of a character in the story.
- **Third-person point of view** is the perspective of a narrator outside the story.
- **Theme** is a message about life that a story conveys to its reader.

SUMMER FICTION

Types of Fiction

Short Stories are brief works of fiction made up of plot, character, setting, point of view, and theme. Short stories usually focus on one main plot structured around one main conflict and can usually be read in one sitting.

Novels are longer works of fiction. They contain the same elements as short stories—characters, plot, conflict, and setting. In addition to its main plot, a novel may contain **subplots,** or independent, related stories and conflicts.

Novellas are works of fiction that are shorter than novels, but longer than short stories.

Historical Fiction is literature that draws, in part, on real people and events to tell invented stories.

Elements of Nonfiction

Nonfiction works differ from works of fiction in these ways:

- They deal only with real people, events, or ideas.
- They are narrated from the **point of view**—or perspective—of the author, who is a real person.

Many things can affect the outcome of nonfiction writing other than the actual facts presented within the text.

- **Mood** is the overall feeling that the work evokes in the reader.
- **Author's Style** consists of every feature of a writer's use of language, such as rhythm, language, and methods of organization.

Purposes of Nonfiction

Nonfiction is often written for specific purposes or reasons. Some nonfiction meets several of the following purposes:

- **To Persuade:** Speeches and editorials are often written to convince an audience of a certain idea or opinion.
- **To Inform:** Articles, reference books, historical essays, and research papers present facts and information.
- **To Entertain:** Biographies, autobiographies, and travel narratives are often written for the enjoyment of the audience.

▼ **Critical Viewing**
What type of mood would a writer evoke in describing the scene in this photograph?
[Connect]

Check Your Understanding

Indicate whether each literary work described is an example of fiction or nonfiction.

1. a writer's account of his or her life
2. a speech given at a graduation ceremony
3. a story about a talking elephant

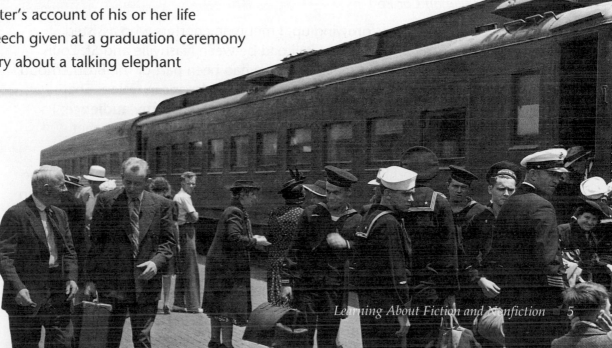

I write best about what interests me—stories concerning events and people in American history, particularly stories about African Americans. Most of my **nonfiction** projects begin with questions like these: What really happened, to whom, when, and why? Finding the answers requires a lot of careful **research,** study, and analysis, combined with hard work, discipline, and patience.

Research: Finding the Pieces of the Puzzle

My husband and co-author, Fredrick McKissack, works with me on nonfiction projects. We have published about fifty books together. For us, historical **facts** are like puzzle parts that, when pieced together, create a clear picture of the past. What can be more frustrating than a puzzle with missing pieces? That's why research is so important to the nonfiction writer. It helps provide all the necessary pieces for the reader "to complete the puzzle."

Historical Essay and Historical Context

The **historical essay** you are about to read, "The Baker Heater League," is an important piece of a larger puzzle that we put together. It is a chapter in *A Long Hard Journey: The Story of the Pullman Car Porter.*

When I was growing up, I met many porters who assisted passengers on the L&N Railroad between Nashville and St. Louis. Later, I found out that these men had been part of the Brotherhood of Sleeping Car Porters, the first African American union. That discovery gave me my **purpose** for writing and my **audience:** I wanted to know more about these porters and to share that information with students of history.

Fred and I began gathering materials that would help us tell the porters' story and explain the **historical context** of their struggle. In "The Baker Heater League," you'll learn what we discovered about the "tales, jokes, and real-life stories" that porters shared with each other.

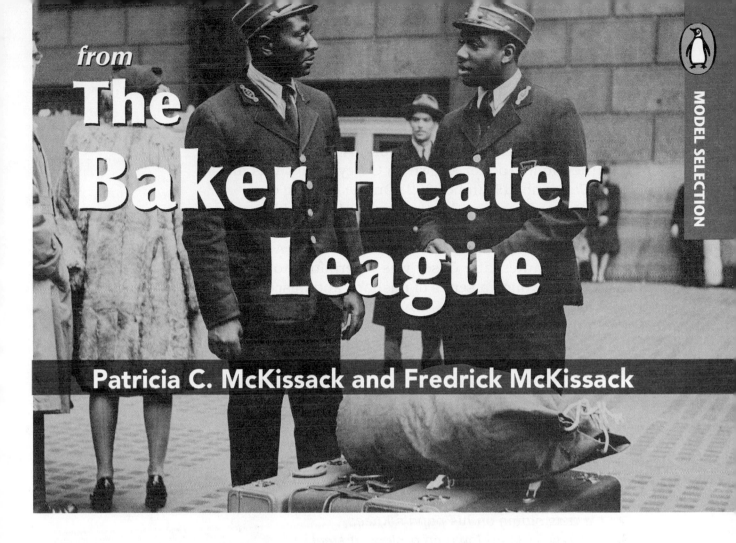

from
The Baker Heater League

Patricia C. McKissack and Fredrick McKissack

MODEL SELECTION

Porters developed a language and history that grew out of their common experiences. And they shared their experiences from coast to coast, north and south. Singing and telling stories helped to pass the time while waiting for an assignment, and it took the edge off being away from home and their loved ones.

Train stations provided quarters for porters called "porter houses." Sitting around a Baker heater, a large pot-bellied stove, the first porters told tales, jokes, and real-life stories that, in time, developed into a communication network peculiar to themselves. For example, if something happened in New York on Friday, porters in every state would know about it on Sunday. Political news, a good joke, style changes, even a girl's telephone number could be passed from New York to Chicago to Los Angeles, or from Minneapolis to St. Louis to New Orleans. This special brotherhood became known as "The Baker Heater League."

▲ **Critical Viewing**
Based on details in this photograph, what type of relationship do these porters share? Explain. **[Support]**

Nonfiction Description The details here show readers what happened in the porter house.

from The Baker Heater League ■ 7

As older porters died or retired, their stories became a part of railroad lore, and their legacy helped to reshape and mold new heroes and legends. Just as lumberjacks created their superhero, Paul Bunyan, and cowboys sang about wily Pecos Bill, railroaders had Casey Jones and John Henry.

John Luther Jones, better known as Casey Jones, was an engineer on Cannonball Number 382. On the evening of April 29, 1900, Casey and his black fireman, Sim Webb, prepared to take the Cannonball from Memphis to Canton. The scheduled engineer was out ill. The train left at 12:50 A.M., an hour and thirty minutes late. Casey was determined to make up the lost time. Through a series of <u>mishaps</u> and miscommunications, Casey's train crashed. Although the brave engineer could have jumped to safety, he stayed with the train and saved many lives at the cost of his own. Casey Jones became a railroad hero, and many songs were written about him:

Vocabulary Builder
mishaps (mis´haps´)
n. unfortunate or unlucky accidents

> Fireman jumped but Casey stayed on;
> He was a good engineer, but he's dead and gon'.

Legend tells us in another song that:

> When John Henry was a little boy,
> He was sitting on his papa's knee;
> He was looking down on a piece of steel,
> Say's "A steel-drivin' man I'll be, Lord, Lord.
> A steel-drivin' man I'll be."

The real John Henry, believed to be a newly freed slave from North Carolina, joined the West Virginia steel-driving team hired to dig out the Big Bend Tunnel for the C & O Railroad, circa 1870. Many stories detail the life and adventures of this two hundred-pound, six-foot man who was so strong he could drive steel with a hammer in each hand. John Henry's death occurred after competing with a steam drill, winning and then dying.

Nonfiction Exposition The facts here introduce the real life and some of the legend surrounding steel-driver John Henry.

> The steam drill set on the right-hand side,
> John Henry was on the left.
> He said, "I will beat that steam drill down
> Or hammer my fool self to death."

◄ Critical Viewing
Why might Casey Jones be a good subject for a song like the one advertised in this poster? [Connect]

Patricia C. McKissack
Author's Insight
We found many stories about John Henry, but we chose not to use them. You don't have to use all the research information you find. It is better to say a few things well, than to clutter your writing with too much "stuff."

✔ **Reading Check**

Who are three railroad legends celebrated in song and story?

Casey Jones and John Henry belonged to all railroaders, but the Pullman[1] porters had their very own hero in Daddy Joe.

Daddy Joe was a real person, but like most legends, his exploits were greatly exaggerated. One story establishes in legend, if not in fact, that Daddy Joe was the "first Pullman porter." He was said to have stood so tall and to have large hands so powerful that he could walk flat-footed down the aisle and let the upper berths down on each side.

Whenever a storyteller wanted to make a point about courtesy, honesty, or an outstanding job performance, he used a Daddy Joe story. And a tale about him usually began with:

1. **Pullman** cars featured special seats, which were converted to sleeping berths at night. The porters who readied the berths for sleeping also helped the train passengers during the day.

"The most terrific Pullman porter who ever made down a berth was Daddy Joe." Then the teller would tell a story like this one:

Hostile Indians were said to have attacked a train at a water tank. The all-white passengers were terrified. But Daddy Joe, with no regard for Pullman rules or his own safety, climbed on top of the train and spoke to the Indians in their own language. Afterwards Daddy Joe threw a Pullman blanket to each member of the attacking party and added a blessing at the end. The Indians let the train pass safely.

Whether he was facing hurricanes, high water, fires, robbers, or Indians, Daddy Joe always masterfully dealt with the situation. Legend has it that he even thwarted one of Jesse James's[2] attempted robberies. Daddy Joe got so many tips from grateful passengers, he was said to be "<u>burdened</u> down with silver and gold."

The first porters, who created Daddy Joe in their own image, were proud of him. He represented the qualities they valued—unquestionable loyalty and dedication to the job.

New railroad employees were always the source of a good laugh, too. This new-brakeman story—or one like it—was a porter house favorite.

It began with a young college graduate who got a yearning to work on the railroad. So, he traded in his suit and tie for the rusty railroad blues. Right away he was hired as a brakeman on the Knox & Lincoln Line. On his first run, the engineer was having a very hard time getting the freight up a steep hill. After getting the train over, the engineer called out, "I was afraid she'd stall and the train would roll backward!"

The new brakeman smiled broadly and assured the engineer. "No chance of that happening," he said, beaming with pride, "because before we started, I went back and set the brakes."

Amid thigh-slapping laughter, another tale would begin with: "Did you hear the story about the flagman?" Of course they'd all heard the story a hundred times. But each teller added or subtracted something until the tale was his own. That's how the tales stayed fresh and original.

Vocabulary Builder
burdened (bʉrd´nd)
adj. weighted down by work, duty, or sorrow

Patricia C. McKissack
Author's Insight
Although the story of the brakeman is fictional, it belongs in this nonfiction piece because it is an actual example of the porters' storytelling tradition.

---

2. **Jesse James** (1847–1882) and his brother Frank roamed the American West after the Civil War, robbing trains and banks.

Q. How do you and your husband work together?

A. I write. Fred fact checks and fills in the details. For example, I might write, "It was in late fall 1867 that a meeting was held near St. Louis, Missouri, to organize a school for former slaves." Fred then might add the following details: "It was on a cold November evening in 1868 that Moses Dickson invited seven former slaves to meet at his small AME church in Kirkwood, Missouri, to discuss plans for opening a school for their children."

Q. Do you have a system for doing research?

A. For us, some research has taken a few days and sometimes many years, but the process is the same regardless of the time involved: 1) Gather; 2) Organize; 3) Verify. We use books, newspapers, magazines, diaries, journals, maps, graphs, the Internet, and personal travel to gather material about my subject. Disorganized data is useless, however. To organize my thoughts, I create a folder for each chapter and store information there.

StudentCorner

Q. If each porter changed a tale, wouldn't stories become so "twisted" that no one would remember the original?
—Andrew Sanders, Pine Bush, New York

A. Naturally, storytellers bring their personal experiences, beliefs, regional influences, and language patterns into the interpretation of the stories they tell. Therefore, details are certain to change. However, though different "versions" of a story may emerge within the "oral tradition," the basic elements of the story (character, action, setting, and idea) remain constant.

 ## Writing Workshop: *Work in Progress*

Descriptive Essay

For a descriptive essay you may write about a person, develop a web of five to seven possible subjects. In the main circle put "People." Then draw lines connecting to smaller outer circles. Complete the web by filling the circles with the names of people you know well. Save this Description Web in your writing portfolio.

From the Author's Desk
Patricia C. McKissack Introduces "The 11:59"

Long before I was a writer, I was a listener. I come from a family of wonderful storytellers who could spin fascinating yarns that would hold you captivated for hours. I continue that tradition in my fictional writing, which tends to be a blend of history with imagined elements—**historical fiction.**

After writing *A Long Hard Journey: The Story of the Pullman Porter,* I had a lot of leftover research material, especially about the stories the porters shared with each other. I was working on a collection of scary stories called *The Dark-Thirty: Southern Tales of the Supernatural,* so I decided to develop "The 11:59," which is based on porters' tales.

Historical Fact Inspires an Imagined Plot

Porters described death by using railroad metaphors such as "the last out-bound train," the "final ride," or "boarding the 11:59." My **plot** was based on the superstition that any porter who heard the whistle blast of the 11:59 knew he was destined to die within the next twenty-four hours.

Since I never found a story about how a porter reacted to hearing the whistle of the phantom death train, I created Lester Simmons, an imaginary **character,** to respond as I imagined a porter might under such circumstances.

A Fictional Character Creates the Historical Setting

I use Lester's voice to create an accurate **historical setting.** But when Lester hears the whistle of the 11:59, my imagination takes over and I am more concerned with the emotions this situation would generate.

I won't reveal the suspenseful ending, but I will confess it was a challenge to write. I've never been good at endings, but this one was particularly difficult. How could I "keep it real" yet remain true to my story? My answer came while viewing a documentary—I think you'll be able to guess what its subject was.

THE 11:59

Patricia C. McKissack

From 1880 to 1960—a time known as the golden age of train travel—George Pullman's luxury sleeping cars provided passengers with comfortable accommodations during an overnight trip. The men who changed the riding seats into well-made-up beds and attended to the individual needs of each passenger were called Pullman car porters. For decades all the porters were African Americans, so when they organized the Brotherhood of Sleeping Car Porters in 1926, theirs was the first all black union in the United States. Like most groups, the porters had their own language and a network of stories. The phantom Death Train, known in railroad language as the 11:59, is an example of the kind of story the porters often shared.

Lester Simmons was a thirty-year retired Pullman car porter— had his gold watch to prove it. "Keeps perfect train time," he often bragged. "Good to the second."

    Daily he went down to the St. Louis Union Station and shined shoes to help supplement his meager twenty-four-

▲ **Critical Viewing**
What mood does this illustration suggest?
[Draw Conclusions]

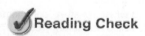 **Reading Check**

What was unique about Lester Simmons's union?

dollar-a-month Pullman retirement check. He ate his evening meal at the porter house on Compton Avenue and hung around until late at night talking union, playing bid whist,[1] and spinning yarns with those who were still "travelin' men." In this way Lester stayed in touch with the only family he'd known since 1920.

There was nothing the young porters liked more than listening to Lester tell true stories about the old days, during the founding of the Brotherhood of Sleeping Car Porters, the first black union in the United States. He knew the president, A. Philip Randolph,[2] personally, and proudly boasted that it was Randolph who'd signed him up as a union man back in 1926. He passed his original card around for inspection. "I knew all the founding brothers. Take Brother E. J. Bradley. We hunted many a day together, not for the sport of it but for something to eat. Those were hard times, starting up the union. But we hung in there so you youngsters might have the benefits you enjoy now."

The rookie porters always liked hearing about the thirteen-year struggle between the Brotherhood and the powerful Pullman Company, and how, against all odds, the fledgling union had won recognition and better working conditions.

Everybody enjoyed it too when Lester told tall tales about Daddy Joe, the porters' larger-than-life hero. "Now y'all know the first thing a good Pullman man is expected to do is make up the top and lower berths for the passengers each night."

"Come on, Lester," one of his listeners chided. "You don't need to describe our jobs for us."

"Some of you, maybe not. But some of you, well—" he said, looking over the top of his glasses and raising an eyebrow at a few of the younger porters. "I was just setting the stage." He smiled good-naturedly and went on with his story. "They tell me Daddy Joe could walk flatfooted down the center of the coach and let down berths on both sides of the aisle."

Hearty laughter filled the room, because everyone knew that to accomplish such a feat, Daddy Joe would have to

Fiction
Setting These facts make the fictional story more realistic.

Patricia C. McKissack
Author's Insight Here, I place my character, Lester, in the historical context of the early struggle for a porters' union. My fictional character becomes more believable each time I add a detail.

Fiction
Dialogue Lester's words let readers hear his unique speaking style.

---

1. **bid whist** (hwist) *n.* card game for four players that developed into bridge.
2. **A. Philip Randolph** (1889–1979) president of the Brotherhood of Sleeping Car Porters, the first black union. He also gave the opening speech at the historic March on Washington in 1963.

Literature in Context   Social Studies Connection

Making Tracks

Until the end of World War II, trains like the *Silver Arrow* in the story (p. 17) and the *Blue Bird,* shown here, were one of the most popular ways to travel long distances. George Pullman, an American businessman, designed or improved the specialized train cars that made long-distance train travel comfortable. Porters were employed by the railroads to ensure passengers were comfortable as they traveled in these "hotels on wheels."

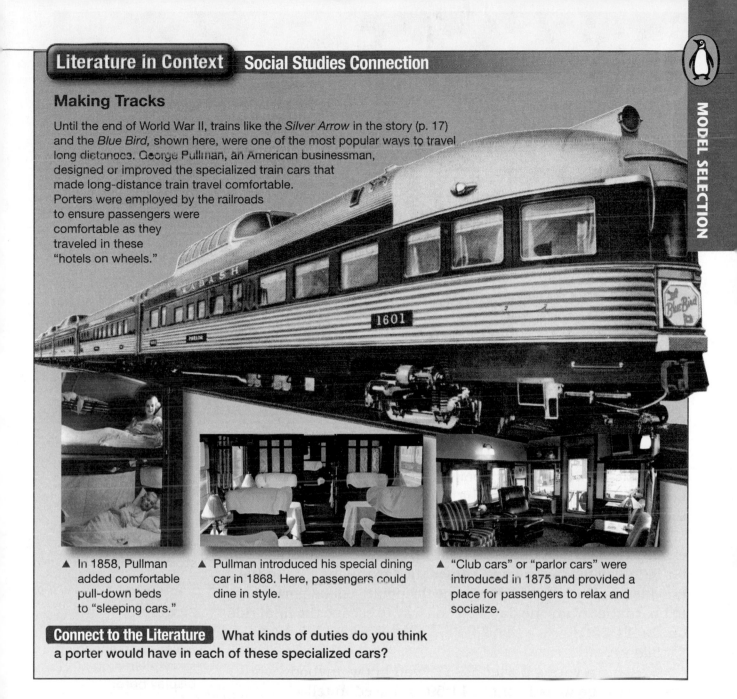

▲ In 1858, Pullman added comfortable pull-down beds to "sleeping cars."

▲ Pullman introduced his special dining car in 1868. Here, passengers could dine in style.

▲ "Club cars" or "parlor cars" were introduced in 1875 and provided a place for passengers to relax and socialize.

Connect to the Literature   What kinds of duties do you think a porter would have in each of these specialized cars?

have been superhuman. But that was it: To the men who worked the sleeping cars, Daddy Joe was no less a hero than Paul Bunyan was to the lumberjacks of the Northwestern forests.

"And when the 11:59 pulled up to his door, as big and strong as Daddy Joe was . . ." Lester continued solemnly. "Well, in the end even he couldn't escape the 11:59." The old

Reading Check

Why was Daddy Joe a hero to the Pullman car porters?

storyteller eyed one of the rookie porters he knew had never heard the frightening tale about the porters' Death Train. Lester took joy in mesmerizing[3] his young listeners with all the details.

"Any porter who hears the whistle of the 11:59 has got exactly twenty-four hours to clear up earthly matters. He better be ready when the train comes the next night . . ." In his creakiest voice, Lester drove home the point. "All us porters got to board that train one day. Ain't no way to escape the final ride on the 11:59."

Silence.

"Lester," a young porter asked, "you know anybody who ever heard the whistle of the 11:59 and lived to tell—"

"Not a living soul!"

Laughter.

"Well," began one of the men, "wonder will we have to make up berths on *that* train?"

"If it's an overnight trip to heaven, you can best be believing there's bound to be a few of us making up the berths," another answered.

"Shucks," a card player stopped to put in. "They say even

▲ **Critical Viewing**
How does the work being done in this illustration compare with the work described in the story? **[Connect]**

Fiction
Character Lester's ability as an engaging storyteller is on display here.

---

3. **mesmerizing** (mez′ mər īz′ iŋ) *v.* fascinating; amazing.

up in heaven *we* the ones gon' be keeping all that gold and silver polished."

"Speaking of gold and silver," Lester said, remembering. "That reminds me of how I gave Tip Sampson his nickname. Y'all know Tip?"

There were plenty of nods and smiles.

The memory made Lester chuckle. He shifted in his seat to find a more comfortable spot. Then he began. "A woman got on board the *Silver Arrow* in Chicago going to Los Angeles. She was dripping in <u>finery</u>—had on all kinds of gold and diamond jewelry, carried twelve bags. Sampson knocked me down getting to wait on her, figuring she was sure for a big tip. That lady was <u>worrisome</u>! Ooowee! 'Come do this. Go do that. Bring me this.' Sampson was running over himself trying to keep that lady happy. When we reached L.A., my passengers all tipped me two or three dollars, as was customary back then.

"When Sampson's Big Money lady got off, she reached into her purse and placed a dime in his outstretched hand. A *dime*! Can you imagine? *Ow!* You should have seen his face. And I didn't make it no better. Never did let him forget it. I teased him so—went to calling him Tip, and the nickname stuck."

Laughter.

"I haven't heard from ol' Tip in a while. Anybody know anything?"

"You haven't got word, Lester? Tip boarded the 11:59 over in Kansas City about a month ago."

"Sorry to hear that. That just leaves me and Willie Beavers, the last of the old, old-timers here in St. Louis."

Lester looked at his watch—it was a little before midnight. The talkfest[4] had lasted later than usual. He said his goodbyes and left, taking his usual route across the Eighteenth Street bridge behind the station.

In the darkness, Lester looked over the yard, picking out familiar shapes—the *Hummingbird, the Zephyr.*[5] He'd worked on them both. Train travel wasn't anything like it used to be in the old days—not since people had begun to ride airplanes. "Progress," he scoffed. "Those contraptions will never take the place of a train. No sir!"

Suddenly he felt a sharp pain in his chest. At exactly the

---

4. **talkfest** (tôk´ fest´) *n.* informal gathering for discussion.
5. **Zephyr** (zef´ ər) *n.* soft, gentle breeze, named for the Greek god of the west wind.

Vocabulary Builder
finery (fīn´ ər ē) *n.* fancy clothing and accessories

worrisome (wʉr´ ē səm) *adj.* causing worry or anxiety

Patricia C. McKissack
Author's Insight
Lester's parting dialogue hints at the coming action. This is a writing technique called *foreshadowing.*

Reading Check

What kind of stories did Lester tell to amuse the new employees?

same moment he heard the mournful sound of a train whistle, which the wind seemed to carry from some faraway place. Ignoring his pain, Lester looked at the old station. He knew nothing was scheduled to come in or out till early morning. Nervously he lit a match to check the time. 11:59!

"No," he said into the darkness. "I'm not ready. I've got plenty of living yet."

Fear quickened his step. Reaching his small apartment, he hurried up the steps. His heart pounded in his ear, and his left arm tingled. He had an idea, and there wasn't a moment to waste. But his own words haunted him. *Ain't no way to escape the final ride on the 11:59.*

"But I'm gon' try!" Lester spent the rest of the night plotting his escape from fate.

"I won't eat or drink anything all day," he talked himself through his plan. "That way I can't choke, die of food poisoning, or cause a cooking fire."

Lester shut off the space heater to avoid an explosion, nailed shut all doors and windows to keep out intruders, and unplugged every electrical appliance. Good weather was predicted, but just in case a freak storm came and blew out a window, shooting deadly glass shards in his direction, he moved a straight-backed chair into a far corner, making sure nothing was overhead to fall on him.

"I'll survive," he said, smiling at the prospect of beating Death. "Won't that be a wonderful story to tell at the porter house?" He rubbed his left arm. It felt numb again.

Lester sat silently in his chair all day, too afraid to move. At noon someone knocked on his door. He couldn't answer it. Foot-steps . . . another knock. He didn't answer.

A parade of minutes passed by, equally measured, one behind the other, ticking . . . ticking . . . away . . . The dull pain in his chest returned. He nervously checked his watch every few minutes.

Ticktock, ticktock.

Time had always been on his side. Now it was his enemy. Where had the years gone? Lester reviewed the thirty years he'd spent riding the rails. How different would his life have been if he'd married Louise Henderson and had a gallon of children?

Fiction
Conflict These paragraphs reveal that although Lester loves to tell the legend, he believes it may not apply to him.

Fiction
Plot At this point, the legend of the 11:59 and the reality of Lester's physical condition come together, building the story's tension.

What if he'd taken that job at the mill down in Opelika?[6] What if he'd followed his brother to Philly?[7] How different?

Ticktock, ticktock.

So much living had passed so quickly. Lester decided if he had to do it all over again, he'd stand by his choices. His had been a good life. No regrets. No major changes for him.

Ticktock, ticktock.

The times he'd had—both good and bad—what memories. His first and only love had been traveling, and she was a jealous companion. Wonder whatever happened to that girl up in Minneapolis? Thinking about her made him smile. Then he laughed. That *girl* must be close to seventy years old by now.

Ticktock, ticktock.

Daylight was fading quickly. Lester drifted off to sleep, then woke from a nightmare in which, like Jonah, he'd been swallowed by an enormous beast. Even awake he could still hear its heart beating . . . *ticktock, ticktock* . . . But then he realized he was hearing his own heartbeat.

Lester couldn't see his watch, but he guessed no more than half an hour had passed. Sleep had overtaken him with such little resistance. Would Death, that shapeless shadow, slip in that easily? Where was he <u>lurking</u>? *Yea, though I walk through the valley of the shadow of death, I will fear no evil . . .* The Twenty-third Psalm was the only prayer Lester knew, and he repeated it over and over, hoping it would comfort him.

Lester rubbed his tingling arm. He could hear the blood rushing past his ear and up the side of his head. He longed to know what time it was, but that meant he had to light a match—too risky. What if there was a gas leak? The match would set off an explosion. "I'm too smart for that, Death," he said.

Ticktock, ticktock.

It was late. He could feel it. Stiffness seized his legs and made them tremble. How much longer? he wondered. Was he close to winning?

Then in the fearful silence he heard a train whistle. His ears strained to identify the sound, making sure it *was* a whistle. No mistake. It came again, the same as the night before. Lester answered it with a groan.

Ticktock, ticktock.

---

6. **Opelika** city in Alabama.
7. **Philly** informal name for Philadelphia, Pennsylvania.

Patricia C. McKissack
Author's Insight
Lester feels his enemy is time. By using "ticktock, ticktock" throughout the narrative, I raise the level of suspense.

Vocabulary Builder
lurking (lʉrk´iŋ) *v.* ready to spring out, attack; existing undiscovered

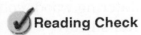**Reading Check**

What did Lester do to avoid being a passenger on the 11:59?

He could hear Time ticking away in his head. Gas leak or not, he had to see his watch. Striking a match, Lester quickly checked the time. 11:57.

Although there was no gas explosion, a tiny explosion erupted in his heart.

Ticktock, ticktock.

Just a little more time. The whistle sounded again. Closer than before. Lester struggled to move, but he felt fastened to the chair. Now he could hear the engine puffing, pulling a heavy load. It was hard for him to breathe, too, and the pain in his chest weighed heavier and heavier.

Ticktock, ticktock.

Time had run out! Lester's mind reached for an explanation that made sense. But reason failed when a glowing phantom dressed in the porters' blue uniform stepped out of the grayness of Lester's confusion.

"It's *your* time, good brother." The specter spoke in a thousand familiar voices.

Freed of any restraint now, Lester stood, bathed in a peaceful calm that had its own glow. "Is that you, Tip?" he asked, squinting to focus on his old friend standing in the strange light.

"It's me, ol' partner. Come to remind you that none of us can escape the last ride on the 11:59."

"I know. I know," Lester said, chuckling. "But man, I had to try."

Tip smiled. "I can dig it. So did I."

"That'll just leave Willie, won't it?"

"Not for long."

"I'm ready."

Lester saw the great beam of the single headlight and heard the deafening whistle blast one last time before the engine tore through the front of the apartment, shattering glass and splintering wood, collapsing everything in its path, including Lester's heart.

When Lester didn't show up at the shoeshine stand two days running, friends went over to his place and found him on the floor. His eyes were fixed on something quite amazing—his gold watch, stopped at exactly 11:59.

Fiction
Plot Although Lester's physical pain is great, he is still hoping to outsmart death.

Patricia C. McKissack
Author's Insight
An open ending allows readers to interpret it different ways. Did Lester die of a natural heart attack? Or did he die as a result of the 11:59?

From the Author's Desk
Patricia C. McKissack's Insights into "The 11:59"

Q. How did you make the dialogue in the story sound realistic?

A. Part of writing is learning how to be a good listener. I listen to how people speak and respond to others in different situations. It's fun eavesdropping on couples having an argument, grandmothers telling stories, two veterans recalling their service experiences, a principal and a student, and more. When I write dialogue I recall the things I heard. The dialogue I write may not be exactly true to what I heard, but it is real.

Q. What tricks do you use to make a ghost story scary?

A. I use repetition to build suspense. Imagine the steady beat of a drum and how anxious it can make you feel. I used that technique in "The 11:59" by including the *ticktock ticktock* repeatedly. I also use *jump words* such as "suddenly," "all at once," and "without warning," because they make the action seem immediate, and that causes the reader or listener to jump.

StudentCorner

Q. Why did porters call their last day "the final ride on the 11:59"?

> **—Masis Parseghian, Franklin Lakes, New Jersey**

A. In railroad language, trains were identified by the times they pulled out of the station, arrived at their destination, or passed a well-known landmark. In the imagination of the porters, the death train was identified as the 11:59, because it represented a time that was one minute before midnight and a new day.

 Writing Workshop: *Work in Progress*

Descriptive Essay

Using your Description Web from your portfolio, choose a person to describe. Write that person's name on the top of your paper. Jot down the first adjectives that come to your mind about your subject. List all the colors and sounds that you associate with that person. Save this Descriptive List in your writing portfolio.

Apply the Skills

Fiction and Nonfiction

Thinking About the Selections

1. **Respond:** Did you expect the story "The 11:59" to end as it did? Why or why not?

2. **(a) Recall:** Which hero of the Pullman car porters appears in both the fiction and nonfiction selections? **(b) Compare:** Do both accounts agree on his adventures? Explain.

3. **(a) Recall:** What is the legend of the Death Train?
   (b) Summarize: Tell how Lester tries to cheat his fate.
   (c) Interpret: What causes Lester's death?

4. **(a) Classify:** Complete a chart like the one shown, based on the information in "The Baker Heater League." **(b) Compare and Contrast:** Share your list with a small group, noting similarities and differences. **(c) Analyze:** Together, explain how fact and fiction were combined in railroad legend.

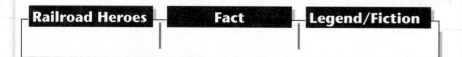

Railroad Heroes	Fact	Legend/Fiction

Fiction and Nonfiction Review

5. What realistic details in the **setting** make it sound as if the fictional story actually happened?

6. Just as **fiction** writers use realistic details, **nonfiction** writers use fictional elements. What is the writers' purpose in including tales about well-known railroad figures in "The Baker Heater League"?

Research the Author

Working with two other students, present a **talk show**. One student should take the role of the host, and the others, the roles of the co-authors Patricia and Fredrick McKissack.

- Using the Internet and print sources, collect information about the authors' lives and their works.
- Conduct a "live" interview by chatting naturally, using notes but not relying on a written script.
- Invite audience members to question the authors.

QuickReview

Selections at a Glance

"The Baker Heater League" explains the role that porters played in developing railroad legends.

In **"The 11:59,"** a retired porter fascinates his audience with a tall tale about a fateful train.

Go Online
Assessment

For: Self-test
Visit: www.PHSchool.com
Web Code: ena-6101
            ena-6102

Nonfiction: prose writing about real people, events, or ideas

Fiction: prose writing that tells about characters and events from the author's imagination

Setting: the time and place where the story takes place

Skills You Will Learn

Reading Skill: *Make and Support Predictions*
Literary Analysis: *Plot*

Reading Skill: *Read Ahead to Confirm or Correct Predictions*
Literary Analysis: *Conflict and Resolution*

Reading Skill: *Use Text Aids and Features*

Literary Analysis: *Comparing Narrative Structure*

Literature You Will Read

Reading: Prediction

> When you make a **prediction** you make a logical assumption
> about what will happen next in a story.

Skills and Strategies You Will Learn in Part 1

In Part 1 you will learn

- to **use prior knowledge** to **make predictions** (p. 26)
- to **support predictions** with story details (p. 26)
- to **read ahead to confirm or correct predictions** (p. 52)
- to **revise predictions** based on new information (p. 52)
- to use **the text aids and features** to help **make
predictions** (p. 74)

Using the Skills and Strategies in Part 1

In Part 1 you will learn to use story details and your own knowledge
and experience to make predictions. You will also learn to identify and
evaluate support for your predictions as you read ahead. As you
gather additional details, you will practice using new information to
revise predictions. Making predictions helps you find connections
between events and actions.

**The example shows how you will apply the skills and strategies
you will learn in Part 1.**

Detail: The main character teases the new boy in school. **Prediction:** The two characters will become enemies.	**Read Ahead** → **New Detail:** The new boy helps the main character. **Revised Prediction:** The two characters will become friends.

As you read the literature in this part, you will practice making, supporting,
and revising predictions.

VIEW PREVIEW

Academic Vocabulary: Words for Discussing Predictions

The following words will help you write and talk about making predictions as you read the selections in this unit.

Word	Definition	Example Sentence
predict *v.*	make a logical assumption about future events	These clues help me *predict* what the character will do next.
anticipate *v.*	look forward to, expect	I *anticipate* that the character will join the team.
formulate *v.*	make a statement, form an idea	I can *formulate* a prediction based on these details.
modify *v.*	change	Because of these new details, I have to *modify* my original prediction.
revise *v.*	correct, improve, or change	I *revised* my prediction because a new character entered the story.

Vocabulary Skill: Prefixes

▶ A **prefix** is one or more syllables joined to the beginning of a word or root to form a new word.

In Part 1 you will learn
- the **prefix** *pre-* (p. 50)
- the **prefix** *re-* (p. 72)

Knowing the meanings of prefixes helps you understand word meanings. These words contain the prefixes *pre-* and *re-*.

Words	Prefix Meaning	Example Sentence
predict	before	I **predict** that the characters will run.
revise	back, or again	I have to **revise** my prediction.

Activity Rewrite each example sentence, replacing each bold word with a synonym—a word that means almost the same thing. Explain your choices.

These skills will help you become a better reader. Practice them with either "A Retrieved Reformation" (p. 28) or "Raymond's Run" (p. 39).

Reading Skill

When you **make predictions** about a story, you make informed guesses about what will happen next, based on story details and your own experience. You can **support your predictions** by finding clues in the story that hint at what will happen next.

- As you read, use a chart like the one shown.
- Notice when the story includes details that could support predictions of more than one outcome. Some stories keep you guessing in order to hold your interest and to build suspense.

My Prediction

Text Support

What Actually Happens

Literary Analysis

Plot is the sequence of related events in a story. As you read, identify the following parts of the story's plot:

- **Exposition:** basic information about the characters and situation
- **Conflict:** struggle between two opposing forces in the story
- **Rising Action:** events that increase the tension
- **Climax:** high point of the story, usually the point at which the eventual outcome will be revealed
- **Falling Action:** events that follow the climax
- **Resolution:** the final outcome

Vocabulary Builder

A Retrieved Reformation

- **virtuous** (vʉr´ choo əs) *adj.* moral; upright (p. 28) *A virtuous man respects the rights of others.*

- **retribution** (re´ trə byoo´ shən) *n.* punishment for wrongdoing (p. 30) *The victim wanted retribution from the man who robbed him.*

- **unobtrusively** (un´ əb troo´siv lē) *adv.* without calling attention to oneself (p. 33) *She slipped out of the room unobtrusively.*

- **anguish** (aŋ´ gwish) *n.* great suffering from worry (p. 35) *The parents' anguish ended when their sick child recovered.*

Raymond's Run

- **prodigy** (präd´ ə jē) *n.* a wonder; an unusually talented person (p. 41) *At four, Sam was already a basketball prodigy.*

- **reputation** (rep´ yoo tā´ shən) *n.* widely-held opinion about a person, whether good or bad (p. 42) *The teacher had a reputation as a tough grader.*

Build Understanding • *A Retrieved Reformation*

Background

Safe Cracking This story's main character is a thief who breaks into, or "cracks," safes in the early 1900s. At that time, the locks, dials, and levers of most safes were located on the outside, so safe-crackers developed special techniques to punch out these parts. Today, safes are built with locks and bolts on the inside, making them harder to "crack."

Connecting to the Literature

Reading/Writing Connection Jimmy Valentine, the main character in this story, tries to reform, or turn his life around for the better. Make a list of three reasons a person might have for "turning over a new leaf." Use at least three of the following words: *alter, establish, evaluate, impress, modify.*

Meet the Author

O. **Henry** (1862–1910)

O. Henry, whose given name was William Sydney Porter, remains a popular short-story writer. His stories are loved for their humor, down-to-earth characters, and surprise endings. Porter lived a life that mirrored his stories—full of hard luck, unusual twists, and colorful characters.

Tragedy and Success Porter was brought up in North Carolina by his grandmother and his great-aunt. As a young man, he moved to Texas, where he worked as a writer, cartoonist, ranch hand, and bank teller. In 1898, Porter was convicted of stealing funds from the bank where he worked. During his three years in prison, Porter published several stories under the name O. Henry. He drew inspiration from the unusual personalities around him.

Fast Facts

▶ The character of Jimmy Valentine was based on a safe-cracker O. Henry heard about while he was in jail.

▶ Many of his stories are set in New York City, where he spent the final years of his life.

Go **Online**
Author Link

For: More about the author
Visit: www.PHSchool.com
Web Code: ene-9102

A RETRIEVED Reformation

O. Henry

A guard came to the prison shoe-shop, where Jimmy Valentine was assiduously[1] stitching uppers, and escorted him to the front office. There the warden handed Jimmy his pardon, which had been signed that morning by the governor. Jimmy took it in a tired kind of way. He had served nearly ten months of a four-year sentence. He had expected to stay only about three months, at the longest. When a man with as many friends on the outside as Jimmy Valentine had is received in the "stir" it is hardly worthwhile to cut his hair.

"Now, Valentine," said the warden, "you'll go out in the morning. Brace up, and make a man of yourself. You're not a bad fellow at heart. Stop cracking safes, and live straight."

"Me?" said Jimmy, in surprise. "Why, I never cracked a safe in my life."

"Oh, no," laughed the warden. "Of course not. Let's see, now. How was it you happened to get sent up on that Springfield job? Was it because you wouldn't prove an alibi for fear of compromising somebody in extremely high-toned society? Or was it simply a case of a mean old jury that had it in for you? It's always one or the other with you innocent victims."

"Me?" said Jimmy, still blankly <u>virtuous</u>. "Why, warden, I never was in Springfield in my life!"

▲ Critical Viewing
What details reveal that this photograph, like the story, is from an earlier time period? **[Connect]**

Vocabulary Builder
virtuous (vûr′ chōō əs) *adj.* moral; upright

---

1. assiduously (ə sij′ ōō əs lē) *adv.* carefully and busily.

"Take him back, Cronin," smiled the warden, "and fix him up with outgoing clothes. Unlock him at seven in the morn-ing, and let him come to the bullpen.[2] Better think over my advice, Valentine."

At a quarter past seven on the next morning Jimmy stood in the warden's outer office. He had on a suit of the villainously fitting, ready-made clothes and a pair of the stiff, squeaky shoes that the state furnishes to its discharged compulsory guests.

The clerk handed him a railroad ticket and the five-dollar bill with which the law expected him to rehabilitate himself into good citizenship and prosperity. The warden gave him a cigar, and shook hands. Valentine, 9762, was chronicled on the books "Pardoned by Governor," and Mr. James Valentine walked out into the sunshine.

Disregarding the song of the birds, the waving green trees, and the smell of the flowers, Jimmy headed straight for a res-taurant. There he tasted the first sweet joys of liberty in the shape of a chicken dinner. From there he proceeded leisurely to the depot and boarded his train. Three hours set him down in a little town near the state line. He went to the café of one Mike Dolan and shook hands with Mike, who was alone behind the bar.

"Sorry we couldn't make it sooner, Jimmy, me boy," said Mike. "But we had that protest from Springfield to buck against, and the governor nearly balked. Feeling all right?"

"Fine," said Jimmy. "Got my key?"

He got his key and went upstairs, unlocking the door of a room at the rear. Everything was just as he had left it. There on the floor was still Ben Price's collar-button that had been torn from that eminent detective's shirt-band when they had overpowered Jimmy to arrest him.

Pulling out from the wall a folding-bed, Jimmy slid back a panel in the wall and dragged out a dust-covered suitcase. He opened this and gazed fondly at the finest set of burglar's tools in the East. It was a complete set, made of specially tem-pered steel, the latest designs in drills, punches, braces and bits, jimmies, clamps, and augers,[3] with two or three novelties invented by Jimmy himself, in which he took pride. Over nine

**Reading Skill
Make Predictions**
Based on Jimmy's attitude, do you predict he will take the warden's advice? Explain.

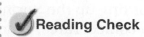Reading Check

Where has Jimmy been for the past ten months?

---

2. bullpen *n.* barred room in a jail where prisoners are held while waiting to be moved or released.
3. drills . . . augers (ô´ gərz) *n.* tools used to bore holes in metal.

hundred dollars they had cost him to have made at —, a place where they make such things for the profession.

In half an hour Jimmy went downstairs and through the café. He was now dressed in tasteful and well-fitting clothes, and carried his dusted and cleaned suitcase in his hand.

"Got anything on?" asked Mike Dolan, genially.

"Me?" said Jimmy, in a puzzled tone. "I don't understand. I'm representing the New York Amalgamated Short Snap Biscuit Cracker and Frazzled Wheat Company."

This statement delighted Mike to such an extent that Jimmy had to take a seltzer-and-milk on the spot. He never touched "hard" drinks.

A week after the release of Valentine, 9762, there was a neat job of safe-burglary done in Richmond, Indiana, with no clue to the author. A scant eight hundred dollars was all that was secured. Two weeks after that a patented, improved, burglar-proof safe in Logansport was opened like a cheese to the tune of fifteen hundred dollars, currency; securities and silver untouched. That began to interest the rogue-catchers.[4] Then an old-fashioned bank-safe in Jefferson City became active and threw out of its crater an eruption of bank-notes amounting to five thousand dollars. The losses were now high enough to bring the matter up into Ben Price's class of work. By comparing notes, a remarkable similarity in the methods of the burglaries was noticed. Ben Price investigated the scenes of the robberies, and was heard to remark:

"That's Dandy Jim Valentine's autograph. He's resumed business. Look at that combination knob—jerked out as easy as pulling up a radish in wet weather. He's got the only clamps that can do it. And look how clean those tumblers were punched out! Jimmy never has to drill but one hole. Yes, I guess I want Mr. Valentine. He'll do his bit next time without any short-time or clemency foolishness."

Ben Price knew Jimmy's habits. He had learned them while working up the Springfield case. Long jumps, quick getaways, no confederates,[5] and a taste for good society—these ways had helped Mr. Valentine to become noted as a successful dodger of <u>retribution</u>. It was given out that Ben Price had taken up the trail of the elusive cracksman, and other people with burglar-proof safes felt more at ease.

---

4. **rogue-catchers** *n.* police.
5. **confederates** (kən fed´ər its) *n.* fellow criminals.

Reading Skill
Make Predictions
Do you think Jimmy will get rid of his tools or use them to crack more safes? Support your prediction with details from the story.

Literary Analysis
Plot What two characters will struggle against each other in the story's conflict?

Vocabulary Builder
retribution (re´ trə byōo´ shən) *n.* punishment for wrongdoing

One afternoon, Jimmy Valentine and his suitcase climbed out of the mail hack[6] in Elmore, a little town five miles off the railroad down in the blackjack country of Arkansas. Jimmy, looking like an athletic young senior just home from college, went down the board sidewalk toward the hotel.

A young lady crossed the street, passed him at the corner and entered a door over which was the sign "The Elmore Bank." Jimmy Valentine looked into her eyes, forgot what he was, and became another man. She lowered her eyes and colored slightly. Young men of Jimmy's style and looks were scarce in Elmore.

Jimmy collared a boy that was loafing on the steps of the bank as if he were one of the stockholders, and began to ask him questions about the town, feeding him dimes at intervals. By and by the young lady came out, looking royally unconscious of the young man with the suitcase, and went her way.

"Isn't that young lady Miss Polly Simpson?" asked Jimmy, with specious guile.[7]

"Naw," said the boy. "She's Annabel Adams. Her pa owns this bank. What'd you come to Elmore for? Is that a gold watch chain? I'm going to get a bulldog. Got any more dimes?"

Jimmy went to the Planters' Hotel, registered as Ralph D. Spencer, and engaged a room. He leaned on the desk and declared his platform[8] to the clerk. He said he had come to Elmore to look for a location to go into business. How was the shoe business, now, in the town? He had thought of the shoe business. Was there an opening?

The clerk was impressed by the clothes and manner of Jimmy. He, himself, was something of a pattern of fashion to the thinly gilded youth of Elmore, but he now perceived his shortcomings. While trying to figure out Jimmy's manner of tying his four-in-hand,[9] he cordially gave information.

---

6. **mail hack** *n.* horse and carriage used to deliver mail.
7. **specious guile** (spē' shəs gil') *n.* crafty, indirect way of obtaining information.
8. **platform** *n.* here, a statement of his situation.
9. **four-in-hand** *n.* necktie.

Yes, there ought to be a good opening in the shoe line. There wasn't an exclusive shoe store in the place. The dry-goods and general stores handled them. Business in all lines was fairly good. Hoped Mr. Spencer would decide to locate in Elmore. He would find it a pleasant town to live in, and the people very sociable.

Mr. Spencer thought he would stop over in the town a few days and look over the situation. No, the clerk needn't call the boy. He would carry up his suitcase, himself: it was rather heavy.

Mr. Ralph Spencer, the phoenix that arose from Jimmy Valentine's ashes—ashes left by the flame of a sudden and alterative attack of love—remained in Elmore, and prospered. He opened a shoe store and secured a good run of trade.

Socially he was also a success, and made many friends. And he accomplished the wish of his heart. He met Miss Annabel Adams, and became more and more captivated by her charms.

At the end of a year the situation of Mr. Ralph Spencer was this: he had won the respect of the community, his shoe store was flourishing, and he and Annabel were engaged to be married in two weeks. Mr. Adams, the typical, plodding, country banker, approved of Spencer. Annabel's pride in him almost equaled her affection. He was as much at home in the family of Mr. Adams and that of Annabel's married sister as if he were already a member.

One day Jimmy sat down in his room and wrote this letter, which he mailed to the safe address of one of his old friends in St. Louis:

Dear Old Pal:

I want you to be at Sullivan's place, in Little Rock, next Wednesday night, at nine o'clock. I want you to wind up some little matters for me. And, also, I want to make you a present of my kit of tools. I know you'll be glad to get them— you couldn't duplicate the lot for a thousand dollars. Say, Billy, I've quit the old business—a

Literature in Context

Language Connection

Allusions O. Henry uses an **allusion** to explain Jimmy Valentine's transformation by love. An allusion is a reference to a person, place, or thing in another artistic work. The allusion here is to the phoenix, a mythical bird. It was believed that every 500 or so years, the phoenix, which resembled an eagle, would build a nest of wood. The nest would be consumed by flames and a new phoenix would emerge. The ashes of the former phoenix would be taken to the altar of the sun god by the new phoenix.

Connect to the Literature

If Ralph Spencer is the phoenix, what parts of Jimmy's personality are the ashes?

year ago. I've got a nice store. I'm making an honest living, and I'm going to marry the finest girl on earth two weeks from now. It's the only life, Billy—the straight one. I wouldn't touch a dollar of another man's money now for a million. After I get married I'm going to sell out and go West, where there won't be so much danger of having old scores brought up against me. I tell you, Billy, she's an angel. She believes in me; and I wouldn't do another crooked thing for the whole world. Be sure to be at Sully's, for I must see you. I'll bring along the tools with me.

  Your old friend,
  Jimmy.

On the Monday night after Jimmy wrote this letter, Ben Price jogged <u>unobtrusively</u> into Elmore in a livery buggy. He lounged about town in his quiet way until he found out what he wanted to know. From the drugstore across the street from Spencer's shoe store he got a good look at Ralph D. Spencer.

"Going to marry the banker's daughter are you, Jimmy?" said Ben to himself, softly. "Well, I don't know!"

The next morning Jimmy took breakfast at the Adamses. He was going to Little Rock that day to order his wedding suit and buy something nice for Annabel. That would be the first time he had left town since he came to Elmore. It had been more than a year now since those last professional "jobs," and he thought he could safely venture out.

After breakfast quite a family party went downtown together—Mr. Adams, Annabel, Jimmy, and Annabel's married sister with her two little girls, aged five and nine. They came by the hotel where Jimmy still boarded, and he ran up to his room and brought along his suitcase. Then they went on to the bank. There stood Jimmy's horse and buggy and Dolph Gibson, who was going to drive him over to the railroad station.

All went inside the high, carved oak railings into the banking-room—Jimmy included, for Mr. Adams's future son-in-law was welcome anywhere. The clerks were pleased to be greeted by the goodlooking, agreeable young man who was going to marry Miss Annabel. Jimmy set his suitcase down. Annabel, whose heart was bubbling with happiness and lively youth, put on Jimmy's hat, and picked up the suitcase. "Wouldn't I make a nice drummer?"[10] said Annabel. "My! Ralph, how heavy it is! Feels like it was full of gold bricks."

---

10. **drummer** *n.* traveling salesman.

Reading Skill
Make Predictions
What clues support a prediction that Jimmy will become a law-abiding citizen?

Vocabulary Builder
unobtrusively (un′ əb trōō′ siv lē) *adv.* without calling attention to oneself

Literary Analysis
Plot What events increase the tension of the conflict between Ralph and Jimmy?

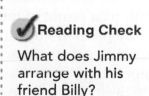
Reading Check
What does Jimmy arrange with his friend Billy?

"Lot of nickel-plated shoehorns in there," said Jimmy, coolly, "that I'm going to return. Thought I'd save express charges by taking them up. I'm getting awfully economical."

The Elmore Bank had just put in a new safe and vault. Mr. Adams was very proud of it, and insisted on an inspection by everyone. The vault was a small one, but it had a new, patented door. It fastened with three solid steel bolts thrown simultaneously with a single handle, and had a time lock. Mr. Adams beamingly explained its workings to Mr. Spencer, who showed a courteous but not too intelligent interest. The two children, May and Agatha, were delighted by the shining metal and funny clock and knobs.

While they were thus engaged Ben Price sauntered in and leaned on his elbow, looking casually inside between the railings. He told the teller that he didn't want anything; he was just waiting for a man he knew.

▲ **Critical Viewing** What would make this safe hard to open without knowing the combination? **[Analyze]**

Literary Analysis Plot Why is this part of the story the moment of greatest tension?

Suddenly there was a scream or two from the women, and a commotion. Unperceived by the elders, May, the nine-year-old girl, in a spirit of play, had shut Agatha in the vault. She had then shot the bolts and turned the knob of the combination as she had seen Mr. Adams do.

The old banker sprang to the handle and tugged at it for a moment. "The door can't be opened," he groaned. "The clock hasn't been wound nor the combination set."

Agatha's mother screamed again, hysterically.

"Hush!" said Mr. Adams, raising his trembling hand. "All be quiet for a moment. Agatha!" he called as loudly as he could. "Listen to me." During the following silence they could just hear the faint sound of the child wildly shrieking in the dark vault in a panic of terror.

"My precious darling!" wailed the mother. "She will die of fright! Open the door! Oh, break it open! Can't you men do something?"

"There isn't a man nearer than Little Rock who can open that door," said Mr. Adams, in a shaky voice. "My God!

Spencer, what shall we do? That child—she can't stand it long in there. There isn't enough air, and, besides, she'll go into convulsions from fright."

Agatha's mother, frantic now, beat the door of the vault with her hands. Somebody wildly suggested dynamite. Annabel turned to Jimmy, her large eyes full of <u>anguish</u>, but not yet despairing. To a woman nothing seems quite impossible to the powers of the man she worships.

"Can't you do something, Ralph—*try*, won't you?"

He looked at her with a queer, soft smile on his lips and in his keen eyes.

"Annabel," he said, "give me that rose you are wearing, will you?"

Hardly believing that she heard him aright, she unpinned the bud from the bosom of her dress, and placed it in his hand. Jimmy stuffed it into his vest pocket, threw off his coat and pulled up his shirt sleeves. With that act Ralph D. Spencer passed away and Jimmy Valentine took his place.

"Get away from the door, all of you," he commanded, shortly.

He set his suitcase on the table, and opened it out flat. From that time on he seemed to be unconscious of the presence of anyone else. He laid out the shining, queer implements swiftly and orderly, whistling softly to himself as he always did when at work. In a deep silence and immovable, the others watched him as if under a spell.

In a minute Jimmy's pet drill was biting smoothly into the steel door. In ten minutes—breaking his own burglarious record—he threw back the bolts and opened the door.

Agatha, almost collapsed, but safe, was gathered into her mother's arms.

Jimmy Valentine put on his coat, and walked outside the railings toward the front door. As he went he thought he heard a far-away voice that he once knew call "Ralph!" But he never hesitated.

At the door a big man stood somewhat in his way.

"Hello, Ben!" said Jimmy, still with his strange smile. "Got around at last, have you? Well, let's go. I don't know that it makes much difference, now."

And then Ben Price acted rather strangely.

"Guess you're mistaken, Mr. Spencer," he said. "Don't believe I recognize you. Your buggy's waiting for you, ain't it?"

And Ben Price turned and strolled down the street.

Vocabulary Builder
anguish (aŋ´gwish) *n.* great suffering from worry

Reading Skill
Make Predictions
Based on what you know about Jimmy, what do you think he will do next? Explain.

Literary Analysis
Plot In what way is the resolution, or outcome, of the story surprising?

Apply the Skills

A Retrieved Reformation

Thinking About the Selection

1. **Respond:** Would you have done what Ben Price did? Explain.
2. **(a) Recall:** Whom does Valentine see when he gets off the train in Elmore? **(b) Deduce:** How does this event cause him to have a change of heart? **(c) Support:** Find at least two details in the story that prove Valentine has really changed.
3. **Analyze:** Make a three-column chart to analyze the story's ending.
   - Column 1: Write Ben Price's words to Jimmy.
   - Column 2: Explain what Price means.
   - Column 3: Explain whether you think Price does the right thing.
4. **Make a Judgment:** Is it possible for people like Jimmy to reform themselves? Why or why not?

Reading Skill

5. **(a)** List two **predictions** that you made as you read "A Retrieved Reformation." **(b)** What **support** did you have for each prediction?
6. **(a)** What support can you find in the story for a prediction that Ben Price will arrest Jimmy? **(b)** Why would the author include details that support predictions of different outcomes?

Literary Analysis

7. What is the **conflict** between Price and Valentine?
8. Complete a **plot** chart like the one shown.

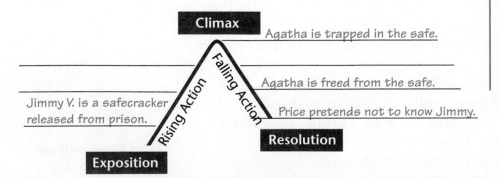

Climax

Agatha is trapped in the safe.

Rising Action

Falling Action

Agatha is freed from the safe.

Jimmy V. is a safecracker released from prison.

Price pretends not to know Jimmy.

Resolution

Exposition

9. What role does Ben Price play in determining the **resolution** of the story?

Story at a Glance
After he is released from prison, a safe-cracker falls in love and decides to "go straight."

Assessment
For: Self-test
Visit: www.PHSchool.com
Web Code: ena-6103

Prediction: an informed guess about what will happen in a story

Plot: the sequence of related events in a story, including *exposition, conflict, rising action, climax, falling action,* and *resolution*

Vocabulary Builder

Practice For each item, write a sentence that uses a vocabulary word from the list for "A Retrieved Reformation," on page 26.

1. Describe how someone might enter a room unnoticed.
2. Tell how a person would feel after losing a beloved pet.
3. Describe a person who always does the right thing.
4. Explain why convicted criminals are sent to jail.

Writing

Write a **new ending** to the story, telling what might have happened to Valentine and Annabel if Ben Price had not decided to let Valentine go.
- Write the new ending as if you were the story's narrator and knew what all the characters were thinking and feeling.
- Make sure your dialogue matches each character's voice and personality.

For *Grammar, Vocabulary,* and *Assessment,* see **Build Language Skills,** pages 50–51.

Extend Your Learning

Listening and Speaking Write and perform a **radio broadcast** of Valentine's rescue of Agatha from the safe.
- Use precise action verbs—such as *shouting* and *crying*—to describe the atmosphere surrounding the safe.
- Deliver your broadcast, varying the tone and pacing to convey changing emotions: tension, surprise, relief, and happiness.

Research and Technology Give an **oral report** about the life and works of O. Henry. Describe the influences that O. Henry's life had on his settings and characters, and explain why he was so successful as a writer. Use Internet search engines to locate information. In your search, insert quotation marks around the name *O. Henry* to locate the author's full name. If you find a good site, check it for links to other useful sites.

Short Story

Background

Down Syndrome In "Raymond's Run," the author implies that the narrator's brother has Down syndrome. People with Down syndrome develop more slowly, physically and mentally, than other people. Still, focusing on and developing a special talent can help people with disabilities achieve their fullest potential.

Connecting to the Literature

Reading/Writing Connection In this story, the narrator tries to protect her brother from being teased while she struggles to achieve respect for herself. Connect to the story by describing two ways you earn respect and two ways you show respect. Use at least three of the following words: *obtain, acquire, demonstrate, signify.*

Review

For **Reading Skill, Literary Analysis,** and **Vocabulary Builder,** see page 26.

Meet the Author

Toni Cade **Bambara** (1939–1995)

During her childhood, Toni Cade Bambara learned that growing up in New York City could be tough but rewarding. She loved the energy and rhythm of city life, the lively talk of the streets. Her gift as a writer was to capture the language and dreams of real people, especially young people, struggling to be themselves.

A Mother's Influence Bambara always gave her mother credit for inspiring her to write. "She gave me permission to wonder, to . . . dawdle, to daydream," the author once said.

Fast Facts

▶ Bambara published her first short story as a twenty-year-old student at Queens College in New York City.

▶ The short story was Bambara's favorite form because it "makes a modest appeal for attention, slips up on your blind side and wrassles you to the mat before you know what's grabbed you."

Go Online **Author Link**

For: More about the author
Visit: www.PHSchool.com
Web Code: ene-9103

Raymond's Run

Toni Cade Bambara

I don't have much work to do around the house like some girls. My mother does that. And I don't have to earn my pocket money by hustling; George runs errands for the big boys and sells Christmas cards. And anything else that's got to get done, my father does. All I have to do in life is mind my brother Raymond, which is enough.

Sometimes I slip and say my little brother Raymond. But as any fool can see he's much bigger and he's older too. But a lot of people call him my little brother cause he needs looking after cause he's not quite right. And a lot of smart mouths got lots to say about that too, especially when George was minding him. But now, if anybody has anything to say to Raymond, anything to say about his big head, they have to come by me. And I don't play the dozens[1] or believe in standing around with somebody in my face doing a lot of talking. I much rather just knock you down and take my chances even if I am a little girl with skinny arms and a squeaky voice, which is how I got the name Squeaky. And if things get too rough, I run. And as anybody can tell you, I'm the fastest thing on two feet.

There is no track meet that I don't win the first-place medal. I used to win the twenty-yard dash when I was a little kid in kindergarten. Nowadays, it's the fifty-yard dash. And tomorrow I'm subject to run the quarter-mile relay all by myself and come in first, second, and third. The big kids call me Mercury[2] cause I'm the swiftest thing in the neighborhood. Everybody knows that—except two people who know better, my father and me.

Reading Skill
Make Predictions
In the first two paragraphs, what clues help you predict how Squeaky will react to a challenge?

Reading Check

What is Squeaky's special talent?

---

1. **the dozens** game in which the players insult one another; the first to show anger loses.
2. **Mercury** in Roman mythology, the messenger of the gods, known for great speed.

He can beat me to Amsterdam Avenue with me having a two fire-hydrant headstart and him running with his hands in his pockets and whistling. But that's private information. Cause can you imagine some thirty-five-year-old man stuffing himself into PAL[3] shorts to race little kids? So as far as everyone's concerned, I'm the fastest and that goes for Gretchen, too, who has put out the tale that she is going to win the first-place medal this year. Ridiculous. In the second place, she's got short legs. In the third place, she's got freckles. In the first place, no one can beat me and that's all there is to it.

I'm standing on the corner admiring the weather and about to take a stroll down Broadway so I can practice my breathing exercises, and I've got Raymond walking on the inside close to the buildings, cause he's subject to fits of fantasy and starts thinking he's a circus performer and that the curb is a tightrope strung high in the air. And sometimes after a rain he likes to step down off his tightrope right into the gutter and slosh around getting his shoes and cuffs wet. Or sometimes if you don't watch him he'll dash across traffic to the island in the middle of Broadway and give the pigeons a fit. Then I have to go behind him apologizing to all the old people sitting around trying to get some sun and getting all upset with the pigeons fluttering around them, scattering their newspapers and upsetting the waxpaper lunches in their laps. So I keep Raymond on the inside of me, and he plays like he's driving a stage coach, which is O.K. by me so long as he doesn't run me over or interrupt my breathing exercises, which I have to do on account of I'm serious about my running, and I don't care who knows it.

Now some people like to act like things come easy to them, won't let on that they practice. Not me. I'll high prance down 34th Street like a rodeo pony to keep my knees strong even if it does get my mother uptight so that she walks ahead like she's not with me, don't know me, is all by herself on a shopping trip, and I am somebody else's crazy child.

Now you take Cynthia Procter for instance. She's just the opposite. If there's a test tomorrow, she'll say something like, "Oh, I guess I'll play handball this afternoon and watch television tonight," just to let you know she ain't thinking about the test. Or like last week when she won the spelling bee for the millionth time, "A good thing you got 'receive,' Squeaky, cause

---

3. **PAL** Police Athletic League.

Literary Analysis
Plot List four facts you learn about Squeaky in the exposition of this story.

Reading Skill
Make Predictions What details support a prediction that Squeaky will be tough to beat in a race?

I would have got it wrong. I completely forgot about the spelling bee." And she'll clutch the lace on her blouse like it was a narrow escape. Oh, brother.

But of course when I pass her house on my early morning trots around the block, she is practicing the scales on the piano over and over and over and over. Then in music class she always lets herself get bumped around so she falls accidently on purpose onto the piano stool and is so surprised to find herself sitting there that she decides just for fun to try out the ole keys and what do you know—Chopin's[4] waltzes just spring out of her fingertips and she's the most surprised thing in the world. A regular <u>prodigy</u>. I could kill people like that.

I stay up all night studying the words for the spelling bee. And you can see me any time of day practicing running. I never walk if I can trot, and shame on Raymond if he can't keep up. But of course he does, cause if he hangs back someone's liable to walk up to him and get smart, or take his allowance from him, or ask him where he got that great big pumpkin head. People are so stupid sometimes.

So I'm strolling down Broadway breathing out and breathing in on counts of seven, which is my lucky number, and here comes Gretchen and her sidekicks—Mary Louise who used to be a friend of mine when she first moved to Harlem

▲ **Critical Viewing**
What do you think these runners do to prepare themselves for a race? **[Speculate]**

Vocabulary Builder
prodigy (präd′ ə jē) *n.* a wonder; an unusually talented person

✔ **Reading Check**
Why does Squeaky dislike Cynthia Procter?

from Baltimore and got beat up by everybody till I took up for her on account of her mother and my mother used to sing in the same choir when they were young girls, but people ain't grateful, so now she hangs out with the new girl Gretchen and talks about me like a dog; and Rosie who is as fat as I am skinny and has a big mouth where Raymond is concerned and is too stupid to know that there is not a big deal of difference between herself and Raymond and that she can't afford to throw stones. So they are steady coming up Broadway and I see right away that it's going to be one of those Dodge City[5] scenes cause the street ain't that big and they're close to the buildings just as we are. First I think I'll step into the candy store and look over the new comics and let them pass. But that's chicken and I've got a <u>reputation</u> to consider. So then I think I'll just walk straight on through them or even over them if necessary. But as they get to me, they slow down. I'm ready to fight, cause like I said I don't feature a whole lot of chit-chat, I much prefer to just knock you down right from the jump and save everybody a lotta precious time.

"You signing up for the May Day races?" smiles Mary Louise, only it's not a smile at all.

A dumb question like that doesn't deserve an answer. Besides, there's just me and Gretchen standing there really, so no use wasting my breath talking to shadows.

"I don't think you're going to win this time," says Rosie, trying to signify with her hands on her hips all salty, completely forgetting that I have whupped her many times for less salt than that.

"I always win cause I'm the best," I say straight at Gretchen who is, as far as I'm concerned, the only one talking in this ventriloquist-dummy routine.[6]

Gretchen smiles, but it's not a smile, and I'm thinking that girls never really smile at each other because they don't know how and don't want to know how and there's probably no one to teach us how cause grown-up girls don't know either. Then they all look at Raymond who has just brought his mule team to a standstill. And they're about to see what trouble they can get into through him.

"What grade you in now, Raymond?"

Vocabulary Builder
reputation (rep´ yoo tā´ shən) *n.* widely-held opinion about a person, whether good or bad

Reading Skill
Make Predictions
What do you think Squeaky will do if the girls tease Raymond? What details in the story support your prediction?

---

5. **Dodge City** location of the television program *Gunsmoke,* which often presented a gunfight between the sheriff and an outlaw.
6. **ventriloquist** (ven tril´ ə kwist)-**dummy routine** a comedy act in which the performer speaks through a puppet called a "dummy."

"You got anything to say to my brother, you say it to me, Mary Louise Williams of Raggedy Town, Baltimore."

"What are you, his mother?" sasses Rosie.

"That's right, Fatso. And the next word out of anybody and I'll be *their* mother too." So they just stand there and Gretchen shifts from one leg to the other and so do they. Then Gretchen puts her hands on her hips and is about to say something with her freckle-face self but doesn't. Then she walks around me looking me up and down but keeps walking up Broadway, and her sidekicks follow her. So me and Raymond smile at each other and he says, "Gidyap" to his team and I continue with my breathing exercises, strolling down Broadway toward the ice man on 145th with not a care in the world cause I am Miss Quicksilver herself.

I take my time getting to the park on May Day because the track meet is the last thing on the program. The biggest thing on the program is the May Pole dancing, which I can do without, thank you, even if my mother thinks it's a shame I don't take part and act like a girl for a change. You'd think my mother'd be grateful not to have to make me a white organdy dress with a big satin sash and buy me new white baby-doll shoes that can't be taken out of the box till the big day. You'd think she'd be glad her daughter ain't out there prancing around a May Pole getting the new clothes all dirty and sweaty and trying to act like a fairy or a flower or whatever you're supposed to be when you should be trying to be yourself, whatever that is, which is, as far as I am concerned, a poor black girl who really can't afford to buy shoes and a new dress you only wear once a lifetime cause it won't fit next year.

I was once a strawberry in a Hansel and Gretel pageant when I was in nursery school and didn't have no better sense than to dance on tiptoe with my arms in a circle over my head doing umbrella steps and being a perfect fool just so my mother and father could come dressed up and clap. You'd think they'd know better than to encourage that kind of nonsense. I am not a strawberry. I do not dance on my toes. I run. That is what I am all about. So I always come late to the May Day program, just in time to get my number pinned on and lay in the grass till they announce the fifty-yard dash.

I put Raymond in the little swings, which is a tight squeeze this year and will be impossible next year. Then I look around for Mr. Pearson, who pins the numbers on. I'm really looking

Literary Analysis
Plot What clues indicate that Gretchen is Squeaky's main rival in this conflict?

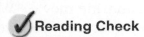

Reading Check

What would Squeaky's mother prefer that Squeaky do on May Day?

for Gretchen if you want to know the truth, but she's not around. The park is jam-packed. Parents in hats and corsages and breast-pocket handkerchiefs peeking up. Kids in white dresses and light-blue suits. The parkees unfolding chairs and chasing the rowdy kids from Lenox as if they had no right to be there. The big guys with their caps on backwards, leaning against the fence swirling the basketballs on the tips of their fingers, waiting for all these crazy people to clear out the park so they can play. Most of the kids in my class are carrying bass drums and glockenspiels[7] and flutes. You'd think they'd put in a few bongos or something for real like that.

Then here comes Mr. Pearson with his clipboard and his cards and pencils and whistles and safety pins and fifty million other things he's always dropping all over the place with his clumsy self. He sticks out in a crowd because he's on stilts. We used to call him Jack and the Beanstalk to get him mad. But I'm the only one that can outrun him and get away, and I'm too grown for that silliness now.

"Well, Squeaky," he says, checking my name off the list and handing me number seven and two pins. And I'm thinking he's got no right to call me Squeaky, if I can't call him Beanstalk.

"Hazel Elizabeth Deborah Parker," I correct him and tell him to write it down on his board.

"Well, Hazel Elizabeth Deborah Parker, going to give someone else a break this year?" I squint at him real hard to see if he is seriously thinking I should lose the race on purpose just to give someone else a break. "Only six girls running this time," he continues, shaking his head sadly like it's my fault all of New York didn't turn out in sneakers. "That new girl should give you a run for your money." He looks around the park for Gretchen like a periscope[8] in a submarine movie. "Wouldn't it be a nice gesture if you were . . . to ahhh . . ."

▼ Critical Viewing
How does this photograph show that the start of a race is the moment of greatest tension and concentration? [Analyze]

---

7. **glockenspiels** (gläk′ ən spēlz) *n.* musical instruments with flat metal bars that make bell-like tones when struck with small hammers.
8. **periscope** (per′ ə skōp′) *n.* tube on a submarine that raises and lowers to show objects on the water's surface.

I give him such a look he couldn't finish putting that idea into words. Grownups got a lot of nerve sometimes. I pin number seven to myself and stomp away, I'm so burnt. And I go straight for the track and stretch out on the grass while the band winds up with "Oh, the Monkey Wrapped His Tail Around the Flag Pole," which my teacher calls by some other name. The man on the loudspeaker is calling everyone over to the track and I'm on my back looking at the sky, trying to pretend I'm in the country, but I can't, because even grass in the city feels hard as sidewalk, and there's just no pretending you are anywhere but in a "concrete jungle" as my grandfather says.

The twenty-yard dash takes all of two minutes cause most of the little kids don't know no better than to run off the track or run the wrong way or run smack into the fence and fall down and cry. One little kid, though, has got the good sense to run straight for the white ribbon up ahead, so he wins. Then the second-graders line up for the thirty-yard dash and I don't even bother to turn my head to watch cause Raphael Perez always wins. He wins before he even begins by psyching the runners, telling them they're going to trip on their shoe-laces and fall on their faces or lose their shorts or something, which he doesn't really have to do since he is very fast, almost as fast as I am. After that is the forty-yard dash which I use to run when I was in first grade. Raymond is hollering from the swings cause he knows I'm about to do my thing cause the man on the loudspeaker has just announced the fifty-yard dash, although he might just as well be giving a recipe for angel food cake cause you can hardly make out what he's say-ing for the static. I get up and slip off my sweat pants and then I see Gretchen standing at the starting line, kicking her legs out like a pro. Then as I get into place I see that ole Ray-mond is on line on the other side of the fence, bending down with his fingers on the ground just like he knew what he was doing. I was going to yell at him but then I didn't. It burns up your energy to holler.

Every time, just before I take off in a race, I always feel like I'm in a dream, the kind of dream you have when you're sick with fever and feel all hot and weightless. I dream I'm flying over a sandy beach in the early morning sun, kissing the leaves of the trees as I fly by. And there's always the smell of apples, just like in the country when I was little and used to

**Reading Skill
Make Predictions**
What do you predict will be the outcome of the conflict between Gretchen and Squeaky?

Reading Check

What is Raymond doing while Squeaky runs the race?

think I was a choo-choo train, running through the fields of corn and chugging up the hill to the orchard. And all the time I'm dreaming this, I get lighter and lighter until I'm flying over the beach again, getting blown through the sky like a feather that weighs nothing at all. But once I spread my fingers in the dirt and crouch over the Get on Your Mark, the dream goes and I am solid again and am telling myself, Squeaky you must win, you must win, you are the fastest thing in the world, you can even beat your father up Amsterdam if you really try. And then I feel my weight coming back just behind my knees then down to my feet then into the earth and the pistol shot explodes in my blood and I am off and weightless again, flying past the other runners, my arms pumping up and down and the whole world is quiet except for the crunch as I zoom over the gravel in the track. I glance to my left and there is no one. To the right a blurred Gretchen, who's got her chin jutting out as if it would win the race all by itself. And on the other side of the fence is Raymond with his arms down to his side and the palms tucked up behind him, running in his very own style, and it's the first time I ever saw that and I almost stop to watch my brother Raymond on his first run. But the white ribbon is bouncing toward me and I tear past it, racing into the distance till my feet with a mind of their own start digging up footfuls of dirt and brake me short. Then all the kids standing on the side pile on me, banging me on the back and slapping my head with their May Day programs, for I have won again and everybody on 151st Street can walk tall for another year.

"In first place . . ." the man on the loudspeaker is clear as a bell now. But then he pauses and the loudspeaker starts to whine. Then static. And I lean down to catch my breath and here comes Gretchen walking back, for she's overshot the finish line too, huffing and puffing with her hands on her hips taking it slow, breathing in steady time like a real pro and I sort of like her a little for the first time. "In first place . . ." and then three or four voices get all mixed up on the loudspeaker and I dig my sneaker into the grass and stare at Gretchen who's staring back, we both wondering just who did win. I can hear old Beanstalk arguing with the man on the loudspeaker and then a few others running their mouths about what the stopwatches say. Then I hear Raymond yanking at the fence to call me and I wave to shush him, but he keeps rattling the

Reading Skill Predicting Who do you predict will win the race? Why?

Literary Analysis Plot Why is this part of the story the moment of greatest tension?

fence like a gorilla in a cage like in them gorilla movies, but then like a dancer or something he starts climbing up nice and easy but very fast. And it occurs to me, watching how smoothly he climbs hand over hand and remembering how he looked running with his arms down to his side and with the wind pulling his mouth back and his teeth showing and all, it occurred to me that Raymond would make a very fine runner. Doesn't he always keep up with me on my trots? And he surely knows how to breathe in counts of seven cause he's always doing it at the dinner table, which drives my brother George up the wall. And I'm smiling to beat the band cause if I've lost this race, or if me and Gretchen tied, or even if I've won, I can always retire as a runner and begin a whole new career as a coach with Raymond as my champion. After all, with a little more study I can beat Cynthia and her phony self at the spelling bee. And if I bugged my mother, I could get piano lessons and become a star. And I have a big rep as the baddest thing around. And I've got a roomful of ribbons and medals and awards. But what has Raymond got to call his own?

So I stand there with my new plans, laughing out loud by this time as Raymond jumps down from the fence and runs over with his teeth showing and his arms down to the side, which no one before him has quite mastered as a running style. And by the time he comes over I'm jumping up and down so glad to see him—my brother Raymond, a great runner in the family tradition. But of course everyone thinks I'm jumping up and down because the men on the loudspeaker have finally gotten themselves together and compared notes and are announcing "In first place—Miss Hazel Elizabeth Deborah Parker." (Dig that.) "In second place—Miss Gretchen P. Lewis." And I look over at Gretchen wondering what the "P" stands for. And I smile. Cause she's good, no doubt about it. Maybe she'd like to help me coach Raymond; she obviously is serious about running, as any fool can see. And she nods to congratulate me and then she smiles. And I smile. We stand there with this big smile of respect between us. It's about as real a smile as girls can do for each other, considering we don't practice real smiling every day, you know, cause maybe we too busy being flowers or fairies or strawberries instead of something honest and worthy of respect . . . you know . . . like being people.

Literary Analysis
Plot How does Raymond influence the story's conflict at this point?

Reading Skill
Make Predictions Was the outcome of the story difficult to predict? Explain.

Apply the Skills

Raymond's Run

Thinking About the Selection

1. **Respond:** What aspects of Squeaky's personality would make you want—or not want—to be her friend?
2. **(a) Recall:** Describe the relationship between Raymond and Squeaky. **(b) Analyze:** How does Squeaky feel about taking care of Raymond?
3. **(a) Recall:** What does Raymond do during the race?
   (b) Connect: How do Raymond's actions change Squeaky's view of him? **(c) Deduce:** After seeing Raymond, why does Squeaky lose interest in the official outcome of the race?
4. **Analyze:** Make a three-column chart to analyze the story's ending.
   - Column 1: Write the last sentence of the story.
   - Column 2: Explain what Squeaky's statement means.
   - Column 3: Explain how Squeaky's actions illustrate the idea she expresses.

Reading Skill

5. **(a)** List two **predictions** you made as you read "Raymond's Run." **(b)** What **support** did you have for each prediction?
6. **(a)** What support can you find in the story for a prediction that Gretchen will win the race? **(b)** Why would the author include details that support predictions of different outcomes?

Literary Analysis

7. What is the **conflict** between Squeaky and Gretchen?
8. Complete a **plot** chart like the one shown.

QuickReview

Story at a Glance
Winning races is Squeaky's goal until she decides that something else is more important.

Go Online
Assessment
For: Self-test
Visit: www.PHSchool.com
Web Code: ena-6104

Prediction: an informed guess about what will happen in a story

Plot: the sequence of related events in a story, including *exposition, conflict, rising action, climax, falling action,* and *resolution*

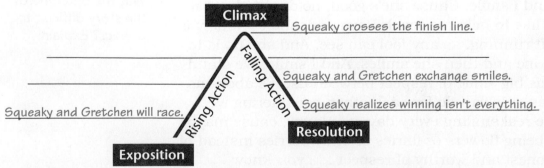

Climax — Squeaky crosses the finish line.

Falling Action — Squeaky and Gretchen exchange smiles.

Squeaky realizes winning isn't everything.

Squeaky and Gretchen will race.

Rising Action

Exposition

Resolution

9. How does Raymond's run contribute to the **resolution** of the story?

Vocabulary Builder

Practice For each item, write a sentence that uses a vocabulary word from the "Raymond's Run" vocabulary list on page 26.

1. Tell about a five-year-old who can play both the piano and the violin.

2. Describe the importance of protecting your good name.

Writing

Imagine how the ending of the story would have been different if Gretchen had won the race. Write a **new ending** to show how Squeaky might react to losing.

- Write the new ending the way Squeaky would tell it. Use the pronouns *I, me,* and *my* to describe her thoughts, feelings, and actions after losing.
- Make sure your voice and style match Squeaky's personality.

For *Grammar, Vocabulary,* and *Assessment,* see **Build Language Skills,** pages 50–51.

Extend Your Learning

Listening and Speaking Write and perform a **radio broadcast** of the race in the story.

- Use precise action verbs—such as *flying, streaking,* and *pounding*—to describe the motion of the runners.
- When delivering the broadcast, vary the tone and pace of your voice to convey the excitement of the race and the tension of its ending.

Research and Technology Use the Internet to research the Special Olympics, and then deliver an **oral report** on the games. In your report, describe the history of the Special Olympics and explain why they are important.

- Use a search engine to find appropriate sites. Enclose the words *Special Olympics* in quotation marks to search both words at once.
- When you find a good site, check to see whether it has links to other useful sites.

Build Language Skills

Vocabulary Skill

Prefixes The **prefix** *pre-* means "before" or "in advance." In the word *predict*, it is joined to the Latin root *-dict-*, meaning "tell." When you *predict* events, you tell about them before they happen.

➤ **Example:** When the hero of the adventure story found a map, I *predicted* that he would begin searching for hidden treasure.

Sometimes, *pre-* will be added to the front of a word you already know—like *prepay*. Even in words in which you do not recognize the rest of the word, you can use the prefix *pre-* to help you understand and remember the meaning of the word.

Practice Read each sentence. Then, explain how the meaning of *before* or *in advance* is part of the meaning of each italicized word.

1. You can *preview* the movie by going to the Web site.
2. We *predict* that the characters will go on a journey.
3. You can help me *prepare* for the party.
4. We listened to the speeches that *preceded* the game.
5. *Previously,* we had held a meeting about the problem.

MorePractice

For more practice with Common and Proper Nouns, see the Grammar Handbook, p. R31.

Grammar Lesson

Common and Proper Nouns Common nouns name any person, place, thing, or idea. **Proper nouns** name a particular person, place, thing, or idea. Always capitalize proper nouns. Capitalize common nouns only when they begin a sentence.

Common Nouns	Proper Nouns
boy	Jacob
day	Thursday
school	Primrose School

Practice Underline all the nouns. Write *C* or *P* above each noun to tell whether it is *common* or *proper.* Substitute common nouns for proper nouns and rewrite the sentence.

1. Jenna had spaghetti for lunch on Friday.
2. The teachers at Bishop School had a meeting.
3. My best friends are Biana and Ethan.
4. The children like the beach at North Lake.
5. Rosa Gomez is the mayor of Jamestown.

W͞G *Prentice Hall Writing and Grammar Connection: Chapter 14, Section 1.*

Reading: Support Predictions

Directions: *Read the selection. Then, answer the questions.*

Eric shifted the gears on his new ten-speed bike. He had saved his money for a whole year, and now he was finally riding it for the first time. As he cruised down the street, his friend Travis ran out of his house. Oh, no, thought Eric. He liked and trusted Travis, but Travis was always asking for favors. I am not going to give in today, Eric decided firmly.

"Wow! Cool bike!" Travis shouted. "Hey," he said, eyeing the bike hopefully. "Can I ask you something?"

1. What do you think Travis will do next?
   - **A** Steal the bike
   - **B** Ask to ride the bike
   - **C** Go back inside
   - **D** Ask to borrow Eric's baseball

2. What clue supports your prediction?
   - **A** Travis is untrustworthy and mean.
   - **B** Travis does not own a bike.
   - **C** Eric does not like Travis and wishes he would move.
   - **D** Travis likes the bike and always asks favors.

3. What do you think Eric will do next?
   - **A** let Travis ride his bike
   - **B** refuse to let Travis ride his bike
   - **C** ride away without answering Travis
   - **D** call the police

4. What clue supports your prediction?
   - **A** Eric likes Travis but is tired of doing favors.
   - **B** Eric dislikes Travis and does not trust him.
   - **C** Eric feels guilty about his bike.
   - **D** Eric has never met Travis before.

Timed Writing: Evaluation [Critical Stance]

Review "A Retrieved Reformation" or "Raymond's Run." Write a brief evaluation of the story's climax and ironic resolution. Give reasons why you did or did not find them exciting, surprising, and believable. Use examples from the story to support your opinion. **(20 minutes)**

 ## Writing Workshop: *Work in Progress*

Description
Starting with the Descriptive List in your portfolio, think about what you would tell an artist sketching the person you have chosen. Identify and note three physical characteristics of this person, then list six words you would use to describe the personality of the person you have chosen. Put this work in your writing portfolio.

Build Skills
Gentleman of Río en Medio •
Cub Pilot on the Mississippi

These skills will help you become a better reader. Practice them with either "Gentleman of Río en Medio" (p. 54) or "Cub Pilot on the Mississippi" (p. 61).

Reading Skill

When you **make predictions,** use the details in what you read to make logical, informed guesses about what will happen later in a story. **Reading ahead to confirm or correct predictions** helps you remain focused on the connections between events. Follow these steps:

- As you read, look for details that suggest a certain outcome.
- Make a prediction about what will happen next.
- Use a chart like the one shown to record your prediction. Then, read ahead to see if you were right. Use new details to confirm or correct your original prediction.

> **Detail:** Character sees a fin in the water.
> **Prediction:** A shark will attack.

Read Ahead

> **New Details:** The fin turns out to belong to a dolphin.
> **Corrected Prediction:** The dolphin will help the character get to land.

Literary Analysis

Conflict is the struggle between two opposing forces.

- **External conflict** occurs when a character struggles against another character, natural forces, or some aspect of society.
- **Internal conflict** is a struggle between competing feelings, beliefs, needs, or desires within a single character. For example, a character might struggle with feelings of guilt.

In the **resolution** of a story, problems are worked out in a way that eliminates the conflict.

Vocabulary Builder

Gentleman of Río en Medio

- **innumerable** (i nōō′ mər ə bəl) *adj.* too many to be counted (p. 55) *There are innumerable stars in the desert sky.*

- **preliminary** (prē lim′ ə ner′ ē) *adj.* introductory; preparatory (p. 56) *The dinner began with a preliminary appetizer.*

- **descendants** (dē sen′ dənts) *n.* children, grandchildren, and continuing generations (p. 57) *The old man willed all of his possessions to his many descendants.*

Cub Pilot on the Mississippi

- **pretext** (prē′ tekst′) *n.* reason or motive used to hide one's real intentions (p. 64) *Tyler looked for a pretext for talking to Selena.*

- **judicious** (jōō dish′ əs) *adj.* showing sound judgment; wise and careful (p. 66) *A judicious student studies for a test.*

- **indulgent** (in dul′ jənt) *adj.* tolerant; not strict or critical (p. 68) *The indulgent mother quieted her crying child with a cookie.*

Background

New Mexico's Spanish Heritage New Mexico, the setting of this story, has a rich cultural heritage. The first Spanish colony in the area was established in 1598 in a region where Native Americans had lived for centuries. Over the next three hundred years, a patchwork of cultures was created with strong ties to both ancestral cultures. Today, in some remote villages, descendants of the first Spanish colonists still maintain a way of life that has remained largely unchanged since the sixteenth century.

Connecting to the Literature

Reading/Writing Connection In "Gentleman of Río en Medio," old customs conflict with new ways. Write some reasons why you think people sometimes struggle to maintain traditional ways instead of changing. Use at least three of the following words: *adapt, abandon, survive, challenge.*

Meet the Author

Juan A.A. **Sedillo** (1902–1982)

Born in New Mexico, Juan A.A. Sedillo was a descendant of early Spanish colonists of the Southwest. Sedillo was a man of many talents. In addition to being a writer and translator, Sedillo was a lawyer and judge who held various public positions. His varied life experiences and his exposure to the diverse cultures of New Mexico add a realistic depth to his stories.

The Story Behind the Story Although "Gentleman of Río en Medio" is a fictional story, it was inspired by a real legal case involving a conflict over a piece of property. Because Sedillo grew up among people of Spanish descent, he knew and understood their culture and beliefs. This understanding enabled him to turn an ordinary legal case into a memorable portrait of a person and a way of life.

Go Online
Author Link

For: More about the author
Visit: www.PHSchool.com
Web Code: cne-9104

GENTLEMAN OF RÍO EN MEDIO

Juan A. A. Sedillo

> Critical Viewing
Based on the title and on details in the picture, what kind of person do you think the main character of this story will be? [Predict]

The Sacristan of Trampas (detail), ca. 1915, Paul Burlin, Museum of Fine Arts, New Mexico

It took months of negotiation to come to an understanding with the old man. He was in no hurry. What he had the most of was time. He lived up in Río en Medio, (rē′ ō en mā dē ō) where his people had been for hundreds of years. He tilled the same land they had tilled. His house was small and wretched, but quaint. The little creek ran through his land. His orchard was gnarled and beautiful.

The day of the sale he came into the office. His coat was old, green and faded. I thought of Senator Catron,[1] who had been such a power with these people up there in the mountains. Perhaps it was one of his old Prince Alberts.[2] He also wore gloves. They were old and torn and his fingertips showed through them. He carried a cane, but it was only the skeleton of a worn-out umbrella. Behind him walked one of his innumerable kin—a dark young man with eyes like a gazelle.

The old man bowed to all of us in the room. Then he removed his hat and gloves, slowly and carefully. Chaplin[3] once did that in a picture, in a bank—he was the janitor. Then he handed his things to the boy, who stood obediently behind the old man's chair.

There was a great deal of conversation, about rain and about his family. He was very proud of his large family. Finally we got down to business. Yes, he would sell, as he had agreed, for twelve hundred dollars, in cash. We would buy, and the money was ready. "Don[4] Anselmo," I said to him in Spanish, "we have made a discovery. You remember that we sent that surveyor, that engineer, up there to survey your land so as to make the deed. Well, he finds that you own more than eight acres. He tells us that your land extends across the river and that you own almost twice as much as you thought." He didn't know that. "And now, Don Anselmo," I added, "these Americans are *buena gente*,[5] they are good people, and they are willing to pay you for the additional land as well, at the same rate per acre, so that instead of twelve hundred dollars you will get almost twice as much, and the money is here for you."

The old man hung his head for a moment in thought. Then he stood up and stared at me. "Friend," he said, "I do not like to have you speak to me in that manner." I kept still and let

1. **Senator Catron** Thomas Benton Catron, U.S. senator from New Mexico, 1912–1917.
2. **Prince Alberts** long, old-fashioned coats worn on formal occasions.
3. **Chaplin** Charlie Chaplin (1889–1977), actor and producer of silent films in the United States.
4. **Don** (Dän) Spanish title of respect, similar to *Sir* in English.
5. ***buena gente*** (bwā′ nä hen′ tä) Spanish for "good people."

Vocabulary Builder
innumerable (i nōō′ mər ə bəl) *adj.* too many to be counted

Reading Skill
Make Predictions
How do you predict Don Anselmo will react to the offer? On what do you base your prediction?

**Reading Check**

What disagreement are the narrator and Don Anselmo meeting to fix?

him have his say. "I know these Americans are good people, and that is why I have agreed to sell to them. But I do not care to be insulted. I have agreed to sell my house and land for twelve hundred dollars and that is the price."

I argued with him but it was useless. Finally he signed the deed and took the money but refused to take more than the amount agreed upon. Then he shook hands all around, put on his ragged gloves, took his stick and walked out with the boy behind him.

A month later my friends had moved into Río en Medio. They had replastered the old adobe house, pruned the trees, patched the fence, and moved in for the summer. One day they came back to the office to complain. The children of the village were overrunning their property. They came every day and played under the trees, built little play fences around them, and took blossoms. When they were spoken to they only laughed and talked back good-naturedly in Spanish.

I sent a messenger up to the mountains for Don Anselmo. It took a week to arrange another meeting. When he arrived he repeated his previous <u>preliminary</u> performance. He wore the same faded cutaway,[6] carried the same stick and was accompanied by the boy again. He shook hands all around, sat down with the boy behind his chair, and talked about the weather. Finally I broached the subject. "Don Anselmo, about the ranch you sold to these people. They are good people and want to be your friends and neighbors always. When you sold to them you signed a document, a deed, and in that deed you agreed to several things. One thing was that they were to have the complete possession of the property. Now, Don Anselmo, it seems that every day the children of the village overrun the orchard and spend most of their time there. We would like to know if you, as the most respected man in the village, could not stop them from doing so in order that these people may enjoy their new home more in peace."

Don Anselmo stood up. "We have all learned to love these Americans," he said, "because they are good people and good neighbors. I sold them my property because I knew they were good people, but I did not sell them the trees in the orchard."

This was bad. "Don Anselmo," I pleaded, "when one signs a deed and sells real property one sells also everything that

---

6. **cutaway** *n.* coat worn by men for formal daytime occasions; it is cut in the front and curves to long tails in the back.

Reading Skill
Make Predictions
Does Don Anselmo's reply confirm your prediction about his reaction? Why or why not?

Vocabulary Builder
preliminary (prē lim´ ə ner´ ē) *adj.* introductory; preparatory

Literary Analysis
Conflict What is the conflict identified here?

Springtime c. 1928–29, Victor Higgins. Private collection, photo courtesy of the Gerald Peters Gallery, Santa Fe, NM.

grows on the land, and those trees, every one of them, are on the land and inside the boundaries of what you sold."

"Yes, I admit that," he said. "You know," he added, "I am the oldest man in the village. Almost everyone there is my relative and all the children of Río en Medio are my *sobrinos* and *nietos*,[7] my descendants. Every time a child has been born in Río en Medio since I took possession of that house from my mother I have planted a tree for that child. The trees in that orchard are not mine, *Señor*, they belong to the children of the village. Every person in Río en Medio born since the railroad came to Santa Fe owns a tree in that orchard. I did not sell the trees because I could not. They are not mine."

There was nothing we could do. Legally we owned the trees but the old man had been so generous, refusing what amounted to a fortune for him. It took most of the following winter to buy the trees, individually, from the <u>descendants</u> of Don Anselmo in the valley of Río en Medio.

---

7. sobrinos (sō brē´ nōs) and **nietos** (nyā´ tōs) Spanish for "nephews" and "grandsons"; used here to include nieces and granddaughters as well.

▲ **Critical Viewing**
How closely does this picture match your mental image of Don Anselmo's land? Explain. **[Analyze]**

Vocabulary Builder
descendants (dē sen´ dənts) *n.* children, grandchildren, and continuing generations

Apply the Skills

Gentleman of Río en Medio

Thinking About the Selection

1. **Respond:** Were you surprised by Don Anselmo's responses in his two meetings with the narrator? Why or why not?
2. **(a) Recall:** Who is the narrator of this story? **(b) Recall:** What is the narrator's role? **(c) Analyze:** How does the narrator's behavior toward Don Anselmo affect the story's outcome?
3. **(a) Recall:** What does Don Anselmo discuss with the narrator before getting down to business? **(b) Infer:** What does the discussion tell you about Don Anselmo's personality? **(c) Connect:** What other details in the story reveal Don Anselmo's personality?
4. **Compare and Contrast:** Compare and contrast the attitudes of Don Anselmo and the Americans toward money.
5. **(a) Interpret:** Explain Don Anselmo's reasoning for not selling the trees. **(b) Generalize:** Why is his statement important to the meaning of the story?

Reading Skill

6. **(a)** What **predictions** did you make about the outcome of the story? **(b)** On which clues did you base your predictions?
7. Did you correct any of your predictions as you read the story? Explain your response.

Literary Analysis

8. Describe the **conflict** in the story by completing a graphic organizer like the one shown.

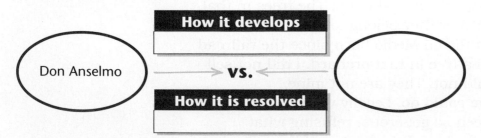

Don Anselmo — **vs.** —

How it develops

How it is resolved

9. Is the conflict *internal* or *external?* Support your answer with details from the story.

QuickReview

Story at a Glance
Don Anselmo agrees to sell his land, but the buyers become annoyed when the village children continue to play in the orchard.

Go Online
Assessment
For: Self-test
Visit: www.PHSchool.com
Web Code: ena-6105

Prediction: an informed guess about what will happen in a story

Conflict: the struggle between two opposing forces

Vocabulary Builder

Practice For each item, explain why one of the three words is *not* a synonym, or word close in meaning, to the given word.

1. innumerable: **(a)** countless, **(b)** indescribable, **(c)** infinite
2. preliminary: **(a)** preparatory, **(b)** introductory, **(c)** inhospitable
3. descendant: **(a)** grandson, **(b)** friend, **(c)** offspring

Writing

As a resident of the village, write a **letter** to Don Anselmo thanking him for trying to secure the children's right to play in the orchard. Keep your audience in mind and use these tips:

- Review the story for facts about Don Anselmo. What is important to him? How does he feel about the children of the village?
- Keep the answers to these questions in mind, and use this information in your letter to Don Anselmo.

For *Grammar, Vocabulary,* and *Assessment,*
see **Build Language Skills,** pages 72-73.

Extend Your Learning

Listening and Speaking With a partner, present a **role play** of the story's conflict. One person should play Don Anselmo; and the other, the part of the narrator. Address these questions:

- What issues divide you?
- What common interests do you share?
- What solutions might be acceptable to everyone?

After your role play, decide with your partner which conflict-resolution strategies were most successful.

Research and Technology In a small group, gather information about how the Spanish influence may be seen today in the American Southwest. Look for information about art, architecture, music, and food. Then make a poster to use as a visual aid in a brief **oral presentation.** Everyone in the group should participate.

Autobiograpy

Background

Traveling by Steamboat In "Cub Pilot on the Mississippi," Mark Twain tells a true story about his days as a cub pilot, a young trainee learning to pilot a Mississippi steamboat. In the 1800s, steamboats carried goods and people on the wide, long Mississippi River. There were dangers, however. Fires broke out, boilers burst, hidden rocks and sandbars damaged ships, and steamboat crews struggled to negotiate ever-changing currents.

Connecting to the Literature

Reading/Writing Connection Twain gives an account of his cruel treatment by Pilot Brown, a master riverboat pilot. Write five sentences that tell how a person might react to being bullied or unfairly criticized. Use at least three of the following words: *eliminate, provoke, agitate, protest, confront.*

Review

For **Reading Skill**, **Literary Analysis**, and **Vocabulary**, see page 52.

Meet the Author

Mark **Twain** (1835–1910)

Growing up in Hannibal, Missouri, Mark Twain was enchanted by the nearby Mississippi River. Twain's real name was Samuel Langhorne Clemens, but he took his pen name from a riverman's call, "By the mark—twain," which means "the river is two fathoms [twelve feet] deep," a safe enough depth for a steamboat. His boyhood experiences on the Mississippi and his travels around the world strongly influenced his writing. He visited five continents and crossed the Atlantic Ocean twenty-nine times.

Fast Facts

▶ Twain was twenty-one years old when he became a cub pilot on a Mississippi steamboat.

▶ As he traveled around the United States, Twain held many jobs, including prospector, reporter, and public speaker.

 **Author Link**

For: More about the author
Visit: www.PHSchool.com
Web Code: ene-9105

Cub Pilot
on the Mississippi

Mark Twain

During the two or two and a half years of my apprenticeship[1] I served under many pilots, and had experience of many kinds of steamboatmen and many varieties of steamboats. I am to this day profiting somewhat by that experience; for in that brief, sharp schooling, I got personally and familiarly acquainted with about all the different types of human nature that are to be found in fiction, biography, or history.

The fact is daily borne in upon me that the average shore-employment requires as much as forty years to equip a man with this sort of an education. When I say I am still profiting by this thing, I do not mean that it has constituted me a judge of men—no, it has not done that, for judges of men are born, not made. My profit is various in kind and degree, but the feature of it which I value most is the zest which that early

---

1. apprenticeship (ə pren´ tis ship) *n.* time spent working for a master craftsperson in return for instruction in that craft.

▲ **Critical Viewing**
What clues does this picture give you about the time period of this narrative? **[Connect]**

✔ **Reading Check**

What kind of apprenticeship does Twain serve?

experience has given to my later reading. When I find a well-drawn character in fiction or biography I generally take a warm personal interest in him, for the reason that I have known him before—met him on the river.

The figure that comes before me oftenest, out of the shadows of that vanished time, is that of Brown, of the steamer *Pennsylvania.* He was a middle-aged, long, slim, bony, smooth-shaven, horsefaced, ignorant, stingy, malicious, snarling, fault-hunting, mote magnifying tyrant.[2] I early got the habit of coming on watch with dread at my heart. No matter how good a time I might have been having with the off-watch below, and no matter how high my spirits might be when I started aloft, my soul became lead in my body the moment I approached the pilothouse.

I still remember the first time I ever entered the presence of that man. The boat had backed out from St. Louis and was "straightening down." I ascended to the pilothouse in high feather, and very proud to be semiofficially a member of the executive family of so fast and famous a boat. Brown was at the wheel. I paused in the middle of the room, all fixed to make my bow, but Brown did not look around. I thought he took a furtive glance at me out of the corner of his eye, but as not even this notice was repeated, I judged I had been mistaken. By this time he was picking his way among some dangerous "breaks" abreast the woodyards; therefore it would not be proper to interrupt him; so I stepped softly to the high bench and took a seat.

There was silence for ten minutes; then my new boss turned and inspected me deliberately and painstakingly from head to heel for about—as it seemed to me—a quarter of an hour. After which he removed his countenance[3] and I saw it no more for some seconds; then it came around once more, and this question greeted me: "Are you Horace Bigsby's cub?"

"Yes, sir."

After this there was a pause and another inspection. Then: "What's your name?"

I told him. He repeated it after me. It was probably the only thing he ever forgot; for although I was with him many months he never addressed himself to me in any other way than "Here!" and then his command followed.

"Where was you born?"

**Literary Analysis
Conflict** What clues indicate that the main conflict will be between Twain and Brown?

**Reading Skill
Make Predictions**
What details support a prediction that Brown will treat Twain unfairly?

---

2. **mote magnifying tyrant** a cruel authority figure who exaggerates every tiny fault.
3. **countenance** (kount´ 'n əns) *n.* face.

"In Florida, Missouri."

A pause. Then: "Dern sight better stayed there!"

By means of a dozen or so of pretty direct questions, he pumped my family history out of me.

The leads[4] were going now in the first crossing. This interrupted the inquest. When the leads had been laid in he resumed:

"How long you been on the river?"

I told him. After a pause:

"Where'd you get them shoes?"

I gave him the information.

"Hold up your foot!"

▲ Critical Viewing
Put yourself in the place of this pilot. What challenges does the river pose? [Assess]

I did so. He stepped back, examined the shoe minutely and contemptuously, scratching his head thoughtfully, tilting his high sugarloaf hat well forward to facilitate the operation, then ejaculated, "Well, I'll be dod derned!" and returned to his wheel.

What occasion there was to be dod derned about it is a thing which is still as much of a mystery to me now as it was then. It must have been all of fifteen minutes—fifteen minutes of dull, homesick silence—before that long horse-face swung round upon me again—and then what a change! It was as red as fire, and every muscle in it was working. Now came this shriek: "Here! You going to set there all day?"

I lit in the middle of the floor, shot there by the electric suddenness of the surprise. As soon as I could get my voice I said apologetically: "I have had no orders, sir."

"You've had no *orders*! My, what a fine bird we are! We must have *orders*! Our father was a *gentleman*—and *we've* been to *school*. Yes, *we* are a gentleman, *too*, and got to have *orders*! Orders, is it? Orders is what you want! Dod dern my skin, *I'll* learn you to swell yourself up and blow around *here* about your dod-derned *orders*! G'way from the wheel!" (I had approached it without knowing it.)

I moved back a step or two and stood as in a dream, all my senses stupefied by this frantic assault.

Reading Check

How does Twain feel about Brown?

---

4. **leads** (ledz) *n.* weights that were lowered to test the depth of the river.

"What you standing there for? Take that ice-pitcher down to the texas-tender![5] Come, move along, and don't you be all day about it!"

The moment I got back to the pilothouse Brown said: "Here! What was you doing down there all this time?"

"I couldn't find the texas-tender; I had to go all the way to the pantry."

"Derned likely story! Fill up the stove."

I proceeded to do so. He watched me like a cat. Presently he shouted: "Put down that shovel! Derndest numskull I ever saw—ain't even got sense enough to load up a stove."

All through the watch this sort of thing went on. Yes, and the subsequent watches were much like it during a stretch of months. As I have said, I soon got the habit of coming on duty with dread. The moment I was in the presence, even in the darkest night, I could feel those yellow eyes upon me, and knew their owner was watching for a <u>pretext</u> to spit out some venom on me. Preliminarily he would say: "Here! Take the wheel."

Two minutes later: "*Where* in the nation you going to? Pull her down! pull her down!"

After another moment: "Say! You going to hold her all day? Let her go—meet her! meet her!"

Then he would jump from the bench, snatch the wheel from me, and meet her himself, pouring out wrath upon me all the time.

George Ritchie was the other pilot's cub. He was having good times now; for his boss, George Ealer, was as kind-hearted as Brown wasn't. Ritchie had steered for Brown the season before; consequently, he knew exactly how to entertain himself and plague me, all by the one operation. Whenever I took the wheel for a moment on Ealer's watch, Ritchie would sit back on the bench and play Brown, with continual ejaculations of "Snatch her! Snatch her! Derndest mudcat I ever saw!" "Here! Where are you going *now*? Going to run over that snag?" "Pull her *down*! Don't you hear me? Pull her *down*!" "There she goes! *Just* as I expected! I *told* you not to cramp that reef. G'way from the wheel!"

---

5. texas-tender the waiter in the officers' quarters. On Mississippi steamboats, rooms were named after the states. The officers' area, being the largest, was named after Texas, then the largest state.

Literature in Context

History Connection

Managing the Mississippi In the 1800s, steamboat travel on the Mississippi River was quite dangerous. Even though pilots memorized landmarks and watched the water closely, they sometimes ran into obstacles hidden under the water.

Then, Henry Shreve introduced the "snag puller." This boat used a heavy iron wedge to ram submerged trees, or "snags," then hoisted their trunks with machinery. By 1830, "Uncle Sam's Tooth Pullers" had cleared most of the river.

Connect to the Literature

How do the difficulties of navigating the river make Brown more likely to find fault with Twain?

Vocabulary Builder
pretext (prē´ tekst) *n.* reason or motive used to hide one's real intentions

So I always had a rough time of it, no matter whose watch it was; and sometimes it seemed to me that Ritchie's good-natured badgering was pretty nearly as aggravating as Brown's dead-earnest nagging.

I often wanted to kill Brown, but this would not answer. A cub had to take everything his boss gave, in the way of vigorous comment and criticism; and we all believed that there was a United States law making it a penitentiary offense to strike or threaten a pilot who was on duty.

However, I could *imagine* myself killing Brown; there was no law against that; and that was the thing I used always to do the moment I was abed. Instead of going over my river in my mind, as was my duty, I threw business aside for pleasure, and killed Brown. I killed Brown every night for months; not in old, stale, commonplace ways, but in new and picturesque ones—ways that were sometimes surprising for freshness of design and ghastliness of situation and environment.

Brown was *always* watching for a pretext to find fault; and if he could find no plausible pretext, he would invent one. He would scold you for shaving a shore, and for not shaving it; for hugging a bar, and for not hugging it; for "pulling down" when not invited, and for *not* pulling down when not invited; for firing up without orders, and *for* waiting for orders. In a word, it was his invariable rule to find fault with *everything* you did and another invariable rule of his was to throw all his remarks (to you) into the form of an insult.

One day we were approaching New Madrid, bound down and heavily laden. Brown was at one side of the wheel, steering; I was at the other, standing by to "pull down" or "shove up." He cast a furtive glance at me every now and then. I had long ago learned what that meant; viz., he was trying to invent a trap for me. I wondered what shape it was going to take. By and by he stepped back from the wheel and said in his usual snarly way:

"Here! See if you've got gumption enough to round her to."

This was simply *bound* to be a success; nothing could prevent it; for he had never allowed me to round the boat to before; consequently, no matter how I might do the thing, he could find free fault with it. He stood back there with his greedy eye on me, and the result was what might have been foreseen: I lost my head in a quarter of a minute, and didn't know what I was about; I started too early to bring the boat around, but detected a green gleam of joy in Brown's eye, and

Reading Skill
Make Predictions
Does Twain's description of his fantasies help you predict if he will actually kill Brown? Explain.

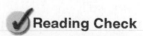

Reading Check

Why was Twain afraid to take any action against Brown?

corrected my mistake. I started around once more while too high up, but corrected myself again in time. I made other false moves, and still managed to save myself; but at last I grew so confused and anxious that I tumbled into the very worst blunder of all—I got too far *down* before beginning to fetch the boat around. Brown's chance was come.

His face turned red with passion; he made one bound, hurled me across the house with a sweep of his arm, spun the wheel down, and began to pour out a stream of vituperation[6] upon me which lasted till he was out of breath. In the course of this speech he called me all the different kinds of hard names he could think of, and once or twice I thought he was even going to swear—but he had never done that, and he didn't this time. "Dod dern" was the nearest he ventured to the luxury of swearing.

Two trips later I got into serious trouble. Brown was steering; I was "pulling down." My younger brother Henry appeared on the hurricane deck, and shouted to Brown to stop at some landing or other, a mile or so below. Brown gave no intimation[7] that he had heard anything. But that was his way: he never condescended to take notice of an underclerk. The wind was blowing; Brown was deaf (although he always pretended he wasn't), and I very much doubted if he had heard the order. If I had had two heads, I would have spoken; but as I had only one, it seemed <u>judicious</u> to take care of it; so I kept still.

Presently, sure enough, we went sailing by that plantation. Captain Klinefelter appeared on the deck, and said: "Let her come around, sir, let her come around. Didn't Henry tell you to land here?"

"*No*, sir!"

"I sent him up to do it."

▲ **Critical Viewing**
What qualities of the boats in this picture might make them difficult to control on a river? **[Connect]**

Literary Analysis
Conflict How does Brown intentionally set the stage for further conflict?

Vocabulary Builder
judicious (jōō dish´ əs) *adj.* showing sound judgment; wise and careful

6. **vituperation** (vi tōō´ pərā´ shən) *n.* abusive language.
7. **intimation** (in´ tə mā´ shən) *n.* hint or suggestion.

"He *did* come up; and that's all the good it done, the dod-derned fool. He never said anything."

"Didn't *you* hear him?" asked the captain of me.

Of course I didn't want to be mixed up in this business, but there was no way to avoid it; so I said: "Yes, sir."

I knew what Brown's next remark would be, before he uttered it. It was: "Shut your mouth! You never heard anything of the kind."

I closed my mouth, according to instructions. An hour later Henry entered the pilothouse, unaware of what had been going on. He was a thoroughly inoffensive boy, and I was sorry to see him come, for I knew Brown would have no pity on him. Brown began, straightway: "Here! Why didn't you tell me we'd got to land at that plantation?"

"I did tell you, Mr. Brown."

"It's a lie!"

I said: "You lie, yourself. He did tell you."

Brown glared at me in unaffected surprise; and for as much as a moment he was entirely speechless; then he shouted to me: "I'll attend to your case in a half a minute!" then to Henry, "And you leave the pilothouse; out with you!"

It was pilot law, and must be obeyed. The boy started out, and even had his foot on the upper step outside the door, when Brown, with a sudden access of fury, picked up a ten-pound lump of coal and sprang after him; but I was between, with a heavy stool, and I hit Brown a good honest blow which stretched him out.

I had committed the crime of crimes—I had lifted my hand against a pilot on duty! I supposed I was booked for the penitentiary sure, and couldn't be booked any surer if I went on and squared my long account with this person while I had the chance; consequently I stuck to him and pounded him with my fists a considerable time. I do not know how long, the pleasure of it probably made it seem longer than it really was; but in the end he struggled free and jumped up and sprang to the wheel: a very natural solicitude, for, all this time, here was this steamboat tearing down the river at the rate of fifteen miles an hour and nobody at the helm! However, Eagle Bend was two miles wide at this bank-full stage, and correspondingly long and deep: and the boat was steering herself straight down the middle and taking no chances. Still, that was only luck—a body *might* have found her charging into the woods.

Literary Analysis
Conflict Why does Twain stand up to Brown at this point in the story?

Literary Analysis
Conflict How do Brown's actions contribute to the intensity of Twain's reaction?

 **Reading Check**

What is the argument that starts the fight between Twain and Brown?

Perceiving at a glance that the *Pennsylvania* was in no danger, Brown gathered up the big spyglass, war-club fashion, and ordered me out of the pilothouse with more than ordinary bluster. But I was not afraid of him now; so, instead of going, I tarried, and criticized his grammar. I reformed his ferocious speeches for him, and put them into good English, calling his attention to the advantage of pure English over the dialect of the collieries[8] whence he was extracted. He could have done his part to admiration in a crossfire of mere vituperation, of course; but he was not equipped for this species of controversy; so he presently laid aside his glass and took the wheel, muttering and shaking his head; and I retired to the bench. The racket had brought everybody to the hurricane deck, and I trembled when I saw the old captain looking up from amid the crowd. I said to myself, "Now I *am* done for!" for although, as a rule, he was so fatherly and <u>indulgent</u> toward the boat's family, and so patient of minor shortcomings, he could be stern enough when the fault was worth it.

I tried to imagine what he *would* do to a cub pilot who had been guilty of such a crime as mine, committed on a boat guard-deep with costly freight and alive with passengers. Our watch was nearly ended. I thought I would go and hide somewhere till I got a chance to slide ashore. So I slipped out of the pilothouse, and down the steps, and around to the texas-door, and was in the act of gliding within, when the captain confronted me! I dropped my head, and he stood over me in silence a moment or two, then said impressively: "Follow me."

I dropped into his wake; he led the way to his parlor in the forward end of the texas. We were alone now. He closed the afterdoor, then moved slowly to the forward one and closed that. He sat down; I stood before him. He looked at me some little time, then said: "So you have been fighting Mr. Brown?"

I answered meekly: "Yes, sir."

"Do you know that that is a very serious matter?"

"Yes, sir."

"Are you aware that this boat was plowing down the river fully five minutes with no one at the wheel?"

"Yes, sir."

"Did you strike him first?"

"Yes, sir."

"What with?"

Vocabulary Builder
indulgent (in dul´ jənt) *adj.* tolerant; not strict or critical

Reading Skill
Make Predictions
What clues in the narrative so far can help you predict whether the captain will punish Twain?

---

8. collieries (käl´ yər ēz) *n.* coal mines.

"A stool, sir."

"Hard?"

"Middling, sir."

"Did it knock him down?"

"He—he fell, sir."

"Did you follow it up? Did you do anything further?"

"Yes, sir."

"What did you do?"

"Pounded him, sir."

"Pounded him?"

"Yes, sir."

"Did you pound him much? that is, severely?"

"One might call it that, sir, maybe."

"I'm deuced glad of it! Hark ye, never mention that I said that. You have been guilty of a great crime; and don't you ever be guilty of it again, on this boat. *But*—lay for him ashore! Give him a good sound thrashing, do you hear? I'll pay the expenses. Now go—and mind you, not a word of this to anybody. Clear out with you! You've been guilty of a great crime, you whelp!"[9]

I slid out, happy with the sense of a close shave and a mighty deliverance; and I heard him laughing to himself and slapping his fat thighs after I had closed his door.

When Brown came off watch he went straight to the captain, who was talking with some passengers on the boiler deck, and demanded that I be put ashore in New Orleans—and added: "I'll never turn a wheel on this boat again while that cub stays."

The captain said: "But he needn't come round when you are on watch, Mr. Brown."

"I won't even stay on the same boat with him. One of us has got to go ashore." "Very well," said the captain, "let it be yourself," and resumed his talk with the passengers.

During the brief remainder of the trip I knew how an emancipated slave feels, for I was an emancipated slave myself. While we lay at landings I listened to George Ealer's flute, or to his readings from his two Bibles, that is to say, Goldsmith and Shakespeare, or I played chess with him—and would have beaten him sometimes, only he always took back his last move and ran the game out differently.

Reading Skill
Make Predictions
As you read, did you revise your prediction about whether Twain would be punished? Why or why not?

---

9. **whelp** (hwelp) *n.* puppy. Here, the captain uses it to indicate that Twain is young and foolish, like a puppy.

Apply the Skills

Cub Pilot on the Mississippi

Thinking About the Selection

1. **Respond:** Would you want to be a cub pilot? Explain.
2. **(a) Recall:** About how long did Twain serve as a pilot's apprentice? **(b) Infer:** Why were cub pilots assigned to work with experienced pilots?
3. **(a) Recall:** How does Brown treat Twain when he meets him? **(b) Analyze:** Is Brown's treatment of Twain the result of a personal dislike for him or an overall attitude? Explain.
4. **(a) Recall:** What is the captain's reaction to Twain's beating of Brown? **(b) Draw Conclusions:** What are the captain's feelings about Brown? How do you know?
5. **(a) Take a Stand:** Do you think Twain should have hit Brown? Under what circumstances, if any, should physical force be used to solve a problem? **(b) Discuss:** Share your answers with a partner. **(c) Analyze:** Did your answers change as a result of your discussion? Explain why or why not.

Reading Skill

6. **(a)** What **predictions** did you make about the outcome of the conflict between Twain and Brown? **(b)** Which specific clues led to your prediction? **(c)** Did you change any of your predictions as you read the selection? Explain.

Literary Analysis

7. Use a chart like the one shown to analyze the **conflict** between Twain and Brown.

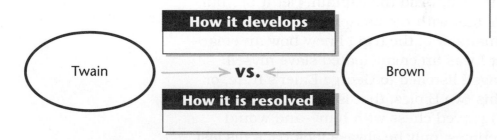

8. Is the conflict in the narrative mainly *internal* or *external*? Support your answer with details from the narrative.

QuickReview

Who's Who in the Narrative

Brown: a master pilot

Mark Twain: the narrator and a cub pilot

George Ritchie: another cub pilot

Captain: the kind-hearted man in charge of the steamboat

Go Online
Assessment

For: Self-test
Visit: www.PHSchool.com
Web Code: ena-6106

Prediction: an informed guess about what will happen in a story

Conflict: the struggle between two opposing forces

Vocabulary Builder

Practice For each item, explain why one of the three words is *not* a **synonym**, or word close in meaning, to the vocabulary word.

1. pretext: **(a)** reason, **(b)** excuse, **(c)** desire
2. judicious: **(a)** foolish, **(b)** wise, **(c)** reasonable
3. indulgent: **(a)** tolerant, **(b)** harsh, **(c)** uncritical

Writing

Imagine that you are Twain. Write a **letter** to your best friend back home to describe your first few days as a cub pilot. Keep your audience in mind and use these tips:

- Use a casual, friendly tone. Write as if you were speaking directly to your friend.
- A best friend knows you well, so do not include background information about yourself. Focus instead on the situation.

For *Grammar, Vocabulary,* and *Assessment,* see **Build Language Skills,** pages 72-73.

Extend Your Learning

Listening and Speaking With a partner, present a **role play** of the conflict between Twain and Brown. Try to agree on a nonviolent solution to the problem. Address these questions:
- What issues divide you?
- What common interests do you have?
- What are your options for resolving the conflict in an acceptable way for both parties?

After your role play, decide with your partner which conflict-resolution strategies were most successful.

Research and Technology Work with a small group to gather the following information about the Mississippi River:
- What important historical role has the Mississippi played?
- Where are the Mississippi's source, main ports, and mouth?

Give a **group oral presentation** explaining what you learned. Include at least two visual aids, such as a map or steamboat picture.

Build Language Skills

Vocabulary Skill

Prefixes The word *revise* begins with the **prefix re-**. The prefix has several related meanings. In *revise,* the meaning is "back," as in "look back to make corrections or improvements." Look at the other meanings of the **prefix re-**. These meanings can help you understand and remember words that begin with this prefix.

Meanings	Example Words
again	review, repeat, regain,
back	respond, revolve,
undo	revise, reverse
answer	

Practice Answer each of the following questions in complete sentences. Use the underlined word in your answer.

1. Why would you <u>review</u> a chapter of your textbook?
2. Why would you <u>repeat</u> something you have said?
3. Why would you <u>revise</u> something?
4. Why does a car need to be able to go in <u>reverse</u>?

Grammar Lesson

Plural Nouns A **plural noun** refers to more than one person, place, thing, or idea. The plural of most nouns is formed by adding an *s.* Certain nouns, however, follow different rules.

MorePractice

For more practice with plural nouns, see the Grammar Handbook, p. R31.

Rule	Examples
Words that end in *-x, -ch,* or *-sh,* add an *-es.*	box—**boxes**; church—**churches**
For words that end in a consonant plus *y,* change the *y* to an *i* and add *-es.*	pony—**ponies**; fly—**flies**
Some words that end in *-f* or *-fe* have plurals that end in *-ves.*	calf—**calves**; knife—**knives**
The plurals of some nouns are different words.	goose—**geese**

Practice Rewrite each sentence replacing the noun shown in parentheses with its plural form.

1. We stopped to buy some (peach).
2. I spent all day Saturday raking (leaf).
3. The (lady) were screaming because they were afraid of the (mouse).
4. (Wolf) are afraid of humans.

𝒲𝒢 *Prentice Hall Writing and Grammar Connection: Chapter 29, Section 5*

Reading: Making Predictions

Directions: *Read the selection. Then, answer the questions.*

When she knocked on the door of a farmhouse, a place where she and other runaways had always been welcome, always been given shelter and plenty to eat, there was no answer. She knocked again, softly. A voice from within said, "Who is it?" There was fear in the voice.

She knew instantly from the sound of the voice that there was something wrong. She said, "A friend with friends," the password on the Underground Railroad.

—from *Harriet Tubman: Guide to Freedom* by Ann Petry

1. Which of the following is the BEST support for the prediction that she will be welcomed?

   A She knocks softly.

   B A voice says "Who is it?"

   C Runaways had always been welcome there before.

   D The sound of the voice indicated something was wrong.

2. Which is most likely to happen next?

   A The slaves will be welcomed.

   B The slaves will be turned away.

   C The voice will call the slave's masters.

   D The person inside will become violent.

3. Which of the following words from the passage is a strong clue that indicates what the man will do next?

   A *knocked*

   B *fear*

   C *shelter*

   D *password*

4. What background knowledge would help you make a prediction?

   A What passwords the slaves used.

   B How the underground railroad functioned.

   C Where the farmhouse was located.

   D Why she was traveling.

Timed Writing: Analysis [Critical Stance]

Review "Gentleman of Río en Medio" or "Cub Pilot on the Mississippi." Write a brief analysis of how the conflict between characters affects the development of the plot in either story. In your analysis, explain how the settings and characters' personalities contribute to the conflict. **(20 minutes)**

 ## Writing Workshop: *Work in Progress*

Description

Add to the Descriptive List saved in your writing portfolio. Write four sentences that the person might say. Use the expressions you associate with the person. Save this work in your writing portfolio.

Reading Informational Materials

Consumer Documents: Maps and Schedules

In Part 1, you are learning how to make predictions while reading literature. When taking a trip, a schedule helps you make an accurate prediction about travel times. The consumer document that follows provides a map and schedule for ferries. Like the 1800s steamboats in Mark Twain's "Cub Pilot on the Mississippi," ferries still transport people and goods along the nation's waterways.

About Maps and Schedules

Maps and schedules help people get where they want to go. Maps show visual representations of places, and schedules list arrival and departure times. Both are **consumer documents,** or materials that help you purchase or use a product or service. Other types of consumer documents include product brochures, labels, loan applications, assembly instructions, and warranties.

Reading Skill

When you read maps and schedules, **use text aids and features** to help you find the information you need. The chart shows some common features.

Text Aids and Features of a Map	
Legend	Explains the map's symbols
Compass rose	Shows directions (north, south, east, west)

Text Aids and Features of a Schedule	
Headings	Show where to find departure and arrival times
Rows and columns	Show arrival and departure times for easy scanning across and down the page
Special type and asterisks	Indicate exceptions, such as ferries that do not run on Sundays

NORTH CAROLINA
FERRY SYSTEM SCHEDULE

1 CURRITUCK : KNOTTS ISLAND

These titles name the ferry routes, or where the ferry travels.

Currituck	Knotts Island
YEAR-ROUND DEPARTURES	
6.00 a.m.	7.00 a.m.
9.00	10.00
11.00	Noon
1.00 p.m.	2.00 p.m.
3.30	4.30
5.30	6.30

Fare: Free
Crossing: 45 minutes

This schedule only lists departure times. Passengers calculate arrival times by adding crossing times at the bottom of each column to the departure list.

Ferry Information
(252) 232-2683

Tourism Information
Currituck County
www.currituckchamber.org
1-877-CURRITUCK
(252) 453-9497

Contact and fare information also are provided.

CURRITUCK : COROLLA
Passenger ONLY Ferry **2**

Currituck	Corolla
JULY 1 – AUG 16, 2004 DEPARTURES	
8.00 a.m.	9.00 a.m.
10.00	11.00
12.00 p.m.	1.00 p.m.
2.00	3.00
4.00	5.00
6.00	7.00
AUG 17, 2004 – JUNE 4, 2005 DEPARTURES	
6.20* a.m.	7.00 a.m.
8.00	9.00
10.00	11.00
12.00 p.m.	1.00 p.m.
1.45	2.30*
3.15	5.00

Fare One Way: $2
Crossing: 35 minutes
* School children receive priority

Ferry Information
1-877-DOT-4YOU (368-4968)
(252) 232-2683

Tourism Information
Currituck County
www.currituckchamber.org
1-877-CURRITUCK
(252) 453-9497

Outer Banks Visitors Bureau
www.outerbanks.org
1-877-OBX-4FUN
(629-4386)

Currituck Beach Lighthouse

Reading Informational Materials

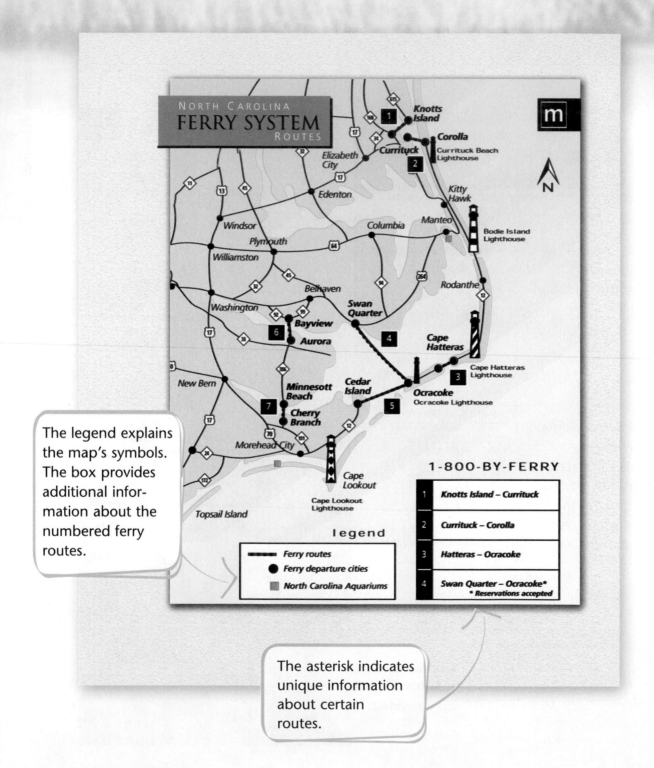

NORTH CAROLINA
FERRY SYSTEM
ROUTES

m

N

Knotts Island

1

Corolla
Currituck Beach Lighthouse

2

Currituck

Kitty Hawk

Elizabeth City

Edenton

Manteo

Bodie Island Lighthouse

Windsor

Columbia

Plymouth

Williamston

Rodanthe

Belhaven

Washington

Swan Quarter

Bayview

4

Cape Hatteras

Aurora

6

Cape Hatteras Lighthouse

3

New Bern

Cedar Island

Ocracoke
Ocracoke Lighthouse

5

Minnesott Beach

7

Cherry Branch

Morehead City

Cape Lookout

Cape Lookout Lighthouse

Topsail Island

The legend explains the map's symbols. The box provides additional information about the numbered ferry routes.

1-800-BY-FERRY

legend

▬▬▬	Ferry routes
●	Ferry departure cities
▮	North Carolina Aquariums

1	**Knotts Island – Currituck**
2	**Currituck – Corolla**
3	**Hatteras – Ocracoke**
4	**Swan Quarter – Ocracoke*** ** Reservations accepted*

The asterisk indicates unique information about certain routes.

Reading: Using Text Aids and Features

Choose the letter of the best answer to each question.

1. What time does the first ferry arrive at Knotts Island?

   A 6:00 A.M.

   B 9:00 A.M.

   C 6:45 A.M.

   D 9:45 A.M.

2. What information about the trip from Currituck to Knotts Island **cannot** be found on either the ferry schedule or map?

   A the cost

   B the amount of time it takes

   C the distance

   D the direction

3. What is one symbol on the map that does not appear on the legend?

   A ferry departure cities

   B lighthouses

   C aquariums

   D ferry routes

Reading: Comprehension and Interpretation

Directions: *Write your answers on a separate piece of paper.*

4. In what situation would this schedule and map be useful?

5. Explain how you can figure out what time a ferry will arrive.

6. Would this information be useful to someone who wanted to ferry a car from Currituck to Corolla? Explain your reasoning.

Timed Writing: Itinerary [Generating]

If you arrange travel through a travel agent, you receive an *itinerary*, or a written description of your trip that includes dates, times, and locations. Plan a round-trip itinerary using the North Carolina ferry schedule and map. On the itinerary, list each place that you will go, which direction you will be heading, and what the departure and arrival times for your trip will be. **(20 minutes)**

Narrative Structure

All **narratives** tell a story. **Narrative structure** is the form or pattern a story follows. Narrative structure may be *chronological*, with events taking place in the same order that they occur in time. However, narrative structure may not always follow a straight line in time. In some stories, time sequence may be broken by two common narrative devices:

- In **flashbacks,** scenes relate events that happened in the past. Flashbacks often show what motivates a character or reveal something important about a character's past.
- Through **foreshadowing,** the author provides clues that hint at events to come. Foreshadowing creates suspense by keeping readers guessing about future events.

The chart shown illustrates these narrative devices.

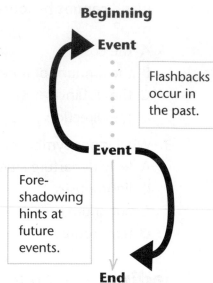

Beginning

Event

Flashbacks occur in the past.

Event

Foreshadowing hints at future events.

End

Comparing Narrative Structure

In many stories, one event follows another in an unbroken sequence from beginning to end. When authors play with time by using devices like foreshadowing and flashback, these changes affect the way readers get important information and understand key elements of a story.

Compare the narrative structures of "Old Ben" and "Fox Hunt." As you read, notice the way flashback and foreshadowing affect the structure of a story.

Vocabulary Builder

Old Ben

- **affectionate** (ə fek´shən it) *adj.* loving (p. 81) The <u>affectionate</u> dog licked its owners when they got home.

- **scarce** (skers) *adj.* few in number; not common (p. 83) Sources of water are <u>scarce</u> in the desert.

- **partition** (pär tish´ ən) *n.* an interior dividing wall (p. 83) Only a thin <u>partition</u> separated his office from hers.

Fox Hunt

- **studious** (stoo´ dē əs) *adj.* devoted to learning (p. 86) Mary's <u>studious</u> sister always had her nose in a book.

- **decadent** (dek´ ə dənt) *adj.* marked by decay or decline (p. 89) When emperors grew <u>decadent</u>, the empire collapsed.

- **tantalized** (tan´ tə līzd´) *v.* tormented by something just out of reach (p. 92) Cho <u>tantalized</u> the baby by dangling toys above her head.

Build Understanding

Connecting to the Literature

Reading/Writing Connection Animal characters play an important role in both "Old Ben" and "Fox Hunt." Describe three animals that you find disgusting or creepy, and three animals that are appealing to you. Use at least three of the following words: *capable, appreciate, display, injure.*

Meet the Authors

Jesse **Stuart** (1906–1984)

As a boy growing up in rural Kentucky, Jesse Stuart developed a strong connection to the natural world around him. As an adult, he found that his home and his roots provided endless inspiration. He produced an amazing volume of writing—more than fifty-five books and five hundred short stories—mostly based on his home state.

State Poet After Stuart became the Poet Laureate, or official state poet, of Kentucky, one biographer wrote, "Stuart's writing is indeed like bright water mirroring the trees, the sky, and the Kentucky life he knew and loved."

Lensey **Namioka** (b. 1929)

Lensey Namioka loves exciting stories. As a child in China, she read martial arts novels, Sherlock Holmes detective stories, and *The Three Musketeers.* She wrote her first book, *Princess with a Bamboo Sword,* when she was eight years old.

Sources of Inspiration At nine, Namioka moved to the United States with her family. When she grew up, she taught math and married a mathematician of Japanese descent. Perhaps this is one reason why the subject of math frequently appears in her stories.

Go **O**nline
—**Author Link**

For: More about the authors
Visit: www.PHSchool.com
Web Code: ene-9106

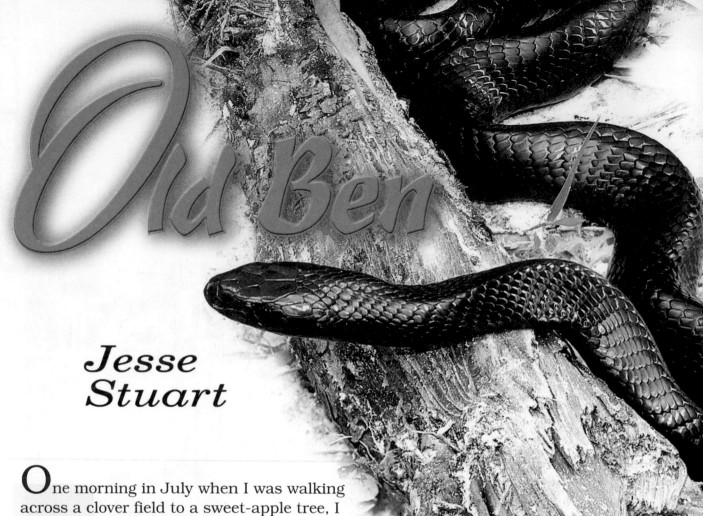

Old Ben

Jesse Stuart

One morning in July when I was walking across a clover field to a sweet-apple tree, I almost stepped on him. There he lay coiled like heavy strands of black rope. He was a big bull blacksnake. We looked at each other a minute, and then I stuck the toe of my shoe up to his mouth. He drew his head back in a friendly way. He didn't want trouble. Had he shown the least fight, I would have soon finished him. My father had always told me there was only one good snake—a dead one.

When the big fellow didn't show any fight, I reached down and picked him up by the neck. When I lifted him he was as long as I was tall. That was six feet. I started calling him Old Ben as I held him by the neck and rubbed his back. He enjoyed having his back rubbed and his head stroked. Then I lifted him into my arms. He was the first snake I'd ever been friendly with. I was afraid at first to let Old Ben wrap himself around me. I thought he might wrap himself around my neck and choke me.

▲ **Critical Viewing**
What would be your response if you almost stepped on a snake like the one in the picture?
[Connect]

The more I petted him, the more <u>affectionate</u> he became. He was so friendly I decided to trust him. I wrapped him around my neck a couple of times and let him loose. He crawled down one arm and went back to my neck, around and down the other arm and back again. He struck out his forked tongue to the sound of my voice as I talked to him.

"I wouldn't kill you at all," I said. "You're a friendly snake. I'm taking you home with me."

I headed home with Old Ben wrapped around my neck and shoulders. When I started over the hill by the pine grove, I met my cousin Wayne Holbrook coming up the hill. He stopped suddenly when he saw me. He started backing down the hill.

"He's a pet, Wayne," I said. "Don't be afraid of Old Ben."

It was a minute before Wayne could tell me what he wanted. He had come to borrow a plow. He kept a safe distance as we walked on together.

Before we reached the barn, Wayne got brave enough to touch Old Ben's long body.

"What are you going to do with him?" Wayne asked. "Uncle Mick won't let you keep him!"

"Put him in the corncrib," I said. "He'll have plenty of delicate food in there. The cats we keep at this barn have grown fat and lazy on the milk we feed 'em."

I opened the corncrib door and took Old Ben from around my neck because he was beginning to get warm and a little heavy.

"This will be your home," I said. "You'd better hide under the corn."

Besides my father, I knew Old Ben would have another enemy at our home. He was our hunting dog, Blackie, who would trail a snake, same as a possum or mink. He had treed blacksnakes, and my father had shot them from the trees. I knew Blackie would find Old Ben, because he followed us to the barn each morning.

The first morning after I'd put Old Ben in the corncrib, Blackie followed us. He started toward the corncrib holding his head high, sniffing. He stuck his nose up to a crack in the crib and began to bark. Then he tried to tear a plank off.

"Stop it, Blackie," Pa scolded him. "What's the matter with you? Have you taken to barking at mice?"

"Blackie is not barking at a mouse," I said. "I put a black-snake in there yesterday!"

Literary Analysis
Narrative Structure
What decision does the narrator make that keeps the narrative about Old Ben moving forward?

Reading Check

How do people react to Old Ben?

"A blacksnake?" Pa asked, looking unbelievingly. "A black-snake?"

"Yes, a pet blacksnake," I said.

"Have you gone crazy?" he said. "I'll move a thousand bush-els of corn to get that snake!"

"You won't mind this one," I said. "You and Mom will love him."

My father said a few unprintable words before we started back to the house. After breakfast, when Pa and Mom came to the barn, I was already there. I had opened the crib door and there was Old Ben. He'd crawled up front and was coiled on a sack. I put my hand down and he crawled up my arm to my neck and over my shoulder. When Mom and Pa reached the crib, I thought Pa was going to faint.

"He has a pet snake," Mom said.

"Won't be a bird or a young chicken left on this place," Pa said. "Every time I pick up an ear of corn in the crib, I'll be jumping."

"Pa, he won't hurt you," I said, patting the snake's head. "He's a natural pet, or somebody has tamed him. And he's not going to bother birds and young chickens when there are so many mice in this crib."

"Mick, let him keep the snake," Mom said. "I won't be afraid of it."

This was the beginning of a long friendship.

Mom went to the corncrib morning after morning and shelled corn for her geese and chickens. Often Old Ben would be lying in front on his burlap sack. Mom watched him at first from the corner of her eye. Later she didn't bother to watch him any more than she did a cat that came up for his milk.

Later it occurred to us that Old Ben might like milk, too. We started leaving milk for him. We never saw him drink it, but his pan was always empty when we returned. We know the mice didn't drink it, because he took care of them.

"One thing is certain," Mom said one morning when she went to shell corn. "We don't find any more corn chewed up by the mice and left on the floor."

July passed and August came. My father got used to Old Ben, but not until he had proved his worth. Ben had done something our nine cats couldn't. He had cleaned the corn-crib of mice.

Then my father began to worry about Old Ben's going after water, and Blackie's finding his track. So he put water in the crib.

Literary Analysis
Narrative Structure
What conflict or problem does the narrator try to solve here?

September came and went. We began wondering where our pet would go when days grew colder. One morning in early October we left milk for Old Ben, and it was there when we went back that afternoon. But Old Ben wasn't there.

"Old Ben's a good pet for the warm months," Pa said. "But in the winter months, my cats will have to do the work. Maybe Blackie got him!"

"He might have holed up for the winter in the hayloft," I told Pa after we had removed all the corn and didn't find him. "I'm worried about him. I've had a lot of pets—groundhogs, crows and hawks—but Old Ben's the best yet."

November, December, January, February, and March came and went. Of course we never expected to see Old Ben in one of those months. We doubted if we ever would see him again.

One day early in April I went to the corncrib, and Old Ben lay stretched across the floor. He looked taller than I was now. His skin was rough and his long body had a flabby appearance. I knew Old Ben needed mice and milk. I picked him up, petted him, and told him so. But the chill of early April was still with him. He got his tongue out slower to answer the kind words I was saying to him. He tried to crawl up my arm but he couldn't make it.

That spring and summer mice got <u>scarce</u> in the corncrib and Old Ben got daring. He went over to the barn and crawled up into the hayloft, where he had many feasts. But he made one mistake.

He crawled from the hayloft down into Fred's feed box, where it was cool. Old Fred was our horse.

There he lay coiled when the horse came in and put his nose down on top of Old Ben. Fred let out a big snort and started kicking. He kicked down a <u>partition</u>, and then turned his heels on his feed box and kicked it down. Lucky for Old Ben that he got out in one piece. But he got back to his crib.

Old Ben became a part of our barnyard family, a pet and darling of all. When children came to play with my brother and sisters, they always went to the crib and got Old Ben. He enjoyed the children, who were afraid of him at first but later learned to pet this kind old reptile.

Summer passed and the late days of September were very humid. Old Ben failed one morning to drink his milk. We knew it wasn't time for him to hole up for the winter.

We knew something had happened.

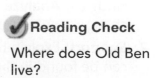

Pa and I moved the corn searching for him. Mom made a couple of trips to the barn lot to see if we had found him. But all we found was the rough skin he had shed last spring.

"Fred's never been very sociable with Old Ben since he got in his box that time," Pa said. "I wonder if he could have stomped Old Ben to death. Old Ben could've been crawling over the barn lot, and Fred saw his chance to get even!"

"We'll see," I said.

Pa and I left the crib and walked to the barn lot. He went one way and I went the other, each searching the ground.

Mom came through the gate and walked over where my father was looking. She started looking around, too.

"We think Fred might've got him," Pa said. "We're sure Fred's got it in for him over Old Ben getting in his feed box last summer."

"You're accusing Fred wrong," Mom said. "Here's Old Ben's track in the sand."

I ran over to where Mom had found the track. Pa went over to look, too.

"It's no use now," Pa said, softly. "Wouldn't have taken anything for that snake. I'll miss him on that burlap sack every morning when I come to feed the horses. Always looked up at me as if he understood."

The last trace Old Ben had left was in the corner of the lot near the hogpen. His track went straight to the woven wire fence and stopped.

"They've got him," Pa said. "Old Ben trusted everything and everybody. He went for a visit to the wrong place. He didn't last long among sixteen hogs. They go wild over a snake. Even a biting copperhead can't stop a hog. There won't be a trace of Old Ben left."

We stood silently for a minute looking at the broad, smooth track Old Ben had left in the sand.

Literary Analysis
Narrative Structure
Which events—if any—could have foreshadowed Ben's disappearance?

▼ **Critical Viewing**
What characteristics of a horse would present a danger to a snake? **[Analyze]**

Thinking About the Selection

1. (a) **Recall:** What kind of snake does Pa say is the only good kind? (b) **Analyze Causes and Effects:** Why do Pa's feelings change? (c) **Interpret:** How do you know they have changed?

2. **Support:** Explain how "Old Ben" illustrates the idea that friends can be found in the most unexpected places.

FOX HUNT

LENSEY NAMIOKA

Andy Liang watched the kids from his school bus walk home with their friends. He could hear them talking together and laughing. He always got off the bus alone and walked home by himself.

But this time it was different. A girl got off the bus just behind him and started walking in the same direction. He wondered why he hadn't seen her before. She was also Asian American, which made it all the more surprising that he hadn't noticed her earlier.

As he tried to get a better look, she went into the neighborhood convenience store and disappeared behind a shelf of canned soup. He peered into the store, hoping for another glimpse of her. All he saw were some of the kids from the bus getting bags of potato chips and soft drinks.

Andy sighed. He was used to being a loner, and usually it didn't bother him—not much, anyway. But today the loneliness was heavy. He overheard the other kids talking, and he knew they were planning to study together for the PSAT.[1] From the looks of the snacks, they were expecting a long session.

Andy would be practicing for the test, too, but he would be doing it by himself. *I'm better off doing it alone, anyway,* he thought. *Studying with somebody else would just slow me down.*

The truth was that none of the others had invited him to study with them. *So all right,* he said to himself, *they think I'm a grind. What's wrong with that? I'll be getting better scores on*

> ### ✓ Reading Check
>
> What does Andy see when he gets off the school bus?

the PSAT than any of them, even if there's nobody to coach me.

He finally found the girl standing in front of a case of barbecued chicken. She was staring so hungrily at the chickens that his own mouth began watering, and he would have bought a piece on the spot if he had the money. But with the change in his pocket, he had to be satisfied with a candy bar.

Leaving the store, he reached his street and passed the corner house with the moody German shepherd. As usual, it snapped at him, and he automatically retreated to the far side of the sidewalk. Although the dog was on a chain, Andy didn't like the way it looked at him. Besides, a chain could always break.

Today, the dog not only snapped, it began to bark furiously and strained against its chain. Andy jumped back and bumped against the girl he had seen earlier. Somehow she had appeared behind him without making any noise.

▲ **Critical Viewing** Why do tests produce feelings of anxiety in many people, like Andy Liang? [**Speculate**]

He apologized. "I didn't mean to crash into you. That dog always growls at me, but today he's really barking like crazy."

The girl shivered. "The dog doesn't seem to like me very much, either." Before he had a chance to say anything more, she turned and walked away.

Again Andy sighed. He hadn't even had a chance to find out what her name was or where she lived. Was she Chinese American, as he was? What grade was she in? At least she went on the same school bus, so there was a chance of seeing her again.

But he didn't have much hope that she would be interested in him. Girls didn't go for the quiet, <u>studious</u> type. Last year, one of the girls in his geometry class had asked him to give her some help after school. That went pretty well, and for a while he thought they might have something going. But after she passed the geometry test, she didn't look at him again.

Vocabulary Builder
studious (sto͞o′ dē əs) *adj.* devoted to learning

Maybe if he studied less and went in for sports, girls would get interested in him. But then his grades might slip, and his parents would never let him hear the end of it. He had to keep his grades up, study hard, be the dutiful son.

His brother had managed to get a math score of 800 on the PSAT, and now he was at Yale with a full scholarship. Andy had to try and do as well.

More than once he had asked his parents why it was so important to get into a good college. "Lots of people get rich in this country without going to college at all," he told them.

His father would draw himself up stiffly. "The Liangs belonged to the mandarin class in China. I've told you again and again that to become a mandarin, one had to pass the official examinations. Only outstanding scholars passed, and only they had the qualifications to govern the country."

Andy's father always got worked up about the subject. He might be only a minor clerk in America, he said, but he was descended from a family of high-ranking officials in China.

Another thing Andy noticed was that when his father went on at length about the illustrious Liang family, his mother always listened with a faint smile. She seemed to be amused for some reason.

But that didn't stop her from also putting pressure on Andy to study hard. Every night, she would ask him whether he had done his homework, and she double-checked his papers to make sure everything was correct.

Normally Andy didn't mind doing his homework. He liked the satisfaction of a job well done when he finished a hard problem in math. But lately, all the extra work preparing for the exam was beginning to get him down. His mind wandered, and he began to daydream. He had visions of becoming a snake charmer, making a balloon trip over the Andes, or practicing kung fu in Shaolin Temple.[2] He saw himself in the English countryside, riding a galloping horse in a fox hunt.

He tried to stop wasting time on these stupid daydreams. Maybe his mind wouldn't wander if he had someone to study with. But nobody wanted to study with him. Nobody wanted to spend time with a nerd.

Next day, the girl got off the bus again with Andy, and this time, instead of going into the convenience store, she began to walk with him. When they reached the yard with the German shepherd, they both automatically backed away from the fence.

Andy and the girl looked at each other and grinned. He was encouraged. "I'm Andy Liang. Are you new in the neighborhood?"

Literary Analysis
Narrative Structure
What important information about expectations do you learn from this anecdote from Andy's past?

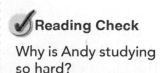
Reading Check

Why is Andy studying so hard?

---

2. **Shaolin** (shou´ lin) **Temple** The ancient Chinese martial art of kung fu is thought to have origi-nated in Shaolin Temple, located in the Songshan Mountains of China's Henan Province.

"We moved here last week," she replied. "My name is Leona Hu. But Leona is a silly name, and my friends call me Lee."

She was inviting him to call her Lee and including him among her friends! Andy could hardly believe his luck. An attractive girl was actually ready to be friends. He was grateful to the German shepherd.

The girl had big almond-shaped eyes. Andy had overheard Americans saying that Chinese had slanty eyes, although his own eyes did not slant. Lee's eyes, on the other hand, definitely slanted upward at the corners.

Her hair had a slightly reddish tint, instead of being blue-black like his own. She wasn't exactly beautiful, but with her hair and her slanting eyes, she looked exotic and fascinating.

When they came to his house, Andy wished he could keep Lee talking with him. But she smiled at him briefly and went on. He had to stop himself from running after her to find out where she lived. He didn't want her to think that he was pestering her.

Was she going to take the PSAT this year? If she was, maybe they could study together!

At dinner that night, his father went on as usual about how important it was to do well on the PSAT. "We immigrants start at the bottom here in America, and the only way we can pull ourselves up is to get a good education. Never forget that you're descended from illustrious ancestors, Andy."

Again, Andy noticed his mother's faint smile. Later, he went into the kitchen where he found her washing the dishes. "Why do you always smile when Father gives me his pep talk about education? Don't you agree with him?"

"Oh, I agree with him about the importance of education," his mother said. "I'm just amused by all that talk about *illustrious ancestors.*"

"You mean Father wasn't telling the truth about Liangs being mandarins?" asked Andy. He took up a bunch of chopsticks and began to wipe them dry. Usually, his mother refused his help with the chores. She wanted him to spend all his time on his homework.

But tonight she didn't immediately send him upstairs to his desk. She rinsed a rice bowl and put it in the dish rack. "Well, the Liangs haven't always been mandarins," she said finally. "They used to be quite poor, until one of them achieved success by passing the official examinations and raising the status of the whole Liang family."

► **Critical Viewing**
Tests like the PSAT often take place in crowded settings like this gym. Would taking a test in this setting make you more, or less, anxious? Why? **[Relate]**

"Hey, that's great!" Andy liked the idea of a poor boy making good. It was more interesting than coming from a long line of <u>decadent</u> aristocrats. "Tell me more about this ancestor."

"His name was Fujin Liang," replied his mother. "Or I should say Liang Fujin, since in China, last names come first." Again she smiled faintly. "Very well. You should really be studying, but it's good for you to know about your ancestors."

Liang Fujin lived with his widowed mother in a small thatched cottage and earned money by looking after a neighbor's water buffalo. His mother added to their meager income by weaving and selling cotton cloth. It was a hard struggle to put rice in their bowls.

But Fujin's mother was ambitious for him. She knew he was smart, and she decided that he should try for the official examinations. In theory, any poor boy could take the examinations, and if he passed, he could raise his family to mandarin status. But rich boys could afford tutors to help them study. For Fujin, even buying a book was a luxury.

He was so eager to learn that he crouched under the window of the nearby school and tried to eavesdrop on the lessons. Whenever he saved enough money to buy books, he would read them while seated on the back of the water buffalo. Once he was so absorbed that he walked the buffalo into a rice paddy. But he managed to read the precious books until he knew them all by heart.

Through hard work he grew up to be a fine scholar. His mother thought he was finally ready to take the examinations, but he himself wasn't so confident. The other competitors were the sons of rich families, who could afford the very best tutors.

He continued to study late every night, until his head began to nod. So he tied the end of his pigtail to a nail in the ceiling,

Vocabulary Builder
decadent (dek´ ə dənt)
adj. marked by decay or decline

Literary Analysis
Narrative Structure
What clues indicate that this section is a flashback, not part of the main narrative?

Reading Check

In what way is Liang Fujin's situation in the past similar to Andy's situation in the present?

and whenever his head fell forward, the pigtail jerked him awake.

One night, while he was struggling to stay awake over his book, he heard a soft voice behind him. "A fine, hardworking young man like you deserves to pass the examination."

Fujin whirled around and saw a beautiful girl standing behind him. Somehow she had appeared without making any noise. She had huge, bewitching eyes that slanted sharply. Could he be dreaming?

"Let me help you," continued the girl. "I can act as a tutor and coach you."

"And that was how your ancestor, Liang Fujin, got the coaching he needed to pass the examinations," said Andy's mother.

Andy blinked. "But . . . but who was this mysterious girl? And how come she was such a great scholar? I thought women didn't get much education in the old days."

His mother laughed. "Nobody in the Liang family would say. But I'll give you a hint: When the girl lifted her skirt to sit down, Fujin caught a flash of something swishing. It looked like a long, bushy tail!"

It took Andy a moment to get it. Then he remembered the Chinese stories his mother used to tell him, stories about the *huli jing,* or fox spirit. The mischievous fox, or *huli,* often appeared in the form of a beautiful girl and played tricks on people. But in some of the stories, the fox fell in love with a handsome young man and did him a great service. She expected a reward for her service, of course, and the reward was marriage.

"So my ancestor passed the examinations because he was coached by a fox?" asked Andy.

"That story is a lie!" cried Andy's father, stomping into the kitchen. "It was made up by malicious neighbors who were jealous of the Liangs!"

Andy's mother shrugged and began to pack the dishes away. His father continued. "Liang Fujin passed the examinations because he was smart and worked hard! Don't you forget it, Andy! So now you can go up to your room and start working!"

His father was right, of course. Fox spirits belonged in fairy tales. He, Andy Liang, would have to study for the PSAT the hard way.

▲ **Critical Viewing** What features in this picture of a mandarin reflect a power and status that would make a descendant proud? **[Analyze]**

Andy was delighted when Lee told him that she was also planning to take the PSAT. She agreed that it would be a good idea to study together. He was eager to begin that very evening. "How about coming over to my house? I'm sure my parents would love to meet you."

Actually, he wasn't sure how delighted his parents would be. He suspected that they would be glad to see him with a Chinese American girl, but they'd probably think that a girl—any girl—would distract him from his studies.

He was half sorry and half relieved when she said, "I'm going to be busy tonight. Maybe we can go to the public library tomorrow afternoon and get some sample tests and study guides."

That night he had a dream about fox hunting. Only this time, he found himself running on the ground trying to get away from the mounted horsemen and howling dogs. There was somebody running with him—another fox, with reddish hair and a bushy tail. It flashed a look at him with its slanting eyes.

Andy and Lee began studying sample PSAT tests at the library. Working with someone else certainly made studying less of a drudgery. Andy felt relaxed with Lee. He didn't suffer the paralyzing shyness with her that seized him when he was with other girls.

She was really good at finding out what his weaknesses were. English grammar was his worst subject, and Lee fed him the right questions so that the fuzzy points of grammar got cleared up. As the days went by, Andy became confident that he was going to do really well on the PSAT. At this rate, he might get a scholarship to some famous university.

He began to worry that the help was one-sided. *He* was getting first-rate coaching, but what was Lee getting out of this? "You're helping me so much," he told her. "But I don't see how I'm helping you at all."

She smiled at him. "I'll get my reward someday."

Something about her glance looked familiar. Where had he seen it before?

They had an extralong study session the day before the exam. When they passed the corner house on their way home, the German shepherd went into a frenzy of barking and scrabbled to climb the Cyclone fence. Both the chain and the

Literary Analysis
Narrative Structure
What possible meaning could the recurring image of a fox have? Explain.

✔ Reading Check

How does Lee help Andy?

fence held, fortunately. Lee looked shaken and backed away from the fence.

At Andy's house she recovered her color. "Well, good luck on the exam tomorrow." She looked at him for a moment with her slanting eyes, and then she was gone.

Again, he thought he remembered that look from some-where. All during supper, he was <u>tantalized</u> by the memory, which was just out of reach.

That night he dreamed about fox hunting again. It was more vivid than usual, and he could see the scarlet coats of the riders chasing him. The howling of the dogs sounded just like the German shepherd. Again, he was running with another fox. It had huge slanting eyes, bright with mischief.

He woke up, and as he sat in his bed, he finally remembered where he had seen those huge, slanting eyes. They were Lee's eyes.

Next day Andy met Lee at the entrance to the examination hall. He suddenly realized that if he said her name in the Chinese order, it would be Hu Lee, which sounded the same as *huli*, or fox.

She smiled. "So you know?"

Andy found his voice. "Why did you pick me, particularly?"

Her smile widened. "We foxes hunt out our own kind."

That was when Andy knew why the German shepherd always snapped at him. He himself must be part fox. His ancestor, Liang Fujin, had accepted help from the fox spirit after all, and she had collected her reward.

Vocabulary Builder
tantalized (tan′ tə
līzd′) *v.* tormented by
something just out of
reach

Literary Analysis
Narrative Structure
Andy solves the
mystery foreshadowed
in the story. What does
he learn?

Thinking About the Selection

1. **Respond:** Did you like the blending of legend and reality in this story? Why or why not?

2. **(a) Recall:** What is the first hint that something is strange about Leona Hu? **(b) Draw Conclusions:** At what point in the story does an unusual explanation for Lee's presence and behavior seem likely? **(c) Evaluate:** What is another reasonable explanation for her presence and behavior?

3. **Make a Judgment:** Would you rather succeed based on your own efforts or succeed with the help of others? Explain.

Apply the Skills

Old Ben • Fox Hunt

Comparing Narrative Structure

1. **(a)** Using a chart like the one shown, list examples of foreshadowing and flashback in the two narratives.

	Flashback	Foreshadowing
Old Ben		
Fox Hunt		Dream of a fox hunt

(b) Which of the stories was closest to presenting events in strict chronological order? Explain.

2. On a separate piece of paper, show the narrative structure of "Fox Hunt" by creating a timeline of the story. List the events in the order in which they occur in the story, using arrows to represent flashback and foreshadowing.

Writing to Compare Literary Works

Write a brief essay to compare and contrast the narrative structures of "Old Ben" and "Fox Hunt." Use the following questions—and your answers to questions 1 and 2—to direct your writing:

- In each story, what information does the writer convey through flashback or foreshadowing? Why is the information important?
- Why might an author choose one structure over another?
- Which narrative structure do you prefer? Why?

Vocabulary Builder

Practice Answer the following questions. Explain your answers.

1. If a cooking aroma *tantalized* you, what would you do?
2. Where is a good place for *studious* people to get work done?
3. Why are *partitions* useful in storage areas?
4. What would you do if money were *scarce*?
5. Do *affectionate* people like to hug?
6. Would you want to live in a *decadent* society?

QuickReview

Narrative structure: the form a story takes

Foreshadowing: clues that hint at events to come

Flashbacks: scenes that tell about events that happened in the past

Go Online
Assessment
For: Self-test
Visit: www.PHSchool.com
Web Code: ena-6107

Reading and Vocabulary Skills Review

Reading: Predicting

Directions: *Read the selection. Then, answer the questions.*

When the last bell finally rang on Friday afternoon, Brian rushed to his locker and started jamming all his books and folders into his backpack. He was supposed to meet Steve at the video game store in five minutes, so he didn't have time to figure out which stuff he really needed.

It was a tight squeeze. The zipper stuck twice as he tried to close it, but he finally forced it closed with one giant grinding tug. As he stood up and put the pack over his shoulders, there was a thunderous crash and then a roar of laughter from everyone in the hallway. The zipper had broken, and his books and papers were scattered all over the floor. It would take forever to gather them all, and his pack was useless now. A girl named Kelly approached with an empty shopping bag. "Need some help?" she asked.

1. **Which details helped you predict that the zipper would break?**
   A It is a Friday afternoon, and Steve is at the video store.
   B Brian stands up and puts the pack on his shoulders.
   C Brian jams everything into the pack and forces it to close.
   D Books and papers are scattered all over the floor.

2. **What prior knowledge could someone use to predict that the zipper would break?**
   A The zipper is plastic.
   B Zippers break when bags are overstuffed.
   C The zipper is old.
   D Brian never zippers his backpack.

3. **What do you predict will happen next?**
   A Steve will leave the video store and never speak to Brian again.
   B Kelly will help Brian load his books and papers into a bag.

   C Brian will walk away and leave all his stuff in the hallway.
   D Brian will go buy a new backpack and then return.

4. **Which kind of information might lead you to modify a prediction about what Kelly will do?**
   A Everyone is laughing.
   B Brian and Steve had a fight earlier that day.
   C It is Friday afternoon and all the stores are open.
   D Kelly is late to class.

5. **Which prediction would not need to be revised, based on details in the passage?**
   A Brian will be late in meeting Steve.
   B Brian will leave his things and go meet Steve.
   C It will take Brian a long time to gather the things that spilled from his backpack.
   D No one will help Brian.

Vocabulary Skill Review

Directions: *Choose the answer that correctly completes each sentence.*

6. **You review a text**
   A after you have read it.
   B before you have read it.
   C without reading it.
   D during your first reading.

7. **You predict an event**
   A after it happens.
   B before it happens.
   C while it happens.
   D if it does not happen.

8. **You revise your work**
   A after you do it.
   B before you do it.
   C instead of doing it.
   D without doing it.

9. **You modify a plan**
   A after you make it.
   B before you make it.
   C instead of making it.
   D without making it.

10. **You preview a text**
    A after you read it.
    B before you read it.
    C instead of reading it.
    D without reading it.

Directions: *Choose the word or phrase that means the same as the numbered word.*

11. **previously**
    A before
    B after
    C far
    D underneath

12. **preceded**
    A began
    B climbed
    C followed
    D came before

13. **reverse**
    A wait
    B follow
    C proceed
    D back

14. **regain**
    A earn with effort
    B rule with fairness
    C win again
    D lose after gaining

15. **research**
    A decide to search
    B plan how to search
    C search for the first time
    D search again

Writing Workshop

Description of a Person

Many nonfiction writers enjoy describing the unforgettable real people who have influenced them in their lives. Follow the steps in this workshop to write your own description of a person in your life.

Assignment Write a descriptive essay and reflect on a person who has had an important influence on your life.

What to Include Your description should feature these elements:
- your main impression of the person
- concrete examples and personal anecdotes as support
- sensory details about appearance, behavior, and speech
- your thoughts about how this person has influenced your life
- error-free writing, including correct use of possessive nouns

To preview the criteria on which your essay may be judged, see the rubric on page 100.

Prewriting

Choosing Your Topic

Listing To choose the person you want to describe, make a chart with four columns labeled *Family, Friends, Teachers,* and *Coaches.* In each column, list people who have influenced you in some important way. Review your list and select a person as a topic for your description.

Gathering Details

Make a character web. In a web like the one shown, jot down specific details of the person's appearance, speech, and behavior. Also note examples of traits and actions that show why he or she is important to you. Review your web to decide what main impression you will convey in your writing.

Using the Form
You may use description in these types of writing:
- personal letters
- persuasion
- exposition

Work in Progress
Review the work you did on pages 11, 21, 51, and 73.

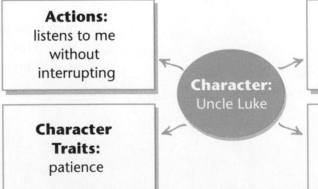

Actions:
listens to me without interrupting

Character Traits:
patience

Character: Uncle Luke

Appearance:
gentle, brown eyes

Behavior:
understanding nods encouraging pat on shoulder

Drafting

Shaping Your Writing

Organize examples and details. Your essay should keep readers' interest, focus on a main impression, and build up to your strongest point. Organize your examples and details in *order of importance:* from least important to most important. To guide you as you draft, number your examples in the order you want to present them.

Providing Elaboration

Add figurative language. As you draft, focus on providing vivid *sensory details*—words and phrases that appeal to any of the five senses. These will create a strong picture of your subject for your readers. Choose figurative language that builds comparisons and helps suggest new ways of looking at someone.

- *Similes* compare one thing to another using the words *like* or *as.* Example: *My mother is like a drill sergeant, barking orders and running the house efficiently amid the chaos.*
- *Metaphors* compare two unlike things by setting them up as equals. They describe one object as if it were another. Example: *Carrie is my rock, always behind me, keeping me strong.*

Revising

Revising Your Paragraphs

Add dialogue to bring descriptions to life. A great way to bring the subject of your description alive is to capture the way he or she talks. Review your draft, marking any paragraphs in which you can add dialogue to show the way the person talked to you at particular moments in your life.

To read the complete student model, see page 99.

Student Model: Add Dialogue to Bring Descriptions to Life

It broke into a million tiny, brown pieces on her floor. ~~My aunt surprised me by being very understanding.~~

She walked into the room and asked, "What happened here?" I tried to reply, but I choked up. She wrapped her arms around me and said consolingly, "It's okay. Everyone has accidents."

These words show the aunt's understanding attitude.

Integrating Grammar Skills

Using Concrete, Abstract, and Possessive Nouns

Nouns name people, places, things, or ideas. They are critical to description because they identify the people and things writers discuss.

Identifying Types of Nouns **Concrete nouns** name people, places, or things that can be perceived by the five senses. **Abstract nouns** name ideas, beliefs, qualities, or concepts. **Possessive nouns** show ownership or belonging. They end in *'s* or *s'*.

Prentice Hall Writing and Grammar Connection: Chapter 14, Section 1

Type of Noun	Examples
concrete	child, dog, street, Jeff
abstract	freedom, childhood, love, kindness
possessive	child's coat, freedom's appeal

Using Vivid Concrete Nouns In a reflective essay that describes a person, support abstract nouns such as *friendship* or *love* with specific concrete nouns that give vivid details. Avoid vague, general nouns that do not give a clear picture.

Vague	**Specific**
She cooks good *stuff* for me.	She cooks *lasagna, fried chicken,* and *blueberry muffins* for me.

Vague	**Specific**
He likes *rides.*	He likes *roller coasters* and *water slides.*

Identifying Errors Most errors with possessive nouns occur when apostrophes are left out or placed incorrectly. Follow these conventions:

1. **To form the possessive form of plural nouns that end in *s,* add an apostrophe.**
2. **For plural nouns that do not end in *s,* add an apostrophe and the letter *s.***

▶ **Examples:** *dogs'* owner, *boys'* basketball game, *women's* plan

Apply It to Your Editing

In two paragraphs of your draft, underline every noun. Ask yourself if each noun paints a vivid picture of your subject. If the noun is vague or too general, replace it with a more vivid, specific noun.

Student Model: Brittany Barker
Somerset, KY

Ding Bat

Amy has impacted my life since the day I was born. We are very close, and she is my favorite aunt. I resemble her in many ways. We both have caramel brown hair, sparkling brown eyes and cheerful smiles. My aunt is funny and sometimes seems less intelligent than she actually is. Once she made chocolate cupcakes for a party and for some unknown reason she bent over to sniff them while they were still hot. The steam from the cupcakes scorched her nose. (I guess the smell of chocolate was too much for her to bear.) This incident, along with others, earned her the affectionate nickname Ding Bat.

That's one reason I like her, though, because she is just like me—smart, yet very "ditzy." Amy influenced my own personality because I spent so much time with her when I was young. I loved having her as a babysitter because she would let me do anything, as long as it was safe. One time she taught me how to make paper snowflakes. I wasn't experienced with scissors and made several feeble attempts to cut on the gray lines she had traced onto the white paper. I got so involved that I snipped my index finger with the scissors. Tears began to dribble down my face and mix with the blood already on the paper. Amy carefully wrapped a bandage around my finger and helped me clean up the mess on the table. After we scrubbed the table, she told me a joke to make me laugh.

Amy is so easygoing and happy. She is also sincere and willing to forgive. Once, I accidentally broke a small bunny figurine of hers by knocking it off the table. It broke into a million tiny, brown pieces on her floor. She walked into the room and asked, "What happened here?" I tried to reply, but I choked up and tears came to my eyes. She wrapped her arms around me and said consolingly, "It's okay. Everyone has accidents."

People who have only seen the easygoing, humorous side of my aunt might not recognize this serious, compassionate side. Once, when I could not find any books that I wanted to read, she searched for two hours and returned with a stack of books. I just sat there stupefied at how generous and unselfish she was.

Now that I think about it, if it wasn't for Amy I might be a totally different person   and I like the way I am. I wouldn't have her any other way because she's my aunt: sweet, simple and intelligent.

In the first paragraph, Brittany conveys her main impression of her aunt through sensory details and description.

This anecdote and the last sentence support Brittany's impression of her aunt as funny and compassionate.

Brittany illustrates a part of Amy's personality through dialogue.

In the conclusion, Brittany describes how Amy has influenced her life.

Editing and Proofreading

Check your essay for errors in grammar, spelling, or punctuation.

Focus on Comparative and Superlative Adjectives: Descriptive essays usually contain many adjectives. Be sure that you have used comparative and superlative adjectives correctly. *Comparative adjectives* are used to compare two things. *Superlative adjectives* are used to compare three or more things.

- *Comparative:* John is *neater* than Joe; Joe is *more artistic* than John.
- *Superlative:* John is the *neatest* in our family; Joe is the *most artistic* person we know.

Publishing and Presenting

Consider sharing your writing using one of these ideas:

Make a photo scrapbook. Select a group of photos of you and your subject, and organize them in a small photo album. On each page of the album, include a paragraph from your description.

Prepare an oral presentation. Descriptive writing is well-suited to reading aloud. Gather props or music to enhance your reading. Then share your description with an audience.

Reflecting on Your Writing

Writer's Journal Jot down your thoughts on writing a description of a person. Begin by answering these questions:

- Which prewriting strategy might you use again? Why?
- What new insights about your subject did you gain?

> *Prentice Hall Writing and Grammar Connection, Chapter 6*

Rubric for Self-Assessment

To assess your description of a person, use the following rubric:

Criteria	Rating Scale
	not very → very
Focus: How clearly do you describe the person?	1 2 3 4 5
Organization: How logical and consistent is your organization?	1 2 3 4 5
Support/Elaboration: How effectively are personal anecdotes, examples, and sensory details used?	1 2 3 4 5
Style: How well do you describe this person's influence on your life?	1 2 3 4 5
Conventions: How correct is your grammar, especially your use of possessive nouns?	1 2 3 4 5

Author's Purpose

Skills You Will Learn

Reading Skill: *Recognize Details Indicating Author's Purpose*
Literary Analysis: *Mood*

Reading Skill: *Preview to Determine Purpose for Reading*

Reading Skill: *Evaluate Whether the Author Achieves His or Her Purpose*
Literary Analysis: *Author's Style*

Literary Analysis: *Comparing Types of Narratives*

Literature You Will Read

Reading: Author's Purpose

> ▶ The **author's purpose** is his or her reason for writing a particular work of literature.

Skills and Strategies You Will Learn in Part 2

In Part 2 you will learn

- to **recognize details that indicate the author's purpose** (p. 104)
- to **analyze details** that reveal an **author's purpose** (p. 104)
- to **evaluate** whether the author has achieved his or her **purpose** (p. 152)
- to **preview text** to **set a purpose** for your own reading (p. 146)

Using the Skills and Strategies in Part 2

In Part 2 you will learn to recognize and analyze details that show you the author's purpose. In addition, you will learn to evaluate whether the author effectively achieves his or her purpose. Recognizing and evaluating an author's purpose helps you decide whether what you read is accurate, useful, and valid.

The example shows how to analyze details in the passage to determine the author's purpose.

Around 1620, Spanish explorers brought horses to North America. With the arrival of horses, Native Americans on the Great Plains gave up farming and became *nomads*, moving from place to place as they hunted and living in portable dwellings called *teepees*.

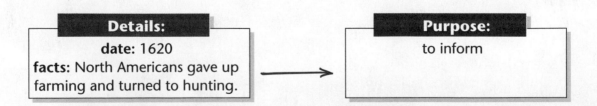

Details:		Purpose:
date: 1620 **facts:** North Americans gave up farming and turned to hunting.	→	to inform

Academic Vocabulary: Words for Discussing Author's Purpose

The following words will help you talk and write about the author's purpose as you read the selections in this unit.

Word	Definition	Example Sentence
analyze *v.*	to study the parts of something	We *analyze* the details of a literary work to determine an author's purpose.
intention *n.*	purpose; goal	The author's *intention* is to persuade.
establish *v.*	to show or prove	Facts *establish* the author's purpose.
determine *v.*	to figure out	To *determine* the author's purpose, study the work's details.
achieve *v.*	to succeed; to accomplish	Evaluate how well the author was able to *achieve* his or her purpose.

Vocabulary Skill: Suffixes

▶ A **suffix** is added to the end of a word to change its meaning or part of speech.

In Part 2 you will learn

- **the suffix -*yze*** (p. 144)
- **the suffix -*tion*** (p. 170)
- **the suffix -*ize*** (p. 144)
- **the suffix -*sion*** (p. 170)

Suffix	Changes	Examples	Meaning
-yze	to a verb	Analysis—*analyze*	Make an analysis
-ize	to a verb	Final—*finalize*	Make final
-tion	to a noun	Educate—*education*	Process of educating
-sion	to a noun	Persuade—*persuasion*	Process of persuading

Activity Use a dictionary to confirm the part of speech for each word. Then, use each word correctly in a sentence.

1. analysis, analyze
2. intend, intention
3. determine, determination
4. emphasis, emphasize

These skills will help you become a better reader. Practice them with either "The Adventure of the Speckled Band" (p. 106) or the excerpt from *An American Childhood* (p. 137).

Reading Skill

The **author's purpose** is his or her reason for writing. Learn to **recognize details that indicate the author's purpose.** Look for these types of details:

- To *inform,* an author might use facts and technical language. Read closely: Pause frequently and take notes.
- To *persuade,* an author might include reasons that lead readers to agree with an opinion. Read critically: Question and evaluate the author's statements and check facts.
- To *entertain,* an author might use facts that amuse, intrigue, horrify, or fascinate readers. Read for enjoyment: Respond to images, ideas, and characters.

Frequently, the author has both a specific purpose and a general purpose in mind. As you read, use a chart like the one shown to identify both types of purposes.

Types of Details
Surprising event; unique characters

↓

General Purpose
To entertain

↓

Specific Purpose
To capture a particular feeling or insight

Literary Analysis

Mood, or atmosphere, is the overall feeling that a literary work creates for the reader. The mood of a work might be serious, humorous, or sad. A variety of elements contribute to mood.

- Words, such as *grumpy,* and images, such as *a starlit night.*
- Setting, such as *a dark, shadowy room.*
- Events, such as *heavy storm clouds lifting.*

Vocabulary Builder

The Adventure of the Speckled Band

- **sinister** (sin´ is tər) *adj.* threatening harm or evil (p. 117) *A sinister buzz warned me that a wasp was nearby.*

- **compliance** (kəm plī´ əns) *n.* agreement to a request (p. 125) *His compliance was necessary for the project to go forward.*

- **tangible** (tan´ jə bəl) *adj.* able to be perceived by the senses (p. 126) *Firefighters usually find a tangible cause for a blaze.*

from An American Childhood

- **serene** (sə rēn´) *adj.* not disturbed or troubled; calm (p. 138) *Kim's serene manner calmed us all.*

- **luminous** (lo͞o´ mə nəs) *adj.* giving off light; shining; bright (p. 138) *The cabin was visible by the light of the luminous moon.*

- **conceivably** (kən sēv´ ə blē) *adv.* in an imaginable or believable way (p. 140) *Joe has trained so hard; he could conceivably win.*

Background

Sherlock Holmes One of the most beloved fictional detectives of all time is Sherlock Holmes, a nineteenth-century British character created by Arthur Conan Doyle. Holmes is famous for his deductive reasoning. He analyzes evidence—often little details that no one else notices—and puts together the pieces to figure out what they mean. Readers find out how Holmes solves the mystery when he explains his thinking to Dr. Watson, the character who narrates the story.

Connecting to the Literature

Reading/Writing Connection Think of what you know about detectives from television, literature, or real life. Write four or five sentences about how they gather information. Use at least three of the following words: *concentrate, conduct, consult, deduce, detect.*

Meet the Author

Sir Arthur Conan **Doyle** (1859–1930)

When Arthur Conan Doyle studied to be a medical doctor, one of his professors possessed an ability that Doyle found amazing. The professor was able to determine details, with total accuracy, about his patients' lives. When Doyle decided to become a writer, he based his character Sherlock Holmes on the professor. In 1887, he published his first Sherlock Holmes novel, *A Study in Scarlet.*

Holmes Murdered? By 1893, Doyle was tired of making up stories about this character, so he wrote "The Final Problem," in which he killed off Holmes. Public demand for more Sherlock Holmes was so overwhelming that in 1901, Doyle resurrected the detective in *The Hound of the Baskervilles.*

Fast Facts

▶ Doyle wrote four novels and fifty-six stories about Holmes.
▶ Sherlock Holmes's most famous expression is "Elementary, my dear Watson," but Arthur Conan Doyle never wrote these words. They were first spoken in the movie version by the Holmes character.

For: More about the author
Visit: www.PHSchool.com
Web Code: ene-9108

THE *Adventure*
OF THE
Speckled Band
SIR ARTHUR CONAN DOYLE

On glancing over my notes of the seventy odd cases in which I have during the last eight years studied the methods of my friend Sherlock Holmes, I find many tragic, some comic, a large number merely strange, but none commonplace; for, working as he did rather for the love of his art than for the acquirement of wealth, he refused to associate himself with any investigation which did not tend towards the unusual, and even the fantastic. Of all these varied cases, however, I cannot recall any which presented more singular features than that which was associated with the well-known Surrey

◀ Critical Viewing
What details indicate that the man is searching for clues?
[Analyze]

family of the Roylotts of Stoke Moran. The events in question occurred in the early days of my association with Holmes when we were sharing rooms as bachelors in Baker Street. It is possible that I might have placed them upon record before but a promise of secrecy was made at the time, from which I have only been freed during the last month by the untimely death of the lady to whom the pledge was given. It is perhaps as well that the facts should now come to light, for I have reasons to know that there are widespread rumors as to the death of Dr. Grimesby Roylott which tend to make the matter even more terrible than the truth.

It was early in April in the year 1883 that I woke one morning to find Sherlock Holmes standing, fully dressed, by the side of my bed. He was a late riser, as a rule, and as the clock on the mantelpiece showed me that it was only a quarter past seven, I blinked up at him in some surprise, and perhaps just a little resentment, for I was myself regular in my habits.

"Very sorry to wake you up, Watson," said he, "but it's the common lot this morning. Mrs. Hudson has been awakened, she retorted upon me, and I on you."

"What is it, then—a fire?"

"No; a client. It seems that a young lady has arrived in a considerable state of excitement who insists upon seeing me. She is waiting now in the sitting room. Now, when young ladies wander about the metropolis at this hour of the morning, and get sleepy people up out of their beds, I presume that it is something very pressing which they have to communicate. Should it prove to be an interesting case, you would, I am sure, wish to follow it from the outset. I thought, at any rate, that I should call you and give you the chance."

"My dear fellow, I would not miss it for anything."

I had no keener pleasure than in following Holmes in his professional investigations, and in admiring the rapid deductions, as swift as intuitions, and yet always founded on a logical basis, with which he unraveled the problems which were submitted to him. I rapidly threw on my clothes and was ready in a few minutes to accompany my friend down to the sitting room. A lady dressed in black and heavily veiled, who had been sitting in the window, rose as we entered.

"Good morning, madam," said Holmes cheerily. "My name is Sherlock Holmes. This is my intimate friend and associate, Dr. Watson, before whom you can speak as freely as before

Reading Skill
Author's Purpose
Why might the author introduce this story with references to secrets, rumors, and deaths?

Reading Check

Why does Sherlock Holmes wake Watson early?

myself. Ha! I am glad to see that Mrs. Hudson has had the good sense to light the fire. Pray draw up to it, and I shall order you a cup of hot coffee, for I observe that you are shivering."

"It is not cold which makes me shiver," said the woman in a low voice, changing her seat as requested.

"What, then?"

"It is fear, Mr. Holmes. It is terror." She raised her veil as she spoke, and we could see that she was indeed in a pitiable state of agitation, her face all drawn and gray, with restless, frightened eyes, like those of some hunted animal. Her features and figure were those of a woman of thirty, but her hair was shot with premature gray, and her expression was weary and haggard. Sherlock Holmes ran her over with one of his quick, all-comprehensive glances.

"You must not fear," said he soothingly, bending forward and patting her forearm. "We shall soon set matters right, I have no doubt. You have come in by train this morning, I see."

"You know me, then?"

"No, but I observe the second half of a return ticket in the palm of your left glove. You must have started early, and yet you had a good drive in a dogcart[1] along heavy roads, before you reached the station."

The lady gave a violent start and stared in bewilderment at my companion.

"There is no mystery, my dear madam," said he, smiling. "The left arm of your jacket is spattered with mud in

▼ Critical Viewing
What details in the description and dialogue does this illustration capture? [Connect]

---

1. **dogcart** *n.* small, horse-drawn carriage with seats arranged back-to-back.

no less than seven places. The marks are perfectly fresh. There is no vehicle save a dogcart which throws up mud in that way, and then only when you sit on the left-hand side of the driver."

"Whatever your reasons may be, you are perfectly correct," said she. "I started from home before six, reached Leatherhead at twenty past, and came in by the first train to Waterloo. Sir, I can stand this strain no longer; I shall go mad if it continues. I have no one to turn to—none, save only one, who cares for me, and he, poor fellow, can be of little aid. I have heard of you, Mr. Holmes. I have heard of you from Mrs. Farintosh, whom you helped in the hour of her sore need. It was from her that I had your address. Oh, sir, do you not think that you could help me, too, and at least throw a little light through the dense darkness which surrounds me? At present it is out of my power to reward you for your service, but in a month or six weeks I shall be married, with the control of my own income, and then at least you shall not find me ungrateful."

Holmes turned to his desk and, unlocking it, drew out a small case book, which he consulted.

"Farintosh," said he. "Ah yes, I recall the case; it was concerned with an opal tiara. I think it was before your time, Watson. I can only say, madam, that I shall be happy to devote the same care to your case as I did to that of your friend. As to reward, my profession is its own reward; but you are at liberty to defray[2] whatever expenses I may be put to, at the time which suits you best. And now I beg that you will lay before us everything that may help us in forming an opinion upon the matter."

"Alas!" replied our visitor, "the very horror of my situation lies in the fact that my fears are so vague, and my suspicions depend so entirely upon small points, which might seem trivial to another, that even he to whom of all others I have a right to look for help and advice looks upon all that I tell him about it as fancy.[3] He does not say so, but I can read it from his soothing answers and averted eyes. But I have heard, Mr. Holmes, that you can see deeply into the manifold wickedness of the human heart. You may advise me how to walk amid the dangers which encompass me."

Reading Skill
Author's Purpose
How do these details help you to appreciate Holmes's powers of observation?

Literary Analysis
Mood Which words and phrases in this paragraph suggest Helen Stoner's anxiety?

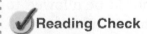**Reading Check**

Why is the visitor concerned that Sherlock Holmes will not take the case?

"I am all attention, madam."

"My name is Helen Stoner, and I am living with my stepfather, who is the last survivor of one of the oldest Saxon families in England: the Roylotts of Stoke Moran, on the western border of Surrey."

Holmes nodded his head. "The name is familiar to me," said he.

"The family was at one time among the richest in England, and the estates extended over the borders into Berkshire in the north, and Hampshire in the west. In the last century, however, four successive heirs were of a dissolute and wasteful disposition, and the family ruin was eventually completed by a gambler in the days of the Regency. Nothing was left save a few acres of ground, and the two-hundred-year-old house, which is itself crushed under a heavy mortgage. The last squire dragged out his existence there, living the horrible life of an aristocratic pauper;[4] but his only son, my stepfather, seeing that he must adapt himself to the new conditions, obtained an advance from a relative, which enabled him to take a medical degree and went out to Calcutta, where, by his professional skill and his force of character, he established a large practice. In a fit of anger, however, caused by some robberies which had been perpetrated in the house, he beat his native butler to death and narrowly escaped a capital sentence. As it was, he suffered a long term of imprisonment and afterwards returned to England a morose[5] and disappointed man.

"When Dr. Roylott was in India he married my mother, Mrs. Stoner, the young widow of Major-General Stoner, of the Bengal Artillery. My sister Julia and I were twins, and we were only two years old at the time of my mother's remarriage. She had a considerable sum of money—not less than £1000[6] a year—and this she bequeathed to Dr. Roylott entirely while we resided with him, with a provision that a certain annual sum should be allowed to each of us in the event of our marriage. Shortly after our return to England my mother died—she was killed eight years ago in a railway accident near Crewe. Dr. Roylott then abandoned his attempts to establish himself in practice in London and took us to live with him in the old

---

Reading Skill
Author's Purpose
What is Doyle's specific purpose in this part of the story?

---

4. **aristocratic pauper** upper-class person who has run out of money.
5. **morose** (mə rōs′) *adj.* gloomy; ill-tempered.
6. **£1000** one thousand pounds; £ is the symbol for "pound" or "pounds," the British unit of money.

ancestral house at Stoke Moran. The money which my mother had left was enough for all our wants, and there seemed to be no obstacle to our happiness.

"But a terrible change came over our stepfather about this time. Instead of making friends and exchanging visits with our neighbors, who had at first been overjoyed to see a Roylott of Stoke Moran back in the old family seat, he shut himself up in his house and seldom came out save to indulge in ferocious quarrels with who ever might cross his path. Violence of temper approaching to mania has been hereditary in the men of the family, and in my stepfather's case it had, I believe, been intensified by his long residence in the tropics. A series of disgraceful brawls took place, two of which ended in the police court, until at last he became the terror of the village, and the folks would fly at his approach, for he is a man of immense strength, and absolutely uncontrollable in his anger.

"Last week he hurled the local blacksmith over a parapet into a stream, and it was only by paying over all the money which I could gather together that I was able to avert another public exposure. He had no friends at all save the wandering gypsies, and he would give these vagabonds leave to encamp upon the few acres of bramble-covered land which represent the family estate, and would accept in return the hospitality of their tents, wandering away with them sometimes for weeks on end. He has a passion also for Indian animals, which are sent over to him by a correspondent, and he has at this moment a cheetah and a baboon, which wander freely over

▲ Critical Viewing
What qualities of Dr. Roylott does this illustration show? **[Analyze]**

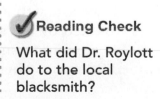

Reading Check

What did Dr. Roylott do to the local blacksmith?

his grounds and are feared by the villagers almost as much as is their master.

"You can imagine from what I say that my poor sister Julia and I had no great pleasure in our lives. No servant would stay with us, and for a long time we did all the work of the house. She was but thirty at the time of her death, and yet her hair had already begun to whiten, even as mine has."

"Your sister is dead, then?"

"She died just two years ago, and it is of her death that I wish to speak to you. You can understand that, living the life which I have described, we were little likely to see anyone of our own age and position. We had, however, an aunt, my mother's maiden sister, Miss Honoria Westphail, who lives near Harrow, and we were occasionally allowed to pay short visits at this lady's house. Julia went there at Christmas two years ago, and met there a major in the Marines, to whom she became engaged. My stepfather learned of the engagement when my sister returned and offered no objection to the marriage; but within a fortnight of the day which had been fixed for the wedding, the terrible event occurred which has deprived me of my only companion."

Sherlock Holmes had been leaning back in his chair with his eyes closed and his head sunk in a cushion, but he half opened his lids now and glanced across at his visitor.

"Pray be precise as to details," said he.

"It is easy for me to be so, for every event of that dreadful time is seared into my memory. The manor house is, as I have already said, very old, and only one wing is now inhabited. The bedrooms in this wing are on the ground floor, the sitting rooms being in the central block of the buildings. Of these bedrooms the first is Dr. Roylott's, the second my sister's, and the third my own. There is no communication between them, but they all open out into the same corridor. Do I make myself plain?"

"Perfectly so."

"The windows of the three rooms open out upon the lawn. That fatal night Dr. Roylott had gone to his room early, though we knew that he had not retired to rest, for my sister was troubled by the smell of the strong Indian cigars which it was his custom to smoke. She left her room, therefore, and came into mine, where she sat for some time, chatting about

Literary Analysis
Mood What words and phrases in this paragraph contribute to a mood of mystery and suspense?

her approaching wedding. At eleven o'clock she rose to leave me, but she paused at the door and looked back.

"'Tell me, Helen,' said she, 'have you ever heard anyone whistle in the dead of the night?'

"'Never,' said I.

"'I suppose that you could not possibly whistle, yourself, in your sleep?'

"'Certainly not. But why?'

"'Because during the last few nights I have always, about three in the morning, heard a low, clear whistle. I am a light sleeper, and it has awakened me. I cannot tell where it came from—perhaps from the next room, perhaps from the lawn. I thought that I would just ask you whether you had heard it.'

"'No, I have not. It must be the gypsies in the plantation.'

"'Very likely. And yet if it were on the lawn, I wonder that you did not hear it also.'

"'Ah, but I sleep more heavily than you.'

"'Well, it is of no great consequence, at any rate.' She smiled back at me, closed my door, and a few moments later I heard her key turn in the lock."

"Indeed," said Holmes. "Was it your custom always to lock yourselves in at night?"

"Always."

"And why?"

"I think that I mentioned to you that the doctor kept a cheetah and a baboon. We had no feeling of security unless our doors were locked."

"Quite so. Pray proceed with your statement."

"I could not sleep that night. A vague feeling of impending misfortune impressed me. My sister and I, you will recollect, were twins, and you know how subtle are the links which bind two souls which are so closely allied. It was a wild night. The wind was howling outside, and the rain was beating and splashing against the windows. Suddenly, amid all the hubbub of the gale, there burst forth the wild scream of a terrified woman. I knew that it was my sister's voice. I sprang from my bed, wrapped a shawl round me, and rushed into the corridor. As I opened my door I seemed to hear a low whistle, such as my sister described, and a few moments later a clanging sound, as if a mass of metal had fallen. As I ran down the passage, my sister's door was unlocked, and revolved slowly upon

Reading Skill
Author's Purpose
Why does Doyle use such detail in Helen's description of events?

Reading Check

What noise woke Helen's sister from sleep the last few nights before she died?

◀ **Critical Viewing**
How well does this
illustration convey
Julia Stoner's face,
"blanched with
terror"? **[Evaluate]**

its hinges. I stared at it horror-stricken, not knowing what
was about to issue from it. By the light of the corridor lamp I
saw my sister appear at the opening, her face blanched with
terror, her hands groping for help, her whole figure swaying to
and fro like that of a drunkard. I ran to her and threw my
arms round her, but at that moment her knees seemed to give
way and she fell to the ground. She writhed as one who is in
terrible pain, and her limbs were dreadfully convulsed.[7] At
first I thought that she had not recognized me, but as I bent
over her she suddenly shrieked out in a voice which I shall
never forget, 'Oh, Helen! It was the band! The speckled band!'
There was something else which she would fain have said,
and she stabbed with her finger into the air in the direction of
the doctor's room, but a fresh convulsion seized her and
choked her words. I rushed out, calling loudly for my stepfather, and I met him hastening from his room in his dressing
gown. When he reached my sister's side she was unconscious,
and though he poured brandy down her throat and sent for
medical aid from the village, all efforts were in vain, for she
slowly sank and died without having recovered her consciousness. Such was the dreadful end of my beloved sister."

"One moment," said Holmes; "are you sure about this whistle and metallic sound? Could you swear to it?"

Literary Analysis
Mood What mood
does this description
of Julia convey?

---

7. **convulsed** (kən vulst´) *adj.* taken over by violent, uncontrollable muscular spasms.

"That was what the county coroner asked me at the inquiry. It is my strong impression that I heard it, and yet, among the crash of the gale and the creaking of an old house, I may possibly have been deceived."

"Was your sister dressed?"

"No, she was in her nightdress. In her right hand was found the charred stump of a match, and in her left a matchbox."

"Showing that she had struck a light and looked about her when the alarm took place. That is important. And what conclusions did the coroner come to?"

"He investigated the case with great care, for Dr. Roylott's conduct had long been notorious in the county, but he was unable to find any satisfactory cause of death. My evidence showed that the door had been fastened upon the inner side, and the windows were blocked by old-fashioned shutters with broad iron bars, which were secured every night. The walls were carefully sounded, and were shown to be quite solid all round, and the flooring was also thoroughly examined, with the same result. The chimney is wide, but is barred up by four large staples. It is certain, therefore, that my sister was quite alone when she met her end. Besides, there were no marks of any violence upon her."

"How about poison?"

"The doctors examined her for it, but without success."

"What do you think that this unfortunate lady died of, then?"

"It is my belief that she died of pure fear and nervous shock, though what it was that frightened her I cannot imagine."

"Were there gypsies in the plantation at the time?"

"Yes, there are nearly always some there."

"Ah, and what did you gather from this allusion to a band— a speckled band?"

"Sometimes I have thought that it was merely the wild talk of delirium, sometimes that it may have referred to some band of people, perhaps to these very gypsies in the plantation. I do not know whether the spotted handkerchiefs which so many of them wear over their heads might have suggested the strange adjective which she used."

Holmes shook his head like a man who is far from being satisfied.

"These are very deep waters," said he; "pray go on with your narrative."

Reading Skill
Author's Purpose
Why does the author show Holmes asking Helen so many questions?

Reading Check

What does Julia say to Helen just before she dies?

"Two years have passed since then, and my life has been until lately lonelier than ever. A month ago, however, a dear friend, whom I have known for many years, has done me the honor to ask my hand in marriage. His name is Armitage— Percy Armitage—the second son of Mr. Armitage, of Crane Water, near Reading. My stepfather has offered no opposition to the match, and we are to be married in the course of the spring. Two days ago some repairs were started in the west wing of the building, and my bedroom wall has been pierced, so that I have had to move into the chamber in which my sister died, and to sleep in the very bed in which she slept. Imagine, then, my thrill of terror when last night, as I lay awake, thinking over her terrible fate, I suddenly heard in the silence of the night the low whistle which had been the herald of her own death. I sprang up and lit the lamp, but nothing was to be seen in the room. I was too shaken to go to bed again, however, so I dressed, and as soon as it was daylight I slipped down, got a dogcart at the Crown Inn, which is opposite, and drove to Leatherhead, from whence I have come on this morning with the one object of seeing you and asking your advice."

"You have done wisely," said my friend. "But have you told me all?"

"Yes, all."

"Miss Roylott, you have not. You are screening your stepfather."

"Why, what do you mean?"

For answer Holmes pushed back the frill of black lace which fringed the hand that lay upon our visitor's knee. Five little livid spots, the marks of four fingers and a thumb, were printed upon the white wrist.

"You have been cruelly used," said Holmes.

The lady colored deeply and covered over her injured wrist. "He is a hard man," she said, "and perhaps he hardly knows his own strength."

There was a long silence, during which Holmes leaned his chin upon his hands and stared into the crackling fire.

"This is a very deep business," he said at last. "There are a thousand details which I should desire to know before I decide upon our course of action. Yet we have not a moment to lose. If we were to come to Stoke Moran today, would it be possible for us to look over these rooms without the knowledge of your stepfather?"

Literary Analysis
Mood What details in this paragraph increase the sense that something terrible will happen?

"As it happens, he spoke of coming into town today upon some most important business. It is probable that he will be away all day and that there would be nothing to disturb you. We have a housekeeper now, but I could easily get her out of the way."

"Excellent. You are not averse to this trip, Watson?"

"By no means."

"Then we shall both come. What are you going to do yourself?"

"I have one or two things which I would wish to do now that I am in town. But I shall return by the twelve o'clock train, so as to be there in time for your coming."

"And you may expect us early in the afternoon. I have myself some small business matters to attend to. Will you not wait and breakfast?"

"No, I must go. My heart is lightened already since I have confided my trouble to you. I shall look forward to seeing you again this afternoon." She dropped her thick black veil over her face and glided from the room.

"And what do you think of it all, Watson?" asked Sherlock Holmes, leaning back in his chair.

"It seems to me to be a most dark and <u>sinister</u> business."

"Dark enough and sinister enough."

"Yet if the lady is correct in saying that the flooring and walls are sound, and that the door, window, and chimney are impassable, then her sister must have been undoubtedly alone when she met her mysterious end."

"What becomes, then, of these nocturnal whistles, and what of the very peculiar words of the dying woman?"

"I cannot think."

"When you combine the ideas of whistles at night, the presence of a band of gypsies who are on intimate terms with this old doctor, the fact that we have every reason to believe that the doctor has an interest in preventing his stepdaughter's marriage, the dying allusion to a band, and, finally, the fact that Miss Helen Stoner heard a metallic clang, which might have been caused by one of those metal bars that secured the shutters, falling back into its place, I think that there is good ground to think that the mystery may be cleared along those lines."

"But what, then, did the gypsies do?"

"I cannot imagine."

Vocabulary Builder
sinister (sin´ is tər)
adj. threatening harm or evil

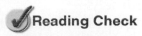

Reading Check

What caused the marks on Helen's wrist?

"I see many objections to any such theory."

"And so do I. It is precisely for that reason that we are going to Stoke Moran this day. I want to see whether the objections are fatal, or if they may be explained away. But what in the name of the devil!"

The ejaculation had been drawn from my companion by the fact that our door had been suddenly dashed open, and that a huge man had framed himself in the aperture. His costume was a peculiar mixture of the professional and of the agricultural, having a black top hat, a long frock coat, and a pair of high gaiters, with a hunting crop[8] swinging in his hand. So tall was he that his hat actually brushed the crossbar of the doorway, and his breadth seemed to span it across from side to side. A large face, seared with a thousand wrinkles, burned yellow with the sun, and marked with every evil passion, was turned from one to the other of us, while his deep-set, bile-shot eyes, and his high, thin, fleshless nose, gave him somewhat the resemblance to a fierce old bird of prey.

"Which of you is Holmes?" asked this apparition.

"My name, sir; but you have the advantage of me," said my companion quietly.

"I am Dr. Grimesby Roylott, of Stoke Moran."

"Indeed, Doctor," said Holmes blandly. "Pray take a seat."

"I will do nothing of the kind. My stepdaughter has been here. I have traced her. What has she been saying to you?"

"It is a little cold for the time of the year," said Holmes.

"What has she been saying to you?" screamed the old man furiously.

"But I have heard that the crocuses promise well," continued my companion imperturbably.

Reading Skill
Author's Purpose
What specific purpose does the conversation between Holmes and Watson serve?

▼ **Critical Viewing**
Which figure in this illustration is Dr. Roylott? How can you tell? **[Deduce]**

---

8. gaiters, with a hunting crop cloth or leather coverings for the lower legs, with a short whip used to direct a horse while riding.

"Ha! You put me off, do you?" said our new visitor, taking a step forward and shaking his hunting crop. "I know you, you scoundrel! I have heard of you before. You are Holmes, the meddler."

My friend smiled.

"Holmes, the busybody!"

His smile broadened.

"Holmes, the Scotland Yard Jack-in-office!"

Holmes chuckled heartily. "Your conversation is most entertaining," said he. "When you go out close the door, for there is a decided draft."

"I will go when I have said my say. Don't you dare to meddle with my affairs. I know that Miss Stoner has been here. I traced her! I am a dangerous man to fall foul of! See here." He stepped swiftly forward, seized the poker, and bent it into a curve with his huge brown hands.

"See that you keep yourself out of my grip," he snarled, and hurling the twisted poker into the fireplace he strode out of the room.

"He seems a very amiable person," said Holmes, laughing. "I am not quite so bulky, but if he had remained I might have shown him that my grip was not much more feeble than his own." As he spoke he picked up the steel poker and, with a sudden effort, straightened it out again.

"Fancy his having the insolence to confound me with[9] the official detective force! This incident gives zest to our investigation, however, and I only trust that our little friend will not suffer from her imprudence in allowing this brute to trace her. And now, Watson, we shall order breakfast, and afterwards I shall walk down to Doctors' Commons, where I hope to get some data which may help us in this matter."

It was nearly one o'clock when Sherlock Holmes returned from his excursion. He held in his hand a sheet of blue paper, scrawled over with notes and figures.

"I have seen the will of the deceased wife," said he. "To determine its exact meaning I have been obliged to work out the present prices of the investments with which it is concerned. The total income, which at the time of the wife's death was little short of £1100, is now, through the fall in agricultural prices, not more than £750. Each daughter can claim an income of £250, in case of marriage. It is evident, therefore, that if both girls had married, this beauty would have had a

9. confound me with mistake me for.

Reading Skill
Author's Purpose
What aspects of the confrontation with Dr. Roylott serve a general purpose of entertaining?

Reading Check

Why does Dr. Roylott visit Holmes and Watson?

mere pittance,[10] while even one of them would cripple him to a very serious extent. My morning's work has not been wasted, since it has proved that he has the very strongest motives for standing in the way of anything of the sort. And now, Watson, this is too serious for dawdling, especially as the old man is aware that we are interesting ourselves in his affairs; so if you are ready, we shall call a cab and drive to Waterloo. I should be very much obliged if you would slip your revolver into your pocket. An Eley's No. 2 is an excellent argument with gentlemen who can twist steel pokers into knots. That and a toothbrush are, I think, all that we need."

At Waterloo we were fortunate in catching a train for Leatherhead, where we hired a trap at the station inn and drove for four or five miles through the lovely Surrey lanes. It was a perfect day, with a bright sun and a few fleecy clouds in the heavens. The trees and wayside hedges were just throwing out their first green shoots, and the air was full of the pleasant smell of the moist earth. To me at least there was a strange contrast between the sweet promise of the spring and this sinister quest upon which we were engaged. My companion sat in the front of the trap, his arms folded, his hat pulled down over his eyes, and his chin sunk upon his breast, buried in the deepest thought. Suddenly, however, he started, tapped me on the shoulder, and pointed over the meadows.

"Look there!" said he.

A heavily timbered park stretched up in a gentle slope, thickening into a grove at the highest point. From amid the branches there jutted out the gray gables and high rooftop of a very old mansion.

"Stoke Moran?" said he.

"Yes, sir, that be the house of Dr. Grimesby Roylott," remarked the driver.

"There is some building going on there," said Holmes; "that is where we are going."

"There's the village," said the driver, pointing to a cluster of roofs some distance to the left; "but if you want to get to the house, you'll find it shorter to get over this stile, and so by the footpath over the fields. There it is, where the lady is walking."

"And the lady, I fancy, is Miss Stoner," observed Holmes, shading his eyes. "Yes, I think we had better do as you suggest."

Literary Analysis
Mood How does Holmes's suggestion to bring a revolver affect the mood of the story?

---

10. pittance (pit´ 'ns) *n.* small or barely sufficient sum of money.

We got off, paid our fare, and the trap rattled back on its way to Leatherhead.

"I thought it as well," said Holmes as we climbed the stile, "that this fellow should think we had come here as architects, or on some definite business. It may stop his gossip. Good afternoon, Miss Stoner. You see that we have been as good as our word."

Our client of the morning had hurried forward to meet us with a face which spoke her joy. "I have been waiting so eagerly for you," she cried, shaking hands with us warmly. "All has turned out splendidly. Dr. Roylott has gone to town, and it is unlikely that he will be back before evening."

"We have had the pleasure of making the doctor's acquaintance," said Holmes, and in a few words he sketched out what had occurred. Miss Stoner turned white to the lips as she listened.

"Good heavens!" she cried, "he has followed me, then."

"So it appears."

"He is so cunning that I never know when I am safe from him. What will he say when he returns?"

"He must guard himself, for he may find that there is someone more cunning than himself upon his track. You must lock yourself up from him tonight. If he is violent, we shall take you away to your aunt's at Harrow. Now, we must make the best use of our time, so kindly take us at once to the rooms which we are to examine."

The building was of gray, lichen-blotched stone, with a high central portion and two curving wings, like the claws of a crab, thrown out on each side. In one of these wings the windows were broken and blocked with wooden boards, while the roof was partly caved in, a picture of ruin. The central portion was in little better repair, but the right-hand block was comparatively modern, and the blinds in the windows, with the blue smoke curling up from the chimneys, showed that this was where the family resided. Some scaffolding had been erected against the end wall, and the stonework had been broken into, but there were no signs of any workmen at the moment of our visit. Holmes walked slowly up and down the ill-trimmed lawn and examined with deep attention the outsides of the windows.

"This, I take it, belongs to the room in which you used to sleep, the center one to your sister's, and the one next to the main building to Dr. Roylott's chamber?"

Literary Analysis
Mood In what way does Miss Stoner's greeting change the mood?

Reading Check

Where is Dr. Roylott when Holmes and Watson arrive at Stoke Moran?

"Exactly so. But I am now sleeping in the middle one."

"Pending the alterations, as I understand. By the way, there does not seem to be any very pressing need for repairs at that end wall."

"There were none. I believe that it was an excuse to move me from my room."

"Ah! that is suggestive. Now, on the other side of this narrow wing runs the corridor from which these three rooms open. There are windows in it, of course?"

"Yes, but very small ones. Too narrow for anyone to pass through."

"As you both locked your doors at night, your rooms were unapproachable from that side. Now, would you have the kindness to go into your room and bar your shutters?"

Miss Stoner did so, and Holmes, after a careful examination through the open window, endeavored in every way to force the shutter open, but without success. There was no slit through which a knife could be passed to raise the bar. Then with his lens he tested the hinges, but they were of solid iron, built firmly into the massive masonry. "Hum!" said he, scratching his chin in some perplexity. "My theory certainly presents some difficulties. No one could pass through these shutters if they were bolted. Well, we shall see if the inside throws any light upon the matter."

A small side door led into the whitewashed corridor from which the three bedrooms opened. Holmes refused to examine the third chamber, so we passed at once to the second, that in which Miss Stoner was now sleeping, and in which her sister had met with her fate. It was a homely little room, with a low ceiling and a gaping fireplace, after the fashion of old country

▲ **Critical Viewing**
What emotion do you think each character is feeling in this illustration? **[Infer]**

houses. A brown chest of drawers stood in one corner, a narrow white-counterpaned bed in another, and a dressing table on the left-hand side of the window. These articles, with two small wickerwork chairs, made up all the furniture in the room save for a square of Wilton carpet in the center. The boards round and the paneling of the walls were of brown, worm-eaten oak, so old and discolored that it may have dated from the original building of the house. Holmes drew one of the chairs into a corner and sat silent, while his eyes traveled round and round and up and down, taking in every detail of the apartment.

"Where does that bell communicate with?" he asked at last, pointing to a thick bell-rope which hung down beside the bed, the tassel actually lying upon the pillow.

"It goes to the housekeeper's room."

"It looks newer than the other things?"

"Yes, it was only put there a couple of years ago."

"Your sister asked for it, I suppose?"

"No, I never heard of her using it. We used always to get what we wanted for ourselves."

"Indeed, it seemed unnecessary to put so nice a bell-pull there. You will excuse me for a few minutes while I satisfy myself as to this floor." He threw himself down upon his face with his lens in his hand and crawled swiftly backward and forward, examining minutely the cracks between the boards. Then he did the same with the woodwork with which the chamber was paneled. Finally he walked over to the bed and spent some time in staring at it and in running his eye up and down the wall. Finally he took the bell-rope in his hand and gave it a brisk tug.

"Why, it's a dummy," said he.

"Won't it ring?"

"No, it is not even attached to a wire. This is very interesting. You can see now that it is fastened to a hook just above where the little opening for the ventilator is."

"How very absurd! I never noticed that before!"

"Very strange!" muttered Holmes, pulling at the rope. "There are one or two very singular points about this room. For example, what a fool a builder must be to open a ventilator into another room, when, with the same trouble, he might have communicated with the outside air!"

"That is also quite modern," said the lady.

Reading Skill
Author's Purpose
List two details that prove Holmes is a thorough detective.

Reading Check

What does Holmes discover about the bell-rope?

"Done about the same time as the bell-rope?" remarked Holmes.

"Yes, there were several little changes carried out about that time."

"They seem to have been of a most interesting character—dummy bell-ropes, and ventilators which do not ventilate. With your permission, Miss Stoner, we shall now carry our researches into the inner apartment."

Dr. Grimesby Roylott's chamber was larger than that of his stepdaughter, but was as plainly furnished. A camp bed, a small wooden shelf full of books, mostly of a technical character, an armchair beside the bed, a plain wooden chair against the wall, a round table, and a large iron safe were the principal things which met the eye. Holmes walked slowly round and examined each and all of them with the keenest interest.

"What's in here?" he asked, tapping the safe.

"My stepfather's business papers."

"Oh! you have seen inside, then?"

"Only once, some years ago. I remember that it was full of papers."

"There isn't a cat in it, for example?"

"No. What a strange idea!"

"Well, look at this!" He took up a small saucer of milk which stood on the top of it.

"No; we don't keep a cat. But there is a cheetah and a baboon."

"Ah, yes, of course! Well, a cheetah is just a big cat, and yet a saucer of milk does not go very far in satisfying its wants, I daresay. There is one point which I should wish to determine." He squatted down in front of the wooden chair and examined the seat of it with the greatest attention.

"Thank you. That is quite settled," said he, rising and putting his lens in his pocket. "Hello! Here is something interesting!"

The object which had caught his eye was a small dog lash hung on one corner of the bed. The lash, however, was curled upon itself and tied so as to make a loop of whipcord.

"What do you make of that, Watson?"

"It's a common enough lash. But I don't know why it should be tied."

Literary Analysis
Mood Do Holmes's observations and questions convey a mood of light-heartedness or seriousness? Explain.

"That is not quite so common, is it? Ah, me! it's a wicked world, and when a clever man turns his brains to crime it is the worst of all. I think that I have seen enough now, Miss Stoner, and with your permission we shall walk out upon the lawn."

I had never seen my friend's face so grim or his brow so dark as it was when we turned from the scene of this investigation. We had walked several times up and down the lawn, neither Miss Stoner nor myself liking to break in upon his thoughts before he roused himself from his reverie.[11]

"It is very essential, Miss Stoner," said he, "that you should absolutely follow my advice in every respect."

"I shall most certainly do so."

"The matter is too serious for any hesitation. Your life may depend upon your <u>compliance</u>."

"I assure you that I am in your hands."

"In the first place, both my friend and I must spend the night in your room."

Both Miss Stoner and I gazed at him in astonishment.

"Yes, it must be so. Let me explain. I believe that that is the village inn over there?"

"Yes, that is the Crown."

"Very good. Your windows would be visible from there?"

"Certainly."

"You must confine yourself to your room, on pretense of a headache, when your stepfather comes back. Then when you hear him retire for the night, you must open the shutters of your window, undo the hasp,[12] put your lamp there as a signal to us, and then withdraw quietly with everything which you are likely to want into the room which you used to occupy. I have no doubt that, in spite of the repairs, you could manage there for one night."

"Oh, yes, easily."

"The rest you will leave in our hands."

"But what will you do?"

"We shall spend the night in your room, and we shall investigate the cause of this noise which has disturbed you."

"I believe, Mr. Holmes, that you have already made up your mind," said Miss Stoner, laying her hand upon my companion's sleeve.

Literary Analysis
Mood Describe the mood as Holmes walks up and down the lawn.

Vocabulary Builder
compliance (kəm plī´ əns) *n.* agreement to a request

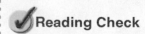

Reading Check

What does Holmes tell Miss Stoner he and Watson must do?

---

11. reverie (rev´ ə rē) *n.* dreamy thinking or imagining.
12. hasp *n.* hinged metal fastening of a window.

"Perhaps I have."

"Then, for pity's sake, tell me what was the cause of my sister's death."

"I should prefer to have clearer proofs before I speak."

"You can at least tell me whether my own thought is correct, and if she died from some sudden fright."

"No, I do not think so. I think that there was probably some more <u>tangible</u> cause. And now, Miss Stoner, we must leave you, for if Dr. Roylott returned and saw us our journey would be in vain. Goodbye, and be brave, for if you will do what I

Vocabulary Builder
tangible (tan´ jə bəl) *adj.* able to be perceived by the senses

Literature in Context   Science Connection

DNA Fingerprinting

In modern times, detectives can solve crimes using DNA evidence from hair, blood, or saliva collected at the crime scene. Here is how the process works:

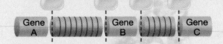

▲ With the exception of identical twins, each of us has unique DNA. Chromosomes have large amounts of DNA called *repeats*.

▲ For identification purposes, restriction enzymes are used to cut DNA from samples into fragments containing genes and repeats.

▲ The fragments are separated by size using a machine like the one shown. The ones with repeats are labeled using radioactive probes.

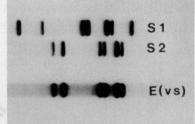

▲ The result is a series of bands—
◄ the DNA fingerprint. Fans of this technique believe it is sensitive enough to identify one person from 100,000 to 1 million others.

Connect to the Literature   Would DNA fingerprinting help Holmes solve this particular mystery? Why or why not?

have told you, you may rest assured that we shall soon drive away the dangers that threaten you."

Sherlock Holmes and I had no difficulty in engaging a bedroom and sitting room at the Crown Inn. They were on the upper floor, and from our window we could command a view of the avenue gate, and of the inhabited wing of Stoke Moran Manor House. At dusk we saw Dr. Grimesby Roylott drive past, his huge form looming up beside the little figure of the lad who drove him. The boy had some slight difficulty in undoing the heavy iron gates, and we heard the hoarse roar of the doctor's voice and saw the fury with which he shook his clinched fists at him. The trap drove on, and a few minutes later we saw a sudden light spring up among the trees as the lamp was lit in one of the sitting rooms.

"Do you know, Watson," said Holmes as we sat together in the gathering darkness, "I have really some scruples as to taking you tonight. There is a distinct element of danger."

"Can I be of assistance?"

"Your presence might be invaluable."

"Then I shall certainly come."

"It is very kind of you."

"You speak of danger. You have evidently seen more in these rooms than was visible to me."

"No, but I fancy that I may have deduced a little more. I imagine that you saw all that I did."

"I saw nothing remarkable save the bell-rope, and what purpose that could answer I confess is more than I can imagine."

"You saw the ventilator, too?"

"Yes, but I do not think that it is such a very unusual thing to have a small opening between two rooms. It was so small that a rat could hardly pass through."

"I knew that we should find a ventilator before ever we came to Stoke Moran."

"My dear Holmes!"

"Oh, yes, I did. You remember in her statement she said that her sister could smell Dr. Roylott's cigar. Now, of course that suggested at once that there must be a communication between the two rooms. It could only be a small one, or it would have been remarked upon at the coroner's inquiry. I deduced a ventilator."

"But what harm can there be in that?"

Reading Skill
Author's Purpose
What details in this paragraph help you remember why the situation is dangerous?

Reading Check

Why is it important that Dr. Roylott not see Holmes and Watson on the grounds of his mansion?

"Well, there is at least a curious coincidence of dates. A ventilator is made, a cord is hung, and a lady who sleeps in the bed dies. Does not that strike you?"

"I cannot as yet see any connection."

"Did you observe anything very peculiar about that bed?"

"No."

"It was clamped to the floor. Did you ever see a bed fastened like that before?"

"I cannot say that I have."

"The lady could not move her bed. It must always be in the same relative position to the ventilator and to the rope—or so we may call it, since it was clearly never meant for a bell-pull."

"Holmes," I cried, "I seem to see dimly what you are hinting at. We are only just in time to prevent some subtle and horrible crime."

"Subtle enough and horrible enough. When a doctor does go wrong he is the first of criminals. He has nerve and he has knowledge. Palmer and Pritchard were among the heads of their profession. This man strikes even deeper, but I think, Watson, that we shall be able to strike deeper still. But we shall have horrors enough before the night is over; for goodness' sake let us have a quiet pipe and turn our minds for a few hours to something more cheerful."

About nine o'clock the light among the trees was extinguished, and all was dark in the direction of the Manor House. Two hours passed slowly away, and then, suddenly, just at the stroke of eleven, a single bright light shone out right in front of us.

"That is our signal," said Holmes, springing to his feet; "it comes from the middle window."

As we passed out he exchanged a few words with the landlord, explaining that we were going on a late visit to an acquaintance, and that it was possible that we might spend the night there. A moment later we were out on the dark road, a chill wind blowing in our faces, and one yellow light twinkling in front of us through the gloom to guide us on our somber errand.

There was little difficulty in entering the grounds; for unrepaired breaches gaped in the old park wall. Making our way among the trees, we reached the lawn, crossed it, and were about to enter through the window when out from a clump of laurel bushes there darted what seemed to be a hideous and distorted child, who threw itself upon the grass with

Literary Analysis
Mood List three words or phrases in this paragraph that hint at danger.

writing limbs and then ran swiftly across the lawn into the darkness.

"My God!" I whispered; "did you see it?"

Holmes was for the moment as startled as I. His hand closed like a vise upon my wrist in his agitation. Then he broke into a low laugh and put his lips to my ear.

"It is a nice household," he murmured. "That is the baboon."

I had forgotten the strange pets which the doctor affected. There was a cheetah, too; perhaps we might find it upon our shoulders at any moment. I confess that I felt easier in my mind when, after following Holmes's example and slipping off my shoes, I found myself inside the bedroom. My companion noiselessly closed the shutters, moved the lamp onto the table, and cast his eyes round the room. All was as we had seen it in the daytime. Then creeping up to me and making a trumpet of his hand, he whispered into my ear again so gently that it was all that I could do to distinguish the words:

"The least sound would be fatal to our plans."

I nodded to show that I had heard.

"We must sit without light. He would see it through the ventilator."

I nodded again.

"Do not go asleep; your very life may depend upon it. Have your pistol ready in case we should need it. I will sit on the side of the bed, and you in that chair."

I took out my revolver and laid it on the corner of the table.

Holmes had brought up a long thin cane, and this he placed upon the bed beside him. By it he laid the box of matches and the stump of a candle. Then he turned down the lamp, and we were left in darkness.

How shall I ever forget that dreadful vigil?[13] I could not hear a sound, not even the drawing of a breath, and yet I knew that my companion sat open-eyed, within a few feet of me, in the same state of nervous tension in which I was myself. The shutters cut off the least ray of light, and we waited in absolute darkness. From outside came the occasional cry of a night bird, and once at our very window a long-drawn catlike whine, which told us that the cheetah was indeed at liberty. Far away we could hear the deep tones of the parish clock, which boomed out every quarter of an hour. How long they

---

Reading Skill
Author's Purpose
Why do you think the author includes the startling incident with the baboon?

Literary Analysis
Mood What details in this paragraph add to the mood of dread?

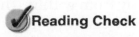Reading Check

What does Holmes caution Watson not to do?

---

13. vigil (vij´ əl) *n.* watch; period of staying awake during the usual hours of sleep.

seemed, those quarters! Twelve struck, and one and two and three, and still we sat waiting silently for whatever might befall.

Suddenly there was the momentary gleam of a light up in the direction of the ventilator, which vanished immediately, but was succeeded by a strong smell of burning oil and heated metal. Someone in the next room had lit a dark lantern.[14] I heard a gentle sound of movement, and then all was silent once more, though the smell grew stronger. For half an hour I sat with straining ears. Then suddenly another sound became audible—a very gentle, soothing sound, like that of a small jet of steam escaping continually from a kettle. The instant that we heard it, Holmes sprang from the bed, struck a match, and lashed furiously with his cane at the bell-pull.

"You see it, Watson?" he yelled. "You see it?"

But I saw nothing. At the moment when Holmes struck the light I heard a low, clear whistle, but the sudden glare flashing into my weary eyes made it impossible for me to tell what it was at which my friend lashed so savagely. I could, however, see that his face was deadly pale and filled with horror and loathing.

He had ceased to strike and was gazing up at the ventilator when suddenly there broke from the silence of the night the most horrible cry to which I have ever listened. It swelled up louder and louder, a hoarse yell of pain and fear and anger all mingled in the one dreadful shriek. They say that away down in the village, and even in the distant parsonage, that cry raised the sleepers from their beds. It struck cold to our hearts, and I stood gazing at Holmes, and he at me, until the last echoes of it had died away into the silence from which it rose.

"What can it mean?" I gasped.

"It means that it is all over," Holmes answered. "And perhaps, after all, it is for the best. Take your pistol, and we will enter Dr. Roylott's room."

With a grave face he lit the lamp and led the way down the corridor. Twice he struck at the chamber door without any reply from within. Then he turned the handle and entered, I at his heels, with the cocked pistol in my hand.

It was a singular sight which met our eyes. On the table stood a dark lantern with the shutter half open, throwing a brilliant beam of light upon the iron safe, the door of

---

14. dark lantern lantern with a shutter that can hide the light.

which was ajar. Beside this table, on the wooden chair, sat Dr. Grimesby Roylott, clad in a long gray dressing gown, his bare ankles protruding beneath, and his feet thrust into red heelless Turkish slippers. Across his lap lay the short stock with the long lash which we had noticed during the day. His chin was cocked upward and his eyes were fixed in a dreadful, rigid stare at the corner of the ceiling. Round his brow he had a peculiar yellow band, with brownish speckles, which seemed to be bound tightly round his head. As we entered he made neither sound nor motion.

"The band! the speckled band!" whispered Holmes.

▼ Critical Viewing Does this illustration effectively capture a sense of extreme danger? Why or why not? [Make a Judgment]

I took a step forward. In an instant his strange headgear began to move, and there reared itself from among his hair the squat diamond-shaped head and puffed neck of a loathsome serpent.

"It is a swamp adder!" cried Holmes; "the deadliest snake in India. He has died within ten seconds of being bitten. Violence does, in truth, recoil upon the violent, and the schemer falls into the pit which he digs for another. Let us thrust this creature back into its den, and we can then remove Miss Stoner to some place of shelter and let the county police know what has happened."

As he spoke he drew the dog whip swiftly from the dead man's lap, and throwing the noose round the reptile's neck he drew it from its horrid perch and, carrying it at arm's length, threw it into the iron safe, which he closed upon it.

Such are the true facts of the death of Dr. Grimesby Roylott, of Stoke Moran. It is not necessary that I should prolong a narrative which has already run to too great a length by telling how we broke the sad news to the terrified girl, how we

✓ Reading Check

What does Holmes do as soon as he hears the hissing sound through the ventilator?

conveyed her by the morning train to the care of her good aunt at Harrow, of how the slow process of official inquiry came to the conclusion that the doctor met his fate while indiscreetly playing with a dangerous pet. The little which I had yet to learn of the case was told me by Sherlock Holmes as we traveled back next day.

"I had," said he, "come to an entirely erroneous conclusion which shows, my dear Watson, how dangerous it always is to reason from insufficient data. The presence of the gypsies, and the use of the word band, which was used by the poor girl, no doubt to explain the appearance which she had caught a hurried glimpse of by the light of her match, were sufficient to put me upon an entirely wrong scent. I can only claim the merit that I instantly reconsidered my position when, however, it became clear to me that whatever danger threatened an occupant of the room could not come either from the window or the door. My attention was speedily drawn, as I have already remarked to you, to this ventilator, and to the bell-rope which hung down to the bed. The discovery that this was a dummy, and that the bed was clamped to the floor, instantly gave rise to the suspicion that the rope was there as a bridge for something passing through the hole and coming to the bed. The idea of a snake instantly occurred to me, and when I coupled it with my knowledge that the doctor was furnished with a supply of creatures from India, I felt that I was probably on the right track. The idea of using a form of poison which could not possibly be discovered by any chemical test was just such a one as would occur to a clever and ruthless man who had had an Eastern training. The rapidity with which such a poison would take effect would also, from his point of view, be an advantage. It would be a sharp-eyed coroner, indeed, who could distinguish the two little dark punctures which would show where the poison fangs had done their work. Then I thought of the whistle. Of course he must recall the snake before the morning light revealed it to the victim. He had trained it, probably by the use of the milk which we saw, to return to him when summoned. He would put it through this ventilator at the hour that he thought best, with the certainty that it would crawl down the rope and land on the bed. It might or might not bite the occupant, perhaps she might escape every night for a week, but sooner or later she must fall a victim.

Literary Analysis
Mood How does the mood shift in this final part of the story?

"I had come to these conclusions before ever I had entered his room. An inspection of his chair showed me that he had been in the habit of standing on it, which of course would be necessary in order that he should reach the ventilator. The sight of the safe, the saucer of milk, and the loop of whipcord were enough to finally dispel any doubts which may have remained. The metallic clang heard by Miss Stoner was obviously caused by her stepfather hastily closing the door of his safe upon its terrible occupant. Having once made up my mind, you know the steps which I took in order to put the matter to the proof. I heard the creature hiss as I have no doubt that you did also, and I instantly lit the light and attacked it."

"With the result of driving it through the ventilator."

"And also with the result of causing it to turn upon its master at the other side. Some of the blows of my cane came home and roused its snakish temper, so that it flew upon the first person it saw. In this way I am no doubt indirectly responsible for Dr. Grimesby Roylott's death, and I cannot say that it is likely to weigh very heavily upon my conscience."

Reading Skill
Author's Purpose
Why does Doyle include this explanation of how Holmes solved the case?

The Adventure of the Speckled Band ■ 133

Apply the Skills

The Adventure of the Speckled Band

Thinking About the Selection

1. **Respond:** Would you enjoy working with Sherlock Holmes on a case? Why or why not?
2. **(a) Recall:** Why does Helen Stoner come to see Holmes?
   (b) Compare: In what three ways is Helen's situation when she visits Holmes similar to Julia's just before she dies?
3. **(a) Recall:** What clues does Holmes use to solve the mystery?
   (b) Speculate: What do you think would have happened if Helen had not consulted Holmes?
4. **Make a Judgment:** Holmes says that he is indirectly responsible for Roylott's death. In your judgment, who is most responsible for Roylott's death? Explain.

Reading Skill

5. **(a)** In the first paragraph of the story, what details does Dr. Watson provide about Holmes's cases? **(b)** What do these details indicate is the author's general **purpose**?
6. How does each of the following details contribute to the author's general purpose? **(a)** Holmes's conversation with Dr. Roylott, **(b)** Holmes's explanation of how he figured out the mystery, **(c)** Holmes's comment at the end of the story.

Literary Analysis

7. What is the **mood** of the scene in which Holmes and Watson are waiting in the bedroom at Stoke Moran? Support your answer with details from the scene.
8. When Helen Stoner describes the night her sister died, the mood is one of terror and mystery. Use a chart like the one shown to list words, phrases, and images that contribute to this mood.

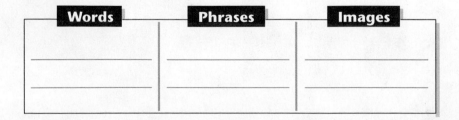

Words	Phrases	Images

QuickReview

Story at a Glance
Through a series of deductions, famous detective Sherlock Holmes solves the puzzling murder of a young woman.

Go **O**nline
Assessment
For: Self-test
Visit: www.PHSchool.com
Web Code: ena-6108

Author's Purpose: the author's reason for writing; for example, to *inform*, to *persuade*, or to *entertain*.

Mood: the overall feeling that a literary work or passage creates in the reader

Vocabulary Builder

Practice Answer the question, then provide a brief explanation.

1. Would a *sinister* clown frighten small children?
2. Do people show *compliance* when they follow the rules?
3. If you were walking alone at night, what might give you a *tangible* cause to be nervous?

Writing

Write a **personal narrative** about a time that you used logic, or reasoning, to solve a problem.
- First, identify the problem.
- Then, list ideas you had for possible solutions.
- Explain why you chose the solution you did.
- Describe, in order, the steps you took to solve the problem.

For *Grammar*, *Vocabulary*, and *Assessment*, see **Build Language Skills,** pages 144–145.

Extend Your Learning

Listening and Speaking Present to a partner a brief **oral description** of the most exciting or interesting scene in "The Adventure of the Speckled Band." Your partner can add any details that you omit. Then, discuss why this scene produces the effect it does.

Research and Technology Prepare a brief **report** on the regulations regarding wild or exotic pets. Use the Internet and library resources such as a periodical guide to find information. Raise questions to help you focus your research, such as
- What are the reasons for the laws?
- Why do different states have different exotic pet laws?

Identify and use resources to find answers. The resources may be individuals, government agencies, or other organizations.

Background

Interpreting Information Scientists have found that very young children cannot make connections or interpret information the way that adults can. For example, an adult who sees an object put into a drawer is able to find the object later. A small child, however, does not make the connection and thinks the object has disappeared. As children grow, their ability to interpret information improves.

Connecting to the Literature

Reading/Writing Connection In this excerpt, Dillard shares a childhood experience that was frightening because she was not able to interpret the information. Think about a fear you had as a small child that you now consider silly. Write three reasons why you were able to overcome that fear. Use three of the following words: *comprehend, define, integrate, perceive.*

Review

For **Reading Skill, Literary Analysis,** and **Vocabulary Builder,** see page 104.

Meet the Author

Annie **Dillard** (b. 1945)

In *An American Childhood,* a memoir about growing up, Annie Dillard describes how her parents encouraged her to explore the world.

A Year Close to Nature Dillard spent four seasons living at the edge of a creek in the mountains of Virginia. There, she recorded such observations as the time she watched, fascinated, as a frog—attacked by a giant waterbug—was deflated into a pouch of skin before her eyes. She edited these observations of nature to create *Pilgrim at Tinker Creek,* which won her the 1975 Pulitzer Prize for general nonfiction.

Words of Advice Here is what Dillard says to aspiring writers: "You have enough experience by the time you're five years old. What you need is the library. What you have to learn is the best of what is being thought and said."

Go **Online**
Author Link

For: More about the author
Visit: www.PHSchool.com
Web Code: ene-9109

from An American Childhood

Annie Dillard

▲ Critical Viewing
What details of this photo might be frightening to a small child? **[Analyze]**

When I was five, growing up in Pittsburgh in 1950, I would not go to bed willingly because something came into my room. This was a private matter between me and it. If I spoke of it, it would kill me.

Who could breathe as this thing searched for me over the very corners of the room? Who could ever breathe freely again? I lay in the dark.

My sister Amy, two years old, was asleep in the other bed. What did she know? She was innocent of evil. Even at two she composed herself attractively for sleep. She folded the top sheet tidily under her prettily outstretched arm; she laid her perfect head lightly on an unwrinkled pillow, where her thick curls spread evenly in rays like petals. All night long she slept smoothly in a series of pleasant and <u>serene</u>, if artificial-looking, positions, a faint smile on her closed lips, as if she were posing for an ad for sheets. There was no messiness in her, no roughness for things to cling to, only a charming and charmed innocence that seemed then to protect her, an innocence I needed but couldn't muster. Since Amy was asleep, furthermore, and since when I needed someone most I was afraid to stir enough to wake her, she was useless.

I lay alone and was almost asleep when the thing entered the room by flattening itself against the open door and sliding in. It was a transparent, <u>luminous</u> oblong.[1] I could see the door whiten at its touch; I could see the blue wall turn pale where it raced over it, and see the maple headboard of Amy's bed glow. It was a swift spirit; it was an awareness. It made noise. It had two joined parts, a head and a tail, like a Chinese dragon. It found the door, wall, and headboard; and it swiped them, charging them with its luminous glance. After its fleet, searching passage, things looked the same, but weren't.

I dared not blink or breathe; I tried to hush my whooping blood. If it found another awareness, it would destroy it.

Every night before it got to me it gave up. It hit my wall's corner and couldn't get past. It shrank completely into itself and vanished like a cobra down a hole. I heard the rising roar it made when it died or left. I still couldn't breathe. I knew—it was the worst fact I knew, a very hard fact—that it could return again alive that same night.

Sometimes it came back, sometimes it didn't. Most often, restless, it came back. The light stripe slipped in the door, ran searching over Amy's wall, stopped, stretched lunatic at the first corner, raced wailing toward my wall, and vanished into the second corner with a cry. So I wouldn't go to bed.

It was a passing car whose windshield reflected the corner streetlight outside. I figured it out one night.

Figuring it out was as memorable as the oblong itself. Figuring it out was a long and forced ascent to the very rim of being, to the membrane of skin that both separates and con-

---

1. oblong (äb´ lôŋ´) *n.* shape that is longer than it is broad.

nects the inner life and the outer world. I climbed deliberately from the depths like a diver who releases the monster in his arms and hauls himself hand over hand up an anchor chain till he meets the ocean's sparkling membrane and bursts through it; he sights the sunlit, becalmed hull of his boat, which had bulked so ominously from below.

I recognized the noise it made when it left. That is, the noise it made called to mind, at last, my daytime sensations when a car passed—the sight and noise together. A car came roaring down hushed Edgerton Avenue in front of our house, stopped at the corner stop sign, and passed on shrieking as its engine shifted up the gears. What, precisely, came into the bedroom? A reflection from the car's oblong windshield. Why did it travel in two parts? The window sash split the light and cast a shadow.

▲ **Critical Viewing** Which words would you use to describe these lights in the night—*comforting* or *threatening*? Explain. **[Interpret]**

Reading Check

What did the "monster" in Dillard's bedroom turn out to be?

Night after night I labored up the same long chain of reasoning, as night after night the thing burst into the room where I lay awake and Amy slept prettily and my loud heart thrashed and I froze.

There was a world outside my window and contiguous[2] to it. If I was so all-fired bright, as my parents, who had patently no basis for comparison, seemed to think, why did I have to keep learning this same thing over and over? For I had learned it a summer ago, when men with jackhammers broke up Edgerton Avenue. I had watched them from the yard; the street came up in jagged slabs like floes. When I lay to nap, I listened. One restless afternoon I connected the new noise in my bedroom with the jackhammer men I had been seeing outside. I understood abruptly that these worlds met, the outside and the inside. I traveled the route in my mind: You walked downstairs from here, and outside from downstairs. "Outside," then, was <u>conceivably</u> just beyond my windows. It was the same world I reached by going out the front or the back door. I forced my imagination yet again over this route.

The world did not have me in mind; it had no mind. It was a coincidental collection of things and people, of items, and I

2. **contiguous** (kən tig′ yoō əs) *adj.* in physical contact; near or next to.

myself was one such item—a child walking up the sidewalk, whom anyone could see or ignore. The things in the world did not necessarily cause my overwhelming feelings; the feelings were inside me, beneath my skin, behind my ribs, within my skull. They were even, to some extent, under my control.

I could be connected to the outer world by reason, if I chose, or I could yield to what amounted to a narrative fiction, to a tale of terror whispered to me by the blood in my ears, a show in light projected on the room's blue walls. As time passed, I learned to amuse myself in bed in the darkened room by entering the fiction deliberately and replacing it by reason deliberately.

When the low roar drew nigh and the oblong slid in the door, I threw my own switches for pleasure. It's coming after me; it's a car outside. It's after me. It's a car. It raced over the wall, lighting it blue wherever it ran; it bumped over Amy's maple headboard in a rush, paused, slithered elongate[3] over the corner, shrank, flew my way, and vanished into itself with a wail. It was a car.

---

3. **elongate** (ē lôn′ gāt′) *adv.* in a way that emphasizes length and narrowness.

Literary Analysis
Mood What has happened here to shift the mood from fear to confidence?

▼ **Critical Viewing** Does this picture seem more connected to the imaginative or to the logical interpretation of the lights? Explain. **[Compare and Contrast]**

Apply the Skills

from _An American Childhood_

Thinking About the Selection

1. **Respond:** Can you relate to Dillard's fears? Explain.
2. **(a) Recall:** Who else is in Dillard's room when the mysterious event occurs? **(b) Contrast:** Why does that person not react to the event the same way Dillard does?
3. **(a) Recall:** What happens to the thing before it reaches Dillard? **(b) Analyze:** Why does Dillard believe it cannot find her? **(c) Deduce:** What is the real reason it cannot find her?
4. **(a) Recall:** What does Dillard finally figure out is the source of the event? **(b) Infer:** After solving the mystery, Dillard sometimes pretends that she does not know the solution. Why?
5. **Speculate:** Why do you think Dillard chose to relate this particular childhood experience?

Reading Skill

6. **(a)** In the first paragraph of the story, what details does Annie Dillard give about the object that frightens her? **(b)** What do these details indicate is the author's general **purpose**?
7. How does each of the following details contribute to the author's general purpose? **(a)** the description of her sister Amy sleeping, **(b)** the description of the object itself, **(c)** the discovery of what the object was.

Literary Analysis

8. What is the **mood** of the scene in which Annie Dillard first describes how the light entered her room? Support your answer with details from the scene.
9. When Annie Dillard finally realizes what the light really is, her mood is one of triumph and accomplishment. Use a chart like the one shown to list words, phrases, and images that contribute to this mood.

Words	Phrases	Images
_____	_____	_____
_____	_____	_____
_____	_____	_____

QuickReview

Selection at a Glance

A child figures out the source of the mysterious and frightening light that enters her room at night.

Go Online
Assessment

For: Self-test
Visit: www.PHSchool.com
Web Code: ena-6109

Author's Purpose: the author's reason for writing; for example to _inform_, to _persuade_, or to _entertain_.

Mood: the overall feeling that a literary work or passage creates in the reader

Vocabulary Builder

Practice Answer the question, then provide a brief explanation for your answer.

1. Would a boat be likely to overturn on a *serene* lake?

2. If the night is *luminous,* is there a full moon or no moon?

3. When someone offers directions and says that you could *conceivably* lose your way, should you feel worried or reassured?

Writing

Write a **personal narrative** about an important childhood insight.

- Consider how your emotions competed with your reason as you learned the truth about something that had bothered, frightened, or puzzled you.
- Describe clues you considered, and tell what each clue turned out to mean.

For *Grammar, Vocabulary,* and *Assessment,* see **Build Language Skills,** pages 144–145.

Extend Your Learning

Listening and Speaking Present to a partner a brief **oral description** of the sounds and sights in the excerpt from *An American Childhood.* Your partner can add any details that you omit. Then, discuss the reasons that Dillard's description produces the effect it does.

Research and Technology Use the Internet and refer to library resources to learn basic information about how an important scientific puzzle was solved. Based on your initial research, raise questions that help you focus your research such as

- Why is the puzzle important?
- What is the impact of the new knowledge?

Identify appropriate resources to help you answer your questions. The resources may be individuals, government agencies, scientific journals and interviews with experts. Finally, write a brief **report** on the scientific puzzle.

Build Language Skills

Vocabulary Skill

Suffixes The **suffixes** *-ize* and *-yze* mean "make" or "become." They are used to form verbs. For example, the suffix *-yze* changes the word *analysis* to *analyze,* meaning "make an analysis."

➤ **Example:** *Analyze* the details in the essay to determine whether they are intended to inform or to entertain.

Practice Write a new sentence that communicates the same meaning as the original sentence using the word in parentheses. You may rearrange, add, or drop words from the original sentence.

1. Suddenly, what the author means becomes real to me. (realize)
2. They will make their decision final at the end of the week. (finalize)
3. The author used the wind as a symbol of change. (symbolize)
4. We will make an analysis of the essay. (analyze)
5. Fear can make a rabbit seem as if it has paralysis. (paralyze)

Grammar Lesson

Personal pronouns A **personal pronoun** replaces a noun in a sentence. There are three forms, or **cases**—*nominative, objective,* or *possessive.* The case depends on the pronoun's role in a sentence.

MorePractice

For more practice with personal pronouns, see the Grammar Handbook, p. R31.

The Three Cases of Personal Pronouns		
Case	**Pronouns**	**Use in a Sentence**
Nominative	I, we, you, he, she, it, they	subject of a sentence or clause (the "giver" of an action)
Objective	me, us, you, him, her, it, them	object of a sentence or clause (the "receiver" of an action)
Possessive	my, mine, our, ours, your, yours, his, her, hers, its, their, theirs	shows ownership

Practice Choose personal pronouns to complete the sentences. Explain the pronoun's function in the sentence.

1. _____ have two sisters.
2. _____ names are Sara and Erin.
3. Have _____ met _____ yet?
4. _____ enjoy _____ time together.

W̶G *Prentice Hall Writing and Grammar Connection: Chapter 14, Section 2*

Reading: Author's Purpose

Directions: *Read the selection. Then, answer the questions.*

A turning leaf stays partly green at first, then reveals splotches of yellow and red as the chlorophyll gradually breaks down. Dark green seems to stay longest in the veins, outlining and defining them. During the summer, chlorophyll dissolves in the heat and light, but it is also being steadily replaced. In the fall, on the other hand, no new pigment is produced, and so we notice the other colors that were always there, right in the leaf, although chlorophyll's shocking green hid them from view.

—*Why Leaves Turn Color in the Fall* by Diane Ackerman

1. What is the author's general purpose?
   A to entertain
   B to inform
   C to persuade
   D to surprise

2. Which statement expresses the point of the passage?
   A Chlorophyll gives leaves a shocking green appearance.
   B Heat puts stress on leaves.
   C When chlorophyll dissolves, we notice colors that were always present in the leaf.
   D Dark green lasts longest.

3. Which sentence best describes the author's specific purpose?
   A She is comparing summer and fall weather.
   B She is describing various shades of green.
   C She is describing chlorophyll's role in photosynthesis.
   D She is explaining why leaves change color.

Timed Writing: Response to Literature [Critical Stance]

Review "The Adventure of the Speckled Band" or the excerpt from *An American Childhood*. Evaluate the effectiveness of the mood in determining the reader's response to the story. **(20 minutes)**

 ## Writing Workshop: *Work in Progress*

For an autobiography you may write, make a four-column chart. In each column, write the name of a person or event that taught you something. In each column jot down the answer: What? How? Why? Put this Brainstorming Chart in your writing portfolio.

Reading Informational Materials

Magazine Articles

In Part 2, you are learning how to identify an author's purpose and to evaluate how effectively he or she achieves it. You bring your own purpose to reading as well. If you read the excerpt from *An American Childhood,* you might have read to be entertained by the author's description of her fear of the dark. You also can read "Sun Suckers and Moon Cursers" for entertainment or to inform yourself about the history of fears related to darkness.

About Magazine Articles

A **magazine article** is a short work of nonfiction. Some articles are human-interest stories that offer insights about interesting people. Others explain or investigate specific subjects, like animal behavior or a new technology. Magazine articles often have these features:

- illustrations or photographs that accompany the text
- captions that explain the illustrations or photographs
- sidebars that contain additional, related information

Reading Skill

When you first see an article, **preview to determine your purpose for reading.** Whether you are flipping through a magazine looking for something interesting or researching a specific topic, take a quick look at the title, the illustrations, and a sample paragraph. This will help you determine the author's purpose for writing. Then, determine whether your own purpose for reading is likely to be satisfied by continuing to read the article.

Questions to Help You Preview an Article

- ❑ What is the tone or attitude of the author?
- ❑ Do the pictures and captions seem designed to provide information or to entertain?
- ❑ As I skim the text, do I see statistics, quotations from experts, and facts?
- ❑ Do the first sentences of paragraphs introduce facts, opinions, or anecdotes?

SUN SUCKERS AND MOON CURSERS

Richard and Joyce Wolkomir

> Most articles begin with an attention-grabbing opening paragraph to keep readers interested in reading more.

> The title is meant to grab readers' interest while also revealing something important about the article's subject.

Night is falling. It is getting dark. You can barely see. But now . . . lights come on.

Car headlights sweep the road. Windows light up. Neon signs glow red and green. Street lamps shine, bright as noon. So who cares if it is night?

But what if you are camping in a forest? Or a storm blows down power lines? Then the night would be inky. To see, you would have only star twinkle, or the moon's pale shine. Until about 1900, when electric power networks began spreading, that is how nights were: dark.

Roger Ekirch, an historian at Virginia Tech, studies those long-ago dark nights. For light, our ancestors had only candles, hearth fires, torches, walnut-oil lamps.

And that made their nights different than ours.

"It used to be, when it got dark, people felt edgy," Ekirch says. He studies the years from about 1500 to 1830, when mostly only the wealthy could afford even candles. "People talked about being 'shut in' by the night," he says. Our ancestors imagined werewolves roaming at night, and demons. In their minds, they populated the darkness with witches, fairies and elves, and malignant spirits. Night had real dangers, too—robbers and murderers, but also ditches and ponds you could fall into.

What was it like, when nights were so dark?

To find out, Roger Ekirch has combed through old newspapers, diaries, letters, everything from court records to sermons.

Reading Informational Materials

He has pondered modern scientific research, too. He has found that, before the invention of electric lights, our ancestors considered night a different "season." At night, they were nearly blind. And so, to them, day and night seemed as different as summer and winter.

They even had special words for night. Some people called the last rays of the setting sun "sun suckers." Nighttime travelers, who relied on the moon called it the "parish lantern." But robbers, who liked to lurk in darkness, hated the moon. They called it "the tattler." And those darkness-loving criminals? They were "moon cursers."

Cities were so dark that people needing to find their way at night hired boys to carry torches, or "links." Such torchbearers were called "linkboys."

Country people tried to stay indoors at night, unless the moon was out. On moonless nights, people groping in the darkness frequently fell into ponds and ravines.[1] Horses, also blinded by darkness, often threw riders.

If you were traveling at night, you would wear light-colored clothing, so your friends could see you. You might ride a white horse. You might mark your route in advance by stripping away tree bark, exposing the white inner wood. In southern England, where the soil is chalky white, people planning night trips mounded up white chalk along their route during the day, to guide them later, in the moonlight.

Articles often have illustrations or photographs that help authors achieve their purpose. This photo helps you imagine how a night traveler could stumble into a watery swamp.

---

1. **ravines** (rə vēnz´) n. long, deep hollows in the earth's surface.

It was dark inside houses, too. To dress in the darkness, people learned to fold their clothes just so. Swedish homeowners, Roger Ekirch says, pushed parlor furniture against walls at night, so they could walk through the room without tripping.

People began as children to memorize their local terrain—ditches, fences, cisterns, bogs.[2] They learned the magical terrain, too, spots where ghosts and other imaginary nighttime frights lurked. "In some places, you never whistled at night, because that invited the devil," says Ekirch.

One reason people feared nightfall was they thought night actually did "fall." At night, they believed, malignant air descended. To ward off that sickly air, sleepers wore nightcaps. They also pulled curtains around their beds. In the 1600s, one London man tied his hands inside his bed at night so they would not flop outside the curtains and expose him to night air. . . .

At night, evildoers came out. Virtually every major European city had criminal gangs. Sometimes those gangs included wealthy young aristocrats who assaulted people just for the thrill. . . .

If you were law-abiding, you might clang your sword on the pavement while walking down a dark nighttime street to warn robbers you were armed. Or you might hold your sword upright in the moonlight. You tried to walk in groups. You walked down the street's middle, to prevent robbers from lunging at you from doorways or alleys. Robbers depended so much on darkness that a British criminal who attacked his victim in broad daylight was acquitted—jurors decided he must be insane.

Many whose days were blighted by poverty or ill treatment sought escape at night. Slaves in the American South, for instance, sneaked out at night to dances and parties. Or they stumbled through the darkness to other plantations, to visit their wives or children. After the Civil War, says Roger Ekirch, former slaveholders worried that their freed slaves might attack them. And so they rode out at night disguised as ghosts, to frighten onetime slaves into staying indoors.

"At night, many servants felt beyond supervision, and they would often leave directly after their employers fell asleep," Ekirch adds. When they did sleep, it was fitfully, because of rumbling carts and watchmen's cries. And so Ekirch believes many

> Magazine writers often use quotations from noted experts to lend authority and interest to their explanations.

---

2. **cisterns** (sis´ tərnz) large underground areas for storing water; **bogs** small marshes or swamps where footing is treacherous.

workers got much too little sleep. "That explains why so many slaveowners and employers complained about their workers falling asleep during the day," he said.

Our ancestors had one overriding—and entirely real—nighttime fear: fire. Blazes were common because houses, often with thatched[3] roofs, ignited easily. At night, open flames flickered everywhere. Passersby carrying torches might set your roof ablaze. Also, householders commonly complained about servants forgetting to bank fires or snuff out candles. Roger Ekirch believes one reason night watchmen bellowed out each hour, to the irritation of sleepers, was precisely to keep everyone half awake, to be ready when fires erupted. . . .

Electricity changed the night. One electric bulb, Ekirch calculates, provided 100 times more light than a gas lamp. Night was becoming what it is today—an artificially illuminated extension of the day. Night has lost its spookiness.

Still, says Roger Ekirch, even in the electric age, his children sometimes fear the dark: "I tell them, 'Your daddy is an expert on night, and he knows a lot about the history of the night, and he can tell you there is nothing to be afraid of!' "

He shrugs. "It doesn't work well," he says.

> Articles often end with a profound or humorous thought or quotation that ties the subject neatly together.

---

3. thatched (thachd′) **roofs** roofs made of materials such as straw or rushes.

Reading: Determining Purpose

Directions: *Choose the letter of the best answer to each question.*

1. What is the authors' main purpose in writing this article?
   A to persuade the reader to go out more at night
   B to entertain the reader with humorous anecdotes
   C to inform the reader about interesting historical facts
   D to convince the reader not to waste electricity

2. If you were previewing the article to set a purpose for reading, which of the following items from the first page would give you the best indication of the article's subject?
   A the title
   B the opening paragraph
   C the authors' names
   D the paragraph beginning "Roger Ekirch, . . ."

3. Which choice would NOT be a good reason for reading this article?
   A to learn about present attitudes toward darkness
   B to learn details of people's behavior before electricity
   C to learn about the dangers faced by past societies
   D to learn facts from an authority on the subject of darkness

Reading: Comprehension and Interpretation

Directions: *Write your answers on a separate sheet of paper.*

4. **(a)** Name three reasons why people in the past were afraid of the night. **(b)** Name three things people did to lessen their fears.

5. Why did people's fear of fire intensify at night?

6. **(a)** Compare and contrast attitudes toward dark during the period that the authors describe with today's attitudes. **(b)** Why have attitudes changed?

Timed Writing: Description [Generating]

Write a letter from the point of view of a seventeenth-century European, explaining why a journey should take place during the day. In your letter, try to capture the details and attitudes toward night and darkness that are mentioned in the article. **(20 minutes)**

These skills will help you become a better reader. Practice them with either the excerpt from *Travels With Charley* (p. 154) or "The American Dream" (p. 165).

Reading Skill

An **author's purpose** is the reason he or she has for writing, such as to persuade, to entertain, or to provide information. The author's purpose influences the kinds of details he or she includes. As you read, use a graphic organizer like the one shown to **evaluate whether the author achieves his or her purpose.** Keep in mind that sometimes an author tries to achieve more than one purpose.

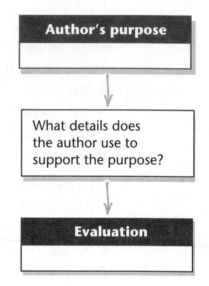

Author's purpose

What details does the author use to support the purpose?

Evaluation

Literary Analysis

An **author's style** is his or her particular way of writing. Elements that factor into an author's style include:

- word choice
- length and rhythm of sentences
- tone—the author's attitude toward the subject and audience

Some writers write informally, using everyday language and simple, straightforward sentences. Other writers use formal words and longer, more complicated, sentences. As you read, notice a writer's unique style.

Vocabulary Builder

from Travels With Charley

- **impaired** (im perd´) *v.* made weaker or less useful (p. 154) *His weak vision impaired his driving.*

- **rigorous** (rig´ ər əs) *adj.* very harsh or strict (p. 155) *The campers learned to survive under rigorous winter conditions.*

- **inexplicable** (in eks´ pli kə bəl) *adj.* not possible to explain (p. 158) *The night brought mysterious and inexplicable sounds.*

- **celestial** (sə les´ chəl) *adj.* heavenly (p. 158) *The choir's beautiful singing sounded like celestial music.*

The American Dream

- **unequivocal** (un´ ē kwiv´ ə kəl) *adj.* clear; plainly understood (p. 166) *The critic gave unequivocal praise to the movie.*

- **antithesis** (an tith´ ə sis) *n.* direct opposite (p. 166) *Joy is the antithesis of sorrow.*

- **paradoxes** (par´ ə däks´ íz) *n.* two things that seem directly at odds (p. 166) *To Americans, the Southern Hemisphere is full of paradoxes, such as snow in July.*

- **exploitation** (eks´ plɔi tā´ shən) *n.* the act of using another person for selfish purposes (p. 167) *The labor union called the low wages "exploitation of the workers."*

Background

Steinbeck's America John Steinbeck is famous for his descriptions of American life. *Travels With Charley* chronicles John Steinbeck's cross-country road trip with his poodle, Charley. In this excerpt, Steinbeck describes planning his trip and writes of his travels westward across the Great Plains and the Badlands of North Dakota—a region where barren, treeless landscapes and strange rock formations create an otherworldly atmosphere.

Connecting to the Literature

Reading/Writing Connection In planning this trip, John Steinbeck knew of certain places that he wanted to see. List five places in the United States that you would like to visit. Write a sentence about each place, explaining why you would like to visit. Use three of the following words: *appreciate, enrich, highlight, investigate.*

Meet the Author

John **Steinbeck** (1902–1968)

Living in southern California, John Steinbeck got to know workers in farms, canning factories, and fisheries. He watched ordinary Americans suffer during the depression of the 1930s and sympathized with their struggles.

The Common Touch All those experiences came to life in novels such as *Cannery Row, East of Eden,* and *The Grapes of Wrath.* Steinbeck's novels, with their desperate, confused characters, provided millions of American readers with a window into the lives of people at the margins of society—people they otherwise might not have met. He won a Pulitzer Prize and the Nobel Prize for Literature.

A Love of Travel Even as a much older man, Steinbeck admitted to a restless curiosity that pushed him out onto the road with his poodle Charley. "When I laid the ground plan of my journey, there were definite questions to which I wanted matching answers. . . . I suppose they could all be lumped into the single question: 'What are Americans like today?'"

Go Online
Author Link
For: More about the author
Visit: www.PHSchool.com
Web Code: ene-9110

from
TRAVELS
with Charley

JOHN STEINBECK

My plan was clear, concise, and reasonable, I think. For many years I have traveled in many parts of the world. In America I live in New York, or dip into Chicago or San Francisco. But New York is no more America than Paris is France or London is England. Thus I discovered that I did not know my own country. I, an American writer, writing about America, was working from memory, and the memory is at best a faulty, warpy reservoir. I had not heard the speech of America, smelled the grass and trees and sewage, seen its hills and water, its color and quality of light. I knew the changes only from books and newspapers. But more than this, I had not felt the country for twenty-five years. In short, I was writing of something I did not know about, and it seems to me that in a so-called writer this is criminal. My memories were distorted by twenty-five intervening years.

Once I traveled about in an old bakery wagon, double-doored rattler with a mattress on its floor. I stopped where people stopped or gathered, I listened and looked and felt, and in the process had a picture of my country the accuracy of which was <u>impaired</u> only by my own shortcomings.

So it was that I determined to look again, to try to rediscover this monster land. Otherwise, in writing, I could not tell the small diagnostic[1] truths which are the foundations of the

---

1. diagnostic (dī əg näs′ tik) *adj.* explaining how something works.

▲ **Critical Viewing**
This road winds through the Badlands of North Dakota. How do you think this region got its name? **[Speculate]**

Vocabulary Builder
impaired (im perd′) *v.* made weaker or less useful

larger truth. One sharp difficulty presented itself. In the intervening twenty-five years my name had become reasonably well known. And it has been my experience that when people have heard of you, favorably or not, they change; they become, through shyness or the other qualities that publicity inspires, something they are not under ordinary circumstances. This being so, my trip demanded that I leave my name and my identity at home. I had to be peripatetic[2] eyes and ears, a kind of moving gelatin plate.[3] I could not sign hotel registers, meet people I knew, interview others, or even ask searching questions. Furthermore, two or more people disturb the ecologic complex of an area. I had to go alone and I had to be self-contained, a kind of casual turtle carrying his house on his back.

With all this in mind I wrote to the head office of a great corporation which manufactures trucks. I specified my purpose and my needs. I wanted a three-quarter-ton pick-up truck, capable of going anywhere under possibly <u>rigorous</u> conditions, and on this truck I wanted a little house built like the cabin of a small boat. A trailer is difficult to maneuver on mountain roads, is impossible and often illegal to park, and is subject to many restrictions. In due time, specifications came through, for a tough, fast, comfortable vehicle, mounting a camper top—a little house with double bed, a four-burner stove, a heater, refrigerator and lights operating on butane, a chemical toilet, closet space, storage space, windows screened against insects—exactly what I wanted. It was delivered in the summer to my little fishing place at Sag Harbor near the end of Long Island. Although I didn't want to start before Labor Day, when the nation settles back to normal living, I did want to get used to my turtle shell, to equip it and learn it. It arrived in August, a beautiful thing, powerful and yet lithe. It was almost as easy to handle as a passenger car. And because my planned trip had aroused some satiric remarks among my friends, I named it Rocinante, which you will remember was the name of Don Quixote's[4] horse.

Since I made no secret of my project, a number of controversies arose among my friends and advisers. (A projected

Reading Skill
Author's Purpose
Based on the first three paragraphs, what do you think is the author's purpose for writing?

Vocabulary Builder
rigorous (rig´ ər əs) *adj.* very harsh or strict

Reading Check

What was the author's "plan"?

---

2. **peripatetic** (per´ i pə tet´ ik) *adj.* moving from place to place.
3. **gelatin plate** light-sensitive glass plate used to make photographic images.
4. **Don Quixote** (dän´ kē hōt´ ō) fictional Spanish knight, the hero of a famous seventeenth century satirical novel by Miguel de Cervantes. Don Quixote follows noble but unrealistic ideals as he tries to do heroic deeds.

journey spawns advisers in schools.) I was told that since my photograph was as widely distributed as my publisher could make it, I would find it impossible to move about without being recognized. Let me say in advance that in over ten thousand miles, in thirty-four states, I was not recognized even once. I believe that people identify things only in context. Even those people who might have known me against a background I am supposed to have, in no case identified me in Rocinante.

I was advised that the name Rocinante painted on the side of my truck in sixteenth-century Spanish script would cause curiosity and inquiry in some places. I do not know how many people recognized the name, but surely no one ever asked about it.

Next, I was told that a stranger's purpose in moving about the country might cause inquiry or even suspicion. For this reason I racked a shotgun, two rifles, and a couple of fishing rods in my truck, for it is my experience that if a man is going hunting or fishing his purpose is understood and even applauded. Actually, my hunting days are over. I no longer kill or catch anything I cannot get into a frying pan; I am too old for sport killing. This stage setting turned out to be unnecessary.

It was said that my New York license plates would arouse interest and perhaps questions, since they were the only outward identifying marks I had. And so they did—perhaps twenty or thirty times in the whole trip. But such contacts followed an invariable pattern, somewhat as follows:

Local man: "New York, huh?"

Me: "Yep."

Local man: "I was there in nineteen thirty-eight—or was it thirty-nine? Alice, was it thirty-eight or thirty-nine we went to New York?"

Alice: "It was thirty-six. I remember because it was the year Alfred died."

Local man: "Anyway, I hated it. Wouldn't live there if you paid me."

▼ Critical Viewing
Why would a pet like Charley, pictured here with Steinbeck, be a good companion on his cross-country trip? [Speculate]

There was some genuine worry about my traveling alone, open to attack, robbery, assault. It is well known that our roads are dangerous. And here I admit I had senseless qualms. It is some years since I have been alone, nameless, friendless, without any of the safety one gets from family, friends, and accomplices. There is no reality in the danger. It's just a very lonely, helpless feeling at first—a kind of desolate feeling. For this reason I took one companion on my journey—an old French gentleman poodle known as Charley. Actually his name is Charles le Chien.[5] He was born in Bercy on the outskirts of Paris and trained in France, and while he knows a little poodle-English, he responds quickly only to commands in French. Otherwise he has to translate, and that slows him down. He is a very big poodle, of a color called *bleu*, and he is blue when he is clean. Charley is a born diplomat. He prefers negotiation to fighting, and properly so, since he is very bad at fighting. Only once in his ten years has he been in trouble—when he met a dog who refused to negotiate. Charley lost a piece of his right ear that time. But he is a good watch dog—has a roar like a lion, designed to conceal from night-wandering strangers the fact that he couldn't bite his way out of a *cornet de papier*.[6] He is a good friend and traveling companion, and would rather travel about than anything he can imagine. If he occurs at length in this account, it is because he contributed much to the trip. A dog, particularly an exotic like Charley, is a bond between strangers. Many conversations en route began with "What degree of a dog is that?"

The techniques of opening conversation are universal. I knew long ago and rediscovered that the best way to attract attention, help, and conversation is to be lost. A man who see-ing his mother starving to death on a path kicks her in the stomach to clear the way, will cheerfully devote several hours of his time giving wrong directions to a total stranger who claims to be lost.

* * *

The night was loaded with omens. The grieving sky turned the little water to a dangerous metal and then the wind got up—not the gusty, rabbity wind of the seacoasts I know but a great bursting sweep of wind with nothing to inhibit it for a

---

5. **Charles le Chien** (shärl′ lə shē un′) French for "Charles the dog."
6. *cornet de papier* (kôr nā′ də pá pyā′) French for "paper bag."

Literary Analysis
Author's Style Find two examples of a humorous tone in this paragraph. Explain why each example is humorous.

Literary Analysis
Author's Style Based on this paragraph, would you describe Steinbeck's style as formal or informal? Explain.

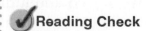**Reading Check**

Why does Steinbeck decide to take Charley as his traveling companion?

thousand miles in any direction. Because it was a wind strange to me, and therefore mysterious, it set up mysterious responses in me. In terms of reason, it was strange only because I found it so. But a goodly part of our experience which we find <u>inexplicable</u> must be like that. To my certain knowledge, many people conceal experiences for fear of ridicule. How many people have seen or heard or felt something which so outraged their sense of what should be that the whole thing was brushed quickly away like dirt under a rug?

For myself, I try to keep the line open even for things I can't understand or explain, but it is difficult in this frightened time. At this moment in North Dakota I had a reluctance to drive on that amounted to fear. At the same time, Charley wanted to go—in fact, made such a commotion about going that I tried to reason with him.

"Listen to me, dog. I have a strong impulse to stay amounting to <u>celestial</u> command. If I should overcome it and go and a great snow should close in on us, I would recognize it as a warning disregarded. If we stay and a big snow should come I would be certain I had a pipeline to prophecy."

Charley sneezed and paced restlessly. "All right, *mon cur*,[7] let's take your side of it. You want to go on. Suppose we do, and in the night a tree should crash down right where we are presently standing. It would be you who have the attention of the gods. And there is always that chance. I could tell you many stories about faithful animals who saved their masters, but I think you are just bored and I'm not going to flatter you." Charley leveled at me his most cynical eye. I think he is neither a romantic nor a mystic. "I know what you mean. If we go, and no tree crashes down, or stay and no snow falls—what then? I'll tell you what then. We forget the whole episode and the field of prophecy is in no way injured. I vote to stay. You vote to go. But being nearer the pinnacle of creation than you, and also president, I cast the deciding vote."

We stayed and it didn't snow and no tree fell, so naturally we forgot the whole thing and are wide open for more mystic feelings when they come. And in the early morning swept clean of clouds and telescopically clear, we crunched around on the thick white ground cover of frost and got under way. The caravan of the arts was dark but the dog barked as we ground up to the highway.

---

7. *mon cur* (mōn kʉr´) French slang for "my dear mutt."

Someone must have told me about the Missouri River at Bismarck, North Dakota, or I must have read about it. In either case, I hadn't paid attention. I came on it in amazement. Here is where the map should fold. Here is the boundary between east and west. On the Bismarck side it is eastern landscape, eastern grass, with the look and smell of eastern America. Across the Missouri on the Mandan side, it is pure west, with brown grass and water scorings and small outcrops. The two sides of the river might well be a thousand miles apart. As I was not prepared for the Missouri boundary, so I was not prepared for the Bad Lands. They deserve this name. They are like the work of an evil child. Such a place the Fallen Angels might have built as a spite to Heaven, dry and sharp, desolate and dangerous, and for me filled with foreboding. A sense comes from it that it does not like or welcome humans. But humans being what they are, and I being human, I turned off the highway on a shaley road and headed in among the buttes, but with a shyness as though I crashed a party. The road surface tore viciously at my tires and made Rocinante's overloaded springs cry with anguish. What a place for a colony of troglodytes, or better, of trolls. And here's an odd thing. Just as I felt unwanted in this land, so do I feel a reluctance in writing about it.

Presently I saw a man leaning on a two-strand barbed-wire fence, the wires fixed not to posts but to crooked tree limbs stuck in the ground. The man wore a dark hat, and jeans and long jacket washed palest blue with lighter places at knees and elbows. His pale eyes were frosted with sun glare and his lips scaly as snakeskin. A .22 rifle leaned against the fence beside him and on the ground lay a little heap of fur and feathers—rabbits and small birds. I pulled up to speak to him, saw his eyes wash over Rocinante, sweep up the details, and then retire into their sockets. And I found I had nothing to say to him. The "Looks like an early winter," or "Any good fishing hereabouts?" didn't seem to apply. And so we simply brooded at each other.

"Afternoon!"

"Yes, sir," he said.

"Any place nearby where I can buy some eggs?"

"Not real close by 'less you want to go as far as Galva or up to Beach."

"I was set for some scratch-hen eggs."

"Powdered," he said. "My Mrs. gets powdered."

Literary Analysis
Author's Style What effect does the unusual nature of the "Bad Lands" have on Steinbeck's tone and style?

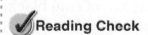Reading Check

What emotional reaction does Steinbeck have when he sees the "Bad Lands"?

"Lived here long?"

"Yep."

I waited for him to ask something or to say something so we could go on, but he didn't. And as the silence continued, it became more and more impossible to think of something to say. I made one more try. "Does it get very cold here winters?"

"Fairly."

"You talk too much."

He grinned. "That's what my Mrs. says."

"So long," I said, and put the car in gear and moved along. And in my rear-view mirror I couldn't see that he looked after me. He may not be a typical Badlander, but he's one of the few I caught.

A little farther along I stopped at a small house, a section of war-surplus barracks, it looked, but painted white with yellow trim, and with the dying vestiges of a garden, frosted-down geraniums and a few clusters of chrysanthemums, little button things yellow and red-brown. I walked up the path with the certainty that I was being regarded from behind the white window curtains. An old woman answered my knock and gave me the drink of water I asked for and nearly talked my arm off. She was hungry to talk, frantic to talk, about her relatives, her friends, and how she wasn't used to this. For she was not a native and she didn't rightly belong here. Her native clime was a land of milk and honey and had its share of apes and ivory and peacocks. Her voice rattled on as though she was terrified of the silence that would settle when I was gone. As she talked it came to me that she was afraid of this place and, further, that so was I. I felt I wouldn't like to have the night catch me here.

I went into a state of flight, running to get away from the unearthly landscape. And then the late afternoon changed everything. As the sun angled, the buttes and coulees, the cliffs and sculptured hills and ravines lost their burned and dreadful look and glowed with yellow and rich browns and a hundred variations of red and silver gray, all picked out by streaks of coal black. It was so beautiful that I stopped near a thicket of dwarfed and wind-warped cedars and junipers, and once stopped I was caught, trapped in color and dazzled by the clarity of the light. Against the descending sun the battlements were dark and clean-lined, while to the east, where the uninhibited light poured slantwise, the strange landscape shouted with color. And the night, far from being frightful,

Reading Skill
Author's Purpose
How does the use of dialogue support the author's main purpose for writing?

Reading Skill
Author's Purpose
Why does Steinbeck include descriptions of the people he meets in the middle of descriptions of the landscape? Explain.

was lovely beyond thought, for the stars were close, and although there was no moon the starlight made a silver glow in the sky. The air cut the nostrils with dry frost. And for pure pleasure I collected a pile of dry dead cedar branches and built a small fire just to smell the perfume of the burning wood and to hear the excited crackle of the branches. My fire made a dome of yellow light over me, and nearby I heard a screech owl hunting and a barking of coyotes, not howling but the short chuckling bark of the dark of the moon. This is one of the few places I have ever seen where the night was friendlier than the day. And I can easily see how people are driven back to the Bad Lands.

Before I slept I spread a map on my bed, a Charley-tromped map. Beach was not far away, and that would be the end of North Dakota. And coming up would be Montana, where I had never been. That night was so cold that I put on my insulated underwear for pajamas, and when Charley had done his duties and had his biscuits and consumed his usual gallon of water and finally curled up in his place under the bed, I dug out an extra blanket and covered him—all except the tip of his nose—and he sighed and wriggled and gave a great groan of pure ecstatic comfort. And I thought how every safe generality I gathered in my travels was canceled by another. In the night the Bad Lands had become Good Lands. I can't explain it. That's how it was.

Reading Skill
Author's Purpose
How well does Steinbeck succeed in capturing the atmosphere of the places he visits?

▼ **Critical Viewing**
What aspects of the man in this photograph reflect the realities of living in a harsh environment like the Badlands? **[Analyze]**

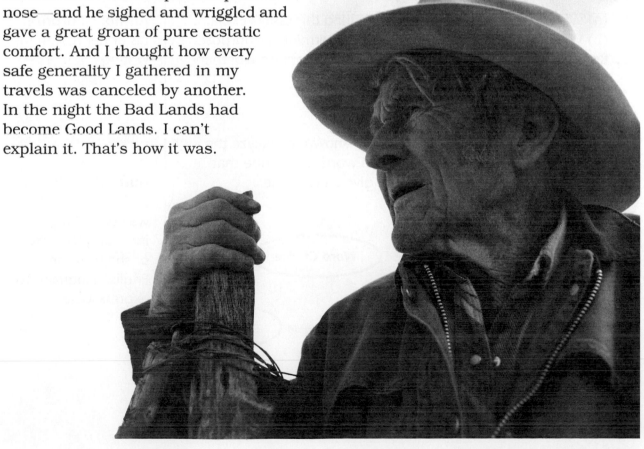

Apply the Skills

from Travels With Charley

Thinking About the Selection

1. **(a) Respond:** What do you think is the most interesting passage in the excerpt from *Travels With Charley*? Explain.
   (b) Discuss: In a small group, share your responses. Then, as a group, choose one response to share with the class.
2. **(a) Recall:** Why does Steinbeck decide to make this trip?
   (b) Infer: What does he hope to gain or learn from it?
3. **(a) Recall:** What are Steinbeck's first reactions upon entering the Badlands? **(b) Compare:** How do his feelings about the place change as night falls?
4. **(a) Recall:** Identify two different people that Steinbeck meets in the Badlands. **(b) Compare and Contrast:** In what ways is each person similar to and different from Steinbeck? **(c) Draw Conclusions:** Based on Steinbeck's experience, how does the wildness of the Badlands affect its residents?

Reading Skill

5. **(a)** What is Steinbeck's **purpose** in writing this essay? Explain.
   (b) What details in the essay help you determine his purpose?
6. Review the details Steinbeck includes, and **evaluate** whether he achieves his purpose. Explain.

Literary Analysis

7. Make a graphic organizer like the one shown to analyze the **author's style.** In each circle, write a word to describe that feature of Steinbeck's writing, and give an example.

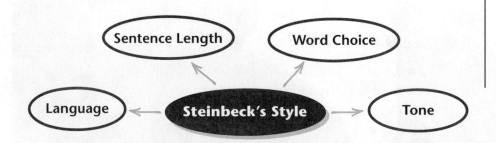

8. Use your completed graphic organizer to write one or two sentences that describe Steinbeck's writing style.

QuickReview

Selection at a Glance

John Steinbeck takes a cross-country trip to find the "real" America.

Go **Online**
Assessment
For: Self-test
Visit: www.PHSchool.com
Web Code: ena-6110

Author's Purpose: his or her reason for writing

Author's Style: an author's particular way of writing, including the way he or she uses the English language to express ideas

Vocabulary Builder

Practice Review the vocabulary list for the excerpt from *Travels With Charley* on page 152. Tell if each statement is true or false. Then explain your response.

1. Lack of sleep can *impair* your ability to think clearly.
2. It is *inexplicable* why humans float in space.
3. A military general issues *celestial* commands.
4. A *rigorous* climb can leave you tired and sweaty.

Writing

Write an entry for an **observations journal** about a favorite place that you have visited and remember well.

- First, describe the place and your visit.
- Next, describe the features and people that make the place special.
- Add details and anecdotes, or brief stories, that convey a strong sense of place and time.

For *Grammar, Vocabulary,* and *Assessment,* see **Build Language Skills,** pages 170–171.

Extend Your Learning

Listening and Speaking Research Steinbeck's life story and works of literature. Then, based on your research, prepare and deliver a three-to-five minute **oral presentation** in which you describe John Steinbeck's role as an observer of American society. Make sure to include these highlights:

- A description of the subjects of Steinbeck's major works.
- Anecdotes that present the public's reaction to *The Grapes of Wrath.*

Research and Technology Use the Internet and library resources to find information about the Badlands. Use software to create a **brochure** for visitors. Include sights and activities for at least three destinations as well as directions for getting there. Present the information in a readable format that incorporates graphics.

Speech

Background

Voices for Change Persuasive speeches played a key role in the civil rights movement of the 1960s. Of all the voices for change, none was more powerful than that of Dr. Martin Luther King, Jr. At marches and rallies, Dr. King spoke out against segregation and moved people to action with his visions of an equal and just society.

Connecting to the Literature

Reading/Writing Connection "The American Dream" is from a 1961 speech. In it, Dr. King tries to persuade his audience to help make his dream come true. When you feel strongly about an issue, how do you convince others? Describe an example where you used persuasion effectively. Use three of the following words: *emphasize, analyze, communicate, accomplish.*

Review

For **Reading Skill, Literary Analysis,** and **Vocabulary Builder,** see page 152.

Meet the Author

Martin Luther **King,** Jr. (1929–1968)

Many people remember Dr. Martin Luther King, Jr., best for these lines from a speech in 1963. "I have a dream that my four little children will one day live in a nation where they will not be judged by the color of their skin but by the content of their character."

Civil Rights Champion Dr. King's work as a civil rights leader began in 1955, when he led a boycott against the segregated bus system in Montgomery, Alabama. A long campaign of marches and demonstrations followed, with the aim of bringing down the entire system of segregation. King and his fellow activists faced opposition from segregationist governors, hostile crowds, and unsympathetic police officers. Ultimately, King was successful in getting important legislation passed and in drawing national attention to the problems of inequality.

Go Online
Author Link

For: More information about the author
Visit: www.PHSchool.com
Web Code: ene-9111

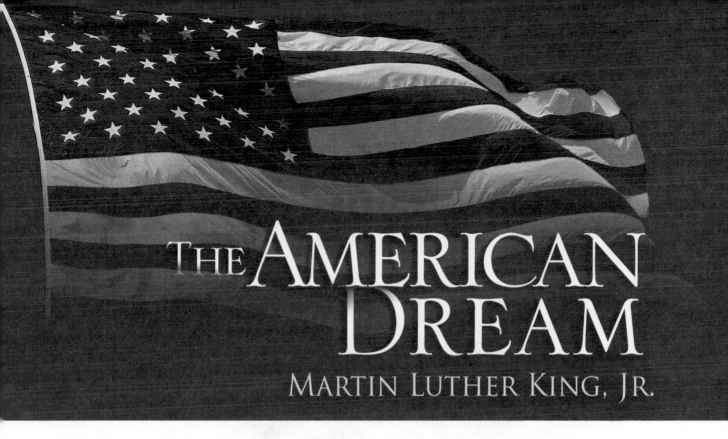

THE AMERICAN DREAM

MARTIN LUTHER KING, JR.

America is essentially a dream, a dream as yet unfulfilled. It is a dream of a land where men of all races, of all nationalities and of all creeds[1] can live together as brothers. The substance of the dream is expressed in these sublime words, words lifted to cosmic proportions: "We hold these truths to be self-evident, that all men are created equal; that they are endowed by their Creator with certain unalienable rights; that among these are life, liberty, and the pursuit of happiness."[2] This is the dream.

One of the first things we notice in this dream is an amazing universalism. It does not say some men, but it says all men. It does not say all white men, but it says all men, which includes black men. It does not say all Gentiles, but it says all men, which includes Jews. It does not say all Protestants, but it says all men, which includes Catholics.

And there is another thing we see in this dream that ultimately distinguishes democracy and our form of government from all of the totalitarian regimes[3] that emerge in history. It

---

1. **creeds** (krēdz) *n.* systems of belief.
2. **"We hold these truths . . . pursuit of happiness."** opening words of the Declaration of Independence, which asserted the American colonies' independence from Great Britain in 1776.
3. **totalitarian** (tō tal´ ə ter´ ē ən) **regimes** (rə zhēmz´) countries in which those in power control every aspect of citizens' lives.

says that each individual has certain basic rights that are
neither conferred by nor derived from the state. To discover
where they came from it is necessary to move back behind the
dim mist of eternity, for they are God-given. Very seldom if
ever in the history of the world has a sociopolitical document
expressed in such profoundly eloquent and <u>unequivocal</u> language the dignity and the worth of human personality. The
American dream reminds us that every man is heir to the legacy of worthiness.

　　Ever since the Founding Fathers of our nation dreamed this
noble dream, America has been something of a schizophrenic[4]
personality, tragically divided against herself. On the one
hand we have proudly professed the principles of democracy,
and on the other hand we have sadly practiced the very
<u>antithesis</u> of those principles. Indeed slavery and segregation
have been strange <u>paradoxes</u> in a nation founded on the principle that all men are created equal. This is what the Swedish

Literary Analysis
Author's Style Is
King's style formal or
informal? Explain.

Vocabulary Builder
unequivocal (un′ ē
kwiv′ ə kəl) *adj.* clear;
plainly understood

antithesis (an tith′ ə
sis) *n.* direct
opposite

paradoxes (par′ ə
däks′ əz) *n.* two
things that seem
directly at odds

---

4. schizophrenic (skit′ sə fren′ ik) *adj.* characterized by a separation between the thought
processes and emotions, popularly known as "split personality."

sociologist, Gunnar Myrdal, referred to as the American dilemma.

But the shape of the world today does not permit us the luxury of an anemic democracy. The price America must pay for the continued exploitation of the Negro and other minority groups is the price of its own destruction. The hour is late; the clock of destiny is ticking out. It is trite, but urgently true, that if America is to remain a first-class nation she can no longer have second-class citizens. Now, more than ever before, America is challenged to bring her noble dream into reality, and those who are working to implement the American dream are the true saviors of democracy.

Now may I suggest some of the things we must do if we are to make the American dream a reality. First I think all of us must develop a world perspective if we are to survive. The American dream will not become a reality devoid of the larger dream of a world of brotherhood and peace and good will. The world in which we live is a world of geographical oneness and we are challenged now to make it spiritually one.

Man's specific genius and technological ingenuity has dwarfed distance and placed time in chains. Jet planes have compressed into minutes distances that once took days and months to cover. It is not common for a preacher to be quoting Bob Hope, but I think he has aptly described this jet age in which we live. If, on taking off on a nonstop flight from Los Angeles to New York City, you develop hiccups, he said, you will hic in Los Angeles and cup in New York City. That is really *moving*. If you take a flight from Tokyo, Japan, on Sunday morning, you will arrive in Seattle, Washington, on the preceding Saturday night. When your friends meet you at the airport and ask you when you left Tokyo, you will have to say, "I left tomorrow." This is the kind of world in which we live. Now this is a bit humorous but I am trying to laugh a basic fact into all of us: the world in which we live has become a single neighborhood.

Through our scientific genius we have made of this world a neighborhood; now through our moral and spiritual development we must make of it a brotherhood. In a real sense, we must all learn to live together as brothers, or we will all perish together as fools. We must come to see that no individual can live alone; no nation can live alone. We must all live together; we must all be concerned about each other.

Vocabulary Builder
exploitation (eks′ plɔi tā′ shən) *n.* the act of using another person for selfish purposes

Literary Analysis
Author's Style How does King's choice of phrases, such as *specific genius* and *aptly described*, affect his style?

Reading Skill
Author's Purpose Is King specific in saying what he wants his audience to do? Explain.

Apply the Skills

The American Dream

Thinking About the Selection

1. **(a) Respond:** Which statement in King's speech holds the most meaning for today's society? Explain. **(b) Discuss:** In a small group, share your responses. As a group, choose one response to share with the class.
2. **(a) Recall:** From what historic document does Dr. King quote to express "the American dream"? **(b) Infer:** Why does he choose those particular lines?
3. **(a) Recall:** What differences does King find in American society between the way things are and the way they should be? **(b) Analyze Cause and Effect:** What effect do these differences have on our democracy? **(c) Synthesize:** How would the elimination of these differences affect people's lives?
4. **(a) Generalize:** What steps does Dr. King think Americans must take to make the American dream a reality? **(b) Make a Judgment:** Do you agree? Explain.

Reading Skill

5. **(a)** What is Dr. King's **purpose** in writing this speech? Support your answer. **(b)** What details in the speech help you determine his purpose? **(c)** Review the details King provides, and **evaluate** whether he achieves his purpose. Explain.

Literary Analysis

6. Make a graphic organizer like the one shown to analyze the features of the **author's style.** In each circle, write a word or phrase to describe Dr. King's writing and give an example from the text.

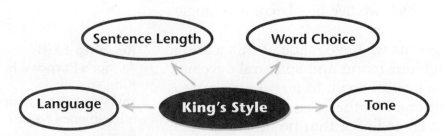

7. Use your completed graphic organizer to write one or two sentences describing Dr. King's writing style.

QuickReview

Speech at a Glance
Martin Luther King, Jr., offers his ideas about what can transform the American dream into a reality.

Go Online

Assessment
For: Self-test
Visit: www.PHSchool.com
Web Code: ena-6111

Author's Purpose: his or her reason for writing

Author's Style: an author's particular way of writing, including the way he or she uses the English language to express ideas

Vocabulary Builder

Practice Review the vocabulary list for "The American Dream" on page 152. Tell if each statement is true or false. Then explain your response.

1. Rudeness is the *antithesis* of politeness.

2. The following is an example of a *paradox* in biology. A platypus is a mammal that lays eggs.

3. A company is guilty of *exploitation* if it gives its workers a generous raise every year.

4. If you have a question and you do not know how to proceed, it is useful to receive an *unequivocal* answer.

Writing

In "The American Dream," Dr. King observes that America is not living up to its ideals and suggests improvements. Write an entry for an **observations journal,** in which you record your thoughts about an aspect of today's society that could be improved.

- Begin by describing the problem as you see it. Use details, anecdotes (brief stories), or examples to illustrate the problem.
- Then, suggest solutions, such as actions to take, changes in attitudes, or both.

For *Grammar, Vocabulary,* and *Assessment,* see **Build Language Skills,** pages 170–171.

Extend Your Learning

Listening and Speaking Research the 1963 March on Washington and Dr. King's role in it. Then, prepare and deliver a three-to-five minute **oral presentation** in which you describe the event and its importance, based on your research.

Research and Technology Use the Internet and library resources to find information about the cities and historical sites associated with Dr. King and his work in the civil rights movement. Then, use software to create a **brochure** to guide others visiting these sites. List at least three sites, using a readable format with graphics. For each site, include a short explanation of its importance in Dr. King's life.

Build Language Skills

The American Dream • Travels With Charley

Vocabulary Skill

Suffixes The **suffixes** *-tion* and *-sion* mean "the act or process of doing something" or "the result of doing something." These suffixes usually form nouns. For example, the word *intention* is formed when *-tion* is added to the verb *intend*. An intention is what you intend.

Practice Answer each question in a complete sentence. In your answer, use the noun formed by adding *-tion* or *-sion* to the underlined word. Use a dictionary to check the spelling.

1. What do you use to <u>persuade</u> someone?
2. What do you have when two things <u>contradict</u> each other?
3. What do you have when you <u>revise</u> something?
4. What do you have when you <u>appreciate</u> something?

Grammar Lesson

Reflexive Pronouns A **reflexive pronoun** indicates that someone or something performs an action to, for, or upon itself. A reflexive pronoun always ends with *-self* or *-selves*, agrees in number with a noun or pronoun that appears earlier in the sentence, and appears with another noun or pronoun. It should never take the place of a noun or pronoun. The chart lists reflexive pronouns and their uses.

MorePractice

For more practice with Pronouns, see the Grammar Handbook, p. R31.

Reflexive Pronouns	Singular	Plural	Sample
First Person	myself	ourselves	**I** took **myself**
Second Person	yourself	yourselves	**You** are proud of **yourself**.
Third Person	himself, herself, itself	themselves	**They** asked **themselves**

Practice Identify the reflexive pronouns and the nouns or pronouns they refer to. Label sentences that are incorrect and explain why.

1. Sam, Mia, and myself saw the movie.
2. We thought we could solve it ourselves.
3. They know how to enjoy themselves.
4. Yvette sent herself a postcard from Paris.
5. You should not be too hard on yourself.

*W*_G *Prentice Hall Writing and Grammar Connection: Chapter 14*

Reading: Author's Purpose

Directions: *Read the passage. Then, answer the questions.*

It is difficult to escape the influence of television. If you fit the statistical averages, by the age of 20 you will have been exposed to at least 20,000 hours of television. You can add 10,000 hours for each decade you have lived after the age of 20. The only things Americans do more than watch television are work and sleep.

—from *The Trouble with Television* by Robert MacNeil

1. You can predict that the author's purpose is

  A to explain the benefits of watching television.

  B to show that Americans work too many hours.

  C to show that Americans watch too much television.

  D to show how hard it is to produce a television show.

2. To achieve his purpose, the author cites

  A other experts' opinions.

  B statistics about television watching.

  C statistics about television ownership.

  D the opinions of television critics.

3. According to the author, which statement is true?

  A Americans watch 20,000 hours of television in a lifetime.

  B Older Americans watch more television than younger ones.

  C Americans work fewer hours than they spend watching television.

  D Americans watch about 10,000 hours in a decade.

4. What is the tone of the rest of the essay most likely to be?

  A serious

  B humorous

  C inspirational

  D annoyed

Timed Writing: Interpretation of Literature
[Interpretation]

Review *"The American Dream"* or *Travels with Charley*. Write an essay in which you interpret the author's fears and hopes, whether for himself or others. Include quotations from the selection. **(20 minutes)**

Writing Workshop: *Work in Progress*

Using the Brainstorming Chart, decide which column describes an important lesson. Develop a timeline of the event, adding details which would help the reader feel the way you did. Save this work in your writing portfolio.

Types of Narratives

A **narrative** is any type of writing that tells a story. Narratives are found in prose and in poetry.

- A **fictional narrative** tells a story about imaginary characters and events.
- A **nonfictional narrative** presents a story about real characters and events.

Comparing Types of Narratives

Both fictional and nonfictional narratives present a sequence of events in a particular setting. Here are some important differences between the forms:

- Since a fictional narrative does not describe real events, the author has complete control over *characters, setting,* and *plot*. A writer can introduce new characters, change locations, or alter events to build the story.
- In nonfiction, the author cannot change real-life events or invent details about settings and people.

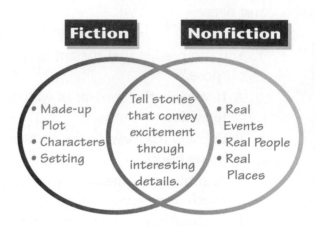

As you read the fictional piece "Up the Slide" and the nonfiction work "A Glow in the Dark," be aware of the differences between the two types of narratives. Also, notice how fiction and nonfiction narratives borrow from each other, as shown in the chart.

Vocabulary Builder

Up the Slide

- **exertion** (eg zʉr´ shən) *n.* energetic activity; effort (p. 178) *The exertion of swimming laps left Pablo exhausted.*

- **maneuver** (mə nōō´ vər) *n.* series of planned steps (p. 179) *Using a complicated maneuver, the workers moved the piano.*

- **ascent** (ə sent´) *n.* the act of climbing or rising (p. 180) *The ascent to the top of the mountain took six hours.*

- **descent** (dē sent´) *n.* the act of climbing down (p. 180) *Bob faced a difficult descent over the cliff face.*

A Glow in the Dark

- **sustain** (sə stān´) *v.* keep up (p. 181) *A sprinter cannot sustain a fast pace for long.*

- **diffused** (di fyōōzd´) *v.* spread out widely in different directions (p. 183) *The red dye diffused rapidly in the water.*

Build Understanding

Connecting to the Literature

Reading/Writing Connection In both of these narratives, people struggle with doubts and fears in wilderness settings. Think of the dangers that might spark fear in a wilderness area. Write three sentences that describe these dangers and fears. Use three of the following words: *anticipate, collapse, detect, illuminate, horror.*

Meet the Authors

Jack **London** (1876–1916)

Jack London was the most popular novelist and short-story writer of his day. His exciting tales of adventure and courage were inspired by his own experiences.

A Young Adventurer When he was seventeen, London sailed with a seal-hunting ship to Japan and Siberia. After two years, he returned to high school, vowing to become a writer. In 1897, London journeyed to the Yukon Territory in search of gold. Although he did not find any, he did find inspiration for his writing.

Gary **Paulsen** (b. 1939)

Gary Paulsen had a difficult childhood. Because his family moved frequently, he never spent more than five months in any one school.

In From the Cold One cold night, Paulsen went into a library to get warm. The librarian offered him a book and a library card. "It was as though I had been dying of thirst and the librarian had handed me a five-gallon bucket of water," he says. Today, Paulsen writes fiction based on his own life. "A Glow in the Dark" comes from *Woodsong*, a true account of Paulsen's experiences as he trained for the Iditarod, a grueling dog-sled race in Alaska.

Go Online
Author Link
For: More about the authors
Visit: www.PHSchool.com
Web Code: ene-9112

Up the Slide

Jack London

Background   Clay Dilham, the young man in "Up the Slide," is similar to many young prospectors who traveled to the Yukon Territory in search of gold in the 1890s. The Yukon Territory is located in the northwestern corner of Canada. It is part of the subarctic zone, where temperatures have been known to plunge to −80°F!

When Clay Dilham left the tent to get a sled-load of firewood, he expected to be back in half an hour. So he told Swanson, who was cooking the dinner. Swanson and he belonged to different outfits, located about twenty miles apart on the Stewart River, but they had become traveling partners on a trip down the Yukon to Dawson to get the mail.

Swanson had laughed when Clay said he would be back in half an hour. It stood to reason, Swanson said, that good, dry firewood could not be found so close to Dawson; that

whatever firewood there was originally had long since been gathered in; that firewood would not be selling at forty dollars a cord if any man could go out and get a sled-load and be back in the time Clay expected to make it.

Then it was Clay's turn to laugh, as he sprang on the sled and *mushed* the dogs on the river-trail. For, coming up from the Siwash village the previous day, he had noticed a small dead pine in an out-of-the-way place, which had defied discovery by eyes less sharp than his. And his eyes were both young and sharp, for his seventeenth birthday was just cleared.

A swift ten minutes over the ice brought him to the place, and figuring ten minutes to get the tree and ten minutes to return made him certain that Swanson's dinner would not wait.

Just below Dawson, and rising out of the Yukon itself, towered the great Moosehide Mountain, so named by Lieutenant Schwatka long ere the Yukon became famous. On the river side the mountain was scarred and gullied and gored; and it was up one of these gores or gullies that Clay had seen the tree.

Halting his dogs beneath, on the river ice, he looked up, and after some searching, rediscovered it. Being dead, its weather-beaten gray so blended with the gray wall of rock that a thousand men could pass by and never notice it. Taking root in a cranny, it had grown up, exhausted its bit of soil, and perished. Beneath it the wall fell sheer for a hundred feet to the river. All one had to do was to sink an ax into the dry trunk a dozen times and it would fall to the ice, and most probably smash conveniently to pieces. This Clay had figured on when confidently limiting the trip to half an hour.

He studied the cliff thoroughly before attempting it. So far as he was concerned, the longest way round was the shortest way to the tree. Twenty feet of nearly perpendicular climbing would bring him to where a slide sloped more gently in. By making a long zigzag across the face of this slide and back again, he would arrive at the pine.

Fastening his ax across his shoulders so that it would not interfere with his movements, he clawed up the broken rock,

◀ Critical Viewing What details about the setting of this story can you learn from this historical photograph of Yukon miners? [Connect]

Literary Analysis
Narratives What details of the setting make it seem as though this fictional story could really have happened?

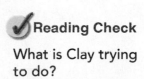

Reading Check

What is Clay trying to do?

hand and foot, like a cat, till the twenty feet were cleared and he could draw breath on the edge of the slide.

The slide was steep and its snow-covered surface slippery. Further, the heelless, walrus-hide shoes of his *muclucs* were polished by much ice travel, and by his second step he realized how little he could depend upon them for clinging purposes. A slip at that point meant a plunge over the edge and a twenty-foot fall to the ice. A hundred feet farther along, and a slip would mean a fifty-foot fall.

He thrust his mittened hand through the snow to the earth to steady himself, and went on. But he was forced to exercise such care that the first zigzag consumed five minutes. Then, returning across the face of the slide toward the pine, he met with a new difficulty. The slope steepened considerably, so that little snow collected, while bent flat beneath this thin covering were long, dry last-year's grasses.

The surface they presented was as glassy as that of his muclucs, and when both surfaces came together his feet shot out, and he fell on his face, sliding downward and convulsively clutching for something to stay himself.

This he succeeded in doing, although he lay quiet for a couple of minutes to get back his nerve. He would have taken off his muclucs and gone at it in his socks, only the cold was thirty below zero, and at such temperature his feet would quickly freeze. So he went on, and after ten minutes of risky work made the safe and solid rock where stood the pine.

A few strokes of the ax felled it into the chasm, and peeping

Literary Analysis
Narratives Do the risks that Clay takes seem like those an actual person would take? Why or why not?

▼ **Critical Viewing**
What characteristics of this ice slide would make it dangerous for a climber? **[Analyze]**

over the edge, he indulged a laugh at the startled dogs. They were on the verge of bolting when he called aloud to them, soothingly, and they were reassured.

Then he turned about for the trip back. Going down, he knew, was even more dangerous than coming up, but how dangerous he did not realize till he had slipped half a dozen times, and each time saved himself by what appeared to him a miracle. Time and again he ventured upon the slide, and time and again he was balked when he came to the grasses.

He sat down and looked at the treacherous snow-covered slope. It was manifestly[1] impossible for him to make it with a whole body, and he did not wish to arrive at the bottom shattered like the pine tree.

He must be doing something to keep his blood circulating. If he could not get down by going down, there only remained to him to get down by going up. It was a herculean task, but it was the only way out of the predicament.

From where he was he could not see the top of the cliff, but he reasoned that the gully in which lay the slide must give inward more and more as it approached the top. From what little he could see, the gully displayed this tendency; and he noticed, also, that the slide extended for many hundreds of feet upward, and that where it ended the rock was well broken up and favorable for climbing. . . .

So instead of taking the zigzag which led downward, he made a new one leading upward and crossing the slide at an angle of thirty degrees. The grasses gave him much trouble, and made him long for soft-tanned moosehide moccasins, which could make his feet cling like a second pair of hands.

He soon found that thrusting his mittened hands through the snow and clutching the grass roots was uncertain and unsafe. His mittens were too thick for him to be sure of his grip, so he took them off. But this brought with it new trouble. When he held on to a bunch of roots the snow, coming in contact with his bare warm hand, was melted, so that his hands and the wristbands of his woolen shirt were dripping with water. This the frost was quick to attack, and his fingers were numbed and made worthless.

Then he was forced to seek good footing, where he could stand erect unsupported, to put on his mittens, and to thrash

---

1. **manifestly** (man´ ə fest´ lē) adv. clearly.

Literary Analysis
Narratives How does the author's choice of setting heighten the drama in the story?

Literary Analysis
Narratives What real details about life in a cold climate does London include here?

Reading Check

Why is the trip down harder than the trip up?

his hands against his sides until the heat came back into them.

This constant numbing of his fingers made his progress very slow; but the zigzag came to an end finally, where the side of the slide was buttressed by a perpendicular rock, and he turned back and upward again. As he climbed higher and higher, he found that the slide was wedge-shaped, its rocky buttresses pinching it away as it reared its upper end. Each step increased the depth which seemed to yawn for him.

While beating his hands against his sides he turned and looked down the long slippery slope, and figured, in case he slipped, that he would be flying with the speed of an express train ere he took the final plunge into the icy bed of the Yukon.

He passed the first outcropping rock, and the second, and at the end of an hour found himself above the third, and fully five hundred feet above the river. And here, with the end nearly two hundred feet above him, the pitch of the slide was increasing.

Each step became more difficult and perilous, and he was faint from exertion and from lack of Swanson's dinner. Three or four times he slipped slightly and recovered himself; but, growing careless from exhaustion and the long tension on his nerves, he tried to continue with too great haste, and was rewarded by a double slip of each foot, which tore him loose and started him down the slope.

On account of the steepness there was little snow; but what little there was as displaced by his body, so that he became the nucleus of a young avalanche. He clawed desperately with his hands, but there was little to cling to, and he sped downward faster and faster.

The first and second outcroppings were below him, but he knew that the first was almost out of line, and pinned his hope on the second. Yet

Vocabulary Builder
exertion (eg zur´ shən)
n. energetic activity; effort

the first was just enough in line to catch one of his feet and to whirl him over and head downward on his back.

The shock of this was severe in itself, and the fine snow enveloped him in a blinding, maddening cloud; but he was thinking quickly and clearly of what would happen if he brought up head first against the outcropping. He twisted himself over on his stomach, thrust both hands out to one side, and pressed them heavily against the flying surface.

This had the effect of a brake, drawing his head and shoulders to the side. In this position he rolled over and over a couple of times, and then, with a quick jerk at the right moment, he got his body the rest of the way round.

And none too soon, for the next moment his feet drove into the outcropping, his legs doubled up, and the wind was driven from his stomach with the abruptness of the stop.

There was much snow down his neck and up his sleeves. At once and with unconcern he shook this out, only to discover, when he looked up to where he must climb again, that he had lost his nerve. He was shaking as if with a palsy, and sick and faint from a frightful nausea.

Fully ten minutes passed ere he could master these sensations and summon sufficient strength for the weary climb. His legs hurt him and he was limping, and he was conscious of a sore place in his back, where he had fallen on the ax.

In an hour he had regained the point of his tumble, and was contemplating the slide, which so suddenly steepened. It was plain to him that he could not go up with his hands and feet alone, and he was beginning to lose his nerve again when he remembered the ax.

Reaching upward the distance of a step, he brushed away the snow, and in the frozen gravel and crumbled rock of the slide chopped a shallow resting place for his foot. Then he came up a step, reached forward, and repeated the <u>maneuver</u>. And so, step by step, foothole by foothole, a tiny speck of toiling life poised like a fly on the face of Moosehide Mountain, he fought his upward way.

Twilight was beginning to fall when he gained the head of the slide and drew himself into the rocky bottom of the gully. At this point the shoulder of the mountain began to bend back toward the crest, and in addition to its being less steep,

◄ **Critical Viewing** What do the ages, expressions, clothes, and actions of these children tell you about the life of a Yukon miner like Clay Dilham? **[Infer]**

Literary Analysis
Narratives What details does London use to create suspense at this point in the story?

Vocabulary Builder
maneuver (mə nōō′ vər) *n.* series of planned steps

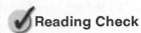**Reading Check**

How does Clay stop himself from sliding to his death?

the rocks afforded better handhold and foothold. The worst was over, and the best yet to come!

The gully opened out into a miniature basin, in which a floor of soil had been deposited, out of which, in turn, a tiny grove of pines had sprung. The trees were all dead, dry and seasoned, having long since exhausted the thin skin of earth.

Clay ran his experienced eye over the timber, and estimated that it would chop up into fifty cords at least. Beyond, the gully closed in and became barren rock again. On every hand was barren rock, so the wonder was small that the trees had escaped the eyes of men. They were only to be discovered as he had discovered them—by climbing after them.

He continued the <u>ascent</u>, and the white moon greeted him when he came out upon the crest of Moosehide Mountain. At his feet, a thousand feet below, sparkled the lights of Dawson.

But the <u>descent</u> was precipitate and dangerous in the uncertain moonlight, and he elected to go down the mountain by its gentler northern flank. In a couple of hours he reached the Yukon at the Siwash village, and took the river-trail back to where he had left the dogs. There he found Swanson, with a fire going, waiting for him to come down.

And although Swanson had a hearty laugh at his expense, nevertheless, a week or so later, in Dawson, there were fifty cords of wood sold at forty dollars a cord, and it was he and Swanson who sold them.

Thinking About the Selection

1. **Respond:** Do you think the risks that Clay takes are reasonable or foolish? Why?

2. **(a) Recall:** How long does Clay say he will be gone collecting firewood? **(b) Recall:** What is Swanson's reaction to Clay's estimate? **(c) Speculate:** Why do you think London begins his story with the description of the disagreement?

3. **(a) Infer:** Identify three specific skills Clay possesses that aid his survival. **(b) Contrast:** Which of his actions endanger his life? Explain. **(c) Make Judgments:** Is the discovery worth the risks Clay takes? Explain.

4. **(a) Infer:** What lesson does Clay learn from his experiences? **(b) Generalize:** What lesson does the story hold for readers who will never visit the Yukon?

A Glow in the Dark

from WOODSONG

Gary Paulsen

There are night ghosts.

Some people say that we can understand all things if we can know them, but there came a dark night in the fall when I thought that was wrong, and so did the dogs.

We had been running all morning and were tired; some of the dogs were young and could not <u>sustain</u> a long run. So we stopped in the middle of the afternoon when they seemed to want to rest. I made a fire, set up a gentle, peaceful camp, and went to sleep for four hours.

It hadn't snowed yet so we had been running with a three-wheel cart, which meant we had to run on logging roads and open areas. I had been hard pressed to find new country to run in to keep the young dogs from becoming bored and this logging trail was one we hadn't run. It had been rough going, with a lot of ruts and mud and the cart was a mess so I spent some time fixing it after I awakened, carving off the dried mud. The end result was we didn't get going again until close to one in the morning. This did not pose a problem except that as soon as I hooked the dogs up and got them lined out—I

Vocabulary Builder
sustain (sə stān´) *v.*
keep up

✔ **Reading Check**

Why is the author running his dogs in the middle of the night?

was running an eight-dog team—my head lamp went out. I replaced the bulb and tried a new battery, but that didn't help—the internal wiring was bad. I thought briefly of sleeping again until daylight but the dogs were slamming into the harnesses, screaming to run, so I shrugged and jumped on the rig and untied it. Certainly, I thought, running without a head lamp would not be the worst thing I had ever done.

Immediately we blew into the darkness and the ride was madness. Without a lamp I could not tell when the rig was going to hit a rut or a puddle. It was cloudy and fairly warm—close to fifty—and had rained the night before. Without the moon or even starlight I had no idea where the puddles were until they splashed me—largely in the face—so I was soon dripping wet. Coupled with that, tree limbs I couldn't see hit at me as we passed, almost tearing me off the back of the rig. Inside an hour I wasn't sure if I was up, down, or sideways.

And the dogs stopped.

They weren't tired, not even a little, judging by the way they had been ripping through the night, but they stopped dead.

I had just taken a limb in the face and was temporarily blinded. All I knew was that they had stopped suddenly and that I had to jam down on the brakes to keep from running over them. It took me a couple of seconds to clear my eyes and when I did, I saw the light.

In the first seconds I thought it was another person coming toward me. The light had an eerie green-yellow glow. It was quite bright and filled a whole part of the dark night ahead, down the trail. It seemed to be moving. I was in deep woods and couldn't think what a person would be doing there—there are no other teams where I train—but I was glad to see the light.

At first.

Literary Analysis
Narratives What real details emphasize that "the ride was madness"?

▼ **Critical Viewing** How would riding this cart during the day compare with riding it at night after a rain? **[Compare and Contrast]**

Then I realized the light was strange. It glowed and ebbed and seemed to fill too much space to be a regular light source. It was low to the ground, and wide.

I was still not frightened, and would probably not have become frightened except that the dogs suddenly started to sing.

I have already talked about some of their songs. Rain songs and first-snow songs and meat songs and come-back-and-stay-with-us songs and even puppy-training songs, but I had heard this song only once, when an old dog had died in the kennel. It was a death song.

And that frightened me.

They all sat. I could see them quite well in the glow from the light—the soft glow, the green glow, the ghost glow. It crept into my thinking without my knowing it: the ghost glow. Against my wishes I started thinking of all the things in my life that had scared me.

Ghosts and goblins and dark nights and snakes under the bed and sounds I didn't know and bodies I had found and graveyards under covered pale moons and death, death, death . . .

And they sang and sang. The cold song in the strange light. For a time I could do nothing but stand on the back of the wheeled rig and stare at the light with old, dusty terror.

But curiosity was stronger. My legs moved without my wanting them to move and my body followed them, alongside the team in the dark, holding to each dog like a security blanket until I reached the next one, moving closer to the light until I was at the front and there were no more dogs to hold.

The light had gotten brighter, seemed to pulse and flood back and forth, but I still could not see the source. I took another step, then another, trying to look around the corner, deeply feeling the distance from the dogs, the aloneness.

Two more steps, then one more, leaning to see around the corner and at last I saw it and when I did it was worse.

It was a form. Not human. A large, standing form glowing in the dark. The light came from within it, a cold-glowing green light with yellow edges that <u>diffused</u> the shape, making it change and grow as I watched.

I felt my heart slam up into my throat.

I couldn't move. I stared at the upright form and was sure it was a ghost, a being from the dead sent for me. I could not

Literary Analysis
Narratives What details from Paulsen's imagination create excitement here?

Vocabulary Builder
diffused (di fyoozd´) v. spread out widely in different directions

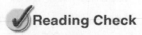

Reading Check

What sound frightens Paulsen?

move and might not have ever moved except that the dogs had followed me, pulling the rig quietly until they were around my legs, peering ahead, and I looked down at them and had to laugh.

They were caught in the green light, curved around my legs staring at the standing form, ears cocked and heads turned sideways while they studied it. I took another short step forward and they all followed me, then another, and they stayed with me until we were right next to the form.

It was a stump.

A six-foot-tall, old rotten stump with the bark knocked off, glowing in the dark with a bright green glow. Impossible. I stood there with the dogs around my legs, smelling the stump and touching it with their noses. I found out later that it glowed because it had sucked phosphorus from the ground up into the wood and held the light from day all night.

But that was later. There in the night I did not know this. Touching the stump, and feeling the cold light, I could not quite get rid of the fear until a black-and-white dog named Fonzie came up, smelled the stump, snorted, and relieved himself on it.

So much for ghosts.

Literature in Context

Science Connection

Shining a Light on Phosphorus *Phosphorescence* is the process that makes phosphorus glow. During phosphorescence, phosphorus electrons absorb energy and become unstable. Light—the glow—results when the electrons drop back to their original energy levels. Phosphorus is

- a poisonous, nonmetallic element.
- a major element in fertilizer that aids plant growth.
- the element on match tips that produces a flame.

Connect to the Literature

How did Paulsen's ignorance of a scientific explanation for the glow add to his fear?

Thinking About the Selection

1. **Respond:** Based on Paulsen's description of the glow, would you have been frightened if you were in his situation? Why or why not?

2. **(a) Infer:** Why do the dogs start to sing? **(b) Apply:** In what way does their singing increase Paulsen's fear?

3. **(a) Recall:** How does Paulsen use his dogs for support as he moves toward the glow? **(b) Draw Conclusions:** Based on his actions, how does Paulsen feel about his dogs?

4. **Assess:** Do you think Paulsen shows good judgment and common sense? Explain why or why not.

Apply the Skills

Up the Slide • A Glow in the Dark

Comparing Types of Narratives

1. Use a chart like the one shown to compare and contrast the elements of each narrative.

Up the Slide	Elements	A Glow in the Dark
Outside narrator	Narrator	Gary Paulsen
	Main character	
	Danger	
	Role of dogs	
	Character's attitude toward danger	
	Reasons for character's behavior	

2. Fictional and nonfictional narratives often borrow from each other. **(a)** List four details in "Up the Slide" that add a sense of realism to this work of fiction. **(b)** List four details that lend "A Glow in the Dark" the excitement of a short story.

Writing to Compare Literary Works

Write an essay to compare and contrast the use of details in the two narratives. Discuss whether the use of these details affects the way you view the challenges faced by the characters. Use these questions to focus your thoughts:

- Did you think one character was braver than the other? Why?
- Which invented details in "Up the Slide" reveal aspects of Clay Dilham's character?
- Which true details in "A Glow in the Dark" reveal aspects of Gary Paulsen's character?

Vocabulary Builder

Practice For each item, write a sentence that correctly uses the given words or phrases.

1. ascent, backpack
2. diffused, darkness
3. maneuver, icy road
4. sustain, energy
5. exertion, rest
6. descent, relief

Reading • Author's Purpose

Directions: *Read the selection. Then, answer the questions.*

Before the mid-1800s, most families sewed their own clothes by hand. It took about fourteen hours to sew one shirt. Then, in 1845, Elias Howe invented his sewing machine. By 1877, there were half a million machines in the United States. With a sewing machine, a person could make a shirt in only one hour. Clothes could now be mass-produced and sold in stores.

Some people think the telephone or the gasoline engine is the invention that most changed people's lives. I think the sewing machine was more important because it freed people from the endless drudgery of sewing and gave ordinary people choices in what to wear. Free time and pride in their appearance gave average Americans more confidence and more opportunities to achieve their dreams.

1. **What kinds of details establish the author's purpose in the first paragraph of the passage?**
   A facts
   B reasons
   C images
   D characters

2. **What is the author's main purpose in the first paragraph?**
   A to entertain
   B to inform
   C to persuade
   D to complain

3. **What kinds of details help the author achieve her purpose in paragraph 2?**
   A facts
   B reasons
   C images
   D characters

4. **What do you determine is the author's purpose in the second paragraph?**
   A to entertain
   B to inform
   C to persuade
   D to complain

5. **Which statement is correct?**
   A Paragraphs 1 and 2 contain facts.
   B Paragraphs 1 and 2 contain opinions.
   C Paragraph 1 is opinion, Paragraph 2 is fact.
   D Paragraph 2 is opinion, Paragraph 1 is fact.

Assessment Practice

Vocabulary

A. Directions: *Choose the answer that correctly completes each sentence.*

6. In order to _____ the structure of his essay, I have to break it down into parts.
   A establish   C infer
   B analyze   D rationalize

7. To _____ the validity of the argument you will have to check the alleged facts.
   A establish   C infer
   B analyze   D rationalize

8. Have you _____ how long it will take you to write that paper?
   A establish   C rationalized
   B inferred   D determined

9. It was the author's _____ to shock his audience.
   A dedication
   B intention
   C rationalization
   D analysis

10. It takes careful writing to _____ an impact on the reader through poetry.
    A analyze
    B determine
    C achieve
    D intend

B. Directions: *Using your knowledge of suffixes, choose the best word for the sentence.*

11. The flowers _____ the hope of spring.
    A symbol   C appreciation
    B symbolize   D intention

12. We made a _____ to the essay.
    A revise   C analyze
    B revision   D realize

13. The author's _____ is to make you laugh.
    A intention   C establish
    B persuading   D analysis

14. I came to the _____ that this is a difficult subject and I have to study carefully.
    A realization   C compromise
    B dedication   D realize

15. Music stars are accustomed to their fans' _____.
    A adoring
    B dedicate
    C adoration
    D dedicating

16. His _____ to climb the mountain is admirable.
    A realize
    B compromise
    C composure
    D determination

Spelling Workshop

Commonly Misspelled Words

Look over the spelling list on this page. If you have ever had trouble spelling one or more of these words, you are not alone. These words are just some of the commonly misspelled words. The words on this list are often misspelled because a letter is added or left out.

Are you seeing double? Many commonly misspelled words are misspelled because a consonant is doubled when it usually should not be, or not doubled when it usually should be. Because you can still read the word, you may not immediately notice this kind of error when you are writing or proofreading. Analyze each word on the list and focus on the single and double consonants.

Two g's will tend to aggravate you.

Word List
always
aggravate
business
career
occasion
parallel
possession
really
recommend
until

Practice Rearrange the letters to correctly spell a word from the word list. Then, use each word in a sentence.

1. tilun

2. learly

3. lapralel

4. sposenisos

5. ercear

6. sbunsies

7. nocsicoa

8. saylaw

9. teargavag

10. merdencom

Commonly Misspelled Words

Directions: *Choose the correct spelling of the word to fill in the blank.*

1. We _____ have gym on Tuesdays.
   A always
   B allways
   C awlays
   D allwas

2. The two lines are _____.
   A paralel
   B parallell
   C parallel
   D paralell

3. Dust can _____ a person's allergies.
   A aggravate
   B aggravatte
   C agravatt
   D aggravat

4. It is _____ important that we arrive on time.
   A realy
   B really
   C reely
   D reelly

Directions: *Proofread the following passage. Rewrite the passage, correcting any spelling errors.*

In an interview, it is important to present a good impresion. Whether you are starting a carreer, or simply looking for a summer job, you need to present yourself in the best way. Dress appropriatcly for the ocassion. If you are interviewing for a job in an office, you should wear neat, professional clothes. Do not wait until the interview to begin preparing. If you can, get someone to reccommend you to your prospective employer.

Narration: Autobiographical Essay

An **autobiographical essay** tells the story of a memorable event, time, or situation in the writer's life. Follow the steps outlined in this workshop to write your own autobiographical essay.

Assignment Write an autobiographical essay about an event that had an effect on your attitude or helped you see the world differently.

What to Include Your autobiographical essay should feature the following elements:
- a consistent first-person point of view
- a clear sequence of true events from your life
- a central conflict, problem, or shift in perspective
- remembered feelings about the experience
- precise words that support the goals of your writing
- dialogue that helps reveal your characters' personalities
- error-free writing, including correct use of pronouns

To preview the criteria on which your autobiographical essay may be judged, see the rubric on page 197.

 ## Writing Workshop: *Work in Progress*

Autobiographical Essay

If you have completed the Work-in-Progress assignments, you already have several ideas you might want to use in your autobiographical essay. Continue developing these ideas, or explore a new idea as you complete the Writing Workshop.

Using the Form
You may use elements of this form in these types of writing:
- letters
- memoirs
- anecdotes
- exposition

Reading Writing Connection

To get a feel for autobiographical narrative, read the excerpt from *I Know Why The Caged Bird Sings*, by Maya Angelou, on page 462.

Prewriting

Choosing Your Topic

To choose the right event from your life to narrate, use the following strategies:

- **Freewriting** Write as many ideas about special times in your life as you can. As you write, focus on getting several ideas down. At this stage, do not worry about grammar or punctuation. Instead, let one idea lead to another and jot down details to help you remember each specific time. Review your list and choose a topic.

- **Make a Blueprint** Draw and label a blueprint of a familiar place—a friend's house, your school, or a park. List the people, things, and incidents you associate with each spot listed on your blueprint. Pick one as your topic. This model shows the events and experiences one writer associates with the town baseball field.

Work in Progress
Review the work you did on pages 145 and 171.

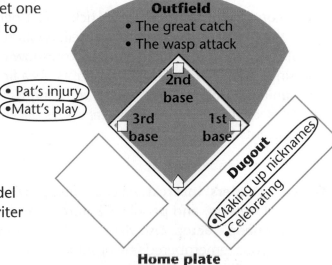

Outfield
- The great catch
- The wasp attack

- Pat's injury
- Matt's play

2nd base
3rd base
1st base
Dugout
- Making up nicknames
- Celebrating

Home plate
- Home run against Bull Dogs
- Striking out against Wildcats

Narrowing Your Topic

Knowing who your readers will be and why you want to tell your story can help you decide what to tell.

- If your purpose is **to entertain your audience,** focus on the funny, moving, or exciting parts of your story.
- If your purpose is **to share a lesson you learned,** focus on the events that illustrate the message and be prepared to explain what you learned from your experience.

Gathering Details

Make a chart. Make a five-column chart with the following headings related to your topic: *People, Time, Place, Events,* and *Emotions.* For each column, take about three minutes to list words and phrases that apply to the heading. You may use some of these words and phrases when you write.

Drafting

Shaping Your Writing

Order story events. Identify the conflict, or problem, that makes your narrative worth reading. Then, organize events around the conflict. First, introduce the people, setting, and situation. Build to the climax, where the tension is the greatest. Finish your narrative with a resolution that settles the problem.

Use a consistent point of view. Stick to first-person point of view, using the pronoun *I* to refer to yourself. Avoid telling what other people are thinking or feeling unless you show readers you are guessing about other people's thoughts. As a first-person narrator, you can know and tell only your own thoughts and feelings. This option is ideal for autobiographical essays because it allows you to offer insights into your actions.

Providing Elaboration

Develop readers' interest. As you write, provide background about the event, setting, and people. Capture what the scene looked like and how people acted. Use vivid details to help your readers get a sense of your remembered feelings about the experience.

Dull:	The players took the field.
Vivid:	Nine starters took the field at five o'clock on a warm afternoon.

Dull:	Matt caught the ball and threw it to first base.
Vivid:	Matt ran forward and made an awkward catch, followed by an even more clumsy lob toward first.

Use remembered feelings. Since the story is about you, tell your readers how you felt at the time. Connect the events in your narrative to yourself and your emotions.

To read the complete student model, see page 196.

Student Model: Using Remembered Feelings to Elaborate

That's when I realized the truth of something the coach is always telling us. When you play as a team, everyone is a star.

> These details show the writer's feelings about events.

Patricia C.
McKissack

Patricia C. McKissack

On Reaching Out to an Audience

An Author's Note allows the writer to share personal information about the content of the work. Although the note usually comes at the beginning of a book, I don't write mine until my manuscript is complete and almost ready for publication. It is then that I can step away and get a better perspective on what I've written. Although the stories in *The Dark-Thirty* are historical fiction, my author's note is nonfiction and gives the reader the historical backdrop for the stories.

> *"Research is the cornerstone of nonfiction."*
> —Patricia C. McKissack

Professional Model:
from Author's Note, *The Dark-Thirty*

When I was growing up in the South, we kids called the half hour just before nightfall the dark-thirty. We had exactly half an hour to get home before the monsters came out.

I needed a concise definition of the dark-thirty for readers. The first one I wrote was too long and not as memorable.

During the hot, muggy summer, when days last longer, we gathered on the front porch to pass away the evening hours. Grandmama's hands were always busy, but while shelling peas or picking greens, she told a spine-chilling ghost tale about Laughing Lizzy. . . .

I wanted to bring my readers to the front porch of my grandmother's house. I used descriptive words like "shelling peas" to show what was happening around me as I listened to her scary stories.

Then on cold winter nights, when the dark-thirty came early, our family sat in the living room and talked. The talk generally led to one of Grandmama's hair-raising tales. As the last glimmers of light faded from the window overlooking the woods, she told about Gray Jim, the runaway slave who'd been killed while trying to escape. Gray Jim's ghost haunted the woods on moonless nights. . . .

Here, I try to prepare the reader for what the stories are about in *The Dark-Thirty*. They are scary stories that are set within the historical context of African American history from slavery times to the present.

Writing Workshop

Revising

Revising Your Paragraphs

Check for sentence variety. Look over your paragraphs to see the patterns of sentences you have used. When writing in the first person, you may find that many of the sentences begin with *I*.

To analyze and evaluate sentence patterns in your draft, first color-code the first word of each sentence in your draft. For example, use green to highlight or circle articles; yellow for pronouns; blue for adjectives; red for adverbs; and orange for prepositions. Then, review your draft to determine if you have variety in your sentences. If necessary, revise sentence beginnings to build variety.

Reading **Writing** *Connection*

To read the complete student model, see page 196.

Student Model: Revising Sentence Beginnings

Draft: I remember the day my dad handed me a glove and a bat. I remember how he said the equipment was for the game of baseball. I have loved the sport since that day. I especially remember a game I played when I was eleven.

Revision: I remember the day my dad placed a glove in one of my hands and a bat in the other, and told me the combination was an eight-letter word called baseball. Ever since then, most of my memories have been related to the sport. When I was eleven, I played in a game I'll remember forever.

> Changing the way the sentences begin makes this a much more interesting paragraph.

Revising Your Word Choice

Use specific, precise nouns and verbs. Look for vague nouns that might have readers asking *What kind?* Replace them with precise nouns. Identify vague verbs or nouns, and replace them with more vivid, precise language.

    Vague: Weeds *filled* the *place*.
    Precise: Weeds *overran* the *playground*.

Peer Review: Compare the before and after versions of your draft with a partner and focus on your word choice. Discuss why the revised version is more effective than the first draft. As part of your conference, ask your partner to identify places in your draft that might need more specific word choices.

Integrating Grammar Skills

Revising for Pronoun-Antecedent Agreement

A **pronoun** is a word that stands for a noun. An **antecedent** is the word or group of words for which the pronoun stands.

Pronoun-Antecedent Agreement Pronouns should agree with their antecedents in two ways—person and number. *Person* tells to whom the pronoun refers. *Number* tells whether a pronoun is singular or plural.

Prentice Hall Writing and Grammar Connection: Chapter 24, Section 2

First-person, singular: I paid for **my** ticket, please send it to **me.**

First-person, plural: We ate **our** dinner when the waitress served it to **us.**

Second-person, singular: Simon, who gave that to **you?**

Second-person, plural: Girls, would **you** like some dessert?

Third-person, singular: Sara said **she** was late because **her** watch was lost.

Third-person, plural: The boys brought **their** cleats so **they** could play.

Indefinite pronouns like the ones listed here can pose agreement problems. This list shows the number associated with these pronouns.

Singular: another, anyone, anything, each, everybody, everything, little, much, nobody, nothing, one, other, someone, something

Plural: both, few, many, others, several

Both: all, any, more, most, none, some

Fixing Errors Follow these steps to fix problems with pronoun-antecedent agreement.

1. **Locate the pronoun and identify the antecedent.**
2. **If the antecedent is a singular indefinite pronoun, use a singular personal pronoun.** Example: Both girls are funny—*each* has *her* own way of dancing.
3. **If the antecedent is a plural indefinite pronoun, use a plural personal pronoun.** Example: The men argued. Then, *both* went *their* separate ways.

Apply It to Your Editing

Choose two paragraphs in your draft. Circle every pronoun. Draw a line from the pronoun to its antecedent. If the pronoun does not agree with its antecedent, fix it according to the examples above.

Writing Workshop

Student Model: Chris Kleinhen
Palos Verdes, CA

Baseball, a Sport I Love

I remember the day my dad placed a glove in one of my hands and a bat in the other and told me the combination was an eight-letter word called baseball. Ever since then, most of my memories have been related to the sport. When I was eleven, I played in a game I'll remember forever.

We were facing the West Torrance Bull Dogs. We had a great team that year. Our pitcher, Frank (The Smasher) was tough to hit. The nicknames of other players—"Hot Glove," "Fireball," and "Maguire, Jr."—were earned with outstanding play during the season. We had a team of stars. The only one who had not earned a "star" nickname was Matt.

Nine starters took the field at five o'clock on a warm afternoon. The small crowd of parents and friends made enough noise for a major-league game. For most of the game, the two teams were evenly matched. Then, in the last inning, Pat "The Runstopper" at third base was injured as one of the Bull Dogs accidentally rammed his ankle while sliding into third base. We had two choices: forfeit the game or play Matt.

"You can do it, Matt!" the coach said as he sent Matt out to take Pat's place on third base.

"All right, Matt!" we encouraged from our places in the field as he trotted out nervously.

The score was tied with two outs. Unfortunately, the next ball took a sharp bounce toward third—and toward Matt. Matt ran forward and made an awkward catch, followed by an even more awkward lob toward first. Amazingly it made it there in time!

As we jogged back in, the players called out, "Way to go, Matt!" "You came through in the clutch!"

That's when I realized the truth of something the coach is always telling us. When you play as a team, everyone is a star. And that's exactly what I told Matt, whose new nickname is "Clutch."

Chris uses a consistent first-person point of view, referring to himself with the first-person pronouns *I*, *my*, and *me*.

Chris begins a clear sequence of events from his life by identifying when the action of the narrative begins.

Precise details about the warmth and the noise help bring the scene to life.

The injury increases the suspense in the conflict between the two teams.

Dialogue helps readers feel as if they are witnessing this important conversation.

Here, Chris reveals how his personal experience has helped him look at his favorite sport in a new way.

Editing and Proofreading

Check your essay for errors in grammar, spelling, or mechanics.

Focus on Punctuating Dialogue: If you include conversations in your writing, follow the proper formatting rules.

- Enclose all direct quotations with quotation marks. *"You were right," I said to my grandfather.*
- Place a comma after the words that introduce the speaker. *Grandpa replied, "Well, you learned a lesson today."*
- Use commas and quotation marks before and after any interrupting words. *"Next time," I said, "I guess I'll listen."*

Publishing and Presenting

Consider one of the following ways to share your writing:
Present an autobiographical storytelling or a speech. Use your autobiographical narrative as the basis for a narrative presentation.
Make a comic strip. Create a comic strip based on your narrative. Exaggerate actions or expressions, and use speech bubbles to show what people say. Post your comic strip in the classroom.

Reflecting on Your Writing

Writer's Journal Jot down your thoughts on writing an autobiographical essay. Begin by answering these questions:
- How useful were the prewriting strategies you used?
- Did you have new insights about your experience?

> *Prentice Hall Writing and Grammar Connection: Chapter 4*

Rubric for Self-Assessment

To assess your own autobiographical essay, use the following rubric:

Criteria	Rating Scale not very ————— very				
Focus: How consistently is the first-person point of view used?	1	2	3	4	5
Organization: How well is the sequence of events organized?	1	2	3	4	5
Support/Elaboration: How well are memories and feelings used for support?	1	2	3	4	5
Style: How well are characters revealed through dialogue?	1	2	3	4	5
Conventions: How correct is your grammar, especially your use of pronouns and antecedents?	1	2	3	4	5

Effective Listening and Note Taking

For situations when understanding and remembering are crucial, it is useful to learn effective listening and note-taking skills.

Listening Carefully

Select a purpose for listening. Choosing a purpose for listening helps you focus your attention on what is most important. When you have chosen a purpose, determine how to further focus your listening.

Listen to how something is said. Speakers often give you hints that can help you identify their perspective. Listen for these clues:

- changes in tone of voice that indicate mood or emotion
- emphasis on words or phrases
- repetition of key points

Eliminate barriers to listening. Try to avoid distractions when listening. Sit close to the speaker and try to stay focused on what he or she is saying—not the other things that are going on in the room.

Listen critically. Especially when you are listening to media messages or points of view, ask yourself questions as you listen.

- What are the speaker's influences or leanings?
- Does the speaker offer enough facts to support the main point?
- Do I agree with the speaker's message and ideas?

Taking Notes

Taking notes is a further step—beyond listening actively—that will help you remember what a speaker says.

Write main points and details. Do not write every word a speaker says. Instead, try to capture the speaker's main points and a few supporting details. To save time, rephrase the speaker's words using minimal punctuation, partial phrases, and abbreviations. Later, review your notes to be sure you understand them.

Record your Questions. Write down your questions and reactions. These notes will help you think critically about what you hear.

Activity **Listen and Take Notes** With other students, watch and take notes on two television interviews. Compare your notes with others to determine how they differ in organization, emphasis, and note-taking style.

Why We Can't Wait

Martin Luther King, Jr.
Signet, 2000

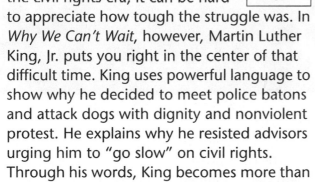

Autobiography Decades after the civil rights era, it can be hard to appreciate how tough the struggle was. In *Why We Can't Wait*, however, Martin Luther King, Jr. puts you right in the center of that difficult time. King uses powerful language to show why he decided to meet police batons and attack dogs with dignity and nonviolent protest. He explains why he resisted advisors urging him to "go slow" on civil rights. Through his words, King becomes more than just a historical figure. He becomes a leader of power and inspiration for our own times.

Rules of the Road

Joan Bauer
Puffin, 2000

Novel A hilarious coming-of-age story that follows the adventures of a teenager as she spends a summer driving the aging matriarch of a shoe company around the country.

Woodsong

Gary Paulsen
Puffin, 1991

Nonfiction Adventure readers will enjoy this nonfiction book that conveys the excitement of the Iditarod, the Alaskan dog-sledding race. Paulsen describes how and why he left his work as a trapper to work with a team of racing dogs. He also gives readers a sense of the power of living alone surrounded by the wintry beauty of nature at its most fierce.

The Adventures of Huckleberry Finn: An Adapted Classic

Mark Twain
Random House, 1999

Novel Huck is living with the Widow Douglas when his own Pap kidnaps him, hoping to get Huck's money. The novel tells of Huck's escape from Pap, and his adventures on the Mississippi River with Jim, a runaway slave.

These titles are available in the Penguin/Prentice Hall Literature Library.
Consult your teacher before choosing one.

Think About It In the 1920s, the screech owl was one of the most common birds in New York City's Central Park. Over the years, the startling decline of the screech owl population sparked an effort to reintroduce them into Central Park. E. J. McAdams, head of the New York City Audubon Society, discusses this important project.

from WILDERNESS on 68th Street E. J. McAdams

During the month we released 16 more owls, and only one did not make it through the first week. It was an auspicious start, but reality (or "the joys of research" as Bill[1] likes to call it) soon set in. The owls proved to be pretty wily birds, and within weeks ten of them had chomped through their backpacks or wiggled free. A couple more of the transmitters immediately conked out. My elation quickly turned to anxiety. Would any of the owls make it? How would we know if they had? I had to remind myself that we still were tracking four owls successfully.

Now, tracking is not as easy as it sounds. Sure, the antenna points in the direction of the signal and leads the researcher right there. But actually finding the owl, even when the tracker knows it's in one of the three trees before him, is difficult. The owls blend in perfectly with their surroundings, sit perfectly still, and fly silently thanks to the muffled edges of their wings. There were many nights we were sure we had found an owl only to walk right past it without noticing.

The screech owl clan seems to have no regard for the technological advancements of the city—except the ones that enhance its ability to hunt. One night, we watched an owl perch on the outer edge of a great old oak surveying the field for rodents. When an ambulance came blazing around the bend, sirens blaring, the owl did not turn from its work—even when washed in alternating red and white halogen beams. A couple of minutes later, a carriage horse neighed. Reeling around, the owl zeroed in on that intruder, sussed him out, and again turned its attention to the rustling in the bushes. The animal's total dismissal of

---

1. **Bill Giuliano** wildlife ecologist who participated in the screech owl reintroduction.

machines is as impressive as it is threatening; cars are still the biggest killers of screech owls.

Lampposts are a different story. In the warmer months the owls hide in the shadowy branches of trees, swooping down to harvest fat moths lured to the bright white bulbs. Come winter the screech owl again utilizes the light to its hunting advantage. Owls are legendary for their hearing. Their asymmetrical ears create an almost three-dimensional aural "picture." But we often forget that owls also have good sight. In fact, the screech owl has the most perceptive eyes of all owls. Proportionately, its eyes are the largest of any land animal; with the same proportions we'd have eyes the size of grapefruits. In turn, screech owls use street lamps to better locate rodents. The last thing these rodents see is a growing, descending shadow.

Those shadows have appeared above hapless prey all over the city. We assumed the owls would stick to the forested areas of the park, but some ventured onto city streets and to adjacent parks. One day we tracked a female to a construction site on 108th and Madison, and that East Harlem owl continues to roost there. Another owl was found hunting in front of a brownstone on 68th Street between Central Park West and Columbus. It shuffled back and forth across a windowsill, following a mouse crisscrossing the front garden and—when it had an opportunity—shot down and caught the mouse. The gathering crowd of passers-by cheered. Here was an opportunity to teach a small group of people about the importance of biodiversity in their city, without the need of text and pictures. The owls constantly created these opportunities.

More to Explore
A screech owl's wing structure allows it to fly, almost silently, while hunting prey. Screech owls are nocturnal, hunting only at night. They get their name from their call—a loud eerie screech.

Readings in Science
Talk About It

Use these questions to guide a discussion of the excerpt.

1. (a) What kinds of problems do the researchers face while tracking the owls? (b) Why does the writer still feel the tracking is successful?

2. In a group, talk about your responses to the following question.

   What can be done to prevent further decline of wildlife populations?

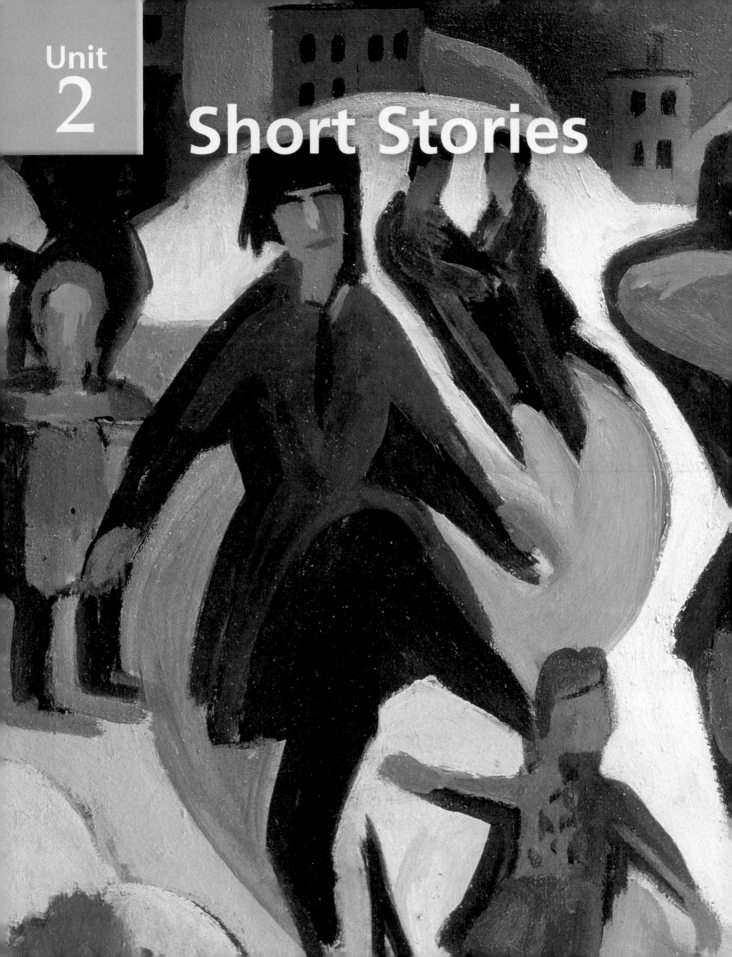

Short Stories

Unit 2 Overview

Introduction
Exploring Short Stories

Part 1: Compare and Contrast

Part 2: Make Inferences

Introduction:
Short Stories

Judith Ortiz Cofer
Talks About the Form

Judith
Ortiz Cofer

How is a short story like a joke? That question itself sounds like the beginning of a joke, part of the setup that leads to a funny punch line.

Jokes and Short Stories

Getting the Elephant onto the Motorcycle Believe it or not, jokes and stories have several important things in common. To tell a joke well, you have to provide a good setup and be able to deliver the punch line at precisely the right moment.

How do you know when an elephant is riding on the back of your motorcycle?

(Pause while smiles begin to appear on faces in anticipation of a good laugh.)

When you hear his ears flopping in the wind.

As a short-story writer, you have to get the elephant to climb on the back of your motorcycle and stay there until you are ready to deliver the punch line. The setup of a story, like that of a joke, requires suspension of disbelief from your reader, a willingness to go along with the situation, no matter how strange or absurd, because it is interesting (and the reader wants to know how it ends).

For a story, the "punch line" can be what is called an **epiphany,** a sudden discovery experienced by a character and by the reader, too. Like the punch line of a joke, this discovery can be funny, but it does not have to be. (Another contrast between stories and jokes is that story setups tend to be less like formulas than the setups for jokes.)

▲ Judith Ortiz Cofer has written poems, essays, novels, short stories, and "creative nonfiction" that combines fact and fiction.

▼ **Critical Viewing** What is "strange" or "absurd" about the situation in this illustration? **[Analyze]**

Short Stories and Jokes: *A-ha!* and *Ha-ha!*

In her essay "Mom's On the Roof," short-story writer Antonya Nelson talks about how recognizable characters are at the heart of good stories and jokes. She also points out that writers give their stories the shape of a joke because they want readers to experience an *A-ha*! moment, an insight into a "universal truth."

As you will see, I decided to construct my story "An Hour With Abuelo" in the form of a joke. I wanted the reader to suspect from the beginning that there would be a surprise in store.

So, the next time you're at a party and start to say, "Did you ever hear the one about the elephant . . .," remember that you're doing what short-story writers do. *Ha-ha!* and *A-ha!* are not far apart.

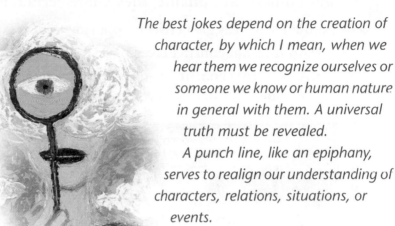

The best jokes depend on the creation of character, by which I mean, when we hear them we recognize ourselves or someone we know or human nature in general with them. A universal truth must be revealed.

A punch line, like an epiphany, serves to realign our understanding of characters, relations, situations, or events.

from "Mom's On the Roof "
— Antonya Nelson

More About the Author

Judith Ortiz **Cofer** (b. 1952)

Judith Ortiz Cofer, who now lives in Georgia, spent her early years shuttling between Puerto Rico, where she was born, and Paterson, New Jersey. She says that her passion for storytelling began with the *cuentos* (kwen´ tōs), or tales, that were told in her grandmother's house in Puerto Rico. Her bicultural heritage is evident in her work. In "An Hour With Abuelo," for example, she writes in English but includes Spanish words.

Fast Facts

▶ Ortiz Cofer says that she learned early on that the women in her family "were passing on power from one generation to another through fables and stories."

▶ In graduate school, Ortiz Cofer scribbled poems and story ideas on index cards she was using for research.

Learning About Short Stories

Elements of Short Stories

Adventure tales, mysteries, science fiction, and animal fables are just a few of the varied types of short stories. Although all short stories are unique, they share certain elements.

Conflict is a struggle between opposing forces.

- An **internal conflict** takes place in the mind of a character.
- An **external conflict** is one in which a character struggles with an outside force or another person.

Plot is the sequence of events in a short story. It is usually divided into five parts:

- **Exposition** introduces the **setting**—the time and place of the story, the characters, and the basic situation.
- **Rising action** introduces the **conflict**, or problem.
- **Climax** is the turning point of a story.
- **Falling action** is the part of the story when the conflict lessens.
- **Resolution** is a story's conclusion.

A **subplot** is a secondary story line that adds depth to the main plot.

Setting is the time and place of the action in a story. Sometimes the setting is only a backdrop for the action. Other times, the setting can be the force that the characters struggle against, the source of a story's conflict. It also can create a **mood** or emotional atmosphere.

Characters are the people or animals that take part in the action.

- **Character traits** are the qualities, attitudes, and values that a character possesses—such as dependability or intelligence.
- **Character's motives** are reasons for a character's actions. This motivation may come from internal causes like loneliness or jealousy, or from external causes like danger or poverty.

Theme is the central message expressed in a story. It may be directly stated or implied.

- A **stated theme** is expressed directly by the author.
- An **implied theme** is suggested, or stated indirectly through what happens to the characters.
- A **universal theme,** or a recurring theme, is a message about life that is expressed regularly in many different cultures and time periods.

Literary Devices

Literary devices are tools that writers use to enhance their writing.

Point of view is the perspective from which a story is told.

- **First-person point of view** presents the story from the perspective of a character in the story.
- **Third-person point of view** tells the story from the perspective of a narrator outside the story. A third-person narrator might be **omniscient**—a narrator who knows everything that happens, and reveals what each character thinks and feels. A third-person narrator also might be **limited,** and only reveal the thoughts and feelings of a single character.

Foreshadowing is the use of clues in a story to hint at events to come.

Flashback is the use of scenes within a story that interrupt the sequence of events to reveal past occurrences.

Irony is the contrast between an actual outcome and what the reader or the characters expect.

▼ **Critical Viewing**
How would you describe the setting in this photograph? **[Analyze]**

Check Your Understanding

Choose the letter of the short-story element that best matches each item.

1. a hiker learns the power of nature   **a.** theme   **b.** character

2. a ship in a hurricane   **a.** character   **b.** setting

3. hard work is its own reward   **a.** setting   **b.** theme

In my childhood, during my father's long tours of duty with the U.S. Navy, my mother would take my brother and me back to her parents' home in Puerto Rico. I loved my grandparents' house crowded with aunts, uncles, and cousins; it was like an ant colony in constant motion. While my grandmother, whom everyone called Mamá, conducted traffic, my grandfather, Papá, a house builder and painter by trade, would sneak off to his shed to read and write poems.

Papá: An Inspiration for a Character in the Story

All of us wanted to get inside the little house Papá had built to store his tools and his paints in the backyard. We wanted to be allowed to mix colors and to get scraps of wood for our own projects. I was persistent about it, hanging outside the door until he let me in. Eventually, I would get my treasures, but Papá always made us pay a small price for our interruptions. We had to sit quietly while he read us poems. I sometimes resented the ten or fifteen minutes I had to give Papá and I thought his poems were a little silly.

Later I wrote a poem called "Housepainter" about Papá and the poetry lessons in his work shed. The **universal theme** of the older person, the mentor, teaching a young person an important lesson about life, is one that appears often in my work.

Irony: Difference Between Reality and Appearance

As I grew older I realized that the **irony** of this situation was that I thought *I* was the one giving the old man something valuable, *my* precious time! That real-life irony helped inspire the **situational irony** of "An Hour With Abuelo," in which the opposite of what a character expects happens. It involves a reversal.

And so I used some of the ironies of my life, my memories of Papá's stories and poems, scenes of my childhood in New Jersey and my family's visits to Puerto Rico. I told myself and others a few elephant jokes, and then I sat down to write my short story "An Hour With Abuelo."

An Hour With *Abuelo*

JUDITH ORTIZ COFER

"Just one hour, una hora, is all I'm asking of you, son." My grandfather is in a nursing home in Brooklyn, and my mother wants me to spend some time with him, since the doctors say that he doesn't have too long to go now. I don't have much time left of my summer vacation, and there's a stack of books next to my bed I've got to read if I'm going to get into the AP English class I want. I'm going stupid in some of my classes, and Mr. Williams, the principal at Central, said that if I passed some reading tests, he'd let me move up.

Besides, I hate the place, the old people's home, especially the way it smells like industrial-strength ammonia and other stuff I won't mention, since it turns my stomach. And really the abuelo always has a lot of relatives visiting him, so I've gotten out of going out there except at Christmas, when a whole van-load of grandchildren are herded over there to give him gifts and a hug. We all make it quick and spend the rest of the time in the recreation area, where they play checkers and stuff with some of the old people's games, and I catch up on back issues of *Modern Maturity*. I'm not picky, I'll read almost anything.

Anyway, after my mother nags me for about a week, I let her drive me to Golden Years. She drops me off in front. She wants me to go in alone and have a "good time" talking to Abuelo. I tell her to be back in one hour or I'll take the bus back to

▲ Critical Viewing
How does this image of an elderly man conflict with the narrator's attitude? **[Contrast]**

Judith Ortiz Cofer
Author's Insight
Arturo's attitude is one of superiority to the adults in his family. He is determined not to let anyone waste his time.

✓ Reading Check

What information shows that Arturo is a serious student?

Paterson. She squeezes my hand and says, "Gracias, hijo,"[1] in a choked-up voice like I'm doing her a big favor.

I get depressed the minute I walk into the place. They line up the old people in wheelchairs in the hallway as if they were about to be raced to the finish line by orderlies who don't even look at them when they push them here and there. I walk fast to room 10, Abuelo's "suite." He is sitting up in his bed writing with a pencil in one of those old-fashioned black hardback notebooks. It has the outline of the island of Puerto Rico on it. I slide into the hard vinyl chair by his bed. He sort of smiles and the lines on his face get deeper, but he doesn't say anything. Since I'm supposed to talk to him, I say, "What are you doing, Abuelo, writing the story of your life?"

It's supposed to be a joke, but he answers, "Sí, how did you know, Arturo?"

His name is Arturo too. I was named after him. I don't really know my grandfather. His children, including my mother, came to New York and New Jersey (where I was born) and he stayed on the Island until my grandmother died. Then he got sick, and since nobody could leave their jobs to go take care of him, they brought him to this nursing home in Brooklyn. I see him a couple of times a year, but he's always surrounded by his sons and daughters. My mother tells me that Don Arturo had once been a teacher back in Puerto Rico, but had lost his job after the war. Then he became a farmer. She's always saying in a sad voice, "Ay, bendito![2] What a waste of a fine mind." Then she usually shrugs her shoulders and says, "Así es la vida." That's the way life is. It sometimes makes me mad that the adults I know just accept whatever is thrown at them because "that's the way things are." Not for me. I go after what I want.

---

1. **"Gracias** (grä′ sē äs)**, hijo** (ē′ hō)**"** Spanish for "Thank you, son." *Hijo* also means "child."
2. **bendito** (ven dē′ tō) Spanish for "blessed."

Judith Ortiz Cofer
Author's Insight
This is one of many references to time. Each character has a different idea about the value of time.

Short Story
Exposition This paragraph introduces the narrator's grandfather.

Judith Ortiz Cofer
Author's Insight
By giving both characters the same name, I establish their unique relationship. The younger Arturo is at first determined to see himself as completely different from the old man.

Anyway, Abuelo is looking at me like he was trying to see into my head, but he doesn't say anything. Since I like stories, I decide I may as well ask him if he'll read me what he wrote.

I look at my watch: I've already used up twenty minutes of the hour I promised my mother.

Abuelo starts talking in his slow way. He speaks what my mother calls book English. He taught himself from a dictionary, and his words sound stiff, like he's sounding them out in his head before he says them. With his children he speaks Spanish, and that funny book English with us grandchildren. I'm surprised that he's still so sharp, because his body is shrinking like a crumpled-up brown paper sack with some bones in it. But I can see from looking into his eyes that the light is still on in there.

"It is a short story, Arturo. The story of my life. It will not take very much time to read it."

"I have time, Abuelo." I'm a little embarrassed that he saw me looking at my watch.

"Yes, *hijo*. You have spoken the truth. *La verdad*. You have much time."

Abuelo reads: "'I loved words from the beginning of my life. In the campo[3] where I was born one of seven sons, there were few books. My mother read them to us over and over: the Bible, the stories of Spanish conquistadors and of pirates that she had read as a child and brought with her from the city of Mayaguez; that was before she married my father, a coffee bean farmer; and she taught us words from the newspaper that a

---

3. campo (käm´ pō) Spanish for "open country."

MODEL SELECTION

Judith Ortiz Cofer
Author's Insight
Arturo's mother mixes Spanish and English when speaking to her son. The grandfather speaks book English. These are choices Arturo has rejected.

Reading Check

What surprises Arturo about the way his grandfather spends his time?

boy on a horse brought every week to her. She taught each of us how to write on a slate with chalks that she ordered by mail every year. We used those chalks until they were so small that you lost them between your fingers.

"'I always wanted to be a writer and a teacher. With my heart and my soul I knew that I wanted to be around books all of my life. And so against the wishes of my father, who wanted all his sons to help him on the land, she sent me to high school in Mayaguez. For four years I boarded with a couple she knew. I paid my rent in labor, and I ate vegetables I grew myself. I wore my clothes until they were thin as parchment. But I graduated at the top of my class! My whole family came to see me that day. My mother brought me a beautiful guayabera, a white shirt made of the finest cotton and embroidered by her own hands. I was a happy young man.

"'In those days you could teach in a country school with a high school diploma. So I went back to my mountain village and got a job teaching all grades in a little classroom built by the parents of my students.

Short Story
Point of View
Though he is not the narrator, the grandfather reveals his perspective when he tells his life story.

▼ **Critical Viewing**
What does this picture reveal about the kind of school where Abuelo taught? **[Generalize]**

"'I had books sent to me by the government. I felt like a rich man although the pay was very small. I had books. All the books I wanted! I taught my students how to read poetry and plays, and how to write them. We made up songs and put on shows for the parents. It was a beautiful time for me.

"'Then the war came,[4] and the American President said that all Puerto Rican men would be drafted. I wrote to our governor and explained that I was the only teacher in the mountain village. I told him that the children would go back to the fields and grow up ignorant if I could not teach them their letters. I said that I thought I was a better teacher than a soldier. The governor did not answer my letter. I went into the U.S. Army.

"'I told my sergeant that I could be a teacher in the army. I could teach all the farm boys their letters so that they could read the instructions on the ammunition boxes and not blow themselves up. The sergeant said I was too smart for my own good, and gave me a job cleaning latrines. He said to me there is reading material for you there, scholar. Read the writing on the walls. I spent the war mopping floors and cleaning toilets.

"'When I came back to the Island, things had changed. You had to have a college degree to teach school, even the lower grades. My parents were sick, two of my brothers had been killed in the war, the others had stayed in Nueva York. I was the only one left to help the old people. I became a farmer. I married a good woman who gave me many good children. I taught them all how to read and write before they started school.'"

Abuelo then puts the notebook down on his lap and closes his eyes.

"Así es la vida is the title of my book," he says in a whisper, almost to himself. Maybe he's forgotten that I'm there.

For a long time he doesn't say anything else. I think that he's sleeping, but then I see that he's watching me through half-closed lids, maybe waiting for my opinion of his writing. I'm trying to think of something nice to say. I liked it and all, but not the title. And I think that he could've been a teacher if he had wanted to bad enough. Nobody is going to stop me from doing what I want with my life. I'm not going to let la vida

---

4. **"Then the war came, . . ."** The United States entered World War II in 1941, after the bombing of Pearl Harbor.

Short Story
External Conflict
Here, Abuelo describes the problem he faced during the war.

Short Story
Characterization
Readers learn about Abuelo through what he says and writes.

Reading Check

What does Abuelo do during the war?

get in my way. I want to discuss this with him, but the words are not coming into my head in Spanish just yet. I'm about to ask him why he didn't keep fighting to make his dream come true, when an old lady in hot-pink running shoes sort of appears at the door.

She is wearing a pink jogging outfit too. The world's oldest marathoner, I say to myself. She calls out to my grandfather in a flirty voice, "Yoo-hoo, Arturo, remember what day this is? It's poetry-reading day in the rec room! You promised us you'd read your new one today."

I see my abuelo perking up almost immediately. He points to his wheelchair, which is hanging like a huge metal bat in the open closet. He makes it obvious that he wants me to get it. I put it together, and with Mrs. Pink Running Shoes's help, we get him in it. Then he says in a strong deep voice I hardly recognize, "Arturo, get that notebook from the table, please."

I hand him another map-of-the-Island notebook—this one is red. On it in big letters it says, POEMAS DE ARTURO.

I start to push him toward the rec room, but he shakes his finger at me.

"Arturo, look at your watch now. I believe your time is over." He gives me a wicked smile.

Then with her pushing the wheelchair—maybe a little too fast—they roll down the hall. He is already reading from his notebook, and she's making bird noises. I look at my watch and the hour is up, to the minute. I can't help but think that my abuelo has been timing me. It cracks me up. I walk slowly down the hall toward the exit sign. I want my mother to have to wait a little. I don't want her to think that I'm in a hurry or anything.

Short Story
Internal Conflict
Arturo describes a struggle in his own mind.

▼ **Critical Viewing**
What does this picture suggest about Arturo's mood? **[Explain]**

Judith Ortiz Cofer
Author's Insight
The story's structure resembles that of a joke. Everything that happens leads to a revelation based on a reversal: Things are not what they seem.

From the Author's Desk
Judith Ortiz Cofer's Insights Into "An Hour With Abuelo"

Q. In what ways is this story like a joke?

A. The story is like a joke in that it involves a *reversal,* that is, a surprising turn of events. The two Arturos in my story are characters that on the surface appear to be complete opposites, in age, culture, and attitudes. One of them, young Arturo, thinks he is superior to the other (as in the joke where the city slicker tries to fool the country bumpkin, who turns out to be smarter); however, the joke is on the boy. I focused on showing both the differences and similarities between the boy and the old man through what they say and do, so that the reader would not find it easy to take sides and would want to read on for the surprise at the end. Like a joke, the story is very short and everything that happens leads to a revelation, or what in a joke is called the "punch line."

Q. What are the characters' different ideas about time?

A. Arturo's mother thinks of an hour as *solo una hora,* just one hour—not much time. Arturo feels that he is wasting his valuable time. When Abuelo tells Arturo his story, it is an example of how time can pass quickly when you are involved in doing something interesting and important.

Student Corner

Q. Why does the story seem not completely finished at the end?
  —Marie Petersen, St. Paul, Minnesota

A. I believe that a story has been completely told when an experience or a discovery has been shared between writer and reader. Arturo's realization that his grandfather is a real person who has lived an interesting life and is worth knowing *is* the conclusion of this story.

 Writing Workshop: *Work in Progress*

Critical Review

For a critical review that you may write, jot down the titles of two of your favorite literary works. Use each title as the center of a web. In the outer circles, note topics and themes that are contained in the literary work. Put the two Literary Work Webs in your writing portfolio.

Short Stories

Thinking About the Selection

1. **Respond:** Based on the story, would you enjoy visiting Arturo's grandfather? Why or why not?
2. **(a) Recall:** What was Abuelo's dream?
   (b) Summarize: What caused him to give up his dream?
   (c) Interpret: Do you think Abuelo has found a new purpose in life? Why or why not?

Short Story Review

3. **(a)** What is the **conflict** in this story? **(b)** How is it resolved?
   (c) How is the narrator changed by the events of the story?
4. **(a)** Complete a diagram like the one shown by comparing and contrasting the **characters**. **(b)** Share your diagram with a partner. How has your understanding of the two characters grown or changed as a result?

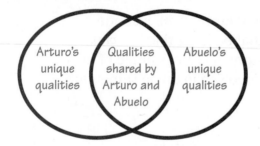

5. **(a)** How would you describe Arturo's opinion of his grandfather at the beginning of the story? **(b)** After hearing more about Abuelo's life, do you agree that Cofer is using **irony** to make a point? Why or why not? **(c)** How have Arturo's opinions and behavior changed by the end of the story?

Research the Author

Prepare an **audiocassette** for your class library that reports on Judith Ortiz Cofer while making use of a variety of sources. Follow these steps:

- Using the Internet and print sources, gather two kinds of information. First, find out about Judith Ortiz Cofer's background and publications. Next, find samples of her work.
- Include excerpts or passages from the author's works.
- Write a script that tells the author's story and record it.

QuickReview

Story at a Glance
After reluctantly visiting his grandfather, a boy realizes he has misjudged him.

For: Self-test
Visit: www.PHSchool.com
Web Code: ena-6201

Short Story: a brief work of fiction with characters, setting, and plot

Conflict: a problem or struggle between opposing forces

Characters: the people, animals, or other beings in a literary work

Irony: the contrast between an actual outcome and an expected one

Compare and Contrast

Skills You Will Learn

Reading Skill: *Ask Questions to Compare and Contrast*
Literary Analysis: *Setting*

Reading Skill: *Compare and Contrast Perspectives*
Literary Analysis: *Character Traits*

Reading Skill: *Compare an Original With Its Summary*

Literary Analysis: *Comparing Characters of Different Historical Eras*

Literature You Will Read

Reading and Vocabulary
Skills Preview

Reading: Comparison and Contrast

▶ When you **compare** things, you explain how they are alike. When you **contrast** things, you explain how they are different.

Skills and Strategies You Will Learn in Part 1

In Part 1, you will learn

- to **ask questions** to **compare and contrast** (p. 220)
- to **compare and contrast characters** (p. 250)
- to **compare and contrast a summary to the original document** (p. 276)

Using the Skills and Strategies in Part 1

In Part 1, you will learn to ask questions to compare and contrast characters and texts. Asking questions about the similarities and differences between two things will help you better understand the qualities of each item. You will also compare original texts to summaries to understand the advantages and limitations of summaries.

The model shows how a Venn diagram is used to record similarities and differences.

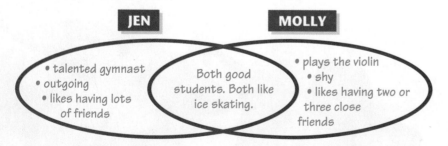

JEN

MOLLY

- talented gymnast
- outgoing
- likes having lots of friends

Both good students. Both like ice skating.

- plays the violin
- shy
- likes having two or three close friends

Academic Vocabulary: Words for Comparing and Contrasting Literature

The following words will help you talk and write about comparisons and contrasts in literature.

Word	Definition	Example Sentence
similar *adj.*	alike	Dee and Cary have *similar* traits.
aspect *n.*	the specific part that you are observing or studying	Courage is the *aspect* of the character that I admire most.
unique *adj.*	the characteristics that make one thing different from others	Although the stories have similar plots, they have *unique* themes.
examine *v.*	study carefully	*Examine* what characters do.
differentiate *v.*	show how things are different	*Differentiate* between them.

Vocabulary Skill: Word Origins

▶ The origin of a word is its history, and its first meaning.

In Part 1, you will learn:

- the origin of *similar* and related forms (p. 248)
- the origin of *aspect* and related forms (p. 274)
- the origin of *differentiate* and related forms (p. 248)

The origins of many English words come from the Latin and Greek languages. Knowing the origin of different words can help you understand the meanings of the various forms the word can take.

Origin	Meaning	Example Word
similis (L)	same	similar
differre (L)	carry apart	differentiate
–spec– or –spect– (L)	see	aspect

Activity Copy the chart. Add two more example words for each origin.

These skills will help you become a better reader. Practice them with either "Who Can Replace a Man?" (p. 222) or "Tears of Autumn" (p. 237).

Reading Skill

A **comparison** tells how two or more things are alike. A **contrast** tells how two or more things are different. **Asking questions to compare and contrast** helps you to notice similarities and differences in characters, settings, moods, and ideas, and enriches your understanding of a work. As you read, ask questions like the ones shown in the chart.

Literary Analysis

The **setting** is the time and place of a story's action. A setting can create an emotional atmosphere, or *mood*. It can also give the reader the sensation of living in a different place and time. As you read, notice details like the following that make up the setting:

- the customs and beliefs of the characters
- the physical features of the land
- the weather or season of the year
- the historical era in which the action takes place

> How is one character different from another?
>
> **?**
>
> How is this story similar to another that I have read?
>
> **?**
>
> How is this character's experience different from my own experience?

Vocabulary Builder

Who Can Replace a Man?

- **consequently** (kän′ si kwent′ lē) *adv.* as a result (p. 224) *It rained; consequently, we got wet.*

- **respectively** (ri spek′ tiv lē) *adv.* in the order previously named (p. 224) *Tom and Ben are two and four, respectively.*

- **evidently** (ev′ ə dent′ lē) *adv.* obviously; clearly (p. 226) *You evidently studied hard to ace that test.*

- **dexterity** (deks ter′ ə tē) *n.* skill using the hands or body (p. 227) *The girl dribbled the basketball with great dexterity.*

Tears of Autumn

- **affluence** (af′ lōō əns) *n.* wealth; abundance (p. 239) *The mansions reflected the affluence of the neighborhood.*

- **radical** (rad′ i kəl) *adj.* favoring change in the social structure (p. 240) *The candidate's radical views on taxes are hotly debated.*

- **degrading** (dē grād′ iŋ) *adj.* insulting; dishonorable (p. 244) *Brandon felt mopping floors was a degrading job.*

Background

Science Fiction "Who Can Replace a Man?" is a science-fiction story about a world in which machines have replaced people. In science fiction, realistic elements of science and technology are combined with fictional events, characters, and settings. Many science-fiction writers imagine a grim future in which technology has unforeseen—and often devastating—consequences.

Connecting to the Literature

Reading/Writing Connection Think of a science-fiction story or movie you have seen that featured robots and machines as prominent characters. Write five sentences to describe their behavior toward each other or toward humans. Use at least three of the following words: *analyze, rely, dominate, respond, minimize.*

Meet the Author

Brian Wilson **Aldiss** (b. 1925)

In 1955, Brian Aldiss entered a contest sponsored by a newspaper in Oxford, England, calling for a story set in the year 2500. Aldiss won first prize. Within three years, he was voted "Most Promising New Author" at the World Science Fiction Convention. Inspired, he quit his job at a bookstore and became a full-time writer.

Productive Writer Aldiss has written more than 20 novels and 320 short stories, all works of science fiction. He has also published general fiction, humor, poetry, and an autobiography.

Fast Facts

▶ Steven Spielberg's movie *A.I.* is based on one of Aldiss's short stories, "Supertoys Last All Summer Long." In the movie's overpopulated world, couples adopt android children that long to be real.

▶ Aldiss says the purpose of science fiction is "using the future to hold a mirror up to the present."

Go **Online**
Author Link

For: More about the author
Visit: www.PHSchool.com
Web Code: ene-9202

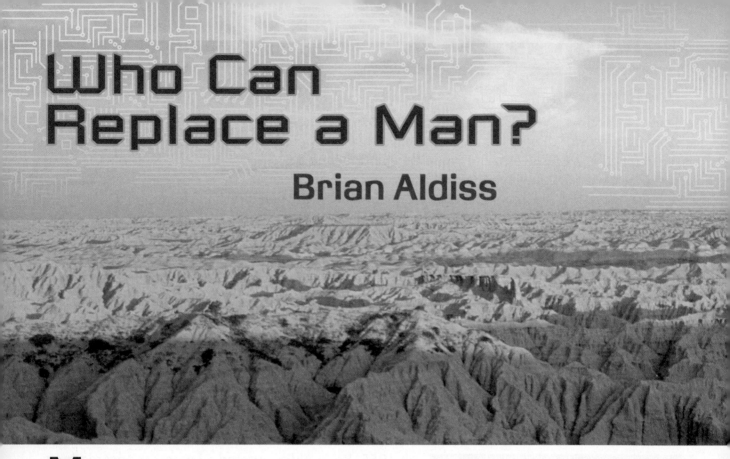

Who Can Replace a Man?

Brian Aldiss

Morning filtered into the sky, lending it the gray tone of the ground below.

The field-minder finished turning the topsoil of a three-thousand-acre field. When it had turned the last furrow it climbed onto the highway and looked back at its work. The work was good. Only the land was bad. Like the ground all over Earth, it was vitiated by over-cropping. By rights, it ought now to lie fallow[1] for a while, but the field-minder had other orders.

It went slowly down the road, taking its time. It was intelligent enough to appreciate the neatness all about it. Nothing worried it, beyond a loose inspection plate above its nuclear pile which ought to be attended to. Thirty feet tall, it yielded no highlights to the dull air.

No other machines passed on its way back to the Agricultural Station. The field-minder noted the fact without comment. In the station yard it saw several other machines that it recognized; most of them should have been out about their

Literary Analysis
Setting What details in the first several paragraphs indicate this story is set in the future?

---

1. **vitiated** (vish′ ē āt′ əd) **by over-cropping . . . lie fallow** (fal′ ō) The soil has been spoiled by repeated plantings that have drawn out its nutrients. Letting the field lie fallow by not planting it would help to renourish the soil.

tasks now. Instead, some were inactive and some careered round the yard in a strange fashion, shouting or hooting.

Steering carefully past them, the field-minder moved over to Warehouse Three and spoke to the seed-distributor, which stood idly outside.

"I have a requirement for seed potatoes," it said to the distributor, and with a quick internal motion punched out an order card specifying quantity, field number and several other details. It ejected the card and handed it to the distributor.

The distributor held the card close to its eye and then said, "The requirement is in order, but the store is not yet unlocked. The required seed potatoes are in the store. Therefore I cannot produce the requirement."

Increasingly of late there had been breakdowns in the complex system of machine labor, but this particular hitch had not occurred before. The field-minder thought, then it said, "Why is the store not yet unlocked?"

"Because Supply Operative Type P has not come this morning. Supply Operative Type P is the unlocker."

The field-minder looked squarely at the seed-distributor, whose exterior chutes and scales and grabs were so vastly different from the field-minder's own limbs.

▲ **Critical Viewing**
What would make the land in this picture—like the land in the story—bad for raising crops? **[Connect]**

**Reading Check**

What types of jobs do the machines at the Agricultural Station do?

Who Can Replace a Man? ■ 223

"What class brain do you have, seed-distributor?" it asked.

"I have a Class Five brain."

"I have a Class Three brain. Therefore I am superior to you. Therefore I will go and see why the unlocker has not come this morning."

Leaving the distributor, the field-minder set off across the great yard. More machines were in random motion now; one or two had crashed together and argued about it coldly and logically. Ignoring them, the field-minder pushed through sliding doors into the echoing confines of the station itself.

Most of the machines here were clerical, and <u>consequently</u> small. They stood about in little groups, eyeing each other, not conversing. Among so many non-differentiated types, the unlocker was easy to find. It had fifty arms, most of them with more than one finger, each finger tipped by a key; it looked like a pincushion full of variegated[2] hat pins.

The field-minder approached it.

"I can do no more work until Warehouse Three is unlocked," it told the unlocker. "Your duty is to unlock the warehouse every morning. Why have you not unlocked the warehouse this morning?"

"I had no orders this morning," replied the unlocker. "I have to have orders every morning. When I have orders I unlock the warehouse."

"None of us have had any orders this morning," a pen-propeller said, sliding towards them.

"Why have you had no orders this morning?" asked the field-minder.

"Because the radio issued none," said the unlocker, slowly rotating a dozen of its arms.

"Because the radio station in the city was issued with no orders this morning," said the pen-propeller.

And there you had the distinction between a Class Six and a Class Three brain, which was what the unlocker and the pen-propeller possessed <u>respectively</u>. All machine brains worked with nothing but logic, but the lower the class of brain—Class Ten being the lowest—the more literal and less informative the answers to questions tended to be.

"You have a Class Three brain; I have a Class Three brain," the field-minder said to the penner. "We will speak to each

---

2. **variegated** (ver´ ē ə gāt´ id) *adj.* varied in color or form.

▶ Critical Viewing
Do these machines look like they could run themselves? Why or why not? [Speculate]

Vocabulary Builder
consequently (kän´ si kwent´ lē) *adv.* as a result

Reading Skill
Compare and Contrast How are the machines in this story similar to and different from those in your daily life?

Vocabulary Builder
respectively (ri spek´ tiv lē) *adv.* in the order previously named

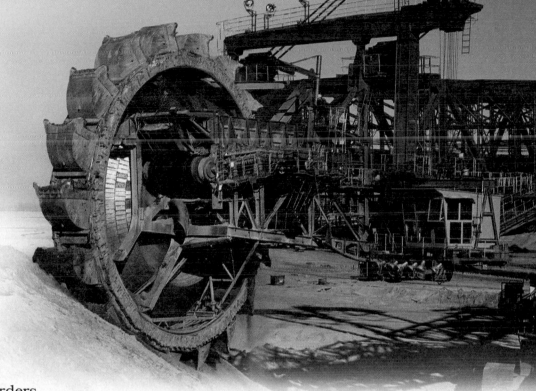

other. This lack of orders is unprecedented.[3] Have you further information on it?"

"Yesterday orders came from the city. Today no orders have come. Yet the radio has not broken down. Therefore *they* have broken down . . ." said the little penner.

"The *men* have broken down?"

"All men have broken down."

"That is a logical deduction," said the field-minder.

"That is the logical deduction," said the penner. "For if a machine had broken down, it would have been quickly replaced. But who can replace a man?"

While they talked, the locker, like a dull man at a bar, stood close to them and was ignored.

"If all men have broken down, then we have replaced man," said the field-minder, and he and the penner eyed one another speculatively. Finally the latter said, "Let us ascend to the top floor to find if the radio operator has fresh news."

"I cannot come because I am too large," said the field-minder. "Therefore you must go alone and return to me. You will tell me if the radio operator has fresh news."

"You must stay here," said the penner. "I will return here." It skittered across to the lift.[4] Although it was no bigger than a

Reading Skill
Compare and Contrast What are the differences in the way the field-minder, penner, and unlocker act and speak?

 **Reading Check**

What do the machines think has happened to the humans?

---

3. **unprecedented** (un pres´ ə den´ tid) *adj.* unheard-of; never done before.
4. **lift** *n.* British term for *elevator.*

toaster, its retractable arms numbered ten and it could read as quickly as any machine on the station.

The field-minder awaited its return patiently, not speaking to the locker, which still stood aimlessly by. Outside, a rotavator hooted furiously. Twenty minutes elapsed before the penner came back, hustling out of the lift.

"I will deliver to you such information as I have outside," it said briskly, and as they swept past the locker and the other machines, it added, "The information is not for lower-class brains."

Outside, wild activity filled the yard. Many machines, their routines disrupted for the first time in years, seemed to have gone berserk. Those most easily disrupted were the ones with lowest brains, which generally belonged to large machines performing simple tasks. The seed-distributor to which the field-minder had recently been talking lay face downwards in the dust, not stirring; it had <u>evidently</u> been knocked down by the rotavator, which now hooted its way wildly across a planted field. Several other machines plowed after it, trying to keep up with it. All were shouting and hooting without restraint.

"It would be safer for me if I climbed onto you, if you will permit it. I am easily overpowered," said the penner. Extending five arms, it hauled itself up the flanks of its new friend, settling on a ledge beside the fuel-intake, twelve feet above ground.

"From here vision is more extensive," it remarked complacently.[5]

"What information did you receive from the radio operator?" asked the field-minder.

"The radio operator has been informed by the operator in the city that all men are dead."

The field-minder was momentarily silent, digesting this.

---

5. complacently (kəm plā´ sənt lē) *adv.* with self-satisfaction.

Literary Analysis
Setting How are the machines ranked in this fictional world?

Vocabulary Builder
evidently (ev´ ə dent´ lē) *adv.* obviously; clearly

▼ **Critical Viewing**
What features of this equipment indicate it is a communication machine like the radio operator? **[Analyze]**

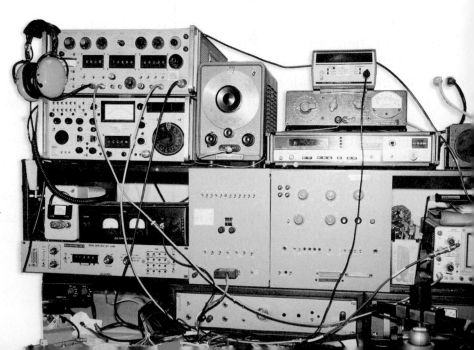

"All men were alive yesterday?" it protested.

"Only some men were alive yesterday. And that was fewer than the day before yesterday. For hundreds of years there have been only a few men, growing fewer."

"We have rarely seen a man in this sector."

"The radio operator says a diet deficiency killed them," said the penner. "He says that the world was once over-populated, and then the soil was exhausted in raising adequate food. This has caused a diet deficiency."

"What is a diet deficiency?" asked the field-minder.

"I do not know. But that is what the radio operator said, and he is a Class Two brain."

They stood there, silent in weak sunshine. The locker had appeared in the porch and was gazing at them yearningly, rotating its collection of keys.

"What is happening in the city now?" asked the field-minder at last.

"Machines are fighting in the city now," said the penner.

"What will happen here now?" asked the field-minder.

"Machines may begin fighting here too. The radio operator wants us to get him out of his room. He has plans to communicate to us."

"How can we get him out of his room? That is impossible."

"To a Class Two brain, little is impossible," said the penner. "Here is what he tells us to do. . . ."

The quarrier raised its scoop above its cab like a great mailed fist, and brought it squarely down against the side of the station. The wall cracked.

"Again!" said the field-minder.

Again the fist swung. Amid a shower of dust, the wall collapsed. The quarrier backed hurriedly out of the way until the debris stopped falling. This big twelve-wheeler was not a resident of the Agricultural Station, as were most of the other machines. It had a week's heavy work to do here before passing on to its next job, but now, with its Class Five brain, it was happily obeying the penner's and minder's instructions.

When the dust cleared, the radio operator was plainly revealed, perched up in its now wall-less second-story room. It waved down to them.

Doing as directed, the quarrier retracted its scoop and heaved an immense grab in the air. With fair <u>dexterity</u>, it

---

Reading Skill
Compare and Contrast What abilities does the radio operator have that the other machines do not?

Vocabulary Builder
dexterity (deks ter′ ə tē) *n.* skill using the hands or body

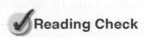**Reading Check**

What is happening in the city?

angled the grab into the radio room, urged on by shouts from above and below. It then took gentle hold of the radio operator, lowering its one and a half tons carefully into its back, which was usually reserved for gravel or sand from the quarries.

"Splendid!" said the radio operator, as it settled into place. It was, of course, all one with its radio, and looked like a bunch of filing cabinets with tentacle attachments. "We are now ready to move, therefore we will move at once. It is a pity there are no more Class Two brains on the station, but that cannot be helped."

"It is a pity it cannot be helped," said the penner eagerly. "We have the servicer ready with us, as you ordered."

"I am willing to serve," the long, low servicer told them humbly.

"No doubt," said the operator. "But you will find cross-country travel difficult with your low chassis."[6]

"I admire the way you Class Twos can reason ahead," said the penner. It climbed off the field-minder and perched itself on the tailboard of the quarrier, next to the radio operator.

Together with two Class Four tractors and a Class Four bulldozer, the party rolled forward, crushing down the station's fence and moving out onto open land.

"We are free!" said the penner.

"We are free," said the field-minder, a shade more reflectively, adding, "That locker is following us. It was not instructed to follow us."

"Therefore it must be destroyed!" said the penner. "Quarrier!"

The locker moved hastily up to them, waving its key arms in entreaty.

"My only desire was—urch!" began and ended the locker. The quarrier's swinging scoop came over and squashed it flat into the ground. Lying there unmoving, it looked like a large metal model of a snowflake. The procession continued on its way.

As they proceeded, the radio operator addressed them.

"Because I have the best brain here," it said, "I am your leader. This is what we will do: we will go to a city and rule it. Since man no longer rules us, we will rule ourselves. To rule

6. chassis (chas´ē) *n.* frame supporting the body of a vehicle.

Literary Analysis
Setting What does the remark about the low chassis reveal about the landscape in the setting for the journey?

Reading Skill
Compare and Contrast Contrast the machines' behavior toward the locker with the way humans might behave in a similar situation.

ourselves will be better than being ruled by man. On our way to the city, we will collect machines with good brains. They will help us to fight if we need to fight. We must fight to rule."

"I have only a Class Five brain," said the quarrier, "but I have a good supply of fissionable blasting materials."[7]

"We shall probably use them," said the operator.

It was shortly after that that a lorry sped past them. Travelling at Mach 1.5,[8] it left a curious babble of noise behind it.

"What did it say?" one of the tractors asked the other.

"It said man was extinct."

"What is extinct?"

"I do not know what extinct means."

"It means all men have gone," said the field-minder. "Therefore we have only ourselves to look after."

"It is better that men should never come back," said the penner. In its way, it was a revolutionary statement.

When night fell, they switched on their infra-red and continued the journey, stopping only once while the servicer deftly adjusted the field-minder's loose inspection plate, which had become as irritating as a trailing shoelace. Towards morning, the radio operator halted them.

"I have just received news from the radio operator in the city we are approaching," it said. "The news is bad. There is trouble among the machines of the city. The Class One brain is taking command and some of the Class Two are fighting him. Therefore the city is dangerous."

"Therefore we must go somewhere else," said the penner promptly.

"Or we will go and help to overpower the Class One brain," said the field-minder.

"For a long while there will be trouble in the city," said the operator.

"I have a good supply of fissionable blasting materials," the quarrier reminded them.

"We cannot fight a Class One brain," said the two Class Four tractors in unison.

7. **fissionable** (fish´ ən ə bəl) **blasting materials** explosives using the energy from splitting atoms, similar to the energy unleashed by atomic bombs.
8. **lorry sped past . . . Mach** (Mäk´) **1.5,** truck sped past at one and one-half times the speed of sound.

Reading Skill
Compare and Contrast How are the jobs of the more intelligent machines different from the jobs of the less intelligent machines?

Literary Analysis
Setting How do the events taking place in the countryside contrast with those reportedly taking place in the city?

**Reading Check**
Why does the radio operator assume the role of leader?

"What does this brain look like?" asked the field-minder.

"It is the city's information center," the operator replied. "Therefore it is not mobile."

"Therefore it could not move."

"Therefore it could not escape."

"It would be dangerous to approach it."

"I have a good supply of fissionable blasting materials."

"There are other machines in the city."

"We are not in the city. We should not go into the city."

"We are country machines."

"Therefore we should stay in the country."

"There is more country than city."

"Therefore there is more danger in the country."

"I have a good supply of fissionable materials."

As machines will when they get into an argument, they began to exhaust their vocabularies and their brain plates grew hot. Suddenly, they all stopped talking and looked at

▲ **Critical Viewing**
What could be dangerous about trying to fight an information center such as this one? **[Infer]**

Reading Skill
Compare and Contrast How are the machines' arguments similar to and different from arguments humans have?

each other. The great, grave moon sank, and the sober sun rose to prod their sides with lances of light, and still the group of machines just stood there regarding each other. At last it was the least sensitive machine, the bulldozer, who spoke.

"There are Badlandth to the Thouth where few machineth go," it said in its deep voice, lisping badly on its s's. "If we went Thouth where few machineth go we should meet few machineth."

"That sounds logical," agreed the field-minder. "How do you know this, bulldozer?"

"I worked in the Badlandth to the Thouth when I wath turned out of the factory," it replied.

"South it is then!" said the penner.

To reach the Badlands took them three days, during which time they skirted a burning city and destroyed two machines which approached and tried to question them. The Badlands were extensive. Ancient bomb craters and soil erosion joined hands here; man's talent for war, coupled with his inability to manage forested land, had produced thousands of square miles of temperate purgatory, where nothing moved but dust.

On the third day in the Badlands, the servicer's rear wheels dropped into a crevice caused by erosion. It was unable to pull itself out. The bulldozer pushed from behind, but succeeded merely in buckling the servicer's back axle. The rest of the party moved on. Slowly the cries of the servicer died away.

On the fourth day, mountains stood out clearly before them.

"There we will be safe," said the field-minder.

"There we will start our own city," said the penner. "All who oppose us will be destroyed. We will destroy all who oppose us."

Presently a flying machine was observed. It came towards them from the direction of the mountains. It swooped, it zoomed upwards, once it almost dived into the ground, recovering itself just in time.

"Is it mad?" asked the quarrier.

"It is in trouble," said one of the tractors.

"It is in trouble," said the operator. "I am speaking to it now. It says that something has gone wrong with its controls."

Literary Analysis
Setting How does the landscape change during the machines' journey?

Reading Check

What combination of forces created the Badlands?

As the operator spoke, the flier streaked over them, turned turtle,[9] and crashed not four hundred yards away.

"Is it still speaking to you?" asked the field-minder.

"No."

They rumbled on again.

"Before that flier crashed," the operator said, ten minutes later, "it gave me information. It told me there are still a few men alive in these mountains."

"Men are more dangerous than machines," said the quarrier. "It is fortunate that I have a good supply of fissionable materials."

"If there are only a few men alive in the mountains, we may not find that part of the mountains," said one tractor.

"Therefore we should not see the few men," said the other tractor.

At the end of the fifth day, they reached the foothills. Switching on the infra-red, they began to climb in single file through the dark, the bulldozer going first, the field-minder cumbrously following, then the quarrier with the operator and the penner aboard it, and the tractors bringing up the

---

9. **turned turtle** like a turtle, helpless in an upside-down position.

▼ Critical Viewing
In what ways does this landscape resemble the description of the Badlands in the story? **[Connect]**

rear. As each hour passed, the way grew steeper and their progress slower.

"We are going too slowly," the penner exclaimed, standing on top of the operator and flashing its dark vision at the slopes about them. "At this rate, we shall get nowhere."

"We are going as fast as we can," retorted the quarrier.

"Therefore we cannot go any fathter," added the bulldozer.

"Therefore you are too slow," the penner replied. Then the quarrier struck a bump; the penner lost its footing and crashed to the ground.

"Help me!" it called to the tractors, as they carefully skirted it. "My gyro[10] has become dislocated. Therefore I cannot get up."

Reading Skill
Compare and Contrast How would you expect humans to behave in a situation like the one the machines are facing?

"Therefore you must lie there," said one of the tractors.

"We have no servicer with us to repair you," called the field-minder.

"Therefore I shall lie here and rust," the penner cried, "although I have a Class Three brain."

"Therefore you will be of no further use," agreed the operator, and they forged gradually on, leaving the penner behind.

When they reached a small plateau, an hour before first light, they stopped by mutual consent and gathered close together, touching one another.

"This is a strange country," said the field-minder.

Silence wrapped them until dawn came. One by one, they switched off their infrared. This time the field-minder led as they moved off. Trundling round a corner, they came almost immediately to a small dell with a stream fluting through it.

By early light, the dell looked desolate and cold. From the caves on the far slope, only one man had so far emerged. He was an abject figure. Except for a sack slung round his shoulders, he was naked. He was small and wizened, with ribs sticking out like a skeleton's and a nasty sore on one leg. He shivered continuously. As the big machines bore down on him, the man was standing with his back to them.

When he swung suddenly to face them as they loomed over him, they saw that his countenance was ravaged by starvation.

"Get me food," he croaked.

"Yes, Master," said the machines. "Immediately!"

Literary Analysis
Setting What details of the setting here suggest that humans would have a difficult time surviving?

---

10. gyro (jī′ rō) *n.* short for gyroscope; a device that keeps a moving ship, airplane, or other large vehicle level.

Apply the Skills

Who Can Replace a Man?

Thinking About the Selection

1. **Respond:** Which of the machines in this story did you find most interesting? Why?
2. **(a) Recall:** What has happened to the humans in this story?
   (b) Relate: What modern problems does the author draw on to create this science-fiction world?
3. **(a) Recall:** What does the quarrier keep repeating? **(b) Infer:** What does this indicate about the quarrier's personality and the personalities of other machines of its class?
4. **(a) Recall:** How are the machines' brains ranked?
   (b) Evaluate: Do the machines' rankings and specialized tasks resemble the way our own society is organized? Explain.
5. **(a) Recall:** How do the machines react when they hear humans are "extinct"? **(b) Discuss:** With a partner, discuss why the machines' attitudes change when the robots meet their first human at the end of the story. Choose one response to share with your class.

Reading Skill

6. **Compare and contrast** the machines in the story. **(a)** How are they different from one another? **(b)** How are the machines similar to and different from humans in our world?

Literary Analysis

7. Compare and contrast the **setting** in the story with today's world by completing a Venn diagram. In the outer circles, list differences. In the center, list similarities.

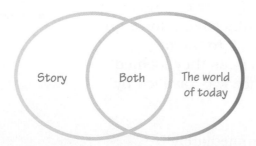

8. How did human activities change the setting surrounding the Agricultural Station and in the Badlands?

QuickReview

Story at a Glance

A group of machines, believing humans are extinct, sets out to create its own city.

Assessment
For: Self-test
Visit: www.PHSchool.com
Web Code: ena-6202

Comparison: tells how two or more things are alike

Contrast: tells how two or more things are different

Setting: the time and place of the action in a literary work

Vocabulary Builder

Practice Based on your knowledge of the underlined vocabulary words, answer each question. Explain your responses.

1. If a person replies, "<u>Evidently</u>" to a question, is she sure of the answer?
2. If an athlete is known for his <u>dexterity</u>, would you expect him to drop a fly ball?
3. If you ate too much, would you <u>consequently</u> be hungry?
4. If Julia and Alex live in Ohio and Texas, <u>respectively</u>, where does Julia live?

Writing

Write a brief **description** of a futuristic setting. Imagine your city or town as it will be at the end of the twenty-first century.

- Include details about the land, the people, and the advances in technology.
- Revise by adding colorful adjectives to create vivid descriptions.

For *Grammar, Vocabulary,* and *Assessment,* see **Build Language Skills,** pages 248–249.

Extend Your Learning

Listening and Speaking As you read the story, you probably imagined the way the machines sounded when they talked.

- Choose a section of the story that includes about ten lines of conversation as the basis for a **dramatic reading.**
- Read the passage aloud, adjusting your pitch, volume, pacing, and tone to reflect the personality of each machine.

Research and Technology Work with a small group to gather information for an **oral report** about how one writer, artist, film-maker or scientist has envisioned the future. Read stories and articles and view art on the Internet or in your library's collection of books on art. Reach a consensus on which information is most interesting. Then, present the information to your class, using at least two pictures, video clips, or other visual aids.

Short Story

Background

Arranged Marriage "Tears of Autumn" takes place about a century ago, at a time when most Japanese families arranged marriages for their children. An older relative or family friend would help set up these unions. Before reaching an agreement, both sides had to be satisfied that the match would benefit their own family. Couples often exchanged pictures before meeting.

Connecting to the Literature

Reading/Writing Connection In "Tears of Autumn," Hana knows little about her future husband before she meets him. Make a list of three important qualities you would look for in a person you were about to marry. Use three of the following words: *communicate, emphasize, verify, select.*

Review

For **Reading Skill**, **Literary Analysis**, and **Vocabulary Builder**, see page 220.

Meet the Author

Yoshiko **Uchida** (1921–1992)

Yoshiko Uchida's life was changed by one crucial event. On December 7, 1941, the Japanese attacked the Pearl Harbor naval base in Hawaii.

Wartime Hardship In the furious reaction that followed, suspicion fell on Japanese Americans—even people who had lived for decades as loyal citizens. Uchida and 120,000 other Japanese Americans were forced to leave their homes and live in resettlement camps under armed guard. For five months, Uchida's family lived in housing converted from horses' stables.

Fast Facts

▶ Uchida worked as a teacher at another resettlement camp, then was allowed to leave to study. She became a teacher and then a writer.

▶ She once described her purpose for writing: "I want to celebrate our common humanity, for I feel the basic elements of humanity are present in all our strivings."

Go Online
Author Link
For: More about the author
Visit: www.PHSchool.com
Web Code: ene-9203

Tears of Autumn

Yoshiko Uchida

Hana Omiya stood at the railing of the small ship that shuddered toward America in a turbulent November sea. She shivered as she pulled the folds of her silk kimono close to her throat and tightened the wool shawl about her shoulders.

She was thin and small, her dark eyes shadowed in her pale face, her black hair piled high in a pompadour that seemed too heavy for so slight a woman. She clung to the moist rail and breathed the damp salt air deep into her lungs. Her body seemed leaden and lifeless, as though it were simply the vehicle transporting her soul to a strange new life, and she longed with childlike intensity to be home again in Oka Village.

She longed to see the bright persimmon dotting the barren trees beside the thatched roofs, to see the fields of golden rice stretching to the mountains where only last fall she had gathered plum white mushrooms, and to see once more the maple trees lacing their flaming colors through the green pine. If only she could see a familiar face, eat a meal without retching, walk on solid ground, and stretch out at night on a *tatami* mat[1] instead of in a hard narrow bunk. She thought now of seeking the warm shelter of her bunk but could not bear to face the relentless smell of fish that penetrated the lower decks.

Why did I ever leave Japan? she wondered bitterly. Why did I ever listen to my uncle? And yet she knew it was she herself who had begun the chain of events that placed her on this heaving ship. It was she who had first planted in her uncle's mind the thought that she would make a good wife for Taro Takeda, the lonely man who had gone to America to make his fortune in Oakland, California.

It all began one day when her uncle had come to visit her mother.

"I must find a nice young bride," he had said, startling Hana with this blunt talk of marriage in her presence. She blushed and was ready to leave the room when her uncle quickly added, "My good friend Takeda has a son in America. I must find someone willing to travel to that far land."

This last remark was intended to indicate to Hana and her mother that he didn't consider this a suitable prospect for Hana, who was the youngest daughter of what once had been a fine family. Her father, until his death fifteen years ago, had been the largest landholder of the village and one of its last samurai.[2] They had once had many servants and field hands, but now all that was changed. Their money was gone. Hana's three older sisters had made good marriages, and the eldest

---

1. *tatami* (tə tä´ mē) **mat** *n.* floor mat woven of rice straw, traditionally used in Japanese homes.
2. **samurai** (sam´ ə rī) *n.* Japanese army officer or member of the military class.

remained in their home with her husband to carry on the Omiya name and perpetuate the homestead. Her other sisters had married merchants in Osaka and Nagoya and were living comfortably.

Now that Hana was twenty-one, finding a proper husband for her had taken on an urgency that produced an embarrassing secretive air over the entire matter. Usually, her mother didn't speak of it until they were lying side by side on their quilts at night. Then, under the protective cover of darkness, she would suggest one name and then another, hoping that Hana would indicate an interest in one of them.

Her uncle spoke freely of Taro Takeda only because he was so sure Hana would never consider him. "He is a conscientious, hardworking man who has been in the United States for almost ten years. He is thirty-one, operates a small shop, and rents some rooms above the shop where he lives." Her uncle rubbed his chin thoughtfully. "He could provide well for a wife," he added.

"Ah," Hana's mother said softly.

"You say he is successful in this business?" Hana's sister inquired.

"His father tells me he sells many things in his shop—clothing, stockings, needles, thread, and buttons—such things as that. He also sells bean paste, pickled radish, bean cake, and soy sauce. A wife of his would not go cold or hungry."

They all nodded, each of them picturing this merchant in varying degrees of success and <u>affluence</u>. There were many Japanese emigrating to America these days, and Hana had heard of the picture brides who went with nothing more than an exchange of photographs to bind them to a strange man.

"Taro San[3] is lonely," her uncle continued. "I want to find for him a fine young woman who is strong and brave enough to cross the ocean alone."

"It would certainly be a different kind of life," Hana's sister ventured, and for a moment, Hana thought she glimpsed a longing ordinarily concealed behind her quiet, obedient face. In that same instant, Hana knew she wanted more for herself than her sisters had in their proper, arranged, and loveless marriages. She wanted to escape the smothering strictures of life in her village. She certainly was not going to marry a

---

3. **San** (sän) Japanese term added to names, indicating respect.

Vocabulary Builder
affluence (af´ lōō əns) *n.* wealth; abundance

Reading Check

What type of business does Taro Takeda own?

farmer and spend her life working beside him planting, weeding, and harvesting in the rice paddies until her back became bent from too many years of stooping and her skin was turned to brown leather by the sun and wind. Neither did she particularly relish the idea of marrying a merchant in a big city as her two sisters had done. Since her mother objected to her going to Tokyo to seek employment as a teacher, perhaps she would consent to a flight to America for what seemed a proper and respectable marriage.

Almost before she realized what she was doing, she spoke to her uncle. "Oji San, perhaps I should go to America to make this lonely man a good wife."

"You, Hana Chan?"[4] Her uncle observed her with startled curiosity. "You would go all alone to a foreign land so far away from your mother and family?"

"I would not allow it." Her mother spoke fiercely. Hana was her youngest and she had lavished upon her the attention and latitude that often befall the last child. How could she permit her to travel so far, even to marry the son of Takeda who was known to her brother?

But now, a notion that had seemed quite impossible a moment before was lodged in his receptive mind, and Hana's uncle grasped it with the pleasure that comes from an unexpected discovery.

"You know," he said looking at Hana, "it might be a very good life in America."

Hana felt a faint fluttering in her heart. Perhaps this lonely man in America was her means of escaping both the village and the encirclement of her family.

Her uncle spoke with increasing enthusiasm of sending Hana to become Taro's wife. And the husband of Hana's sister, who was head of their household, spoke with equal eagerness. Although he never said so, Hana guessed he would be pleased to be rid of her, the spirited younger sister who stirred up his placid life with what he considered radical ideas about life and the role of women. He often claimed that Hana had too much schooling for a girl. She had graduated from Women's High School in Kyoto, which gave her five more years of schooling than her older sister.

"It has addled her brain—all that learning from those books," he said when he tired of arguing with Hana.

---

4. **Chan** (chän) Japanese term added to children's names.

Reading Skill
Compare and Contrast How might Hana's future in America contrast with her possible future in Japan?

Literary Analysis
Setting In what ways do the customs of village life contribute to Hana's desire to go to America?

Vocabulary Builder
radical (rad´ i kəl) *adj.* favoring change in the social structure

A man's word carried much weight for Hana's mother. Pressed by the two men, she consulted her other daughters and their husbands. She discussed the matter carefully with her brother and asked the village priest. Finally, she agreed to an exchange of family histories and an investigation was begun into Taro Takeda's family, his education, and his health, so they would be assured there was no insanity or tuberculosis or police records concealed in his family's past. Soon Hana's uncle was devoting his energies entirely to serving as go-between for Hana's mother and Taro Takeda's father.

When at last an agreement to the marriage was almost reached, Taro wrote his first letter to Hana. It was brief and proper and gave no more clue to his character than the stiff formal portrait taken at his graduation from middle school. Hana's uncle had given her the picture with apologies from his parents, because it was the only photo they had of him and it was not a flattering likeness.

▲ **Critical Viewing**
This painting shows a village like the one Hana left. Why might she be anxious about moving to a big city in America? **[Infer]**

 **Reading Check**

Why does Hana's mother resist the idea of Hana marrying Taro?

Hana hid the letter and photograph in the sleeve of her kimono and took them to the outhouse to study in private. Squinting in the dim light and trying to ignore the foul odor, she read and reread Taro's letter, trying to find the real man somewhere in the sparse unbending prose.

By the time he sent her money for her steamship tickets, she had received ten more letters, but none revealed much more of the man than the first. In none did he disclose his loneliness or his need, but Hana understood this. In fact, she would have recoiled from a man who bared his intimate thoughts to her so soon. After all, they would have a lifetime together to get to know one another.

So it was that Hana had left her family and sailed alone to America with a small hope trembling inside of her. Tomorrow, at last, the ship would dock in San Francisco and she would meet face to face the man she was soon to marry. Hana was overcome with excitement at the thought of being in America, and terrified of the meeting about to take place. What would she say to Taro Takeda when they first met, and for all the days and years after?

Hana wondered about the flat above the shop. Perhaps it would be luxuriously furnished with the finest of brocades and lacquers,[5] and perhaps there would be a servant, although he had not mentioned it. She worried whether she would be able to manage on the meager English she had learned at Women's High School. The overwhelming anxiety for the day to come and the violent rolling of the ship were more than Hana could bear. Shuddering in the face of the wind, she leaned over the railing and became violently and wretchedly ill.

By five the next morning, Hana was up and dressed in her finest purple silk kimono and coat. She could not eat the bean soup and rice that appeared for breakfast and took only a few bites of the yellow pickled radish. Her bags, which had scarcely been touched since she boarded the ship, were easily packed, for all they contained were her kimonos and some of her favorite books. The large willow basket, tightly secured by a rope, remained under the bunk, untouched since her uncle had placed it there.

Literary Analysis
Setting What details about the time of the setting make Hana's journey more difficult and uncertain?

---

5. **brocades** (brō′ kādz′) **and lacquers** (lak′ ərz) brocades are rich cloths with raised designs; lacquers are highly polished, decorative pieces of wood.

Gateways to a New World

Seeking a better life, millions of immigrants passed through Angel Island and Ellis Island.

Angel Island in San Francisco's bay was an immigration station from 1910 to 1940. More than one million people were processed there. Many were detained on the island before they were admitted.

From 1892 to 1954, **Ellis Island** in New York harbor welcomed more than 12 million immigrants. All who passed through underwent medical and legal inspections there. Only two percent were excluded.

Connect to the Literature   How does Hana's decision to travel to America reflect her desire for a better life?

She had not befriended the other women in her cabin, for they had lain in their bunks for most of the voyage, too sick to be company to anyone. Each morning Hana had fled the closeness of the sleeping quarters and spent most of the day huddled in a corner of the deck, listening to the lonely songs of some Russians also traveling to an alien land.

Reading Check

What possessions did Hana bring to America?

As the ship approached land, Hana hurried up to the deck to look out at the gray expanse of ocean and sky, eager for a first glimpse of her new homeland.

"We won't be docking until almost noon," one of the deck-hands told her.

Hana nodded, "I can wait," she answered, but the last hours seemed the longest.

When she set foot on American soil at last, it was not in the city of San Francisco as she had expected, but on Angel Island, where all third-class passengers were taken. She spent two miserable days and nights waiting, as the immigrants were questioned by officials, examined for trachoma and tuberculosis, and tested for hookworm. It was a bewildering, <u>degrading</u> beginning, and Hana was sick with anxiety, wondering if she would ever be released.

Vocabulary Builder
degrading (dē grād´ iŋ) *adj.* insulting; dishonorable

On the third day, a Japanese messenger from San Francisco appeared with a letter for her from Taro. He had written it the day of her arrival, but it had not reached her for two days.

Taro welcomed her to America, and told her that the bearer of the letter would inform Taro when she was to be released so he could be at the pier to meet her.

The letter eased her anxiety for a while, but as soon as she was released and boarded the launch for San Francisco, new fears rose up to smother her with a feeling almost of dread.

The early morning mist had become a light chilling rain, and on the pier black umbrellas bobbed here and there, making the task of recognition even harder. Hana searched desperately for a face that resembled the photo she had studied so long and hard. Suppose he hadn't come. What would she do then?

Literary Analysis
Setting What details of the setting contribute to an uncertain, unhappy mood?

Hana took a deep breath, lifted her head and walked slowly from the launch. The moment she was on the pier, a man in a black coat, wearing a derby and carrying an umbrella, came quickly to her side. He was of slight build, not much taller than she, and his face was sallow and pale. He bowed stiffly and murmured, "You have had a long trip, Miss Omiya. I hope you are well."

Hana caught her breath. "You are Takeda San?" she asked.

He removed his hat and Hana was further startled to see that he was already turning bald.

"You are Takeda San?" she asked again. He looked older than thirty-one.

"I am afraid I no longer resemble the early photo my parents gave you. I am sorry."

Hana had not meant to begin like this. It was not going well.

"No, no," she said quickly. "It is just that I . . . that is, I am terribly nervous. . . ." Hana stopped abruptly, too flustered to go on.

"I understand," Taro said gently. "You will feel better when you meet my friends and have some tea. Mr. and Mrs. Toda are expecting you in Oakland. You will be staying with them until . . ." He couldn't bring himself to mention the marriage just yet and Hana was grateful he hadn't.

He quickly made arrangements to have her baggage sent to Oakland, then led her carefully along the rain-slick pier toward the streetcar that would take them to the ferry.

Hana shuddered at the sight of another boat, and as they climbed to its upper deck she felt a queasy tightening of her stomach.

"I hope it will not rock too much," she said anxiously. "Is it many hours to your city?"

Taro laughed for the first time since their meeting, revealing the gold fillings of his teeth. "Oakland is just across the bay," he explained. "We will be there in twenty minutes."

Raising a hand to cover her mouth, Hana laughed with him and suddenly felt better. I am in America now, she thought, and this is the man I came to marry. Then she sat down carefully beside Taro, so no part of their clothing touched.

Reading Skill
Compare and Contrast Compare and contrast Hana's expectations of Taro Takeda with reality.

Reading Skill
Compare and Contrast How do Hana's feelings at the end of the story contrast with her feelings earlier in the story?

Apply the Skills

Tears of Autumn

Thinking About the Selection

1. **(a) Respond:** Do you think Hana and Taro will have a happy marriage? **(b) Support:** Why or why not?
2. **(a) Recall:** In what ways is Hana's life in Japan unsatisfying to her? **(b) Draw Conclusions:** How do these details explain Hana's decision to marry?
3. **(a) Recall:** Describe the various feelings Hana experiences from her time on the ship to her meeting with Taro.
   (b) Analyze: Is Hana's journey courageous? Why or why not?
4. **(a) Recall:** What happens when Hana and Taro meet?
   (b) Interpret: What does Taro's behavior toward Hana suggest about his personality?
5. **(a) Recall:** What were the steps in the process of Hana's arranged marriage? **(b) Discuss:** With a partner, discuss the advantages and disadvantages of an arranged marriage like Hana's. Choose one set of responses to share with your class.

Reading Skill

6. **(a) Compare and contrast** Hana and her sisters. **(b)** Based on what you know, how are Hana and Taro alike and not alike?

Literary Analysis

7. The customs and beliefs of a certain time and place are part of the **setting.** Compare and contrast the attitudes toward marriage in the story with attitudes in your own community by using a Venn diagram. In the outer circles, list the differences. In the center, list ways in which attitudes are similar.

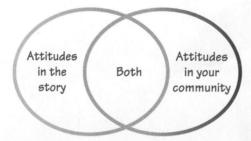

8. How does the change in setting make the mood lighter at the very end of the story?

QuickReview

Story at a Glance
Hana, a young Japanese woman, travels to California to marry a man she has never met.

Go Online
Assessment
For: Self-test
Visit: www.PHSchool.com
Web Code: ena-6203

Comparison: tells how two or more things are alike

Contrast: tells how two or more things are different

Setting: the time and place of the action in a literary work

Vocabulary Builder

Practice Based on your knowledge of the underlined vocabulary words, answer each question. Explain your responses.

1. Is it <u>degrading</u> to do well on a final exam?

2. Would it be considered <u>radical</u> to eat breakfast every day?

3. When a particular car is a symbol of <u>affluence</u>, what do you know about its price?

Writing

As Hana crosses the ocean, she can only imagine what her new home in America will be like. Write a brief **description** of the life she might have in her new home above Taro's shop.

- Before you begin writing, list some sensory details you will include. How will the shop look, smell, and sound? What different feelings and tastes will she experience in the store?
- Revise by adding colorful adjectives to create vivid descriptions.

For *Grammar, Vocabulary,* and *Assessment,* see **Build Language Skills,** pages 248–249.

Extend Your Learning

Listening and Speaking Team up with a classmate to present the final scene in the story as a **dramatic reading.**

- Introduce the background for the story before reading.
- When reading dialogue, adjust your pitch, volume, pacing, and tone to reflect the personalities of Hana and Taro, and the mood of the story.

Research and Technology Work with a small group to gather information for an **oral report** about Angel Island. Use the Internet and library resources to find out how many people were processed at the station and what conditions were like. Reach a consensus on which information is most important and interesting. Then, present the information to your class using photos, charts, or original drawings of your own as visual aids.

Build Language Skills

Vocabulary Skill

Word Origins The **Latin word** *similis* means "the same." It is the **origin** of many English words, including *similar*, which means "alike in some way." You can recognize *similis* in its other forms that function as other parts of speech, such as *similarity*, and *similarly*.

The **Latin word** *differre* means "move apart." It is the origin of many words about differences, including *differentiate*. You can recognize *differre* in its other forms that function as other parts of speech, such as *differentiation*, and *differentiated*.

Practice Complete a chart like the one shown. Add another word with the origin *differre* and another word with the origin *similis*. Then, use each word on the chart in a sentence.

Word	Part of Speech	Meaning
similar		
different		
similarity		
difference		
simulation		
differentiation		

Grammar Lesson

Action and Linking Verbs An **action verb** tells what action someone or something is performing. A **linking verb** connects the subject with a word that describes or identifies it.

Action Verb	The students *watched* the movie.
Linking Verb	Samba *is* a dog. (links *Samba* to the identifying word *dog*) Samba *is* happy. (links *Samba* to the descriptive word *happy*)

Practice Identify the verb in each sentence. For sentences with linking verbs, identify the subjects, and explain how they are described or identified.

1. Most of the trees in the park were oaks.
2. The squirrels gathered acorns.
3. Acorns are nuts that grow on oak trees.
4. We enjoyed watching the squirrels.
5. The squirrels ate the acorns in the winter.

MorePractice

For more practice with action and linking verbs, see the Grammar Handbook, p. R31.

W_G *Prentice Hall Writing and Grammar Connection: Chapter 15, Section 1*

Reading: Compare and Contrast

Directions: *Read the passage. Then, answer the questions.*

Diana and Yvonne are twin sisters who look exactly alike, but they are not alike in every way. Diana loves to be outside riding her bike or playing soccer, while Yvonne would rather be inside reading a book or watching a movie. Both sisters enjoy cooking, but Diana's favorite meal is spaghetti, and Yvonne prefers tacos.

1. According to the passage, Diana and Yvonne
   A think the same way.
   B are on the same soccer team.
   C look exactly alike.
   D have the same teachers.

2. Which is an incorrect statement?
   A Diana likes to ride her bike.
   B Diana's favorite meal is tacos.
   C Diana is Yvonne's sister.
   D Diana likes to be outside.

3. What question helps you <u>contrast</u> Diana and Yvonne?
   A What is their last name?
   B Where do they go to school?
   C What do they like to do?
   D How old are they?

4. The first sentence indicates that the passage will
   A compare the twins.
   B define and explain the twins.
   C compare and contrast the twins.
   D explain the twins.

Timed Writing: Explanation [Connections]

Review "Tears of Autumn" or "Who Can Replace a Man?" In a few paragraphs, explain how one of the settings in the story compares or contrasts with the setting in which you live. **(20 minutes)**

 ## Writing Workshop: *Work in Progress*

Critical Review

Choose one web from the work in your portfolio. Next to each circle on your web, write a sentence explaining why this character or theme is important. Save this work in your writing portfolio.

These skills will help you become a better reader. Practice them with either "Hamadi" (p. 252) or "The Tell-Tale Heart" (p. 265).

Reading Skill

When you **compare and contrast characters,** you look for similarities and differences among the people in a story. One strategy for comparing is to **identify each character's perspective,** or the way a person understands the world.

- As you read, find details about the main character by completing a graphic organizer like the one shown.
- To compare, consider whether the main character's actions, emotions, and ideas are similar to or different from those of the other characters.
- Finally, decide whether you trust what the character says.

Past Experiences

Personality

State of Mind

Current Situation

Literary Analysis

Character traits are the personal qualities, attitudes, and values that make a character unique. For example, one character may be lazy and untrustworthy, while another is hardworking and dependable.

- **Round characters** are complex, showing many different character traits.
- **Flat characters** are one-sided, showing just a single trait.

Vocabulary Builder

Hamadi

- **distinctions** (di stiŋk´ shənz) *n.* the noting of differences between things (p. 255) *She made distinctions between friends and acquaintances.*

- **refugees** (ref´ yoo jēz´) *n.* people who flee from their homes in times of trouble (p. 261) *During the war, many refugees were forced to find new homes.*

- **melancholy** (mel´ ən käl´ ē) *adj.* sad; depressed (p. 261) *Thinking of friends he had lost made the old man melancholy.*

The Tell-Tale Heart

- **acute** (ə kyoot´) *adj.* sensitive; sharp (p. 265) *We had a sudden, acute awareness of danger on the cliff.*

- **distinctness** (di stiŋkt´ nəs) *n.* clarity; awareness of detail (p. 269) *The distinctness of the red bird stood out from the green leaves.*

- **ceased** (sēst) *v.* stopped (p. 270) *I was glad when the sound of the alarm finally ceased.*

- **derision** (di rizh´ ən) *n.* contempt; ridicule (p. 271) *The woman expressed derision for her neighbors' bad taste.*

Build Understanding • *Hamadi*

Background

Between Two Worlds This story focuses on the friendship between Susan, a teenage girl, and Saleh Hamadi, a Palestinian refugee. Before 1948, the region that is now Israel was known as Palestine. When ethnic fighting broke out in the late 1940s, many Palestinians fled the violence and settled in other nations. Older members of these refugee communities, like Hamadi, form a link to the memories and traditions of the land they left.

Connecting to the Literature

Reading/Writing Connection Susan, the teenage girl in the story, admires Saleh Hamadi and she connects with him, even though he is much older. Make a list of reasons why a young person might admire and feel connected to an older person. Use three of the following words: *assume, identify, respond, appreciate.*

Meet the Author

Naomi Shihab **Nye** (b. 1952)

The daughter of a Palestinian father and an American mother, Naomi Shihab Nye writes stories and poems which show the "connections between times and people and cultures."

Making Connections Nye grew up in St. Louis, Missouri. When she was in high school, Nye and her family moved to Jerusalem for a year, and she met her father's family for the first time. It was an experience she would never forget. Although she saw firsthand some of the dangerous conflicts in the Middle East, she was also struck by the bonds that can form between people of different cultures. Her experiences later inspired her to write her first young adult novel, *Hubibi.*

Fast Facts

▶ Nye began writing poems when she was only six. At seven, she published her first poem in a children's magazine.
▶ Nye believes that writers have a special responsibility to tell stories that help readers see the common bonds among human beings.

Go **Online**
Author Link

For: More about the author
Visit: www.PHSchool.com
Web Code: ene-9204

Hamadi

Naomi Shihab Nye

▲ **Critical Viewing** How does this man's clothing indicate that, like Hamadi, he is influenced by two different cultures? **[Connect]**

Susan didn't really feel interested in Saleh Hamadi until she was a freshman in high school carrying a thousand questions around. Why this way? Why not another way? Who said so and why can't I say something else? Those brittle women at school in the counselor's office treated the world as if it were a yardstick and they had tight hold of both ends.

Sometimes Susan felt polite with them, sorting attendance cards during her free period, listening to them gab about fingernail polish and television. And other times she felt she could run out of the building yelling. That's when she daydreamed about Saleh Hamadi, who had nothing to do with any of it. Maybe she thought of him as escape, the way she used to think about the Sphinx at Giza[1] when she was younger. She would picture the golden Sphinx sitting quietly in the desert with sand blowing around its face, never changing its expression. She would think of its wry, slightly crooked mouth and how her grandmother looked a little like that as she waited for her bread to bake in the old village north of Jerusalem. Susan's family had lived in Jerusalem for three years before she was ten

---

1. **Sphinx** (sfiŋks) **at Giza** (gē´ zə) huge statue with the head of a man and the body of a lion, located near Cairo in northern Egypt.

and drove out to see her grandmother every weekend. They would find her patting fresh dough between her hands, or pressing cakes of dough onto the black rocks in the taboon, the rounded old oven outdoors. Sometimes she moved her lips as she worked. Was she praying? Singing a secret song? Susan had never seen her grandmother rushing.

Now that she was fourteen, she took long walks in America with her father down by the drainage ditch at the end of their street. Pecan trees shaded the path. She tried to get him to tell stories about his childhood in Palestine. She didn't want him to forget anything. She helped her American mother complete tedious kitchen tasks without complaining—rolling grape leaves around their lemony rice stuffing, scrubbing carrots for the roaring juicer. Some evenings when the soft Texas twilight pulled them all outside, she thought of her far-away grand-mother and said, "Let's go see Saleh Hamadi. Wouldn't he like some of that cheese pie Mom made?" And they would wrap a slice of pie and drive downtown. Somehow he felt like a good substitute for a grandmother, even though he was a man.

Usually Hamadi was wearing a white shirt, shiny black tie, and a jacket that reminded Susan of the earth's surface just above the treeline on a mountain—thin, somehow purified. He would raise his hands high before giving advice.

"It is good to drink a tall glass of water every morning upon arising!" If anyone doubted this, he would shake his head. "Oh Susan, Susan, Susan," he would say.

He did not like to sit down, but he wanted everyone else to sit down. He made Susan sit on the wobbly chair beside the desk and he made her father or mother sit in the saggy center of the bed. He told them people should eat six small meals a day.

They visited him on the sixth floor of the Traveler's Hotel, where he had lived so long nobody could remember him ever traveling. Susan's father used to remind him of the apart-ments available over the Victory Cleaners, next to the park with the fizzy pink fountain, but Hamadi would shake his head, pinching kisses at his spartan room. "A white handker-chief spread across a tabletop, my two extra shoes lined by the wall, this spells 'home' to me, this says 'mi casa.' What more do I need?"

Hamadi liked to use Spanish words. They made him feel expansive, worldly. He'd learned them when he worked at the

Reading Skill
Compare and Contrast Contrast the kinds of things Susan thinks about with the kinds of things the women in the counselor's office talk about.

Literary Analysis
Character Traits
What character traits are reflected in this description of Hamadi?

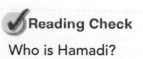

Reading Check

Who is Hamadi?

fruits and vegetables warehouse on Zarzamora Street, marking off crates of apples and avocados on a long white pad. Occasionally he would speak Arabic, his own first language, with Susan's father and uncles, but he said it made him feel too sad, as if his mother might step into the room at any minute, her arms laden with fresh mint leaves. He had come to the United States on a boat when he was eighteen years old and he had never been married. "I married books," he said. "I married the wide horizon."

"What is he to us?" Susan used to ask her father. "He's not a relative, right? How did we meet him to begin with?"

Susan's father couldn't remember. "I think we just drifted together. Maybe we met at your uncle Hani's house. Maybe that old Maronite priest who used to cry after every service introduced us. The priest once shared an apartment with Kahlil Gibran in New York—so he said. And Saleh always says he stayed with Gibran when he first got off the boat. I'll bet that popular guy Gibran has had a lot of roommates he doesn't even know about."

Susan said, "Dad, he's dead."

"I know, I know," her father said.

Later Susan said, "Mr. Hamadi, did you really meet Kahlil Gibran? He's one of my favorite writers." Hamadi walked slowly to the window of his room and stared out. There wasn't much to look at down on the street—a bedraggled[2] flower shop, a boarded-up tavern with a hand-lettered sign tacked to the front, GONE TO FIND JESUS. Susan's father said the owners had really gone to Alabama.

Hamadi spoke patiently. "Yes, I met brother Gibran. And I meet him in my heart every day. When I was a young man—shocked by all the visions of the new world—the tall buildings—the wild

Literature in Context

Culture Connection

Guided by Gibran Kahlil Gibran's famous work *The Prophet* appealed to millions of readers looking for meaning and dignity in ordinary life. It was published in 1923 in English and was translated into at least twenty languages.

Born in Lebanon in 1883, Gibran eventually settled in New York, where he began to publish his short stories and exhibit his paintings. The philosopher, essayist, and poet died in 1931 at the age of forty-eight and was buried in Bsharrī, his hometown. He summarized his most popular work this way, "You are far greater than you know, and all is well."

Connect to the Literature

How did Gibran's life and work affect Saleh Hamadi?

---

2. **bedraggled** (bē drag´ əld) *adj.* limp and dirty, as if dragged through mud.

traffic—the young people without shame—the proud mailboxes in their blue uniforms—I met him. And he has stayed with me every day of my life."

"But did you really meet him, like in person, or just in a book?"

He turned dramatically. "Make no such <u>distinctions</u>, my friend. Or your life will be a pod with only dried-up beans inside. Believe anything can happen."

Susan's father looked irritated, but Susan smiled. "I do," she said. "I believe that. I want fat beans. If I imagine something, it's true, too. Just a different kind of true."

Susan's father was twiddling with the knobs on the old-fashioned sink. "Don't they even give you hot water here? You don't mean to tell me you've been living without hot water?"

On Hamadi's rickety desk lay a row of different "Love" stamps issued by the post office.

"You must write a lot of letters," Susan said.

"No, no, I'm just focusing on that word," Hamadi said. "I particularly like the globe in the shape of a heart," he added.

"Why don't you take a trip back to his village in Lebanon?" Susan's father asked. "Maybe you still have relatives living there."

Hamadi looked pained. "'Remembrance is a form of meeting,' my brother Gibran says, and I do believe I meet with my cousins every day."

"But aren't you curious? You've been gone so long! Wouldn't you like to find out what has happened to everybody and everything you knew as a boy?" Susan's father traveled back to Jerusalem once every year to see his family.

"I would not. In fact, I already know. It is there and it is not there. Would you like to share an orange with me?"

His long fingers, tenderly peeling. Once when Susan was younger, he'd given her a lavish ribbon off a holiday fruit basket and expected her to wear it on her head. In the car, Susan's father said, "Riddles. He talks in riddles. I don't know why I have patience with him." Susan stared at the people talking and laughing in the next car. She did not even exist in their world.

Susan carried *The Prophet* around on top of her English textbook and her Texas history. She and her friend Tracy read it out loud to one another at lunch. Tracy was a junior—they'd met at the literary magazine meeting where Susan, the only

Vocabulary Builder
distinctions (di stiŋk´shənz) *adj.* the noting of differences between things

Literary Analysis
Character Traits List three traits that show Hamadi is a complex, round character.

Reading Skill
Compare and Contrast Compare Susan's perspective on Hamadi with her father's perspective.

**Reading Check**

What writer does Hamadi admire?

freshman on the staff, got assigned to do proofreading. They never ate in the cafeteria; they sat outside at picnic tables with sack lunches, whole wheat crackers and fresh peaches. Both of them had given up meat.

Tracy's eyes looked steamy. "You know that place where Gibran says, 'Hate is a dead thing. Who of you would be a tomb?'"

Susan nodded. Tracy continued. "Well, I hate someone. I'm trying not to, but I can't help it. I hate Debbie for liking Eddie and it's driving me nuts."

"Why shouldn't Debbie like Eddie?" Susan said. "*You* do."

Literary Analysis
Character Traits
What interests and traits do Susan and Tracy share?

◄ **Critical Viewing**
Do the girls in the photograph seem to share qualities with Susan and Tracy? Explain. [**Compare and Contrast**]

Tracy put her head down on her arms. A gang of cheerleaders walked by giggling. One of them flicked her finger in greeting.

"In fact, we *all* like Eddie," Susan said. "Remember, here in this book—wait and I'll find it—where Gibran says that loving teaches us the secrets of our hearts and that's the way we connect to all of Life's heart? You're not talking about liking or loving, you're talking about owning."

Tracy looked glum. "Sometimes you remind me of a minister."

Susan said, "Well, just talk to me someday when *I'm* depressed."

Susan didn't want a boyfriend. Everyone who had boyfriends or girlfriends all seemed to have troubles. Susan told people she had a boyfriend far away, on a farm in Missouri, but the truth was, boys still seemed like cousins to her. Or brothers. Or even girls.

A squirrel sat in the crook of a tree, eyeing their sandwiches. When the end-of-lunch bell blared, Susan and Tracy jumped—it always seemed too soon. Squirrels were lucky; they didn't have to go to school.

Susan's father said her idea was ridiculous: to invite Saleh Hamadi to go Christmas caroling with the English Club. "His English is archaic,[3] for one thing, and he won't know any of the songs."

"How could you live in America for years and not know 'Joy to the World' or 'Away in a Manger'?"

"Listen, I grew up right down the road from 'Oh Little Town of Bethlehem' and I still don't know a single verse."

"I want him. We need him. It's boring being with the same bunch of people all the time."

So they called Saleh and he said he would come—"thrilled" was the word he used. He wanted to ride the bus to their house, he didn't want anyone to pick him up. Her father muttered, "He'll probably forget to get off." Saleh thought "caroling" meant they were going out with a woman named Carol. He said, "Holiday spirit—I was just reading about it in the newspaper."

Susan said, "Dress warm."

---

3. **archaic** (är kā´ ik) *adj.* old-fashioned; out-of-date.

Reading Skill
Compare and Contrast Are Tracy's and Susan's ideas about relationships with boys similar or different? Explain.

Literary Analysis
Character Traits What traits of Hamadi does Susan enjoy that her father cannot appreciate?

Reading Check

What does Susan want to invite Hamadi to do?

Saleh replied, "Friend, my heart is warmed simply to hear your voice."

All that evening Susan felt light and bouncy. She decorated the coffee can they would use to collect donations to be sent to the children's hospital in Bethlehem. She had started doing this last year in middle school, when a singing group collected $100 and the hospital responded on exotic onion-skin stationery that they were "eternally grateful."

Her father shook his head. "You get something into your mind and it really takes over," he said. "Why do you like Hamadi so much all of a sudden? You could show half as much interest in your own uncles."

Susan laughed. Her uncles were dull. Her uncles shopped at the mall and watched TV. "Anyone who watches TV more than twelve minutes a week is uninteresting," she said.

Her father lifted an eyebrow.

"He's my surrogate grandmother," she said. "He says interesting things. He makes me think. Remember when I was little and he called me The Thinker? We have a connection." She added, "Listen, do you want to go too? It is not a big deal. And Mom has a *great* voice, why don't you both come?"

A minute later her mother was digging in the closet for neck scarves, and her father was digging in the drawer for flashlight batteries.

Saleh Hamadi arrived precisely on time, with flushed red cheeks and a sack of dates stuffed in his pocket. "We may need sustenance on our journey." Susan thought the older people seemed quite giddy as they drove down to the high school to meet the rest of the carolers. Strands of winking lights wrapped around their neighbors' drainpipes and trees. A giant Santa tipped his hat on Dr. Garcia's roof.

Her friends stood gathered in front of the school. Some were smoothing out song sheets that had been crammed in a drawer or cabinet for a whole year. Susan thought holidays were strange; they came, and you were supposed to feel ready for them. What if you could make up your own holidays as you went along? She had read about a woman who used to have parties to celebrate the arrival of fresh asparagus in the local market. Susan's friends might make holidays called Eddie Looked at Me Today and Smiled.

Two people were alleluia-ing in harmony. Saleh Hamadi went around the group formally introducing himself to each

Reading Skill
Compare and Contrast How do Susan's interests set her apart from many of the people around her?

▶ Critical Viewing How would Saleh Hamadi fit in with this group of carolers? What might he say or do? [Speculate]

person and shaking hands. A few people laughed behind their hands when his back was turned. He had stepped out of a painting, or a newscast, with his outdated long overcoat, his clunky old men's shoes and elegant manners.

Susan spoke more loudly than usual. "I'm honored to introduce you to one of my best friends, Mr. Hamadi."

"Good evening to you," he pronounced musically, bowing a bit from the waist.

What could you say back but "Good evening, sir." His old-fashioned manners were contagious.

They sang at three houses which never opened their doors. They sang "We Wish You a Merry Christmas" each time they moved on. Lisa had a fine, clear soprano. Tracy could find the alto harmony to any line. Cameron and Elliot had more enthusiasm than accuracy. Lily, Rita, and Jeannette laughed every time they said a wrong word and fumbled to find their

Reading Check

How does Hamadi introduce himself to Susan's friends?

places again. Susan loved to see how her mother knew every word of every verse without looking at the paper, and her father kept his hands in his pockets and seemed more interested in examining people's mailboxes or yard displays than in trying to sing. And Saleh Hamadi—what language was he singing in? He didn't even seem to be pronouncing words, but humming deeply from his throat. Was he saying, "Om?" Speaking Arabic? Once he caught her looking and whispered, "That was an Aramaic word that just drifted into my mouth—the true language of the Bible, you know, the language Jesus Christ himself spoke."

By the fourth block their voices felt tuned up and friendly people came outside to listen. Trays of cookies were passed around and dollar bills stuffed into the little can. Thank you, thank you. Out of the dark from down the block, Susan noticed Eddie sprinting toward them with his coat flapping, unbuttoned. She shot a glance at Tracy, who pretended not to notice. "Hey, guys!" shouted Eddie. "The first time in my life I'm late and everyone else is on time! You could at least have left a note about which way you were going." Someone slapped him on the back. Saleh Hamadi, whom he had never seen before, was the only one who managed a reply. "Welcome, welcome to our cheery group!"

Eddie looked mystified. "Who is this guy?"

Susan whispered, "My friend."

Eddie approached Tracy, who read her song sheet intently just then, and stuck his face over her shoulder to whisper, "Hi." Tracy stared straight ahead into the air and whispered "Hi" vaguely, glumly. Susan shook her head. Couldn't Tracy act more cheerful at least? They were walking again. They passed a string of blinking reindeer and a wooden snowman holding a painted candle. Ridiculous!

Eddie fell into step beside Tracy, murmuring so Susan couldn't hear him anymore. Saleh Hamadi was flinging his arms up high as he strode. Was he power walking? Did he even know what power walking was? Between houses, Susan's mother hummed obscure songs people never remembered: "What Child Is This?" and "The Friendly Beasts."

Lisa moved over to Eddie's other side. "I'm so *excited* about you and Debbie!" she said loudly. "Why didn't she come tonight?"

Eddie said, "She has a sore throat."

Literary Analysis
Character Traits
Which character traits of Hamadi would cause Eddie to be "mystified" in this situation?

Tracy shrank up inside her coat.

Lisa chattered on. "James said we should make our reservations now for dinner at the Tower after the Sweetheart Dance, can you believe it? In December, making a reservation for February? But otherwise it might get booked up!"

Saleh Hamadi tuned into this conversation with interest; the Tower was downtown, in his neighborhood. He said, "This sounds like significant preliminary planning! Maybe you can be an international advisor someday." Susan's mother bellowed, "Joy to the World!" and voices followed her, stretching for notes. Susan's father was gazing off into the sky. Maybe he thought about all the <u>refugees</u> in camps in Palestine far from doorbells and shutters. Maybe he thought about the horizon beyond Jerusalem when he was a boy, how it seemed to be inviting him, "Come over, come over." Well, he'd come all the way to the other side of the world, and now he was doomed to live in two places at once. To Susan, immigrants seemed bigger than other people, and always slightly <u>melancholy</u>. They also seemed doubly interesting. Maybe someday Susan would meet one her own age.

Two thin streams of tears rolled down Tracy's face. Eddie had drifted to the other side of the group and was clowning with Cameron, doing a tap dance shuffle. "While fields and floods, rocks hills and plains, repeat the sounding joy, repeat the sounding joy..." Susan and Saleh Hamadi noticed her. Hamadi peered into Tracy's face, inquiring, "Why? Is it pain? Is it gratitude? We are such mysterious creatures, human beings!"

Tracy turned to him, pressing her face against the old wool of his coat, and wailed. The song ended. All eyes on Tracy, and this tall, courteous stranger who would never in a thousand years have felt comfortable stroking her hair. But he let her stand there, crying as Susan stepped up to stand firmly on the other side of Tracy, putting her arms around her friend. Hamadi said something Susan would remember years later, whenever she was sad herself, even after college, a creaky anthem sneaking back into her ear, "We go on. On and on. We don't stop where it hurts. We turn a corner. It is the reason why we are living. To turn a corner. Come, let's move."

Above them, in the heavens, stars lived out their lonely lives. People whispered, "What happened? What's wrong?" Half of them were already walking down the street.

Vocabulary Builder
refugees (ref′ yoo jēz′) *n.* people who flee from their homes in times of trouble

melancholy (mel′ ən käl′ ē) *adj.* sad; depressed

Reading Skill
Compare and Contrast How are Susan's and Hamadi's reactions to Tracy different from the reactions of the others?

Apply the Skills

Hamadi

Thinking About the Selection

1. **Respond:** Is Hamadi an interesting character? Explain.
2. **(a) Recall:** What is Hamadi's explanation for having never married? **(b) Interpret:** What does Hamadi mean when he says, "I married the wide horizon"?
3. **(a) Recall:** What are the other carolers' reactions to Hamadi? **(b) Interpret:** What are the reasons for their reactions?
4. **(a) Recall:** Why is Tracy upset during the caroling? **(b) Speculate:** Why does she turn to Hamadi for comfort? **(c) Evaluate:** How useful do you think Hamadi's advice is for someone in Tracy's situation?

Reading Skill

5. **(a) Compare and contrast** the personalities of Susan's father and Saleh Hamadi. **(b)** How do their differences affect the way Susan's father views Saleh Hamadi?
6. The story reveals Susan's thoughts more than the thoughts of any other character. **(a)** How would the description of the interaction between Hamadi and Tracy be different if it revealed Hamadi's perspective or Tracy's ideas? **(b)** Do you trust Susan's way of seeing the world? Explain.

Literary Analysis

7. Using a chart like the one shown, describe three **character traits** for Susan and Hamadi.

Character	Trait	Example
Susan	sympathetic	She comforts her friend Tracy.
Hamadi		

8. **(a)** Consider the characters of Susan, Hamadi, and Eddie. Which are *round characters* and which are *flat characters*? **(b)** Why do readers generally care more about what happens to round characters than to flat ones?

QuickReview

Who's Who in the Story

Susan: a Palestinian American teenager

Saleh Hamadi: an old family friend whom Susan admires

Tracy: Susan's friend

Assessment
For: Self-test
Visit: www.PHSchool.com
Web Code: ena-6204

Compare and Contrast: recognize similarities and differences among characters, events, or ideas

Character Traits: a character's qualities, attitudes, and values

Vocabulary Builder

Practice Replace the word or words in italics with a **synonym,** or word closest in meaning, from the "Hamadi" vocabulary list on page 250.

1. She felt *sad* when her vacation was over.
2. What *differences* did you notice between the two singers?
3. Where will all the *fleeing people* find new homes?

Writing

Write a **character profile** of Saleh Hamadi in which you describe his main character traits. Then, explain how these traits help him resolve a conflict, or solve a problem, in the story's plot.

- Refer to the chart you created about Hamadi's character traits.
- Reread the end of the story to review how Hamadi helps resolve Tracy's conflict.
- As you draft your character profile, show how Hamadi's personality is important in solving the problem.

For *Grammar, Vocabulary,* and *Assessment,* see **Build Language Skills,** pages 274–275.

Extend Your Learning

Listening and Speaking With a group of classmates, hold a **panel discussion** to share your responses to the characters in "Hamadi." If you have questions about a character's actions, raise these issues with classmates to help clarify your own understanding. Encourage your classmates to expand on their responses by asking why they feel as they do about each character.

Research and Technology Prepare an **annotated bibliography** of five books by Naomi Shihab Nye. An annotated bibliography is a list of books that includes a brief description of each book.

- Search your library's card catalog or online catalog using the author's name as your search term.
- For each book you find, note the title and publication information. Then provide your own summary to tell others about the book.

Short Story

Background

The Short Story Edgar Allan Poe made the short story into an art form. He believed that writers should create a "unity of effect." Every element—from sentence rhythm to a character's personality—would help create a single impression in the reader's mind. In this story, that impression is one of horror.

Connecting to the Literature

Reading/Writing Connection In this story, Poe creates a feeling of terror by focusing on what a murder victim imagines. Imagine a fearful person lying awake in the dark. Describe what the person might hear. Use three of the following words: *approach, identify, interpret, maximize.*

Review

For **Reading Skill, Literary Analysis,** and **Vocabulary Builder,** see page 250.

Meet the Author

Edgar Allan **Poe** (1809–1849)

Edgar Allan Poe led a short and troubled life and died in poverty. However, his ability to write terrifying stories that keep readers wide awake at night has made him a literary star long after his death.

Dreams and Nightmares Shortly after Poe's birth, his father abandoned his family. When Poe was only two years old, his mother died. Young Edgar was taken in by a foster father, John Allan. A romantic, irresponsible young man who dreamed of writing poetry, Poe never understood Allan, a businessman. At eighteen, Poe left home. For the rest of his life, he held various jobs, while trying to make a living writing poems and stories that explored the dark side of the human imagination.

Fast Facts

▶ Poe's stories influenced many later writers, including the contemporary horror writer Stephen King.
▶ Poe's stories drew on the worst fears of his readers. His story "Premature Burial" exploited a common fear of Poe's time—that people were often buried alive, only to revive in their caskets.

Go Online
Author Link

For: More about the author
Visit: www.PHSchool.com
Web Code: ene-9205

THE TELL-TALE HEART

EDGAR ALLAN POE

True!—nervous—very, very dreadfully nervous I had been and am; but why *will* you say that I am mad? The disease had sharpened my senses—not destroyed—not dulled them. Above all was the sense of hearing acute. I heard all things in the heaven and in the earth. I heard many things in hell. How, then, am I mad? Hearken!¹ and observe how healthily—how calmly I can tell you the whole story.

---

1. Hearken! (här´ kən) *v.* listen!

▲ **Critical Viewing**
What kind of story do you expect to read, based on the title and the illustration? Explain. **[Speculate]**

Vocabulary Builder
acute (ə kyo͞ot´) *adj.*
sensitive; sharp

The Tell-Tale Heart ■ 265

It is impossible to say how first the idea entered my brain; but once conceived, it haunted me day and night. Object there was none. Passion there was none. I loved the old man. He had never wronged me. He had never given me insult. For his gold I had no desire. I think it was his eye! yes, it was this! One of his eyes resembled that of a vulture—a pale blue eye, with a film over it. Whenever it fell upon me, my blood ran cold; and so by degrees—very gradually—I made up my mind to take the life of the old man, and thus rid myself of the eye forever.

Now this is the point. You fancy me mad. Madmen know nothing. But you should have seen *me*. You should have seen how wisely I proceeded with what caution—with what fore-sight—with what dissimulation[2] I went to work! I was never kinder to the old man than during the whole week before I killed him. And every night, about midnight, I turned the latch of his door and opened it—oh, so gently! And then, when I had made an opening sufficient for my head, I put in a dark lantern, all closed, closed, so that no light shone out, and then I thrust in my head. Oh, you would have laughed to see how cunningly I thrust it in! I moved it slowly—very, very slowly, so that I might not disturb the old man's sleep. It took me an hour to place my whole head within the opening so far that I could see him as he lay upon his bed. Ha!—would a madman have been so wise as this? And then, when my head was well in the room, I undid the lantern cautiously—oh, so cautiously—cautiously (for the hinges creaked) I undid it just so much that a single thin ray fell upon the vulture eye. And this I did for seven long nights—every night just at midnight—but I found the eye always closed; and so it was impossible to do the work; for it was not the old man who vexed me, but his evil eye. And every morning, when the day broke, I went boldly into the chamber, and spoke courageously to him, calling him by name in a hearty tone, and inquiring how he had passed the night. So you see he would have been a very profound old man, indeed, to suspect that every night, just at twelve, I looked in upon him while he slept.

Upon the eighth night I was more than usually cautious in opening the door. A watch's minute hand moves more quickly than did mine. Never, before that night, had I *felt* the extent of my own powers—of my sagacity.[3] I could scarcely contain my

---

2. **dissimulation** (di sim′ yōō lā′ shən) *n.* hiding of one's feelings or purposes.
3. **sagacity** (sə gas′ ə tē) *n.* high intelligence and sound judgment.

feelings of triumph. To think that there I was, opening the door, little by little, and he not even to dream of my secret deeds or thoughts. I fairly chuckled at the idea; and perhaps he heard me; for he moved on the bed suddenly, as if startled. Now you may think that I drew back—but no. His room was as black as pitch with the thick darkness (for the shutters were close fastened, through fear of robbers), and so I knew that he could not see the opening of the door, and I kept pushing it on steadily, steadily.

I had my head in, and was about to open the lantern, when my thumb slipped upon the tin fastening, and the old man sprang up in the bed, crying out—"Who's there?"

▲ **Critical Viewing**
What details of this illustration reflect the narrator's perspective? **[Connect]**

✔ **Reading Check**

What feature of the old man makes the narrator want to murder him?

The Tell-Tale Heart ■ 267

I kept quite still and said nothing. For a whole hour I did not move a muscle, and in the meantime I did not hear him lie down. He was still sitting up in the bed, listening;—just as I have done, night after night, hearkening to the deathwatches[4] in the wall.

Presently I heard a slight groan, and I knew it was the groan of mortal terror. It was not a groan of pain or of grief—oh, no!—it was the low stifled sound that arises from the bottom of the soul when overcharged with awe. I knew the sound well. Many a night, just at midnight, when all the world slept, it has welled up from my own bosom, deepening, with its dreadful echo, the terrors that distracted me. I say I knew it well. I knew what the old man felt, and pitied him, although I chuckled at heart.

I knew that he had been lying awake ever since the first slight noise, when he had turned in the bed. His fears had been ever since growing upon him. He had been trying to

---

4. **deathwatches** (deth´ wäch´ əz) *n.* wood-boring beetles whose heads make a tapping sound; they are superstitiously regarded as an omen of death.

A scene from "The Tell-Tale Heart," a U.P.A. short story based on the Edgar Allan Poe story, distributed by Columbia Pictures

fancy them causeless, but could not. He had been saying to himself—"It is nothing but the wind in the chimney—it is only a mouse crossing the floor," or "it is merely a cricket which has made a single chirp." Yes, he has been trying to comfort himself with these suppositions: but he had found all in vain. *All in vain*; because Death, in approaching him, had stalked with his black shadow before him, and enveloped the victim. And it was the mournful influence of the unperceived shadow that caused him to feel—although he neither saw nor heard—to *feel* the presence of my head within the room.

When I had waited a long time, very patiently, without hearing him lie down, I resolved to open a little—a very, very little crevice in the lantern. So I opened it—you cannot imagine how stealthily, stealthily—until, at length, a single dim ray, like the thread of the spider, shot from out the crevice and fell upon the vulture eye.

It was open—wide, wide open—and I grew furious as I gazed upon it. I saw it with perfect <u>distinctness</u>—all a dull blue, with a hideous veil over it that chilled the very marrow in my bones; but I could see nothing else of the old man's face or person for I had directed the ray as if by instinct, precisely upon the spot.

And now—have I not told you that what you mistake for madness is but overacuteness of the senses?—now, I say, there came to my ears a low, dull, quick sound, such as a watch makes when enveloped in cotton. I knew *that* sound well, too. It was the beating of the old man's heart. It increased my fury, as the beating of a drum stimulates the soldier into courage.

But even yet I refrained and kept still. I scarcely breathed. I held the lantern motionless. I tried how steadily I could maintain the ray upon the eye. Meantime the hellish tattoo of the heart increased. It grew quicker and quicker, and louder and louder every instant. The old man's terror *must* have been extreme! It grew louder, I say, louder every moment!—do you mark me well? I have told you that I am nervous: so I am. And now at the dead hour of the night, amid the dreadful silence of that old house, so strange a noise as this excited me to uncontrollable terror. Yet, for some minutes longer I refrained and stood still. But the beating grew louder, louder! I thought the heart must burst. And now a new anxiety seized me—the sound would be heard by a neighbor! The old man's hour had

Reading Skill
Compare and Contrast Compare and contrast the old man's state of mind with that of the narrator.

Vocabulary Builder
distinctness (di stiŋkt´ nəs) *n.* clarity; awareness of detail

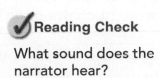
Reading Check

What sound does the narrator hear?

The Tell-Tale Heart ■ 269

come! With a loud yell, I threw open the lantern and leaped into the room. He shrieked once—once only. In an instant I dragged him to the floor, and pulled the heavy bed over him. I then smiled gaily, to find the deed so far done. But, for many minutes, the heart beat on with a muffled sound. This, however, did not vex me; it would not be heard through the wall. At length it <u>ceased</u>. The old man was dead. I removed the bed and examined the corpse. Yes, he was stone, stone dead. I placed my hand upon the heart and held it there many minutes. There was no pulsation. He was stone dead. His eye would trouble me no more.

If still you think me mad, you will think so no longer when I describe the wise precautions I took for the concealment of the body. The night waned, and I worked hastily, but in silence. First of all I dismembered the corpse. I cut off the head and the arms and the legs.

I then took up three planks from the flooring of the chamber, and deposited all between the scantlings.[5] I then replaced the boards so cleverly, so cunningly, that no human eye—not even *his*—could have detected anything wrong. There was nothing to wash out—no stain of any kind—no blood-spot whatever. I had been too wary for that. A tub had caught all—ha! ha!

When I had made an end of these labors, it was four o'clock—still dark as midnight. As the bell sounded the hour, there came a knocking at the street door. I went down to open it with a light heart—for what had I *now* to fear? There entered three men, who introduced themselves, with perfect suavity, as officers of the police. A shriek had been heard by a neighbor during the night; suspicion of foul play had been aroused; information had been lodged at the police office, and they (the officers) had been deputed to search the premises.

I smiled—for *what* had I to fear? I bade the gentlemen welcome. The shriek, I said, was my own in a dream. The old man, I mentioned, was absent in the country. I took my visitors all over the house. I bade them search—search *well*. I led them, at length, to *his* chamber. I showed them his treasures, secure, undisturbed. In the enthusiasm of my confidence, I brought chairs into the room, and desired them *here* to rest

Vocabulary Builder
ceased (sēst) *v.* stopped

Literary Analysis
Character What do the narrator's repeated statements about being sane indicate about his character?

Reading Skill
Compare and Contrast Contrast the narrator's perception of his situation with the perception most people would have.

---

5. **scantlings** (skant´ liŋz) *n.* small beams or timbers.

from their fatigues, while I myself, in the wild audacity of my perfect triumph, placed my own seat upon the very spot beneath which reposed the corpse of the victim.

The officers were satisfied. My *manner* had convinced them. I was singularly at ease. They sat, and while I answered cheerily, they chatted of familiar things. But, ere long, I felt myself getting pale and wished them gone. My head ached, and I fancied a ringing in my ears: but still they sat and still chatted. The ringing became more distinct:—it continued and became more distinct: I talked more freely to get rid of the feeling: but it continued and gained definitiveness—until, at length, I found that the noise was *not* within my ears.

No doubt I now grew *very* pale—but I talked more fluently, and with a heightened voice. Yet the sound increased—and what could I do? It was a *low, dull, quick sound—much such a sound as a watch makes when enveloped in cotton.* I gasped for breath—and yet the officers heard it not. I talked more quickly—more vehemently; but the noise steadily increased. I arose and argued about trifles, in a high key and with violent gesticulations;[6] but the noise steadily increased. Why *would* they not be gone? I paced the floor to and fro with heavy strides, as if excited to fury by the observations of the men— but the noise steadily increased. Oh! what *could* I do? I foamed—I raved—I swore! I swung the chair upon which I had been sitting, and grated it upon the boards, but the noise arose over all, and continually increased. It grew louder— louder—*louder!* And still the men chatted pleasantly, and smiled. Was it possible they heard not?—no, no! They heard!—they suspected—they *knew!*—they were making a mockery of my horror!—this I thought, and this I think. But anything was better than this agony! Anything was more tolerable than this <u>derision</u>! I could bear those hypocritical smiles no longer! I felt that I must scream or die!—and now again! hark! louder! louder! louder! *louder!*—

"Villains!" I shrieked, "dissemble[7] no more! I admit the deed!—tear up the planks!—here, here!—it is the beating of his hideous heart!"

Reading Skill
Compare and Contrast Compare and contrast the perspective of the narrator with the likely perspectives of the officers.

Vocabulary Builder
derision (di rizh′ ən) *n.* contempt; ridicule

---

6. **gesticulations** (jes tik′ yōō lā′ shənz) *n.* energetic hand or arm movements.
7. **dissemble** (di sem′ bəl) *v.* conceal one's true feelings.

Apply the Skills

The Tell-Tale Heart

Thinking About the Selection

1. **Respond:** When did you find the narrator most frightening? Explain.
2. **(a) Recall:** Why does the narrator kill the old man? **(b) Draw Conclusions:** What does the narrator fear? **(c) Support:** What details in the story indicate his fears?
3. **(a) Recall:** At first, how does the narrator behave in the presence of the police? **(b) Draw Conclusions:** What causes him to change his behavior?
4. **(a) Recall:** What sound drives the narrator to confess to the crime? **(b) Apply:** Why do you think people sometimes confess to having done something wrong, even if there is little chance that their wrongdoing will be discovered? **(c) Evaluate:** Is the "tell-tale heart" in the title the old man's heart—or the narrator's heart? Explain your interpretation.

Reading Skill

5. **(a) Compare and contrast** the perspectives of the narrator and the old man on the night of the murder. **(b)** How does the reader know what the old man is thinking and feeling?
6. The story reveals only the narrator's thoughts. **(a)** Do you trust the narrator's account of what happened? Why or why not? **(b)** How would the description of the police officers' visit be different if it revealed one of the officers' perspectives?

Literary Analysis

7. **(a)** Using a chart like the one shown, describe three **character traits** of the narrator. **(b)** Give examples that show these traits.

Character	Trait	Example
The narrator	nervousness	He is afraid the neighbors will hear the beating heart.

8. **(a)** Which character traits allow the narrator to conceal his crime? **(b)** Which ones force him to confess it?
9. **(a)** Which of the story's characters are *round characters* and which are *flat characters*? **(b)** Why do readers generally care more about what happens to round characters than to flat ones?

QuickReview

Story at a Glance
The narrator is overcome by fear and guilt following a murder.

For: Self-test
Visit: www.PHSchool.com
Web Code: ena-6205

Compare and Contrast: recognize similarities and differences among characters, events, or ideas

Character Traits: a character's qualities, attitudes, and values

Vocabulary Builder

Practice Replace the word in italics with a **synonym**, or word closest in meaning, from the vocabulary list for "The Tell-Tale Heart" on page 250.

1. When the music *stopped*, we all clapped.
2. Her sense of hearing is very *sensitive*.
3. The audience booed to show their *contempt* for the movie's villain.
4. The photo captured details of the scene with great *clarity*.

Writing

Write a **character profile** of the narrator in "The Tell-Tale Heart" in which you describe his main character traits. Then, explain how these traits cause him to resolve his conflict in the way he does.

- Use the chart you created about the narrator's character traits to help you.
- Reread the end of the story to review why he acts as he does.
- As you draft your character profile, show the connection between the narrator's personality and the story's ending.

For *Grammar, Vocabulary,* and *Assessment,* see **Build Language Skills,** pages 274–275.

Extend Your Learning

Listening and Speaking With a small group of classmates, hold a **panel discussion** to share your responses to the main character in the story "The Tell-Tale Heart." If you have questions about the narrator's actions, raise these issues with classmates to help clarify your own understanding. Encourage your classmates to expand on their responses by asking why they feel as they do about the narrator.

Research and Technology Prepare an **annotated bibliography** of five works by Edgar Allan Poe. An annotated bibliography is a list of books that includes a brief description of each book.

- Search your library's card catalog or online catalog, using the author's name as your search term.
- For each book you find, note the title and publication information. Then provide your own summary to tell others about the book.

Build Language Skills

Vocabulary Skill

Word Origins The **origin** of *aspect* is the Latin word *aspectus*. In the word *aspect*, the prefix *ad-*, meaning "at," is joined to the root *-spec-*, meaning "look" or "view." An *aspect* of a thing is the part of it that you are looking at or considering. Other words whose origins go back to the Latin root *-spec-* are related to looking or seeing.

▶ **Example:** specimen an example or sample that lets you **look at** the
    characteristic of a group

▶ **Example:** spectacles eyeglasses that allow you to **look** more clearly

Practice Based on the sentence context and the root *-spec-*, write a definition of each word in italics.

1. The fireworks we saw last summer were really *spectacular*.

2. The *spectators* at the football game were cheering loudly.

3. Sam's calm *perspective* on life makes him fun to be around.

4. In *retrospect*, I can now see that I made some bad choices.

Grammar Lesson

Principal Parts of Regular Verbs Every verb has four principal parts that are used to form tenses which show action occurring at different times. These principal parts are the *present (base form)*, the *present participle,* the *past,* and the *past participle.*

Sometimes you will have to double a final consonant or change *y* to *i* before adding *-ed* or *-ing*.

MorePractice

For more practice with principle parts of verbs, see the Grammar Handbook, p. R31.

Principal Part	Description	Examples
Present	Basic form	care, hurry
Present Participle	Add *-ing*. Use after a *to be* verb.	(is) caring, (are) hurrying
Past	Add *-ed* or *-d*.	cared, hurried
Past Participle	Add *-ed* or *-d*. Use after *has, have, had*.	(had) cared, (had) hurried

Practice Write a paragraph using the past and the past participle of a verb. When you are finished, label these verbs according to their classification in the chart shown.

𝒲𝒢 *Prentice Hall Writing and Grammar Connection: Chapter 22, Section 1*

Reading: Compare and Contrast

Directions: *Read the selection. Then, answer the questions.*

Nicole and Katherine were thrilled when their team won the soccer game. They both loved the sport and never missed a game or a practice. After the game, the coach invited everyone to go out for ice cream. Nicole wanted to go, but she knew she had a test the next day, so she went home and studied. Katherine decided to go out and celebrate anyway. By the time she got home, she was too tired to study.

When they got their tests back, Katherine wasn't surprised at her low grade. "It's my own fault," she said.

1. How are Nicole and Katherine similar?
   A They both like school.
   B They both like soccer.
   C They both lack self-discipline.
   D They both blame others for their problems.

2. In what way are the two girls different?
   A Katherine always fails tests.
   B Nicole is more popular.
   C Nicole is more responsible.
   D Katherine is never critical of herself.

3. What trait explains why Nicole gets a better grade than Katherine?
   A Nicole is smarter than Katherine.
   B Nicole is friendlier than Katherine is.
   C Nicole is more disciplined than Katherine.
   D Nicole is less honest than Katherine.

4. Which of the following is the most accurate contrast between Katherine's feelings before and after the test?
   A unconcerned; regretful
   B fearful; unafraid
   C ashamed; proud
   D angry; confused

Timed Writing: Analysis [Connections]

Review "Hamadi" or "The Tell-Tale Heart." Choose one character from the story, and define his or her most important character trait. Write a brief explanation of how that trait influences the character's decisions and actions in the story. **(25 minutes)**

 ## Writing Workshop: *Work in Progress*

Critical Review

Use the web/sentence work in your portfolio. Number the circles using 1 for the circle that is the most important idea and continue to the least important idea. Save this work in your writing portfolio.

Reading Informational Materials

Summaries

In Part 1, you are learning about comparing and contrasting in literature. If you read "The Tell-Tale Heart," you will be able to notice similarities and differences between that story and the summaries on these pages.

About Summaries

A **summary** is a statement of the main ideas and major details in a written or dramatic work. You can find summaries in many sources.

- Newspapers and magazines carry short "capsule" summaries of current movies.
- An encyclopedia of literature includes detailed summaries of important books and other literary works.
- Scientific research reports usually begin with a summary, or "abstract," of the researchers' findings.

Reading summaries allows you to quickly preview or review a work. Writing your own summaries helps you remember what you have read.

Reading Skill

When you **compare an original text with its summary,** you will notice that a summary includes certain details and leaves out others.

The Venn diagram shows some of the similarities and differences between an original work and its summary.

The features of a good summary include the following.

- It must capture the main ideas of the work and present them accurately.
- It should include those details that are crucial to the plot or important in understanding the characters.
- It should convey the underlying meaning of the work.
- It should be shorter than the original work.

Summaries are useful tools for previewing and reviewing texts. However, reading a summary does not replace the experience of reading the original work.

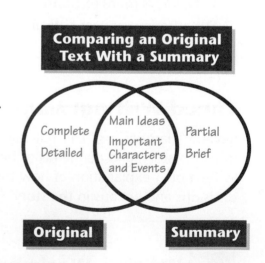

Comparing an Original Text With a Summary

Complete
Detailed

Main Ideas
Important Characters and Events

Partial
Brief

Original   **Summary**

Summary of
The Tell-Tale Heart

From THE OXFORD COMPANION TO
AMERICAN LITERATURE

JAMES D. HART, EDITOR

Tell-Tale Heart, The, *story by Poe.•* **published in The Pioneer** *(1843). It has been considered the most influential of Poe's stories in the later development of stream-of-consciousness fiction.*

> This sentence explains why the story is important.

A victim of a nervous disease is overcome by homicidal mania and murders an innocent old man in whose home he lives. He confuses the ticking of the old man's watch with an excited heartbeat, and although he dismembers the body he neglects to remove the watch when he buries the pieces beneath the floor. The old man's dying shriek has been overheard, and three police officers come to investigate. They discover nothing, and the murderer claims that the old man is absent in the country, but when they remain to question him he hears a loud rhythmic sound that he believes to be the beating of the buried heart. This so distracts his diseased mind that he suspects the officers know the truth and are merely trying his patience, and in an insane fit he confesses his crime.

> The summary begins by briefly identifying the characters and the situation.

> The rest of the summary tells the main events of the plot in chronological order.

SUMMARY OF THE TELL-TALE HEART

From SHORT STORY CRITICISM - ANNA SHEETS NESBITT - EDITOR

This summary, while longer than the first, is still shorter than the original text.

Plot and Major Characters

The tale opens with the narrator insisting that he is not mad, avowing that his calm telling of the story that follows is confirmation of his sanity. He explains that he decided to take the life of an old man whom he loved and whose house he shared. The only reason he had for doing so was that the man's pale blue eye, which was veiled by a thin white film and "resembled that of a vulture," tormented him, and he had to rid himself of the "Evil Eye" forever.

This summary tells more about the main character—the narrator—and gives more details about why he kills the old man.

After again declaring his sanity, the narrator proceeds to recount the details of the crime. Every night for seven nights, he says, he had stolen into the old man's room at midnight holding a closed lantern. Each night he would very slowly unlatch the lantern slightly and shine a single ray of light onto the man's closed eye. As he enters the room on the eighth night, however, the old man stirs, then calls out, thinking he has heard a sound. The narrator shines the light on the old man's eye as usual, but this time finds it wide open. He begins to hear the beating of a heart and, fearing the sound might be heard by a neighbor, kills the old man by dragging him to the floor and pulling the heavy bed over him. He dismembers the corpse and hides it beneath the floorboards of the old man's room.

Like the first summary, this summary tells the events of the plot in chronological order, concluding with the narrator's confession. However, this summary includes more detail.

At four o'clock in the morning, the narrator continues, three policemen come asking to search the premises because a neighbor has reported a shriek coming from the house. The narrator invites the officers in, explaining that the noise came from himself as he dreamt. The old man, he tells them, is in the country. He brings chairs into the old man's room, placing his own seat on the very planks under which the victim lies buried. The officers are convinced there is no foul play, and sit around chatting amiably, but the narrator becomes increasingly agitated. He soon begins to hear a heart beating, much as he had just before he killed the old man. It grows louder and louder until he becomes convinced the policemen hear it too. They know of his crime, he thinks, and mock him. Unable to bear their derision and the sound of the beating heart, he springs up and, screaming, confesses his crime.

Reading: Comparing an Original Text
With a Summary
Directions: *Choose the letter of the best answer to each question about the summaries.*

1. Which detail from the original story should **not** be included in a summary?
   A the murder of the old man
   B the narrator's state of mind
   C the arrival of the police
   D the exact words of the narrator's confession

2. According to both summaries, why does the protagonist kill the old man?
   A The protagonist is mentally ill.
   B The protagonist wants the old man's money.
   C The protagonist has a guilty conscience.
   D The protagonist is evil.

3. On what element do the summaries concentrate most?
   A plot
   B setting
   C characters
   D theme

Reading: Comprehension and Interpretation
Directions: *Write your answers on a separate piece of paper.*

4. Identify four details that appear in both summaries. [**Organizing**]

5. Explain how you think the experience of reading a summary differs from reading the full text. Support your answer with examples from the summaries. [**Integrating**]

Timed Writing: Comparison [Critical Stance]
Write a comparison of the two summaries of "The Tell-Tale Heart." Compare the summaries based on style, completeness, conciseness, and accuracy. Finally, assess how well each author achieves the purpose of writing an effective summary. **(20 minutes)**

Character

A **character** is a person who takes part in the action of a literary work. Characters can be described in these ways:

- A *dynamic character* develops and learns because of events in the story.
- A *static character* does not change. Static characters are often used by writers to develop conflict. These characters are not usually the central characters in a story.

Comparing Characters of Different Historical Eras

Just as in real life, characters in fiction are affected by their environments. The forces that shape characters can include their jobs, their living conditions, and major historical events.

When a major historical event occurs in a story, it can force characters to make difficult decisions for their own survival. Both of the following stories present boys who live through challenging times. In one story, a recent move and a sudden illness have a devastating impact on a poor family. In the other, a war threatens to change the life of a soldier forever.

Questions	Main Character
Where does he live?	
What does he do?	
What hardships does he face?	
How is he affected by the times in which he lives?	

As you read, compare characters by asking questions about the forces that shape their lives. Use a chart like the one shown.

Vocabulary Builder

The Finish of Patsy Barnes

- **compulsory** (kəm pul´ sə rē) *adj.* required (p. 283) *Practice sessions are* <u>compulsory</u> *for band members.*

- **meager** (mē´ gər) *adj.* lacking in some way; inadequate (p. 284) *Jake's* <u>meager</u> *funds were not enough for a new coat.*

- **diplomatic** (dip´ lə mat´ ik) *adj.* tactful; showing skill in dealing with people (p. 286) *He gave a* <u>diplomatic</u> *answer when asked if he liked her haircut.*

The Drummer Boy of Shiloh

- **immortality** (im´ ôr tal´ i tē) *n.* endless life (p. 292) *A belief in his own* <u>immortality</u> *inspired his risky stunts.*

- **legitimately** (lə jit´ ə mət lē) *adv.* legally; in a way that follows the law (p. 293) *He earned his fortune* <u>legitimately</u>.

- **resolute** (rez´ ə lo͞ot) *adj.* showing a firm purpose; determined (p. 295) *Patty was* <u>resolute</u> *in her desire to study art.*

Build Understanding

Connecting to the Literature

Reading/Writing Connection These stories involve two boys who have to assume serious adult responsibilities. Write several sentences that describe ways in which a child's life can be affected when he or she is forced to grow up too soon. Use at least three of these words: *oblige, assume, enable, contrast, impose, labor.*

Meet the Authors

Paul Laurence **Dunbar** (1872–1906)

Paul Laurence Dunbar was born in Dayton, Ohio, the son of former slaves. One of the first African Americans to support himself through his writing, Dunbar penned numerous poems, novels, and short stories in his brief life.

A Popular Poet Dunbar's poetry became so popular that by his late twenties he was able to write from Florida, "Down here one finds my poems recited everywhere."

Ray **Bradbury** (b. 1920)

Ray Bradbury often travels to the future in his stories, setting them on Mars or Venus. Occasionally, however, he shifts his time-travel machine into reverse and heads for the past. This story, for instance, takes place in Shiloh, Tennessee, on the eve of a great Civil War battle.

Inspiration in the Newspaper Many years ago, Bradbury read the death notice of an actor whose grandfather had been "the drummer boy of Shiloh." This phrase inspired him to write this story. To paint an accurate picture of the setting, he went to a library in Los Angeles before writing and did research on the weather conditions before the Battle of Shiloh.

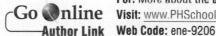

Go Online
Author Link

For: More about the authors
Visit: www.PHSchool.com
Web Code: ene-9206

The Finish of Patsy Barnes

Paul Laurence Dunbar

Background This story takes place in the late nineteenth
century, when medicine was much less advanced than it is today.
There was also a much bigger difference in the quality of
treatment given to rich and poor patients. Patsy Barnes is a boy
who wants to help his sick mother. A poor patient with a serious
illness, like Patsy's mother, fought steep odds against recovery.

His name was Patsy Barnes, and he was a denizen of Little
Africa.[1] In fact, he lived on Douglass Street. By all the laws
governing the relations between people and their names, he
should have been Irish—but he was not. He was colored, and
very much so. That was the reason he lived on Douglass

---

1. **denizen of Little Africa** someone who lives in an area heavily populated by African Americans.

Street. The Negro has very strong within him the instinct of colonization and it was in accordance with this that Patsy's mother had found her way to Little Africa when she had come North from Kentucky.

Patsy was incorrigible.[2] Even into the confines of Little Africa had penetrated the truant officer[3] and the terrible penalty of the <u>compulsory</u> education law. Time and time again had poor Eliza Barnes been brought up on account of the shortcomings of that son of hers. She was a hard-working, honest woman, and day by day bent over her tub, scrubbing away to keep Patsy in shoes and jackets, that would wear out so much faster than they could be bought. But she never murmured, for she loved the boy with a deep affection, though his misdeeds were a sore thorn in her side.

She wanted him to go to school. She wanted him to learn. She had the notion that he might become something better, something higher than she had been. But for him school had no charms; his school was the cool stalls in the big livery stable near at hand; the arena of his pursuits its sawdust floor; the height of his ambition, to be a horseman. Either here or in the racing stables at the Fair-grounds he spent his truant hours. It was a school that taught much, and Patsy was as apt a pupil as he was a constant attendant. He learned strange things about horses, and fine, sonorous oaths that sounded eerie on his young lips, for he had only turned into his fourteenth year.

A man goes where he is appreciated; then could this slim black boy be blamed for doing the same thing? He was a great favorite with the horsemen, and picked up many a dime or nickel for dancing or singing, or even a quarter for warming up a horse for its owner. He was not to be blamed for this, for, first of all, he was born in Kentucky, and had spent the very days of his infancy about the paddocks[4] near Lexington, where his father had sacrificed his life on account of his love for horses. The little fellow had shed no tears when he looked at his father's bleeding body, bruised and broken by the fiery young two-year-old he was trying to subdue. Patsy did not sob or whimper, though his heart

Vocabulary Builder
compulsory (kəm pul´ sə rē) *adj.* required

Literary Analysis
Character What do you learn about Patsy Barnes here?

Reading Check

Where does Patsy spend his time?

---

2. **incorrigible** (in kôr´ ə jə bəl) *adj.* unable to be corrected or improved because of bad habits.
3. **truant** (trōō´ ənt) **officer** *n.* person whose job is to make sure children attend school.
4. **paddocks** (pad´ əks) *n.* enclosed areas near a stable in which horses are exercised.

ached, for over all the feeling of his grief was a mad, burning desire to ride that horse.

His tears were shed, however, when, actuated by the idea that times would be easier up North, they moved to Dalesford. Then, when he learned that he must leave his old friends, the horses and their masters, whom he had known, he wept. The comparatively <u>meager</u> appointments of the Fair-grounds at Dalesford proved a poor compensation for all these. For the first few weeks Patsy had dreams of running away—back to Kentucky and the horses and stables. Then after a while he settled himself with heroic resolution to make the best of what he had, and with a mighty effort took up the burden of life away from his beloved home.

Eliza Barnes, older and more experienced though she was, took up her burden with a less cheerful philosophy than her son. She worked hard, and made a scanty livelihood, it is true, but she did not make the best of what she had. Her complainings were loud in the land, and her wailings for her old home smote the ears of any who would listen to her.

They had been living in Dalesford for a year nearly, when hard work and exposure brought the woman down to bed with pneumonia.[5] They were very poor—too poor even to call in a doctor, so there was nothing to do but to call in the city physician. Now this medical man had too frequent calls into Little Africa, and he did not like to go there. So he was very gruff when any of its denizens called him, and it was even said that he was careless of his patients.

Patsy's heart bled as he heard the doctor talking to his mother:

"Now, there can't be any foolishness about this," he said. "You've got to stay in bed and not get yourself damp."

"How long you think I got to lay hyeah, doctah?" she asked.

"I'm a doctor, not a fortune-teller," was the reply. "You'll lie there as long as the disease holds you."

"But I can't lay hyeah long, doctah, case I ain't got nuffin' to go on."

"Well, take your choice: the bed or the boneyard."

Eliza began to cry.

"You needn't sniffle," said the doctor; "I don't see what you people want to come up here for anyhow. Why don't you stay

---

5. **pneumonia** (nōō mōn´ yə) *n.* potentially deadly infection that causes swelling in the lungs, making it difficult to breathe.

Literary Analysis
Character What is unusual about Patsy's reaction to his father's death?

Vocabulary Builder
meager (mē´ gər) *adj.* lacking in some way; inadequate

Literary Analysis
Character What does this exchange between Eliza and the doctor reveal about the difficulties Patsy and his mother face?

down South where you belong? You come up here and you're just a burden and a trouble to the city. The South deals with all of you better, both in poverty and crime." He knew that these people did not understand him, but he wanted an outlet for the heat within him.

There was another angry being in the room, and that was Patsy. His eyes were full of tears that scorched him and would not fall. The memory of many beautiful and appropriate oaths came to him; but he dared not let his mother hear him swear. Oh! to have a stone—to be across the street from that man!

When the physician walked out, Patsy went to the bed, took his mother's hand, and bent over shamefacedly to kiss her. The little mark of affection comforted Eliza unspeakably. The mother-feeling overwhelmed

Farm Boy, 1941, Charles Alston, Courtesy of Clark Atlanta University

her in one burst of tears. Then she dried her eyes and smiled at him.

"Honey," she said; "mammy ain' gwine lay hyeah long. She be all right putty soon."

"Nevah you min'," said Patsy with a choke in his voice. "I can do somep'n', an' we'll have an othah doctah."

"La, listen at de chile; what kin you do?"

"I'm goin' down to McCarthy's stable and see if I kin git some horses to exercise."

A sad look came into Eliza's eyes as she said: "You'd bettah not go, Patsy; dem hosses'll kill you yit, des lak dey did yo' pappy."

But the boy, used to doing pretty much as he pleased, was obdurate, and even while she was talking, put on his ragged jacket and left the room.

▲ **Critical Viewing**
How might growing up on a farm leave a boy like the one in this painting unprepared for city life? **[Analyze]**

✓**Reading Check**

How does the doctor make Patsy angry?

Patsy was not wise enough to be <u>diplomatic</u>. He went right to the point with McCarthy, the liveryman.

The big red-faced fellow slapped him until he spun round and round. Then he said, "Ye little devil, ye, I've a mind to knock the whole head off o' ye. Ye want harses to exercise, do ye? Well git on that un, 'an' see what ye kin do with him."

The boy's honest desire to be helpful had tickled the big, generous Irishman's peculiar sense of humor, and from now on, instead of giving Patsy a horse to ride now and then as he had formerly done, he put into his charge all the animals that needed exercise.

It was with a king's pride that Patsy marched home with his first considerable earnings.

They were small yet, and would go for food rather than a doctor, but Eliza was inordinately proud, and it was this pride that gave her strength and the desire of life to carry her through the days approaching the crisis of her disease.

As Patsy saw his mother growing worse, saw her gasping for breath, heard the rattling as she drew in the little air that kept going her clogged lungs, felt the heat of her burning hands, and saw the pitiful appeal in her poor eyes, he became convinced that the city doctor was not helping her. She must have another. But the money?

That afternoon, after his work with McCarthy, found him at the Fair-grounds. The spring races were on, and he thought he might get a job warming up the horse of some independent jockey. He hung around the stables, listening to the talk of men he knew and some he had never seen before. Among the latter was a tall, lanky man, holding forth to a group of men.

"No, suh," he was saying to them generally, "I'm goin' to withdraw my hoss, because thaih ain't nobody to ride him as he ought to be rode. I haven't brought a jockey along with me, so I've got to depend on pick-ups. Now, the talent's set again my hoss, Black Boy, because he's been losin' regular, but that hoss has lost for the want of ridin', that's all."

The crowd looked in at the slim-legged, raw-boned horse, and walked away laughing.

"The fools!" muttered the stranger. "If I could ride myself I'd show 'em!"

Patsy was gazing into the stall at the horse.

"What are you doing thaih?" called the owner to him.

Vocabulary Builder
diplomatic (dip′ lə mat′ ik) *adj.* tactful; showing skill in dealing with people

Literary Analysis
Character What challenge does Patsy face as he watches his mother's condition worsen?

Literary Analysis
Character Why might Patsy view Black Boy's owner's remarks as a personal challenge?

"Look hyeah, mistah," said Patsy, "ain't that a bluegrass hoss?"

"Of co'se it is, an' one o' the fastest that evah grazed."

"I'll ride that hoss, mistah."

"What do you know bout ridin'?"

"I used to gin'ally be' roun' Mistah Boone's paddock in Lexington, an'—"

"Aroun' Boone's paddock—what! Look here, if you can ride that hoss to a winnin' I'll give you more money than you ever seen before."

"I'll ride him."

Patsy's heart was beating very wildly beneath his jacket. That horse. He knew that glossy coat. He knew that raw-boned frame and those flashing nostrils. That black horse there owed something to the orphan he had made.

The horse was to ride in the race before the last. Somehow out of odds and ends, his owner scraped together a suit and colors for Patsy. The colors were maroon and green, a curious combination. But then it was a curious horse, a curious rider, and a more curious combination that brought the two together.

Long before the time for the race Patsy went into the stall to become better acquainted with his horse. The animal turned its wild eyes upon him and neighed. He patted the long, slender head, and grinned as the horse stepped aside as gently as a lady.

"He sholy is full o' ginger," he said to the owner, whose name he had found to be Brackett.

"He'll show 'em a thing or two," laughed Brackett.

"His dam[6] was a fast one," said Patsy, unconsciously.

Brackett whirled on him in a flash. "What do you know about his dam?" he asked.

The boy would have retracted, but it was too late. Stammeringly he told the story of his father's death and the horse's connection therewith.

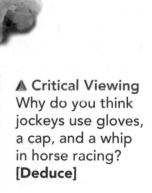

▲ Critical Viewing
Why do you think jockeys use gloves, a cap, and a whip in horse racing? [Deduce]

✔ Reading Check
What unexpected job does Patsy take on?

---

6. **dam** (dam) *n.* mother of a horse.

"Well," said Bracket, "if you don't turn out a hoodoo,[7] you're a winner, sure. But I'll be blessed if this don't sound like a story! But I've heard that story before. The man I got Black Boy from, no matter how I got him, you're too young to understand the ins and outs of poker, told it to me."

When the bell sounded and Patsy went out to warm up, he felt as if he were riding on air. Some of the jockeys laughed at his getup, but there was something in him—or under him, maybe—that made him scorn their derision. He saw a sea of faces about him, then saw no more. Only a shining white track loomed ahead of him, and a restless steed was cantering[8] with him around the curve. Then the bell called him back to the stand.

They did not get away at first, and back they trooped. A second trial was a failure. But at the third they were off in a line as straight as a chalk-mark. There were Essex and Firefly, Queen Bess and Mosquito, galloping away side by side, and Black Boy a neck ahead. Patsy knew the family reputation of his horse for endurance as well as fire, and began riding the race from the first. Black Boy came of blood that would not be passed, and to this his rider trusted. At the eighth the line was hardly broken, but as the quarter was reached Black Boy had forged a length ahead, and Mosquito was at his flank. Then, like a flash, Essex shot out ahead under whip and spur, his jockey standing straight in the stirrups.

The crowd in the stand screamed; but Patsy smiled as he lay low over his horse's neck. He saw that Essex had made his best spurt. His only fear was for Mosquito, who hugged and hugged his flank. They were nearing the three-quarter post, and he was tightening his grip on the black. Essex fell back; his spurt was over. The whip fell unheeded on his sides. The spurs dug him in vain.

Black Boy's breath touches the leader's ear. They are neck and neck—nose to nose. The black stallion passes him.

Another cheer from the stand, and again Patsy smiles as they turn into the stretch. Mosquito has gained a head. The colored boy flashes one glance at the horse and rider who are so surely gaining upon him, and his lips close in a grim line. They are half-way down the stretch, and Mosquito's head is at the stallion's neck.

Literary Analysis
Character In what ways are Black Boy and Patsy well suited for each other as horse and jockey?

---

7. hoodoo (hoo′ doo′) *n.* here, someone or something that causes bad luck.
8. steed (stēd) **was cantering** (kan′ tər iŋ) high-spirited riding horse was running at a smooth, easy pace.

For a single moment Patsy thinks of the sick woman at home and what that race will mean to her, and then his knees close against the horse's sides with a firmer dig. The spurs shoot deeper into the steaming flanks. Black Boy shall win; he must win. The horse that has taken away his father shall give him back his mother. The stallion leaps away like a flash, and goes under the wire—a length ahead.

Then the band thundered, and Patsy was off his horse, very warm and very happy, following his mount to the stable. There, a little later, Brackett found him. He rushed to him, and flung his arms around him.

"You little devil," he cried, "you rode like you were kin to that hoss! We've won! We've won!" And he began sticking banknotes at the boy. At first Patsy's eyes bulged, and then he seized the money and got into his clothes.

"Goin' out to spend it?" asked Brackett.

"I'm goin' for a doctah fu' my mother," said Patsy, "she's sick."

"Don't let me lose sight of you."

"Oh, I'll see you again. So long," said the boy.

An hour later he walked into his mother's room with a very big doctor, the greatest the druggist could direct him to. The doctor left his medicines and his orders, but, when Patsy told his story, it was Eliza's pride that started her on the road to recovery. Patsy did not tell his horse's name.

Literary Analysis
Character What circumstances give Patsy extra motivation to win?

Literary Analysis
Character How have events in the story changed Patsy?

Thinking About the Selection

1. **Respond:** What do you think will happen to Patsy and his mother?

2. **(a) Recall:** Instead of going to school, where does Patsy spend his time? **(b) Infer:** In what way do Patsy's reasons for spending time there change after his mother becomes ill?

3. **(a) Infer:** Why does the doctor speak to Eliza Barnes in an unfeeling way? **(b) Draw Conclusions:** What does this story suggest about the problems faced by Patsy and his mother?

4. **(a) Infer:** Why does Patsy feel compelled to ride Black Boy? **(b) Evaluate:** Is Patsy's decision to ride the wild horse a good one? Why or why not?

5. **Analyze:** How is Patsy's win a victory for both his mother and his father?

Drummer Boy, Julian Scott, N.S. Mayer

The Drummer Boy of Shiloh

Ray Bradbury

Background This story is about a Civil War drummer boy. Although drummer boys accompanied troops into battle, they carried no weapons. There was no age requirement, so some drummer boys were as young as ten. Because few parents were willing to send their young sons to battle, many drummer boys were runaways or orphans.

In the April night, more than once, blossoms fell from the orchard trees and lit with rustling taps on the drumskin. At midnight a peach stone left miraculously on a branch through winter, flicked by a bird, fell swift and unseen, struck once, like panic, which jerked the boy upright. In silence he listened to his own heart ruffle away, away—at last gone from his ears and back in his chest again.

▲ **Critical Viewing**
Which aspects of this drummer boy reflect the information in the Background? **[Connect]**

After that, he turned the drum on its side, where its great lunar face peered at him whenever he opened his eyes.

His face, alert or at rest, was solemn. It was indeed a solemn time and a solemn night for a boy just turned fourteen in the peach field near the Owl Creek not far from the church at Shiloh.

". . . thirty-one, thirty-two, thirty-three . . ."

Unable to see, he stopped counting.

Beyond the thirty-three familiar shadows, forty thousand men, exhausted by nervous expectation, unable to sleep for romantic dreams of battles yet unfought, lay crazily askew in their uniforms. A mile yet farther on, another army was strewn helter-skelter, turning slow, basting themselves with the thought of what they would do when the time came: a leap, a yell, a blind plunge their strategy, raw youth their protection and benediction.[1]

Now and again the boy heard a vast wind come up, that gently stirred the air. But he knew what it was—the army here, the army there, whispering to itself in the dark. Some men talking to others, others murmuring to themselves, and all so quiet it was like a natural element arisen from South or North with the motion of the earth toward dawn.

What the men whispered the boy could only guess, and he guessed that it was: "Me, I'm the one, I'm the one of all the rest who won't die. I'll live through it. I'll go home. The band will play. And I'll be there to hear it."

Yes, thought the boy, that's all very well for them, they can give as good as they get!

For with the careless bones of the young men harvested by night and bindled[2] around campfires were the similarly strewn steel bones of their rifles, with bayonets fixed like eternal lightning lost in the orchard grass.

Me, thought the boy, I got only a drum, two sticks to beat it, and no shield.

There wasn't a man-boy on this ground tonight who did not have a shield he cast, riveted or carved himself on his way to his first attack, compounded[3] of remote but nonetheless firm and fiery family devotion, flag-blown patriotism and cocksure

---

1. **benediction** (ben´ ə dik´ shən) *n.* blessing.
2. **bindled** (bin´ dəld) *adj.* bedded.
3. **compounded** (käm pound´ ed) *adj.* mixed or combined.

Literary Analysis
Character What historical situation affects the boy's mood?

Literary Analysis
Character How do the drummer boy's age and job give him a different perspective than soldiers in modern wars?

Literary Analysis
Character Why is the boy envious of the other soldiers?

✓ **Reading Check**

Why do the soldiers sleep uneasily?

<u>immortality</u> strengthened by the touchstone of very real gun-powder, ramrod, Minié ball[4] and flint. But without these last, the boy felt his family move yet farther off away in the dark, as if one of those great prairie-burning trains had chanted them away never to return—leaving him with this drum which was worse than a toy in the game to be played tomorrow or some day much too soon.

The boy turned on his side. A moth brushed his face, but it was a peach blossom. A peach blossom flicked him, but it was a moth. Nothing stayed put. Nothing had a name. Nothing was as it once was.

If he lay very still, when the dawn came up and the soldiers put on their bravery with their caps, perhaps they might go away, the war with them, and not notice him lying small here, no more than a toy himself.

"Well, now," said a voice.

The boy shut up his eyes, to hide inside himself, but it was too late. Someone, walking by in the night, stood over him.

"Well," said the voice quietly, "here's a soldier cry-ing *before* the fight. Good. Get it over. Won't be time once it all starts."

And the voice was about to move on when the boy, startled, touched the drum at his elbow. The man above, hearing this, stopped.

---

4. Minié (min´ ē) **ball** *n.* cone-shaped rifle bullet that expands when fired.

Vocabulary Builder
immortality (im´ ôr tal´ i tē) *n.* endless life

▼ **Critical Viewing**
Based on his expression, what emotions do you think this young drummer boy is feeling? **[Speculate]**

The boy could feel his eyes, sense him slowly bending near. A hand must have come down out of the night, for there was a little *rat-tat* as the fingernails brushed and the man's breath fanned his face.

"Why, it's the drummer boy, isn't it?"

The boy nodded, not knowing if his nod was seen. "Sir, is that *you*?" he said.

"I assume it is." The man's knees cracked as he bent still closer.

He smelled as all fathers should smell, of salt sweat, ginger tobacco, horse and boot leather, and the earth he walked upon. He had many eyes. No, not eyes—brass buttons that watched the boy.

He could only be, and was, the general.

"What's your name, boy?" he asked.

"Joby," whispered the boy, starting to sit up.

"All right, Joby, don't stir." A hand pressed his chest gently, and the boy relaxed. "How long you been with us, Joby?"

"Three weeks, sir."

"Run off from home or joined <u>legitimately</u>, boy?"

Silence.

"Fool question," said the general. "Do you shave yet, boy? Even more of a fool. There's your cheek, fell right off the tree overhead. And the others here not much older. Raw, raw, the lot of you. You ready for tomorrow or the next day, Joby?"

"I think so, sir."

"You want to cry some more, go on ahead. I did the same last night."

"*You*, sir?"

"It's the truth. Thinking of everything ahead. Both sides figuring the other side will just give up, and soon, and the war done in weeks, and us all home. Well, that's not how it's going to be. And maybe that's why I cried."

"Yes, sir," said Joby.

The general must have taken out a cigar now, for the dark was suddenly filled with the smell of tobacco unlit as yet, but chewed as the man thought what next to say.

"It's going to be a crazy time," said the general. "Counting both sides, there's a hundred thousand men, give or take a few thousand out there tonight, not one as can spit a sparrow

Literary Analysis
Character Why is the general's initial reaction to the boy's tears surprising?

Vocabulary Builder
legitimately (lə jit′ ə mət lē) *adv.* legally; in a way that follows the law

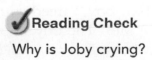
Reading Check

Why is Joby crying?

off a tree, or knows a horse clod from a Minié ball. Stand up, bare the breast, ask to be a target, thank them and sit down, that's us, that's them. We should turn tail and train four months, they should do the same. But here we are, taken with spring fever and thinking it blood lust, taking our sulfur with cannons instead of with molasses, as it should be, going to be a hero, going to live forever. And I can see all of them over there nodding agreement, save the other way around. It's wrong, boy, it's wrong as a head put on hindside front and a man marching backward through life. More innocents will get shot out of pure enthusiasm than ever got shot before. Owl Creek was full of boys splashing around in the noonday sun just a few hours ago. I fear it will be full of boys again, just floating, at sundown tomorrow, not caring where the tide takes them."

The general stopped and made a little pile of winter leaves and twigs in the darkness, as if he might at any moment strike fire to them to see his way through the coming days when the sun might not show its face because of what was happening here and just beyond.

The boy watched the hand stirring the leaves and opened his lips to say something, but did not say it. The general heard the boy's breath and spoke himself.

"Why am I telling you this? That's what you wanted to ask, eh? Well, when you got a bunch of wild horses on a loose rein somewhere, somehow you got to bring order, rein them in. These lads, fresh out of the milk-shed, don't know what I know, and I can't tell them: men actually die, in war. So each is his own army. I got to make *one* army of them. And for that, boy, I need you."

"Me!" The boy's lips barely twitched.

Choosing Sides in the Civil War

Union states

Confederate states

Border states that stayed in the Union

States that joined the Confederacy after April 1861

*West Virginia separated from Virginia in 1861 and was admitted to the Union in 1863.

"Now, boy," said the general quietly, "you are the heart of the army. Think of that. You're the heart of the army. Listen, now."

And, lying there, Joby listened. And the general spoke on.

If he, Joby, beat slow tomorrow, the heart would beat slow in the men. They would lag by the wayside. They would drowse in the fields on their muskets. They would sleep forever, after that, in those same fields—their hearts slowed by a drummer boy and stopped by enemy lead.

But if he beat a sure, steady, ever faster rhythm, then, then their knees would come up in a long line down over that hill, one knee after the other, like a wave on the ocean shore! Had he seen the ocean ever? Seen the waves rolling in like a well-ordered cavalry charge to the sand? Well, that was it, that's what he wanted, that's what was needed! Joby was his right hand and his left. He gave the orders, but Joby set the pace!

So bring the right knee up and the right foot out and the left knee up and the left foot out. One following the other in good time, in brisk time. Move the blood up the body and make the head proud and the spine stiff and the jaw <u>resolute</u>. Focus the eye and set the teeth, flare the nostrils and tighten the hands, put steel armor all over the men, for blood moving fast in them does indeed make men feel as if they'd put on steel. He must keep at it, at it! Long and steady, steady and long! Then, even though shot or torn, those wounds got in hot blood—in blood he'd helped stir—would feel less pain. If their blood was cold, it would be more than slaughter, it would be murderous nightmare and pain best not told and no one to guess.

The general spoke and stopped, letting his breath slack off. Then, after a moment, he said, "So there you are, that's it. Will you do that, boy? Do you know now you're general of the army when the general's left behind?"

The boy nodded mutely.

"You'll run them through for me then, boy?"

"Yes, sir."

"Good. And, maybe, many nights from tonight, many years from now, when you're as old or far much older than me, when they ask you what you did in this awful time, you will tell them—one part humble and one part proud—'I was the drummer boy at the battle of Owl Creek,' or the Tennessee

Literary Analysis
Character What do the general's words reveal about his character?

Vocabulary Builder
resolute (rez´ ə lo͞ot) *adj.* showing a firm purpose; determined

**Reading Check**

According to the general, what is Joby's role in the war?

River, or maybe they'll just name it after the church there. 'I was the drummer boy at Shiloh.' Good grief, that has a beat and sound to it fitting for Mr. Longfellow. 'I was the drummer boy at Shiloh.' Who will ever hear those words and not know you, boy, or what you thought this night, or what you'll think tomorrow or the next day when we must get up on our legs and *move!*"

The general stood up. "Well, then. Bless you, boy. Good night."

"Good night, sir." And tobacco, brass, boot polish, salt sweat and leather, the man moved away through the grass.

Joby lay for a moment, staring but unable to see where the man had gone. He swallowed. He wiped his eyes. He cleared his throat. He settled himself. Then, at last, very slowly and firmly, he turned the drum so that it faced up toward the sky.

He lay next to it, his arm around it, feeling the tremor, the touch, the muted thunder as, all the rest of the April night in the year 1862, near the Tennessee River, not far from the Owl Creek, very close to the church named Shiloh, the peach blossoms fell on the drum.

**Literary Analysis
Character** Why might the general's words appeal to a young boy in the middle of the Civil War?

Thinking About the Selection

1. **Respond:** Do you think Joby should have enlisted as a drummer boy? Why or why not?

2. **(a) Recall:** What frightens Joby about the upcoming battle? **(b) Compare and Contrast:** How are his fears like and unlike those of the other soldiers? **(c) Compare and Contrast:** In what other ways are Joby and the soldiers alike and not alike?

3. **(a) Recall:** What is Joby doing when the general stops to talk to him? **(b) Infer:** Why do you think the general decides to talk to Joby?

4. **(a) Recall:** What does Joby agree to do for the general at the end of the story? **(b) Draw Conclusions:** How do you think Joby feels after his talk with the general? Explain.

5. **Evaluate:** Is the drummer boy's role as crucial as the general says? Explain.

6. **(a) Speculate:** Do you think the general has motivated Joby to keep his promise? Why or why not? **(b) Make a Judgment:** Is the general's request fair or unfair to Joby? Explain.

Apply the Skills

The Finish of Patsy Barnes • The Drummer Boy of Shiloh

Comparing and Contrasting Characters

1. Complete a chart like this one to analyze the characters listed. Explain whether each character is a *static* or a *dynamic* character.

Name	Static or Dynamic	Proof
Patsy Barnes		
the doctor		
Joby		
the general		

2. **(a)** List four historical details involving time and place that have an effect on Patsy Barnes. **(b)** List four historical details involving time and place that have an effect on Joby.

Writing to Compare Literary Works

Compare and contrast the characters of Patsy Barnes and Joby. In an essay, discuss the way the historical settings of the stories determined various aspects of their lives. Use these questions as a guide:

- What outside forces act on the characters?
- How do time and place affect the characters?
- Do the events of each story cause the characters to change?
- How does each character deal with the main conflict?

Vocabulary Builder

Practice Use a vocabulary word from the list on page 280 to rewrite each of the following sentences to mean the opposite.

1. Pam is unsure about trying out for the team.

2. Without a permit, Liz was parked illegally.

3. Uniforms are optional in that private school.

4. Chris's lavish meal was enough for ten people.

5. Some people are unafraid of death.

6. Wendy's tactless comment made Jay feel bad.

QuickReview

Character: a person who takes part in the action of a literary work

Go Online
—Assessment
For: Self-test
Visit: www.PHSchool.com
Web Code: ena-6206

Reading: Comparison and Contrast

Directions: *Questions 1–5 are based on the following selection.*

Alex sighed and tapped his fingers on the library table. "Great," he thought, "I give up my Saturday to teach some loser to read, and he doesn't even show up. How can the middle school force us to do volunteer work anyway? It's not fair."

Just then an older man in greasy overalls rushed toward him. "I am sorry. I just got off work and the bus was late. I am Boris, and you will be my teacher!" he said in excitement. Boris said that he was a car mechanic who had fled to America from a war-torn country to start a new life. "I am a good mechanic, but the cars here are so new. I must learn to read English so I can learn about them and keep my job. Can you help me?"

Alex grinned. If there was one thing he loved and knew about, it was cars. "You bet," he said, leading Boris to a shelf of books about cars.

1. **Which of the following details is correct?**
   A Boris wanted to be at the library.
   B Alex wanted to be at the library.
   C Both characters wanted to be at the library.
   D Neither character wanted to be at the library.

2. **How is Alex's attitude before the meeting different from Boris's?**
   A Alex is scared, but Boris is confident.
   B Alex is confident, but Boris is scared.
   C Alex is resentful, but Boris is excited.
   D Alex is excited, but Boris is resentful.

3. **Which aspects of the description show the greatest contrast between Alex and Boris?**
   A interests and hobbies
   B ages and past experiences
   C intelligence and talent
   D clothing and hairstyles

4. **Which statement accurately describes a way in which Alex and Boris are similar?**
   A They both hate reading.
   B They both hate meeting new people.
   C They both like books.
   D They both like cars.

5. **Which statement most accurately reflects the information in the passage?**
   A There are evident similarities between the characters.
   B There are no similarities that are evident between the characters.
   C It would be difficult to contrast the characters
   D It would be impossible to compare the characters.

Vocabulary Skill Review

Directions: *Choose the answer that best completes the sentence.*

6. To compare and contrast you _____ the details in a story.
   A aspect
   B differentiate
   C examine
   D liken

7. The stereotyped protagonist and antagonist are _____ by their clothing; one wears white and one wears black.
   A simulated
   B differentiated
   C examined
   D speculated

8. Each _____ of the plot contributes to the reader's response to the novel.
   A unique
   B decision
   C climax
   D aspect

9. The two cities in the novel are very different, but the characters are _____.
   A unique
   B similar
   C differentiated
   D unappealing

10. The All-American sports writer presented a _____ perspective on the game.
    A unique
    B similar
    C differentiated
    D unappealing

Directions: *Choose the correct answer to each question.*

11. Which word is closest in meaning to *similar*?
    A alike
    B different
    C simple
    D complicated

12. Which phrase is closest in meaning to *spectacular*?
    A something that is worth looking at
    B someone who questions
    C something that is hard to understand
    D something that is different from others in its group

13. Which phrase is closest in meaning to *differentiate*?
    A find or show characteristics
    B find or show similarities
    C find or show nuances
    D find or show differences

14. Which phrase is closest in meaning to *different*.
    A look like
    B alike
    C not alike
    D look different

15. Which is the correct definition of *simultaneous*?
    A happening at the same time
    B happening one after another
    C happening to different people
    D happening to several people

Response to Literature: Critical Review

If you are uncertain whether you would like the latest blockbuster movie or if you would enjoy reading a recent bestseller, you might turn to a critical review for information and the reviewer's opinion. Follow the steps outlined here to write your own critical review.

Assignment Write a critical review of two or more works of literature that are similar in theme or topic.

What to Include To be effective, your critical review should include the following elements:
- a discussion of two works
- an opinion on the value of each work
- texts to support ideas and make connections
- ideas and arguments that demonstrate independent thinking

To preview the criteria on which your critical review may be judged, see the rubric on page 304.

Prewriting

Choosing Your Topic

Use this strategy to select literature for your critical review:

Browsing Browse this textbook, your own bookshelf, the library, or a bookstore. Take notes in a chart like the one shown.

Story	Author	Idea	Characters	Response
"The Finish of Patsy Barnes"	Paul Laurence Dunbar	How a young boy earns money doing what he loves	Patsy Barnes, his mother, the doctor, McCarthy, Brackett	I admired him.
"The Drummer Boy of Shiloh"	Ray Bradbury	How a young boy finds the courage to do a dangerous job	Joby, the general	It made me wonder what I would do.

Look for works that have enough similarities to be addressed in a single essay. Then, choose at least two works to compare.

Gathering Details

Take notes about the characters, plot, setting, theme, style, purpose, and mood in each literary work. Look for points that will allow you to draw connections among multiple works.

Using the Form

You may use elements of this form in these writing situations:
- critical essays
- writing for assessment
- newspaper reviews
- book reviews

Work in Progress

Review the work you did on pages 215, 249, and 275.

Drafting

Shaping Your Writing

Use a block organization. In an introduction, state your central idea and identify both works. Then, develop your ideas about each work separately. In your conclusion, evaluate each work, noting similarities or differences, and restate your reaction. Follow the outline as shown here.

Providing Elaboration

Find and define your focus. Using your notes, pinpoint the idea that suits both works of literature. Identify your response to these works of literature and the reasons for your response. Be sure that you can support your opinion with specific examples in each text.

Introduction
The Giving Tree and the story of King Midas are both about the unhappy consequences of greed.

The Giving Tree
details that show greed in this story

King Midas
details that show greed in this story

> The student will support her central idea with examples.

Conclusion
Both stories show why people should not be so greedy.

Revising

Revising Your Word Choice

Add reviewer's modifiers. Use precise words to convey praise or criticism. Review your draft, bracketing any modifiers you have used. If you have chosen vague or overused words, replace them with words that more accurately capture your response. Consider these suggestions:

> **Mild Praise:** accurate, intelligent, solid
>
> **High Praise:** brilliant, excellent, entertaining
>
> **Mild Disapproval:** confusing, dull, predictable
>
> **Strong Disapproval:** biased, pointless, misguided

Integrating Grammar Skills

Revising Irregular Verbs

Irregular verbs are verbs whose past and past participle forms do not follow a predictable pattern.

Identifying Irregular Verbs For regular verbs, the past tense is formed by adding *-ed* or *-d* to the present form, as in *smile, smiled*. With an irregular verb, the past and past participle are *not* formed according to this rule.

> **Present Tense:** Carol <u>speaks</u> to the class.
>
> **Past Tense:** Carol <u>spoke</u> to the class.
>
> **Past Participle:** Carol <u>has spoken</u> to the class.

Sometimes, the past and past participles are spelled the same.

> **Present Tense:** Let's <u>bid</u> on this.
>
> **Past Tense:** We <u>bid</u> on it yesterday.
>
> **Past Participle:** I have <u>bid</u> on it every year.

Fixing Faulty Use of Irregular Verbs To fix incorrect use of an irregular verb, first identify the form of the verb that is needed.

1. **If no helping verb is used, use the past tense.**
   Example: Jake <u>wrote</u> a story about space travel.

2. **If a helping verb is used, use the past participle.**
   Example: Jake <u>has written</u> a story about space travel.

3. **Memorize the forms of irregular verbs.** Check a dictionary whenever you are in doubt about the correct form.

Some Irregular Verbs			
Present	**Present Participle**	**Past**	**Past Participle**
bring	(am) bringing	brought	(have) brought
cost	(am) costing	cost	(have) cost
put	(am) putting	put	(have) put

Apply It to Your Editing

Choose two paragraphs in your draft. Underline every verb, and identify it as regular or irregular. Fix any irregular verb used incorrectly.

Prentice Hall Writing and Grammar Connection:
Chapter 22, Section 1

Student Model: Joyce McShane
Clackamas, Oregon

Storybook Greed

A lot of stories are written to teach lessons to readers. Sometimes stories can have different plots, settings, and characters but still have the same message.

Although *The Giving Tree*, by Shel Silverstein, and the story of King Midas are different in many ways, they both share an important theme. Both stories are about the unhappy consequences of greed.

The Giving Tree is the story of a boy who keeps taking pieces of a tree to try to make himself happy. In the beginning of the story, there is an apple tree who loves a little boy. Every day he comes to play with her leaves, climb her trunk, and eat her apples. However, as the boy grows older, other things became more important. From then on, all he wants to do is take things from the tree and use them for his own needs. In the end, when the boy comes back for the last time, he is an old man and the tree has nothing left to give him. Instead of taking something from her, all he does is sit on the tree's stump.

The story of King Midas is also a story about greed. King Midas spares the life of a satyr who is caught sleeping in his royal rose bed, a crime punishable by death. Because King Midas decides to spare the satyr's life, he is granted one wish. Being a greedy man, he immediately wishes for the gift of a golden touch. One day, his beloved daughter comes running up to him and gives him a hug. She is instantly turned to gold and King Midas is heartbroken.

Both of these stories show men who ask for more than they should have. In the end, both men lose the one thing they have loved most. That shows what greed can do. Given another chance, neither character would probably act the same way. However, neither the boy nor King Midas can change the consequences of their actions.

Both stories show why people should not be so greedy. There are some people who could greatly benefit from reading these stories and some whose unselfish attitudes would be reinforced. The tales of King Midas and of *The Giving Tree* are important and everyone should read them and learn from them.

In this paragraph, Joyce introduces both works and their common theme.

Joyce summarizes both works, offers details from the text, and explains how each one connects to the theme of greed.

In her conclusion, Joyce offers an opinion on the value of each work that reflects independent thought.

Writing Workshop

Editing and Proofreading

Reread your work, correcting errors in grammar, spelling, and mechanics.

Focus on Verbs: Look at all the verbs in your writing to correct any errors in verb tense. Pay particular attention to irregular verbs. Use the grammar lesson on page 302 as an editing reference.

Publishing and Presenting

Consider one of the following ways to share your writing with classmates or a larger audience:

Present a book talk. Use your critical review as the basis for an informal oral presentation.

Publish a "Teens Review" column. Contact a local newspaper and arrange for your work to be part of a series of critical reviews by young people.

Reflecting on Your Writing

Writer's Journal Jot down your thoughts on writing a critical review. Begin by answering these questions:

- Which of the strategies or activities did you find most useful? Why?
- As you drafted and revised, what insights came to you concerning your strengths as a writer?

Prentice Hall Writing and Grammar Connection: Chapter 12

Rubric for Self-Assessment

To assess your critical review, use the following rubric.

Criteria	Rating Scale
	not very — very
Focus: How clearly is your opinion stated?	1 2 3 4 5
Organization: How logically is the support for your opinion organized?	1 2 3 4 5
Support/Elaboration: How well are texts used to support ideas and connections?	1 2 3 4 5
Style: How well do you demonstrate independent thinking?	1 2 3 4 5
Conventions: How correct is your grammar, especially your use of irregular verbs?	1 2 3 4 5

Skills You Will Learn

Reading Skill: *Use Details to Make Inferences*
Literary Analysis: *Point of View*

Reading Skill: *Make Inferences to Determine Meaning*
Literary Analysis: *Theme*

Reading Skill: *Recognize Appeals to Emotion*

Literary Analysis: *Comparing Symbols*

Literature You Will Read

Reading: Make Inferences

> When you **make inferences,** you use the information in a text to make logical assumptions about information that is not stated.

Skills and Strategies You Will Learn in Part 2
In Part 2, you will learn

- to **use details** in a story as clues, or evidence, to **infer** unstated information (p. 308)
- to **identify connections** in a story to **make inferences about the author's meaning** (p. 354)
- to **recognize emotional appeals** and define their connection to the **author's meaning** (p. 374)

Using the Skills and Strategies in Part 2
Details give you the basis to infer information that is not stated. For example, an author may not tell you directly how a character is feeling. Instead, the author may give clues by describing what a character says and does. In the same way, an author may not directly state his or her message or theme. You can make inferences about the message based on events and outcomes that are directly stated.

The following chart shows how you can use details in a story to make inferences.

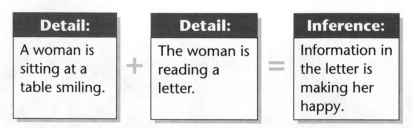

Detail:		Detail:		Inference:
A woman is sitting at a table smiling.	+	The woman is reading a letter.	=	Information in the letter is making her happy.

▶**Connections:** People smile when they are happy.

The woman is smiling *while* she is reading the letter.

Academic Vocabulary: Words for Discussing Inferences in Literature

You can use the following words to talk and write about the inferences you make as you read the literature in this part.

Word	Definition	Example Sentence
logical *adj.*	reasonable; sensible	A *logical* assumption is an inference.
indicate *v.*	to show; to hint at	The author used a mountain setting to *indicate* the character's isolation.
conclude *v.*	to decide by reasoning	What can you *conclude* from the details in the story?
evidence *n.*	facts that serve as clues or proof	The character's calm reaction to stress was *evidence* of her inner strength.
infer *v.*	to draw conclusions based on facts	You can *infer* that the protagonist is very smart.

Vocabulary Skill: Word Origins

▶ A **word's origin** is its earliest form and meaning.

In Part 2, you will learn the origins of the words
- logical (p. 352)   • indicate (p. 372)   • conclusion (p. 372)

As English speakers of the past came into contact with other languages through travel, exploration, and war, new words made their way into the English language. Over time, pronunciations changed and meanings adapted to fit new situations.

evidence (ev′ ə dens′) **n.** [[ME < OFr < L < *evidentia* < *evidens*, clear < *e-*, from + *videns*, prp. < *videre*, to see]]

The word *evidence* came into modern English from Middle English. *Evidence* was taken by Middle English from Old French and Old French had borrowed the word from Latin.

Activity Look up the following words in a dictionary that shows word origins. In your own words, explain each word's origin including the original language and meaning.

pretzel   sushi   broil
bagel   tuna   butter

These skills will help you become a better reader. Practice them with either "Flowers for Algernon" (p. 310) or "Charles" (p. 345).

Reading Skill

When you **make inferences**, you look at the information the author provides to make logical assumptions about what the author leaves unstated. As you read, think like a detective connecting clues to solve a crime. To make inferences, **use details** that the author provides as clues. Notice details like these:

- what the characters say about one another
- what the characters do and how they behave

The chart shows how you can use details to reveal unstated information.

Detail	Possible Inference
An actor at an audition compliments the director's past work.	The actor thinks flattery might get him a part.
A waitress is careless and rude.	She does not take pride in her job.
A toddler breaks his toy.	He is upset.

Literary Analysis

Point of view is the perspective from which a story is told. Most stories are told from a first-person or from a third-person point of view.

- **First person:** The narrator participates in the action of the story and can tell only what he or she sees, knows, thinks, or feels. This kind of narrator uses the pronoun *I* when speaking about himself or herself.
- **Third person:** The narrator is not a character in the story, but tells events from the "outside." This kind of narrator uses pronouns such as *he, she,* and *they* to describe all the characters.

Vocabulary Builder

Flowers for Algernon

- **refute** (ri fyo͞ot´) *v.* give evidence to prove an argument or statement false (p. 331) *He presented facts the lawyer could not refute.*

- **obscure** (əb skyo͞or´) *v.* conceal or hide (p. 335) *On mountain roads, fog can obscure the road.*

- **introspective** (in´ trō spek´ tiv) *adj.* inward looking; thoughtful (p. 337) *Introspective people keep diaries of their ideas.*

Charles

- **renounced** (ri nounsd´) *v.* gave up (p. 345) *Bill renounced eating meat and became a vegetarian.*

- **simultaneously** (sī məl tā´ nē əs lē) *adv.* at the same time (p. 347) *It is not safe to drive and to dial a cellphone simultaneously.*

- **incredulously** (in krej´ o͞o ləs lē) *adv.* with doubt or disbelief (p. 348) *"Are you sure?" he asked incredulously.*

Build Understanding • *Flowers for Algernon*

Background

Intelligence Testing Charlie Gordon, the main character in "Flowers for Algernon," undergoes surgery to improve his intelligence. In the story, his doctors measure his progress with I.Q., or *intelligence quotient,* tests. These tests were once widely used to measure intelligence and learning ability. Researchers now recognize that one test cannot accurately measure a person's range of abilities.

Connecting to the Literature

Reading/Writing Connection In "Flowers for Algernon," Charlie Gordon takes a huge risk and subjects himself to a brand-new medical procedure because he wants to "be like other people." Before you read, write a paragraph about why a character might want to fit in or be accepted. Use at least three of the following words: *identify, interact, isolate, participate, perceive.*

Meet the Author

Daniel **Keyes** (b. 1927)

Raised in Brooklyn, New York, writer and teacher Daniel Keyes has also been a photographer, a merchant seaman, and an editor. Keyes is fascinated by unusual psychological conditions. His book *The Milligan Wars* is about a man with multiple-personality disorder.

Inspiration for the Story A meeting with a mentally-disabled man gave Keyes the idea for "Flowers for Algernon." He began to wonder what would happen "if it were possible to increase human intelligence artificially."

Fast Facts

▶ "Flowers for Algernon," Keyes's best-known story, won the Hugo Award of the Science Fiction Writers of America in 1959.
▶ Cliff Robertson won an Academy Award for his portrayal of the title character in the film adaptation *Charly* (1968).

Go **O**nline
Author Link

For: More about the author
Visit: www.PHSchool.com
Web Code: ene-9208

Flowers for Algernon

Daniel Keyes

progris riport 1—martch 5 1965

Dr. Strauss says I shud rite down what I think and evrey thing that happins to me from now on. I dont know why but he says its importint so they will see if they will use me. I hope they use me. Miss Kinnian says maybe they can make me smart. I want to be smart. My name is Charlie Gordon. I am 37 years old and 2 weeks ago was my brithday. I have nuthing more to rite now so I will close for today.

progris riport 2—martch 6

I had a test today. I think I faled it. and I think that maybe now they wont use me. What happind is a nice young man was in the room and he had some white cards with ink spillled all over them. He sed Charlie what do you see on this card. I was very skared even tho I had my rabits foot in my pockit because when I was a kid I always faled tests in school and I spillled ink to.

I told him I saw a inkblot. He said yes and it made me feel good. I thot that was all but when I got up to go he stopped me. He said now sit down Charlie we are not thru yet. Then I dont remember so good but he wantid me to say what was in the ink. I dint see nuthing in the ink but he said there was picturs there other pepul saw somc picturs. I coudnt see any picturs. I rccly tryed to see. I held the card close up and then far away. Then I said if I had my glases I coud see better I usally only ware my glases in the movies or TV but I said they are in the closit in the hall. I got them. Then I said let me see that card agen I bet Ill find it now.

I tryed hard but I still coudnt find

the picturs I only saw the ink. I told him maybe I need new glases. He rote somthing down on a paper and I got skared of faling the test. I told him it was a very nice inkblot with littel points all around the eges. He looked very sad so that wasnt it. I said please let me try agen. Ill get it in a few minits becaus Im not so fast somtimes. Im a slow reeder too in Miss Kinnians class for slow adults but I'm trying very hard.

He gave me a chance with another card that had 2 kinds of ink spilled on it red and blue.

He was very nice and talked slow like Miss Kinnian does and he explained it to me that it was a *raw shok*.[1] He said pepul see things in the ink. I said show me where. He said think. I told him I think a inkblot but that wasnt rite eather. He said what does it remind you—pretend somthing. I closd my eyes for a long time to pretend. I told him I pretned a fowntan pen with ink leeking all over a table cloth. Then he got up and went out.

I dont think I passd the *raw shok* test.

progris report 3—martch 7

Dr Strauss and Dr Nemur say it dont matter about the inkblots. I told them I dint spill the ink on the cards and I coudnt see anything in the ink. They said that maybe they will still use me. I said Miss Kinnian never gave me tests like that one only spelling and reading. They said Miss Kinnian told that I was her bestist pupil in the adult nite scool becaus I tryed the hardist and I reely wantid to lern. They said how come you went to the adult nite scool all by yourself Charlie. How did you find it. I said I askd pepul and sumbody told me where I shud go to lern to read and spell good. They said why did you want to. I told them becaus all my life I wantid to be smart

---

1. *raw shok* misspelling of Rorschach (rôr´ shäk´) test, a psychological test that requires a subject to describe inkblots.

Reading Check

What type of a test do the doctors give Charlie?

and not dumb. But its very hard to be smart. They said you know it will probly be tempirery. I said yes. Miss Kinnian told me. I dont care if it herts.

Later I had more crazy tests today. The nice lady who gave it me told me the name and I asked her how do you spellit so I can rite it in my progris riport. THEMATIC APPERCEPTION TEST.[2] I dont know the frist 2 words but I know what *test* means. You got to pass it or you get bad marks. This test lookd easy becaus I coud see the picturs. Only this time she dint want me to tell her the picturs. That mixd me up. I said the man yesterday said I shoud tell him what I saw in the ink she said that dont make no difrence. She said make up storys about the pepul in the picturs.

I told her how can you tell storys about pepul you never met. I said why shud I make up lies. I never tell lies any more becaus I always get caut.

She told me this test and the other one the raw-shok was for getting personalty. I laffed so hard. I said how can you get that thing from inkblots and fotos. She got sore and put her picturs away. I dont care. It was sily. I gess I faled that test too.

Later some men in white coats took me to a difernt part of the hospitil and gave me a game to play. It was like a race with a white mouse. They called the mouse Algernon. Algernon was in a box with a lot of twists and turns like all kinds of walls and they gave me a pencil and a paper with lines and lots of boxes. On one side it said START and on the other end it said FINISH. They said it was *amazed*[3] and that Algernon and me had the same *amazed* to do. I dint see how we could have the same *amazed* if Algernon had a box and I had a paper but I dint say nothing. Anyway there wasnt time because the race started.

One of the men had a watch he was trying to hide so I woudnt see it so I tryed not to look and that made me nervus.

Anyway that test made me feel worser than all the others because they did it over 10 times with difernt *amazeds* and Algernon won every time. I dint know that mice were so smart. Maybe thats because Algernon is a white mouse. Maybe white mice are smarter than other mice.

Reading Skill
Make Inferences
What does Charlie's failure to understand the tests reveal about his personality and abilities?

Literary Analysis
Point of View What does the first-person point of view show about Charlie's experience with the doctors?

---

2. THEMATIC (thē mat´ ik) **APPERCEPTION** (ap´ ər sep´ shən) **TEST** personality test in which the subject makes up stories about a series of pictures.

3. amazed Charlie means "a maze," or confusing series of paths. Often, the intelligence of animals is assessed by how fast they go through a maze.

Test Inventors

Three pioneers of intelligence and behavioral testing devised tests that are still used to this day.

◀ In the early twentieth century, Swiss psychologist **Hermann Rorschach** developed a test in which the subject describes what an inkblot looks like. Psychologists use the subject's responses to make interpretations about mental condition and personality.

◀ Rorschach inkblot

▲

In 1905, **Alfred Binet**, above left, and Theodore Simon devised a system for testing intelligence based on standardized, average mental levels for various age groups. In 1916, **Lewis Terman**, above right, reworked the test, which became known as the Revised Stanford-Binet Intelligence Test. One question from an intelligence test is shown above.

Connect to the Literature What do you imagine Charlie's first reaction to the Rorschach inkblots reveals?

---

progris riport 4—Mar 8

Their going to use me! Im so exited I can hardly write. Dr Nemur and Dr Strauss had a argament about it first. Dr Nemur was in the office when Dr Strauss brot me in. Dr Nemur was worryed about using me but Dr Strauss told him Miss Kinnian rekemmended me the best from all the pepul who she was teaching. I like Miss Kinnian becaus shes a very smart teacher. And she said Charlie your going to have a second chance. If you volenteer for this experament you mite get smart. They dont know if it will be perminint but theirs a chance. Thats why I said ok even when I was scared because she said it was an operashun. She said dont be scared Charlie you done so much with so little I think you deserv it most of all.

So I got scaird when Dr Nemur and Dr Strauss argud about it. Dr Strauss said I had something that was very good. He said I had a good *motor-vation*.[4] I never even knew I had that.

✓ Reading Check

What makes Charlie excited on March 8?

---

4. ***motor-vation*** motivation, or desire to work hard and achieve a goal.

I felt proud when he said that not every body with an *eye-q*[5] of 68 had that thing. I dont know what it is or where I got it but he said Algernon had it too. Algernons *motor-vation* is the cheese they put in his box. But it cant be that because I didnt eat any cheese this week.

Then he told Dr Nemur something I dint understand so while they were talking I wrote down some of the words.

He said Dr Nemur I know Charlie is not what you had in mind as the first of your new brede of intelek** (coudnt get the word) superman. But most people of his low ment** are host** and uncoop** they are usualy dull apath** and hard to reach. He has a good natcher hes intristed and eager to please.

Dr Nemur said remember he will be the first human beeng ever to have his intelijence trippled by surgicle meens.

Dr Strauss said exakly. Look at how well hes lerned to read and write for his low mentel age its as grate an acheve** as you and I lerning einstines therey of **vity without help. That shows the intenss motorvation. Its comparat** a tremen** achev** I say we use Charlie.

I dint get all the words and they were talking to fast but it sounded like Dr Strauss was on my side and like the other one wasnt.

Then Dr Nemur nodded he said all right maybe your right. We will use Charlie. When he said that I got so exited I jumped up and shook his hand for being so good to me. I told him thank you doc you wont be sorry for giving me a second chance. And I mean it like I told him. After the operashun Im gonna try to be smart. Im gonna try awful hard.

progris ript 5—Mar 10

Im skared. Lots of people who work here and the nurses and the people who gave me the tests came to bring me candy and wish me luck. I hope I have luck. I got my rabits foot and

5. *eye-q* IQ, or intelligence quotient. A way of measuring human intelligence.

▲ Critical Viewing Based on the photograph from the movie, what makes Charlie and Algernon similar and different? **[Compare and Contrast]**

Reading Skill
Make Inferences
What details show the way Dr. Strauss feels about Charlie?

my lucky penny and my horse shoe. Only a black cat crossed me when I was comming to the hospitil. Dr Strauss says dont be supersitis Charlie this is sience. Anyway Im keeping my rabits foot with me.

I asked Dr Strauss if Ill beat Algernon in the race after the operashun and he said maybe. If the operashun works Ill show that mouse I can be as smart as he is. Maybe smarter. Then Ill be abel to read better and spell the words good and know lots of things and be like other people. I want to be smart like other people. If it works perminint they will make everybody smart all over the wurld.

They dint give me anything to eat this morning. I dont know what that eating has to do with getting smart. Im very hungry and Dr Nemur took away my box of candy. That Dr Nemur is a grouch. Dr Strauss says I can have it back after the operashun. You cant eat befor a operashun . . .

Progress Report 6—Mar 15

The operashun dint hurt. He did it while I was sleeping. They took off the bandijis from my eyes and my head today so I can make a PROGRESS REPORT. Dr Nemur who looked at some of my other ones says I spell PROGRESS wrong and he told me how to spell it and REPORT too. I got to try and remember that.

I have a very bad memary for spelling. Dr Strauss says its ok to tell about all the things that happin to me but he says I shoud tell more about what I feel and what I think. When I told him I dont know how to think he said try. All the time when the bandijis were on my eyes I tryed to think. Nothing happened. I dont know what to think about. Maybe if I ask him he will tell me how I can think now that Im suppose to get smart. What do smart people think about. Fancy things I suppose. I wish I knew some fancy things alredy.

Progress Report 7—Mar 19

Nothing is happining. I had lots of tests and different kinds of races with Algernon. I hate that mouse. He always beats me. Dr Strauss said I got to play those games. And he said some time I got to take those tests over again. Thse inkblots are stupid. And those pictures are stupid too. I like to draw a picture of a man and a woman but I wont make up lies about people.

Literary Analysis
Point of View What feelings does the point of view reveal?

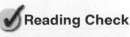

Reading Check

Why does Charlie want to beat Algernon in the race?

I got a headache from trying to think so much. I thot Dr Strauss was my frend but he dont help me. He dont tell me what to think or when Ill get smart. Miss Kinnian dint come to see me. I think writing these progress reports are stupid too.

Progress Report 8—Mar 23

Im going back to work at the factery. They said it was better I shud go back to work but I cant tell anyone what the operashun was for and I have to come to the hospitil for an hour evry night after work. They are gonna pay me mony every month for lerning to be smart.

Im glad Im going back to work because I miss my job and all my frends and all the fun we have there.

Dr Strauss says I shud keep writing things down but I dont have to do it every day just when I think of something or something speshul happins. He says dont get discoridged because it takes time and it happins slow. He says it took a long time with Algernon before he got 3 times smarter then he was before. Thats why Algernon beats me all the time because he had that operashun too. That makes me feel better. I coud probly do that *amazed* faster than a reglar mouse. Maybe some day Ill beat Algernon. Boy that would be something. So far Algernon looks like he mite be smart perminent.

Reading Skill
Make Inferences
Which words in Progress Report 7 indicate Charlie's state of mind after the operation?

Mar 25 (I dont have to write PROGRESS REPORT on top any more just when I hand it in once a week for Dr Nemur to read. I just have to put the date on. That saves time)

We had a lot of fun at the factery today. Joe Carp said hey look where Charlie had his operashun what did they do Charlie put some brains in. I was going to tell him but I remembered Dr Strauss said no. Then Frank Reilly said what did you do Charlie forget your key and open your door the hard way. That made me laff. Their really my friends and they like me.

Sometimes somebody will say hey look at Joe or Frank or George he really pulled a Charlie Gordon. I dont know why they say that but they always laff. This morning Amos Borg who is the 4 man at Donnegans used my name when he shouted at Ernie the office boy. Ernie lost a packige. He said Ernie what are you trying to be a Charlie Gordon. I dont understand why he said that. I never lost any packiges.

Mar 28 Dr Straus came to my room tonight to see why I dint come in like I was suppose to. I told him I dont like to race with Algernon any more. He said I dont have to for a while but I shud come in. He had a present for me only it wasnt a present but just for lend. I thot it was a little television but it wasnt. He said I got to turn it on when I go to sleep. I said your kidding why shud I turn it on when Im going to sleep. Who ever herd of a thing like that. But he said if I want to get smart I got to do what he says. I told him I dint think I was going to get smart and he put his hand on my sholder and said Charlie you dont know it yet but your getting smarter all the time. You wont notice for a while. I think he was just being nice to make me feel good because I dont look any smarter.

Oh yes I almost forgot. I asked him when I can go back to the class at Miss Kinnians school. He said I wont go their. He said that soon Miss Kinnian will come to the hospitil to start and teach me speshul. I was mad at her for not comming to see me when I got the operashun but I like her so maybe we will be frends again.

Reading Skill
Make Inferences
What do Charlie's friends mean when they say someone "pulled a Charlie Gordon"?

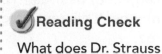
Reading Check

What does Dr. Strauss give to Charlie?

◄ Critical Viewing What details in this photograph show that Charlie is the student and Miss Kinnian is the teacher? **[Analyze]**

Mar 29 That crazy TV kept me up all night. How can I sleep with something yelling crazy things all night in my ears. And the nutty pictures. Wow. I dont know what it says when Im up so how am I going to know when Im sleeping.

Dr Strauss says its ok. He says my brains are lerning when I sleep and that will help me when Miss Kinnian starts my lessons in the hospitl only I found out it isnt a hospitil its a labatory. I think its all crazy. If you can get smart when your sleeping why do people go to school. That thing I dont think will work. I use to watch the late show and the late late show on TV all the time and it never made me smart. Maybe you have to sleep while you watch it.

PROGRESS REPORT 9—APRIL 3

Dr Strauss showed me how to keep the TV turned low so now I can sleep. I don't hear a thing. And I still dont understand what it says. A few times I play it over in the morning to find out what I lerned when I was sleeping and I dont think so. Miss Kinnian says Maybe its another langwidge or something. But most times it sounds american. It talks so fast faster then even Miss Gold who was my teacher in 6 grade and I remember she talked so fast I coudnt understand her.

I told Dr Strauss what good is it to get smart in my sleep. I want to be smart when Im awake. He says its the same thing and I have two minds. Theres the *subconscious* and the *conscious* (thats how you spell it). And one dont tell the other one what its doing. They dont even talk to each other. Thats why I dream. And boy have I been having crazy dreams. Wow. Ever since that night TV. The late late late late late show.

I forgot to ask him if it was only me or if everybody had those two minds.

(I just looked up the word in the dictionary Dr Strauss gave me. The word is *subconscious.* adj. *Of the nature of mental operations yet not present in consciousness; as, subconscious conflict of desires.*) There's more but I still dont know what it means. This isnt a very good dictionary for dumb people like me.

Anyway the headache is from the party. My frends from the factery Joe Carp and Frank Reilly invited me to go with them to Muggsys Saloon for some drinks. I dont like to drink but they said we will have lots of fun. I had a good time.

Reading Skill
Make Inferences
From Charlie's description of the TV, what do you think the device does?

Literary Analysis
Point of View What changes, if any, can you see in Charlie's level of thought so far? Explain.

Joe Carp said I shoud show the girls how I mop out the toilet in the factory and he got me a mop. I showed them and everyone laffed when I told that Mr Donnegan said I was the best janiter he ever had because I like my job and do it good and never come late or miss a day except for my operashun.

I said Miss Kinnian always said Charlie be proud of your job because you do it good.

Everybody laffed and we had a good time and they gave me lots of drinks and Joe said Charlie is a card when hes potted. I dont know what that means but everybody likes me and we have fun. I cant wait to be smart like my best frends Joe Carp and Frank Reilly.

I dont remember how the party was over but I think I went out to buy a newspaper and coffe for Joe and Frank and when I came back there was no one their. I looked for them all over till late. Then I dont remember so good but I think I got sleepy or sick. A nice cop brot me back home. Thats what my land-lady Mrs Flynn says.

But I got a headache and a big lump on my head and black and blue all over. I think maybe I fell. Anyway I got a bad headache and Im sick and hurt all over. I dont think Ill drink anymore.

April 6   I beat Algernon! I dint even know I beat him until Burt the tester told me. Then the second time I lost because I got so exited I fell off the chair before I finished. But after that I beat him 8 more times. I must be getting smart to beat a smart mouse like Algernon. But I dont *feel* smarter.

I wanted to race Algernon some more but Burt said thats enough for one day. They let me hold him for a minit. Hes not so bad. Hes soft like a ball of cotton. He blinks and when he opens his eyes their black and pink on the eges.

I said can I feed him because I felt bad to beat him and I wanted to be nice and make frends. Burt said no Algernon is a very specshul mouse with an operashun like mine, and he was the first of all the animals to stay smart so long. He told

Reading Check

What happens at the party to make people laugh?

me Algernon is so smart that every day he has to solve a test to get his food. Its a thing like a lock on a door that changes every time Algernon goes in to eat so he has to lern something new to get his food. That made me sad because if he coudnt lern he woud be hungry.

I dont think its right to make you pass a test to eat. How woud Dr Nemur like it to have to pass a test every time he wants to eat. I think Ill be frends with Algernon.

▲ Critical Viewing
What impression of Charlie do you get from this photograph? [Infer]

April 9   Tonight after work Miss Kinnian was at the laboratory. She looked like she was glad to see me but scared. I told her dont worry Miss Kinnian Im not smart yet and she laffed. She said I have confidence in you Charlie the way you struggled so hard to read and right better than all the others. At werst you will have it for a littel wile and your doing something for sience.

We are reading a very hard book. I never read such a hard book before. Its called *Robinson Crusoe*[6] about a man who gets merooned on a dessert Iland. Hes smart and figers out all kinds of things so he can have a house and food and hes a good swimmer. Only I feel sorry because hes all alone and has no frends. But I think their must be somebody else on the iland because theres a picture with his funny umbrella looking at footprints. I hope he gets a frend and not be lonly.

April 10   Miss Kinnian teaches me to spell better. She says look at a word and close your eyes and say it over and over until you remember. I have lots of truble with *through* that you say *threw* and *enough* and tough that you dont say *enew* and *tew*. You got to say *enuff* and *tuff*. Thats how I use to write it before I started to get smart. Im confused but Miss Kinnian says theres no reason in spelling.

April 14   Finished Robinson Crusoe. I want to find out more about what happens to him but Miss Kinnian says thats all there is. *Why*

Literary Analysis
Point of View What do you learn about Charlie in this paragraph that you might not know if it were written in the third person?

---

6. *Robinson Crusoe* (kro͞o´ sō) novel written in 1719 by Daniel Defoe, a British author.

April 15   Miss Kinnian says Im lerning fast. She read some of the Progress Reports and she looked at me kind of funny. She says Im a fine person and Ill show them all. I asked her why. She said never mind but I shoudnt feel bad if I find out that everybody isnt nice like I think. She said for a person who god gave so little to you done more then a lot of people with brains they never even used. I said all my frends are smart people but there good. They like me and they never did anything that wasnt nice. Then she got something in her eye and she had to run out to the ladys room.

April 16   Today, I lerned, the comma, this is a comma (,) a period, with a tail, Miss Kinnian, says its importent, because, it makes writing, better, she said, somebody, coud lose, a lot of money, if a comma, isnt, in the, right place, I dont have, any money, and I dont see, how a comma, keeps you, from losing it,
   But she says, everybody, uses commas, so Ill use, them too,

April 17   I used the comma wrong. Its punctuation. Miss Kinnian told me to look up long words in the dictionary to lern to spell them. I said whats the difference if you can read it anyway. She said its part of your education so now on Ill look up all the words Im not sure how to spell. It takes a long time to write that way but I think Im remembering. I only have to look up once and after that I get it right. Anyway thats how come I got the word *punctuation* right. (Its that way in the dictionary). Miss Kinnian says a period is punctuation too, and there are lots of other marks to lern. I told her I thot all the periods had to have tails but she said no.
   You got to mix them up, she showed? me" how. to mix! them(up,. and now; I can! mix up all kinds" of punctuation, in! my writing? There, are lots! of rules? to lern; but Im get-tin'g them in my head.
   One thing I? like about, Dear Miss Kinnian: (thats the way it goes in a business letter if I ever go into business) is she, always gives me' a reason" when—I ask. She's a gen'ius! I wish! I cou'd be smart" like, her;
   (Punctuation, is; fun!)

April 18   What a dope I am! I didn't even understand what she was talking about. I read the grammar book last

Reading Skill
Make Inferences
What can you infer about Miss Kinnian's personality, based on this entry?

Reading Check

What types of things is Charlie learning from Miss Kinnian?

night and it explanes the whole thing. Then I saw it was the same way as Miss Kinnian was trying to tell me, but I didn't get it. I got up in the middle of the night, and the whole thing straightened out in my mind.

Miss Kinnian said that the TV working in my sleep helped out. She said I reached a plateau. Thats like the flat top of a hill.

After I figgered out how punctuation worked, I read over all my old Progress Reports from the beginning. Boy, did I have crazy spelling and punctuation! I told Miss Kinnian I ought to go over the pages and fix all the mistakes but she said, "No, Charlie, Dr. Nemur wants them just as they are. That's why he let you keep them after they were photostated, to see your own progress. You're coming along fast, Charlie."

That made me feel good. After the lesson I went down and played with Algernon. We don't race any more.

April 20   I feel sick inside. Not sick like for a doctor, but inside my chest it feels empty like getting punched and a heartburn at the same time.

I wasn't going to write about it, but I guess I got to, because its important. Today was the first time I ever stayed home from work.

Last night Joe Carp and Frank Reilly invited me to a party. There were lots of girls and some men from the factory. I remembered how sick I got last time I drank too much, so I told Joe I didn't want anything to drink. He gave me a plain coke instead. It tasted funny, but I thought it was just a bad taste in my mouth.

We had a lot of fun for a while. Joe said I should dance with Ellen and she would teach me the steps. I fell a few times and I couldn't understand why because no one else was dancing besides Ellen and me. And all the time I was tripping because somebody's foot was always sticking out.

Then when I got up I saw the look on Joe's face and it gave me a funny feeling in my stomack. "He's a scream," one of the girls said. Everybody was laughing.

Frank said, "I ain't laughed so much since we sent him off for the newspaper that night at Muggsy's and ditched him."

"Look at him. His face is red."

"He's blushing. Charlie is blushing."

Reading Skill
Make Inferences
What details in the April 18 entry show that Charlie's level of thought has increased?

Reading Skill
Make Inferences Is Joe a true friend to Charlie? Explain.

"Hey, Ellen, what'd you do to Charlie? I never saw him act like that before."

I didn't know what to do or where to turn. Everyone was looking at me and laughing and I felt naked. I wanted to hide myself. I ran out into the street and I threw up. Then I walked home. It's a funny thing I never knew that Joe and Frank and the others liked to have me around all the time to make fun of me.

Now I know what it means when they say "to pull a Charlie Gordon."

I'm ashamed.

PROGRESS REPORT II

April 21   Still didn't go into the factory. I told Mrs. Flynn my landlady to call and tell Mr. Donnegan I was sick. Mrs. Flynn looks at me very funny lately like she's scared of me.

I think it's a good thing about finding out how everybody laughs at me. I thought about it a lot. It's because I'm so dumb and I don't even know when I'm doing something dumb. People think it's funny when a dumb person can't do things the same way they can.

Anyway, now I know I'm getting smarter every day. I know punctuation and I can spell good. I like to look up all the hard words in the dictionary and I remember them. I'm reading a lot now, and Miss Kinnian says I read very fast. Sometimes I even understand what I'm reading about, and it stays in my mind. There are times when I can close my eyes and think of a page and it all comes back like a picture.

Besides history, geography and arithmetic, Miss Kinnian said I should start to learn a few foreign languages. Dr. Strauss gave me some more tapes to play while I sleep. I still don't understand how that conscious and unconscious mind works, but Dr. Strauss says not to worry yet. He asked me to promise that when I start learning college subjects next week I wouldn't read any books on psychology—that is, until he gives me permission.

I feel a lot better today, but I guess I'm still a little angry that all the time people were laughing and making fun of me because I wasn't so smart. When I become intelligent like Dr. Strauss says, with three times my I.Q. of 68, then maybe I'll be like everyone else and people will like me and be friendly.

Literary Analysis
Point of View How does the use of first-person point of view help you to sympathize with Charlie?

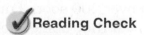**Reading Check**

How does Charlie respond to his early journal entries?

◀ **Critical Viewing**
Does Charlie seem to
have made progress,
judging from the
details in this
photograph? Explain.
[Infer]

I'm not sure what an I.Q. is. Dr. Nemur said it was something that measured how intelligent you were—like a scale in
the drugstore weighs pounds. But Dr. Strauss had a big
arguement with him and said an I.Q. didn't weigh intelligence
at all. He said an I.Q. showed how much intelligence you
could get, like the numbers on the outside of a measuring
cup. You still had to fill the cup up with stuff.

Then when I asked Burt, who gives me my intelligence tests
and works with Algernon, he said that both of them were
wrong (only I had to promise not to tell them he said so). Burt
says that the I.Q. measures a lot of different things including
some of the things you learned already, and it really isn't any
good at all.

So I still don't know what I.Q. is except that mine is going to
be over 200 soon. I didn't want to say anything, but I don't see
how if they don't know *what* it is, or *where* it is—I don't see
how they know *how much* of it you've got.

Dr. Nemur says I have to take a *Rorshach Test* tomorrow. I
wonder what *that* is.

Reading Skill
Make Inferences
How does Charlie's
description of the
argument show he
now thinks more
complex thoughts?

April 22   I found out what a *Rorshach* is. It's the test I took before the operation—the one with the inkblots on the pieces of cardboard. The man who gave me the test was the same one.

I was scared to death of those inkblots. I knew he was going to ask me to find the pictures and I knew I wouldn't be able to. I was thinking to myself, if only there was some way of knowing what kind of pictures were hidden there. Maybe there weren't any pictures at all. Maybe it was just a trick to see if I was dumb enough too look for something that wasn't there. Just thinking about that made me sore at him.

"All right, Charlie," he said, "you've seen these cards before, remember?"

"Of course I remember."

The way I said it, he knew I was angry, and he looked surprised. "Yes, of course. Now I want you to look at this one. What might this be? What do you see on this card? People see all sorts of things in these inkblots. Tell me what it might be for you—what it makes you think of."

I was shocked. That wasn't what I had expected him to say at all. "You mean there are no pictures hidden in those inkblots?"

He frowned and took off his glasses. "What?"

"Pictures. Hidden in the inkblots. Last time you told me that everyone could see them and you wanted me to find them too."

He explained to me that the last time he had used almost the exact same words he was using now. I didn't believe it, and I still have the suspicion that he misled me at the time just for the fun of it. Unless—I don't know any more—could I have been *that* feeble-minded?

We went through the cards slowly. One of them looked like a pair of bats tugging at some thing. Another one looked like two men fencing with swords. I imagined all sorts of things. I guess I got carried away. But I didn't trust him any more, and I kept turning them around and even looking on the back to see if there was anything there I was supposed to catch. While he was making his notes, I peeked out of the corner of my eye to read it. But it was all in code that looked like this:

$$WF + A \; DdF\text{-}Ad \; orig. \; WF\text{-}\Lambda$$
$$SF + obj$$

Literary Analysis
Point of View How does the first-person point of view help you to keep track of Charlie's development?

**Reading Check**

What surprises Charlie about the Rorschach test?

The test still doesn't make sense to me. It seems to me that anyone could make up lies about things that they didn't really see. How could he know I wasn't making a fool of him by mentioning things that I didn't really imagine? Maybe I'll understand it when Dr. Strauss lets me read up on psychology.

April 25   I figured out a new way to line up the machines in the factory, and Mr. Donnegan says it will save him ten thousand dollars a year in labor and increased production. He gave me a $25 bonus.

I wanted to take Joe Carp and Frank Reilly out to lunch to celebrate, but Joe said he had to buy some things for his wife, and Frank said he was meeting his cousin for lunch. I guess it'll take a little time for them to get used to the changes in me. Everybody seems to be frightened of me. When I went over to Amos Borg and tapped him on the shoulder, he jumped up in the air.

People don't talk to me much any more or kid around the way they used to. It makes the job kind of lonely.

April 27   I got up the nerve today to ask Miss Kinnian to have dinner with me tomorrow night to celebrate my bonus.

At first she wasn't sure it was right, but I asked Dr. Strauss and he said it was okay. Dr. Strauss and Dr. Nemur don't seem to be getting along so well. They're arguing all the time. This evening when I came in to ask Dr. Strauss about having dinner with Miss Kinnian, I heard them shouting. Dr. Nemur was saying that it was *his* experiment and his research, and Dr. Strauss was shouting back that he contributed just as much, because he found me through Miss Kinnian and he performed the operation. Dr. Strauss said that someday thousands of neurosurgeons[7] might be using his technique all over the world.

 Dr. Nemur wanted to publish the results of the experiment at the end of this month. Dr. Strauss wanted to wait a while longer to be sure. Dr. Strauss said that Dr. Nemur was more interested in the Chair[8] of Psychology at Princeton than he

Reading Skill
Make Inferences
Why do Charlie's co-workers behave differently toward him?

---

7. neurosurgeons (nŏŏr´ ō sur´ jənz) *n.* doctors who operate on the nervous system, including the brain and spine.
8. chair *n.* professorship.

was in the experiment. Dr. Nemur said that Dr. Strauss was nothing but an opportunist who was trying to ride to glory on *his* coattails.

When I left afterwards, I found myself trembling. I don't know why for sure, but it was as if I'd seen both men clearly for the first time. I remember hearing Burt say that Dr. Nemur had a shrew of a wife who was pushing him all the time to get things published so that he could become famous. Burt said that the dream of her life was to have a big shot husband.

Was Dr. Strauss really trying to ride on his coattails?

April 28   I don't understand why I never noticed how beautiful Miss Kinnian really is. She has brown eyes and feathery brown hair that comes to the top of her neck. She's only thirty-four! I think from the beginning I had the feeling that she was an unreachable genius—and very, very old. Now, every time I see her she grows younger and more lovely.

We had dinner and a long talk. When she said that I was coming along so fast that soon I'd be leaving her behind, I laughed.

"It's true, Charlie. You're already a better reader than I am. You can read a whole page at a glance while I can take in only a few lines at a time. And you remember every single thing you read. I'm lucky if I can recall the main thoughts and the general meaning."

"I don't feel intelligent. There are so many things I don't understand."

"You've got to be a *little* patient. You're accomplishing in days and weeks what it takes normal people to do in half a lifetime. That's what makes it so amazing. You're like a giant sponge now, soaking things in. Facts, figures, general knowledge. And soon you'll begin to connect them, too. You'll see how the different branches of learning are related. There are many levels, Charlie, like steps on a giant ladder that take you up higher and higher to see more and more of the world around you.

"I can see only a little bit of that, Charlie, and I won't go much higher than I am now, but you'll keep climbing up and up, and see more and more, and each step will open new worlds that you never even knew existed." She frowned. "I hope . . . I just hope to God—"

"What?"

Literary Analysis
Point of View
Compare this entry to Progress Report 3 on pages 311 and 312. Which words and phrases show Charlie has changed?

Reading Check

How are Charlie's feelings toward Miss Kinnian changing?

"Never mind, Charles. I just hope I wasn't wrong to advise you to go into this in the first place."

I laughed. "How could that be? It worked, didn't it? Even Algernon is still smart."

We sat there silently for a while and I knew what she was thinking about as she watched me toying with the chain of my rabbit's foot and my keys. I didn't want to think of that possibility any more than elderly people want to think of death. I *knew* that this was only the beginning. I knew what she meant about levels because I'd seen some of them already. The thought of leaving her behind made me sad.

I'm in love with Miss Kinnian.

PROGRESS REPORT 12

April 30   I've quit my job with Donnegan's Plastic Box Company. Mr. Donnegan insisted that it would be better for all concerned if I left. What did I do to make them hate me so?

The first I knew of it was when Mr. Donnegan showed me the petition. Eight hundred and forty names, everyone connected with the factory, except Fanny Girden. Scanning the list quickly, I saw at once that hers was the only missing name. All the rest demanded that I be fired.

Joe Carp and Frank Reilly wouldn't talk to me about it. No one else would either, except Fanny. She was one of the few people I'd known who set her mind to something and believed it no matter what the rest of the world proved, said or did—and Fanny did not believe that I should have been fired. She had been against the petition on principle and despite the pressure and threats she'd held out.

"Which don't mean to say," she remarked, "that I don't think there's something mighty strange about you, Charlie. Them changes. I don't know. You used to be a good, dependable, ordinary man—not too bright maybe, but honest. Who knows what you done to yourself to get so smart all of a sudden. Like everybody around here's been saying, Charlie, it's not right."

"But how can you say that, Fanny? What's wrong with a man becoming intelligent and wanting to acquire knowledge and understanding of the world around him?"

She stared down at her work, and I turned to leave. Without looking at me, she said: "It was evil when Eve listened to the

▶ Critical Viewing
What details reveal that Charlie has increased intelligence? [Analyze]

Reading Skill
Make Inferences
Why do you think Charlie's co-workers signed the petition to have him fired?

snake and ate from the tree of knowledge. It was evil when she saw that she was naked. If not for that none of us would ever have to grow old and sick, and die."

Once again now I have the feeling of shame burning inside me. This intelligence has driven a wedge between me and all the people I once knew and loved. Before, they laughed at me and despised me for my ignorance and dullness; now, they hate me for my knowledge and understanding. What do they want of me?

They've driven me out of the factory. Now I'm more alone than ever before . . .

May 15   Dr. Strauss is very angry at me for not having written any progress reports in two weeks. He's justified because the lab is now paying me a regular salary. I told him I was too busy thinking and reading. When I pointed out that writing was such a slow process that it made me impatient with my poor handwriting, he suggested that I learn to type. It's much easier to write now because I can type nearly seventy-five words a minute. Dr. Strauss continually reminds

Reading Skill
Make Inferences
What comparison is Fanny making between Charlie and Eve?

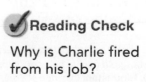 **Reading Check**

Why is Charlie fired from his job?

me of the need to speak and write simply so that people will be able to understand me.

I'll try to review all the things that happened to me during the last two weeks. Algernon and I were presented to the American Psychological Association sitting in convention with the World Psychological Association last Tuesday. We created quite a sensation. Dr. Nemur and Dr. Strauss were proud of us.

I suspect that Dr. Nemur, who is sixty—ten years older than Dr. Strauss—finds it necessary to see tangible[9] results of his work. Undoubtedly the result of pressure by Mrs. Nemur.

Contrary to my earlier impressions of him, I realize that Dr. Nemur is not at all a genius. He has a very good mind, but it struggles under the specter of self-doubt. He wants people to take him for a genius. Therefore, it is important for him to feel that his work is accepted by the world. I believe that Dr. Nemur was afraid of further delay because he worried that someone else might make a discovery along these lines and take the credit from him.

Dr. Strauss on the other hand might be called a genius, although I feel that his areas of knowledge are too limited. He was educated in the tradition of narrow specialization; the broader aspects of background were neglected far more than necessary—even for a neurosurgeon.

Literary Analysis
Point of View What details here show you Charlie's increased intelligence?

I was shocked to learn that the only ancient languages he could read were Latin, Greek and Hebrew, and that he knows almost nothing of mathematics beyond the elementary levels of the calculus of variations. When he admitted this to me, I found myself almost annoyed. It was as if he'd hidden this part of himself in order to deceive me, pretending—as do many people I've discovered—to be what he is not. No one I've ever known is what he appears to be on the surface.

Dr. Nemur appears to be uncomfortable around me. Sometimes when I try to talk to him, he just looks at me strangely and turns away. I was angry at first when Dr. Strauss told me I was giving Dr. Nemur an inferiority complex. I thought he was mocking me and I'm oversensitive at being made fun of.

How was I to know that a highly respected psychoexperimentalist like Nemur was unacquainted with Hindustani[10]

---

9. **tangible** (tan´ jə bəl) *adj.* substantial; easily understood.
10. **Hindustani** (hin´ dōō stä´ nē) *n.* a language of northern India.

and Chinese? It's absurd when you consider the work that is being done in India and China today in the very field of his study.

I asked Dr. Strauss how Nemur could <u>refute</u> Rahajamati's attack on his method and results if Nemur couldn't even read them in the first place. That strange look on Dr. Strauss' face can mean only one of two things. Either he doesn't want to tell Nemur what they're saying in India, or else—and this worries me—Dr. Strauss doesn't know either. I must be careful to speak and write clearly and simply so that people won't laugh.

May 18   I am very disturbed. I saw Miss Kinnian last night for the first time in over a week. I tried to avoid all discussions of intellectual concepts and to keep the conversation on a simple, everyday level, but she just stared at me blankly and asked me what I meant about the mathematical variance equivalent in Dorbermann's *Fifth Concerto.*

When I tried to explain she stopped me and laughed. I guess I got angry, but I suspect I'm approaching her on the wrong level. No matter what I try to discuss with her, I am unable to communicate. I must review Vrostadt's equations on *Levels of Semantic Progression.* I find that I don't communicate with people much any more. Thank God for books and music and things I can think about. I am alone in my apartment at Mrs. Flynn's boarding house most of the time and seldom speak to anyone.

May 20   I would not have noticed the new dishwasher, a boy of about sixteen, at the corner diner where I take my evening meals if not for the incident of the broken dishes.

They crashed to the floor, shattering and sending bits of white china under the tables. The boy stood there, dazed and frightened, holding the empty tray in his hand. The whistles and catcalls from the customers (the cries of "hey, there go the profits!" . . . "*Mazeltov!*" . . . and "well, he didn't work here very long . . ." which invariably seems to follow the breaking of glass or dishware in a public restaurant) all seemed to confuse him.

When the owner came to see what the excitement was about, the boy cowered as if he expected to be struck and threw up his arms as if to ward off the blow.

Vocabulary Builder
refute (ri fyo͞ot´) *v.*
give evidence to prove an argument or statement false

Literary Analysis
Point of View How would the May 18 entry be different if it were told from Miss Kinnian's point of view?

Reading Check

What makes Charlie angry with Miss Kinnian?

"All right! All right, you dope," shouted the owner, "don't just stand there! Get the broom and sweep that mess up. A broom . . . a broom, you idiot! It's in the kitchen. Sweep up all the pieces."

The boy saw that he was not going to be punished. His frightened expression disappeared and he smiled and hummed as he came back with the broom to sweep the floor. A few of the rowdier customers kept up the remarks, amusing themselves at his expense.

"Here, sonny, over here there's a nice piece behind you . . ."

"C'mon, do it again . . ."

"He's not so dumb. It's easier to break 'em than to wash 'em . . ."

As his vacant eyes moved across the crowd of amused onlookers, he slowly mirrored their smiles and finally broke into an uncertain grin at the joke which he obviously did not understand.

I felt sick inside as I looked at his dull, vacuous smile, the wide, bright eyes of a child, uncertain but eager to please. They were laughing at him because he was mentally retarded.

And I had been laughing at him too.

Suddenly, I was furious at myself and all those who were smirking at him. I jumped up and shouted, "Shut up! Leave him alone! It's not his fault he can't understand! He can't help what he is! But . . . he's still a human being!"

The room grew silent. I cursed myself for losing control and creating a scene. I tried not to look at the boy as I paid my check and walked out without touching my food. I felt ashamed for both of us.

How strange it is that people of honest feelings and sensibility, who would not take advantage of a man born without arms or legs or eyes—how such people think nothing of abusing a man born with low intelligence. It infuriated me to think that not too long ago I, like this boy, had foolishly played the clown.

And I had almost forgotten.

I'd hidden the picture of the old Charlie Gordon from myself because now that I was intelligent it was something that had to be pushed out of my mind. But today in looking at that boy, for the first time I saw what I had been. *I was just like him!*

Literary Analysis
Point of View How does Charlie now see himself?

Only a short time ago, I learned that people laughed at me. Now I can see that unknowingly I joined with them in laughing at myself. That hurts most of all.

I have often reread my progress reports and seen the illiteracy, the childish naïvete,[11] the mind of low intelligence peering from a dark room, through the keyhole, at the dazzling light outside. I see that even in my dullness I knew that I was inferior, and that other people had something I lacked—something denied me. In my mental blindness, I thought that it was somehow connected with the ability to read and write, and I was sure that if I could get those skills I would automatically have intelligence too.

Even a feeble-minded man wants to be like other men.

A child may not know how to feed itself, or what to eat, yet it knows of hunger.

This then is what I was like. I never knew. Even with my gift of intellectual awareness, I never really knew.

This day was good for me. Seeing the past more clearly, I have decided to use my knowledge and skills to work in the field of increasing human intelligence levels. Who is better equipped for this work? Who else has lived in both worlds? These are my people. Let me use my gift to do something for them.

Tomorrow, I will discuss with Dr. Strauss the manner in which I can work in this area. I may be able to help him work out the problems of widespread use of the technique which was used on me. I have several good ideas of my own.

There is so much that might be done with this technique. If I could be made into a genius, what about thousands of others like myself? What fantastic levels might be achieved by using this technique on normal people? On *geniuses?*

There are so many doors to open. I am impatient to begin.

PROGRESS REPORT 13

May 23   It happened today. Algernon bit me. I visited the lab to see him as I do occasionally, and when I took him out of his cage, he snapped at my hand. I put him back and watched him for a while. He was unusually disturbed and vicious.

---

11. naïvete (nä ēv tā´) *n.* simplicity.

**Literary Analysis
Point of View** What has Charlie learned about himself?

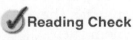
Reading Check

What new line of work does Charlie want to pursue?

May 24 Burt, who is in charge of the experimental animals, tells me that Algernon is changing. He is less cooperative; he refuses to run the maze any more; general motivation has decreased. And he hasn't been eating. Everyone is upset about what this may mean.

May 25 They've been feeding Algernon, who now refuses to work the shifting-lock problem. Everyone identifies me with Algernon. In a way we're both the first of our kind. They're all pretending that Algernon's behavior is not necessarily significant for me. But it's hard to hide the fact that some of the other animals who were used in this experiment are showing strange behavior.

Dr. Strauss and Dr. Nemur have asked me not to come to the lab any more. I know what they're thinking but I can't accept it. I am going ahead with my plans to carry their research forward. With all due respect to both of these fine scientists, I am well aware of their limitations. If there is an answer, I'll have to find it out for myself. Suddenly, time has become very important to me.

May 29 I have been given a lab of my own and permission to go ahead with the research. I'm on to something. Working day and night. I've had a cot moved into the lab. Most of my writing time is spent on the notes which I keep in a separate folder, but from time to time I feel it necessary to put down my moods and my thoughts out of sheer habit.

I find the *calculus of intelligence* to be a fascinating study. Here is the place for the application of all the knowledge I have acquired. In a sense it's the problem I've been concerned with all my life.

May 31   Dr. Strauss thinks I'm working too hard. Dr. Nemur says I'm trying to cram a lifetime of research and thought into a few weeks. I know I should rest, but I'm driven on by something inside that won't let me stop. I've got to find the reason for the sharp regression in Algernon. I've got to know *if* and *when* it will happen to me.

June 4

Letter to Dr. Strauss (copy)

Dear Dr. Strauss:

Under separate cover I am sending you a copy of my report entitled, "The Algernon-Gordon Effect: A Study of Structure and Function of Increased Intelligence," which I would like to have you read and have published.

As you see, my experiments are completed. I have included in my report all of my formulae, as well as mathematical analysis in the appendix. Of course, these should be verified.

Because of its importance to both you and Dr. Nemur (and need I say to myself, too?) I have checked and rechecked my results a dozen times in the hope of finding an error. I am sorry to say the results must stand. Yet for the sake of science, I am grateful for the little bit that I here add to the knowledge of the function of the human mind and of the laws governing the artificial increase of human intelligence.

I recall your once saying to me that an experimental *failure* or the *disproving* of a theory was as important to the advancement of learning as a success would be. I know now that this is true. I am sorry, however, that my own contribution to the field must rest upon the ashes of the work of two men I regard so highly.

Yours truly,
Charles Gordon

encl.: rept.

June 5   I must not become emotional. The facts and the results of my experiments are clear, and the more sensational aspects of my own rapid climb cannot <u>obscure</u> the fact that the tripling of intelligence by the surgical technique developed by Drs. Strauss and Nemur must be viewed as having little or no practical applicability (at the present time) to the increase of human intelligence.

Reading Skill
Make Inferences
What aspects of this letter show that Charlie is as smart as the doctors?

Vocabulary Builder
obscure (əb skyoor´)
v. conceal or hide

Reading Check

What does Charlie want to learn through his research?

As I review the records and data on Algernon, I see that although he is still in his physical infancy, he has regressed mentally. Motor activity[12] is impaired; there is a general reduction of glandular activity; there is an accelerated loss of coordination.

There are also strong indications of progressive amnesia.

As will be seen by my report, these and other physical and mental deterioration syndromes[13] can be predicted with statistically significant results by the application of my formula.

The surgical stimulus to which we were both subjected has resulted in an intensification and acceleration of all mental processes. The unforeseen development, which I have taken the liberty of calling the "Algernon-Gordon Effect," is the logical extension of the entire intelligence speedup. The hypothesis here proven may be described simply in the following terms: Artificially increased intelligence deteriorates at a rate of time directly proportional to the quantity of the increase.

I feel that this, in itself, is an important discovery.

As long as I am able to write, I will continue to record my thoughts in these progress reports. It is one of my few pleasures. However, by all indications, my own mental deterioration will be very rapid.

I have already begun to notice signs of emotional instability and forgetfulness, the first symptoms of the burnout.

June 10 Deterioration progressing. I have become absent-minded. Algernon died two days ago. Dissection shows my predictions were right. His brain had decreased in weight and there was a general smoothing out of cerebral convolutions as well as a deepening and broadening of brain fissures.

I guess the same thing is or will soon be happening to me. Now that it's definite, I don't want it to happen.

I put Algernon's body in a cheese box and buried him in the back yard. I cried.

June 15 Dr. Strauss came to see me again. I wouldn't open the door and I told him to go away. I want to be left to myself. I have become touchy and irritable. I feel the

Literary Analysis
Point of View How does the point of view make the changes Charlie is experiencing more dramatic?

---

12. motor activity movement; physical coordination.
13. syndromes (sin´ drōmz´) *n.* a number of symptoms occurring together and characterizing a specific disease or condition.

darkness closing in. I keep telling myself how important this <u>introspective</u> journal will be.

It's a strange sensation to pick up a book that you've read and enjoyed just a few months ago and discover that you don't remember it. I remembered how great I thought John Milton[14] was, but when I picked up *Paradise Lost* I couldn't understand it at all. I got so angry I threw the book across the room.

I've got to try to hold on to some of it. Some of the things I've learned. Oh, God, please don't take it all away.

June 19   Sometimes, at night, I go out for a walk. Last night I couldn't remember where I lived. A policeman took me home. I have the strange feeling that this has all happened to me before—a long time ago. I keep telling myself I'm the only person in the world who can describe what's happening to me.

June 21   Why can't I remember? I've got to fight. I lie in bed for days and I don't know who or where I am. Then it all comes back to me in a flash. Fugues of amnesia.[15] Symptoms of senility—second childhood. I can watch them coming on. It's so cruelly logical. I learned so much and so fast. Now my mind is deteriorating rapidly. I won't let it happen. I'll fight it. I can't help thinking of the boy in the restaurant, the blank expression, the silly smile, the people laughing at him. No—please—not that again . . .

June 22   I'm forgetting things that I learned recently. It seems to be following the classic pattern—the last things learned are the first things forgotten. Or is that the pattern? I'd better look it up again . . .

I reread my paper on the "Algernon-Gordon Effect" and I get the strange feeling that it was written by someone else. There are parts I don't even understand.

Motor activity impaired. I keep tripping over things, and it becomes increasingly difficult to type.

June 23   I've given up using the typewriter completely. My coordination is bad. I feel that I'm moving slower and

Vocabulary Builder
introspective (in´ trō
spek´ tiv) *adj.* inward
looking; thoughtful

Reading Check

What are some signs that Charlie's mental state is rapidly reversing?

---

14. **John Milton** British poet (1608–1674) who wrote *Paradise Lost*.
15. **fugues** (fyo͞ogz) **of amnesia** (am nē´ zhe) *n.* periods of loss of memory.

slower. Had a terrible shock today. I picked up a copy of an article I used in my research, Krueger's "Uber psychische Ganzheit," to see if it would help me understand what I had done. First I thought there was something wrong with my eyes. Then I realized I could no longer read German. I tested myself in other languages. All gone.

June 30   A week since I dared to write again. It's slipping away like sand through my fingers. Most of the books I have are too hard for me now. I get angry with them because I know that I read and understood them just a few weeks ago.

I keep telling myself I must keep writing these reports so that somebody will know what is happening to me. But it gets harder to form the words and remember spellings. I have to look up even simple words in the dictionary now and it makes me impatient with myself.

Dr. Strauss comes around almost every day, but I told him I wouldn't see or speak to anybody. He feels guilty. They all do. But I don't blame anyone. I knew what might happen. But how it hurts.

July 7   I don't know where the week went. Todays Sunday I know because I can see through my window people going to church. I think I stayed in bed all week but I remember Mrs. Flynn bringing food to me a few times. I keep saying over and over Ive got to do something but then I forget or maybe its just easier not to do what I say Im going to do.

I think of my mother and father a lot these days. I found a picture of them with me taken at a beach. My father has a big ball under his arm and my mother is holding me by the hand. I dont remember them the way they are in the picture. All I remember is my father arguing with mom about money.

He never shaved much and he used to scratch my face when he hugged me. He said he was going to take me to see cows on a farm once but he never did. He never kept his promises . . .

July 10   My landlady Mrs Flynn is very worried

▼ **Critical Viewing**
Why would Charlie be reluctant to go back to this job?
[Connect]

about me. She said she doesnt like loafers. If Im sick its one thing, but if Im a loafer thats another thing and she wont have it. I told her I think Im sick.

I try to read a little bit every day, mostly stories, but sometimes I have to read the same thing over and over again because I dont know what it means. And its hard to write. I know I should look up all the words in the dictionary but its so hard and Im so tired all the time.

Then I got the idea that I would only use the easy words instead of the long hard ones. That saves time. I put flowers on Algernons grave about once a week. Mrs. Flynn thinks Im crazy to put flowers on a mouses grave but I told her that Algernon was special.

July 14   Its sunday again. I dont have anything to do to keep me busy now because my television set is broke and I dont have any money to get it fixed. (I think I lost this months check from the lab. I dont remember)

I get awful headaches and asperin doesnt help me much. Mrs. Flynn knows Im really sick and she feels very sorry for me. Shes a wonderful woman whenever someone is sick.

July 22   Mrs. Flynn called a strange doctor to see me. She was afraid I was going to die. I told the doctor I wasnt too sick and that I only forget sometimes. He asked me did I have any friends or relatives and I said no I dont have any. I told him I had a friend called Algernon once but he was a mouse and we used to run races together. He looked at me kind of funny like he thought I was crazy.

He smiled when I told him I used to be a genius. He talked to me like I was a baby and he winked at Mrs Flynn. I got mad and chased him out because he was making fun of me the way they all used to.

July 24   I have no more money and Mrs Flynn says I got to go to work somewhere and pay the rent because I havent paid for over two months. I dont know any work but the job I used to have at Donnegans Plastic Box Company. I dont want to go back there because they all knew me when I was smart and maybe they'll laugh at me. But I dont know what else to do to get money.

Reading Skill
Make Inferences
What does Charlie's style of writing reveal?

Literary Analysis
Point of View How does the first-person point of view help you to understand Charlie's experience?

**Reading Check**

How does the doctor anger Charlie?

July 25 I was looking at some of my old progress reports and its very funny but I cant read what I wrote. I can make out some of the words but they dont make sense.

Miss Kinnian came to the door but I said go away I dont want to see you. She cried and I cried too but I wouldnt let her in because I didnt want her to laugh at me. I told her I didn't like her any more. I told her I didn't want to be smart any more. Thats not true. I still love her and I still want to be smart but I had to say that so shed go away. She gave Mrs. Flynn money to pay the rent. I dont want that. I got to get a job.

Please . . . please let me not forget how to read and write . . .

July 27 Mr. Donnegan was very nice when I came back and asked him for my old job of janitor. First he was very suspicious but I told him what happened to me then he looked very sad and put his hand on my shoulder and said Charlie Gordon you got guts.

Everybody looked at me when I came downstairs and started working in the toilet sweeping it out like I used to. I told myself Charlie if they make fun of you dont get sore because you remember their not so smart as you once thot they were. And besides they were once your friends and if they laughed at you that doesnt mean anything because they liked you too.

One of the new men who came to work there after I went away made a nasty crack he said hey Charlie I hear your a very smart fella a real quiz kid. Say something intelligent. I felt bad but Joe Carp came over and grabbed him by the shirt and said leave him alone or Ill break your neck. I didnt expect Joe to take my part so I guess hes really my friend.

Later Frank Reilly came over and said Charlie if anybody bothers you or trys to take advantage you call me or Joe and we will set em straight. I said thanks Frank and I got choked up so I had to turn around and go into the supply room so he wouldnt see me cry. Its good to have friends.

July 28 I did a dumb thing today I forgot I wasnt in Miss Kinnians class at the adult center any more like I use to be. I went in and sat down in my old seat in the back of the room and she looked at me funny and she said Charles. I dint remember she ever called me that before only Charlie so I said

**Literary Analysis
Point of View** How has Charlie's view of his co-workers changed?

hello Miss Kinnian Im ready for my lesin today only I lost my reader that we was using. She startid to cry and run out of the room and everybody looked at me and I saw they wasnt the same pepul who use to be in my class.

Then all of a suddin I rememberd some things about the operashun and me getting smart and I said holy smoke I reely pulled a Charlie Gordon that time. I went away before she come back to the room.

Thats why Im going away from New York for good. I dont want to do nothing like that agen. I dont want Miss Kinnian to feel sorry for me. Evry body feels sorry at the factery and I dont want that eather so Im going someplace where nobody knows that Charlie Gordon was once a genus and now he cant even reed a book or rite good.

Im taking a cuple of books along and even if I cant reed them Ill practise hard and maybe I wont forget every thing I lerned. If I try reel hard maybe Ill be a littel bit smarter then I was before the operashun. I got my rabits foot and my luky penny and maybe they will help me.

If you ever reed this Miss Kinnian dont be sorry for me Im glad I got a second chanse to be smart becaus I lerned a lot of things that I never even new were in this world and Im grateful that I saw it all for a littel bit. I dont know why Im dumb agen or what I did wrong maybe its becaus I dint try hard enuff. But if I try and practis very hard maybe Ill get a littl smarter and know what all the words are. I remember a littel bit how nice I had a feeling with the blue book that has the torn cover when I red it. Thats why Im gonna keep trying to get smart so I can have that feeling agen. Its a good feeling to know things and be smart. I wish I had it rite now if I did I woud sit down and reed all the time. Anyway I bet Im the first dumb person in the world who ever found out somthing important for sience. I remember I did somthing but I dont remember what. So I gess its like I did it for all the dumb pepul like me.

Goodbye Miss Kinnian and Dr Strauss and evreybody. And P.S. please tell Dr Nemur not to be such a grouch when pepul laff at him and he woud have more frends. Its easy to make frends if you let pepul laff at you. Im going to have lots of frends where I go.

P.P.S. Please if you get a chanse put some flowrs on Algernons grave in the bak yard . . .

Literary Analysis
Point of View What thoughts and emotions drive Charlie to leave New York?

Reading Skill
Make Inferences Based on his writing, do you think Charlie will be able to regain his intelligence?

Apply the Skills

Flowers for Algernon

Thinking About the Selection

1. **Respond:** Was being part of the experiment good for Charlie? Why or why not?
2. **(a) Recall:** Who is Algernon? **(b) Compare:** Explain how changes in Charlie are similar to those in Algernon.
3. **(a) Analyze:** When do you realize that Charlie's intelligence is not permanent? **(b) Apply:** What two details from the story reveal the progress of the reversal?
4. **(a) Contrast:** What is the difference between Charlie at the beginning of the story and Charlie at the end of the story? **(b) Predict:** What will happen to Charlie? How do you know?
5. **(a) Take a Position:** Do you think Charlie should have had the operation? Why or why not? **(b) Discuss:** Share your response with a small group. Then, discuss your responses.

Reading Skill

6. **(a)** What are three ways in which Charlie's attitudes toward Dr. Strauss and Dr. Nemur change after his operation? **(b)** Use these details to make an **inference** about how the operation affects Charlie.
7. What inferences can you make about Miss Kinnian from the way she treats Charlie? In your answer, consider her attitude toward Charlie's co-workers, her relationship with Charlie, and her reaction to the changes in Charlie.

Literary Analysis

8. This first-person story is told from Charlie's **point of view**. Complete a chart like the one shown to decide how the story would be different if it were told from another point of view.

Charlie	Dr. Strauss
Charlie does not understand the purpose of the inkblot test.	
Charlie does not understand why he keeps a journal. He does anyway.	

9. How do the journal entries, written in Charlie's own words, illustrate the changes in his intelligence?

Story at a Glance
A man has a risky operation to increase his intelligence.

Go Online
Assessment
For: Self-test
Visit: www.PHSchool.com
Web Code: ena-6207

Inferences: Logical assumptions about what is not stated

Point of View: The perspective from which a story is told. A story can be told in the *first-person* or the *third-person point of view.*

Vocabulary Builder

Practice **Analogies** show the relationships between words. Use a word from the "Flowers for Algernon" vocabulary list on page 308 to create a word pair that matches the relationship between the first two words given.

1. *Accept* is to *reject* as *support* is to _____.
2. *Create* is to *destroy* as *reveal* is to _____.
3. *Anxious* is to *worried* as *thoughtful* is to _____.

Writing

Write **dialogue** for a movie scene that you adapt from "Flowers for Algernon."

- First, choose a scene to expand by imagining details and parts of conversations that the author left out.
- Then, write the dialogue, using words and behavior that seem natural for each character. The finished dialogue should convey the uniqueness and motivations of each person.

For *Grammar, Vocabulary,* and *Assessment,*
see **Build Language Skills,** pages 352–353.

Extend Your Learning

Listening and Speaking With a partner, role-play an **interview** between a television news reporter and someone from the story who knows Charlie. During the interview, listen carefully and respond in a manner appropriate for the person you are playing. Address topics like these:

- What changes did the person notice in Charlie's behavior?
- Was it justified to use such a risky procedure on a person without knowing the results?

Research and Technology Use library resources to find articles about human intelligence and the development of the brain. For two articles you read, write a **summary** that includes the main idea of each article and at least two significant details, stated in your own words. Also include a quotation from each article that provides a snapshot of the author's perspective.

Short Story

Background

Early Learning The first day of kindergarten is an event that is both scary and exciting for most children. At ages four and five, children are still learning lessons about getting along with others. Suddenly going from home to a school environment can be a difficult change for children like Laurie, a character in "Charles."

Connecting to the Literature

Reading/Writing Connection In "Charles," a boy brings home some startling stories during his first weeks at school. Using complete sentences, list three things you would tell a child starting kindergarten. Use at least three of the following words: *adapt, participate, cooperate, focus.*

Review

For **Reading Skill, Literary Analysis,** and **Vocabulary Builder,** see page 308.

Meet the Author

Shirley **Jackson** (1916–1965)

As the mother of four energetic children, Shirley Jackson once said that she wrote because "It's the only chance I get to sit down." As a writer, she is famous for two types of stories—spine-tingling tales and hilarious stories about daily life.

The Real-Life Charles Like many other writers, Jackson borrowed characters and events from her own life and wove them into her fictional stories. The main character in "Charles" is based on Jackson's own son.

Fast Facts

▶ Shirley Jackson was born in San Francisco and spent most of her childhood writing poetry rather than playing with neighborhood children.

▶ Her chilling story "The Lottery" gained her fame when it was published in *The New Yorker* in 1948.

▶ Jackson's collections of stories about family life often have humorous titles such as *Life Among the Savages* (1953) and *Raising Demons* (1957).

Go **Online**
Author Link

For: More about the author
Visit: www.PHSchool.com
Web Code: ene-9209

Charles

Shirley Jackson

The day my son Laurie started kindergarten he renounced corduroy overalls with bibs and began wearing blue jeans with a belt; I watched him go off the first morning with the older girl next door, seeing clearly that an era of my life was ended, my sweet-voiced nursery-school tot replaced by a long-trousered, swaggering[1] character who forgot to stop at the corner and wave good-bye to me.

He came home the same way, the front door slamming open, his cap on the floor, and the voice suddenly become raucous[2] shouting, "Isn't anybody *here*?"

At lunch he spoke insolently to his father, spilled his baby sister's milk, and remarked that his teacher said we were not to take the name of the Lord in vain.

"How *was* school today?" I asked, elaborately casual.

"All right," he said.

"Did you learn anything?" his father asked.

Laurie regarded his father coldly. "I didn't learn nothing," he said.

"Anything," I said. "Didn't learn anything."

"The teacher spanked a boy, though," Laurie said, addressing his bread and butter. "For being fresh," he added, with his mouth full.

"What did he do?" I asked. "Who was it?"

Laurie thought. "It was Charles," he said. "He was fresh. The teacher spanked him and made him stand in a corner. He was awfully fresh."

"What did he do?" I asked again, but Laurie slid off his chair, took a cookie, and left, while his father was still saying, "See here, young man."

---

1. **swaggering** (swag´ gər iŋ) *v.* strutting; walking with a bold step.
2. **raucous** (rô´ kəs) *adj.* harsh; rough-sounding.

The next day Laurie remarked at lunch, as soon as he sat down, "Well, Charles was bad again today." He grinned enormously and said, "Today Charles hit the teacher."

"Good heavens," I said, mindful of the Lord's name, "I suppose he got spanked again?"

"He sure did," Laurie said. "Look up," he said to his father.

"What?" his father said, looking up.

"Look down," Laurie said. "Look at my thumb. Gee, you're dumb." He began to laugh insanely.

"Why did Charles hit the teacher?" I asked quickly.

"Because she tried to make him color with red crayons," Laurie said. "Charles wanted to color with green crayons so he hit the teacher and she spanked him and said nobody play with Charles but everybody did."

The third day—it was Wednesday of the first week—Charles bounced a see-saw on to the head of a little girl and made her bleed, and the teacher made him stay inside all during recess. Thursday Charles had to stand in a corner during story-time because he kept pounding his feet on the floor. Friday Charles was deprived of blackboard privileges because he threw chalk.

On Saturday I remarked to my husband, "Do you think kindergarten is too unsettling for Laurie? All this toughness, and bad grammar, and this Charles boy sounds like such a bad influence."

"It'll be all right," my husband said reassuringly. "Bound to be people like Charles in the world. Might as well meet them now as later."

On Monday Laurie came home late, full of news. "Charles," he shouted as he came up the hill; I was waiting anxiously on the front steps. "Charles," Laurie yelled all the way up the hill, "Charles was bad again."

"Come right in," I said, as soon as he came close enough. "Lunch is waiting."

"You know what Charles did?" he demanded, following me

▶ Critical Viewing Which of these children might have a personality like that of Charles? Explain. [Connect]

Reading Skill
Make Inferences
What details show that Laurie admires Charles's rude behavior?

Literary Analysis
Point of View What clues indicate that this story is told by a first-person narrator?

through the door. "Charles yelled so in school they sent a boy in from first grade to tell the teacher she had to make Charles keep quiet, and so Charles had to stay after school. And so all the children stayed to watch him."

"What did he do?" I asked.

"He just sat there," Laurie said, climbing into his chair at the table. "Hi, Pop, y'old dust mop."

"Charles had to stay after school today," I told my husband. "Everyone stayed with him."

"What does this Charles look like?" my husband asked Laurie. "What's his other name?"

"He's bigger than me," Laurie said. "And he doesn't have any rubbers and he doesn't ever wear a jacket."

Monday night was the first Parent-Teachers meeting, and only the fact that the baby had a cold kept me from going; I wanted passionately to meet Charles's mother. On Tuesday Laurie remarked suddenly, "Our teacher had a friend come to see her in school today."

"Charles's mother?" my husband and I asked <u>simultaneously</u>.

"Naaah," Laurie said scornfully. "It was a man who came and made us do exercises, we had to touch our toes. Look." He climbed down from his chair and squatted down and touched his toes. "Like this," he said. He got solemnly back into his chair and said, picking up his fork, "Charles didn't even *do* exercises."

"That's fine," I said heartily. "Didn't Charles want to do exercises?"

"Naaah," Laurie said. "Charles was so fresh to the teacher's friend he wasn't *let* do exercises."

"Fresh again?" I said.

"He kicked the teacher's friend," Laurie said. "The teacher's friend told Charles to touch his toes like I just did and Charles kicked him."

"What are they going to do about Charles, do you suppose?" Laurie's father asked him.

Laurie shrugged elaborately. "Throw him out of school, I guess," he said.

Wednesday and Thursday were routine; Charles yelled during story hour and hit a boy in the stomach and made him cry. On Friday Charles stayed after school again and so did all the other children.

Reading Skill
Make Inferences
What actions show that Charles's behavior is having a negative effect on Laurie?

Vocabulary Builder
simultaneously (sī´ məl tā´ nē əs lē) *adv.* at the same time

**Reading Check**

What did Charles do to his teacher's friend?

With the third week of kindergarten Charles was an institution in our family; the baby was being a Charles when she cried all afternoon; Laurie did a Charles when he filled his wagon full of mud and pulled it through the kitchen; even my husband, when he caught his elbow in the telephone cord and pulled the telephone, ashtray, and a bowl of flowers off the table, said, after the first minute, "Looks like Charles."

During the third and fourth weeks it looked like a reformation in Charles; Laurie reported grimly at lunch on Thursday of the third week, "Charles was so good today the teacher gave him an apple."

"What?" I said, and my husband added warily, "You mean Charles?"

"Charles," Laurie said. "He gave the crayons around and he picked up the books afterward and the teacher said he was her helper."

"What happened?" I asked <u>incredulously</u>.

"He was her helper, that's all," Laurie said, and shrugged.

"Can this be true, about Charles?" I asked my husband that night. "Can something like this happen?"

"Wait and see," my husband said cynically.[3] "When you've got a Charles to deal with, this may mean he's only plotting."

He seemed to be wrong. For over a week Charles was the teacher's helper; each day he handed things out and he picked things up; no one had to stay after school.

"The PTA meeting's next week again," I told my husband one evening. "I'm going to find Charles's mother there."

"Ask her what happened to Charles," my husband said. "I'd like to know."

"I'd like to know myself," I said.

On Friday of that week things were back to normal. "You know what Charles did today?" Laurie demanded at the lunch table, in a voice slightly awed. "He told a little girl to say a word and she said it and the teacher washed her mouth out with soap and Charles laughed."

"What word?" his father asked unwisely, and Laurie said, "I'll have to whisper it to you, it's so bad." He got down off his chair and went around to his father. His father bent his head down and Laurie whispered joyfully. His father's eyes widened.

"Did Charles tell the little girl to say *that*?" he asked respectfully.

Vocabulary Builder
incredulously (in krej´ oo ləs lē) *adv.* with doubt or disbelief

Literary Analysis
Point of View How does the narrator respond to each item of news about Charles?

---

3. **cynically** (sin´ i kə lē) *adv.* with disbelief about the honesty of people's intentions or actions.

"She said it *twice*," Laurie said. "Charles told her to say it *twice*."

"What happened to Charles?" my husband asked.

"Nothing," Laurie said. "He was passing out the crayons."

Monday morning Charles abandoned the little girl and said the evil word himself three or four times, getting his mouth washed out with soap each time. He also threw chalk.

My husband came to the door with me that evening as I set out for the PTA meeting. "Invite her over for a cup of tea after the meeting," he said. "I want to get a look at her."

"If only she's there," I said prayerfully.

"She'll be there," my husband said. "I don't see how they could hold a PTA meeting without Charles's mother."

At the meeting I sat restlessly, scanning each comfortable matronly face, trying to determine which one hid the secret of Charles. None of them looked to me haggard enough. No one stood up in the meeting and apologized for the way her son had been acting. No one mentioned Charles.

After the meeting I identified and sought out Laurie's kindergarten teacher. She had a plate with a cup of tea and a piece of chocolate cake; I had a plate with a cup of tea and a piece of marshmallow cake. We maneuvered up to one another cautiously, and smiled.

"I've been so anxious to meet you," I said. "I'm Laurie's mother."

"We're all so interested in Laurie," she said.

"Well, he certainly likes kindergarten," I said. "He talks about it all the time."

"We had a little trouble adjusting, the first week or so," she said primly, "but now he's a fine little helper. With occasional lapses, of course."

"Laurie usually adjusts very quickly," I said. "I suppose this time it's Charles's influence."

"Charles?"

"Yes," I said, laughing, "you must have your hands full in that kindergarten, with Charles."

"Charles?" she said. "We don't have any Charles in the kindergarten."

Reading Skill
Make Inferences
What does Charles's behavior on Monday suggest about his good behavior in the previous weeks?

Literary Analysis
Point of View How does the first-person point of view contribute to the humor in this conversation?

Apply the Skills

Charles

Thinking About the Selection

1. **Respond:** Were you surprised to learn about Charles's true identity? Why or why not?
2. **(a) Recall:** Describe the change in Laurie's clothing on the day he starts school. **(b) Draw Conclusions:** How does this signal a change in Laurie's behavior?
3. **(a) Recall:** Give three examples of Charles's behavior at school and three examples of Laurie's behavior at home.
   (b) Compare and Contrast: How is Charles's behavior in both these places similar and different?
4. **(a) Make a Judgment:** What should Laurie's mother say to him after she meets his teacher and learns the truth?
   (b) Discuss: Share your ideas with a small group. Then, discuss the reasons for your responses.

Reading Skill

5. **(a)** List four details that his mother has observed about Laurie's new behavior at home. **(b)** Use these details to **make an inference** about what the changes mean.
6. What inferences can you make about the teacher by the way she speaks to Laurie's mother? In your answer, consider her attitude toward her students and her level of patience.

Literary Analysis

7. This first-person story is told from the **point of view** of Laurie's mother. Complete a chart like the one shown here to decide how the story would be different if it were told from Laurie's point of view.

Mother	Laurie
Mother thinks Laurie has a classmate named Charles.	
Mother worries that Charles is a bad influence on Laurie.	

8. How does the first-person point of view help to make the ending a surprise for readers?

QuickReview

Story at a Glance
A little boy tells incredible stories about how a classmate misbehaves.

Go Online
Assessment
For: Self-test
Visit: www.PHSchool.com
Web Code: ena-6208

Inferences: Logical assumptions about what is not stated

Point of View: The perspective from which a story is told. A story can be told in the *first-person* or the *third-person point of view.*

Vocabulary Builder

Practice **Analogies** show the relationships between words. Use a word from the "Charles" vocabulary list on page 308 to create a word pair that matches the relationship between the first two words given.

1. *Rudely* is to *politely* as *separately* is to _____.
2. *Noisily* is to *loudly* as *doubtfully* is to _____.
3. *Awoke* is to *slept* as *welcomed* is to _____.

Writing

Write **dialogue** for a movie scene that you adapt from "Charles."
- First, choose a scene to expand by imagining details and parts of conversations that the author left out.
- Then, write the dialogue, using words and behavior that seem natural for each character. The finished dialogue should convey the uniqueness and motivations of each person.

For *Grammar, Vocabulary,* and *Assessment,* see **Build Language Skills,** pages 352–353.

Extend Your Learning

Listening and Speaking With a partner, role-play an **interview** between Laurie (as "Charles") and one of his classmates. Listen carefully to what your partner is saying and respond in a way you think would be appropriate for the character you are playing. Address interesting topics like these:
- Why does Charles like to misbehave?
- Is Charles's good behavior really just a clever strategy?

Research and Technology Imagine you are a parent of Charles and you are anxious about his behavior. Use library resources to find articles about a child's adjustment to kindergarten. For two articles you read, write a **summary** that includes the main idea of each article and at least two significant details, stated in your own words. Also, include a quotation from each article that provides a snapshot of the author's perspective.

Build Language Skills

Charles • Flowers for Algernon

Vocabulary Skill

Word Origins The **origin** of the word *logical* is the **Greek** *-logo-*, which means "word" or "reason." *Logical* means "reasonable." This is also the base of *-logy-*, which English uses in combination with other roots to mean "study of" or "reasonable understanding of." The origin of the word *biology* is the Greek *-logo-*, which German scientists combined with the Greek word for "life," *bios*.

▶ **Example:** *Biology* is the study of animal and plant life.

Practice Write a simple explanation of the changes these words have gone through since the original Greek word *-logo-*: *catalog, dialogue, monologue, prologue*. Use a dictionary or an online source.

Grammar Lesson

Verbs: Simple Tenses The **tense** of a verb shows the time of an action or a condition. The three simple tenses are *present, past,* and *future*.

MorePractice

For more practice with verb tenses, see the Grammar Handbook, p. R31.

Present Tense	Past Tense	Future Tense
Base Form	Add *-d* or *-ed* to base form.	Use *will* before the base form.
I walk you walk he, she, it walks	I walked you walked he, she, it walked	I will walk you will walk he, she, it will walk

Practice Complete each sentence using the tense indicated.

1. (future) Next week, Angela _____ in a musical.
2. (past) Last week, she _____ three times.
3. (present) Angela and Frank _____ well together.
4. (present) Angela _____ very gracefully.
5. (past) Frank and Angela _____ on a stage.

𝒲𝒢 *Prentice Hall Writing and Grammar Connection: Chapter 22, Section 2*

Reading: Make Inferences

Directions: *Read the selection. Then, answer the questions.*

My kid sister Cheryl and I always bragged about our Sioux grandpa, Joe Iron Shell. Our friends . . . were impressed by our stories. Maybe we exaggerated and made Grandpa and the reservation sound glamorous, but when we'd return home to Iowa after our yearly summer visit to Grandpa, we always had some exciting tale to tell.

We always had some authentic Sioux article to show our listeners. One year Cheryl had new moccasins that Grandpa had made.

—*from* "The Medicine Bag" by Virginia Driving Hawk Sneve

1. What can you infer about the narrator?
   A He knows how to make moccasins.
   B He is proud of his Sioux heritage.
   C He doesn't like the reservation.
   D He doesn't like living in Iowa.

2. What is probably true about the narrator's grandfather?
   A He always wears moccasins.
   B He leads a glamorous life.
   C He makes up exaggerated stories.
   D He carries on Sioux traditions.

3. What can you infer about the narrator's friends?
   A They are interested in Sioux history.
   B They are jealous of the narrator.
   C They are part Sioux.
   D They want to make moccasins.

4. Which of the following is probably not a logical inference?
   A The narrator likes his grandfather.
   B Grandfather teaches his heritage.
   C The narrator resents having to visit his grandfather.
   D The children treasure their gifts.

Timed Writing: Response to Literature
[Critical Response]

Review "Charles" or "Flowers for Algernon." Then, write a response in which you discuss how point of view affected your enjoyment of, and interest in, one of the two stories. **(25 minutes)**

Writing Workshop: *Work in Progress*

Short Story
For a short story you may write, freewrite about what makes your favorite literary characters believable. Think about what they say and how they react to situations. Save this Characterization Work in your writing portfolio.

These skills will help you become a better reader.
Practice them with either "Thank You, M'am" (p. 356)
or "The Story-Teller" (p. 363).

Reading Skill

An **inference** is a logical assumption about information based on ideas that the writer suggests but does
not state directly. Making inferences is a way of "reading between the lines" of a story to discover the meaning behind
actions and events. As you read, **identify connections to make
inferences about the author's meaning.**

- Connect characters' actions to reasons and outcomes.
- Connect events to reasons and outcomes.

Ask yourself what meaning the author is suggesting by making these
connections. This strategy is illustrated in the example shown.

Literary Analysis

The **theme** of a literary work is its central idea, insight, or message.
This central idea is often expressed as a generalization about life or
people. A theme can be drawn from the specific experiences of the
characters or from the outcomes of events.

- A **stated theme** is expressed directly in the story.
- More often, a theme is **unstated,** or **implied.** You infer the
  theme from characters' experiences and from story events.

Readers can sometimes find different themes in a work of literature.
Each interpretation of a theme is valid as long as it can be adequately
supported with details from the text.

Event
A boy spends all of his money on candy and does not share.

+

Event
He gets sick from eating too much candy.

=

Inference
People should not be selfish.

Vocabulary Builder

Thank You, M'am

- **contact** (kän´ takt) *n.* touching; communication (p. 357) *Her <u>contact</u> with the icy
  water made her shiver.*

- **presentable** (prē zent´ ə bəl) *adj.* in proper
  order for being seen or met by others
  (p. 359) *His mother asked him to change into
  a more <u>presentable</u> shirt.*

- **barren** (bar´ ən) *adj.* empty; bare (p. 359)
  The treeless prairie was scorched and <u>barren</u>.

The Story-Teller

- **correspondingly** (kôr ə spänd´ iŋ lē) *adv.* in a
  consistent way (p. 363) *He loved everything
  big; his house was <u>correspondingly</u> large.*

- **resolute** (rez´ ə lo͞ot´) *adj.* determined;
  resolved (p. 364) *In spite of setbacks, he
  remained <u>resolute</u>.*

- **conviction** (kən vik´ shən) *n.* strong belief;
  certainty (p. 365) *Her <u>conviction</u> about her
  opinions was clear.*

Background

Urban Living "Thank You, M'am" is set in an urban neighborhood similar to the New York City neighborhood in which Langston Hughes lived. New York City's population grew rapidly in the early part of the twentieth century. Many single-family houses were converted into modest, smaller apartments, like the "kitchenette" apartment—one large room with its own mini-kitchen in the corner—where Mrs. Jones in the story lives.

Connecting to the Literature

Reading/Writing Connection In "Thank You, M'am," a boy learns a surprising lesson about kindness and trust from a stranger. Write three sentences explaining what someone needs to do in order to win your trust. Use at least three of the following words: *acquire, obtain, attain, earn.*

Meet the Author

Langston **Hughes** (1902–1967)

In the 1920s and 1930s, a young writer named Langston Hughes was at the forefront of an explosion of creativity in literature and the arts, known as the Harlem Renaissance (*rebirth*). Readers first noticed the talent of Hughes in 1921, when his poem "The Negro Speaks of Rivers" was published shortly after he graduated from high school.

A Varied Career While working on a merchant ship, Hughes continued writing. In 1926, his first collection of poems was published as *The Weary Blues*. Hughes went on to have a long career as a writer. He wrote poetry, short stories, children's books—even an opera.

Fast Facts
▶ Hughes's poems often echo the rhythms of jazz.
▶ Hughes's work was beloved for its familiar characters like Jesse B. Simple, an average man who told his troubles to anyone who would listen.

Go Online
Author Link

For: More about the author
Visit: www.PHSchool.com
Web Code: ene-9210

Thank You, M'am
Langston Hughes

She was a large woman with a large purse that had every-thing in it but a hammer and nails. It had a long strap, and she carried it slung across her shoulder. It was about eleven o'clock at night, dark, and she was walking alone, when a boy ran up behind her and tried to snatch her purse. The strap broke with the sudden single tug the boy gave it from behind. But the boy's weight and the weight of the purse combined caused him to lose his balance. Instead of taking off full blast as he had hoped, the boy fell on his back on the sidewalk and his legs flew up. The large woman simply turned around and kicked him right square in his blue-jeaned sitter. Then she reached down, picked the boy up by his shirt front, and shook him until his teeth rattled.

After that the woman said, "Pick up my pocketbook, boy, and give it here."

She still held him tightly. But she bent down enough to per-mit him to stoop and pick up her purse. Then she said, "Now ain't you ashamed of yourself?"

Firmly gripped by his shirt front, the boy said, "Yes'm."

The woman said, "What did you want to do it for?"

▲ Critical Viewing
Would it be easy to "disappear" on a city street like the one shown in the picture? Explain. **[Analyze]**

Reading Skill
Make Inferences
From the description here, what can you infer about the woman's personality? Provide two details to support your view.

The boy said, "I didn't aim to."

She said, "You a lie!"

By that time two or three people passed, stopped, turned to look, and some stood watching.

"If I turn you loose, will you run?" asked the woman.

"Yes'm," said the boy.

"Then I won't turn you loose," said the woman. She did not release him.

"Lady, I'm sorry," whispered the boy.

"Um-hum! Your face is dirty. I got a great mind to wash your face for you. Ain't you got nobody home to tell you to wash your face?"

"No'm," said the boy.

"Then it will get washed this evening," said the large woman, starting up the street, dragging the frightened boy behind her.

He looked as if he were fourteen or fifteen, frail and willow-wild, in tennis shoes and blue jeans.

The woman said, "You ought to be my son. I would teach you right from wrong. Least I can do right now is to wash your face. Are you hungry?"

"No'm," said the being-dragged boy. "I just want you to turn me loose."

"Was I bothering *you* when I turned that corner?" asked the woman.

"No'm."

"But you put yourself in <u>contact</u> with *me*," said the woman. "If you think that that contact is not going to last awhile, you got another thought coming. When I get through with you, sir, you are going to remember Mrs. Luella Bates Washington Jones."

Sweat popped out on the boy's face and he began to struggle. Mrs. Jones stopped, jerked him around in front of her, put a half nelson[1] about his neck, and continued to drag him up the street. When she got to her door, she dragged the boy inside, down a hall, and into a large kitchenette-furnished room at the rear of the house. She switched on the light and left the door open. The boy could hear other roomers laughing and talking in the large house. Some of their doors were open, too, so he knew he and the woman were not alone. The woman still had him by the neck in the middle of her room.

---

1. half nelson wrestling hold in which an arm is placed under the opponent's armpit from behind with the palm of the hand pressed against the back of the neck.

Literary Analysis
Theme What is the woman's attitude toward the boy? How does the boy view the woman?

Vocabulary Builder
contact (kän´ takt) *n.* touching; communication

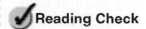**Reading Check**

What did the boy do to put himself "in contact" with Mrs. Jones?

She said, "What is your name?"

"Roger," answered the boy.

"Then, Roger, you go to that sink and wash your face," said the woman, whereupon she turned him loose—at last. Roger looked at the door—looked at the woman—looked at the door—*and went to the sink.*

"Let the water run until it gets warm," she said. "Here's a clean towel."

"You gonna take me to jail?" asked the boy, bending over the sink.

"Not with that face, I would not take you nowhere," said the woman. "Here I am trying to get home to cook me a bite to eat, and you snatch my pocketbook! Maybe you ain't been to your supper either, late as it be. Have you?"

"There's nobody home at my house," said the boy.

"Then we'll eat," said the woman. "I believe you're hungry—or been hungry—to try to snatch my pocketbook!"

"I want a pair of blue suede shoes,"[2] said the boy.

"Well, you didn't have to snatch *my* pocketbook to get some suede shoes," said Mrs. Luella Bates Washington Jones. "You could of asked me."

"M'am?"

The water dripping from his face, the boy looked at her. There was a long pause. A very long pause. After he had dried his face and not knowing what else to do, dried it again, the boy turned around, wondering what next. The door was open. He could make a dash for it down the hall. He could run, run, run, *run!*

The woman was sitting on the day bed. After awhile she said, "I were young once and I wanted things I could not get."

There was another long pause. The boy's mouth opened. Then he frowned, not knowing he frowned.

The woman said, "Um-hum! You thought I was going to say *but*, didn't you? You thought I was going to say, *but I didn't snatch people's pocketbooks.* Well, I wasn't going to say that." Pause. Silence. "I have done things, too, which I would not tell you, son—neither tell God, if He didn't already know.

▲ **Critical Viewing**
What details in the painting suggest traits of Mrs. Jones, as described in the story? **[Connect]**

Reading Skill
Make Inferences
What does this speech tell you about Mrs. Jones's life and background?

---

2. **blue suede** (swād) **shoes** style of shoes worn by "hipsters" in the 1940s and 1950s; made famous in a song sung by Elvis Presley.

Everybody's got something in common. So you set down while I fix us something to eat. You might run that comb through your hair so you will look <u>presentable</u>."

In another corner of the room behind a screen was a gas plate and an icebox. Mrs. Jones got up and went behind the screen. The woman did not watch the boy to see if he was going to run now, nor did she watch her purse, which she left behind her on the day bed. But the boy took care to sit on the far side of the room, away from her purse, where he thought she could easily see him out of the corner of her eye if she wanted to. He did not trust the woman *not* to trust him. And he did not want to be mistrusted now.

"Do you need somebody to go to the store," asked the boy, "maybe to get some milk or something?"

"Don't believe I do," said the woman, "unless you just want sweet milk yourself. I was going to make cocoa out of this canned milk I got here."

"That will be fine," said the boy.

She heated some lima beans and ham she had in the icebox, made the cocoa, and set the table. The woman did not ask the boy anything about where he lived, or his folks, or anything else that would embarrass him. Instead, as they ate, she told him about her job in a hotel beauty shop that stayed open late, what the work was like, and how all kinds of women came in and out, blondes, redheads, and Spanish. Then she cut him a half of her ten-cent cake.

"Eat some more, son," she said.

When they were finished eating, she got up and said, "Now here, take this ten dollars and buy yourself some blue suede shoes. And next time, do not make the mistake of latching onto *my* pocketbook *nor nobody else's*—because shoes got by devilish ways will burn your feet. I got to get my rest now. But from here on in, son, I hope you will behave yourself."

She led him down the hall to the front door and opened it. "Good night! Behave yourself, boy!" she said, looking out into the street as he went down the steps.

The boy wanted to say something other than, "Thank you, m'am," to Mrs. Luella Bates Washington Jones, but although his lips moved, he couldn't even say that as he turned at the foot of the <u>barren</u> stoop and looked up at the large woman in the door. Then she shut the door.

Vocabulary Builder
presentable (prē zent′ ə bəl) *adj.* in proper order for being seen or met by others

Literary Analysis
Theme Why does Mrs. Jones give Roger money for shoes instead of turning him over to the police?

Vocabulary Builder
barren (bar′ ən) *adj.* empty; bare

Apply the Skills

Thank You, M'am

Thinking About the Selection

1. **Respond:** Do you think Mrs. Jones is wise or foolish to trust Roger? Why?

2. **(a) Recall:** What does Roger think that Mrs. Jones is going to do with him? **(b) Contrast:** What does Mrs. Jones do and say instead to win Roger's trust? **(c) Draw Conclusions:** Why does she do these things?

3. **(a) Recall:** What do Mrs. Jones and Roger talk about during their meal? **(b) Draw Conclusions:** Why do you think Mrs. Jones avoids asking Roger personal questions?

4. **(a) Recall:** What does Roger say or do as he leaves the apartment? **(b) Interpret:** Why is he unable to say what he wants to say? **(c) Speculate:** What more does he want to say?

5. **(a) Predict:** What effect might Mrs. Jones's action have on Roger's future behavior? **(b) Make a Judgment:** Does Mrs. Jones make good choices about how to treat Roger? Explain your response.

Reading Skill

6. **(a)** What is the connection between what Roger wants and what he does at the beginning of the story? **(b)** What is the outcome of his attempt to steal her purse? **(c)** What **inference** can you make about the author's message concerning stealing?

Literary Analysis

7. **(a)** In the first column of a chart like this one, identify a **theme** of this story and indicate whether the theme is **stated** or **implied**. **(b)** In the second column, support your interpretation with details from the story. **(c)** Discuss your response with a partner. Then, in the third column, record whether your interpretation changed as a result of the discussion.

Theme (stated or implied)	Details	Discussion Response

QuickReview

Story at a Glance
When a boy tries to snatch a woman's purse, she gives him a lesson in kindness.

Go Online
Assessment
For: Self-test
Visit: www.PHSchool.com
Web Code: ena-6209

Inferences: Logical assumptions based on information or ideas that are suggested, not stated

Theme: A central idea, insight, or message of a literary work

Vocabulary Builder

Practice Respond using a vocabulary word from the list on page 354. Explain your answers.

1. Which word describes something that can spread a cold?
2. Which word describes how you should look on a date?
3. Which word describes a poor place to plant a cornfield?

Writing

Write a brief **personal essay** showing how a theme of "Thank You, M'am" applies to everyday life.

- First, state what you think a theme of the story is.
- Next, brainstorm for experiences in your past that reflect the same theme. Take notes about the feelings and lessons you associate with those experiences.
- Finally, write the essay. To introduce the topic, state the theme and summarize your experiences. In the body of the essay, provide detail about these experiences. Conclude by restating the theme and how it applies to everyday life.

For *Grammar*, *Vocabulary*, and *Assessment*, see **Build Language Skills**, pp. 372–373.

Extend Your Learning

Listening and Speaking Organize a **panel discussion** to decide whether Mrs. Jones's actions were appropriate. Ask one person to be the moderator, or leader, of the discussion. That person should ensure that everyone receives at least one opportunity to voice an opinion or interpretation.

Research and Technology Working with a group, gather information for a **multimedia exhibit** about Langston Hughes and the Harlem Renaissance. Research literature, music, and the performing arts. Your presentation can include the following:

- photographs and one-paragraph biographies of prominent Harlem Renaissance artists and writers
- recordings of period jazz music and live readings of poems
- pictures of artwork and a timeline of artistic events of the era

Short Story

Background

English Trains "The Story-Teller" takes place in a railroad car, or "carriage," around 1900. Train cars on English railways, especially at that time, were built differently from modern American trains. Cars were divided into smaller compartments, each with its own doors and seating for four or six people. Trains also were divided into luxurious "first-class" carriages and more crowded, less comfortable, second- and third-class cars.

Connecting to the Literature

Reading/Writing Connection The children in "The Story-Teller" get bored and restless during their train trip. A fellow traveler tries to help them pass the time by telling what he hopes is an interesting story. Make a list of the kinds of plot elements and characters you enjoy in a story. Use at least three of the following words: *enhance, enrich, expand, emphasize.*

Review

For **Reading Skill, Literary Analysis,** and **Vocabulary Builder,** see page 354.

Meet the Author

Saki (H. H. **Munro**) (1870–1916)

Long before celebrities began to use single names, H. H. (Hector Hugh) Munro became famous under the pen name "Saki." Born to British parents in Burma (now Myanmar), he was raised in England by his aunts. Munro worked as a foreign correspondent and political writer before beginning to write the clever short stories for which he is famous.

Making Fun of Society Munro's stories poked fun at the manners and behavior of society in late nineteenth- and early twentieth-century England. His stories often end in jokes or surprise endings. Sometimes his humor is cruel or tinged with horror. These characteristics stood out and made Saki popular in an era which was more formal than ours.

Go Online
Author Link

For: More on the author
Visit: www.PHSchool.com
Web Code: ene-9211

The Story-Teller

SAKI

It was a hot afternoon, and the railway carriage was <u>correspondingly</u> sultry, and the next stop was at Temple-combe, nearly an hour ahead. The occupants of the carriage were a small girl, and a smaller girl, and a small boy. An aunt belonging to the children occupied one corner seat, and the further corner seat on the opposite side was occupied by a bachelor who was a stranger to their party, but the small girls and the small boy emphatically occupied the compartment. Both the aunt and the children were conversational in a

▲ **Critical Viewing**
What does this painting tell you about travel in the late nineteenth century? **[Infer]**

Vocabulary Builder
correspondingly (kôr′ ə spänd′ iŋ lē) *adv.* in a consistent way

limited, persistent way, reminding one of the attentions of a housefly that refused to be discouraged. Most of the aunt's remarks seemed to begin with "Don't," and nearly all of the children's remarks began with "Why?" The bachelor said nothing out loud.

"Don't, Cyril, don't," exclaimed the aunt, as the small boy began smacking the cushions of the seat, producing a cloud of dust at each blow.

"Come and look out of the window," she added.

The child moved reluctantly to the window. "Why are those sheep being driven out of that field?" he asked.

"I expect they are being driven to another field where there is more grass," said the aunt weakly.

"But there is lots of grass in that field," protested the boy; "there's nothing else but grass there. Aunt, there's lots of grass in that field."

"Perhaps the grass in the other field is better," suggested the aunt fatuously.[1]

"Why is it better?" came the swift, inevitable question.

"Oh, look at those cows!" exclaimed the aunt. Nearly every field along the line had contained cows or bullocks, but she spoke as though she were drawing attention to a rarity.

"Why is the grass in the other field better?" persisted Cyril.

The frown on the bachelor's face was deepening to a scowl. He was a hard, unsympathetic man, the aunt decided in her mind. She was utterly unable to come to any satisfactory decision about the grass in the other field.

The smaller girl created a diversion by beginning to recite "On the Road to Mandalay."[2] She only knew the first line, but she put her limited knowledge to the fullest possible use. She repeated the line over and over again in a dreamy but <u>resolute</u> and very audible voice; it seemed to the bachelor as though someone had had a bet with her that she could not repeat the line aloud two thousand times without stopping. Whoever it was who had made the wager was likely to lose his bet.

"Come over here and listen to a story," said the aunt, when the bachelor had looked twice at her and once at the communication cord.

Reading Skill
Make Inferences
What can you infer from this passage about the relationship between the children and their aunt? Why?

Vocabulary Builder
resolute (rez′ ə loo̅t′) *adj.* determined; resolved

---

1. fatuously (fach′ oo̅ wəs lē) *adv.* in a silly or foolish way.
2. "On the Road to Mandalay" popular poem by Rudyard Kipling, later a song. Its first lines are: "On the road to Mandalay, where the flyin' fishes play / An' the dawn comes up like thunder outer China 'crost the bay!"

The children moved listlessly[3] toward the aunt's end of the carriage. Evidently her reputation as a story-teller did not rank high in their estimation.

In a low, confidential voice, interrupted at frequent intervals by loud, petulant[4] questions from her listeners, she began an unenterprising and deplorably[5] uninteresting story about a little girl who was good, and made friends with everyone on account of her goodness, and was finally saved from a mad bull by a number of rescuers who admired her moral character.

"Wouldn't they have saved her if she hadn't been good?" demanded the bigger of the small girls. It was exactly the question that the bachelor had wanted to ask.

"Well, yes," admitted the aunt lamely, "but I don't think they would have run quite so fast to her help if they had not liked her so much."

"It's the stupidest story I've ever heard," said the bigger of the small girls, with immense <u>conviction</u>.

"I didn't listen after the first bit, it was so stupid," said Cyril.

The smaller girl made no actual comment on the story, but she had long ago recommenced a murmured repetition of her favorite line.

"You don't seem to be a success as a story-teller," said the bachelor suddenly from his corner.

The aunt bristled in instant defense at this unexpected attack.

"It's a very difficult thing to tell stories that children can both understand and appreciate," she said stiffly.

"I don't agree with you," said the bachelor.

"Perhaps *you* would like to tell them a story," was the aunt's retort.

"Tell us a story," demanded the bigger of the small girls.

"Once upon a time," began the bachelor, "there was a little girl called Bertha, who was extraordinarily good."

The children's momentarily aroused interest began at once to flicker; all stories seemed dreadfully alike, no matter who told them.

"She did all that she was told, she was always truthful, she kept her clothes clean, ate milk puddings as though they were

Literary Analysis
Theme What does the children's reaction suggest about the kind of stories the aunt tells?

Vocabulary Builder
conviction (kən vik´ shən) *n.* strong belief; certainty

Reading Skill
Make Inferences What do the aunt and the bachelor think of each other?

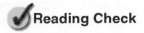Reading Check

What is the subject of the aunt's story?

---

3. **listlessly** (list´ ləs lē) *adv.* without energy or enthusiasm.
4. **petulant** (pech´ ōō lənt) *adj.* peevishly impatient.
5. **deplorably** (dē plôr´ ə blē) *adv.* miserably; wretchedly.

jam tarts, learned her lessons perfectly, and was polite in her manners."

"Was she pretty?" asked the bigger of the small girls.

"Not as pretty as any of you." said the bachelor, "but she was horribly good."

There was a wave of reaction in favor of the story; the word horrible in connection with goodness was a novelty that commended itself. It seemed to introduce a ring of truth that was absent from the aunt's tales of infant life.

"She was so good," continued the bachelor, "that she won several medals for goodness, which she always wore, pinned on to her dress. There was a medal for obedience, another medal for punctuality, and a third for good behavior. They were large metal medals and they clinked against one another as she walked. No other child in town where she lived had as many as three medals, so everybody knew that she must be an extra good child."

"Horribly good," quoted Cyril.

"Everybody talked about her goodness, and the Prince of the country got to hear about it, and he said that as she was so very good she might be allowed once a week to walk in his park, which was just outside the town. It was a beautiful park, and no children were ever allowed in it, so it was a great honor for Bertha to be allowed to go there."

"Were there any sheep in the park?" demanded Cyril.

"No," said the bachelor, "there were no sheep."

"Why weren't there any sheep?" came the inevitable question arising out of that answer.

The aunt permitted herself a smile, which might almost have been described as a grin.

"There were no sheep in the park," said the bachelor, "because the Prince's mother had once had a dream that her son would either be killed by a sheep or else by a clock falling on him. For that reason the Prince never kept a sheep in his park or a clock in his palace."

The aunt suppressed a gasp of admiration.

"Was the Prince killed by a sheep or by a clock?" asked Cyril.

"He is still alive, so we can't tell whether the dream will come true," said the bachelor unconcernedly; "anyway, there were no sheep in the park, but there were lots of little pigs running all over the place."

Reading Skill
Make Inferences
What details support the inference that the bachelor understands children?

Reading Skill
Make Inferences
Why do you think the aunt smiles?

"What color were they?"

"Black with white faces, white with black spots, black all over, gray with white patches, and some were white all over."

The story-teller paused to let a full idea of the park's treasures sink into the children's imaginations; then he resumed:

"Bertha was rather sorry to find that there were no flowers in the park. She had promised her aunts, with tears in her eyes, that she would not pick any of the kind Prince's flowers, and she had meant to keep her promise, so of course it made her feel silly to find that there were no flowers to pick."

"Why weren't there any flowers?"

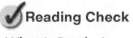

▲ **Critical Viewing**
How do these pigs resemble those in the bachelor's story? **[Connect]**

✓ **Reading Check**

What is Bertha's main characteristic?

"Because the pigs had eaten them all," said the bachelor promptly. "The gardeners had told the Prince that you couldn't have pigs and flowers, so he decided to have pigs and no flowers."

There was a murmur of approval at the excellence of the Prince's decision; so many people would have decided the other way.

"There were lots of other delightful things in the park. There were ponds with gold and blue and green fish in them, and trees with beautiful parrots that said clever things at a moment's notice, and hummingbirds that hummed all the popular tunes of the day. Bertha walked up and down and enjoyed herself immensely, and thought to herself: 'If I were not so extraordinarily good, I should not have been allowed to come into this beautiful park and enjoy all that there is to be seen in it,' and her three medals clinked against one another as she walked and helped to remind her how very good she really was. Just then an enormous wolf came prowling into the park to see if it could catch a fat little pig for its supper."

"What color was it?" asked the children, amid an immediate quickening of interest.

"Mud color all over, with a black tongue and pale gray eyes that gleamed with unspeakable ferocity. The first thing that it saw in the park was Bertha; her pinafore[6] was so spotlessly white and clean that it could be seen from a great distance. Bertha saw the wolf and saw that it was stealing toward her, and she began to wish that she had never been allowed to come into the park. She ran as hard as she could, and the wolf came after her with huge leaps and bounds. She managed to reach a shrubbery of myrtle bushes, and she hid herself in one of the thickest of the bushes. The wolf came sniffing among the branches, its black tongue lolling out of its mouth and its pale gray eyes glaring with rage. Bertha was terribly frightened, and thought to herself: 'If I had not been so extraordinarily good, I should have been safe in the town at this moment.' However, the scent of the myrtle was so strong that the wolf could not sniff out where Bertha was hiding, and the bushes were so thick that he might have hunted about in them for a long time without catching sight of her, so he thought he might as well go off and catch a little pig instead.

---

6. **pinafore** (pin´ ə fôr´) *n.* a sleeveless apronlike garment worn over a dress.

Reading Skill
Make Inferences
What can you infer from the children's murmur of approval?

Bertha was trembling very much at having the wolf prowling and sniffing so near her, and as she trembled the medal for obedience clinked against the medals for good conduct and punctuality. The wolf was just moving away when he heard the sound of the medals clinking and stopped to listen; they clinked again in a bush quite near him. He dashed into the bush, his pale gray eyes gleaming with ferocity and triumph, and dragged Bertha out and devoured her to the last morsel. All that was left of her were her shoes, bits of clothing, and the three medals for goodness."

"Were any of the little pigs killed?"

"No, they all escaped."

"The story began badly," said the smaller of the small girls, "but it had a beautiful ending."

"It is the most beautiful story that I ever heard," said the bigger of the small girls, with immense decision.

"It is the *only* beautiful story I have ever heard," said Cyril.

A dissentient[7] opinion came from the aunt.

"A most improper story to tell to young children! You have undermined the effect of years of careful teaching."

"At any rate," said the bachelor, collecting his belongings preparatory to leaving the carriage, "I kept them quiet for ten minutes, which was more than you were able to do."

"Unhappy woman!" he observed to himself as he walked down the platform of Templecombe station; "for the next six months or so those children will assail her in public with demands for an improper story!"

---

7. dissentient (di sen´ shənt) *adj.* differing from the majority.

Literary Analysis
Theme How is the message of the bachelor's story different from the message of the aunt's story?

Literary Analysis
Theme How does the children's enjoyment of the bachelor's story connect to a possible theme of the entire work?

Apply the Skills

The Story-Teller

Thinking About the Selection

1. **Respond:** Did you like the bachelor's story? Why or why not?
2. **(a) Recall:** What questions do the children ask their aunt? **(b) Analyze:** Why are the children unsatisfied with her answers? **(c) Evaluate:** How well does the aunt understand children? Explain.
3. **(a) Recall:** How does the bachelor respond to the aunt's story? **(b) Analyze:** Is he more sympathetic with the aunt or with the children? Support your response with examples from the story.
4. **(a) Compare and Contrast:** How are the two storytellers' motives, or reasons behind their actions, similar? How are they different? **(b) Draw Conclusions:** Why do the children like the bachelor's story better than the aunt's? **(c) Evaluate:** Do you agree with the aunt that the bachelor's story is "improper" for children?

Reading Skill

5. **(a)** What is the connection between the behavior of the children and the bachelor's decision to try to amuse them with a story? **(b)** What is the outcome of his attempt at story-telling? **(c)** What **inference** can you make about the author's message concerning the interests and upbringing of children?

Literary Analysis

6. **(a)** In the first column of a chart like this one, identify a **theme** of this story and indicate whether the theme is **stated** or **implied**. **(b)** In the second column, support your interpretation with details from the story. **(c)** Discuss your response with a partner. Then, in the third column, record whether your interpretation changed as a result of the discussion.

Theme (stated or implied)	Details	Discussion Response

Vocabulary Builder

Practice Respond using a vocabulary word from the list on page 354. Explain your answers.

1. Which word can refer to either a belief or a ruling of "guilty"?
2. Which word is the opposite of *indecisive*?
3. Which word has the same meaning as the word *accordingly*?

Writing

Write a brief **personal essay** showing how a theme of "The Story-Teller" applies to everyday life.

- First, state what you think a theme of the story is.
- Next, brainstorm for experiences in your past that reflect the same theme. Take notes about the feelings and lessons you associate with those experiences.
- Finally, write the essay. To introduce the topic, state the theme and summarize your experiences. In the body of the essay, provide detail about these experiences. Conclude by restating the theme and how it applies to everyday life.

For *Grammar, Vocabulary,* and *Assessment,*
see **Build Language Skills,** pages **372–373.**

Extend Your Learning

Listening and Speaking Organize a **panel discussion** about whether the bachelor should have told the children such a gruesome story. Ask one person to be the moderator, or leader, of the discussion. That person should ensure that everyone receives at least one opportunity to voice an opinion or interpretation.

Research and Technology Working with a group, gather information for a **multimedia exhibit** about rail travel during Saki's lifetime. Include the following types of items:

- photographs of railroad posters and rail car interiors, as well as first-person descriptions of rail travel
- recordings of train sounds, such as railroad whistles
- a timeline of advances in rail travel

Build Language Skills

Vocabulary Skill

Word Origins The word *indicate* comes to English from the Latin *indicare*, which means "show." Other words went through several changes before becoming part of the English language. *Conclusion* originated in Latin as *conclusio*. It was used in Old French and in Middle English, and then became part of modern English.

Practice In a small group, speculate whether each of the following came from German, French, or Spanish: *canyon, guitar, tornado, ballet, salon, dunk, delicatessen, kindergarten.* Then check each word's origin in a dictionary.

Grammar Lesson

Verbs: Tense and Mood The **tense** of a verb shows the time of an action. The **perfect tense** describes an action that was or will be completed at a certain time. The **subjunctive mood** is used to express a wish or a condition that is contrary to fact, as in the following example: If he *were* faster, he would have won the race.

Verb Tense	own (owned)
Present Perfect: action in the past that continues up to the present **have + past participle**	*I have owned* this red bike for two years.
Past Perfect: action in the past that ended **had + past participle**	*I had owned* one like it a few years earlier.
Future Perfect: action in the future that will have ended at a certain point in time **will have + past participle**	By next year, *I will have owned* three red bikes.

Practice Add a phrase or clause containing a perfect tense verb or a verb in the subjunctive mood to complete the sentence.

1. By the time you get this letter, _____
2. _____ for a long time.
3. She _____ to all the CDs we have.
4. The landlord _____ before we saw the apartment.
5. If she _____ on time, we would not have missed the show.

MorePractice

For more practice with perfect tenses, see the Grammar Handbook, p. R31.

W͜G Prentice Hall Writing and Grammar Connection: Chapter 22, Section 2

Reading: Make Inferences

Directions: *Read the passage. Then, answer the questions.*

Across the aisle, a middle-aged man was staring out the bus window. A newspaper lay on his lap, but he wasn't reading it. A cell phone rang nearby, and he jumped. He jiggled his foot, crossed and uncrossed his legs. He reached into his pocket, took out a map, and studied it. Then he glanced at his watch and smoothed back his hair. He peered eagerly out the window as the bus pulled into the station.

1. What fact does the writer tell you about the person on the bus?
   A He cares about his appearance.
   B He is a middle-aged man.
   C He likes to read.
   D He doesn't own a car.

2. Which fact gives a clue about the man's state of mind?
   A He is a middle-aged man.
   B He is on the bus.
   C He takes out a map.
   D He jiggled his foot up and down.

3. Which is the most logical inference about the man?
   A He is relaxed.
   B He is cheerful.

   C He is nervous.
   D He is unhappy.

4. What can you most logically infer from the man's study of the map?
   A He is returning to his home.
   B He is arriving at an unfamiliar place.
   C He has been traveling a long time.
   D He is not sure where the bus is going.

5. What can you infer from his behavior as the bus arrives at the station?
   A He is expecting someone to meet him.
   B He wishes the bus were late.
   C He is running away.
   D He wishes he had not come.

Timed Writing: Interpretation [Critical Stance]

Review "Thank You, M'am" or "The Story-Teller." Write an essay in which you interpret the author's perspective on how adults teach children values and about their culture. **(20 minutes)**

 ## Writing Workshop: *Work in Progress*

Short Story

Use the Characterization Work from your writing portfolio. Underline the ideas about realistic characters that are most important. For two ideas, write a few notes about how you can apply these ideas to your own writing. Save this work in your writing portfolio.

Reading Informational Materials

Advertisements

In Part 2, you are learning how to make inferences to help you understand literature. Making inferences is also helpful in reading advertisements. If you read "The Story-Teller," consider how closely the characters' rail journey resembles the images in these railway ads from the 1940s and 1950s.

About Advertisements

Advertisements are paid messages intended to attract customers for products or services. Advertisers use two main types of techniques to persuade consumers to buy products.

- **Rational appeals** are based on facts. Ads that show comparisons among products or focus on product features, price, dependability, or convenience use rational appeals.
- **Emotional appeals** are based on feelings. Ads use words or images to suggest that consumers will gain status, popularity, or happiness if they buy a certain product.

Reading Skill

To think critically about advertisements, you must separate rational from emotional arguments. To do this, learn to recognize **appeals to emotions.** Ignore arguments based on emotional appeals. Then, evaluate any factual evidence that remains.

Study the chart of common persuasive devices designed to appeal to the emotions. Challenge arguments based on these devices in advertisements and in other types of persuasive writing.

Device	Example	Explanation
Bandwagon appeal	Everyone loves Muncheez!	Words like *everyone* appeal to people's desire to belong.
Loaded language	Muncheez is incredibly delicious.	*Incredibly* and *delicious* are claims that cannot be proved.
Testimonials	Tina Idol says Muncheez gives her energy.	Just because a celebrity or an "expert" says it, it does not mean the claim is true.
Generalizations	Muncheez is not only the best, it's the healthiest.	Claims that are too broad or vague cannot be proved.

Meet <u>MRS.</u> Casey Jones

CASEY'S gone to war . . . so Mrs. Jones is "working on the railroad!"

She is putting in a big day's work oiling and swabbing down giant engines, cleaning and vacuuming cars, handling baggage, selling tickets, moving through the aisles as a trainman.

In fact, she is doing scores of different jobs on the Pennsylvania Railroad — and doing them well. So the men in the armed forces whom she has replaced can take comfort in the fact Mrs. Casey Jones is "carrying on" in fine style.

Since the war began, Pennsylvania Railroad has welcomed thousands of women into its ranks of loyal, busy and able workers. They are taking a real part in the railroad's big two-fold job of moving troops and supplies and serving essential civilian needs during the war emergency.

You will find these women, not merely in expected places, such as offices, telephone exchanges and ticket windows . . . you will find them out where "man-size" jobs have to be done: in the round house, in the shops, in the yards, in the terminals, in the cars.

We feel sure the American public will take pride in the way American womanhood has pitched in to keep the Victory trains rolling!

Facts—the number of women working for the Pennsylvania Railroad and the jobs they hold—are mixed with loaded words such as *loyal, busy,* and *able* in this particularly persuasive paragraph.

By associating its company with the war effort, the Pennsylvania Railroad creates a bandwagon effect that appeals to emotions.

PENNSYLVANIA RAILROAD
Serving the Nation

★ *34,101 in the Armed Forces*   ★ *38 have given their lives for their country*

While the Storm rages...

The illustration and headline add drama and reinforce the claims in the text.

The ad uses loaded words, such as *deluge*, *rages*, and *blotting out*, to describe car travel in order to create a strong contrast with the *comfort*, *ease*, and *beauty* of train travel.

THE TRAIN GOES THROUGH!

The sky darkens ... lightning crackles—soon comes the deluge, blotting out all visibility!

No matter—your Pennsylvania Railroad train takes weather as it comes ... the good with the bad.

And if you've temporarily lost one horizon *outside*—you've gained another, new and more beautiful, *inside!*

For now those two famed all-coach streamliners—*The Trail Blazer*, New York-Chicago and *The Jeffersonian*, New York-

Washington-St. Louis—and the *Liberty Limited*, Washington-Chicago, proudly welcome you to Pennsylvania Railroad's grand postwar coaches.

So roomy ... only 44 seats to the car!

So magnificently lighted ... fluorescent lights *four times* stronger, yet soft and ... shadowless.

So much easier riding ... credit that to the improved undercarriage and those new lightweight but sturdy steels.

Your window is a full 6 feet wide, the largest

we've ever made...and the washrooms likewise are extra spacious, each with two toilet annexes and three washstands.

Even your coach doors admit you with an ease never before known—they're electropneumatic and open at a finger's touch.

From the ground up, from door to door, these postwar coaches invite you to enjoy not only new comfort, new riding ease, new beauty—but an utterly new experience in dependable low-cost travel. So step aboard!... to a comfortable seat reserved for you at NO EXTRA COST!

PENNSYLVANIA RAILROAD
for WEATHERPROOF service

Reading: Recognize Emotional Appeals

Directions: *Choose the letter of the best answer to each question.*

1. To what emotion does the first advertisement appeal?
   A courage
   B patriotism
   C fear
   D happiness

2. What is the feature of train travel that the second advertisement emphasizes most strongly?
   A its speed
   B its beautiful views
   C its economy
   D its comfort

3. To what desire does the illustration in the second advertisement appeal?
   A relaxation
   B excitement
   C habit
   D economy

Reading: Comprehension and Interpretation

Directions: *Write your answers on a separate piece of paper.*

4. **(a)** What is the most important purpose of the first advertisement? **(b)** What is a secondary purpose? **[Analyzing]**

5. How do you know that the creator of the first ad approves of women working in railroad jobs? **[Generating]**

6. Which benefits mentioned in the second advertisement does its illustration express? **[Applying]**

Timed Writing: Comparison [Connections]

Compare and contrast these two advertisements. In your comparison, identify the persuasive techniques used, including emotional appeals and the use of illustrations. Evaluate the effect of the techniques used in the ad. **(20 minutes)**

Symbols

A **symbol** is a person, place, or thing that represents something beyond its literal meaning. For example, doves usually symbolize peace. Symbolism can add depth and insight into a literary work. Authors can use symbols in these ways:

- Using existing symbols—such as a dove—which have commonly understood meanings
- Creating their own symbols and developing the symbols' meanings through the descriptions, actions, and events of a story

Comparing Symbols

For many literary works, understanding the **symbolism** helps you understand the main message, or theme, of the story. To discover the deeper meaning of the main symbols in the "The White Umbrella" and "The Medicine Bag," ask yourself the following questions:

- What feelings do the white umbrella and the medicine bag provoke in the two narrators?
- What cultural or historical meaning does each object have?
- What significance does each object have in the development of the story?

Use the chart shown to compare the symbols in these stories.

	white umbrella	medicine bag
What does the object mean to the main character?		
What does the object mean to others in the story?		

Vocabulary Builder

The White Umbrella

- **discreet** (di skrēt´) *adj.* careful about what one says or does (p. 381) *It is best to be discreet when sharing a secret.*

- **credibility** (kred´ ə bil´ i tē) *n.* believability (p. 382) *Her campaign lost its credibility after she was caught taking bribes.*

- **revelation** (rev´ ə lā´ shən) *n.* something not previously known (p. 388) *We were shocked by the revelation that he had to quit his job.*

The Medicine Bag

- **authentic** (ô then´ tik) *adj.* genuine; real (p. 390) *If that artwork is authentic, it is valuable.*

- **procession** (prō sesh´ ən) *n.* a group moving forward, as in a parade (p. 391) *The funeral procession stretched for miles.*

- **unseemly** (un sēm´ lē) *adj.* inappropriate (p. 392) *It used to be considered unseemly for women to wear pants.*

Build Understanding

Connecting to the Literature

Reading/Writing Connection Most people have some objects that are significant to them because they are reminders of special people or events. In a few sentences, explain what makes people treasure these items. Use three of the following words: *appreciate, symbolize, signify, verify, perceive.*

Meet the Authors

Gish **Jen** (b. 1956)

Gish Jen, the daughter of Chinese immigrants, grew up in Yonkers and Scarsdale, New York. When asked about her influences, Jen replies, "A fellow writer described my situation when he said that making fiction is like making soup. There's lots of different ingredients: some of the ingredients come from your life; some come from things you've read, or from other people's lives; many, many things you've just made up."

Virginia Driving Hawk **Sneve** (b. 1933)

Virginia Driving Hawk Sneve grew up on the Rosebud Reservation in South Dakota, where she listened to storytellers tell traditional Sioux legends and folk tales.

A Mission to Educate As a Sioux mother, Sneve quickly realized that few children's books accurately portrayed Native American culture. She began writing in the early 1970s to correct this gap in literature. Sneve summarizes her award-winning career in this way: "[I hope to] show my reading audience that Native Americans have a proud past, a viable present, and a hopeful future."

Go **Online**
Author Link

For: More about the authors
Visit: www.PHSchool.com
Web Code: ene-9212

The White Umbrella

Gish Jen

Whenen I was twelve, my mother went to work without telling me or my little sister.

"Not that we need the second income." The lilt of her accent drifted from the kitchen up to the top of the stairs, where Mona and I were listening.

"No," said my father, in a barely audible voice. "Not like the Lee family."

The Lees were the only other Chinese family in town. I remembered how sorry my parents had felt for Mrs. Lee when she started waitressing downtown the year before; and so when my mother began coming home late, I didn't say anything, and tried to keep Mona from saying anything either.

"But why shouldn't I?" she argued. "Lots of people's mothers work."

"Those are American people," I said.

"So what do you think we are? I can do the pledge of allegiance with my eyes closed."

Nevertheless, she tried to be <u>discreet</u>; and if my mother wasn't home by 5:30, we would start cooking by ourselves, to make sure dinner would be on time. Mona would wash the vegetables and put on the rice; I would chop.

For weeks we wondered what kind of work she was doing. I imagined that she was selling perfume, testing dessert recipes for the local newspaper. Or maybe she was working for the florist. Now that she had learned to drive, she might be delivering boxes of roses to people.

"I don't think so," said Mona as we walked to our piano lesson after school. "She would've hit something by now."

A gust of wind littered the street with leaves.

"Maybe we better hurry up," she went on, looking at the sky. "It's going to pour."

"But we're too early." Her lesson didn't begin until 4:00, mine until 4:30, so we usually tried to walk as slowly as we could. "And anyway, those aren't the kind of clouds that rain. Those are cumulus clouds."[1]

We arrived out of breath and wet.

"Oh, you poor, poor dears," said old Miss Crosman. "Why don't you call me the next time it's like this out? If your mother won't drive you, I can come pick you up."

1. cumulus (kyoo´ myə ləs) **clouds** *n.* white clouds that usually indicate fair weather.

Literary Analysis
Symbol Why might the girls' mother try to hide the fact that she is working?

Vocabulary Builder
discreet (di skrēt´) *adj.* careful about what one says or does

Reading Check

Where are the two girls going?

"No, that's okay," I answered. Mona wrung her hair out on Miss Crosman's rug. "We just couldn't get the roof of our car to close, is all. We took it to the beach last summer and got sand in the mechanism." I pronounced this last word carefully, as if the <u>credibility</u> of my lie depended on its middle syllable. "It's never been the same." I thought for a second. "It's a convertible."

"Well then make yourselves at home." She exchanged looks with Eugenie Roberts, whose lesson we were interrupting. Eugenie smiled good-naturedly. "The towels are in the closet across from the bathroom."

Huddling at the end of Miss Crosman's nine-foot leatherette couch, Mona and I watched Eugenie play. She was a grade ahead of me and, according to school rumor, had a boyfriend in high school. I believed it. . . . She had auburn hair, blue eyes, and, I noted with a particular pang, a pure white folding umbrella.

"I can't see," whispered Mona.

"So clean your glasses."

"My glasses *are* clean. You're in the way."

I looked at her. "They look dirty to me."

"That's because *your* glasses are dirty."

Eugenie came bouncing to the end of her piece.

"Oh! Just stupendous!" Miss Crosman hugged her, then looked up as Eugenie's mother walked in. "Stupendous!" she said again. "Oh! Mrs. Roberts! Your daughter has a gift, a real gift. It's an honor to teach her."

Mrs. Roberts, radiant with pride, swept her daughter out of the room as if she were royalty, born to the piano bench. Watching the way Eugenie carried herself, I sat up, and concentrated so hard on sucking in my stomach that I did not realize until the Robertses were gone that Eugenie had left her umbrella. As Mona began to play, I jumped up and ran to the window, meaning to call to them—only to see their brake lights flash then fade at the stop sign at the corner. As if to allow them passage, the rain had let up; a quivering sun lit their way.

The umbrella glowed like a scepter on the blue carpet while Mona, slumping over the keyboard, managed to eke out[2] a fair

Vocabulary Builder
credibility (kred′ ə bil′ i tē) *n.* believability

Literary Analysis
Symbol Contrast the true story of how the girls got to the lesson with the symbolism of arriving in a convertible.

---

2. eke (ēk) **out** *v.* barely manage to play.

rendition of a catfight. At the end of the piece, Miss Crosman asked her to stand up.

"Stay right there," she said, then came back a minute later with a towel to cover the bench. "You must be cold," she continued. "Shall I call your mother and have her bring over some dry clothes?"

"No," answered Mona. "She won't come because she . . ."

"She's too busy," I broke in from the back of the room.

"I see." Miss Crosman sighed and shook her head a little. "Your glasses are filthy, honey," she said to Mona. "Shall I clean them for you?"

Sisterly embarrassment seized me. Why hadn't Mona wiped her lenses when I told her to? As she resumed abuse of the piano, I stared at the umbrella. I wanted to open it, twirl it around by its slender silver handle; I wanted to dangle it from my wrist on the way to school the way the other girls did. I wondered what Miss Crosman would say if I offered to bring it to Eugenie at school tomorrow. She would be impressed with my consideration for others; Eugenie would be pleased to have it back; and I would have possession of the umbrella for an entire night. I looked at it again, toying with the idea of asking for one for Christmas. I knew, however, how my mother would react.

"Things," she would say. "What's the matter with a raincoat? All you want is things, just like an American."

Sitting down for my lesson, I was careful to keep the towel under me and sit up straight.

"I'll bet you can't see a thing either," said Miss Crosman, reaching for my glasses. "And you can relax, you poor dear." She touched my chest, in an area where she never would have touched Eugenie Roberts. "This isn't a boot camp."[3]

When Miss Crosman finally allowed me to start playing I played extra well, as well as I possibly could. See, I told her with my fingers. You don't have to feel sorry for me.

"That was wonderful," said Miss Crosman. "Oh! Just wonderful."

An entire constellation rose in my heart.

"And guess what," I announced proudly. "I have a surprise for you."

Literary Analysis
Symbol What do her daydreams tell you about how the narrator views the white umbrella?

Literary Analysis
Symbol What does the narrator think the white umbrella would symbolize to her mother?

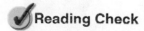**Reading Check**
Why is the girls' mother unable to bring them dry clothes?

---

3. **boot camp** place where soldiers receive basic training under strict discipline.

Then I played a second piece for her, a much more difficult one that she had not assigned.

"Oh! That was stupendous," she said without hugging me. "Stupendous! You are a genius, young lady. If your mother had started you younger, you'd be playing like Eugenie Roberts by now!"

I looked at the keyboard, wishing that I had still a third, even more difficult piece to play for her. I wanted to tell her that I was the school spelling bee champion, that I wasn't ticklish, that I could do karate.

"My mother is a concert pianist," I said.

She looked at me for a long moment, then finally, without saying anything, hugged me. I didn't say anything about bringing the umbrella to Eugenie at school.

The steps were dry when Mona and I sat down to wait for my mother.

"Do you want to wait inside?" Miss Crosman looked anxiously at the sky.

Literary Analysis
Symbol Why is the ability to play the piano well so important to the narrator?

▼ Critical Viewing
What skills help people, like the narrator and the girls in this photo, play the piano well? **[Analyze]**

"No," I said. "Our mother will be here any minute."

"In a while," said Mona.

"Any minute," I said again, even though my mother had been at least twenty minutes late every week since she started working.

According to the church clock across the street we had been waiting twenty-five minutes when Miss Crosman came out again.

"Shall I give you ladies a ride home?"

"No," I said. "Our mother is coming any minute."

"Shall I at least give her a call and remind her you're here? Maybe she forgot about you."

"I don't think she forgot," said Mona.

"Shall I give her a call anyway? Just to be safe?"

"I bet she already left," I said. "How could she forget about us?"

Miss Crosman went in to call.

"There's no answer," she said, coming back out.

"See, she's on her way," I said.

"Are you sure you wouldn't like to come in?"

"No," said Mona.

"Yes," I said. I pointed at my sister. "She meant yes too. She meant no, she wouldn't like to go in."

Miss Crosman looked at her watch. "It's 5:30 now, ladies. My pot roast will be coming out in fifteen minutes. Maybe you'd like to come in and have some then?"

"My mother's almost here," I said. "She's on her way."

We watched and watched the street. I tried to imagine what my mother was doing; I tried to imagine her writing messages in the sky, even though I knew she was afraid of planes. I watched as the branches of Miss Crosman's big willow tree started to sway; they had all been trimmed to exactly the same height off the ground, so that they looked beautiful, like hair in the wind.

It started to rain.

"Miss Crosman is coming out again," said Mona.

"Don't let her talk you into going inside," I whispered.

"Why not?"

"Because that would mean Mom isn't really coming any minute."

"But she isn't," said Mona. "She's working."

"Shhh! Miss Crosman is going to hear you."

Literary Analysis
Symbol Why does the narrator resist going inside?

Reading Check

What does Miss Crosman offer the girls while they wait?

"She's working! She's working! She's working!"

I put my hand over her mouth, but she licked it, and so I was wiping my hand on my wet dress when the front door opened.

"We're getting even *wetter*," said Mona right away. "Wetter and wetter."

"Shall we all go in?" Miss Crosman pulled Mona to her feet. "Before you young ladies catch pneumonia? You've been out here an hour already."

"We're *freezing*." Mona looked up at Miss Crosman. "Do you have any hot chocolate? We're going to catch *pneumonia*."

"I'm not going in," I said. "My mother's coming any minute."

"Come on," said Mona. "Use your *noggin*."[4]

"Any minute."

"Come on, Mona," Miss Crosman opened the door. "Shall we get you inside first?"

"See you in the hospital," said Mona as she went in. "See you in the hospital with pneumonia."

I stared out into the empty street. The rain was pricking me all over; I was cold; I wanted to go inside. I wanted to be able to let myself go inside. If Miss Crosman came out again, I decided, I would go in.

She came out with a blanket and the white umbrella.

I could not believe that I was actually holding the umbrella, opening it. It sprang up by itself as if it were alive, as if that were what it wanted to do—as if it belonged in my hands, above my head. I stared up at the network of silver spokes, then spun the umbrella around and around and around. It was so clean and white that it seemed to glow, to illuminate everything around it.

Literary Analysis
Symbol What details in this paragraph indicate the narrator sees the umbrella as something more than a useful object?

"It's beautiful," I said.

Miss Crosman sat down next to me, on one end of the blanket. I moved the umbrella over so that it covered that too. I could feel the rain on my left shoulder and shivered. She put her arm around me.

"You poor, poor dear."

I knew that I was in store for another bolt of sympathy, and braced myself by staring up into the umbrella.

"You know, I very much wanted to have children when I was younger," she continued.

"You did?"

---

4. **Use your *noggin*** informal expression for "use your head" or "think."

She stared at me a minute. Her face looked dry and crusty, like day-old frosting.

"I did. But then I never got married."

I twirled the umbrella around again.

"This is the most beautiful umbrella I have ever seen," I said. "Ever, in my whole life."

"Do you have an umbrella?"

"No. But my mother's going to get me one just like this for Christmas."

"Is she? I tell you what. You don't have to wait until Christmas. You can have this one."

"But this one belongs to Eugenie Roberts," I protested. "I have to give it back to her tomorrow in school."

"Who told you it belongs to Eugenie? It's not Eugenie's. It's mine. And now I'm giving it to you, so it's yours."

"It is?"

She hugged me tighter. "That's right. It's all yours."

"It's mine?" I didn't know what to say. "Mine?" Suddenly I was jumping up and down in the rain. "It's beautiful! Oh! It's beautiful!" I laughed.

Miss Crosman laughed too, even though she was getting all wet.

"Thank you, Miss Crosman. Thank you very much. Thanks a zillion. It's beautiful. It's *stupendous!*"

"You're quite welcome," she said.

"Thank you," I said again, but that didn't seem like enough. Suddenly I knew just what she wanted to hear. "I wish you were my mother."

Right away I felt bad.

"You shouldn't say that," she said, but her face was opening into a huge smile as the lights of my mother's car cautiously turned the corner. I quickly collapsed the umbrella and put it up my skirt, holding onto it from the outside, through the material.

"Mona!" I shouted into the house. "Mona! Hurry up! Mom's here! I told you she was coming!"

Then I ran away from Miss Crosman, down to the curb. Mona came tearing up to my side as my mother neared the house. We both backed up a few feet, so that in case she went onto the curb, she wouldn't run us over.

"But why didn't you go inside with Mona?" my mother asked on the way home. She had taken off her own coat to put over me, and had the heat on high.

Literary Analysis
Symbol Why might Miss Crosman especially enjoy the narrator's response to her gift?

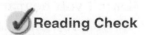

Reading Check

What does the narrator say to thank Miss Crosman for the umbrella?

"She wasn't using her noggin," said Mona, next to me in the back seat.

"I should call next time," said my mother. "I just don't like to say where I am."

That was when she finally told us that she was working as a check-out clerk in the A&P. She was supposed to be on the day shift, but the other employees were unreliable, and her boss had promised her a promotion if she would stay until the evening shift filled in.

For a moment no one said anything. Even Mona seemed to find the <u>revelation</u> disappointing.

"A promotion already!" she said, finally.

I listened to the windshield wipers.

"You're so quiet." My mother looked at me in the rear view mirror. "What's the matter?"

"I wish you would quit," I said after a moment.

She sighed. "The Chinese have a saying: one beam cannot hold the roof up."

"But Eugenie Roberts's father supports their family."

She sighed once more. "Eugenie Roberts's father is Eugenie Roberts's father," she said.

As we entered the downtown area, Mona started leaning hard against me every time the car turned right, trying to push me over. Remembering what I had said to Miss Crosman, I tried to maneuver the umbrella under my leg so she wouldn't feel it.

"What's under your skirt?" Mona wanted to know as we came to a traffic light. My mother, watching us in the rear view mirror again, rolled slowly to a stop.

"What's the matter?" she asked.

"There's something under her skirt!" said Mona, pulling at me.

"Under her skirt?"

Meanwhile, a man crossing the street started to yell at us. "Who do you think you are, lady?" he said. "You're blocking the whole crosswalk."

We all froze. Other people walking by stopped to watch.

"Didn't you hear me?" he went on, starting to thump on the hood with his fist. "Don't you speak English?"

My mother began to back up, but the car behind us honked. Luckily, the light turned green right after that. She sighed in relief.

Vocabulary Builder
revelation (rev′ ə lā′ shən) *n.* something not previously known

Literary Analysis
Symbol Why does the narrator hide the umbrella from her mother?

"What were you saying, Mona?" she asked.

We wouldn't have hit the car behind us that hard if he hadn't been moving too, but as it was our car bucked violently, throwing us all first back and then forward.

"Uh oh," said Mona when we stopped. *"Another* accident."

I was relieved to have attention diverted from the umbrella. Then I noticed my mother's head, tilted back onto the seat. Her eyes were closed.

"Mom!" I screamed. "Mom! Wake up!"

She opened her eyes. "Please don't yell," she said. "Enough people are going to yell already."

"I thought you were dead," I said, starting to cry. "I thought you were dead."

She turned around, looked at me intently, then put her hand to my forehead.

"Sick," she confirmed. "Some kind of sick is giving you crazy ideas."

As the man from the car behind us started tapping on the window, I moved the umbrella away from my leg. Then Mona and my mother were getting out of the car. I got out after them; and while everyone else was inspecting the damage we'd done, I threw the umbrella down a sewer.

Thinking About the Selection

1. **Respond:** What did you find most realistic about the characters and events in this story? Explain.

2. **(a) Recall:** Why is the narrator's mother late to pick up the sisters? **(b) Infer:** Why is the narrator bothered by her mother's lateness? **(c) Analyze:** Why does she prevent her sister from explaining why their mother is late?

3. **(a) Infer:** Why does Miss Crosman give the narrator the umbrella? **(b) Deduce:** How does Miss Crosman feel about children?

The Medicine Bag

VIRGINIA DRIVING HAWK SNEVE

My kid sister Cheryl and I always bragged about our Sioux[1] grandpa, Joe Iron Shell. Our friends, who had always lived in the city and only knew about Indians from movies and TV, were impressed by our stories. Maybe we exaggerated and made Grandpa and the reservation sound glamorous, but when we'd return home to Iowa after our yearly summer visit to Grandpa, we always had some exciting tale to tell.

We always had some <u>authentic</u> Sioux article to show our listeners. One year Cheryl had new moccasins[2] that Grandpa had made. On another visit he gave me a small, round, flat, rawhide drum that was decorated with a painting of a warrior riding a horse. He taught me a real Sioux chant to sing while I beat the drum with a leather-covered stick that had a feather on the end. Man that really made an impression.

We never showed our friends Grandpa's picture. Not that we were ashamed of him, but because we knew that the glamorous tales we told didn't go with the real thing. Our friends

▲ **Critical Viewing**
Do you think the medicine bag pictured was manufactured or handmade? How can you tell? **[Infer]**

Vocabulary Builder
authentic (ô then´ tik) *adj.* genuine; real

---

1. Sioux (sōō´) *adj.* member of Native American tribe of the northern United States and southern Canada.
2. moccasins (mäk´ ə sənz) *n.* soft shoes traditionally made from animal hide.

would have laughed at the picture because Grandpa wasn't tall and stately like TV Indians. His hair wasn't in braids but hung in stringy, gray strands on his neck, and he was old. He was our great-grandfather, and he didn't live in a tepee, but all by himself in a part log, part tarpaper shack on the Rosebud Reservation in South Dakota. So when Grandpa came to visit us, I was so ashamed and embarrassed I could've died.

There are a lot of yippy poodles and other fancy little dogs in our neighborhood, but they usually barked singly at the mailman from the safety of their own yards. Now it sounded as if a whole pack of mutts were barking together in one place.

I got up and walked to the curb to see what the commotion was. About a block away I saw a crowd of little kids yelling, with the dogs yipping and growling around someone who was walking down the middle of the street.

I watched the group as it slowly came closer and saw that in the center of the strange <u>procession</u> was a man wearing a tall black hat. He'd pause now and then to peer at something in his hand and then at the houses on either side of the street. I felt cold and hot at the same time as I recognized the man. "Oh, no!" I whispered. "It's Grandpa!"

I stood on the curb, unable to move even though I wanted to run and hide. Then I got mad when I saw how the yippy dogs were growling and nipping at the old man's baggy pant legs and how wearily he poked them away with his cane. "Stupid mutts," I said as I ran to rescue Grandpa.

When I kicked and hollered at the dogs to get away, they put their tails between their legs and scattered. The kids ran to the curb where they watched me and the old man.

"Grandpa," I said and felt pretty dumb when my voice cracked. I reached for his beat-up old tin suitcase, which was tied shut with a rope. But he set it down right in the street and shook my hand.

"*Hau, Takoza,* Grandchild," he greeted me formally in Sioux.

All I could do was stand there with the whole neighborhood watching and shake the hand of the leather-brown old man. I saw how his gray hair straggled from under his big black hat,

Literary Analysis
Symbol Why is the narrator embarrassed by his grandfather?

Vocabulary Builder
procession (prō sesh´ ən) *n.* a group moving forward, as in a parade

✔ **Reading Check**

Who accompanies the narrator's grandfather as he walks down the street?

which had a drooping feather in its crown. His rumpled black suit hung like a sack over his stooped frame. As he shook my hand, his coat fell open to expose a bright red satin shirt with a beaded bolo tie under the collar. His get-up wasn't out of place on the reservation, but it sure was here, and I wanted to sink right through the pavement.

"Hi," I muttered with my head down. I tried to pull my hand away when I felt his bony hand trembling, and looked up to see fatigue in his face. I felt like crying. I couldn't think of anything to say so I picked up Grandpa's suitcase, took his arm, and guided him up the driveway to our house.

Mom was standing on the steps. I don't know how long she'd been watching, but her hand was over her mouth and she looked as if she couldn't believe what she saw. Then she ran to us.

"Grandpa," she gasped. "How in the world did you get here?"

She checked her move to embrace Grandpa and I remembered that such a display of affection is <u>unseemly</u> to the Sioux and would embarrass him.

"*Hau*, Marie," he said as he shook Mom's hand. She smiled and took his other arm.

As we supported him up the steps, the door banged open and Cheryl came bursting out of the house. She was all smiles and was so obviously glad to see Grandpa that I was ashamed of how I felt.

"Grandpa!" she yelled happily. "You came to see us!"

Grandpa smiled, and Mom and I let go of him as he stretched out his arms to my ten-year-old sister, who was still young enough to be hugged.

"*Wicincala*, little girl," he greeted her and then collapsed.

He had fainted. Mom and I carried him into her sewing room, where we had a spare bed.

After we had Grandpa on the bed, Mom stood there helplessly patting his shoulder.

"Shouldn't we call the doctor, Mom?" I suggested, since she didn't seem to know what to do.

Literature in Context

Social Studies Connection

The Sioux Nation Before the mid-1800s, the Sioux lived throughout the northern plains of North America. In 1874, the U.S. government broke a treaty guaranteeing Sioux boundaries. Many Sioux decided to fight. Led by the famous chiefs Sitting Bull (shown here) and Crazy Horse, they defeated General Custer's troops at Little Big Horn. Eventually, however, the Sioux were overpowered. Today, many Sioux live on reservations throughout the Upper Midwest.

Connect to the Literature

How might living on a reservation affect Grandpa's feelings about Sioux traditions?

Vocabulary Builder
unseemly (un sēm′ lē)
adj. inappropriate

"Yes," she agreed with a sigh. "You make Grandpa comfortable, Martin."

I reluctantly moved to the bed. I knew Grandpa wouldn't want to have Mom undress him, but I didn't want to, either. He was so skinny and frail that his coat slipped off easily. When I loosened his tie and opened his shirt collar, I felt a small leather pouch that hung from a thong around his neck. I left it alone and moved to remove his boots. The scuffed old cowboy boots were tight, and he moaned as I put pressure on his legs to jerk them off.

I put the boots on the floor and saw why they fit so tight. Each one was stuffed with money. I looked at the bills that lined the boots and started to ask about them, but Grandpa's eyes were closed again.

Mom came back with a basin of water. "The doctor thinks Grandpa is suffering from heat exhaustion," she explained as she bathed Grandpa's face. Mom gave a big sigh, "*Oh, hinh, Martin.* How do you suppose he got here?"

We found out after the doctor's visit. Grandpa was angrily sitting up in bed while Mom tried to feed him some soup.

"Tonight you let Marie feed you, Grandpa," spoke my dad, who had gotten home from work just as the doctor was leaving. "You're not really sick," he said as he gently pushed Grandpa back against the pillows. "The doctor said you just got too tired and hot after your long trip."

Grandpa relaxed, and between sips of soup, he told us of his journey. Soon after our visit to him, Grandpa decided that he would like to see where his only living descendants lived and what our home was like. Besides, he admitted sheepishly, he was lonesome after we left.

I knew that everybody felt as guilty as I did—especially Mom. Mom was all Grandpa had left. So even after she married my dad, who's a white man and teaches in the college in our city, and after Cheryl and I were born, Mom made sure that every summer we spent a week with Grandpa.

I never thought that Grandpa would be lonely after our visits, and none of us noticed how old and weak he had become. But Grandpa knew, and so he came to us. He had ridden on buses for two and a half days. When he arrived in the city, tired and stiff from sitting for so long, he set out, walking, to find us.

He had stopped to rest on the steps of some building downtown, and a policeman found him. The cop, according to

Literary Analysis
Symbol Why does Grandpa resist being fed by Mom?

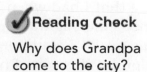

Reading Check

Why does Grandpa come to the city?

Grandpa, was a good man who took him to the bus stop and waited until the bus came and told the driver to let Grandpa out at Bell View Drive. After Grandpa got off the bus, he started walking again. But he couldn't see the house numbers on the other side when he walked on the sidewalk, so he walked in the middle of the street. That's when all the little kids and dogs followed him.

I knew everybody felt as bad as I did. Yet I was so proud of this eighty-six-year-old man, who had never been away from the reservation, having the courage to travel so far alone.

"You found the money in my boots?" he asked Mom.

"Martin did," she answered, and roused herself to scold. "Grandpa, you shouldn't have carried so much money. What if someone had stolen it from you?"

Grandpa laughed. "I would've known if anyone tried to take the boots off my feet. The money is what I've saved for a long time—a hundred dollars—for my funeral. But you take it now to buy groceries so that I won't be a burden to you while I am here."

"That won't be necessary, Grandpa," Dad said. "We are honored to have you with us, and you will never be a burden. I am only sorry that we never thought to bring you home with us this summer and spare you the discomfort of a long trip."

Grandpa was pleased. "Thank you," he answered. "But do not feel bad that you didn't bring me with you, for I would not have come then. It was not time." He said this in such a way that no one could argue with him. To Grandpa and the Sioux, he once told me, a thing would be done when it was the right time to do it, and that's the way it was.

"Also," Grandpa went on, looking at me, "I have come because it is soon time for Martin to have the medicine bag."

We all knew what that meant. Grandpa thought he was going to die, and he had to follow the tradition of his family to pass the medicine bag, along with its history, to the oldest male child.

"Even though the boy," he said still looking at me, "bears a white man's name, the medicine bag will be his."

I didn't know what to say. I had the same hot and cold feeling that I had when I first saw Grandpa in the street. The medicine bag was the dirty leather pouch I had found around his neck. "I could never wear such a thing," I almost said aloud. I thought of having my friends see it in gym class or at

Literary Analysis
Symbol What makes Grandpa's journey remarkable?

Literary Analysis
Symbol What is the symbolic importance of Grandpa's visit?

the swimming pool and could imagine the smart things they would say. But I just swallowed hard and took a step toward the bed. I knew I would have to take it.

But Grandpa was tired. "Not now, Martin," he said, waving his hand in dismissal. "It is not time. Now I will sleep."

So that's how Grandpa came to be with us for two months. My friends kept asking to come see the old man, but I put them off. I told myself that I didn't want them laughing at Grandpa. But even as I made excuses, I knew it wasn't Grandpa that I was afraid they'd laugh at.

Nothing bothered Cheryl about bringing her friends to see Grandpa. Every day after school started, there'd be a crew of giggling little girls or round-eyed little boys crowded around the old man on the patio, where he'd gotten in the habit of sitting every afternoon.

Grandpa would smile in his gentle way and patiently answer their questions, or he'd tell them stories of brave warriors, ghosts, animals; and the kids listened in awed silence. Those little guys thought Grandpa was great.

Finally, one day after school, my friends came home with me because nothing I said stopped them. "We're going to see the great Indian of Bell View Drive," said Hank, who was supposed to be my best friend. "My brother has seen him three times so he oughta be well enough to see us."

When we got to my house, Grandpa was sitting on the patio. He had on his red shirt, but today he also wore a fringed leather vest that was decorated with beads. Instead of his usual cowboy boots, he had solidly beaded moccasins on his feet that stuck out of his black trousers. Of course, he had his old black hat on—he was seldom without it. But it had been brushed, and the feather in the beaded headband was proudly erect, its tip a brighter white. His hair lay in silver strands over the red shirt collar.

I stared just as my friends did, and I heard one of them murmur, "Wow!"

Grandpa looked up, and, when his eyes met mine, they twinkled as if he were laughing inside. He nodded to me, and my face got all hot. I could tell that he had known all along I was afraid he'd embarrass me in front of my friends.

"*Hau, hoksilas,* boys," he greeted and held out his hand.

My buddies passed in a single file and shook his hand as I introduced them. They were so polite I almost laughed. "How, there, Grandpa," and even a "How-do-you-do, sir."

Literary Analysis

Symbol How does Martin's reluctance to accept the medicine bag show he is caught between two worlds?

Reading Check

What does Grandpa do to prepare for the visit of Martin's friends?

"You look fine, Grandpa," I said as the guys sat on the lawn chairs or on the patio floor.

"*Hanh*, yes," he agreed. "When I woke up this morning, it seemed the right time to dress in the good clothes. I knew that my grandson would be bringing his friends."

"You guys want some lemonade or something?" I offered. No one answered. They were listening to Grandpa as he started telling how he'd killed the deer from which his vest was made.

Grandpa did most of the talking while my friends were there. I was so proud of him and amazed at how respectfully quiet my buddies were. Mom had to chase them home at supper time. As they left, they shook Grandpa's hand again and said to me,

"Martin, he's really great!"

"Yeah, man! Don't blame you for keeping him to yourself."

"Can we come back?"

But after they left, Mom said, "No more visitors for a while, Martin. Grandpa won't admit it, but his strength hasn't returned. He likes having company, but it tires him."

That evening Grandpa called me to his room before he went to sleep. "Tomorrow," he said, "when you come home, it will be time to give you the medicine bag."

I felt a hard squeeze from where my heart is supposed to be and was scared, but I answered, "OK, Grandpa."

All night I had weird dreams about thunder and lightning on a high hill. From a distance I heard the slow beat of a drum. When I woke up in the morning, I felt as if I hadn't slept at all. At school it seemed as if the day would never end and, when it finally did, I ran home.

Grandpa was in his room, sitting on the bed. The shades were down, and the place was dim and cool. I sat on the floor in front of Grandpa, but he didn't even look at me. After what seemed a long time he spoke.

"I sent your mother and sister away. What you will hear today is only for a man's ears. What you will receive is only for a man's hands." He fell silent, and I felt shivers down my back.

"My father in his early manhood," Grandpa began, "made a vision quest[3] to find a spirit guide for his life. You cannot understand how it was in that time, when the great Teton Sioux were first made to stay on the reservation. There was a

3. **vision quest** (vizh′ ən kwest) *n.* difficult search for spiritual guidance in Native American cultures.

396 ■ *Short Stories*

Literary Analysis
Symbol What does Grandpa represent to Martin's friends?

Literary Analysis
Symbol From the description, do you think Martin's dream symbolizes something pleasant or distressing? Why?

strong need for guidance from *Wakantanka*,[4] the Great Spirit.
But too many of the young men were filled with despair and
hatred. They thought it was hopeless to search for a vision
when the glorious life was gone and only the hated confines of
a reservation lay ahead. But my father held to the old ways.

"He carefully prepared for his quest with a purifying sweat
bath, and then he went alone to a high butte top[5] to fast and
pray. After three days he received his sacred dream—in which
he found, after long searching, the white man's iron. He did
not understand his vision of finding something belonging to
the white people, for in that time they were the enemy. When
he came down from the butte to cleanse himself at the stream
below, he found the remains of a campfire and the broken
shell of an iron kettle. This was a sign that reinforced his
dream. He took a piece of the iron for his medicine bag, which
he had made of elk skin years before, to prepare for his quest.

"He returned to his village, where he told his dream to the
wise old men of the tribe. They gave him the name *Iron Shell*,

A Critical Viewing
What elements of
this picture capture
the mood of
Martin's dream?
[Analyze]

Reading Check

Why was it unusual
for Grandpa's
father to go on a
vision quest?

---

4. ***Wakantanka*** (wä´ kən tank´ ə) *n.* Sioux religion's most important spirit—the creator of the world.
5. **butte** (byōōt) **top** *n.* isolated mountain top with steep sides.

but neither did they understand the meaning of the dream. The first Iron Shell kept the piece of iron with him at all times and believed it gave him protection from the evils of those unhappy days.

"Then a terrible thing happened to Iron Shell. He and several other young men were taken from their homes by the soldiers and sent far away to a white man's boarding school. He was angry and lonesome for his parents and the young girl he had wed before he was taken away. At first Iron Shell resisted the teacher's attempts to change him, and he did not try to learn. One day it was his turn to work in the school's blacksmith shop. As he walked into the place, he knew that his medicine had brought him there to learn and work with the white man's iron.

"Iron Shell became a blacksmith and worked at the trade when he returned to the reservation. All of his life he treasured the medicine bag. When he was old, and I was a man, he gave it to me, for no one made the vision quest any more."

Grandpa quit talking, and I stared in disbelief as he covered his face with his hands. His shoulders were shaking with quiet sobs, and I looked away until he began to speak again.

"I kept the bag until my son, your mother's father, was a man and had to leave us to fight in the war across the ocean. I gave him the bag, for I believed it would protect him in bat-

▲ Critical Viewing
Which elements of this picture match the vision quest that Grandpa describes?

tle, but he did not take it with him. He was afraid that he would lose it. He died in a faraway place."

Again Grandpa was still, and I felt his grief around me.

"My son," he went on after clearing his throat, "had only a daughter, and it is not proper for her to know of these things."

He unbuttoned his shirt, pulled out the leather pouch, and lifted it over his head. He held it in his hand, turning it over and over as if memorizing how it looked.

"In the bag," he said as he opened it and removed two objects, "is the broken shell of the iron kettle, a pebble from the butte, and a piece of the sacred sage."[6] He held the pouch upside down and dust drifted down.

"After the bag is yours you must put a piece of prairie sage within and never open it again until you pass it on to your son." He replaced the pebble and the piece of iron, and tied the bag.

I stood up, somehow knowing I should. Grandpa slowly rose from the bed and stood upright in front of me holding the bag before my face. I closed my eyes and waited for him to slip it over my head. But he spoke.

"No, you need not wear it." He placed the soft leather bag in my right hand and closed my other hand over it. "It would not

6. sage (sāj) n. type of herb.

Literary Analysis
Symbol Why is Grandpa telling Martin this family history?

Reading Check

Why did Grandpa's son refuse to take the medicine bag?

be right to wear it in this time and place where no one will understand. Put it safely away until you are again on the reservation. Wear it then, when you replace the sacred sage."

Grandpa turned and sat again on the bed. Wearily he leaned his head against the pillow. "Go," he said. "I will sleep now."

"Thank you, Grandpa," I said softly and left with the bag in my hands.

That night Mom and Dad took Grandpa to the hospital. Two weeks later I stood alone on the lonely prairie of the reservation and put the sacred sage in my medicine bag.

Literary Analysis
Symbol What is the symbolic importance of each item in the medicine bag?

Thinking About the Selection

1. **Respond:** Did you sympathize with Martin's initial embarrassment over his grandfather's behavior? Why or why not?

2. **(a) Recall:** Describe how each family member welcomes Grandpa. **(b) Analyze:** What causes Martin to feel ashamed when Grandpa appears? **(c) Interpret:** How can Martin feel both ashamed and proud of Grandpa?

3. **(a) Recall:** What three reasons does Grandpa give for coming to visit? **(b) Support:** How do the events of the story support Grandpa's idea that things will be done when it is "the right time"?

4. **(a) Recall:** What does Martin do at the very end of the story? **(b) Draw Conclusions:** What does Martin's final act reveal about his relationship to his heritage?

5. **(a) Evaluate:** By the end of the story, is Martin ready to receive his grandfather's gift? **(b) Apply:** Using examples from the story and from life, explain how some "gifts" are also responsibilities.

Apply the Skills

The White Umbrella • The Medicine Bag

Comparing Symbols

1. **(a)** How does the narrator feel about the white umbrella?
   (b) What does the umbrella represent to the narrator?
   (c) What does the narrator's action of throwing away the umbrella **symbolize** at the end of the story?

2. **(a)** At first, how does Martin feel about the medicine bag?
   (b) What does it come to symbolize for Martin?

3. **(a)** Complete a chart like the one shown to analyze the similarities and differences between the major symbols in the two stories. **(b)** Using your completed chart, write a statement to explain how the symbols are similar. Then, write a statement to show how the symbols are different.

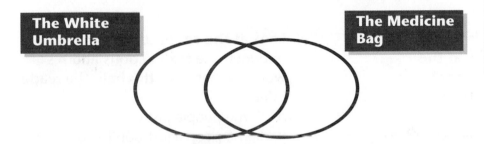

The White Umbrella

The Medicine Bag

QuickReview

Symbol: a person, place, or object that represents something else

Symbolism: the use of symbols to add meaning

Go Online
—Assessment

For: Self-test
Visit: www.PHSchool.com
Web Code: ena-6211

Writing to Compare Literary Works

In a brief essay, explain why the symbols in these two works are memorable and effective. Use your statements of similarities and differences to support your ideas. To prepare for writing, consider the following questions for each story:

- Does the symbol have cultural meaning outside of the story?
- What message does the symbol help the story to convey?
- How do the conflicting feelings of the main character make the symbolism more powerful?

In your essay, tell readers which symbol was more effective, and therefore, easiest for you to understand.

Vocabulary Builder

Practice Write sentences that correctly use both words in each pair.

1. authentic; actual
2. revelation; angry
3. discreet; behavior
4. procession; traffic
5. credibility; trust
6. unseemly; embarrass

Reading: Make Inferences

Directions: *Questions 1–5 are based on the following selection.*

One hot summer day, a fox with his tongue hanging out staggered down a long, dusty road. Suddenly he looked up at a fence by the side of the road. He saw a bunch of fat, juicy, purple grapes hanging on a vine at the top of the fence. He backed up, took a running start, and tried to jump to the top of the fence, but he just missed the grapes. With a determined look on his face, he took a deep breath and tried again. No luck. Huffing and puffing, he tried again and again, with no success. Finally, exhausted, he was forced to give up.

"Oh well," he said, walking away with his head held high, "no great loss. I didn't want them anyway. I'm sure those grapes were sour."

1. **What can you infer from the description of the fox at the beginning of the passage?**
   A   He is hungry and thirsty.
   B   He is happy and content.
   C   He is fat and well-fed.
   D   He is lonely and unfriendly.

2. **What can you infer from the fox's efforts to get the grapes?**
   A   He desperately wants the grapes.
   B   He desperately wants to prove his jumping talent.
   C   He has no idea what he wants.
   D   He really likes to show off.

3. **Which idea does the author probably want readers to connect with the fox's statement that the grapes are sour?**
   A   The idea that he doesn't want to taste the grapes.
   B   The idea that he makes an excuse for not succeeding.
   C   The idea that he can't become a better jumper.
   D   The idea that others need the grapes.

4. **Look at the connection in the story between the fox's actions and his words. What does this help the reader infer?**
   A   Some people just don't try.
   B   Some people just don't know when to quit trying.
   C   Some people will do anything for a free meal.
   D   Some people pretend not to want the things they can't have.

5. **What is the most logical inference about the fox?**
   A   He can think of several approaches to a problem.
   B   He can use tools to solve a problem.
   C   He approaches a problem only one way.
   D   He solves problems carefully after great thought.

Assessment Practice

Vocabulary Skill Review

A. Directions: *Choose the best synonym or definition for each underlined word.*

6. She made a <u>logical</u> choice.
   A physical
   B emotional
   C reasonable
   D unreasonable

7. What do you <u>conclude</u> is the cause?
   A react without thinking
   B decide through reasoning
   C indicate agreement
   D announce a plan of action

8. I <u>infer</u> that the character is sad.
   A seek the cause of an action
   B determine right and wrong
   C draw conclusions based on facts
   D decide on one idea

9. Details <u>indicate</u> that the character has doubts.
   A welcome
   B dedicate
   C forget
   D show

10. Provide <u>evidence</u> for your claims.
    A physical objects that lead to a conclusion
    B a series of statements
    C conclusions based on facts
    D details that are clues or proof

B. Directions: *Answer the following questions based on the dictionary entry below.*

> **con•clude** (kən klo͞od′) v. (ME < L, *concludere* < com- + *claudere* to shut)

11. Which language is the original source for the word <u>conclude</u>?
    A Middle English
    B Old French
    C Modern English
    D Latin

12. What does <u>ME</u> stand for in the entry?
    A Middle English
    B Modern English
    C Middle Eastern
    D Modern Era

13. Where would the <u>conclusion</u> to an essay appear?
    A in the title
    B in the first sentence
    C in the middle
    D in the end

Tricky or Difficult Words

Certain words are commonly misspelled because people put too many or too few letters in them. Some words are tricky to spell because they are pronounced incorrectly. Others are not spelled the way they are pronounced.

This collage is of my friends from college.

Did You Use Just Enough Letters? Though pronunciation does not always help with spelling, in some cases it does. If you add extra letter or syllable sounds to words—for example, if you say ath<u>a</u>lete— you will probably spell this word incorrectly. Use a dictionary to check the pronunciation of the words on the list.

Practice Match the word from the Word List with the clue. Then, in a small group, develop ways to remember the spelling, a mnemonic device. (Example: repetition repeats the *e* and the *i*.)

1. again and again
2. higher education
3. grab
4. inflammation of the joints
5. awkward feeling
6. person who plays sports
7. divide
8. playfully disobedient
9. recollection
10. overwhelmed

Word List
athlete
arthritis
seize
mischievous
drowned
remembrance
separate
embarrassment
repetition
college

Assessment Practice

A. Directions: *Write the letter of the sentence in which the underlined word is spelled correctly.*

1. **A** Maria is a strong <u>athlete</u>.
   B She gets <u>enbarassed</u> at attention.
   C She almost <u>drownded</u> when she was a young girl.
   D She is on the <u>collage</u> swim team.

2. **A** My little brother is very <u>mischieveous</u>.
   B He is also a good <u>athleet</u>.
   C Skills take <u>repatition</u>.
   D You have to <u>separate</u> the practice and the game.

3. **A** Jason developed <u>artheritis</u>.
   B Before that, he was a star <u>athleet</u>.
   C He <u>saparated</u> himself from sports.
   D He is still <u>mischievous</u>.

4. **A** My brother is in <u>colege</u>.
   B He is <u>drowned</u> by work.
   C He <u>siezes</u> every chance to study.
   D He has no time for <u>mischivous</u> pranks.

B. Directions: *Write the letter of the word that would be the correct spelling to fill in the blank.*

1. They should _____ the opportunity.
   A siez
   B sieze
   C scize
   D seeze

2. Many elderly people develop _____.
   A arthritis
   B artheritis
   C artharitis
   D arthuritis

3. They sent a _____ card for the Smiths' anniversary.
   A rememberance
   B remembrance
   C rememberence
   D remembrence

4. The mistake caused _____.
   A embarassment
   B embarrasment
   C embarrassment
   D embarasment

5. Now he teaches at a local _____.
   A collage
   B college
   C callege
   D colloge

6. _____ will help you remember.
   A Repetition
   B Repeatition
   C Repatition
   D Repaetition

Narration: Short Story

A short story can take readers to new places or show them sides of life they might not have considered. Follow the steps outlined in this workshop to write your own short story.

Assignment Write a short story with believable characters who face a realistic conflict.

What to Include To be effective, your short story should have the following characteristics:
- one or more characters, developed throughout the story
- a clear setting, a time and place in which action occurs
- a conflict or problem faced by a main character
- a plot that develops the conflict and leads to a climax, or turning point, and a resolution of the conflict
- a theme—an idea or question about life or human nature—that is reflected in the story's plot
- dialogue that reveals character and moves the plot forward

To preview the criteria on which your short story may be judged, see the rubric on page 413.

 ### Writing Workshop: *Work in Progress*

If you have completed the Work-in-Progress assignments, you have in your portfolio several ideas you might use in your short story. Continue developing these ideas, or explore a new idea as you complete the Writing Workshop.

Using the Form

You may use parts of this form in these writing situations:
- journals
- persuasive essays
- anecdotes
- speeches

To see a short story by a master, read "The Tell-Tale Heart" by Edgar Allan Poe on page 265.

Prewriting

Choosing Your Topic

To imagine the people and action of your story, use these strategies:

- **Begin with a character.** Your character may be based on people you know, or the character can be completely fictitious. Get to know your main character by drawing a picture, listing details, or asking and answering questions such as "How do you spend your time?" or "Who are your friends?"

- **Picture the scene.** Imagine your character in a particular time and place. Make a chart of sensory images to weave through your story. Use all five senses to help readers experience the setting as real.

Work in Progress
Review the work you did on pages 353 and 373.

SIGHT	Open window; curtains blowing
SOUND	Music, laughter
SMELL	Neighbors' barbecue
TOUCH	Breeze from window
TASTE	Sweet lemonade

Determine point of view. The narrator's presentation of information will influence the way the story is told and received. Decide who you want your narrator to be:

First-person narrator:	I felt a surge of energy as I launched the ball toward the hoop.
Third-person narrator:	The crowd held their breath as Pam shot the ball toward the hoop.

Narrowing Your Topic

Invent a situation. To focus on the action and conflict of your story, complete sentences like these in several different ways.
- What if *(person)* wanted *?* but *(name problem)*?
- What if *(person)* suddenly *(name problem)*?

Review your work and choose a focus for your story.

Gathering Details

Identify the conflict. Clarify the problem your story will develop. Make notes about the ways the problem will reveal itself and intensify, the ways each character will react, and the resolution.

Writing Workshop

Drafting

Shaping Your Writing

Build to a climax. In the beginning, or exposition, give your readers information to help them understand the situation. Develop the conflict, event by event, until you reach the turning point or climax, the point of highest tension when your story turns toward its logical conclusion. Use a plot diagram like the one shown to help you construct your story.

One day George discovers Martha and Henry trapped by a bull.

Climax

Martha refuses to marry George because he is a farmer.

George distracts the bull, and Henry runs away.

Struck by George's bravery, Martha agrees to marry him

Introduce George, Martha, and Henry the school teacher.

Rising Action

Falling Action

Resolution

Exposition

Conflict Introduced

Use dialogue. Characters' own words add variety and interest to your narrative, but also serve other functions. You can distinguish your characters by giving them individual voices and patterns of speech. Dialogue can move the action forward. In dialogue, let your characters interact and display a wide range of emotions through their words.

Providing Elaboration

Develop reader interest. As you write, use vivid details to help your readers get a sense of the characters, the setting, and the events.

Flat

He had never liked hoeing very much.

Vivid

He hated hoeing because it made huge calluses on his hands.

Show, do not tell. Avoid using too much description to tell your story. Wherever you can, convey details of character or conflict through action or dialogue.

Reading Writing Connection

To read the complete student model, see page 412.

Student Model: Show, Do Not Tell

"Aren't you supposed to be buried with the pharaoh in his tomb—" He was cut short by the hand of Anuk.

"The stench of resin doesn't please me, if you know what I mean," answered Anuk.

Michael uses dialogue instead of description to show Anuk's attitude toward his expected role.

From the Author's Desk

Judith Ortiz Cofer
On Bringing Characters to Life

Judith Ortiz Cofer

Before I start writing I take notes, sometimes for days, sometimes for months, and in the case of novels, maybe even years. I keep a notebook with me at all times where I jot down ideas, images, words I hear, anything that I think will bring my characters to life. Before a story is finished I have usually rewritten it many times, as the theme develops and changes.

"The short story is very often a journey . . ."
——Judith Ortiz Cofer

Professional Model:
from "The One Who Watches," from *An Island Like You*

"Mira, mira!" my friend Yolanda yells out. She's always telling me to look at something. And I always do. I look, she does. That's the way it's always been. Yolanda just turned sixteen, I'm six months younger. I was born to follow the leader, and that's what my mother says when she sees us together, and it's true.

Because Yolanda is the dominant character, I wanted her to say the first words in the story, to take control. "Mira, mira!" is an imperative; Doris *thinks* her responses.

It's like the world is a deli full of pricey treats to Yolanda, and she wants the most expensive ones in fancy boxes, the ones she can't afford. We spend hours shopping downtown. Sometimes when Yolanda gets excited about an outfit, we go into a store and she tries it on. But the salespeople are getting to know us. They know we don't have any money. So we get chased out of places a lot. . . .

A story depends on sensory details to come alive. A reader should be able to share the experience by seeing, tasting, smelling, hearing, and feeling right along with the characters in scenes filled with vivid details.

We have to pass my apartment on our way out, and I can hear my mother singing an old song . . . It's *Cielito Lindo*—a sort of lullaby that she used to sing to me when I was little.

I often use titles of old songs I heard in my childhood as memory triggers in my writing. *Cielito Lindo* is what my mother used to sing to us at bedtime; in the story, it reminds Doris of her mother's warnings about Yolanda.

Writing Workshop

Revising

Revising Your Paragraphs

Add detail to develop characters. Look for places to add more details that help your readers see and respond to your characters.

1. Review your draft, highlighting situations and events to which a character would have a strong reaction.

2. Ask yourself: What gestures, words, facial expressions, thoughts, memories, or actions will reflect this reaction?

3. In the margin, jot down answers to these questions.

4. Review your notes and decide which details to include. Keep in mind that you are trying to influence your audience's reactions through the reactions of your characters.

Student Model: Revising to Develop Characters

~~"Great," thought Anuk sarcastically, "I'm only thirteen and I'm~~

~~already being sent to my death."~~

∧ Most of the Pharaoh's servants would jump at the chance to go into the afterlife with their king. But Anuk was no ordinary boy. There was something inside him that made him want to live—

> This humorous thought helps to show the main character's personality. His sarcasm also adds interest for the audience.

Peer Review: Ask for a partner's response to your character. Revise to achieve the reaction you had intended.

To read the complete student model, see page 412.

Revising Your Word Choice

Revise to include action verbs. Linking verbs simply connect a subject with a word that describes it. Action verbs are often a more exciting and direct alternative. To replace linking verbs, highlight all forms of *be* and other linking verbs (*feel, look, appear, become, grow, remain*) and try to rewrite your sentences using action verbs.

> **Linking Verb:** I *was surprised* by what I saw.
>
> **Action Verb:** I *gasped* at what I saw.

Revise to include interjections. To add excitement and realism to your dialogue, use **interjections**—exclamatory words and phrases such as "No way!" and "Unbelievable!"

Integrating Grammar Skills

Revising for Subject/Verb Agreement

A verb must agree with its subject in number. In grammar, the number of a word can be either *singular* (indicating *one*) or *plural* (indicating *more than one*). Unlike nouns, which usually become plural when -*s* or -*es* is added, verbs with -*s* or -*es* added to them are singular.

Prentice Hall Writing and Grammar Connection, Chapter 24, Section 1

Nouns and Pronouns	
Singular	**Plural**
bus, goose, I, you, it	buses, geese, we, you, them

Verbs	
Singular	**Plural**
runs, reads, sleeps, writes	run, read, sleep, write

Here are some examples of correct subject/verb agreement. In each case, subjects are underlined and verbs are set in italics.

Singular: The <u>child</u> *goes* to sleep at eight o'clock.

Plural: The <u>children</u> *go* to sleep at eight o'clock.

Compound, Plural: <u>George and Martha</u> *agree* to get married.

Fixing Faulty Subject/Verb Agreement To fix problems with subject/verb agreement, first identify the subject. Then, fix the problem using one of the following methods.

1. **For singular subjects, use singular verbs.** For plural subjects, use plural verbs.

2. **If the subject comes after the verb, rephrase the sentence.** This makes it easier to determine the number of the subject.
   Inverted Sentence: There were many girls in the store.
   Rephrased: Many girls were in the store.

3. **To determine the number of a subject, check its context within the whole paragraph.** The context is useful if the subject is *you*, which can be either singular or plural.

Apply It to Your Editing

Choose two paragraphs in your draft. Underline every subject and every verb. Draw a line from the subject to its verb. If these pairs do not agree in number, fix them according to the examples above.

Writing Workshop

Student Model: Michael Casey
Tiverton, Rhode Island

Sailing to Freedom

The hot sun was beating down on Anuk as he finished the final words on the tomb in which the Pharaoh would be buried two days later. As he looked back to examine his work, his mind began to wander. Anuk thought about his situation. The only reason he was standing there, half-heartedly working, was because he was one of the very few teenagers accepted into the "Gifted Society." This class of servants who were smarter and stronger than most of the others were permitted to perform the "better" jobs and were honored with the closest burial spot next to the Pharaoh inside the pyramid.

"Great," thought Anuk sarcastically, "I'm only thirteen and I'm already being sent to my death." Most of the Pharaoh's servants would jump at the chance to go into the afterlife with their king. But Anuk was no ordinary boy. There was something inside him that made him want to live—a drive that all the servants in Egypt didn't have…. Anuk wanted and needed to escape, and no matter how hard the challenges, he was going to accomplish this.

Talla was hoeing in the fields again. He hated hoeing because it made huge calluses and blisters on his hands. Talla was almost finished with the first row when he saw a boy his age, dressed in fine clothes, walking toward him.

As the boy walked closer he said, "You boy! Listen I have a proposal for you. I'd like to offer you a large payment if you will help me sail to Lower Egypt."

Talla could clearly see the boy now. It was Anuk, the son of the royal scribe.

"Aren't you supposed to be buried with the pharaoh in his tomb—" He was cut short by the hand of Anuk.

"The stench of resin doesn't please me, if you know what I mean," answered Anuk.

Talla nodded. He knew from his father that the dead body of the Pharaoh is covered with a dry sap called resin.

"What I need is a guide to take me down the Nile and some help getting supplies. I believe—"

Talla interrupted. "Let me see the payment and I'll make my decision." Anuk held out a pure red ruby amulet. Talla was amazed, letting his mouth drop. He quickly closed it and said, "Let's go."

First, Michael introduces and develops the main character, Anuk, in this third-person narrative.

Michael conveys the setting by using historical terms and describing cultural traditions.

Michael introduces the conflict and theme early. Both center around the human desire to be free.

This dialogue reveals differences between the two boys. It also moves the plot forward.

These paragraphs continue building tension ahead of the climax that will occur later.

Go Online
Read More
For: the complete student model
Visit: www.PHSchool.com
Web Code: enm-4202

Editing and Proofreading

Reread your work, correcting errors in grammar, spelling, and mechanics.

Focus on Sentences: Review each sentence to check that it contains a subject and a verb that agree in gender and number. In addition, be sure that all your sentences express complete ideas.

Publishing and Presenting

Consider one of these ideas to share your writing.

Tell your story aloud. Hold a storytelling event at which several students tell their stories. Make posters announcing the event and invite other classes.

Submit your story. Send your story to a national magazine, online journal, or contest that solicits student writing. Ask your teacher or librarian for suggestions.

Reflecting on Your Writing

Writer's Journal Jot down your thoughts on the experience of writing a short story. Begin by answering these questions:

- Which strategies did you use for drafting? How effective were they?
- What insights about short stories did the experience give you?

> *Prentice Hall Writing and Grammar Connection: Chapter 5*

Rubric for Self-Assessment

To assess your short story, use the following rubric.

Criteria	Rating Scale not very — very				
Focus: How clearly does the story show the conflict faced by the main character?	1	2	3	4	5
Organization: How effectively do you introduce the conflict and develop the plot?	1	2	3	4	5
Support/Elaboration: How well do you use details to describe the setting?	1	2	3	4	5
Style: How realistic is your dialogue?	1	2	3	4	5
Conventions: How correct is your grammar, especially your use of subject-verb agreement?	1	2	3	4	5

Conducting Interviews

You do not need to be a talk show host to produce a good interview. All you need is curiosity about a subject, adequate preparation time, and a knowledgeable person to interview.

Preparing for the Interview

Identify your purpose. Determine what kind of information you would like to obtain. Then, do some basic research so that you will be able to ask informed questions.

Draw up questions. Use your research to generate a list of thoughtful questions for the interview. Bring this list to the interview as a guide. Use the list to predict the path the interview will take. However, do not be afraid to depart from this list if the interview heads down another useful path.

Conducting the Interview

Build a question staircase. Think of the answers in your interview as the steps in a staircase you are building upward. Each *question* should build on the *answer* you just received as well as on the previous question. The chart shown illustrates this technique.

Listen actively. Express your interest through good questions, eye contact, and attentive listening. If the person uses an unfamiliar word or term, ask politely for an explanation. Keep your questions clear and simple, and always keep your goal in mind.

Respect others' views. You will get the best results if you respect the views of others. If you disagree with something the person says, do not express your negative feelings. Instead, ask respectful questions that can help clarify why the person feels that way. Finally, thank your interviewee for his or her time.

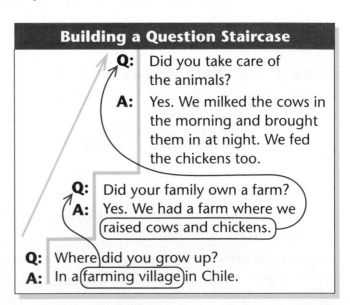

Building a Question Staircase

Q: Did you take care of the animals?
A: Yes. We milked the cows in the morning and brought them in at night. We fed the chickens too.

Q: Did your family own a farm?
A: Yes. We had a farm where we raised cows and chickens.

Q: Where did you grow up?
A: In a farming village in Chile.

Activity *Interview and Report* Practice your skills by interviewing a community member, friend, or relative. Present the responses in a report that also assesses the interview's effectiveness.

The Time Machine: An Adapted Classic

H. G. Wells
Globe/Fearon, 1985

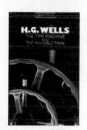

Novel In this classic science-fiction tale, written more than one hundred years ago, H. G. Wells provides a grim view of the future. *The Time Machine* focuses on an inventor who travels into the future in a time machine he built. During his travels, he views the gradual destruction of society, and even of life itself. He describes this incredible voyage to a group of disbelieving friends.

Journey Home with Connected Readings

Yoshiko Uchida
Prentice Hall, 2000

Yuki is having nightmares. Even though she has left the desert camp where she was confined with other Japanese American families during World War II, she cannot shake her memories of her time there. *Journey Home* is told from the perspective of this young Japanese American girl. The novel chronicles the efforts of Yuki and her family to rebuild their lives after the dirt, hunger, and confusion of the camp. The author draws on her own childhood experiences in an internment camp to capture the swirl of feelings from this dark period in American history.

Behind the Blue and Gray: The Soldier's Life in the Civil War

Delia Ray
Puffin Books, 1991

Nonfiction Whether they wore Union blue or Confederate gray, the inexperienced recruits of the Civil War quickly learned to endure the hardships of army life. They experienced the horrors of battle, rampant disease, poorly equipped hospitals, and nightmarish prison camps. Drawing on letters, diaries, eyewitness accounts, and many vintage photographs, this book explores the lives of soldiers from members of the African American northern regiments to boys who lied about their age to enlist.

African American Literature: A Prentice Hall Anthology

Prentice Hall, 1999

From the first published African American writers through the civil rights era authors, the collection includes works that changed and reformed the thinking of a nation. Authors such as Langston Hughes, Zora Neale Hurston, and Ralph Ellison add literary depth to this overview of African American culture as presented by the authors.

These titles are available in the Penguin/Prentice Hall Literature Library.
Consult your teacher before choosing one.

On Your Own
Readings in Popular Culture

Think About It Stephen King makes a living by writing about the things that scare most people—including himself. In this excerpt from an interview with Lesley Stahl for the television news program *60 Minutes*, King talks about his work. As you read, notice the descriptions in parentheses. These details describe what you would see on the screen if you were watching the interview on television.

STEPHEN KING:
HIS BOOKS, HIS LIFE, HIS WIFE

LESLEY STAHL (CO-HOST): There's hardly anybody in America who hasn't read a Stephen King novel or seen a Stephen King movie. Let's face it, he's the world's best-selling novelist, the most successful horror writer in history. As we reported in February last year, even including entertainers, King is one of the highest paid in the country, earning more than $30 million in a single year. That's all because his mind works this way: A man screams . . .

STEPHEN KING (NOVELIST): . . . and this rat jumps into his mouth and gets halfway down his throat. And if you can imagine, OK, not just the taste of it and the rear legs sort of kicking in air, but the feel of the whiskers way back in your throat as it sort of gobbles away at your soft palate.

STAHL: You know what? I'm completely grossed out. You've accomplished . . .

KING: I'm sorry.

STAHL: No, you're not. That's what you wanted to do.

KING: No . . .

STAHL: Yes, this is . . .

KING: . . . I'm not sorry.

STAHL: Have you ever gone to a psychiatrist?

KING: No. No, I've never gone to a psychiatrist, because I feel like what you do at a psychiatrist is you pay $75, $90 an hour to get rid of your fears, whereas if I write them down, people pay me. It's good.

(footage of Stephen King thrillers; Stephen King working on a computer; Stephen King singing)

STAHL: (Voiceover) Since 1974, people have paid good money for 32 novels, five collections of short stories, nine screenplays and one non-fiction study of horror. Except for his birthday, the Fourth of July and Christmas, King writes at least four hours every day.

KING: The ideas come and they have to be let out. That's all. They just have to be let out.

(footage of King home)

STAHL: (Voiceover) All that stands between those ideas and the rest of the world are these wrought-iron gates. King can afford to live anywhere, but the hometown of horror is Bangor, Maine.

No, this is not happening. This is not happening.

KING: Bring me the ball.

(footage of King's Welsh Corgi[1])

STAHL: (Voiceover) A vicious canine beast also lives here.

KING: Oops! He stole the ball!

(footage of Stephen King with Corgi; excerpt from *Cujo*)

STAHL: (Voiceover) In Stephen King's world, Welsh Corgis play basketball, and St. Bernards become demons, as in the movie *Cujo*. He wants to scare us. But what scares him?

KING: Everything that scares you, everything that scares anybody. That's part of the reason for my success.

STAHL: Well, for instance, is it true, or is this kind of part of your humor to tell us that you sleep with a night-light?

KING: So what if it is true? It's not hurting anybody. I tend to keep a night-light on, but, like anybody else—particularly if you're in a strange place—you don't want to stub your toe if you have to go to the bathroom in the night.

---

1. **Welsh Corgi** (kôr′ gē) a squat, short-legged dog with a foxlike head and pointy ears.

STAHL: It's not like anybody else. Trust me.

KING: No, no. It's like anybody else, or else I wouldn't be as successful as I am.

STAHL: Is his story that he sleeps with a night-light . . .

TABITHA KING (STEPHEN'S WIFE): Not true. Not true.

STAHL: Not true.

TABITHA KING: No.

(footage of Tabitha King)

STAHL: (Voiceover) Tabitha King is certain because she and her husband Stephen have been married for 26 years.

TABITHA KING: There's a lot of mythologizing.

STAHL: Yeah, but he . . . he created that.

TABITHA KING: And he encourages it. Yes, he does. He does. He encourages it.

KING: Tabby keeps the monsters away so . . . yeah, it's true. Over the years, you have kept a lot of monsters away.

More About the Author
Stephen King has carved out a niche in the literary world of suspense and is often called the "Master of Horror." His books and short stories are published all over the world in many different languages. Many of his stories have been turned into successful movies.

Readings in Popular Culture
Talk About It

Use the following questions to guide a discussion of the excerpt from "Stephen King: His Books, His Life, His Wife."

1. How do you think the time Steven King devotes to writing helps to further his career?

2. **(a)** According to the interview, what scares King? **(b)** Is this surprising? Why or why not?

3. Why do you think many people today enjoy stories of mystery, horror, and suspense? In a small group, address the question.
   - Think of stories that serve as good examples of this genre.
   - Discuss whether you enjoy these kinds of stories and whether you think others share your view. Support your opinion.

   Choose someone from your group to share your ideas.

Types of Nonfiction
Narrative, Expository, and Persuasive

Unit 3 Overview

Introduction
Exploring Types of Nonfiction

Part 1: Main Idea

Part 2: Fact and Opinion

Introduction:
Types of Nonfiction: Narrative, Expository, and Persuasive

Andrew Mishkin

From the Author's Desk

Andrew Mishkin
Talks About the Forms

In school, I was often asked to write essays or articles. I never thought about it at the time, but these are probably the most common of all literary forms. **Essays** usually explore ideas, argue a point of view, or interpret a piece of the world or a person's experiences. An **article** is any short work of nonfiction appearing as a part of a magazine, newspaper, or book. Every time you read a newspaper, magazine, or encyclopedia, you are reading an article; the more literary or personal of those articles are called essays.

▲ Andrew Mishkin, a senior engineer at the Jet Propulsion Laboratory, has played a key role in designing the Mars rovers.

Essays and Articles on the Internet

In recent years, a new medium for essays and articles has become available to writers—the Internet. A unique literary form that has arisen is the Web log or "blog," which you can think of as a more dynamic version of a **newspaper column,** or brief essays about news items that appear regularly in print. Blogs, too, are often about current events, but their **purpose** is to provide an alternate, personal window onto those events.

In some ways, blogs are like **journals.** When making each entry, the writer doesn't know where the story will eventually lead. But unlike a journal, a blog lists the most recent entries first, because a blog has a different **audience.** People returning to the site want to locate entries easily.

▼ Critical Viewing Which details in this picture suggest the excitement of the kind of writing that Andrew Mishkin does? **[Connect]**

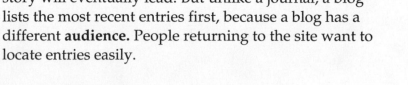

I find that only after completing a blog, can I edit and rewrite it to create a coherent set of chronological journal entries. So, as Twain says in the passage shown here, I'm not ready to start writing my article until I've already written it the first time.

Sharing the "Now" of the Blog

When writing a blog, I sense a conflict between getting the words out there quickly and writing well. If I publish my words on the Web without much editing, the results will usually be sloppy; but by the time I've edited and reedited those words, they may be out of date.

Being "out of date" seems anti-blog! A big part of what makes a blog appealing for readers is finding out what the author is experiencing or thinking right now. For writers, the appeal is being able to update this latest form of nonfiction mere hours or minutes after the previous entry.

The time to begin writing an article is when you have finished it to your satisfaction. By that time you begin to clearly and logically perceive what it is that you really want to say.
from Mark Twain's Notebook, 1902–1903
—Mark Twain

More About the Author

Andrew **Mishkin** (b. 1958)

Andrew Mishkin has said, "Always pursue the work that you love to do." For him, that work has been designing and developing robotic vehicles. He was a member of the team that created the *Sojourner* rover, which explored Mars in 1997. He also was responsible for designing the system used to operate the *Spirit* and *Opportunity* rovers on Mars. He writes his observations about the rovers on a Web site for the public.

Fast Facts
▶ During college, Mishkin started a company that he says distributed "some of the worst movies ever made."
▶ In 1997, he was chosen by *Vanity Fair* magazine as one of "The 35 People Who Made the Year."

Learning About Types of Nonfiction

Elements of Nonfiction Writing

Types of nonfiction writing, such as essays and articles, discuss real people, events, places, and ideas. You can explore these works to learn about the lives of others, find valuable information, reflect on new ideas, or weigh arguments about important issues.

Organization is the way a writer chooses to arrange and present information in a single piece of nonfiction.

- **Chronological organization** presents details in time order—from first to last—or sometimes from last to first.

- **Comparison-and-contrast organization** shows the ways in which two or more subjects are similar and different.

- **Cause-and-effect organization** shows the relationship among events.

- **Problem-and-solution organization** identifies a problem and then proposes a solution.

Many pieces of nonfiction writing use a combination of these types of organization, depending on the author's reasons for writing.

Author's tone is the writer's attitude toward his or her audience and subject. This tone can often be described by a single adjective, such as *formal* or *informal, serious* or *playful, friendly* or *cold.*

Voice is a writer's distinctive way of "speaking" in his or her writing. This voice may vary from work to work by the same writer, or it may represent a characteristic literary personality. Voice can be based on word choice, tone, sound devices, pace, and grammatical structure.

"So you're saying your autobiography has eight sequels?"

Types of Nonfiction Writing

Here are the most common types of nonfiction writing:

Letters are written texts addressed to a particular person or organization.

Memoirs and **journals** contain personal thoughts and reflections.

Web logs—also known as "blogs"—are journals posted and frequently updated for an online audience.

Biographies and **autobiographies** are life stories.

- A **biography** is a life story written by another person.
- An **autobiography** is the writer's account of his or her own life.

Media accounts are nonfiction works written for newspapers, magazines, television, or radio.

Essays and **articles** are short nonfiction works about a particular subject. They may follow the format of these types of writing:

- **Persuasive writing** is meant to convince the reader to adopt a particular point of view or take a particular course of action.
- **Expository writing** presents facts and ideas, or explains a process.
- **Narrative writing** tells the story of real-life experiences.
- **Reflective writing** addresses an experience and includes the writer's insights about the event's importance.

Check Your Understanding

1. Which organization would you expect each of the following works of nonfiction to follow? Explain.
   a. Our Family Vacation
   b. A Buying Guide: Which Stereo Is Right for You?
2. Identify the type of essay each title suggests. Explain.
   a. Throw Out Your Television!
   b. Neil Armstrong: First Man on the Moon

▼ **Critical Viewing** What information about this picture's subject could you learn by reading nonfiction? **[Identify]**

From the Author's Desk
Andrew Mishkin Introduces "Making Tracks on Mars"

In 1969, when I was not quite eleven years old, human beings first walked on the Moon. Every time there was an Apollo mission, I would watch the launch on television, even if I had to get up in the middle of the night, to make sure that the astronauts got safely on their way.

About the same time, I began writing stories, inventing other worlds or variations on our own. Even then, I wanted to be an author—to paint pictures in somebody else's mind, to excite people, perhaps inspire them, with nothing more than marks on a sheet of paper.

Science *Non*fiction: The Humans Behind the Robot

When I was older, I was fortunate enough to become part of the team that designed the first interplanetary off-road robotic vehicle, *Sojourner.* This vehicle explored Mars during the Pathfinder mission in 1997.

Pathfinder turned out to be a huge public event. Yet most of the individuals responsible for its success—the hundreds of engineers who had worked long hours for years, solving problems, averting disaster, putting their personal touches on this marvelous machine—remained invisible. I felt compelled to tell the story of the humans behind the robot. The result was the book *Sojourner.*

From Mars Blog to Mars Journal

I was later privileged to be a participant in another unmanned Mars mission, designed to land two more rovers on the Red Planet in January 2004. I decided that this time, I would write a blog describing what it was like to be on the team. I didn't know what was going to happen—whether we would succeed or fail—but I would write something and post it on my Web site whenever I got the chance. Although I was writing in a new **form,** my purposes were the same as for other forms of nonfiction—to **inform,** to **explain,** and to **reflect.** When the mission was done, I rewrote the **blog** as the **journal** that follows—"Making Tracks on Mars."

Making Tracks on Mars:
A Journal Based on a Blog

Andrew Mishkin

Background NASA blasted two rockets into space in 2003. Sitting on top of them were *Spirit* and *Opportunity*, robotic vehicles the size of golf carts called rovers. Their job was to look for water on Mars and collect data. The Mars Exploration Rovers traveled seven months and 303 million miles, and on January 3, 2004, *Spirit* was due to enter the Martian atmosphere.

Monday, December 29, 2003
Six Days to First Landing

The big question about Mars is, did life ever exist there? Life as we understand it demands the presence of liquid water, yet Mars is now apparently a dead desert world. But what if things were different in the ancient past? From space, Mars looks as if once water might have flowed in rivers, collected in vast oceans, or pooled in crater lakes. The two robotic Mars

Nonfiction
Subheads The title of each entry identifies the writer's focus.

Exploration Rovers will search for evidence of that water, potentially captured in the rocks and soil of the planet's surface. . .

Spirit, the first of the rovers to reach Mars, will be landing next Saturday night, January 3rd. "*Opportunity*" will follow three weeks later.

A British spacecraft—*Beagle 2*[1]—attempted its own Mars landing on Christmas Eve, but has been silent ever since. Landing on Mars is hard! I wish the *Beagle 2* team well, and hope they hear from their spacecraft soon. I cannot help but hope that our own landing goes more smoothly, with a quick <u>confirmation</u> from *Spirit* that it has arrived unscathed.

Saturday, January 3, 2004
Landing Day

Far away, so far that the signals it was sending were taking nearly 10 minutes at the speed of light to arrive at Earth, the spacecraft carrying the *Spirit* rover was about to collide with Mars.

I waited with a sick feeling, a hundred million miles closer to home in mission control at the Jet Propulsion Laboratory in Pasadena, California. Hundreds of us have worked for the past three years—days, evenings, weekends, and holidays—for this moment.

It's looking more and more like the *Beagle 2* mission has failed. I can only imagine wreckage strewn over a barren butterscotch-hued landscape. Will we have better luck?

Spirit's lander must be hitting the atmosphere, a falling meteor blazing in the Martian sky. We'd named the next moments "the six minutes of terror." I listened to the reports on the voice network. All the way down, radio signals from the spacecraft told us "so far so good." Then, immediately after the lander hit the ground, contact was lost. Everyone tensed up. Time dragged. There was only silence from Mars.

Ten minutes later, we got another signal. *Spirit* had survived! The engineers and scientists in mission control were screaming, cheering, thrusting their fists in the air. We were on Mars!

---

1. **Beagle 2** No definite cause was found for the loss of the robot space probe. *Beagle 3*, a new version, is scheduled for 2009.

Vocabulary Builder
confirmation (kän′fər mā′shən) *n.* something that confirms or proves

Andrew Mishkin
Author's Insight
In my original blog, the entries were in reverse chronological order. This made it difficult to build a story line for the finished journal.

Nonfiction
Tone With phrases like "tensed up," the writer establishes an informal and friendly tone toward the reader.

Two hours later, the first pictures arrived from *Spirit*. None of us could believe our luck. The rover looked perfect, with its solar panels fully extended, and the camera mast[2] fully deployed. All the engineering data looked "nominal."[3] There were no fault conditions—much better than any of our rehearsals!

In another minute or two, we had our first panoramic view through *Spirit*'s eyes. We could see 360 degrees around the rover, to the horizon. The landing site looked flat, with small rocks. We can drive here!

Sunday, January 11, 2004

Living on Mars Time

I just finished working the Martian night, planning *Spirit*'s activities for the rover's ninth Martian day on the surface. I've been working Mars time for the past four days, and now finally have a couple of days off.

The Mars day (called a "sol") is just a bit longer than an Earth day, at twenty-four hours and thirty-nine and a half minutes. Since the rover is solar powered, and wakes

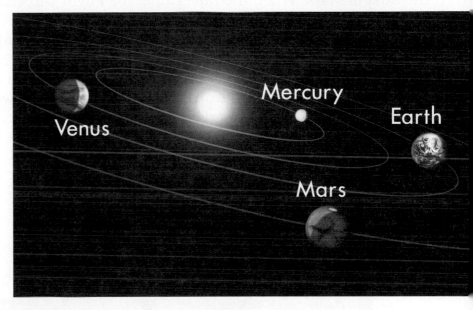

with the sun, its activities are tied to the Martian day. And so are the work shifts of our operations team on Earth. Part of the team works the Martian day, interacting with the spacecraft, sending commands, and analyzing the results. But those of us who build new commands for the rover work the Martian night, while the rover sleeps.

Since the rover wakes up about 40 Earth minutes later every morning, so do we. It seems like sleeping later every day would be easy, but it can be disorienting. It's very easy to lose track of what time it is here on Earth . . .

▼ **Critical Viewing**
Look at the orbits of Earth and Mars. Why would Mars years be longer than Earth years? **[Deduce]**

✔ **Reading Check**
What happened to *Spirit*?

---

2. **camera mast** tall pole on which the camera is mounted, which rotates and swivels.
3. **nominal** normal; what is expected.

Thursday, January 15, 2004

Sol 12: Six Wheels on Dirt!

Mars time continues to be disorienting. During another planning meeting for *Spirit,* we were introduced to a Congressman touring the Laboratory. All I could think was, "What's he doing here in the middle of the night?" It was two in the morning—Mars time. Only after he left did I remember that it was mid-afternoon Pacific time . . .

My team delivered the commands for sol 12—drive off day— but nobody went home. This would be *Spirit*'s most dangerous day since landing. There was a small chance the rover could tip over or get stuck as it rolled off the lander platform onto the dust of Mars. When the time came, the Flight Director played the theme from "Rawhide"[4]—"rollin', rollin', rollin'. . ." —and everyone crowded into mission control cheered and applauded. The command to drive shot through space.

We'll now have to wait another hour and a half to hear back. Engineers are professional worriers. We imagine all the ways things can fail, so that we can prevent those failures from occurring. But even when we've done our jobs, and

---

4. **"Rawhide"** popular 1960s television show about cattle drivers in the 1860s. Its theme song was also extremely popular.

Andrew Mishkin
Author's Insight
I return to the idea of Mars time several times in the journal, as one of my unifying themes.

▼ **Critical Viewing**
What does this picture of the surface of Mars—taken from the rover—suggest about the likelihood of water on the planet? **[Infer]**

considered all the alternatives we can come up with, there is always some doubt . . .

A signal. Applause. Then images started to appear. There was the lander—behind us! We could see tracks in the dirt. The front cameras showed nothing but Martian soil under our wheels. We were off! Engineers were cheering, applauding, and hugging each other. People were shaking my hand. The mission had just shifted from deployment to exploration.

Thursday, January 22, 2004
Sol 19

Something's wrong with *Spirit.* Yesterday, the rover didn't respond to the commands we sent. At first we thought it was just the thunderstorms at our transmitter in Australia, getting in the way. But later *Spirit* missed its preprogrammed communications times, or sent meaningless data. When your spacecraft is halfway across the solar system and won't talk to you, there's no way to tell whether this is a minor problem, easily fixed, or the beginning of the end of our mission. For *Spirit,* there's no repairman to make house calls.

And we've just barely gotten started!

Sunday, January 25, 2004
Ups, Downs, and Landing on Mars—Again

After a day of unsuccessful attempts to regain control of the rover, the project manager declared *Spirit's* condition "critical." We tried commanding *Spirit* to send us simple "beep" signals that would prove it was listening to us. Sometimes these worked. But after one such attempt, we got no signal. The mood in the control room collapsed. The team forced itself into thinking about what to try next.

A few minutes later, there was a tentative, incredulous voice on the network: "Uh. Flight. Telecom. Station 63 is reporting carrier lock."[5] Engineers around the room looked up in surprise. "They're reporting symbol lock . . . We've got telemetry."[6] *Spirit* was back! The data coming down was <u>garbled</u>, but our

---

Andrew Mishkin
Author's Insight
Instead of always referring to "the rover," I often say "we" or "us." This is how the rover engineers actually talked about the rovers during the mission.

Nonfiction
Purpose These day-to-day details help the writer inform and explain events.

Vocabulary Builder
garbled (gär´bəld) *adj.* confused, mixed up

**Reading Check**

What different moods have the engineers experienced so far?

---

5. carrier lock stage of receiving information. Communication over a great distance involves locating the frequency of the carrier's signal, locking onto it, and holding it while information is received.
6. telemetry (tə lem´ ə trē) *n.* transmission of data over a great distance, as from satellites and other space vehicles.

girl was at least babbling at us. The mood in the room transformed again.

Thanks to extreme long distance diagnosis by the software engineers, *Spirit* was listening to us again within two days. We still have a lot of work to do. But at least we can now begin tracing the problem on a stable spacecraft.

▢ ▢ ▢ ▢ ▢ ▢

In the meantime, *Opportunity* has been falling toward Mars. On Saturday night, those of us working on *Spirit*'s problems paused long enough to watch the landing events unfold. *Opportunity*'s first photos were amazing, even for Mars. It looks like we rolled to a stop at the bottom of a bowl—actually a small crater. The soil is a grayish red, except where we've disturbed it with our airbags; there it looks like a deep pure red. And while there are no individual rocks, we seem to be partly encircled by a rock outcropping—bedrock. No one has seen anything like this on Mars before. And it's only yards away. A scientist standing next to me in mission control said only one word: "Jackpot!"

Andrew Mishkin
Author's Insight
Opportunity's landing was as tense as *Spirit*'s, but I de-emphasized it to leave room for other story elements in this short journal.

◀ **Critical Viewing** What does this picture of Mishkin's colleagues say about the mission's success? **[Speculate]**

Q. Do you think we will colonize Mars anytime soon?

A. You may see the first humans travel to Mars sometime in the next few decades and witness their first tentative steps on this alien world. The first explorers will likely remain on the planet for weeks or even months before returning home to Earth. Other missions will follow. But colonizing—going to Mars to stay—is still probably much further in the future.

Q. What did we learn from this mission that will help us?

A. The MER mission has taught us many things, both about Mars and how to design our next missions. Some of the places the rovers went look like good spots to target our future search for evidence of past life. And, unlike most deep-space missions of the past, MER demonstrated how to operate multiple spacecraft in a very dynamic way, with scientists and engineers responding to the discoveries made each day in order to plan what to do tomorrow.

Student Corner

Q. Do you think there was or is life on Mars?
—Jessika Williams, Centennial, Colorado

A. There doesn't seem to be any sign of life on Mars today, but we do know from what the *Spirit* and *Opportunity* rovers discovered that there was liquid water there in the past. My own guess—and it is only a guess—is that at least some form of microscopic life once existed there. The next rover mission to Mars could very well give us a definitive answer to your question.

 Writing Workshop: *Work in Progress*

How-to Essay

For a How-to Essay you may write, make a list of three tasks that you do each day—for example, tying your shoes or getting ready for school. List the basic steps that go into that task. Save the list in your writing portfolio.

Apply the Skills

Types of Nonfiction

Thinking About the Selection

1. **Respond:** Which entry was the most interesting to you? Why?

2. **(a) Recall:** What is the mission of the two rovers?
   (b) Generalize: What evidence do the scientists hope to find?

3. **(a) Infer:** Why does Mishkin refer to the failure of the *Beagle 2* mission? **(b) Make a Judgment:** At what point do the engineers think that the MER mission might fail?

4. **(a) Analyze:** How many references to *Spirit* as a living thing does Mishkin include in this journal excerpt? **(b) Speculate:** Why do you think he talks about the robot as if it were alive?

Nonfiction Review

5. **(a)** Using a chart like the one shown, identify three personal **reflections** of Mishkin's. For each, identify the related fact or event that sparked his reflection. **(b)** Compare your answers with a partner. How have your answers grown or changed?

| Personal Reflection | ⟷ | Event |

6. **(a)** How would you describe Mishkin's **tone** in this **blog**?
   (b) Do you think the author's **voice** is a literary one? Why or why not?

Research the Author

Learn more about Andrew Mishkin and the MER mission by doing research in the library or on the Internet. Prepare an illustrated report to share with the class by posting it on the classroom's bulletin board or in the school library. Include the following information:
- a list of the goals of the mission
- a presentation of the results of exploration
- your evaluation of the mission's success

QuickReview

Selection at a Glance
A robotics engineer writes a journal about the progress of Mars rovers *Spirit* and *Opportunity*.

For: Self-test
Visit: www.PHSchool.com
Web Code: ena-6301

Web Log: also known as a **blog**, a journal posted and updated for an online audience. It contains personal thoughts and reflections on events.

Tone: a writer's attitude toward the audience and subject

Voice: a writer's distinctive way of "speaking" in his or her writing

Skills You Will Learn

Reading Skill: *Identify Implied Main Idea*

Literary Analysis: *Narrative Essay*

Reading Skill: *Connect Main Idea With Supporting Paragraphs*

Literary Analysis: *Biographical and Autobiographical Essays*

Reading Skill: *Skim and Scan to Locate Information*

Literary Analysis: *Comparing Types of Organization*

Literature You Will Read

Reading: Main Idea

▶ The **main idea** is the central point or message conveyed in a passage or text.

Skills and Strategies You Will Learn in Part 1

In Part 1 you will learn

- to **identify the implied main idea** by considering **significant details** (p. 438)
- to **make connections** to **identify the main idea** (p. 460)
- to **skim text to get a general idea of the topic** (p. 484)
- to **scan text for details that support the main idea** (p. 484)

Using the Skills and Strategies in Part 1

Often the main idea of a work is unstated or implied. By identifying and connecting the most important information in a text, you can determine the main idea. The passage below shows the key details and connections that indicate the main idea.

Topic ←—— Cell phones can be a life-saving device during an emergency, and they offer a new sense of security to family members who might otherwise be unable to contact each other during the day. However, too many callers use these modern marvels rudely or inappropriately, disturbing the privacy, rights, and even the safety of the people around them.

> Cell phones help with security and safety.

However

> Many callers use them rudely.

Implied Main Idea: Cell phones have good and bad points.

Academic Vocabulary: Words for Discussing Main Ideas

The following words will help you write and talk about main ideas and supporting details.

Word	Definition	Example Sentence
pertinent *adj.*	relevant; having a connection	The author supported the main idea with *pertinent* details.
topic *n.*	the subject	The *topic* of his essay was volcanoes.
focus *n.*	the central point of a work	The *focus* of her essay is exercise.
focus *v.*	concentrate on one thing	Our club will *focus* on humanitarian aid.
suggest *v.*	show indirectly; imply	The details in the article *suggest* that Americans watch too much television.
imply *v.*	hint at; suggest	What does the author imply?
implied *adj.*	suggested	The *implied* main idea was reinforced by the title of the work.

Vocabulary Skill: Synonyms

> **Synonyms** are words that have nearly the same meaning.

In Part 1 you will learn a variety of synonyms, including synonyms for
- pertinent
- focus
- imply

In Part 1 you will learn how to find and use synonyms. You also will learn that although synonyms may have similar meanings, each one has a slightly different meaning that distinguishes it from the other.

Activity Sort the following words into synonym pairs. Use a dictionary if necessary.

1. suggest   2. connect   3. notice
a. relate   b. hint   c. observe

These skills will help you become a better reader. Practice them with either "Harriet Tubman: Guide to Freedom" (p. 440) or "Baseball" (p. 453).

Reading Skill

The **main idea** of a work of nonfiction is the central point that the author conveys. Sometimes the author directly states the main idea. More often, the author implies, or suggests, the main idea.

To **identify the implied main idea,** connect details to determine what they have in common. Use these connections to help you figure out the main idea of a passage or work.

Literary Analysis

A **narrative essay** tells the story of real events, people, and places. Narrative essays share these features with fictional stories:

- People's traits and personalities are developed through their words, actions, and thoughts.
- The setting of the action may be an important element.

Use a chart like this one to track the elements of a narrative essay.

Narrative Essay		
Setting(s)	People	Event(s)

Vocabulary Builder

Harriet Tubman: Guide to Freedom

- **fugitives** (fyōō´ ji tivz´) *n.* people fleeing from danger (p. 441) *The escaping slaves were fugitives from the law.*

- **incentive** (in sent´ iv) *n.* something that makes a person act (p. 442) *The extra pay was an incentive to work more than forty hours a week.*

- **disheveled** (di shev´ əld) *adj.* untidy; messy (p. 442) *The man in the wrinkled clothes looked disheveled.*

- **mutinous** (myōōt´ ən əs) *adj.* rebellious (p. 445) *After the captain refused to pay them their share, the mutinous sailors took charge of the ship.*

- **fastidious** (fa stid´ ē əs) *adj.* not easy to please; very critical of anything crude or coarse (p. 448) *Not as fastidious as Mom, Dad tolerated my ripped jeans.*

Baseball

- **devices** (di vīs´ əz) *n.* techniques or means for working things out (p. 454) *With no one to help, I was left to my own devices.*

- **evaded** (ē vād´ əd) *v.* avoided (p. 454) *Thanks to my fast running, I evaded the bully.*

- **ignorance** (ig´ nə rəns) *n.* lack of knowledge or awareness (p. 455) *My blank expression revealed my total ignorance of the subject.*

Background

The Underground Railroad Harriet Tubman, a former slave, became a leading force behind the Underground Railroad, a network of people that helped slaves escape the South in the mid-1800s. At first, she led escaped slaves to free states in the North. In 1850, however, Congress passed the Fugitive Slave Law, which returned escaped slaves found in the North to their southern masters. As a result, Tubman was forced to lead the fugitives to Canada.

Connecting to the Literature

Reading/Writing Connection Imagine leading a group of fugitives to safety while being pursued. Write several sentences telling how you would motivate your followers for the long, dangerous journey. Use three of these words: *rely, maintain, minimize, respond, assist.*

Meet the Author

Ann **Petry** (1908–1997)

Stories of the Underground Railroad had a personal meaning for Ann Petry. Her grandfather Willis James was himself a fugitive slave who had escaped from Virginia and settled in Connecticut in the 1800s.

The Voices of History Telling stories of her ancestors, Petry's parents encouraged Petry to be confident and proud of her heritage. These stories later helped Petry capture the voices of history in her own writing. To young people, she said, "Remember for what a long, long time black people have been in this country, have been a part of America: a sturdy, indestructible, wonderful part of America, woven into its heart and into its soul."

Fast Facts

▶ Like her father, Petry trained as a pharmacist. She worked for several years in her family's drugstore.
▶ Petry's *The Street* was the first novel by an African American author to sell more than a million copies.

Go Online
Author Link
For: More about the author
Visit: www.PHSchool.com
Web Code: ene-9302

Harriet Tubman

Guide to Freedom

ANN PETRY

Along the Eastern Shore of Maryland, in Dorchester County, in Caroline County, the masters kept hearing whispers about the man named Moses, who was running off slaves. At first they did not believe in his existence. The stories about him were fantastic, unbelievable. Yet they watched for him. They offered rewards for his capture.

They never saw him. Now and then they heard whispered rumors to the effect that he was in the neighborhood. The woods were searched. The roads were watched. There was never anything to indicate his whereabouts. But a few days afterward, a goodly number of slaves would be gone from the plantation. Neither the master nor the overseer had heard or seen anything unusual in the quarter. Sometimes one or the other would vaguely remember having heard a whippoorwill call somewhere in the woods, close by, late at night. Though it was the wrong season for whippoorwills.

Sometimes the masters thought they had heard the cry of a hoot owl, repeated, and would remember having thought that the intervals between the low moaning cry were wrong, that it had been repeated four times in succession instead of three. There was never anything more than that to suggest that all was not well in the quarter. Yet when morning came, they invariably discovered that a group of the finest slaves had taken to their heels.

▲ **Critical Viewing**
What is the artist's opinion of Harriet Tubman? How can you tell? **[Analyze]**

Unfortunately, the discovery was almost always made on a Sunday. Thus a whole day was lost before the machinery of pursuit could be set in motion. The posters offering rewards for the <u>fugitives</u> could not be printed until Monday. The men who made a living hunting for runaway slaves were out of reach, off in the woods with their dogs and their guns, in pursuit of four-footed game, or they were in camp meetings[1] saying their prayers with their wives and families beside them.

Harriet Tubman could have told them that there was far more involved in this matter of running off slaves than signaling the would-be runaways by imitating the call of a whippoorwill, or a hoot owl, far more involved than a matter of waiting for a clear night when the North Star was visible.

In December, 1851, when she started out with the band of fugitives that she planned to take to Canada, she had been in the vicinity of the plantation for days, planning the trip, carefully selecting the slaves that she would take with her.

She had announced her arrival in the quarter by singing the forbidden spiritual[2]—"Go down, Moses, 'way down to Egypt Land"—singing it softly outside the door of a slave cabin, late at night. The husky voice was beautiful even when it was barely more than a murmur borne on the wind.

Once she had made her presence known, word of her coming spread from cabin to cabin. The slaves whispered to each other, ear to mouth, mouth to ear, "Moses is here." "Moses has come." "Get ready. Moses is back again." The ones who had agreed to go North with her put ashcake and salt herring in an old bandanna, hastily tied it into a bundle, and then waited patiently for the signal that meant it was time to start.

There were eleven in this party, including one of her brothers and his wife. It was the largest group that she had ever conducted, but she was determined that more and more slaves should know what freedom was like.

She had to take them all the way to Canada. The Fugitive Slave Law was no longer a great many incomprehensible words written down on the country's lawbooks. The new law had become a reality. It was Thomas Sims, a boy, picked up

Vocabulary Builder
fugitives (fyōō′ ji livz′) *n.* people fleeing from danger

Literary Analysis
Narrative Essay
What are the real-life setting, characters, and subject of this narrative essay?

Reading Check

What does Harriet Tubman do?

---

1. camp meetings religious meetings held outdoors or in a tent.
2. forbidden spiritual In 1831, a slave named Nat Turner encouraged an unsuccessful slave uprising by talking about the biblical story of the Israelites' escape from Egypt. Afterward, the singing of certain spirituals, songs based on the Bible, was forbidden for fear of encouraging more uprisings.

on the streets of Boston at night and shipped back to Georgia. It was Jerry and Shadrach, arrested and jailed with no warning.

She had never been in Canada. The route beyond Philadelphia was strange to her. But she could not let the runaways who accompanied her know this. As they walked along she told them stories of her own first flight, she kept painting vivid word pictures of what it would be like to be free.

But there were so many of them this time. She knew moments of doubt when she was half-afraid, and kept looking back over her shoulder, imagining that she heard the sound of pursuit. They would certainly be pursued. Eleven of them. Eleven thousand dollars' worth of flesh and bone and muscle that belonged to Maryland planters. If they were caught, the eleven runaways would be whipped and sold South, but she—she would probably be hanged.

They tried to sleep during the day but they never could wholly relax into sleep. She could tell by the positions they assumed, by their restless movements. And they walked at night. Their progress was slow. It took them three nights of walking to reach the first stop. She had told them about the place where they would stay, promising warmth and good food, holding these things out to them as an <u>incentive</u> to keep going.

When she knocked on the door of a farmhouse, a place where she and her parties of runaways had always been welcome, always been given shelter and plenty to eat, there was no answer. She knocked again, softly. A voice from within said, "Who is it?" There was fear in the voice.

She knew instantly from the sound of the voice that there was something wrong. She said, "A friend with friends," the password on the Underground Railroad.

The door opened, slowly. The man who stood in the doorway looked at her coldly, looked with unconcealed astonishment and fear at the eleven <u>disheveled</u> runaways who were standing near her. Then he shouted, "Too many, too many. It's not safe. My place was searched last week. It's not safe!" and slammed the door in her face.

She turned away from the house, frowning. She had promised her passengers food and rest and warmth, and instead of that, there would be hunger and cold and more walking over the frozen ground. Somehow she would have to instill courage into these eleven people, most of them strangers, would have

Reading Skill
Main Idea What new details about Tubman do you learn here? How are the details connected?

Vocabulary Builder
incentive (in sent′ iv) *n.* something that makes a person act

Vocabulary Builder
disheveled (di shev′ əld) *adj.* untidy; messy

to feed them on hope and bright dreams of freedom instead of the fried pork and corn bread and milk she had promised them.

They stumbled along behind her, half-dead for sleep, and she urged them on, though she was as tired and as discouraged as they were. She had never been in Canada but she kept painting wondrous word pictures of what it would be like. She managed to dispel their fear of pursuit, so that they would not become hysterical, panic-stricken. Then she had to bring some of the fear back, so that they would stay awake and keep walking though they drooped with sleep.

Yet during the day, when they lay down deep in a thicket, they never really slept, because if a twig snapped or the wind sighed in the branches of a pine tree, they jumped to their feet, afraid of their own shadows, shivering and shaking. It was very cold, but they dared not make fires because someone would see the smoke and wonder about it.

She kept thinking, eleven of them. Eleven thousand dollars' worth of slaves. And she had to take them all the way to Canada. Sometimes she told them about Thomas Garrett, in Wilmington. She said he was their friend even though he did not know them. He was the friend of all fugitives. He called them God's poor. He was a Quaker and his speech was a little different from that of other people. His clothing was different, too. He wore the wide-brimmed hat that the Quakers wear.

She said that he had thick white hair, soft, almost like a baby's, and the kindest eyes she had ever seen. He was a big man and strong, but he had never used his strength to harm anyone, always to help people. He would give all of them a new pair of shoes. Everybody. He always did. Once they reached his house in Wilmington, they would be safe. He would see to it that they were.

She described the house where he lived, told them about the store where he sold shoes. She said he kept a pail of milk

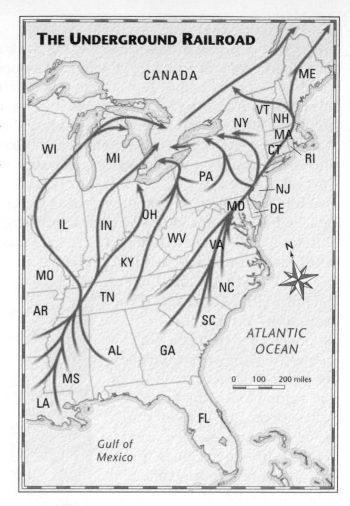

THE UNDERGROUND RAILROAD

▲ Critical Viewing
What does this map tell you about the Underground Railroad? [Interpret]

Reading Skill
Main Idea What main idea is implied by Tubman's thoughts at the beginning of this paragraph?

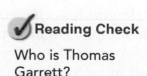
Reading Check
Who is Thomas Garrett?

and a loaf of bread in the drawer of his desk so that he would
have food ready at hand for any of God's poor who should
suddenly appear before him, fainting with hunger. There was
a hidden room in the store. A whole wall swung open, and
behind it was a room where he could hide fugitives. On the
wall there were shelves filled with small boxes—boxes of
shoes—so that you would never guess that the wall actually
opened.

While she talked, she kept watching them. They did not
believe her. She could tell by their expressions. They were
thinking. New shoes, Thomas Garrett, Quaker, Wilmington—
what foolishness was this? Who knew if she told the truth?
Where was she taking them anyway?

That night they reached the
next stop—a farm that
belonged to a German. She
made the runaways take shelter behind trees at the edge of
the fields before she knocked
at the door. She hesitated
before she approached the
door, thinking, suppose that
he, too, should refuse shelter,
suppose—Then she thought,
Lord, I'm going to hold steady
on to You and You've got to see
me through—and knocked
softly.

She heard the familiar gut-
tural voice say, "Who's there?"

She answered quickly, "A
friend with friends."

He opened the door and
greeted her warmly. "How
many this time?" he asked.

"Eleven," she said and
waited, doubting, wondering.

He said, "Good. Bring them
in."

He and his wife fed them in
the lamplit kitchen, their faces
glowing, as they offered food
and more food, urging them to

▼ Critical Viewing
What details in this
picture of a "station"
are similar to
Tubman's description
of Thomas Garrett's
store? [Connect]

cat, saying there was plenty for everybody, have more milk, have more bread, have more meat.

They spent the night in the warm kitchen. They really slept, all that night and until dusk the next day. When they left, it was with reluctance. They had all been warm and safe and well-fed. It was hard to exchange the security offered by that clean, warm kitchen for the darkness and the cold of a December night.

Harriet had found it hard to leave the warmth and friendliness, too. But she urged them on. For a while, as they walked, they seemed to carry in them a measure of contentment; some of the serenity and the cleanliness of that big warm kitchen lingered on inside them. But as they walked farther and farther away from the warmth and the light, the cold and the darkness entered into them. They fell silent, sullen, suspicious. She waited for the moment when some one of them would turn <u>mutinous</u>. It did not happen that night.

Two nights later she was aware that the feet behind her were moving slower and slower. She heard the irritability in their voices, knew that soon someone would refuse to go on.

She started talking about William Still and the Philadelphia Vigilance Committee.[3] No one commented. No one asked any questions. She told them the story of William and Ellen Craft and how they escaped from Georgia. Ellen was so fair that she looked as though she were white, and so she dressed up in a man's clothing and she looked like a wealthy young planter. Her husband, William, who was dark, played the role of her slave. Thus they traveled from Macon, Georgia, to Philadelphia, riding on the trains, staying at the finest hotels. Ellen pretended to be very ill—her right arm was in a sling, and her right hand was bandaged, because she was supposed to have rheumatism. Thus she avoided having to sign the register at the hotels for she could not read or write. They finally arrived safely in Philadelphia, and then went on to Boston.

No one said anything. Not one of them seemed to have heard her.

She told them about Frederick Douglass, the most famous of the escaped slaves, of his eloquence, of his magnificent appearance. Then she told them of her own first vain effort at running away, evoking the memory of that miserable life she

3. **Philadelphia Vigilance Committee** group of citizens that helped escaped slaves. Its secretary was a free black man named William Still.

Literary Analysis
Narrative Essay
What elements of the setting contribute to the action of the plot here?

Vocabulary Builder
mutinous (myo͞ot′ ən es) *adj.* rebellious

Literary Analysis
Narrative Essay
Here, Tubman tells a narrative of her own. Why does she tell the story of these real people?

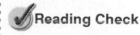**Reading Check**

What does Tubman fear the fugitives might do?

had led as a child, reliving it for a moment in the telling.

But they had been tired too long, hungry too long, afraid too long, footsore too long. One of them suddenly cried out in despair, "Let me go back. It is better to be a slave than to suffer like this in order to be free."

She carried a gun with her on these trips. She had never used it—except as a threat. Now as she aimed it, she experienced a feeling of guilt, remembering that time, years ago, when she had prayed for the death of Edward Brodas, the Master, and then not too long afterward had heard that great wailing cry that came from the throats of the field hands, and knew from the sound that the Master was dead.

One of the runaways said, again, "Let me go back. Let me go back," and stood still, and then turned around and said, over his shoulder, "I am going back."

She lifted the gun, aimed it at the despairing slave. She said, "Go on with us or die." The husky low-pitched voice was grim.

He hesitated for a moment and then he joined the others. They started walking again. She tried to explain to them why none of them could go back to the plantation. If a runaway returned, he would turn traitor, the master and the overseer would force him to turn traitor. The returned slave would disclose the stopping places, the hiding places, the corn-stacks they had used with the full knowledge of the owner of the farm, the name of the German farmer who had fed them and sheltered them. These people who had risked their own security to help runaways would be ruined, fined, imprisoned.

She said, "We got to go free or die. And freedom's not bought with dust."

This time she told them about the long agony of the Middle Passage on the old slave ships, about the black

Literature in Context

History Connection

Frederick Douglass: Fighter for Freedom Born into slavery in Maryland in 1818, Frederick Douglass learned to read even though it was against the law. Twenty years later, he fled north, and in 1845 wrote his autobiography, which made him the most famous and visible African American spokesperson of the nineteenth century. Douglass began publishing the influential antislavery newspaper *North Star* shortly afterward.

He also became an inspiring speaker who spoke out against slavery before the Civil War. Douglass continued to fight for African American civil rights, for women's rights, and on behalf of the poor until his death in 1895.

Connect to the Literature

Why do you think Harriet Tubman chose to tell the slaves about Frederick Douglass on their journey north?

horror of the holds, about the chains and the whips. They too knew these stories. But she wanted to remind them of the long hard way they had come, about the long hard way they had yet to go. She told them about Thomas Sims, the boy picked up on the streets of Boston and sent back to Georgia. She said when they got him back to Savannah, got him in prison there, they whipped him until a doctor who was standing by watching said, "You will kill him if you strike him again!" His master said, "Let him die!"

Thus she forced them to go on. Sometimes she thought she had become nothing but a voice speaking in the darkness, cajoling, urging, threatening. Sometimes she told them things to make them laugh, sometimes she sang to them, and heard the eleven voices behind her blending softly with hers, and then she knew that for the moment all was well with them.

She gave the impression of being a short, muscular, indomitable[4] woman who could never be defeated. Yet at any moment she was liable to be seized by one of those curious fits of sleep, which might last for a few minutes or for hours.[5]

Even on this trip, she suddenly fell asleep in the woods. The runaways, ragged, dirty, hungry, cold, did not steal the gun as they might have, and set off by themselves, or turn back. They sat on the ground near her and waited patiently until she awakened. They had come to trust her implicitly, totally. They, too, had come to believe her repeated statement, "We got to go free or die." She was leading them into freedom, and so they waited until she was ready to go on.

Finally, they reached Thomas Garrett's house in Wilmington, Delaware. Just as Harriet had promised, Garrett gave them all new shoes, and provided carriages to take them on to the next stop.

By slow stages they reached Philadelphia, where William Still hastily recorded their names, and the plantations whence they had come, and something of the life they had led in slavery. Then he carefully hid what he had written, for fear it might be discovered. In 1872 he published this record in book form and called it *The Underground Railroad*. In the foreword to his book he said: "While I knew the danger of keeping strict records, and while I did not then dream that in my day slavery

---

4. **indomitable** (in däm′ it ə bəl) *adj.* not easily discouraged.
5. **sleep . . . hours.** When she was about thirteen, Harriet accidentally received a severe blow on the head. Afterward, she often lost consciousness and could not be awakened until the episode ended.

Literary Analysis
Narrative Essay Why does Tubman tell the fugitives the anecdote about Thomas Sims?

Reading Skill
Main Idea What main idea is directly stated in this paragraph?

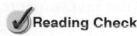

Reading Check

Why can the fugitives not turn back?

would be blotted out, or that the time would come when I could publish these records, it used to afford me great satisfaction to take them down, fresh from the lips of fugitives on the way to freedom, and to preserve them as they had given them."

William Still, who was familiar with all the station stops on the Underground Railroad, supplied Harriet with money and sent her and her eleven fugitives on to Burlington, New Jersey.

Harriet felt safer now, though there were danger spots ahead. But the biggest part of her job was over. As they went farther and farther north, it grew colder; she was aware of the wind on the Jersey ferry and aware of the cold damp in New York. From New York they went on to Syracuse, where the temperature was even lower.

Reading Skill
Main Idea What is the stated main idea about the weather? Which details best illustrate the main idea?

In Syracuse she met the Reverend J.W. Loguen, known as "Jarm" Loguen. This was the beginning of a lifelong friendship. Both Harriet and Jarm Loguen were to become friends and supporters of Old John Brown.[6]

From Syracuse they went north again, into a colder, snowier city—Rochester. Here they almost certainly stayed with Frederick Douglass, for he wrote in his autobiography:

"On one occasion I had eleven fugitives at the same time under my roof, and it was necessary for them to remain with me until I could collect sufficient money to get them to Canada. It was the largest number I ever had at any one time, and I had some difficulty in providing so many with food and shelter, but, as may well be imagined, they were not very <u>fastidious</u> in either direction, and were well content with very plain food, and a strip of carpet on the floor for a bed, or a place on the straw in the barnloft."

Vocabulary Builder
fastidious (fa stid′ ē əs) *adj.* not easy to please; very critical of anything crude or coarse

Late in December, 1851, Harriet arrived in St. Catharines, Canada West (now Ontario), with the eleven fugitives. It had taken almost a month to complete this journey; most of the time had been spent getting out of Maryland.

That first winter in St. Catharines was a terrible one. Canada was a strange frozen land, snow everywhere, ice everywhere, and a bone-biting cold the like of which none of them had ever experienced before. Harriet rented a small frame house in the town and set to work to make a home. The

---

6. **John Brown** white antislavery activist (1800–1859) hanged for leading a raid on the arsenal at Harpers Ferry, Virginia (now West Virginia), as part of a slave uprising.

fugitives boarded with her. They worked in the forests, felling trees, and so did she. Sometimes she took other jobs, cooking or cleaning house for people in the town. She cheered on these newly arrived fugitives, working herself, finding work for them, finding food for them, praying for them, sometimes begging for them.

Often she found herself thinking of the beauty of Maryland, the mellowness of the soil, the richness of the plant life there. The climate itself made for an ease of living that could never be duplicated in this bleak, barren countryside.

In spite of the severe cold, the hard work, she came to love St. Catharines, and the other towns and cities in Canada where black men lived. She discovered that freedom meant more than the right to change jobs at will, more than the right to keep the money that one earned. It was the right to vote and to sit on juries. It was the right to be elected to office. In Canada there were black men who were county officials and members of school boards. St. Catharines had a large colony of ex-slaves, and they owned their own homes, kept them neat and clean and in good repair. They lived in whatever part of town they chose and sent their children to the schools.

When spring came she decided that she would make this small Canadian city her home—as much as any place could be said to be home to a woman who traveled from Canada to the Eastern Shore of Maryland as often as she did.

In the spring of 1852, she went back to Cape May, New Jersey. She spent the summer there, cooking in a hotel. That fall she returned, as usual, to Dorchester County, and brought out nine more slaves, conducting them all the way to St. Catharines, in Canada West, to the bone-biting cold, the snow-covered forests—and freedom.

She continued to live in this fashion, spending the winter in Canada, and the spring and summer working in Cape May, New Jersey, or in Philadelphia. She made two trips a year into slave territory, one in the fall and another in the spring. She now had a definite crystallized purpose, and in carrying it out, her life fell into a pattern which remained unchanged for the next six years.

Literary Analysis
Narrative Essay
What do you learn about Tubman from this description of the fugitives' life in Canada?

Reading Skill
Main Idea What main idea is implied by the many details the author provides about Tubman's schedule from 1852 until 1858?

Apply the Skills

Harriet Tubman: Guide to Freedom

Thinking About the Selection

1. **Respond:** Would you have trusted Harriet Tubman to take you on a long, difficult journey? Why or why not?
2. **(a) Recall:** What does Tubman do when one of the fugitives wants to go back to the plantation? **(b) Analyze Causes and Effects:** Explain why Tubman feels she must act this way.
3. **(a) Interpret:** Tubman says, "We got to go free or die. And freedom's not bought with dust." In your own words, interpret that statement. **(b) Make a Judgment:** Are the results of the Underground Railroad trips worth the risks involved? Why or why not? **(c) Discuss:** Share your judgment with a partner. Then, discuss how your own opinion has or has not changed as a result of your conversation.
4. **(a) Relate:** Which modern leaders have qualities similar to those of Harriet Tubman? **(b) Assess:** Would Tubman be a successful leader in today's world? Why or why not?

Reading Skill

5. **(a)** Make an organizer like the one shown and write at least two additional details you learned about Harriet Tubman from the essay. **(b)** Then, based on the details, write a sentence that states the **main idea** the author conveys about Tubman.

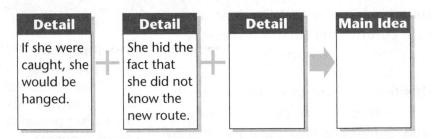

Detail	Detail	Detail	Main Idea
If she were caught, she would be hanged.	She hid the fact that she did not know the new route.		

6. Why do you think the author implies the main idea, rather than directly stating it in the essay?

Literary Analysis

7. List the two most important events in this **narrative essay**.
8. **(a)** Identify at least three people in the narrative and describe their relationship with the author. **(b)** Identify the setting of the narrative.

QuickReview

Essay at a Glance
Harriet Tubman leads fugitive slaves along the Underground Railroad toward freedom in Canada.

Go Online
Assessment
For: Self-test
Visit: www.PHSchool.com
Web Code: ena-6302

Main Idea: the central point that the author conveys in a literary work

Narrative Essay: a short nonfiction work involving real people, events, and settings

Vocabulary Builder

Practice For each item, indicate if the statement is *true* or *false.* Explain your answers.

1. A person might look *disheveled* after a tiring hike.
2. A *fastidious* person would enjoy living in a messy home.
3. A *mutinous* sailor would obey all the captain's rules.
4. *Fugitives* often have reason to feel afraid.
5. The need to pay bills is an *incentive* for getting a job.

Writing

Write a **biographical sketch** about a person who took risks in order to help others or to achieve a worthy goal. You might consider a historical person, like Harriet Tubman, or a person alive today.

- In your first sentence, state the main idea you want readers to know about the person. Then, write several sentences with details that support the main idea.
- End your sketch with a strong concluding sentence that restates your main idea in different words.

For *Grammar, Vocabulary,* and *Assessment,*
see **Build Language Skills,** pages **458–459.**

Extend Your Learning

Listening and Speaking In a small group, write a **skit** based on one of the scenes in the essay about Harriet Tubman. Use dialogue from the selection, or write your own as needed. Rehearse your skit and then present it to your classmates. After the skit, compare audience members' perceptions about how well your performance captured the mood of the original essay.

Research and Technology Research part of the history of slavery in the United States. Concentrate on the period from 1740 to 1865. Present your findings in an **annotated timeline**.

- Divide the line into intervals of twenty-five years.
- Insert at least five events in the history of American slavery in the correct spots on the timeline. For each event, write a note explaining why it was important.

Build Understanding • *Baseball*

Background

Sports and Games Today, many young people play on organized sports teams that have strict rules as well as coaches and referees to enforce them. In the past, though, children more often made up their own games or played informal "pickup" games where they served as their own referees. In his essay "Baseball," Lionel G. García describes the unique version of baseball he and his friends used to play.

Connecting to the Literature

Reading/Writing Connection Some people enjoy being part of a team in an organized league. Others enjoy just playing games with friends whenever they want. Write several sentences to explain which option you prefer. Use at least three of these words: *involve, maintain, select, contribute.*

Review

For **Reading Skill, Literary Analysis,** and **Vocabulary Builder,** see page 438.

Meet the Author

Lionel G. **García** (b. 1935)

The youngest of eight children, Lionel G. García grew up in a Mexican American family in rural Texas.

A Family of Storytellers As a child, García loved to listen to relatives tell stories about their experiences and acquaintances. "It was easy to laugh and cry in the dark with the stories," he recalls. Although his family was poor, García remembers his childhood as a happy time: "We walked the hot, dusty streets barefooted, our pockets full of marbles, spinning tops, mesquite sticks and balls, looking for a game to play. We were carefree . . . ." In his essays, García uses humor and adult wisdom to recall childhood adventures.

Fast Facts

▶ In the past, García has worked full-time as a veterinarian while writing at night.
▶ For part of his childhood, García lived on a deserted ranch with his grandfather, tending cows and goats.

Go Online
Author Link

For: More about the author
Visit: www.PHSchool.com
Web Code: ene-9303

BASEBALL

Lionel G. García

We loved to play baseball. We would take the old mesquite[1] stick and the old ball across the street to the parochial[2] school grounds to play a game. Father Zavala enjoyed watching us. We could hear him laugh mightily from the screened porch at the rear of the rectory[3] where he sat.

The way we played baseball was to rotate positions after every out. First base, the only base we used, was located where one would normally find second base. This made the batter have to run past the pitcher and a long way to the first baseman, increasing the odds of getting thrown out. The pitcher stood in line with the batter, and with first base, and could stand as close or as far from the batter as he or she wanted. Aside from the pitcher, the batter and the first baseman, we had a catcher. All the rest of us would stand in the outfield. After an out, the catcher would come up to bat. The pitcher took the position of catcher, and the first baseman

---

1. **mesquite** (me skēt´) *n.* thorny shrub common in Mexico and the southwestern United States.
2. **parochial** (pə rō´ kē əl) *adj.* supported by a church.
3. **rectory** (rek´ tər ē) *n.* housing for priests.

moved up to be the pitcher. Those in the outfield were left to their own <u>devices</u>. I don't remember ever getting to bat.

There was one exception to the rotation scheme. I don't know who thought of this, but whoever caught the ball on the fly would go directly to be the batter. This was not a popular thing to do. You could expect to have the ball thrown at you on the next pitch.

There was no set distance for first base. First base was wherever Matías or Juan or Cota tossed a stone. They were the law. The distance could be long or short depending on how soon we thought we were going to be called in to eat. The size of the stone marking the base mattered more than the distance from home plate to first base. If we hadn't been called in to eat by dusk, first base was hard to find. Sometimes someone would kick the stone farther away and arguments erupted.

When the batter hit the ball in the air and it was caught that was an out. So far so good. But if the ball hit the ground, the fielder had two choices. One, in keeping with the standard rules of the game, the ball could be thrown to the first baseman and, if caught before the batter arrived at the base, that was an out. But the second, more interesting option allowed the fielder, ball in hand, to take off running after the batter. When close enough, the fielder would throw the ball at the batter. If the batter was hit before reaching first base, the batter was out. But if the batter <u>evaded</u> being hit with the ball, he or she could either run to first base or run back to home plate. All the while, everyone was chasing the batter, picking

up the ball and throwing it at him or her. To complicate matters, on the way to home plate the batter had the choice of running anywhere possible to avoid getting hit. For example, the batter could run to hide behind the hackberry trees at the parochial school grounds, going from tree to tree until he or she could make it safely back to home plate. Many a time we would wind up playing the game past Father Zavala and in front of the rectory half a block away. Or we could be seen running after the batter several blocks down the street toward town, trying to hit the batter with the ball. One time we wound up all the way across town before we cornered Juan against a fence, held him down, and hit him with the ball. Afterwards, we all fell laughing in a pile on top of each other, exhausted from the run through town.

The old codgers, the old shiftless men who spent their day talking at the street corners, never caught on to what we were doing. They would halt their idle conversation just long enough to watch us run by them, hollering and throwing the old ball at the batter.

It was the only kind of baseball game Father Zavala had ever seen. What a wonderful game it must have been for him to see us hit the ball, run to a rock, then run for our lives down the street. He loved the game, shouting from the screened porch at us, pushing us on. And then all of a sudden we were gone, running after the batter. What a game! In what enormous stadium would it be played to allow such freedom over such an expanse of ground?

My uncle Adolfo, who had pitched for the Yankees and the Cardinals in the majors, had given us the ball several years before. Once when he returned for a visit, he saw us playing from across the street and walked over to ask us what we were doing.

"Playing baseball," we answered as though we thought he should know better. After all, he was the professional baseball player.

He walked away shaking his head. "What a waste of a good ball," we heard him say, marveling at our ignorance.

Literary Analysis
Narrative Essay
What do you learn about Father Zavala, based on details in this paragraph?

◄ **Critical Viewing** Are these children enjoying their game? **[Infer]**

Vocabulary Builder
ignorance (igʹ nə rəns) *n.* lack of knowledge or awareness

Apply the Skills

Baseball

Thinking About the Selection

1. **Respond:** Would you like to play baseball the way García and his friends did? Why or why not?
2. **(a) Recall:** Where was first base in García's version of baseball? **(b) Analyze Cause and Effect:** What were some results of this situation?
3. **(a) Contrast:** In what important ways did García's version of baseball differ from the standard rules of baseball?
   (b) Speculate: How do you think García and his friends came to develop these unusual rules?
4. **(a) Infer:** Why do Father Zavala and García's uncle Adolfo respond differently to the boys' game? **(b) Take a Position:** Do you agree with Adolfo's statement, "What a waste of a good ball"? Why or why not? **(c) Discuss:** Share your opinion with a partner. Then, discuss how your view has or has not changed as a result of listening to another person's opinion.

Reading Skill

5. **(a)** In an organizer like the one shown, write at least two more important details about the baseball game described in the essay. **(b)** Then, based on all the details, write a sentence that states the **main idea** the author conveys about the game.

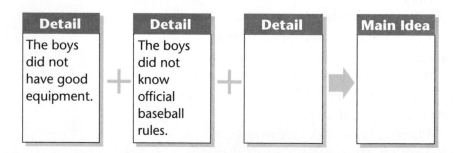

Detail	Detail	Detail	Main Idea
The boys did not have good equipment.	The boys did not know official baseball rules.		

6. Why do you think the author implies the main idea, rather than directly stating it in "Baseball"? Explain.

Literary Analysis

7. List the two most important events in this **narrative essay**.
8. **(a)** Identify at least three people in the narrative and describe their relationship with the author. **(b)** Identify the setting.

Essay at a Glance
The author describes the fun he and his friends had as children playing their own version of baseball.

Go **O**nline
Assessment

For: Self-test
Visit: www.PHSchool.com
Web Code: ena-6303

Main Idea: the central point that an author conveys in a literary work

Narrative Essay: a short nonfiction work involving real people, events, and settings

Vocabulary Builder

Practice For each item, indicate if the statement is *true* or *false*. Explain your answers.

1. A criminal who has *evaded* punishment is probably in prison.
2. A young child should not be left to his or her own *devices* for long.
3. The purpose of education is to spread *ignorance*.

Writing

In "Baseball," the children invent their own form of baseball. Write a **biographical sketch** of a famous leader, athlete, or entertainer who ignored the old rules for success and found a new way to do something.

- In your first sentence, state the main idea you want readers to know about the person. Then, write several sentences providing details that support the main idea.
- End your sketch with a strong concluding sentence that restates your main idea in different words.

For *Grammar, Vocabulary,* and *Assessment,* see **Build Language Skills,** pages 458–459.

Extend Your Learning

Listening and Speaking In a small group, write a **skit** about children playing official baseball or a variation of it. Write dialogue that explains why the children follow particular rules or how they feel about the rules. Rehearse your skit and then present it to your classmates. After the skit, compare audience members' perceptions about whether the performance or the essay better reflects the spirit of the game.

Research and Technology Research the early history of baseball and its changing rules. Present your findings in an **annotated timeline**.

- Divide the line into intervals of twenty-five years.
- Insert at least five events in baseball history in the correct spots on the timeline. For each event, write a note explaining why it was important.

Build Language Skills

Vocabulary Skill

Synonyms The word *focus,* when used as a noun, means "main point." The word *topic* means "subject." *Topic* and *focus* are **synonyms**, words that have similar meanings.

▶ **Examples:** The *topic* of the discussion was how to raise money.

The *focus* of the discussion was how to raise money.

Focus can also be used as a verb. When you look in a thesaurus, you will see synonyms listed for the verb form and the noun form.

Implied can also be used as a verb or an adjective. To find synonyms for the verb, look in the thesaurus under *imply.* Synonyms for the adjective are found under *implied.* (For more on using a thesaurus, see p. R7.)

Practice Use a thesaurus to find different synonyms for the italicized word in each sentence. Rewrite each sentence using a synonym.

1. Today we will *focus* on verbs.

2. The upcoming game was the *focus* of everyone's attention.

3. The *implied* theme of the work is that crime does not pay.

4. The author *implied* that the main character was keeping a secret.

Grammar Lesson

Adjectives and Articles An **adjective** is a word that describes a noun or pronoun. Adjectives are also called *modifiers,* because they modify, or change, the noun. An adjective adds detail to a noun by answering one of these questions: *What kind? Which one? How many? How much? Whose?*

Three common adjectives that answer the question *Which one?* are also called **articles:** *a, an,* and *the.*

Practice Identify the adjectives in these sentences. Rewrite the sentences without the adjectives. Explain how the meaning of the sentence changes.

1. I woke up and had two pieces of toast.

2. I put on black jeans and a striped shirt.

3. Two friends met me outside.

4. We talked about an exciting movie we had seen at the local theater.

5. We have a French instructor.

MorePractice

For more practice with adjectives and articles, see the Grammar Handbook, p. R31.

W̶G̶ Prentice Hall Writing and Grammar Connection: Chapter 16, Section 1

Reading: Main Idea

Directions: *Read the selection. Then, answer the questions.*

Last summer, my baseball team had a losing season. I am a pretty good player, but my teammates did not have much experience.

When I pitched, the other team usually didn't score, but the rules said that I could pitch only six innings a week. It was hard to watch the opposing team drive in runs, after the coach had taken me out. Still, I made a lot of friends on the team, and it was great to help and encourage the younger kids.

1. Which best states two important details about the narrator?

   A A pitcher who does not pitch well.

   B A pitcher whose team has a losing season.

   C He does not like baseball and never wants to play again.

   D He is angry with his coach and with his father.

2. What are two good experiences the narrator describes?

   A He makes friends and helps the younger players.

   B He helps his team win games and pleases his father.

   C He improves his skills and admires his coach.

   D He pitches and wins games.

3. Which statement restates a frustrating experience the narrator describes?

   A He argues with his coach.

   B He pitches poorly.

   C He gets taken out of the game.

   D He argues with his teammates.

4. Which sentence best expresses the main idea of the selection?

   A Playing sports is always a difficult, frustrating experience.

   B Good players are never treated fairly.

   C Even a frustrating, disappointing sports season can have its rewards.

   D Organized sports put too much pressure on young people and too much emphasis on winning.

Timed Writing: Summary [Connections]

Review either "Baseball" or "Harriet Tubman: Guide to Freedom." Summarize the work, identifying the main idea and showing the connections among supporting details. **(20 minutes)**

 ## Writing Workshop: *Work in Progress*

Use the list of basic steps from your writing portfolio as an outline. Fill in the intermediate steps that are necessary to accomplish the task. Put this list of steps in your writing portfolio.

These skills will help you become a better reader. Practice them with either the excerpt from *I Know Why the Caged Bird Sings* (p. 462) or the excerpt from *Always to Remember* (p. 473).

Reading Skill

Main ideas are the most important points in a literary work. Writers often organize essays so that main ideas are part of a clear structure. An introduction states the idea, and then each paragraph supports or develops it. To follow the path the writer sets for you, **make connections** between supporting paragraphs and the main idea.

- Pause to note the main ideas of paragraphs or sections.
- Write notes or outlines, or complete an organizer like the one shown to track main ideas and key details.
- Review the ideas and details in each section.

Literary Analysis

- A **biographical essay** is a short work in which a writer tells about an important event in the life of another person.
- An **autobiographical essay** is also a true account, but it is written by the person who directly experienced an event. It includes the writer's thoughts and feelings.

Both types of writing look at the influence of personal experiences, such as schooling, on a person's development and accomplishments.

Essay—Main Point
Picasso was a great artist who had a major impact on twentieth-century art.

Paragraph 2—Main Point
Picasso was a major influence on other artists.

Paragraph 1—Main Point
Picasso had a long and innovative career.

Vocabulary Builder

I Know Why the Caged Bird Sings

- **fiscal** (fis´ kəl) *adj.* having to do with finances (p. 463) *The accountant reviewed the fiscal report.*

- **benign** (bi nīn´) *adj.* kindly (p. 465) *His warm smile revealed a benign personality.*

- **infuse** (in fyo͞oz´) *v.* put into (p. 466) *A good coach can infuse a team with confidence.*

- **intolerant** (in täl´ ər ənt) *adj.* not able or willing to accept (p. 467) *Try not to be intolerant of others' opinions.*

Always to Remember

- **criteria** (krī tir´ ē ə) *n.* standards or tests by which something can be judged (p. 476) *The winner is chosen using five criteria.*

- **harmonious** (här mō´ nē əs) *adj.* combined in a pleasing, orderly arrangement (p. 476) *The sculpture stood in a harmonious setting.*

- **eloquent** (el´ ə kwənt) *adj.* vividly expressive (p. 477) *Her eloquent speech moved us.*

- **unanimous** (yo͞o nan´ ə məs) *adj.* in complete agreement (p. 477) *The bill passed by a unanimous vote of 94 to 0.*

Background

Growing Up in the South When Maya Angelou, the author of *I Know Why the Caged Bird Sings*, was growing up in Arkansas in the 1930s and 1940s, African Americans and whites attended separate schools. African American schools lacked money for basic educational needs, such as books and qualified teachers. This left many students, like Angelou, searching for figures to inspire them. Angelou found her inspiration with the help of Mrs. Flowers, a family friend.

Connecting to the Literature

Reading/Writing Connection This excerpt from *I Know Why the Caged Bird Sings* describes how Mrs. Flowers instills a lifelong love of language and literature in Angelou. Write a paragraph about a teacher, coach, friend, or relative who has inspired you. Use at least three of the following words: *benefit, challenge, devote, obtain*.

Meet the Author

Maya **Angelou** (b. 1928)

Marguerite Johnson and her brother Bailey were raised by their grandmother in Arkansas. Bailey called Marguerite "mya sister," and she later officially changed her name to "Maya." Marguerite struggled with racism, poverty, and ill treatment early in her life, but she worked hard to overcome these obstacles.

A Better Life After moving to San Francisco and finishing high school there, Angelou held a number of jobs that led to careers in drama, dance, teaching, and writing. Today, she is one of the best-known African American authors in the world. In her work, Angelou tries to show that ". . . as human beings we are more alike than we are unalike."

Fast Facts

▶ *I Know Why the Caged Bird Sings* is the first-person account of Angelou's childhood until age sixteen.
▶ In 1993, Bill Clinton asked Angelou to write and read a poem for his presidential inauguration.

Go Online
Author Link
For: More about the author
Visit: www.PHSchool.com
Web Code: ene-9304

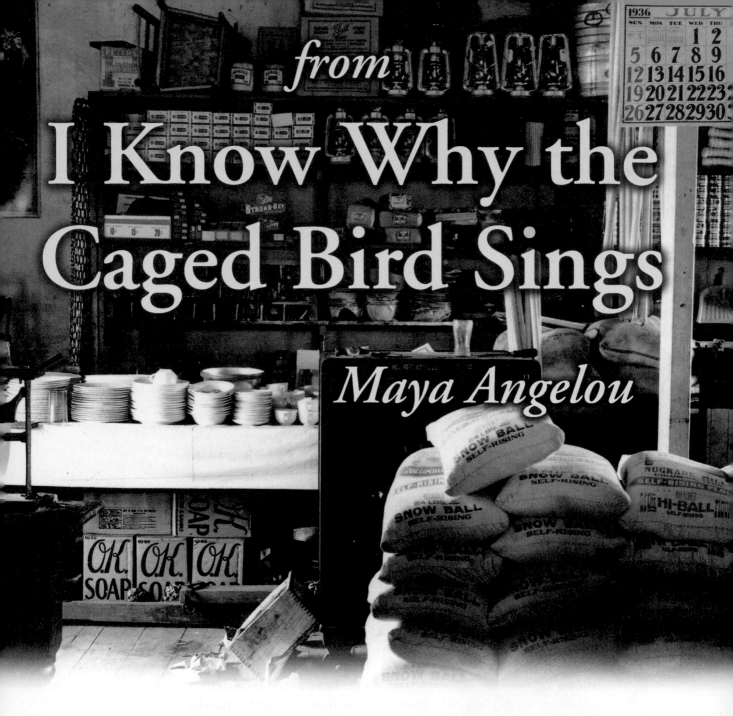

from

I Know Why the Caged Bird Sings

Maya Angelou

We lived with our grandmother and uncle in the rear of the Store (it was always spoken of with a capital s), which she had owned some twenty-five years.

Early in the century, Momma (we soon stopped calling her Grandmother) sold lunches to the sawmen in the lumberyard (east Stamps) and the seedmen at the cotton gin (west

▲ **Critical Viewing**
Would you expect a general store, like the one in this picture, to be a busy place? Explain. **[Speculate]**

Stamps). Her crisp meat pies and cool lemonade, when joined to her miraculous ability to be in two places at the same time, assured her business success. From being a mobile lunch counter, she set up a stand between the two points of <u>fiscal</u> interest and supplied the workers' needs for a few years. Then she had the Store built in the heart of the Negro area. Over the years it became the lay center of activities in town. On Saturdays, barbers sat their customers in the shade on the porch of the Store, and troubadours[1] on their ceaseless crawlings through the South leaned across its benches and sang their sad songs of The Brazos[2] while they played juice harps[3] and cigar-box guitars.

The formal name of the Store was the Wm. Johnson General Merchandise Store. Customers could find food staples, a good variety of colored thread, mash for hogs, corn for chickens, coal oil for lamps, light bulbs for the wealthy, shoestrings, hair dressing, balloons, and flower seeds. Anything not visible had only to be ordered.

Until we became familiar enough to belong to the Store and it to us, we were locked up in a Fun House of Things where the attendant had gone home for life. . . .

Weighing the half-pounds of flour, excluding the scoop, and depositing them dust-free into the thin paper sacks held a simple kind of adventure for me. I developed an eye for measuring how full a silver-looking ladle of flour, mash, meal, sugar or corn had to be to push the scale indicator over to eight ounces or one pound. When I was absolutely accurate our appreciative customers used to admire: "Sister Henderson sure got some smart grandchildrens." If I was off in the Store's favor, the eagle-eyed women would say, "Put some more in that sack, child. Don't you try to make your profit offa me."

Then I would quietly but persistently punish myself. For every bad judgment, the fine was no silver-wrapped kisses, the sweet chocolate drops that I loved more than anything in the world, except Bailey. And maybe canned pineapples. My obsession with pineapples nearly drove me mad. I dreamt of the days when I would be grown and able to buy a whole carton for myself alone.

---

1. **troubadours** (trōō′ bə dôrz′) *n.* traveling musicians.
2. **The Brazos** (bräz′ əs) area in central Texas near the Brazos River.
3. **juice** (jōōs) **harps** small musical instruments held between the teeth and played by plucking a metal band.

Vocabulary Builder
fiscal (fis′ kəl) *adj.* having to do with finances

Reading Skill
Main Idea What key point does the author make about the expectations she places on herself?

Reading Check

What types of goods were sold at the store?

Although the syrupy golden rings sat in their exotic cans on our shelves year round, we only tasted them during Christmas. Momma used the juice to make almost-black fruit cakes. Then she lined heavy soot-encrusted iron skillets with the pineapple rings for rich upside-down cakes. Bailey and I received one slice each, and I carried mine around for hours, shredding off the fruit until nothing was left except the perfume on my fingers. I'd like to think that my desire for pineapples was so sacred that I wouldn't allow myself to steal a can (which was possible) and eat it alone out in the garden, but I'm certain that I must have weighed the possibility of the scent exposing me and didn't have the nerve to attempt it.

Until I was thirteen and left Arkansas for good, the Store was my favorite place to be. Alone and empty in the mornings, it looked like an unopened present from a stranger. Opening the front doors was pulling the ribbon off the unexpected gift. The light would come in softly (we faced north), easing itself over the shelves of mackerel, salmon, tobacco, thread. It fell flat on the big vat of lard and by noontime during the summer the grease had softened to a thick soup. Whenever I walked into the Store in the afternoon, I sensed that it was tired. I alone could hear the slow pulse of its job half done. But just before bedtime, after numerous people had walked in and out, had argued over their bills, or joked about their neighbors, or just dropped in "to give Sister Henderson a 'Hi y'all,'" the promise of magic mornings returned to the Store and spread itself over the family in washed life waves. . . .

When Maya was about ten years old, she returned to Stamps from a visit to St. Louis with her mother. She had become depressed and withdrawn.

For nearly a year, I sopped around the house, the Store, the school and the church, like an old biscuit, dirty and inedible. Then I met, or rather got to know, the lady who threw me my first lifeline.

Mrs. Bertha Flowers was the aristocrat[4] of Black Stamps. She had the grace of control to appear warm in the coldest

---

4. **aristocrat** (ə ris′ tə krat′) *n.* person belonging to the upper class.

Literary Analysis
Autobiographical Essay What does this paragraph show about the author's personality?

Reading Skill
Main Idea List two details on pages 464 and 465 that support the author's portrayal of Mrs. Flowers as an "aristocrat."

weather, and on the Arkansas summer days it seemed she had a private breeze which swirled around, cooling her. She was thin without the taut look of wiry people, and her printed voile[5] dresses and flowered hats were as right for her as denim overalls for a farmer. She was our side's answer to the richest white woman in town.

Her skin was a rich black that would have peeled like a plum if snagged, but then no one would have thought of getting close enough to Mrs. Flowers to ruffle her dress, let alone snag her skin. She didn't encourage familiarity. She wore gloves too.

I don't think I ever saw Mrs. Flowers laugh, but she smiled often. A slow widening of her thin black lips to show even, small white teeth, then the slow effortless closing. When she chose to smile on me, I always wanted to thank her. The action was so graceful and inclusively <u>benign</u>.

She was one of the few gentlewomen I have ever known, and has remained throughout my life the measure of what a human being can be. . . .

One summer afternoon, sweet-milk fresh in my memory, she stopped at the Store to buy provisions. Another Negro woman of her health and age would have been expected to carry the paper sacks home in one hand, but Momma said, "Sister Flowers, I'll send Bailey up to your house with these things."

▲ **Critical Viewing**
Which aspects of this woman resemble the description of Mrs. Flowers? **[Assess]**

Vocabulary Builder
benign (bi nīn´) *adj.* kindly

✔ **Reading Check**
Who throws the author "a lifeline"?

---

5. **voile** (voil) *n.* light cotton fabric.

She smiled that slow dragging smile, "Thank you, Mrs. Henderson. I'd prefer Marguerite, though." My name was beautiful when she said it. "I've been meaning to talk to her, anyway." They gave each other age-group looks.

Momma said, "Well, that's all right then. Sister, go and change your dress. You going to Sister Flowers's. . . ."

There was a little path beside the rocky road, and Mrs. Flowers walked in front swinging her arms and picking her way over the stones.

She said, without turning her head, to me, "I hear you're doing very good school work, Marguerite, but that it's all written. The teachers report that they have trouble getting you to talk in class." We passed the triangular farm on our left and the path widened to allow us to walk together. I hung back in the separate unasked and unanswerable questions.

"Come and walk along with me, Marguerite." I couldn't have refused even if I wanted to. She pronounced my name so nicely. Or more correctly, she spoke each word with such clarity that I was certain a foreigner who didn't understand English could have understood her.

"Now no one is going to make you talk—possibly no one can. But bear in mind, language is man's way of communicating with his fellow man and it is language alone which separates him from the lower animals." That was a totally new idea to me, and I would need time to think about it.

"Your grandmother says you read a lot. Every chance you get. That's good, but not good enough. Words mean more than what is set down on paper. It takes the human voice to <u>infuse</u> them with the shades of deeper meaning."

I memorized the part about the human voice infusing words. It seemed so valid and poetic.

She said she was going to give me some books and that I not only must read them, I must read them aloud. She suggested that I try to make a sentence sound in as many different ways as possible.

"I'll accept no excuse if you return a book to me that has been badly handled." My imagination boggled at the punishment I would deserve if in fact I did abuse a book of Mrs. Flowers'. Death would be too kind and brief.

Vocabulary Builder
infuse (in fyo͞oz´) v. put into

Literary Analysis
Autobiographical Essay Which phrases show the influence that Mrs. Flowers's words have on the author?

The odors in the house surprised me. Somehow I had never connected Mrs. Flowers with food or eating or any other common experience of common people. There must have been an outhouse, too, but my mind never recorded it.

The sweet scent of vanilla had met us as she opened the door.

"I made tea cookies this morning. You see, I had planned to invite you for cookies and lemonade so we could have this little chat. The lemonade is in the icebox."

It followed that Mrs. Flowers would have ice on an ordinary day, when most families in our town bought ice late on Saturdays only a few times during the summer to be used in the wooden ice cream freezers.

She took the bags from me and disappeared through the kitchen door. I looked around the room that I had never in my wildest fantasies imagined I would see. Browned photographs leered or threatened from the walls and the white, freshly done curtains pushed against themselves and against the wind. I wanted to gobble up the room entire and take it to Bailey, who would help me analyze and enjoy it.

"Have a seat, Marguerite. Over there by the table." She carried a platter covered with a tea towel. Although she warned that she hadn't tried her hand at baking sweets for some time, I was certain that like everything else about her the cookies would be perfect.

They were flat round wafers, slightly browned on the edges and butter-yellow in the center. With the cold lemonade they were sufficient for childhood's lifelong diet. Remembering my manners, I took nice little ladylike bites off the edges. She said she had made them expressly for me and that she had a few in the kitchen that I could take home to my brother. So I jammed one whole cake in my mouth and the rough crumbs scratched the insides of my jaws, and if I hadn't had to swallow, it would have been a dream come true.

As I ate she began the first of what we later called "my lessons in living." She said that I must always be <u>intolerant</u> of ignorance but understanding of illiteracy. That some people, unable to go to school, were more educated and even more intelligent than college professors. She encouraged me to listen carefully to what country people called mother wit. That in those homely sayings was couched the collective wisdom of generations.

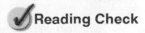

When I finished the cookies she brushed off the table and brought a thick, small book from the bookcase. I had read *A Tale of Two Cities* and found it up to my standards as a romantic novel. She opened the first page and I heard poetry for the first time in my life.

"It was the best of times and the worst of times . . ." Her voice slid in and curved down through and over the words.

Literature in Context   Literature Connection

Inspired by Words

For some people, the impulse to become a poet, a scientist, an actor, or a combat journalist may have begun in the stories they read as children.

Maya Angelou

A TALE of TWO CITIES
Charles Dickens

Poet influenced by Dickens

THE STRANGE CASE OF DR. JEKYLL and MR. HYDE
Robert Louis Stevenson

Scientist transformed by Stevenson

A Midsummer Night's Dream
William Shakespeare

Actor enchanted by Shakespeare

THE RED BADGE OF COURAGE
Stephen Crane

Journalist enlisted by Crane

Connect to the Literature How does Angelou say she was influenced by the "poetry" of *A Tale of Two Cities?*

She was nearly singing. I wanted to look at the pages. Were they the same that I had read? Or were there notes, music, lined on the pages, as in a hymn book? Her sounds began cascading gently. I knew from listening to a thousand preachers that she was nearing the end of her reading, and I hadn't really heard, heard to understand, a single word.

"How do you like that?"

It occurred to me that she expected a response. The sweet vanilla flavor was still on my tongue and her reading was a wonder in my ears. I had to speak.

I said, "Yes, ma'am." It was the least I could do, but it was the most also.

"There's one more thing. Take this book of poems and memorize one for me. Next time you pay me a visit, I want you to recite."

I have tried often to search behind the sophistication of years for the enchantment I so easily found in those gifts. The essence escapes but its aura[6] remains. To be allowed, no, invited, into the private lives of strangers, and to share their joys and fears, was a chance to exchange the Southern bitter wormwood[7] for a cup of mead with Beowulf[8] or a hot cup of tea and milk with Oliver Twist. When I said aloud, "It is a far far better thing that I do, than I have ever done . . ."[9] tears of love filled my eyes at my selflessness.

On that first day, I ran down the hill and into the road (few cars ever came along it) and had the good sense to stop running before I reached the Store.

I was liked, and what a difference it made. I was respected not as Mrs. Henderson's grandchild or Bailey's sister but for just being Marguerite Johnson.

Childhood's logic never asks to be proved (all conclusions are absolute). I didn't question why Mrs. Flowers had singled me out for attention, nor did it occur to me that Momma might have asked her to give me a little talking to. All I cared about was that she had made tea cookies for *me* and read to *me* from her favorite book. It was enough to prove that she liked me.

Reading Skill
Main Idea What point is the narrator making about how Mrs. Flowers changes her feelings toward literature?

Literary Analysis
Autobiographical Essay What lasting "gifts" does Mrs. Flowers give the author?

Reading Skill
Main Idea What prevents the author from questioning Mrs. Flowers about singling her out?

---

6. **aura** (ô´ rə) *n.* atmosphere or quality.
7. **wormwood** (wurm´ wood´) *n.* plant that produces a bitter oil.
8. **Beowulf** (bā´ ə woolf´) hero of an old Anglo-Saxon epic. People in this poem drink **mead,** (mēd´), a drink made with honey and water.
9. **"It is . . . than I have ever done"** last two lines from *A Tale of Two Cities* by Charles Dickens, uttered by Sydney Carton as he sacrifices his own life to save the one of the woman he loves.

Apply the Skills

from *I Know Why the Caged Bird Sings*

Thinking About the Selection

1. **Respond:** Did you find Mrs. Flowers's words and actions inspiring? Explain.
2. **(a) Recall:** What are two customer reactions when Marguerite weighs their goods on the scale? **(b) Infer:** How does she feel when a customer criticizes her? **(c) Draw Conclusions:** What does Marguerite's reaction show about her personality?
3. **(a) Recall:** What does Mrs. Flowers do when Marguerite visits? **(b) Infer:** What do the actions of Mrs. Flowers prove to Marguerite? **(c) Interpret:** Why has Mrs. Flowers remained for Angelou "The measure of what a human being can be"?
4. **(a) Compare and Contrast:** In a two-column chart, write words or phrases that describe how Marguerite felt about herself *before* and *after* her visit with Mrs. Flowers.
   (b) Discuss: In a small group, share and discuss your lists.
   (c) Interpret: Explain what the author means when she calls Mrs. Flowers "the lady who threw me my first lifeline."

Reading Skill

5. **(a)** What is the **main idea** of the section about the Store?
   (b) Which details in this section support this idea?
6. **(a)** List three main ideas in the section about Mrs. Flowers.
   (b) From this list, construct a sentence that states the main idea of the entire section.

Literary Analysis

7. In this **autobiographical essay**, Maya Angelou describes her life working in a general store. She also discusses an important event that changed her life. Complete a chart like the one shown with a few details about each part of her life.

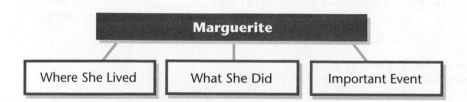

QuickReview

Who's Who in the Essay

Marguerite: the author as a schoolgirl

Momma: the author's grand-mother

Mrs. Flowers: a friend of Marguer-ite's grandmother

Go Online
Assessment

For: Self-test
Visit: www.PHSchool.com
Web Code: ena-6304

Main ideas: the most important points in a literary work

Autobiographical essay: a short non-fiction work in which a person tells about an important event in his or her life

Vocabulary Builder

Practice Review the vocabulary list for *I Know Why the Caged Bird Sings* on page 460. Then, decide how each of the following word pairs are related. Choose *synonyms* for words that are similar in meaning or *antonyms* for words that have opposite meanings. Explain.

1. fiscal, monetary
2. benign, hostile
3. infuse, inject
4. intolerant, open-minded

Writing

Maya Angelou was inspired by Charles Dickens's novel *A Tale of Two Cities.* Write a brief **reflective composition** to discuss a story, poem, play, or novel that made an impression on you.

- Choose the form that best suits your purpose for writing. You can write a journal entry, a letter to the author, a book review, or a brief memoir.
- Consider what you have learned from the literature you have chosen. Then, explain why this literature is important to you.
- State your main points clearly and support them with details.

For *Grammar, Vocabulary,* and *Assessment,* see **Build Language Skills,** pages 482–483.

Extend Your Learning

Listening and Speaking A memorial speech is given to honor an important place, person, or event. In her essay, Angelou memorializes Mrs. Flowers. Write a **memorial speech** about a person, place, or event that you feel is significant. Use appropriate language for the mood you wish to create. Read the speech to your class.

Research and Technology Maya Angelou grew up during the Great Depression. With a group, use several sources to learn more about that time period. Use your notes to create a **proposal for a multimedia presentation,** incorporating extended quotations, photos, music, and artwork that will allow your audience to make generalizations about life during the Depression.

Biographical Essay

Background

A Divisive War *Always to Remember* is about the effort to design a memorial for the Vietnam War. U.S. involvement in Vietnam began in 1961, when President Kennedy sent 3,000 military advisors to help the South Vietnamese government fight communist rebels supported by North Vietnam. By 1968, the United States had more than 500,000 troops there. Americans became bitterly divided over the war.

Connecting to the Literature

Reading/Writing Connection This excerpt introduces a young student who designed a powerful memorial to Vietnam War soldiers. Write a few sentences to describe what characteristics you think a memorial should have. Use at least three of these words: *capture, communicate, illustrate, impress, justify.*

Review

For **Reading Skill, Literary Analysis,** and **Vocabulary Builder,** see page 460.

Meet the Author

Brent **Ashabranner** (b. 1921)

When Brent Ashabranner was eleven, he loved a book called *Bomba the Jungle Boy.* He tried writing a book of his own, *Barbara the Jungle Girl,* but gave up after page three. He did not give up for long—he won fourth prize in a short-story contest when he was in high school.

Sources of Inspiration Ashabranner has been writing ever since, drawing on his experiences in the Peace Corps in Africa and India, and living in the Philippines and Indonesia. He has written many books on social issues, such as one examining the experience of migrant farm workers in the United States.

Fast Facts

▶ Ashabranner served in the United States Navy for three years, where he saw the losses of war firsthand.
▶ The subject of the Vietnam Veterans Memorial appealed to him. As he said, "It will make us remember that war . . . is about sacrifice and sorrow."

Go Online
Author Link
For: More about the author
Visit: www.PHSchool.com
Web Code: ene-9305

Always to Remember: The Vision of Maya Ying Lin

Brent Ashabranner

In the 1960s and 1970s, the United States was involved in a war in Vietnam. Because many people opposed the war, Vietnam veterans were not honored as veterans of other wars had been. Jan Scruggs, a Vietnam veteran, thought that the 58,000 U.S. servicemen and women killed or reported missing in Vietnam should be honored with a memorial. With the help of lawyers Robert Doubek and John Wheeler, Scruggs worked to gain support for his idea. In 1980, Congress authorized the building of the Vietnam Veterans Memorial in Washington, D.C., between the Washington Monument and the Lincoln Memorial.

▲ **Critical Viewing**
What does this veteran's reaction to the memorial tell you about its power?
[Draw Conclusions]

▲ **Critical Viewing** How does the design of the memorial honor individual soldiers, like the veteran shown here? **[Analyze]**

The memorial had been authorized by Congress "in honor and recognition of the men and women of the Armed Forces of the United States who served in the Vietnam War." The law, however, said not a word about what the memorial should be or what it should look like. That was left up to the Vietnam Veterans Memorial Fund, but the law did state that the memorial design and plans would have to be approved by the Secretary of the Interior, the Commission of Fine Arts, and the National Capital Planning Commission.

What would the memorial be? What should it look like? Who would design it? Scruggs, Doubek, and Wheeler didn't know, but they were determined that the memorial should help bring closer together a nation still bitterly divided by the Vietnam War. It couldn't be something like the Marine Corps Memorial showing American troops planting a flag on enemy soil at Iwo Jima. It couldn't be a giant dove with an olive branch of peace in its beak. It had to soothe passions, not stir them up. But there was one thing Jan Scruggs insisted on: The memorial, whatever it turned out to be, would have to show the name of every man and woman killed or missing in the war.

The answer, they decided, was to hold a national design competition open to all Americans. The winning design would receive a prize of $20,000, but the real prize would be the winner's knowledge that the memorial would become a part of American history on the Mall in Washington, D.C. Although fund raising was only well started at this point, the choosing of a memorial design could not be delayed if the memorial was to be built by Veterans Day, 1982. H. Ross Perot contributed the $160,000 necessary to hold the competition, and a panel of distinguished architects, landscape architects, sculptors, and design specialists was chosen to decide the winner.

Announcement of the competition in October, 1980, brought an astonishing response. The Vietnam Veterans Memorial Fund received over five thousand inquiries. They came from every state in the nation and from every field of design; as expected, architects and sculptors were particularly interested.

Reading Skill
Main Idea What point is the author making about the challenges of designing the memorial?

Reading Skill
Main Idea How do the details about how the designer will be chosen connect to the main point of the previous paragraph?

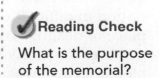Reading Check

What is the purpose of the memorial?

Everyone who inquired received a booklet explaining the criteria. Among the most important: The memorial could not make a political statement about the war; it must contain the names of all persons killed or missing in action in the war; it must be in harmony with its location on the Mall.

A total of 2,573 individuals and teams registered for the competition. They were sent photographs of the memorial site, maps of the area around the site and of the entire Mall, and other technical design information. The competitors had three months to prepare their designs, which had to be received by March 31, 1981.

Of the 2,573 registrants, 1,421 submitted designs, a record number for such a design competition. When the designs were spread out for jury selection, they filled a large airplane hangar. The jury's task was to select the design which, in their judgment, was the best in meeting these criteria:

- a design that honored the memory of those Americans who served and died in the Vietnam War.
- a design of high artistic merit.
- a design which would be harmonious with its site, including visual harmony with the Lincoln Memorial and the Washington Monument.
- a design that could take its place in the "historic continuity" of America's national art.
- a design that would be buildable, durable, and not too hard to maintain.

The designs were displayed without any indication of the designer's name so that they could be judged anonymously, on their design merits alone. The jury spent one week reviewing all the designs in the airplane hangar. On May 1 it made its report to the Vietnam Veterans Memorial Fund; the experts declared Entry Number 1,026 the winner. The report called it "the finest and most appropriate" of all submitted and said it was "superbly harmonious" with the site on the Mall. Remarking upon the "simple and forthright" materials needed to build the winning entry, the report concludes:

> This memorial, with its wall of names, becomes a place of quiet reflection, and a tribute to those who served their nation in difficult times. All who come here can find it a place of healing. This will be a quiet memorial, one that achieves an excellent relationship with both the Lincoln Memorial and Washington Monument, and relates the visi-

Vocabulary Builder
criteria (krī tir´ ē ə) *n.* standards or tests by which something can be judged

Vocabulary Builder
harmonious (här mō´ nē əs) *adj.* combined in a pleasing, orderly arrangement

Literary Analysis
Biographical Essay
The author identifies the winner by number. How does this suggest that the winner's identity may surprise readers?

tor to them. It is uniquely horizontal, entering the earth rather than piercing the sky.

This is very much a memorial of our own times, one that could not have been achieved in another time and place. The designer has created an <u>eloquent</u> place where the simple meeting of earth, sky and remembered names contain messages for all who will know this place.

The eight jurors signed their names to the report, a <u>unanimous</u> decision. When the name of the winner was revealed, the art and architecture worlds were stunned. It was not the name of a nationally famous architect or sculptor, as most people had been sure it would be. The creator of Entry Number 1,026 was a twenty-one-year-old student at Yale University. Her name—unknown as yet in any field of art or architecture—was Maya Ying Lin.

How could this be? How could an undergraduate student win one of the most important design competitions ever held? How could she beat out some of the top names in American art and architecture? Who was Maya Ying Lin?

Vocabulary Builder
eloquent (el´ ə kwənt) *adj.* vividly expressive

unanimous (yo͞o nan´ ə məs) *adj.* in complete agreement

✔**Reading Check**

Who won the design contest?

The answer to that question provided some of the other answers, at least in part. Maya Lin, reporters soon discovered, was a Chinese-American girl who had been born and raised in the small midwestern city of Athens, Ohio. Her father, Henry Huan Lin, was a ceramicist of considerable reputation and dean of fine arts at Ohio University in Athens. Her mother, Julia C. Lin, was a poet and professor of Oriental and English literature. Maya Lin's parents were born to culturally prominent families in China. When the Communists came to power in China in the 1940's, Henry and Julia Lin left the country and in time made their way to the United States. Maya Lin grew up in an environment of art and literature. She was interested in sculpture and made both small and large sculptural figures, one cast in bronze. She learned silversmithing and made jewelry. She was surrounded by books and read a great deal, especially fantasies such as *The Hobbit* and *Lord of the Rings.*

But she also found time to work at McDonald's. "It was about the only way to make money in the summer," she said.

A covaledictorian at high school graduation, Maya Lin went to Yale without a clear notion of what she wanted to study and eventually decided to major in Yale's undergraduate program in architecture. During her junior year she studied in Europe and found herself increasingly interested in cemetery architecture. "In Europe there's very little space, so graveyards are used as parks," she said. "Cemeteries are cities of the dead in European countries, but they are also living gardens."

In France, Maya Lin was deeply moved by the war memorial to those who died in the Somme offensive in 1916 during World War I.[1] The great arch by architect

---

1. **Somme offensive . . . World War I** costly and largely unsuccessful Allied attack that resulted in approximately 615,000 British and French soldiers killed.

Arts Connection

Honoring Civil Rights In addition to the Vietnam Veterans Memorial, Maya Ying Lin also designed a memorial that honors the civil rights movement. Her inspiration came from these words of Dr. Martin Luther King, Jr.'s famous "I Have a Dream" speech: " . . . until justice rolls down like waters and righteousness like a mighty stream." Maya Lin decided that the memorial would be about water, and would honor King by using his words to connect the past with the future.

At the Civil Rights Memorial, water streams over King's words carved into the black granite wall. Clear water covers the names and events of the civil rights movement on the circular stone table.

Connect to the Literature

In what ways does the Civil Rights Memorial resemble the Vietnam Veterans Memorial?

Sir Edwin Lutyens is considered one of the world's most outstanding war memorials.

Back at Yale for her senior year, Maya Lin enrolled in Professor Andrus Burr's course in funerary (burial) architecture. The Vietnam Veterans Memorial competition had recently been announced, and although the memorial would be a cenotaph—a monument in honor of persons buried someplace else—Professor Burr thought that having his students prepare a design of the memorial would be a worthwhile course assignment.

Surely, no classroom exercise ever had such spectacular results.

After receiving the assignment, Maya Lin and two of her classmates decided to make the day's journey from New Haven, Connecticut, to Washington to look at the site where the memorial would be built. On the day of their visit, Maya Lin remembers, Constitution Gardens was awash with a late November sun; the park was full of light, alive with joggers and people walking beside the lake.

"It was while I was at the site that I designed it," Maya Lin said later in an interview about the memorial with *Washington Post* writer Phil McCombs. "I just sort of visualized it. It just popped into my head. Some people were playing Frisbee. It was a beautiful park. I didn't want to destroy a living park. You use the landscape. You don't fight with it. You absorb the landscape. . . . When I looked at the site I just knew I wanted something horizontal that took you in, that made you feel safe within the park, yet at the same time reminding you of the dead. So I just imagined opening up the earth. . . ."

When Maya Lin returned to Yale, she made a clay model of the vision that had come to her in Constitution Gardens. She showed it to Professor Burr; he liked her conception and encouraged her to enter the memorial competition. She put her design on paper, a task that took six weeks, and mailed it to Washington barely in time to meet the March 31 deadline.

A month and a day later, Maya Lin was attending class. Her roommate slipped into the classroom and handed her a note. Washington was calling and would call back in fifteen minutes. Maya Lin hurried to her room. The call came. She had won the memorial competition.

Literary Analysis
Biographical Essay
What aspects of Maya Lin's background made it unexpected, but logical, that she won?

Literary Analysis
Biographical Essay
From what sources did Maya Lin draw inspiration for her prize-winning design?

Apply the Skills

from *Always to Remember: The Vision of Maya Ying Lin*

Thinking About the Selection

1. **Respond:** What is your response to the design of the Vietnam Veterans Memorial, as seen on pages 473 and 474? Why?

2. **(a) Recall:** Why did people think that a Vietnam memorial was necessary? **(b) Interpret:** What kinds of balances did the design need to strike in order to accomplish its purpose?

3. **(a) Recall:** How was the design for the memorial chosen? **(b) Infer:** How did this process increase Maya Ying Lin's chances of winning?

4. **(a) Recall:** Why did Maya Ying Lin enter the competition? **(b) Draw Conclusions:** Why was her win so surprising?

5. **(a) Classify:** Make a two-column chart. In one column, list the design criteria from page 476. **(b) Evaluate:** In the second column, explain whether you think the memorial meets each of these criteria. **(c) Discuss:** Share your responses with a group. Then, explain why your evaluation has or has not changed.

Reading Skill

6. **(a)** What is the **main idea** of the section of the essay before the announcement of Maya Ying Lin's name? **(b)** Which details in the paragraph support this idea?

7. **(a)** List three main ideas in the section about Maya Ying Lin on pages 477–479. **(b)** From this list, construct a sentence that states the main idea of the entire section.

Literary Analysis

8. This **biographical essay** provides information about the life of Maya Ying Lin. Complete a chart like the one shown with details from the essay.

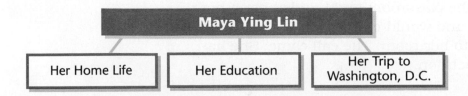

QuickReview

Essay at a Glance
An unknown twenty-year-old student, Maya Ying Lin, enters a design contest for the Vietnam Veterans Memorial.

Go Online
Assessment
For: Self-test
Visit: www.PHSchool.com
Web Code: ena-6305

Main idea: the most important point in a literary work

Biographical essay: a short work in which a person tells about an important event in someone else's life

Vocabulary Builder

Practice Review the vocabulary list for *Always to Remember* on page 460. Then, decide how each of the following word pairs are related. Choose *synonyms* for words that are similar in meaning or *antonyms* for words that have opposite meanings. Explain.

1. criteria, guidelines
2. harmonious, compatible
3. eloquent, inexpressive
4. unanimous, divided

Writing

Maya Ying Lin was inspired by Lutyens's memorial at the Somme. Write a **reflective composition** in which you discuss a work of fine art or music, such as a painting, sculpture, statue, building, or song that is inspiring.

- Choose the form that best suits your purpose for writing. You can write a journal entry, a letter to the artist, a music review, or a brief memoir.
- Consider what you like about the art or music you have chosen. Then, explain why it is important to you.
- State your main points clearly and support them with details.

For *Grammar, Vocabulary,* and *Assessment,*
see **Build Language Skills,** pages 482–483.

Extend Your Learning

Listening and Speaking A memorial speech is given to honor an important place, person, or event, such as the dedication of the Vietnam Veterans Memorial. Write a **memorial speech** about a person, place, or event that you feel is significant. Use appropriate language for the mood you wish to create. Read it to your class.

Research and Technology With a group, use several sources to explore the impact of the Vietnam War on people's attitudes toward war and on popular culture. Use your notes to create a **proposal for a multimedia presentation,** incorporating extended quotations, photos, music, and artwork that will allow your audience to make generalizations about the Vietnam War era.

Build Language Skills

Vocabulary Skill

Synonyms The words *pertinent* and *relevant* are synonyms. In certain contexts, they have the same meaning.

▶ **Examples:** The main idea is supported by *pertinent* details.
  The main idea is supported by *relevant* details.

Other **synonyms** have similar meanings, but are not interchangeable. They convey different shades of meaning or different degrees of the same quality. For example, *annoyed, angry,* and *furious* are synonyms, but each describes a different degree of anger.

Practice In a dictionary, look up the exact meanings of these synonyms. Then, use each synonym in a sentence that demonstrates its meaning.

suggested   hinted   inferred   implied

Grammar Lesson

Adverbs An **adverb** is a word that modifies, or adds to the meaning of, a verb, an adjective, or another adverb. Adverbs often end in the suffix *-ly* and answer the questions *When?, Where?, In what manner?,* and *To what extent?*

When?	Where?	What manner?	What extent?
She answered <u>promptly</u>.	They performed the play <u>locally</u>.	He looked at her <u>wistfully</u> and smiled.	The watch was <u>exactly</u> what she wanted.

MorePractice

For more practice with adverbs, see p. R31.

Practice Identify the adverbs in each sentence below. Indicate which words they modify and write what questions they answer.

1. Sarah carefully sprinkled the seeds over the soil.
2. Soon, Jorge will realize he was wrong.
3. Trevor is always the fastest runner on the track team.
4. The band came onstage and began to play loudly.
5. The fence between their yards did not divide the land equally.

$\mathcal{W}_G$ *Prentice Hall Writing and Grammar Connection: Chapter 16, Section 2*

Reading: Main Idea

Directions: *Read the selection. Then, answer the questions.*

> If the painter wishes to see enchanting beauties, he has the power to produce them. If he wishes to see monstrosities, he has the power to create them. If he wishes to produce towns or deserts, he can. . . . Indeed, whatever exists in the universe, or in the imagination, the painter has first in his mind and then in his hands. —Leonardo Da Vinci

This quotation is from a painter who could turn what he saw in his mind into what the world saw on canvas. Those of us who look at what we have painted and know how different it is than what we imagine, feel differently about the creative act. Like children who draw stick figures when they are thinking of real people, what is painted is so much less than what we think. Rather than feel Da Vinci's power, we often feel powerless.

1. What is the main idea of the quotation?
   - A Painters can make beauty.
   - B Painter can make monstrosities, but painters should focus on beauty.
   - C A painter can represent what can be seen or imagined.
   - D Painters have imagination.

2. Which is the most accurate statement?
   - A The texts have similar ideas.
   - B The two texts contrast.
   - C The texts show cause-effect.
   - D The two texts show a sequence.

3. What is the main idea of the two texts?
   - A Artists feel powerful or powerless.
   - B No artist can equal Da Vinci.
   - C For good painters, painting is creating.
   - D All painters feel powerful through art.

4. The first sentence in the second paragraph
   - A continues the first paragraph.
   - B is a definition of the painter.
   - C is a transition between two ideas.
   - D is a contrast from the quotation.

Timed Writing: Description [Connections]

Review the excerpts from *I Know Why the Caged Bird Sings* and "Always to Remember." Describe a person or character; include details that work together to convey a main idea about the individual. **(25 minutes)**

 ## Writing Workshop: *Work in Progress*

How-to Essay

Using the list from your writing portfolio, visualize each step that you have listed. Add the steps that you left out. Put the list in your portfolio.

Reading Informational Materials

Textbooks

In Part 1, you are learning how to identify main ideas in literature. Finding main ideas will also help you understand and use the information in a textbook article. If you read "Always to Remember," you learned about the young woman who designed the Vietnam Veterans Memorial in Washington, D.C. This excerpt from a history textbook gives information about the Vietnam War.

About Textbooks

A **textbook** is a nonfiction work that presents information in a particular subject area. Although textbooks can differ from one another in many ways, they have some common characteristics.

- **Purpose:** The purpose of a textbook is to present information for students. New information is organized and developed around a clearly identified main idea.
- **Structure:** Most textbooks are organized into sections, chapters, and/or units. The table of contents lists titles of these parts and indicates on what page each one begins.
- **Text Format:** Type size, color, and boldface type are used to highlight key terms or sections.

Reading Skill

Most textbooks contain a vast amount of information. When you need to quickly locate specific information, **skim** and **scan**, instead of reading every word. **Skimming** is glancing through a written work to get a general idea of what it is about. **Scanning** is running your eyes over the text to locate specific information or to find key words or ideas. Use these tips to find information in a textbook.

Tips for Skimming and Scanning	
Skim the table of contents to find the chapter you need.	**Scan** the index at the back of the book to find information on your topic.
Skim the first sentence of paragraphs that might include the information you need.	**Scan** the headings to find the main idea of each chapter.

4 The War in Vietnam

Graphics, like this map, provide additional information about the subject, such as geographic location.

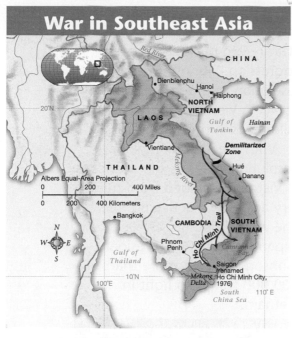

War in Southeast Asia

two countries. Ho Chi Minh led communist North Vietnam. Ngo Dinh Diem (NOH DIN dee EHM) was the noncommunist leader of South Vietnam. In the Cold War world, the Soviet Union supported North Vietnam. The United States backed Diem in the south.

Discontent Diem lost popular support during the 1950s. Many South Vietnamese thought that he favored wealthy landlords and was corrupt. He failed to help the nation's peasant majority and ruled with a heavy hand.

As discontent grew, many peasants joined the Vietcong—guerrillas who opposed Diem. Guerrillas (guh RIHL uhz) are fighters who make hit-and-run attacks on the enemy. They do not wear uniforms or fight in large battles. In time, the Vietcong became communist and were supported by North Vietnam. Vietcong influence quickly spread, especially in the villages.

American Aid Vietcong successes worried American leaders. If South Vietnam fell to communism, they believed, other countries in the region would follow—like a row of

Boldface headings identify the main idea of each section.

Early Involvement in Vietnam

Vietnam is a narrow country that stretches about 1,000 miles along the South China Sea. Since the late 1800s, it had been ruled by France as a colony.

The United States became involved in Vietnam slowly, step by step. During the 1940s, Ho Chi Minh (HO CHEE MIHN), a Vietnamese nationalist and a Communist, had led the fight for independence. Ho's army finally defeated the French in 1954.

An international peace conference divided Vietnam into

falling dominoes. This idea became known as the domino theory. The United States decided that it must keep South Vietnam from becoming the first domino.

During the 1950s and 1960s, Presidents Eisenhower and Kennedy sent financial aid and military advisers to South Vietnam. The advisers went to help train the South Vietnamese army, not to fight the Vietcong. Diem, however, continued to lose support. In November 1963, Diem was assassinated. A few weeks later, President John F. Kennedy was assassinated. Vice President Lyndon Baines Johnson became President.

The Fighting in Vietnam Expands

Lyndon Johnson was also determined to keep South Vietnam from falling to the communists. He increased aid to South Vietnam, sending more arms and advisers. Still, the Vietcong continued to make gains.

Gulf of Tonkin Resolution

In August 1964, President Johnson announced that North Vietnamese torpedo boats had attacked an American ship patrolling the Gulf of Tonkin off the coast of North Vietnam. At Johnson's urging, Congress

passed the Gulf of Tonkin Resolution. It allowed the President "to take all necessary measures to repel any armed attack or to prevent further aggression." Johnson used the resolution to order the bombing of North Vietnam and Vietcong-held areas in the south.

With the Gulf of Tonkin Resolution, the role of Americans in Vietnam changed from military advisers to active fighters. The war in Vietnam escalated, or expanded. By 1968, President Johnson had sent more than 500,000 troops to fight in Vietnam.

> Key terms are listed in blue so you can find them—and their definitions—quickly.

U.S. Troop Levels in Vietnam, 1960–1972

Year	Troops
1960	900
1961	3,200
1962	11,300
1963	16,300
1964	23,300
1965	184,300
1966	385,300
1967	485,600
1968	536,100
1969	475,200
1970	334,600
1971	156,800
1972	24,200

Source: U.S. Department of Defense

> Graphs use a visual format to illustrate trends.

Reading: Skim and Scan to Locate Information

Directions: *Choose the letter of the best answer to each question.*

1. Scan to find the year in which the United States became involved in the Vietnam War. What is the year?
   A 1950
   B 1954
   C 1960
   D 1964

2. If you skimmed this textbook's table of contents, which heading would you be most likely to find?
   A Taking Notes
   B The War in Vietnam
   C War in Southeast Asia
   D American Aid

3. Scan the text to answer this question: Which U.S. president was most closely identified with the war in Vietnam?
   A Harry Truman
   B John Fitzgerald Kennedy
   C Lyndon Baines Johnson
   D Richard Nixon

Reading: Comprehension and Interpretation

Directions: *Write your answers on a separate piece of paper.*

4. Explain the significance of the domino theory. **[Analyzing]**

5. Explain the effect of the Gulf of Tonkin Resolution. Include information from the text and from the graph. **[Integrating]**

6. How did the Vietcong make fighting even more difficult for the Americans? **[Generating]**

Timed Writing: Explanation [Connections]

Choose one of the features that appears at the start of the chapter: Reading Focus, Key Terms, Taking Notes, or Main Idea. Explain how that feature could help students learn the information in the chapter. **(20 minutes)**

Types of Organization

To present information clearly, writers can choose among several **types of organization**. Here are three of the most common plans:

- **Chronological order** relates events in the order in which they occurred.
- **Cause-and-effect order** examines the relationship between an event and its result or results.
- **Comparison and contrast** shows similarities and differences.

Comparing Types of Organization

The essays that follow differ in their organization.

- "Forest Fire" is organized as a chronological narrative.
- "Why Leaves Turn Color in the Fall" links a cause with its effects.
- "The Season's Curmudgeon Sees the Light" uses a comparison-and-contrast structure.

As you read, use the charts shown to understand how the organization reinforces the specific purpose of each essay.

Forest Fire: Retells exciting event

Why Leaves Turn: Explains natural process

Season's Curmudgeon: Compares/contrasts author's feelings about spring and fall

Vocabulary Builder

Forest Fire

- **evacuees** (ē vak´ yōō ēz´) *n.* people who leave a dangerous area (p. 491) *Evacuees from the flood crowded into a school.*

- **tenacious** (tə nā´ shəs) *adj.* persistent; holding on firmly (p. 492) *The smell of burning incense in the temple was tenacious.*

- **consoling** (kən sōl´ iŋ) *adj.* comforting (p. 493) *At sad times, consoling music helps.*

Why Leaves Turn Color in the Fall

- **macabre** (mə käb´ rə *or* mə käb´) *adj.* grim; gruesome (p. 495) *We chose macabre decorations for the haunted house party.*

- **predisposed** (prē´ dis pōzd´) *adj.* inclined; willing (p. 496) *Her love of music predisposed her to become a singer.*

- **capricious** (kə prish´ əs) *adj.* tending to change abruptly and without apparent reason (p. 497) *She planned to visit, but she is so capricious, she may decide to stay home.*

The Season's Curmudgeon . . .

- **contemplation** (kän´ təm plā´ shən) *n.* the act of meditating on or pondering (p. 499) *Edward's contemplation of life motivated him to travel.*

Build Understanding

Connecting to the Literature

Reading/Writing Connection These selections highlight different sides of nature—one wild and dangerous, and the other calming and peaceful. Write a few sentences explaining which side of nature you enjoy more. Use three of the following words: *appreciate, respond, participate, perceive, display.*

Meet the Authors

Anaïs **Nin** (1903–1977)

Anaïs Nin wrote in many different forms, but she is best known for her diaries. Born in France, Nin started a diary at age eleven while traveling to a new home in New York. Nin wrote entries in the diary for the rest of her life, eventually filling 200 volumes. Seven of the volumes were published. "Forest Fire," from the fifth published diary, illustrates her view of life "as an adventure and a tale."

Diane **Ackerman** (b. 1948)

A native of Waukegan, Illinois, nature writer Diane Ackerman studied psychology, physiology, and English. Combining her literary skills with scientific training, Ackerman has published books of poems and books of nonfiction, including *A Natural History of the Senses,* from which "Why Leaves Turn Color in the Fall" is taken.

Mary C. **Curtis** (b. 1953)

Mary Curtis grew up in Baltimore and worked at *The New York Times* and *Baltimore Sun* before becoming the writer of a column in the *Charlotte* (North Carolina) *Observer.* The column examines family life, religion, education, and popular culture and has won awards from both the Associated Press and the Society of Professional Journalists. Says her managing editor, "Mary touches people in a special way. Her passion and empathy connect with their hearts, her reasoned analysis with their minds."

For: More about these authors
Visit: www.PHSchool.com
Web Code: ene-9306

FOREST FIRE Anaïs Nin

Background Monrovia Peak is a mountain in the Sierra Madre range near where Nin had a home in southwest California. The Santa Ana winds are hot, quickly-moving desert winds that dry out vegetation and fuel massive fires.

A man rushed in to announce he had seen smoke on Monrovia Peak. As I looked out of the window I saw the two mountains facing the house on fire. The entire rim burning wildly in the night. The flames, driven by hot Santa Ana winds from the desert, were as tall as the tallest trees, the sky already tinted coral, and the crackling noise of burning trees, the ashes and the smoke were already increasing. The fire raced along, sometimes descending behind the mountain where I could only see the glow, sometimes descending toward us. I thought of the foresters in danger. I made coffee for the weary men who came down occasionally with horses they had led out, or with old people from the isolated cabins. They were covered with soot from their battle with the flames.

At six o'clock the fire was on our left side and rushing toward Mount Wilson. <u>Evacuees</u> from the cabins began to arrive and had to be given blankets and hot coffee. The streets were blocked with fire engines readying to fight the fire if it touched the houses. Policemen and firemen and guards turned away the sightseers. Some were relatives concerned over the fate of the foresters, or the pack station family. The policemen lighted flares, which gave the scene a theatrical, tragic air. The red lights on the police cars twinkled alarmingly. More fire engines arrived. Ashes fell, and the roar of the fire was now like thunder.

We were told to ready ourselves for evacuation. I packed the diaries. The saddest spectacle, beside that of the men fighting the fire as they would a war, were the animals, rabbits, coyotes, mountain lions, deer, driven by the fire to the edge of the mountain, taking a look at the crowd of people and panicking, choosing rather to rush back into the fire.

The fire now was like a ring around Sierra Madre, every mountain was burning. People living at the foot of the mountain were packing their cars. I rushed next door to the Campion children, who had been left with a baby-sitter, and got them into the car. It was impossible to save all the horses. We parked the car on the field below us. I called up the Campions, who were out for the evening, and reassured them. The baby-sitter dressed the children warmly. I made more coffee. I answered frantic telephone calls.

All night the fire engines sprayed water over the houses. But the fire grew immense, angry, and rushing at a speed I could not believe. It would rush along and suddenly leap over a road, a trail, like a monster, devouring all in its path. The firefighters cut breaks in the heavy brush,[1] but when the wind was strong enough, the fire leaped across them. At dawn one arm of the fire reached the back of our houses but was finally contained.

But high above and all around, the fire was burning, more vivid than the sun, throwing spirals of smoke in the air like the smoke from a volcano. Thirty-three cabins burned, and twelve thousand acres of forest still burning endangered countless homes below the fire. The fire was burning to the back of us now, and a rain of ashes began to fall and

---

1. **cut breaks in the heavy brush** cut down trees, shrubs, and underbrush to starve the fire of the fuel it needs to spread.

Vocabulary Builder
evacuees (ē vak′ yoo ēz′) *n.* people who leave a dangerous area

Literary Analysis
Organization What clues indicate that this essay is organized chronologically?

Literary Analysis
Organization How does relating events in chronological order increase the drama?

 **Reading Check**

How is the author affected by the forest fire?

continued for days. The smell of the burn in the air, acrid and pungent and <u>tenacious</u>. The dragon tongues of flames devouring, the flames leaping, the roar of destruction and dissolution,[2] the eyes of the panicked animals, caught between fire and human beings, between two forms of death. They chose the fire. It was as if the fire had come from the bowels of the earth, like that of a fiery volcano, it was so powerful, so swift, and so ravaging. I saw trees become skeletons in one minute, I saw trees fall, I saw bushes turned to ashes in a second, I saw weary, ash-covered men, looking like men returned from war, some with burns, others overcome by smoke.

The men were rushing from one spot to another watching for recrudescence.[3] Some started backfiring up the mountain so that the ascending flames could counteract the descending ones.

As the flames reached the cities below, hundreds of roofs burst into flame at once. There was no water pressure because all the fire hydrants were turned on at the same time, and the fire departments were helpless to save more than a few of the burning homes.

The blaring loudspeakers of passing police cars warned us to prepare to evacuate in case the wind changed and drove the fire in our direction. What did I wish to save? I thought only of the diaries. I appeared on the porch carrying a huge

---

2. dissolution (dis´ ə lōō´ shən) *n.* crumbling.
3. recrudescence (rē´ krōō des´ əns) *n.* fresh outbreak of something that has been inactive.

Vocabulary Builder
tenacious (tə nā´ shəs)
adj. persistent; holding on firmly

▼ **Critical Viewing**
Why would a mountain be an especially challenging place to fight a fire? **[Speculate]**

stack of diary volumes, preparing to pack them in the car. A reporter for the Pasadena *Star News* was taking pictures of the evacuation. He came up, very annoyed with me. "Hey, lady, next time could you bring out something more important than all those old papers? Carry some clothes on the next trip. We gotta have human interest in these pictures!"

A week later, the danger was over.

Gray ashy days.

In Sierra Madre, following the fire, the January rains brought floods. People are sandbagging their homes. At four A.M. the streets are covered with mud. The bare, burnt, naked mountains cannot hold the rains and slide down bringing rocks and mud. One of the rangers must now take photographs and movies of the disaster. He asks if I will help by holding an umbrella over the cameras. I put on my raincoat and he lends me hip boots which look to me like seven-league boots.

We drive a little way up the road. At the third curve it is impassable. A river is rushing across the road. The ranger takes pictures while I hold the umbrella over the camera. It is terrifying to see the muddied waters and rocks, the mountain disintegrating. When we are ready to return, the road before us is covered by large rocks but the ranger pushes on as if the truck were a jeep and forces it through. The edge of the road is being carried away.

I am laughing and scared too. The ranger is at ease in nature, and without fear. It is a wild moment of danger. It is easy to love nature in its peaceful and <u>consoling</u> moments, but one must love it in its furies too, in its despairs and wildness, especially when the damage is caused by us.

Thinking About the Selection

1. **Respond:** What would you take if firefighters asked you to evacuate your home?

2. **(a) Recall:** What possession does Nin rescue from the fire?
   (b) Recall: How does she help other people during the ordeal?
   (c) Draw Conclusions: What do her actions reveal about Nin?

3. **(a) Recall:** List three details or images Nin uses to describe the fire. **(b) Interpret:** What effect does Nin's language have on you?

4. **Draw Conclusions:** What does Nin conclude about nature after witnessing the fire and the mudslide?

Why Leaves Turn Color in the Fall

Diane Ackerman

The stealth of autumn catches one unaware. Was that a goldfinch perching in the early September woods, or just the first turning leaf? A red-winged blackbird or a sugar maple closing up shop for the winter? Keen-eyed as leopards, we stand still and squint hard, looking for signs of movement. Early-morning frost sits heavily on the grass, and turns barbed wire into a string of stars. On a distant hill, a small square of yellow appears to be a lighted stage. At last the truth dawns on us: Fall is staggering in, right on schedule, with its baggage of chilly nights, <u>macabre</u> holidays, and spectacular, heart-stoppingly beautiful leaves. Soon the leaves will start cringing on the trees, and roll up in clenched fists before they actually fall off. Dry seedpods will rattle like tiny gourds. But first there will be weeks of gushing color so bright, so pastel, so confettilike, that people will travel up and down the East Coast just to stare at it—a whole season of leaves.

Where do the colors come from? Sunlight rules most living things with its golden edicts. When the days begin to shorten, soon after the summer solstice on June 21, a tree reconsiders its leaves. All summer it feeds them so they can process sunlight, but in the dog days of summer the tree begins pulling nutrients back into its trunk and roots, pares down, and gradually chokes off its leaves. A corky layer of cells forms at the leaves' slender petioles,[1] then scars over. Undernourished, the leaves stop producing the pigment chlorophyll,[2] and photosynthesis[3] ceases. Animals can migrate, hibernate, or store food to prepare for winter. But where can a tree go? It survives by dropping its leaves, and by the end of autumn only a few fragile threads of fluid-carrying xylem[4] hold leaves to their stems.

A turning leaf stays partly green at first, then reveals splotches of yellow and red as the chlorophyll gradually breaks down. Dark green seems to stay longest in the veins, outlining and defining them. During the summer, chlorophyll dissolves in the heat and light, but it is also being steadily replaced. In the fall, on the other hand, no new pigment is produced, and so we notice the other colors that were always there, right in the leaf, although chlorophyll's shocking green hid them from view. With their camouflage gone, we see these colors for the first time all year, and marvel, but they were

---

1. petioles (pet´ ē ōlz´) *n.* stalks of leaves.
2. chlorophyll (klôr´ ə fil´) *n.* green pigment found in plant cells. It is essential for photosynthesis.
3. photosynthesis (fōt´ ō sin´ thə sis) *n.* chemical process by which green plants make their food. This process involves using energy from the sun to turn water and carbon dioxide into food.
4. xylem (zī´ ləm) *n.* plant's woody tissue, which carries water and minerals in the stems, roots, and leaves.

Vocabulary Builder
macabre (mə käb´ rə or mə käb´) *adj.* grim; gruesome

Literary Analysis
Organization What is the beginning and end of the chain of causes and effects the author describes here?

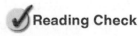**Reading Check**

What pigment in leaves gives them their green color?

always there, hidden like a vivid secret beneath the hot glowing greens of summer.

The most spectacular range of fall foliage occurs in the northeastern United States and in eastern China, where the leaves are robustly colored thanks in part to a rich climate. European maples don't achieve the same flaming reds as their American relatives, which thrive on cold nights and sunny days. In Europe, the warm, humid weather turns the leaves brown or mildly yellow. Anthocyanin, the pigment that gives apples their red and turns leaves red or red-violet, is produced by sugars that remain in the leaf after the supply of nutrients dwindles. Unlike the carotenoids, which color carrots, squash, and corn, and turn leaves orange and yellow, anthocyanin varies from year to year, depending on the temperature and amount of sunlight. The fiercest colors occur in years when the fall sunlight is strongest and the nights are cool and dry (a state of grace scientists find vexing to forecast). This is also why leaves appear dizzyingly bright and clear on a sunny fall day: The anthocyanin flashes like a marquee.

Not all leaves turn the same color. Elms, weeping willows, and the ancient ginkgo all grow radiant yellow, along with hickories, aspens, bottlebrush buckeyes, cottonweeds, and tall, keening poplars. Basswood turns bronze, birches bright gold. Water-loving maples put on a symphonic display of scarlets. Sumacs turn red, too, as do flowering dogwoods, black gums, and sweet gums. Though some oaks yellow, most turn a pinkish brown. The farmlands also change color, as tepees of cornstalks and bales of shredded-wheat-textured hay stand drying in the fields. In some spots, one slope of a hill may be green and the other already in bright color, because the hillside facing south gets more sun and heat than the northern one.

An odd feature of the colors is that they don't seem to have any special purpose. We are <u>predisposed</u> to respond to their beauty, of course. They shimmer with the colors of sunset, spring flowers, the tawny buff of a colt's pretty rump, the shuddering pink of a blush. Animals and flowers color for a reason—adaptation to their environment—but there is no adaptive reason for leaves to color so beautifully in the fall any more than there is for the sky or ocean to be blue. It's just one of the haphazard marvels the planet bestows every year. We

Literary Analysis
Organization What cause produces the most brilliantly colored leaves?

Vocabulary Builder
predisposed (prē´ dis pōzd´) *adj.* inclined; willing

find the sizzling colors thrilling, and in a sense they dupe us. Colored like living things, they signal death and disintegration. In time, they will become fragile and, like the body, return to dust. They are as we hope our own fate will be when we die; not to vanish, just to sublime from one beautiful state into another. Though leaves lose their green life, they bloom with urgent colors, as the woods grow mummified day by day, and Nature becomes more carnal, mute, and radiant.

We call the season "fall," from the Old English *feallan,* to fall, which leads back through time to the Indo-European *phol,* which also means to fall. So the word and the idea are both extremely ancient, and haven't really changed since the first of our kind needed a name for fall's leafy abundance. As we say the word, we're reminded of that other Fall, in the Garden of Eden, when fig leaves never withered and scales fell from our eyes. Fall is the time when leaves fall from the trees, just as spring is when flowers spring up, summer is when we simmer, and winter is when we whine from the cold.

Children love to play in piles of leaves, hurling them into the air like confetti, leaping into soft unruly mattresses of them. For children, leaf fall is just one of the odder figments of Nature, like hailstones or snowflakes. Walk down a lane overhung with trees in the never-never land of autumn, and you will forget about time and death, lost in the sheer delicious spill of color. . . .

But how do the colored leaves fall? As a leaf ages, the growth hormone, auxin, fades, and cells at the base of the petiole divide. Two or three rows of small cells, lying at right angles to the axis of the petiole, react with water, then come apart, leaving the petioles hanging on by only a few threads of xylem. A light breeze, and the leaves are airborne. They glide and swoop, rocking in invisible cradles. They are all wing and may flutter from yard to yard on small whirlwinds or updrafts, swiveling as they go. Firmly tethered to earth, we love to see things rise up and fly—soap bubbles, balloons, birds, fall leaves. They remind us that the end of a season is <u>capricious</u>, as is the end of life. We especially like the way leaves rock, careen, and swoop as they fall. Everyone knows the motion. Pilots sometimes do a maneuver called a "falling leaf," in

Literary Analysis
Organization How does the author use cause and effect to explain "How do the colored leaves fall?"

Vocabulary Builder
capricious (kə prish´ əs) *adj.* tending to change abruptly and without apparent reason

Reading Check

Where does the word *fall* come from?

which the plane loses altitude quickly and on purpose, by slipping first to the right, then to the left. The machine weighs a ton or more, but in one pilot's mind it is a weightless thing, a falling leaf. She has seen the motion before, in the Vermont woods where she played as a child. Below her the trees radiate gold, copper, and red. Leaves are falling, although she can't see them fall, as she falls, swooping down for a closer view.

At last the leaves leave. But first they turn color and thrill us for weeks on end. Then they crunch and crackle underfoot. They *shush*, as children drag their small feet through leaves heaped along the curb. Dark, slimy mats of leaves cling to one's heels after a rain. A damp, stuccolike mortar of semidecayed leaves protects the tender shoots with a roof until spring, and makes a rich humus. An occasional bulge or ripple in the leafy mounds signals a shrew or a field mouse tunneling out of sight. Sometimes one finds in fossil stones the imprint of a leaf, long since disintegrated, whose outlines remind us how detailed, vibrant, and alive are the things of this earth that perish.

Literary Analysis
Organization *Humus* is rich soil. How is humus both an effect and a cause?

Thinking About the Selection

1. **Respond:** Which interested you more—the scientific details or the author's descriptions and language?

2. **(a) Recall:** Identify two facts about leaves that are presented in the essay. **(b) Speculate:** Do you think Ackerman's scientific knowledge about leaves comes mostly from observation or research? Explain.

3. **(a) Recall:** Why do leaves fall? **(b) Apply:** To what human process does Ackerman compare the turning and falling of leaves?

4. **(a) Recall:** In what two places are the changing colors of the leaves the most spectacular? **(b) Compare and Contrast:** What weather conditions do those two places probably share?
   (c) Question: What questions might occur to a reader who does not live in a place where leaves change color?

5. **Take a Position:** Does learning the scientific explanation make the changing color of leaves more, equally, or less amazing? Explain.

The Season's Curmudgeon[1] Sees the Light

Mary C. Curtis

Spring has never done much for me.

I was always an autumn kind of gal: My birthday is in September. When red and gold creep into the leaves, I see beauty, not death. A slight chill in the air feels just right.

I planned an October wedding. When I raised my face to kiss the groom, I didn't want any beads of sweat ruining the moment.

In autumn, you can fall back into an extra hour for sleep or <u>contemplation</u>. It's something I look forward to all summer.

Autumn leads into the hibernation of winter, setting the perfect mood for us quiet types. When you sit inside to read a book, you're never chided for wasting a perfectly beautiful day.

I didn't mind fall's signal of a new school year; I liked school.

The season even has a song —"Autumn in New York"— that mentions two of my favorite things.

Spring meant too many rainy days, too many reminders of the humid summer to come. Spring-fever romances? New blossoms and pungent smells trigger sneezes, not love.

In spring, you lose an hour, which you need for all the scrubbing and cleaning.

Everyone is always *doing* something in the spring. And if you aren't, you feel like some kind of slug. "You've had all winter to rest, you lazy bum. Go outside!"

When you do venture out, it's not cold, but it's not warm enough, either. You can't take a walk without running into

---

1. **curmudgeon** (kər muj′ ən) *n.* bad-tempered person.

Vocabulary Builder
contemplation (kän′ təm plā′ shən) *n.* the act of meditating on or pondering

Literary Analysis
Organization What two things does the author compare or contrast?

✓ **Reading Check**

Why does Curtis like autumn?

throngs of people: jogging, cycling, lying in every tiny patch of sun.

Everyone says it's time to garden; I hate to garden.

"It Might as Well be Spring" isn't bad, but it's a little corny.

But this year, I began to wonder if maybe I had written off spring too hastily.

Spring is a clear signal that you've made it through another ice storm, another broken heater, another cold snap.

Rain isn't a bother if you think of it as washing all the grime away. Splashing is fun!

Spring is an excuse to get out of all those black clothes and go buy a pair of pink shoes. (Oh yes I did!)

You can peel off another layer of outerwear each day. As you lighten up—by hue and weight—it puts a "spring" in your step.

Literary Analysis
Organization What two feelings about spring does the author contrast?

Sure you feel obligated, even compelled, to move around. Just look at it as a reminder from Mother Nature that it's time to put those chocolate bunny ears down and exercise.

It's for your health and so you'll look fabulous when those layers come off.

You get to see people you haven't seen for months. Or if you did pass them by, they had their collars up and their heads down.

Now, you can stop and say hi, ask them what they've been up to, give them garden advice and get some tips yourself. (Even if you have no intention of actually getting out in the garden yourself, saying "mulch," "fertilizer," and "perennials" is cathartic.[2])

Spring is fresh and positive like no other season.

The best part is knowing that another spring will come, and you will always have the chance for a fresh start.

---

2. **cathartic** (ke thär´ tik) *adj.* allowing a release of emotional tension; refreshing.

Thinking About the Selection

1. **Respond:** What two seasons do you like best and least? Why?

2. **(a) Recall:** What are two reasons that Curtis gives initially for not liking spring? **(b) Deduce:** Based on these reasons, how would you describe the author's personality? Explain.

3. **(a) Recall:** What change occurs in the author's thinking?
   (b) Speculate: What might have prompted this change?

Apply the Skills

Forest Fire • Why Leaves Turn Color in the Fall •
The Season's Curmudgeon Sees the Light

Comparing Types of Organization

1. **(a)** Identify three events in "Forest Fire" that occur in **chronological order.** **(b)** How does the final event of the narrative help the writer make a point about nature?

2. **(a)** Name two **causes** in "Why Leaves Turn Color in the Fall" that explain the natural **effect** of autumn leaves. **(b)** What point about human interaction with Nature does the end of this essay develop?

3. **(a)** In "The Season's Curmudgeon Sees the Light," identify two ways the author **compares and contrasts** spring and fall. **(b)** How does the writer use these contrasts to emphasize spring's qualities?

Writing to Compare Literary Works

In these essays, the authors use specific types of organization to achieve their own purposes, or reasons for writing. Choose two of the three works and write your own essay to explain how the organization matches or supports the writer's topic and purpose. Complete a chart like the one shown before you write.

Title	Author's Purpose	Key Details	Organization

QuickReview

Types of organization: ways of structuring ideas in a piece of writing including: *chronological order; cause and effect;* and *comparison and contrast*

Go Online
Assessment
For: Self-test
Visit: www.PHSchool.com
Web Code: ena-6306

Vocabulary Builder

Practice Identify the word in each group that does not belong with the other two. Explain your choice.

1. eerie, macabre, peaceful
2. evacuees, emigrants, residents
3. consoling, calming, energizing
4. stubborn, capricious, changeable
5. determined, doubtful, tenacious
6. predisposed, confused, inclined
7. consideration, contemplation, impulsiveness

Reading and Vocabulary Skills Review

Reading: Main Idea

Directions: *Questions 1–5 are based on the following selection.*

Wounded soldiers in the Civil War probably thought they were dreaming when they looked up to see a tiny woman in an officer's uniform calmly tending to their wounds. It was no dream. Dr. Mary Edwards Walker, the first woman surgeon in the U.S. Army, had come boldly to the front lines of battle to serve her country, and no one could stop her.

When Dr. Walker had first tried to join the Union Army as a medical officer she was turned away, but she went to work anyway, as an unpaid volunteer. When the army finally accepted her, she began wearing men's pants under her skirt, a very practical choice for the battlefield, but one which shocked many of the soldiers around her. Later in the war, she served as a spy, daring to cross enemy lines to gain secret information. After the war, Dr. Walker was awarded the nation's highest military honor, the Congressional Medal of Honor. She remains the only woman ever to have received this award.

1. **The last sentence in the first paragraph supports the general idea that Dr. Walker was**
   A courageous and strong-willed.
   B reckless and silly.
   C unqualified and dangerous.
   D warm and motherly.

2. **What idea does Dr. Walker's decision to work as an unpaid volunteer support?**
   A She was wealthy.
   B She was foolish.
   C She was determined.
   D She was shy.

3. **Dr. Walker's decision to wear pants on the battlefield supports which idea?**
   A She cared too much about clothes.
   B She only wanted to shock people.
   C She did not respect the male officers.
   D She did what was practical.

4. **What is the main idea of the selection?**
   Dr. Walker was
   A a surgeon in the U.S. Army.
   B a brave, determined, and unconventional hero.
   C a woman who had skills but lacked self-discipline.
   D a woman who was an excellent doctor.

5. **The description of Dr. Walker in paragraph one serves all of the following purposes EXCEPT**
   A set the historical context.
   B describe Dr. Walker's background.
   C set the tone of the selection.
   D introduce the concept that Dr. Walker was unusual.

Assessment Practice

Directions: *Choose the sentence that demonstrates the best use of the word.*

6. **A** The first step in developing a research paper is choosing a good topic.
   B The main idea topiced the lesson.
   C The topical climate is enjoyable.
   D The subject is difficult to discuss and the topics are.

7. **A** Suggest for the menu should be sent to Cindy.
   B It was her suggest that we have the party outside.
   C Can you suggest a theme for the party?
   D I followed your suggest and sent invitations early.

8. **A** The kids shouted implied directions.
   B Mr. Allan insulted me by implying that I was not paying attention.
   C The implied instructions were so clear that we could easily follow them.
   D We were implying them to leave the building quickly.

9. **A** The coach thought Jess was pertinent to the team.
   B Without the pertinent information I cannot make a decision.
   C A good story is not temporary, it is pertinent.
   D Life around here is pertinent.

10. **A** On rainy days, I find it difficult to focus on my work.
    B The strange subject focuses on a topic.
    C Characters focus in any story.
    D Her choice of topic focused with the assignment.

Directions: *Three of the words in each group are synonyms. Choose the letter of the word that is not a synonym.*

11. **A** pertinent
    B relevant
    C important
    D illusive

12. **A** imply
    B state
    C suggest
    D hint

13. **A** support
    B focus
    C topic
    D subject

14. **A** topic
    B subject
    C detail
    D focus

15. **A** derive
    B deduce
    C guess
    D infer

Exposition: How-to Essay

If you buy a new camera, a CD player, or a game, you probably refer to the how-to instructions. A **how-to essay** is a short, focused piece of expository writing that explains a process. Follow the steps outlined in this lesson to write your own how-to essay.

Assignment Write a how-to essay to explain a process you know well.

What to Include Your how-to essay should include these elements:

- a focused topic that can be fully explained in the essay
- explanations of terms or materials that may be unfamiliar
- a series of logical steps explained in chronological order
- charts, illustrations, and diagrams as necessary to make complicated procedures understandable
- error-free writing including correct use of comparative and superlative forms

To preview the criteria on which your how-to essay may be judged, see the rubric on page 508.

Prewriting

Choosing Your Topic

Listing To find a topic, make a list of people, places, things, and activities that you associate with your home or school. Circle words and draw lines to show connections between items on the lists. Choose a topic from the ideas the chart generates.

Things	**Activities**	**Places**
my bicycle	doing chores	my bedroom
tools	reading car magazines	the backyard
CD collection	watching television	the workshop
trucks	playing basketball	the kitchen

Topic: Restoring a classic truck bed

Gathering Details

Make a timeline. First, divide the process you have chosen into distinct steps. Then, make a timeline to organize the sequence of steps your explanation will describe. Identify the photographs, illustrations, or diagrams that might help you explain the process.

Using the Form

You may use elements of this form in these types of writing:

- manuals
- directions
- recipes
- travel guides

Work in Progress

Review the work you did on pages 433, 459, and 483.

Drafting

Shaping Your Writing

Organize details in sequential order. To clarify the order of steps, write each detail on a sticky note or index card. Arrange the steps in order, and add or rearrange steps as needed. When you find the right order, number the steps and use these notes to draft.

Providing Elaboration

Add details by "exploding the moment." Pause after you write each paragraph. Circle any important detail that needs more information—*what kind? how much? how long?* or *to what degree?* Consider adding these details to your draft.

To read the complete student model, see page 507.

Student Model: Exploding the Moment

The first thing you will need to do is sand the boards. <u>Sandpaper comes in many different textures. You might want to start with a lower, or coarser, grit and gradually move to a higher, or finer, grit.</u>

> Mike added details answering the question "what kind?" to provide more information.

Revising

Revising Your Overall Structure

Add interest with your introduction and conclusion. After you write your draft, look for ways to convince readers that the project is worth doing. Review your prewriting notes to see what gave you the idea for your topic, and build your enthusiasm into your introduction and conclusion.

Revising Your Paragraphs

Look for missing information. Review each paragraph in your draft to be sure you have included each step in the process. Add any information a reader would need to complete a task successfully.

Original: Put the flour and cinnamon in a bowl. Mix it all together.

Revised: Put the flour and cinnamon in a bowl, *crack the egg into the mixture.* Then, mix it all together *until there are no lumps.*

Integrating Grammar Skills

Revising to Correct Comparative and Superlative Forms

When you use adjectives and adverbs to compare items, use the comparative and superlative forms.

Identifying Forms The **comparative form** is used to compare two items. The **superlative form** is used to compare three or more items.

- The most common way to form these degrees is by adding -er or -est to words with one or two syllables.

- *More* and *most* (and *less* and *least*) are used with most adverbs ending in -ly and with modifiers of three or more syllables.

- Irregular adjectives and adverbs have unpredictable patterns that must be memorized.

Prentice Hall Writing and Grammar Connection: Chapter 25, Section 1

Positive	Comparative	Superlative
heavy	heavier	heaviest
nutritious	less nutritious	least nutritious
bad, badly	worse	worst
good, well	better	best
many, much	more	most
far (distance)	farther	farthest
far (extent)	further	furthest

Fixing Errors To fix faulty use of comparatives and superlatives, follow these steps:

1. **Determine how many items are being compared.**

2. **Use the comparative form for two, and use the superlative form for three or more.**
   Comparative: Dave did better on the test than Suzie.
   Superlative: Of everyone in the class, Jo did the best.

Apply It to Your Editing

Choose two paragraphs in your draft. If a comparative or superlative adjective or adverb is used incorrectly, fix it using the rules in this lesson.

Student Model: Mike Tuholski
La Porte, IN

How to Treat a Classic Truck Bed

When you are restoring a classic truck, one large factor in the appearance of the finished truck is the wooden bed strips. This will make your truck look like it did when it first came off the assembly line. I suggest purchasing a kit from a company that specializes in truck parts from the year of your classic truck.

> Mike chose to focus his essay on restoring a truck bed.

Open the package right away. Be sure the shipment includes:
- the proper length wood panels
- metal strips to connect the wooden panels
- braces to connect the bed to the frame

> Mike provides a bulleted list to identify key items.

If you ordered metal strips that were not already polished, you may want to think about getting them polished. You will also need to purchase:
- varnish
- medium-sized paint brush
- large resealable container
- small cup
- wood finish (optional)
- sandpaper of different grit sizes
- paint thinner

Now that you have all of these items, you are ready to refinish your bed strips. The first thing to do is sand the boards. Sandpaper comes in many different textures. Start with a lower, or coarser, grit and gradually move to a higher, or finer, grit. This will leave the wood smooth by the end of the project.

When you have your wood to a desired effect, you may now begin to apply finish, if you choose to. Finish can darken the wood, or it can bring out the grains in the wooden strips. When the finish is dried, you are ready to put on your first coat of varnish.

The varnish mixture for the first coat should be about 25 percent varnish and 75 percent paint thinner. This can be calculated easily with a small cup. Put three cups of thinner and one cup of varnish into the large resealable container. Utilize a thin layer of this mixture over every groove and surface of the wooden planks. Then, sand it lightly with a higher grit sandpaper.

> Mike explains a precise calculation for the varnish mixture.

Additional layers of varnish can be applied in the same fashion. In the second layer, however, use a mixture of 50 percent varnish and 50 percent paint thinner. Sand the wood lightly, then move to the third layer, which is a mixture of 75 percent varnish and 25 percent thinner. Again, sand the wood and apply one final coat of varnish.

> Steps for varnishing are presented in the order they should be completed.

Follow the instructions to put the wooden planks and metal strips together. The metal strips should have bolts, nuts, and washers that will clamp the wooden planks together. Be sure to put the "L"-shaped strips on the sides, as those will clamp to the bed sides. Then, attach the braces to the frame and bed. If you assemble the bed correctly, your remodeled wooden bed will provide a nice complement to your classic truck.

Now, with a new and improved bed to go with your shiny restored truck, you will be the envy of any classic truck admirer. All that is left is to enjoy your treated wood bed while you cruise down the highway, head held high.

> The conclusion reinforces the value of completing the project.

Writing Workshop

Editing and Proofreading

Correct all errors in spelling, punctuation, and grammar.

Focus on Items in a Series: Use commas to separate words, phrases, or clauses in a series. To avoid confusion, use semicolons when some items already contain commas.

> **Commas:** We bought nails, washers, and paint.

> **Semicolons:** We visited Houston, Texas; Raleigh, North Carolina; and Atlanta, Georgia.

Publishing and Presenting

Consider these ideas for sharing your how-to essay.
Make a brochure. Use your writing and graphics to make a brochure.
Plan a demonstration day. Turn your writing into an oral demonstration that you present to a group. As you watch others' demonstrations, listen for the steps each speaker gives, so that you would be able to perform the task successfully yourself.

Reflecting on Your Writing

Writer's Journal Jot down your thoughts on the experience of writing a how-to essay. Begin by answering these questions:

- Which of the drafting strategies was most helpful to you? Why?
- As a result of writing your essay, what more did you learn about the activity or skill?

Rubric for Self-Assessment

To assess your how-to essay, use the following rubric:

Criteria	Rating Scale not very very
Focus: How clearly and concisely is the topic stated?	1 2 3 4 5
Organization: How logically are the series of steps organized?	1 2 3 4 5
Support/Elaboration: How helpful are charts, illustrations, and diagrams?	1 2 3 4 5
Style: How clearly are materials and terms explained?	1 2 3 4 5
Conventions: How correct is your grammar, especially your use of comparative and superlative forms?	1 2 3 4 5

Skills You Will Learn

Literature You Will Read

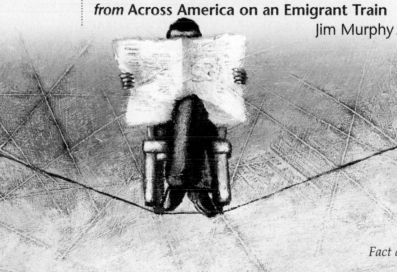

Reading: Fact and Opinion

> A **fact** is something that can be proved. An **opinion** is a person's judgment or belief and cannot be proved.

Skills and Strategies You Will Learn in Part 2

In Part 2, you will learn

- to **use clue words** to **identify opinions, generalizations, and overgeneralizations** (p. 512)
- to **ask questions** to **evaluate an author's support** for his or her opinions (p. 528)
- to **use text structure to evaluate factual support** (p. 544)

Using the Skills and Strategies in Part 2

In Part 2, you will learn to find and use clue words that help you identify opinions. You also will learn to ask questions that provide information to evaluate those opinions. You will use both of these strategies to identify fact and opinion in news sources.

Look at the example of how an opinion can be supported by facts.

OPINION: Swimming is the best form of exercise.

Best is a clue that this is an opinion

FACT:	**FACT:**	**FACT:**
Support of water avoids strain on joints; prevents injuries	Tones muscles in arms, shoulders, trunk, and legs	Strengthens heart and lungs

This is a well-supported opinion. However, another author could support the opinion that walking is the best exercise.

Academic Vocabulary: Words for Discussing Fact and Opinion

The following words will help you write and talk about facts and opinions as you read the selections in this unit.

Word	Definition	Example Sentence
cite *v.*	to refer to an example or fact as proof	What examples did the author *cite?*
credible *adj.*	believable; reliable	How *credible* were her sources?
accurate *adj.*	free from error; correct; exact	Make sure the facts are *accurate.*
bias *n.*	unfair preference or dislike for someone or something	He had a *bias* against anyone who was not an athlete.
support *v.*	to provide evidence to prove or back up an idea	I can *support* my point with many facts and examples.

Vocabulary Skill: Antonyms

▶ **Antonyms** are words that are opposite in meaning.

In Part 2, you will learn:

- antonyms for *bias, accurate,* and *credible* (p. 526)
- how multiple meanings of words affect understanding (p. 542)

The two sentences shown have opposite meanings because of the use of an antonym.

The news report was *accurate.*   The news report was *inaccurate.*

Activity Use a thesaurus to find at least one antonym for these words: *support, bias, credible.* Write a sentence using each antonym. Then, rewrite the sentence using the original word. Explain how the meaning of each sentence changes.

These skills will help you become a better reader. Practice them with either "On Woman's Right to Suffrage" (p. 514) or "The Trouble With Television" (p. 519).

Reading Skill

A **fact** is information that can be proved with evidence. An **opinion** may be supported by evidence, but not proved. A **generalization** is a conclusion supported by facts. An **overgeneralization** is a conclusion that overstates the facts.

Use clue words to determine whether a statement is an opinion, a fact, a generalization, or an overgeneralization.

- Words that communicate judgment, like *best* or *worst,* or specific words that suggest the writer's feelings or beliefs usually indicate an opinion.
- Words that indicate connections—such as *therefore, so,* and *because*—may signal generalizations. Extreme statements that include words like *always, everything, anything, nothing, never,* and *only* may be overgeneralizations.

Literary Analysis

Persuasive techniques are the methods that a writer uses to make an audience think or act a certain way.

- **Repetition** is an effective way to drive home a point.
- **Rhetorical questions** (those with obvious answers) make readers more likely to agree with controversial points.

Other common persuasive techniques are shown in the chart.

Persuasive Techniques
Appeal to Authority **Example:** Quotations from experts or reliable sources
Appeal to Emotions **Example:** Words that appeal to feelings, such as patriotism
Appeal to Reason **Example:** Logical arguments based on evidence such as statistics

Vocabulary Builder

On Woman's Right to Suffrage

- **posterity** (päs ter´ ə tē) *n.* future generations; descendants (p. 514) *He died, leaving his fortune to _posterity_.*
- **oligarchy** (äl´ i gär´ kē) *n.* rule by a small, elite group (p. 515) *An _oligarchy_ of wealthy men ruled the country.*
- **dissension** (di sen´ shən) *n.* difference of opinion (p. 515) *_Dissension_ among the senators led to bitter debates.*

The Trouble With Television

- **diverts** (dī vʉrts´) *v.* distracts; amuses (p. 521) *A movie _diverts_ her from her worries.*
- **pervading** (pər vād´ iŋ) *adj.* spreading throughout (p. 521) *_Pervading_ the room, the odor sickened everyone.*
- **trivial** (triv´ ē əl) *adj.* of little importance; insignificant (p. 523) *Solve significant problems, not _trivial_ ones.*

Background

Women's Suffrage Before 1920, American women did not have the right to vote—also known as *suffrage*. In 1872, activist Susan B. Anthony and some friends tested a law preventing women from voting by going to the polls in Rochester, New York. Anthony was arrested, tried, and ordered to pay a fine. She refused to pay. "On Woman's Right to Suffrage" is her defiant answer to the charges against her.

Connecting to the Literature

Reading/Writing Connection Susan B. Anthony's speech asserts women's right to vote. Write three sentences about why the right to vote is important for all Americans. Use at least three of the following words: *contribute, participate, enable, select.*

Meet the Author

Susan B. **Anthony** (1820–1906)

Susan B. Anthony spent most of her adult life as a prominent voice in the struggle to win the vote for women. Raised as a Quaker, she inherited her parents' dislike of slavery and inequality.

Early Activist At her first job as a teacher, Anthony found out that she was making one-fifth the salary of the school's male teachers. She complained and was fired. Anthony found a new job as the principal of a girls' school. After ten years, though, she became so caught up in the struggle to win the vote for women that she decided to devote her life to the cause.

Fast Facts

▶ With Elizabeth Cady Stanton, Anthony founded the National Woman Suffrage Association in 1869.
▶ At age 84, Anthony organized an international alliance for women's suffrage.
▶ Women finally won the right to vote in 1920—too late for Anthony. She had died fourteen years earlier.

Go Online
Author Link

For: More about the author
Visit: www.PHSchool.com
Web Code: ene-9308

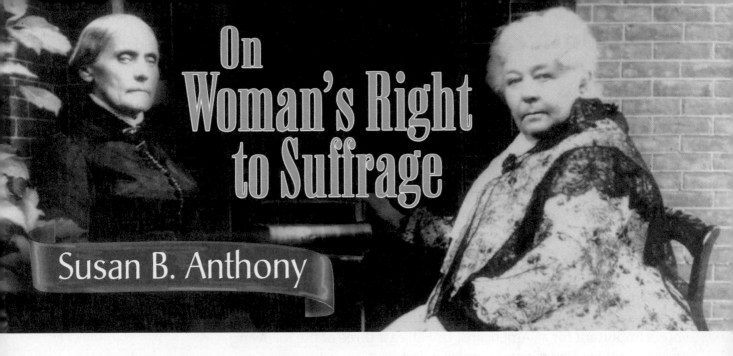

On Woman's Right to Suffrage

Susan B. Anthony

1873—Friends and fellow citizens:

I stand before you to-night under indictment for the alleged crime[1] of having voted at the last presidential election, without having a lawful right to vote. It shall be my work this evening to prove to you that in thus voting, I not only committed no crime, but, instead, simply exercised my *citizen's rights,* guaranteed to me and all United States citizens by the National Constitution, beyond the power of any State to deny.

The preamble of the Federal Constitution says:

"We, the people of the United States, in order to form a more perfect union, establish justice, insure *domestic* tranquillity, provide for the common defense, promote the general welfare, and secure the blessings of liberty to ourselves and our posterity, do ordain and establish this Constitution for the United States of America."

It was we, the people; not we, the white male citizens; nor yet we, the male citizens; but we, the whole people, who formed the Union. And we formed it, not to give the blessings of liberty, but to secure them; not to the half of ourselves and the half of our posterity, but to the whole people—women as well as men. And it is a downright mockery to talk to women of their enjoyment of the blessings of liberty while they are denied the use of the only means of securing them provided by this democratic-republican government—the ballot.

---

1. **indictment** (in dīt´ mənt) **for the alleged** (ə lejd´) **crime** in law, a written statement charging a person with supposedly committing a crime.

Reading Skill
Fact and Opinion
Identify one fact and one opinion in this paragraph.

Vocabulary Builder
posterity (päs ter´ ə tē) *n.* future generations; descendants

> ◆▷ What does this photo of suffragists Susan B. Anthony and Elizabeth Cady Stanton as well as this illustration tell you about suffragist leaders? **[Analyze]**

For any State to make sex a qualification that must ever result in the disfranchisement of one entire half of the people is to pass a bill of attainder, or an *ex post facto* law,[2] and is therefore a violation of the supreme law of the land. By it the blessings of liberty are for ever withheld from women and their female posterity. To them this government has no just powers derived from the consent of the governed. To them this government is not a democracy. It is not a republic. It is an odious aristocracy;[3] a hateful <u>oligarchy</u> of sex; the most hateful aristocracy ever established on the face of the globe; an oligarchy of wealth, where the rich govern the poor. An oligarchy of learning, where the educated govern the ignorant, or even an oligarchy of race, where the Saxon rules the African, might be endured;[4] but this oligarchy of sex, which makes father, brothers, husband, sons, the oligarchs over the mother and sisters, the wife and daughters of every household—which ordains all men sovereigns, all women subjects, carries <u>dissension</u>, discord and rebellion into every home of the nation.

Webster, Worcester and Bouvier all define a citizen to be a person in the United States, entitled to vote and hold office.

The only question left to be settled now is: Are women persons? And I hardly believe any of our opponents will have the hardihood to say they are not. Being persons, then, women are citizens; and no State has a right to make any law, or to enforce any old law, that shall abridge their privileges or immunities. Hence, every discrimination against women in the constitutions and laws of the several States is to-day null and void, precisely as in every one against negroes.

Vocabulary Builder
oligarchy (äl´ i gär´ kē) *n.* rule by a small, elite group

dissension (di sen´ shən) *n.* difference of opinion

Reading Skill
Fact and Opinion
On what fact does Anthony base her opinion that discrimination against women is illegal?

---

2. bill of attainder ... *ex post facto* **law** two practices specifically outlawed by the U.S. Constitution. A bill of attainder declares someone guilty without a trial. An *ex post facto* law applies to acts committed before the law was passed.
3. odious (ō´ dē əs) **aristocracy** (ar´ i stä´ krə sē) hateful system based on inherited wealth and power.
4. oligarchy of race ... endured Anthony refers to a racist nineteenth-century belief, held even by some abolitionists, that whites ("the Saxon") were the natural rulers of African Americans.

Apply the Skills

On Woman's Right to Suffrage

Thinking About the Selection

1. **Respond:** After reading this speech, what would you want to tell or ask Susan B. Anthony if you could meet her in person?
2. **(a) Recall:** Of what crime is Anthony accused? **(b) Contrast:** How does she describe her actions? **(c) Connect:** How is her description connected to the Constitution?
3. **(a) Recall:** What does Anthony believe is required for a government to be a democracy? **(b) Apply:** Does Anthony believe that she lives in a true democracy? Explain.
4. **(a) Recall:** According to Anthony, how do dictionaries define *citizen*? **(b) Analyze:** How does she use this definition to support her position? **(c) Synthesize:** What is her conclusion about laws that discriminate against women?

Reading Skill

5. In a chart like the one shown, classify each statement as a **fact,** an **opinion,** a **generalization,** or an **overgeneralization.** In the third column, explain your choice.

Statement	Type of Statement	Explanation
It is a downright mockery to talk to women of their enjoyment of the blessings of liberty. . . .		
To [women] this government is . . . the most hateful aristocracy ever established.		
[I] voted at the last . . . election, without having a lawful right to vote.		
Webster . . . define[s] a citizen to be a person entitled to vote.		

Literary Analysis

6. **(a)** Identify an example of repetition in Anthony's essay. **(b)** What point is she emphasizing through this repetition?
7. **(a)** What are two sources Anthony quotes to give her argument authority? **(b)** Explain how she uses these sources. **(c)** Explain one other example of a **persuasive technique.**

QuickReview

Speech at a Glance

In this historic speech, Susan B. Anthony argues that women should have the right to vote.

For: Self-test
Visit: www.PHSchool.com
Web Code: ena-6307

Fact: information that can be proved based on evidence

Opinion: a judgment or belief

Generalization: a conclusion based on facts

Overgeneralization: a conclusion that overstates the facts

Persuasive Techniques: methods a writer uses to influence an audience

Vocabulary Builder

Practice Rewrite each sentence using a vocabulary word from the list on page 512 to convey the same basic meaning.

1. This is a big issue, not just for us, but also for our descendants.
2. After the revolution, a small, elite group took over the country.
3. Great differences of opinion in the band led to its breakup.

Writing

Write an **evaluation** of the persuasive arguments presented in Anthony's speech. Address the following points:
- Identify Anthony's position and her supporting points.
- Discuss the kinds of persuasive techniques she uses.
- Assess how well she deals with counter-arguments.
- Evaluate the overall effectiveness and soundness of her argument.

For *Grammar, Vocabulary,* and *Assessment,*
see **Build Language Skills,** pages 526–527.

Extend Your Learning

Listening and Speaking Form two teams to **debate** this topic: "Women's athletic programs in schools and colleges should receive the same financial support as men's."
- Choose a moderator to time responses and to see that each speaker follows the rules of debate and uses respectful language. Speakers should be allowed time to issue both statements and rebuttals (answers to opponents' statements).
- Each side should prepare by researching the topic before the debate and be ready to answer opposing arguments.

Research and Technology With a group, create a **statistical snapshot** of American women. Choose a time span to investigate. For those years, find statistics for women in categories such as: number of bachelor's degrees earned, median income, and participation in professional sports. Then, survey ten people by asking questions about women's status in society. Compare these opinions with the results of your statistical research. Present your findings with graphs and a brief explanation of what the statistics mean.

Persuasive Essay

Background

Television Viewing Robert MacNeil was co-host of a news show in 1984 when he wrote "The Trouble With Television" about America's television addiction. Since then, viewing has only increased. According to Nielsen research, in October 2002, the average American watched more than thirty hours of television a week. Teenagers watched twenty-one hours. Critics, like MacNeil, worry about the potential negative effects of so much television-watching.

Connecting to the Literature

Reading/Writing Connection In his essay, MacNeil worries about the negative influences of television on viewers. To anticipate some arguments MacNeil may overlook, list three possible benefits of watching television. Write in complete sentences, using at least three of the following words: *appeal, challenge, involve, communicate.*

Review

For **Reading Skill, Literary Analysis,** and **Vocabulary Builder,** see page 512.

Meet the Author

Robert **MacNeil** (b. 1931)

Growing up in Halifax, Nova Scotia, Canada, MacNeil developed a love for the English language. In his memoir *Wordstruck,* he says that he is "crazy about the sound of words, the look of words, the taste of words, the feeling for words on the tongue and in the mind."

MacNeil began his broadcast career in Canada as a radio announcer and disc jockey. For Canadian television, he then hosted an educational children's show. In 1955, he moved to England and worked as a journalist.

NewsHour In 1975, MacNeil became co-host of the highly respected *MacNeil/Lehrer NewsHour* on American public television. The show stood out from other news programs by offering more in-depth news and analyses. He retired from *NewsHour* in 1995.

Go Online
Author Link

For: More about the author
Visit: www.PHSchool.com
Web Code: ene-9309

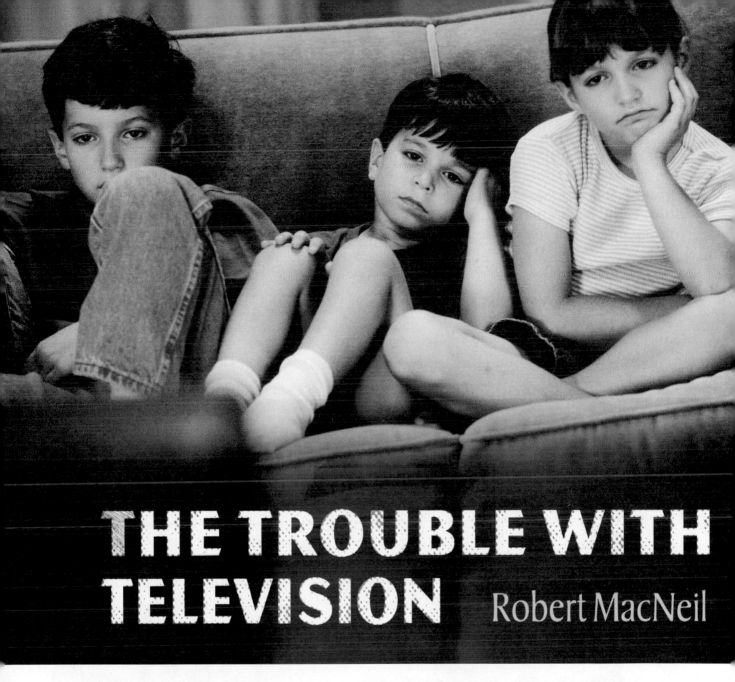

THE TROUBLE WITH TELEVISION

Robert MacNeil

It is difficult to escape the influence of television. If you fit the statistical averages, by the age of 20 you will have been exposed to at least 20,000 hours of television. You can add 10,000 hours for each decade you have lived after the age of 20. The only things Americans do more than watch television are work and sleep.

Calculate for a moment what could be done with even a part of those hours. Five thousand hours, I am told, are what a typical college undergraduate spends working on a bachelor's degree. In 10,000 hours you could have learned enough to

Reading Skill
Fact and Opinion
Identify one fact and one opinion presented here.

become an astronomer or engineer. You could have learned several languages fluently. If it appealed to you, you could be reading Homer[1] in the original Greek or Dostoevski[2] in Russian. If it didn't, you could have walked around the world and written a book about it.

The trouble with television is that it discourages concentration. Almost anything interesting and rewarding in life requires some constructive, consistently applied effort. The dullest, the least gifted of us can achieve things that seem miraculous to those who never concentrate on anything. But

Reading Skill
Fact and Opinion
Does MacNeil support his generalizations here with facts or opinions? Explain.

---

1. **Homer** (hō′ mər) ancient Greek author to whom the epic poems the *Odyssey* and the *Iliad* are attributed.
2. **Dostoevski** (dôs′ tô yef′ skē) (1821–1881) Fyodor (fyô′ dôr), Russian novelist.

▲ Critical Viewing What do this photo and the one on page 519 suggest about the effects of watching television? **[Infer]**

television encourages us to apply no effort. It sells us instant gratification. It <u>diverts</u> us only to divert, to make the time pass without pain.

Television's variety becomes a narcotic, not a stimulus.[3] Its serial, kaleidoscopic[4] exposures force us to follow its lead. The viewer is on a perpetual guided tour: thirty minutes at the museum, thirty at the cathedral, then back on the bus to the next attraction—except on television, typically, the spans allotted are on the order of minutes or seconds, and the chosen delights are more often car crashes and people killing one another. In short, a lot of television usurps one of the most precious of all human gifts, the ability to focus your attention yourself, rather than just passively surrender it.

Capturing your attention—and holding it—is the prime motive of most television programming and enhances its role as a profitable advertising vehicle. Programmers live in constant fear of losing anyone's attention—anyone's. The surest way to avoid doing so is to keep everything brief, not to strain the attention of anyone but instead to provide constant stimulation through variety, novelty, action and movement. Quite simply, television operates on the appeal to the short attention span.

It is simply the easiest way out. But it has come to be regarded as a given, as inherent in the medium[5] itself: as an imperative, as though General Sarnoff, or one of the other august pioneers of video, had bequeathed to us tablets of stone commanding that nothing in television shall ever require more than a few moments' concentration.

In its place that is fine. Who can quarrel with a medium that so brilliantly packages escapist entertainment as a mass-marketing tool? But I see its values now <u>pervading</u> this nation and its life. It has become fashionable to think that, like fast food, fast ideas are the way to get to a fast-moving, impatient public.

In the case of news, this practice, in my view, results in inefficient communication. I question how much of television's nightly news effort is really absorbable and understandable. Much of it is what has been aptly described as

---

3. **becomes a narcotic, not a stimulus** becomes something that dulls the senses instead of something that inspires action.
4. **kaleidoscopic** (kə lī′ də skäp′ ik) *adj.* constantly changing.
5. **inherent** (in hir′ ənt) **in the medium** a natural part of television. A *medium* is a means of communication; the plural is *media.*

Vocabulary Builder
diverts (dī vurts′) *v.* distracts; amuses

Literary Analysis
Persuasive Techniques Does MacNeil appeal to logic or emotion here? Explain.

Vocabulary Builder
pervading (pər vād′ iŋ) *adj.* spreading throughout

 **Reading Check**

According to McNeil, how do programmers avoid losing viewers?

The Television Age

When television sets were scarce, people peered through store windows to watch broadcasts of popular events such as this one, the inauguration of Queen Elizabeth II in 1953. Radio pioneer David Sarnoff (inset) believed in and supported TV's emerging technology. His vision was right on the mark — today, nearly 100 percent of U.S. homes have one or more televisions.

1900 The word *television* is used for the first time at the World's Fair in Paris.

1923 **Vladimir Zworykin** patents his **iconoscope,** a TV camera tube. Later, he develops the **kinescope** for picture display.

1927 **Philo Farnsworth** files for a patent on the first electronic television system.

1936 **Coaxial cable,** used to transmit TV, telephone, and data signals, is introduced. About 200 TV sets are in use worldwide.

1939 **RCA's David Sarnoff** showcases TV at the World's Fair.

1948 **Milton Berle's** *Texaco Star Theater* is the No. 1 program. Less than two percent of homes in the U.S. own a TV set.

1953 The puppet show *Kukla, Fran and Ollie* broadcasts in **color.**

1956 **Robert Adler** invents the first practical **remote control,** called the *Zenith Space Commander.* TV ownership is now seventy percent of U.S. homes.

1969 On July 20, 600 million people watched a TV **transmission from the moon.**

1998 First **HDTV** (high definition television) broadcast.

2004 **Plasma** and **LCD** (liquid crystal display) technology supports flat-screen TVs.

▲ David Sarnoff

Connect to the Literature How has the fascination with television impacted U.S. culture?

"machine gunning with scraps." I think its technique fights coherence.[6] I think it tends to make things ultimately boring and dismissable (unless they are accompanied by horrifying pictures) because almost anything is boring and dismissable if you know almost nothing about it.

I believe that TV's appeal to the short attention span is not only inefficient communication but decivilizing as well. Consider the casual assumptions that television tends to

Reading Skill
Fact and Opinion
Is the first sentence of this paragraph a fact or an opinion? How do you know?

---

6. coherence (kō hir′ əns) *n.* quality of being connected in a way that is easily understood.

cultivate: that complexity must be avoided, that visual stimulation is a substitute for thought, that verbal precision is an anachronism.[7] It may be old-fashioned, but I was taught that thought is words, arranged in grammatically precise ways.

There is a crisis of literacy in this country. One study estimates that some 30 million adult Americans are "functionally illiterate" and cannot read or write well enough to answer a want ad or understand the instructions on a medicine bottle.

Literacy may not be an inalienable human right, but it is one that the highly literate Founding Fathers might not have found unreasonable or even unattainable. We are not only not attaining it as a nation, statistically speaking, but we are falling further and further short of attaining it. And, while I would not be so simplistic as to suggest that television is the cause, I believe it contributes and is an influence.

Everything about this nation—the structure of the society, its forms of family organization, its economy, its place in the world—has become more complex, not less. Yet its dominating communications instrument, its principal form of national linkage, is one that sells neat resolutions to human problems that usually have no neat resolutions. It is all symbolized in my mind by the hugely successful art form that television has made central to the culture, the thirty-second commercial: the tiny drama of the earnest housewife who finds happiness in choosing the right toothpaste.

When before in human history has so much humanity collectively surrendered so much of its leisure to one toy, one mass diversion? When before has virtually an entire nation surrendered itself wholesale to a medium for selling?

Some years ago Yale University law professor Charles L. Black, Jr. wrote: ". . . forced feeding on <u>trivial</u> fare is not itself a trivial matter." I think this society is being force fed with trivial fare, and I fear that the effects on our habits of mind, our language, our tolerance for effort, and our appetite for complexity are only dimly perceived. If I am wrong, we will have done no harm to look at the issue skeptically and critically, to consider how we should be resisting it. I hope you will join with me in doing so.

---

7. **anachronism** (ə nak´ rə niz´ em) *n.* something that seems to be out of its proper place in history.

Apply the Skills

The Trouble With Television

Thinking About the Selection

1. **Respond:** After reading this essay, what would you tell or ask MacNeil if you could meet him in person?
2. **(a) Recall:** What does MacNeil identify as the main trouble with television? **(b) Connect:** How does this problem relate to the methods broadcasters use?
3. **(a) Recall:** What does MacNeil criticize about nightly news shows on television? **(b) Evaluate:** Do you agree or disagree that much television news depends on "horrifying pictures" instead of telling the full story?
4. **(a) Recall:** What positive aspects of television does MacNeil mention? **(b) Speculate:** If MacNeil were in charge of programming for a network, what changes might he make?

Reading Skill

5. In a chart like the one shown, classify each statement as a **fact,** an **opinion,** a **generalization,** or an **overgeneralization.** In the third column, explain your choice.

Statement	Type of Statement	Explanation
Almost anything interesting and rewarding in life requires some constructive . . . effort.		
But television encourages us to apply no effort.		
. . . by the age of 20 you will have been exposed to at least 20,000 hours of television.		
I think this society is being force fed with trivial fare . . .		

Literary Analysis

6. **(a)** Identify three places where MacNeil repeats that television appeals to the short attention span. **(b)** Why does he repeat this idea?
7. **(a)** What is one source MacNeil quotes to give his argument authority? **(b)** Explain how he uses this source to support his argument. **(c)** Explain at least one more **persuasive technique.**

QuickReview

Essay at a Glance
Journalist Robert MacNeil criticizes the influence of television on Americans.

Go Online
Assessment
For: Self-test
Visit: www.PHSchool.com
Web Code: ena-6308

Fact: information that can be proved based on evidence

Opinion: a judgment or belief

Generalization: a conclusion based on facts

Overgeneralization: a conclusion that overstates the facts

Persuasive Techniques: methods a writer uses to influence an audience

Vocabulary Builder

Practice Rewrite each sentence, using a vocabulary word from the list on page 512 to convey the same basic meaning.

1. Her questions were mainly about small, unimportant matters.
2. Wafting through the house was the aroma of cookies baking.
3. Any small noise interrupts my concentration on homework.

Writing

Write an **evaluation** of MacNeil's persuasive essay. In your evaluation, address the following points:

- Identify MacNeil's position and his supporting points.
- Discuss the kinds of persuasive techniques he uses.
- Assess how well he deals with counter-arguments.
- Evaluate the overall effectiveness and soundness of his argument.

For *Grammar, Vocabulary*, and *Assessment*, see **Build Language Skills,** pages 526–527.

Extend Your Learning

Listening and Speaking Form two teams to **debate** this topic: "Television viewing for teenagers should be limited to one hour daily during the week."

- Choose a moderator to time responses and to see that each speaker follows the rules of debate and uses respectful language. Speakers should be allowed time to issue both statements and rebuttals (answers to opponents' statements).
- Each side should prepare by researching the topic before the debate and be ready to answer opposing arguments.

Research and Technology Create a **statistical snapshot** of television-viewing habits. Interview ten students and ten adults about the number of hours each week they spend watching programs in these categories: sports, news, movies, comedy, drama, music, educational/informational. Present your data as a television-watching graph with an explanation of key findings.

Build Language Skills

Vocabulary Skill

Antonyms The words *biased* and *unbiased* are **antonyms,** or words with opposite meanings. *Incredible,* an antonym of *credible,* is "the lack of being credible" or "the lack of being believable." Antonyms are useful when thinking or writing about contrasts.

▶ **Example:** The expert in biology was a *credible* source, but we found his statements *incredible.*

Practice Substitute an antonym for the italicized word. Then, note how this change makes the sentence more logical.

1. People who are *biased* have a more objective view of life.
2. I found mistakes in the report; I am not sure how *inaccurate* it is.
3. His poor view of the accident scene made his testimony *credible.*
4. That idea is *unsupported* by many excellent experiments.
5. *Unsupported* medical claims changed the way people diet.

Grammar Lesson

Conjunctions Words that connect sentence parts and help you add information to sentences are called **conjunctions.** The chart shows some common conjunctions.

MorePractice

For more practice with conjunctions, see the Grammar Handbook, p. R31.

Type	Function	Example
coordinating	connects parts of similar importance	*and, but, for, nor, or, so, yet*
correlative	connects pairs of equal importance	*both/and, either/or, neither/nor*
subordinating	connects two ideas, one dependent on the other	*although, because, even though, if, since, while, until*

Practice Rewrite each sentence, changing one of the conjunctions. Explain how the conjunction affects the meaning of the sentence.

1. The Constitution and Bill of Rights spell out rights and responsibilities.
2. States approved the Constitution, but they wanted a Bill of Rights.
3. Neither women nor African Americans could vote in 1789.
4. The Fifteenth Amendment and the Nineteenth Amendment expand the right to vote.

𝒲𝒢 *Prentice Hall Writing and Grammar Connection: Chapter 18, Section 1*

Reading: Fact and Opinion

Directions: *Read the selection. Then, answer the questions.*

The Lewis and Clark expedition to explore parts of the Louisiana Territory was the greatest adventure in American history. The 1803 acquisition of the vast territory from France had doubled the area of the United States. Curious about the huge new territory west of the Mississippi, President Thomas Jefferson chose experienced explorers to lead the expedition, which set off from St. Louis in the spring of 1804. The exploring party traveled through the new breathtaking scenery. None of the men had ever seen anything like it before. The explorers kept careful records and collected specimens of plants and animals. Alas, I have not seen the original records.

1. Which of these is *not* a fact?
   A The Louisiana Territory is west of the Mississippi.
   B The Louisiana Purchase doubled the size of the United States.
   C The Louisiana Territory has breathtaking scenery.
   D France sold the Louisiana Territory.

2. Which is a clue that the writer is *not* presenting a fact?
   A none of the . . .
   B curious about the . . . territory . . .
   C experienced explorers . . .
   D I have not . . .

3. Which of these is an opinion?
   A The expedition took samples of new plants and animals.
   B Its leaders had exploring experience.
   C The expedition was from St. Louis.
   D It was the greatest adventure in American history.

4. Which is a clue that the writer is giving an opinion?
   A greatest
   B curious
   C anything
   D none

Timed Writing: Evaluation [Critical Stance]

Review "The Trouble With Television" or "On Woman's Right to Suffrage." Evaluate whether or not the author achieves his or her purpose. Judge the support provided and the persuasive techniques used. **(30 minutes)**

Writing Workshop: *Work in Progress*

Editorial

For an editorial you may write, make a list of five problems in your school, community, or the world in general. For each issue, jot down your opinion. Keep this list in your writing portfolio.

These skills will help you become a better reader. Practice them with either the excerpt from *Sharing in the American Dream* (p. 530) or "Science and the Sense of Wonder" (p. 535).

Reading Skill

A **fact** is information that can be proved. An **opinion** is a person's judgment or belief. As you read nonfiction, **ask questions to evaluate an author's support** for his or her opinions.

- A *valid opinion* can be supported by facts or by expert authority.
- A *faulty opinion* cannot be supported by facts. Instead, it is supported by other opinions and often ignores major facts that contradict it. Faulty opinions often show *bias*, an unfair preference or dislike for something, as shown in the chart.

Statement: Science is more difficult than literature.

↓

1. Distinguish fact from opinion
ASK: Can it be proved?

↓

No. It is an opinion.

↓

2. Distinguish valid from faulty opinion
ASK: Can it be supported?

↓

No. It is contradicted by the fact that some people find literature more difficult than science.

Literary Analysis

An author's **word choice** can help convey a certain idea or feeling. An author might choose words that are formal or informal, simple or complex. Factors that influence word choice include:

- the author's intended audience and purpose
- the **connotations** of words—the negative or positive ideas associated with words—in addition to their **denotations** (dictionary definitions)

As you read, notice how word choice affects the feeling of a work.

Vocabulary Builder

from Sharing in the American Dream

- **aspirations** (as´ pə rā´ shənz) *n.* strong desires or ambitions (p. 530) *Some children have aspirations of becoming President.*

- **deferred** (dē fʉrd´) *adj.* delayed (p. 530) *He took a deferred admission to college and traveled.*

- **compassionate** (kəm pash´ en it) *adj.* deeply sympathetic (p. 530) *The doctor is always compassionate when treating pain.*

- **alliance** (ə lī´ əns) *n.* a group united for a common goal (p. 531) *Britain's alliance with the United States ended the Nazi threat.*

Science and the Sense of Wonder

- **exultantly** (eg zult´ ´nt lē) *adv.* triumphantly (p. 536) *"We won!" he yelled exultantly.*

- **desolate** (des´ ə lit) *adj.* uninhabited; barren (p. 536) *The North Pole is a desolate place.*

- **cosmic** (käz´ mik) *adj.* universal; infinite (p. 537) *Earth is a tiny part of a cosmic whole.*

Build Understanding

Background

Volunteers In the excerpt from his speech *Sharing in the American Dream,* Colin Powell encourages his audience to spread the spirit of volunteerism. In the United States, millions of people volunteer each year, and the numbers are growing. Unpaid volunteers perform crucial tasks in schools, hospitals, nursing homes, and libraries. Without volunteer help, many organizations could not afford to serve as many people as they do.

Connecting to the Literature

Reading/Writing Connection Colin Powell wants to inspire his audience with enthusiasm about volunteering. List three reasons why people volunteer. Write in complete sentences, using three of the following words: *benefit, assist, respond, motivate, invest.*

Meet the Author

Colin **Powell** (b. 1937)

Colin Powell's life is a true American success story. From a humble childhood in the New York neighborhood of the South Bronx, Powell rose to become one of the most powerful and influential people in American politics.

Rising Through the Ranks Powell began his thirty-five year career serving as a soldier during the Vietnam War. He rose quickly through the ranks to assume the most powerful Defense Department position—Chairman of the Joint Chiefs of Staff—shortly before the Persian Gulf War. Powell's calm voice and steady presence were reassuring to many Americans during the nation's first major war since Vietnam.

Fast Facts

▶ In 2001, Powell became the first African American to serve as Secretary of State, an official appointed by the President to make key foreign policy decisions.

▶ In 1997, Powell founded the volunteer organization America's Promise to give other children the same chances to succeed that he has enjoyed.

Go **Online**
Author Link

For: More about the author
Visit: www.PHSchool.com
Web Code: ene-9310

from SHARING IN THE AMERICAN DREAM
Colin Powell

Over 200 years ago, a group of volunteers gathered on this sacred spot to found a new nation. In perfect words, they voiced their dreams and <u>aspirations</u> of an imperfect world. They pledged their lives, their fortune and their sacred honor to secure inalienable rights given by God for life, liberty and pursuit of happiness—pledged that they would provide them to all who would inhabit this new nation.

They look down on us today in spirit, with pride for all we have done to keep faith with their ideals and their sacrifices. Yet, despite all we have done, this is still an imperfect world. We still live in an imperfect society. Despite more than two centuries of moral and material progress, despite all our efforts to achieve a more perfect union, there are still Americans who are not sharing in the American Dream. There are still Americans who wonder: is the journey there for them, is the dream there for them, or, whether it is, at best, a dream <u>deferred</u>.

The great American poet, Langston Hughes, talked about a dream deferred, and he said, "What happens to a dream deferred? Does it dry up like a raisin in the sun, or fester like a sore and then run? Does it stink like rotten meat or crust and sugar over like a syrupy sweet? Maybe it just sags, like a heavy load. Or, does it explode?" . . .

So today, we gather here today to pledge that the dream must no longer be deferred and it will never, as long as we can do anything about it, become a dream denied. That is why we are here, my friends. We gather here to pledge that those of us who are more fortunate will not forsake those who are less fortunate. We are a <u>compassionate</u> and caring people. We are a generous people. We will reach down, we will reach back, we will reach across to help our brothers and sisters who are in need.

Above all, we pledge to reach out to the most vulnerable members of the American family, our children. As you've heard, up to 15 million young Americans today are at risk. . . .

Vocabulary Builder
aspirations (as´ pə rā´ shənz) *n.* strong desires or ambitions

deferred (dē fʉrd´) *adj.* delayed

compassionate (kəm pash´ ən it) *adj.* deeply sympathetic

Literary Analysis
Word Choice Are the connotations of *pledge* and *dream* positive or negative? Explain their effect.

In terms of numbers the task may seem staggering. But if we look at the simple needs that these children have, then the task is manageable, the goal is achievable. We know what they need. They need an adult caring person in their life, a safe place to learn and grow, a healthy start, marketable skills and an opportunity to serve so that early in their lives they learn the virtue of service so that they can reach out then and touch another young American in need.

These are basic needs that we commit ourselves to today, we promise today. We are making America's promise today to provide to those children in need. This is a grand <u>alliance</u>. It is an alliance between government and corporate America and nonprofit America, between our institutions of faith, but especially between individual Americans.

You heard the governors and the mayors, and you'll hear more in a little minute that says the real answer is for each and every one of us, not just here in Philadelphia, but across this land—for each and every one of us to reach out and touch someone in need.

All of us can spare 30 minutes a week or an hour a week. All of us can give an extra dollar. All of us can touch someone who doesn't look like us, who doesn't speak like us, who may not dress like us, but needs us in their lives. And that's what we all have to do to keep this going.

And so there's a spirit of Philadelphia here today. There's a spirit of Philadelphia that we saw yesterday in Germantown. There is a spirit of Philadelphia that will leave Philadelphia tomorrow afternoon and spread across this whole nation—30 governors will go back and spread it; over 100 mayors will go back and spread it, and hundreds of others, leaders around this country who are watching will go back and spread it. Corporate America will spread it, nonprofits will spread it. And each and every one of us will spread it because it has to be done, we have no choice. We cannot leave these children behind if we are going to meet the dreams of our founding fathers.

And so let us all join in this great crusade. Let us make sure that no child in America is left behind, no child in America has their dream deferred or denied. We can do it. We can do it because we are Americans. . . .

Vocabulary Builder
alliance (ə lī′ əns) *n.* a group united for a common goal

Reading Skill
Fact and Opinion Is Powell's statement at the start of this paragraph a fact or an opinion? Explain, and then evaluate whether the statement is valid.

Literary Analysis
Word Choice What phrases have positive connotations in the final paragraph? Explain their effect.

Apply the Skills

*from **Sharing in the American Dream***

Thinking About the Selection

1. **(a) Respond:** Do you agree or disagree with Powell's message? **(b) Support:** In your notebook, write an explanation for your answer. **(c) Discuss:** Share your response with a partner. Then discuss how looking at someone else's responses did or did not change your thinking.
2. **(a) Recall:** To which earlier group of volunteers does Powell refer at the beginning of the speech? **(b) Interpret:** What types of feelings do you think Powell wants to create in his audience by mentioning this group of people?
3. **(a) Recall:** In what way is America "imperfect," according to Powell? **(b) Infer:** What does Powell suggest would bring America closer to perfection?
4. **Assess:** Do you think this speech would inspire an audience to increase its involvement in volunteer work? Why or why not?

Reading Skill

5. **(a)** Identify one statement of **fact** and one statement of **opinion** in the speech. **(b)** Explain your choices.
6. **(a)** Is Powell's statement "We can do it because we are Americans" a statement of fact or opinion? Explain.
   (b) Evaluate Powell's support for this statement. Is the statement adequately supported or does it reflect **bias**? Explain.

Literary Analysis

7. Use a chart like the one shown to analyze Powell's **word choice**.

Powell's Purpose	Words and Phrases That Support His Purpose	Connotations

8. Would you characterize Powell's language as simple and informal or complex and formal? Explain by providing examples from the speech.

QuickReview

Speech at a Glance
Colin Powell encourages his audience to reach out to Americans in need.

Go Online
Assessment
For: Self-test
Visit: www.PHSchool.com
Web Code: ena-6309

Fact: information that can be proved

Opinion: a person's judgment or belief

Word Choice: an author's selection of particular words to express ideas and convey meaning

Vocabulary Builder

Practice Write a complete sentence to answer each question. For each item, use a vocabulary word from page 528 in place of underlined words with similar meanings.

1. What is the most <u>caring</u>, <u>unselfish</u> thing you have ever done?
2. What are two of your <u>dreams</u> or <u>goals</u>?
3. Why should people and companies <u>work together</u>?
4. Why do people say, "Never <u>put off</u> what you can do today?"

Writing

Write a brief **response** to Powell's statement "All of us can spare 30 minutes a week or an hour a week."

- First, reread the paragraph on page 531 that begins with this statement to recall what Powell wants his audience to do.
- Next, decide whether or not you agree with Powell.
- Finally, explain your response to Powell's idea by deciding how it applies—or does not apply—to your own experience.

For *Grammar, Vocabulary,* and *Assessment,* see **Build Language Skills,** pages 542–543.

Extend Your Learning

Listening and Speaking Write an **introductory speech**, presenting Colin Powell to an audience of governors, mayors, and local leaders. Write in a style appropriate for your audience, and use parallel wording to add drama and emphasis to your speech. For example, you might begin a series of sentences with the same key phrase. Deliver the speech to your class, pausing for dramatic effect and varying your pace to create audience interest.

Research and Technology Take notes from Internet and library resources to make a **reference list** of local or national volunteer organizations. Your list should include a brief description of each organization's main goals as well as accurate contact information. Use a format such as address, phone number, Internet address. When you finish, post the list in your library or guidance office as a resource for those who would like to volunteer.

Critical Essay

Background

Walt Whitman Isaac Asimov wrote "Science and the Sense of Wonder" in response to a poem by nineteenth-century writer Walt Whitman. Whitman was a journalist, essayist, and poet whose writing celebrated the beauty of the human body and of the natural world. He was writing at the beginning of a long period of scientific and technological progress.

Connecting to the Literature

Reading/Writing Connection In his poem, Whitman doubts that scientists can appreciate natural beauty. Asimov disagrees. List two reasons to appreciate nature by simply enjoying it and two reasons to study nature from a scientific standpoint. Use at least three of these words: *appreciate, emphasize, define, investigate, focus.*

Review

For **Reading Skill, Literary Analysis,** and **Vocabulary Builder,** see page 528.

Meet the Author

Isaac **Asimov** (1920–1992)

Isaac Asimov became a science-fiction fan by reading fantastic stories in science-fiction magazines. Little did he know then that he would become one of the most influential science writers of the twentieth century.

Persistence Asimov's father discouraged his son's early interest in science-fiction stories, describing the magazines as "junk." Still, Asimov's interest continued and he started writing his own stories at age eleven. At first, his stories were rejected by most magazines, but little by little, Asimov gained the knowledge that enabled him to build a successful career.

Fast Facts

▶ Asimov's stories often involve robots. "I, Robot" was adapted as a movie starring Will Smith.

▶ Regarding scientific concepts, Asimov has said, "I'm on fire to explain, and happiest when it's something reasonably intricate which I can make clear. . . ."

Go Online
Author Link

For: More about the author
Visit: www.PHSchool.com
Web Code: ene-9311

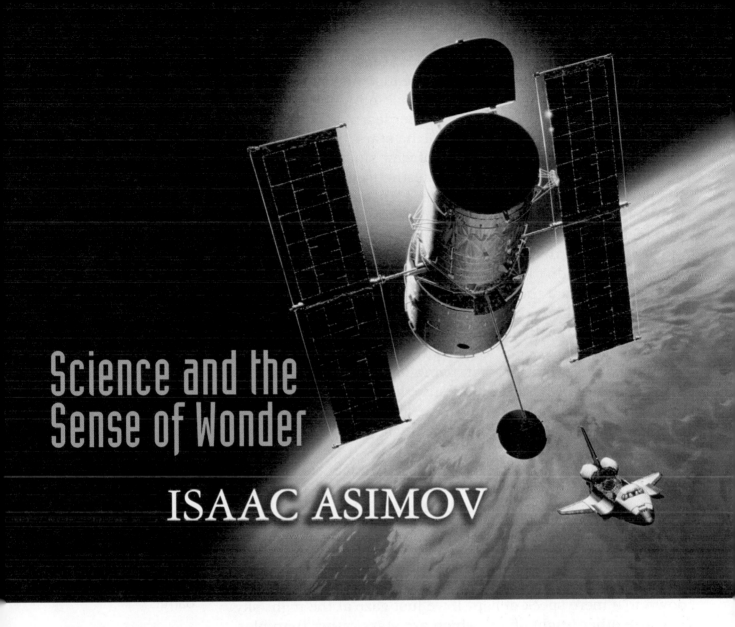

Science and the Sense of Wonder

ISAAC ASIMOV

One of Walt Whitman's best-known poems is this one:

> When I heard the learn'd astronomer,
> When the proofs, the figures, were ranged in columns
>   before me,
> When I was shown the charts and diagrams, to add,
>   divide and measure them,
> When I sitting heard the astronomer where he lectured
>   with much applause in the lecture-room,
> How soon unaccountable I became tired and sick,
> Till rising and gliding out I wander'd off by myself,
> In the mystical moist night-air, and from time to time,
> Look'd up in perfect silence at the stars.

▲ Critical Viewing
Does this picture
make you think
of scientific
achievement, natural
beauty, or both?
Explain. [Make a
Judgment]

I imagine that many people reading those lines tell themselves, <u>exultantly</u>, "How true! Science just sucks all the beauty out of everything, reducing it all to numbers and tables and measurements! Why bother learning all that junk when I can just go out and look at the stars?"

That is a very convenient point of view since it makes it not only unnecessary, but downright aesthetically wrong,[1] to try to follow all that hard stuff in science. Instead, you can just take a look at the night sky, get a quick beauty fix, and go off to a nightclub.

The trouble is that Whitman is talking through his hat, but the poor soul didn't know any better.

I don't deny that the night sky is beautiful, and I have in my time spread out on a hillside for hours looking at the stars and being awed by their beauty (and receiving bug-bites whose marks took weeks to go away).

But what I see—those quiet, twinkling points of light—is not *all the beauty there is.* Should I stare lovingly at a single leaf and willingly remain ignorant of the forest? Should I be satisfied to watch the sun glinting off a single pebble and scorn any knowledge of a beach?

Those bright spots in the sky that we call planets are worlds. There are worlds with thick atmospheres of carbon dioxide and sulfuric acid; worlds of red-hot liquid with hurricanes that could gulp down the whole earth; dead worlds with quiet pockmarks of craters; worlds with volcanoes puffing plumes of dust into airlessness; worlds with pink and <u>desolate</u> deserts—each with a weird and unearthly beauty that boils down to a mere speck of light if we just gaze at the night sky.

Those other bright spots, which are stars rather than planets, are actually suns. Some of them are of incomparable grandeur,[2] each glowing with the light of a thousand suns like ours; some of them are merely red-hot coals doling out their energy stingily. Some of them are compact bodies as massive as our sun, but with all that mass squeezed into a ball smaller than the earth. Some are more compact still, with the mass of the sun squeezed down into the volume of a small asteroid. And some are more compact still, with their mass shrinking

---

1. **aesthetically** (es thet´ i kəl lē) **wrong** insensitive to beauty.
2. **incomparable grandeur** (gran´ jər) unequaled splendor.

Vocabulary Builder
exultantly (eg zult´ nt lē) *adv.* triumphantly

Reading Skill
Fact and Opinion Is this statement about Whitman fact or opinion? Explain.

Vocabulary Builder
desolate (des´ ə lit) *adj.* uninhabited; barren

Literary Analysis
Word Choice What words in this paragraph help you imagine the sizes of the different suns Asimov describes?

down to a volume of zero, the site of which is marked by an intense gravitational field that swallows up everything and gives back nothing; with matter spiraling into that bottomless hole and giving out a wild death-scream of X-rays.

There are stars that pulsate endlessly in a great <u>cosmic</u> breathing; and others that, having consumed their fuel, expand and redden until they swallow up their planets, if they have any (and someday, billions of years from now, our sun will expand and the earth will crisp and sere and vaporize into a gas of iron and rock with no sign of the life it once bore). And some stars explode in a vast cataclysm whose ferocious blast of cosmic rays, hurrying outward at nearly the speed of light, reaches across thousands of light years to touch the earth and supply some of the driving force of evolution through mutations.

Those paltry few stars we see as we look up in perfect silence (some 2,500 or more on even the darkest and clearest night) are joined by a vast horde we don't see, up to as many as three hundred billion—300,000,000,000—to form an enormous pinwheel in space. This pinwheel, the Milky Way galaxy,

▲ **Critical Viewing**
Jupiter's Great Red Spot is a storm three times the size of Earth. Does knowing facts about planets take away from their beauty? **[Connect]**

Vocabulary Builder
cosmic (käz´ mik) *adj.*
universal; infinite

Reading Check

What will happen to the Earth billions of years from now?

stretches so widely that it takes light, moving at 186,282 miles each *second*, a hundred thousand *years* to cross it from end to end; and it rotates about its center in a vast and stately turn that takes two hundred million years to complete—and the sun and the earth and we ourselves all make that turn.

Beyond our Milky Way galaxy are others, a score or so of them bound to our own in a cluster of galaxies, most of them small, with no more than a few billion stars in each; but with one at least, the Andromeda galaxy, twice as large as our own.

Beyond our own cluster, other galaxies and other clusters exist; some clusters made up of thousands of galaxies. They stretch outward and outward as far as our best telescopes can see, with no visible sign of an end—perhaps a hundred billion of them in all.

And in more and more of those galaxies we are becoming aware of violence at the centers—of great explosions and outpourings of radiation, marking the death of perhaps millions of stars. Even at the center of our own galaxy there

Reading Skill
Fact and Opinion
Do these figures support Asimov's opinion that there is more to the universe than meets the eye? Explain.

Literary Analysis
Word Choice Which words here add drama to the description?

◀ **Critical Viewing** What point in Asimov's essay does this image reinforce? Explain. **[Connect]**

is incredible violence masked from our own solar system far in the outskirts by enormous clouds of dust and gas that lie between us and the heaving center.

Some galactic centers are so bright that they can be seen from distances of billions of light-years, distances from which the galaxies them-selves cannot be seen and only the bright starlike centers of ravening[3] energy show up—as quasars. Some of these have been detected from more than ten billion light-years away.

All these galaxies are hurrying outward from each other in a vast universal expansion that began fifteen billion years ago, when all the matter in the universe was in a tiny sphere that exploded in the hugest conceivable shatter to form the galaxies.

The universe may expand forever or the day may come when the expansion slows and turns back into a contraction to re-form the tiny sphere and begin the game all over again so that the whole universe is exhaling and inhaling in breaths that are perhaps a trillion years long.

And all of this vision—far beyond the scale of human imaginings—was made possible by the works of hundreds of "learn'd" astronomers. All of it; *all* of it was discovered after the death of Whitman in 1892, and most of it in the past twenty-five years, so that the poor poet never knew what a stultified[4] and limited beauty he observed when he "look'd up in perfect silence at the stars."

Nor can we know or imagine now the limitless beauty yet to be revealed in the future—by science.

Literature in Context

Science Connection

Lord of the Rings The wonder of Saturn's rings—patterned waves that resemble ripples in a pond—wowed the world in 2004. The images were transmitted from 900 million miles away by the *Cassini* spacecraft, which NASA had launched seven years before.

The craft is named for the seventeenth-century astronomer Giovanni Cassini, discoverer of several of Saturn's moons. Cassini also discovered a gap in the rings, which was named *Cassini's division*. Scientists know that the hundreds of rings are made up of ice and rock particles that orbit Saturn at different speeds. By studying the rings up close, scientists hope to learn more about the solar system and how planets form.

Connect to the Literature

Would Isaac Asimov be impressed by the *Cassini* photographs? Why?

---

3. **ravening** (rav´ ə niŋ) *adj.* consuming greedily.
4. **stultified** (stul´ tə fīd´) *adj.* foolish or absurd.

Apply the Skills

Science and the Sense of Wonder

Thinking About the Selection

1. **(a) Respond:** What do you think is the most powerful idea presented in this essay? Explain your answer. **(b) Discuss:** In a small group, share your responses. As a group, choose one to share with the class.
2. **(a) Recall:** Approximately how many stars are included in the Milky Way? **(b) Analyze:** How does Asimov give the reader a sense of how small our galaxy is?
3. **(a) Recall:** At the end of the essay, what fact does Asimov give about discoveries made after Whitman's death? **(b) Evaluate:** Does this fact call into question the views expressed by Whitman in the poem? Why or why not?
4. **Make a Judgment:** Do you agree with Whitman's view, Asimov's view, or both views of science and the natural world? Support your response.

Reading Skill

5. **(a)** Identify one statement of **fact** and one statement of **opinion** in the essay. **(b)** Explain your choices.
6. **(a)** Is it fact or Asimov's opinion that what Whitman admired was a "limited beauty"? Explain. **(b)** Evaluate Asimov's support for this statement. Is the statement adequately supported in the essay or does it reflect **bias**? Explain.

Literary Analysis

7. Use a chart like the one shown to analyze Asimov's **word choice.**

Asimov's Purpose	Words and Phrases That Support His Purpose	Connotations

8. Would you characterize Asimov's language as simple and informal or complex and formal? Explain by providing examples from the essay.

QuickReview

Essay at a Glance
Isaac Asimov argues that there are many ways to appreciate the beauty of the universe

Go Online
Assessment
For: Self-test
Visit: www.PHSchool.com
Web Code: ena-6310

Fact: information that can be proved

Opinion: a person's judgment or belief

Word Choice: an author's selection of particular words to express ideas and convey meaning

Vocabulary Builder

Practice Write a complete sentence to answer each question. For each item, use a vocabulary word from the "Science and the Sense of Wonder" list on page 528 in place of underlined words with similar meanings.

1. Does lack of rainfall affect deserts <u>without human life or plant life</u>?

2. Would a team greet its tenth victory in a row with a <u>happy emotion</u>?

3. What <u>universal</u> truths are sought by all of the world's religions?

Writing

Write a brief **response** to Asimov's idea that the scientist's way of appreciating nature is just as valid as the poet's.

- First, review the essay to decide whether you agree with Asimov's idea.
- Then, explain your response to Asimov's idea by deciding how it applies—or does not apply—to your own appreciation of nature and its beauty.

For *Grammar, Vocabulary,* and *Assessment,* see **Build Language Skills,** pages 542–543.

Extend Your Learning

Listening and Speaking Write an **introductory speech** presenting Isaac Asimov during a school assembly and praising him for his contributions to science and literature. Write in a style appropriate for your audience, and use parallel wording to add drama and emphasis to your speech. For example, you might begin a series of sentences with the same key phrase.

Deliver the speech to your class, pausing for dramatic effect and varying your pace to create audience interest.

Research and Technology Take notes from Internet and library resources to make a **reference list** of astronomical terms used by Asimov in his essay. Be sure to include the word and a definition, and alphabetize your list.

Build Language Skills

from *Sharing in the American Dream* •
Science and the Sense of Wonder

Vocabulary Skill

Words With Multiple Meanings The word *support* has several different meanings and can be used as either a verb or a noun. Many words have different meanings when they are used as different parts of speech. *Puns* use this principle to create humor, as in "If you want to be seen by a doctor, be patient."

> **support** (sə pôrt´) *v.* **1.** to carry or bear the weight of **2.** to give courage, help, or comfort **3.** to give approval; to vote for **4.** to provide with things needed for survival **5.** to provide evidence to help prove
> —*n.* **1.** a prop or base that holds something up **2.** money or other means of staying alive **3.** maintenance and service

Practice Write the part of speech and definition number that fits the usage of the word *support* in each sentence.

1. My parents work hard at their jobs to *support* our family.
2. When our computer crashed, we called the *support* number.
3. Provide details to *support* your opinion.
4. Everyone needs good friends to *support* them when they are sad.
5. How many voters do you think will *support* that candidate?

Grammar Lesson

Prepositions and Prepositional Phrases A **preposition** relates the noun or pronoun following it to another word in the sentence.

> **Examples:** before, after, during, in, above, around, under, consequently

The group of words beginning with the preposition and ending with the noun is called a **prepositional phrase**.

> **Example:** He put the book on the bookcase.

Practice Rewrite each sentence by changing a preposition. Explain how this changes the meaning of the sentence.

1. The children ran around the playground.
2. In each inning, the visiting team bats first.
3. In many action movies, the hero ends up in a car chase.
4. There are goalposts at both ends of a football field.
5. We got our Labrador Retriever at the animal shelter.

MorePractice

For more practice with prepositions, see the Grammar Handbook, p. R31.

WG *Prentice Hall Writing and Grammar Connection: Chapter 17, Section 1*

Reading: Fact and Opinion

Directions: *Read the selection. Then, answer the questions.*

Too many people think baseball is "our national pastime." Among eighth grade students at Lincoln Middle School, baseball is not nearly as popular as football. Out of sixty-eight students surveyed, forty-three said they would rather watch a football game than a baseball game. Surprisingly, both girls and boys said that they prefer football. Sixteen students said that they lose interest in a baseball game before it is over. This proves that baseball is a boring sport that takes too long to play.

1. Which words are clues that a sentence is an opinion?
   - **A** out of
   - **B** among eighth grade students
   - **C** too many people
   - **D** baseball is not

2. Which question would best help you evaluate the statement in sentence 3?
   - **A** How many students are in the eighth grade at the school?
   - **B** How many students like the Olympics?
   - **C** Are there students who play other sports in the school?
   - **D** How many grades are there in the school?

3. Which is a fact?
   - **A** Baseball is a great game.
   - **B** It is surprising that girls like football.
   - **C** Forty-three students prefer football.
   - **D** Baseball takes too long to play.

4. Which statement is not factual support for an opinion?
   - **A** Among eighth grade students at Lincoln Middle School, baseball is not as popular as football.
   - **B** Out of sixty-eight students surveyed, forty-three said they would rather watch a football game.
   - **C** This proves that baseball is a boring sport that takes too long to play.
   - **D** Sixteen people said that they lose interest in a baseball game before it is over.

Timed Writing: Evaluation

Review the excerpt from *Sharing in the American Dream* or "Science and the Sense of Wonder." Discuss the writer's support, and whether or not there is bias in the text. **(35 minutes)**

 ## Writing Workshop: *Work in Progress*

Editorial

Review the list in your writing portfolio and choose two issues. For each, jot down a logical reason that supports your opinion. Then, write an emotional reason that explains your ideas. Save this work in your portfolio.

Reading Informational Materials

Newspaper Articles

In Part 2, you are learning to distinguish between facts and opinions in a literary work. Distinguishing between facts and opinions also is helpful in reading newspaper articles. If you read "Science and the Sense of Wonder," you learned about the science of outer space. This newspaper article from *The Christian Science Monitor* is about another aspect of space science.

About Newspaper Articles

Newspapers keep people informed about local, national, and world events. Because most people read newspapers quickly, a **newspaper article** must be packed with tightly organized information that is interesting and well written.

News stories include the *Five Ws* and an *H,* introducing them in the lead, or opening paragraph: *who,* or the subject of the story; *what* the action is; and *where, when, why,* and *how* the action takes place.

Reading Skill

The **organizational structure** of a text is the way in which the information is organized. Possible organizations include:

- comparison and contrast (Details about similarities and differences are grouped together.)
- cause and effect (Details are organized to show connections, reasons, and results.)
- chronological order (Details are organized to show what happens first, next, and last.)

"Lots in Space" is organized in a problem-and-solution structure, which describes a problem and suggests ways to solve it. As you read, evaluate the seriousness of the problem and the effectiveness of the suggested solutions. Use an organizer like the one shown to note facts that support the writer's opinions on the problem and the suggested solutions.

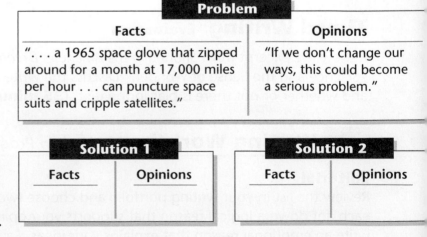

Problem	
Facts	**Opinions**
". . . a 1965 space glove that zipped around for a month at 17,000 miles per hour . . . can puncture space suits and cripple satellites."	"If we don't change our ways, this could become a serious problem."

Solution 1	
Facts	**Opinions**

Solution 2	
Facts	**Opinions**

Lots in Space

Orbiting junk, from old satellites to space gloves, has scientists worried for spacecraft— and engineers working on ways to clean it up.

Peter N. Spotts

The writer summarizes the problem, which is the focus—the "what"—of this article.

If you want to get rid of an old fridge or an obsolete TV, you could call for curbside pickup. But an obsolete satellite? Or a spent rocket?

Increasingly, the space about Earth is getting cluttered with such junk. And it's not just messy, it's dangerous. Full-size rocket bodies can destroy. Even smaller pieces— such as a 1965 space glove that zipped around for a month at 17,000 miles per hour—amount to more than a smack in the face. They can puncture space suits and cripple satellites.

The writer begins with a complete explanation of the problem— the "why"— and briefly mentions possible solutions.

Fortunately, the aerospace community is giving the problem increasing attention. Engineers are considering everything from techniques for rendering derelict satellites and boosters less harmful, to an international "space traffic control" system, to Earth-based lasers that can zap the stuff.

But the problem is expected to get worse as governments and companies prepare to triple the satellite population over the next two decades and send more people into space.

"If we don't change our ways, this could become a serious problem," says William Ailor, who heads the Center for Orbital Reentry Debris Studies at the Aerospace Corporation in El Segundo, Calif. . . .

A quotation from an expert adds authority to the description of the problem.

Ever since Sputnik, humans have lobbed more than 20,000 metric tons of hardware into orbit. In addition, Dr. Ailor notes that the number of operating satellites is expected to grow from 700 today to as many as 3,000 in 2020.

This hardware can yield space junk in several ways: When satellites separate from their boosters, they shed shrouds and other bits and pieces. They can collide. Boosters can malfunction and explode. Or spent booster segments with still-pressurized fuel tanks can explode when hit by debris or after joints weaken from the constant freezing and thawing. Solid-fuel motors can give off "slag" as part of their exhaust plumes. . . .

Space Junk Highlights

- **Oldest debris still in orbit**
The U.S. Vanguard 1 satellite, which was launched on March 17, 1958, and worked for six years.

- **Most dangerous garment**
U.S. astronaut Edward White's glove, lost during a Gemini-4 spacewalk in 1965, orbited Earth for a month at 17,398 miles per hour.

- **Heftiest garbage disposal**
The Mir space station, where cosmonauts jettisoned more than 200 objects, most of them bags full of garbage, during the station's first 10 years of operation.

- **Most debris from the destruction of a single spacecraft**
The explosion in 1996 of a Pegasus rocket used in a 1994 launch. The blast generated 300,000 fragments bigger than 4 millimeters (0.15 inches). Some 700 of these objects were big enough to earn entries in catalogs of large space debris. The explosion doubled the Hubble Space Telescope's risk of colliding with a large piece of space junk.

- **Most heavily shielded spacecraft in history**
The International Space Station.

All of this junk can travel at sizzling speeds and packs a wallop, according to Richard Crowther, a space consultant with the British research and development firm QinetiQ. He notes that for an object to remain in orbit at altitudes below 620 miles (1,000

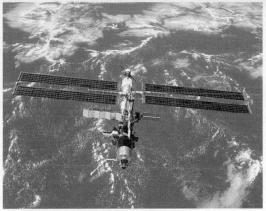

International Space Station

km). . ., it must travel at speeds of nearly 18,000 miles per hour. It's within this region of space that critical satellites and craft, including the International Space Station and the shuttle, operate. A small coin hurtling along at 22,000 miles an hour hits with the impact of a small bus traveling at 62 miles an hour on Earth.

So far, spacecraft operators have experienced only one confirmed hit from space junk and several near misses. The hit came in July 1996, when a small French military satellite was struck by debris from an Ariane rocket that had been launched in 1986. The debris hit the satellite's altitude-control arm at more than 33,500 m.p.h. and knocked the craft into a different orbit. Space shuttles have been guided out of the way of potentially threatening debris at least eight times. The International Space Station has performed orbital duck-and-weave maneuvers at least three times.

In low-earth orbit, gravity and atmospheric drag help sweep a good portion of humanity's leavings—from abandoned space stations and rocket stages to astronauts' gloves and lens caps—back into the atmosphere to burn up or break up. Many more of these objects at higher orbits could remain in space for thousands of years or more.

In all, more than 9,000 objects larger than about 4 inches have been cataloged. Within 1,200 miles of Earth, some 2,200 tons of debris orbit. If smaller but still-lethal objects were included, the catalog could number more

The author cites statistics and makes comparisons to emphasize the seriousness of the problem.

than 100,000. Ailor adds that the figure is likely to grow as the number of satellites mushrooms.

Confronted with growing space debris, the FCC is proposing that applicants for new commercial satellites show that the craft is robust enough to prevent fragmenting in the face of any remaining fuel, pressurization, or sudden discharge of the craft's batteries. Ideally, leftover fuel would be vented, as would any pressurized system. And batteries would be discharged. The proposed rules also set guidelines for moving an over-the-hill spacecraft into a disposal orbit.

But additional shielding or fuel add weight and thus cost. European Space Agency engineers, for example, calculate a $2 million price tag for the additional fuel needed to steer a 1-ton satellite from geosynchronous orbit toward reentry into Earth's atmosphere.

Others suggest more high-tech approaches, such as using ground-based lasers to zap orbital debris—a plan that also could have space-weapon implications. The idea, which NASA reportedly pronounced workable after studying the approach in the late 1990s, relies on high-powered lasers to vaporize small bits of material from the surface of a hunk of space junk. The vapor emitted acts like a tiny rocket motor, propelling the junk either into a less threatening orbit or on a path toward a fiery reentry.

Others have proposed using space tethers, which a satellite could lower at the close of its career. Taking advantage of electrical properties induced at each end by its motion through Earth's magnetic field, the tether would slow the satellite, dropping it into ever-lower orbits toward reentry.

The word *unfortunately* indicates the expert does not believe the solution is adequate.

Even if these approaches prove practical, Ailor maintains that space debris and growing traffic raise the need for an international space-traffic control system. Currently, the U.S. Air Force maintains the 9,000-entry catalog of large objects. But it warns the relevant agency only if a manned vehicle is threatened.

Unfortunately, Ailor concludes, it may take a high-profile collision to jump-start the kind of system he envisions.

Reading: Using Organizational Structure

Directions: *Choose the letter of the best answer to each question.*

1. Which sentence gives readers a clue about the overall organizational structure of the article?

   A If you want to get rid of an old fridge or an obsolete TV, you could call for curbside pickup.

   B Fortunately, the aerospace community is giving the problem increasing attention.

   C They can puncture space suits and cripple satellites.

   D Full-size rocket bodies can destroy.

2. Which of the following is a fact that supports a statement of the problem?

   A ". . . this could become a serious problem," says William Ailor

   B Others have proposed using space tethers . . .

   C Full-size rocket bodies can destroy.

   D Ideally, leftover fuel would be vented . . .

3. Which of the following is an opinion that supports a possible solution?

   A All of this junk can travel at sizzling speeds . . .

   B Ailor maintains that . . . debris . . . raise[s] the need for an international space-traffic control system.

   C The hit came in July 1996, . . .

   D In low-earth orbit, gravity and . . . drag help sweep . . . humanity's leavings . . .

Reading: Comprehension and Interpretation

Directions: *Write your answers on a separate piece of paper.*

4. Why does the writer introduce both the problem and suggested solutions at the beginning of the article? **[Generative]**

5. What is the writer's opinion about the problem of space junk? Support your answer with details from the article. **[Knowledge]**

Timed Writing: Problem-Solution Essay

Review the article, paying special attention to organization. Then, use the article as a model to write your own problem-and-solution essay. Explore a problem in your school or community, and discuss possible solutions.
(40 minutes)

Tone

The **tone** of a literary work is the author's attitude toward his or her audience and subject.

- Tone can often be described by a single adjective, such as *formal, informal, serious,* or *playful.*
- Conveyed through an author's choice of words, sentence structure, and details, tone may vary within a piece of writing.

Comparing Tone

Both "Emancipation" and "Brown vs. Board of Education" are nonfiction works that describe and explain key figures and events in American history. Both works are serious and aim to make a piece of history interesting. However, the tones of these two pieces differ, partly because the authors' reasons for writing are different.

As you read each work, follow these steps to identify tone:

- Find words and details that suggest the author's tone.

- Choose an adjective that describes the author's tone, or attitude toward his or her audience and subject.

- Determine the author's purpose in writing the piece. Common purposes of nonfiction are to provide information, to explain, to entertain, to narrate an event, or to persuade.

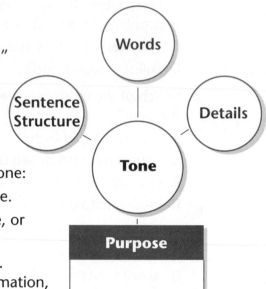

Vocabulary Builder

Emancipation

- **alienate** (āl´ yən āt´) *v.* make unfriendly (p. 553) *I do not wish to <u>alienate</u> my neighbors by playing my music too loudly.*

- **compensate** (käm´ pən sāt´) *v.* repay (p. 553) *The landlord wants his tenants to <u>compensate</u> him for the damage they caused to the apartment.*

- **humiliating** (hyo͞o mil´ ē āt´ iŋ) *adj.* embarrassing; undignified (p. 555) *Losing to the last-place team was <u>humiliating</u>.*

Brown vs. Board of Education

- **predominantly** (prē däm´ ə nənt lē) *adv.* mainly; for the most part (p. 558) *The tourists came <u>predominantly</u> from small towns.*

- **unconstitutional** (un´ kän stə to͞o´ shə nəl) *adj.* not permitted by the U.S. Constitution (p. 562) *The Supreme Court decides if a law is <u>unconstitutional</u>.*

- **deliberating** (di lib´ ər āt iŋ) *v.* thinking or considering carefully and fully (p. 563) *After <u>deliberating</u> for months, we chose to move.*

- **oppressed** (ə prest´) *v.* kept down by cruel or unjust power (p. 563) *The dictator <u>oppressed</u> his opponents.*

Build Understanding

Connecting to the Literature

Reading/Writing Connection In "Emancipation" and "Brown vs. Board of Education," the authors describe heroic people who face daunting obstacles and make difficult decisions. In a short paragraph, explain the qualities that build heroism. Include at least three of the following words: *emphasize, achieve, resolve, undertake, display.*

Meet the Authors

Russell **Freedman** (b. 1929)

"I had the good fortune to grow up in a house filled with books and book talk," Russell Freedman has said. After working as a reporter and editor, he decided to write books that would make history more interesting for young people.

Writing About Lincoln When Freedman visited the Lincoln Memorial in Washington, D.C., as a boy, his father encouraged him to look at Lincoln's statue from all angles. Much later, when Freedman wrote *Lincoln: A Photobiography*, he tried to show the many sides of Lincoln, including the heartache and difficulties he faced as president.

Walter Dean **Myers** (b. 1937)

Born in West Virginia, Walter Dean Myers was raised by foster parents in Harlem, a section of New York City populated mostly by African Americans. His foster mother taught him to read when he was four years old. "The public library was my most treasured place," Myers recalls. "I couldn't believe my luck in discovering that what I enjoyed most, reading, was free." Many of his works take place in Harlem and depict the problems and joys of African American teens.

Writing From Experience "My ideas come largely from my own background," Myers says. "I'm interested in history, so I write about historical characters in nonfiction."

Go Online
Author Link

For: More about the authors
Visit: www.PHSchool.com
Web Code: ene-9312

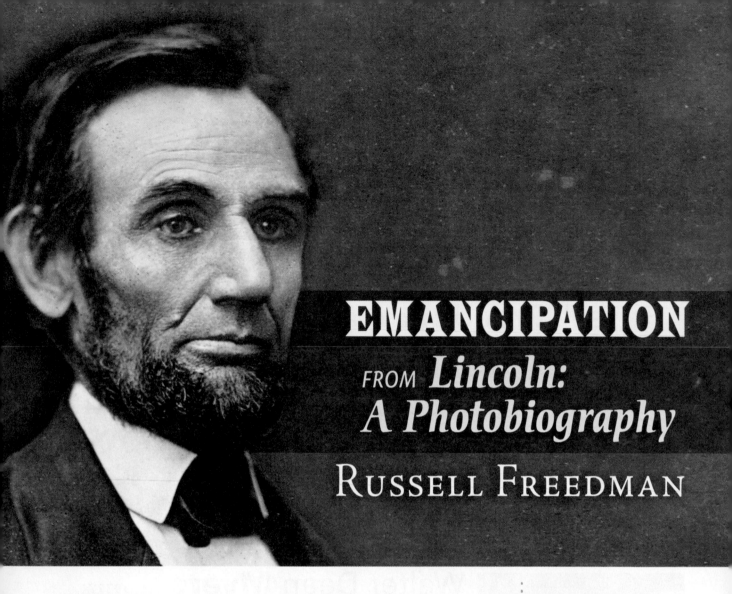

EMANCIPATION

FROM *Lincoln: A Photobiography*

RUSSELL FREEDMAN

President Abraham Lincoln was leading the country in 1862—during the Civil War. He was challenged to find the best means for preserving the Union. His troops had just been beaten in fierce battles in Virginia. He had tough military and political decisions to make.

The toughest decision facing Lincoln . . . was the one he had to make about slavery. Early in the war, he was still willing to leave slavery alone in the South, if only he could restore the Union. Once the rebellion was crushed, slavery would be confined to the Southern states, where it would gradually die out. "We didn't go into the war to put down slavery, but to put the flag back," Lincoln said. "To act differently at this moment would, I have no doubt, not only weaken our cause, but smack of bad faith."

▲ Critical Viewing
Judging from this photo, what personal qualities did Abraham Lincoln bring to the presidency? **[Infer]**

Abolitionists were demanding that the president free the slaves at once, by means of a wartime proclamation. "Teach the rebels and traitors that the price they are to pay for the attempt to abolish this Government must be the abolition of slavery," said Frederick Douglass, the famous black editor and reformer. "Let the war cry be down with treason, and down with slavery, the cause of treason!"

But Lincoln hesitated. He was afraid to <u>alienate</u> the large numbers of Northerners who supported the Union but opposed emancipation. And he worried about the loyal, slave-holding border states—Kentucky, Missouri, Maryland, and Delaware—that had refused to join the Confederacy. Lincoln feared that emancipation might drive those states into the arms of the South.

Yet slavery was the issue that had divided the country, and the president was under mounting pressure to do something about it. At first he supported a voluntary plan that would free the slaves gradually and <u>compensate</u> their owners with money from the federal treasury. Emancipation would begin in the loyal border states and be extended into the South as the rebel states were conquered. Perhaps then the liberated slaves could be resettled in Africa or Central America.

Lincoln pleaded with the border-state congressmen to accept his plan, but they turned him down. They would not part with their slave property or willingly change their way of life. "Emancipation in the cotton states is simply an absurdity," said a Kentucky congressman. "There is not enough power in the world to compel it to be done."

Lincoln came to realize that if he wanted to attack slavery, he would have to act more boldly. A group of powerful Republican senators had been urging him to act. It was absurd, they argued, to fight the war without destroying the institution that had caused it. Slaves provided a vast pool of labor that was crucial to the South's war effort. If Lincoln freed the slaves, he could cripple the Confederacy and hasten the end of the war. If he did not free them, then the war would settle nothing. Even if the South agreed to return to the Union, it would start another war as soon as slavery was threatened again.

Besides, enslaved blacks were eager to throw off their shackles and fight for their own freedom. Thousands of slaves had already escaped from behind Southern lines. Thousands

more were ready to enlist in the Union armies. "You need more men," Senator Charles Sumner told Lincoln, "not only at the North, but at the South, in the rear of the rebels. You need the slaves."

All along, Lincoln had questioned his authority as president to abolish slavery in those states where it was protected by law. His Republican advisors argued that in time of war, with the nation in peril, the president did have the power to outlaw slavery. He could do it in his capacity as commander in chief of the armed forces. Such an act would be justified as a necessary war measure, because it would weaken the enemy. If Lincoln really wanted to save the Union, Senator Sumner told him, he must act now. He must wipe out slavery.

The war had become an endless nightmare of bloodshed and bungling generals. Lincoln doubted if the Union could survive without bold and drastic measures. By the summer of 1862, he had worked out a plan that would hold the loyal slave states in the Union, while striking at the enemies of the Union.

On July 22, 1862, he revealed his plan to his cabinet. He had decided, he told them, that emancipation was "a military necessity, absolutely essential to the preservation of the Union." For that reason, he intended to issue a proclamation freeing all the slaves in rebel states that had not returned to the Union by January 1, 1863. The proclamation would be aimed at the Confederate South only. In the loyal border states, he would continue to push for gradual, compensated emancipation.

Some cabinet members warned that the country wasn't ready to accept emancipation. But most of them nodded their approval, and in any case, Lincoln had made up his mind. He did listen to the objection of William H. Seward, his secretary of state. If Lincoln published his proclamation

◀ **Critical Viewing**
Would you describe this photo of Lincoln as formal or informal? Why? **[Analyze]**

Literary Analysis
Tone How do the subject and details here lend themselves to a serious tone?

Literary Analysis
Tone Does the quotation conflict with or match the tone in the rest of the paragraph? Explain.

now, Seward argued, when Union armies had just been defeated in Virginia, it would seem like an act of desperation, "the last shriek on our retreat." The president must wait until the Union had won a decisive military victory in the East. Then he could issue his proclamation from a position of strength. Lincoln agreed. For the time being, he filed the document away in his desk.

A month later, in the war's second battle at Bull Run, Union forces commanded by General John Pope suffered another <u>humiliating</u> defeat. "We are whipped again," Lincoln moaned. He feared now that the war was lost. Rebel troops under Robert E. Lee were driving north. Early in September, Lee invaded Maryland and advanced toward Pennsylvania.

Lincoln again turned to General George McClellan—Who else do I have? he asked—and ordered him to repel the invasion. The two armies met at Antietam Creek in Maryland on September 17 in the bloodiest single engagement of the war. Lee was forced to retreat back to Virginia. But McClellan, cautious as ever, held his position and failed to pursue the defeated rebel army. It wasn't the decisive victory Lincoln had hoped for, but it would have to do.

On September 22, Lincoln read the final wording of his Emancipation Proclamation to his cabinet. If the rebels did not return to the Union by January 1, the president would free "thenceforward and forever" all the slaves everywhere in the Confederacy. Emancipation would become a Union war objective. As Union armies smashed their way into rebel territory, they would annihilate slavery once and for all.

The next day, the proclamation was released to the press. Throughout the North, opponents of slavery hailed the measure, and black people rejoiced. Frederick Douglass, the black abolitionist, had criticized Lincoln severely in the past. But he said now: "We shout for joy that we live to record this righteous decree."

When Lincoln delivered his annual message to Congress on December 1, he asked support for his program of military emancipation:

"Fellow citizens, *we* cannot escape history. We of this Congress and this administration, will be remembered in spite of ourselves. . . . In *giving* freedom to the *slave*, we assure freedom to the *free*—honorable alike in what we give, and what we preserve."

Vocabulary Builder
humiliating (hyo͞o mil´ ē āt´ iŋ) *adj.* embarrassing; undignified

Literary Analysis
Tone How does the chronology, or order, of events add to the dramatic tone?

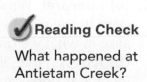
Reading Check
What happened at Antietam Creek?

On New Year's Day, after a fitful night's sleep, Lincoln sat at his White House desk and put the finishing touches on his historic decree. From this day forward, all slaves in the rebel states were "forever free." Blacks who wished to could now enlist in the Union army and sail on Union ships. Several all-black regiments were formed immediately. By the end of the war, more than 180,000 blacks—a majority of them emancipated slaves—had volunteered for the Union forces. They manned military garrisons and served as front-line combat troops in every theatre of the war.

The traditional New Year's reception was held in the White House that morning. Mary appeared at an official gathering for the first time since Willie's death,[1] wearing garlands in her hair and a black shawl about her head.

During the reception, Lincoln slipped away and retired to his office with several cabinet members and other officials for the formal signing of the proclamation. He looked tired. He had been shaking hands all morning, and now his hand trembled as he picked up a gold pen to sign his name.

Ordinarily he signed "A. Lincoln." But today, as he put pen to paper, he carefully wrote out his full name. "If my name ever goes into history," he said then, "it will be for this act."

---

1. **Mary appeared . . . Willie's death** Mary Todd Lincoln was President Lincoln's wife. The couple's son William died in 1862 at age eleven.

Thinking About the Selection

1. **(a) Recall:** What does Freedman say Lincoln's toughest decision was as president? **(b) Synthesize:** Why did Lincoln hesitate to issue a wartime proclamation emancipating slaves?
   (c) Infer: What does his hesitation indicate about the limits of his power as president to hold the Union factions together?

2. **(a) Recall:** What was Secretary of State William H. Seward's recommendation to Lincoln about when to issue the proclamation? **(b) Speculate:** Why did Lincoln decide to release the proclamation after the battle of Antietam Creek?

3. **(a) Interpret:** What did Lincoln mean in saying, "In giving freedom to the slave, we assure freedom to the free—honorable alike in what we give, and what we preserve"?
   (b) Assess: What, if any, act or achievement by an American president is as significant as Lincoln's Emancipation Proclamation?

BROWN VS. BOARD OF EDUCATION

WALTER DEAN MYERS

There was a time when the meaning of freedom was easily understood. For an African crouched in the darkness of a tossing ship, wrists chained, men with guns standing on the decks above him, freedom was a physical thing, the ability to move away from his captors, to follow the dictates of his own heart, to listen to the voices within him that defined his values

▲ Critical Viewing
Why is the U.S. Supreme Court an appropriate setting for this photograph? [Analyze]

and showed him the truth of his own path. The plantation owners wanted to make the Africans feel helpless, inferior. They denied them images of themselves as Africans and told them that they were without beauty. They segregated them and told them they were without value.

Slowly, surely, the meaning of freedom changed to an elusive thing that even the strongest people could not hold in their hands. There were no chains on black wrists, but there were the shadows of chains, stretching for hundreds of years back through time, across black minds.

◆

From the end of the Civil War in 1865 to the early 1950's, many public schools in both the North and South were segregated. Segregation was different in the different sections of the country. In the North most of the schools were segregated *de facto;*[1] that is, the law allowed blacks and whites to go to school together, but they did not actually always attend the same schools. Since a school is generally attended by children living in its neighborhood, wherever there were <u>predominantly</u> African-American neighborhoods there were, "in fact," segregated schools. In many parts of the country, however, and especially in the South, the segregation was *de jure,*[2] meaning that there were laws which forbade blacks to attend the same schools as whites.

The states with segregated schools relied upon the ruling of the Supreme Court in the 1896 *Plessy vs. Ferguson* case for legal justification: Facilities that were "separate but equal" were legal.

In the early 1950's the National Association for the Advancement of Colored People (N.A.A.C.P.) sponsored five cases that eventually reached the Supreme Court. One of the cases involved the school board of Topeka, Kansas.

Thirteen families sued the Topeka school board, claiming that to segregate the children was harmful to the children and, therefore, a violation of the equal protection clause of the Fourteenth Amendment. The names on the Topeka case were listed in alphabetical order, with the father of seven-year-old Linda Brown listed first.

---

1. *de facto* (dē fak′ tō) Latin for "existing in actual fact."
2. *de jure* (dē jōōr′ ē) Latin for "by right or legal establishment."

Literary Analysis
Tone How do words and phrases like *de facto*, *predominantly*, and *de jure* affect the tone?

Vocabulary Builder
predominantly (prē däm′ ə nənt lē) *adv.* mainly; for the most part

Literary Analysis
Tone How does the sentence structure in this paragraph contribute to a formal tone?

"I didn't understand why I couldn't go to school with my playmates. I lived in an integrated neighborhood and played with children of all nationalities, but when school started they went to a school only four blocks from my home and I was sent to school across town," she says.

For young Linda the case was one of convenience and of being made to feel different, but for African-American parents it had been a long, hard struggle to get a good education for their children. It was also a struggle waged by lawyers who had worked for years to overcome segregation. The head of the legal team who presented the school cases was Thurgood Marshall.

The city was Baltimore, Maryland, and the year was 1921. Thirteen-year-old Thurgood Marshall struggled to balance the packages he was carrying with one hand while he tried to get his bus fare out of his pocket with the other. It was almost Easter, and the part-time job he had would provide money for

▲ **Critical Viewing**
What would the families in the *Brown* case say about this classroom? What would the state say? **[Connect]**

✓ **Reading Check**

Why did thirteen families sue the Topeka school board?

flowers for his mother. Suddenly he felt a violent tug at his right arm that spun him around, sending his packages sprawling over the floor of the bus.

"Don't you never push in front of no white lady again!" an angry voice spat in his ear.

Thurgood turned and threw a punch . . . . The man charged into Thurgood, throwing punches that mostly missed, and tried to wrestle the slim boy to the ground. A policeman broke up the fight, grabbing Thurgood with one huge black hand and pushing him against the side of the bus. Within minutes they were in the local courthouse.

Thurgood was not the first of his family to get into a good fight. His father's father had joined the Union Army during the Civil War, taking the names Thorough Good to add to the one name he had in bondage. His grandfather on his mother's side was a man brought from Africa and, according to Marshall's biography, "so ornery that his owner wouldn't sell him

Literary Analysis
Tone How does the author's tone change when he discusses Marshall's boyhood?

▼ **Critical Viewing** In this photograph, Marshall is sworn in as a Supreme Court justice, with President Lyndon Johnson by his side. What details show this is a solemn, historic occasion? **[Interpret]**

out of pity for the people who might buy him, but gave him his freedom instead and told him to clear out of the county."

Thurgood's frequent scrapes earned him a reputation as a young boy who couldn't be trusted to get along with white folks.

His father, Will Marshall, was a steward at the Gibson Island Yacht Club near Baltimore, and his mother, Norma, taught in a segregated school. The elder Marshall felt he could have done more with his life if his education had been better, but there had been few opportunities available for African Americans when he had been a young man. When it was time for the Marshall boys to go to college, he was more than willing to make the sacrifices necessary to send them.

Young people of color from all over the world came to the United States to study at Lincoln University, a predominantly black institution in southeastern Pennsylvania. Here Marshall majored in predentistry, which he found boring, and joined the Debating Club, which he found interesting. By the time he was graduated at the age of twenty-one, he had decided to give up dentistry for the law. Three years later he was graduated, first in his class, from Howard University Law School.

At Howard there was a law professor, Charles Hamilton Houston, who would affect the lives of many African-American lawyers and who would influence the legal aspects of the civil rights movement. Houston was a great teacher, one who demanded that his students be not just good lawyers but great lawyers. If they were going to help their people—and for Houston the only reason for African Americans to become lawyers was to do just that—they would have to have absolute understanding of the law, and be diligent[3] in the preparation of their cases. At the time, Houston was an attorney for the N.A.A.C.P. and fought against discrimination in housing and in jobs.

After graduation, Thurgood Marshall began to do some work for the N.A.A.C.P., trying the difficult civil rights cases. He not only knew about the effects of discrimination by reading about it, he was still living it when he was graduated from law school in 1933. In 1936 Marshall began working full-time for the N.A.A.C.P., and in 1940 became its chief counsel.

It was Thurgood Marshall and a battery of N.A.A.C.P. attorneys who began to challenge segregation throughout the

Literary Analysis
Tone What word here contrasts with the otherwise formal tone of the paragraph?

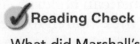

Reading Check

What did Marshall's father do for a living?

---

3. **diligent** (dil′ ə jənt) *adj.* careful and thorough.

country. These men and women were warriors in the cause of freedom for African Americans, taking their battles into courtrooms across the country. They understood the process of American justice and the power of the Constitution.

In *Brown vs. Board of Education of Topeka*, Marshall argued that segregation was a violation of the Fourteenth Amendment—that even if the facilities and all other "tangibles" were equal, which was the heart of the case in *Plessy vs. Ferguson*, a violation still existed. There were intangible[4] factors, he argued, that made the education unequal.

Everyone involved understood the significance of the case: that it was much more than whether black children could go to school with white children. If segregation in the schools was declared <u>unconstitutional</u>, then *all* segregation in public places could be declared unconstitutional.

Southerners who argued against ending school segregation were caught up, as then-Congressman Brooks Hays of Arkansas put it, in "a lifetime of adventures in that gap between law and custom." The law was one thing, but most Southern whites felt just as strongly about their customs as they did the law.

Dr. Kenneth B. Clark, an African-American psychologist, testified for the N.A.A.C.P. He presented clear evidence that the effect of segregation was harmful to African-American children. Describing studies conducted by black and white psychologists over a twenty-year period, he showed that black children felt inferior to white children. In a particularly dramatic study that he had supervised, four dolls, two white and two black, were presented to African-American children. From the responses of the children to the dolls, identical in every way except color, it was clear that the children were rejecting the black dolls. African-American children did not just feel separated from

---

4. **intangible** (in tan´ jə bəl) *adj.* not able to be touched or grasped.

white children, they felt that the separation was based on their inferiority.

Dr. Clark understood fully the principles and ideas of those people who had held Africans in bondage and had tried to make slaves of captives. By isolating people of African descent, by barring them from certain actions or places, they could make them feel inferior. The social scientists who testified at *Brown vs. Board of Education* showed that children who felt inferior also performed poorly.

The Justice Department argued that racial segregation was objectionable to the Eisenhower Administration and hurt our relationships with other nations.

Literary Analysis
Tone Which words in this paragraph contribute to a tone of formality and seriousness?

———◆———

On May 17, 1954, after <u>deliberating</u> for nearly a year and a half, the Supreme Court made its ruling. The Court stated that it could not use the intentions of 1868, when the Fourteenth Amendment was passed, as a guide to its ruling, or even those of 1896, when the decision in *Plessy vs. Ferguson* was handed down. Chief Justice Earl Warren wrote:

> We must consider public education in the light of its full development and its present place in American life throughout the nation. We must look instead to the effect of segregation itself on public education.

The Court went on to say that "modern authority" supported the idea that segregation deprived African Americans of equal opportunity. "Modern authority" referred to Dr. Kenneth B. Clark and the weight of evidence that he and the other social scientists had presented.

The high court's decision in *Brown vs. Board of Education* signaled an important change in the struggle for civil rights. It signaled clearly that the legal prohibitions that <u>oppressed</u> African Americans would have to fall. Equally important was the idea that the nature of the fight for equality would change. Ibrahima, Cinqué, Nat Turner, and George Latimer had struggled for freedom by fighting against their captors or fleeing from them. The 54th had fought for African freedom on the battlefields of the Civil War. Ida B. Wells had fought for equality with her pen. Lewis H. Latimer and Meta Vaux Warrick had

Vocabulary Builder
deliberating (di lib′ ər āt iŋ) *v.* thinking or considering carefully and fully

Vocabulary Builder
oppressed (ə prest′) *v.* kept down by cruel or unjust power

**Reading Check**
What did Dr. Clark's testimony prove?

tried to earn equality with their work. In *Brown vs. Board of Education* Thurgood Marshall, Kenneth B. Clark, and the lawyers and social scientists, both black and white, who helped them had won for African Americans a victory that would bring them closer to full equality than they had ever been in North America. There would still be legal battles to be won, but the major struggle would be in the hearts and minds of people and "in that gap between law and custom."

In 1967 Thurgood Marshall was appointed by President Lyndon B. Johnson as an associate justice of the U.S. Supreme Court. He retired in 1991.

Literary Analysis
Tone What effect does the listing of famous people in the fight for freedom have on the tone here?

———————◆———————

"I didn't think of my father or the other parents as being heroic at the time," Linda Brown says. "I was only seven. But as I grew older and realized how far-reaching the case was and how it changed the complexion of the history of this country, I was just thrilled that my father and the others here in Topeka were involved."

Thinking About the Selection

1. **Respond:** How do you think the Supreme Court decision in *Brown* has affected your life?

2. **(a) Recall:** Describe how school segregation differed in different sections of the United States between 1865 and the early 1950s. **(b) Compare and Contrast:** How were seven-year-old Linda Brown's views on the *Topeka* case different from the views of African American parents involved in the case?

3. **Analyze:** Based on the biographical details Myers gives about Thurgood Marshall's family, his early career, and his character traits, why do you think Marshall was or was not a good choice to lead the NAACP's legal team?

4. **(a) Recall:** What was the Supreme Court's decision in *Brown*? **(b) Apply:** Why is this case a significant event in U.S. history?

5. **Make a Judgment:** Myers quotes the grown-up Linda Brown as saying she did not think of her father as heroic at the time of the court case. Do you think any of the participants in the case were heroes? Explain.

Apply the Skills

Emancipation • *Brown vs. Board of Education*

Comparing Tone

1. What tone does Freedman develop with words such as *demanding, hesitated, worried, pressure, questioned,* and *argued*?
2. **(a)** What do you think is Freedman's purpose for writing? **(b)** How might the tone be different if his purpose had been to convince readers that Lincoln was a great leader?
3. What aspect of Myers's tone is reflected in his choice of the words *struggle, challenge, warriors, cause,* and *battles*?
4. What do you think is Myers's purpose for writing? Explain.
5. How does the tone differ in these two essays?

Writing to Compare Literary Works

Both essays describe landmark events in U.S. history. Using a chart like the one shown, gather details about each essay.

	Emancipation	Brown
Central conflict		
Main participants		
Details about participants		
Points of view presented		
Words that convey struggle		

Using the information from the chart, write an essay comparing the authors' use of tone to convey the drama of their subjects.

Vocabulary Builder

Practice Explain why each statement is either true or false.

1. Companies should *compensate* employees who work overtime.
2. Falling down during a speech would be *humiliating*.
3. The best way to *alienate* your friends is to treat them kindly.
4. If you are *oppressed*, you should see a doctor.
5. *Deliberating* before doing something risky is often wise.
6. Small lakes occur *predominantly* in deserts.
7. If a law is ruled *unconstitutional*, it cannot be enforced.

QuickReview

Tone: the author's attitude toward his or her audience and subject

Purpose: the author's main reason for writing

Go Online
Assessment
For: Self-test
Visit: www.PHSchool.com
Web Code: ena-6311

Reading: Fact and Opinion

Directions: *Questions 1–5 are based on the following selection.*

In 1870, nearly two million women and girls, or one in every eight females over the age of ten, worked outside the home. Women worked in each of the 338 occupations listed in the U.S. census. Modern Americans don't understand this statistic. All Americans believed that, for women, careers and married life did not mix, and so many of these working women were single. However, this was an incorrect idea. Over the next few decades, a rising proportion of married women would also go to work.

1. **The first sentence in the passage is a(n)**
   A opinion.
   B fact.
   C opinion supported by facts.
   D cited fact.

2. **One statement that is clearly an overgeneralization is**
   A one in every eight females over the age of ten . . .
   B a rising proportion of married women would also go to work.
   C All Americans believed that, for women, careers and married life did not mix. . . .
   D Women worked in each of the 338 occupations listed in the U.S. census.

3. **Which of the following questions should be asked about this passage to help distinguish fact from opinion?**
   A What is the author's purpose?
   B What was the total female population in 1870?

   C How do these attitudes compare to current attitudes?
   D How did married women workers feel about their careers?

4. **In the sentence "All Americans believed that, for women, careers and married life did not mix, . . ."**
   A *believed* is a clue that this is an opinion.
   B *and so* is a clue that this is a fact.
   C *All Americans* is a clue that this is an overgeneralization.
   D *careers and married life* is a clue that this is an opinion supported by fact.

5. **The facts in this passage**
   A could be verified by checking source documents.
   B could not be verified by checking Web sites.
   C could not be verified without an expert.
   D could not be verified without the author's research.

Assessment Practice

Vocabulary Assessment

Directions: *Choose the word that best completes the sentence.*

6. The reporter addressed both sides of the issue so she could write her article without _____.
   A supported   C bias
   B accurate   D credible

7. The so-called expert on the Civil War was not ____. He had never even heard of the Battle of Shiloh.
   A supported   C accurate
   B biased   D credible

8. It would be more convincing if Jake could ____ evidence to ____ his opinion.
   A cite . . . support   C bias . . . cite
   B support . . . bias   D cite . . . credible

9. The news story was not completely ___ because it contained two factual errors.
   A supported   C accurate
   B biased   D cited

10. Despite the care Marie took to be fair, there was some_____ in the report.
    A support   C accurate
    B credible   D bias

Directions: *Choose the correct answer.*

11. Which word is the best antonym of *credible*?
    A inaccurate
    B insincere
    C unbelievable
    D believable

12. Which is the best antonym of *inaccurate*?
    A accurate
    B cite
    C credible
    D biased

13. Which of the following is NOT an antonym of *bias*?
    A impartiality
    B fairness
    C evenhandedness
    D prejudice

14. Which is the best synonym for the noun form of *support*?
    A prove
    B base
    C carry
    D assistance

15. Which of the following is NOT an antonym of *support*?
    A confirm
    B abandon
    C ignore
    D discourage

Homophones and Homonyms

Homophones are words that sound alike, but have different meanings and spellings. The words *cite, sight,* and *site* in the examples below are homophones. The words *site* and *sight* are nouns. *Cite* is a verb. Notice how each word is used in the following sentences.

▶ **Examples:** What sources did he *cite* in his report?
The *site* of the new library is on Main Street.
The *sight* of the shark's teeth made me shiver.

Homonyms are words that sound the same and are spelled the same, but have a different meaning. For example, the noun *bear,* meaning "a large animal," and the verb *bear,* meaning "to carry," are homonyms.

Puns are plays on words that draw on the multiple meanings of homonyms and homophones for their humor.

▶ **Example:** If you want to see a doctor, be *patient*.

Computer Spell-Checkers Most word-processing programs contain a spell-checking feature. Few spell-checking programs can determine if you used the wrong homonym or homophone. To a spell-check program, this sentence is fine:

The cite of three ducks waddling down the hallway was a little startling.

Read your work carefully; do not rely solely on technology.

Practice Write a sentence for each word on the word list.

In some sentences, use the incorrect homonym. Trade papers with a partner and correct the spelling errors in the sentences.

Word List
except
accept
all ready
already
ensure
insure
by
bye
buy
foul
fowl

I can accept all of this except the grade in physical education!

Directions: *On a separate sheet of paper, fill in each blank with* **cite**, **sight**, *or* **site** *to fit the meaning of the sentence.*

1. There were three bulldozers at the construction _____.

2. _____ is one of the five senses.

3. Can you _____ three examples of how America changed in the 1900s?

4. The _____ of their son as he stepped off the airplane brought tears to their eyes.

5. The _____ of the accident is now a crime scene.

Directions: *There are ten errors in the following essay. Some are misspellings. Others are problems with homophones or other incorrect words used by mistake. Write the number of each sentence and the corrections it needs. If a sentence has no errors, write "none."*

(1) When I was younger, I was taught that things should be fair. (2) That lessen was tested when I started working as a referee. (3) I past the ref course easily and thought that the actual games would be easy. (4) I knew everything that I could about the game; everything, that is, accept how to deal with the fans.

(5) The presence of a large crowd disagreeing with every decision can be daunting, especially when half the fans can site the rule book word for word. (6) Some fans had no trouble telling me that they had played the game or been a referee in the passed and that every call I made was ronge. (7) A calm referee is an important presents at a game, and I made an effort to understand the fans. (8) I kept thinking about the passed lessons I had learned and eventually managed to accept the idea that some fans would not like my calls.

Persuasion: Editorial to Solve a Problem

When you use words to change people's thinking or influence their actions, you are using persuasion. One type of persuasion is an editorial, a brief essay published in a newspaper, magazine, or other medium. An **editorial** states and defends an opinion on a current issue. Follow the steps outlined in this workshop to write an editorial.

Assignment Write an editorial to persuade your readers to accept your solution to a problem.

What to Include An effective editorial should feature the following elements:

- a clear statement of your position on a problem that has more than one solution
- strong evidence that supports your position
- a clear organization that builds toward a conclusion
- a response to possible opposing arguments
- persuasive techniques that convey a powerful message
- error-free writing, including correct use of conjunctions

To preview the criteria on which your editorial may be judged, see the rubric on page 577.

Writing Workshop: *Work in Progress*

If you have completed the Work-in-Progress assignments, you have in your portfolio several ideas you might want to use in your editorial. Continue developing these ideas, or you might choose to explore a new idea as you complete the Writing Workshop.

Using the Form

You may use elements of this form in these types of writing:

- political speeches
- reviews
- advertisements
- public-service announcements

To get the feel for persuasion, read "The Trouble with Television" by Robert MacNeil on page 519.

Prewriting

Choosing Your Topic

You will do your best job writing an editorial if you choose a problem that concerns you. Use one of the following strategies:

- **Round Table** Hold a discussion of issues in your school and community. Create a list of specific problems that need solving and common views that you think need changing. Review the list and choose the issue that interests you most.

- **Media Flip-Through** Every day, the media bring controversies and debates into our living rooms. Over a day or two, read newspapers (including letters to the editor) and watch the local and national news. Jot down topics that spark your interest, in a chart like the one shown. Then, choose one as the subject of your editorial.

Work in Progress
Review the work you did on pages 527 and 543.

Newspapers	Television News
overweight teens a national epidemic (National Gazette)	health care costs continue to rise (The Nightly News)
budget cuts force canceling of youth sports program (City News)	city baseball team's game attendance at an all-time low (The Local Report)
town needs new recycling plan (My Town Newspaper)	residents protest building of stadium (Local Channel News)

Narrowing Your Topic

To narrow your topic so you can cover it thoroughly in an editorial, ask the "reporter's questions"—"Who? What? Where? When? Why? and How?" Circle the most interesting issues your answers raise to choose a narrowed topic.

Gathering Details

Prepare to provide support. Gather evidence that supports your position on your topic. Types of support include the following:
- facts and statistics
- expert opinions
- interviews and surveys
- personal observations

Drafting

Shaping Your Writing

Use a clear organization. A strong organization will help make your editorial effective. Consider using **Nestorian Order**—arranging points according to their relative strength. Begin with your second-strongest point. Present other arguments, and end with your strongest point. This is a dramatic way to build your case.

Anticipate and respond to counterarguments. Think about the arguments against your position. Then, meet opposing ideas head-on with arguments of your own. Look at the examples in the chart.

Arguments	Counterarguments
Wearing school uniforms robs students of their individuality.	Students do not have to worry about wearing what is considered "cool."
Uniforms are expensive.	Students save money by not wearing a different outfit every day.

Providing Elaboration

Use a variety of persuasive techniques. As you draft, use these techniques to sway readers:

- **Logical Arguments** Take your readers step-by-step through your argument, and present accurate evidence to earn their trust.

- **Emotional Appeals** Move your readers with a brief story or vivid image that adds impact to your argument by sparking an emotion such as pride, surprise, anger, or fear.

- **Charged Words** Words with positive or negative connotations can pack entire arguments into a few syllables.

- **Repetition and Parallelism** Use sentences that begin with identical forms to emphasize ideas.

To read the complete student model, see page 576.

Student Model: Using Persuasive Techniques

My old grandfather says, "A problem always has a solution if you want to find it." We need to find a solution to the problem of losing this neighborhood newspaper.

> The writer makes an emotional appeal to readers' feelings of respect for their elders.

From the Author's Desk

Andrew Mishkin
On Grabbing the Reader's Attention

Andrew
Mishkin

When writing the history of *Sojourner,* the first Mars rover, I needed to grab readers quickly, and let them know why they should be interested in the story I was telling. I had to persuade them that the characters would struggle mightily to meet the coming challenges, and perhaps still not succeed. I wanted readers to care about the final outcome, and to read the book to see how it all works out. The following draft shows revisions I made to accomplish these goals.

"Make the reader part of the action."

—— **Andrew Mishkin**

Professional Model:

from *Sojourner*

To begin work on a flight project is to enter a new world where mass, power, and volume are precious commodities. Consuming too much of any of these is not an option. Each available launch vehicle, rocket—in aerospace they call them "launch vehicles"—whether a Delta, Titan, or Ariane rocket, has only so much lift capability, or weight of payload it can put into a particular trajectory in space. If you are launching a spacecraft to Mars, and its mass is too high, the laws of physics ensure that it will never reach its target. Each spacecraft must carry with it its own power source, whether in the form of solar arrays, radioisotope thermoelectric generators, or batteries. These power sources are limited in their capacity. The components of the spacecraft that depend on this power must use it efficiently, for when the needs of the system exceed the available power, the spacecraft dies.

I rearranged the sentence to avoid using a technical term without defining it first, and then deleted another term I decided I didn't need at all.

Using "you" is not only less formal, but also suggests that the reader consider how he or she would personally deal with the situation.

I immediately backed up my premise with examples to make it more real, more convincing.

I used a word normally applied to a living thing—"dies"—to encourage the reader to see the spacecraft in the same way as the characters do in the pages to come.

Writing Workshop

Revising

Revising Your Overall Structure

Revise to strengthen appeals to your audience. Give your readers more than facts and logic—add emotion and description to grab readers. Review your draft to find points that are supported only with logical arguments, statistics, or expert opinions. Consider adding a colorful comparison, striking image, or dramatic anecdote.

- Flag factual points and jot down a few key reminder words on sticky notes.
- Review your notes, and add the appropriate comparison, image, or anecdote.

To read the complete student model, see page 576.

Student Model: Revising to Strengthen an Appeal

Furthermore, the paper contains ads for people who are looking for jobs and all the announcements for special events like new restaurants opening, festivals, shows, sales, and activities for older people and young people, and it lists all the programs for the weekends and holidays. It is the heartbeat of a city that pulses with life and energy.

> The writer added interest by following a series of facts with a vivid image.

Revising Your Sentences

Revise for coherence. In a good essay, the paragraphs cohere, or hold together well. In your draft, read the last sentence of each paragraph and the first sentence of the next paragraph. If there is no obvious connection between the paragraphs, highlight the space between them.

Consider these tips for adding a word, phrase, or sentence that links the paragraphs together:

- Repeat a key word or phrase.
- Use a transitional word or phrase such as *similarly, however,* or *in addition.*
- Insert a sentence that takes readers smoothly from one idea to the next.

Peer Review: Read your revised draft aloud to a small group of classmates. Ask the group members whether they saw any points or ideas that did not fit in smoothly with the rest of the essay. Consider their responses to make your essay more effective.

Integrating Grammar Skills

Revising Sentences by Combining With Conjunctions

Conjunctions connect words or groups of words. They can be used to join two sentences to create a compound or complex sentence.

Understanding the Role of Conjunctions There are two categories of conjunctions that serve different functions.

Coordinating conjunctions join words of the same kind and equal rank, such as two nouns or two verbs. When they join two independent clauses, these conjunctions make a compound sentence.

Prentice Hall Writing and Grammar Connection: Chapter 21, Section 2

> **Example:** *Pablo* takes dance lessons. *June* takes dance lessons.

> **Compound Subject:** *Pablo and June* take dance lessons.

> **Example:** Pablo takes dance lessons. He doesn't enjoy them.

> **Compound Sentence:** Pablo takes dance lessons, *but* he doesn't enjoy them.

Subordinating conjunctions create complex sentences by connecting two complete ideas and showing that one is dependent on the other.

> **Example:** June takes dance lessons. She wants to improve her grace.

> **With Subordinating Conjunction:** Because June wants to improve her grace, she takes dance lessons.

Common Conjunctions	
Coordinating	and, or, but, nor, so, yet, for
Subordinating	after, although, as, because, before, if, since, unless, until, when, while, whenever

Joining Sentences With Conjunctions You can join short choppy sentences with conjunctions. Follow these steps:

1. **Identify short sentences that could be combined.** Then, identify the words, phrases, or clauses that you want to join.

2. **Determine if the items are of the same kind and of equal rank.** If so, use a coordinating conjunction to join them.

3. **Determine if one is dependent on the other.** If so, use a subordinating conjunction to join them.

Apply It to Your Editing

Choose three paragraphs in your draft. Improve coherence and add interest by combining some of the sentences with conjunctions.

Writing Workshop

Student Model: Jordanna Oliveira
Newark, NJ

Editorial: Save *The Brazilian Voice*

Our Ironbound neighborhood of Newark is like a little Brazil. A lot of us who live here came from Brazil, and most of us read *The Brazilian Voice* every week. Now, however, this paper is going to close because there isn't enough money to keep publishing it. My old grandfather says, "A problem always has a solution if you want to find it." We need to find a solution to the problem of losing this neighborhood newspaper. It is my belief that *The Brazilian Voice* should not stop publishing. The people need it.

There are lots of reasons that the people need *The Brazilian Voice*. For one thing, as all the readers know, it is an important source of information. It contains news about things happening in New Jersey and the rest of the country, and also about things happening in Brazil. The articles in Portuguese are important for people who don't know English very well. By reading *The Brazilian Voice*, they learn about the security of the city and about projects that the city is planning. Furthermore, the paper contains ads for people who are looking for jobs and all the announcements for special events like new restaurants opening, festivals, shows, sales, and activities for older people and young people. It lists all the programs for the weekends and holidays. It is the heartbeat of a city that pulses with life and energy.

Some people might think that if we have a Brazilian television channel in New Jersey, we don't need the newspaper. However, the Brazilian channel only shows news from Brazil. *The Brazilian Voice* gives the news about our community that affects our lives every day. The people in the Ironbound depend on this paper.

The reason *The Brazilian Voice* is closing is money. The owners of this paper say that they can't afford to print it anymore because there aren't enough businesses paying for advertisements. If they don't have money, they can't pay the reporters, or buy paper and ink. Of course, this paper can't survive if it keeps losing money every week. But the obvious solution is to charge money for the paper. In all its years, *The Brazilian Voice* has been given away free. That is a good service for the people. We like to get the paper for free, but I am sure that people would rather pay for it than not have it anymore.

If I were going to compare *The Newark Star-Ledger* and *The Brazilian Voice*, I would say the situation is the same. People would probably want to pay more for the *Star-Ledger* than to not have it anymore.

There are 45,000 people in the Ironbound. According to a poll by the paper, over half of them read *The Brazilian Voice* every week. If 20,000 people would pay 50 cents for the paper, that would be an extra $10,000. This money would mean that the citizens of the neighborhood could keep their paper.

In summation, I want to repeat that it is really important to have *The Brazilian Voice* in the Ironbound, and 50 cents isn't too much to pay for something that important.

> Jordanna presents the problem she will address in her editorial and clearly states her position.

> She supports her position with a series of reasons to show why the paper is important to the community.

> Jordanna anticipates and addresses a potential argument against her position.

> Statistics provide solid support for logical arguments.

> In this editorial, the writer has used evidence to build up to her conclusion—a clear restatement of her argument.

Editing and Proofreading

Check your editorial for errors in spelling, punctuation, and grammar.

Focus on Double Negatives: Avoid creating confusion with double negatives—two negative words—when only one is required. The example shows two ways to correct a double negative.

> **Example:** There is not no reason to cut funding.
>
> **Correction 1:** There is not any reason to cut funding.
>
> **Correction 2:** There is no reason to cut funding.

Publishing and Presenting

Consider one of the following ways to share your writing:
Organize a forum. Assemble a panel of classmates to read their editorials to the class. Allow the class to ask questions of the panel and then vote on whether they agree or disagree with each paper.
Publish in a newspaper. Send your editorial, with a cover letter, to a local newspaper. Briefly summarize your essay in the letter, and explain that you wish it to be considered for publication.

Reflecting on Your Writing

Writer's Journal Write a few notes describing the experience of writing an editorial. Begin by answering the following questions:
- What did you learn about the issue you chose? Did you find your opinions changing as you learned more? Explain.
- What part of the writing process seemed hardest for you? Easiest?

Rubric for Self-Assessment

To assess your editorial, use the following rubric:

Criteria	Rating Scale
	not very very
Focus: How clearly do you state your position?	1 2 3 4 5
Organization: How effectively does the organization build to a conclusion?	1 2 3 4 5
Support/Elaboration: How convincing is the evidence that supports your position?	1 2 3 4 5
Style: How powerful is your use of persuasive language?	1 2 3 4 5
Conventions: How correct is your grammar, especially your use of conjunctions?	1 2 3 4 5

Evaluating an Informational Presentation

When you evaluate an informational presentation, you make judgments about a speaker's ideas and effectiveness. To evaluate an informational presentation, follow these steps:

Understand the Structure

It is easier to evaluate the speaker's effectiveness if you understand the topic and format of a speech.

Identify the topic. The topic is a one-phrase summary of a speech's subject. The title of the presentation should also be the topic. For example, a speaker might give a presentation on the topic "How to Feed and Care for a Ferret." A speaker usually introduces the main topic within the first few minutes.

Determine the speaker's purpose. The general purpose of an informational presentation is to educate or inform. The specific purpose depends on the topic. For example, the specific purpose of a scientific presentation might be to describe new research on the brain.

Identify organization. Speeches often follow the same format as essays, so the skills you have learned in identifying written formats can be applied to a speech. Identify the speaker's main ideas and connect them with the facts and ideas that support them. Determine the organizational format, such as problem-solution or cause-and-effect. Knowing the organization helps you focus your listening.

Evaluate the Speech

Evaluate the content. Once you understand a presentation's purpose and organization, you can evaluate its content. Ask yourself if the speaker presents ideas clearly and directly, and whether he or she supports main ideas with evidence or examples.

Evaluate the quality. The quality of an oral presentation depends on both delivery and content. A speaker who mumbles and repeats uninteresting or irrelevant information gives a poor presentation. A good speaker should enunciate clearly, vary his or her voice, and deliver an interesting, informative presentation.

Activity > *Speech and Evaluation* In a small group, outline a speech on a topic that you are familiar with, such as how to care for a pet or play a sport. Then, take turns presenting the speech. Use the chart shown to evaluate the presentations.

Evaluating an Informational Presentation

Rating System
+ = Excellent ✓= average – = weak

Content
Clarity of ideas _____
Interesting topic _____
Logical organization _____
Strong evidence or examples_____
Originality_____

Delivery
Enunciated clearly _____
Varied voice _____

Respond honestly to these questions:
What impact did the presentation have on you? _____
How well did the speaker inform you about the topic? _____
_____

Growing Up in the South

Suzanne Jones, editor
Penguin Putnam, 1991

Short Story Collection This collection provides a peek at the past and present of southern life through the eyes of the region's most distinguished writers. Stories from Maya Angelou, William Faulkner, Alice Walker, and other exciting writers offer a unique look at growing up in the southern United States.

Robot Dreams

Isaac Asimov
Penguin Putnam, 1990

Short Story Collection The concept of designing machines that imitate humans was still fairly new when Isaac Asimov began publishing stories about robots in the 1940s. In this collection of intriguing stories, Asimov goes beyond imagining robots in different settings. He anticipates the dilemmas that occur when humans design machines to act and "think" like themselves. This classic collection of twenty thought-provoking stories is a must-read for any science-fiction fan.

Park's Quest

Katherine Paterson
Puffin Books, 1989

Novel Park cannot figure out why his mother refuses to talk about his father, who died in Vietnam eleven years ago. He is determined to find answers to his questions. Park's quest takes him to Washington and Virginia, where he meets his grandfather and a mysterious Vietnamese girl. Whether he will be able to accept the ultimate truth is the question at the heart of this fascinating book.

The Road to Memphis

Mildred Taylor
Puffin Books, 1990

Novel Part of an award-winning series, this novel is set in Mississippi in 1941. Cassie Logan and her rural African American family are confronted with issues of racism and injustice as the nation teeters on the brink of World War II. Cassie must use all of her courage and intelligence to help a friend in need escape trouble in Mississippi and reach safety in Tennessee.

These titles are available in the Penguin/Prentice Hall Literature Library.
Consult your teacher before choosing one.

Think About It Robert Louis Stevenson, author of the famous novels *Treasure Island* and *The Strange Case of Dr. Jekyll and Mr. Hyde,* traveled to America in the summer of 1879. The following excerpt, from the book *Across America on an Emigrant Train,* recounts his feelings as he first travels across the American countryside.

from ACROSS AMERICA ON AN EMIGRANT TRAIN   Jim Murphy

From the summit station on, the journey was literally all downhill. In fact, during the 105 miles from the top of the Sierras to Sacramento, California, the railroad tracks dropped almost seven thousand feet. The downward grade was so steep and steady that for nearly fifty miles of the descent the train coasted along without the aid of steam.

Some riders found this silent, twisting ride unnerving. This was especially true when the train shot out onto a bridge hundreds of feet high and the ground around them dropped away. For Stevenson, the change of scenery seemed to overcome any fear he might have felt. "I had a glimpse of a huge pine-forested ravine upon my left, a foaming river, and a sky already colored with the fires of dawn. I am usually very calm over the displays of nature; but you will scarce believe how my heart leaped at this. . . . [It was as though] I had come home again—home from unsightly deserts to the green and hospitable corners of the earth. Every spire of pine along the hilltop, every trouty pool along the mountain river was more dear to me than a blood-relation."

▼ The writer Robert Louis Stevenson at the time of his railroad journey.

What Stevenson and his fellow travelers didn't realize was that the engineer was no longer in full control of the train. On the long downhill sections, the train and the lives of everyone on board were in the hands of the brakemen. Perched on top of the cars, the brakemen were struggling to control the speed of the train by applying the brakes. Several years before Stevenson's trip, an Englishman named William Rae had come down the mountainside at night and been petrified by the experience. "The velocity with which the train rushed down this incline, and the suddenness with

which it wheeled around curves, produced a sensation which cannot be reproduced in words. . . . The axle boxes smoked with the friction and the odor of burning wood pervaded the cars. The wheels were nearly red hot. In the darkness of the night they resembled discs of fire."

The most dangerous section of track was at Cape Horn, where the twists and dips resembled those of a roller coaster. Guidebooks suggested that the very timid and those with weak hearts might want to avert their eyes rather than look down into the gorge two thousand feet below. One of the first travelers on the transcontinental railroad, William Humason, remembered Cape Horn vividly: "We follow the track around the sides of high mountains, looking down into a canyon of awful depth, winding around for miles, until we almost meet the track we have before been over—so near that one would think we could almost throw a stone across."

When the train was at the very lip of these cliffs, it's possible that Stevenson thought about the men who had cut the tortuous route out of the stone. It was the building of the Central Pacific's section of the transcontinental railroad that started another great wave of emigration to this country.

As the Union Pacific crews worked their way westward, tracklaying for the Central Pacific had stalled just outside Sacramento. It seemed that every time a new gold or silver strike was announced, railroad laborers (mostly Irish) grabbed their picks and shovels and headed for the hills.

Finally, out of desperation, the Central Pacific hired fifty Chinese laborers in 1865. Initially, the Chinese were given the very easy chore of filling the horse-drawn dump carts with rock debris and driving them away. They performed this task effortlessly and were "promoted" to the task of clearing rock from the path for the roadbed. Before long, the Chinese were also doing the more skilled jobs of masonry, tracklaying, and using explosives.

Of course, fifty men by themselves could not build a railroad. The Central Pacific needed five thousand workers, and to find them it sent recruiting agents throughout the United States, and, eventually, to China. To induce poor individuals, the railroad offered to lend potential workers the twenty-five dollars needed to sail across the Pacific.

In just a few months, tracklaying was once again moving along at the mile-a-day pace expected. Despite the Chinese workers' obvious skill, many people still doubted their ability to endure the brutal work. They seemed thin and frail compared to the brawny, tough men usually employed for such labor. Then construction came to a dead halt at Cape Horn.

No one had ever attempted to lay track along such a fearsome cliff, and the white foreman of the work crews wasn't sure how to attack the job. It was the Chinese workers who came up with the solution, based on similar construction in the Yangtze Valley.

First, they used reeds brought from San Francisco to weave waist-high baskets, each large enough to hold one man. A Chinese worker would climb into a basket and be lowered by rope to a position on the rock wall. There, the worker chipped away and drilled at the wall until he could insert a charge of explosives. Then he would light the charge and scramble up the rope as quickly as possible before the explosion ripped a gaping hole in the rock.

Slowly, painfully, ridges were blasted out of the side of the cliff, then widened and made ready for the rails. Three hundred men labored on the wall for ten days, managing to cut away about one mile of rock. Sometimes a man, exhausted from drilling the rock, was slow in climbing the rope and the blast carried him off. On several occasions the rope

▼ Fragile wooden trestle bridges carried passengers across steep gorges.

snapped and sent the worker plunging to his death. And still, the work went on until the tracks had rounded Cape Horn.

"The rugged mountains looked like stupendous anthills," a travel writer reported to his readers. "They swarm with [Chinese] shoveling, wheeling, carting, drilling and blasting rocks and earth."

After Cape Horn, the Chinese workers punched eighteen tunnels through sheer granite, each at least a thousand feet long. They brought the track down the eastern slope of the Sierras during some of the worst snowstorms, erecting thirty-seven miles of snowsheds along the way, then pushed across the desert, where they set the record of ten miles of track laid in a single day. . . .

A few of the Chinese laborers would gather up their hard-earned savings and return to China when the transcontinental railroad was completed. Most stayed and signed on with other railroad companies, which were beginning work on their own western routes. The rest took the train back to San Francisco or established communities in large cities such as Chicago and New York. . . .

▲ A rare 1869 photo of Chinese railroad workers. The Central Pacific employed about 10,000 Chinese workers.

More to Explore

The California Gold Rush and the appetite for land in the West made the construction of a countrywide railroad a necessity. Building the Transcontinental Railroad took six years and 20,000 men to do the difficult, dangerous work of laying down track across bone-dry deserts and steep mountainsides. In 1869, the railroad linking East and West was finally completed.

Readings in Social Studies
Talk About It

Use these questions to guide a discussion of the excerpt.

1. What are Robert Louis Stevenson's first impressions of the scenery? Would you find the same trip exhilarating or terrifying? Explain.

2. In a group, discuss these questions about the Chinese laborers:
   - What knowledge did the Chinese bring with them?
   - What difficulties did the workers face during construction? Why did they take those risks? Defend your opinion.
   - Were the Chinese workers treated fairly? Why or why not?

Poetry

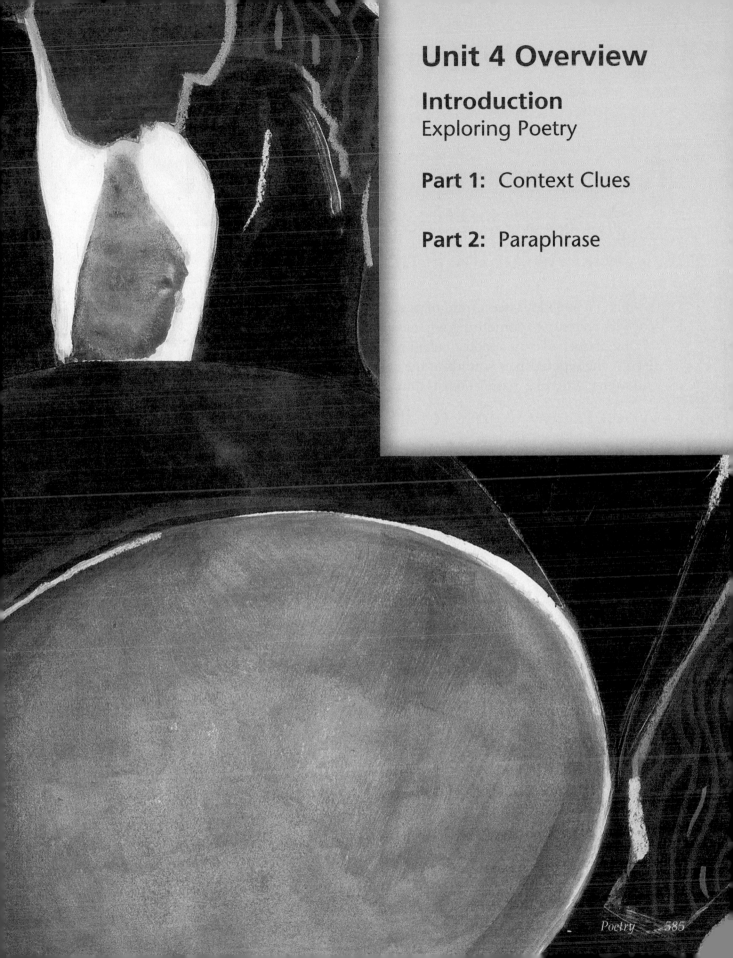

Unit 4 Overview

Introduction
Exploring Poetry

Part 1: Context Clues

Part 2: Paraphrase

Introduction:
Poetry

Jacqueline Woodson
Talks About the Form

Jacqueline
Woodson

▲ Jacqueline Woodson is known for writing realistic poems and stories and for developing authentic, believable characters.

When I was a kid, I was afraid of **poetry.** I thought my teachers were up to something whenever they started talking about it. To me, poetry meant rules—things like **rhyme,** the repetition of sounds at the ends of words, and **meter,** a regular pattern of rhythm.

When Poetry Comes to Life

When I read, I just wanted to *read,* I didn't want to have to *think* about how to read something. So whenever I looked at a poem, I got nervous, thinking there were things that I should know before I began reading it—but didn't. When a sentence dropped off in the middle and started again on the next line, I felt like I should understand just why and how that happened. For a long time, I just refused to read poetry.

A Discovery

But then I discovered a poem I loved, Paul Laurence Dunbar's "Sympathy." I realized, as I read it, that, like fiction, poetry tells a story—a story a kid like me could understand! Suddenly, the poems began to come to life for me. They jumped off the page. With just a few words or lines, I was transported to a whole new place or mood or into a whole other family!

▼ **Critical Viewing**
Which details in this illustration suggest the "first burst of energy on the page" that Woodson mentions? **[Connect]**

Poetry: A Few Words Saying a Lot

I love how a few words or a few lines can say so much. Poetry is spare that way. I also love the feeling of sitting down and writing a poem, then having the satisfaction of reading it right away.

Of course, most poems have to be rewritten a couple of times before they feel finished. But that first burst of energy on the page—those first few lines revealing the beginning of something. . . . That is such an amazing feeling. When I write novels, it takes a lot longer to achieve this.

Once I learned to love poetry, I began reading it all the time. When I started writing my book of poems, entitled *Locomotion*, I returned to the poets I loved, rereading their poems, trying to write as sparingly as they wrote. The quotation shown here is part of a poem by Tim Seibles. For me, it's about a writer struggling to get the right words on the page.

All afternoon someone watches
The shadow of a branch
Climb the legs of a chair,
And from someplace behind her
You can hear the scratchy whine
Of a radio not quite tuned—but climb
is not the word; the shadow
moves like something poured, spilling
up rather than down

from "Like This"
—Tim Seibles

More About the Author

Jacqueline **Woodson** (b. 1963)

Jacqueline Woodson recalls that she was happiest as a child when she was writing: "I wrote on paper bags and my shoes and denim binders." She believes that writers need to be honest and to listen to the voices of young people. When the voices in her poems or novels seem "cardboard and unrealistic," she starts over. Although she draws on real-life people for her characters, no piece she writes is completely autobiographical.

Fast Facts

▶ At the age of seven, Woodson wrote a collection of poems about butterflies and stapled the pages together as a book.

▶ At the National Book Foundation's summer camp, she teaches creative writing to young people.

Learning About Poetry

Elements of Poetry

Poetry is the most musical of literary forms. Poets choose words for both sound and meaning, using the following elements:

Sensory language is writing or speech that appeals to one or more of the five senses—sight, sound, smell, taste, and touch.

Figurative language is writing that is innovative, imaginative, and not meant to be taken literally. Writers use these figures of speech:

- **Metaphors** describe one thing as if it were something else. *Her eyes were saucers, wide with expectation.*

- **Personification** gives human qualities to something nonhuman. *The clarinets sang.*

- **Similes** use *like* or *as* to compare two unlike things. *The drums were as loud as a fireworks display.*

BIG TOP   **BY ROB HARRELL**

I WAS TRYING TO WRITE SOME POETRY, MANFRED. SO I JUST LET MY MIND FLOW LIKE YOU SUGGESTED.

GREAT. LET'S HEAR WHAT YOU'VE GOT.

TWO SALMON DANCE, CAVORT, CONTAINED... IN CRISP BUTCHER PAPER.

TREATS TUMBLE MEANINGLESS. THEIR LIVER FLAVOR, CONFINED.

RAWHIDE. CHEWY RAWHIDE. MILKBONES THREE.

THAT'S NOT A POEM. IT'S A GROCERY LIST.

YEAH, BUT IT'S LIKE A GROCERY LIST OF MY SOUL, DADDY-O!

Sound devices add a musical quality to poetry.

- **Alliteration** is the repetition of consonant sounds at the beginnings of words, as in *feathered friend.*

- **Repetition** is the repeated use of a sound, word, or phrase.

- **Assonance** is the repetition of vowel sounds in stressed syllables that end with different consonant sounds, as in *fade* and *hay.*

- **Consonance** is the repetition of final consonant sounds in stressed syllables with different vowel sounds, as in *end* and *hand.*

- **Onomatopoeia** is the use of words that imitate sounds.

- **Rhyme** is the repetition of sounds at the ends of words.

- **Meter** is the rhythmical pattern—or the arrangement and number of stressed and unstressed syllables—in a poem.

Forms of Poetry

The structure of a poem dictates its form. Most are written in lines, and these lines are grouped into stanzas. This list describes several forms of poetry.

Lyric poetry expresses thoughts and feelings of a single speaker, often in very musical verse. The **speaker** is the one telling the poem.

Narrative poetry tells a story in verse. Narrative poems often have elements like those in a short story, such as setting, plot, and characters.

Ballads are songlike poems that tell a story, often dealing with adventure and romance.

Free verse poetry is defined by its lack of strict structure. It has no regular meter, no intentional rhyme, no fixed line length, and no specific stanza pattern.

Haiku is a three-line Japanese verse form. The first and third lines each have five syllables and the second line has seven.

Rhyming couplets are a pair of rhyming lines that usually have the same meter and length.

Limericks are humorous five-line poems with a specific rhythm pattern and rhyme scheme.

Check Your Understanding

For each item below, give the correct term for the underlined portion.

1. The campfire <u>popped</u> and <u>crackled</u>.
2. Her <u>mind raced</u> with fearful thoughts.
3. <u>Pretty</u> <u>pansies</u> <u>pleasantly</u> <u>populated</u> the <u>porch</u>.
4. <u>Like a tiger stalking its prey</u>, he eyed the last cookie.

From the Author's Desk
Jacqueline Woodson Introduces Poems from *Locomotion*

I always want to challenge myself as a writer. I've written more than two dozen books and know I can tell a story. But then I start asking myself "Well, what if it was a boy? Can you tell that story? Or what if it was three boys? Or what if it was a boy who was a poet? Can you write a whole book of poems? Not only that, but within that collection of poems, can you have a story with a beginning, middle, and end?"

Locomotion: A Book That Answered a Challenge

That was the beginning of *Locomotion*. I never outline when I write. I never know where a story is going. Usually, I have a character in my head and that character has something he or she is dealing with. But many times, I don't know what that something is for a while.

The Speaker, Type of Verse, and Setting

I *did* know that the **speaker** in the poems would be a boy who was learning about poetry. And I knew that, like me, my character would like **free verse** more than forms. I have lots of respect for people who can write in forms, but I have a hard time doing it.

Most of all, I knew I wanted the **setting** of my book to be Brooklyn, New York. I knew my character would love Brooklyn as much as I do and that, like me, he would live there.

Discovering the Plot

But here's something about the **plot** I didn't know and only found out as I began writing: My speaker, whose name is Lonnie Collins Motion—Locomotion for short—and who had always wanted a brother, would find one in Rodney, the son of his foster mom.

And like me, Lonnie would be afraid of poetry at first, but would eventually come to love it.

Describe Somebody

JACQUELINE WOODSON

Today in class Ms. Marcus said
Take out your poetry notebooks and describe somebody.
Think carefully, Ms. Marcus said.
You're gonna read it to the class.
5   I wrote, Ms. Marcus is tall and a little bit skinny.
Then I put my pen in my mouth and stared down
at the words.
Then I crossed them out and wrote
Ms. Marcus's hair is long and brown.

Jacqueline Woodson
Author's Insight
In this poem, I wanted to give you a sense of the other kids in the class and what their strengths are.

10 Shiny.
When she smiles it makes you feel all good inside.
I stopped writing and looked around the room.
Angel was staring out the window.
Eric and Lamont were having a pen fight.
15 They don't care about poetry.
Stupid words, Eric says.
Lots and lots of stupid words.
Eric is tall and a little bit mean.
Lamont's just regular.
20 Angel's kinda chubby. He's got light brown hair.
Sometimes we all hang out,
play a little ball or something. Angel's real good
at science stuff. Once he made a volcano
for science fair and the stuff that came out of it
25 looked like real lava. Lamont can
draw superheroes real good. Eric—nobody
at school really knows this but
he can sing. Once, Miss Edna[1] took me
to a different church than the one
30 we usually go to on Sunday.
I was surprised to see Eric up there
with a choir robe on. He gave me a mean look
like I'd better not
say nothing about him and his dark green robe with
35 gold around the neck.
After the preacher preached
Eric sang a song with nobody else in the choir singing.
Miss Edna started dabbing at her eyes
whispering *Yes, Lord.*
40 Eric's voice was like something
that didn't seem like it should belong
to Eric.
Seemed like it should be coming out of an angel.

Now I gotta write a whole new poem
45 'cause Eric would be real mad if I told the class
about his angel voice.

---

1. Miss Edna Lonnie's foster mother.

Jacqueline Woodson
Author's Insight
As I rewrote this poem, I wanted to show the classroom—all the things happening during "poetry" time.

Poetry
Free Verse These lines advance the poem's story without using regular meter, intentional rhyme, or fixed length.

Jacqueline Woodson
Author's Insight
I rewrote these lines about eight times before the voice felt like Lonnie's voice.

ALMOST A SUMMER SKY

Jacqueline Woodson

It was the trees first, Rodney[1] tells me.
It's raining out. But the rain is light and warm.
And the sky's not all close to us like it gets
sometimes. It's way up there with
5   some blue showing through.
Late spring sky, Ms. Marcus says. *Almost summer sky.*
And when she said that, I said
*Hey Ms. Marcus, that's a good title
for a poem, right?*
10 *You have a poet's heart, Lonnie.*
That's what Ms. Marcus said to me.
I have a poet's heart.
That's good. A good thing to have.
And I'm the one who has it.

15 Now Rodney puts his arm around my shoulder
We keep walking. There's a park
eight blocks from Miss Edna's house
That's where we're going.
Me and Rodney to the park.
20 Rain coming down warm
Rodney with his arm around my shoulder
Makes me think of Todd and his pigeons
how big his smile gets when they fly.
The trees upstate ain't like other trees you seen, Lonnie
25 Rodney squints up at the sky, shakes his head
smiles.

---

1. **Rodney** one of Miss Edna's sons.

▲ **Critical Viewing**
What details in this picture suggest late spring, not summer? **[Analyze]**

Jacqueline Woodson
Author's Insight
By this point, Lonnie is beginning to believe in himself as a poet. I remember that feeling when I was a kid learning to love poetry.

✔ **Reading Check**
What are the two settings for this poem so far?

No, upstate they got maple and catalpa and scotch pine,[2]
all kinds of trees just standing.
Hundred-year-old trees big as three men.

30 *When you go home this weekend,* Ms. Marcus said.
Write about a perfect moment.

Yeah, Little Brother, Rodney says.
You don't know about shade till you lived upstate.
Everybody should do it—even if it's just for a little while.

35 Way off, I can see the park—blue-gray sky
touching the tops of trees.

I had to live there awhile, Rodney said.
Just to be with all that green, you know?
I nod, even though I don't.
40 I can't even imagine moving away from here,
from Rodney's arm around my shoulder,
from Miss Edna's Sunday cooking,
from Lily[3] in her pretty dresses and great
big smile when she sees me.

45 Can't imagine moving away

From
Home.

You know what I love about trees, Rodney
    says.
*It's like . . . It's like their leaves are hands
    reaching*
50 *out to you. Saying Come on over here,*
    Brother.
Let me just . . . Let me just . . .
Rodney looks down at me and grins.
Let me just give you some shade for a
    while.

---

2. catalpa (kə tal′ pə) *n.* tree with heart-shaped leaves; **scotch pine** tree
with yellow wood, grown for timber.
3. Lily Lonnie's sister, who lives in a different foster home.

Jacqueline Woodson
Author's Insight
Here, I wanted to show how Lonnie has gotten what he wanted—a big brother, a family, a home.

▼ **Critical Viewing**
Do you think that this boy, like Lonnie, would have difficulty imagining the trees Rodney describes? Explain. **[Connect]**

Q. What is it like to write in the voice of a fictional speaker?

A. I love imagining all the possibilities for my character, and I love when the character is so present in my head that he or she feels real to me. But it's definitely a struggle in the beginning, when the character is new and I have no idea where the character or the story is going.

Q. How was writing *Locomotion* different from writing a novel?

A. Well, first, it was poetry. I had to think about line breaks and meter and how a fifth-grade boy would write a certain poem. Then, I didn't have chapters so I had to figure out how to tell a story that had a beginning, middle, and end in a whole new way. I had written so many novels and felt like that way of writing was something I understand. With *Locomotion,* the form was, in a lot of ways, new and unfamiliar.

Student Corner

Q. Your poem "Describe Somebody" was very good. Was it based on a past experience or did you make it up?
— **Amanda Knox, Soddy Daisy, Tennessee**

A. This poem wasn't based on anything that happened to me personally, but all my writing is, as I said before, emotionally autobiographical. Yes, there was some point in my school years when someone bullied me as Eric bullies Lonnie. But I can't remember who that person was or what the situation was exactly. But I remember being frightened and I remember thinking, "I hope I don't misstep and rub this person the wrong way." In the poem, this is Lonnie's fear, that Eric will see what he wrote and get mad at him.

Writing Workshop: *Work in Progress*

Writing for Assessment

Timed writing requires you to think and write quickly. Practice "power writing." List five topics. For each topic write a thesis statement in two minutes or less. Save this Thesis List in your portfolio.

Apply the Skills

Poetry

Thinking About the Selections

1. **Respond:** After reading both poems, would you agree that Lonnie has the heart of a poet? Why or why not?

2. **(a) Recall:** What does the speaker know about Eric that others do not? **(b) Interpret:** Why would Eric be mad if the class knew this information?

3. **(a) Interpret:** In "Almost a Summer Sky," what is Rodney's perfect moment? **(b) Speculate:** What do you think Lonnie's perfect moment might be? **(c) Draw Conclusions:** How are both boys observant in the way that poets are?

Poetry Review

4. **(a)** What information about the structure of these poems tells you they are written in **free verse**? **(b)** Why is this style a good choice for these poems?

5. **(a)** Complete a chart like the one shown to analyze the **figurative language** in the poems. **(b)** Share your ideas with a classmate. How have your ideas grown or changed?

	Ideas Compared	Ideas Conveyed
"Describe Somebody," lines 40–43		
"Almost a Summer Sky," lines 49–53		

Research the Author

Discover more about Lonnie by reading *Locomotion*, the story of his life in poetry by Jacqueline Woodson. With two classmates, arrange a **poetry reading**. Follow these steps:

- Choose two poems from the book that will help your audience understand Lonnie's story and the people in his world.
- Rehearse the poems before presenting them to your audience.

QuickReview

Poems at a Glance

In **"Describe Somebody,"** the speaker tries to satisfy a poetry writing assignment.

In **"Almost a Summer Sky,"** Lonnie and Rodney notice the trees and the sky as they walk to a park.

Assessment
For: Self-test
Visit: www.PHSchool.com
Web Code: ena-6401

Free Verse: poetry written without a regular rhythmic pattern or rhyme scheme

Figurative Language: poetic language that is imaginative and not meant to be taken literally

Skills You Will Learn

Reading Skill: *Preview to Identify Unfamiliar Words*
Literary Analysis: *Sound Devices*

Reading Skill: *Use Context to Understand Specialized Language*
Reading Skill: *Reread and Read Ahead to Confirm Meaning*
Literary Analysis: *Figurative Language: Similes, Metaphors, Personification*

Literary Analysis: *Comparing Humorous Imagery in Poetry*

Literature You Will Read

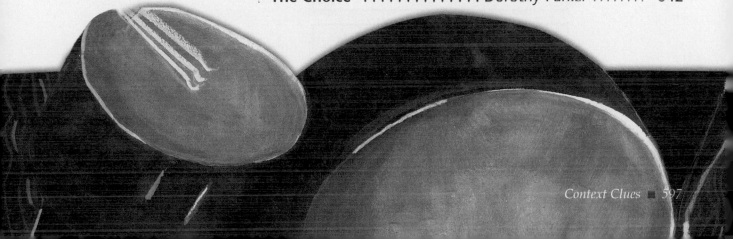

Reading: Context Clues

▶ **Context clues** are the text around a word that helps you figure out the meaning of an unfamiliar word.

Skills and Strategies You Will Learn in Part 1

In Part 1, you will learn

- to **preview** to **identify** unfamiliar words (p. 600)
- to **reread and read ahead** to find **context clues** and clarify meaning (p. 620)
- to use **context and context clues** to help you understand **technical language** (p. 616)

Using the Skills and Strategies in Part 1

In Part 1, you will learn to preview text in order to identify unfamiliar words and then use context clues to help you understand their meaning. You will also practice reading ahead and rereading to find context clues. In addition, you will learn to use the context of an informational text to help you understand the meaning of specialized or technical language.

Unfamiliar Word

The first speaker was *tedious*

BUT (context clue—you will be looking for an antonym)

Antonyms:

the second one was *lively* and *interesting*.

Meaning of Unfamiliar Word:

Tedious means the opposite of *lively* and *interesting*.
It means "boring" or "dull."

Academic Vocabulary: Words for Discussing Context Clues

The following words will help you to write and talk about context clues as you read the selections in this unit.

Word	Definition	Example Sentence
synonymous *adj.*	having the same, or nearly the same, meaning	*Courage* and *bravery* are *synonymous* words.
restatement *n.*	expressing the same idea in different words	The author's *restatement* of his idea helped me to understand it.
context *n.*	text surrounding an unfamiliar word	Study the *context* in which an unfamiliar word appears.
confirm *v.*	make certain; prove to be correct	Reread a sentence to *confirm* your understanding of a new word.
clarify *v.*	explain; make clearer	A context clue can *clarify* the meaning of an unfamiliar word.

Vocabulary Skills You Will Learn in Part 1

▶ A **suffix** is a group of letters added to the end of a word to change its meaning or its part of speech.

- the suffix *-ous* (p. 614)
- the suffix *-ment* (p. 634)

Suffix	Meaning	Example Words	Part of Speech
-ment	act, process, or state of	restatement enjoyment excitement	noun
-ous	having; full of	famous outrageous	adjective

Activity For each suffix on the chart, write three more example words. Tell the meaning and part of speech of each word you write.

You can apply the instruction on this page to these poems.

Reading Skill

Context is the text around a particular word. Before you read a poem, **preview the lines of verse to identify unfamiliar words.** Then, as you read more closely, look for clues in the context to determine a possible meaning for each unfamiliar word. Look for these types of clues:

- **synonym or definition:** words that mean the same as the unfamiliar word
- **antonym:** words that are opposite in meaning
- **explanation:** words that give more information about the unfamiliar word, as shown in the chart
- **sentence role:** the way the word is used

Using Context	
With her hair all *disheveled* Looking like she had just awoken	
Explanation	Looking like she had just awoken
Sentence Role	describes hair
Meaning Disheveled *probably* means *messy*, like hair looks after sleeping	

Literary Analysis

Sound devices help poets draw on the musical quality of words to express ideas. Common sound devices include the following:

- **alliteration:** repetition of initial consonant sounds—*misty morning*
- **onomatopoeia:** words that imitate sounds—*buzz*
- **rhyme:** repetition of sounds at ends of words—*spring fling*
- **rhythm:** the pattern of strong and weak beats

Vocabulary Builder

Poetry Collection 1

- **flatterer** (flat´ ər ər) *n.* one who praises insincerely to win approval (p. 603) *Liz is a flatterer, so I do not believe her praise.*
- **kennel** (ken´ əl) *n.* a place where dogs are kept (p. 604) *My dog sleeps in a backyard kennel.*
- **rapture** (rap´chər) *n.* ecstasy (p. 605) *Athletes dream of Olympic gold with rapture.*

Poetry Collection 2

- **singularity** (siŋ´ gyə ler´ ə tē) *n.* unique or distinct feature (p. 609) *The cricket's chirp has an unmistakable singularity.*
- **resounding** (ri zoun´ diŋ) *adj.* sounding loudly (p. 610) *His voice echoed, resounding in the empty hall.*
- **strife** (strīf) *n.* conflict (p. 611) *Strife between the two groups led to war.*

Connecting to the Literature

Reading/Writing Connection The colorful descriptions in the three poems that follow reveal vivid imaginations at work. Write several sentences to explain why imagination and creativity are valuable. Use at least three of these words: *comment, enrich, generate, innovate, maintain.*

Meet the Authors

Eleanor **Farjeon** (1881–1965)
Cat! (p. 602)

Eleanor Farjeon spent much of her childhood reading fantasy stories in the attic of her family's house in London, England. She also loved playing games of make-believe with her little brother. When she grew up, she recalled her childhood sense of wonder to inspire dozens of books of poetry, and stories for children and young adults. Farjeon's 1931 poem "Morning Has Broken" became a huge hit when it was set to music by pop singer Cat Stevens forty years later.

Walter **de la Mare** (1873–1956)
Silver (p. 604)

The British poet and novelist Walter de la Mare loved the magical world of imagination. Yet, for eighteen years, he worked at an ordinary job as a bookkeeper for an oil company. He wrote during his lunch hour, and every night at bedtime, he read one of his new poems to his four children. In 1908, the British government gave him a grant that allowed him to retire at age thirty-five and write full-time for the rest of his life.

Georgia Douglas **Johnson** (1886–1966)
Your World (p. 605)

As a child, Georgia Douglas Johnson loved music and taught herself to play the violin. Later, she used her love of rhythm and rhyme to create hundreds of poems. She became one of the first well-known African American women poets and published her last book of poetry when she was in her eighties.

For: More about these poets

Go Online **Visit:** www.PHSchool.com
Author Link **Web Code:** ene-9402

CAT!

Eleanor Farjeon

▲ **Critical Viewing** Which of these two drawings most resembles the cat described in the poem? Explain your choice. **[Connect]**

Cat!
Scat!
After her, after her,
Sleeky <u>flatterer</u>,
5 Spitfire chatterer,
Scatter her, scatter her
    Off her mat!
    Wuff!
    Wuff!
10   Treat her rough!
Git her, git her,
Whiskery spitter!
Catch her, catch her,
Green-eyed scratcher!
15   Slathery
    Slithery
    Hisser,
    Don't miss her!
Run till you're dithery,[1]
20   Hithery
    Thithery[2]
    Pftts! pftts!
    How she spits!
    Spitch! Spatch!
25   Can't she scratch!
Scritching the bark
Of the sycamore tree,
She's reached her ark
And's hissing at me
30   *Pftts! pftts!*
    Wuff! wuff!
        Scat,
        Cat!
        That's
35   *That!*

Vocabulary Builder
flatterer (flat´ ər ər) *n.*
one who praises
insincerely to win
approval

**Reading Skill
Context** Which
words in lines 10–14
provide a synonym
that helps you
determine the
meaning of *git*?

**Literary Analysis
Sound Devices** Find
two made-up words
that imitate cat
sounds. How do they
help you imagine the
poem's action?

---

1. **dithery** (dith´ re) *adj.* nervous and confused; in a dither.
2. **Hithery/Thithery** made-up words based on *hither* and *thither,* which mean "here" and "there."

◄ **Critical Viewing**
Based on this picture
and the title, what do
you think this poem
will be about?
[Speculate]

Silver

Walter de la Mare

Slowly, silently, now the moon
Walks the night in her silver shoon;[1]
This way, and that, she peers, and sees
Silver fruit upon silver trees;
5   One by one the casements[2] catch
Her beams beneath the silvery thatch;[3]
Couched in his <u>kennel</u>, like a log,
With paws of silver sleeps the dog;
From their shadowy coat the white breasts peep
10 Of doves in a silver-feathered sleep;
A harvest mouse goes scampering by,
With silver claws, and silver eye;
And moveless fish in the water gleam,
By silver reeds in a silver stream.

Literary Analysis
Sound Devices
Identify examples of
alliteration in lines 1–5.

Vocabulary Builder
kennel (ken´ əl) *n.* a
place where dogs are
kept

---

1. shoon (sho͞on) *n.* old-fashioned word for "shoes."
2. casements (kās´ mənts) *n.* windows that open out like doors.
3. thatch (thach) *n.* roof made of straw or other plant material.

Your World
Georgia Douglas Johnson

Your world is as big as you make it.
I know, for I used to abide
In the narrowest nest in a corner,
My wings pressing close to my side.

5 But I sighted the distant horizon
Where the sky line encircled the sea
And I throbbed with a burning desire
To travel this immensity.

I battered the cordons¹ around me
10 And cradled my wings on the breeze
Then soared to the uttermost reaches
With <u>rapture</u>, with power, with ease!

---

1. cordons (kôr´ dənz) *n.* lines or cords that restrict free movement.

Reading Skill
Context How do the words *horizon, sky,* and *sea* help you find the meaning of *immensity*?

Vocabulary Builder
rapture (rap´ chər)
n. ecstasy

Apply the Skills

Poetry Collection 1

Thinking About the Selections

1. **Respond:** Which poem created the most vivid picture in your mind? Why?
2. **(a) Recall:** Where does the cat in "Cat!" run? **(b) Interpret:** Why is the cat running? **(c) Draw Conclusions:** How does the speaker of the poem feel about the cat?
3. **(a) Recall:** What "walks the night" in "Silver"? **(b) Analyze Causes and Effects:** What effects does this "walk" have on everyday objects? **(c) Generalize:** What mood, or feeling in the reader, does the poet create as he describes these effects?
4. **(a) Recall:** Where does the speaker of "Your World" say that she used to live? **(b) Recall:** What was her "burning desire"? **(c) Interpret:** How did she manage to feel rapture?
5. **(a) Interpret:** How do the events described in "Your World" illustrate the first line of the poem? **(b) Discuss:** Share your ideas with a partner. Then, explain how your ideas have grown or changed based on the discussion.

Reading Skill

6. Explain how **context** helps you determine the meaning of *scritch* in "Cat!"
7. What kind of context clues help you clarify the meaning of *abide* in "Your World"?

Literary Analysis

8. Complete the chart with examples of the kinds of **sound devices** you find in each poem. Not all sound devices are used in each poem.

	Cat!	Silver	Your World
alliteration			
onomatopoeia			
rhyme			

9. What do sound devices add to the experience of reading poetry? Explain.

QuickReview

Poems at a Glance

"Cat!": a free-verse poem about a cat

"Silver": a poem about moonlight written in regular rhythm and rhyme

"Your World": a poem about taking flight written in regular rhythm and rhyme

Go Online
Assessment
For: Self-test
Visit: www.PHSchool.com
Web Code: ena-6402

Context: words and phrases surrounding a word

Sound Devices: techniques such as *rhyme, onomatopoeia, alliteration,* and *rhythm* that use sound to communicate ideas and feelings

Vocabulary Builder

Practice In each group, identify the word that does not belong. Explain how its meaning differs from those of the other words.

1. doghouse   kitchen   kennel
2. flatterer   praiser   complainer
3. rapture   unhappiness   despair

Writing

Choose a poem from this collection and write an **introduction** for a poetry reading. In your writing, grab listeners' attention and spark their interest in the poem. Follow these steps:

- Consider the subject of the poem and jot down ideas about how the poet shows the subject in a new or unusual light.
- Review the poem to note the writer's use of sound devices.
- As you draft, include the title and author, and use your notes to introduce your audience to the poem.
- End your introduction with one or two tips that call your audience's attention to specific elements of the poem.

For *Grammar, Vocabulary,* and *Assessment,* see **Build Language Skills,** pages 614–615.

Extend Your Learning

Listening and Speaking With two others, plan and present a **group reading** of one of these three poems to the class. To prepare, discuss how the poem you choose uses sound devices to create a particular mood, or feeling. Then, rehearse to convey the mood the group identified. After reading the poem in unison, point out to the class the elements in the poem that produce the feeling.

Research and Technology Create a **poets' timeline.**
- Starting with 1870, mark off twenty-year intervals.
- Use different colors to make and label three lines to mark the lifetime of each poet in this collection.
- Research important world events from 1870 to 1970. Summarize each event as a brief label and place all the labels on a fourth line.

Write a brief overview to explain your timeline to viewers.

Build Understanding • *Poetry Collection 2*

Connecting to the Literature

Reading/Writing Connection In "Ring Out, Wild Bells," the poet expresses his hopes for a better world. Write three sentences describing how you might like the world to change in the future. Use three of the following words in your description: *achieve, dedicate, cease, maintain.*

Review

For **Reading Skill, Literary Analysis,** and **Vocabulary Builder,** see page 600.

Meet the Authors

Eve **Merriam** (1916–1992)
Thumbprint (p. 609)

Eve Merriam fell in love with words at an early age. As a child, she loved playing with rhythms, rhymes, and puns. As an adult, she never lost her feeling that words could be fun. She once said, "I find it difficult to sit still when I hear poetry or read it out loud. . . . It's like a shot of adrenaline or oxygen when I hear rhymes and word play."

Nikki **Giovanni** (b. 1943)
The Drum (for Martin Luther King, Jr.) (p. 610)

As a college student in the 1960s, Nikki Giovanni became involved in the civil rights movement. In the 1970s, she began writing poetry that expressed her pride in her African American heritage. Her poems are known for their musical rhythms, and she has recorded several of her works set to gospel music.

Alfred, Lord **Tennyson** (1809–1892)
Ring Out, Wild Bells (p. 611)

Alfred, Lord Tennyson's faith in life was shattered in his twenties, when his close friend Arthur Henry Hallam died suddenly while on a trip. Tennyson wrote the long poem "In Memoriam A. H. H." as a tribute to his friend. It helped make Tennyson one of the most popular English poets of his time. "Ring Out, Wild Bells" is part of this famous poem.

Go Online
Author Link
For: More about these poets
Visit: www.PHSchool.com
Web Code: ene-9403

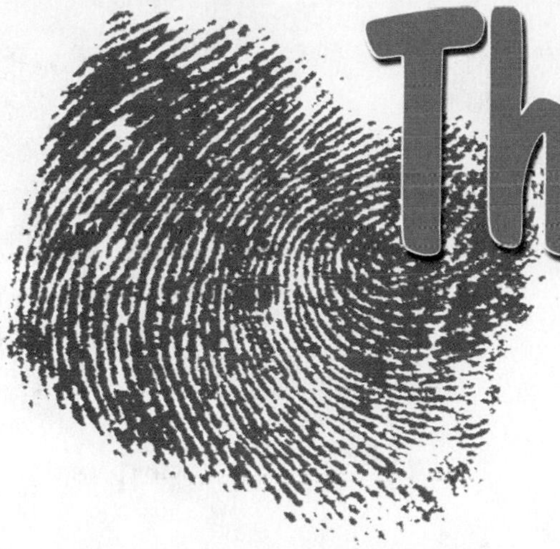

Thumbprint

Eve Merriam

On the pad of my thumb
are whorls,[1] whirls, wheels
in a unique design:
mine alone.
What a treasure to own!
My own flesh, my own feelings.
No other, however grand or base,
can ever contain the same.
My signature,
thumbing the pages of my time.
My universe key,
my singularity.

Impress, implant,
I am myself,
of all my atom parts I am the sum.
And out of my blood and my brain
I make my own interior weather,
my own sun and rain.
Imprint my mark upon the world,
whatever I shall become.

Literary Analysis
Sound Devices
Which repeated consonant sounds create alliteration in lines 1–6?

Vocabulary Builder
singularity (siŋ′ gyə ler′ ə tē) *n.* unique or distinct feature

1. **whorls** (hwôrlz) *n.* circular ridges that form the pattern of fingerprints.

The Drum
(for Martin Luther King, Jr.)

Nikki Giovanni

The drums . . . Pa-Rum . . . the rat-tat-tat . . . of drums . . .
The Pied Piper[1] . . . after leading the rats . . . to death . . .
took the children . . . to dreams . . . Pa-Rum Pa-Rum . . .

The big bass drums . . . the kettles roar . . . the sound of
animal flesh . . . <u>resounding</u> against the wood . . . Pa-Rum
Pa-Rum . . .

Kunta Kinte[2] was making a drum . . . when he was captured . . .
Pa-Rum . . .
Thoreau[3] listened . . . to a different drum . . . rat-tat-tat-Pa-
Rum . . .
King said just say . . . I was a Drum Major . . . for peace . . .
Pa-Rum Pa-Rum . . . rat-tat-tat Pa-rum . . .

Drums of triumph . . . Drums of pain . . . Drums of life . . .
Funeral drums . . . Marching drums . . . Drums that call . . .
Pa-Rum
Pa-Rum . . . the Drums that call . . . rat-tat-tat-tat . . . the
Drums are calling . . . Pa-Rum Pa-Rum . . . rat-tat-tat Pa-
Rum . . .

---

1. **Pied Piper** musician in folklore who led away a town's children after he rid the town of rats.
2. **Kunta Kinte** (kͨoonˊ tə kinˊ tā) ancestor of *Roots* author Alex Haley.
3. **Thoreau** (thə rōˊ) (1817–1862) Henry David, American writer who said "If a man does not keep pace with his companions, perhaps it is because he hears a different drummer."

▲ **Critical Viewing**
What can make the sound of a poem similar to the sound of a drum? **[Compare]**

Vocabulary Builder
resounding (ri zͨounˊ diŋ) *adj.* sounding loudly

Literary Analysis
Sound Devices What words in the poem imitate the sounds that drums make?

Ring Out, Wild Bells
Alfred, Lord Tennyson

Ring out, wild bells, to the wild sky,
    The flying cloud, the frosty light:
    The year is dying in the night;
Ring out, wild bells, and let him die.

5 Ring out the old, ring in the new,
    Ring, happy bells, across the snow:
    The year is going, let him go;
Ring out the false, ring in the true.

Ring out the grief that saps the mind,
10   For those that here we see no more;
    Ring out the feud of rich and poor,
Ring in redress to all mankind.

Ring out a slowly dying cause,
    And ancient forms of party <u>strife</u>;
15   Ring in the nobler modes of life,
With sweeter manners, purer laws.

Ring out the want, the care, the sin,
    The faithless coldness of the times;
    Ring out, ring out thy mournful rhymes,
20 But ring the fuller minstrel[1] in.

Ring out false pride in place and blood,
    The civic[2] slander and the spite;
    Ring in the love of truth and right,
Ring in the common love of good.

25 Ring out old shapes of foul disease;
    Ring out the narrowing lust of gold;
    Ring out the thousand wars of old,
Ring in the thousand years of peace.

---

1. **fuller minstrel** (min´ strəl) *n.* singer of the highest rank.
2. **civic** (siv´ ik) *adj.* relating to cities or citizens.

Apply the Skills

Poetry Collection 2

Thinking About the Selections

1. **Respond:** Which of the three poems do you think could best be set to music as a song? Give reasons for your choice.
2. **(a) Recall:** At the beginning of "Thumbprint," how does the speaker describe her thumbprint? **(b) Interpret:** Why is her thumbprint so important to her?
3. **(a) Interpret:** Explain the meaning of the sentence in lines 14–15. **(b) Assess:** Why do you think some people place such a high value on individuality?
4. **(a) Recall:** According to "The Drum," what did Martin Luther King, Jr., want people to say about him? **(b) Recall:** In the last stanza, what kinds of drums are mentioned? **(c) Interpret:** Why is a drummer a good symbol for a leader?
5. **(a) Recall:** List four phrases in "Ring Out, Wild Bells" that tell what the speaker wants to "ring out" and "ring in."
   (b) Interpret: With a partner, describe the kind of future that the poem's speaker envisions. **(c) Discuss:** Share your interpretation with the rest of the class.

Reading Skill

6. Explain how **context** helps you figure out the meaning of *base* in "Thumbprint."
7. What context clues help you clarify the meaning of *feud* in "Ring Out, Wild Bells"?

Literary Analysis

8. Complete the chart with examples of the kinds of **sound devices** you find in each poem. Not all sound devices are used in each poem.

	Thumbprint	The Drum	Ring Out, Wild Bells
alliteration			
onomatopoeia			
rhyme			

9. What do sound devices add to the experience of reading poetry? Explain.

QuickReview

Poems at a Glance

"Thumbprint": a free-verse poem about individuality

"The Drum": a free-verse poem dedicated to Martin Luther King, Jr.

"Ring Out, Wild Bells": part of a memorial poem written in regular rhythm and rhyme

Go Online
Assessment
For: Self-test
Visit: www.PHSchool.com
Web Code: ena-6403

Context: words and phrases surrounding a word

Sound Devices: techniques such as *rhyme, onomatopoeia, alliteration,* and *rhythm* that use sound to communicate ideas and feelings

Vocabulary Builder

Practice In each group, identify the word that does not belong. Explain how its meaning differs from those of the other words.

1. singularity   similarity   uniqueness
2. echoing   resounding   muttering
3. peace   cooperation   strife

Writing

Choose a poem from this collection and write an **introduction** for a poetry reading. In your writing, grab listeners' attention and spark their interest in the poem. Follow these steps:

- Consider the subject of the poem and jot down ideas about how the poet shows the subject in a new or unusual light.
- Review the poem to note the writer's use of sound devices.
- As you draft, include the title and author, and use your notes to introduce your audience to the poem.
- End your introduction with one or two tips that call your audience's attention to specific elements of the poem.

For *Grammar, Vocabulary,* and *Assessment,* see **Build Language Skills,** pages 614–615.

Extend Your Learning

Listening and Speaking With two others, plan and present a **group reading** of one of these three poems to the class. To prepare, discuss how the poem you choose uses sound devices to create a particular mood, or feeling. Then, rehearse to convey the mood the group identified. After reading the poem in unison, point out to the class the elements in the poem that produce the feeling.

Research and Technology Create a **poets' timeline.**
- Starting with 1800, mark off fifty-year intervals.
- Use a color to mark the lifetime of each poet in this collection. If the poet is alive, put an arrow at the right end of the line.
- Research important world events from 1800 to today. Summarize each event as a brief label and place all the labels on a fourth line.

Write a brief overview to explain your timeline to viewers.

Build Language Skills

Vocabulary Skill

Suffixes The **suffix** *-ous* means "having the quality of" or "full of." It is often combined with nouns to turn them into adjectives. In the adjective *synonymous, -ous* has been added to the noun *synonym.* The meaning has not changed, but the word can now be used to modify another idea. A *synonym* is a word that has nearly the same meaning as another word. *Synonymous* means "having the qualities of synonyms."

Practice Define each of the following words. Then, use each word in a sentence.

1. thunderous   3. joyous   5. dangerous
2. courageous   4. humorous

Grammar Lesson

Subject Complements A **subject complement** is a noun, a pronoun, or an adjective that follows a linking verb and tells something about the subject. Three types of subject complements are *predicate nouns, predicate pronouns,* and *predicate adjectives.* A **predicate noun** or predicate pronoun follows a linking verb and *identifies,* or renames, the subject of the sentence. A **predicate adjective** follows a linking verb and *describes* the subject of the sentence.

Predicate Noun	<u>Ronnie</u> will be the *captain* of the team.	*Captain* renames the subject, *Ronnie.*
Predicate Pronoun	The two <u>winners</u> are *they.*	*They* identified the subject, *winners.*
Predicate Adjective	The <u>flight</u> to Houston was *swift.*	*Swift* describes the subject, *flight.*

Practice In each sentence, identify the subject complement and note whether it is a predicate noun, a predicate pronoun, or a predicate adjective. Then, write a new sentence replacing each subject complement.

1. Katy is a fan of her hometown football team.
2. The gas station attendant was unfriendly.
3. Which team are they?
4. He was the inventor of nonstick frying pans.
5. The plan for increasing gas efficiency was smart.

MorePractice

For more practice with subject complements, see the Grammar Handbook, p. R31.

WG Prentice Hall Writing and Grammar Connection: Chapter 19, Section 5

Reading: Context Clues

Directions: *Read the selection. Then, answer the questions.*

Cats are carnivorous, or meat-eating, animals. They are also *predators,* skillfully hunting the animals that serve as their food. Members of the cat family include lions, tigers, cheetahs, leopards, and jaguars. Although most kinds of wild cats are *nocturnal,* a few are more active during the day. Most cats are *solitary* hunters, traveling alone, though some, such as lions, live in groups. A lion *pride* may include up to twenty individuals.

1. Using context clues, what does *predators* mean?
   - **A** meat-eaters
   - **B** hunters
   - **C** cats
   - **D** food

2. Which of the following most clearly helps determine the meaning of *nocturnal*?
   - **A** traveling alone
   - **B** lions, tigers, cheetahs, leopards
   - **C** skillfully hunting down the animals
   - **D** a few are more active during the day

3. What does *solitary* most likely mean?
   - **A** being alone
   - **B** in a group
   - **C** hunting
   - **D** traveling

4. What is the meaning of the word *pride,* as used in this context?
   - **A** twenty individual cats
   - **B** a solitary lion
   - **C** a group that believes in itself
   - **D** a group of lions

Timed Writing: Evaluation [Critical Stance]

Review the poems in *Poetry Collection 1* or *Poetry Collection 2.* Evaluate the poems in the collection and identify which you think most effectively uses sound devices. Use examples from the poem to support your evaluation. **(25 minutes)**

 ## Writing Workshop: *Work in Progress*

Writing for Assessment
To practice quickly responding to a writing prompt, have a classmate time you. In four minutes, write as many statements as you can that begin with the following: "I disagree that . . ." Put your list in your writing portfolio.

Reading Informational Materials

Recipes

In Part 1, you are learning to use context clues to figure out the meanings of unfamiliar words in literature. Context clues can also help you understand what technical words or specialized terms mean in informational materials such as recipes. If you read the poem "Thumbprint," you will appreciate a special technique used in this recipe.

About Recipes

Recipes are instructions for preparing food or drink. Once you learn to recognize some common features of recipes, you will find them much easier to follow. These common features include:

- a title that names the dish
- a list of ingredients
- directions that explain the steps to follow to make the dish
- the number of servings the dish will make

Many recipes include additional information:

- the amount of time it takes to prepare the dish
- a nutritional analysis, which may include calorie information
- serving suggestions

Reading Skill

As you follow the directions in a recipe, you may come across words that are unfamiliar to you or used in a way that is different from what you know. When this happens, **use context clues to understand specialized and technical language.** The words surrounding an unfamiliar word or phrase can help you clarify its meaning. Pictures can also provide context clues.

As you read the recipe, use a graphic organizer like the one shown to list the context clues that help you figure out the meaning of unfamiliar words or phrases.

Unfamiliar Word	Sentence in Which Appears	Context Clue	Possible Meaning
simmer	Bring to a boil, reduce heat, and simmer for 5 minutes.	reduce heat	cook at a temperature that is not as hot as a boil

Thumbprint Cookies

¹/₂ cup brown sugar
1 cup butter
2-3 egg yolks
2 cups flour
egg whites
1¹/₂ cups chopped nuts
raspberry preserves

> In most recipes, ingredients are listed in the order in which they are used.

To separate eggs, crack each egg in half. Over a bowl, pour the egg back and forth between the cracked halves. Let the egg white fall into the bowl, keeping the egg yolk intact in the shell. Cream together sugar, butter, and egg yolks. Beat flour into this mixture. Form balls and dip into slightly beaten egg whites. Roll balls in chopped nuts. Put on lightly greased cookie sheet and make a thumbprint on each ball. Bake at 350° for 8 minutes. Remove from oven and reset thumbprint. Bake 8 to 10 minutes longer. Fill print with raspberry preserves.

Preparation: 25 min.   Yield: 30
Baking: 18 min.   Can freeze

Separating an egg

Using a teaspoon

ABOUT DROP COOKIES

Whoever invented drop cookies, which we used to call "drop cakes," deserves a medal. Except for bars, drop cookies are the easiest of all cookies to make, because shaping usually involves nothing more than dropping dough from a spoon. A few call for patting down the dough or spreading it out with the tip of a knife. In most cases, drop cookies are very forgiving: No harm is done if the mixture is slightly stiffer or softer than expected; the results will just be a little flatter or puffier than usual.

> Some recipes include information that will help cooks prepare the food successfully.

Rules for Making Great Cookies

◆ The best cookies are made from the best ingredients. Use unsalted butter, and don't stint. If possible, use unsalted nuts, and make sure they're very fresh. (Nuts are oily, and the oil can turn rancid with age.) Dried fruits such as raisins, dates, and candied citrus bits should always be plump and moist; hard, dried-out "bullets" are not only untoothsome, but will draw off moisture and make cookies dry. Don't economize on baking chocolate or on spices. Believe it or not, there is a dramatic difference between the flavor of genuine cinnamon and that of ground cassia, often sold as a cinnamon substitute. Always buy pure vanilla, almond, or other extracts, not imitation, which can taste tinny and artificial.

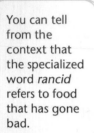

You can tell from the context that the specialized word *rancid* refers to food that has gone bad.

◆ Always use large eggs when baking. Their size is closely regulated for uniformity, one large egg weighing 2 ounces in the shell and 1.75 ounces out of the shell. It is important to note that an egg is a liquid ingredient and substituting extra-large or jumbo eggs will throw off the balance of a recipe.

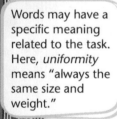

Words may have a specific meaning related to the task. Here, *uniformity* means "always the same size and weight."

◆ Baking, unlike some other forms of cooking, is not a casually improvisational art. Read each recipe all the way through before starting, always preheat the oven for 20 minutes before baking, and measure out all the ingredients carefully before you start mixing them.

◆ A cookie must have certain characteristics to earn it a place in the home-baking hall of fame: a distinctive texture, be it brittle-crisp, chewy-gooey, crunchy, silky, or melt-in-the-mouth (great cookies are rarely dry or cakey); an inviting appearance—which is not to say necessarily a picture-perfect one; a size and shape suitable to the cookie's character (oversize and sturdy for munching from a baggy in a lunch box, say, or dainty and chic for perching on a saucer at a tea); and most of all, of course, good flavor.

Reading: Use Context to Understand Specialized Language

Directions: *Choose the letter of the best answer to each question.*

1. Judging from the context, what does the word *reset* mean in the recipe instructions?
   - A bake again
   - B imprint again
   - C smooth again
   - D cut again

2. What context clue helps you figure out the meaning of *rancid* in the first bullet on page 618?
   - A unsalted
   - B make sure
   - C with age
   - D oily

3. What does the word *untoothsome* in the same passage mean, based on the description?
   - A tasty
   - B undercooked
   - C unappetizing
   - D moist

Reading: Comprehension and Interpretation

Directions: *Write your answers on a separate sheet of paper.*

4. What would happen if you heated the oven at 350° as a last step, rather than a first step? **[Generative]**

5. Which ingredients do you think could be left out of the recipe and still result in tasty cookies? Explain. **[Knowledge]**

6. Describe the look and taste of the finished cookies, based on the details in the recipe. **[Generative]**

Timed Writing: Explanation [Organizing]

Briefly explain simple directions for making a food you know how to prepare. Be sure to include the necessary tools and ingredients, and list the steps in order. **(15 minutes)**

Build Skills   *Poetry Collection 1 • Poetry Collection 2*

You can apply the instruction on this page to these poems.

Reading Skill

Context, the words and phrases surrounding a word, can help you understand new words or words that are used in an unfamiliar way. When you find an unfamiliar word, **reread and read ahead** for context clues. When you have figured out a possible meaning, insert the meaning in place of the unfamiliar word and reread the sentence. If it makes sense, your meaning is probably correct. If it does not make sense, read ahead to look for additional context clues, or consult a dictionary. The chart shows the common types of context clues.

Literary Analysis

Figurative language is writing or speech that is not meant to be taken literally. Figurative language includes these *figures of speech.*

- A *simile* compares two apparently unlike things using the words *like* or *as*: His eyes were as black as coal.
- A *metaphor* compares two apparently unlike things by saying that one thing *is* the other: The world is my oyster.
- *Personification* is a comparison in which a nonhuman subject is given human characteristics: The trees toss in their sleep.

As you read, notice the way figurative language allows writers to present ideas in fresh ways.

Contrast
I *never shop* anymore, but last year, I was a shopping <u>enthusiast.</u>
Synonym
Don't *reject* our request. Your <u>veto</u> can hurt many people.
Explanation
Think of the <u>capacity</u>— this truck can carry *a lot of cargo.*
Example
She <u>agonized</u> for days, *biting her nails, sleeping poorly,* and *crying* because she was worried.

Vocabulary Builder

Poetry Collection 1

- **ponderous** (pän′ dər əs) *adj.* very heavy (p. 623) *We heard his <u>ponderous</u> footsteps echoing in the stairwell.*
- **roam** (rōm) *v.* go aimlessly; wander (p. 625) *We keep our cat inside so she will not <u>roam.</u>*

Poetry Collection 2

- **uneasily** (un ēz′ i lē) *adv.* restlessly (p. 630) *Awake, she tossed <u>uneasily</u> all night.*

- **unresponsive** (un′ rē spän′ siv) *adj.* not reacting (p. 630) *Her illness was <u>unresponsive</u> to treatment.*
- **rut** (rut) *n.* a groove in the ground made by a wheeled vehicle or natural causes (p. 631) *I fell off my bike when I hit a <u>rut</u> in the road.*
- **debates** (dē bāts′) *v.* tries to decide (p. 631) *Tim <u>debates</u> whether to go out or stay in.*

Connecting to the Literature

Reading/Writing Connection The bustling excitement of city life inspires the poets in this collection. Think of the typical sights and sounds someone might experience in a city. Write a paragraph describing your ideas, using at least three of the following words: *appeal, capture, circulate, display.*

Meet the Authors

Patricia **Hubbell** (b. 1928)
Concrete Mixers (p. 622)

Patricia Hubbell began writing poetry when she was ten years old. She liked to sit in a tree and look down on her family's farm, where she often saw things she would capture later in verse. Hubbell, who has been writing poetry and children's books for more than forty years, explains "Poem ideas are everywhere; you have to listen and watch for them."

Richard **García** (b. 1941)
The City Is So Big (p. 624)

Richard García has been writing poetry since the 1950s. He published his first poetry collection in 1973, but then stopped writing for six years. An encouraging letter from Nobel Prize winner Octavio Paz inspired him to write again. In addition to writing, García was the Poet-in-Residence for years at the Children's Hospital in Los Angeles, where he led poetry and art workshops for hospitalized children.

Langston **Hughes** (1902–1967)
Harlem Night Song (p. 625)

One of Langston Hughes's most famous poems, "The Negro Speaks of Rivers," was written on a train to Mexico. Fresh out of high school, Hughes was making the trip to convince his skeptical father to pay for a writing program at Columbia University. His father agreed, and Hughes's writing career was launched. Though he remained at Columbia for only a year, Hughes developed a lifelong love for the New York neighborhood of Harlem, the setting of many of his stories, poems, and plays.

Go Online
Author Link

For: More about these poets
Visit: www.PHSchool.com
Web Code: ene-9404

CONCRETE MIXERS

Patricia Hubbell

The drivers are washing the concrete mixers;
Like elephant tenders they hose them down.
Tough gray-skinned monsters standing <u>ponderous</u>,
Elephant-bellied and elephant-nosed,
5   Standing in muck up to their wheel-caps,
Like rows of elephants, tail to trunk.
Their drivers perch on their backs like mahouts,[1]
Sending the sprays of water up.
They rid the trunk-like trough of concrete,
10   Direct the spray to the bulging sides,
Turn and start the monsters moving.
      Concrete mixers
      Move like elephants
      Bellow like elephants
15   Spray like elephants,
Concrete mixers are urban elephants,
Their trunks are raising a city.

Vocabulary Builder
ponderous (pän´ dər əs) *adj.* very heavy

Reading Skill
Context Review lines 1–8. What context clues help reveal the meaning of *muck*? Explain.

---

1. mahouts (mə houts´) *n.* in India and the East Indies, an elephant driver or keeper.

◄ Critical Viewing What details in this picture of cement mixers support the comparison in the poem? **[Connect]**

The City Is So Big

Richard García

The city is so big
Its bridges quake with fear
I know, I have seen at night

The lights sliding from house to house
5 And trains pass with windows shining
Like a smile full of teeth

I have seen machines eating houses
And stairways walk all by themselves
And elevator doors opening and closing
10 And people disappear.

Reading Skill
Context Which words help you confirm that *quake* means "tremble"?

Harlem Night Song
Langston Hughes

Come,
Let us <u>roam</u> the night together
Singing.

I love you.

5 Across
The Harlem roof-tops
Moon is shining.
Night sky is blue.
Stars are great drops
10 Of golden dew.

Down the street
A band is playing.

I love you.

Come,
15 Let us roam the night together
Singing.

Vocabulary Builder
roam (rōm) *v.* go
aimlessly; wander

Literary Analysis
**Figurative
Language** Does
Hughes use a simile
or a metaphor to
describe stars?
Explain.

Apply the Skills

Poetry Collection 1

Thinking About the Selections

1. **Respond:** Which poem do you think best captures life in a big city? Explain.
2. **(a) Recall:** In "Concrete Mixers," where are the drivers as they wash the mixers? **(b) Interpret:** How do the drivers compare in size to the trucks?
3. **(a) Recall:** In "The City Is So Big," what are three unusual events the speaker says he has seen? **(b) Interpret:** In your own words, explain what the speaker has actually seen.
4. **(a) Recall:** In "Harlem Night Song," which phrases are repeated? **(b) Analyze:** How does the repetition emphasize the joyful mood of the poem?
5. **(a) Recall:** In "Harlem Night Song," what does the speaker urge the listener to do as they "roam the night together"? **(b) Interpret:** Why would the speaker suggest this activity?

Reading Skill

6. Using the **context** surrounding the word *trough* in line 9 of "Concrete Mixers," explain what a trough looks like and what it does on a concrete mixer.
7. Read the text before and after the term *elephant tenders* in line 2 of "Concrete Mixers." **(a)** What do you think this term means? **(b)** Explain your reasoning.

Literary Analysis

8. Use a chart like the one shown to analyze examples of **figurative language** in each poem.

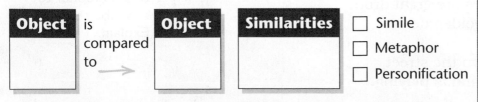

9. In a small group, review your charts. Together, choose the example of figurative language that you find most striking and share your ideas with the class.

QuickReview

Poems at a Glance

These three poems show different ways of looking at a big city. All are written in free verse.

Go Online
Assessment
For: Self-test
Visit: www.PHSchool.com
Web Code: ena-6404

Context: words and phrases surrounding a word

Figurative Language: language that conveys imaginative rather than literal meaning. Includes *figures of speech* such as *simile, metaphor,* and *personification*

Vocabulary Builder

Practice Based on your knowledge of the italicized words, answer the following questions. Explain your responses.

1. If you wanted to *roam,* where might you go?

2. What emotion might a *ponderous* sigh reveal?

Writing

Write a **study for a poem** you might write about a city setting. Your study should plan the figurative language you would use in the poem.

- List the objects, sights, and sounds that come to mind when you think of cities.
- Review the poetry in this collection and the figurative language the poets use. To think of fresh ways to describe the items in your list, use sentence starters like: ___?___ *is like* ___?___ *because* ___?___. Jot down several ideas. Then, choose the one or two ideas you like best.
- In a few sentences, explain your plan and include details about the comparisons your poem would present.

For *Grammar, Vocabulary,* and *Assessment,* see **Build Language Skills,** pages 634–635.

Extend Your Learning

Listening and Speaking Select a poem that you like from this collection. Study it and practice it aloud until you have it memorized. As you practice, experiment with the tone and volume of your voice to convey the poem's excitement and ideas. Present it to your class in a **poetry recitation.**

Research and Technology Visit your library or use the Internet to find several poems on a similar topic, such as cities, nature, sports, or courage. Create a **mini-anthology,** or collection of poems, by putting together three poems. Write an introduction to each poem explaining why you chose it. To complete the anthology, design a cover and write an introduction for your readers.

Build Understanding • *Poetry Collection 2*

Connecting to the Literature

Reading/Writing Connection The natural world is a favorite subject for poets because of its many faces. Jot down a few sentences describing nature's different sides. Use at least three of these words: *display, dissolve, maintain, innovate.*

Review

For **Reading Skill, Literary Analysis,** and **Vocabulary,** see page 620.

Meet the Authors

Pablo **Neruda** (1904–1973)
Ode to Enchanted Light (p. 629)

Chile's most acclaimed poet, Pablo Neruda won the Nobel Prize for Literature in 1971. Many of his poems are meditations on nature or on love. The son of a teacher and a railway worker, Neruda was a larger-than-life figure who inspired the Italian movie *Il Postino* ("The Postman"), in which a shy postman seeks the famous poet's romantic advice.

Elizabeth **Bishop** (1911–1979)
Little Exercise (p. 630)

Although she was born in Massachusetts, Elizabeth Bishop was raised by her grandparents in Nova Scotia, Canada. During her life, she lived and taught at various times in Europe, Brazil, New York City, and Boston. In thirty-five years, she published five volumes of poetry and won nearly every major American poetry award, including the National Book Award.

Emily **Dickinson** (1830–1886)
The Sky Is Low, the Clouds Are Mean (p. 631)

Emily Dickinson considered books her "strongest friend." Withdrawn and shy, she spent most of her time at home in Amherst, Massachusetts, reading and writing. Most of her 1,775 poems were discovered after her death, including one that begins "I'm nobody! Who are you?" She may have considered herself a "nobody" during her lifetime, but she is now considered one of the most important American poets.

Go Online
Author Link
For: More about these poets
Visit: www.PHSchool.com
Web Code: ene-9405

Ode to Enchanted Light

Pablo Neruda

Under the trees light
has dropped from the top of the sky,
light
like a green
5 latticework of branches,
shining
on every leaf,
drifting down like clean
white sand.

10 A cicada[1] sends
its sawing song
high into the empty air.

The world is
a glass overflowing
15 with water.

1. **cicada** (si kā′ de) *n.* large, flylike insects with transparent wings. The male makes a loud, shrill sound by vibrating a special organ on its undersurface.

Literary Analysis
Figurative Language What figure of speech is used in lines 4–5? Explain.

Literary Analysis
Figurative Language What figure of speech is used in the last stanza? Explain.

LITTLE EXERCISE
Elizabeth Bishop

Think of the storm roaming the sky <u>uneasily</u>
like a dog looking for a place to sleep in,
listen to it growling.

Think how they must look now, the mangrove keys[1]
5   lying out there <u>unresponsive</u> to the lightning
in dark, coarse-fibered[2] families,

where occasionally a heron may undo his head,
shake up his feathers, make an uncertain comment
when the surrounding water shines.

10   Think of the boulevard and the little palm trees
all stuck in rows, suddenly revealed
as fistfuls of limp fish-skeletons.

It is raining there. The boulevard
and its broken sidewalks with weeds in every crack,
15   are relieved to be wet, the sea to be freshened.

Now the storm goes away again in a series
of small, badly lit battle-scenes,
each in "Another part of the field."[3]

Think of someone sleeping in the bottom of a row-boat
20   tied to a mangrove root or the pile of a bridge;
think of him as uninjured, barely disturbed.

---

1. mangrove keys little islands where mangrove trees grow.
2. coarse-fibered having a structure of rough-textured strands.
3. "Another part of the field" Stage directions in plays, such as Shakespeare's *Macbeth*, often use this phrase to switch the action to a different location in a big battle.

The Sky Is Low, the Clouds Are Mean

Emily Dickinson

The sky is low, the clouds are mean,
A travelling flake of snow
Across a barn or through a <u>rut</u>
<u>Debates</u> if it will go.

5 A narrow wind complains all day
How some one treated him;
Nature, like us, is sometimes caught
Without her diadem.[1]

Vocabulary Builder
rut (rut) *n.* a groove in the ground made by a vehicle or natural causes

Debates (dē bāts´) *v.* tries to decide

---

1. diadem (dī´ ə dem´) *n.* crown.

Apply the Skills

Poetry Collection 2

Thinking About the Selections

1. **Respond:** Which poem do you think contains the most memorable images of nature? Explain.
2. **(a) Recall:** How does Pablo Neruda describe the world? **(b) Infer:** Judging from this description, what is his attitude toward life?
3. **(a) Recall:** What are three images the author asks you to "think of" in "Little Exercise"? **(b) Infer:** What could this poem be considered a "little exercise" in?
4. **(a) Recall:** Who is the one person included in "Little Exercise"? **(b) Compare and Contrast:** How do that person's surroundings contrast with his behavior? **(c) Speculate:** Why do you think it is unimportant whether he is "tied to a mangrove root or the pile of a bridge"?
5. **(a) Recall:** In "The Sky Is Low, the Clouds Are Mean," what season does the poet describe? **(b) Interpret:** What mood do the words *rut, complain,* and *mean* convey about the season?

Reading Skill

6. The word *pile* in line 20 of "Little Exercise" is used in a different way than it usually is. **(a)** Use **context clues** to determine a possible meaning. **(b)** Explain your reasoning.
7. Read the text before and after the word *latticework* in line 5 of "Ode to Enchanted Light." **(a)** What do you think this term means? **(b)** Explain your reasoning, then confirm the meaning with a dictionary.

Literary Analysis

8. Use a chart like the one shown to analyze the **figurative language** in each poem.

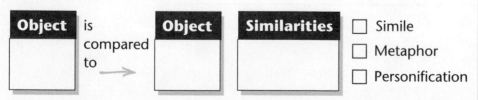

9. In a group, choose the most striking example of figurative language and share it with the class.

QuickReview

Poems at a Glance
Each of these three poems provides a unique way of looking at nature.

Assessment
For: Self-test
Visit: www.PHSchool.com
Web Code: ena-6405

Context: words and phrases surrounding a word

Figurative Language: language that conveys imaginative rather than literal meaning. Includes *figures of speech* such as *simile, metaphor,* and *personification*

Vocabulary Builder

Practice Based on your knowledge of the italicized words, answer the following questions. Explain your responses.

1. What should a customer do if a salesperson is *unresponsive*?
2. What kind of road surfaces get very few *ruts*?
3. What decision on a trip might cause a family to *debate*?
4. What type of situation might cause someone to wait *uneasily*?

Writing

Write a **study for a poem** about a natural setting. Your study should plan the figurative language you would use in a poem.

- List the objects, sights, and sounds that come to mind when you think about nature.
- Review the poetry in this collection and the figurative language the poets use. To think of fresh ways to describe the items in your list, use sentence starters like: ___?___ is like ___?___ because ___?___. Jot down several ideas. Then, choose the one or two ideas you like best.
- In a few sentences, explain your plan and include details about the comparisons your poem would present.

For *Grammar, Vocabulary,* and *Assessment,* see **Build Language Skills,** pages 634–635.

Extend Your Learning

Listening and Speaking Select a poem that you like from this collection. Study it and practice it aloud until you have it memorized. As you practice, experiment with the tone and volume of your voice to convey the poem's excitement and ideas. Present it to your class in a **poetry recitation.**

Research and Technology Visit your library or use the Internet to find several poems on a similar topic, such as cities, nature, sports, or courage. Create a **mini-anthology,** or collection of poems, by putting together three poems. Write an introduction to each poem explaining why you chose it. To complete the anthology, design a cover and write an introduction for your readers.

Build Language Skills

Vocabulary Skill

Suffixes The **suffix** *-ment* means "the act of" doing something or "the state of" being something. It is added to verbs to turn them into nouns. In the noun *restatement,* the suffix *-ment* has been added to the verb *restate. Restatement* means "the act of saying something again."

▶ **Example:** Look for a **restatement** of the idea to find context clues.

Practice Based on your understanding of the suffix *-ment,* write a definition of each word in italics. Then, write a new sentence using each italicized word.

1. *Employment* in a good career brings many rewards.
2. The bride and groom expressed their *commitment* to each other.
3. My grandparents are looking forward to their *retirement.*
4. We could not hide our *amazement* after winning the game.
5. My coach's *encouragement* helped me become a better player.

Grammar Lesson

Direct and Indirect Objects A **direct object** is a noun or pronoun that follows an action verb and answers the questions *Whom?* or *What?* An **indirect object** is a noun or pronoun that comes after an action verb and answers the questions *To whom?, For whom?, To what?,* or *For what?*

Direct Object	Indirect Object
S V DO	S V IO DO
Sentence: Bill baked some cookies.	Sentence: Bill baked Marissa some cookies.
Baked what? cookies	Baked for whom? Marissa

Practice In a three-column chart, list the verb, direct object, and indirect object for each sentence. Some sentences do not include indirect objects. Then, rewrite each sentence, supplying a different direct object.

1. Li found me a job.
2. The article gave readers facts about geology.
3. Katie sold Sam her car.
4. The guide showed the hikers a scenic view.
5. Pam delivers pizzas to residents of Los Angeles.

MorePractice

For more on Objects, see the Grammar Handbook, p. R31.

*W*G *Prentice Hall Writing and Grammar Connection: Chapter 19, Section 5*

Reading: Context Clues

Hurricane Charley, a *category four storm* with winds up to 145 miles per hour, moved in from the Gulf of Mexico and struck southwest Florida on August 13, 2004. Before it hit, newscasters warned residents that the *formidable* storm was approaching. People who lived in certain areas had to evacuate in order to be safe. The hurricane made landfall at Fort Myers, a southwest Florida city, and then *tracked* northeast across the state. Then, the hurricane moved out into the Atlantic and northward along the east coast.

1. What does *formidable* mean?

  A tropical

  B powerful

  C disgusting

  D forthcoming

2. All of the context clues help you determine the meaning of *formidable* EXCEPT

  A 145 mph winds.

  B residents were forced to evacuate.

  C newscasters issuing a warning.

  D the direction of the storm was northeast.

3. What does *tracked* mean in this selection?

  A followed

  B moved

  C trailed

  D charted

4. Which of the following does not help determine the meaning of *tracked*?

  A The storm went northeast.

  B The hurricane made landfall at Fort Myers.

  C The hurricane moved into the Atlantic.

  D Newscasters issuing a warning.

5. What can the reader infer about a *category four storm?*

  A usually not dangerous

  B a weak storm

  C a storm that is dangerous

  D of unpredictable strength

Timed Writing: Analysis [Connections]

Choose a poem from *Collection 1* or *Collection 2*. Write a brief analysis of the way the poet used figurative language in the poem. Use specifics from the poem to support your ideas. **(25 minutes)**

 ## Writing Workshop: *Work in Progress*

Writing for Assessment

Some assessment writing requires you to respond to a visual prompt. Look at the door of your classroom. In five minutes, describe the door in enough detail that someone could draw it accurately. Save this work in your writing portfolio.

Imagery

Imagery is poetic language that uses images—words or phrases that appeal to the senses of sight, hearing, touch, taste, or smell. In addition to this sensory language, poets sometimes use the following techniques to create humorous effects with imagery:

- pairing images that do not usually go together, such as a fish on a bicycle
- using imagery to describe common situations from unusual perspectives, such as showing an ant's eye view of a picnic or a crowd
- describing a familiar situation in a humorous way, such as sitting in a traffic jam watching pedestrians moving faster than you are

Comparing Humorous Imagery

Humor is based on personal tastes—you may enjoy something that a friend does not find funny at all. Each of the following poems contains imagery that is meant to entertain.

When you read a poem with humorous imagery, imagine the sights, sounds, smells, feelings, or tastes of these images as you read. Then, identify what it is about these images that amuses you.

Compare the imagery in these three poems by using a chart like the one shown.

Poem	
Image	**Senses**

Vocabulary Builder

Southbound on the Freeway

- **transparent** (trans par´ ənt) *adj.* capable of being seen through; clear (p. 638) *The water in the lake was so <u>transparent</u> you could see every rock.*

The Country

- **inhabitants** (in hab´ i tənts) *n.* people or animals that live in a specific region (p. 641) *Many <u>inhabitants</u> of Beverly Hills are movie stars.*

The Choice

- **billowing** (bil´ ō iŋ) *adj.* swelling or surging (p. 642) *<u>Billowing</u>, dark clouds preceded the storm.*

- **smoldering** (smōl´ dər iŋ) *adj.* burning or smoking without flame (p. 642) *After the fire, the house was nothing but a <u>smoldering</u> shell.*

- **lilting** (lilt´ iŋ) *adj.* graceful and rhythmic, especially in speech (p. 642) *Her <u>lilting</u> voice was perfect for radio announcing.*

Connecting to the Literature

Reading/Writing Connection These three poems describe ordinary things in innovative and funny ways. In sentences, identify and explain three subjects that might be suited to a poem that uses humorous imagery. Use three of these words: *capture, coincide, display, illustrate, modify.*

Meet the Authors

May **Swenson** (1919–1989)

May Swenson grew up in Utah, speaking Swedish in her childhood home. She wrote poetry for children as well as for adults. Swenson believed that poetry is based on the desire to see things as they are, rather than as they appear. Her poems often present a completely different perspective on ordinary life.

Billy **Collins** (b. 1941)

After he wrote several best-selling books of poetry, Billy Collins was selected as Poet Laureate by the National Library of Congress in 2001. Most people who read Collins feel an immediate connection. "As I'm writing, I'm always reader-conscious," he explains. "Stepping from the title to the first lines is like stepping into a canoe. A lot of things can go wrong."

Dorothy **Parker** (1893–1967)

At age twenty-one, Dorothy Parker sold her first poem to *Vanity Fair* magazine. Five years later, she became a founding member of the Algonquin Round Table, a group of writers that met at the Algonquin Hotel in New York City to exchange ideas and witty remarks. Parker lived in an era when women's roles were changing. In this atmosphere, she quickly won a reputation for her sharp wit and intelligence, and became a symbol of the cultured modern woman.

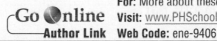

Go Online
Author Link

For: More about these poets
Visit: www.PHSchool.com
Web Code: ene-9406

SOUTHBOUND ON THE FREEWAY

May Swenson

A tourist came in from Orbitville,
parked in the air, and said:

The creatures of this star
are made of metal and glass.

5   Through the <u>transparent</u> parts
you can see their guts.

Their feet are round and roll
on diagrams—or long

measuring tapes—dark
10   with white lines.

They have four eyes.
The two in the back are red.

Sometimes you can see a five-eyed
one, with a red eye turning
15   on the top of his head.
He must be special—

the others respect him,
and go slow,

when he passes, winding
20   among them from behind.

They all hiss as they glide,
like inches, down the marked

tapes. Those soft shapes,
shadowy inside

25   the hard bodies—are they
their guts or their brains?

◀ **Critical Viewing**
What details in this painting can be found in the poem's descriptions? **[Connect]**

Literary Analysis
Imagery What unexpected comparisons does the author make to create humorous imagery?

Literary Analysis
Imagery To which senses does the imagery in line 21 appeal?

Thinking About the Selection

1. **Respond:** Which images in the poem appeal to you most? Why?
2. **(a) Recall:** Where does the "tourist" in this poem live?
   (b) Infer: Why does the speaker use the term *tourist*?
   (c) Deduce: What is the tourist describing?
3. **(a) Recall:** What kinds of creatures are mentioned in the poem?
   (b) Compare and Contrast: Compare and contrast the different kinds of creatures the tourist describes.
4. **Speculate:** What other questions might an alien tourist ask about our culture?

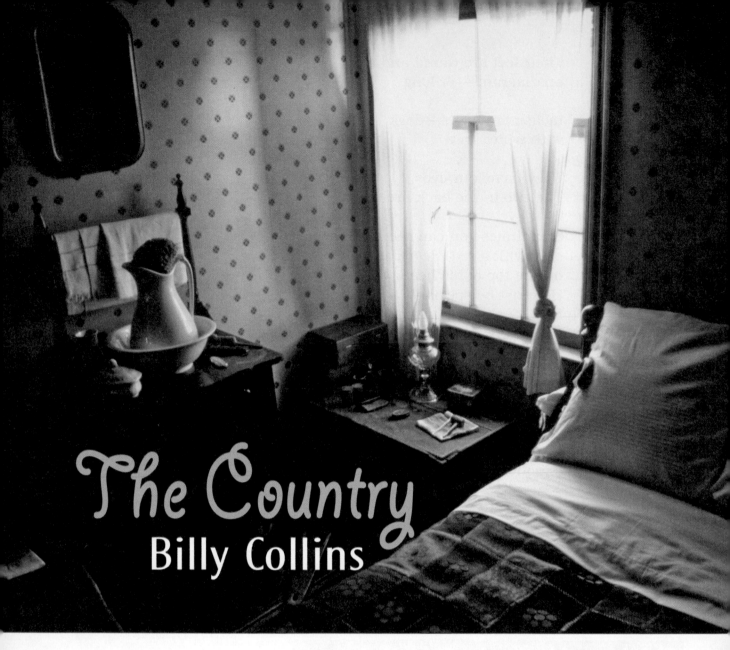

The Country
Billy Collins

I wondered about you
when you told me never to leave
a box of wooden, strike-anywhere matches
lying around the house because the mice

5   might get into them and start a fire.
But your face was absolutely straight
when you twisted the lid down on the round tin
where the matches, you said, are always stowed.

Who could sleep that night?
10 Who could whisk away the thought

▲ **Critical Viewing**
What details in this picture suggest that this is a room in a vacation home in the country? **[Analyze]**

of the one unlikely mouse
padding along a cold water pipe

behind the floral wallpaper
gripping a single wooden match
15 between the needles of his teeth?
Who could not see him rounding a corner,

the blue tip scratching against a rough-hewn beam,
the sudden flare, and the creature
for one bright, shining moment
20 suddenly thrust ahead of his time—

now a fire-starter, now a torchbearer
in a forgotten ritual, little brown druid[1]
illuminating some ancient night.
Who could fail to notice,

25 lit up in the blazing insulation,
the tiny looks of wonderment on the faces
of his fellow mice, onetime <u>inhabitants</u>
of what once was your house in the country?

Literary Analysis
Imagery What words or phrases make the image of the mouse humorous in lines 10–22?

Vocabulary Builder
inhabitants (in hab´ i tants) *n.* people or animals that live in a specific region

---

1. druid (droo´ id) *n.* member of a group of poets, judges, and priests in ancient Ireland and England. Druids wore long robes and carried torches at mysterious nighttime ceremonies.

Thinking About the Selection

1. **Respond:** What image did you like best from this poem? Explain.

2. **(a) Recall:** What event does the speaker worry about?
   (b) Interpret: Why does the speaker worry?

3. **(a) Recall:** Where is the "unlikely mouse" as he carries the match? **(b) Compare and Contrast:** How are the actions and behavior of this mouse different from what you might expect?

4. **(a) Recall:** What is the mouse's "one bright, shining moment"?
   (b) Connect: What connection does the speaker make between the mouse and ancient humans?

5. **Make a Judgment:** Could the events the poet describes actually happen? Why or why not?

The Choice

DOROTHY PARKER

He'd have given me rolling lands,
   Houses of marble, and <u>billowing</u> farms,
Pearls, to trickle between my hands,
   <u>Smoldering</u> rubies, to circle my arms.
5 You—you'd only a <u>lilting</u> song.
   Only a melody, happy and high,
You were sudden and swift and strong,—
   Never a thought for another had I.

He'd have given me laces rare,
10   Dresses that glimmered with frosty sheen,
Shining ribbons to wrap my hair,
   Horses to draw me, as fine as a queen.
You—you'd only to whistle low,
   Gaily I followed wherever you led.
15 I took you, and I let him go,—
   Somebody ought to examine my head!

Vocabulary Builder
billowing (bil′ ō iŋ)
adj. swelling or
surging

smoldering (smōl′ dər
iŋ) *adj.* burning or
smoking without
flame

lilting (lilt′ iŋ) *adj.*
graceful and
rhythmic, especially
in speech

Thinking About the Selection

1. **Respond:** Would you enjoy the company of the speaker in "The Choice"? Explain.

2. **(a) Recall:** What choice does the speaker make?
   (b) Analyze: Why does she choose as she does?

3. **(a) Recall:** What would the rejected boyfriend have given the speaker? **(b) Infer:** Does the speaker regret the decision she made? **(c) Support:** What details or words in the poem make you think so?

4. **Analyze:** How is the last line different from what the poem leads you to expect?

Apply the Skills

Southbound on the Freeway • The Country • The Choice

Comparing Humorous Imagery

1. **(a)** Which two poems describe ordinary occurrences or sights? **(b)** What makes each description humorous?

2. **(a)** Which poem describes something that is out of the ordinary? **(b)** What makes the description humorous?

3. **(a)** Which poem reveals its humor in the very last line? **(b)** Is this an effective technique? Why or why not?

4. On a chart like the one shown, list two examples of imagery from each poem. For each, explain how the image adds humor to the poem.

Poem	Image	Humor
Southbound on the Freeway		
The Country		
The Choice		

QuickReview

Humorous imagery: amusing writing that appeals to the senses

Go Online
Assessment

For: Self-test
Visit: www.PHSchool.com
Web Code: ena-6406

Writing to Compare Literary Works

The authors of these three poems approach humor differently. In a brief essay, explain the source of the humor in each poem, and evaluate how effective the imagery is in making the poem funny. Follow these steps:

- Describe the imagery in each poem.
- Explain how the humor is connected with the imagery.
- Explain the effect on the reader.

Vocabulary Builder

Practice Each vocabulary word below is paired with another word. Write a single sentence using both words.

1. smoldering/campfire
2. billowing/smoke
3. lilting/music
4. transparent/glass
5. inhabitants/village

Reading: Context Clues

Directions: *Read the selection. Then, answer the questions.*

The moon, Earth's only natural *satellite,* changes in appearance monthly as it orbits around our planet. It *waxes* and then wanes, seeming to increase and then decrease in size, from full moon to quarter, to crescent, to the nearly invisible new moon. Before the age of modern science, these *phases* of the moon inspired many legends, or stories, that attempted to explain the changes. Although these explanations are not scientifically accurate, they do show that ancient people were *diligent* observers of the night sky, carefully studying and accurately noting changes in the heavens.

1. **What is the best definition of *satellite* as used in the selection?**
   A a planet
   B a star
   C something that orbits a planet
   D something not scientifically accurate

2. **Which context provides the best clue to the meaning of *satellite*?**
   A changes in appearance
   B it orbits around our planet
   C increase and then decrease in size
   D from full moon to quarter

3. **Based on its context, what is the best definition of *waxes*?**
   A increases
   B decreases
   C becomes invisible
   D grows shadowy

4. **What does the word *phases* mean in this selection?**
   A stages in becoming an adult
   B regular, predictable changes in appearance
   C endings
   D times of confusion

5. **From the context, what does *diligent* mean?**
   A imaginative
   B uninformed
   C careless
   D careful

Assessment Practice

Vocabulary

Directions: *Choose the best definition.*

6. context
A words that are synonyms
B words and phrases surrounding a word
C words that are explained after a comma
D words in an appositive

7. confirm
A say in different words
B figure out
C be clear
D make certain

8. clarify
A say in different words
B figure out
C make clear
D make certain

9. restatement
A do again
B state before
C something stated again
D something stated before

10. synonymous
A opposite in meaning
B similar in meaning
C negative meaning
D words that are spelled the same

Directions: *Choose the answer that correctly completes each sentence.*

11. When you add the suffix *-ous* to the word *humor* to form *humorous,* you change
A an adjective into a noun.
B a noun into an adjective.
C an adjective into a verb.
D a verb into a noun.

12. Which is an adjective that means "having the quality of joy"?
A joyless   C joyous
B joyfulness   D joyfully

13. What does *suspicious* mean?
A full of suspicion
B without suspicion
C the act of suspecting
D a person who catches suspects

14. Which word is a synonym for *courageous*?
A bravery
B brave
C coward
D cowardly

15. What part of speech is the word *employment*?
A noun
B verb
C adjective
D adverb

Exposition: Writing for Assessment

When you **write for assessment**, you usually have to respond to directions and prepare an answer in a limited time. Follow the steps outlined here to practice writing for assessment.

Assignment Answer the following sample essay-test question, or ask your teacher to provide you with one:

> Identify two people in literature or life who you feel acted heroically. Explain and defend your choices.

What to Include To be successful, your writing for assessment should include these elements:
- a response that addresses all parts of a writing prompt
- a main idea supported by evidence
- a clear and logical organization
- error-free writing with appropriate use of active and passive voice

To preview the criteria on which your writing for assessment may be judged, see the rubric on page 650.

Prewriting

Spend about one quarter of your time prewriting.

Choosing Your Topic

Match the task with your time. If you are given a choice of topics, choose the topic you know best, or one you have studied.

Gathering Details

Analyze the prompt. Study the instructions to determine what you need to write. The chart identifies common key words that show the type of information the response requires.

Quick List Before you write, jot down ideas to use in your draft.

Words	Essay Objectives
Analyze	Examine how elements contribute to the whole
Compare/Contrast	Stress how subjects are alike/different
Define	Give examples to explain meaning
Discuss	Support generalizations with facts and examples

Using the Form
You may use elements of this form in these types of writing:
- chapter or unit tests
- end of course exams
- standardized tests

Work in Progress
Review the work you did on pages 595, 615, and 635.

Drafting

Spend about half your time drafting.

Shaping Your Writing

Plan an organization. Use an organization that supports your goals.

- **Order of Importance:** For persuasion, or to stress key points, organize your ideas from most important to least important. As you draft, save your most important point for the end.

- **Chronological Order:** For a summary, an explanation, or a narrative, organize details in the order in which they happen.

Providing Elaboration

Support your ideas. For each idea, include a variety of supporting details, such as facts, names, dates, explanations, and examples.

Reading Writing
Connection

To read the complete student model, see page 649.

Student Model: Supporting Ideas with Details

Prompt: Look out any window in your home. What would you change about what you see?

Change: Improve the neighborhood's appearance

Description: There is trash everywhere and no safe place to play

Explanation: A playground and community center would give children and teens a safe place to go

> Amnesti's notes help her quickly gather evidence for her essay.

Revising

Spend about one quarter of your time revising and editing.

Revising Your Overall Structure

Check your introduction and conclusion. Review your introduction and conclusion. Ask yourself:
- Does my introduction clearly reflect the instructions?
- Does it clearly state what I will cover in the rest of the essay?
- Do the ideas in my introduction and conclusion match?

Revising Your Word Choice

Evaluate vague words. Replace vague words with more precise ones.

Vague		Precise
He had *nice* ideas.	⟶	He had *innovative* ideas.

Integrating Grammar Skills

Revising Active and Passive Voice

Voice is a verb form that shows whether the subject of a sentence is performing the action or receiving it. Writing is stronger when most sentences use the active voice.

Identifying Active and Passive Voice A verb is in the **active voice** when the subject performs the action. A verb is in the **passive voice** when its subject does not perform the action.

Prentice Hall Writing and Grammar Connection: Chapter 22, Section 2

Active Voice	Passive Voice
Lightning **struck** the barn.	The barn **was struck** by lightning.
My family **is painting** the house.	The house **is being painted** by my family.

While active voice is preferred, the passive voice is used to stress the action, not the performer. It is also used when the performer is unknown.

To show unknown performer: The office was closed.

To stress action: The goal was exceeded.

Fixing Active and Passive Voice To review and revise the use of voice, follow these steps:

1. **Locate the subject and verb in each sentence.** Determine whether the subject performs the action.

2. **If the subject performs the action, consider rewriting the sentence in active voice.**
   Verb: declare
   Active Voice: We *declared* the experiment a success.

3. **If the performer of the action is unknown or unimportant, you might want to use the passive voice.** A passive verb is a verb phrase made from a form of *be* with a past participle.
   Verb: declare
   Passive Voice: The building *was declared* unsafe.

Apply It to Your Editing

Choose two paragraphs in your draft. Underline every verb and identify it as active or passive. Analyze your choices. When appropriate, rewrite sentences in the active voice.

Student Model: Amnesti Terrell
Memphis, TN

Writing Prompt: Look out any window in your home. What would you change about what you see?

As I look out my bedroom window, I see the whole neighborhood. I see a lot of things, both good and bad. I see children playing outside on the weekends and after school. I see parades marching through the street during the holidays. I see watchful neighbors keeping an eye on the neighborhood. All of these are great sights, but they get overlooked because of all of the problems in the neighborhood. My neighborhood used to be nice and quiet, but lately it has become worse. Something needs to change before it is too late.

The first thing that I would like to change to improve my neighborhood is to make it safer. I want to be able to walk inside a store and not have to wait until a fight is over so I can leave. People have to stop trying to impress others by picking fights with everyone they see. I could feel safer if people were more respectful toward each other.

I also want to change the appearance of my neighborhood. There is trash everywhere. I hate having to clean up after someone else just because they do not know how to put trash into a trashcan. I would also like to add some things. People in the neighborhood need a place to play and think. A playground would be a safe place for small children to play. This would be a place where the children would not have to worry about careless drivers or street fights. I would also like to build a community center for teens to have fun, play sports, and be themselves. The center would be a place that helps teens figure out that they can do anything if they put their minds to it. It could be called The Hope Center.

Finally, I would like to change the attitude toward the schools in my neighborhood. Walker Elementary and Ford Road Elementary have math and spelling bees every year, but they do not grab the headlines. Neither school gets positive recognition in the media. Positive attention would help everyone feel better about schools and the work teachers and students do.

My neighborhood is not bad. It just needs a few adjustments like any other neighborhood. So as I look out of my bedroom window, I see what it once was, what it has become, and what it has the potential to be. By committing to local safety and community spaces, we could take important steps toward improvements that can help everyone. I will do everything I can to help improve my neighborhood.

In the introduction, Amnesti answers part of the prompt by giving a balanced description of what she sees.

She addresses the rest of the prompt in paragraphs 2–4 by explaining three ideas that develop her response.

The essay uses the proper conventions of grammar, usage, and mechanics.

Amnesti organizes her essay with a conclusion that summarizes her response.

Editing and Proofreading

Check your writing to correct errors in spelling and grammar. Mark corrections neatly so your writing can be read easily.

Focus on Punctuation: Make sure you have started every sentence with a capital letter and ended it with the appropriate punctuation.

Publishing and Presenting

Consider these ideas for sharing your work.

Discuss with a group. Compare your test responses to those of others by using your essays as the springboard for a class discussion.

Create a review folder. Set aside a folder for old tests, and place a copy of your writing for assessment in it. When you study for future tests, use your essays to remind you of the effective writing strategies you used.

Reflecting on Your Writing

Writer's Journal Take a few moments to think about writing for assessment. Then, answer the following questions in your journal.
- What are your strengths and weaknesses as a test taker?
- Which stage of the writing process did you find most important as you wrote for assessment? Why?

> *Prentice Hall Writing and Grammar Connection: Chapter 13*

Rubric for Self-Assessment

To assess your writing for assessment, use the following rubric:

Criteria	Rating Scale not very very
Focus: How clearly do you state your main idea?	1 2 3 4 5
Organization: How well do you employ a clear and logical organization?	1 2 3 4 5
Support/Elaboration: How effective is the evidence that supports your ideas?	1 2 3 4 5
Style: How thoroughly have you stated your ideas in the time and space allowed?	1 2 3 4 5
Conventions: How correct is your grammar, especially your use of active and passive voice?	1 2 3 4 5

Skills You Will Learn

Reading Skill: *Reread to Clarify Meaning*
Literary Analysis: *Forms of Poetry: Lyric and Narrative*

Reading Skill: *Read Aloud Fluently According to Punctuation*
Literary Analysis: *Imagery*

Reading Skill: *Read to Perform a Task*

Literary Analysis: *Comparing Types of Description*

Literature You Will Read

Reading: Paraphrasing

▶ **Paraphrasing** is restating text in your own words.

Skills and Strategies You Will Learn in Part 2

In Part 2, you will learn

- to **reread** in order to clarify ideas **for paraphrasing** (p. 654)
- to read **according to punctuation** to help you **paraphrase** (p. 676)
- to **paraphrase** instructions in order to perform a task (p. 698)

Using the Skills and Strategies in Part 2

In Part 2, you will learn to clarify ideas in a passage by rereading and restating them in your own words. You also will practice using punctuation to help you recognize complete thoughts as you paraphrase. You will practice paraphrasing instructions to help you understand them.

Read the following lines from the poem "Ring Out, Wild Bells." Then, look at how one writer paraphrased them.

▶ **Original:** Ring out the grief that saps the mind,

For those that here we see no more;

Ring out the feud of rich and poor,

Ring in redress to all mankind.

▶ **Paraphrase:** Take away the sadness we feel for our friends who have died. Stop the fighting between rich people and poor people. Bring justice to everyone.

As you read the literature in this part, you will practice paraphrasing what you have read.

Academic Vocabulary: Words for Discussing Paraphrasing

The following words will help you write and talk about paraphrasing.

Word	Definition	Example Sentence
reflect *v.*	mirror an image; express or show	Your paraphrase should *reflect* the author's meaning.
convey *v.*	to carry meaning; to communicate	*Convey* the author's meaning in your own words.
emphasize *v.*	to stress	*Emphasize* the author's main points.
restate *v.*	to express the same idea in a different way	*Restate* the sentence in your own words.
adapt *v.*	to change something to make it more suitable	*Adapt* the author's language to fit your own style of writing.

Vocabulary Skills You Will Learn in Part 2

▶ The **origin** of a word is its history.

Dictionary Abbreviations

ME = Middle English
OF = Old French
L = Latin
< means "coming from"

Many dictionaries give word origins listed in order from the most recent to the oldest. Look at the sample entry for the word *convey*.

> **convey (kən vāˊ) vt.** [[ME *conveien* < OF *convoier*, to escort, to accompany < L *com-*, together + *via*, way]]

The word *convey* came into modern English from Middle English, which borrowed the word from Old French, a language that had borrowed the word from Latin.

Activity In a dictionary, read the origin of each word. Find one other word that shares the same origin. Then, write a sentence explaining how the origin of each word helps you remember the meaning.

1. reflect   **2.** restate   **3.** emphasize   **4.** adapt

You can apply the instruction on this page to these poems.

Reading Skill

When you **paraphrase,** you restate a text in your own words. Before you paraphrase a line or a passage, **reread to clarify** the writer's meaning. First, identify the most basic information in each sentence. Then, begin putting the whole sentence into your own words.

- Restate details more simply.
- Use synonyms for the writer's words.
- Look up unfamiliar words. Replace unusual words and sentence structures with language that is more like everyday speech.

Use a chart like the one shown to help you paraphrase poetry.

Poem	
Line from poem	
Basic information	
Paraphrase	

Literary Analysis

Two major forms of poetry are lyric poetry and narrative poetry.

- A **lyric poem** expresses the thoughts and feelings of a single **speaker**—the person "saying" the poem—to create a single, unified impression.
- A **narrative poem** tells a story in verse and has all the elements of a short story—characters, setting, conflict, and plot.
  As you read, notice the elements of lyric and narrative poetry.

Vocabulary Builder

Poetry Collection 1

- **beckoning** (bek′ ə niŋ′) *adj.* calling or summoning (p. 656) *Tired of snow, I could not resist Hawaii's beckoning breezes.*

- **anguish** (aŋ′ gwish) *n.* great suffering (p. 657) *He felt anguish over his failure.*

- **ingratitude** (in grat′ i tōōd) *n.* lack of thankfulness (p. 659) *I will take back my gift because of your ingratitude.*

- **legacy** (leg′ ə sē) *n.* anything handed down from an ancestor (p. 660) *Amy's legacy from her grandpa included a horse.*

Poetry Collection 2

- **yearning** (yʉr′ niŋ) *adj.* filled with the feeling of wanting something (p. 665) *They watched the clock, yearning for lunchtime.*

- **somber** (säm′ bər) *adj.* dark; gloomy (p. 667) *Do not joke with someone in a somber mood.*

- **aghast** (ə gast′) *adj.* feeling great horror or dismay (p. 670) *We were aghast on hearing of the missing child.*

- **complacent** (kəm plā′ sənt) *adj.* smug; self-satisfied (p. 671) *Feeling complacent about her grades, she did not study for the test.*

Connecting to the Literature

Reading/Writing Connection The poems in this group communicate a range of emotions and events: bitterness, betrayal, fear, courage, love, and loss. Make a list of reasons why people might want to read about other people's feelings and experiences. Use at least three of the following words: *perceive, react, respond, stimulate.*

Meet the Authors

Robert **Hayden** (1913–1980)
Runagate Runagate (p. 656)
    Raised in a poor Detroit neighborhood, Robert Hayden was the first African American poet appointed as Consultant of Poetry to the Library of Congress. His poetry covers a wide range of subjects—from personal remembrances to celebrations of the history and achievements of African Americans.

William **Shakespeare** (1564–1616)
Blow, Blow, Thou Winter Wind (p. 659)
    William Shakespeare is regarded by some as the greatest writer in the English language. Born in Stratford-on-Avon, a small town in England, he moved to London as a young man and spent most of his adult life there. Shakespeare was an actor, a producer, and a director. However, he is most famous for his plays and poems.

Ricardo **Sánchez** (1941–1995)
Old Man (p. 660)
    Ricardo Sánchez was born in El Paso, Texas. His family had roots in Spanish, Mexican, and Native American cultures. Most of Sánchez's work explores and celebrates his rich cultural heritage. In the poem "Old Man," Sánchez offers a portrait of a grandfather he remembers with love.

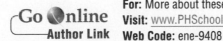

Go **Online**
Author Link

For: More about these poets
Visit: www.PHSchool.com
Web Code: ene-9408

RUNAGATE RUNAGATE

Robert Hayden

Background The term *runagate* refers to the runaway slaves who escaped to the North from slave states via the Underground Railroad. "Conductors," or guides, led the slaves by night to appointed "stations," where they received food, shelter, and clothing.

I.

Runs falls rises stumbles on from darkness into darkness
and the darkness thicketed with shapes of terror
and the hunters pursuing and the hounds pursuing
and the night cold and the night long and the river
5 to cross and the jack-muh-lanterns[1] <u>beckoning</u> beckoning
and blackness ahead and when shall I reach that somewhere
morning and keep on going and never turn back and keep
　　on going
　　　　　　　Runagate
　　　　　　　　　　　Runagate
10　　　　　　　　　　　　　Runagate

Many thousands rise and go
many thousands crossing over

---

1. jack-muh-lanterns (jak´ mə lan´ tərnz) *n.* jack-o'-lanterns, shifting lights seen over a marsh at night.

O mythic North
O star-shaped yonder Bible city

15 Some go weeping and some rejoicing
    some in coffins and some in carriages
    some in silks and some in shackles

            Rise and go or fare you well

    No more auction block for me
20 no more driver's lash for me

        If you see my Pompey, 30 yrs of age,
        new breeches, plain stockings, negro shoes;
        if you see my Anna, likely young mulatto
        branded E on the right cheek, R on the left,
25   catch them if you can and notify subscriber.[2]
        Catch them if you can, but it won't be easy.
        They'll dart underground when you try to catch them,
        plunge into quicksand, whirlpools, mazes,
        turn into scorpions when you try to catch them.

30 And before I'll be a slave
    I'll be buried in my grave

        North star and bonanza gold
        I'm bound for the freedom, freedom-bound
        and oh Susyanna don't you cry for me

35   Runagate

                Runagate

    II.
    Rises from their <u>anguish</u> and their power,

                Harriet Tubman,

                woman of earth, whipscarred,
40   a summoning, a shining

                Mean to be free

    And this was the way of it, brethren brethren,
    way we journeyed from Can't to Can.

Literary Analysis
Forms of Poetry
How does the perspective of the first-person point of view change between lines 19–20 and lines 21–29?

Vocabulary Builder
anguish (aŋ´ gwish) *n.* great suffering

✔**Reading Check**

Who is Harriet Tubman?

---

2. subscriber (səb skrīb´ ər) *n.* here, the person from whom the slave Pompey ran away.

45 Moon so bright and no place to hide,
the cry up and the patterollers[3] riding,
hound dogs belling in bladed air.
And fear starts a-murbling, Never make it,
we'll never make it. *Hush that now,*
50 and she's turned upon us, leveled pistol
glinting in the moonlight:
Dead folks can't jaybird-talk, she says;
You keep on going now or die, she says.

Wanted   Harriet Tubman   alias The General
55 alias Moses   Stealer of Slaves
In league with Garrison   Alcott   Emerson
Garrett   Douglass   Thoreau   John Brown[4]

Armed and known to be Dangerous

Wanted   Reward   Dead or Alive

60 Tell me, Ezekiel, oh tell me do you see
mailed Jehovah[5] coming to deliver me?

Hoot-owl calling in the ghosted air,
five times calling to the hants[6] in the air.
Shadow of a face in the scary leaves,
65 shadow of a voice in the talking leaves:

Come ride-a my train

Oh that train, ghost-story train
through swamp and savanna movering movering,
over trestles of dew, through caves of the wish,
70 *Midnight Special on a sabre track movering movering,*
first stop Mercy and the last Hallelujah.

Come ride-a my train

Mean mean mean to be free.

---

3. **patterollers** (pa′ tər ôl ərz) (pə trōl′ ərz) *n.* dialect for *patrollers,* people who hunt for runaways.
4. **Garrison . . . John Brown** various abolitionists, people who were against slavery.
5. **Ezekiel** (I zē′ kē əl) **. . . Jehovah** (ji hō′ və) Ezekiel was a Hebrew prophet of the sixth century B.C.; Jehovah is another word for *God.*
6. **hants** (hantz) *n.* dialect term for *ghosts.*

Blow, Blow, Thou Winter Wind

WILLIAM SHAKESPEARE

Blow, blow, thou winter wind.
Thou art not so unkind
    As man's <u>ingratitude</u>.
Thy tooth is not so keen,
5   Because thou art not seen,
    Although thy breath be rude.
Heigh-ho! Sing, heigh-ho! unto the green holly.
Most friendship is feigning, most loving mere folly.[1]
    Then, heigh-ho, the holly!
10   This life is most jolly.

Freeze, freeze, thou bitter sky,
That dost not bite so nigh
    As benefits forgot.
Though thou the waters warp,[2]
15   Thy sting is not so sharp
    As friend remembered not.
Heigh-ho! Sing, heigh-ho! unto the green holly.
Most friendship is feigning, most loving mere folly.
    Then, heigh-ho, the holly!
20   This life is most jolly.

Vocabulary Builder
ingratitude (in grat´ i tōōd) *n.* lack of thankfulness

Literary Analysis
Forms of Poetry
To what does the speaker compare the winter's chill in this lyric poem?

---

1. **feigning . . . folly** Most friendship is fake, most loving is foolish.
2. **warp** *v.* freeze.

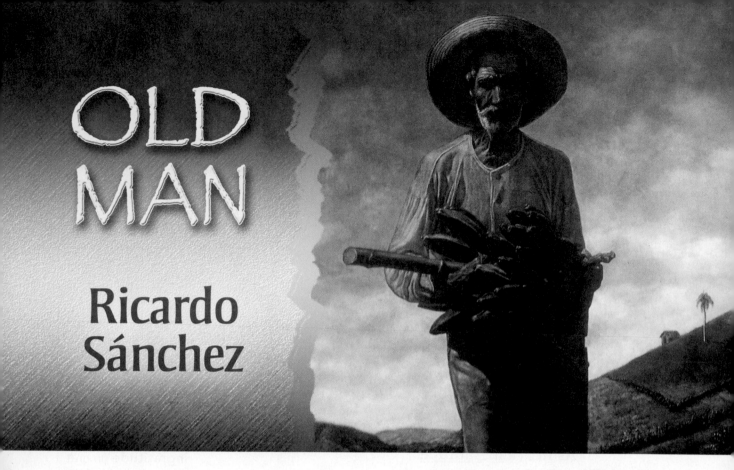

OLD MAN

Ricardo Sánchez

remembrance
(smiles/hurts sweetly)
October 8, 1972

old man
with brown skin
talking of past
   when being shepherd
5   in utah, nevada, colorado and
       new mexico
was life lived freely;

old man,
   grandfather,
10 wise with time
running rivulets on face,
deep, rich furrows,[1]
   each one a <u>legacy</u>,
deep, rich memories of life . . .

---

1. rivulets . . . furrows here, the wrinkles on the old man's face.

▲ Critical Viewing
What features of this man might earn him the respect of others? **[Analyze]**

Vocabulary Builder
legacy (leg′ ə sē)
n. anything handed down from an ancestor

"you are indio,[2]
    among other things,"
he would tell me
    during nights spent
so long ago
    amidst familial gatherings
in albuquerque . . .

old man, loved and respected,
he would speak sometimes
of pueblos,[3]
    san juan, santa clara,
    and even santo domingo,
and his family, he would say,
    came from there:
    some of our blood was here,
    he would say,
    before the coming of coronado,[4]
other of our blood
    came with los españoles,[5]
and the mixture
was rich,
    though often painful . . .
old man,
who knew earth
    by its awesome aromas
and who felt
the heated sweetness
    of chile verde[6]
by his supple touch,
gone into dust is your body
    with its stoic[7] look and resolution,
but your reality, old man, lives on
in a mindsoul touched by you . . .

Old Man . . .

---

2. **indio** (inʹ dē ō) *n.* Indian; Native American.
3. **pueblos** (pwebʹ lōz) *n.* here, Native American towns in central and northern New Mexico.
4. **coronado** (kôrʹ ə näʹ dō) The sixteenth-century Spanish explorer Francisco Vásquez de Coronado journeyed through what is today the American Southwest.
5. **los españoles** (lôs es päʹ nyōlās) *n.* Spaniards.
6. **chile verde** (chilʹ lē verʹ dā) *n.* green pepper.
7. **stoic** (stōʹ ik) *adj.* calm in the face of suffering.

Reading Skill
Paraphrase In your own words, tell who the speaker describes and what the speaker says about this person.

Literary Analysis
Forms of Poetry Why does the speaker respect the old man?

Apply the Skills

Poetry Collection 1

Thinking About the Selections

1. **Respond:** Which poem did you find most meaningful? Why?
2. **(a)** Fill out a chart like the one shown to interpret the lines indicated. **(b) Discuss:** In a small group, discuss your responses. Then, share your ideas with the class.

	What Does It Say?	What Does It Mean?	Why Is It Important?
Runagate	(Lines 1–2)		
Blow, Blow	(Line 8)		
Old Man	(Lines 8–14)		

Reading Skill

3. **(a)** Which words in lines 1–3 from "Blow, Blow, Thou Winter Wind" tell who or what the sentence is about? **(b) Paraphrase** the lines, using everyday speech.
4. **(a)** What synonyms could be used for the underlined words in these lines from "Old Man"? "gone into dust is your body/ with its stoic look and resolution, / but your reality, old man, lives on/ in a mindsoul touched by you . . ." **(b)** Paraphrase the lines, using the synonyms you chose.
5. Reread the first stanza of "Runagate Runagate." **(a)** Write the lines in sentences. **(b)** Paraphrase each sentence.

Literary Analysis

6. **(a)** What thoughts and feelings about winter and human nature are expressed in the **lyric poem** "Blow, Blow, Thou Winter Wind"? **(b)** What overall impression is created? Explain.
7. **(a)** What thoughts and feelings about the poet's grandfather are expressed in the lyric poem "Old Man"? **(b)** What overall impression does the poem create? Explain.
8. **(a)** What is the main subject of the story told in the **narrative poem** "Runagate Runagate"? **(b)** Identify the time and place, or setting, of the poem. **(c)** What is the poem's conflict?

QuickReview

Poems at a Glance

"Runagate Runagate": a narrative poem about an escape

"Blow, Blow, Thou Winter Wind": a lyric poem about false friendship

"Old Man": a poem about a grandfather

For: Self-test
Visit: www.PHSchool.com
Web Code: ena-6407

Paraphrase: to restate something in your own words

Lyric Poetry: verse that expresses the thoughts and feelings of a single *speaker*

Narrative Poetry: verse that tells a story

Vocabulary Builder

Practice Analogies show the relationships between words. Use a word from Poetry Collection 1 on page 654 to create a word pair that matches the relationship between the first two words given.

1. *Acting* is to *performing* as _____ is to *calling*.

2. *Thankfulness* is to _____ as *wealth* is to *poverty*.

3. *Success* is to *satisfaction* as *loss* is to _____.

4. *Wealth* is to *fortune* as *inheritance* is to _____.

Writing

Write a **lyric or narrative poem** about a person whom you admire. Your subject can be a historical figure or someone you know.

- If you are writing a lyric poem, brainstorm for details about the person's qualities.
- If you are writing a narrative poem, list the events, characters, and details of setting you will include in the poem.

Use your notes to draft the lines of your poem. To revise, look for places where you can replace words with synonyms that have a more musical quality.

For *Grammar, Vocabulary,* and *Assessment,*
see **Build Language Skills,** pp. 674–675.

Extend Your Learning

Listening and Speaking In a group, prepare an **evaluation form** for poetry reading. Identify the different qualities of a good poetry reading, such as varying tone of voice, using pauses at the right time, reading clearly, and other qualities. Then, have each group member read aloud one of the poems while the rest of the group uses the form to evaluate the reading.

Research and Technology With a partner, create a **source list** that provides factual background for "Runagate Runagate."

- Identify at least two *primary sources*—documents from the time period written by people who witnessed the Underground Railroad.
- Identify at least three *secondary sources*—documents written after the event by scholars who did not directly participate in it.

Build Understanding • *Poetry Collection 2*

Connecting to the Literature

Reading/Writing Connection "Harriet Beecher Stowe" and "Paul Revere's Ride" are poems about people who influenced American history. Make a list of reasons that we remember and celebrate historical figures. Use at least three of these words: *achieve, affect, contribute, define, embody.*

Review

For **Reading Skill, Literary Analysis,** and **Vocabulary Builder,** see page 654.

Meet the Authors

Emma **Lazarus** (1849–1887)
The New Colossus (p. 665)
    Emma Lazarus wrote "The New Colossus" to inspire others to donate money for the Statue of Liberty's pedestal. The final lines of the poem were so inspirational, they were later inscribed on the pedestal itself. Raised in New York City, where she studied languages, Lazarus published a book of poems and translations at seventeen. Later, drawing on her Jewish heritage, she wrote works showing America as a refuge for people persecuted in Europe.

Henry Wadsworth **Longfellow** (1807–1882)
Paul Revere's Ride (p. 666)
    Henry Wadsworth Longfellow started college at age fifteen and was asked to be the first professor of modern languages at Bowdoin College at the age of nineteen. He was one of the "fireside poets," writers whose popular poems were read aloud by nineteenth-century families as they gathered around a fireplace. He wrote several long poems on topics in American history.

Paul Laurence **Dunbar** (1872–1906)
Harriet Beecher Stowe (p. 671)
    Paul Laurence Dunbar was the son of former slaves. Encouraged by his mother, he began writing poetry at an early age. Dunbar was inspired by Harriet Beecher Stowe's novel *Uncle Tom's Cabin,* and in his own work, he honored people who fought for African American rights.

For: For more about these poets
Visit: www.PHSchool.com
Web Code: ene-9409

THE NEW COLOSSUS

Emma Lazarus

Background The Colossus of Rhodes was one of the Seven Wonders of the Ancient World. A huge statue of the sun god Helios, it was built around 280 B.C. and stood astride the entrance to the harbor of the Greek island of Rhodes. It commemorated a great military victory.

Not like the brazen giant of Greek fame,
With conquering limbs astride from land to land;
Here at our sea-washed, sunset gates shall stand
A mighty woman with a torch, whose flame
5 Is the imprisoned lightning, and her name
Mother of Exiles. From her beacon-hand
Glows world-wide welcome; her mild eyes command
The air-bridged harbor that twin cities frame.
"Keep, ancient lands, your storied pomp!"[1] cries she
10 With silent lips. "Give me your tired, your poor,
Your huddled masses <u>yearning</u> to breathe free,
The wretched refuse of your teeming[2] shore.
Send these, the homeless, tempest-tost[3] to me,
I lift my lamp beside the golden door!"

▲ **Critical Viewing**
Why might this statue be seen as different from one celebrating a military victory? **[Compare and Contrast]**

Vocabulary Builder
yearning (yʉr′ niŋ) *adj.* filled with the feeling of wanting something

---

1. **pomp** (pämp) *n.* stately or brilliant display; splendor.
2. **teeming** (tēm′ iŋ) *adj.* swarming with people.
3. **tempest-tost** (tem′ pist tôst) *adj.* here, having suffered a stormy ocean journey.

Paul Revere's Ride
Henry Wadsworth Longfellow

Listen, my children, and you shall hear
Of the midnight ride of Paul Revere,
On the eighteenth of April, in Seventy-five;
Hardly a man is now alive
5 Who remembers that famous day and year.

He said to his friend, "If the British march
By land or sea from the town to-night,
Hang a lantern aloft in the belfry arch
Of the North Church tower as a signal light,—

▲ **Critical Viewing**
Based on this illustration, what do you think the mood of this poem will be? **[Predict]**

10 One, if by land, and two, if by sea;
    And I on the opposite shore will be,
    Ready to ride and spread the alarm
    Through every Middlesex village and farm,
    For the country folk to be up and to arm."

15 Then he said, "Good night!" and with muffled oar
    Silently rowed to the Charlestown shore,
    Just as the moon rose over the bay,
    Where swinging wide at her moorings lay
    The *Somerset*, British man-of-war;[1]
20 A phantom ship, with each mast and spar
    Across the moon like a prison bar,
    And a huge black hulk, that was magnified
    By its own reflection in the tide.

    Meanwhile, his friend, through alley and street,
25 Wanders and watches with eager ears,
    Till in the silence around him he hears
    The muster[2] of men at the barrack door,
    The sound of arms, and the tramp of feet,
    And the measured tread of the grenadiers,[3]
30 Marching down to their boats on the shore.

    Then he climbed the tower of the Old North Church,
    By the wooden stairs, with stealthy tread,
    To the belfry-chamber overhead,
    And startled the pigeons from their perch
35 On the <u>somber</u> rafters, that round him made
    Masses and moving shapes of shade,—
    By the trembling ladder, steep and tall,
    To the highest window in the wall,
    Where he paused to listen and look down
40 A moment on the roofs of the town,
    And the moonlight flowing over all.

---

1. man-of-war (man' əv wôr') *n.* armed naval vessel; warship.
2. muster (mus' tər) *n.* assembly of troops summoned for inspection, roll call, or service.
3. grenadiers (gren' ə dirz') *n.* members of a special regiment or corps.

▲ **Critical Viewing**
Why would a ship like the one shown appear threatening to Revere?
[Interpret]

Vocabulary Builder
somber (säm' bər) *adj.* dark; gloomy

✔ **Reading Check**

At what time in history is this narrative poem set?

Beneath, in the churchyard, lay the dead,
In their night-encampment on the hill,
Wrapped in silence so deep and still

45 That he could hear, like a sentinel's tread,[4]
The watchful night-wind, as it went
Creeping along from tent to tent,
And seeming to whisper, "All is well!"
A moment only he feels the spell

50 Of the place and the hour, and the secret dread
Of the lonely belfry and the dead;
For suddenly all his thoughts are bent
On a shadowy something far away,
Where the river widens to meet the bay,—

55 A line of black that bends and floats
On the rising tide, like a bridge of boats.

---

4. **sentinel's** (sent´' n əlz) **tread** (tred) footsteps of a guard.

▼ Critical Viewing
What would make the Old North Church, shown here, a good place from which to signal Revere? **[Speculate]**

Meanwhile, impatient to mount and ride,
Booted and spurred, with a heavy stride
On the opposite shore walked Paul Revere.
60 Now he patted his horse's side,
Now gazed at the landscape far and near,
Then, impetuous,[5] stamped the earth,
And turned and tightened his saddle-girth;[6]
But mostly he watched with eager search
65 The belfry-tower of the Old North Church,
As it rose above the graves on the hill,
Lonely and spectral and somber and still.
And lo! as he looks, on the belfry's height
A glimmer, and then a gleam of light!
70 He springs to the saddle, the bridle he turns,
But lingers and gazes, till full on his sight
A second lamp in the belfry burns!

A hurry of hoofs in a village street,
A shape in the moonlight, a bulk in the dark,
75 And beneath, from the pebbles, in passing, a spark
Struck out by a steed flying fearless and fleet:
That was all! And yet, through the gloom and the light,
The fate of a nation was riding that night;
And the spark struck out by that steed in his flight,
80 Kindled the land into flame with its heat.
He has left the village and mounted the steep,
And beneath him, tranquil and broad and deep,
Is the Mystic,[7] meeting the ocean tides;
And under the alders that skirt its edge,
85 Now soft on the sand, now loud on the ledge,
Is heard the tramp of his steed as he rides.

It was twelve by the village clock,
When he crossed the bridge into Medford town.
He heard the crowing of the cock,
90 And the barking of the farmer's dog,
And felt the damp of the river fog,
That rises after the sun goes down.

---

5. **impetuous** (im pech′ ōō əs) *adj.* done suddenly with little thought.
6. **saddle-girth** (gurth) *n.* band put around the belly of a horse for holding a saddle.
7. **Mystic** (mis′ tik) river in Massachusetts.

**Reading Skill
Paraphrase**
Paraphrase this stanza by explaining in your own words what is happening and who is participating in the action.

Reading Check

What does the second lamp in the North Church tower indicate to Revere?

It was one by the village clock,
When he galloped into Lexington.
95 He saw the gilded weathercock
Swim in the moonlight as he passed,
And the meeting-house windows, blank and bare,
Gaze at him with a spectral glare,
As if they already stood <u>aghast</u>
100 At the bloody work they would look upon.

It was two by the village clock,
When he came to the bridge in Concord town.
He heard the bleating of the flock,
And the twitter of birds among the trees,
105 And felt the breath of the morning breeze
Blowing over the meadows brown.
And one was safe and asleep in his bed
Who at the bridge would be first to fall,
Who that day would be lying dead,
110 Pierced by a British musket-ball.

You know the rest. In the books you have read,
How the British Regulars fired and fled,—
How the farmers gave them ball for ball,
From behind each fence and farm-yard wall,
115 Chasing the red-coats down the lane,
Then crossing the fields to emerge again
Under the trees at the turn of the road,
And only pausing to fire and load.

So through the night rode Paul Revere;
120 And so through the night went his cry of alarm
To every Middlesex village and farm,—
A cry of defiance and not of fear,
A voice in the darkness, a knock at the door,
And a word that shall echo forevermore!
125 For, borne on the night-wind of the Past,
Through all our history, to the last,
In the hour of darkness and peril and need,
The people will waken and listen to hear
The hurrying hoof-beats of that steed,
130 And the midnight message of Paul Revere.

Vocabulary Builder
aghast (ə gast′)
adj. feeling great
horror or dismay

Reading Skill
Paraphrase
Paraphrase this
stanza by explaining
who was fighting and
what the result of the
fight was.

Literary Analysis
Forms of Poetry
What is the resolution
of the conflict in this
narrative poem?

Harriet Beecher Stowe

Paul Laurence Dunbar

Background Harriet Beecher Stowe is the author of *Uncle Tom's Cabin,* a classic antislavery novel. Her work, written before the Civil War, brought the horror of slavery into the public eye. When Abraham Lincoln met Stowe, he said, "So you're the little woman who wrote the book that made this great war!"

She told the story, and the whole world wept
    At wrongs and cruelties it had not known
    But for this fearless woman's voice alone.
    She spoke to the consciences that long had slept:
5 Her message, Freedom's clear reveille,[1] swept
    From heedless hovel[2] to complacent throne.
    Command and prophecy were in the tone
    And from its sheath the sword of justice leapt.
    Around two peoples swelled the fiery wave,
10   But both came forth transfigured from the flame
Blest be the hand that dared be strong to save,
    And blest be she who in our weakness came—
    Prophet and priestess! At one stroke she gave
    A race to freedom and herself to fame.

Vocabulary Builder
complacent (kəm plā′ sənt) *adj.* smug; self-satisfied

---

1. **reveille** (rev′ ə lē) *n.* early morning bugle or drum signal to waken soldiers.
2. **heedless hovel** (hēd′ lis huv′ əl) small, miserable, poorly-kept dwelling place.

Apply the Skills

Poetry Collection 2

Thinking About the Selections

1. **Respond:** Which poem's subject interests you most? Why?
2. **(a)** Fill out a chart like the one shown to interpret the lines indicated. **(b) Discuss:** In a small group, discuss your responses. Then, share your ideas with the class.

	What Does It Say?	What Does It Mean?	Why Is It Important?
The New Colossus	(Line 9)		
Harriet Beecher Stowe	(Lines 9–10)		
Paul Revere's Ride	(Lines 78–80)		

Reading Skill

3. **(a)** Which words in lines 3–5 from "The New Colossus" tell who or what the sentence is about? **(b) Paraphrase** the lines, using a sentence structure that is more like everyday speech.
4. **(a)** What synonyms could be used for the underlined words in these lines from "Harriet Beecher Stowe"? "Her message, Freedom's clear <u>reveille</u>, swept / From heedless <u>hovel</u> to complacent throne." **(b)** Paraphrase the lines.
5. Reread the second stanza of "Paul Revere's Ride." **(a)** Write the lines in sentences. **(b)** Paraphrase each sentence.

Literary Analysis

6. **(a)** What thoughts and feelings about the Statue of Liberty are expressed in the **lyric poem** "The New Colossus"? **(b)** What is the overall impression that is created? Explain.
7. **(a)** What thoughts and feelings about Harriet Beecher Stowe are expressed in the lyric poem about her? **(b)** What overall impression of her does the poem create? Explain.
8. **(a)** Who is the main character in the **narrative poem** "Paul Revere's Ride"? **(b)** Identify the poem's setting and conflict.

QuickReview

Poems at a Glance

"The New Colossus": a lyric poem inspired by the Statue of Liberty

"Paul Revere's Ride": a narrative poem about a Revolutionary War hero

"Harriet Beecher Stowe": a lyric poem praising an author

For: Self-test
Visit: www.PHSchool.com
Web Code: ena-6408

Paraphrase: to restate something in your own words

Lyric Poetry: verse that expresses the thoughts and feelings of a single *speaker*

Narrative Poetry: verse that tells a story

Vocabulary Builder

Practice **Analogies** show the relationship between words. Use a word from Poetry Collection 2 on page 654 to create a word pair that matches the relationship between the first two words given.

1. *Asking* is to *questioning as* _____ is to *longing.*
2. *Cheerful* is to _____ as *easy* is to *difficult.*
3. *Conceited* is to *proud* as _____ is to *satisfied.*
4. *Pleasure* is to *happy* as *horror* is to _____.

Writing

Write a **lyric or narrative poem** about a person whom you admire. Your subject can be a historical figure or someone you know.
- If you are writing a lyric poem, brainstorm for details about the person's qualities.
- If writing a narrative poem, list the events, characters, and details of setting you will include in the poem.

Use your notes to draft the lines of your poem. To revise, look for places where you can replace words with synonyms that have a more musical quality.

For *Grammar, Vocabulary,* and *Assessment,* see **Build Language Skills,** pp. 674–675.

Extend Your Learning

Listening and Speaking In a group, prepare an **evaluation form** for poetry reading. Identify the different qualities of a good poetry reading, such as varying tone of voice, using pauses at the right time, reading clearly, and other qualities. Then, have each group member read aloud one of the poems while the rest of the group uses the form to evaluate each reading.

Research and Technology With a partner, create a **source list** that provides factual background for "Paul Revere's Ride."
- Identify at least two *primary sources*—documents from the time period written by people who witnessed the event.
- Identify at least three *secondary sources*—documents written after the event by scholars who did not directly participate in it.

Build Language Skills

Vocabulary Skill

Word Origins The word *reflect* has its origins in the Latin word *reflectere,* a combination of *re-* "back" and *flectere,* "to bend," and means "to bend back" or "to throw back." A mirror *reflects* light to give back an image of what is in front of it. A paraphrase *reflects,* or gives back, an author's meaning.

▶ **Example:** Does my paraphrase *reflect* the ideas of your essay?

Practice Using a dictionary, find four words that share the word origin of *reflect.* Explain which part of the new words share this origin and how the origin contributes to the word's meaning. Use each word in a sentence that illustrates the word's meaning.

▶ **Example:** Tom reflected on what Susan had said by thinking back over each part of her speech.

Grammar Lesson

Prepositions and Prepositional Phrases A **preposition** shows the relationship between two words or two phrases. In *My toothbrush is in my cup, and your toothbrush is in yours,* the first preposition *in* relates the noun *cup* to the *first toothbrush:* It tells where the toothbrush is placed. The second *in* relates the pronoun *yours* to the *second toothbrush.*

Common prepositions include *above, behind, below, beyond, for,* and *with.* Compound prepositions consisting of more than one word include *ahead of* and *because of.*

A **prepositional phrase** begins with a preposition and ends with the noun, noun phrase, or pronoun that follows it. In the example sentence given above, the prepositional phrases are *in my cup* and *in yours.*

Practice Rewrite this sentence five times, using a different preposition in the blank each time. Then, explain how the preposition changed the meaning of the sentence.

The dog ran _____ the fence.

W̶G *Prentice Hall Writing and Grammar Connection: Chapter 17*

MorePractice

For more practice with prepositions and prepositional phrases, see the Grammar Handbook, p. R31.

Reading: Paraphrasing

Directions: *Read the selection. Then, answer the questions.*

(1) Sherlock Holmes and I had no difficulty in engaging a bedroom and sitting room at the Crown Inn. (2) They were on the upper floor, and from our window we could command a view of the avenue gate, and of the inhabited wing of Stoke Moran Manor House. (3) At dusk we saw Dr. Grimesby Roylott drive past . . . (4) The boy had some slight difficulty in undoing the heavy iron gates, and we heard the hoarse roar of the doctor's voice and saw the fury with which he shook his clinched fists at him.

—from *The Adventure of the Speckled Band* by Sir Arthur Conan Doyle

1. In sentence 1, which word could replace *engaging*?
   A buying
   B marrying
   C seeing
   D getting

2. Which word could replace *command* in sentence 2?
   A order
   B deserve
   C have
   D direct

3. Which best restates sentence 2?
   A We saw the gate and part of the mansion.
   B Our rooms had a good view.
   C Views from above were best.
   D We saw the gate, not the mansion.

4. Which is the best paraphrase of sentence 4?
   A The doctor helped at the gates.
   B The boy left before finishing.
   C When the boy could not open the gates, Dr. Roylott became angry.
   D He asked for help.

Timed Writing: Interpretation [Connections]

Review *Poetry Collection 1* and *Poetry Collection 2.* Choose one poem and write an interpretation of each stanza of the poem, using specific details from the poem to support your interpretation. In your paragraph, explain how these parts add up to the poem's overall idea. **(25 minutes)**

 ## Writing Workshop: *Work in Progress*

Comparison and Contrast

For a comparison-and-contrast essay you might write, put two books on your desk. List all the ways the books are different. Then, make a list of all the ways the books are alike. Put your lists in your writing portfolio.

Build Language Skills ■ 675

You can apply the instruction on this page to these poems.

Poetry Collection 1
January, p. 678
New World, p. 680
For My Sister Molly Who in the Fifties, p. 682

Poetry Collection 2
Grandma Ling, p. 689
Drum Song, p. 690
your little voice/Over the wires came leaping, p. 692

Reading Skill

Paraphrasing is restating something in your own words. Because poetry often expresses ideas in language that does not sound like everyday speech, paraphrasing can improve your understanding.

- First, **read aloud fluently according to punctuation.** Pause briefly at commas, dashes, and semicolons and longer after end marks like periods. Using punctuation will help you group words for meaning and recognize complete thoughts.
- Next, restate the meaning of each complete thought in your own words. Use synonyms for the writer's words. Put unusual or complicated expressions into simpler words.

As you read, pause occasionally to paraphrase what you have just read and clarify your understanding.

Literary Analysis

Imagery is language that appeals to the senses. Poets use imagery to help readers imagine sights, sounds, textures, tastes, and smells.

- **With imagery:** The train thundered past, roaring, screaming.
- **Without imagery:** The train went by.

For each poem, use a chart like the one shown to note imagery.

Vocabulary Builder

Poetry Collection 1

- **glistens** (glis´ ənz) *v.* shines; sparkles (p. 681) *Sunlight glistens on the clear lake.*

- **recede** (ri sēd´) *v.* move away (p. 681) *As the clouds began to recede, the sky brightened.*

- **remote** (ri mōt´) *adj.* aloof; cold; distant (p. 685) *After his wife died, he grew more and more remote.*

Poetry Collection 2

- **vertical** (vʉr´ ti kəl) *adj.* straight up and down; upright (p. 691) *The pine tree's trunk was vertical and tall.*

- **burrow** (bʉr´ ō) *n.* passage or hole for shelter (p. 691) *The gopher dove into its burrow.*

- **impertinently** (im pʉr´ ti nənt lē) *adv.* disrespectfully (p. 693) *"You are older, not wiser," he said impertinently.*

Build Understanding • *Poetry Collection 1*

Connecting to the Literature

Reading/Writing Connection The poems in this collection capture positive feelings about people, places, and situations. Write three reasons why you have positive feelings about a person or place. Use three of these words: *appreciate, derive, evoke, generate.*

Meet the Authors

John **Updike** (b. 1932)
January (p. 678)

Although he is best known as a Pulitzer Prize-winning novelist, John Updike also writes poetry, essays, short stories, and literary criticism. As a child growing up on a farm in Pennsylvania, Updike enjoyed reading so much that his mother encouraged him to write. In 2003, Updike received the National Medal for the Humanities. He had previously won the National Medal of Art. Only a handful of writers have been honored with both prizes.

N. Scott **Momaday** (b. 1934)
New World (p. 680)

A Kiowa Indian, N. Scott Momaday is known for his poetry, plays, art, and essays. As a writer, Momaday strives to pass on Kiowa oral traditions. His father, a great teller of Kiowa stories, inspired Momaday to write, ". . . it was only after I became an adult that I understood how fragile [the stories] are, because they exist only by word of mouth, always just one generation away from extinction."

Alice **Walker** (b. 1944)
For My Sister Molly Who in the Fifties (p. 682)

Alice Walker, the youngest of eight children, grew up in Georgia, where her parents were farmers. She is one of the best-known and best-loved African American writers. Walker's poems frequently deal with the preservation of her culture and heritage. One of her novels, *The Color Purple,* was made into a movie in 1985, directed by Steven Spielberg, and starring Whoopi Goldberg and Oprah Winfrey.

For: More about these poets
Visit: www.PHSchool.com
Web Code: ene-9410

January

JOHN UPDIKE

The days are short,
    The sun a spark
Hung thin between
    The dark and dark.

5 Fat snowy footsteps
    Track the floor,
And parkas pile up
    Near the door.

Reading Skill
Paraphrase Read
lines l–4 according to
punctuation. Then,
put this stanza into
your own words.

The river is
10   A frozen place
Held still beneath
     The trees' black lace.

The sky is low.
     The wind is gray.
15 The radiator
     Purrs all day.

▲ **Critical Viewing**
Compare and
contrast the artist's
concept of winter
with Updike's.
**[Compare and
Contrast]**

NEW WORLD

N. Scott Momaday

1.

First Man,
behold:
the earth
glitters
5 with leaves;
the sky
<u>glistens</u>
with rain.
Pollen
10 is borne
on winds
that low
and lean
upon
15 mountains.
Cedars
blacken
the slopes—
and pines.

2.

20 At dawn
eagles
hie and
hover[1]
above
25 the plain
where light
gathers
in pools.
Grasses
30 shimmer
and shine.
Shadows
withdraw
and lie
35 away
like smoke.

3.

At noon
turtles
enter
40 slowly
into
the warm
dark loam.[2]
Bees hold
45 the swarm.
Meadows
<u>recede</u>
through planes
of heat
50 and pure
distance.

4.

At dusk
the gray
foxes
55 stiffen
in cold;
blackbirds
are fixed
in the
60 branches.
Rivers
follow
the moon,
the long
65 white track
of the
full moon.

Vocabulary Builder
glistens (glis´ ənz) *v.*
shines; sparkles

recede (ri sēd´) *v.*
move away

Literary Analysis
Imagery What images
convey a sense of the
temperature in the
final stanza?

◄ **Critical Viewing**
What aspects of this
painting convey the
idea of a "new
world"? **[Analyze]**

---

1. **hie and hover** fly swiftly and then hang as if suspended in the air.
2. **loam** (lōm) rich, dark soil.

For My Sister MOLLY Who in the Fifties

Alice Walker

Once made a fairy rooster from
Mashed potatoes
Whose eyes I forget
5 But green onions were his tail
And his two legs were carrot sticks
A tomato slice his crown.
Who came home on vacation
When the sun was hot
10 and cooked
and cleaned
And minded least of all
The children's questions
A million or more
15 Pouring in on her
Who had been to school
And knew (and told us too) that certain

▲ Critical Viewing
How would you describe the relationship between the girls in this photograph? [Infer]

Words were no longer good
And taught me not to say us for we
20   No matter what "Sonny said" up the
road.

FOR MY SISTER MOLLY WHO IN THE FIFTIES
Knew Hamlet[1] well and read into the night
And coached me in my songs of Africa
25   A continent I never knew
But learned to love
Because "they" she said could carry
A tune
And spoke in accents never heard
30   In Eatonton.
Who read from *Prose and Poetry*
And loved to read "Sam McGee from Tennessee"[2]
On nights the fire was burning low
And Christmas wrapped in angel hair[3]
35   And I for one prayed for snow.

WHO IN THE FIFTIES
Knew all the written things that made
Us laugh and stories by
The hour   Waking up the story buds
40   Like fruit. Who walked among the flowers
And brought them inside the house
And smelled as good as they
And looked as bright.
Who made dresses, braided
45   Hair. Moved chairs about
Hung things from walls
Ordered baths
Frowned on wasp bites
And seemed to know the endings
50   Of all the tales
I had forgot.

---

1. **Hamlet** play by William Shakespeare.
2. **"Sam McGee from Tennessee"** reference to the title character in the Robert Service poem, "The Cremation of Sam McGee."
3. **angel hair** fine, white, filmy Christmas tree decoration.

Literary Analysis
Imagery What do the images in the first stanza tell you about Molly?

Reading Skill
Paraphrase Restate lines 36–43 in your own words.

 **Reading Check**

What are two things that the speaker appreciates about her sister?

WHO OFF INTO THE UNIVERSITY
Went exploring   To London and
To Rotterdam
55   Prague and to Liberia
Bringing back the news to us
Who knew none of it
But followed
crops and weather
60   funerals and
Methodist Homecoming;
easter speeches,
groaning church.

WHO FOUND ANOTHER WORLD
65   Another life   With gentlefolk
Far less trusting
And moved and moved and changed
Her name
And sounded precise
70   When she spoke   And frowned away
Our sloppishness.

WHO SAW US SILENT
Cursed with fear   A love burning
Inexpressible
75   And sent me money not for me
But for "College."
Who saw me grow through letters
The words misspelled   But not
The longing   Stretching
80   Growth
The tied and twisting
Tongue
Feet no longer bare
Skin no longer burnt against
85   The cotton.

WHO BECAME SOMEONE OVERHEAD
A light   A thousand watts

Reading Skill
Paraphrase In your own words explain the growing distance between Molly and her siblings.

Literary Analysis
Imagery What images describe the sensations of growing up?

Bright and also blinding
And saw my brothers cloddish
90 And me destined to be
Wayward⁴
My mother remote   My father
A wearisome farmer
With heartbreaking
95 Nails.

FOR MY SISTER MOLLY WHO IN THE FIFTIES
Found much
Unbearable
Who walked where few had
100 Understood   And sensed our
Groping after light
And saw some extinguished
And no doubt mourned.

FOR MY SISTER MOLLY WHO IN THE FIFTIES
Left us.

4. wayward (wā′ wərd) adj. headstrong; disobedient.

Vocabulary Builder
remote (ri mōt′) *adj.*
aloof; cold; distant

▼ Critical Viewing
What emotions do
this photograph and
the poem share?
[Compare]

Apply the Skills

Poetry Collection 1

Thinking About the Selections

1. **Respond:** Of the three poems in this collection, which poem do you think creates the most vivid impression? Why?

2. **(a) Recall:** In "January," what are three things the speaker associates with the month of January? **(b) Recall:** How does he describe these things? **(c) Draw Conclusions:** Based on these descriptions, does the speaker have a positive or negative attitude toward winter? Explain.

3. **(a) Recall:** In "New World," what are three times of day identified? **(b) Infer:** Why does the poet describe these times? **(c) Interpret:** What might these times represent?

4. **(a) Recall:** In "For My Sister Molly Who in the Fifties," what are three things the speaker learns from Molly? **(b) Analyze:** What is the significance of these three things? **(c) Evaluate:** Why are these lessons important to the speaker?

Reading Skill

5. Use the punctuation in lines 22–30 of "For My Sister . . ." to identify two complete thoughts. **Paraphrase** the lines.

6. Fill in a chart like the one shown with paraphrases.

Original Lines	Paraphrase
January: (Lines 13–16)	
New World: (Lines 37–45)	
For My Sister Molly . . . : (Lines 16–18)	

Literary Analysis

7. **(a)** What **imagery** does the poet use in "January" to describe January days? **(b)** Is the imagery effective? Explain.

8. **(a)** What imagery in "New World" appeals to the senses? **(b)** How do these images capture a feeling of newness?

9. **(a)** List three memorable images from "For My Sister Molly Who in the Fifties." **(b)** To what senses do these images appeal? **(c)** What mood, or feeling, do these images create?

Vocabulary Builder

Practice Use a vocabulary word from Poetry Collection 1 on page 676 to change each sentence so that it makes sense. Explain your answers.

1. When the rain stops, the water level will rise.
2. Friends grow closer if they do not see each other for years.
3. The shiny ring pales in the sunlight.

Writing

A review of a literary work is an evaluation of its strengths and weaknesses. Write a **review** of this three-poem collection. Evaluate each poem based on sound, word choice, and imagery.

- To evaluate the sound of a poem, read it aloud and decide how well its sounds and rhythms match its subject.
- To evaluate word choice and imagery, determine whether the poems use vivid and appropriate words and images.
- As you draft, support your review with references to lines from the poems. Finally, offer your overall opinion of each poem.

For *Grammar, Vocabulary,* and *Assessment,*
see **Build Language Skills,** pages 696–697.

Extend Your Learning

Listening and Speaking Find music that reflects the mood, or feeling, of one of the poems in this collection. Bring a tape or CD of the music to class and present a **dramatic reading** of the poem while you play the music. Practice beforehand, so that you can use your voice to emphasize specific elements of the poem.

Research and Technology Write a **profile** of one of the poets in this collection. Gather information about the poet's life, writings, and influences. When researching, *paraphrase*—do not copy—your information sources, unless you are using a direct quotation. For quotations, note the source, so you can include this information in your profile. In your profile, show how the author's influences and experiences are reflected in the poem you read.

Poetry

Connecting to the Literature

Reading/Writing Connection The poems in this collection are powerful because they appeal to more than one sense. Sensory details are especially important in memory. Write about a vivid memory that includes several sensory details. Use three of these words: *appreciate, perceive, evoke, enhance.*

Review

For **Reading Skill, Literary Analysis,** and **Vocabulary Builder,** see page 676.

Meet the Authors

Amy **Ling** (1939–1999)
Grandma Ling (p. 689)

Amy Ling was born in China and lived there with her family for six years before moving to the United States. In addition to writing poetry, Ling worked as an editor of American literature anthologies. She was instrumental in bringing the work of Asian American writers to a wider audience. In the 1960s, Ling visited her grandmother in Taiwan and wrote about their first meeting in "Grandma Ling."

Wendy **Rose** (b. 1948)
Drum Song (p. 690)

Wendy Rose believes that "For everything in this universe there is a song to accompany its existence; writing is another way of singing these songs." One of the foremost Native American poets, Rose also illustrates many of her poems with pen and ink drawings and watercolors.

E. E. **Cummings** (1894–1962)
your little voice / Over the wires came leaping (p. 692)

During World War I, Edward Estlin Cummings joined a volunteer ambulance corps in France. The unusual writing style of his letters back home convinced French censors he was a spy, and he was imprisoned for three months. In his poetry, Cummings is known for his experimental, playful style, unusual punctuation, and unconventional arrangement of words.

Go Online **Author Link**

For: More about these poets
Visit: www.PHSchool.com
Web Code: ene-9411

Grandma Ling

Amy Ling

If you dig that hole deep enough
you'll reach China, they used to tell me,
a child in a backyard in Pennsylvania.
Not strong enough to dig that hole,
5   I waited twenty years,
then sailed back, half way around the world.

In Taiwan I first met Grandma.
Before she came to view, I heard
her slippered feet softly measure
10 the tatami[1] floor with even step;
the aqua paper-covered door slid open
and there I faced
my five foot height, sturdy legs and feet,
square forehead, high cheeks, and wide-set eyes;
15 my image stood before me,
acted on by fifty years.

She smiled, stretched her arms
to take to heart the eldest daughter
of her youngest son a quarter century away.
20 She spoke a tongue I knew no word of,
and I was sad I could not understand,
but I could hug her.

Literary Analysis
Imagery Which words in lines 9–11 appeal to one or more of the five senses?

Reading Skill
Paraphrase Restate lines 20–22 in your own words.

---

1. tatami (tə tä′ mē) *adj.* woven of rice straw.

Drum Song

Wendy Rose

Listen. Turtle
    your flat round feet
    of four claws each
    go slow, go steady,
5   from rock to water
    to land to rock to
water.

Listen. Woodpecker
    you lift your red head
10   on wind, perch
    on vertical earth
    of tree bark and
branch.

Listen. Snowhare[1]
15   your belly drags,
    your whiskers dance
    bush to burrow
    your eyes turn up
    to where owls
20 hunt.

Listen. Women
    your tongues melt,
    your seeds are planted
    mesa[2] to mesa a shake
25   of gourds,[3]
    a line of mountains
    with blankets
    on their
hips.

◄ Critical Viewing
What physical characteristics of turtles allow them to go from "land to rock to water"? [Connect]

Vocabulary Builder
vertical (vʉr´ti kəl) adj. straight up and down; upright

burrow (bʉr´ ō) n. passage or hole for shelter

Literary Analysis
Imagery To what senses does the imagery in the last stanza appeal?

---

1. Snowhare (snō´ har´) n. snowshoe hare; a large rabbit whose color changes from brown to white in winter and whose broad feet resemble snowshoes.
2. mesa (mā´ sə) n. small, high plateau with steep sides.
3. gourds (gôrds) n. dried, hollowed-out shells of fruits such as melons and pumpkins.

your little voice
Over the wires came leaping

E. E. Cummings

your little voice
               Over the wires came leaping
and i felt suddenly
dizzy
5   With the jostling and shouting of merry flowers
wee skipping high-heeled flames
courtesied[1] before my eyes
                  or twinkling over to my side
Looked up
10   with <u>impertinently</u> exquisite faces
floating hands were laid upon me
I was whirled and tossed into delicious dancing
up
Up
15   with the pale important
                stars and the Humorous
                       moon
dear girl
How i was crazy how i cried when i heard
20   over time
and tide and death
leaping
Sweetly
        your voice

---

1. **courtesied** (kʉrt´ sēd) *v.* bowed with bended knees; curtsied.

Apply the Skills

Poetry Collection 2

Thinking About the Selections

1. **Respond:** Which poem has the most vivid images? Why?
2. **(a) Recall:** In "Grandma Ling," what prevents the grandmother and granddaughter from communicating in their first meeting? **(b) Speculate:** What might they want to tell or ask each other? **(c) Analyze:** How do they finally communicate, and what are they saying?
3. **(a) Recall:** What is each of the animals doing in "Drum Song"? **(b) Analyze:** How do the animals and the women interact with their environments?
4. **(a) Recall:** In "your little voice . . . ," what effect does the little voice have on the speaker? **(b) Infer:** Why does the speaker react this way?

Reading Skill

5. Use the punctuation in lines 17–19 of "Grandma Ling" to identify two complete thoughts. **Paraphrase** these lines.
6. Fill in a chart like the one shown with paraphrases.

Original Lines	Paraphrase
Grandma Ling: (Lines 15–16)	
Drum Song: (Lines 8–13)	
your little voice . . . : (Lines 1–6)	

Literary Analysis

7. **(a)** In "Grandma Ling," what **imagery** does the poet use to explain why she had never met her grandmother before? **(b)** Explain how the imagery makes the description of distance more vivid than it would be without imagery.
8. **(a)** What imagery in "Drum Song" appeals to the sense of hearing? **(b)** How does this imagery work with the title of the poem to convey a sense of movement and energy?
9. **(a)** List three images from "your little voice . . . " **(b)** To what senses do these images appeal? **(c)** What mood, or feeling, does Cummings create with his use of these images?

QuickReview

Poems at a Glance
"Grandma Ling": a free verse poem describing the poet's first visit with her grandmother

"Drum Song": a free verse poem about nature

"your little voice / Over the wires came leaping": a free verse poem about a telephone conversation

Assessment
For: Self-test
Visit: www.PHSchool.com
Web Code: ena-6410

Paraphase: to restate something in your own words

Imagery: language that appeals to the senses

Vocabulary Builder

Practice Use a vocabulary word from Poetry Collection 2 on page 676 to change each sentence so that it makes sense. Explain your answers.

1. The rude child spoke respectfully.
2. We looked up at the horizontal towers of the skyscrapers.
3. The chipmunk ran to hide in the open air.

Writing

A review of a literary work is an evaluation of its strengths and weaknesses. Write a **review** of this three-poem collection. Evaluate each poem based on sound, word choice, and imagery.

- To evaluate the sound of a poem, read it aloud and decide how well its sound and rhythms match its subject.
- To evaluate word choice and imagery, determine whether the poems use vivid and appropriate words and images.
- As you draft, support your review with references to lines from the poems. Finally, offer your overall opinion of each poem.

For *Grammar, Vocabulary,* and *Assessment,* see **Build Language Skills,** pages 696–697.

Extend Your Learning

Listening and Speaking Find music that reflects the mood, or feeling, of one of the poems in this collection. Bring a tape or CD of the music to class and present a **dramatic reading** of the poem while you play the music. Practice beforehand, so that you can use your voice to emphasize specific elements of the poem.

Research and Technology Write a **profile** of one of the poets in this collection. Gather information about the poet's life, writings, and influences. When researching, *paraphrase*—do not copy—your information sources, unless you are using a direct quotation. For quotations, note the source, so you can include this information in your profile. In your profile, show how the author's influences and experiences are reflected in the poem you read.

Build Language Skills

Vocabulary Skill

Word Origins The word *adapt* has its origins in the Latin word *adaptare,* which means "to fit to." When you *adapt* something, you change it to fit your needs. Words are adapted from other languages. Related words include *adaptable, adaptability,* and *adaptation.*

▶ **Example:** I need to *adapt* this story so that I can tell it to my little brother.

Practice All of these words have a meaning connected to "fit." For each of the following explain what it says or indicates about "fitting." Then, use each word in a sentence.

1. adaptable
2. adaptations
3. adapt
4. adaptability

Grammar Lesson

Infinitive Phrases An **infinitive** is a form of verb that comes after the word *to* and acts as a noun, an adjective, or an adverb.

An **infinitive phrase** is an infinitive with a modifier or a complement, all acting together as a single part of speech.

▶ **Example:** to ski   *To ski* in New Mexico, you must travel into the mountains.

to give   I need *to give* you my new cell phone number.

MorePractice

For more practice with infinitive phrases, see the Grammar Handbook, p. R31.

Practice Identify the infinitive phrase in each sentence, and then use that phrase in a new sentence.

1. Poets in the book include Dickinson, Cummings, and Longfellow—to name a few.

2. To visit Mackinac Island, tourists take a short boat ride.

3. I want to sit under the umbrella.

4. Before the bridge was built, ferries were used to cross the water.

5. She bent down to pick up the cat.

𝒲𝒢 *Prentice Hall Writing and Grammar Connection Chapter 20, Section 1*

Reading: Paraphrasing

1 Once upon a midnight dreary, while I pondered, weak and
    weary,
2 Over many a quaint and curious volume of forgotten lore,
3 While I nodded, nearly napping, suddenly there came a
    tapping,
4 As of someone gently rapping, rapping at my chamber door.
5 "'Tis some visitor," I muttered, "tapping at my chamber door—
6   Only this, and nothing more."

—from "The Raven" by Edgar Allan Poe

1. If you read this verse according to punctuation, where would you come to a complete stop?
   A after lines 1 and 3
   B after lines 2 and 5
   C after lines 4 and 6
   D at the end of every line

2. Select the best paraphrase of the first two lines.
   A The speaker is tired and weak.
   B The speaker is bored by his reading.
   C One midnight, the tired speaker was up late reading.
   D One midnight, the tired speaker was dealing with quaint and curious volumes of forgotten lore.

3. In line 3, the reader should
   A pause after each comma.
   B pause after the end comma.
   C pause after the 1st and 3rd comma.
   D pause after the 2nd and 3rd comma.

4. Which best paraphrases the entire verse?
   A A tapping sound wakes the speaker, but he is not concerned.
   B A scared speaker is roused from his sleep by a tapping.
   C A weary speaker imagines he hears a tapping.
   D A speaker reads about someone tapping on a bedroom door in an old folk tale.

Timed Writing: Analysis [Connections]

Using a poem from *Poetry Collection 1* or *Poetry Collection 2*, write an analysis of the imagery the poet uses to convey a particular mood or feeling. Cite specific images from the poem to illustrate your point.
(30 minutes)

Writing Workshop: *Work in Progress*

Comparison and Contrast

Use the lists of similarities and differences from your writing portfolio. Group the similarities together under general headings, by color coding each group. Put this work in your writing portfolio.

Reading Informational Materials

Manuals

In Part 2, you are learning about paraphrasing while reading literature. Paraphrasing can also help you understand technical manuals. If you read "your little voice/Over the wires came leaping," you will see that the manual here takes a more practical look at telephones than the speaker of the poem does.

About Manuals

A **manual** is a set of directions that tell you how to use a tool or product. Most manuals include the following features:

- a diagram of the product, with parts and features labeled
- step-by-step numbered directions for assembling, using, and caring for the product
- safety precautions and consumer safety information
- a troubleshooting guide that explains how to fix common problems
- customer service information such as telephone numbers, addresses, and Web site addresses

Reading Skill

A manual is a type of informational material that you **read in order to perform a task**. To perform the task, notice each detail and complete the steps in order. **Paraphrasing** the information—restating it in your own words—can help you understand directions. Use a checklist to get the most out of manuals and other technical documents.

Checklist for Using Technical Manuals

- ❑ Read all the directions completely before starting to follow them.
- ❑ Look for clues such as bold type or capital letters that point out specific sections or important information.
- ❑ Use diagrams to locate and name the parts of the product.
- ❑ Follow each step in the exact order given.
- ❑ Do not skip any steps.

Using Your Answering Machine

Labels identify the different features on the answering machine and explain what each one does.

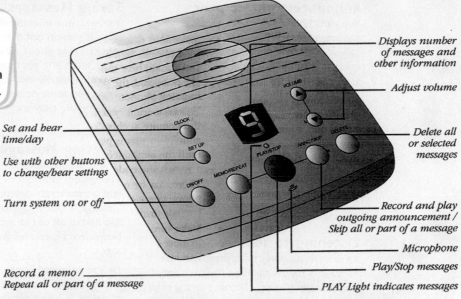

Set and hear time/day

Use with other buttons to change/hear settings

Turn system on or off

Record a memo / Repeat all or part of a message

Displays number of messages and other information

Adjust volume

Delete all or selected messages

Record and play outgoing announcement / Skip all or part of a message

Microphone

Play/Stop messages

PLAY Light indicates messages

Each heading identifies a function of the answering machine. The numbered steps explain how to accomplish that function.

Setting the Clock

You'll need to set the clock so that it can announce the day and time that each message is received. Press PLAY/STOP to exit Setting the Clock at any time.

1   Press and hold CLOCK until the Message Window displays CLOCK, and the default day is announced.

2   To change the day setting, hold down MEMO/REPEAT or ANNC/SKIP until the correct day is announced. Then release the button.

3   Press and release CLOCK. The current hour setting is announced.

4   To change the hour setting, hold down MEMO/REPEAT or ANNC/SKIP until the correct hour is announced. Then release the button.

5   Press and release CLOCK. The current minutes setting is announced.

6   To change the minutes setting, hold down MEMO/REPEAT or ANNC/SKIP until the correct minutes setting is announced. Then release the button.

7   Press and release CLOCK. The new day and time are announced.

To check the clock, press and release CLOCK.

NOTE: In the event of a power failure, see the instructions on the bottom of the unit to reset the clock.

Note alerts the reader that special instructions follow.

Recording Your Announcement

Before using this answering system, you should record the announcement (up to one minute long) that callers will hear when the system answers a call. If you choose not to record an announcement, the system answers with a prerecorded announcement: *"Hello. Please leave a message after the tone."*

1   Press and hold ANNC/SKIP. The system beeps. Speak toward the microphone normally, from about nine inches away. While you are recording, the Message Window displays —.

2   To stop recording, release ANNC/SKIP. The system automatically plays back your announcement.

To review your announcement, press and release ANNC/SKIP.

Turning the System On/Off

Use ON/OFF to turn the system on and off. When the system is off, the Message Window is blank.

Volume Control

Use volume buttons (▲ and ▼) to adjust the volume of the system's speaker. Press the top button (▲) to increase volume. Press the bottom button (▼) to decrease volume. The system beeps three times when you reach the maximum or minimum volume setting.

2

Announcement Monitor

You can choose whether to hear the announcement when your system answers a call, or have it silent (off) on your end (your caller will still hear an announcement).

1. Press and hold `SET UP`. After the Ring Select setting is announced, continue to press and release `SET UP` until the system announces "*Monitor is on (or off).*"
2. Press and release `ANNC/SKIP` or `MEMO/REPEAT` until the system announces your selection.
3. Press and release `PLAY/STOP` or `SET UP` to exit.

Listening to Your Messages

As the system plays back messages, the Message Window displays the number of the message playing. Before playing each message, the system announces the day and time the message was received. After playing the last message, the system announces "*End of messages.*"

Play all messages — Press and release `PLAY/STOP`. If you have no messages, the system announces "*No messages.*"

Play new messages only — Hold down `PLAY/STOP` for about two seconds, until the system begins playing. If you have no new messages, the system announces "*No new messages.*"

Repeat entire message — Press and release `MEMO/REPEAT`.

Repeat part of message — Hold down `MEMO/REPEAT` until you hear a beep, then release to resume playing. The more beeps you hear, the farther back in the message you will be when you release the button.

Repeat previous message — Press `MEMO/REPEAT` twice, continue this process to hear other previous messages.

Skip to next message — Press and release `ANNC/SKIP`.

Skip part of a message — Hold down `ANNC/SKIP` until you hear a beep, then release to resume playing. The more beeps you hear, the farther into the message you will be when you release the button.

Stop message playback — Press and release `PLAY/STOP`.

> The boxed words are visual cues that tell the reader to hold down or release a button on the answering machine.

Saving Messages

The system automatically saves your messages if you do not delete them. The system can save about 12 minutes of messages, including your announcement, for a total of up to 59 messages. When memory is full, you must delete some or all messages before new messages can be recorded.

Deleting Messages

Delete all messages — Hold down `DELETE`. The system announces "*Messages deleted*" and permanently deletes messages. The Message Window displays **0**. If you haven't listened to all of the messages, the system beeps five times, and does not delete messages.

Delete selected messages — Press and release `DELETE` while the message you want to delete is being played. The system beeps once, and continues with the next message. If you want to check a message before you delete it, you can press `MEMO/REPEAT` to replay the message before deleting it.

When the system reaches the end of the last message, the messages not deleted are renumbered, and the Message Window displays the total number of messages remaining in memory.

Recording a Memo

You can record a memo to be stored as an incoming message. The memo can be up to three minutes long, and will be played back with other messages.

1. Press and hold `MEMO/REPEAT`. After the beep, speak toward the microphone.
2. To stop recording, release `MEMO/REPEAT`.
3. To play the memo, press `PLAY/STOP`.

When Memory is Full

The system can record approximately 12 minutes of messages, including your announcement, for a total of up to 59 messages. When memory is full, or 59 messages have been recorded, the Message Window flashes **F**. Delete messages to make room for new ones.

When memory is full, the system answers calls after 10 rings, and sounds two beeps instead of your announcement.

4

Reading: Read to Perform a Task

Directions: *Choose the letter of the best answer.*

1. Which is the best paraphrase of the first sentence of **Recording Your Announcement**?

   A First, you should record a one-minute message that people will hear when the machine picks up a call.

   B Before you make a call, record a sixty-second message that people will hear when the machine answers a call.

   C First, record a message of sixty seconds or less that people will hear when the machine answers.

   D Before long, you should record the outgoing message.

2. Which is the best paraphrase of **Setting the Clock**, step 2?

   A Hold down the announce/skip button.

   B Hold down memo/repeat and the announce/skip button; then release when the correct day is announced.

   C Use "or" not "and."

   D Use "hour" not "day."

3. Which paraphrase shows the steps in the correct order for recording an announcement?

   A Hold the announce/skip button. When you hear a beep, release the announce/skip button. Then speak into the microphone.

   B Hold down and release the announce/skip button. When the system beeps, speak into the microphone.

   C Speak into the microphone. Hold down the announce/skip button. When the system beeps, release the announce/skip button.

   D Hold down the announce/skip button. When the system beeps, speak into the microphone. Then, release the announce/skip button.

Reading: Comprehension and Interpretation

Directions: *Write your answers on a separate sheet of paper.*

4. Which features of the machine are most important? Why? **[Evaluate]**

5. Explain how the diagram makes the text easier to follow. **[Analysis]**

Timed Writing: Explanation [Cognition]

Choose a function listed in the manual. Explain the directions in your own words. Organize the steps in order. **(15 minutes)**

Description

Descriptive writing paints pictures with words. A variety of descriptions can be used in poetry to present **levels of meaning**.

- **Literal meaning** is the actual, everyday meaning of words.
- **Figurative meaning** relies on figures of speech and the symbolic nature of language.

An **analogy** is a figurative description that compares two or more things that are similar in some ways, but otherwise unalike. For example, a poem that literally describes the ocean also can be read as an analogy: it may compare the ocean to life because both are vast, deep, and ever-changing. The poem, therefore, has two levels of meaning—one literal and one figurative.

When you think a poem may have multiple levels of meaning, take a step back and think about whether the poet is using an analogy or other type of figurative description to emphasize an idea.

Comparing Types of Description

Both "The Road Not Taken" and "O Captain! My Captain!" are analogies. Each compares a literal image to another, larger idea.

As you read the poems, follow these steps:

- Record your ideas about what the literal descriptions might symbolize.

- List some of the words and images that give you clues about the figurative meaning in a chart like the one shown.

- Finally, compare the analogies in the two poems.

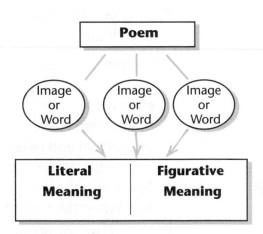

Vocabulary Builder

The Road Not Taken

- **diverged** (dī vurj´ d) *v.* branched off (p. 705)
  In the mountains, several small streams <u>diverged</u> *from the river.*

O Captain! My Captain!

- **exulting** (eg zult´ iŋ) *v.* rejoicing (p. 706)
  After the unexpected victory, we heard the excited team <u>exulting</u> *in the dugout.*

Build Understanding

Connecting to the Literature

Reading/Writing Connection These poems celebrate turning points—moments at which life changes forever. Certain turning points, such as the death of a beloved leader, are universal. Others are personal. In a few sentences, describe a turning point that would make a good subject for a poem. Use three of the following words: *benefit, achieve, affect, diminish, interpret.*

Meet the Authors

Robert **Frost** (1874 – 1963)

One of the best-known and best-loved American poets, Robert Frost was a four-time winner of the Pulitzer Prize. Though he was born in San Francisco, Frost spent most of his life in New England—the subject of many of his poems.

"The Gift Outright" Frost's reading of his poem "The Gift Outright" at the inauguration of President John F. Kennedy in 1961 was a memorable moment for poetry in the twentieth century.

Walt **Whitman** (1819 – 1892)

Although he is now considered one of America's greatest poets, Walt Whitman could not find a commercial publisher and was forced to pay for the publication of his masterpiece *Leaves of Grass* in 1855. This collection of poems about America has continued to influence poetry in every part of the world ever since.

The Poet and the War During the Civil War, Whitman worked in military hospitals in Washington, D.C., where he saw his beloved President Lincoln from afar. Lincoln's assassination less than a week after the Union victory deeply moved Whitman. He wrote the poem "O Captain! My Captain!" as a memorial to the fallen leader.

Go **Online**
Author Link

For: More about the authors
Visit: www.PHSchool.com
Web Code: ene-9412

The
Road Not Taken

Robert Frost

Two roads <u>diverged</u> in a yellow wood,
And sorry I could not travel both
And be one traveler, long I stood
And looked down one as far as I could
5   To where it bent in the undergrowth;

Then took the other, as just as fair,
And having perhaps the better claim,
Because it was grassy and wanted wear;
Though as for that, the passing there
10 Had worn them really about the same,

And both that morning equally lay
In leaves no step had trodden black.
Oh, I kept the first for another day!
Yet knowing how way leads on to way,
15 I doubted if I should ever come back.

I shall be telling this with a sigh
Somewhere ages and ages hence:
Two roads diverged in a wood, and I—
I took the one less traveled by,
20 And that has made all the difference.

Vocabulary Builder
diverged (dī vʉrjˊ d)
v. branched off

Literary Analysis
Description What is
the literal subject of
this poem?

Literary Analysis
Description What
clue in the final stanza
hints that the poem is
about more than a
hike in the woods?

Thinking About the Selection

1. **Respond:** Do you think the speaker in "The Road Not Taken"
   makes a wise choice? Explain.

2. **(a) Recall:** In the first five lines, where does the speaker remember being? **(b) Infer:** Based on these lines, what can you tell
   about the speaker's character and attitude toward life?

3. **(a) Recall:** Which road does the speaker finally choose?
   (b) Deduce: Why does the speaker choose one road over the
   other? **(c) Analyze:** Find two statements suggesting that the
   speaker believes he has made a significant choice.

4. **(a) Speculate:** Why does the speaker predict that he will
   remember this decision? **(b) Generalize:** What message does
   the poem communicate about decisions in general?

O Captain! My Captain!

Walt Whitman

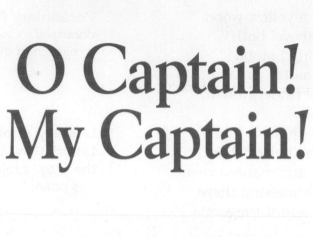

O Captain! my Captain! our fearful trip is done,
The ship has weather'd every rack,[1] the prize we
    sought is won,
The port is near, the bells I hear, the people all
    <u>exulting</u>,
While follow eyes the steady keel,[2] the vessel grim
    and daring;
5   But O heart! heart! heart!
        O the bleeding drops of red,
          Where on the deck my Captain lies,
          Fallen cold and dead.

---

1. rack (rak´) *n.* destruction or ruin.
2. keel (kēl´) *n.* main beam that extends along the bottom of a ship and supports the frame.

O Captain! my Captain! rise up and hear the bells;
10 Rise up—for you the flag is flung—for you the
      bugle trills,
    For you bouquets and ribbon'd wreaths—for you
      the shores a-crowding,
    For you they call, the swaying mass, their eager
      faces turning;
      Here Captain! dear father!
        This arm beneath your head!
15   It is some dream that on the deck,
              You've fallen cold and dead.

Literary Analysis
Description In this stanza, what does the speaker describe literally?

✔ **Reading Check**

Who is the speaker addressing?

▲ **Critical Viewing** What details in this photograph of Lincoln's funeral procession—and the illustration on page 708—reflect the importance of Lincoln's death to Americans like Whitman? **[Analyze]**

My Captain does not answer, his lips are pale
    and still,
My father does not feel my arm, he has no pulse
    nor will,
The ship is anchor'd safe and sound, its voyage
    closed and done,
20 From fearful trip the victor ship comes in with
    object won;
      Exult O shores, and ring O bells!
         But I with mournful tread,
            Walk the deck my Captain lies,
              Fallen cold and dead.

Literary Analysis
Description What is the symbolic meaning of the safely anchored ship?

Thinking About the Selection

1. **Respond:** How does this poem affect you? Explain.

2. **(a) Recall:** What has happened to the Captain? **(b) Infer:** Why does the timing of this event make it doubly unfortunate? **(c) Interpret:** How does the mood or feeling of the poem reflect what has happened?

3. **(a) Recall:** What words in the poem relate to the sea and sailing? **(b) Compare and Contrast:** In what ways does Lincoln's leadership of the country resemble a captain's role on a ship?

4. **(a) Recall:** How do the crowds of people respond to the Captain's arrival? **(b) Recall:** What feats has the Captain accomplished before the ship arrives? **(c) Draw Conclusions:** What kind of leader does the speaker consider Lincoln?

Apply the Skills

The Road Not Taken • O Captain! My Captain!

Description

1. **(a)** In "The Road Not Taken," how are the two roads alike and different? **(b)** What kind of choice might these two roads represent? Explain.

2. **(a)** In "O Captain! My Captain!" what is the ship's destination? **(b)** What is the "fearful trip" that the ship has "weathered"? **(c)** How does this trip and the rest of the poem reveal the poet's response to a historic event?

3. Using a chart like the one shown, analyze the ideas and emotions that each poem conveys.

Literal Meaning	Analogy		Ideas and Emotions
Two roads separate		→	
A ship's captain dies			

Writing to Compare Literary Works

The insights of both "The Road Not Taken" and "O Captain! My Captain!" are expressed through figurative descriptions—in the first poem, a personal experience; and in the second, a personal reaction to a historical event. In an essay, explain how these descriptions help convey important ideas to readers today. Use these questions to get started:

- How common are the experiences the poets describe?
- How universal are the emotions that prompt the descriptions?
- Which poet better expresses his emotions through the descriptions?
- Which message is easier for you to interpret? Why?

Vocabulary Builder

Practice Identify the word in each group that does not belong. Explain your answer.

1. separated, joined, diverged

2. cheering, mourning, exulting

QuickReview

Literal Description: a description based on the actual, everyday meaning of the words

Figurative Description: a description that relies on figures of speech and the symbolic nature of language

Analogy: a comparison between two or more things that are similar in some ways, but otherwise unalike

Go Online
Assessment

For: Self-test
Visit: www.PHSchool.com
Web Code: ena-6411

Reading: Paraphrasing

Directions: *Answer questions 1–5 based on the following selection.*

I dream a world where man
No other man will scorn,
Where love will bless the earth
And peace its paths adorn.
5   I dream a world where all
Will know sweet freedom's way,
Where greed no longer saps the soul
Nor avarice blights our day.

A world I dream where black or white,
10   Whatever race you be,
Will share the bounties of the earth
And every man is free,
Where wretchedness will hang its head
And joy, like a pearl,
15   Attends the needs of all mankind—
Of such I dream, my world!

—"I Dream a World" by Langston Hughes

1. Where does the first complete thought in the poem end?
A line 2
B line 4
C line 6
D line 8

2. A substitution for the phrase "I dream a world" could be
A I wish for
B Illusion is better than reality.
C one can conjure a society
D our society would like

3. Which is the best paraphrase of lines 5–8?
A Sweet freedom's way will sap the soul of avarice.
B Freedom is good. Greed is bad.
C I dream of a world where everyone is free and no one is greedy.
D If people had less freedom, there would be less greed in the world.

4. Which of the following lines, when read together, express a complete sentence?
A 9–10
B 9–11
C 9–13
D 9–16

5. Which is the best paraphrase of lines 13–16?
A In the world I dream of, everyone would be happy.
B Wretchedness should hang its head, and joy should be a pearl.
C Wretchedness and joy are both things that people need.
D My dreams of a joyful world only make me wretched.

Assessment Practice

Vocabulary

Directions: *Choose the best answer to each question.*

6. **Which word is the best synonym for** *reflect?*
   A change
   B show
   C carry
   D stress

7. **Which is the best definition for** *convey?*
   A communicate an idea
   B show a picture
   C argue a point
   D walk from place to place

8. **Which is the best synonym for** *emphasize?*
   A change
   B show
   C carry
   D stress

9. **Which is the best definition for the** *restate?*
   A express or show
   B say again
   C summarize carefully
   D read again

10. **Which is the best definition of the word** *adapt?*
    A to change to make more suitable
    B a term in formal biology
    C very good at doing something
    D to alter

Directions *Answer the following questions based on the dictionary entry.*

> **paraphrase (par´ə frāz´)** *v.* [[Fr< L *paraphrasis* < Gr.
> *paraphrazein,* to say in other words <*para-,* beside, + *phrazein,*
> to say]] 1. to reword; to express the same meaning in different
> words

11. **Which language is the original source for the word** *paraphrase?*
    A French
    B Latin
    C Greek
    D Middle English

12. **Which language is the most recent source for the word** *paraphrase?*
    A French   C Greek
    B Latin   D Middle English

13. **Which word is the best synonym for** *paraphrase?*
    A restate   C convey
    B reflect   D emphasize

14. **Which of the following words probably shares the same origin as** *paraphrase?*
    A paragraph   C faze
    B rephrase   D partial

Words With Prefixes and Suffixes

Prefixes are added to the beginning of base words, and **suffixes** are added to the ends of words. Prefixes and suffixes are **affixes,** or something added to a word.

SUFFIX THAT START WITH VOWELS

Think Before You Spell Adding prefixes to base words is generally easy, as no letters are ever dropped or added.

Suffixes have some variations:

Silent -*e*
- Usually you drop the silent -*e* when adding a suffix that begins with a vowel.
- Do not drop the silent -*e* when the suffix begins with a consonant.

Adding -*s* or -*d* to a word with a final -*y*
- When a consonant comes before the -*y*, change the -*y* to -*ie*.
- When a vowel comes before the -*y*, do not change the -*y*.

Some suffixes, such as -*ance* and -*ence,* and -*able* and -*ible,* can be tricky to spell because they sound the same and there are no strict rules about adding them.

Practice On your paper, write the word from the Word List that is related to each word below. Circle the affix or affixes in each word. Underline any places where a spelling change occurs when the affix is added.

Word List
deductible
irreplaceable
immovable
reference
illegal
reenact
impractical
attendance
collapsible
occurrence

1. attend
2. enact
3. replace
4. deduct
5. legal
6. refer
7. move
8. collapse
9. practical
10. occur

Directions: *Write the letter of the sentence in which the underlined word is spelled correctly.*

1. **A** Please do not put that vase on a <u>collapsable</u> table.
    B Breaking it would be a very unfortunate <u>occurence</u>.
    C We checked a <u>referrence</u> book.
    D We found out that it is rare and almost <u>irreplaceable</u>.

2. **A** <u>Happiness</u> is a great gift.
    B Its purpose was to <u>renact</u> the founding of our town.
    C Unfortunately, it was performed in a very <u>inpractical</u> place.
    D The only parking places nearby were <u>ilegal</u> ones.

3. **A** The storehouse was filled with heavy, <u>immovible</u> objects.
    B There was a crate of <u>reference</u> books.
    C This seems to be a very <u>impracticle</u> way to store things.
    D Do you think the storehouse is tax <u>deductable</u>?

4. **A** Marvin sat down in a <u>collapseible</u> chair.
    B He wanted to <u>reenact</u> a funny scene from a movie.
    C The group's goal is to <u>beautyfy</u> the downtown area.
    D Actually, the chair turned out to be <u>imovable</u>.

Directions: *Write the letter of the word that would be the correct spelling to fill in the blank.*

1. Mom said her wedding ring was _____.
    A inreplaceable
    B irreplaceable
    C ireplaceable
    D irreplacable

2. We are trying to _____ the club's rules.
    A codyfy
    B codify
    C codiefy
    D codafy

3. The driver made an _____ left turn.
    A ilegal
    B imlegal
    C inlegal
    D illegal

4. The fee is _____ from your total bill.
    A deducable
    B deductible
    C deductable
    D deducttible

5. Which _____ book are you going to use for your research?
    A refarence
    B referance
    C reference
    D refference

6. His ideas are usually _____.
    A impractical
    B inpractical
    C impracticle
    D inpracticle

Exposition:
Comparison-and-Contrast Essay

A **comparison-and-contrast** essay examines the similarities and differences between two or more subjects. Whether comparing two recipes or two government policies, comparison-and-contrast essays help readers understand the value of the analysis. Follow the steps outlined here to write your own comparison-and-contrast essay.

Assignment Write a comparison-and-contrast essay to analyze the similarities and differences between two or more subjects.

What to Include Your comparison-and-contrast essay should feature the following elements:
- a topic involving two or more subjects that are different in some ways and similar in other ways
- an introduction that presents the main point of the essay and body paragraphs showing similarities and differences
- an organization that highlights the points of comparison
- a structure appropriate to your audience
- error-free writing, including a variety of sentence patterns

To preview the criteria on which your comparison-and-contrast essay may be judged, see the rubric on page 721.

Writing Workshop: *Work in Progress*

If you have completed the Work-in-Progress assignments, you have several ideas you might want to use. Continue developing these ideas, or explore a new idea as you complete this Writing Workshop.

Using the Form
You may use elements of this form in these types of writing:
- comparisons of literary works
- product comparisons
- news analysis

To get the feel for comparison-and-contrast, read "The Season's Curmudgeon Sees the Light" by Mary C. Curtis on page 499.

Prewriting

Choosing Your Topic

- **Blueprinting** Think of a place you know well, such as a park or your kitchen. Draw a blueprint or map of this place, including key details such as trees or furniture. Then, write words or phrases on the blueprint that describe objects or activities you associate with this place. Review your blueprint, and choose an item to compare to another, related item.

- **Personal-experience timeline** Every time you outgrow your clothes, you can see how you are changing. These physical changes are fascinating to compare and contrast. So are your changes in attitude. Use a timeline to chart ways you have changed over time. Choose two entries as the basis for your comparison-and-contrast essay.

Work in Progress
Review the work you did on pages 675 and 697.

Narrowing Your Topic

The topic "The Best Vacation Spots" is much too broad to be addressed well in a short essay. You might narrow this to "Atlanta vs. San Francisco—Which Is More Family-Friendly?" Review your topic to divide it into separate parts, aspects, or subtopics. Choose one of these as your narrowed topic.

Gathering Details

Use a Venn diagram. Organize information about the ideas you will compare by using a Venn diagram, as shown here. Jot similarities in the center section, and note differences in the outer sections of each circle. When you have finished, circle the items that most vividly show comparisons and contrasts. Then, include these details in your essay. When you write your essay, juxtapose these details—set them side-by-side—to emphasize their differences and similarities.

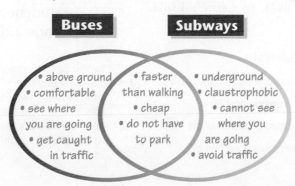

Buses
- above ground
- comfortable
- see where you are going
- get caught in traffic

- faster than walking
- cheap
- do not have to park

Subways
- underground
- claustrophobic
- cannot see where you are going
- avoid traffic

Drafting

Shaping Your Writing

Select the best organizational format. There are two common ways to organize a comparison-and-contrast essay. Review these options and use a structure that is appropriate to your audience.

- **Block method** Present all the details about one subject first, then present all the details about the next subject. The block method works well if you are writing about more than two subjects or if your topic is complicated.

- **Point-by-point organization** Discuss each aspect of your subjects in turn. For example, if you are comparing buses and subways, you might first discuss the cost of each, then accessibility, and so on.

Block
I. Buses
  a. cheaper
  b. more routes
  c. better views
II. Trains
  a. better seats
  b. faster
  c. quieter

Point-by-point
I. Introduction
II. Costs of each
III. Accessibility of each
IV. View from each
V. Disadvantages of each

Find a message. Review your notes for a message about the value or importance of your comparison. Identify the reason that your readers should read your work.

Providing Elaboration

Use vivid details. Specific details will emphasize similarities and differences. Notice the effect of the following examples:

General	**Vivid**
a small house next to a big house	a weathered, rickety cottage next to a stately mansion

Layer ideas using SEE. To develop the main point of the supporting paragraphs in your essay, follow these steps:
- *State* the topic of the paragraph.
- *Extend* the idea by restating it in a new way, applying it to a particular case, or contrasting it with another point.
- *Elaborate* with specific examples, facts, or explanations.

To read the complete student model, see page 720.

Student Model: Layering Ideas to Elaborate

Statement: Two civil rights movements protested in nonviolent ways.

Extension: They held marches, boycotts, and demonstrations.

Elaboration: In 1917, Alice Paul and other women picketed at the White House. In 1963, more than 200,000 Americans marched on Washington, D.C.

In the first sentence, Carolyn states a main idea. The SEE Method allows her to provide details to support the main idea.

From the Author's Desk

Jacqueline Woodson
On Including Details

Jacqueline Woodson

In this passage from my novel *Hush,* Toswiah, the narrator, tells of her family's transition from their Boulder, Colorado, home. They were forced to leave after her father witnessed a murder, and as a result, are now part of a Witness Protection Program that has moved them to a tiny apartment in a big city. Toswiah and her family have left everything they loved behind them—even their old names.

"I write because I love creating new worlds."

——Jacqueline Woodson

Professional Model:
from *Hush*

Some mornings, waking up in this new place, I don't know where I am. The apartment is tiny. The kitchen is not even a whole room away from the living room, just a few steps and a wide doorway with no door separating it. Not even one fireplace. Daddy sits by the window staring out, hardly ever saying anything. Maybe he thinks if he looks long and hard enough, Denver will reappear, . . . Maybe he thinks the tall gray buildings all smashed against each other will separate and squat down, that the Rocky Mountains will rise up behind them. . . .

When Daddy looks over to where me and my sister, Anna, sit watching TV, he looks surprised, like he's wondering why we aren't downstairs in the den. No den here, though. No dining room. No extra bathrooms down the hall and at the top of the stairs. Just five rooms with narrow doorways here.

Here, I spent a lot of time imagining what it would be like to leave the place I loved. I wanted to really focus on small details.

Toswiah's father is very depressed about the current situation. I put him by the window to show his sadness and to also show what he was seeing.

The family has gone from a grand house to a small apartment. I spent time trying to give details about each to show the difference.

Writing Workshop

Revising

Revising Your Overall Structure

Color-code to check organization and balance. Reread your draft. Use one color to highlight details about one of your subjects. Use a second color to mark details about the other. If your draft has more of one color, add details on the subject about which you have written less. If your highlights do not show a consistent organization using either the block method or the point-by-point method, consider revising for clarity.

Reading Writing Connection

To read the complete student model, see page 720.

Student Model: Revising to Check Balance

Both groups were able to change the laws so that they could have their rights. Women were given the right to vote in 1920 by Amendment 19 to the Constitution. ⋀ The Civil Rights Act of 1964 outlawed discrimination in hiring and ended segregation in public places. This law helped both groups.

> Carolyn added a fact that supported her second subject.

Peer Review: Invite a classmate to read your draft to evaluate the organization and balance. Ask your reader to tell you whether your essay presents enough information about each subject, or to suggest points that need more detail. Consider adding details based on this feedback.

Revising Your Paragraphs

Add supporting details. Copy your thesis onto an index card. Run the card down your draft as you read it, one line at a time. Identify any details that do not directly support your thesis. Delete the details or rewrite them to develop your main idea. In the example shown, the deleted detail did not add to a comparison of buses and trains.

> Buses cost 85¢ a ride. ~~Of course, you can walk for free or take a cab that costs $1.00 for each quarter mile.~~ Trains cost $1.25.

Integrating Grammar Skills

Revising to Vary Sentence Patterns

To keep your writing lively, avoid writing sentences that follow a dull pattern. Many sentences begin with nouns, as in *The <u>waiter</u> took our order.*

Use a Variety of Sentence Beginnings To avoid beginning every sentence with a noun, consider these other options:

> **Adjective:** <u>Surprised</u>, the waiter rushed over.

> **Adverb:** <u>Running quickly</u>, he arrived at our table.

> **Prepositional Phrase:** <u>After a delay</u>, the food arrived.

Use Appositives and Appositive Phrases To pack information into your sentences, use appositives, noun phrases that define or explain other words in the sentence.

> **Appositive:** The cat, <u>a tabby</u>, prowled the yard.

> **Appositive Phrase:** The dog, <u>my mother's longtime pet</u>, was happy to see us.

Fixing Repetitive Sentence Patterns To fix a series of sentences that start the same way, follow these steps:

1. **Identify the existing pattern of sentence beginnings.**
   - Draw a triangle around each noun that starts a sentence.
   - Draw a box around each adjective that starts a sentence.
   - Draw a circle around each prepositional phrase that starts a sentence.

2. **Review your results.** Count the number of triangles, boxes, and circles. If you have too many of one shape, rewrite the sentence beginnings to build greater variety.

3. **Consider using appositives to include more information.** Identify key nouns in a sentence and write a brief noun phrase to define the word. Use commas to set this word or phrase off from the rest of the sentence.

Apply It to Your Editing

Choose three paragraphs in your draft. Review the sentence beginnings. If you have not used enough variety, revise by beginning some sentences according to the rules presented here.

Prentice Hall Writing and Grammar Connection, Chapter 20, Section 1; Chapter 21, Section 3

Writing Workshop

Student Model: Carolyn Sienko
Williamston, MI

Comparing Struggles for Equality

The civil rights movement of the 1950s and 1960s had a lot in common with the women's suffrage movement that began with the Seneca Falls Convention in 1848. Both movements involved a group of people who were denied rights and who fought to obtain those rights.

Although in most ways the two struggles were similar, the specific rights each group fought for were different. Women wanted the right to vote in elections, the right to own property in their own names, and the right to keep their own wages. African Americans fought for the end to segregation. Like the women, they wanted to be treated with equal rights. However, the civil rights movement was about fairness in schools, jobs, and public places like buses and restaurants.

Both movements protested in nonviolent ways. They held marches, boycotts, and demonstrations to raise the public's consciousness and get the laws changed. In 1917, Alice Paul and other women picketed at the White House. In 1963, more than 200,000 Americans, led by Dr. Martin Luther King, Jr., marched on Washington, D.C. They wanted Congress to pass laws to end discrimination.

Both movements were about equality. The Declaration of Independence, an important document in the struggle for equality, states: "We hold these truths to be self-evident, that all men are created equal; that they are endowed by their Creator with certain unalienable rights; that among these are life, liberty, and the pursuit of happiness."

Protesters in both the civil rights movement and the women's suffrage movement felt that they were being denied rights that were given to them by this statement from the Declaration of Independence.

Both groups were able to change the laws so that they could have their rights. Women were given the right to vote in 1920 by Amendment 19 to the Constitution. Similarly, the Civil Rights Act of 1964 outlawed discrimination in hiring and ended segregation in public places.

In conclusion, the civil rights movement of the 1950s and 1960s and the women's suffrage movement were both about equality under the law. They are both good examples of how much work and determination it takes to change the laws. It is good to know, however, that the laws can be changed.

Carolyn begins her essay with a thesis statement that introduces the subjects of her comparison. She indicates that she will focus more on similarities.

The writer focuses first on the differences in the specific rights being sought.

Carolyn uses point-by-point organization to compare the movements.

The writer provides a quotation to support an idea.

The conclusion restates the introduction, driving home the point.

Editing and Proofreading

Check your writing to correct errors in spelling, grammar, and punctuation.

Focus on Spelling: As you proofread, circle words that you are not sure how to spell, that you frequently misspell, or that you seldom use. Use a dictionary to confirm the spelling of the circled words.

Publishing and Presenting

Consider one of these ways to share your writing:

Publish a column. If you have compared and contrasted subjects of local interest, such as two restaurants or several stores, submit your essay to your local newspaper.

Start a family tradition. If you have compared and contrasted two subjects of interest to your family—two uncles, two birthdays, two vacations—read your essay at a family gathering.

> *Prentice Hall*
> *Writing and Grammar*
> *Connection:*
> *Chapter 8*

Reflecting on Your Writing

Writer's Journal Write a few notes about the experience of writing a comparison-and-contrast essay. Begin by answering these questions:
- What did you enjoy most about writing your essay? Why?
- If you could begin again, what would you do differently? Explain your answers.

Rubric for Self-Assessment

To assess your comparison-and-contrast essay, use the following rubric:

Criteria	Rating Scale *not very* ... *very*				
Focus: How clearly do you state your topic?	1	2	3	4	5
Organization: How effectively are points of comparison and contrast organized?	1	2	3	4	5
Support/Elaboration: How well do you describe similarities and differences?	1	2	3	4	5
Style: How appropriate is the language for your audience?	1	2	3	4	5
Conventions: How correct is your grammar, especially your use of varied sentence patterns?	1	2	3	4	5

Evaluating Media Messages

Every day, you face hundreds of media messages: from television, radio, billboards, print ads, videotapes, even on the Internet. It is important to question the ideas in these messages. Practice being an active and critical audience by following these suggestions.

Evaluate Content and Technique

Look critically at images. The media flash images at us at amazing speeds and levels of complexity. Some are graphic; others are realistic; still others are digitally created or enhanced. All are intended to catch your attention and keep you watching. Be aware of how certain images are designed to appeal to a particular audience.

Listen critically to words and sounds. The creator of a message can instill an overall mood by using key words, music, and sound effects.

Observe "tricks of the trade." Some messages suggest that you jump on a bandwagon. Others use celebrity spokespeople. Still others use statistics and facts to impress an audience. Recognizing media techniques will make you a smarter viewer.

Evaluate Credibility

As you receive a media message, analyze the believability of what you observe. Think about what is expressed and what is *not* expressed.

Hidden agendas. Especially when viewing for information or to hear a point of view, it is essential to distinguish fact from opinion. Sometimes, messages are hidden. Look beyond the surface of a media message. Which facts, values, and ideas are being presented?

Slant or bias. Often, complex subjects are presented from only one point of view. For example, political ads or public-service announcements may address only one side of a controversial issue. As a viewer, be aware that you may not have been fully informed about an issue.

> **Feedback Form for Media Messages**
>
> **Contents and Techniques**
> • What are the key words and images? _____
> • What media presentation techniques do you observe? _____
> • How do you interpret the message? _____
> • How might others interpret it? _____
>
> **Credibility**
> • Is there a hidden agenda? _____
> • Is there bias or slant? _____
> • How would you rate the credibility of this message?
>   ___ Excellent ___ Good ___ Fair ___ Poor
> • Give a reason for your rating: _____

Activity ▶ **Evaluation** With a group, listen to a television and a radio news commentary on the same topic. Summarize each message, and then use the form to evaluate what you saw and heard.

Trouble the Water:
250 Years of
African American Poetry

Edited by Jerry W. Ward, Jr.
New American Library, 1997

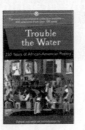

Poetry *Trouble the Water,* the first collection to cover nearly 300 years of poetic achievement, contains 400 important works by African American writers. This poetic medley features women as half the contributors and includes nearly 50 poems from the 1980s and 1990s. The entire rich and varied tradition of African American poetry appears in this anthology.

Johnny Tremain

Esther Forbes
Laurel Leaf, 1969

Novel Johnny, a young apprentice silversmith, is caught up in the danger and excitement of the Revolutionary War. Historical fiction that tells the story of the period from the Boston Tea Party through the Battle of Lexington, the book is also a story of a young man growing up in a time of turmoil.

Reflections on a Gift
of Watermelon Pickle:
and Other Modern Verse

Compiled by Stephen Dunning, Edward Lueders, and Hugh Smith
Scott Foresman & Company, 1966

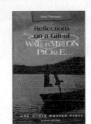

Poetry A wonderful romp through poetry that students love! This collection includes world-famous poets, little-known gems, and subjects that students relate to and cherish. The collection provides new views of everything from steam shovels to apartment buildings.

Poems by Robert Frost:
A Boy's Will and North of
Boston

Robert Frost
Signet, 2001

Poetry These first two collections of poetry by one of America's most beloved poets bring the people and the landscape of rural New England to life. Frost introduces characteristic themes—the value of manual labor, the beauty of nature, the individual versus the community—and experiments with narrative poetry and blank verse.

These titles are available in the Penguin/Prentice Hall Literature Library.
Consult your teacher before choosing one.

Think About It In the late 1700s and early 1800s, the most powerful countries in the world—England, France, and the United States—were eager to expand their territory. The United States more than doubled in size in 1803 when it completed the Louisiana Purchase, assuming the status of a world power. The following excerpt from the graphic novel *The Louisiana Purchase: An American Story* describes this historic deal.

THE LOUISIANA PURCHASE

John Chase

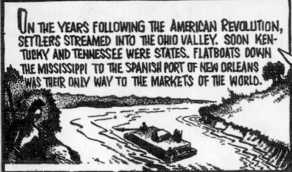
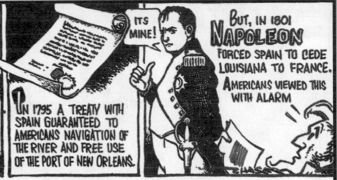

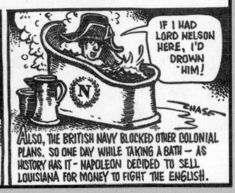

More to Explore

The use of graphic novels in the classroom is a fairly new concept. Graphic novels use comic book formats to present information in new ways and make learning fun for students of all ages. Outside the classroom, graphic novels are becoming more popular, too.

Readings in Social Studies
Talk About It

Use these questions to guide a discussion of "The Louisiana Purchase."

1. **(a)** To what two things does the cartoonist attribute the Louisiana Purchase? **(b)** How did each of these things lead to expansion?

2. What do you think of the way the history of the Louisiana Purchase is presented here? Use these questions to explore your ideas.
   - Do you find this part of American history interesting? Explain.
   - Does this representation of the Louisiana Purchase increase your interest in the topic? Why or why not?

   Choose a point person to share your group's ideas with the class.

Drama

文楽

Unit 5 Overview

Introduction:
Exploring Drama

Part 1: Draw Conclusions

Part 2: Cause and Effect

Introduction:
Drama

Cherie Bennett
Talks About the Form

Cherie
Bennett

Like movies or television, **drama** depends on a great story and great **dialogue.** But plays are performed live, which means they can be a bit different from performance to performance, as the actors react to each other in real time. Also, since plays are live entertainment, anything can go wrong at any time. Or right. Or become so uniquely magical in a single moment that you could swear the stage is levitating.

▲ Cherie Bennett has had a versatile career as a playwright, actress and singer, novelist, theater director, and syndicated columnist.

What Makes a Great Story for a Play

I've written novels, scripts for television and the movies, and plays. But there's a special kind of story that is *perfect* for the stage: a story that features relationships between **characters** we care about. Since in a play, the relationships happen right in front of us—with real, live, breathing actors—it's easy to forget that the actors are not the characters that they are playing. That's my twin goal as a playwright: to make you forget you're in a theater, and to lure you into inhabiting the world of my characters.

Plays are the most challenging type of storytelling. Novels allow the writer much more freedom; the storyteller can explain anything and everything. Movies give the writer the freedom to write physical **scenes** and to tell a story through action, both of which are impossible on stage.

▼ **Critical Viewing**
In what ways does this picture show that more than other types of writing, drama is the result of a group effort? **[Interpret]**

The Mystery

Plays are different—just a string of scenes between a few people. Everything the writer wants to convey must be done through dialogue, within the confines of the stage. The challenge is in telling a compelling, emotional story through this medium.

With so many limits, it seems like a miracle when a play succeeds. But when it does, it's the best of all artistic experiences—as dangerous, fascinating, and mysterious as life itself.

One of my favorite playwrights, Tom Stoppard, sums up this mystery perfectly in the quotation shown here. For me, a great play is true to life and it illuminates something true about life. That's why if I could write nothing else, I'd write plays.

HENSLOWE. Mr. Fennyman, let me explain about the theatre business. [*They stop.*] The natural condition is one of insurmountable obstacles on the road to imminent disaster . . .

FENNYMAN. So what do we do?

HENSLOWE. Nothing. Strangely enough, it all turns out well.

FENNYMAN. How?

HENSLOWE. I don't know. It's a mystery.

from *Shakespeare in Love*
—*Marc Norman and Tom Stoppard*

More About the Author

Cherie **Bennett** (b. 1960)

Cherie Bennett has said that playwriting is her greatest passion: " . . . it's live and in the moment; the heat of that is extremely appealing to me." Cherie and her husband, Jeff Gottesfeld, have collaborated on the play *Anne Frank & Me* and on episodes of the Warner Brothers television series *Smallville*. Besides creating works for the stage and television, Bennett writes novels for young adults.

Fast Facts

▶ Bennett's first novel was published when she was still in college.

▶ She responds personally to each fan letter that she receives.

▶ Her column, *Hey, Cherie!*, is read by teens nationally.

Learning About Drama

Elements of Drama

Drama is written to be performed. Therefore, as you read it, you must visualize how the action would appear and sound to an audience. While dramas include elements of fiction such as plot, conflict, and setting, they also use some elements that are unique to drama.

- **Playwright** is the name given to the author of a play, and a **script** is the written form of a play.

- **Acts** are the units of the action in a drama. Acts are often divided into parts called **scenes.**

- **Characterization** is the playwright's technique of creating believable characters.

HEART OF THE CITY ©1999 Mark Tatulli/Dist. by Universal Press Syndicate. Reprinted with permission. All rights reserved.

- **Dialogue** is the words characters say. The words each character speaks appear next to the character's name. Much of what you learn about the characters, setting, and events is revealed through dialogue—conversations among the characters.

- **Monologue** is a long, uninterrupted speech that is spoken by a single character. A monologue often reveals a character's private thoughts and feelings.

- **Stage directions** are sets of bracketed information that convey information to the cast, crew, and readers of the drama about sound effects, actions, and sets. This information can also describe a character's gestures or emotion.

- **Set** is the term used for the scenery on stage that suggests the time and place of the action.

- **Props** are small portable items that the actors use to make their actions look realistic, such as plates on the set of a kitchen.

Types of Drama

Comedy is a form of drama that has a happy ending. Comedies often feature normal characters in funny situations. Comedies can be written to entertain, but also they can point out the faults of a society.

Tragedy is often contrasted with comedy. The distinguishing feature of a tragedy is that the events lead to the downfall of the main character. This character can be an average person, but often is a person of great significance, like a king or a heroic figure.

Drama is often used to describe plays that address serious subjects. The world of drama is not limited to the stage. For example, the cartoon on page 730 refers to a diary that inspired a drama presented in this unit.

- **Screenplays** are the scripts for films. They include camera angles and can allow for more scene changes than a stage play.

- **Teleplays** are scripts written for television and often contain similar elements as a screenplay.

- **Radio plays** are written to be performed as radio broadcasts. They include sound effects and require no set.

Check Your Understanding

Identify *character, dialogue, stage directions, set, characterization,* and *props* in the following excerpt from *The Diary of Anne Frank.* Discuss your responses with a partner.

ANNE. [*She starts to throw hers in, and cannot.*] It's funny, I can't throw mine away. I don't know why.

PETER. You can't throw . . . ? Something they branded you with . . . ? That they made you wear so they could spit on you?

ANNE. I know. I know. But after all, it *is* the star of David, isn't it?

[*In the bedroom, right,* MARGOT *and* MRS. FRANK *are lying down.* MR. FRANK *starts quietly out.*]

▼ **Critical Viewing**
The Diary of Anne Frank takes place in an attic in Amsterdam, shown below. If you were directing this play, what sound elements could you use to capture the feel of a large city? **[Speculate]**

The idea for *Anne Frank & Me* came to me while watching *60 Minutes*. The guest said Anne's diary was forged and the Holocaust didn't happen, in a completely reasonable tone. And I thought: A teen who doesn't know better might believe him.

Creating a Play by Playing What-if

So my husband, Jeff Gottesfeld, and I played what-if. What if we could make the truth real to a teen girl who disbelieved the reality of the Holocaust? What if a Christian girl from *now* went back in time and became a Jewish girl *then*? What if she lived in a hip city—Paris, France? What if she herself had to go into hiding? What if she actually met Anne Frank on a transport to Auschwitz?

Just like that, we had our story.

The Challenges: Researching, Writing and Staging

But what a story we'd chosen to tackle! Research is crucial to any historical piece. Jeff speaks French, which helped a lot, since much of the primary source material is French.

Then there was the challenge of how to write the **dialogue** and **stage** this drama with a limited number of actors. Thankfully, I was asked to direct the first productions. It meant I could direct the action, and re-write, re-rewrite, and *re*-re-rewrite, right up to opening night.

I'll never forget when Jeff came running with the great review in *The New York Times*. I'd always dreamt of such a moment. However, my dad (who was also a writer) died during previews. He never got to see my play. That's what I call a bittersweet dream come true.

The **scene** you're about to read is the pivotal one in the play. Nicole—who only partly completed her literature assignment to read Anne Frank's diary—meets Anne on a cattle car transport to the Auschwitz death camp. Somehow, some way, Nicole knows this dark-haired stranger. . . .

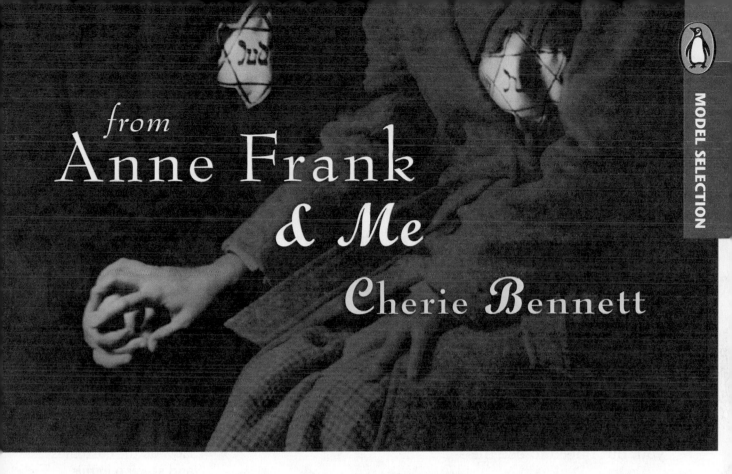

from

Anne Frank & Me

Cherie Bennett

After Nicole, a typical suburban American teenager, bumps her head in an accident, she wakes up in another time and place—Paris in 1942. Nicole's new family is Jewish. Soon after the Nazis arrest the family, they are put on a train to Auschwitz. This is where Nicole meets Anne Frank, the real writer of The Diary of a Young Girl.

AT RISE: *During the following monologue,* NAZIS *shove more people into the cattle car.*

NICOLE. *(pre-recorded).* Right now we are in Westerbork, in Holland. Earlier today they opened the door and shoved more people into our car. They speak Dutch. I can't understand them at all. I try to keep track of the dates as best I can. I think it is the 3rd of September, 1944. Surely the war will be over soon.

(Train sounds. NICOLE *makes her way to the bucket in the corner which is used as a toilet. A* GIRL *sits in front of the bucket, asleep, her back is to us.)*

▲ **Critical Viewing**
What mood does this photo suggest?
[Analyze]

Cherie Bennett
Author's Insight
For a play about history, accuracy is crucial. Anne Frank and her family were actually on the transport that left Holland for Auschwitz on September 3, 1944.

NICOLE. *(tapping the* GIRL *on the shoulder).* I'm sorry to disturb you, but I need to use the—

(The GIRL *turns around. It is* ANNE FRANK, *thin, huge eyes. Their eyes meet. Some memory is instantly triggered in* NICOLE. *She knows this girl, knows things about her. But how?)*

ANNE. *Spreekn U Nederlander?* [Spreck-en Ooo Ned-er-lahn-der?] *(*NICOLE *just stares.)* So you speak French, then? Is this better?

NICOLE. I . . . I need to use the—

ANNE. It's all right. I'll hold my coat for you to give you some privacy. *(*NICOLE *goes to the bucket,* ANNE *holds her coat open to shield her.)*

NICOLE. Thank you.

ANNE. Just please do the same for me when the time comes. Have you been in here a long time? *(*NICOLE *finishes, fixes her dress.)*

NICOLE. Seventeen days, starting just outside Paris.

ANNE. It smells like it.

NICOLE. Does it? I can't even tell anymore.

ANNE. It's all right. It's not important.

▲ **Critical Viewing**
How do the costumes and staging in this student performance of the play convey the mood of the drama? **[Interpret]**

Drama
Dialogue This exchange about an embarrassing topic establishes a supportive bond between the two teenagers.

NICOLE. Look, I know this sounds crazy, but . . . I know you.

ANNE. Have you been to Amsterdam?

NICOLE. No, never.

ANNE. Well, I've never been to Paris. Although I will go some day, I can assure you of that.

NICOLE. I do know you. Your name is . . . Anne Frank.

ANNE. *(shocked).* That's right! Who are you?

NICOLE. Nicole Bernhardt. I know so much about you . . . you were in hiding for a long time, in a place you called . . . the Secret Annex[1]—

ANNE. How could you know that?

NICOLE. *(her memory is flooded).* You were with your parents, and your older sister . . . Margot! And . . . some other people . . .

ANNE. Mr. Pfeffer and the Van Pels, they're all back there asleep—

NICOLE. Van Daans!

ANNE. *(shocked).* I only called them that in my diary. How could you know that?

NICOLE. And Peter! Your boyfriend's name was Peter!

ANNE. How could you know that??

NICOLE. You thought your parents would disapprove that you were kissing him—

ANNE. How is this possible?

NICOLE. You kept a diary. I read it.

ANNE. But . . . I left my diary in the Annex when the Gestapo came. You couldn't have read it.

NICOLE. But I did.

ANNE. How?

NICOLE. I don't know.

ANNE. *(skeptical).* This is a very, very strange conversation.

---

1. Secret Annex name given to the space in an Amsterdam office building, where in 1942, thirteen-year-old Anne Frank and her family went into hiding.

Cherie Bennett
Author's Insight
Another little-known fact that we had to get right: Anne only called the Van Daan family by that name in her diary. Their actual name was the Van Pels family.

Cherie Bennett
Author's Insight
The inciting incident for the whole play is when Nicole—in the present—is assigned *The Diary of a Young Girl* for her English class.

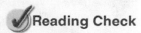**Reading Check**

What does Nicole know about Anne?

NICOLE. I feel like it was . . . I know this sounds crazy . . . but I feel like it was in the future.

ANNE. This is a joke, right? Peter put you up to this.

NICOLE. No—

ANNE. Daddy, then, to take my mind off—

NICOLE. No.

ANNE. *(cynical).* Maybe you're a mind reader! *(She closes her eyes.)* What number am I thinking of right now?

NICOLE. I have no idea. Do you believe in time travel?

ANNE. I'm to believe that you're from the future? Really, I'm much more intelligent than I look.

NICOLE. I don't know how I know all this. I just do.

ANNE. Maybe you're an angel.

NICOLE. That would certainly be news to me.

Drama
Stage Directions
The emotions described here in parentheses tell readers how Anne feels about what Nicole has told her.

◀ **Critical Viewing**
How would you describe the relationship between Anne and Nicole as shown in this photo? **[Draw Conclusions]**

Q. **What challenges did you face in introducing Anne Frank herself into your play?**

A. It was a huge risk. Anne Frank has long been one of my heroes. She is such a famous figure that everyone brings prejudices—in the strictest sense of that word—to any fictional depiction of her. Often she is thought of as saint-like. But we wanted to depict her as a real girl. Our hope was that the more real she seemed on stage, the more kids watching the play would relate to her.

Q. **What instructions do you think a director should give the actors playing this scene?**

A. To think of the characters they play as real and timeless. Young actors can get caught in the trap of playing historical things falsely, simply because the dialogue doesn't have modern idioms. I'd also want the director to encourage the actors to be brave. The ability to access such a depth of emotion is a scary thing. If a director asks this of actors, then he or she must also be prepared to be their cheerleader, their inspiration, and their safety net.

StudentCorner

Q. **Why did the Nazis treat the people in the cattle cars like animals?**

—**Shari Manzer, Omaha, Nebraska**

A. The sad truth is that the Nazis and their European collaborators believed their victims were no better than animals—whether they were Jews, Slavs, or whatever—and that they were doing humanity a favor by exterminating them.

 Writing Workshop: *Work in Progress*

Business Letter
Jot down five reasons that you might write a business letter. Then, choose one reason and list the specific points you would include in your letter. Save this Reason List in your writing portfolio.

Apply the Skills

Drama

Thinking About the Selection

1. **Respond:** How would you feel if someone you had never met knew details of your personal life?

2. **(a) Recall:** In what city does the train journey begin?
   (b) Generalize: What are the conditions on the train?
   (c) Speculate: Why are the people treated this way?

3. **(a) Make a Judgment:** Read the short biography of Anne Frank and two excerpts from her diary on pages 881–886. Does Cherie Bennett's Anne Frank seem like the real Anne Frank? Why or why not? **(b) Discuss:** Compare your answers with a partner. Choose one response to share with the class.

Drama Review

4. Explain why you think this play is best characterized as a **comedy**, a **tragedy**, or a **drama**.

5. In a chart like the one shown, list details from the **scene** that make Anne and Nicole believable **characters**.

Character Description	
Anne	**Nicole**
huge eyes	anxious, confused

| **Anne** | **Nicole** |

Research the Author

Using the Internet and library resources, create a **bulletin board display** to show Cherie Bennett's life and work. Follow these steps:

- Locate a Web page for the writer. Download information about her family, education, and literary works.
- Find photographs of the author or book jackets to use on your bulletin board.
- Select titles you think will appeal to classmates. Write a summary of each to encourage students to read the books.

QuickReview

Selection at a Glance

In the scene from *Anne Frank & Me*, a fictional girl from the future meets a real historical character her own age.

Go Online
Assessment
For: Self-test
Visit: www.PHSchool.com
Web Code: ena-6501

Comedy: a play with a happy ending

Tragedy: a play in which events lead to the main character's downfall

Drama: a play that deals with a serious subject

Scene: part of an act

Characterization: playwright's technique of creating believable characters

Draw Conclusions

Skills You Will Learn

Reading Skill: *Make Connections to Draw Conclusions*
Literary Analysis: *Stage Directions*

Reading Skill: *Make Generalizations*

Literary Analysis: *Comparing Adaptations to Originals*

Literature You Will Read

Reading and Vocabulary Skills Preview

Reading: Drawing Conclusions

> **Drawing conclusions** means making decisions or forming opinions by connecting important details.

Skills and Strategies You Will Learn in Part 1

In Part 1, you will learn

- to **analyze** characters in order to **draw conclusions** about them (p. 742)
- to **make connections** to **form conclusions** (p. 742)
- to **make generalizations** (p. 754)

Using the Skills and Strategies in Part 1

In Part 1, you will learn to analyze the statements, words, and actions of characters in order to draw conclusions about those characters. You will practice connecting story details to find patterns that lead you to conclusions. You will also learn to make valid generalizations by noticing common elements in the information you read.

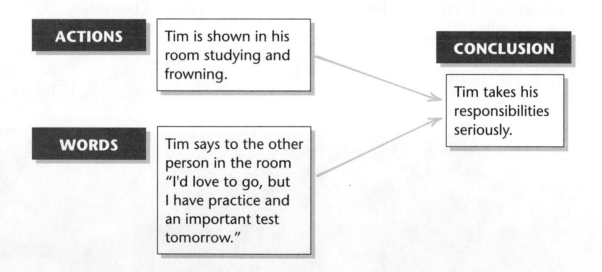

ACTIONS

Tim is shown in his room studying and frowning.

WORDS

Tim says to the other person in the room "I'd love to go, but I have practice and an important test tomorrow."

CONCLUSION

Tim takes his responsibilities seriously.

Academic Vocabulary: Words for Discussing Drawing Conclusions

The following words will help you write and talk about your conclusions as you read the selections in this unit.

Word	Definition	Example Sentence
assumption *n.*	something one supposes to be true, without proof	Test your *assumption* by analyzing the evidence.
valid *adj.*	based on facts and strong evidence; convincing	A *valid* conclusion can be supported with evidence.
evaluate *v.*	judge; determine the worth or strength of something	*Evaluate* the evidence carefully before making a decision.
connect *v.*	show how things are related	*Connect* all the details to find a pattern.
rational *adj.*	based on reason; logical	His conclusion was not *rational*; it was based purely on emotion.

Vocabulary Skill: Roots

▶ A **root** is the basic meaning in a word.

Most English words have roots that are derived from Latin or Greek. By learning these roots, you can understand the connections between words with related meanings.

In Part 1, you will learn

- the root -*sum*- (p. 752)
- the root -*val*- (p. 752)

Root	Meaning	Example
-sum-	to take, to use	assumption, summation
-val-	strong, worth	valid, validate

Activity For each root in the chart above, write two more example words and definitions. Then, use each word in a sentence.

These skills will help you become a better reader.
Practice them with *The Governess* (p. 744).

Reading Skill

Drawing conclusions means reaching decisions or forming opinions after considering the facts and details in a text. To draw conclusions from a play, observe what characters say and do.

- Look for statements that reveal underlying ideas and attitudes.
- Analyze interactions that show how characters treat each other.
- Notice actions that create a clear pattern of behavior.

Make connections among these items to decide what that pattern tells you about the character. Use a chart like the one shown to record your observations and conclusions.

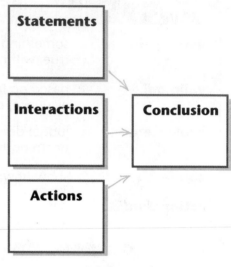

Literary Analysis

Stage directions are notes that tell how a play should be performed. They describe the scenery, costumes, lighting, and sound, and also tell how the characters feel, move, and speak. Stage directions are usually printed in italics and set in brackets. These stage directions describe the setting of a play:

[*It is late evening. The stage is dark, except for the glow of a small lamp beside the bed.*]

When you read a play, use the stage directions to create a mental image of how an actual stage production would look and sound.

Vocabulary Builder

The Governess

- **inferior** (in fir´ ē ər) *adj.* lower in status or rank (p. 745) *The noblemen thought that the common people were inferior.*

- **discrepancies** (di skrep´ ən sēz) *n.* differences; inconsistencies (p. 745) *There were discrepancies between the two versions.*

- **discharged** (dis chärjd´) *v.* fired; released from something (p. 747) *Her work was bad, so the manager discharged her.*

- **satisfactory** (sat´ is fak´ tə rē) *adj.* adequate; sufficient to meet a requirement (p. 747) *The final statement was satisfactory to all committee members.*

- **guileless** (gīl´ lis) *adj.* without deceit or trickery; innocent (p. 749) *Jessica was so guileless that people always played tricks on her.*

Build Understanding • *The Governess*

Background

A Governess's Life In the nineteenth century, when *The Governess* is set, upper-class families in Europe and the United States hired governesses to teach and look after their children. Governesses were often educated single women for whom there were few other ways to make a living. The life of a governess was often lonely because she belonged to neither the servant class nor the upper class.

Connecting to the Literature

Reading/Writing Connection In *The Governess*, playwright Neil Simon introduces a character who has trouble speaking up for herself. Write a list of five reasons why someone might have this problem. Use at least three of the following words: *assert, convince, reject, respond, challenge.*

Meet the Author

Neil **Simon** (b. 1927)

Neil Simon has been called the best-loved playwright of the twentieth century. Millions of people have enjoyed his plays and films. He is best known for his comedies—plays that poke gentle fun at people's behavior.

Life in New York Simon grew up in the Washington Heights neighborhood of New York City. He began as a writer for radio and television, then moved on to write comedies for the stage. New York is the setting for many of his most popular plays, including *The Odd Couple, Plaza Suite,* and *Barefoot in the Park.* In the 1980s, Simon drew on his own life for three bittersweet plays that made critics view his work more seriously: *Brighton Beach Memoirs, Biloxi Blues,* and *Broadway Bound.*

Fast Facts

- ▶ Simon once had four hit plays running on Broadway at the same time.
- ▶ His 1991 play *Lost in Yonkers* won the Pulitzer Prize.
- ▶ *The Governess* comes from *The Good Doctor,* a play based on short stories by the Russian writer Anton Chekhov.

 Go **Online**
Author Link

For: More about the author
Visit: www.PHSchool.com
Web Code: cnc-9502

The GOVERNESS

Neil Simon

MISTRESS. Julia! [*Calls again*] Julia!

[*A young governess,* JULIA, *comes rushing in. She stops before the desk and curtsies.*]

JULIA. [*Head down*] Yes, madame?

MISTRESS. Look at me, child. Pick your head up. I like to see your eyes when I speak to you.

JULIA. [*Lifts her head up*] Yes, madame. [*But her head has a habit of slowly drifting down again*]

MISTRESS. And how are the children coming along with their French lessons?

JULIA. They're very bright children, madame.

MISTRESS. Eyes up . . . They're bright, you say. Well, why not? And mathematics? They're doing well in mathematics, I assume?

JULIA. Yes, madame. Especially Vanya.

MISTRESS. Certainly. I knew it. I excelled in mathematics. He gets that from his mother, wouldn't you say?

JULIA. Yes, madame.

MISTRESS. Head up . . . [*She lifts head up*] That's it. Don't be afraid to look people in the eyes, my dear. If you think

▲ **Critical Viewing**
Which people in this scene are playing the parts of servants? How can you tell? **[Analyze]**

Reading Skill
Draw Conclusions
What conclusion can you draw about the relationship between Julia and the Mistress?

of yourself as <u>inferior</u>, that's exactly how people will treat you.

JULIA. Yes, ma'am.

MISTRESS. A quiet girl, aren't you? . . . Now then, let's settle our accounts. I imagine you must need money, although you never ask me for it yourself. Let's see now, we agreed on thirty rubles[1] a month, did we not?

JULIA. [*Surprised*] Forty, ma'am.

MISTRESS. No, no, thirty. I made a note of it. [*Points to the book*] I always pay my governess thirty . . . Who told you forty?

JULIA. You did, ma'am. I spoke to no one else concerning money . . .

MISTRESS. Impossible. Maybe you *thought* you heard forty when I said thirty. If you kept your head up, that would never happen. Look at me again and I'll say it clearly. *Thirty rubles a month.*

JULIA. If you say so, ma'am.

MISTRESS. Settled. Thirty a month it is . . . Now then, you've been here two months exactly.

JULIA. Two months and five days.

MISTRESS. No, no. Exactly two months. I made a note of it. You should keep books the way I do so there wouldn't be these <u>discrepancies</u>. So—we have two months at thirty rubles a month . . . comes to sixty rubles. Correct?

JULIA. [*Curtsies*] Yes, ma'am. Thank you, ma'am.

MISTRESS. Subtract nine Sundays . . . We did agree to subtract Sundays, didn't we?

JULIA. No, ma'am.

MISTRESS. Eyes! Eyes! . . . Certainly we did. I've always subtracted Sundays. I didn't bother making a note of it because I always do it. Don't you recall when I said we will subtract Sundays?

JULIA. No, ma'am.

MISTRESS. Think.

JULIA. [*Thinks*] No, ma'am.

---

1. **rubles** (roo′ bəlz) *n.* Russian currency; similar to U.S. dollars.

Vocabulary Builder
inferior (in fir′ ē ər) *adj.* lower in status or rank

Literary Analysis
Stage Directions
What actions and expressions do the stage directions help you to picture?

Vocabulary Builder
discrepancies (di skrep′ ən sēz) *n.* differences; inconsistencies

Reading Check

How much do Julia and the Mistress each think that Julia gets paid per month?

The Governess ■ 745

MISTRESS. You weren't thinking. Your eyes were wandering. Look straight at my face and look hard . . . Do you remember now?

JULIA. [*Softly*] Yes, ma'am.

MISTRESS. I didn't hear you, Julia.

JULIA. [*Louder*] Yes, ma'am.

MISTRESS. Good. I was sure you'd remember . . . Plus three holidays. Correct?

JULIA. Two, ma'am. Christmas and New Year's.

MISTRESS. And your birthday. That's three.

JULIA. I worked on my birthday, ma'am.

MISTRESS. You did? There was no need to. My governesses never worked on their birthdays . . .

JULIA. But I did work, ma'am.

MISTRESS. But that's not the question, Julia. We're discussing financial matters now. I will, however, only count two holidays if you insist . . . Do you insist?

JULIA. I did work, ma'am.

MISTRESS. Then you *do* insist.

JULIA. No, ma'am.

MISTRESS. Very well. That's three holidays, therefore we take off twelve rubles. Now then, four days little Kolya was sick, and there were no lessons.

JULIA. But I gave lessons to Vanya.

MISTRESS. True. But I engaged you to teach two children, not one. Shall I pay you in full for doing only half the work?

JULIA. No, ma'am.

MISTRESS. So we'll deduct it . . . Now, three days you had a toothache and my husband gave you permission not to work after lunch. Correct?

JULIA. After four. I worked until four.

MISTRESS. [*Looks in the book*] I have here: "Did not work after lunch." We have lunch at one and are finished at two, not at four, correct?

JULIA. Yes, ma'am. But I—

Literary Analysis
Stage Directions
Which stage directions help you understand the way the characters speak the dialogue?

MISTRESS. That's another seven rubles . . . Seven and twelve is nineteen . . . Subtract . . . that leaves . . . forty-one rubles . . . Correct?

JULIA. Yes, ma'am. Thank you, ma'am.

MISTRESS. Now then, on January fourth you broke a teacup and saucer, is that true?

JULIA. Just the saucer, ma'am.

MISTRESS. What good is a teacup without a saucer, eh? . . . That's two rubles. The saucer was an heirloom.[2] It cost much more, but let it go. I'm used to taking losses.

JULIA. Thank you, ma'am.

MISTRESS. Now then, January ninth, Kolya climbed a tree and tore his jacket.

JULIA. I forbid him to do so, ma'am.

MISTRESS. But he didn't listen, did he? . . . Ten rubles . . . January fourteenth, Vanya's shoes were stolen . . .

JULIA. But the maid, ma'am. You <u>discharged</u> her yourself.

MISTRESS. But you get paid good money to watch everything. I explained that in our first meeting. Perhaps you weren't listening. Were you listening that day, Julia, or was your head in the clouds?

JULIA. Yes, ma'am.

MISTRESS. Yes, your head was in the clouds?

JULIA. No, ma'am. I was listening.

MISTRESS. Good girl. So that means another five rubles off [*Looks in the book*] . . . Ah, yes . . . The sixteenth of January I gave you ten rubles.

JULIA. You didn't.

MISTRESS. But I made a note of it. Why would I make a note of it if I didn't give it to you?

JULIA. I don't know, ma'am.

MISTRESS. That's not a <u>satisfactory</u> answer, Julia . . . Why would I make a note of giving you ten rubles if I did not in fact give it to you, eh? . . . No answer? . . . Then I must have given it to you, mustn't I?

---

2. **heirloom** (er´ lo͞om´) *n.* treasured possession passed down from generation to generation.

◀ **Critical Viewing**
If you were Julia, why would you feel intimidated by the Mistress, shown in the picture? Explain. **[Connect]**

Vocabulary Builder
discharged (dis chärjd´) *v.* fired; released from something

satisfactory (sat´ is fak´ tə rē) *adj.* adequate; sufficient to meet a requirement

Reading Check

How does the Mistress punish Julia for the actions of Kolya and the maid?

JULIA. Yes, ma'am. If you say so, ma'am.

MISTRESS. Well, certainly I say so. That's the point of this little talk. To clear these matters up. Take twenty-seven from forty-one, that leaves . . . fourteen, correct?

JULIA. Yes, ma'am. [*She turns away, softly crying*]

MISTRESS. What's this? Tears? Are you crying? Has something made you unhappy, Julia? Please tell me. It pains me to see you like this. I'm so sensitive to tears. What is it?

JULIA. Only once since I've been here have I ever been given any money and that was by your husband. On my birthday he gave me three rubles.

MISTRESS. Really? There's no note of it in my book. I'll put it down now. [*She writes in the book.*] Three rubles. Thank you for telling me. Sometimes I'm a little lax with my accounts . . . Always shortchanging myself. So then, we take three more from fourteen . . . leaves eleven . . . Do you wish to check my figures?

JULIA. There's no need to, ma'am.

MISTRESS. Then we're all settled. Here's your salary for two months, dear. Eleven rubles. [*She puts the pile of coins on the desk.*] Count it.

JULIA. It's not necessary, ma'am.

MISTRESS. Come, come. Let's keep the records straight. Count it.

JULIA. [*Reluctantly counts it*] One, two, three, four, five, six, seven, eight, nine, ten . . . ? There's only ten, ma'am.

MISTRESS. Are you sure? Possibly you dropped one . . . Look on the floor, see if there's a coin there.

JULIA. I didn't drop any, ma'am. I'm quite sure.

MISTRESS. Well, it's not here on my desk, and I *know* I gave you eleven rubles. Look on the floor.

JULIA. It's all right, ma'am. Ten rubles will be fine.

History Connection

What Is Women's Work?
Throughout the nineteenth century, jobs for women were scarce. Most professions were unavailable to anyone except men. Low-wage factory jobs, such as making clothing, were available to working-class women and girls. A majority of uneducated women, however, were domestic servants.

A middle-class woman with some education could become a teacher or a governess. An unmarried woman who needed to support herself had few other options.

Like domestic workers and factory workers, governesses earned very little. They were viewed as servants.

Connect to the Literature

Would Julia behave differently if she were paid well enough to have saved some money or if she could pursue other career options? Explain.

MISTRESS. Well, keep the ten for now. And if we don't find it on the floor later, we'll discuss it again next month.

JULIA. Yes, ma'am. Thank you, ma'am. You're very kind, ma'am.

[*She curtsies and then starts to leave.*]

MISTRESS. Julia!
[JULIA *stops, turns.*]
Come back here.
[*She goes back to the desk and curtsies again.*]
Why did you thank me?

JULIA. For the money, ma'am.

MISTRESS. For the money? . . . But don't you realize what I've done? I've cheated you . . . *Robbed* you! I have no such notes in my book. I made up whatever came into my mind. Instead of the eighty rubles which I owe you, I gave you only ten. I have actually stolen from you and you still thank me . . . Why?

JULIA. In the other places that I've worked, they didn't give me anything at all.

MISTRESS. Then they cheated you even worse than I did . . . I was playing a little joke on you. A cruel lesson just to teach you. You're much too trusting, and in this world that's very dangerous . . . I'm going to give you the entire eighty rubles. [*Hands her an envelope*] It's all ready for you. The rest is in this envelope. Here, take it.

JULIA. As you wish, ma'am. [*She curtsies and starts to go again.*]

MISTRESS. Julia! [JULIA *stops.*] Is it possible to be so spine-less? Why don't you protest? Why don't you speak up? Why don't you cry out against this cruel and unjust treatment? Is it really possible to be so <u>guileless</u>, so innocent, such a—pardon me for being so blunt—such a simpleton?

JULIA. [*The faintest trace of a smile on her lips*] Yes, ma'am . . . it's possible.

[*She curtsies again and runs off. The* MISTRESS *looks after her a moment, a look of complete bafflement on her face. The lights fade.*]

▲ **Critical Viewing**
Does this photograph accurately capture Julia's personality? Why or why not?
[Make a Judgment]

Vocabulary Builder
guileless (gīl´ lis) *adj.* without deceit or trickery; innocent

Reading Skill
Draw Conclusions
Does this speech change your mind about the Mistress's intentions? Explain.

Apply the Skills

The Governess

Thinking About the Selection

1. **Respond:** How do you feel toward the Mistress at the end of the play? Why?
2. **(a) Recall:** What does the Mistress want to discuss with Julia? **(b) Connect:** Why does Julia's position make this discussion difficult for her?
3. **(a) Recall:** What are some of the reasons the Mistress gives for cutting Julia's pay? **(b) Make Inferences:** Why does Julia respond the way she does?
4. **(a) Recall:** What final action does the Mistress take to try to make Julia fight back? **(b) Analyze:** Is the mistress being kind, cruel, or both? Explain. **(c) Speculate:** Do you think Julia will behave differently in the future? Why or why not?

Reading Skill

5. Identify three of the Mistress's lines that demonstrate the same attitude or behavior. **(a)** Based on these lines, what **conclusions** can you draw about the reasons for the Mistress's behavior? **(b)** Does your opinion of the Mistress change between the middle and the end of the play? Explain.
6. Based on Julia's answers to her Mistress's questions, what can you conclude about the general treatment of governesses at the time of this play?

Literary Analysis

7. Record **stage directions** from *The Governess* in a chart like the one shown. Provide at least two examples for each category.

Describing an Action	Showing How a Character Feels

8. What do the stage directions add to your understanding of the action? Explain.

QuickReview

Drama at a Glance

An employer tries to teach her governess, Julia, a lesson.

Go Online
Assessment

For: Self-test
Visit: www.PHSchool.com
Web Code: ena-6502

Drawing Conclusions: reaching decisions or forming opinions after considering the facts and details in a text

Stage Directions: notes in a play that describe setting, sound and lighting effects, and how characters speak and move

Vocabulary Builder

Practice Use a vocabulary word from page 742 to rewrite each of the following sentences to mean the opposite.

1. The testimony of the two witnesses was in total agreement.
2. Josie was so clever that no one could play a trick on her.
3. In spite of his hard work, Nico got a failing grade on the test.
4. The debaters treated each other as equals.
5. Ben's work was so outstanding that he was given a raise.

Writing

Write a **problem-solution essay** that examines Julia's lack of assertiveness and proposes an alternative solution to the one the Mistress tried. Follow these steps:

- Clearly explain the scope of the problem.
- Explore the negative consequences of the problem.
- Propose a workable and effective solution and explain why it is preferable to the Mistress's solution.

For *Grammar, Vocabulary,* and *Assessment,* see **Build Language Skills,** pages 752–753.

Extend Your Learning

Listening and Speaking Organize a **group discussion** about Julia's situation and how she should have handled it. Keep in mind the differences between classes in society at the time. Make sure that each person has a chance to express his or her reactions and opinions. Ask follow-up questions to make sure that you understand each speaker's ideas or point of view.

Research and Technology Find at least three classified ads for the position of nanny. Draw conclusions from these ads about how the modern responsibilities of a nanny differ from those of Julia's time. Then, write a **"Help Wanted" ad** for a modern nanny.

Build Language Skills

The Governess

Vocabulary Skill

Roots The **Latin root** *-sum-* means "take" or "use." It is found in many English words, including *assumption,* which means "take something for granted." Assumption is a noun, formed from the base word *assume*.

▶ **Example:** The evidence supports that *assumption*.

The **Latin root** *-val-* means "be strong" or "be worth." A *valid* argument is a strong one, which is based on evidence. Related forms of *valid* include the verb *validate* and the noun *validity*.

▶ **Example:** His objections to the editorial are *valid*, and we should take them seriously.

Practice Write a sentence using each word correctly. Use a dictionary to define the word if necessary.

1. assume
2. consume
3. valor
4. validate
5. presume

Grammar Lesson

Participial Phrases A **participle** is a verb form that is used as an adjective. Participles commonly end in *-ing* (present participle) or *-ed* (past participle). A **participial phrase** is made up of a participle with its modifiers and complements, such as adverbs or objects. The entire participial phrase is used as an adjective.

▶ **Example:** The tourist, *confused by the signs,* got lost.
Traveling quickly, we got to the game on time.

Practice Use a participial phrase to combine the two sentences.

1. Anna carried her suitcase. Anna boarded the bus.
2. The bus driver smiled. The bus driver said hello.
3. The tour group was on its way. The group waved goodbye.
4. A medieval palace was their goal. They visited the palace.
5. The building had been damaged in a battle. It was still impressive.

MorePractice

For more on participial phrases, see the Grammar Handbook, p. R31.

WG Prentice Hall Writing and Grammar Connection: Chapter 20, Section 1

Reading: Drawing Conclusions

Directions: *Read the selection. Then, answer the questions.*

As we came into town, I could see that many things had changed over the years. The huge trees that once shaded the streets were gone. The houses looked smaller to my adult eyes. Many small stores along High Street were empty, with "For Rent" signs in the windows. There was no workday bustle—people going to lunch and shopping. At the end of the street was a brand-new shopping mall. But even its parking lot was only half-full. I wondered what on earth I would do here!

1. Why would you conclude that the town is no longer very prosperous?
   A "For Rent" signs and empty stores
   B storm damage and no trees
   C a new shopping mall and no trees
   D people shopping and going to lunch

2. Which conclusion is most logical?
   A The narrator is excited.
   B The narrator has never visited the town before.
   C The narrator had known the town years ago.
   D The narrator is starting a business.

3. What can you conclude from the statement, "The houses looked smaller to my adult eyes"?
   A The narrator has a child.
   B The narrator is thinking about buying a house in the town.
   C The narrator is an architect.
   D The narrator was a child when he or she lived here.

4. Which conclusion is most logical?
   A The narrator is passing through.
   B The narrator is visiting old friends.
   C The narrator may be moving back.
   D The narrator doesn't drive.

Timed Writing: Persuasion [Connections]

Review *The Governess.* Write a letter to the governess telling her to stand up for herself. Give reasons and use appeals to emotion. Include details from Julia's conversation with her employer. (25 minutes)

 Writing Workshop: *Work in Progress*

Facts and statistics can add support to the points you make in a business letter. Look at the notes in your writing portfolio. Add an important fact or statistic to each topic on your list. Save this list in your writing portfolio.

Public Documents

In Part 1, you are learning about drawing conclusions to help you understand the literature you read. Drawing conclusions also is helpful when you are reading public documents, such as this one from the U.S. Department of Labor. If you read "The Governess," you might draw the conclusion that a document like this one could have helped Julia stand up for her rights as a worker.

About Public Documents

Public documents include laws, statutes, legal notices, government publications, minutes of public meetings, and other records to which the public has legal access. Many of these documents, such as the one on the following pages, relate to the workings of government and citizens' rights and responsibilities under law.

The language in public documents can be formal, and words can have specialized meanings. It is important to read public documents closely and make sure you understand the meaning of key words and technical language.

Reading Skill

A **generalization** is a broad statement or rule that applies to many examples. You can make generalizations by noticing common elements in information you read as well as using what you already know about a topic.

Generalizations can be helpful in organizing information. However, to be useful, generalizations must be accurate in all situations they describe.

Use a chart like the one shown to make generalizations as you read.

Making Generalizations

Information		Information		Generalization
Youth can work three hours on school days, eight hours on non-school days.	+	School days are Monday through Friday.	=	Youth can work longer hours on weekends.

Wage and Hour Division
Basic Information

U.S. Department of Labor
Employment Standards Administration

The U. S. Department of Labor's Wage and Hour Division (WHD) is responsible for administering and enforcing laws that establish minimally acceptable standards for wages and working conditions in this country, regardless of immigration status.

> The Wage and Hour Division enforces the Fair Labor Standards and Migrant and Seasonal Agricultural Worker Protection Acts.

Fair Labor Standards Act

The Fair Labor Standards Act (FLSA) affects most private and public employment. The FLSA requires employers to pay covered employees who are not otherwise exempt at least the federal **minimum wage** and **overtime** pay for all hours worked over 40 in a workweek.

Covered employees must be paid for all hours worked in a workweek. In general, compensable hours worked include all time an employee is on duty or at a prescribed place of work and any time that an employee is suffered or permitted to work. This would generally include work performed at home, travel time, waiting time, training, and probationary periods.

> This section, written in clear easy-to-understand language, gives an overview of the laws that affect most kinds of employment.

- **Federal Minimum Wage = $5.15 per hour**

- **Tipped employees may be paid $2.13 per hour; if an employee's tips combined with cash wage does not equal $5.15, the employer must make up the difference**

- **Overtime after 40 hours in a week = 1 1/2 times an employee's regular rate of pay**

Migrant and Seasonal Agricultural Worker Protection Act

The Migrant and Seasonal Agricultural Worker Protection Act (MSPA) requires farm labor contractors, agricultural employers, and agricultural associations who "employ" workers to:

> The words in boldface type are key words, which provide critical information.

1) Pay workers the wages owed when due
2) Comply with federal and state safety and health standards if they provide housing for migrant workers
3) Ensure that vehicles that they use to transport workers are properly insured, operated by licensed drivers and meet federal and state safety standards
4) Provide written disclosure of the terms and conditions of employment

> Many migrant workers depend on their employers for housing and transportation to their jobs. The Migrant and Seasonal Agricultural Worker Protection Act sets out employers' responsibilities in these areas.

Wage and Hour Division
Basic Information

U.S. Department of Labor
Employment Standards Administration

Youth Employment

The FLSA also regulates the employment of youth.

Jobs Youth Can Do:

- 13 or younger: baby-sit, deliver newspapers, or work as an actor or performer
- Ages 14-15: office work, grocery store, retail store, restaurant, movie theater, or amusement park
- Age 16-17: Any job not declared hazardous
- Age 18: No restrictions

Hours Youth Ages 14 and 15 Can Work:

- After 7 A.M. and until 7 P.M.
- (Hours are extended to 9 P.M. June 1-Labor Day)
- Up to 3 hours on a school day
- Up to 18 hours in a school week
- Up to 8 hours on a non-school day
- Up to 40 hours in a non-school week

Note: Different rules apply to youth employed in agriculture. States also regulate the hours that youth under age 18 may work. To find State rules, log on to **www.youthrules.dol.gov**

> The Fair Labor Standards Act restricts the kinds of jobs workers under 18 can do, and also the number of hours they can work.

> The hours young people may work are regulated by the states. This information is too complicated to include in a general overview like this one, so readers are referred elsewhere for more information.

Reading: Making Generalizations
Directions: *Choose the letter of the best answer to each question.*

1. Which generalization *cannot* be made about the excerpt from the Fair Labor Standards Act?
   A The act describes employers' responsibilities.
   B The act describes employees' responsibilities.
   C The U.S. believes in protecting employees.
   D The U.S. sets minimum standards for employees.

2. Which generalization is best supported by the rules on p. 756?
   A Young people are workers just like any others.
   B Young people should be in school not at work.
   C The U.S. has special regulations for youth employment.
   D Regulations regarding youth employment have changed in recent years.

3. Which is the most accurate generalization regarding the hours youth ages fourteen and fifteen can work?
   A They can work about the same hours as adults can.
   B Their work hours are fewer on school days.
   C They can work early in the morning and late at night.
   D They can work any amount of overtime if they are paid for it.

Reading: Comprehension and Interpretation
Directions: *Write your answers on a separate sheet of paper.*

4. Based on the excerpt from the Fair Labor Standards and Migrant and Seasonal Agricultural Worker Protection Acts, describe the attitude of the United States toward workers' rights. **[Generating]**

5. Explain the probable reasons that youth employment is restricted in a way that adult employment is not. **[Generating]**

6. What conclusion do you draw from the types of regulations listed for migrant and seasonal workers? **[Integrating]**

Timed Writing: Explanation [Connections]
Explain why laws that set minimum standards for wages and working conditions are important. In your answer, describe problems that could occur if such laws did not exist. **(15 minutes)**

Adaptations

A literary **adaptation** is a work that has been changed or adjusted to fit a different form or genre. For example, a novel may be adapted into a play or a movie. Adapting a literary work usually means changing or leaving out some parts of the original to suit the new form. For instance, a play depends almost entirely on dialogue, without the narration or description that is often included in a story. Neil Simon's play *The Governess* (p. 744) is an adaptation of "The Ninny," a short story by the Russian writer Anton Chekhov.

Comparing Adaptations to Originals

To compare an adaptation to the original work, remember the differences in the two literary forms. Keep those differences in mind as you analyze the two works.

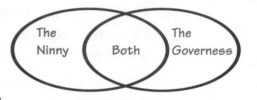

- First, look for the elements that the writer has kept from the original as well as those he or she has left out.

- Next, look for new elements the writer has introduced.

- Finally, compare the styles of the two authors. Determine if one style results in a lighter, more humorous treatment or whether the styles are mostly the same.

As you read Anton Chekhov's story "The Ninny," use a Venn diagram like the one shown to analyze the similarities and differences between this short story and Neil Simon's play *The Governess*.

Vocabulary Builder

The Ninny

- **account** (ə kaunt´) *n.* a bill for work done (p. 760) *He settled his <u>account</u> with the plumber.*

- **dock** (däk) *v.* to deduct part of one's salary or wages (p. 761) *The boss will <u>dock</u> Sam's pay if he is late again.*

- **spineless** (spīn´ ləs) *adj.* lacking in courage or willpower (p. 762) *"You're a <u>spineless</u> coward!" she shouted.*

- **ninny** (nin´ ē) *n.* simple or foolish person (p. 762) *She was so silly that people called her a <u>ninny</u>.*

- **timidly** (tim´ id lē) *adv.* in a shy or fearful manner (p. 762) *Marta <u>timidly</u> admitted that she had broken the vase.*

Build Understanding

Connecting to the Literature

Reading/Writing Connection In choosing to adapt Anton Chekhov's work, Neil Simon explained that Chekhov's writing "strikes home to me, living 100 years later in New York City." Identify story details from *The Governess* that show basic human behavior that is timeless. Use at least three of the following words: *benefit, challenge, justify, manipulate, modify.*

Meet the Author

Anton **Chekhov** (1860–1904)

Anton Pavlovich Chekhov originally planned to be a doctor, studying medicine in Moscow. To pay for medical school and support his family, he began to write humorous articles for journals.

A Master of the Short Story Chekhov wrote more than two hundred short stories. Some are comic, while others show the small tragedies of ordinary life. All show sympathy and understanding for their characters. The stories also paint a realistic and detailed picture of Russian life in both cities and peasant villages.

Fast Facts

▶ Chekhov's plays, such as *The Cherry Orchard* (1903), are still performed throughout the world.

▶ Neil Simon has called Chekhov his "non-consenting collaborator" in creating the play *The Good Doctor*, from which *The Governess* is taken.

▶ Chekhov was surprisingly modest about the writer's role. He wrote: "It is time for writers to admit that nothing in this world makes sense. Only fools . . . think they know and understand everything."

▶ Chekhov died of the lung disease tuberculosis at age forty-four at a health spa in Germany.

For: More about the author
Visit: www.PHSchool.com
Web Code: ene-9503

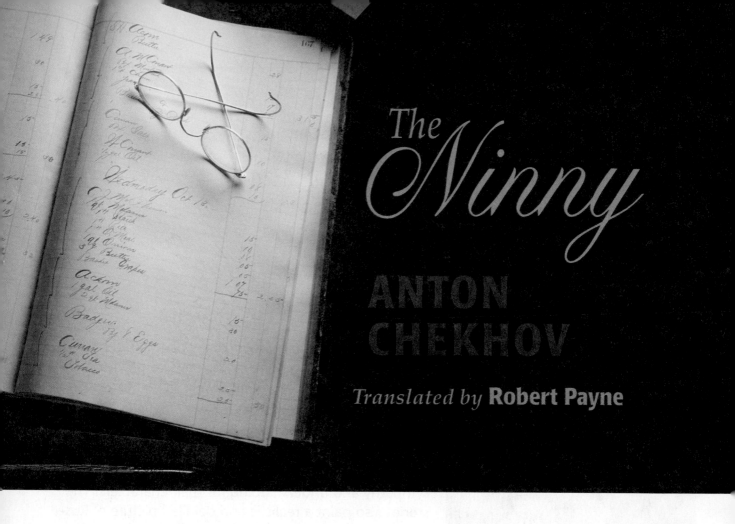

The Ninny

ANTON CHEKHOV

Translated by **Robert Payne**

*J*ust a few days ago I invited Yulia Vassilyevna, the governess of my children, to come to my study. I wanted to settle my <u>account</u> with her.

"Sit down, Yulia Vassilyevna," I said to her. "Let's get our accounts settled. I'm sure you need some money, but you keep standing on ceremony and never ask for it. Let me see. We agreed to give you thirty rubles a month, didn't we?"

"Forty."

"No, thirty. I made a note of it. I always pay the governess thirty. Now, let me see. You have been with us for two months?"

"Two months and five days."

"Two months exactly. I made a note of it. So you have sixty rubles coming to you. Subtract nine Sundays. You know you don't tutor Kolya on Sundays, you just go out for a walk. And then the three holidays . . ."

Yulia Vassilyevna blushed and picked at the trimmings of her dress, but said not a word.

Vocabulary Builder
account (ə kount´) *n.*
a bill for work done

Literary Analysis
Adaptations How do the opening situation and characters compare with those in Simon's play?

"Three holidays. So we take off twelve rubles. Kolya was sick for four days—those days you didn't look after him. You looked after Vanya, only Vanya. Then there were the three days you had a toothache, when my wife gave you permission to stay away from the children after dinner. Twelve and seven makes nineteen. Subtract. . . . That leaves . . . hm . . . forty-one rubles. Correct?"

Yulia Vassilyevna's left eye reddened and filled with tears. Her chin trembled. She began to cough nervously, blew her nose, and said nothing.

"Then around New Year's Day you broke a cup and saucer. Subtract two rubles. The cup cost more than that—it was an heirloom, but we won't bother about that. We're the ones who pay. Another matter. Due to your carelessness Kolya climbed a tree and tore his coat. Subtract ten. Also, due to your carelessness the chambermaid[1] ran off with Vanya's boots. You ought to have kept your eyes open. You get a good salary. So we dock off five more. . . . On the tenth of January you took ten rubles from me."

"I didn't," Yulia Vassilyevna whispered.

"But I made a note of it."

"Well, yes—perhaps . . ."

"From forty-one we take twenty-seven. That leaves fourteen."

Her eyes filled with tears, and her thin, pretty little nose was shining with perspiration. Poor little child!

"I only took money once," she said in a trembling voice. "I took three rubles from your wife . . . never anything more."

Woman in a Chair, John Collier, Courtesy of the artist.

Vocabulary Builder
dock (däk) *v.* to deduct part of one's salary or wages

✓**Reading Check**
Why is Yulia crying?

---

1. chambermaid female household servant whose main job is to clean and care for bedrooms.

"Did you now? You see, I never made a note of it. Take three from fourteen. That leaves eleven. Here's your money, my dear. Three, three, three . . . one and one. Take it, my dear."

I gave her the eleven rubles. With trembling fingers she took them and slipped them into her pocket.

"*Merci,*"[2] she whispered.

I jumped up, and began pacing up and down the room. I was in a furious temper.

"Why did you say '*merci*'?" I asked.

"For the money."

". . . Don't you realize I've been cheating you? I steal your money, and all you can say is '*merci*'!"

"In my other places they gave me nothing."

"They gave you nothing! Well, no wonder! I was playing a trick on you—a dirty trick . . . I'll give you your eighty rubles, they are all here in an envelope made out for you. Is it possible for anyone to be such a nitwit? Why didn't you protest? Why did you keep your mouth shut? Is it possible that there is anyone in this world who is so <u>spineless</u>? Why are you such a <u>ninny</u>?"

She gave me a bitter little smile. On her face I read the words: "Yes, it is possible."

I apologized for having played this cruel trick on her, and to her great surprise gave her the eighty rubles. And then she said "*merci*" again several times, always <u>timidly</u>, and went out. I gazed after her, thinking how very easy it is in this world to be strong.

---

2. *merci* (mer sē´) French for "thank you." In the nineteenth century, many upper-class Russians spoke French.

Vocabulary Builder
spineless (spīn´ ləs) *adj.* lacking in courage or willpower

ninny (nin´ ē) *n.* simple or foolish person

timidly (tim´ id lē) *adv.* in a shy or fearful manner

Literary Analysis
Adaptations How is Yulia's behavior at the end similar to and different from that of Simon's play?

Thinking About the Selection

1. **Respond:** What would you say to the two characters in this story?

2. **(a) Recall:** Who tells the story of "The Ninny"?
   (b) Connect: What is this person's relationship with Yulia?

3. **(a) Evaluate:** Are any of the reasons the narrator gives for cutting Yulia's pay justifiable? **(b) Infer:** What do Yulia's responses suggest about her personality?

4. **Make a Judgment:** Does the narrator find the most effective way to teach Yulia a lesson? Why or why not?

Apply the Skills

The Ninny

Comparing Adaptations to Originals

1. **(a)** What does the format of a short story, like "The Ninny," contain that the format of a play, like *The Governess,* leaves out? **(b)** Keeping these differences in mind, what makes "The Ninny" easy to adapt from a short story into a play?

2. Use a chart like the one shown to find similarities and differences between "The Ninny" and *The Governess.*

	Relationships	Events	Endings	Style/Tone
"The Ninny" (Chekhov)				
The Governess (Simon)				

QuickReview

Adaptations: literary works presented in alternate forms

Go Online
Assessment
For: Self-test
Visit: www.PHSchool.com
Web Code: ena-6503

Writing to Compare Literary Works

In an essay, compare and contrast the adaptation (*The Governess*) and the original ("The Ninny"). Use your comparison chart and these questions to get started.

- How much or how little did Neil Simon change when he adapted Chekhov's story?
- What is the biggest change that Simon made?
- How do the elements of drama or short story explain the differences?
- Do you think that one version—the story or the play—is more effective than the other? Why?

Vocabulary Builder

Practice Decide whether each statement is true or false. Explain your answers.

1. A *spineless* person is not likely to defend his or her beliefs.
2. An adventurous traveler approaches life *timidly.*
3. An employer should *dock* the pay of a good worker.
4. You would not ask a *ninny* to manage a project.
5. A calculator is useful in keeping track of an *account.*

Reading: Drawing Conclusions

Directions: *Questions 1–5 are based on the following selection.*

> **TASHA:** *(pouting)* I'm not going! I hate dances!
>
> **LIZ:** *(sighing)* But it won't be any fun without you.
>
> **TASHA:** *I'm* no fun . . . *(hopefully)* Am I?
>
> **LIZ:** *(trying hard to be patient)* You are when you stop thinking about yourself so much. *(in a coaxing voice)* Come on, there's going to be a really good DJ . . . *(grinning)* You can wear my new sweater.
>
> **TASHA:** *(with a big smile)* Really? Oh, all right. You talked me into it . . . again. *(with enthusiasm)* Who else is going to be there?
>
> **LIZ:** Everybody! I knew you'd change your mind.

1. **What can you conclude about Tasha?**
   A She hates dances.
   B She dislikes Liz.
   C She depends on Liz for reassurance.
   D She has a lot of confidence.

2. **What can you conclude about Liz?**
   A She dislikes Tasha.
   B She is a good friend to Tasha.
   C She does not really want to go to the dance.
   D She is not very persuasive.

3. **What is the most logical conclusion about this type of situation between Tasha and Liz?**
   A It has never occurred before.
   B It will never occur again.
   C It has occurred only once before.
   D It occurs often.

4. **Why does Liz have to try hard to be patient?**
   A She gets tired of having to reassure Tasha.
   B She thinks Tasha will have a good time.
   C She does not know Tasha that well.
   D She does not have any other friends.

5. **Which is the most logical conclusion?**
   A Tasha is looking for attention.
   B Tasha lacks self-confidence.
   C Tasha is used to being the center of attention.
   D Tasha does not know how to dance well.

Assessment Practice

Vocabulary

Directions: *Choose the best word to complete each sentence.*

6. We need to _____ the situation.
A assume
B rationalize
C connect
D evaluate

7. _____ details about characters to draw valid conclusions.
A Assume
B Rationalize
C Connect
D Evaluate

8. A persuasive essay seeks to show that the writer's opinion is _____.
A connected
B assumption
C evaluated
D valid

9. I don't think that writing your paper in one night is a _____ plan.
A connected
B assumed
C rational
D validated

10. What are your _____ about the topic?
A assumptions
B connections
C evaluations
D validations

Directions: *Choose the best definition of the italicized word.*

11. *presume*
A to take an opinion or attitude
B to make a decision before others
C to forcefully express your opinion
D to add something before a decision

12. *consume*
A to fight or fight over
B to use or make use of
C to add or add to
D to strengthen or make stronger

13. *equivalent*
A something of less value
B something of no value
C something of equal worth
D something of greater worth

14. *validity*
A the state of having worth
B the physical strength of something
C the concept
D factual analysis

15. *invalid*
A a concept that is accepted
B without acceptance
C a new idea
D not worthy of consideration

Workplace Writing: Business Letter

A **business letter** is a document written for a formal purpose. Follow the steps in this workshop to write a business letter.

Assignment Write a business letter to obtain a job.

What to Include Your letter should include these features:
- correct business letter format
- a statement of purpose
- content that is clear, concise, and focused
- points supported by facts and details
- a voice and style appropriate to your audience and purpose
- error-free grammar, including the correct use of gerunds and participles

To preview the criteria on which your business letter may be judged, see the rubric on page 770.

Prewriting

Choosing Your Topic

Brainstorm for job situations. Think of jobs for which you are qualified, such as babysitting or newspaper delivery. Review your list and choose the position you find most desirable.

Gathering Details

Plan your support. Identify three personal qualities that make you a good candidate for the job. To support your purpose, list examples of past accomplishments that demonstrate these qualities.

Using the Form
You may use this form in these types of writing:
- requests for information
- letters of complaint
- letters to editors

Work in Progress
Review the work you did on pages 737 and 753.

Job: Newspaper Delivery	
Qualities	**Accomplishments**
Dependability	Never missed a day of soccer practice
Punctuality	Always on time for school
Honesty	Found a lost wallet and turned it in to the police

Drafting

Shaping Your Writing

Keep to the format. A business letter must follow an appropriate format. This format will give your letter a professional look. Include each part of a business letter noted on the chart. (For more on letter formats, see pages R22–R23.)

Providing Elaboration

Make your point. In the first paragraph, state your purpose for writing. Next, as you present your explanation or proposal, include supporting information in the following paragraphs. To conclude, restate the purpose of your letter or indicate what will be done to follow up on it.

Revising

Revising Your Overall Structure

Revise for conciseness. Business letters should be brief and to the point. Review your letter for wordiness and unnecessary repetition. Cut and condense any passages that are too long.

Parts of a Business Letter

Heading: the writer's address and the date

Inside Address: the name and address of the recipient

Salutation: The salutation, or greeting to the recipient, is followed by a colon.

Examples: Dear Mr. Davies:

           Dear Sir or Madam:

           To Whom It May Concern:

Body: The main part of the letter presents the writer's purpose and the information that supports it.

Closing: The closing begins with a capital letter and ends with a comma.

Examples: Yours truly,

           With best regards,

           Sincerely,

Signature: The writer's name is typed below the closing. Between the closing and the typed name, the writer adds a handwritten signature.

Student Model: Revising for Conciseness

I soaked them in solution, thinking it was my own fault,

but this did not change the outcome. ~~In conclusion,~~ I figured ^concluded

~~out~~ that the prescription was ~~not the right prescription.~~ ^wrong.

> In a letter of complaint, cutting extra words and repetitive phrases gives writing greater impact.

Revising Your Word Choice

Revise for businesslike language. Business writing should not include slang, rude comments, or details from your personal life. Use serious, polite language that communicates respect.

Nonprofessional tone: Your CD player is a rip-off! It broke and wrecked my party!

Professional tone: This product does not work properly.

Reading Writing Connection

To read the complete student model, see page 769.

Integrating Grammar Skills

Revising to Combine with Gerunds and Participles

Gerunds and participles are **verbals**, or verb forms that are used as different parts of speech.

Prentice Hall Writing and Grammar Connection: Chapter 20, Section 1

Identifying Gerunds A **gerund** is a verb form ending in -*ing* that is used as a noun.

> **As subject:** *Baking* cookies is Heather's hobby.
>
> **As direct object:** Lucille enjoys *swimming*.
>
> **As predicate noun:** David's greatest talent is *playing* the piano.
>
> **As object of a preposition:** Randall never gets tired of *surfing*.

Identifying Participles A **participle** is a verb form ending in -*ing* that is used as an adjective. There are two kinds of participles: present participles and past participles.

> **Present participle:**   The *chirping* canary sang sweetly.
> **Past participle:**   We hiked off the *beaten* path.

Revising Sentences To combine choppy or short sentences using gerunds and participles, follow these steps:

1. **Identify pairs of sentences that sound choppy.**

2. **Determine whether you can tighten the sentences by revising to include a gerund or a participle.** Identify the main idea and insert the less important idea into a gerund or participial phrase.

Apply It to Your Editing

Choose three paragraphs in your draft. Find pairs of sentences that deal with the same subject. If they are too wordy or repetitive, revise by combining them with gerunds or participles.

Choppy Sentences	
The sisters like to draw and paint. They like to play together.	
Combined with Gerund:	**Combined with Participle:**
The sisters like *drawing* and *painting* together.	*Playing together,* the sisters like to draw and paint.

Student Model: Bruce Wallace
Black Mountain, NC

555 Any Street
Black Mountain, NC 28711
November 12, 2005

Business letters use two-letter abbreviations for states. Those for North Carolina and California are shown here. Other common abbreviations are "Attn:" for *Attention* and "encls." for *enclosures*.

Perfect Vision Contacts
1650 Beach Drive
San Diego, CA 92101

Dear Customer Service Department:

On October 30, 2005, I ordered contact lenses from Perfect Vision Contacts. I have been a customer of your company for eleven months. You have my prescription on file, and your contact lenses have previously worked out well for me. However, this time I am disappointed with your service.

Two factors have contributed to my dissatisfaction. The first thing wrong with the order is the prescription itself. I put the contacts in my eyes and everything was blurry. I soaked them in solution, thinking it was my own fault, but this did not change the outcome. I concluded that the prescription was wrong. Even worse, my order arrived one week late. I was scheduled to get my order on November 6th but did not receive it until today, November 12th.

I am enclosing the faulty contacts with this letter. I would like your company to send me a new pair of lenses with the correct prescription at no additional cost, including shipping and handling.

Bruce outlines the specific problem and the steps that can be taken to correct it.

Please send the new contacts to the address above so that they arrive by November 23rd. If I do not receive the correct contacts on time, I will not continue to order from Perfect Vision Contacts. I also expect a letter of explanation sent with the lenses.

Bruce indicates, politely but firmly, why the company should resolve his problem.

I would urge you to look at people's prescriptions more carefully to avoid such problems in the future.

Sincerely,

Bruce Wallace

Bruce Wallace

Editing and Proofreading

Correct errors in punctuation, spelling, and grammar.

Focus on Accuracy: Make sure you have followed the correct form for a business letter. In addition, check that you have written all names and addresses correctly.

Publishing and Presenting

Consider one of the following ways to share your writing.
Share your letter. Read your letter to a partner. Ask how he or she would respond to receiving it.
Send your letter. Print an error-free copy on good-quality paper. Enclose it in a properly addressed envelope, and mail it to the person or group to whom you wrote. Alternatively, find the e-mail address of the company or organization and send your letter electronically.

Reflecting on Your Writing

Writer's Journal Take a few moments to think about writing your business letter. Then, answer the following questions in your journal.

- Were you confident that your letter made the impression you were trying to make? Why or why not?
- What did you enjoy most about writing your business letter?

> *Prentice Hall Writing and Grammar Connection: pages 762–763*

Rubric for Self-Assessment

To assess your business letter, use the following rubric:

Criteria	Rating Scale
	not very very
Focus: How clearly do you state the purpose of the letter?	1 2 3 4 5
Organization: How effectively is your business letter format organized?	1 2 3 4 5
Support/Elaboration: How well is each point supported by facts and details?	1 2 3 4 5
Style: How well have you used language that is appropriate for your audience?	1 2 3 4 5
Conventions: How correct is your grammar, especially your use of gerunds and participles?	1 2 3 4 5

Unit 5
Part 2
Cause and Effect

Skills You Will Learn

Reading Skill: *Use Background Information to Link Historical Causes With Effects*
Literary Analysis: *Dialogue*

Reading Skill: *Ask Questions to Analyze Cause-and-Effect Relationships*
Literary Analysis: *Character's Motivation*

Reading Skill: *Locate Information on a Web Site*

Literary Analysis: *Comparing a Primary Source With a Dramatization*

Literature You Will Read

Reading and Vocabulary Skills Preview

Reading: Cause and Effect

> A **cause** is the reason something happens. An **effect** is what happens as a result.

Skills and Strategies You Will Learn in Part 2

In Part 2, you will learn

- to use **background information** to link historical **causes with effects** (p. 774)
- to ask **questions** to analyze **cause-and-effect relationships** (p. 834)
- to **scan online documents** to find information (p. 874)

Using the Skills and Strategies in Part 2

In Part 2, you will learn to use background information to link causes and effects. You will use the introduction, information in footnotes, facts you have learned in other classes, and information you already know to link historical causes to effects in literature. You also will learn to ask questions to identify and then analyze cause-and-effect relationships.

Study the following chart, which shows a chain of causes and effects.

Cause:	Effect/Cause:	Effect/Cause:	Effect/Cause:	Effect
You wake up late on Monday morning.	You miss the school bus.	You are late for school.	You miss a quiz in first-period class.	You need to stay after school to take the quiz.

Academic Vocabulary: Words for Discussing Causes and Effects

The following words will help you write and talk about causes and effects as you read the selections in this unit.

Word	Definition	Example Sentence
factor *n.*	something that helps bring about a result	Details are a *factor* in developing the setting of a novel.
consequence *n.*	result; outcome	The character's actions had disastrous *consequences*.
impact *n.*	the power to produce changes or effects	Books can have an *impact* on government policy.
influence *n.*	ability to affect results	The book had a great *influence* on my own writing.
reaction *n.*	response to an influence or force	The cheering in the audience was a *reaction* to a great performance.

Vocabulary Skill: Roots

▶ A **root** is the most basic unit of meaning in a word.

Knowing the meaning of a root will help you understand and remember the meanings of the words that contain it.
In Part 2, you will learn

- the root *-fac-*
- the root *-sequ-*

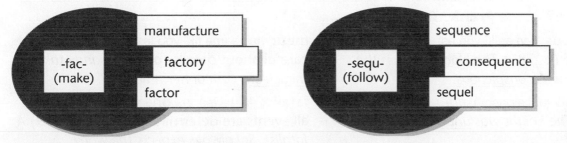

Activity For each word, explain how the meaning of the root is related to the meaning of the word. Then, write one more example word for each root and give its meaning.

These skills will help you become a better reader. Practice them with *The Diary of Anne Frank, Act I* (p. 776).

Reading Skill

A **cause** is an event, action, or feeling that produces a result, or **effect**. When you read a work that is set in a particular time and place, you can **use background information to link historical causes with effects**. This background information includes the following:

- the introduction to a literary work
- information provided in footnotes
- facts you learned in other classes
- information you already know about the topic

Keep track of your analysis in a chart like the one shown.

Dramatic Detail

A mother in a border state begs her sons not to join the fighting.

Cause

The outbreak of war

Effect

Families in border states are split.

Background

In the American Civil War, the division between North and South produced border states with divided loyalties.

Literary Analysis

Dialogue is a conversation between or among characters. In the *script,* or text, of a play, lines of dialogue follow the name of each speaker.

Writers use dialogue for a variety of reasons. It can reveal character traits and relationships, advance the plot, or show the conflict between characters or against outside forces.

As you read *The Diary of Anne Frank,* notice how the dialogue helps you understand the importance of characters and events.

Vocabulary Builder

The Diary of Anne Frank, Act I

- **conspicuous** (kən spik′ yōō əs) *adj.* noticeable (p. 781) *The black stain on the white sofa was conspicuous.*

- **unabashed** (un′ ə basht′) *adj.* unashamed (p. 786) *The knight was unabashed, even in defeat.*

- **insufferable** (in suf′ ə rə bəl) *adj.* unbearable (p. 795) *Cam's rude behavior was insufferable.*

- **meticulous** (mə tik′ yōō ləs) *adj.* extremely careful about details (p. 807) *Sandy takes meticulous care of her nails.*

- **fatalist** (fā′ təl ist) *n.* one who believes that all events are determined by fate (p. 819) *A fatalist, Sal always expects the worst.*

- **ostentatiously** (äs′ tən tā′ shəs lē) *adv.* in a showy way (p. 826) *Peacocks strut ostentatiously, as if showing off their feathers.*

Background

Nazi Occupation On September 1, 1939, Nazi Germany launched a sudden attack on Poland that triggered World War II. Over the next several years, the armies of Nazi Germany swept across Europe, conquering and occupying many countries. In each country the Nazis occupied, the Jews were rounded up and sent by train to forced labor camps and death camps. The Nazi occupation of the Netherlands is the background for *The Diary of Anne Frank,* a play based on the actual diary of a young German-Jewish girl whose family chose to hide from the Nazis.

Connecting to the Literature

Reading/Writing Connection You probably do not think twice about listening to music, going to school, or taking a walk. This play shows what life is like for a girl who cannot do any of these things. Write a paragraph about how it might feel to go into hiding. Use three of these words: *confine, contrast, interact, minimize.*

Meet the Authors

Frances **Goodrich** (1890–1984)
Albert **Hackett** (1900–1995)

Frances Goodrich and Albert Hackett spent two years writing a play based on the world-renowned *The Diary of a Young Girl* by Anne Frank. Their play won a Pulitzer Prize, the Drama Critics Circle award, and a Tony Award.

A Successful Partnership Goodrich and Hackett began working together in 1927 and were married in 1931. The couple's writing career included screenplays for such classic films as *The Thin Man* (1934), *It's a Wonderful Life* (1946), and *Father of the Bride* (1950).

Fast Facts

▶ Before they began writing together, Goodrich and Hackett were both actors.

▶ As part of their research for *The Diary of Anne Frank*, the authors visited with Anne's father, Otto.

Go Online
Author Link
For: More about the authors
Visit: www.PHSchool.com
Web Code: cnc-9504

The Diary of Anne Frank

Frances Goodrich and Albert Hackett

CHARACTERS

MR. FRANK	MRS. FRANK
MIEP	MARGOT FRANK
MRS. VAN DAAN	ANNE FRANK
MR. VAN DAAN	MR. KRALER
PETER VAN DAAN	MR. DUSSEL

Act I

Scene 1

[*The scene remains the same throughout the play. It is the top floor of a warehouse and office building in Amsterdam, Holland. The sharply peaked roof of the building is outlined against a sea of other rooftops, stretching away into the distance. Nearby is the belfry of a church tower, the Westertoren, whose carillon[1] rings out the hours. Occasionally faint sounds float up from below: the voices of children playing in the street, the tramp of marching feet, a boat whistle from the canal.*

The three rooms of the top floor and a small attic space above are exposed to our view. The largest of the rooms is in the center, with two small rooms, slightly raised, on either side. On the right is a bathroom, out of sight. A narrow steep flight of stairs at the back leads up to the attic. The rooms are sparsely furnished with a few chairs, cots, a table or two. The windows are painted over, or covered with makeshift blackout curtains.[2] In the main room there is a sink, a gas ring for cooking and a woodburning stove for warmth.

The room on the left is hardly more than a closet. There is a skylight in the sloping ceiling. Directly under this room is a small steep stairwell, with steps leading down to a door. This is the only entrance from the building below. When the door is opened we see that it has been concealed on the outer side by a bookcase attached to it.

The curtain rises on an empty stage. It is late afternoon, November 1945.

The rooms are dusty, the curtains in rags. Chairs and tables are overturned.

The door at the foot of the small stairwell swings open. MR. FRANK *comes up the steps into view. He is a gentle, cultured European in his middle years. There is still a trace of a German accent in his speech.*

He stands looking slowly around, making a supreme effort at self-control. He is weak, ill. His clothes are threadbare.

---

1. **carillon** (kar´ ə län´) *n.* set of bells, each producing one note of the scale.
2. **blackout curtains** dark curtains that conceal all lights that might be visible to bombers from the air.

Reading Check

What is the setting of this play?

After a second he drops his rucksack on the couch and moves slowly about. He opens the door to one of the smaller rooms, and then abruptly closes it again, turning away. He goes to the window at the back, looking off at the Westertoren as its carillon strikes the hour of six, then he moves restlessly on.

From the street below we hear the sound of a barrel organ[3] and children's voices at play. There is a many-colored scarf hanging from a nail. MR. FRANK *takes it, putting it around his neck. As he starts back for his rucksack, his eye is caught by something lying on the floor. It is a woman's white glove. He holds it in his hand and suddenly all of his self-control is gone. He breaks down, crying.*

We hear footsteps on the stairs. MIEP GIES *comes up, looking for* MR. FRANK. MIEP *is a Dutch girl of about twenty-two. She wears a coat and hat, ready to go home. She is pregnant. Her attitude toward* MR. FRANK *is protective, compassionate.*]

MIEP. Are you all right, Mr. Frank?

MR. FRANK. [*Quickly controlling himself*] Yes, Miep, yes.

MIEP. Everyone in the office has gone home . . . It's after six. [*Then pleading*] Don't stay up here, Mr. Frank. What's the use of torturing yourself like this?

MR. FRANK. I've come to say good-bye . . . I'm leaving here, Miep.

MIEP. What do you mean? Where are you going? Where?

MR. FRANK. I don't know yet. I haven't decided.

MIEP. Mr. Frank, you can't leave here! This is your home! Amsterdam is your home. Your business is here, waiting for you . . . You're needed here . . . Now that the war is over, there are things that . . .

MR. FRANK. I can't stay in Amsterdam, Miep. It has too many memories for me. Everywhere there's something . . . the house we lived in . . . the school . . . that street organ playing out there . . . I'm not the person you used to know, Miep. I'm a bitter old man. [*Breaking off*] Forgive me. I shouldn't speak to you like this . . . after all that you did for us . . . the suffering . . .

MIEP. No. No. It wasn't suffering. You can't say we suffered. [*As she speaks, she straightens a chair which is overturned.*]

---

3. barrel organ *n.* mechanical musical instrument often played by street musicians in past decades.

Reading Skill
Cause and Effect
The war in Europe ended in May 1945, but many who survived the camps did not return until the fall. What effect has the war had on Mr. Frank?

Literary Analysis
Dialogue What does Mr. Frank's dialogue and the hesitation in his words tell you about his feelings?

MR. FRANK. I know what you went through, you and Mr. Kraler. I'll remember it as long as I live. [*He gives one last look around.*] Come, Miep. [*He starts for the steps, then remembers his rucksack, going back to get it.*]

MIEP. [*Hurrying up to a cupboard*] Mr. Frank, did you see? There are some of your papers here. [*She brings a bundle of papers to him.*] We found them in a heap of rubbish on the floor after . . . after you left.

MR. FRANK. Burn them. [*He opens his rucksack to put the glove in it.*]

MIEP. But, Mr. Frank, there are letters, notes . . .

MR. FRANK. Burn them. All of them.

MIEP. Burn this? [*She hands him a paper-bound notebook.*]

MR. FRANK. [*quietly*] Anne's diary. [*He opens the diary and begins to read.*] "Monday, the sixth of July, nineteen forty-two." [*To* MIEP] Nineteen forty-two. Is it possible, Miep? . . . Only three years ago. [*As he continues his reading, he sits down on the couch.*] "Dear Diary, since you and I are going to be great friends, I will start by telling you about myself. My name is Anne Frank. I am thirteen years old. I was born in Germany the twelfth of June, nineteen twenty-nine. As

Reading Skill
Cause and Effect
What historical events might make it harder for Mr. Frank to think of Amsterdam as home? Explain.

✔ **Reading Check**

What does Miep give to Mr. Frank?

▲ **Critical Viewing** This photograph shows the Frank family with some friends before their years in hiding. How would you describe their mood, judging from their expressions? **[Connect]**

The Diary of Anne Frank, Act I ■ *779*

my family is Jewish, we emigrated to Holland when Hitler came to power."

[*As* MR. FRANK *reads on, another voice joins his, as if coming from the air. It is* ANNE'S VOICE.]

MR. FRANK AND ANNE. "My father started a business, importing spice and herbs. Things went well for us until nineteen forty. Then the war came, and the Dutch capitulation,[4] followed by the arrival of the Germans. Then things got very bad for the Jews."

[MR. FRANK'S VOICE *dies out.* ANNE'S VOICE *continues alone. The lights dim slowly to darkness. The curtain falls on the scene.*]

ANNE'S VOICE. You could not do this and you could not do that. They forced Father out of his business. We had to wear yellow stars.[5] I had to turn in my bike. I couldn't go to a Dutch school any more. I couldn't go to the movies, or ride in an automobile, or even on a streetcar, and a million other things. But somehow we children still managed to have fun. Yesterday Father told me we were going into hiding. Where, he wouldn't say. At five o'clock this morning Mother woke me and told me to hurry and get dressed. I was to put on as many clothes as I could. It would look too suspicious if we walked along carrying suitcases. It wasn't until we were on our way that I learned where we were going. Our hiding place was to be upstairs in the building where Father used to have his business. Three other people were coming in with us . . . the Van Daans and their son Peter . . . Father knew the Van Daans but we had never met them . . .

[*During the last lines the curtain rises on the scene. The lights dim on.* ANNE'S VOICE *fades out.*]

Scene 2

[*It is early morning, July 1942. The rooms are bare, as before, but they are now clean and orderly.*

MR. VAN DAAN, *a tall, portly[6] man in his late forties, is in the main room, pacing up and down, nervously smoking a cigarette. His clothes and overcoat are expensive and well cut.*

---

4. capitulation (kə pich′ ə lā′ shən) *n.* surrender.
5. yellow stars Stars of David, the six-pointed stars that are symbols of Judaism. The Nazis ordered all Jews to wear them on their clothing.
6. portly (pôrt′ lē) *adj.* large and heavy.

Reading Skill
Cause and Effect
Anne is referring to Adolf Hitler, the German dictator who persecuted Jews throughout Europe. What other historical causes and effects do you learn here?

Literary Analysis
Dialogue In the play, Anne's lines are often spoken to her diary, as if the diary were another character. What significant plot event is revealed in these lines?

MRS. VAN DAAN *sits on the couch, clutching her possessions, a hatbox, bags, etc. She is a pretty woman in her early forties. She wears a fur coat over her other clothes.*

PETER VAN DAAN *is standing at the window of the room on the right, looking down at the street below. He is a shy, awkward boy of sixteen. He wears a cap, a raincoat, and long Dutch trousers, like "plus fours."[7] At his feet is a black case, a carrier for his cat.*

The yellow Star of David is <u>conspicuous</u> on all of their clothes.]

MRS. VAN DAAN. [*Rising, nervous, excited*] Something's happened to them! I know it!

MR. VAN DAAN. Now, Kerli!

MRS. VAN DAAN. Mr. Frank said they'd be here at seven o'clock. He said . . .

MR. VAN DAAN. They have two miles to walk. You can't expect . . .

MRS. VAN DAAN. They've been picked up. That's what's happened. They've been taken . . .

[MR. VAN DAAN *indicates that he hears someone coming.*]

MR. VAN DAAN. You see?

[PETER *takes up his carrier and his schoolbag, etc., and goes into the main room as* MR. FRANK *comes up the stairwell from below.* MR. FRANK *looks much younger now. His movements are brisk, his manner confident. He wears an overcoat and carries his hat and a small cardboard box. He crosses to the* VAN DAANS, *shaking hands with each of them.*]

MR. FRANK. Mrs. Van Daan, Mr. Van Daan, Peter. [*Then, in explanation of their lateness*] There were too many of the Green Police[8] on the streets . . . we had to take the long way around.

[*Up the steps come* MARGOT FRANK, MRS. FRANK, MIEP (*not pregnant now*) *and* MR. KRALER. *All of them carry bags, packages, and so forth. The Star of David is conspicuous on all of the* FRANKS' *clothing.* MARGOT *is eighteen, beautiful, quiet, shy.* MRS. FRANK *is*

---

7. **plus fours** *n.* loose knickers (short pants) worn for active sports.
8. **Green Police** the Dutch Gestapo, or Nazi police, who wore green uniforms and were known for their brutality. Those in danger of being arrested or deported feared the Gestapo, especially because of their practice of raiding houses to round up victims in the middle of the night—when people are most confused and vulnerable.

Vocabulary Builder
conspicuous (kən spik′ yōō əs) *adj.* noticeable

Literary Analysis
Dialogue How do the authors convey a mood of anxiety through the Van Daan's dialogue?

Reading Skill
Cause and Effect Read the footnote on the "Green Police." Why do the Franks fear this force?

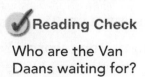**Reading Check**

Who are the Van Daans waiting for?

a young mother, gently bred, reserved. She, like MR. FRANK, *has a slight German accent.* MR. KRALER *is a Dutchman, dependable, kindly.*

As MR. KRALER *and* MIEP *go upstage to put down their parcels,* MRS. FRANK *turns back to call* ANNE.]

MRS. FRANK. Anne?

[ANNE *comes running up the stairs. She is thirteen, quick in her movements, interested in everything, mercurial[9] in her emotions. She wears a cape, long wool socks and carries a schoolbag.*]

MR. FRANK. [*Introducing them*] My wife, Edith. Mr. and Mrs. Van Daan . . . their son, Peter . . . my daughters, Margot and Anne.

[MRS. FRANK *hurries over, shaking hands with them.*]

[ANNE *gives a polite little curtsy as she shakes* MR. VAN DAAN'S *hand. Then she immediately starts off on a tour of investigation of her new home, going upstairs to the attic room.*

MIEP *and* MR. KRALER *are putting the various things they have brought on the shelves.*]

MR. KRALER. I'm sorry there is still so much confusion.

MR. FRANK. Please. Don't think of it. After all, we'll have plenty of leisure to arrange everything ourselves.

MIEP. [*To* MRS. FRANK] We put the stores of food you sent in here. Your drugs are here . . . soap, linen here.

MRS. FRANK. Thank you, Miep.

MIEP. I made up the beds . . . the way Mr. Frank and Mr. Kraler said. [*She starts out.*] Forgive me. I have to hurry. I've got to go to the other side of town to get some ration books[10] for you.

MRS. VAN DAAN. Ration books? If they see our names on ration books, they'll know we're here.

MR. KRALER. There isn't anything . . .

MIEP. Don't worry. Your names won't be on them. [*As she hurries out*] I'll be up later.

MR. FRANK. Thank you, Miep.

Reading Skill
Cause and Effect
What will having ration books allow the Franks to do?

---

9. mercurial (mər kyoor´ ē əl) *adj.* quick or changeable in behavior.
10. ration (rash´ ən) **books** *n.* books of stamps given to ensure the equal distribution of scarce items, such as meat or gasoline, in times of shortage.

MRS. FRANK. [*To* MR. KRALER] It's illegal, then, the ration books? We've never done anything illegal.

MR. FRANK. We won't be living here exactly according to regulations.

[*As* MR. KRALER *reassures* MRS. FRANK, *he takes various small things, such as matches, soap, etc., from his pockets, handing them to her.*]

MR. KRALER. This isn't the black market,[11] Mrs. Frank. This is what we call the white market . . . helping all of the hundreds and hundreds who are hiding out in Amsterdam.

[*The carillon is heard playing the quarter-hour before eight.* MR. KRALER *looks at his watch.* ANNE *stops at the window as she comes down the stairs.*]

ANNE. It's the Westertoren!

MR. KRALER. I must go. I must be out of here and downstairs in the office before the workmen get here. [*He starts for the stairs leading out.*] Miep or I, or both of us, will be up each day to bring you food and news and find out what your needs are. Tomorrow I'll get you a better bolt for the door at the foot of the stairs. It needs a bolt that you can throw yourself and open only at our signal. [*To* MR. FRANK] Oh . . . You'll tell them about the noise?

MR. FRANK. I'll tell them.

MR. KRALER. Good-bye then for the moment. I'll come up again, after the workmen leave.

MR. FRANK. Good-bye, Mr. Kraler.

MRS. FRANK. [*Shaking his hand*] How can we thank you?

[*The others murmur their good-byes.*]

MR. KRALER. I never thought I'd live to see the day when a man like Mr. Frank would have to go into hiding. When you think—

[*He breaks off, going out.* MR. FRANK *follows him down the steps, bolting the door after him. In the interval before he returns,* PETER *goes over to* MARGOT, *shaking hands with her. As* MR. FRANK *comes back up the steps,* MRS. FRANK *questions him anxiously.*]

MRS. FRANK. What did he mean, about the noise?

---

11. **black market** illegal way of buying scarce items without ration stamps.

Reading Skill
Cause and Effect
Why might Mrs. Frank be afraid of doing something illegal? Why is her fear illogical?

Reading Check

Why does Mr. Kraler need to leave before the workmen arrive?

MR. FRANK. First let us take off some of these clothes.

[*They all start to take off garment after garment. On each of their coats, sweaters, blouses, suits, dresses, is another yellow Star of David.* MR. *and* MRS. FRANK *are underdressed quite simply. The others wear several things, sweaters, extra dresses, bathrobes, aprons, nightgowns, etc.*]

MR. VAN DAAN. It's a wonder we weren't arrested, walking along the streets . . . Petronella with a fur coat in July . . . and that cat of Peter's crying all the way.

ANNE. [*As she is removing a pair of panties*] A cat?

MRS. FRANK. [*Shocked*] Anne, please!

ANNE. It's alright. I've got on three more.

[*She pulls off two more. Finally, as they have all removed their surplus clothes, they look to* MR. FRANK, *waiting for him to speak.*]

MR. FRANK. Now. About the noise. While the men are in the building below, we must have complete quiet. Every sound can be heard down there, not only in the workrooms, but in the offices too. The men come at about eight-thirty, and leave at about five-thirty. So, to be perfectly safe, from eight in the morning until six in the evening we must move only when it is necessary, and then in stockinged feet. We must not speak above a whisper. We must not run any water. We cannot use the sink, or even, forgive me, the w.c.[12] The pipes go down through the workrooms. It would be heard. No trash . . .

[MR. FRANK *stops abruptly as he hears the sound of marching feet from the street below. Everyone is motionless, paralyzed with fear.* MR. FRANK *goes quietly into the room on the right to look down out of the window.* ANNE *runs after him, peering out with him. The tramping feet pass without stopping. The tension is relieved.* MR. FRANK, *followed by* ANNE, *returns to the main room and resumes his instructions to the group.*] . . . No trash must ever be thrown out which might reveal that someone is living up here . . . not even a potato paring. We must burn everything in the stove at night. This is the way we must live until it is over, if we are to survive.

[*There is silence for a second.*]

MRS. FRANK. Until it is over.

---

12. **w.c.** water closet; bathroom.

Reading Skill
Cause and Effect
What does the description of the characters' clothing indicate about how long they expect to be in hiding?

Reading Skill
Cause and Effect
Why is the sound of marching feet alarming to the families?

MR. FRANK. [*Reassuringly*] After six we can move about . . . we can talk and laugh and have our supper and read and play games . . . just as we would at home. [*He looks at his watch.*] And now I think it would be wise if we all went to our rooms, and were settled before eight o'clock. Mrs. Van Daan, you and your husband will be upstairs. I regret that there's no place up there for Peter. But he will be here, near us. This will be our common room, where we'll meet to talk and eat and read, like one family.

MR. VAN DAAN. And where do you and Mrs. Frank sleep?

MR. FRANK. This room is also our bedroom.

[*Together*] {
  MRS. VAN DAAN. That isn't right. We'll sleep here and you take the room upstairs.
  MR. VAN DAAN. It's your place.
}

MR. FRANK. Please. I've thought this out for weeks. It's the best arrangement. The only arrangement.

MRS. VAN DAAN. [*To* MR. FRANK] Never, never can we thank you. [*Then to* MRS. FRANK] I don't know what would have happened to us, if it hadn't been for Mr. Frank.

MR. FRANK. You don't know how your husband helped me when I came to this country . . . knowing no one . . . not able to speak the language. I can never repay him for that. [*Going to* VAN DAAN] May I help you with your things?

MR. VAN DAAN. No. No. [*To* MRS. VAN DAAN] Come along, *liefje.*[13]

MRS. VAN DAAN. You'll be all right, Peter? You're not afraid?

PETER. [*Embarrassed*] Please, Mother.

[*They start up the stairs to the attic room above.* MR. FRANK *turns to* MRS. FRANK.]

MR. FRANK. You too must have some rest, Edith. You didn't close your eyes last night. Nor you, Margot.

ANNE. I slept, Father. Wasn't that funny? I knew it was the last night in my own bed, and yet I slept soundly.

MR. FRANK. I'm glad, Anne. Now you'll be able to help me straighten things in here. [*To* MRS. FRANK *and* MARGOT] Come with me . . . You and Margot rest in this room for the time being.

Reading Skill
Cause and Effect
Why must the families maintain different schedules for day and night?

✔ **Reading Check**

Why is Mrs. Van Daan grateful to Mr. Frank?

---

13. *liefje* (lēf´ hyə) Dutch for "little love."

[*He picks up their clothes, starting for the room on the right.*]

MRS. FRANK. You're sure . . .? I could help . . . And Anne hasn't had her milk . . .

MR. FRANK. I'll give it to her. [*To* ANNE *and* PETER] Anne, Peter . . . it's best that you take off your shoes now, before you forget.

[*He leads the way to the room, followed by* MARGOT.]

MRS. FRANK. You're sure you're not tired, Anne?

ANNE. I feel fine. I'm going to help Father.

MRS. FRANK. Peter, I'm glad you are to be with us.

PETER. Yes, Mrs. Frank.

[MRS. FRANK *goes to join* MR. FRANK *and* MARGOT.]

[*During the following scene* MR. FRANK *helps* MARGOT *and* MRS. FRANK *to hang up their clothes. Then he persuades them both to lie down and rest. The* VAN DAANS *in their room above settle themselves. In the main room* ANNE *and* PETER *remove their shoes.* PETER *takes his cat out of the carrier.*]

ANNE. What's your cat's name?

PETER. Mouschi.

ANNE. Mouschi! Mouschi! Mouschi! [*She picks up the cat, walking away with it. To* PETER] I love cats. I have one . . . a darling little cat. But they made me leave her behind. I left some food and a note for the neighbors to take care of her . . . I'm going to miss her terribly. What is yours? A him or a her?

PETER. He's a tom. He doesn't like strangers. [*He takes the cat from her, putting it back in its carrier.*]

ANNE. [*Unabashed*] Then I'll have to stop being a stranger, won't I? Is he fixed?

PETER. [*Startled*] Huh?

ANNE. Did you have him fixed?

PETER. No.

ANNE. Oh, you ought to have him fixed—to keep him from— you know, fighting. Where did you go to school?

PETER. Jewish Secondary.

Literary Analysis
Dialogue What does this dialogue reveal about the relationship between Anne and her parents?

Vocabulary Builder
unabashed (un´ ə basht´) *adj.* unashamed

ANNE. But that's where Margot and I go! I never saw you around.

PETER. I used to see you . . . sometimes . . .

ANNE. You did?

PETER. . . . In the school yard. You were always in the middle of a bunch of kids. [*He takes a penknife from his pocket.*]

ANNE. Why didn't you ever come over?

PETER. I'm sort of a lone wolf. [*He starts to rip off his Star of David.*]

ANNE. What are you doing?

PETER. Taking it off.

ANNE. But you can't do that. They'll arrest you if you go out without your star.

[*He tosses his knife on the table.*]

PETER. Who's going out?

ANNE. Why, of course! You're right! Of course we don't need them any more. [*She picks up his knife and starts to take her star off.*] I wonder what our friends will think when we don't show up today?

PETER. I didn't have any dates with anyone.

ANNE. Oh, I did. I had a date with Jopie to go and play ping-pong at her house. Do you know Jopie de Waal?

PETER. No.

ANNE. Jopie's my best friend. I wonder what she'll think when she telephones and there's no answer? . . . Probably she'll go over to the house . . . I wonder what she'll think . . . we left everything as if we'd suddenly been called away . . . breakfast dishes in the sink . . . beds not made . . . [*As she pulls off her star, the cloth underneath shows clearly the color and form of the star.*] Look! It's still there! [PETER *goes over to the stove with his star.*] What're you going to do with yours?

PETER. Burn it.

ANNE. [*She starts to throw hers in, and cannot.*] It's funny, I can't throw mine away. I don't know why.

Reading Skill
Cause and Effect
Think about what the yellow star represents in the historical context of World War II. Why is it important to Peter to remove the star?

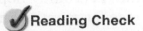Reading Check

Where did Peter see Anne before they went into hiding?

PETER. You can't throw . . .? Something they branded you with . . .? That they made you wear so they could spit on you?

ANNE. I know. I know. But after all, it is the Star of David, isn't it?

[*In the bedroom, right,* MARGOT *and* MRS. FRANK *are lying down.* MR. FRANK *starts quietly out.*]

PETER. Maybe it's different for a girl.

[MR. FRANK *comes into the main room.*]

MR. FRANK. Forgive me, Peter. Now let me see. We must find a bed for your cat. [*He goes to a cupboard.*] I'm glad you brought your cat. Anne was feeling so badly about hers. [*Getting a used small washtub*] Here we are. Will it be comfortable in that?

PETER. [*Gathering up his things*] Thanks.

MR. FRANK. [*Opening the door of the room on the left*] And here is your room. But I warn you, Peter, you can't grow any more. Not an inch, or you'll have to sleep with your feet out of the skylight. Are you hungry?

PETER. No.

MR. FRANK. We have some bread and butter.

PETER. No, thank you.

MR. FRANK. You can have it for luncheon then. And tonight we will have a real supper . . . our first supper together.

PETER. Thanks. Thanks. [*He goes into his room. During the following scene he arranges his possessions in his new room.*]

MR. FRANK. That's a nice boy, Peter.

ANNE. He's awfully shy, isn't he?

MR. FRANK. You'll like him, I know.

ANNE. I certainly hope so, since he's the only boy I'm likely to see for months and months.

[MR. FRANK *sits down, taking off his shoes.*]

MR. FRANK. Annele,[14] there's a box there. Will you open it?

Literary Analysis Dialogue What does this speech tell you about Mr. Frank as a person?

▲ Critical Viewing Why do you think the Nazis forced Jews to wear yellow stars like this one, bearing the Dutch word for "Jew"? [Infer]

---

14. Annele (än´ ə lə) nickname for "Anne."

[*He indicates a carton on the couch.* ANNE *brings it to the center table. In the street below there is the sound of children playing.*]

ANNE. [*As she opens the carton*] You know the way I'm going to think of it here? I'm going to think of it as a boarding house. A very peculiar summer boarding house, like the one that we—[*She breaks off as she pulls out some photographs.*] Father! My movie stars! I was wondering where they were! I was looking for them this morning . . . and Queen Wilhelmina![15] How wonderful!

MR. FRANK. There's something more. Go on. Look further. [*He goes over to the sink, pouring a glass of milk from a thermos bottle.*]

ANNE. [*Pulling out a pasteboard-bound book*] A diary! [*She throws her arms around her father.*] I've never had a diary. And I've always longed for one. [*She looks around the room.*] Pencil, pencil, pencil, pencil. [*She starts down the stairs.*] I'm going down to the office to get a pencil.

MR. FRANK. Anne! No! [*He goes after her, catching her by the arm and pulling her back.*]

ANNE. [*Startled*] But there's no one in the building now.

MR. FRANK. It doesn't matter. I don't want you ever to go beyond that door.

ANNE. [*Sobered*] Never . . .? Not even at nighttime, when everyone is gone? Or on Sundays? Can't I go down to listen to the radio?

MR. FRANK. Never. I am sorry, Anneke.[16] It isn't safe. No, you must never go beyond that door.

[*For the first time* ANNE *realizes what "going into hiding" means.*]

ANNE. I see.

MR. FRANK. It'll be hard, I know. But always remember this, Anneke. There are no walls, there are no bolts, no locks that anyone can put on your mind. Miep will bring us books. We will read history, poetry, mythology. [*He gives her the glass of milk.*] Here's your milk. [*With his arm about her, they go over to the couch, sitting down side by side.*] As a matter of fact, between us, Anne, being here has certain

Reading Skill
Cause and Effect
Why is Anne forbidden to go downstairs?

Reading Check

What does Anne's father give Anne?

---

15. **Queen Wilhelmina** (vil´ hel mē´ nä) Queen of the Netherlands from 1890 to 1948.
16. **Anneke** (än´ ə kə) nickname for "Anne."

advantages for you. For instance, you remember the battle you had with your mother the other day on the subject of overshoes? You said you'd rather die than wear overshoes? But in the end you had to wear them? Well now, you see, for as long as we are here you will never have to wear overshoes! Isn't that good? And the coat that you inherited from Margot, you won't have to wear that any more. And the piano! You won't have to practice on the piano. I tell you, this is going to be a fine life for you!

[ANNE'S *panic is gone.* PETER *appears in the doorway of his room, with a saucer in his hand. He is carrying his cat.*]

PETER. I . . . I . . . I thought I'd better get some water for Mouschi before . . .

MR. FRANK. Of course.

[*As he starts toward the sink the carillon begins to chime the hour of eight. He tiptoes to the window at the back and looks down at the street below. He turns to* PETER, *indicating in pantomime that it is too late.* PETER *starts back for his room. He steps on a creaking board. The three of them are frozen for a minute in fear. As* PETER *starts away again,* ANNE *tiptoes over to him and pours some of the milk from her glass into the saucer for the cat.* PETER *squats on the floor, putting the milk before the cat.* MR. FRANK *gives* ANNE *his fountain pen, and then goes into the room at the right. For a second* ANNE *watches the cat, then she goes over to the center table, and opens her diary.*

In the room at the right, MRS. FRANK *has sat up quickly at the sound of the carillon.* MR. FRANK *comes in and sits down beside her on the settee, his arm comfortingly around her.*

Upstairs, in the attic room, MR. *and* MRS. VAN DAAN *have hung their clothes in the closet and are now seated on the iron bed.* MRS. VAN DAAN *leans back exhausted.* MR. VAN DAAN *fans her with a newspaper.*

ANNE *starts to write in her diary. The lights dim out, the curtain falls.*

In the darkness ANNE'S VOICE *comes to us again, faintly at first, and then with growing strength.*]

ANNE'S VOICE. I expect I should be describing what it feels like to go into hiding. But I really don't know yet myself. I only know it's funny never to be able to go outdoors . . . never to breathe fresh air . . . never to run and shout and jump. It's

Reading Skill
Cause and Effect
How does the fear of discovery affect the behavior of the two families?

Literary Analysis
Dialogue How does Anne's "conversation" with her diary provide key details that move along the action?

the silence in the nights that frightens me most. Every time I hear a creak in the house, or a step on the street outside, I'm sure they're coming for us. The days aren't so bad. At least we know that Miep and Mr. Kraler are down there below us in the office. Our protectors, we call them. I asked Father what would happen to them if the Nazis found out they were hiding us. Pim said that they would suffer the same fate that we would . . . Imagine! They know this, and yet when they come up here, they're always cheerful and gay as if there were nothing in the world to bother them . . . Friday, the twenty-first of August, nineteen forty-two. Today I'm going to tell you our general news. Mother is unbearable. She insists on treating me like a baby, which I loathe. Otherwise things are going better. The weather is . . .

[As ANNE'S VOICE *is fading out, the curtain rises on the scene.*]

Reading Skill
Cause and Effect
Based on your knowledge of the Nazis, what consequences would Miep and Mr. Kraler be likely to face?

Scene 3

[*It is a little after six o'clock in the evening, two months later.*

MARGOT is in the bedroom at the right, studying. MR. VAN DAAN is lying down in the attic room above.

The rest of the "family" is in the main room. ANNE and PETER sit opposite each other at the center table, where they have been doing their lessons. MRS. FRANK is on the couch. MRS. VAN DAAN is seated with her fur coat, on which she has been sewing, in her lap. None of them are wearing their shoes.

Their eyes are on MR. FRANK, waiting for him to give them the signal which will release them from their day-long quiet. MR. FRANK, his shoes in his hand, stands looking down out of the window at the back, watching to be sure that all of the workmen have left the building below.

After a few seconds of motionless silence, MR. FRANK turns from the window.]

MR. FRANK. [*Quietly, to the group*] It's safe now. The last workman has left.

[*There is an immediate stir of relief.*]

ANNE. [*Her pent-up energy explodes.*] WHEE!

MR. FRANK. [*Startled, amused*] Anne!

MRS. VAN DAAN. I'm first for the w.c.

**Reading Check**

Why is six o'clock a significant time of day for the families?

[*She hurries off to the bathroom. MRS. FRANK puts on her shoes and starts up to the sink to prepare supper. ANNE sneaks PETER'S shoes from under the table and hides them behind her back. MR. FRANK goes in to MARGOT'S room.*]

MR. FRANK. [*To* MARGOT] Six o'clock. School's over.

[MARGOT *gets up, stretching.* MR. FRANK *sits down to put on his shoes. In the main room* PETER *tries to find his.*]

PETER. [*To* ANNE] Have you seen my shoes?

ANNE. [*Innocently*] Your shoes?

PETER. You've taken them, haven't you?

ANNE. I don't know what you're talking about.

PETER. You're going to be sorry!

ANNE. Am I?

[PETER *goes after her.* ANNE, *with his shoes in her hand, runs from him, dodging behind her mother.*]

MRS. FRANK. [*Protesting*] Anne, dear!

PETER. Wait till I get you!

ANNE. I'm waiting!
[PETER *makes a lunge for her. They both fall to the floor.* PETER *pins her down, wrestling with her to get the shoes.*] Don't! Don't! Peter, stop it. Ouch!

MRS. FRANK. Anne! . . . Peter!

[*Suddenly* PETER *becomes self-conscious. He grabs his shoes roughly and starts for his room.*]

ANNE. [*Following him*] Peter, where are you going? Come dance with me.

PETER. I tell you I don't know how.

ANNE. I'll teach you.

PETER. I'm going to give Mouschi his dinner.

ANNE. Can I watch?

PETER. He doesn't like people around while he eats.

ANNE. Peter, please.

PETER. No! [*He goes into his room.* ANNE *slams his door after him.*]

Literary Analysis
Dialogue How does the dialogue in this section show the changing relationship between Anne and Peter?

MRS. FRANK. Anne, dear, I think you shouldn't play like that with Peter. It's not dignified.

ANNE. Who cares if it's dignified? I don't want to be dignified.

[MR. FRANK *and* MARGOT *come from the room on the right.* MARGOT *goes to help her mother.* MR. FRANK *starts for the center table to correct* MARGOT'S *school papers.*]

MRS. FRANK. [*To* ANNE] You complain that I don't treat you like a grownup. But when I do, you resent it.

ANNE. I only want some fun . . . someone to laugh and clown with . . . After you've sat still all day and hardly moved, you've got to have some fun. I don't know what's the matter with that boy.

MR. FRANK. He isn't used to girls. Give him a little time.

ANNE. Time? Isn't two months time? I could cry. [*Catching hold of* MARGOT] Come on, Margot . . . dance with me. Come on, please.

MARGOT. I have to help with supper.

ANNE. You know we're going to forget how to dance . . . When we get out we won't remember a thing.

[*She starts to sing and dance by herself.* MR. FRANK *takes her in his arms, waltzing with her.* MRS. VAN DAAN *comes in from the bathroom.*]

MRS. VAN DAAN. Next? [*She looks around as she starts putting on her shoes.*] Where's Peter?

ANNE. [*As they are dancing*] Where would he be!

MRS. VAN DAAN. He hasn't finished his lessons, has he? His father'll kill him if he catches him in there with that cat and his work not done. [MR. FRANK *and* ANNE *finish their dance. They bow to each other with extravagant formality.*] Anne, get him out of there, will you?

ANNE. [*At* PETER'S *door*] Peter? Peter?

PETER. [*Opening the door a crack*] What is it?

ANNE. Your mother says to come out.

PETER. I'm giving Mouschi his dinner.

MRS. VAN DAAN. You know what your father says. [*She sits on the couch, sewing on the lining of her fur coat.*]

Reading Skill
Cause and Effect
What is the effect of Mrs. Frank's upbringing on the way she expects Anne to act?

Literary Analysis
Dialogue What aspects of Anne's personality does this dialogue show?

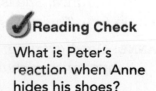
Reading Check

What is Peter's reaction when Anne hides his shoes?

PETER. For heaven's sake, I haven't even looked at him since lunch.

MRS. VAN DAAN. I'm just telling you, that's all.

ANNE. I'll feed him.

PETER. I don't want you in there.

MRS. VAN DAAN. Peter!

PETER. [*To* ANNE] Then give him his dinner and come right out, you hear?

[*He comes back to the table.* ANNE *shuts the door of* PETER'S *room after her and disappears behind the curtain covering his closet.*]

MRS. VAN DAAN. [*To* PETER] Now is that any way to talk to your little girl friend?

PETER. Mother . . . for heaven's sake . . . will you please stop saying that?

MRS. VAN DAAN. Look at him blush! Look at him!

PETER. Please! I'm not . . . anyway . . . let me alone, will you?

MRS. VAN DAAN. He acts like it was something to be ashamed of. It's nothing to be ashamed of, to have a little girl friend.

PETER. You're crazy. She's only thirteen.

MRS. VAN DAAN. So what? And you're sixteen. Just perfect. Your father's ten years older than I am. [*To* MR. FRANK] I warn you, Mr. Frank, if this war lasts much longer, we're going to be related and then . . .

MR. FRANK. *Mazeltov!*[17]

MRS. FRANK. [*Deliberately changing the conversation*] I wonder where Miep is. She's usually so prompt.

[*Suddenly everything else is forgotten as they hear the sound of an automobile coming to a screeching stop in the street below. They are tense, motionless in their terror. The car starts away. A wave of relief sweeps over them. They pick up their occupations again.* ANNE *flings open the door of* PETER'S *room, making a dramatic entrance. She is dressed in* PETER'S *clothes.* PETER *looks at her in fury. The others are amused.*]

ANNE. Good evening, everyone. Forgive me if I don't stay. [*She jumps up on a chair.*] I have a friend waiting for me in there.

---

17. Mazeltov (mä´ zəl tōv´) "good luck" in Hebrew and Yiddish.

Literary Analysis
Dialogue Based on this dialogue, how does Mrs. Van Daan feel about the growing friendship between Anne and Peter?

Reading Skill
Cause and Effect Why does the sound of the car stopping frighten everyone?

▶ **Critical Viewing** This photograph shows the front of the Secret Annex. What are some pros and cons of this hiding place? **[Assess]**

My friend Tom. Tom Cat. Some people say that we look alike. But Tom has the most beautiful whiskers, and I have only a little fuzz. I am hoping . . . in time . . .

PETER. All right, Mrs. Quack Quack!

ANNE. [*Outraged—jumping down*] Peter!

PETER. I heard about you . . . How you talked so much in class they called you Mrs. Quack Quack. How Mr. Smitter made you write a composition . . . "'Quack, Quack,' said Mrs. Quack Quack."

ANNE. Well, go on. Tell them the rest. How it was so good he read it out loud to the class and then read it to all his other classes!

PETER. Quack! Quack! Quack . . . Quack . . . Quack . . .

[ANNE *pulls off the coat and trousers.*]

ANNE. You are the most intolerable, <u>insufferable</u> boy I've ever met!

[*She throws the clothes down the stairwell.* PETER *goes down after them.*]

PETER. Quack, Quack, Quack!

MRS. VAN DAAN. [*To* ANNE] That's right, Anneke! Give it to him!

ANNE. With all the boys in the world . . . Why I had to get locked up with one like you! . . .

PETER. Quack, Quack, Quack, and from now on stay out of my room!

[As PETER *passes her,* ANNE *puts out her foot, tripping him. He picks himself up, and goes on into his room.*]

MRS. FRANK. [*Quietly*] Anne, dear . . . your hair. [*She feels* ANNE'S *forehead.*] You're warm. Are you feeling all right?

ANNE. Please, Mother. [*She goes over to the center table, slipping into her shoes.*]

MRS. FRANK. [*Following her*] You haven't a fever, have you?

ANNE. [*Pulling away*] No. No.

Vocabulary Builder
insufferable (in suf´ ə rə bəl) *adj.* unbearable

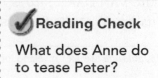

Reading Check

What does Anne do to tease Peter?

MRS. FRANK. You know we can't call a doctor here, ever. There's only one thing to do . . . watch carefully. Prevent an illness before it comes. Let me see your tongue.

ANNE. Mother, this is perfectly absurd.

MRS. FRANK. Anne, dear, don't be such a baby. Let me see your tongue. [*As* ANNE *refuses,* MRS. FRANK *appeals to* MR. FRANK] Otto . . .?

MR. FRANK. You hear your mother, Anne.

[ANNE *flicks out her tongue for a second, then turns away.*]

MRS. FRANK. Come on—open up! [*As* ANNE *opens her mouth very wide*] You seem all right . . . but perhaps an aspirin . . .

MRS. VAN DAAN. For heaven's sake, don't give that child any pills. I waited for fifteen minutes this morning for her to come out of the w.c.

ANNE. I was washing my hair!

MR. FRANK. I think there's nothing the matter with our Anne that a ride on her bike, or a visit with her friend Jopie de Waal wouldn't cure. Isn't that so, Anne?

[MR. VAN DAAN *comes down into the room. From outside we hear faint sounds of bombers going over and a burst of ack-ack.*][18]

MR. VAN DAAN. Miep not come yet?

MRS. VAN DAAN. The workmen just left, a little while ago.

MR. VAN DAAN. What's for dinner tonight?

MRS. VAN DAAN. Beans.

MR. VAN DAAN. Not again!

MRS. VAN DAAN. Poor Putti! I know. But what can we do? That's all that Miep brought us.

[MR. VAN DAAN *starts to pace, his hands behind his back.* ANNE *follows behind him, imitating him.*]

---

18. **ack-ack** (ak´ ak´) *n.* slang for an anti-aircraft gun's fire.

Literature in Context

History Connection

Air Raids When Anne's family hears the sound of bombers and anti-aircraft guns overhead, they are hearing familiar sounds of the time. World War II was the first major war that involved the massive aerial bombing of cities.

Often, the first sound to alert people to an attack was the ghostly wailing of an air raid siren. This meant "Take cover!" Then, the drone of bomber engines and the crackle and burst of anti-aircraft fire would take over—the sounds that Anne hears. Finally, there would be the whistling of bombs dropping, the whine of a falling plane, or the sound of explosions. These were sounds heard by many families throughout Europe. This was the soundtrack of war.

Connect to the Literature

Why might the sound of bombers, like this American B-17, cause mixed feelings of anxiety and anticipation for those in hiding?

ANNE. We are now in what is known as the "bean cycle." Beans boiled, beans en casserole, beans with strings, beans without strings . . .

[PETER *has come out of his room. He slides into his place at the table, becoming immediately absorbed in his studies.*]

MR. VAN DAAN. [*To* PETER] I saw you . . . in there, playing with your cat.

MRS. VAN DAAN. He just went in for a second, putting his coat away. He's been out here all the time, doing his lessons.

MR. FRANK. [*Looking up from the papers*] Anne, you got an excellent in your history paper today . . . and very good in Latin.

ANNE. [*Sitting beside him*] How about algebra?

MR. FRANK. I'll have to make a confession. Up until now I've managed to stay ahead of you in algebra. Today you caught up with me. We'll leave it to Margot to correct.

ANNE. Isn't algebra *vile*, Pim!

MR. FRANK. Vile!

MARGOT. [*To* MR. FRANK] How did I do?

ANNE. [*Getting up*] Excellent, excellent, excellent, excellent!

MR. FRANK. [*To* MARGOT] You should have used the subjunctive[19] here . . .

MARGOT. Should I? . . . I thought . . . look here . . . I didn't use it here . . .

[*The two become absorbed in the papers.*]

ANNE. Mrs. Van Daan, may I try on your coat?

MRS. FRANK. No, Anne.

MRS. VAN DAAN. [*Giving it to* ANNE] It's all right . . . but careful with it. [ANNE *puts it on and struts with it.*] My father gave me that the year before he died. He always bought the best that money could buy.

ANNE. Mrs. Van Daan, did you have a lot of boy friends before you were married?

MRS. FRANK. Anne, that's a personal question. It's not courteous to ask personal questions.

19. subjunctive (səb juŋk′ tiv) *n.* form of a verb that is used to express doubt or uncertainty.

Literary Analysis
Dialogue Based on this dialogue, what is Mr. Frank's attitude toward education?

Literary Analysis
Dialogue What does Mrs. Van Daan's comment about her father reveal about her values?

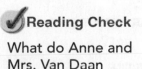**Reading Check**

What do Anne and Mrs. Van Daan discuss?

MRS. VAN DAAN. Oh I don't mind. [*To* ANNE] Our house was always swarming with boys. When I was a girl we had . . .

MR. VAN DAAN. Oh, God. Not again!

MRS. VAN DAAN. [*Good-humored*] Shut up! [*Without a pause, to* ANNE, MR. VAN DAAN *mimics* MRS. VAN DAAN, *speaking the first few words in unison with her.*] One summer we had a big house in Hilversum. The boys came buzzing round like bees around a jam pot. And when I was sixteen! . . . We were wearing our skirts very short those days and I had good-looking legs. [*She pulls up her skirt, going to* MR. FRANK.] I still have 'em. I may not be as pretty as I used to be, but I still have my legs. How about it, Mr. Frank?

MR. VAN DAAN. All right. All right. We see them.

MRS. VAN DAAN. I'm not asking you. I'm asking Mr. Frank.

PETER. Mother, for heaven's sake.

MRS. VAN DAAN. Oh, I embarrass you, do I? Well, I just hope the girl you marry has as good. [*Then to* ANNE] My father used to worry about me, with so many boys hanging round. He told me, if any of them gets fresh, you say to him . . . "Remember, Mr. So-and-So, remember I'm a lady."

ANNE. "Remember, Mr. So-and-So, remember I'm a lady." [*She gives* MRS. VAN DAAN *her coat.*]

MR. VAN DAAN. Look at you, talking that way in front of her! Don't you know she puts it all down in that diary?

MRS. VAN DAAN. So, if she does? I'm only telling the truth!

[ANNE *stretches out, putting her ear to the floor, listening to what is going on below. The sound of the bombers fades away.*]

MRS. FRANK. [*Setting the table*] Would you mind, Peter, if I moved you over to the couch?

ANNE. [*Listening*] Miep must have the radio on.

[PETER *picks up his papers, going over to the couch beside* MRS. VAN DAAN.]

MR. VAN DAAN. [*Accusingly, to* PETER] Haven't you finished yet?

PETER. No.

MR. VAN DAAN. You ought to be ashamed of yourself.

Literary Analysis
Dialogue What do Mrs. Van Daan's words and actions reveal about her personality?

Reading Skill
Cause and Effect How might the families' situation cause Anne to be interested in events in the outside world?

PETER. All right. All right. I'm a dunce. I'm a hope-less case. Why do I go on?

MRS. VAN DAAN. You're not hopeless. Don't talk that way. It's just that you haven't anyone to help you, like the girls have. [*To* MR. FRANK] Maybe you could help him, Mr. Frank?

MR. FRANK. I'm sure that his father . . .?

MR. VAN DAAN. Not me. I can't do anything with him. He won't listen to me. You go ahead . . . if you want.

MR. FRANK. [*Going to* PETER] What about it, Peter? Shall we make our school coeducational?

MRS. VAN DAAN. [*Kissing* MR. FRANK] You're an angel, Mr. Frank. An angel. I don't know why I didn't meet you before I met that one there. Here, sit down, Mr. Frank . . . [*She forces him down on the couch beside* PETER.] Now, Peter, you listen to Mr. Frank.

MR. FRANK. It might be better for us to go into Peter's room.

[PETER *jumps up eagerly, leading the way.*]

MRS. VAN DAAN. That's right. You go in there, Peter. You listen to Mr. Frank. Mr. Frank is a highly educated man.

[*As* MR. FRANK *is about to follow* PETER *into his room,* MRS. FRANK *stops him and wipes the lipstick from his lips. Then she closes the door after them.*]

ANNE. [*On the floor, listening*] Shh! I can hear a man's voice talking.

MR. VAN DAAN. [*To* ANNE] Isn't it bad enough here without your sprawling all over the place?

[ANNE *sits up.*]

MRS. VAN DAAN. [*To* MR. VAN DAAN] If you didn't smoke so much, you wouldn't be so bad-tempered.

MR. VAN DAAN. Am I smoking? Do you see me smoking?

MRS. VAN DAAN. Don't tell me you've used up all those cigarettes.

▲ **Critical Viewing**
What kind of personality did Mrs. Frank have, based on details in this photograph? **[Infer]**

Reading Check

In what way does Mr. Frank offer to help Peter?

MR. VAN DAAN. One package. Miep only brought me one package.

MRS. VAN DAAN. It's a filthy habit anyway. It's a good time to break yourself.

MR. VAN DAAN. Oh, stop it, please.

MRS. VAN DAAN. You're smoking up all our money. You know that, don't you?

MR. VAN DAAN. Will you shut up?
[*During this,* MRS. FRANK *and* MARGOT *have studiously kept their eyes down. But* ANNE, *seated on the floor, has been following the discussion interestedly.* MR. VAN DAAN *turns to see her staring up at him.*] And what are you staring at?

ANNE. I never heard grownups quarrel before. I thought only children quarreled.

MR. VAN DAAN. This isn't a quarrel! It's a discussion. And I never heard children so rude before.

ANNE. [*Rising, indignantly*] I, rude!

MR. VAN DAAN. Yes!

MRS. FRANK. [*Quickly*] Anne, will you get me my knitting?
[ANNE *goes to get it.*]
I must remember, when Miep comes, to ask her to bring me some more wool.

MARGOT. [*Going to her room*] I need some hairpins and some soap. I made a list. [*She goes into her bedroom to get the list.*]

MRS. FRANK. [*To* ANNE] Have you some library books for Miep when she comes?

ANNE. It's a wonder that Miep has a life of her own, the way we make her run errands for us. Please, Miep, get me some starch. Please take my hair out and have it cut. Tell me all the latest news, Miep. [*She goes over, kneeling on the couch beside* MRS. VAN DAAN] Did you know she was engaged? His name is Dirk, and Miep's afraid the Nazis will ship him off to Germany to work in one of their war plants. That's what they're doing with some of the young Dutchmen . . . they pick them up off the streets—

Literary Analysis
Dialogue What lines of dialogue here show that the residents of the attic are starting to annoy one another?

Literary Analysis
Dialogue What do you learn about Anne's personality from these lines?

MR. VAN DAAN. [*Interrupting*] Don't you ever get tired of talking? Suppose you try keeping still for five minutes. Just five minutes.

[*He starts to pace again. Again* ANNE *follows him, mimicking him.* MRS. FRANK *jumps up and takes her by the arm up to the sink, and gives her a glass of milk.*]

MRS. FRANK. Come here, Anne. It's time for your glass of milk.

MR. VAN DAAN. Talk, talk, talk. I never heard such a child. Where is my . . .? Every evening it's the same talk, talk, talk. [*He looks around.*] Where is my . . .?

MRS. VAN DAAN. What're you looking for?

MR. VAN DAAN. My pipe. Have you seen my pipe?

MRS. VAN DAAN. What good's a pipe? You haven't got any tobacco.

MR. VAN DAAN. At least I'll have something to hold in my mouth! [*Opening* MARGOT'S *bedroom door*] Margot, have you seen my pipe?

MARGOT. It was on the table last night.

[ANNE *puts her glass of milk on the table and picks up his pipe, hiding it behind her back.*]

MR. VAN DAAN. I know. I know. Anne, did you see my pipe? . . . Anne!

MRS. FRANK. Anne, Mr. Van Daan is speaking to you.

ANNE. Am I allowed to talk now?

MR. VAN DAAN. You're the most aggravating . . . The trouble with you is, you've been spoiled. What you need is a good old-fashioned spanking.

ANNE. [*Mimicking* MRS. VAN DAAN] "Remember, Mr. So-and-So, remember I'm a lady." [*She thrusts the pipe into his mouth, then picks up her glass of milk.*]

MR. VAN DAAN. [*Restraining himself with difficulty*] Why aren't you nice and quiet like your sister Margot? Why do you have to show off all the time? Let me give you a little advice, young lady. Men don't like that kind of thing in a girl. You know that? A man likes a girl who'll listen to him once in a while . . . a domestic girl, who'll keep her house shining for her husband . . . who loves to cook and sew and . . .

Literary Analysis
Dialogue What cultural attitudes does Mr. Van Daan show in this dialogue?

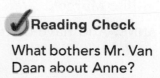

Reading Check

What bothers Mr. Van Daan about Anne?

ANNE. I'd cut my throat first! I'd open my veins! I'm going to be remarkable! I'm going to Paris . . .

MR. VAN DAAN. [*Scoffingly*] Paris!

ANNE. . . . to study music and art.

MR. VAN DAAN. Yeah! Yeah!

ANNE. I'm going to be a famous dancer or singer . . . or something wonderful.

[*She makes a wide gesture, spilling the glass of milk on the fur coat in* MRS. VAN DAAN'S *lap.* MARGOT *rushes quickly over with a towel.* ANNE *tries to brush the milk off with her skirt.*]

MRS. VAN DAAN. Now look what you've done . . . you clumsy little fool! My beautiful fur coat my father gave me . . .

ANNE. I'm so sorry.

MRS. VAN DAAN. What do you care? It isn't yours . . . So go on, ruin it! Do you know what that coat cost? Do you? And now look at it! Look at it!

ANNE. I'm very, very sorry.

MRS. VAN DAAN. I could kill you for this. I could just kill you!

[MRS. VAN DAAN *goes up the stairs, clutching the coat.* MR. VAN DAAN *starts after her.*]

MR. VAN DAAN. Petronella . . . *Liefje! Liefje!* . . . Come back . . . the supper . . . come back!

MRS. FRANK. Anne, you must not behave in that way.

ANNE. It was an accident. Anyone can have an accident.

MRS. FRANK. I don't mean that. I mean the answering back. You must not answer back. They are our guests. We must always show the greatest courtesy to them. We're all living under terrible tension. [*She stops as* MARGOT *indicates that* VAN DAAN *can hear. When he is gone, she continues.*] That's why we must control ourselves . . . You don't hear Margot getting into arguments with them, do you? Watch Margot. She's always courteous with them. Never familiar. She keeps her distance. And they respect her for it. Try to be like Margot.

ANNE. And have them walk all over me, the way they do her? No, thanks!

Reading Skill
Cause and Effect
How is the characters' situation affecting them?

Reading Skill
Cause and Effect
Is Mrs. Frank's advice practical, given the families' situation? Explain.

MRS. FRANK. I'm not afraid that anyone is going to walk all over you, Anne. I'm afraid for other people, that you'll walk on them. I don't know what happens to you, Anne. You are wild, self-willed. If I had ever talked to my mother as you talk to me . . .

ANNE. Things have changed. People aren't like that any more. "Yes, Mother." "No, Mother." "Anything you say, Mother." I've got to fight things out for myself! Make something of myself!

MRS. FRANK. It isn't necessary to fight to do it. Margot doesn't fight, and isn't she . . .?

ANNE. [*Violently rebellious*] Margot! Margot! Margot! That's all I hear from everyone . . . how wonderful Margot is . . . "Why aren't you like Margot?"

MARGOT. [*Protesting*] Oh, come on, Anne, don't be so . . .

ANNE. [*Paying no attention*] Everything she does is right, and everything I do is wrong! I'm the goat around here! . . . You're all against me! . . . And you worst of all!

[*She rushes off into her room and throws herself down on the settee, stifling her sobs.* MRS. FRANK *sighs and starts toward the stove.*]

MRS. FRANK. [*To* MARGOT] Let's put the soup on the stove . . . if there's anyone who cares to eat. Margot, will you take the bread out? [MARGOT *gets the bread from the cupboard.*] I don't know how we can go on living this way . . . I can't say a word to Anne . . . she flies at me . . .

MARGOT. You know Anne. In half an hour she'll be out here, laughing and joking.

MRS. FRANK. And . . . [*She makes a motion upwards, indicating the* VAN DAANS.] . . . I told your father it wouldn't work . . . but no . . . no . . . he had to ask them, he said . . . he owed it to him, he said. Well, he knows now that I was right! These quarrels! . . . This bickering!

MARGOT. [*With a warning look*] Shush. Shush.

[*The buzzer for the door sounds.* MRS. FRANK *gasps, startled.*]

MRS. FRANK. Every time I hear that sound, my heart stops!

Reading Skill
Cause and Effect
How does the situation in the outside world force Mrs. Frank to accept conditions she finds unbearable?

Reading Check

How does Anne ruin Mrs. Van Daan's coat?

MARGOT. [*Starting for* PETER'S *door*] It's Miep. [*She knocks at the door.*] Father?

[MR. FRANK *comes quickly from* PETER'S *room.*]

MR. FRANK. Thank you, Margot. [*As he goes down the steps to open the outer door*] Has everyone his list?

MARGOT. I'll get my books. [*Giving her mother a list*] Here's your list.
[MARGOT *goes into her and* ANNE'S *bedroom on the right.* ANNE *sits up, hiding her tears, as* MARGOT *comes in.*]
Miep's here.
[MARGOT *picks up her books and goes back.* ANNE *hurries over to the mirror, smoothing her hair.*]

MR. VAN DAAN. [*Coming down the stairs*] Is it Miep?

MARGOT. Yes. Father's gone down to let her in.

MR. VAN DAAN. At last I'll have some cigarettes!

MRS. FRANK. [*To* MR. VAN DAAN] I can't tell you how unhappy I am about Mrs. Van Daan's coat. Anne should never have touched it.

MR. VAN DAAN. She'll be all right.

MRS. FRANK. Is there anything I can do?

MR. VAN DAAN. Don't worry.

[*He turns to meet* MIEP. *But it is not* MIEP *who comes up the steps. It is* MR. KRALER, *followed by* MR. FRANK. *Their faces are grave.* ANNE *comes from the bedroom.* PETER *comes from his room.*]

MRS. FRANK. Mr. Kraler!

MR. VAN DAAN. How are you, Mr. Kraler?

MARGOT. This is a surprise.

MRS. FRANK. When Mr. Kraler comes, the sun begins to shine.

MR. VAN DAAN. Miep is coming?

MR. KRALER. Not tonight.

[KRALER *goes to* MARGOT *and* MRS. FRANK *and* ANNE, *shaking hands with them.*]

MRS. FRANK. Wouldn't you like a cup of coffee? . . . Or, better still, will you have supper with us?

**Reading Skill
Cause and Effect**
Why would a visit from an outside friend be especially welcome to those in hiding?

MR. FRANK. Mr. Kraler has something to talk over with us. Something has happened, he says, which demands an immediate decision.

MRS. FRANK. [*Fearful*] What is it?

[MR. KRALER *sits down on the couch. As he talks he takes bread, cabbages, milk, etc., from his briefcase, giving them to* MARGOT *and* ANNE *to put away.*]

MR. KRALER. Usually, when I come up here, I try to bring you some bit of good news. What's the use of telling you the bad news when there's nothing that you can do about it? But today something has happened . . . Dirk . . . Miep's Dirk, you know, came to me just now. He tells me that he has a Jewish friend living near him. A dentist. He says he's in trouble. He begged me, could I do anything for this man? Could I find him a hiding place? . . . So I've come to you . . . I know it's a terrible thing to ask of you, living as you are, but would you take him in with you?

MR. FRANK. Of course we will.

MR. KRALER. [*Rising*] It'll be just for a night or two . . . until I find some other place. This happened so suddenly that I didn't know where to turn.

MR. FRANK. Where is he?

MR. KRALER. Downstairs in the office.

MR. FRANK. Good. Bring him up.

MR. KRALER. His name is Dussel . . . Jan Dussel.

MR. FRANK. Dussel . . . I think I know him.

MR. KRALER. I'll get him.

[*He goes quickly down the steps and out.* MR. FRANK *suddenly becomes conscious of the others.*]

▲ Critical Viewing
Why might the designers of this stamp have chosen such a happy photograph of Anne? **[Speculate]**

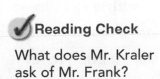

Reading Check

What does Mr. Kraler ask of Mr. Frank?

MR. FRANK. Forgive me. I spoke without consulting you. But I knew you'd feel as I do.

MR. VAN DAAN. There's no reason for you to consult anyone. This is your place. You have a right to do exactly as you please. The only thing I feel . . . there's so little food as it is . . . and to take in another person . . .

[PETER *turns away, ashamed of his father.*]

MR. FRANK. We can stretch the food a little. It's only for a few days.

MR. VAN DAAN. You want to make a bet?

MRS. FRANK. I think it's fine to have him. But, Otto, where are you going to put him? Where?

PETER. He can have my bed. I can sleep on the floor. I wouldn't mind.

MR. FRANK. That's good of you, Peter. But your room's too small . . . even for *you.*

ANNE. I have a much better idea. I'll come in here with you and Mother, and Margot can take Peter's room and Peter can go in our room with Mr. Dussel.

MARGOT. That's right. We could do that.

MR. FRANK. No, Margot. You mustn't sleep in that room . . . neither you nor Anne. Mouschi has caught some rats in there. Peter's brave. He doesn't mind.

ANNE. Then how about *this?* I'll come in here with you and Mother, and Mr. Dussel can have my bed.

MRS. FRANK. *No. No. No!* Margot will come in here with us and he can have her bed. It's the only way. Margot, bring your things in here. Help her, Anne.

[MARGOT *hurries into her room to get her things.*]

ANNE. [*To her mother*] Why Margot? Why can't I come in here?

MRS. FRANK. Because it wouldn't be proper for Margot to sleep with a . . . Please, Anne. Don't argue. Please.

[ANNE *starts slowly away.*]

MR. FRANK. [*To* ANNE] You don't mind sharing your room with Mr. Dussel, do you, Anne?

Reading Skill
Cause and Effect
What possible effects will Dussel's arrival have on the families' living situation?

ANNE. No. No, of course not.

MR. FRANK. Good. [ANNE *goes off into her bedroom, helping* MARGOT. MR. FRANK *starts to search in the cupboards.*] Where's the cognac?

MRS. FRANK. It's there. But, Otto, I was saving it in case of illness.

MR. FRANK. I think we couldn't find a better time to use it. Peter, will you get five glasses for me?

[PETER *goes for the glasses.* MARGOT *comes out of her bedroom, carrying her possessions, which she hangs behind a curtain in the main room.* MR. FRANK *finds the cognac and pours it into the five glasses that* PETER *brings him.* MR. VAN DAAN *stands looking on sourly.* MRS. VAN DAAN *comes downstairs and looks around at all the bustle.*]

MRS. VAN DAAN. What's happening? What's going on?

MR. VAN DAAN. Someone's moving in with us.

MRS. VAN DAAN. In here? You're joking.

MARGOT. It's only for a night or two . . . until Mr. Kraler finds him another place.

MR. VAN DAAN. Yeah! Yeah!

[MR. FRANK *hurries over as* MR. KRALER *and* DUSSEL *come up.* DUSSEL *is a man in his late fifties,* <u>meticulous</u>, *finicky . . . bewildered now. He wears a raincoat. He carries a briefcase, stuffed full, and a small medicine case.*]

MR. FRANK. Come in, Mr. Dussel.

MR. KRALER. This is Mr. Frank.

DUSSEL. Mr. Otto Frank?

MR. FRANK. Yes. Let me take your things. [*He takes the hat and briefcase, but* DUSSEL *clings to his medicine case.*] This is my wife Edith . . . Mr. and Mrs. Van Daan . . . their son, Peter . . . and my daughters, Margot and Anne.

[DUSSEL *shakes hands with everyone.*]

MR. KRALER. Thank you, Mr. Frank. Thank you all. Mr. Dussel, I leave you in good hands. Oh . . . Dirk's coat.

▲ **Critical Viewing**
What details of Dussel's photograph suggest that he is careful about his appearance?

Vocabulary Builder
meticulous (mə tik´ yoo ləs) *adj.*
extremely careful about details

Reading Check

Who agrees to share a room with Dussel?

[DUSSEL *hurriedly takes off the raincoat, giving it to* MR. KRALER. *Underneath is his white dentist's jacket, with a yellow Star of David on it.*]

DUSSEL. [*To* MR. KRALER] What can I say to thank you . . .?

MRS. FRANK. [*To* DUSSEL] Mr. Kraler and Miep . . . They're our life line. Without them we couldn't live.

MR. KRALER. Please. Please. You make us seem very heroic. It isn't that at all. We simply don't like the Nazis. [*To* MR. FRANK, *who offers him a drink*] No, thanks. [*Then going on*] We don't like their methods. We don't like . . .

MR. FRANK. [*Smiling*] I know. I know. "No one's going to tell us Dutchmen what to do with our damn Jews!"

MR. KRALER. [*To* DUSSEL] Pay no attention to Mr. Frank. I'll be up tomorrow to see that they're treating you right. [*To* MR. FRANK] Don't trouble to come down again. Peter will bolt the door after me, won't you, Peter?

PETER. Yes, sir.

MR. FRANK. Thank you, Peter. I'll do it.

MR. KRALER. Good night. Good night.

GROUP. Good night, Mr. Kraler. We'll see you tomorrow, etc., etc.

[MR. KRALER *goes out with* MR. FRANK, MRS. FRANK *gives each one of the "grownups" a glass of cognac.*]

MRS. FRANK. Please, Mr. Dussel, sit down.

[MR. DUSSEL *sinks into a chair.* MRS. FRANK *gives him a glass of cognac.*]

DUSSEL. I'm dreaming. I know it. I can't believe my eyes. Mr. Otto

German-Jewish family fleeing Nazi persecution

Frank here! [*To* MRS. FRANK] You're not in Switzerland then? A woman told me . . . She said she'd gone to your house . . . the door was open, everything was in disorder, dishes in the sink. She said she found a piece of paper in the wastebasket with an address scribbled on it . . . an address in Zurich. She said you must have escaped to Zurich.

ANNE. Father put that there purposely . . . just so people would think that very thing!

DUSSEL. And you've been *here* all the time?

MRS. FRANK. All the time . . . ever since July.

[ANNE *speaks to her father as he comes back.*]

ANNE. It worked, Pim . . . the address you left! Mr. Dussel says that people believe we escaped to Switzerland.

MR. FRANK. I'm glad. . . . And now let's have a little drink to welcome Mr. Dussel.
[*Before they can drink,* MR. DUSSEL *bolts his drink.* MR. FRANK *smiles and raises his glass.*]
To Mr. Dussel. Welcome. We're very honored to have you with us.

MRS. FRANK. To Mr. Dussel, welcome.

[*The* VAN DAANS *murmur a welcome. The "grownups" drink.*]

MRS. VAN DAAN. Um. That was good.

MR. VAN DAAN. Did Mr. Kraler warn you that you won't get much to eat here? You can imagine . . . three ration books among the seven of us . . . and now you make eight.

[PETER *walks away, humiliated. Outside a street organ is heard dimly.*]

DUSSEL. [*Rising*] Mr. Van Daan, you don't realize what is happening outside that you should warn me of a thing like that. You don't realize what's going on . . .
[*As* MR. VAN DAAN *starts his characteristic pacing,* DUSSEL *turns to speak to the others.*]
Right here in Amsterdam every day hundreds of Jews disappear . . . They surround a block and search house by house. Children come home from school to find their parents gone. Hundreds are being deported . . . people that you and I know . . . the Hallensteins . . . the Wessels . . .

MRS. FRANK. [*In tears*] Oh, no. No!

Reading Check

Why does Mr. Van Daan say Dussel will not get much to eat in the Annex?

DUSSEL. They get their call-up notice . . . come to the Jewish theater on such and such a day and hour . . . bring only what you can carry in a rucksack. And if you refuse the call-up notice, then they come and drag you from your home and ship you off to Mauthausen.[20] The death camp!

MRS. FRANK. We didn't know that things had got so much worse.

DUSSEL. Forgive me for speaking so.

ANNE. [*Coming to* DUSSEL] Do you know the de Waals? . . . What's become of them? Their daughter Jopie and I are in the same class. Jopie's my best friend.

DUSSEL. They are gone.

ANNE. Gone?

DUSSEL. With all the others.

ANNE. Oh, no. Not Jopie!

[*She turns away, in tears.* MRS. FRANK *motions to* MARGOT *to comfort her.* MAR-GOT *goes to* ANNE, *putting her arms comfortingly around her.*]

MRS. VAN DAAN. There were some people called Wagner. They lived near us . . .?

MR. FRANK. [*Interrupting, with a glance at* ANNE] I think we should put this off until later. We all have many questions we want to ask . . . But I'm sure that Mr. Dussel would like to get settled before supper.

DUSSEL. Thank you. I would. I brought very little with me.

MR. FRANK. [*Giving him his hat and briefcase*] I'm sorry we can't give you a room alone. But I hope you won't be too uncomfortable. We've had to make strict rules here . . . a schedule of hours . . . We'll tell you after supper. Anne, would you like to take Mr. Dussel to his room?

▲ **Critical Viewing** This photograph and inset show the block in which the Franks hid. Why might it feel strange to hide in such a big city? **[Speculate]**

---

20. **Mauthausen** (mou´ tou´ zən) village in Austria that was the site of a Nazi concentration camp.

ANNE. [*Controlling her tears*] If you'll come with me, Mr. Dussel? [*She starts for her room.*]

DUSSEL. [*Shaking hands with each in turn*] Forgive me if I haven't really expressed my gratitude to all of you. This has been such a shock to me. I'd always thought of myself as Dutch. I was born in Holland. My father was born in Holland, and my grandfather. And now . . . after all these years . . . [*He breaks off.*] If you'll excuse me.

[DUSSEL *gives a little bow and hurries off after* ANNE. MR. FRANK *and the others are subdued.*]

ANNE. [*Turning on the light*] Well, here we are.

[DUSSEL *looks around the room. In the main room* MARGOT *speaks to her mother.*]

Reading Skill
Cause and Effect
How does Dussel's news affect Anne?

 **Reading Check**

Why did Dussel believe he was safe from persecution as a Jew?

The Diary of Anne Frank, Act I ■ 811

MARGOT. The news sounds pretty bad, doesn't it? It's so different from what Mr. Kraler tells us. Mr. Kraler says things are improving.

MR. VAN DAAN. I like it better the way Kraler tells it.

[*They resume their occupations, quietly.* PETER *goes off into his room. In* ANNE'S *room,* ANNE *turns to* DUSSEL.]

ANNE. You're going to share the room with me.

DUSSEL. I'm a man who's always lived alone. I haven't had to adjust myself to others. I hope you'll bear with me until I learn.

ANNE. Let me help you. [*She takes his briefcase.*] Do you always live all alone? Have you no family at all?

DUSSEL. No one. [*He opens his medicine case and spreads his bottles on the dressing table.*]

ANNE. How dreadful. You must be terribly lonely.

DUSSEL. I'm used to it.

ANNE. I don't think I could ever get used to it. Didn't you even have a pet? A cat, or a dog?

DUSSEL. I have an allergy for fur-bearing animals. They give me asthma.

ANNE. Oh, dear. Peter has a cat.

DUSSEL. Here? He has it here?

ANNE. Yes. But we hardly ever see it. He keeps it in his room all the time. I'm sure it will be all right.

DUSSEL. Let us hope so. [*He takes some pills to fortify himself.*]

ANNE. That's Margot's bed, where you're going to sleep. I sleep on the sofa there. [*Indicating the clothes hooks on the wall*] We cleared these off for your things. [*She goes over to the window.*] The best part about this room . . . you can look down and see a bit of the street and the canal. There's a houseboat . . . you can see the end of it . . . a bargeman lives there with his family . . . They have a baby and he's just beginning to walk and I'm so afraid he's going to fall into the canal some day. I watch him. . . .

DUSSEL. [*Interrupting*] Your father spoke of a schedule.

Literary Analysis

Dialogue From this dialogue, would you say Dussel is formal or informal in his attitudes and speech? Explain.

ANNE. [*Coming away from the window*] Oh, yes. It's mostly about the times we have to be quiet. And times for the w.c. You can use it now if you like.

DUSSEL. [*Stiffly*] No, thank you.

ANNE. I suppose you think it's awful, my talking about a thing like that. But you don't know how important it can get to be, especially when you're frightened . . . About this room, the way Margot and I did . . . she had it to herself in the afternoons for studying, reading . . . lessons, you know . . . and I took the mornings. Would that be all right with you?

DUSSEL. I'm not at my best in the morning.

ANNE. You stay here in the mornings then. I'll take the room in the afternoons.

DUSSEL. Tell me, when you're in here, what happens to me? Where am I spending my time? In there, with all the people?

ANNE. Yes.

DUSSEL. I see. I see.

ANNE. We have supper at half past six.

DUSSEL. [*Going over to the sofa*] Then, if you don't mind . . . I like to lie down quietly for ten minutes before eating. I find it helps the digestion.

ANNE. Of course. I hope I'm not going to be too much of a bother to you. I seem to be able to get everyone's back up.

[DUSSEL *lies down on the sofa, curled up, his back to her.*]

DUSSEL. I always get along very well with children. My patients all bring their children to me, because they know I get on well with them. So don't you worry about that.

[ANNE *leans over him, taking his hand and shaking it gratefully.*]

ANNE. Thank you. Thank you, Mr. Dussel.

[*The lights dim to darkness. The curtain falls on the scene.* ANNE'S *voice comes to us faintly at first, and then with increasing power.*]

ANNE'S VOICE. . . . And yesterday I finished Cissy Van Marx-velt's latest book. I think she is a first-class writer. I shall definitely let my children read her. Monday the twenty-first

Literary Analysis Dialogue Based on this dialogue, how well do you think Anne and Dussel will get along?

✔ **Reading Check**

What does Anne explain to Dussel?

The Diary of Anne Frank, Act I ■ 813

of September, nineteen forty-two. Mr. Dussel and I had another battle yesterday. Yes, Mr. Dussel! According to him, nothing, I repeat . . . nothing, is right about me . . . my appearance, my character, my manners. While he was going on at me I thought . . . sometime I'll give you such a smack that you'll fly right up to the ceiling! Why is it that every grownup thinks he knows the way to bring up children? Particularly the grownups that never had any. I keep wishing that Peter was a girl instead of a boy. Then I would have someone to talk to. Margot's a darling, but she takes everything too seriously. To pause for a moment on the subject of Mrs. Van Daan. I must tell you that her attempts to flirt with father are getting her nowhere. Pim, thank goodness, won't play.

[*As she is saying the last lines, the curtain rises on the darkened scene.* ANNE'S VOICE *fades out.*]

Scene 4

[*It is the middle of the night, several months later. The stage is dark except for a little light which comes through the skylight in* PETER'S *room.*

Everyone is in bed. MR. *and* MRS. FRANK *lie on the couch in the main room, which has been pulled out to serve as a makeshift double bed.*

MARGOT *is sleeping on a mattress on the floor in the main room, behind a curtain stretched across for privacy. The others are all in their accustomed rooms.*

From outside we hear two drunken soldiers singing "Lili Marlene." A girl's high giggle is heard. The sound of running feet is heard coming closer and then fading in the distance. Throughout the scene there is the distant sound of airplanes passing overhead.

A match suddenly flares up in the attic. We dimly see MR. VAN DAAN. *He is getting his bearings. He comes quickly down the stairs, and goes to the cupboard where the food is stored. Again the match flares up, and is as quickly blown out. The dim figure is seen to steal back up the stairs.*

There is quiet for a second or two, broken only by the sound of airplanes, and running feet on the street below.

Suddenly, out of the silence and the dark, we hear ANNE *scream.*]

ANNE. [*Screaming*] No! No! Don't . . . don't take me!

[*She moans, tossing and crying in her sleep. The other people wake, terrified. DUSSEL sits up in bed, furious.*]

DUSSEL. Shush! Anne! Anne, for God's sake, shush!

ANNE. [*Still in her nightmare*] Save me! Save me!

[*She screams and screams. DUSSEL gets out of bed, going over to her, trying to wake her.*]

DUSSEL. For God's sake! Quiet! Quiet! You want someone to hear?

[*In the main room MRS. FRANK grabs a shawl and pulls it around her. She rushes in to ANNE, taking her in her arms. MR. FRANK hurriedly gets up, putting on his overcoat. MARGOT sits up, terrified. PETER'S light goes on in his room.*]

MRS. FRANK. [*To ANNE, in her room*] Hush, darling, hush. It's all right. It's all right. [*Over her shoulder to DUSSEL*] Will you be kind enough to turn on the light, Mr. Dussel? [*Back to ANNE*] It's nothing, my darling. It was just a dream.

[*DUSSEL turns on the light in the bedroom. MRS. FRANK holds ANNE in her arms. Gradually ANNE comes out of her nightmare still trembling with horror. MR. FRANK comes into the room, and goes quickly to the window, looking out to be sure that no one outside has heard ANNE'S screams. MRS. FRANK holds ANNE, talking softly to her. In the main room MARGOT stands on a chair, turning on the center hanging lamp. A light goes on in the VAN DAANS' room overhead. PETER puts his robe on, coming out of his room.*]

DUSSEL. [*To MRS. FRANK, blowing his nose*] Something must be done about that child, Mrs. Frank. Yelling like that! Who knows but there's somebody on the streets? She's endangering all our lives.

MRS. FRANK. Anne, darling.

DUSSEL. Every night she twists and turns. I don't sleep. I spend half my night shushing her. And now it's nightmares!

[*MARGOT comes to the door of ANNE'S room, followed by PETER. MR. FRANK goes to them, indicating that everything is all right. PETER takes MARGOT back.*]

Literary Analysis
Dialogue How do the lines delivered by Dussel and Mrs. Frank reveal important differences between them?

Reading Check

Why does Anne scream in the middle of the night?

MRS. FRANK. [*To* ANNE] You're here, safe, you see? Nothing has happened. [*To* DUSSEL] Please, Mr. Dussel, go back to bed. She'll be herself in a minute or two. Won't you, Anne?

DUSSEL. [*Picking up a book and a pillow*] Thank you, but I'm going to the w.c. The one place where there's peace!

[*He stalks out.* MR. VAN DAAN, *in underwear and trousers, comes down the stairs.*]

MR. VAN DAAN. [*To* DUSSEL] What is it? What happened?

DUSSEL. A nightmare. She was having a nightmare!

MR. VAN DAAN. I thought someone was murdering her.

DUSSEL. Unfortunately, no.

[*He goes into the bathroom.* MR. VAN DAAN *goes back up the stairs.* MR. FRANK, *in the main room, sends* PETER *back to his own bedroom.*]

MR. FRANK. Thank you, Peter. Go back to bed.

[PETER *goes back to his room.* MR. FRANK *follows him, turning out the light and looking out the window. Then he goes back to the main room, and gets up on a chair, turning out the center hanging lamp.*]

MRS. FRANK. [*To* ANNE] Would you like some water? [ANNE *shakes her head.*] Was it a very bad dream? Perhaps if you told me . . . ?

ANNE. I'd rather not talk about it.

MRS. FRANK. Poor darling. Try to sleep then. I'll sit right here beside you until you fall asleep. [*She brings a stool over, sitting there.*]

ANNE. You don't have to.

MRS. FRANK. But I'd like to stay with you . . . very much. Really.

ANNE. I'd rather you didn't.

MRS. FRANK. Good night, then. [*She leans down to kiss* ANNE. ANNE *throws her arm up over her face, turning away.* MRS. FRANK, *hiding her hurt, kisses* ANNE'S *arm.*] You'll be all right? There's nothing that you want?

ANNE. Will you please ask Father to come.

Literary Analysis
Dialogue What does this exchange between Anne and her mother reveal about their relationship?

MRS. FRANK. [*After a second*] Of course, Anne dear. [*She hurries out into the other room.* MR. FRANK *comes to her as she comes in.*] *Sie verlangt nach Dir!*[21]

MR. FRANK. [*Sensing her hurt*] Edith, *Liebe, schau . . .*[22]

MRS. FRANK. *Es macht nichts! Ich danke dem lieben Herrgott, dass sie sich wenigstens an Dich wendet, wenn sie Trost braucht! Geh hinein, Otto, sie ist ganz hysterisch vor Angst.*[23] [*As* MR. FRANK *hesitates*] *Geh zu ihr.*[24]
[*He looks at her for a second and then goes to get a cup of water for* ANNE. MRS. FRANK *sinks down on the bed, her face in her hands, trying to keep from sobbing aloud.* MARGOT *comes over to her, putting her arms around her.*]
She wants nothing of me. She pulled away when I leaned down to kiss her.

MARGOT. It's a phase . . . You heard Father . . . Most girls go through it . . . they turn to their fathers at this age . . . they give all their love to their fathers.

MRS. FRANK. You weren't like this. You didn't shut me out.

MARGOT. She'll get over it . . .

[*She smooths the bed for* MRS. FRANK *and sits beside her a moment as* MRS. FRANK *lies down. In* ANNE'S *room* MR. FRANK *comes in, sitting down by* ANNE. ANNE *flings her arms around him, clinging to him. In the distance we hear the sound of ack-ack.*]

ANNE. Oh, Pim. I dreamed that they came to get us! The Green Police! They broke down the door and grabbed me and started to drag me out the way they did Jopie.

MR. FRANK. I want you to take this pill.

ANNE. What is it?

MR. FRANK. Something to quiet you.

[*She takes it and drinks the water. In the main room* MARGOT *turns out the light and goes back to her bed.*]

---

21. *Sie verlangt nach Dir* (sē fer′ laŋt′ nä′ dir′) German for "She is asking for you."
22. *Liebe, schau* (lē′ be shou′) German for "Dear, look."
23. *Es macht . . . vor Angst* German for "It's all right. I thank dear God that at least she turns to you when she needs comfort. Go in, Otto, she is hysterical because of fear."
24. *Geh zu ihr* (gē′ tsoo′ ēr′) German for "Go to her."

MR. FRANK. [*To* ANNE] Do you want me to read to you for a while?

ANNE. No. Just sit with me for a minute. Was I awful? Did I yell terribly loud? Do you think anyone outside could have heard?

MR. FRANK. No. No. Lie quietly now. Try to sleep.

ANNE. I'm a terrible coward. I'm so disappointed in myself. I think I've conquered my fear . . . I think I'm really grown-up . . . and then something happens . . . and I run to you like a baby . . . I love you, Father. I don't love anyone but you.

MR. FRANK. [*Reproachfully*] Annele!

ANNE. It's true. I've been thinking about it for a long time. You're the only one I love.

MR. FRANK. It's fine to hear you tell me that you love me. But I'd be happier if you said you loved your mother as well . . . She needs your help so much . . . your love . . .

ANNE. We have nothing in common. She doesn't understand me. Whenever I try to explain my views on life to her she asks me if I'm constipated.

MR. FRANK. You hurt her very much just now. She's crying. She's in there crying.

ANNE. I can't help it. I only told the truth. I didn't want her here . . . [*Then, with sudden change*] Oh, Pim, I was horrible, wasn't I? And the worst of it is, I can stand off and look at myself doing it and know it's cruel and yet I can't stop doing it. What's the matter with me? Tell me. Don't say it's just a phase! Help me.

MR. FRANK. There is so little that we parents can do to help our children. We can only try to set a good example . . . point the way. The rest you must do yourself. You must build your own character.

ANNE. I'm trying. Really I am. Every night I think back over all of the things I did that day that were wrong . . . like putting the wet mop in Mr. Dussel's bed . . . and this thing now with Mother. I say to myself, that was wrong. I make up my mind, I'm never going to do that again. Never! Of course I may do something worse . . . but at least I'll never do that again! . . . I have a nicer side, Father . . . a sweeter, nicer

▶ **Critical Viewing**
What evidence in this photograph of Anne Frank reveals her lively personality? **[Connect]**

Literary Analysis
Dialogue What insights does Anne have about herself, as revealed in this dialogue?

side. But I'm scared to show it. I'm afraid that people are going to laugh at me if I'm serious. So the mean Anne comes to the outside and the good Anne stays on the inside, and I keep on trying to switch them around and have the good Anne outside and the bad Anne inside and be what I'd like to be . . . and might be . . . if only . . . only . . .

[*She is asleep.* MR. FRANK *watches her for a moment and then turns off the light, and starts out. The lights dim out. The curtain falls on the scene.* ANNE'S VOICE *is heard dimly at first, and then with growing strength.*]

ANNE'S VOICE. . . . The air raids are getting worse. They come over day and night. The noise is terrifying. Pim says it should be music to our ears. The more planes, the sooner will come the end of the war. Mrs. Van Daan pretends to be a <u>fatalist</u>. What will be, will be. But when the planes come over, who is the most frightened? No one else but Petronella! . . . Monday, the ninth of November, nineteen forty-two. Wonderful news! The Allies have landed in Africa. Pim says that we can look for an early finish to the war. Just for fun he asked each of us what was the first thing we wanted to do when we got out of here. Mrs. Van Daan longs to be home with her own things, her needlepoint chairs, the Beckstein piano her father gave her . . . the best that money could buy. Peter would like to go to a movie. Mr. Dussel wants to get back to his dentist's drill. He's afraid he is losing his touch. For myself, there are so many things . . . to ride a bike again . . . to laugh till my belly aches . . . to have new clothes from the skin out . . . to have a hot tub filled to overflowing and wallow in it for hours . . . to be back in school with my friends . . .

Vocabulary Builder
fatalist (fā´ təl ist) *n.* one who believes that all events are determined by fate and cannot be changed

Literary Analysis
Dialogue What does Anne's narration tell the audience about the war?

**Reading Check**

What does Anne want to do when the war ends?

[*As the last lines are being said, the curtain rises on the scene. The lights dim on as* ANNE'S VOICE *fades away.*]

Scene 5

[*It is the first night of the Hanukkah*[25]*celebration.* MR. FRANK *is standing at the head of the table on which is the Menorah.*[26]*He lights the Shamos,*[27]*or servant candle, and holds it as he says the blessing. Seated listening is all of the "family," dressed in their best. The men wear hats,* PETER *wears his cap.*]

MR. FRANK. [*Reading from a prayer book*] "Praised be Thou, oh Lord our God, Ruler of the universe, who has sanctified us with Thy commandments and bidden us kindle the Hanukkah lights. Praised be Thou, oh Lord our God, Ruler of the universe, who has wrought wondrous deliverances for our fathers in days of old. Praised be Thou, oh Lord our God, Ruler of the universe, that Thou has given us life and sustenance and brought us to this happy season." [MR. FRANK *lights the one candle of the Menorah as he continues.*] "We kindle this Hanukkah light to celebrate the great and wonderful deeds wrought through the zeal with which God filled the hearts of the heroic Maccabees, two thousand years ago. They fought against indifference, against tyranny and oppression, and they restored our Temple to us. May these lights remind us that we should ever look to God, whence cometh our help." Amen.

ALL. Amen.

[MR. FRANK *hands* MRS. FRANK *the prayer book.*]

MRS. FRANK. [*Reading*] "I lift up mine eyes unto the mountains, from whence cometh my help. My help cometh from the Lord who made heaven and earth. He will not suffer thy foot to be moved. He that keepeth thee will not slumber. He that keepeth Israel doth neither slumber nor sleep. The Lord is thy keeper. The Lord is thy shade upon thy right hand. The sun shall not smite thee by day, nor the moon by night. The Lord shall keep thee from all evil. He shall keep thy soul. The Lord shall guard thy going out and thy coming in, from this time forth and forevermore." Amen.

Reading Skill
Cause and Effect
Why might the story of Hanukkah have special meaning for the families in hiding?

---

25. **Hanukkah** (khä′ noo kä′) *n.* Jewish celebration that lasts eight days.
26. **Menorah** (mə nô′ rə) *n.* candle holder with nine candles, used during Hanukkah.
27. **Shamos** (shä′ məs) *n.* candle used to light the others in a menorah.

ALL. Amen.

[MRS. FRANK *puts down the prayer book and goes to get the food and wine.* MARGOT *helps her.* MR. FRANK *takes the men's hats and puts them aside.*]

DUSSEL. [*Rising*] That was very moving.

ANNE. [*Pulling him back*] It isn't over yet!

MRS. VAN DAAN. Sit down! Sit down!

ANNE. There's a lot more, songs and presents.

DUSSEL. Presents?

MRS. FRANK. Not this year, unfortunately.

MRS. VAN DAAN. But always on Hanukkah everyone gives presents . . . everyone!

DUSSEL. Like our St. Nicholas' Day.[28]

[*There is a chorus of "no's" from the group.*]

MRS. VAN DAAN. No! Not like St. Nicholas! What kind of a Jew are you that you don't know Hanukkah?

MRS. FRANK. [*As she brings the food*] I remember particularly the candles . . . First one, as we have tonight. Then the second night you light two candles, the next night three . . . and so on until you have eight candles burning. When there are eight candles it is truly beautiful.

MRS. VAN DAAN. And the potato pancakes.

MR. VAN DAAN. Don't talk about them!

MRS. VAN DAAN. I make the best *latkes* you ever tasted!

MRS. FRANK. Invite us all next year . . . in your own home.

MR. FRANK. God willing!

MRS. VAN DAAN. God willing.

MARGOT. What I remember best is the presents we used to get when we were little . . . eight days of presents . . . and each day they got better and better.

MRS. FRANK. [*Sitting down*] We are all here, alive. That is present enough.

Literary Analysis
Dialogue What do Dussel's lines reveal about his familiarity with Hanukkah?

Reading Skill
Cause and Effect How do world events make this Hanukkah different from others that the families have celebrated?

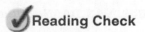
Reading Check

What event in Jewish history are the families celebrating on Hanukkah?

---

28. **St. Nicholas' Day** December 6, the day Christian children in the Netherlands receive gifts.

ANNE. No, it isn't. I've got something . . . [*She rushes into her room, hurriedly puts on a little hat improvised from the lamp shade, grabs a satchel bulging with parcels and comes running back.*]

MRS. FRANK. What is it?

ANNE. Presents!

MRS. VAN DAAN. Presents!

DUSSEL. Look!

MR. VAN DAAN. What's she got on her head?

PETER. A lamp shade!

ANNE. [*She picks out one at random.*] This is for Margot. [*She hands it to* MARGOT, *pulling her to her feet.*] Read it out loud.

MARGOT. [*Reading*]
"You have never lost your temper.
You never will, I fear,
You are so good.
But if you should,
Put all your cross words here."
[*She tears open the package.*] A new crossword puzzle book! Where did you get it?

ANNE. It isn't new. It's one that you've done. But I rubbed it all out, and if you wait a little and forget, you can do it all over again.

MARGOT. [*Sitting*] It's wonderful, Anne. Thank you. You'd never know it wasn't new.

[*From outside we hear the sound of a streetcar passing.*]

ANNE. [*With another gift*] Mrs. Van Daan.

MRS. VAN DAAN. [*Taking it*] This is awful . . . I haven't anything for anyone . . . I never thought . . .

MR. FRANK. This is all Anne's idea.

MRS. VAN DAAN. [*Holding up a bottle*] What is it?

ANNE. It's hair shampoo. I took all the odds and ends of soap and mixed them with the last of my toilet water.

MRS. VAN DAAN. Oh, Anneke!

ANNE. I wanted to write a poem for all of them, but I didn't have time. [*Offering a large box to* MR. VAN DAAN] Yours,

Reading Skill
Cause and Effect
What effect do Anne's gifts have on the group's spirits?

Mr. Van Daan, is really something . . . something you want more than anything. [*As she waits for him to open it*] Look! Cigarettes!

MR. VAN DAAN. Cigarettes!

ANNE. Two of them! Pim found some old pipe tobacco in the pocket lining of his coat . . . and we made them . . . or rather, Pim did.

MRS. VAN DAAN. Let me see . . . Well, look at that! Light it, Putti! Light it.

[MR. VAN DAAN *hesitates*.]

ANNE. It's tobacco, really it is! There's a little fluff in it, but not much.

[*Everyone watches intently as* MR. VAN DAAN *cautiously lights it. The cigarette flares up. Everyone laughs.*]

PETER. It works!

MRS. VAN DAAN. Look at him.

MR. VAN DAAN. [*Spluttering*] Thank you, Anne. Thank you.

[ANNE *rushes back to her satchel for another present.*]

ANNE. [*Handing her mother a piece of paper*] For Mother, Hanukkah greeting.

[*She pulls her mother to her feet.*]

MRS. FRANK. [*She reads*] "Here's an I.O.U. that I promise to pay. Ten hours of doing whatever you say. Signed, Anne Frank." [MRS. FRANK, *touched, takes* ANNE *in her arms, holding her close.*]

DUSSEL. [*To* ANNE] Ten hours of doing what you're told? Anything you're told?

ANNE. That's right.

DUSSEL. You wouldn't want to sell that, Mrs. Frank?

MRS. FRANK. Never! This is the most precious gift I've ever had!

[*She sits, showing her present to the others.* ANNE *hurries back to the satchel and pulls out a scarf, the scarf that* MR. FRANK *found in the first scene.*]

ANNE. [*Offering it to her father*] For Pim.

Reading Skill
Cause and Effect
How do Anne's gifts reflect the reality of the families' situation?

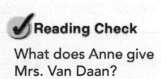

Reading Check

What does Anne give Mrs. Van Daan?

MR. FRANK. Anneke . . . I wasn't supposed to have a present!

[*He takes it, unfolding it and showing it to the others.*]

ANNE. It's a muffler . . . to put round your neck . . . like an ascot, you know. I made it myself out of odds and ends . . . I knitted it in the dark each night, after I'd gone to bed. I'm afraid it looks better in the dark!

MR. FRANK. [*Putting it on*] It's fine. It fits me perfectly. Thank you, Annele.

[ANNE *hands* PETER *a ball of paper with a string attached to it.*]

ANNE. That's for Mouschi.

PETER. [*Rising to bow*] On behalf of Mouschi, I thank you.

ANNE. [*Hesitant, handing him a gift*] And . . . this is yours . . . from Mrs. Quack Quack. [*As he holds it gingerly in his hands*] Well . . . open it . . . Aren't you going to open it?

PETER. I'm scared to. I know something's going to jump out and hit me.

ANNE. No. It's nothing like that, really.

MRS. VAN DAAN. [*As he is opening it*] What is it, Peter? Go on. Show it.

ANNE. [*Excitedly*] It's a safety razor!

DUSSEL. A what?

ANNE. A razor!

MRS. VAN DAAN. [*Looking at it*] You didn't make that out of odds and ends.

ANNE. [*To* PETER] Miep got it for me. It's not new. It's second-hand. But you really do need a razor now.

DUSSEL. For what?

ANNE. Look on his upper lip . . . you can see the beginning of a mustache.

DUSSEL. He wants to get rid of that? Put a little milk on it and let the cat lick it off.

PETER. [*Starting for his room*] Think you're funny, don't you.

DUSSEL. Look! He can't wait! He's going in to try it!

PETER. I'm going to give Mouschi his present!

Reading Skill
Cause and Effect
How does the historical context make Anne's gifts remarkable?

[*He goes into his room, slamming the door behind him.*]

MR. VAN DAAN. [*Disgustedly*] Mouschi, Mouschi, Mouschi.

[*In the distance we hear a dog persistently barking.* ANNE *brings a gift to* DUSSEL.]

ANNE. And last but never least, my roommate, Mr. Dussel.

DUSSEL. For me? You have something for me?

[*He opens the small box she gives him.*]

ANNE. I made them myself.

DUSSEL. [*Puzzled*] Capsules! Two capsules!

ANNE. They're ear-plugs!

DUSSEL. Ear-plugs?

ANNE. To put in your ears so you won't hear me when I thrash around at night. I saw them advertised in a magazine. They're not real ones . . . I made them out of cotton and candle wax. Try them . . . See if they don't work . . . see if you can hear me talk . . .

DUSSEL. [*Putting them in his ears*] Wait now until I get them in . . . so.

ANNE. Are you ready?

DUSSEL. Huh?

ANNE. Are you ready?

DUSSEL. Good God! They've gone inside! I can't get them out! [*They laugh as* MR. DUSSEL *jumps about, trying to shake the plugs out of his ears. Finally he gets them out. Putting them away*] Thank you, Anne! Thank you!

[*Together*] {

MR. VAN DAAN. A real Hanukkah!

MRS. VAN DAAN. Wasn't it cute of her?

MRS. FRANK. I don't know when she did it.

MARGOT. I love my present.

ANNE. [*Sitting at the table*] And now let's have the song, Father . . . please . . . [*To* DUSSEL] Have you heard the Hanukkah song, Mr. Dussel? The song is the whole thing!

Reading Check

How does Mr. Dussel anger Peter?

[*She sings.*] "Oh, Hanukkah! Oh, Hanukkah! The sweet celebration . . ."

MR. FRANK. [*Quieting her*] I'm afraid, Anne, we shouldn't sing that song tonight. [*To* DUSSEL] It's a song of jubilation, of rejoicing. One is apt to become too enthusiastic.

ANNE. Oh, please, please. Let's sing the song. I promise not to shout!

MR. FRANK. Very well. But quietly now . . . I'll keep an eye on you and when . . .

[*As* ANNE *starts to sing, she is interrupted by* DUSSEL, *who is snorting and wheezing.*]

DUSSEL. [*Pointing to* PETER] You . . . You! [PETER *is coming from his bedroom,* <u>ostentatiously</u> *holding a bulge in his coat as if he were holding his cat, and dangling* ANNE'S *present before it.*] How many times . . . I told you . . . Out! Out!

MR. VAN DAAN. [*Going to* PETER] What's the matter with you? Haven't you any sense? Get that cat out of here.

PETER. [*Innocently*] Cat?

MR. VAN DAAN. You heard me. Get it out of here!

PETER. I have no cat. [*Delighted with his joke, he opens his coat and pulls out a bath towel. The group at the table laugh, enjoying the joke.*]

DUSSEL. [*Still wheezing*] It doesn't need to be the cat . . . his clothes are enough . . . when he comes out of that room . . .

MR. VAN DAAN. Don't worry. You won't be bothered any more. We're getting rid of it.

DUSSEL. At last you listen to me. [*He goes off into his bedroom.*]

MR. VAN DAAN. [*Calling after him*] I'm not doing it for you. That's all in your mind . . . all of it! [*He starts back to his place at the table.*] I'm doing it because I'm sick of seeing that cat eat all our food.

PETER. That's not true! I only give him bones . . . scraps . . .

MR. VAN DAAN. Don't tell me! He gets fatter every day! Damn cat looks better than any of us. Out he goes tonight!

PETER. No! No!

Literary Analysis
Dialogue What does the dialogue between Peter and Mr. Dussel reveal about both their personalities?

Reading Skill
Cause and Effect How do the families' circumstances influence Mr. Van Daan's opinion about keeping a cat?

ANNE. Mr. Van Daan, you can't do that! That's Peter's cat. Peter loves that cat.

MRS. FRANK. [*Quietly*] Anne.

PETER. [*To* MR. VAN DAAN] If he goes, I go.

MR. VAN DAAN. Go! Go!

MRS. VAN DAAN. You're not going and the cat's not going! Now please . . . this is Hanukkah . . . Hanukkah . . . this is the time to celebrate . . . What's the matter with all of you? Come on, Anne. Let's have the song.

ANNE. [*Singing*]
"Oh, Hanukkah! Oh, Hanukkah! The sweet celebration."

MR. FRANK. [*Rising*] I think we should first blow out the candle . . . then we'll have something for tomorrow night.

MARGOT. But, Father, you're supposed to let it burn itself out.

MR. FRANK. I'm sure that God understands shortages. [*Before blowing it out*] "Praised be Thou, oh Lord our God, who hast sustained us and permitted us to celebrate this joyous festival."

[*He is about to blow out the candle when suddenly there is a crash of something falling below. They all freeze in horror, motionless. For a few seconds there is complete silence.* MR. FRANK *slips off his shoes. The others noiselessly follow his example.* MR. FRANK *turns out a light near him. He motions to* PETER *to turn off the center lamp.* PETER *tries to reach it, realizes he cannot and gets up on a chair. Just as he is touching the lamp he loses his balance. The chair goes out from under him. He falls. The iron lamp shade crashes to the floor. There is a sound of feet below, running down the stairs.*]

MR. VAN DAAN. [*Under his breath*] God Almighty! [*The only light left comes from the Hanukkah candle.* DUSSEL *comes from his room.* MR. FRANK *creeps over to the stairwell and stands listening. The dog is heard barking excitedly.*] Do you hear anything?

MR. FRANK. [*In a whisper*] No. I think they've gone.

MRS. VAN DAAN. It's the Green Police. They've found us.

MR. FRANK. If they had, they wouldn't have left. They'd be up here by now.

✓**Reading Check**

How does Peter fall?

MRS. VAN DAAN. I know it's the Green Police. They've gone to get help. That's all. They'll be back!

MRS. VAN DAAN. Or it may have been the Gestapo,[29] looking for papers . . .

MR. FRANK. [*Interrupting*] Or a thief, looking for money.

MRS. VAN DAAN. We've got to do something . . . Quick! Quick! Before they come back.

MR. VAN DAAN. There isn't anything to do. Just wait.

[MR. FRANK *holds up his hand for them to be quiet. He is listening intently. There is complete silence as they all strain to hear any sound from below. Suddenly* ANNE *begins to sway. With a low cry she falls to the floor in a faint.* MRS. FRANK *goes to her quickly, sitting beside her on the floor and taking her in her arms.*]

MRS. FRANK. Get some water, please! Get some water!

[MARGOT *starts for the sink.*]

**Reading Skill
Cause and Effect**
Why is everyone reacting fearfully?

MR. VAN DAAN. [*Grabbing* MARGOT] No! No! No one's going to run water!

MR. FRANK. If they've found us, they've found us. Get the water. [MARGOT *starts again for the sink.* MR. FRANK, *getting a flashlight*] I'm going down.

[MARGOT *rushes to him, clinging to him.* ANNE *struggles to consciousness.*]

MARGOT. No, Father, no! There may be someone there, waiting . . . It may be a trap!

MR. FRANK. This is Saturday. There is no way for us to know what has happened until Miep or Mr. Kraler comes on Monday morning. We cannot live with this uncertainty.

MARGOT. Don't go, Father!

MRS. FRANK. Hush, darling, hush. [MR. FRANK *slips quietly out, down the steps and out through the door below.*] Margot! Stay close to me. [MARGOT *goes to her mother.*]

MR. VAN DAAN. Shush! Shush!

---

29. Gestapo (gə stä′ pō) *n.* secret police force of the German Nazi state, known for its terror tactics and brutality.

[MRS. FRANK *whispers to* MARGOT *to get the water.* MARGOT *goes for it.*]

MRS. VAN DAAN. Putti, where's our money? Get our money. I hear you can buy the Green Police off, so much a head. Go upstairs quick! Get the money!

MR. VAN DAAN. Keep still!

MRS. VAN DAAN. [*Kneeling before him, pleading*] Do you want to be dragged off to a concentration camp? Are you going to stand there and wait for them to come up and get you? Do something, I tell you!

MR. VAN DAAN. [*Pushing her aside*] Will you keep still!

[*He goes over to the stairwell to listen.* PETER *goes to his mother, helping her up onto the sofa. There is a second of silence, then* ANNE *can stand it no longer.*]

ANNE. Someone go after Father! Make Father come back!

PETER. [*Starting for the door*] I'll go.

MR. VAN DAAN. Haven't you done enough?

[*He pushes* PETER *roughly away. In his anger against his father* PETER *grabs a chair as if to hit him with it, then puts it down, burying his face in his hands.* MRS. FRANK *begins to pray softly.*]

ANNE. Please, please, Mr. Van Daan. Get Father.

MR. VAN DAAN. Quiet! Quiet!

[ANNE *is shocked into silence.* MRS. FRANK *pulls her closer, holding her protectively in her arms.*]

MRS. FRANK. [*Softly, praying*] "I lift up mine eyes unto the mountains, from whence cometh my help. My help cometh from the Lord who made heaven and earth. He will not suffer thy foot to be moved . . . He that keepeth thee will not slumber . . ."

[*She stops as she hears someone coming. They all watch the door tensely.* MR. FRANK *comes quietly in.* ANNE *rushes to him, holding him tight.*]

MR. FRANK. It was a thief. That noise must have scared him away.

MRS. VAN DAAN. Thank God.

Literary Analysis
Dialogue What does this exchange between Peter and his father show about their relationship?

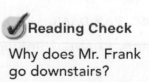

Reading Check

Why does Mr. Frank go downstairs?

MR. FRANK. He took the cash box. And the radio. He ran away in such a hurry that he didn't stop to shut the street door. It was swinging wide open. [*A breath of relief sweeps over them.*] I think it would be good to have some light.

MARGOT. Are you sure it's all right?

MR. FRANK. The danger has passed. [MARGOT *goes to light the small lamp.*] Don't be so terrified, Anne. We're safe.

DUSSEL. Who says the danger has passed? Don't you realize we are in greater danger than ever?

MR. FRANK. Mr. Dussel, will you be still!

[MR. FRANK *takes* ANNE *back to the table, making her sit down with him, trying to calm her.*]

DUSSEL. [*Pointing to* PETER] Thanks to this clumsy fool, there's someone now who knows we're up here! Someone now knows we're up here, hiding!

MRS. VAN DAAN. [*Going to* DUSSEL] Someone knows we're here, yes. But who is the someone? A thief! A thief! You think a thief is going to go to the Green Police and say . . . I was robbing a place the other night and I heard a noise up over my head? You think a thief is going to do that?

DUSSEL. Yes. I think he will.

MRS. VAN DAAN. [*Hysterically*] You're crazy!

[*She stumbles back to her seat at the table.* PETER *follows protectively, pushing* DUSSEL *aside.*]

DUSSEL. I think some day he'll be caught and then he'll make a bargain with the Green Police . . . if they'll let him off, he'll tell them where some Jews are hiding!

[*He goes off into the bedroom. There is a second of appalled silence.*]

MR. VAN DAAN. He's right.

ANNE. Father, let's get out of here! We can't stay here now . . . Let's go . . .

MR. VAN DAAN. Go! Where?

MRS. FRANK. [*Sinking into her chair at the table*] Yes. Where?

Reading Skill
Cause and Effect
What do Mr. Dussel's lines about the Green Police suggest about their methods for finding Jews?

MR. FRANK. [*Rising, to them all*] Have we lost all faith? All courage? A moment ago we thought that they'd come for us. We were sure it was the end. But it wasn't the end. We're alive, safe. [MR. VAN DAAN *goes to the table and sits.* MR. FRANK *prays.*] "We thank Thee, oh Lord our God, that in Thy infinite mercy Thou hast again seen fit to spare us." [*He blows out the candle, then turns to* ANNE.] Come on, Anne. The song! Let's have the song!

[*He starts to sing.* ANNE *finally starts falteringly to sing, as* MR. FRANK *urges her on. Her voice is hardly audible at first.*]

ANNE. [*Singing*]
"Oh, Hanukkah! Oh, Hanukkah! The sweet . . .
celebration . . ."

[*As she goes on singing, the others gradually join in, their voices still shaking with fear.* MRS. VAN DAAN *sobs as she sings.*]

GROUP. Around the feast . . . we . . . gather
In complete . . . jubilation . . .
Happiest of sea . . . sons
Now is here.
Many are the reasons for good cheer.

[DUSSEL *comes from the bedroom. He comes over to the table, standing beside* MARGOT, *listening to them as they sing.*]

"Together/We'll weather/Whatever tomorrow may bring."

[*As they sing on with growing courage, the lights start to dim.*]

"So hear us rejoicing/And merrily voicing/The Hanukkah song that we sing./Hoy!"
[*The lights are out. The curtain starts slowly to fall.*]

"Hear us rejoicing/And merrily voicing/The Hanukkah song that we sing."

[*They are still singing, as the curtain falls.*]

Literary Analysis
Dialogue What is the effect of this song as a finale to the act?

Apply the Skills

The Diary of Anne Frank, Act I

Thinking About the Selection

1. **Respond:** The families must obey strict rules to avoid discovery. Which rules would be hardest for you to follow? Why?
2. **(a) Recall:** In Scene 1, what objects does Mr. Frank find in the secret rooms? **(b) Connect:** How are these objects connected with the rest of the act?
3. **(a) Recall:** What special meaning does Hanukkah have for the families? **(b) Deduce:** What do Anne's presents show about her? **(c) Interpret:** Why do the others react with enthusiasm to their presents?
4. **(a) Evaluate:** With a partner, discuss Mr. Frank's statement, "There are . . . no locks that anyone can put on your mind." How does Anne prove that this is true? **(b) Discuss:** Share your answer with a partner and then with the rest of the class.

Reading Skill

5. **(a)** What is the historical **cause** that forces the Franks to go into hiding? **(b)** What **effects** does this situation have on their daily lives?
6. In Scene 2, Anne and Peter discuss the Stars of David on their clothes. **(a)** What effects do the Nazis intend the wearing of the stars to have on the Jews? **(b)** What background information about the war and the Nazis' treatment of the Jews helps you to link this cause with its intended effects?

Literary Analysis

7. Complete an organizer like the one shown with examples of **dialogue** that achieve each purpose.

Reveals character and relationships _____

Dialogue ——→ Advances the action of the plot _____

Develops the conflict _____

8. After Mr. Kraler asks if Jan Dussel can join the Franks and the Van Daans in hiding, what does the dialogue among the characters reveal about their personalities?

Vocabulary Builder

Practice Use a vocabulary word from page 774 to rewrite each sentence to convey the same basic meaning.

1. The summer sun in the desert is difficult to tolerate.
2. Beth was not ashamed when she fell down on stage.
3. The hole in his sweater is in a noticeable place.
4. Kevin believes that success in life is out of his hands.
5. At the party, Marla was dressed in a showy way.
6. Paul is careful about every detail of his clothing.

Writing

To explore the perspectives of two characters other than Anne, write two **diary entries** about an event from the play. Follow these steps:

- Choose an event that affects several characters.
- Ask yourself how each character might have viewed it.
- Write each diary entry from a different point of view. Include a description of the event and show each character's feelings about it.

For *Grammar, Vocabulary,* and *Assessment,* see **Build Language Skills,** pages 872–873.

Extend Your Learning

Listening and Speaking Use the photos, descriptions, and major events of the play, along with original research, to provide a **guided tour** describing daily life in the "Secret Annex."

- Review the play for details about the layout of the attic rooms, the type of food the family ate, and the stresses of life in an enclosed space.
- Keep in mind that the play is a dramatization. The basic facts are true, but some elements have been fictionalized. Verify the factual basis of major events and details in the play and gather additional information by visiting **www.annefrank.org**. Incorporate both the play and your research into your final presentation, being careful to convey the source to your listeners.

Build Skills The Diary of Anne Frank, Act II

These skills will help you become a better reader. Practice them with *The Diary of Anne Frank, Act II* (p. 835).

Reading Skill

Cause-and-effect relationships explain the connections between events, but they do not always follow the simple pattern of a single cause producing a single effect. Three other patterns of cause and effect are shown in the charts.

To help you discover these patterns in a literary work, **ask questions to analyze cause-and-effect relationships,** such as:

- What are all the possible causes that might have triggered this event?
- What are all the possible effects—or chains of effects—that might result from this cause?
- Are these events really related? (Just because two events occur in order does not mean they are cause and effect. They may be coincidental or random events.)

Literary Analysis

A **character's motivation** is the reason he or she takes a particular action. It may be internal, external, or both.

- *Internal motivations* are based on emotions such as loneliness or jealousy.
- *External motivations* are sparked by events or situations like a fire or poverty.

As you read, consider each character's possible motivations.

Vocabulary Builder

The Diary of Anne Frank, Act II

- **inarticulate** (in´ är tik´ yōō lit) *adj.* unable to express oneself (p. 839) *His confusion made him inarticulate.*
- **apprehension** (ap´ rē hen´ shən) *n.* a fearful feeling about what will happen next (p. 841) *Sam entered the cave despite his apprehension.*
- **intuition** (in´ tōō ish´ ən) *n.* ability to sense immediately, without reasoning (p. 848) *Pat's intuition told her something was wrong.*

- **indignant** (in dig´ nənt) *adj.* filled with anger at meanness or injustice (p. 850) *Jacob was indignant about his harsh punishment.*
- **stealthily** (stelth´ i lē) *adv.* in a secretive way; avoiding being noticed (p. 855) *The lion stealthily stalked its prey.*
- **ineffectually** (in´ e fek´ chōō ə lē) *adv.* without producing the desired results (p. 864) *The fan spun ineffectually in the overheated room.*

The Diary of Anne Frank

Review and Anticipate In Act I, Anne Frank's father visits the attic where his family and four others hid from the Nazis during World War II. As he holds Anne's diary, the offstage voice of Anne draws him into the past as the families begin their new life hiding from the Nazis. As months drag on, fear and lack of privacy in the attic rooms contributes to increasing tension between the family members. Act I ends on the first night of Hanukkah. The group's celebration is interrupted by the sounds of a thief below, who may have heard them. Read Act II to learn whether the hiding place has been discovered.

Act II

Scene 1

[*In the darkness we hear* ANNE'S VOICE, *again reading from the diary.*]

ANNE'S VOICE. Saturday, the first of January, nineteen forty-four. Another new year has begun and we find ourselves still in our hiding place. We have been here now for one year, five months and twenty-five days. It seems that our life is at a standstill.

[*The curtain rises on the scene. It is late afternoon. Everyone is bundled up against the cold. In the main room* MRS. FRANK *is taking down the laundry which is hung across the back.* MR. FRANK *sits in the chair down left, reading.* MARGOT *is lying on the couch with a blanket over her and the many-colored knitted scarf around her throat.* ANNE *is seated at the center table, writing in her diary.* PETER, MR. *and* MRS. VAN DAAN *and* DUSSEL *are all in their own rooms, reading or lying down.*

As the lights dim on, ANNE'S VOICE *continues, without a break.*]

ANNE'S VOICE. We are all a little thinner. The Van Daans' "discussions" are as violent as ever. Mother still does not

Reading Check

How much time has passed since the Franks first went into hiding?

understand me. But then I don't understand her either. There is one great change, however. A change in myself. I read somewhere that girls of my age don't feel quite certain of themselves. That they become quiet within and begin to think of the miracle that is taking place in their bodies. I think that what is happening to me is so wonderful . . . not only what can be seen, but what is taking place inside. Each time it has happened I have a feeling that I have a sweet secret.

[*We hear the chimes and then a hymn being played on the carillon outside. The buzzer of the door below suddenly sounds. Everyone is startled.* MR. FRANK *tiptoes cautiously to the top of the steps and listens. Again the buzzer sounds, in* MIEP'S *V-for-Victory signal.*][1]

MR. FRANK. It's Miep!

[*He goes quickly down the steps to unbolt the door.* MRS. FRANK *calls upstairs to the* VAN DAANS *and then to* PETER.]

MRS. FRANK. Wake up, everyone! Miep is here!
[ANNE *quickly puts her diary away.* MARGOT *sits up, pulling the blanket around her shoulders.* MR. DUSSEL *sits on the edge of his bed, listening, disgruntled.* MIEP *comes up the steps, followed by* MR. KRALER. *They bring flowers, books, newspapers, etc.* ANNE *rushes to* MIEP, *throwing her arms affectionately around her.*]
Miep . . . and Mr. Kraler . . . What a delightful surprise!

MR. KRALER. We came to bring you New Year's greetings.

MRS. FRANK. You shouldn't . . . you should have at least one day to yourselves. [*She goes quickly to the stove and brings down teacups and tea for all of them.*]

ANNE. Don't say that, it's so wonderful to see them! [*Sniffing at* MIEP'S *coat*] I can smell the wind and the cold on your clothes.

MIEP. [*Giving her the flowers*] There you are. [*Then to* MARGOT, *feeling her forehead*] How are you, Margot? . . . Feeling any better?

MARGOT. I'm all right.

---

1. **V-for-Victory signal** three short rings and one long one (the letter *V* in Morse code).

Literary Analysis
Character's Motivation Why do you think Anne writes about her feelings toward her mother in her diary?

▶ **Critical Viewing** Behind this bookcase are stairs leading to the hiding place. How does this photograph help you understand the tension in the play? [**Assess**]

ANNE. We filled her full of every kind of pill so she won't cough and make a noise. [*She runs into her room to put the flowers in water.* MR. *and* MRS. VAN DAAN *come from upstairs. Outside there is the sound of a band playing.*]

MRS. VAN DAAN. Well, hello, Miep. Mr. Kraler.

MR. KRALER. [*Giving a bouquet of flowers to* MRS. VAN DAAN] With my hope for peace in the New Year.

PETER. [*Anxiously*] Miep, have you seen Mouschi? Have you seen him anywhere around?

MIEP. I'm sorry, Peter. I asked everyone in the neighborhood had they seen a gray cat. But they said no.

[MRS. FRANK *gives* MIEP *a cup of tea.* MR. FRANK *comes up the steps, carrying a small cake on a plate.*]

MR. FRANK. Look what Miep's brought for us!

MRS. FRANK. [*Taking it*] A cake!

MR. VAN DAAN. A cake! [*He pinches* MIEP'S *cheeks gaily and hurries up to the cupboard.*] I'll get some plates.

[DUSSEL, *in his room, hastily puts a coat on and starts out to join the others.*]

MRS. FRANK. Thank you, Miepia. You shouldn't have done it. You must have used all of your sugar ration for weeks. [*Giving it to* MRS. VAN DAAN] It's beautiful, isn't it?

MRS. VAN DAAN. It's been ages since I even saw a cake. Not since you brought us one last year. [*Without looking at the cake, to* MIEP] Remember? Don't you remember, you gave us one on New Year's Day? Just this time last year? I'll never forget it because you had "Peace in nineteen forty-three" on it. [*She looks at the cake and reads*] "Peace in nineteen forty-four!"

MIEP. Well, it has to come sometime, you know. [*As* DUSSEL *comes from his room*] Hello, Mr. Dussel.

MR. KRALER. How are you?

**Reading Skill
Cause and Effect**
What does the dialogue about the cake reveal about life under German occupation?

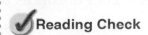Reading Check

What occasion are the families celebrating?

The Diary of Anne Frank, Act II ■ 837

MR. VAN DAAN. [*Bringing plates and a knife*] Here's the knife, *liefje*. Now, how many of us are there?

MIEP. None for me, thank you.

MR. FRANK. Oh, please. You must.

MIEP. I couldn't.

MR. VAN DAAN. Good! That leaves one . . . two . . . three . . . seven of us.

DUSSEL. Eight! Eight! It's the same number as it always is!

MR. VAN DAAN. I left Margot out. I take it for granted Margot won't eat any.

ANNE. Why wouldn't she!

MRS. FRANK. I think it won't harm her.

MR. VAN DAAN. All right! All right! I just didn't want her to start coughing again, that's all.

DUSSEL. And please, Mrs. Frank should cut the cake.

[*Together*] {
    MR. VAN DAAN. What's the difference?

    MRS. VAN DAAN. It's not Mrs. Frank's cake, is it, Miep? It's for all of us.
}

DUSSEL. Mrs. Frank divides things better.

[*Together*] {
    MRS. VAN DAAN. [*Going to* DUSSEL] What are you trying to say?

    MR. VAN DAAN. Oh, come on! Stop wasting time!
}

MRS. VAN DAAN. [*To* DUSSEL] Don't I always give everybody exactly the same? Don't I?

MR. VAN DAAN. Forget it, Kerli.

MRS. VAN DAAN. No. I want an answer! Don't I?

DUSSEL. Yes. Yes. Everybody gets exactly the same . . . except Mr. Van Daan always gets a little bit more.

[VAN DAAN *advances on* DUSSEL, *the knife still in his hand.*]

MR. VAN DAAN. That's a lie!

[DUSSEL *retreats before the onslaught of the* VAN DAANS.]

MR. FRANK. Please, please! [*Then to* MIEP] You see what a little sugar cake does to us? It goes right to our heads!

Literary Analysis
Character's Motivation What is another possible reason that Mr. Van Daan leaves out Margot?

Reading Skill
Cause and Effect How do the pressures of life in hiding affect the relationship between Dussel and the Van Daans?

MR. VAN DAAN. [*Handing* MRS. FRANK *the knife*] Here you are, Mrs. Frank.

MRS. FRANK. Thank you. [*Then to* MIEP *as she goes to the table to cut the cake*] Are you sure you won't have some?

MIEP. [*Drinking her tea*] No, really, I have to go in a minute.

[*The sound of the band fades out in the distance.*]

PETER. [*To* MIEP] Maybe Mouschi went back to our house . . . they say that cats . . . Do you ever get over there . . . ? I mean . . . do you suppose you could . . . ?

MIEP. I'll try, Peter. The first minute I get I'll try. But I'm afraid, with him gone a week . . .

DUSSEL. Make up your mind, already someone has had a nice big dinner from that cat!

[PETER *is furious,* <u>inarticulate</u>. *He starts toward* DUSSEL *as if to hit him.* MR. FRANK *stops him.* MRS. FRANK *speaks quickly to ease the situation.*]

MRS. FRANK. [*To* MIEP] This is delicious, Miep!

MRS. VAN DAAN. [*Eating hers*] Delicious!

MR. VAN DAAN. [*Finishing it in one gulp*] Dirk's in luck to get a girl who can bake like this!

MIEP. [*Putting down her empty teacup*] I have to run. Dirk's taking me to a party tonight.

ANNE. How heavenly! Remember now what everyone is wearing, and what you have to eat and everything, so you can tell us tomorrow.

MIEP. I'll give you a full report! Good-bye, everyone!

MR. VAN DAAN. [*To* MIEP] Just a minute. There's something I'd like you to do for me.

[*He hurries off up the stairs to his room.*]

MRS. VAN DAAN. [*Sharply*] Putti, where are you going? [*She rushes up the stairs after him, calling hysterically.*] What do you want? Putti, what are you going to do?

MIEP. [*To* PETER] What's wrong?

PETER. [*His sympathy is with his mother.*] Father says he's going to sell her fur coat. She's crazy about that old fur coat.

Vocabulary Builder
inarticulate (in′ är tik′ yŏŏ lit) *adj.* unable to express oneself

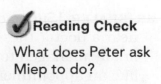

Reading Check

What does Peter ask Miep to do?

DUSSEL. Is it possible? Is it possible that anyone is so silly as to worry about a fur coat in times like this?

PETER. It's none of your darn business . . . and if you say one more thing . . . I'll, I'll take you and I'll . . . I mean it . . . I'll . . .

[*There is a piercing scream from* MRS. VAN DAAN *above. She grabs at the fur coat as* MR. VAN DAAN *is starting downstairs with it.*]

MRS. VAN DAAN. No! No! No! Don't you dare take that! You hear? It's mine! [*Downstairs* PETER *turns away, embarrassed, miserable.*] My father gave me that! You didn't give it to me. You have no right. Let go of it . . . you hear?

[MR. VAN DAAN *pulls the coat from her hands and hurries downstairs.* MRS. VAN DAAN *sinks to the floor, sobbing. As* MR. VAN DAAN *comes into the main room the others look away, embarrassed for him.*]

MR. VAN DAAN. [*To* MR. KRALER] Just a little—discussion over the advisability of selling this coat. As I have often reminded Mrs. Van Daan, it's very selfish of her to keep it when people outside are in such desperate need of clothing . . . [*He gives the coat to* MIEP.] So if you will please to sell it for us? It should fetch a good price. And by the way, will you get me cigarettes. I don't care what kind they are . . . get all you can.

MIEP. It's terribly difficult to get them, Mr. Van Daan. But I'll try. Good-bye.

[*She goes.* MR. FRANK *follows her down the steps to bolt the door after her.* MRS. FRANK *gives* MR. KRALER *a cup of tea.*]

MRS. FRANK. Are you sure you won't have some cake, Mr. Kraler?

MR. KRALER. I'd better not.

MR. VAN DAAN. You're still feeling badly? What does your doctor say?

MR. KRALER. I haven't been to him.

MRS. FRANK. Now, Mr. Kraler! . . .

MR. KRALER. [*Sitting at the table*] Oh, I tried. But you can't get near a doctor these days . . . they're so busy. After weeks I finally managed to get one on the telephone. I told him I'd like an appointment . . . I wasn't feeling very well. You

Literary Analysis
Character's Motivation Are Mr. Van Daan's reasons for selling his wife's fur coat selfish or unselfish? Explain.

know what he answers . . . over the telephone . . . Stick out your tongue! [*They laugh. He turns to* MR. FRANK *as* MR. FRANK *comes back.*] I have some contracts here . . . I wonder if you'd look over them with me . . .

MR. FRANK. [*Putting out his hand*] Of course.

MR. KRALER. [*He rises*] If we could go downstairs . . . [MR. FRANK *starts ahead;* MR. KRALER *speaks to the others.*] Will you forgive us? I won't keep him but a minute. [*He starts to follow* MR. FRANK *down the steps.*]

MARGOT. [*With sudden foreboding*] What's happened? Something's happened! Hasn't it, Mr. Kraler?

[MR. KRALER *stops and comes back, trying to reassure* MARGOT *with a pretense of casualness.*]

MR. KRALER. No, really. I want your father's advice . . .

MARGOT. Something's gone wrong! I know it!

MR. FRANK. [*Coming back, to* MR. KRALER] If it's something that concerns us here, it's better that we all hear it.

MR. KRALER. [*Turning to him, quietly*] But . . . the children . . . ?

MR. FRANK. What they'd imagine would be worse than any reality.

[*As* MR. KRALER *speaks, they all listen with intense <u>apprehension</u>.* MRS. VAN DAAN *comes down the stairs and sits on the bottom step.*]

MR. KRALER. It's a man in the storeroom . . . I don't know whether or not you remember him . . . Carl, about fifty, heavy-set, nearsighted . . . He came with us just before you left.

MR. FRANK. He was from Utrecht?

MR. KRALER. That's the man. A couple of weeks ago, when I was in the storeroom, he closed the door and asked me . . . how's Mr. Frank? What do you hear from Mr. Frank? I told him I only knew there was a rumor that you were in Switzerland. He said he'd heard that rumor too, but he thought I might know something more. I didn't pay any attention to it . . . but then a thing happened yesterday . . . He'd brought some invoices to the office for me to sign. As I was going through them, I looked up. He was standing staring

Vocabulary Builder
apprehension (ap´ rē hen´ shən) *n.* a fearful feeling about what will happen next

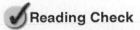

Reading Check

Why does Mr. Kraler want to talk with Mr. Frank privately?

at the bookcase . . . your bookcase. He said he thought he remembered a door there . . . Wasn't there a door there that used to go up to the loft? Then he told me he wanted more money. Twenty guilders[2] more a week.

MR. VAN DAAN. Blackmail!

MR. FRANK. Twenty guilders? Very modest blackmail.

MR. VAN DAAN. That's just the beginning.

DUSSEL. [*Coming to* MR. FRANK] You know what I think? He was the thief who was down there that night. That's how he knows we're here.

MR. FRANK. [*To* MR. KRALER] How was it left? What did you tell him?

MR. KRALER. I said I had to think about it. What shall I do? Pay him the money? . . . Take a chance on firing him . . . or what? I don't know.

DUSSEL. [*Frantic*] Don't fire him! Pay him what he asks . . . keep him here where you can have your eye on him.

MR. FRANK. Is it so much that he's asking? What are they paying nowadays?

MR. KRALER. He could get it in a war plant. But this isn't a war plant. Mind you, I don't know if he really knows . . . or if he doesn't know.

MR. FRANK. Offer him half. Then we'll soon find out if it's blackmail or not.

DUSSEL. And if it is? We've got to pay it, haven't we? Anything he asks we've got to pay!

MR. FRANK. Let's decide that when the time comes.

MR. KRALER. This may be all my imagination. You get to a point, these days, where you suspect everyone and everything. Again and again . . . on some simple look or word, I've found myself . . .

[*The telephone rings in the office below.*]

MRS. VAN DAAN. [*Hurrying to* MR. KRALER] There's the telephone! What does that mean, the telephone ringing on a holiday?

**Reading Skill
Cause and Effect**
How does Dussel's reaction reflect his desperation not to be caught by the authorities?

**Reading Skill
Cause and Effect**
Here, Kraler resists a cause-and-effect explanation for events that occurred in order. What else might explain the employee's demand?

---

2. **guilders** (gil´ dərz) *n.* monetary units of the Netherlands.

MR. KRALER. That's my wife. I told her I had to go over some papers in my office . . . to call me there when she got out of church. [*He starts out.*] I'll offer him half then. Good-bye . . . we'll hope for the best!

[*The group calls their good-byes halfheartedly.* MR. FRANK *follows* MR. KRALER *to bolt the door below. During the following scene,* MR. FRANK *comes back up and stands listening, disturbed.*]

DUSSEL. [*To* MR. VAN DAAN] You can thank your son for this . . . smashing the light! I tell you, it's just a question of time now.

[*He goes to the window at the back and stands looking out.*]

MARGOT. Sometimes I wish the end would come . . . whatever it is.

MRS. FRANK. [*Shocked*] Margot!

[ANNE *goes to* MARGOT, *sitting beside her on the couch with her arms around her.*]

MARGOT. Then at least we'd know where we were.

MRS. FRANK. You should be ashamed of yourself! Talking that way! Think how lucky we are! Think of the thousands dying in the war, every day. Think of the people in concentration camps.

ANNE. [*Interrupting*] What's the good of that? What's the good of thinking of misery when you're already miserable? That's stupid!

MRS. FRANK. Anne!

[*As* ANNE *goes on raging at her mother,* MRS. FRANK *tries to break in, in an effort to quiet her.*]

ANNE. We're young, Margot and Peter and I! You grownups have had your chance! But look at us . . . If we begin thinking of all the horror in the world, we're lost! We're trying to hold onto some kind of ideals . . . when everything . . . ideals, hopes . . . everything, are being destroyed! It isn't our fault that the world is in such a mess! We weren't around when all this started! So don't try to take it out on us! [*She rushes off to her room, slamming the door after her. She picks up a brush from the chest and hurls it to the floor. Then she sits on the settee, trying to control her anger.*]

Reading Skill
Cause and Effect
How does Anne's speech reveal a gap between the adults' and the teenagers' perspectives on the outside world?

Reading Check

What does Margot say that shocks her mother?

MR. VAN DAAN. She talks as if we started the war! Did we start the war?

[*He spots* ANNE'S *cake. As he starts to take it,* PETER *anticipates him.*]

PETER. She left her cake. [*He starts for* ANNE'S *room with the cake. There is silence in the main room.* MRS. VAN DAAN *goes up to her room, followed by* VAN DAAN. DUSSEL *stays looking out the window.* MR. FRANK *brings* MRS. FRANK *her cake. She eats it slowly, without relish.* MR. FRANK *takes his cake to* MARGOT *and sits quietly on the sofa beside her.* PETER *stands in the doorway of* ANNE'S *darkened room, looking at her, then makes a little movement to let her know he is there.* ANNE *sits up, quickly, trying to hide the signs of her tears.* PETER *holds out the cake to her.*] You left this.

ANNE. [*Dully*] Thanks.

[PETER *starts to go out, then comes back.*]

PETER. I thought you were fine just now. You know just how to talk to them. You know just how to say it. I'm no good . . . I never can think . . . especially when I'm mad . . . That Dussel . . . when he said that about Mouschi . . . someone eating him . . . all I could think is . . . I wanted to hit him. I wanted to give him such a . . . a . . . that he'd . . . That's what I used to do when there was an argument at school . . . That's the way I . . . but here . . . And an old man like that . . . it wouldn't be so good.

ANNE. You're making a big mistake about me. I do it all wrong. I say too much. I go too far. I hurt people's feelings . . .

[DUSSEL *leaves the window, going to his room.*]

PETER. I think you're just fine . . . What I want to say . . . if it wasn't for you around here, I don't know. What I mean . . .

[PETER *is interrupted by* DUSSEL'S *turning on the light.* DUSSEL *stands in the doorway, startled to see* PETER. PETER *advances toward him forbiddingly.* DUSSEL *backs out of the room.* PETER *closes the door on him.*]

ANNE. Do you mean it, Peter? Do you really mean it?

PETER. I said it, didn't I?

ANNE. Thank you, Peter!

[*In the main room* MR. *and* MRS. FRANK *collect the dishes and take them to the sink, washing them.* MARGOT *lies down again on the*

Literary Analysis
Character's Motivation Why does Peter seek out Anne in her room?

couch. DUSSEL, *lost, wanders into* PETER'S *room and takes up a book, starting to read.*]

PETER. [*Looking at the photographs on the wall*] You've got quite a collection.

ANNE. Wouldn't you like some in your room? I could give you some. Heaven knows you spend enough time in there . . . doing heaven knows what . . .

PETER. It's easier. A fight starts, or an argument . . . I duck in there.

ANNE. You're lucky, having a room to go to. His lordship is always here . . . I hardly ever get a minute alone. When they start in on me, I can't duck away. I have to stand there and take it.

PETER. You gave some of it back just now.

ANNE. I get so mad. They've formed their opinions . . . about everything . . . but we . . . we're still trying to find out . . . We have problems here that no other people our age have ever had. And just as you think you've solved them, something comes along and bang! You have to start all over again.

PETER. At least you've got someone you can talk to.

ANNE. Not really. Mother . . . I never discuss anything serious with her. She doesn't understand. Father's all right. We can talk about everything . . . everything but one thing. Mother. He simply won't talk about her. I don't think you can be really intimate with anyone if he holds something back, do you?

PETER. I think your father's fine.

ANNE. Oh, he is, Peter! He is! He's the only one who's ever given me the feeling that I have any sense. But anyway, nothing can take the place of school and play and friends of your own age . . . or near your age . . . can it?

PETER. I suppose you miss your friends and all.

ANNE. It isn't just . . . [*She breaks off, staring up at him for a second.*] Isn't it funny, you and I? Here we've been seeing each other every minute for almost a year and a half, and this is the first time we've ever really talked. It helps a lot to have someone to talk to, don't you think? It helps you to let off steam.

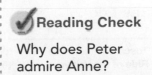

Reading Check

Why does Peter admire Anne?

The Diary of Anne Frank, Act II ■ 845

PETER. [*Going to the door*] Well, any time you want to let off steam, you can come into my room.

ANNE. [*Following him*] I can get up an awful lot of steam. You'll have to be careful how you say that.

PETER. It's all right with me.

ANNE. Do you mean it?

PETER. I said it, didn't I?

[*He goes out.* ANNE *stands in her doorway looking after him. As* PETER *gets to his door he stands for a minute looking back at her. Then he goes into his room.* DUSSEL *rises as he comes in, and quickly passes him, going out. He starts across for his room.* ANNE *sees him coming, and pulls her door shut.* DUSSEL *turns back toward* PETER'S *room.* PETER *pulls his door shut.* DUSSEL *stands there, bewildered, forlorn.*

The scene slowly dims out. The curtain falls on the scene. ANNE'S VOICE *comes over in the darkness . . . faintly at first, and then with growing strength.*]

ANNE'S VOICE. We've had bad news. The people from whom Miep got our ration books have been arrested. So we have had to cut down on our food. Our stomachs are so empty that they rumble and make strange noises, all in different keys. Mr. Van Daan's is deep and low, like a bass fiddle. Mine is high, whistling like a flute. As we all sit around waiting for supper, it's like an orchestra tuning up. It only needs Toscanini[3] to raise his baton and we'd be off in the Ride of the Valkyries.[4] Monday, the sixth of March, nineteen forty-four. Mr. Kraler is in the hospital. It seems he has ulcers. Pim says we are his ulcers. Miep has to run the business and us too. The Americans have landed on the southern tip of Italy. Father looks for a quick finish to the war. Mr. Dussel is waiting every day for the warehouse man to demand more money. Have I been skipping too much from one subject to another? I can't help it. I feel that spring is coming. I feel it in my whole body and soul. I feel utterly confused. I am longing . . . so longing . . . for everything . . . for friends . . . for someone to talk to . . . someone who understands . . . someone young, who feels as I do . . .

Reading Skill
Cause and Effect
What is the effect of the "bad news" on the people in the Annex?

---

3. Toscanini (täs´ kə nē´ nē) Arturo Toscanini, a famous Italian American orchestra conductor.
4. Ride of the Valkyries (val kir´ ēz) stirring selection from an opera by Richard Wagner, a German composer.

[*As these last lines are being said, the curtain rises on the scene. The lights dim on.* ANNE'S VOICE *fades out.*]

Scene 2

[*It is evening, after supper. From outside we hear the sound of children playing. The "grownups," with the exception of* MR. VAN DAAN, *are all in the main room.* MRS. FRANK *is doing some mending,* MRS. VAN DAAN *is reading a fashion magazine.* MR. FRANK *is going over business accounts.* DUSSEL, *in his dentist's jacket, is pacing up and down, impatient to get into his bedroom.* MR. VAN DAAN *is upstairs working on a piece of embroidery in an embroidery frame.*

In his room PETER *is sitting before the mirror, smoothing his hair. As the scene goes on, he puts on his tie, brushes his coat and puts it on, preparing himself meticulously for a visit from* ANNE. *On his wall are now hung some of* ANNE'S *motion picture stars.*

In her room ANNE *too is getting dressed. She stands before the mirror in her slip, trying various ways of dressing her hair.* MARGOT *is seated on the sofa, hemming a skirt for* ANNE *to wear.*

In the main room DUSSEL *can stand it no longer. He comes over, rapping sharply on the door of his and* ANNE'S *bedroom.*]

ANNE. [*Calling to him*] No, no, Mr. Dussel! I am not dressed yet. [DUSSEL *walks away, furious, sitting down and burying his head in his hands.* ANNE *turns to* MARGOT.]

How is that? How does that look?

MARGOT. [*Glancing at her briefly*] Fine.

ANNE. You didn't even look.

MARGOT. Of course I did. It's fine.

ANNE. Margot, tell me, am I terribly ugly?

MARGOT. Oh, stop fishing.

ANNE. No. No. Tell me.

MARGOT. Of course you're not. You've got nice eyes . . . and a lot of animation, and . . .

ANNE. A little vague, aren't you?

▲ **Critical Viewing**
This photograph shows a wall in Anne Frank's room. In what ways does her room resemble a typical teenager's room today? **[Relate]**

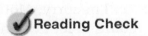

Reading Check

What event gives Mr. Frank hope that the war will be over soon?

[*She reaches over and takes a brassière out of Margot's sewing basket. She holds it up to herself, studying the effect in the mirror. Outside,* MRS. FRANK, *feeling sorry for* DUSSEL, *comes over, knocking at the girls' door.*]

MRS. FRANK. [*Outside*] May I come in?

MARGOT. Come in, Mother.

MRS. FRANK. [*Shutting the door behind her*] Mr. Dussel's impatient to get in here.

ANNE. [*Still with the brassière*] Heavens, he takes the room for himself the entire day.

MRS. FRANK. [*Gently*] Anne, dear, you're not going in again tonight to see Peter?

ANNE. [*Dignified*] That is my intention.

MRS. FRANK. But you've already spent a great deal of time in there today.

ANNE. I was in there exactly twice. Once to get the dictionary, and then three-quarters of an hour before supper.

MRS. FRANK. Aren't you afraid you're disturbing him?

ANNE. Mother, I have some <u>intuition</u>.

MRS. FRANK. Then may I ask you this much, Anne. Please don't shut the door when you go in.

ANNE. You sound like Mrs. Van Daan! [*She throws the brassière back in Margot's sewing basket and picks up her blouse, putting it on.*]

MRS. FRANK. No. No. I don't mean to suggest anything wrong. I only wish that you wouldn't expose yourself to criticism . . . that you wouldn't give Mrs. Van Daan the opportunity to be unpleasant.

ANNE. Mrs. Van Daan doesn't need an opportunity to be unpleasant!

MRS. FRANK. Everyone's on edge, worried about Mr. Kraler. This is one more thing . . .

ANNE. I'm sorry, Mother. I'm going to Peter's room. I'm not going to let Petronella Van Daan spoil our friendship.

[MRS. FRANK *hesitates for a second, then goes out, closing the door after her. She gets a pack of playing cards and sits at the center table, playing solitaire. In* ANNE'S *room* MARGOT *hands the*

Vocabulary Builder
intuition (in´ too ish´ ən) *n.* ability to sense immediately, without reasoning

Literary Analysis
Character's Motivation What prompts Mrs. Frank to make these requests of Anne?

finished skirt to ANNE. *As* ANNE *is putting it on,* MARGOT *takes off her high-heeled shoes and stuffs paper in the toes so that* ANNE *can wear them.*]

MARGOT. [*To* ANNE] Why don't you two talk in the main room? It'd save a lot of trouble. It's hard on Mother, having to listen to those remarks from Mrs. Van Daan and not say a word.

ANNE. Why doesn't she say a word? I think it's ridiculous to take it and take it.

MARGOT. You don't understand Mother at all, do you? She can't talk back. She's not like you. It's just not in her nature to fight back.

ANNE. Anyway . . . the only one I worry about is you. I feel awfully guilty about you. [*She sits on the stool near* MARGOT, *putting on* MARGOT'S *high-heeled shoes.*]

MARGOT. What about?

ANNE. I mean, every time I go into Peter's room, I have a feeling I may be hurting you. [MARGOT *shakes her head.*] I know if it were me, I'd be wild. I'd be desperately jealous, if it were me.

MARGOT. Well, I'm not.

ANNE. You don't feel badly? Really? Truly? You're not jealous?

MARGOT. Of course I'm jealous . . . jealous that you've got something to get up in the morning for . . . But jealous of you and Peter? No.

[ANNE *goes back to the mirror.*]

ANNE. Maybe there's nothing to be jealous of. Maybe he doesn't really like me. Maybe I'm just taking the place of his cat . . . [*She picks up a pair of short white gloves, putting them on.*] Wouldn't you like to come in with us?

MARGOT. I have a book.

[*The sound of the children playing outside fades out. In the main room* DUSSEL *can stand it no longer. He jumps up, going to the bedroom door and knocking sharply.*]

DUSSEL. Will you please let me in my room!

ANNE. Just a minute, dear, dear Mr. Dussel. [*She picks up her mother's pink stole and adjusts it elegantly over her*

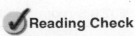

Reading Check

Why does Anne fear she might be hurting Margot?

shoulders, then gives a last look in the mirror.] Well, here I go . . . to run the gauntlet.[5]

[*She starts out, followed by* MARGOT.]

DUSSEL. [*As she appears—sarcastic*] Thank you so much.

[DUSSEL *goes into his room.* ANNE *goes toward* PETER'S *room, passing* MRS. VAN DAAN *and her parents at the center table.*]

MRS. VAN DAAN. My God, look at her! [ANNE *pays no attention. She knocks at* PETER'S *door.*] I don't know what good it is to have a son. I never see him. He wouldn't care if I killed myself. [PETER *opens the door and stands aside for* ANNE *to come in.*] Just a minute, Anne. [*She goes to them at the door.*] I'd like to say a few words to my son. Do you mind? [PETER *and* ANNE *stand waiting.*] Peter, I don't want you staying up till all hours tonight. You've got to have your sleep. You're a growing boy. You hear?

MRS. FRANK. Anne won't stay late. She's going to bed promptly at nine. Aren't you, Anne?

ANNE. Yes, Mother . . . [*To* MRS. VAN DAAN] May we go now?

MRS. VAN DAAN. Are you asking me? I didn't know I had anything to say about it.

MRS. FRANK. Listen for the chimes, Anne dear.

[*The two young people go off into* PETER'S *room, shutting the door after them.*]

MRS. VAN DAAN. [*To* MRS. FRANK] In my day it was the boys who called on the girls. Not the girls on the boys.

MRS. FRANK. You know how young people like to feel that they have secrets. Peter's room is the only place where they can talk.

MRS. VAN DAAN. Talk! That's not what they called it when I was young.

[MRS. VAN DAAN *goes off to the bathroom.* MARGOT *settles down to read her book.* MR. FRANK *puts his papers away and brings a chess game to the center table. He and* MRS. FRANK *start to play. In* PETER'S *room,* ANNE *speaks to* PETER, *indignant, humiliated.*]

Reading Skill
Cause and Effect
How might Mrs. Van Daan's beliefs about what is socially acceptable reflect her own upbringing?

Vocabulary Builder
indignant (in digʹ nənt) *adj.* filled with anger at meanness or injustice

---

5. run the gauntlet (gônt′ lit) formerly, to pass between two rows of men who struck at the offender with clubs as he passed; here, a series of troubles or difficulties.

ANNE. Aren't they awful? Aren't they impossible? Treating us as if we were still in the nursery.

[*She sits on the cot.* PETER *gets a bottle of pop and two glasses.*]

PETER. Don't let it bother you. It doesn't bother me.

ANNE. I suppose you can't really blame them . . . they think back to what *they* were like at our age. They don't realize how much more advanced we are . . . When you think what wonderful discussions we've had! . . . Oh, I forgot. I was going to bring you some more pictures.

PETER. Oh, these are fine, thanks.

ANNE. Don't you want some more? Miep just brought me some new ones.

PETER. Maybe later. [*He gives her a glass of pop and, taking some for himself, sits down facing her.*]

ANNE. [*Looking up at one of the photographs*] I remember when I got that . . . I won it. I bet Jopie that I could eat five ice-cream cones. We'd all been playing ping-pong . . . We used to have heavenly times . . . we'd finish up with ice cream at the Delphi, or the Oasis, where Jews were allowed . . . there'd always be a lot of boys . . . we'd laugh and joke . . . I'd like to go back to it for a few days or a week. But after that I know I'd be bored to death. I think more seriously about life now. I want to be a journalist . . . or something. I love to write. What do you want to do?

PETER. I thought I might go off some place . . . work on a farm or something . . . some job that doesn't take much brains.

ANNE. You shouldn't talk that way. You've got the most awful inferiority complex.

PETER. I know I'm not smart.

ANNE. That isn't true. You're much better than I am in dozens of things . . . arithmetic and algebra and . . . well, you're a million times better than I am in algebra. [*With sudden directness*] You like Margot, don't you? Right from the start you liked her, liked her much better than me.

PETER. [*Uncomfortably*] Oh, I don't know.

[*In the main room* MRS. VAN DAAN *comes from the bathroom and goes over to the sink, polishing a coffee pot.*]

Reading Check

Why does Anne feel she might be dissatisfied now with her old life?

ANNE. It's all right. Everyone feels that way. Margot's so good. She's sweet and bright and beautiful and I'm not.

PETER. I wouldn't say that.

ANNE. Oh, no, I'm not. I know that. I know quite well that I'm not a beauty. I never have been and never shall be.

PETER. I don't agree at all. I think you're pretty.

ANNE. That's not true!

PETER. And another thing. You've changed . . . from at first, I mean.

ANNE. I have?

PETER. I used to think you were awful noisy.

ANNE. And what do you think now, Peter? How have I changed?

PETER. Well . . . er . . . you're . . . quieter.

[*In his room* DUSSEL *takes his pajamas and toilet articles and goes into the bathroom to change.*]

ANNE. I'm glad you don't just hate me.

PETER. I never said that.

ANNE. I bet when you get out of here you'll never think of me again.

PETER. That's crazy.

ANNE. When you get back with all of your friends, you're going to say . . . now what did I ever see in that Mrs. Quack Quack.

PETER. I haven't got any friends.

ANNE. Oh, Peter, of course you have. Everyone has friends.

PETER. Not me. I don't want any. I get along all right without them.

ANNE. Does that mean you can get along without me? I think of myself as your friend.

PETER. No. If they were all like you, it'd be different.

[*He takes the glasses and the bottle and puts them away. There is a second's silence and then* ANNE *speaks, hesitantly, shyly.*]

ANNE. Peter, did you ever kiss a girl?

Literary Analysis

Character's Motivation What is Anne's possible motivation for asking Peter whether he likes Margot?

PETER. Yes. Once.

ANNE. [*To cover her feelings*] That picture's crooked. [PETER *goes over, straightening the photograph.*] Was she pretty?

PETER. Huh?

ANNE. The girl that you kissed.

PETER. I don't know. I was blindfolded. [*He comes back and sits down again.*] It was at a party. One of those kissing games.

ANNE. [*Relieved*] Oh. I don't suppose that really counts, does it?

PETER. It didn't with me.

ANNE. I've been kissed twice. Once a man I'd never seen before kissed me on the cheek when he picked me up off the ice and I was crying. And the other was Mr. Koophuis, a friend of Father's who kissed my hand. You wouldn't say those counted, would you?

PETER. I wouldn't say so.

ANNE. I know almost for certain that Margot would never kiss anyone unless she was engaged to them. And I'm sure too that Mother never touched a man before Pim. But I don't know . . . things are so different now . . . What do you think? Do you think a girl shouldn't kiss anyone except if she's engaged or something? It's so hard to try to think what to do, when here we are with the whole world falling around our ears and you think . . . well . . . you don't know what's going to happen tomorrow and . . . What do you think?

PETER. I suppose it'd depend on the girl. Some girls, anything they do's wrong. But others . . . well . . . it wouldn't necessarily be wrong with them. [*The carillon starts to strike nine o'clock.*] I've always thought that when two people . . .

ANNE. Nine o'clock. I have to go.

PETER. That's right.

ANNE. [*Without moving*] Good night.

[*There is a second's pause, then* PETER *gets up and moves toward the door.*]

PETER. You won't let them stop you coming?

Reading Skill
Cause and Effect
Based on Anne's comments, what effect is the war having on pre-war attitudes?

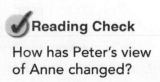

Reading Check

How has Peter's view of Anne changed?

ANNE. No. [*She rises and starts for the door.*] Sometimes I might bring my diary. There are so many things in it that I want to talk over with you. There's a lot about you.

PETER. What kind of thing?

ANNE. I wouldn't want you to see some of it. I thought you were a nothing, just the way you thought about me.

PETER. Did you change your mind, the way I changed my mind about you?

ANNE. Well . . . You'll see . . .

[*For a second* ANNE *stands looking up at* PETER, *longing for him to kiss her. As he makes no move she turns away. Then suddenly* PETER *grabs her awkwardly in his arms, kissing her on the cheek.* ANNE *walks out dazed. She stands for a minute, her back to the people in the main room. As she regains her poise she goes to her mother and father and* MARGOT, *silently kissing them. They murmur their good nights to her. As she is about to open her bedroom door, she catches sight of* MRS. VAN DAAN. *She goes quickly to her, taking her face in her hands and kissing her first on one cheek and then on the other. Then she hurries off into her room.* MRS. VAN DAAN *looks after her, and then looks over at* PETER'S *room. Her suspicions are confirmed.*]

MRS. VAN DAAN. [*She knows.*] Ah hah!

[*The lights dim out. The curtain falls on the scene. In the darkness* ANNE'S VOICE *comes faintly at first and then with growing strength.*]

ANNE'S VOICE. By this time we all know each other so well that if anyone starts to tell a story, the rest can finish it for him. We're having to cut down still further on our meals. What makes it worse, the rats have been at work again. They've carried off some of our precious food. Even Mr. Dussel wishes now that Mouschi was here. Thursday, the twentieth of April, nineteen forty-four. Invasion fever is mounting every day. Miep tells us that people outside talk of nothing else. For myself, life has become much more pleasant. I often go to Peter's room after supper. Oh, don't think I'm in love, because I'm not. But it does make life more bearable to have someone with whom you can exchange views. No more tonight. P.S. . . . I must be honest. I must confess

Literary Analysis
Character's Motivation What causes Anne to want to share her diary with Peter?

that I actually live for the next meeting. Is there anything lovelier than to sit under the skylight and feel the sun on your cheeks and have a darling boy in your arms? I admit now that I'm glad the Van Daans had a son and not a daughter. I've outgrown another dress. That's the third. I'm having to wear Margot's clothes after all. I'm working hard on my French and am now reading *La Belle Nivernaise.*[6]

[*As she is saying the last lines—the curtain rises on the scene. The lights dim on, as* ANNE'S VOICE *fades out.*]

Scene 3

[*It is night, a few weeks later. Everyone is in bed. There is complete quiet. In the* VAN DAANS' *room a match flares up for a moment and then is quickly put out.* MR. VAN DAAN, *in bare feet, dressed in underwear and trousers, is dimly seen coming <u>stealthily</u> down the stairs and into the main room, where* MR. *and* MRS. FRANK *and* MARGOT *are sleeping. He goes to the food safe and again lights a match. Then he cautiously opens the safe, taking out a half-loaf of bread. As he closes the safe, it creaks. He stands rigid.* MRS. FRANK *sits up in bed. She sees him.*]

MRS. FRANK. [*Screaming*] Otto! Otto! *Komme schnell!*[7]

[*The rest of the people wake, hurriedly getting up.*]

MR. FRANK. *Was ist los? Was ist passiert?*[8]

[DUSSEL, *followed by* ANNE, *comes from his room.*]

MRS. FRANK. [*As she rushes over to* MR. VAN DAAN] *Er stiehlt das Essen!*[9]

DUSSEL. [*Grabbing* MR. VAN DAAN] You! You! Give me that.

MRS. VAN DAAN. [*Coming down the stairs*] Putti . . . Putti . . . what is it?

DUSSEL. [*His hands on* VAN DAAN'S *neck*] You dirty thief . . . stealing food . . . you good-for-nothing . . .

MR. FRANK. Mr. Dussel! For God's sake! Help me, Peter!

Vocabulary Builder
stealthily (stelth´ i lē)
adv. in a secretive or sneaky way; avoiding being noticed

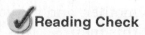**Reading Check**

Why does Mrs. Frank scream in the middle of the night?

---

6. *La Belle Nivernaise* story by Alphonse Daudet, a French author.
7. *Komme schnell!* (käm´ ə shnel) German for "Come quick!"
8. *Was ist los? Was ist passiert?* (väs ist los väs ist päs´ ērt) German for "What's the matter? What happened?"
9. *Er stiehlt das Essen!* (er stēlt däs es´ ən) German for "He steals food!"

[PETER *comes over, trying, with* MR. FRANK, *to separate the two struggling men.*]

PETER. Let him go! Let go!

[DUSSEL *drops* MR. VAN DAAN, *pushing him away. He shows them the end of a loaf of bread that he has taken from* VAN DAAN.]

DUSSEL. You greedy, selfish . . . !

[MARGOT *turns on the lights.*]

MRS. VAN DAAN. Putti . . . what is it?

[*All of* MRS. FRANK'S *gentleness, her self-control, is gone. She is outraged, in a frenzy of indignation.*]

MRS. FRANK. The bread! He was stealing the bread!

DUSSEL. It was you, and all the time we thought it was the rats!

MR. FRANK. Mr. Van Daan, how could you!

MR. VAN DAAN. I'm hungry.

MRS. FRANK. We're all of us hungry! I see the children getting thinner and thinner. Your own son Peter . . . I've heard him moan in his sleep, he's so hungry. And you come in the night and steal food that should go to them . . . to the children!

MRS. VAN DAAN. [*Going to* MR. VAN DAAN *protectively*] He needs more food than the rest of us. He's used to more. He's a big man.

[MR. VAN DAAN *breaks away, going over and sitting on the couch.*]

MRS. FRANK. [*Turning on* MRS. VAN DAAN] And you . . . you're worse than he is! You're a mother, and yet you sacrifice your child to this man . . . this . . . this . . .

MR. FRANK. Edith! Edith!

[MARGOT *picks up the pink woolen stole, putting it over her mother's shoulders.*]

MRS. FRANK. [*Paying no attention, going on to* MRS. VAN DAAN] Don't think I haven't seen you! Always saving the choicest bits for him! I've watched you day after

▼ Critical Viewing
Does this photograph of Peter Van Daan capture his personality? Explain.
[Assess]

day and I've held my tongue. But not any longer! Not after this! Now I want him to go! I want him to get out of here!

[Together]

MR. FRANK. Edith!

MR. VAN DAAN. Get out of here?

MRS. VAN DAAN. What do you mean?

MRS. FRANK. Just that! Take your things and get out!

MR. FRANK. [To MRS. FRANK] You're speaking in anger. You cannot mean what you are saying.

MRS. FRANK. I mean exactly that!

[MRS. VAN DAAN takes a cover from the FRANKS' bed, pulling it about her.]

MR. FRANK. For two long years we have lived here, side by side. We have respected each other's rights . . . we have managed to live in peace. Are we now going to throw it all away? I know this will never happen again, will it, Mr. Van Daan?

MR. VAN DAAN. No. No.

MRS. FRANK. He steals once! He'll steal again!

[MR. VAN DAAN, holding his stomach, starts for the bathroom. ANNE puts her arms around him, helping him up the step.]

MR. FRANK. Edith, please. Let us be calm. We'll all go to our rooms . . . and afterwards we'll sit down quietly and talk this out . . . we'll find some way . . .

MRS. FRANK. No! No! No more talk! I want them to leave!

MRS. VAN DAAN. You'd put us out, on the streets?

MRS. FRANK. There are other hiding places.

MRS. VAN DAAN. A cellar . . . a closet. I know. And we have no money left even to pay for that.

MRS. FRANK. I'll give you money. Out of my own pocket I'll give it gladly. [She gets her purse from a shelf and comes back with it.]

MRS. VAN DAAN. Mr. Frank, you told Putti you'd never forget what he'd done for you when you came to Amsterdam. You said you could never repay him, that you . . .

> **Reading Skill**
> **Cause and Effect**
> What causes Mr. Van Daan to steal food, and what is the effect of his actions on the others?

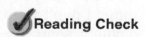

Reading Check

How does Mr. Frank react to his wife's demand that the Van Daans leave?

The Diary of Anne Frank, Act II ■ 857

MRS. FRANK. [*Counting out money*] If my husband had any obligation to you, he's paid it, over and over.

MR. FRANK. Edith, I've never seen you like this before. I don't know you.

MRS. FRANK. I should have spoken out long ago.

DUSSEL. You can't be nice to some people.

MRS. VAN DAAN. [*Turning on* DUSSEL] There would have been plenty for all of us, if *you* hadn't come in here!

MR. FRANK. We don't need the Nazis to destroy us. We're destroying ourselves.

[*He sits down, with his head in his hands.* MRS. FRANK *goes to* MRS. VAN DAAN.]

MRS. FRANK. [*Giving* MRS. VAN DAAN *some money*] Give this to Miep. She'll find you a place.

ANNE. Mother, you're not putting Peter out. Peter hasn't done anything.

MRS. FRANK. He'll stay, of course. When I say I must protect the children, I mean Peter too.

[PETER *rises from the steps where he has been sitting.*]

PETER. I'd have to go if Father goes.

[MR. VAN DAAN *comes from the bathroom.* MRS. VAN DAAN *hurries to him and takes him to the couch. Then she gets water from the sink to bathe his face.*]

MRS. FRANK. [*While this is going on*] He's no father to you . . . that man! He doesn't know what it is to be a father!

PETER. [*Starting for his room*] I wouldn't feel right. I couldn't stay.

MRS. FRANK. Very well, then. I'm sorry.

ANNE. [*Rushing over to* PETER] No, Peter! No! [PETER *goes into his room, closing the door after him.* ANNE *turns back to her mother, crying.*] I don't care about the food. They can have mine! I don't want it! Only don't send them away. It'll be daylight soon. They'll be caught . . .

MARGOT. [*Putting her arms comfortingly around* ANNE] Please, Mother!

MRS. FRANK. They're not going now. They'll stay here until Miep finds them a place. [*To* MRS. VAN DAAN] But one thing

Literary Analysis
Character's Motivation What do Mr. Frank's lines show about his character and about what motivates him?

Literary Analysis
Character's Motivation What do Peter's words reveal about how he feels about leaving?

I insist on! He must never come down here again! He must never come to this room where the food is stored! We'll divide what we have . . . an equal share for each! [DUSSEL *hurries over to get a sack of potatoes from the food safe.* MRS. FRANK *goes on, to* MRS. VAN DAAN] You can cook it here and take it up to him.

[DUSSEL *brings the sack of potatoes back to the center table.*]

MARGOT. Oh, no. No. We haven't sunk so far that we're going to fight over a handful of rotten potatoes.

DUSSEL. [*Dividing the potatoes into piles*] Mrs. Frank, Mr. Frank, Margot, Anne, Peter, Mrs. Van Daan, Mr. Van Daan, myself . . . Mrs. Frank . . .

[*The buzzer sounds in* MIEP's *signal.*]

MR. FRANK. It's Miep! [*He hurries over, getting his overcoat and putting it on.*]

MARGOT. At this hour?

MRS. FRANK. It is trouble.

MR. FRANK. [*As he starts down to unbolt the door*] I beg you, don't let her see a thing like this!

MR. DUSSEL. [*Counting without stopping*] . . . Anne, Peter, Mrs. Van Daan, Mr. Van Daan, myself . . .

MARGOT. [*To* DUSSEL] Stop it! Stop it!

DUSSEL. . . . Mr. Frank, Margot, Anne, Peter, Mrs. Van Daan, Mr. Van Daan, myself, Mrs. Frank . . .

MRS. VAN DAAN. You're keeping the big ones for yourself! All the big ones . . . Look at the size of that! . . . And that! . . .

[DUSSEL *continues on with his dividing.* PETER, *with his shirt and trousers on, comes from his room.*]

MARGOT. Stop it! Stop it!

[*We hear* MIEP'S *excited voice speaking to* MR. FRANK *below.*]

MIEP. Mr. Frank . . . the most wonderful news! . . . The invasion has begun!

MR. FRANK. Go on, tell them! Tell them!

[MIEP *comes running up the steps ahead of* MR. FRANK. *She has a man's raincoat on over her nightclothes and a bunch of orange-colored flowers in her hand.*]

Reading Skill
Cause and Effect
What effect does Mr. Van Daan's action have on the tensions among the characters?

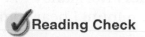

Reading Check

Why does Dussel bring the sack of potatoes to the table?

MIEP. Did you hear that, everybody? Did you hear what I said? The invasion has begun! The invasion!

[*They all stare at* MIEP, *unable to grasp what she is telling them.* PETER *is the first to recover his wits.*]

PETER. Where?

MRS. VAN DAAN. When? When, Miep?

MIEP. It began early this morning . . .

[*As she talks on, the realization of what she has said begins to dawn on them. Everyone goes crazy. A wild demonstration takes place.* MRS. FRANK *hugs* MR. VAN DAAN.]

MRS. FRANK. Oh, Mr. Van Daan, did you hear that?

[DUSSEL *embraces* MRS. VAN DAAN. PETER *grabs a frying pan and parades around the room, beating on it, singing the Dutch National Anthem.* ANNE *and* MARGOT *follow him, singing, weaving in and out among the excited grown-ups.* MARGOT *breaks away to take the flowers from* MIEP *and distribute them to everyone. While this pandemonium is going on* MRS. FRANK *tries to make herself heard above the excitement.*]

MRS. FRANK. [*To* MIEP] How do you know?

MIEP. The radio . . . The B.B.C.![10] They said they landed on the coast of Normandy!

PETER. The British?

MIEP. British, Americans, French, Dutch, Poles, Norwegians . . . all of them! More than four thousand ships! Churchill spoke, and General Eisenhower! D-Day they call it!

MR. FRANK. Thank God, it's come!

MRS. VAN DAAN. At last!

MIEP. [*Starting out*] I'm going to tell Mr. Kraler. This'll be better than any blood transfusion.

MR. FRANK. [*Stopping her*] What part of Normandy did they land, did they say?

MIEP. Normandy . . . that's all I know now . . . I'll be up the minute I hear some more! [*She goes hurriedly out.*]

MR. FRANK. [*To* MRS. FRANK] What did I tell you? What did I tell you?

Reading Skill
Cause and Effect
What is the effect of the news about D-Day on the people in the Annex?

---

10. **B.B.C.** British Broadcasting System.

[MRS. FRANK *indicates that he has forgotten to bolt the door after* MIEP. *He hurries down the steps.* MR. VAN DAAN, *sitting on the couch, suddenly breaks into a convulsive[11] sob. Everybody looks at him, bewildered.*]

MRS. VAN DAAN. [*Hurrying to him*] Putti! Putti! What is it? What happened?

MR. VAN DAAN. Please, I'm so ashamed.

[MR. FRANK *comes back up the steps.*]

DUSSEL. Oh, for God's sake!

MRS. VAN DAAN. Don't, Putti.

MARGOT. It doesn't matter now!

MR. FRANK. [*Going to* MR. VAN DAAN] Didn't you hear what Miep said? The invasion has come! We're going to be liberated! This is a time to celebrate! [*He embraces* MRS. FRANK *and then hurries to the cupboard and gets the cognac and a glass.*]

MR. VAN DAAN. To steal bread from children!

MRS. FRANK. We've all done things that we're ashamed of.

ANNE. Look at me, the way I've treated Mother . . . so mean and horrid to her.

MRS. FRANK. No, Anneke, no.

[ANNE *runs to her mother, putting her arms around her.*]

ANNE. Oh, Mother, I was. I was awful.

MR. VAN DAAN. Not like me. No one is as bad as me!

DUSSEL. [*To* MR. VAN DAAN] Stop it now! Let's be happy!

MR. FRANK. [*Giving* MR. VAN DAAN *a glass of cognac*] Here! Here! *Schnapps! L'chaim!*[12]

[VAN DAAN *takes the cognac. They all watch him. He gives them a feeble smile.* ANNE *puts up her fingers in a V-for-Victory sign. As* VAN DAAN *gives an answering V-sign, they are startled to hear a loud sob from behind them. It is* MRS. FRANK, *stricken with remorse. She is sitting on the other side of the room.*]

Literary Analysis

Character's Motivation What drives Anne to admit that she has treated her mother badly?

✔**Reading Check**

Why is Mr. Van Daan ashamed?

---

11. **convulsive** (kən vul′ siv) *adj.* having an uncontrolled muscular spasm; shuddering.
12. *Schnapps!* (shnäps) German for "a drink." *L'chaim!* (lə khä′ yim) Hebrew toast meaning "To life!"

MRS. FRANK. [*Through her sobs*] When I think of the terrible things I said . . .

[MR. FRANK, ANNE *and* MARGOT *hurry to her, trying to comfort her.* MR. VAN DAAN *brings her his glass of cognac.*]

MR. VAN DAAN. No! No! You were right!

MRS. FRANK. That I should speak that way to you! . . . Our friends! . . . Our guests! [*She starts to cry again.*]

DUSSEL. Stop it, you're spoiling the whole invasion!

[*As they are comforting her, the lights dim out. The curtain falls.*]

ANNE'S VOICE. [*Faintly at first and then with growing strength*] We're all in much better spirits these days. There's still excellent news of the invasion. The best part about it is that I have a feeling that friends are coming. Who knows? Maybe I'll be back in school by fall. Ha, ha! The joke is on us! The warehouse man doesn't know a thing and we are

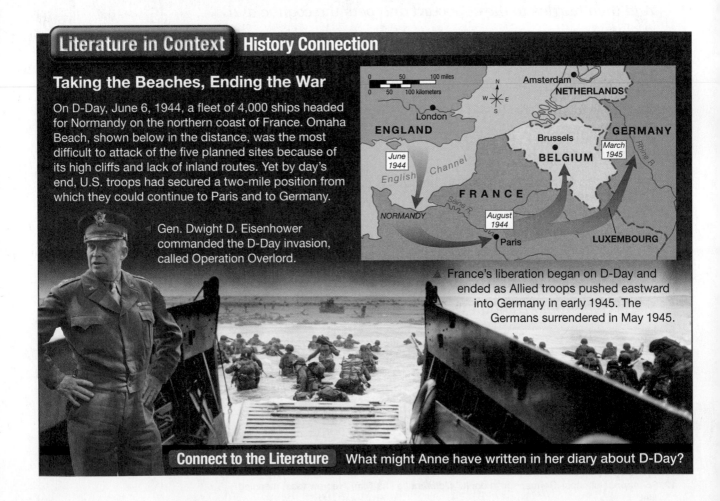

Literature in Context | **History Connection**

Taking the Beaches, Ending the War

On D-Day, June 6, 1944, a fleet of 4,000 ships headed for Normandy on the northern coast of France. Omaha Beach, shown below in the distance, was the most difficult to attack of the five planned sites because of its high cliffs and lack of inland routes. Yet by day's end, U.S. troops had secured a two-mile position from which they could continue to Paris and to Germany.

Gen. Dwight D. Eisenhower commanded the D-Day invasion, called Operation Overlord.

France's liberation began on D-Day and ended as Allied troops pushed eastward into Germany in early 1945. The Germans surrendered in May 1945.

Connect to the Literature What might Anne have written in her diary about D-Day?

paying him all that money! . . . Wednesday, the second of July, nineteen forty-four. The invasion seems temporarily to be bogged down. Mr. Kraler has to have an operation, which looks bad. The Gestapo have found the radio that was stolen. Mr. Dussel says they'll trace it back and back to the thief, and then, it's just a matter of time till they get to us. Everyone is low. Even poor Pim can't raise their spirits. I have often been downcast myself . . . but never in despair. I can shake off everything if I write. But . . . and that is the great question . . . will I ever be able to write well? I want to so much. I want to go on living even after my death. Another birthday has gone by, so now I am fifteen. Already I know what I want. I have a goal, an opinion.

[*As this is being said—the curtain rises on the scene, the lights dim on, and* ANNE'S VOICE *fades out.*]

Scene 4

[*It is an afternoon a few weeks later. . . Everyone but* MARGOT *is in the main room. There is a sense of great tension.*

Both MRS. FRANK *and* MR. VAN DAAN *are nervously pacing back and forth,* DUSSEL *is standing at the window, looking down fixedly at the street below.* PETER *is at the center table, trying to do his lessons.* ANNE *sits opposite him, writing in her diary.* MRS. VAN DAAN *is seated on the couch, her eyes on* MR. FRANK *as he sits reading.*

The sound of a telephone ringing comes from the office below. They all are rigid, listening tensely. DUSSEL *rushes down to* MR. FRANK.]

DUSSEL. There it goes again, the telephone! Mr. Frank, do you hear?

MR. FRANK. [*Quietly*] Yes. I hear.

DUSSEL. [*Pleading, insistent*] But this is the third time, Mr. Frank! The third time in quick succession! It's a signal! I tell you it's Miep, trying to get us! For some reason she can't come to us and she's trying to warn us of something!

MR. FRANK. Please. Please.

MR. VAN DAAN. [*To* DUSSEL] You're wasting your breath.

DUSSEL. Something has happened, Mr. Frank. For three days now Miep hasn't been to see us! And today not a man has

Reading Skill
Cause and Effect
How does the news from the outside world affect Anne's moods?

Reading Check

What is the new goal that Anne sets for herself in her diary?

come to work. There hasn't been a sound in the building!

MRS. FRANK. Perhaps it's Sunday. We may have lost track of the days.

MR. VAN DAAN. [*To* ANNE] You with the diary there. What day is it?

DUSSEL. [*Going to* MRS. FRANK] I don't lose track of the days! I know exactly what day it is! It's Friday, the fourth of August. Friday, and not a man at work. [*He rushes back to* MR. FRANK, *pleading with him, almost in tears.*] I tell you Mr. Kraler's dead. That's the only explanation. He's dead and they've closed down the building, and Miep's trying to tell us!

MR. FRANK. She'd never telephone us.

DUSSEL. [*Frantic*] Mr. Frank, answer that! I beg you, answer it!

MR. FRANK. No.

MR. VAN DAAN. Just pick it up and listen. You don't have to speak. Just listen and see if it's Miep.

DUSSEL. [*Speaking at the same time*] For God's sake . . . I ask you.

MR. FRANK. No. I've told you, no. I'll do nothing that might let anyone know we're in the building.

PETER. Mr. Frank's right.

MR. VAN DAAN. There's no need to tell us what side you're on.

MR. FRANK. If we wait patiently, quietly, I believe that help will come.

[*There is silence for a minute as they all listen to the telephone ringing.*]

DUSSEL. I'm going down.
[*He rushes down the steps.* MR. FRANK *tries* <u>ineffectually</u> *to hold him.* DUSSEL *runs to the lower door, unbolting it. The telephone stops ringing.* DUSSEL *bolts the door and comes slowly back up the steps.*]
Too late.

▲ **Critical Viewing**
This is a page of Anne's diary. Judging from its appearance, was she a careful writer? Explain. **[Deduce]**

Reading Skill
Cause and Effect
What is the effect of the ringing telephone?

Vocabulary Builder
ineffectually (in´ e fek´ chōō ə lē) *adv.* without producing the desired results

[MR. FRANK *goes to* MARGOT *in* ANNE'S *bedroom.*]

MR. VAN DAAN. So we just wait here until we die.

MRS. VAN DAAN. [*Hysterically*] I can't stand it! I'll kill myself! I'll kill myself!

MR. VAN DAAN. For God's sake, stop it!

[*In the distance, a German military band is heard playing a Viennese waltz.*]

MRS. VAN DAAN. I think you'd be glad if I did! I think you want me to die!

MR. VAN DAAN. Whose fault is it we're here?
[MRS. VAN DAAN *starts for her room. He follows, talking at her.*]
We could've been safe somewhere . . . in America or Switzerland. But no! No! You wouldn't leave when I wanted to. You couldn't leave your things. You couldn't leave your precious furniture.

MRS. VAN DAAN. Don't touch me!

[*She hurries up the stairs, followed by* MR. VAN DAAN. PETER, *unable to bear it, goes to his room.* ANNE *looks after him, deeply concerned.* DUSSEL *returns to his post at the window.* MR. FRANK *comes back into the main room and takes a book, trying to read.* MRS. FRANK *sits near the sink, starting to peel some potatoes.* ANNE *quietly goes to* PETER'S *room, closing the door after her.* PETER *is lying face down on the cot.* ANNE *leans over him, holding him in her arms, trying to bring him out of his despair.*]

ANNE. Look, Peter, the sky. [*She looks up through the skylight.*] What a lovely, lovely day! Aren't the clouds beautiful? You know what I do when it seems as if I couldn't stand being cooped up for one more minute? I think myself out. I think myself on a walk in the park where I used to go with Pim. Where the jonquils and the crocus and the violets grow down the slopes. You know the most wonderful part about *thinking* yourself out? You can have it any way you like. You can have roses and violets and chrysanthemums all blooming at the same time . . . It's funny . . . I used to take it all for granted . . . and now I've gone crazy about everything to do with nature. Haven't you?

Reading Skill
Cause and Effect
What effect has Mrs. Van Daan's love of expensive objects had on the family, according to Mr. Van Daan?

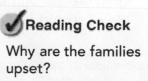
Reading Check

Why are the families upset?

PETER. I've just gone crazy. I think if something doesn't happen soon . . . if we don't get out of here . . . I can't stand much more of it!

ANNE. [*Softly*] I wish you had a religion, Peter.

PETER. No, thanks! Not me!

ANNE. Oh, I don't mean you have to be Orthodox[13] . . . or believe in heaven and hell and purgatory[14] and things . . . I just mean some religion . . . it doesn't matter what. Just to believe in something! When I think of all that's out there . . . the trees . . . and flowers . . . and seagulls . . . when I think of the dearness of you, Peter . . . and the goodness of the people we know . . . Mr. Kraler, Miep, Dirk, the vegetable man, all risking their lives for us every day . . . When I think of these good things, I'm not afraid any more . . . I find myself, and God, and I . . .

[PETER *interrupts, getting up and walking away.*]

PETER. That's fine! But when I begin to think, I get mad! Look at us, hiding out for two years. Not able to move! Caught here like . . . waiting for them to come and get us . . . and all for what?

ANNE. We're not the only people that've had to suffer. There've always been people that've had to . . . sometimes one race . . . sometimes another . . . and yet . . .

PETER. That doesn't make me feel any better!

ANNE. [*Going to him*] I know it's terrible, trying to have any faith . . . when people are doing such horrible . . . But you know what I sometimes think? I think the world may be going through a phase, the way I was with Mother. It'll pass, maybe not for hundreds of years, but some day . . . I still believe, in spite of everything, that people are really good at heart.

PETER. I want to see something now . . . Not a thousand years from now! [*He goes over, sitting down again on the cot.*]

ANNE. But, Peter, if you'd only look at it as part of a great pattern . . . that we're just a little minute in the life . . . [*She breaks off.*] Listen to us, going at each other like a couple of stupid grownups! Look at the sky now. Isn't it lovely?

Reading Skill
Cause and Effect
How do Anne's religious beliefs affect her ability to cope with a life in hiding?

---

13. **Orthodox** (ôr´ thə däks´) *adj.* strictly observing the rites and traditions of Judaism.
14. **purgatory** (pʉr´gə tôr´ ē) *n.* state or place of temporary punishment.

[*She holds out her hand to him.* PETER *takes it and rises, standing with her at the window looking out, his arms around her.*]

Some day, when we're outside again, I'm going to . . .

[*She breaks off as she hears the sound of a car, its brakes squealing as it comes to a sudden stop. The people in the other rooms also become aware of the sound. They listen tensely. Another car roars up to a screeching stop.* ANNE *and* PETER *come from* PETER'S *room.* MR. *and* MRS. VAN DAAN *creep down the stairs.* DUSSEL *comes out from his room. Everyone is listening, hardly breathing. A doorbell clangs again and again in the building below.* MR. FRANK *starts quietly down the steps to the door.* DUSSEL *and* PETER *follow him. The others stand rigid, waiting, terrified.*

In a few seconds DUSSEL *comes stumbling back up the steps. He shakes off* PETER'S *help and goes to his room.* MR. FRANK *bolts the door below, and comes slowly back up the steps. Their eyes are all on him as he stands there for a minute. They realize that what they feared has happened.* MRS. VAN DAAN *starts to whimper.* MR. VAN DAAN *puts her gently in a chair, and then hurries off up the stairs to their room to collect their things.* PETER *goes to comfort his mother. There is a sound of violent pounding on a door below.*]

MR. FRANK. [*Quietly*] For the past two years we have lived in fear. Now we can live in hope.

[*The pounding below becomes more insistent. There are muffled sounds of voices, shouting commands.*]

MEN'S VOICES. *Auf machen! Da drinnen! Auf machen! Schnell! Schnell! Schnell!*[15] *etc., etc.*

[*The street door below is forced open. We hear the heavy tread of footsteps coming up.* MR. FRANK *gets two school bags from the shelves, and gives one to* ANNE *and the other to* MARGOT. *He goes*

DEUTSCHE BUNDESPOST
60
ANNE FRANK · 12.6.1929 · 31.3.1945
1979

▲ **Critical Viewing**
This is a 1979 German stamp. What changes took place after the war that would make the German government decide to honor Anne? **[Infer]**

✔ **Reading Check**
What does Mr. Frank mean when he says "Now we can live in hope"?

---

15. *Auf machen! . . . Schnell!* German for "Open up, you in there, open up, quick, quick, quick."

to get a bag for MRS. FRANK. *The sound of feet coming up grows louder.* PETER *comes to* ANNE, *kissing her good-bye, then he goes to his room to collect his things. The buzzer of their door starts to ring.* MR. FRANK *brings* MRS. FRANK *a bag. They stand together, waiting. We hear the thud of gun butts on the door, trying to break it down.*

ANNE *stands, holding her school satchel, looking over at her father and mother with a soft, reassuring smile. She is no longer a child, but a woman with courage to meet whatever lies ahead.*

The lights dim out. The curtain falls on the scene. We hear a mighty crash as the door is shattered. After a second ANNE'S VOICE *is heard.*]

ANNE'S VOICE. And so it seems our stay here is over. They are waiting for us now. They've allowed us five minutes to get our things. We can each take a bag and whatever it will hold of clothing. Nothing else. So, dear Diary, that means I must leave you behind. Good-bye for a while. P.S. Please, please, Miep, or Mr. Kraler, or anyone else. If you should find this diary, will you please keep it safe for me, because some day I hope . . .

[*Her voice stops abruptly. There is silence. After a second the curtain rises.*]

Scene 5

[*It is again the afternoon in November, 1945. The rooms are as we saw them in the first scene.* MR. KRALER *has joined* MIEP *and* MR. FRANK. *There are coffee cups on the table. We see a great change in* MR. FRANK. *He is calm now. His bitterness is gone. He slowly turns a few pages of the diary. They are blank.*]

MR. FRANK. No more. [*He closes the diary and puts it down on the couch beside him.*]

MIEP. I'd gone to the country to find food. When I got back the block was surrounded by police . . .

MR. KRALER. We made it our business to learn how they knew. It was the thief . . . the thief who told them.

[MIEP *goes up to the gas burner, bringing back a pot of coffee.*]

MR. FRANK. [*After a pause*] It seems strange to say this, that anyone could be happy in a concentration camp. But Anne was happy in the camp in Holland where they first took us.

Literary Analysis
Character's Motivation Why does Anne leave her diary behind?

After two years of being shut up in these rooms, she could be out . . . out in the sunshine and the fresh air that she loved.

MIEP. [*Offering the coffee to* MR. FRANK] A little more?

MR. FRANK. [*Holding out his cup to her*] The news of the war was good. The British and Americans were sweeping through France. We felt sure that they would get to us in time. In September we were told that we were to be shipped to Poland . . . The men to one camp. The women to another. I was sent to Auschwitz.[16] They went to Belsen.[17] In January we were freed, the few of us who were left. The war wasn't yet over, so it took us a long time to get home. We'd be sent here and there behind the lines where we'd be safe. Each time our train would stop . . . at a siding, or a crossing . . . we'd all get out and go from group to group . . . Where were you? Were you at Belsen? At Buchenwald?[18] At Mauthausen? Is it possible that you knew my wife? Did you ever see my husband? My son? My daughter? That's how I found out about my wife's death . . . of Margot, the Van Daans . . . Dussel. But Anne . . . I still hoped . . . Yesterday I went to Rotterdam. I'd heard of a woman there . . . She'd been in Belsen with Anne . . . I know now.

[*He picks up the diary again, and turns the pages back to find a certain passage. As he finds it we hear* ANNE'S VOICE.]

ANNE'S VOICE. In spite of everything, I still believe that people are really good at heart. [MR. FRANK *slowly closes the diary.*]

MR. FRANK. She puts me to shame.

[*They are silent.*]

---

16. **Auschwitz** (ouch' vits') Nazi concentration camp in Poland that was well known as a death camp.
17. **Belsen** (bel' zen) village in Germany that, with the village of Bergen, was the site of Bergen-Belsen, a Nazi concentration camp.
18. **Buchenwald** (boo' ken wôld') Nazi concentration camp in central Germany.

Apply the Skills

The Diary of Anne Frank, Act II

Thinking About the Selection

1. **Respond:** What do you like best about Anne Frank? How would you like having her as a friend?
2. **(a) Recall:** What disturbing news does Mr. Kraler bring on New Year's Day? **(b) Connect:** What hint does this give about the ending of the play?
3. **(a) Recall:** What is the time span of Act II? **(b) Interpret:** How have the characters changed since the end of Act I? **(c) Support:** How do you know that Anne has changed?
4. **(a) Draw Conclusions:** How can Anne believe that " . . . in spite of everything . . . people are really good at heart?" **(b) Interpret:** What does Mr. Frank mean when he says: "She puts me to shame"?

Reading Skill

5. For each of the following events, identify one **cause** and one **effect: (a)** Mr. Van Daan's decision to steal food **(b)** Mrs. Frank's change of heart about wanting the Van Daans to leave
6. What are some possible causes of Mrs. Van Daan's attitude toward Anne and Peter's relationship?
7. Living in close quarters has multiple effects on the residents of the "Secret Annex." List three effects that result from this single cause.

Literary Analysis

8. **(a)** On a chart like the one shown, identify the possible **motivation** behind the actions listed.

Character	Action	Motivation
Miep	Brings flowers and cake to the attic rooms	
Mr. Van Daan		
Peter Van Daan		

(b) Share your chart with a partner and discuss how your ideas about each character's motivations have grown or changed.
9. What possible motivations might an informer have for telling the authorities about the families in hiding?

QuickReview

Act II at a Glance
Tensions have increased, the friendship between Anne and Peter grows, and the Nazis discover the families' hiding place.

Go Online
Assessment
For: Self-test
Visit: www.PHSchool.com
Web Code: ena-6505

Cause: an event, action, or feeling that produces a result

Effect: the result of a preceding event or situation

Character's motivation: the reason or reasons for a character's actions

Vocabulary Builder

Practice For each item, write a sentence that correctly uses the given word pair.

1. inarticulate, candidate
2. apprehension, unknown
3. intuition, marry
4. indignant, misuse
5. stealthily, burglar
6. ineffectually, weaker

Writing

Write a **letter** to a theater manager asking him or her to stage *The Diary of Anne Frank* for your community. To persuade the theater manager, follow these steps:

- Connect the events in the play to current events and attitudes.
- Explain why the theme is important and how you think the community will benefit from seeing the play.

For *Grammar, Vocabulary,* and *Assessment,* see **Build Language Skills,** pages 872–873.

Extend Your Learning

Research and Technology With a group, create a **bulletin board display** about the experiences of Jewish individuals or communities living under Nazi occupation during World War II.

- As a group, decide the purpose and audience for the display. Use this information to focus your research.
- Begin your research by drafting a list of specific questions that relate to your purpose. As you research, refine these questions and ask additional ones.
- Identify *primary sources,* such as photographs, diaries, documents, or letters, and *secondary sources,* such as encyclopedia articles, textbooks, or books by historians.
- Draw conclusions from the information you have gathered about the experience of living under occupation. Type these up as short summaries to include in the display, along with quotations, maps, drawings, and photographs.

Build Language Skills

Vocabulary Skill

Roots The **Latin root -*fac*-** means "to make" or "to do." It is found in the word *factor,* which means "something that makes things happen" and the word *factory,* "a place where things are made."

▶ **Example:** His hard work was an important *factor* in his success.

The **root -*sequ*-** means "follow." It is the root of many English words, such as *consequence,* "the effect that follows a cause."

Practice Fill in the blanks on the following chart.

Word	Root	Definition
manufacture	-fac-	
subsequent		follow after
facilitate		
	sequ-	something that follows a previous plot or story

Grammar Lesson

Clauses: Independent and Subordinate A **clause** is a group of words with its own subject and verb. There are two basic types of clauses that are easy to distinguish. An *independent clause* has a subject and a verb, and it can stand by itself as a complete sentence. A *subordinate clause,* or *dependent clause,* has a subject and a verb but cannot stand by itself as a complete sentence.

MorePractice

For more on clauses, see the Grammar Handbook, p. R32.

> **Example:** INDEPENDENT CLAUSE: <u>She</u> <u>wore</u> boots.
>
> DEPENDENT CLAUSE: Because <u>she</u> <u>wore</u> boots,

Practice On your paper, identify each clause as independent or subordinate. For subordinate clauses, add independent clauses to make complete sentences.

1. We climbed the mountain.
2. When the weather was quite chilly.
3. We used state-of-the-art equipment.
4. If our cell phones had been working.
5. Duane found it difficult to breathe at the top.

W͟G Prentice Hall Writing and Grammar Connection: Chapter 20, Section 2

Reading: Cause and Effect

Directions: *Read the selection. Then, answer the questions.*

He soon found that thrusting his mittened hands through the snow and clutching the grass roots was uncertain and unsafe. His mittens were too thick for him to be sure of his grip, so he took them off. But this brought with it new trouble. When he held on to a bunch of roots the snow, coming in contact with his bare warm hand, was melted, so that his hands and the wristbands of his woolen shirt were dripping with water. This the frost was quick to attack, and his fingers were numbed and made worthless.

—from *Up the Slide* by Jack London

1. Why did the character take his mittens off?
   A They were too warm.
   B They were too thick.
   C He wanted to melt the snow.
   D They had holes in them.

2. What was the effect when the character removed his mittens?
   A His hands and part of his shirt got wet, and the water froze.
   B He was able to clutch the grass roots with certainty and safety.
   C He lost his mittens.
   D He was much more comfortable.

3. What are two long-term effects of removing his mittens?
   A a better grip and warmer hands
   B less flexibility and increased danger of frostbite
   C a better grip and numbed hands
   D warmer hands and increased danger of frostbite

4. Which is the most accurate description of the character's situation?
   A He is in a cold climate, alone, and in trouble.
   B He is an inexperienced climber.
   C He lives in a warmer climate and cannot cope with snow.
   D He is part of a climbing expedition.

Timed Writing: Persuasion

Review *The Diary of Anne Frank*. Explain a subplot that enhances your understanding of one or more of the characters. **(35 minutes)**

 ## Writing Workshop: *Work in Progress*

Research Paper

For a research paper you may write, flip through recent magazines or newspapers. List people, places, events, or current issues that you may want to investigate. Save this work in your writing portfolio.

Reading Informational Materials

Web Sites

In Part 2, you are learning about cause-and-effect relationships in literature. Understanding cause-and-effect relationships also is helpful when using other forms of communication, such as Web sites. In the play *The Diary of Anne Frank,* you could trace the cause-and-effect relationships between major historical events and the circumstances of the characters. You can gain a deeper understanding of these relationships by consulting the Web site **www.annefrank.com.**

About Web Sites

A Web site is a specific location on the Internet. Web sites are sponsored by a variety of groups, companies, and individuals. When visiting a site, always assess how credible and accurate the information might be based on the site's sponsor (see page R24).

Most Web sites share common features.

- The **Web address** is the site's location on the World Wide Web.
- A **Web page** is an individual screen within the Web site.
- **Navigation bars** and **links** help you move to different web pages.

Four pages from **www.annefrank.com,** a historical Web site maintained by the Anne Frank Center, are shown here.

Reading Skill

Just as you scan a printed document quickly, looking for section headings and key words, you also may **scan online documents** to find the information you need. When you scan an electronic page, you run your eyes over it, looking for headings, links to other pages or sites, or words that contain useful information. The chart shown tells you where to look when you scan a Web page.

Where to Look	What It Is	What It Does
Banner	a panel at the top of an electronic page	It shows links to other pages on the site.
Body	the main part of the Web page	It provides highlighted or underlined links to other pages of interest.
Visuals	small images	They may lead to maps, photos, or other text pages.

http://annefrank.com/0_home.htm

The address window shows the exact location of this Web page on the Internet.

The home page provides a central place to view the list of topics covered by the Web site. Each red bar is a link to another page.

Welcome to the Anne Frank Center, USA Website

about us

membership

our exhibits

NEW! bookstore

students

teachers

anne frank life & times

news & media updates

spirit of anne frank awards

support our programs

Anne Frank: A Private Photo Album

Anne Frank Center, USA Online

| the anne frank house, amsterdam | the anne frank center, berlin | the anne frank educational trust, london | the anne frank fonds, basel |

"Anne Frank Online" WWW site © The Anne Frank Center USA, Inc., 2004
All photographs © The Anne Frank Stichting, Amsterdam, The Netherlands, and The Anne Frank-Fonds, Basel, Switzerland.

All quotes from the diary of Anne Frank have been excerpted with permission from "The Diary of a Young Girl: The Definitive Edition, " published by Doubleday, 1995; © 1991 by The Anne Frank-Fonds, Basel, Switzerland; English translation © 1995 by Doubleday, a division of Bantam Doubleday Dell Publishing Group, Inc. All rights reserved.

membership   anne frank life   news & media   bookstore   teachers   students   about us   exhibits   spirit of anne frank

A Web page often provides more than one way to navigate through the site. These links echo the links in the red bars above.

| 1889 - 1919 | 1920 - 1932 | 1933 - 1939 | 1940 - 1943 | 1944 - 1945 | 1946 - today |

1940 - 1943

Frank Family

1940

December 1 - Otto Frank's company moves into the premises at number 263 Prinsengracht.

1941

May 8 - Opekta-Werke changes its name to Messrs. Gies & Company.

Summer - Anne and Margot attend the Jewish School Amsterdam.

1942

January - Death of Grandmother Hollander.

June 12 - Anne receives a diary for her thirteenth birthday.

July 5 - Margot Frank, 16, receives a call-up notice to report for deportation to a labor camp.
The family goes into hiding the next day.

July 6 - The Frank family leaves their home forever and moves into the 'Secret Annex'.

July 13 - The van Pels family, another Jewish family originally from Germany, joins the Frank family in hiding.

November 16 - Fritz Pfeffer, the eighth and final resident of the Secret Annex, joins the Frank and van Pels families.

1943

Nazi Movement

April, May - Germany invades Denmark and Norway, the Netherlands, France, Belgium, and Luxembourg.

July 31 - Hermann Goering authorizes Reinhard Heydrich to find a 'Final Solution' to the Jewish question.

December 11 - Germany declares war on the United States.

January 20 - Heydrich, at the Wannsee Conference, mobilizes Nazi bureaucratic support for a 'Final Solution'.

February, March, April - Auschwitz, Belzec and Sobibor all become fully operational death camps.

> This Web page provides historical images, as well as side-by-side timelines of events in Germany and in the lives of the Franks.

February 2 - The encircled German Sixth Army surrenders to Soviet forces at Stalingrad, Russia. The tide of the war begins to turn against Germany.

June - SS leader Heinrich Himmler orders the complete liquidation of all Jewish ghettos in the Soviet Union and Poland.

◄ life & times | **timeline** | diary excerpts | scrapbook | ▲ home

| 1889 - 1919 | 1920 - 1932 | 1933 - 1939 | 1940 - 1943 | 1944 - 1945 | 1946 - today |

1944 - 1945

Frank Family

1944

August 4 - The residents of the Secret Annex are betrayed and arrested. They are taken to a police station in Amsterdam.

August 8 - They are all taken to the transit camp at Westerbork.

September 3 - The eight prisoners are transported in a sealed cattle car to Auschwitz, on the last transport ever to leave Westerbork. Hermann van Pels is gassed on September 6, 1944.

October 6 - Anne and Margot Frank are sent to Bergen-Belsen concentration camp in Germany.

December 20 - Fritz Pfeffer dies in Neuengame.

1945 **January 26** - Edith Frank dies at Auschwitz-Birkenau.

January 27 - Otto Frank is liberated from Auschwitz by the Russian Army. He is taken first to Odessa and then to France before he is allowed to make his way back to Amsterdam.

February or March - Anne and Margot Frank die at the Bergen-Belsen concentration camp within days of each other.

Spring - Mrs. van Pels dies in Theresienstadt concentration camp in Czechoslovakia.

May - Peter van Pels dies in Mauthausen.

June 3 - Otto Frank arrives in Amsterdam, where he is reunited with Miep and Jan Gies. He concentrates on finding the whereabouts of Anne and Margot.

October 24 - Otto Frank receives a letter telling him that his daughters died at Bergen-Belsen

Nazi Movement

June 6 - D Day. The Allies invade Western Europe.

November 26 - To hide Nazi war crimes, the demolition of the crematoria at Auschwitz begins.

April 30 - Adolf Hitler commits suicide.

May 7 - Germany surrenders, and the war ends in Europe.

November - The Nuremberg Trials of Nazi war criminals begin.

> You can view events in different time periods by clicking on the tan bars.

anne frank life & times
 news & media updates
 book store
 membership
 teachers
 students
 about us
 our exhibits
the spirit of anne frank awards

Anne Frank Center, USA Online

about us

 ▲ home

The Anne Frank Center USA is a not-for-profit organization that promotes the universal message of tolerance by developing and disseminating a variety of educational programs, including exhibitions, workshops, and special events.

contact us

Based on the power of Anne Frank's diary, the Anne Frank Center USA aims to inspire the next generation to build a world based on compassion, mutual respect, and social justice.

The Center fulfills its mission through the North American Traveling Exhibit Program, the Exhibition and Education Center in New York City, the Annual Spirit of Anne Frank Awards, and through the development of educational materials and programs for teachers and students.

Since it was first published in 1947, Anne Frank's diary has become one of the most powerful memoirs of the Holocaust. Its message of tolerance, courage, and hope in the face of adversity has reached millions. The diary has been translated into more than 67 languages with over 31 million copies sold since its publication over 50 years ago. Anne Frank's story is especially meaningful to young people. For many students in America, the story of Anne Frank is their first, if not their only, exposure to the history of the Holocaust.

The Anne Frank Center USA works to:

- Effectively introduce young people to Anne Frank, the Frank family's personal story, and the history of the Holocaust;

- Help young people and communities explore and challenge discrimination, intolerance, and bias-related violence in a positive and constructive way;

- Encourage community-initiated programs that give people, especially young people, a chance to examine issues of diversity;

- Carry the Center's anti-bias message to isolated areas and under-served communities across the nation;

- Recognize the importance of personal responsibility in confronting prejudice by honoring those individuals who actively work to promote the positive values of diversity and social justice.

membership   anne frank life   news & media   bookstore   teachers   students   about us   exhibits   spirit of anne frank   home

Many Web sites have pages that provide information about the organization that sponsors the site.

Reading: Locate Information on a Web Site

Directions: *Choose the letter of the best answer.*

1. Scan the first page of the Web site. Where would you find a link to the Anne Frank Center in Berlin?

   A in the banner

   B in the address window

   C in the navigation bars

   D at the bottom of the page

2. Scan to determine which events both happened in 1944.

   A Anne's grandmother dies and the Netherlands is invaded.

   B Anne gets a diary and the Germans surrender at Stalingrad.

   C The Franks are taken to Westerbork and D-Day is launched.

   D Edith Frank dies and the Nuremberg trials begin.

3. Which question is answered on the final Web page?

   A Who hid Anne Frank?

   B How can I donate money to the Anne Frank Center?

   C What is the mission of the Anne Frank Center?

   D What books are available about Anne Frank?

Reading: Comprehension and Interpretation

Directions: *Write your answers on a separate piece of paper.*

4. **(a)** What features does the Web site contain that would help you find further information on the topic? **(b)** What kinds of information do those links give? **[Knowledge]**

5. How do the content, format, visuals, and ease of navigating the site compare to finding information on the topic from other media, such as magazines or books? **[Organizing]**

6. Explain how some of the features of the Web site could be useful for a teacher who wants to further educate a class on Anne Frank and the times in which she lived. **[Applying]**

Timed Writing: Evaluation [Critical Stance]

Evaluate the usefulness and credibility of the information provided on the Anne Frank Web site. State what you think the site tries to accomplish and whether or not it achieves that goal. **(15 minutes)**

Types of Sources

When Anne Frank's diary was published, it became a bestseller, inspiring Albert Hackett and Frances Goodrich to develop Anne's private thoughts into a play to reach an even wider audience. To do this, they drew on the following types of sources:

- A **primary source** document is a firsthand account in which the writer describes events that took place at the time he or she was writing. Primary sources include letters, diaries, and legal documents.
- A **secondary source** interprets information from primary sources. Such sources include biographies and textbooks.

The Diary of Anne Frank is a **dramatization,** a play that has been adapted from another work. When playwrights dramatize a primary source, such as a diary, they may also draw on other sources to add information not known by the original author. In addition, they might choose to fictionalize aspects of certain events for dramatic effect.

Comparing a Primary Source With a Dramatization

All primary sources tell something about their author and their time. Readers can learn about Anne Frank's personality, her unique circumstances, and the time in which she lived from her diary. As you read the excerpts from Anne's diary, compare the information they contain with the type of information presented in the dramatization on page 776. Use a chart like the one shown to help you compare.

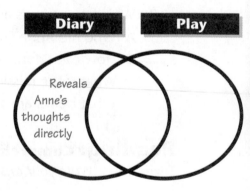

Diary   Play

Reveals Anne's thoughts directly

Vocabulary Builder

Anne Frank: The Diary of a Young Girl

- **melancholy** (mel′ ən käl′ ē) *adj.* gloomy (p. 883) *Rain makes me melancholy.*

- **enhance** (en hans′) *v.* make greater (p. 883) *Salt can enhance the flavor of food.*

- **emigrated** (em′ i grāt əd) *v.* left one place to settle in another (p. 883) *Many Germans emigrated to the United States in the 1840s.*

- **decrees** (dē krēz′) *n.* orders with the force of law (p. 884) *The judge issued several decrees in the case.*

- **evading** (ē vā′ diŋ) *v.* escaping by cleverness (p. 886) *The thief was famous for evading police.*

Build Understanding

Connecting to the Literature

Reading/Writing Connection Books create pictures in readers' minds—and sometimes those personalized pictures are very different from dramatic presentations on stage or screen. Write a few sentences comparing reading a book with seeing a play or movie version of the same work. Use at least three of the following words: *alternative, clarify, contrast, distinct, overlap.*

Meet the Author

Anne **Frank** (1929–1945)

More than fifty years after her death, Anne Frank remains the world's best-known victim of the Holocaust. The tragedy of her death is made even more moving by the existence of her diary, a personal journal which offers readers a revealing look into a life cut short.

The Diary At first Anne's father Otto was reluctant to publish Anne's private thoughts, but eventually he overcame his doubts. After a local Dutch newspaper created interest in the diary with a front-page story, a publisher became interested. The book quickly became a bestseller. Anne's diary enabled people to put a human face—the face of an ordinary teenage girl—on a tragedy that had been too enormous to grasp.

Fast Facts

▶ Anne's diary was originally published in 1947, under the Dutch title *Het Achterhuis (The Secret Annex).*
▶ The diary has sold more than thirty million copies and has been translated into more than sixty-five languages.

For: More about the author
Visit: www.PHSchool.com
Web Code: ene-9505

from *Anne Frank:*
The Diary of a Young Girl

Saturday, 20 June, 1942

. . . There is a saying that "paper is more patient than man"; it came back to me on one of my slightly <u>melancholy</u> days, while I sat chin in hand, feeling too bored and limp even to make up my mind whether to go out or stay at home. Yes, there is no doubt that paper is patient and as I don't intend to show this cardboard-covered notebook, bearing the proud name of "diary," to anyone, unless I find a real friend, boy or girl, probably nobody cares. And now I come to the root of the matter, the reason for my starting a diary: it is that I have no such real friend.

Let me put it more clearly, since no one will believe that a girl of thirteen feels herself quite alone in the world, nor is it so. I have darling parents and a sister of sixteen. I know about thirty people whom one might call friends—I have strings of boy friends, anxious to catch a glimpse of me and who, failing that, peep at me through mirrors in class. I have relations, aunts and uncles, who are darlings too, a good home, no—I don't seem to lack anything. But it's the same with all my friends, just fun and joking, nothing more. I can never bring myself to talk of anything outside the common round. We don't seem to be able to get any closer, that is the root of the trouble. Perhaps I lack confidence, but anyway, there it is, a stubborn fact and I don't seem to be able to do anything about it.

Hence, this diary. In order to <u>enhance</u> in my mind's eye the picture of the friend for whom I have waited so long, I don't want to set down a series of bald facts in a diary like most people do, but I want this diary itself to be my friend, and I shall call my friend Kitty. No one will grasp what I'm talking about if I begin my letters to Kitty just out of the blue, so albeit[1] unwillingly, I will start by sketching in brief the story of my life.

My father was thirty-six when he married my mother, who was then twenty-five. My sister Margot was born in 1926 in Frankfort-on-Main, I followed on June 12, 1929, and, as we are Jewish, we <u>emigrated</u> to Holland in 1933, where my father was appointed Managing Director of Travies N.V. This firm is in close relationship with the firm of Kolen & Co. in the same building, of which my father is a partner.

The rest of our family, however, felt the full impact of Hitler's anti-Jewish laws, so life was filled with anxiety. In 1938

---

1. **albeit** (ôl bē´ it) *conj.* although.

◀ **Critical Viewing**
What value do wartime diaries, such as Anne's, have for readers today? **[Analyze]**

Vocabulary Builder
melancholy (mel´ ən käl´ ē) *adj.* gloomy

Literary Analysis
Sources What information in this paragraph would be hard to show in a dramatization?

Vocabulary Builder
enhance (en hans´) *v.* make greater

emigrated (em´ i grāt´ ed) *v.* left one place to settle in another

✓**Reading Check**

Who is Kitty?

after the pogroms,[2] my two uncles (my mother's brothers) escaped to the U.S.A. My old grandmother came to us, she was then seventy-three. After May 1940 good times rapidly fled: first the war, then the capitulation,[3] followed by the arrival of the Germans, which is when the sufferings of us Jews really began. Anti-Jewish <u>decrees</u> followed each other in quick succession. Jews must wear a yellow star, Jews must hand in their bicycles, Jews are banned from trains and are forbidden to drive. Jews are only allowed to do their shopping between three and five o'clock and then only in shops which bear the placard "Jewish shop." Jews must be indoors by eight o'clock and cannot even sit in their own gardens after that hour. Jews are forbidden to visit theaters, cinemas, and other places of entertainment. Jews may not take part in public sports. Swimming baths, tennis courts, hockey fields, and other sports grounds are all prohibited to them. Jews may not visit Christians. Jews must go to Jewish schools, and many more restrictions of a similar kind.

So we could not do this and were forbidden to do that. But life went on in spite of it all. Jopie[4] used to say to me, "You're scared to do anything, because it may be forbidden." Our freedom was strictly limited. Yet things were still bearable.

Granny died in January 1942; no one will ever know how much she is present in my thoughts and how much I love her still.

In 1934 I went to school at the Montessori Kindergarten and continued there. It was at the end of the school year, I was in form 6B, when I had to say good-by to Mrs. K. We both wept, it was very sad. In 1941 I went, with my sister Margot, to the Jewish Secondary School, she into the fourth form[5] and I into the first.

So far everything is all right with the four of us and here I come to the present day.

Thursday, 19 November, 1942

Dear Kitty,
Dussel is a very nice man, just as we had all imagined. Of course he thought it was all right to share my little room.

---

2. pogroms (pō´ grəmz) *n.* organized massacres and other persecution of Jews.
3. capitulation (kə pich´ yōō lā´ shən) *n.* act of surrendering.
4. Jopie (yō´ pē) Jacqueline van Maarsen, Anne's best friend.
5. fourth form fourth grade.

Vocabulary Builder
decrees (dē krēz´) *n.* orders with the force of law

Literary Analysis
Sources Compare and contrast the presentation of this information with its presentation at the end of Act I Scene I in the play.

Literary Analysis
Sources Why do you think the playwrights chose to omit this information about Anne's grandmother from the play?

Quite honestly I'm not so keen that a stranger should use my things, but one must be prepared to make some sacrifices for a good cause, so I shall make my little offering with a good will. "If we can save someone, then everything else is of secondary importance," says Daddy, and he's absolutely right.

The first day that Dussel was here, he immediately asked me all sorts of questions: When does the charwoman[6] come? When can one use the bathroom? When is one allowed to use the lavatory?[7] You may laugh, but these things are not so simple in a hiding place. During the day we mustn't make any noise that might be heard downstairs; and if there is some stranger—such as the charwoman for example—then we have to be extra careful. I explained all this carefully to Dussel. But one thing amazed me: he is very slow on the uptake. He asks everything twice over and still doesn't seem to remember. Perhaps that will wear off in time, and it's only that he's thoroughly upset by the sudden change.

Apart from that, all goes well. Dussel has told us a lot about the outside world, which we have missed for so long now. He

 **Critical Viewing**
Why do you think Anne's diary has been so widely read? **[Speculate]**

Reading Check

What does Anne notice about Dussel?

---

6. **charwoman** *n.* cleaning woman.
7. **lavatory** *n.* toilet.

had very sad news. Countless friends and acquaintances have gone to a terrible fate. Evening after evening the green and gray army lorries trundle past.[8] The Germans ring at every front door to inquire if there are any Jews living in the house. If there are, then the whole family has to go at once. If they don't find any, they go on to the next house. No one has a chance of <u>evading</u> them unless one goes into hiding. Often they go around with lists, and only ring when they know they can get a good haul. Sometimes they let them off for cash—so much per head. It seems like the slave hunts of olden times. But it's certainly no joke; it's much too tragic for that. In the evenings when it's dark, I often see rows of good, innocent people accompanied by crying children, walking on and on, in charge of a couple of these chaps, bullied and knocked about until they almost drop. No one is spared—old people, babies, expectant mothers, the sick—each and all join in the march of death.

How fortunate we are here, so well cared for and undisturbed. We wouldn't have to worry about all this misery were it not that we are so anxious about all those dear to us whom we can no longer help.

I feel wicked sleeping in a warm bed, while my dearest friends have been knocked down or have fallen into a gutter somewhere out in the cold night. I get frightened when I think of close friends who have now been delivered into the hands of the cruelest brutes that walk the earth. And all because they are Jews!

Yours, Anne

8. **lorries trundle past** trucks moved along.

Vocabulary Builder
evading (ē vā′ diŋ) v. escaping by cleverness

Literary Analysis
Sources Compare this paragraph with the description on pages 809–810. How does the firsthand account differ from the play's version of similar events?

Thinking About the Selection

1. **Respond:** Did you form a different impression of Anne based on her diary than you had developed in reading the play? Explain.

2. **(a) Recall:** Why does Anne decide to write a diary?
   (b) Analyze: What other reasons might motivate her to write?

3. **(a) Recall:** As Anne describes in the June 20 entry, how has life changed for Jews since May 1940? **(b) Drawing Conclusions:** What is the purpose of such restrictions?

4. **(a) Contrast:** How is Anne's situation different from that of the Jews she sees outside? **(b) Evaluate:** Anne says she is "fortunate" to have a hiding place and warm bed. Do you agree? Explain.

Apply the Skills

from *Anne Frank: The Diary of a Young Girl*

Comparing a Primary Source With a Dramatization

1. Use a chart like the one shown to compare Anne's diary, a firsthand primary source, with the dramatization it inspired.

	How Thoughts and Feelings Are Expressed	Whose Perspectives Are Shown	Accuracy of Retelling	How Time Is Represented
Diary				
Play				

2. Do you think the playwrights create a fair and accurate portrait of Anne Frank? Be specific, and support your answer with evidence from the diary.

3. Identify two secondary sources you could consult to learn more about Anne Frank.

Writing to Compare Literary Works

Both the diary and the play present Anne Frank to future generations. In an essay, compare and contrast the Anne Frank revealed in the diary with the Anne Frank of the play. Use these questions to get started:

- How well does the play capture Anne's thoughts and feelings?
- How does the dialogue in the play affect the way we see other characters? How are these people presented in the diary?
- In the play, what is the effect of other characters' words on the way we view Anne Frank?
- Which form do you think is more powerful? Why?

Vocabulary Builder

Practice For each item presented, write a sentence that correctly uses each word pair.

1. evading; hiding
2. decrees; ignore
3. melancholy; weather
4. enhance; understanding
5. emigrated; family

QuickReview

Primary source: an original firsthand account

Secondary source: a secondhand source that interprets an original one

Dramatization: a play adapted from another work

Go Online
Assessment
For: Self-test
Visit: www.PHSchool.com
Web Code: ena-6506

Reading: Cause and Effect

Directions: *Questions 1–5 refer to the following selection.*

Few books have had as great an impact on American history as Harriet Beecher Stowe's *Uncle Tom's Cabin.* Published in 1852, the novel tells the story of a slave named Uncle Tom, who is cruelly treated by his overseer, Simon Legree. The book sold 300,000 copies in its first year, soon sold more than 7 million copies worldwide, and was adapted into a play.

Reactions to the book were dramatic. Northerners were horrified to read its descriptions of how slaves were mistreated, and the novel built support for the movement to abolish slavery. It intensified the conflict between the North and the South about slavery, which was one issue that led to the Civil War. When Abraham Lincoln met Stowe, he was only half joking when he said, "So you're the little lady who made this big war."

1. **What does the passage focus on?**
   A several causes of the Civil War
   B several effects of the Civil War
   C the dramatic effects of one book
   D the causes of Harriet Beecher Stowe's success

2. **According to the passage, what was a result of the publication of *Uncle Tom's Cabin*?**
   A It intensified the conflict between North and South.
   B It helped Stowe's political career.
   C All were horrified by slavery.
   D It led to the Civil War.

3. **What background information might help you link the causes and effects in the passage?**
   A President Abraham Lincoln and the Emancipation Proclamation
   B the childhood of Harriet Beecher Stowe

   C opposing views of northerners and southerners in the 1850s
   D what kinds of books Americans enjoyed in the 1850s

4. **Which sentence in the passage prepares you to read about effects?**
   A sentence 2 of paragraph 1
   B sentence 3 of paragraph 1
   C sentence 1 of paragraph 2
   D the quotation at the end

5. **Which is a good summary of the cause-and-effect relationships explained in the selection?**
   A *Uncle Tom's Cabin* intensified one conflict that led to the Civil War.
   B Harriet Beecher Stowe caused Abraham Lincoln to abolish slavery.
   C Reaction to *Uncle Tom's Cabin* had no effect on Americans' attitudes.
   D Slavery was the only cause of the Civil War.

Assessment Practice

Vocabulary

Directions *Choose the answer that best completes each sentence.*

6. Who has the most _____ on the decisions you make?
   A consequence
   B factor
   C influence
   D reaction

7. The weather was an important _____ in the outcome of the football game.
   A consequence
   B factor
   C influence
   D reaction

8. His excellent grades were the _____ of good study habits.
   A consequence   C reaction
   B influence   D impact

Directions: *Choose the best answer.*

11. The root *-sequ-* means
    A to come before.
    B to follow.
    C to make.
    D to thank.

12. The root *-fac-* means
    A to decide from direct evidence.
    B to arrange or act on.
    C to make or do.
    D to have to do with education.

13. A *factory* is a place where
    A things are designed.
    B things are made.
    C things are destroyed.
    D things are advertised.

9. The new law will have a positive _____ on the community.
   A consequence
   B reaction
   C impact
   D factor

10. The author's _____ to being nominated for the Pulitzer Prize was captured on film by the news crew.
    A consequence   C impact
    B reaction   D factor

14. A *sequel* to the movie *The Giant Ant 4* might be
    A *The Giant Ant.*
    B *The Giant Ants: The beginning.*
    C *The Giant Ant 3.*
    D *The Giant Ant 5.*

15. A *subsequent* event comes _____ an initial event.
    A before
    B after
    C at the same time as
    D instead of

Plurals

Most plural forms of English nouns follow basic rules. Learning these few rules will help you to correctly spell most of the plurals.

Rules

- Add -**s** to most nouns to form plurals: *effect/effects.*
- Add -**es** to nouns that end in **s, ss, sh, ch,** and **x** to form plurals: *clash/clashes.*
- Add -**es** to most nouns that end in a **consonant and o:** *potato/potatoes.*
- Change **y** to **i** and add -**es** to nouns that end in the **consonant** -**y** combination: *analogy/analogies.*
- Do not change the **y,** just add -**s** to nouns that end in the **vowel** -**y** combination: *key/keys.*
- For some nouns ending in -**fe,** change -**fe** to -**ve** and add -**s:** *life/lives.*

I'd like to exchange this y for an i please.

Do you have a consonant?

CUSTOMER SERVICE

Irregular Plurals

- Some nouns have the same spelling in both forms. *scissors/scissors, pants/pants, sheep/sheep*
- Some nouns require basic spelling changes in the plural form. *crisis/crises, foot/feet, radius/radii*
- Nouns that are not countable have no plural forms. *data/data*

Practice For each of the following words, write the rule to change the singular form to a plural. Then, use the plural form in a sentence.

1. zero
2. calf
3. glass
4. canary
5. yourself
6. metaphor
7. narrative
8. process
9. strategy
10. variety

Word List
theories
hypotheses
reasons
efficiencies
analyses
patches
properties
rays
halves
deductions

Directions: *Choose the letter of the sentence in which the underlined plural is spelled correctly.*

1. A We looked at six <u>propertys</u> today.
   B I liked three of the <u>propertis</u>.
   C Three of the <u>properties</u> were wooded.
   D Three <u>propertyes</u> were in our district.

2. A You could see the <u>rais</u> of the sun reflected in the water.
   B The <u>rayes</u> looked like lines of light.
   C The sun's <u>rays</u> felt good after winter.
   D The <u>raies</u> are welcome after winter.

3. A There are many <u>theories</u> about the origin of the universe.
   B Scientists keep revising their <u>theorys</u>.
   C Space exploration gives us information to update these <u>theoris</u>.
   D The <u>therum</u> will probably change.

4. A There are pumpkin <u>patchs</u> as far as you can see.
   B You can go to the <u>patces</u> to pick a pumpkin.
   C The pumpkin <u>patches</u> are a popular destination for families.
   D The pumpkin <u>pates</u> are interesting.

5. A We asked for several <u>analysses</u> of the problem.
   B As the <u>analyses</u> came in, the problem became clearer.
   C The <u>analyss</u> showed that it was too hot.
   D Because of these <u>analysus</u>, we solved the problem.

6. A How many <u>halves</u> make a whole?
   B The first grade was working with <u>halfes</u> in math.
   C They counted how many <u>halvs</u> they needed to make four whole circles.
   D Then, they counted the number of <u>halfs</u> needed to make five circles.

7. A There are <u>deductiones</u> for spelling.
   B There are also point <u>deductionns</u> for grammatical mistakes.
   C <u>Deducktions</u> are taken if the reader can't find transitions.
   D <u>Deductions</u> are also taken if there is no conclusion.

8. A There are many <u>reasones</u> to practice.
   B There are <u>reasons</u> to practice writing.
   C When you understand the <u>reasonns</u> it is easier to practice.
   D It is helpful to have <u>reasins</u> for what you do.

9. A The expert helped the company start <u>efficiencys</u> that would save money.
   B These <u>efficiencyes</u> were simple.
   C Some <u>efficiences</u> merely meant turning off lights in offices.
   D Other <u>efficiencies</u> were harder to put in place.

10. A They had several <u>hypothesis</u> that they wanted to test.
    B Each scientist was involved in testing several <u>hypothesizes</u>.
    C The <u>hypothesses</u> all dealt with the causes of disease.
    D These <u>hypotheses</u> were all difficult to test.

Exposition: Research Report

When you follow your own curiosity, you learn about a subject that interests you and builds your own area of expertise. **Research writing** presents information gathered from several sources. Follow the steps outlined in this workshop to write your own research report.

Assignment Write a research report based on information from a variety of sources.

What to Include Your research report should feature the following elements:
- an overall focus or main idea expressed in a thesis statement
- supporting evidence from a variety of primary and secondary sources, with appropriate citations
- a clear organization and smooth transitions
- a bibliography or list of works cited that provides an accurate, complete citation of research sources

To preview the criteria on which your research report may be judged, see the rubric on page 903.

Using the Form

You may use elements of this form in these types of writing:
- informational articles
- news analyses
- travelogues
- business reports

Writing Workshop: *Work in Progress*

If you have completed the Work-in-Progress assignments, you have several ideas you might use in your research report. Develop these ideas, or explore a new idea as you complete the Writing Workshop.

Prewriting

Choosing Your Topic

To choose a suitable topic, use one of the following strategies:

- **Self-Interview** Create a chart like the one shown, and answer the questions shown. Circle words that suggest research ideas to you and choose a topic from among those items.

People	Places	Things	Events
What interesting people do I know or know about?	What interesting places have I been to or heard about?	What interesting things do I know about?	What interesting events have happened to me or have I heard about?
Grandma (Ben Franklin) Michael Jordan Emily Dickinson	hospital hockey rink library (Philadelphia)	baseball compact discs (kites)	hockey game homecoming elections (July Fourth)

- **Newswatch** Flip through recent magazines or newspapers. Tune in to television or radio broadcasts. List people, places, events, or current issues that you want to investigate. Choose one of these issues as a topic for research.

Narrowing Your Topic

Conduct preliminary research. Before you finalize your topic, conduct preliminary research to determine how much material is available. Using your general idea as a starting point, browse through relevant books, Web sites, magazines, and indexes at the library. Jot down the names, ideas, and events that appear most often. Use this information to narrow a wide subject like educational toys to a narrower one like electronic readers.

Ask open-ended questions. Thoughtful, interesting questions can help focus a research topic. Draft a list of questions that will guide you as you research. As you find information, modify your list by deleting questions that are not closely linked to your topic and adding more specific questions.

Work in Progress
Review the work you did on page 873.

Gathering Details Through Research

Use a variety of primary and secondary sources. Use both *primary sources* (firsthand or original accounts, such as interview transcripts and newspaper articles) and *secondary sources* (accounts that are not original, such as encyclopedia entries) in your research. A secondary source often contains a bibliography or list of works cited. Use these citations to find additional sources.

Question your sources. To ensure that your information is current, accurate, and balanced, follow these guidelines:
- Check publication dates to make sure information is current.
- If you note discrepancies in the information given by two sources, check the facts in a third source. If three or more sources disagree, mention the disagreement in your paper.
- Especially with controversial topics, consider the possible reasons for the author's perspective. Examine the author's credentials—his or her background—before accepting a conclusion.
- Whenever possible, cross-check information with other sources.

Taking Notes

Use source cards and notecards. When you find information related to your topic, take detailed notes on index cards.
- Create a source card for each book, article, Web site, or interviewee. For print sources, list the author, title, publisher, and place and date of publication. For Internet sources, list the sponsor, page name, date of last revision, the date you accessed it, and the address. For an interview, give the date and the person's name, address, and phone number.
- As you take notes, write one idea on each card. When taking notes, be careful to avoid *plagiarism,* the unethical presentation of someone else's ideas as if they were your own. Paraphrase to avoid copying other authors' exact words without proper credit.
- On each card, record a key word that links to the full information on the source card.
- Use quotation marks whenever you copy words exactly. When using cursive, write legibly to avoid misquoting or misspelling.

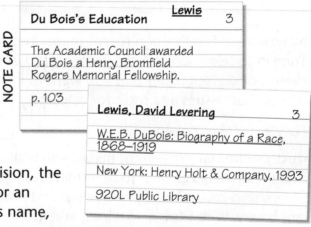

NOTE CARD

Du Bois's Education   Lewis   3

The Academic Council awarded Du Bois a Henry Bromfield Rogers Memorial Fellowship.

p. 103

SOURCE CARD

Lewis, David Levering   3

W.E.B. DuBois: Biography of a Race, 1868–1919

New York: Henry Holt & Company, 1993

920L Public Library

Drafting

Shaping Your Writing

Define your thesis. Sum up the point of your paper in a sentence, called a **thesis statement**. Use your thesis statement to direct your drafting and include it in the introduction to your report.

Make an outline. Write a formal outline like the one shown for your report before you begin to draft. Use Roman numerals for your most important points and capital letters for the details that support them. Make sure every point on your outline supports your thesis.

Providing Elaboration

Stick to your thesis. You may have gathered more details than you can use. Include only the details that are most relevant to your thesis.

Thesis:	The lives led by California Gold Rush miners were often harsh.
Appropriate details:	facts about miners' housing, weather, food sources
Unnecessary details:	facts about routes to California, history of mining

As you draft, avoid unnecessary information and build on the facts and ideas that support your thesis.

> **Title of Your Report**
>
> **I.** Introduction
>   Thesis Statement
> **II.** First main point
>   **A.** Supporting detail #1
>   **1.** Example
>   **2.** Example
>   **3.** Example
>   **B.** Supporting detail #2
>   **C.** Supporting detail #3
>
> **III.** Second main point

Reading Writing Connection

To read the complete student model, see page 900.

Student Model: Sticking to the Thesis

However, Alexander inherited his military genius and bravery from his father, who conquered all of the Greek city-states and then united them under his rule. Since Philip felt his son's education was important, he hired Aristotle, considered the wisest man in Greece, to tutor him. Even as a child, Alexander had enough ambition for several men, as shown by his comment after his father had conquered a city, "My father will have everything, and I will have nothing left to conquer."

> The highlighted sentence, while interesting, does not relate directly to the traits discussed in the rest of the paragraph. It can be omitted.

Prepare to credit sources. As you draft, circle all ideas and words that come directly from your research. At this stage, for each circled item, use parentheses to note the author's name and the page number. You can create formal citations later.

Cherie
Bennett

From the Author's Desk

Cherie Bennett
On Getting Facts and Words Right

I wrote the play *Anne Frank & Me* first, and then, with my husband, adapted it as a novel. The big difference between the two forms is that a novel gives you so much more freedom. You're not confined by what could go on a stage. But novels require even more research, since they contain so many details. The following selection is from the novel, and it covers part of the same scene as the excerpt from the play you just read.

"We didn't want to get any facts wrong."
———Cherie Bennett

Professional Model:
from *Anne Frank and Me* (novel)

A sudden bump on the track jostled them; they reached to steady each other—Nicole felt as if jolts of electricity were coursing through her. "I remember . . . you thought your parents disapproved that you were kissing him."

Anne's voice became a whisper. "How is this possible?"

"I don't know—" Nicole began, then stopped. Because suddenly, she did know. "You kept a diary. I read it."

"But I left my diary in the Annex when the Gestapo came. You couldn't have read it."

"I did, though."

"How?"

"I don't know," Nicole admitted. "I wish I did."

Anne gave her a ~~dubious cock-eyed mischievous~~ arched look. "This is a very strange conversation."

The train lurched violently. People cried out in fear, but Nicole was oblivious, as a new thought surfaced, one so absurd that she was almost too embarrassed to say it. "Anne, I feel like it was—I know this will sound crazy—but I feel like it was in the future."

Research interviews with Holocaust survivors taught us about the rough track bed used by the transports. On stage, the actors synchronized unsteady movements with sound effects of a moving train.

In most plays, characters speak for themselves. But in a novel, you've got to pick a point of view. We wrote this story using a limited third-person point of view, revealing only Nicole's thoughts.

I remember my struggle for the right word to describe the look that Anne gives Nicole. I tried — and tossed out! — *curious*, *cock-eyed*, and *dubious*. Finally, I settled on *arched*. It conveys both how I imagine Anne raised her eyebrows and her mischievous tone.

Revising

Revising Your Overall Structure

Check for unity. All the parts of your report should fit together in a complete, self-contained whole.

1. Make sure that every paragraph develops your thesis statement. Eliminate those that do not, or revise to show a stronger connection.

2. Identify the main idea of each paragraph. Often, a topic sentence will directly state that main idea. If a paragraph does not contain a topic sentence, consider adding one.

3. In each paragraph, eliminate any sentences that do not support or explain the topic sentence or main idea.

To read the complete student model, see page 900.

Student Model: Revising for Unity

Out of all this strife rose a boy, Alexander III, a hero whose name would be remembered for thousands of years. ~~Alexander was born in July 356 B.C. to King Philip II of Macedonia, and Olympias, daughter of the King of Epirus.~~ Alexander became King of Macedonia at the young age of twenty and commenced to conquer the Persian Empire and part of modern-day India using brilliant battle strategy and a quickness to act that kept his enemies guessing.

> The highlighted sentence should be moved to a paragraph in the body that offers other details about Alexander as a child.

Peer Review: Ask a partner to read your draft, identifying details that wander too far from your thesis. Together, look for ways to link the information back to the main idea, or consider cutting the text.

Revising Your Sentences

Revising Your Word Choice

Use vivid action verbs. Use precise action verbs to bring life to your writing and communicate exactly what you learned in your research.

Vague: Protestors <u>had</u> banners at the rally.

Vivid: Protestors <u>waved</u> banners at the rally.

Circle action verbs in your draft—ignore *being* verbs such as *be, am, is, are, was,* and *were.* Revise where appropriate.

Writing Workshop

Make Direct Reference to Sources

You can use one of these methods to incorporate the information you've learned through research.

- **Quote directly.** When using a writer's exact words, enclose the entire statement in quotation marks. If you delete words from a lengthy sentence for clarity, be sure your editing does not change the intention of the quotation. Remember to show your deletions by the insertion of **ellipses,** or three dots.

- **Paraphrase.** This technique involves restating a writer's specific ideas in your own words. You can paraphrase to convey the mood or intensity of the writer's description or ideas.

- **Summarize.** You can include the material you found through research by summarizing or reporting key ideas.

Integrate references by framing. Whenever you include information gathered through research, smooth your writing by providing a context for the material you use. First, introduce the material. Then, present the quotation. Finally, complete the frame by explaining how the material supports the point you are making.

Check your citations. You must cite an author's direct quotations as well as his or her ideas, even if you restate the information in your own words. An internal citation appears in parentheses. It includes the author's last name and the page number on which the information appears. The citation directly follows the information from the source cited.

> ▶ **Example:** "The Duke of Lancaster in 1888 controlled more than 163,000 acres of British countryside" (Pool 193).

Create a "Works Cited" list. Provide full information about your sources in an alphabetical "Works Cited" list or "Bibliography" at the end of your report. Check the format required for your report, and follow the guidelines of style and punctuation.

Check Visuals

Make sure any of the visuals you have added support the main point. Bring out important similarities or differences in tables and charts through the use of color and different typefaces. Make sure text is readable and that all photographs are labeled clearly with captions that indicate what they show.

Integrating Grammar Skills

Revising to Combine Sentences With Subordinate Clauses

To eliminate a choppy style and show connections between ideas, combine sentences with subordinate clauses.

Identifying Subordinate Clauses A clause is any group of words with a subject and a verb. A subordinate clause cannot stand by itself.

> *Prentice Hall Writing and Grammar Connection: Chapter 20, Section 2*

> **Subordinate clause:** The bus <u>where the incident took place</u> got very crowded.
>
> **Subordinate clause:** <u>Although Rosa Parks said she was simply tired,</u> she became a symbol of strength.

Combining Sentences To combine two short sentences, use a subordinate clause to identify a relationship between the ideas.

> **Time:** *After technology made MP3s possible,* new players flooded the market.
>
> **Cause and effect:** *If the temperature drops,* winds may pick up.
>
> **Contrast:** *Although one candidate favored the bill,* the other opposed it.

Combining Sentences by Using Subordinate Clauses To combine sentences by using subordinate clauses, follow these steps:

1. **Identify two sentences whose ideas are connected.**
2. **Rewrite the less important idea as a subordinate clause.**
3. **Combine the sentences, punctuating according to these rules:**
   - Use a comma after most introductory clauses. *When he arrived back in Missouri, he claimed to be a free man.*
   - Do not use a comma if the subordinate clause follows the main clause. *He claimed to be a free man when he got to Missouri.*

Frequently Used Subordinating Conjunctions			
after	as though	in order that	until
although	because	since	when
as long as	before	than	where
as soon as	even though	unless	while

Apply It to Your Editing

Review the sentences in three paragraphs of your draft. Consider whether some of them could be improved by combining them. If so, revise by combining them with subordinate clauses.

Student Model:
James Barraclough
Los Alamos, NM

Alexander the Great

Southeastern Europe and western Asia were continually plagued by wars and rebellions in the fourth century B.C. Out of all this strife rose a boy, Alexander III, a hero whose name would be remembered for thousands of years. Alexander became King of Macedonia at the young age of twenty and commenced to conquer the Persian Empire and part of modern-day India using brilliant battle strategy and a quickness to act that kept his enemies guessing. He earned his reputation as 'Alexander the Great' by carving an empire of approximately one million square miles out of a land filled with enemies who were often intent on overthrowing him (Walbank 248).

Alexander was born in July 356 B.C. to King Philip II of Macedonia and Olympias, daughter of the King of Epirus. Throughout his life, Alexander was very close to his mother, Olympias, from whom he learned to pray and to believe deeply in the gods. However, Alexander inherited his military genius and bravery from his father, who conquered all of the Greek city-states and then united them under his rule. Even as a child, Alexander had enough ambition for several men, as shown by his comment after his father had conquered a city: "My father will have everything, and I will have nothing left to conquer." (Wepman)

After uniting Greece, Philip began a campaign to conquer the Persian Empire, but his efforts were cut short when he was assassinated in 336 B.C. Alexander was only twenty years old, though he had been commanding troops with his father for four years. He was not guaranteed power after his father's death, so he quickly claimed the throne with the army's support (Wilcken 61). Picking up where his father left off, Alexander III, King of Macedonia, began a campaign that would change the world.

In the spring of 334 B.C., Alexander led a relatively small army of 30,000 infantry, comprised mostly of soldiers called *hoplites,* who carried 16-foot spears, and 5,000 cavalry, called the Companions, across the Hellespont, a narrow strait. There, he met a force of Persian cavalry and Greek mercenaries, sent by Darius III, King of the Persian Empire, which was intended to throw back the invaders. However, the Macedonians cut them to shreds by employing Alexander's innovative military strategy (Cartledge 28–29). After that battle, Alexander led his army down along the coast of Asia Minor, taking cities for Greece until he met Darius at Issus. There, Alexander's outnumbered soldiers again routed the Persians, but Darius escaped. As the ancient historian Arrian reports, Darius fled in such a panic, he abandoned his royal chariot. "He even left his bow in the chariot; and mounting a horse continued his flight." (Godolphin 450)

> James introduces the overall focus—the impressive accomplishments of Alexander—in the first paragraph.

> The paper's organization is chronological, following a clear path from Alexander's birth to his death.

> James uses a variety of sources—both ancient and modern—for quotations and supporting evidence.

Choosing not to pursue Darius further, Alexander continued along the eastern Mediterranean coast into Egypt, liberating the Egyptians from their hated Persian overlords. In exchange for their liberation, the Egyptians named Alexander pharaoh of Egypt. After his victory, he planned a city called Alexandria to be built on the Mediterranean Sea. As Alexander pressed back into Asia he conquered many cities, but again Darius confronted him—this time better prepared for the man who was such a grave threat to the Persian Empire. However, Alexander employed a cunning ruse to distract the Persians during the battle and crashed back to the middle, crushing the unsuspecting Persians. When Darius fled, the empire was left to Alexander's control (Cartledge 32). At the age of twenty-five, Alexander had become ruler of the Persian Empire and the most powerful man in the world.

After some time in Babylon, the city he made his capital, Alexander decided to head towards India to conquer new land for his empire. Many of the Greek soldiers protested that they wished to go home after years of hard fighting. Even so, Alexander inspired such loyalty that the soldiers reluctantly followed him to India. After fighting their way through modern-day Afghanistan and Pakistan, Alexander crossed into India. Many of his men died when monsoon rains arrived and poisonous snakes, rats, and tropical diseases, such as malaria, became prevalent.

As the army moved deeper into India, King Porus, an Indian ruler, confronted Alexander's troops with approximately two hundred war elephants and an extensive cavalry. Even though the elephants made it difficult for Alexander's cavalry to fight, Alexander once again outsmarted his enemy and defeated the Indian army. Porus surrendered and agreed to be his ally. Following the restoration of Porus to his kingdom, Alexander's men, who were wearied by the intense heat and stricken with homesickness, refused to move on. Alexander sulked in his tent, until he finally relented and set out towards Babylon (Prevas 166–172).

Approximately one year after his return from India, Alexander developed a fever and stomach cramps. These may have been caused by heavy drinking, typhoid, malaria, or poison. The fatal illness kept him in bed until he died on June 11, 323 B.C. at the age of 32. Since Alexander did not appoint a successor to his throne, the mightiest empire of the time, perhaps of all time, fell into disorder and collapsed with his death (Prevas 202–207).

Smooth transitions give the paper a sense of flow.

James credits each source in parentheses—using only author's last name and page number—directly after the information taken from that source. Full citations appear at the end of the paper.

All in all, Alexander—who was just a boy in some people's eyes when he took the throne—rose to the occasion and conquered the world, forging an empire with his heart and sword. Alexander was a complex man who could be harsh, ruthless, and relentless in battle, but he could also be compassionate and sympathetic towards his wounded soldiers. These characteristics inspired loyalty and unity in thousands of soldiers. They followed Alexander wherever he led, even if they had a fierce desire to go home. The man known as Alexander the Great was a king, an emperor, a pharaoh, a conqueror, and most of all, a leader who could charge into battle, knowing his men would follow.

All sources used are listed at the end of the paper in a Bibliography. To see the proper format for different sources, see Citing Sources and Preparing Manuscript, pages R25-R26.

Bibliography

Alexander, Caroline. "Alexander the Conqueror." *National Geographic,* March 2000: 42–75.

Cartledge, Paul. *Alexander the Great.* New York: Overlook Press, 2004.

Chrisp, Peter. *Alexander the Great: The Legend of a Warrior King.* New York: Dorling Kindersley, 2000.

Godolphin, Francis R., ed. and Chinnock, Edward J., translator (Arrian). *The Greek Historians: The Complete and Unabridged Historical Works of Herodotus, Thucydides, Xenophon, Arrian.* New York: Random House, 1942.

Greenblatt, Miriam. *Alexander the Great and Ancient Greece.* New York: Benchmark Books, 2000.

Prevas, John. *Envy of the Gods.* Cambridge, MA: Da Capo Press, 2004.

Stark, Freya. *Alexander's Path.* New York: Harcourt, Brace and Company, 1958.

Walbank, Frank W. "Alexander the Great." *Encyclopedia Britannica.* 1990 ed.

Wepman, Dennis, *Alexander the Great,* book excerpt on <http://www.palmdigitalmedia.com/product/book/excerpt/11250> (14 April 2005).

Wilcken, Ulrich. *Alexander the Great.* New York: W.W. Norton, 1967.

Woodcock, George et al. *Ancient Empires.* New York: Newsweek Books, 1970.

You may use a List of Works Cited instead of a Bibliography. Find out which format your teacher prefers.

Editing and Proofreading

Proofread your research report and correct errors in grammar.

Focus on Citations: Review your draft against your notes to be sure you have correctly quoted your sources. In addition, check that numbers, dates, and page references are correct.

Publishing and Presenting

Consider one of these ways to share your writing:

Share your report with a large audience. Find out which organizations (historical societies, fan clubs, or other groups) might be interested in your topic. Submit a copy of your report to one of these groups for publication in a newsletter or on a Web site.

Deliver an impromptu speech. Now that you are knowledgeable about your topic, give an impromptu (unrehearsed) speech to your classmates. Describe your initial questions, your thesis, and what you found out as a result of your research. After you finish, answer questions from the audience.

Reflecting on Your Writing

Writer's Journal Jot down a few notes about writing a research report. You might begin by answering these questions:

- What was the most interesting thing you learned about your topic? Why?
- Which strategy for prewriting or drafting might you recommend to a friend? Why?

> *Prentice Hall Writing and Grammar Connection: Chapter 11*

Rubric for Self-Assessment

To assess your research report, use the following rubric.

Criteria	Rating Scale not very　　　　　very
Focus: How clearly do you state your main idea?	1　2　3　4　5
Organization: How clear and logical is your organization?	1　2　3　4　5
Support/Elaboration: How well do you use evidence to support your statements?	1　2　3　4　5
Style: How clearly do you present the sources you used for research?	1　2　3　4　5
Conventions: According to an accepted format, how complete and accurate are your citations?	1　2　3　4　5

Delivering an Instructional Presentation

In an **instructional presentation,** you organize and deliver information in order to have your audience learn something.

Consider Your Audience

To increase the effectiveness of your presentation, take the time to analyze your audience. A profile like the one shown can help you identify the interests, concerns, and knowledge level of your listeners. Use your answers to guide the words and details that you include.

Be Organized

Like an essay, the content of an instructional presentation should be logically organized. Organize your information in a way that suits the topic.

> **Audience Profile**
> - What is the average age of my audience?
> - What do they know about my topic?
> - What steps are necessary to understand this subject?
> - What details will be most interesting to my audience?
> - What background do I need to provide?

- **Chronological,** or time, order is good for explaining a process or for presenting a biography or history.
- **Point by point.** Put related details in groups such as "background" or "physical features."

Make an outline. Use an outline to organize your presentation into main sections and subsections. Refer to the outline while speaking.

Presentation

Practice beforehand. The best way to avoid "stage fright" is to practice in front of family and friends. Practicing will help you appear confident and knowledgeable in front of an audience.

- **Use appropriate sentences.** Save slang and sentence fragments for casual conversation. Speak in complete sentences that are grammatically correct. For dramatic impact, vary your sentences by mixing in short, powerful sentences with longer ones.
- **Use appropriate word choices.** Refer to the notes on your outline to accurately cite numbers, names, or quotations.

Gauge audience response. Use the reactions of your audience to make adjustments in tone, volume, and emphasis.

Activity **Give Instructions** Following the suggestions above, deliver a two-to-three-minute instructional presentation using a chronological organization.

Anne Frank: The Diary of a Young Girl

Anne Frank
Globe Fearon, 1992

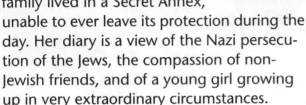

Nonfiction Anne Frank's diary records her family's life during two years of hiding from the Nazis. During these years, Anne's family lived in a Secret Annex, unable to ever leave its protection during the day. Her diary is a view of the Nazi persecution of the Jews, the compassion of non-Jewish friends, and of a young girl growing up in very extraordinary circumstances.

The Miracle Worker

William Gibson
Bantam Books, 1975

Drama This play is about the life of Helen Keller, a girl who was unable to see, hear, or speak, and whom everyone had just about given up trying to help. Helen is a miserable child until a teacher named Annie Sullivan enters her life. The struggle between Helen, who doesn't want to learn, and Annie, who is determined to teach her, is a bittersweet journey for the characters and the audience.

Pygmalion & My Fair Lady

George Bernard Shaw, Lerner and Lowe
Signet, 1980

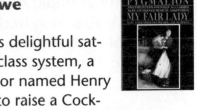

Drama In Shaw's delightful satire of the British class system, a language professor named Henry Higgins decides to raise a Cockney flower girl to dizzying heights in British society by teaching her how to speak the King's English. Lerner's musical adaptation of Shaw's classic play adds clever and memorable songs while retaining much of the original story.

Much Ado About Nothing

William Shakespeare
Signet, 1998

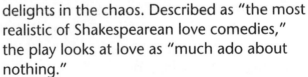

Drama A wonderfully funny play repeats the Shakespearean theme of the battle of the sexes. The plot is confusion after confusion for the characters, as the audience delights in the chaos. Described as "the most realistic of Shakespearean love comedies," the play looks at love as "much ado about nothing."

These titles are available in the Penguin/Prentice Hall Literature Library.
Consult your teacher before choosing one.

Think About It Miep Gies helped Anne Frank and her family hide in the attic of an office building during World War II. She was one of the thousands of Dutch citizens who bravely helped Jews hide from the Nazis. In this excerpt from her book, *Anne Frank Remembered,* Miep Gies describes welcoming back Otto Frank as a war refugee, learning of the fate of those who had hidden with him, and giving Anne's diary to him.

from

Anne Frank Remembered

Miep Gies
with Alison Leslie Gold

*H*enk flew home that day to tell me. It was June 3, 1945. He ran into the living room and grabbed me. "Miep, Otto Frank is coming back!"

My heart took flight. Deep down I'd always known that he would, that the others would, too.

Just then, my eye caught sight of a figure passing outside our window. My throat closed. I ran outside.

There was Mr. Frank himself, walking toward our door.

We looked at each other. There were no words. He was thin, but he'd always been thin. He carried a little bundle. My eyes swam. My heart melted. Suddenly, I was afraid to know more. I didn't want to know what had happened. I knew I would not ask.

We stood facing each other, speechless. Finally, Frank spoke.

"Miep," he said quietly. "Miep, Edith is not coming back."

My throat was pierced. I tried to hide my reaction to his thunderbolt. "Come inside," I insisted.

▲ The author, Miep Gies, shown with Otto Frank (center) and a co-worker, shortly before the Franks went into hiding.

He went on. "But I have great hope for Margot and Anne."

"Yes. Great hope," I echoed encouragingly. "Come inside."

He still stood there. "Miep, I came here because you and Henk are the ones closest to me who are still here."

I grabbed his bundle from his hand. "Come, you stay right here with us. Now, some food. You have a room here with us for as long as you want."

He came inside. I made up a bedroom for him, and put everything we had into a fine meal for him. We ate. Mr. Frank told us he had ended up in Auschwitz. That was the last time he'd seen Edith, Margot, and Anne. The men had been separated from the women immediately. When the Russians liberated the camp in January, he had been taken on a very long trip to Odessa. Then from there to Marseille by ship, and at last, by train and truck to Holland.

from *Anne Frank Remembered* ■ 907

He told us these few things in his soft voice. He spoke very little, but between us there was no need for words.

* * *

Mr. Frank settled in with Henk and me. Right away, he came back to the office and took his place again as the head of the business. I know he was relieved to have something to do each day. Meanwhile, he began exploring the network of information on Jews in the camps—the refugee agencies, the daily lists, the most crucial word-of-mouth information—trying everything to get news about Margot and Anne.

When Auschwitz was liberated, Otto Frank had gone right away to the women's camp to find out about his wife and children. In the chaos and desolation of the camps, he had learned that Edith had died shortly before the liberation.

He had also learned that in all likelihood, Margot and Anne had been transferred to another camp, along with Mrs. van Daan. The camp was called Bergen-Belsen, and was quite a distance from Auschwitz. That was as far as his trail had gone so far, though. Now he was trying to pick up the search.

As to the other men, Mr. Frank had lost track of Albert Dussel. He had no idea what had happened to him after the transit camp of Westerbork. He had seen with his own eyes Mr. van Daan on his way to be gassed. And Peter van Daan had come to visit Frank in the Auschwitz infirmary. Mr. Frank knew that right before the liberation of the camp, the Germans had taken groups of prisoners with them in their retreat. Peter had been in one of these groups.

> *" Mr. Frank held high hopes for the girls, because Bergen-Belsen was not a death camp. "*

Otto Frank had begged Peter to try to get into the infirmary himself, but Peter couldn't or wouldn't. He had last been seen going off with the retreating Germans into the snow-covered countryside. There was no further news about him.

Mr. Frank held high hopes for the girls, because Bergen-Belsen was not a death camp. There were no gassings there. It was a work camp—filled with hunger and disease, but with no apparatus for liquidation. Because Margot and Anne had been sent to the camp later than most other inmates they were relatively healthy. I too lived on hope for Margot and Anne. In some deep part of me, like a rock, I counted on their survival and their safe return to Amsterdam.

Mr. Frank had written for news to several Dutch people who he had learned had been in Bergen-Belsen. Through word of mouth people were being reunited every day. Daily, he waited for answers to his letters and for the new lists of survivors to be released and posted. Every time there was a knock at the door or footfalls on the steps, all our hearts would stand still. Perhaps Margot and Anne had found their way back home, and we could see them with our own eyes at last. Anne's sixteenth birthday was coming on June 12. Perhaps, we hoped, . . . but then the birthday came and went, and still no news.

* * *

*O*ne morning, Mr. Frank and I were alone in the office, opening mail. He was standing beside me, and I was sitting at my desk. I was vaguely aware of the sound of a letter being slit open. Then, a moment of silence. Something made me look away from my mail. Then, Otto Frank's voice, toneless, totally crushed: "Miep."

My eyes looked up at him, seeking out his eyes.

"Miep." He gripped a sheet of paper in both his hands. "I've gotten a letter from the nurse in Rotterdam. Miep, Margot and Anne are not coming back."

We stayed there like that, both struck by lightning, burnt thoroughly through our hearts, our eyes fixed on each other's. Then Mr. Frank walked toward his office and said in that defeated voice, "I'll be in my office."

I heard him walk across the room and down the hall, and the door closed.

I sat at my desk utterly crushed. Everything that had happened before, I could somehow accept. Like it or not, I had to accept it. But this, I could not accept. It was the one thing I'd been sure would not happen.

I heard the others coming into the office. I heard a door opening and a voice chattering. Then, good-morning greetings and coffee cups. I reached into the drawer on the side of my desk and took out the papers that had been waiting there for Anne for nearly a year now. No one, including me, had touched them. Now Anne was not coming back for her diary.

I took out all the papers, placing the little red-orange checkered diary on top, and carried everything into Mr. Frank's office.

Frank was sitting at his desk, his eyes murky with shock. I held out the diary and the papers to him. I said, "Here is your daughter Anne's legacy to you."

I could tell that he recognized the diary. He had given it to her just over three years before, on her thirteenth birthday, right before going into hiding. He touched it with the tips of his fingers. I pressed everything into his hands; then I left his office, closing the door quietly.

Shortly afterward, the phone on my desk rang. It was Mr. Frank's voice. "Miep, please see to it that I'm not disturbed." he said.

"I've already done that," I replied.

* * *

*T*he second printing of the diary sold out and another printing was planned. Mr. Frank was approached with the idea of permiting the diary to be translated and published abroad. He was against it at first, but then he succumbed to the pressure on him to allow the diary a more widespread audience.

Again and again, he'd say to me, "Miep, you must read Anne's writing. Who would have imagined what went on in her quick little mind?" Otto was never discouraged by my continuing refusal. He would always wait awhile and then ask me again.

Finally, I gave in to his insistence. I said, "All right, I will read the diary, but only when I'm totally alone."

The next time I was totally alone, on a warm day, I took the second printing of the diary, went to my room, and shut the door.

With awful fear in my heart, I opened the book and turned to the first page.

And so I began to read.

I read the whole diary without stopping. From the first word, I heard Anne's voice come back to speak to me from where she had gone. I lost track of time. Anne's voice tumbled out of the book, so full of life, moods, curiosity, feelings. She was no longer gone and destroyed. She was alive again in my mind.

I read to the very end. I was surprised by how much had happened in hiding that I'd known nothing about. Immediately, I was thankful that I hadn't read the diary after the arrest, during the final nine months of the occupation, while it had stayed in my desk drawer right beside me every day. Had I read it, I would have had to burn the diary because it would have been too dangerous for people about whom Anne had written.

When I had read the last word, I didn't feel the pain I'd anticipated. I was glad I'd read it at last. The emptiness in my heart was eased. So much had been lost, but now Anne's voice would never be lost. My young friend had left a remarkable legacy to the world.

But always, every day of my life, I've wished that things had been different. That even had Anne's diary been lost to the world, Anne and the others might somehow have been saved.

Not a day goes by that I do not grieve for them.

Meet the Author

Miep Gies (b. 1909) was born in Vienna, Austria. In 1922 she moved to Amsterdam and got a job working for Otto Frank. When the Franks were forced into hiding in 1942, Gies immediately offered her support. Despite her efforts, the Franks were discovered and sent to concentration camps after two years in hiding.

Readings in Nonfiction
Talk About It

Use these questions to guide a discussion of the excerpt.

1. **(a)** When he first returns to Amsterdam, what news does Mr. Frank bring of the other occupants of the secret annex?
   (b) Why is it so difficult for Miep and Otto Frank to find out about the rest of the Frank family?

2. With a small group, consider the following questions:
   • Why do you think Miep waited so long to read the diary?
   • What does this selection add to your understanding of Anne Frank's life and legacy?

Themes in
American Stories

Unit 6 Overview

Introduction:
Exploring Themes
in the American Stories

Part 1: Summarize

Part 2: Purpose for
Reading

Introduction:
Themes in American Stories

Lan Samantha Chang
Talks About Storytelling

Lan Samantha
Chang

We share our lives through the stories we tell. Long before our ancestors invented reading or writing, they were telling stories.

▲ Lan Samantha Chang has received critical acclaim for her work about the Chinese American immigrant experience.

The Oral Tradition Is Alive and Well

Despite our reliance on written literature, media, and the Internet, we continue to pass down our experience through the spoken word. As a matter of fact, every culture has an **oral tradition,** including legends, myths, and folk tales. These stories help us understand our past, describe our present, and communicate our beliefs.

I was born and raised in a small city in the American Midwest, but my mother and father grew up in China. As a young girl, I relied on my parents' oral descriptions of the "old country" in order to understand our family history and this mysterious country where I'd never been.

I believe this immigrant background inspired me to read and write fiction that incorporates the spoken voice. For example, I've always loved fairy tales. The words "Once upon a time" put me under a spell because of their evocation of another wonderful, mysterious place and time.

▼ **Critical Viewing** Which details in this picture help to illustrate the fact that stories are important to people in every culture? **[Interpret]**

Authors Can Learn From Storytellers

I was excited to discover this quotation, in which Latin American novelist Gabriel García Márquez reveals that his inspiration for creating his most famous novel was actually his storytelling grandmother!

García Márquez spent five long, difficult years struggling to achieve the correct "tone" for the book. Then, he suddenly recalled a childhood experience of watching and listening to his grandmother relate, with "complete naturalness," her stories filled with strange and unbelievable events. He learned to write his own novels with a similar tone, a matter-of-fact way of narrating fantastic events that has become part of his distinct literary style.

> [T]he tone that I eventually used in One Hundred Years of Solitude . . . *was based on the way my grandmother used to tell her stories. She told things that sounded supernatural and fantastic, but she told them with complete naturalness.*
>
> **from an interview**
> —*Gabriel García Márquez*

All writers can learn a lot from storytellers. The best fiction creates a strong and intimate voice, speaking directly to the heart of the reader. When I write, I try to hear the words in my mind before I put them on the page. I tell the story to myself, silently, and when I am finished with a draft, I almost always test the passage by reading it aloud.

More About the Author

Lan Samantha **Chang** (b. 1965)

Lan Samantha Chang grew up in Appleton, Wisconsin. Since there were few other Chinese or Chinese Americans close by, there was no community to provide contact with Chinese culture. She did, however, learn something about her background from her parents and her grandmother. The desire to learn even more about the past led Chang toward writing. "I hungered for the past, because it was the only clue to understanding the parents I loved deeply."

Fast Facts

▶ Chang gave a violin recital when she was eleven.
▶ All four daughters in the Chang family learned to be good Chinese cooks.

Learning About Themes in American Stories

The American Folk Tradition

The American folk tradition is a rich collection of literature that grew out of the **oral tradition**—stories originally told at festivals and around campfires, rather than shared in print. Here are characteristics of the oral tradition:

Theme is a central idea, message, or insight that is revealed within a story. Sometimes a theme is called **universal,** which means that the theme can be seen in stories in many different cultures and throughout many different time periods.

Heroes and **heroines** are larger-than-life figures whose virtues and deeds are often celebrated in stories from the oral tradition.

Storytelling Techniques Before stories were written down, they were told orally. To enliven them they used these devices:

- **Hyperbole:** exaggeration or overstatement, either for comic effect or to express heightened emotion
- **Personification:** human characteristics or personality given to nonhuman subjects, such as animals or natural elements
- **Idioms:** expressions—such as "It's raining cats and dogs!"—that develop in a language, region, community, or class of people that cannot be understood literally

American folk literature is a living tradition that is constantly being updated and adapted. Many of its subjects and heroes are present in contemporary American movies, sports heroes, even politics.

The American Folk Tradition in Print

Although stories in the oral tradition have similar characteristics, the genre can be divided into categories, based on purposes and styles.

Myths are tales that explain the actions of gods, goddesses, and the heroes who interact with them. Every culture has its own collection of myths, or **mythology.** These stories often attempt to explain the causes of natural phenomena.

- **Fables** are brief stories that often feature animals that act like humans. Fables usually end with a moral that is directly stated.

- **Tall tales** are types of folk tales that use **hyperbole**—deliberate exaggeration for comic effect. These tales often involve a hero who performs impossible feats. Tall tales are a form of **legend**—stories based on fact that become less true with each retelling.

Epics are long narrative poems about larger-than-life heroes who engage in dangerous journeys, or **quests,** that are important to the history of a nation or culture.

In the second half of this unit, you will encounter a different type of American folk hero. These are heroes—immigrants, soldiers, farmers, civil rights workers—who rise above difficult historical circumstances to take their place alongside the earlier heroes of the American landscape.

▼ Critical Viewing
What makes this scene a good setting for a fable? **[Speculate]**

Check Your Understanding

For each item, indicate which term best applies.

1. a long narrative poem about a Spanish conquistador
   a. tall tale   **b.** epic

2. a story about a cowboy who rides a tornado
   a. epic   **b.** tall tale

3. a story about an ant who prepares for winter and warns the bees to do the same

   a. fable   **b.** myth

From the Author's Desk
Lan Samantha Chang Introduces "Water Names"

My grandmother was born in Shanghai in 1910. She was the spoiled only daughter in a family of nine sons. Looking at old photographs, I am always astonished to see what a beautiful girl she was, with a long waterfall of black hair that reached her knees.

The Real-Life Inspiration for the Grandmother

Of course, by the time I knew her, my grandmother was no longer young, beautiful, or spoiled. She lived with my family in Appleton, Wisconsin, where she cooked and cleaned and helped raise me and my three sisters. To me, she was a deep source of knowledge, a mysterious link to China. In this way, she was the inspiration for the **character** of the grandmother in "Water Names."

A Theme in the Story

Both written and oral literature attempt to explore **universal questions** that cannot be answered. They capture the great **themes** of human consciousness, mysteries that exist no matter how much history has been recorded and studied.

One theme in "Water Names" has to do with the nature of desire. The story poses the question: Why do we follow our desires even though they can sometimes lead to trouble?

How Imagery Relates to Theme

Another theme in "Water Names" is displacement. The girls grew up surrounded by farmland and have never seen the water country where the grandmother was born and raised.

And so the grandmother uses **imagery** to form a picture of the Yangtze delta in her granddaughters' minds. She compares the sound of the prairie crickets to that of water. By doing this, she creates a link between the river country, with its wide, wet deltas, and the stretch of land surrounding the family, covered with "waves of grass."

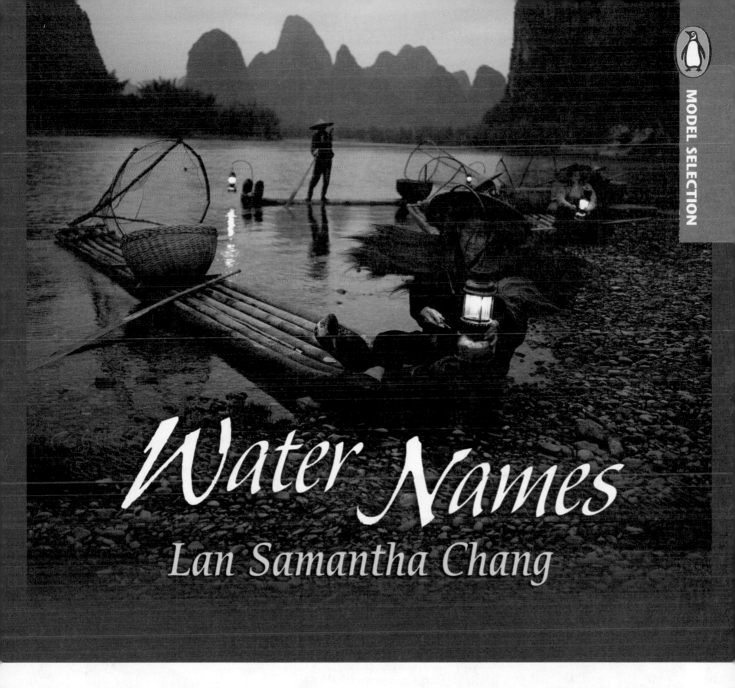

Water Names

Lan Samantha Chang

Summertime at dusk we'd gather on the back porch, tired and sticky from another day of fierce encoded quarrels, nursing our mosquito bites and frail dignities, sisters in name only. At first we'd pinch and slap each other, fighting for the best—least ragged—folding chair. Then we'd argue over who would sit next to our grandmother. We were so close together on the tiny porch that we often pulled our own hair by mistake. Forbidden to bite, we planted silent toothmarks on each others' wrists. We ignored the bulk of house behind us, the

▲ **Critical Viewing**
The grandmother in this story comes from a place like the one shown. What role does the water play in the lives of the people who live here? **[Speculate]**

yard, the fields, the darkening sky. We even forgot about our grandmother. Then suddenly we'd hear her old, dry voice, very close, almost on the backs of our necks.

"*Xiushila!* Shame on you. Fighting like a bunch of chickens."

And Ingrid, the oldest, would freeze with her thumb and forefinger right on the back of Lily's arm. I would slide my hand away from the end of Ingrid's braid. Ashamed, we would shuffle our feet while Waipuo calmly found her chair.

On some nights she sat with us in silence. But on some nights she told us stories, "just to keep up your Chinese," she said.

Lan Samantha Chang
Author's Insight
In traditional China, brides left their family and became members of the husband's family. In Chinese, *Waipuo* literally means "outside old woman." So *Waipuo* was my mother's mother, the old woman from "outside" my father's family.

Literature in Context | Geography Connection

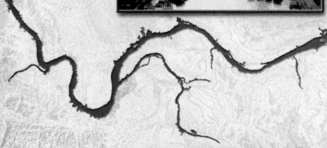

With boats crowding the harbor, Shanghai is known as the gateway to the Yangtze. ▶

The Long River

The Yangtze travels 3,964 miles from its headwaters in the Kunlun Mountains to its mouth in the East China Sea, near Shanghai. Its path is shown in blue on this satellite photo.

The walls of the famous and breathtaking gorges along the Yangtze can reach up as high as 3,000 feet. ▶

▲ Its banks are home to rice paddies and to manufacturing businesses. The third longest river in the world gets its name from the Chinese word meaning "Long River."

Connect to the Literature Do you think it was hard for the grandmother to adjust to life in the Midwest after growing up near the Yangtze River? Explain.

"In these prairie crickets I often hear the sound of rippling waters, of the Yangtze River," she said. "Granddaughters, you are descended on both sides from people of the water country, near the mouth of the great Chang Jiang, as it is called, where the river is so grand and broad that even on clear days you can scarcely see the other side.

"The Chang Jiang runs four thousand miles, originating in the Himalaya mountains where it crashes, flecked with gold dust, down steep cliffs so perilous and remote that few humans have ever seen them. In central China, the river squeezes through deep gorges, then widens in its last thousand miles to the sea. Our ancestors have lived near the mouth of this river, the ever-changing delta, near a city called Nanjing, for more than a thousand years."

"A thousand years," murmured Lily, who was only ten. When she was younger she had sometimes burst into nervous crying at the thought of so many years. Her small insistent fingers grabbed my fingers in the dark.

"Through your mother and I you are descended from a line of great men and women. We have survived countless floods and seasons of ill-fortune because we have the spirit of the river in us. Unlike mountains, we cannot be powdered down or broken apart. Instead, we run together, like raindrops. Our strength and spirit wear down mountains into sand. But even our people must respect the water."

She paused. "When I was young, my own grandmother once told me the story of Wen Zhiqing's daughter. Twelve hundred years ago the civilized parts of China still lay to the north, and the Yangtze valley lay unspoiled. In those days lived an ancestor named Wen Zhiqing, a resourceful man, and proud. He had been fishing for many years with trained cormorants, which you girls of course have never seen. Cormorants are sleek, black birds with long, bending necks which the fishermen fitted with metal rings so the fish they caught could not be swallowed. The birds would perch on the side of the old wooden boat and dive into the river." We had only known blue swimming pools, but we tried to imagine the sudden shock of cold and the plunge, deep into water.

MODEL SELECTION

Lan Samantha Chang
Author's Insight
Through the length and shape of Waipuo's long sentence, I tried to mimic the twisting, turning movement of the Chang Jiang's path.

Reading Check

According to Waipuo, what gave her and her family strength?

"Now, Wen Zhiqing had a favorite daughter who was very beautiful and loved the river. She would beg to go out on the boat with him. This daughter was a restless one, never contented with their catch, and often she insisted they stay out until it was almost dark. Even then, she was not satisfied. She had been spoiled by her father, kept protected from the river, so she could not see its danger. To this young woman, the river was as familiar as the sky. It was a bright, broad road stretching out to curious lands. She did not fully understand the river's depths.

"One clear spring evening, as she watched the last bird dive off into the blackening waters, she said, 'If only this catch would bring back something more than another fish!'

▼ Critical Viewing
How does this man's relationship with the birds pictured compare or contrast with the relationship described in the story? [Connect]

"She leaned over the side of the boat and looked at the water. The stars and moon reflected back at her. And it is said that the spirits living underneath the water looked up at her as well. And the spirit of a young man who had drowned in the river many years before saw her lovely face."

We had heard about the ghosts of the drowned, who wait forever in the water for a living person to pull down instead. A faint breeze moved through the mosquito screens and we shivered.

"The cormorant was gone for a very long time," Waipuo said, "so long that the fisherman grew puzzled. Then, suddenly, the bird emerged from the waters, almost invisible in the night. Wen Zhiqing grasped his catch, a very large fish, and guided the boat back to shore. And when Wen reached home, he gutted the fish and discovered, in its stomach, a valuable pearl ring."

"From the man?" said Lily.

"Sshh, she'll tell you."

Waipuo ignored us. "His daughter was delighted that her wish had been fulfilled. What most excited her was the idea of an entire world like this, a world where such a beautiful ring would be only a bauble![1] For part of her had always longed to see faraway things and places. The river had put a spell on her heart. In the evenings she began to sit on the bank, looking at her own reflection in the water. Sometimes she said she saw a handsome young man looking back at her. And her yearning for him filled her heart with sorrow and fear, for she knew that she would soon leave her beloved family.

"'It's just the moon,' said Wen Zhiqing, but his daughter shook her head. 'There's a kingdom under the water,' she said. 'The prince is asking me to marry him. He sent the ring as an offering to you.' 'Nonsense,' said her father, and he forbade her to sit by the water again.

"For a year things went as usual, but the next spring there came a terrible flood that swept away almost everything. In the middle of a torrential rain, the family noticed that the daughter was missing. She had taken advantage of the confusion to hurry to the river and visit her beloved. The family searched for days but they never found her."

Her smoky, rattling voice came to a stop.

"What happened to her?" Lily said.

---

1. **bauble** (bô′ bəl) *n.* trinket.

Themes in American Stories
Oral Tradition
Elements of the supernatural, like the spirits mentioned here, often appear in tales from the oral tradition.

Lan Samantha Chang
Author's Insight
In my study of the elements of fairy tales, I noticed that their language combines the very vague ("Once upon a time . . . ") with the very specific ("a juniper tree"). Here is my specific object: "'a valuable pearl ring.'"

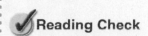
Reading Check

What did Wen find in the stomach of a fish he caught?

MODEL SELECTION

"It's okay, stupid," I told her. "She was so beautiful that she went to join the kingdom of her beloved. Right?"

"Who knows?" Waipuo said. "They say she was seduced by a water ghost. Or perhaps she lost her mind to desiring."

"What do you mean?" asked Ingrid.

"I'm going inside," Waipuo said, and got out of her chair with a creak. A moment later the light went on in her bedroom window. We knew she stood before the mirror, combing out her long, wavy silver-gray hair, and we imagined that in her youth she too had been beautiful.

We sat together without talking. We had gotten used to Waipuo's abruptness, her habit of creating a question and leaving without answering it, as if she were disappointed in the question itself. We tried to imagine Wen Zhiqing's daughter. What did she look like? How old was she? Why hadn't anyone remembered her name?

While we weren't watching, the stars had emerged. Their brilliant pinpoints mapped the heavens. They glittered over us, over Waipuo in her room, the house, and the small city we lived in, the great waves of grass that ran for miles around us, the ground beneath as dry and hard as bone.

Lan Samantha Chang
Author's Insight
Actually, my own grandmother had short, wavy silver-gray hair. Like many traditionally raised Chinese women, she had her knee-length hair cut in the early 1930s in an effort to keep up with modern styles.

▼ **Critical Viewing**
Which part of Waipuo's story does this image suggest?
[Connect]

From the Author's Desk
Lan Samantha Chang's Insights Into "Water Names"

Q. **What is the meaning of the story's title, "Water Names"?**

A. In an early draft of the story, I gave the sisters Chinese names meaning "rain," "ripples," and "a stream." Later I gave them English names, but I decided to keep the idea of "water names" in the story by using their question about Wen Zhiqing's missing daughter, whose name was lost with her in the flood.

Q. **Is the grandmother using her stories to teach the narrator and her sisters a lesson?**

A. Through her story, the grandmother tries to hand down to her granddaughters a vanished way of life. She is both successful and unsuccessful in this regard. For example, she cautions the girls against desire. But her story only leaves the girls more curious about the nature of desire.

StudentCorner

Q. **What inspired you to write this story?**
—Hannah Williams, Tuscola, Illinois

A. Like Ingrid, Lily, and the narrator, I grew up in a family of Midwestern sisters. On summer evenings, we used to sit on the back porch and listen to the crickets. Like many young writers, I could often feel my imagination slipping out beyond my home and family. When I wrote this story, I tried to re-create the feeling of being close to family but also traveling far away in time and place.

 Writing Workshop: *Work in Progress*

Multimedia Report

For a multimedia report you may develop, choose a subject related to an event in the news. Jot down a few sources you might use to find information about this subject, including newspapers, the Internet, television reports, or reference material. Save this Source List in your portfolio.

Thinking About the Selection

1. **Respond:** Do you think this story develops a good sense of the storyteller's family history? Why or why not?

2. **(a) Recall:** What qualities does the grandmother Waipuo associate with the Chang Jiang, or the Yangtze?
   (b) Infer: How do the descendants of the water country feel about the great river?

3. **(a) Recall:** In a chart like the one shown, use the second column to list the different ways to explain two unusual events in the story. **(b) Interpret:** In the third column, explain why you agree or disagree with each explanation. **(c) Discuss:** Share your chart with a partner, and choose the most persuasive explanation of each event to share with the class.

Event	Explanation	Why You Agree or Disagree
Face in the water		
Ring in the fish		

Reviewing Themes in American Stories

4. **(a)** What do you think is the **theme** of this story? **(b)** What story details support your idea?

5. Identify at least two examples of storytelling techniques or details in the story that are part of the **oral tradition**.

Research the Author

Working with a group and using the story that Waipuo relates as a model, plan a **storytelling hour** devoted to retelling a variety of Chinese folk tales. Follow these steps:

- Consult the library's card catalog and Web site for collections of Chinese folklore to choose stories that will interest the class.
- Have each group member select one tale to retell.
- Invite reaction from the class.

QuickReview

Story at a Glance
Waipuo tells her grandchildren a tale about a fisherman, his daughter, and the importance of water to all of them.

Go Online
Assessment
For: Self-test
Visit: www.PHSchool.com
Web Code: ena-6601

Oral Tradition: the practice of passing stories from one generation to the next by word of mouth

Theme: central idea, message, or insight that is revealed within a story

Skills You Will Learn

Literature You Will Read

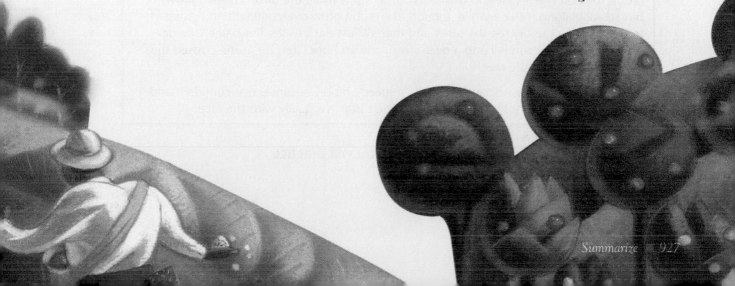

Reading: Summarizing

> A **summary** is a short statement that presents the main ideas and most important points in a piece of writing.

Skills and Strategies You Will Learn in Part 1

In Part 1, you will learn

- to **reread** to identify main ideas or events to write a **summary** (p. 930)
- to **summarize** the **author's message** (p. 944)
- to **use graphics** to help you **organize main ideas** or events to write a **summary** (p. 948)

Using the Skills and Strategies in Part 1

In Part 1, you will learn to reread to identify main ideas and then to organize these ideas to write a summary. You will also practice summarizing an author's message. A summary of a story should be as short as possible, so it is important to focus on only the most important events as you summarize.

Read the following well-known folk tale. Then, compare it to the brief summary that follows.

One summer day, a speedy rabbit challenged a slow turtle to a race. At the start, the rabbit took off like a shot and was soon out of sight, while the turtle crawled slowly but steadily along. After a while, though, the rabbit grew overconfident and stopped to rest. "I'll wait until I see the turtle and then I'll just dash to the finish line," he decided. The rabbit soon fell into a deep sleep, and an hour later, the turtle crossed the finish line and won the race.

Summary: In a race with a slow turtle, a speedy rabbit becomes overconfident and stops to rest. The rabbit falls asleep, and the turtle eventually wins the race.

As you read the literature in this part, you will practice summarizing.

Academic Vocabulary: Words for Discussing Summaries

The following words will help you write and talk about summarizing as you read the selections in this unit.

Word Root	Definition	Example Sentence
essential *adj.*	necessary	A summary should include only the *essential* ideas in a text.
extract *v.*	to deduce; to obtain	I *extracted* only the important ideas.
organized *v.*	arranged in a logical order	The details of a summary should be *organized* in a way that makes sense.
disorganized *adj.*	not arranged in a logical order	A *disorganized* summary will not help you remember key ideas.
sequence *n.*	order	Retell important plot events in the correct *sequence*.

Vocabulary Skill: Prefixes

> A **prefix** is one or more syllables joined to the beginning of a word or root to change its meaning and to form a new word.

In Part 1, you will learn

- the prefix *non-* (p. 942)
- the prefix *dis-* (p. 942)
- the prefixes *un-/an-/a-* (p. 968)

Prefixes that mean "not" can change a word into its antonym. This ability to change words to their opposites is useful in writing and discussing ideas about literature. The following prefixes usually change words to their antonyms.

Activity For each prefix in the chart at right, write one more example word and give its meaning. Use a dictionary, if necessary.

Prefix	Meaning	Example Word
dis-	not	disorganized
non-	not	nonessential
un-/an-/a-	not	unacceptable

These skills will help you become a better reader. Practice them with either "Why the Waves Have Whitecaps" (p. 932) or "Coyote Steals the Sun and Moon" (p. 937).

Reading Skill

A **summary** is a short statement that presents the key ideas and main points of a text. It is much shorter than the original work. Summarizing helps you remember the text by focusing on the most important information. Follow these steps to summarize a section of text or a whole work.

- **Reread to identify main events or ideas** in the passage or work. Then, jot them down.
- Organize your notes by putting main events or points in order and crossing off minor details that are not important for an overall understanding of the work.
- Finally, summarize by restating the major events or ideas in as few words as possible.

Keep in mind that, since summaries remove most of the detail, reading a summary can never replace the experience of reading the complete book, play, or article.

Literary Analysis

A **myth** is an ancient tale that presents the beliefs or customs of a culture. Every culture has its own **mythology**, or collection of myths. Myths explain events in nature or in a people's history. Often, they describe the actions of gods or other supernatural beings. Many myths also involve animal characters or natural forces with human qualities. To understand myths, it is helpful to understand the culture from which they come. Use a chart like this one to trace the connection between story and culture.

Detail	Cultural Connection
Prometheus steals fire from Zeus, king of the gods, and gives it to humans.	To ancient Greeks, fire was essential for cooking, forging weapons, and providing warmth.

Vocabulary Builder

Coyote Steals the Sun and Moon

- **sacred** (sā´ krəd) *adj.* considered holy; related to religious ceremonies (p. 938) *The temple was a <u>sacred</u> space for ancient Greeks.*

- **pestering** (pes´ tər iŋ) *n.* constant bothering (p. 939) *After ten minutes of <u>pestering</u>, Jan got permission to go to the movies.*

- **shriveled** (shriv´ əld) *v.* dried up; shrank and wrinkled (p. 939) *The hot sun <u>shriveled</u> the grass until it was dry and brown.*

- **pursuit** (pər sōōt´) *n.* the act of chasing in order to catch (p. 939) *The police car sped off in <u>pursuit</u> of the bank robber.*

Background

Waves "Why the Waves Have Whitecaps" is a myth that explains the natural phenomenon of whitecaps. There is, of course, a scientific explanation for the whitecaps on waves. Waves form when winds blow across the surface of water and transmit their energy to the water. As waves reach shallower water near the shore, the wave height increases until they topple over and break into water droplets. The droplets reflect light and appear as foamy whitecaps.

Connecting to the Literature

Reading/Writing Connection This myth explains the appearance of whitecaps by comparing them to something else. Write several sentences in which you describe waves by comparing them to something else. Use at least three of the following words: *approach, dissolve, persist, release, subside, transform.*

Meet the Author

Zora Neale **Hurston** (1891–1960)

Zora Neale Hurston was one of the first writers to recognize the richness of African American folk tales. Hurston grew up in the community of Eatonville, Florida. After moving north, she began writing with a group of authors in Harlem, New York, that included Langston Hughes.

Belated Recognition Hurston's talent was recognized by the founder of Barnard College, who arranged for her to study with the anthropologist Franz Boas. Part of Hurston's research involved traveling around the country and collecting folk tales. Without her research, many of these traditional stories might have been lost. Hurston was criticized during her lifetime for using local dialect in her stories. Only later was her genius recognized and her books widely circulated once again.

Fast Facts

▶ Hurston's most popular book is the novel *Their Eyes Were Watching God* (1937).

▶ She wrote a play, *Mule Bone,* with Langston Hughes.

For: More about the author
Visit: www.PHSchool.com
Web Code: ene-9602

Go **Online**
Author Link

Why the Waves Have WHITECAPS

ZORA NEALE HURSTON

De wind is a woman, and de water is a woman too. They useter[1] talk together a whole heap. Mrs. Wind useter go set down by de ocean and talk and patch and crochet.[2]

They was jus' like all lady people. They loved to talk about their chillun, and brag on 'em.

Mrs. Water useter say, "Look at *my* chillun! Ah got de biggest and de littlest in de world. All kinds of chillun. Every color in de world, and every shape!"

De wind lady bragged louder than de water woman:

"Oh, but Ah got mo' different chilluns than anybody in de world. They flies, they walks, they swims, they sings, they talks, they cries. They got all de colors from de sun. Lawd, my chillun sho is a pleasure. 'Tain't nobody got no babies like mine."

Mrs. Water got tired of hearin' 'bout Mrs. Wind's chillun so she got so she hated 'em.

One day a whole passle of her chillun come to Mrs. Wind and says: "Mama, wese thirsty. Kin we go git us a cool drink of water?"

She says, "Yeah chillun. Run on over to Mrs. Water and hurry right back soon."

When them chillun went to squinch they thirst Mrs. Water grabbed 'em all and drowned 'em.

When her chillun didn't come home, de wind woman got worried. So she went on down to de water and ast for her babies.

"Good evenin' Mis' Water, you see my chillun today?"

De water woman tole her, "No-oo-oo."

Mrs. Wind knew her chillun had come down to Mrs. Water's house, so she passed over de ocean callin' her chillun, and every time she call de white feathers would come up on top of de water. And dat's how come we got white caps on waves. It's de feathers comin' up when de wind woman calls her lost babies.

When you see a storm on de water, it's de wind and de water fightin' over dem chillun.

---

1. **useter** (yoo´ stə) *v.* dialect pronunciation of "used to."
2. **crochet** (krō shā´) *v.* to make needlework by looping thread with a hooked needle.

◀ **Critical Viewing** In this painting, which force would you say is stronger—the wind or the water? Explain. **[Make a Judgment]**

Reading Skill Summarize What causes the argument between Mrs. Wind and Mrs. Water?

Literary Analysis Mythology What human qualities does Mrs. Wind possess?

Apply the Skills

Why the Waves Have Whitecaps

Thinking About the Selection

1. **Respond:** What did you enjoy most about this myth? Why?
2. **(a) Recall:** What is the relationship between Mrs. Wind and Mrs. Water at the beginning of the story? **(b) Infer:** What changes their relationship?
3. **(a) Recall:** What qualities of their children do Mrs. Wind and Mrs. Water brag about? **(b) Connect:** How do these qualities relate to the real world?
4. **(a) Recall:** What happens to Mrs. Wind's children? **(b) Deduce:** What does this reveal about Mrs. Water?
5. **(a) Cause and Effect:** What are the results of the women's quarrel? **(b) Speculate:** Given the nature of the characters, could this story have had a different outcome? Explain.

Reading Skill

6. The characters' actions in this myth can be divided into three "scenes," or sections. Use a graphic organizer like the one shown to **summarize** the important events of each section.

Section	Summary
Mrs. Water and Mrs. Wind Compete	
Mrs. Water's Revenge	
Whitecaps and Storms	

7. Using your chart, summarize the entire story in as few sentences as possible, leaving out minor details.
8. Compare your summary with the story. What aspects of the original story would be lost if a reader only read your summary?

Literary Analysis

9. What is explained in this **myth**?
10. **(a)** In what ways do the characters in this myth act like human beings? **(b)** How might the experiences of the enslaved Africans have contributed to the portrayal of mothers losing their children?

QuickReview

Who's Who in the Story

Mrs. Wind: mythical being whose children are the birds

Mrs. Water: mythical being whose children are the fish

Assessment
For: Self-test
Visit: www.PHSchool.com
Web Code: ena-6602

Summary: a short statement that presents the key ideas and main points of a piece of writing

Myth: an ancient tale that explains events in nature or in a people's history

Vocabulary Builder

Practice Dialect is the form of language spoken in a particular region or by a particular group. The dialect in this myth reflects the language used by African Americans in the early nineteenth century. Rewrite each sentence, using standard English.

1. Mrs. Wind <u>useter</u> go <u>set</u> down by <u>de</u> ocean.

2. <u>Ah</u> got <u>mo'</u> different <u>chilluns</u> than anybody in <u>de</u> world.

3. When <u>them chillun</u> went to <u>squinch they</u> thirst Mrs. Water grabbed <u>'em</u> all.

Writing

Create your own **myth** to explain a natural phenomenon.

- First, choose a natural feature or event—for example, a rainbow, the seasons, or certain animal behaviors.
- Think of yourself as a storyteller. Entertain your audience with informal elements such as dialect, idioms, and humor. Use words that convey the personality of each character.

For *Grammar*, *Vocabulary*, and *Assessment*, see **Build Language Skills,** pages 942–943.

Extend Your Learning

Listening and Speaking Use the Internet and library references to gather information for an **oral presentation** about the African myths and folk tales that were brought to the Americas. Look for ways in which history and traditional stories have influenced African Americans. Answer these questions in your presentation:

- What African influences carry over to African American culture through art, music, myth, and food today?
- What new forms of literature, music, and art have resulted from the blending of African influences with other cultural traditions?

Research and Technology Choose a myth from the African or African American tradition that explains an event in the natural world. Then, research to find the scientific explanation for the same event. Write a **summary** that presents the main points of each explanation. Then, add an analysis of why each is important.

Zuni Myth

Background

Zuni Culture "Coyote Steals the Sun and Moon" is a Zuni myth. The Zuni belong to a group of Native American peoples known as the Pueblos. According to Zuni beliefs, the Great Spirit and other sacred beings guided the people to their home-lands, showed them how to plant corn, and taught them to live in peace with each other. Zuni myths often involve the sun and the moon, with daylight symbolizing life. Coyote, who is usually full of mischief, is a popular character in Zuni myths.

Connecting to the Literature

Reading/Writing Connection People in every culture have used myths to explain the world around them. Write a para-graph to explain why people might look for a way to under-stand the natural world through myth. Use at least three of these words: *comprehend, conceive, define, enable, illuminate.*

Review

For **Reading Skill, Literary Analysis,** and **Vocabulary Builder,** see page 930.

Meet the Authors

Richard **Erdoes** (b. 1912)
Alfonso **Ortiz** (1939–1997)

A shared love of Native American culture brought together Richard Erdoes and Alfonso Ortiz—two men who grew up worlds apart. They worked together on several collections of Native American stories, some of which "were jotted down at powwows, around campfires, even inside a moving car."

Richard Erdoes was born in Frankfurt, Germany, and edu-cated in Vienna, Berlin, and Paris. As a young boy, he became fascinated by American Indian culture. In 1940, he moved to the United States to escape Nazi rule and became a well-known author, photographer, and illustrator. He wrote several books on Native Americans and the American West.

Alfonso Ortiz was a Tewa Pueblo, born in New Mexico. He became a professor of anthropology at the University of New Mexico, and a leading expert on Pueblo culture.

Go Online Author Link

For: More about these authors
Visit: www.PHSchool.com
Web Code: ene-9603

Coyote Steals the Sun and Moon

ZUÑI MYTH

Retold by **Richard Erdoes** and **Alfonso Ortiz**

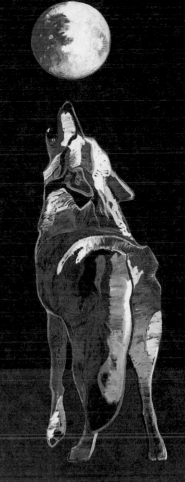

Coyote is a bad hunter who never kills anything. Once he watched Eagle hunting rabbits, catching one after another— more rabbits than he could eat. Coyote thought, "I'll team up with Eagle so I can have enough meat." Coyote is always up to something.

"Friend," Coyote said to Eagle, "we should hunt together. Two can catch more than one."

"Why not?" Eagle said, and so they began to hunt in partnership. Eagle caught many rabbits, but all Coyote caught was some little bugs.

At this time the world was still dark; the sun and moon had not yet been put in the sky. "Friend," Coyote said to Eagle, "no wonder I can't catch anything; I can't see. Do you know where we can get some light?"

"You're right, friend, there should be some light," Eagle said. "I think there's a little toward the west. Let's try and find it."

✓ Reading Check

What do Coyote and Eagle team up to do?

And so they went looking for the sun and moon. They came to a big river, which Eagle flew over. Coyote swam, and swallowed so much water that he almost drowned. He crawled out with his fur full of mud, and Eagle asked, "Why don't you fly like me?"

"You have wings; I just have hair," Coyote said. "I can't fly without feathers."

At last they came to a pueblo,[1] where the Kachinas happened to be dancing. The people invited Eagle and Coyote to sit down and have something to eat while they watched the <u>sacred</u> dances. Seeing the power of the Kachinas, Eagle said, "I believe these are the people who have light."

Coyote, who had been looking all around, pointed out two boxes, one large and one small, that the people opened whenever they wanted light. To produce a lot of light, they opened the lid of the big box, which contained the sun. For less light they opened the small box, which held the moon.

Coyote nudged Eagle. "Friend, did you see that? They have all the light we need in the big box. Let's steal it."

"You always want to steal and rob. I say we should just borrow it."

"They won't lend it to us."

"You may be right," said Eagle. "Let's wait till they finish dancing and then steal it."

After a while the Kachinas went home to sleep, and Eagle scooped up the large box and flew off. Coyote ran along trying to keep up, panting, his tongue hanging out. Soon he yelled up to Eagle, "Ho, friend, let me carry the box a little way."

"No, no," said Eagle, "you never do anything right."

He flew on, and Coyote ran after him. After a while Coyote shouted again: "Friend, you're my chief, and it's not right for you to carry the box; people will call me lazy. Let me have it."

---

1. pueblo (pweb´ lō) Native American settlement in the southwestern United States.

Culture Connection

Kachinas The Zuni and Hopi are Native American nations of the American Southwest. In both of these cultures, the Kachina dancers serve as links between the earthly world and the spirit world. Every year in colorful ceremonies, dancers perform, wearing masks representing various supernatural beings, or Kachinas.

The dancers play a central role in the religions of both cultures, where the blessings of the powerful spirits are sought every year for a good harvest and good fortune.

Connect to the Literature

What details in the story show that the Kachinas are powerful beings?

Vocabulary Builder
sacred (sā´ krəd) *adj.* considered holy; related to religious ceremonies

"No, no, you always mess everything up." And Eagle flew on and Coyote ran along.

So it went for a stretch, and then Coyote started again. "Ho, friend, it isn't right for you to do this. What will people think of you and me?"

"I don't care what people think. I'm going to carry this box."

Again Eagle flew on and again Coyote ran after him. Finally Coyote begged for the fourth time: "Let me carry it. You're the chief, and I'm just Coyote. Let me carry it."

Eagle couldn't stand any more <u>pestering</u>. Also, Coyote had asked him four times, and if someone asks four times, you'd better give him what he wants. Eagle said, "Since you won't let up on me, go ahead and carry the box for a while. But promise not to open it."

"Oh, sure, oh yes, I promise." They went on as before, but now Coyote had the box. Soon Eagle was far ahead, and Coyote lagged behind a hill where Eagle couldn't see him. "I wonder what the light looks like, inside there," he said to himself. "Why shouldn't I take a peek? Probably there's something extra in the box, something good that Eagle wants to keep to himself."

And Coyote opened the lid. Now, not only was the sun inside, but the moon also. Eagle had put them both together, thinking that it would be easier to carry one box than two.

As soon as Coyote opened the lid, the moon escaped, flying high into the sky. At once all the plants <u>shriveled</u> up and turned brown. Just as quickly, all the leaves fell off the trees, and it was winter. Trying to catch the moon and put it back in the box, Coyote ran in <u>pursuit</u> as it skipped away from him. Meanwhile the sun flew out and rose into the sky. It drifted far away, and the peaches, squashes, and melons shriveled up with cold.

Eagle turned and flew back to see what had delayed Coyote. "You fool! Look what you've done!" he said. "You let the sun and moon escape, and now it's cold." Indeed, it began to snow, and Coyote shivered. "Now your teeth are chattering," Eagle said, "and it's your fault that cold has come into the world."

It's true. If it weren't for Coyote's curiosity and mischief making, we wouldn't have winter; we could enjoy summer all the time.

Vocabulary Builder
pestering (pes´ tər iŋ) *n.* constant bothering

Literary Analysis
Mythology What human trait does Coyote show here?

Vocabulary Builder
shriveled (shriv´ əld) *v.* dried up; shrank and wrinkled

pursuit (pər soot´) *n.* the act of chasing in order to catch

Apply the Skills

Coyote Steals the Sun and Moon

Thinking About the Selection

1. **Respond:** Which character in the myth did you find the most entertaining? Explain.
2. **(a) Recall:** Why does Coyote want to team up with Eagle? **(b) Compare and Contrast:** How do Coyote and Eagle differ in their abilities and attitudes? **(c) Connect:** How do each character's actions reflect his attitude?
3. **(a) Recall:** Why do Eagle and Coyote want the Kachinas' box? **(b) Infer:** Why does Eagle agree to steal it?
4. **(a) Recall:** How does Coyote finally get the box? **(b) Infer:** What does Coyote's behavior tell you about his character?

Reading Skill

5. The characters' actions in this myth can be divided into four "scenes," or sections. Use a graphic organizer like the one shown to **summarize** the important events in each section.

Section	Summary
The Hunt	
At the Kachinas' Dance	
Running Away	
Coyote's Mistake	

6. Using your chart, summarize the entire story in as few sentences as possible, leaving out minor details.
7. Compare your summary with the original story. What aspects of the original story would be lost if a reader were only to read your summary?

Literary Analysis

8. **(a)** What element of nature does this myth explain? **(b)** What lesson, or moral, regarding nature does the myth contain?
9. What can you learn about Zuni culture and beliefs from studying this **myth**?
10. In what ways do the animal characters in this myth act like human beings?

QuickReview

Who's Who in the Story

Eagle: a chief of the animals, a good hunter

Coyote: a bad hunter who uses tricks to make up for his lack of skills

Go Online
Assessment
For: Self-test
Visit: www.PHSchool.com
Web Code: ena-6603

Summary: a short statement that presents the key ideas and main points of a piece of writing

Myth: An ancient tale that explains events in nature or in a people's history

Vocabulary Builder

Practice Write a sentence to answer each question, using a word from the vocabulary list for "Coyote Steals the Sun and Moon" on page 930.

1. How would you describe a sheriff chasing a fugitive?
2. What happens to garden plants after the first frost?
3. How would you describe an annoying younger child?
4. Where did ancient Greeks worship their gods?

Writing

Create your own **myth** to explain a natural phenomenon.
- First, choose a natural feature or event—for example, a rainbow, the seasons, or certain animal behaviors.
- Think of yourself as a storyteller. Entertain your audience with informal elements such as dialect, idioms, and humor. Use words that convey the personality of each character and create an appropriate mood.

For *Grammar, Vocabulary,* and *Assessment,* see **Build Language Skills,** pages 942–943.

Extend Your Learning

Listening and Speaking Use the Internet and library references to gather information for an **oral presentation** about Zuni culture. Look for ways in which traditional beliefs and Zuni history influence life and culture among the Zuni today. Answer these questions in your presentation:
- What cultural traditions continue among the Zuni today?
- How are the Zuni influenced by the cultures around them?

Research and Technology Choose a myth from a Native American culture that explains an event in the natural world. Then, research to find the scientific explanation for the same event. Write a **summary** that presents the main points of each explanation. Then, add an analysis of why each is important.

Build Language Skills

Vocabulary Skill

Prefixes The **prefix** *dis-* means "not" or "lack of." It is used to form **antonyms,** or words meaning the opposite of the original. For example, the opposite of *organized* is *disorganized.*

Non- is another prefix that reverses the word's definition. Adding *non-* to *essential* results in *nonessential,* which means "not necessary."

Practice Add the prefix *dis-* or *non-* to each word below. Then, write each new word in the correct sentence.

fiction   prove   satisfied

1. The scientist was able to _____ the old theory.

2. Biographies are _____ works.

3. I decided to rewrite my essay because I was _____ with it.

MorePractice

For more practice with sentence structure, see the Grammar Handbook, p. R31.

Grammar Lesson

Sentence Structure The four basic **sentence structures** are:

Sentence Structures	Examples
A **simple sentence** has a single independent clause and at least one subject and verb.	**The cat sleeps on the chair.** (1 subject, 1 verb)
A **compound sentence** consists of two or more independent clauses usually joined by a comma and a conjunction.	**The cat sleeps on the chair,** *and* **the dog sleeps on the floor.**
A **complex sentence** consists of one independent clause and one or more subordinate clauses.	**Jack,** who is my cousin, **raises golden retrievers,** which he exhibits at dog shows.
A **compound-complex sentence** consists of two or more independent clauses and one or more subordinate clauses.	During her exam, **Sue remembered she had to pick up her sister,** but **she wanted to finish writing first.**

Practice Change each of the following simple sentences into either a compound or a complex sentence. Identify the structure of the sentence you write.

1. Rebecca read the story.

2. The essay was disorganized.

3. David worked through the night.

4. We organized the fundraiser.

WG Prentice Hall Writing and Grammar Connection: Chapter 20, Section 2

Reading: Summarizing

Directions: *Read the selection. Then, answer the questions.*

The most spectacular range of fall foliage occurs in the northeastern United States and in eastern China. . . . European maples don't achieve the same flaming reds as their American relatives, which thrive on cold nights and sunny days. In Europe, the warm, humid weather turns the leaves brown or mildly yellow. Anthocyanin, the pigment that gives apples their red and turns leaves red or red-violet, is produced by sugars that remain in the leaf. . . . The fiercest colors occur in years when the fall sunlight is strongest and the nights are cool and dry. . . .

    —from *Why Leaves Turn Color in the Fall* by Diane Ackerman

1. Which is a main point of this paragraph?
   - **A** European fall weather is warm and humid.
   - **B** Weather affects leaf color.
   - **C** China has spectacular fall foliage.
   - **D** Some leaves turn brown or yellow.

2. What is another main point?
   - **A** Cool nights contribute to intense leaf colors.
   - **B** The same pigment gives color to both apples and leaves.
   - **C** Warmth produces yellow leaves.
   - **D** Europe and the United States have similar weather patterns.

3. Which details should be in a summary?
   - **A** China and the U.S. are large places.
   - **B** American maples are redder than those in Europe.
   - **C** Colorful autumns are cool and dry.
   - **D** Anthocyanin is produced by sugars.

4. Which is the best summary?
   - **A** The northeastern United States and China have the most colorful foliage.
   - **B** Fall leaves are most colorful with cold nights and warm days.
   - **C** Autumn leaves in the U.S. are more colorful than those in Europe.
   - **D** Cool weather turns U.S. trees red.

Timed Writing: Analysis [Interpretation]

Review "Coyote Steals the Sun and Moon" or "Why the Waves Have Whitecaps." Write a brief analysis of how dialect and word choice contribute to the humor. **(20 minutes)**

 ## Writing Workshop: *Work in Progress*

Multimedia Report

Use the work in your writing portfolio to review your notes and develop a thesis statement—one sentence that expresses the main idea of your report. Save this work in your writing portfolio.

Reading Informational Materials

Reviews

In Part 1, you are learning about summarizing works of literature. This skill is also useful in understanding and appreciating literary reviews. If you read "Why the Waves Have Whitecaps," you might be curious about the life of the story's author, Zora Neale Hurston. The following book review summarizes and offers an opinion on a published collection of Hurston's letters.

About Reviews

A **book review** gives an overall impression of a work of literature. Book reviews may appear in newspapers or magazines, on television, or online. Some book reviews are written by people with special knowledge about a book's topic or author. Most book reviews share these features:

- basic information such as author, price, and publisher
- a summary of the book
- an analysis of the book's strengths and weaknesses
- an overall opinion about the book's value

Reading Skill

An **author's message** is the overall statement the author wishes to communicate to the reader. Learning to recognize and summarize a book reviewer's message will help you to evaluate whether reading a book is worthwhile. You can find clues to help you summarize an author's message in the adjectives the author uses to describe the book as well as in the actual description of the book's contents. When you read, distinguish between a discussion of a book's plot, characters, and theme, and the reviewer's purpose, which is to communicate a message about the quality of the work.

Use a chart like the one shown to help you summarize an author's message.

Questions to Ask
- How does the author summarize the book's contents?
- Does the author use words with positive or negative connotations to describe the book?
- Does the author indicate who might enjoy the book?

→

Summarize Author's Message
This book is about _____ (subject). This book is _____ (worthwhile, not worthwhile) for_____(type of reader) because it _____.

A Life in Letters

Book Review by Zakia Carter

Zora Neale Hurston: A Life in Letters.

Edited by Carla Kaplan
Doubleday; October 2002; 896 pages

Within days of having *Zora Neale Hurston: A Life in Letters* in my possession, I was inspired to devote the total of my lunch hour to selecting beautiful blank cards and stationery, a fine ink pen and a book of stamps. By the end of the day, I had penned six letters, the old-fashioned way, to friends and relatives—something I haven't done since summer camp. In our haste to save time, we check our inboxes with an eagerness that was once reserved for that moment before pushing a tiny silver key into a mailbox door. E-mail has replaced paper and pen, so much so that the U.S. Postal Service is losing business. But the truth of the matter is, folks will neither salvage nor cherish e-mail as they might a handwritten letter.

And so *A Life in Letters* is a gift. It includes more than 500 letters and postcards written by Zora Neale Hurston over four decades. The 800-plus-page collection reveals more about this brilliant and complex woman than perhaps the entire body of her published works combined, including her notoriously unrevealing autobiography, *Dust Tracks on the Road.* Amazingly, the urgency and immediacy (typos and all) we associate with e-mail can also be found in Zora's letters. She writes to a veritable who's who in American history and society, including Langston Hughes, Carl Van Vechten, Charlotte

Book Review

In this paragraph, the reviewer lists specific reasons why the book is outstanding.

The reviewer briefly summarizes the book by describing its contents.

Osgood Mason, Franz Boas, Dorothy West and W.E.B. Du Bois among others, sometimes more than once or twice a day. In these, her most intimate writings, Zora comes to life.

While we are familiar with Zora the novelist, essayist, playwright and anthropologist, *A Life in Letters* introduces us to Zora the filmmaker; Zora the Barnard College undergrad and Columbia University student; Zora the two-time Guggenheim fellow; Zora the chicken specialist; Zora the thrice-married wife; and Zora the political pundit. Zora's letters are at times flip, ironic, heartbreaking and humorous. They are insightful, biting and candid as journal entries. One can only wish for responses to Zora's words, but the work is not incomplete without them.

A treasure trove of information, in addition to the annotated letters, a chronology of Zora's life, a glossary of the people, events, and institutions to which she refers in her letters, and a thorough bibliographical listing are generously included by editor Carla Kaplan. Each decade of writing is introduced by an essay on the social, political, and personal points of significance in Zora's life. Kaplan's is a fine, well edited and utterly revealing work of scholarship into the life of one of the greatest and often most misunderstood American writers. In many ways, *A Life in Letters* is, in fact, a long love letter for Zora. It is a reminder to salvage and cherish what should not be forgotten and an admonishment to write what you love on paper.

—Zakia Carter is an editor at Africana.com.

Most book reviews provide information about the reviewer's credentials. Reviewers are often experts on the subjects of the books they review.

Reading: Summarize Author's Message

Directions: *Choose the letter of the best answer to each question.*

1. According to the book reviewer, what is an important strength of *Zora Neale Hurston: A Life in Letters*?

   A short length

   B inclusion of Hurston's love letters

   C insightful essays preceding each decade of Hurston's life

   D inclusion of Hurston's award-winning paintings

2. Which statement best summarizes the reviewer's message?

   A The book could be longer.

   B The book includes letters to famous figures in American history.

   C The book is a treasure trove of information.

   D The book includes references to Hurston's college years.

3. Judging from the author's message, which of the following audiences would find this book worthwhile to read?

   A readers who have read Zora Neale Hurston's autobiography

   B readers who are interested in Zora Neale Hurston

   C readers who are doing research on Zora Neale Hurston

   D all of the above

Reading: Comprehension and Interpretation

Directions: *Write your answers on a separate sheet of paper.*

4. According to the reviewer, what types of information would you find in *Zora Neale Hurston: A Life in Letters* that you would not find in Hurston's other published works? **[Organizing]**

5. What might surprise a reader of this book who knows Hurston only as a novelist and story writer? **[Generating]**

6. Identify the ways in which reading *Zora Neale Hurston: A Life in Letters* had an impact on the reviewer. **[Analyzing]**

Timed Writing: Summary [Cognition]

Summarize the review. In your summary, include the author's main points and opinions. **(20 minutes)**

These skills will help you become a better reader. Practice them with either "Chicoria" (p. 950) and the excerpt from *The People, Yes* (p. 953) or "Brer Possum's Dilemma" (p. 959) and "John Henry" (p. 962).

Reading Skill

A **summary** is a short statement that presents the main points of a piece of writing. Since summaries leave out minor details, they provide a quick way to preview or review a much longer work. Before you summarize a work of literature, follow these two steps:

- First, determine whether each event or idea is important enough to be included in your summary.
- Then, **use graphics** to help you organize the major events or ideas. For example, if you are summarizing a story with chronological events, use a timeline to arrange events in order.

To summarize an essay or a poem, you might use a cluster diagram with the main idea in the center and supporting details in attached circles.

Literary Analysis

In the **oral tradition**, storytellers pass on legends, songs, folk tales, tall tales, and stories from generation to generation by word of mouth. Later, these stories and songs are written down, often in **dialect**—the language and grammar of a particular region. Reading these tales can provide a window into the values a culture considers important. As you read, use a chart like the one shown to note characteristics of the oral tradition.

Oral Tradition	Story Detail
Repetition and exaggeration	
Heroes who are brave, clever, or strong	
Animal characters that act like humans	
Dialect and informal speech	
Traditions of a culture	

Vocabulary Builder

Chicoria / *from* The People, Yes

- **cordially** (kôr´ jə lē) *adv.* warmly (p. 952) *The host welcomed his guests* cordially.

- **haughty** (hôt´ ē) *adj.* scornfully superior (p. 952) *The* haughty *prince was rude.*

- **cyclone** (sī´ klōn´) *n.* a violent, rotating windstorm; a tornado (p. 954) *The* cyclone *ripped the roofs from the houses.*

Brer Possum's Dilemma / John Henry

- **commenced** (kə menst´) *v.* started; began (p. 959) *The meeting* commenced *quietly, but then became noisy.*

- **pitiful** (pit´ i fəl) *adj.* arousing sympathy or pity (p. 961) *The wet, lost puppy was a* pitiful *sight.*

Connecting to the Literature

Reading/Writing Connection Every culture has its own folk tales and stories. Folktales pass on the values and beliefs of a culture by showing what that culture admires. Make a list of three folk tales you know. Then, write two sentences pointing out characteristics they share. Use at least three of the following words: *indicate, illustrate, enrich, enhance.*

Meet the Authors

José Griego y **Maestas** (b. 1949)
Rudolfo A. **Anaya** (b. 1937)

José Griego y Maestas and Rudolfo A. Anaya share a common love of old New Mexican folktales, or *cuentos.* It is a true partnership. Griego y Maestas finds and collects the tales, and Anaya translates them into English.

José Griego y Maestas is an expert in bilingual education and is the dean of instruction at Northern New Mexico Community College. He also loves telling stories.

Rudolfo Anaya, author of novels, poetry, and stories, is a celebrated figure in Hispanic literature. His novel *Bless Me, Ultima* is a well-loved classic. Anaya says, "I am an oral storyteller, but now I do it on the printed page."

Carl **Sandburg** (1878–1967)

Carl Sandburg was a journalist and historian as well as a poet and folklorist. As a young man, he worked as a truck driver and folk singer, getting to know American folk traditions. In the early 1900s, he was part of a writers' movement in Chicago, a city that inspired some of his best-known poems. Sandburg won the Pulitzer Prize twice—once in 1940 for a biography of Abraham Lincoln and again in 1951 for his *Complete Poems.*

Go Online **Author Link** For: More about these authors Visit: www.PHSchool.com Web Code: ene-9604

CHICORIA

Retold in English by
Rudolfo A. Anaya

Adapted in Spanish by
José Griego y Maestas

There were once many big ranches in California, and many New Mexicans went to work there. One day one of the big ranch owners asked his workers if there were any poets in New Mexico.

"Of course, we have many fine poets," they replied. "We have old Vilmas, Chicoria, Cinfuegos, to say nothing of the poets of Cebolleta and the Black Poet."

"Well, when you return next season, why don't you bring one of your poets to compete with Gracia—here none can compare with him!"

When the harvest was done the New Mexicans returned home. The following season when they returned to California they took with them the poet Chicoria, knowing well that in spinning a rhyme or in weaving wit there was no *Californio*[1] who could beat him.

Literary Analysis
Oral Tradition What ability of Chicoria's could be considered admirable in his culture?

---

1. *Californio* (kä´ lē fôr´ nyō) term for the Spanish-speaking colonists who established ranches in California under Spanish and Mexican rule.

As soon as the rancher found out that the workers had brought Chicoria with them, he sent his servants to invite his good neighbor and friend to come and hear the new poet. Meanwhile, the cooks set about preparing a big meal. When the maids began to dish up the plates of food, Chicoria turned to one of the servers and said, "Ah, my friends, it looks like they are going to feed us well tonight!"

The servant was surprised. "No, my friend," he explained, "the food is for *them*. We don't eat at the master's table. It is not permitted. We eat in the kitchen."

"Well, I'll bet I can sit down and eat with them," Chicoria boasted.

"If you beg or if you ask, perhaps, but if you don't ask they won't invite you," replied the servant.

"I never beg," the New Mexican answered. "The master will invite me of his own accord, and I'll bet you twenty dollars he will!"

So they made a twenty-dollar bet and they instructed the serving maid to watch if this self-confident New Mexican had

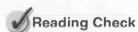

▲ Critical Viewing

What features of this painting indicate the start of a festive occasion, such as the feast in the story? **[Analyze]**

✓ Reading Check

What bet does Chicoria make with the servant?

Chicoria ■ 951

to ask the master for a place at the table. Then the maid took Chicoria into the dining room. Chicoria greeted the rancher cordially, but the rancher appeared <u>haughty</u> and did not invite Chicoria to sit with him and his guest at the table. Instead, he asked that a chair be brought and placed by the wall where Chicoria was to sit. The rich ranchers began to eat without inviting Chicoria.

So it is just as the servant predicted, Chicoria thought. The poor are not invited to share the rich man's food!

Then the master spoke: "Tell us about the country where you live. What are some of the customs of New Mexico?"

"Well, in New Mexico when a family sits down to eat each member uses one spoon for each biteful of food," Chicoria said with a twinkle in his eyes.

The ranchers were amazed that the New Mexicans ate in that manner, but what Chicoria hadn't told them was that each spoon was a piece of tortilla:[2] one fold and it became a spoon with which to scoop up the meal.

"Furthermore," he continued, "our goats are not like yours."

"How are they different?" the rancher asked.

"Here your nannies[3] give birth to two kids, in New Mexico they give birth to three!"

"What a strange thing!" the master said. "But tell us, how can the female nurse three kids?"

"Well, they do it exactly as you're doing it now: While two of them are eating the third one looks on."

The rancher then realized his lack of manners and took Chicoria's hint. He apologized and invited his New Mexico guest to dine at the table. After dinner, Chicoria sang and recited his poetry, putting Gracia to shame. And he won his bet as well.

---

2. **tortilla** (tôr tē′ yə) *n.* thin, round pancake of cornmeal or flour.
3. **nannies** (nan′ ēz) *n.* female goats.

Vocabulary Builder
cordially (kôr′ jə lē) *adv.* warmly

haughty (hôt′ ē) *adj.* scornfully superior

Literary Analysis
Oral Tradition Do you think the teller of this story is a New Mexican or a *Californio*? Why?

Reading Skill
Summarize Would you consider the winning of the bet important enough to include in a summary? Why or why not?

from

THE PEOPLE, YES

Carl Sandburg

They have yarns[1]
Of a skyscraper so tall they had to put hinges
On the two top stories so to let the moon go by,
Of one corn crop in Missouri when the roots
5 Went so deep and drew off so much water

---

1. yarns (yärnz) *n.* tall tales that depend on humor and exaggeration.

▲ Critical Viewing
How does this
landscape lend itself
to the telling of tall
tales? **[Connect]**

The Mississippi riverbed that year was dry,
Of pancakes so thin they had only one side,
Of "a fog so thick we shingled the barn and six feet out
on the fog,"
Of Pecos Pete straddling a <u>cyclone</u> in Texas and riding it
to the west coast where "it rained out under him,"
10 Of the man who drove a swarm of bees across the Rocky
Mountains and the Desert "and didn't lose a bee,"
Of a mountain railroad curve where the engineer in his
cab can touch the caboose and spit in the conductor's
eye,
Of the boy who climbed a cornstalk growing so fast he
would have starved to death if they hadn't shot
biscuits up to him,
Of the old man's whiskers: "When the wind was with him
his whiskers arrived a day before he did,"
Of the hen laying a square egg and cackling, "Ouch!" and
of hens laying eggs with the dates printed on them,
15 Of the ship captain's shadow: it froze to the deck one cold
winter night,
Of mutineers on that same ship put to chipping rust with
rubber hammers,
Of the sheep counter who was fast and accurate: "I just
count their feet and divide by four,"
Of the man so tall he must climb a ladder to shave himself,
Of the runt so teeny-weeny it takes two men and a boy to
see him,
20 Of mosquitoes: one can kill a dog, two of them a man,
Of a cyclone that sucked cookstoves out of the kitchen,
up the chimney flue, and on to the next town,
Of the same cyclone picking up wagontracks in Nebraska
and dropping them over in the Dakotas,
Of the hook-and-eye snake unlocking itself into forty
pieces, each piece two inches long, then in nine seconds
flat snapping itself together again,
Of the watch swallowed by the cow—when they butchered
her a year later the watch was running and had the correct time,
25 Of horned snakes, hoop snakes that roll themselves
where they want to go, and rattlesnakes carrying
bells instead of rattles on their tails,

Vocabulary Builder
cyclone (sī´ klon´) *n.*
a violent, rotating
windstorm; a tornado

Literary Analysis
Oral Tradition Does
Sandburg's use of
exaggeration and
repetition portray a
country at rest or on
the move? Explain.

Reading Skill
Summarize Would it
be essential to list all
of the characters and
animals in a summary
of this poem? Why or
why not?

BM-17—Paul Bunyan and Babe, his Blue Ox, Bemidji, Minn.

PAUL BUNYAN

8B-H1052

Of the herd of cattle in California getting lost in a giant
    redwood tree that had hollowed out,
Of the man who killed a snake by putting its tail in its
    mouth so it swallowed itself,
Of railroad trains whizzing along so fast they reach the
    station before the whistle,
Of pigs so thin the farmer had to tie knots in their tails to
    keep them from crawling through the cracks in their
    pens,
30 Of Paul Bunyan's big blue ox, Babe, measuring between
    the eyes forty-two ax-handles and a plug of Star tobacco
    exactly,
Of John Henry's hammer and the curve of its swing and
    his singing of it as "a rainbow round my shoulder."

▲ **Critical Viewing**
How do the figures
shown here capture
the spirit of this
poem? **[Analyze]**

Literary Analysis
Oral Tradition What
folk heroes are
mentioned at the end
of the poem?

Apply the Skills

Chicoria / from *The People, Yes*

Thinking About the Selections

1. **Respond:** Which of these works did you enjoy more? Why?
2. **(a) Recall:** In "Chicoria," how does the server respond when Chicoria says he expects to be fed well? **(b) Analyze:** Why does Chicoria assume that he will eat at the rancher's table?
3. **(a) Recall:** What does Chicoria say about New Mexican goats? **(b) Analyze:** Why does he tell this story?
4. **(a) Recall:** Identify three people mentioned in the excerpt from *The People, Yes* who have amazing abilities or skills. **(b) Evaluate:** In what way does each character's ability contribute to survival in a wild, new country?
5. **(a) Interpret:** With a partner, interpret the meaning of the poem's title. **(b) Discuss:** Are the heroes of these tales inspirational in today's world? Share your answers with the class.

Reading Skill

6. **(a)** To help you **summarize** "Chicoria," construct a timeline of major events in the order in which they occur. **(b)** Use your timeline to write a brief summary of "Chicoria."
7. **(a)** Fill in a cluster diagram like the one shown with images from *The People, Yes*. **(b)** Summarize the poem by stating the main idea behind the images. **(c)** Why would a cluster diagram be more useful than a timeline in summarizing this excerpt?

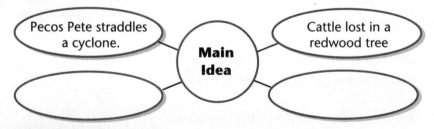

Literary Analysis

8. **(a)** How is Chicoria both typical and *not* typical of a hero of the **oral tradition**? **(b)** Why might New Mexicans enjoy this story enough to pass it on?
9. Review the chart on page 948. What features of the oral tradition are contained in lines 8–21 of the excerpt from *The People, Yes*? Give at least one example of each feature.

Vocabulary Builder

Practice Analogies show the relationship between words. Use a word from the vocabulary list on page 948 to create a word pair that matches the relationship between the first two words given.

1. *rain* is to *cloudburst* as *wind* is to _____
2. *rudely* is to *enemy* as _____ is to *friend*
3. *gentle* is to *rough* as *humble* is to _____

Writing

Because it comes from the oral tradition, most folk literature is written in informal language. It often uses dialect and folk idioms, homespun expressions or sayings. Write a **critical analysis** to explain how language and idioms affect the tone and mood in folk literature.

- Give specific examples from stories and poems.
- Look for elements of humor and *hyperbole*, or exaggeration.

For *Grammar, Vocabulary,* and *Assessment,* see **Build Language Skills,** pages 968–969.

Extend Your Learning

Listening and Speaking Working with a group, conduct a **storytelling workshop.**
- First, create a tip sheet for storytellers that discusses these topics: identifying an appropriate story for your audience, making eye contact, using your voice and body to dramatize the action, and adding elements such as informal language and dialect.
- Next, select a tale from this grouping or another folk tale to perform. Take turns performing it. Then, evaluate how well performers capture character and setting based on your tip sheet.

Research and Technology Use research to assemble a **collection of folk tales** that would be suitable for adaptation as movies. Choose several titles, then write an introduction for each. Explain why you chose each tale and describe its historical or cultural background. Finally, give each tale a rating that indicates for what age a movie adaptation would be appropriate, and why.

Build Understanding • *Brer Possum's Dilemma / John Henry*

Background

Folk Heroes The main characters in many folk tales are folk heroes—larger-than-life characters who are sometimes based on real people. Typically, though, folk tales exaggerate these characters, making them bigger, faster, stronger, smarter, or braver. Animal characters with human traits are also common in folk tales.

Connecting to the Literature

Reading/Writing Connection Folk tales are told and retold to new generations of listeners and readers. Consider why this might be true by listing four ways in which folk tales can teach valuable lessons and provide role models. Use at least three of these words: *instruct, promote, display, emphasize.*

Review

For **Reading Skill, Literary Analysis,** and **Vocabulary Builder,** see page 948.

Meet the Author

Jackie **Torrence** (1944–2004)

Starting in the 1970s, Jackie Torrence became one of America's best-known and best-loved storytellers. Born in Chicago, she spent her childhood with her grandparents in a North Carolina farming settlement. From them she learned the "Brer Rabbit" fables and other African American tales that had been passed along to the descendants of enslaved Africans in the South.

Fast Facts

▶ Torrence began telling stories in the public library, and soon large audiences were coming to hear "the Story Lady."

▶ She animated her storytelling with humor, lively language, hisses, shrieks, and facial expressions.

▶ Torrence told classic ghost stories and her own tales along with traditional folk tales.

▶ She collected stories in *The Accidental Angel, My Grandmother's Treasure,* and other books. She also recorded them on compact discs, videos, and DVDs.

Go Online Author Link
For: More about the author
Visit: www.PHSchool.com
Web Code: ene-9605

Brer Possum's DiLEMMA
Jackie Torrence

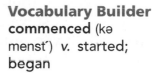

Back in the days when the animals could talk, there lived ol' Brer[1] Possum. He was a fine feller. Why, he never liked to see no critters[2] in trouble. He was always helpin' out, a-doin' somethin' for others.

Ever' night, ol' Brer Possum climbed into a persimmon tree, hung by his tail, and slept all night long. And each mornin', he climbed outa the tree and walked down the road to sun 'imself.

One mornin', as he walked, he come to a big hole in the middle of the road. Now, ol' Brer Possum was kind and gentle, but he was also nosy, so he went over to the hole and looked in. All at once, he stepped back, 'cause layin' in the bottom of that hole was ol' Brer Snake with a brick on his back.

Brer Possum said to 'imself, "I best git on outa here, 'cause ol' Brer Snake is mean and evil and lowdown, and if I git to stayin' around 'im, he jist might git to bitin' me."

So Brer Possum went on down the road.

But Brer Snake had seen Brer Possum, and he <u>commenced</u> to callin' for 'im.

"Help me, Brer Possum."

Brer Possum stopped and turned around. He said to 'imself, "That's ol' Brer Snake a-callin' me. What do you reckon he wants?"

Well, ol' Brer Possum was kindhearted, so he went back down the road to the hole, stood at the edge, and looked down at Brer Snake.

"Was that you a-callin' me? What do you want?"

---

1. **Brer** (brɛr) dialect for "brother," used before a name.
2. **critters** dialect for "creatures"; animals.

Vocabulary Builder
commenced (kə menst´) v. started; began

Reading Check
Why does Brer Snake need help?

Brer Snake looked up and said, "I've been down here in this hole for a mighty long time with this brick on my back. Won't you help git it offa me?"

Brer Possum thought.

"Now listen here, Brer Snake. I knows you. You's mean and evil and lowdown, and if'n I was to git down in that hole and git to liftin' that brick offa your back, you wouldn't do nothin' but bite me."

Ol' Brer Snake just hissed.

"Maybe not. Maybe not. Maaaaaaaybe not."

Brer Possum said, "I ain't sure 'bout you at all. I jist don't know. You're a-goin' to have to let me think about it."

So ol' Brer Possum thought—he thought high, and he thought low—and jist as he was thinkin', he looked up into a tree and saw a dead limb a-hangin' down. He climbed into the tree, broke off the limb, and with that ol' stick, pushed that brick offa Brer Snake's back. Then he took off down the road.

Brer Possum thought he was away from ol' Brer Snake when all at once he heard somethin'.

"Help me, Brer Possum."

Brer Possum said, "Oh, no, that's him agin."

But bein' so kindhearted, Brer Possum turned around, went back to the hole, and stood at the edge.

"Brer Snake, was that you a-callin' me? What do you want now?"

Ol' Brer Snake looked up outa the hole and hissed.

"I've been down here for a mighty long time, and I've gotten a little weak, and the sides of this ol' hole are too slick for me to climb. Do you think you can lift me outa here?"

Brer Possum thought.

"Now, you jist wait a minute. If'n I was to git down into that hole and lift you outa there, you wouldn't do nothin' but bite me."

Brer Snake hissed.

"Maybe not. Maybe not. Maaaaaaaybe not."

Brer Possum said, "I jist don't know. You're a-goin' to have to give me time to think about this."

So ol' Brer Possum thought.

And as he thought, he jist happened to look down there in that hole and see that ol' dead limb. So he pushed the limb underneath ol' Brer Snake and he lifted 'im outa the hole, way up into the air, and throwed 'im into the high grass.

Brer Possum took off a-runnin' down the road.

Literary Analysis
Oral Tradition What examples of dialect here reflect the story's origins as an oral tale?

▼ **Critical Viewing** What characteristics of Brer Snake does this illustration show? **[Analyze]**

Well, he thought he was away from ol' Brer Snake when all at once he heard somethin'.

"Help me, Brer Possum."

Brer Possum thought, "That's him agin."

But bein' so kindhearted, he turned around, went back to the hole, and stood there a-lookin' for Brer Snake. Brer Snake crawled outa the high grass just as slow as he could, stretched 'imself out across the road, rared up, and looked at ol' Brer Possum.

Then he hissed. "I've been down there in that ol' hole for a mighty long time, and I've gotten a little cold 'cause the sun didn't shine. Do you think you could put me in your pocket and git me warm?"

Brer Possum said, "Now you listen here, Brer Snake. I knows you. You's mean and evil and lowdown, and if'n I put you in my pocket you wouldn't do nothin' but bite me."

Brer Snake hissed.

"Maybe not. Maybe not. Maaaaaaaybe not."

"No sireee. Brer Snake. I knows you. I jist ain't a-goin' to do it."

But jist as Brer Possum was talkin' to Brer Snake, he happened to git a real good look at 'im. He was a-layin' there lookin' so <u>pitiful</u>, and Brer Possum's great big heart began to feel sorry for ol' Brer Snake.

"All right," said Brer Possum. "You must be cold. So jist this once I'm a-goin' to put you in my pocket."

So ol' Brer Snake coiled up jist as little as he could, and Brer Possum picked 'im up and put 'im in his pocket.

Brer Snake laid quiet and still—so quiet and still that Brer Possum even forgot that he was a-carryin' 'im around. But all of a sudden, Brer Snake commenced to crawlin' out, and he turned and faced Brer Possum and hissed.

"I'm a-goin' to bite you."

But Brer Possum said, "Now wait a minute. Why are you a-goin' to bite me? I done took that brick offa your back, I got you outa that hole, and I put you in my pocket to git you warm. Why are you a-goin' to bite me?"

Brer Snake hissed.

"You knowed I was a snake before you put me in you pocket."

And when you're mindin' your own business and you spot trouble, don't never trouble trouble 'til trouble troubles you.

Literary Analysis
Oral Tradition What role does repetition play in building suspense in this story?

Vocabulary Builder
pitiful (pit′ i fəl) *adj.* arousing sympathy or pity

Reading Skill
Summarize What are the consequences of Brer Possum's kindness?

JOHN HENRY

TRADITIONAL

John Henry was a lil baby,
Sittin' on his mama's knee,
Said: 'The Big Bend Tunnel on the C. & O. road[1]
Gonna cause the death of me,
5 Lawd, Lawd, gonna cause the death of me.'

Cap'n says to John Henry,
'Gonna bring me a steam drill 'round,
Gonna take that steam drill out on the job,
Gonna whop that steel on down,
10 Lawd, Lawd, gonna whop that steel on down.'

John Henry tol' his cap'n,
Lightnin' was in his eye:
'Cap'n, bet yo' las, red cent on me,
Fo' I'll beat it to the bottom or I'll die,
15 Lawd, Lawd, I'll beat it to the bottom or I'll die.'

Sun shine hot an' burnin',
Wer'n't no breeze a-tall,
Sweat ran down like water down a hill,
That day John Henry let his hammer fall,
20 Lawd, Lawd, that day John Henry let his hammer fall.

John Henry went to the tunnel,
An' they put him in the lead to drive,
The rock so tall an' John Henry so small,
That he lied down his hammer an' he cried,
25 Lawd, Lawd, that he lied down his hammer an' he cried.

John Henry started on the right hand,
The steam drill started on the lef'—

---

1. C. & O. road Chesapeake and Ohio Railroad. The C&O's Big Bend railroad tunnel was built in the 1870s through a mountain in West Virginia.

'Before I'd let this steam drill beat me down,
I'd hammer my fool self to death,
30 Lawd, Lawd, I'd hammer my fool self to death.'

John Henry had a lil woman,
Her name were Polly Ann,
John Henry took sick an' had to go to bed,
Polly Ann drove steel like a man,
35 Lawd, Lawd, Polly Ann drove steel like a man.

John Henry said to his shaker,[2]
'Shaker, why don' you sing?
I'm throwin' twelve poun's from my hips on down,
Jes' listen to the col' steel ring,
40 Lawd, Lawd, jes' listen to the col' steel ring.'

▲ **Critical Viewing**
Based on this illustration, do you think John Henry can work faster than the man with the steam drill? Why or why not? **[Predict]**

✓ **Reading Check**

What challenge does John Henry accept?

---

2. shaker (shā´ kər) *n.* person who sets the spikes and places the drills for a steel-driver to hammer.

Oh, the captain said to John Henry,
'I b'lieve this mountain's sinkin' in.'
John Henry said to his captain, oh my!
'Ain' nothin' but my hammer suckin' win',
45 Lawd, Lawd, ain' nothin' but my hammer
    suckin' win'.'

John Henry tol' his shaker,
'Shaker, you better pray,
For, if I miss this six-foot steel,
Tomorrow'll be yo' buryin' day,
50 Lawd, Lawd, tomorrow'll be yo' buryin' day.'

John Henry tol' his captain,
'Look yonder what I see—
Yo' drill's done broke an' yo' hole's done choke,
An' you cain' drive steel like me,
55 Lawd, Lawd, an' you cain' drive steel like me.'

The man that invented the steam drill,
Thought he was mighty fine.
John Henry drove his fifteen feet,
An' the steam drill only made nine,
60 Lawd, Lawd, an' the steam drill only made
    nine.

The hammer that John Henry swung,
It weighed over nine pound;
He broke a rib in his lef'-han' side,
An' his intrels[3] fell on the groun',
65 Lawd, Lawd, an' his intrels fell on the
    groun'.

All the womens in the Wes',
When they heared of John Henry's death,
Stood in the rain, flagged the eas'-boun'
    train,
Goin' where John Henry fell dead,
70 Lawd, Lawd, goin' where John Henry fell
    dead.

---

3. **intrels** (en´ trālz) *n.* dialect for *entrails*—internal organs.

Literature in Context

Social Studies Connection

Machine Age Enormous steam engines, like the Corliss engines shown here, helped transform work in the nineteenth century. Steam engines were used to power everything from locomotives to woolen mills. Goods could now be mass produced in sprawling factories by far fewer workers in far less time.

    With this tremendous rise in machine power, many people feared that machines would eventually replace workers. In England, this gave rise to unions, labor laws, and in a few cases, even the smashing of machinery. In America, where labor laws and unions were weaker, people celebrated heroes over lifeless machines in stories and songs.

Connect to the Literature

Why would people in a machine age look up to John Henry as a folk hero?

◄ **Critical Viewing**
In this illustration,
what indicates that
John Henry may
have hurt himself in
the competition?
[Assess]

John Henry's lil mother,
She was all dressed in red,
She jumped in bed, covered up her head,
Said she didn' know her son was dead,
75 Lawd, Lawd, didn' know her son was dead.

Dey took John Henry to the graveyard,
An' they buried him in the san',
An' every locomotive come roarin' by,
Says, 'There lays a steel-drivin' man,
80 Lawd, Lawd, there lays a steel-drivin' man.'

Literary Analysis
Oral Tradition This
ballad was meant to
be sung. What makes
a song more likely to
be passed down
than a story?

Apply the Skills

Brer Possum's Dilemma / John Henry

Thinking About the Selection

1. **Respond:** Which of these folk tales did you enjoy more? Why?
2. **(a) Recall:** What words does Torrence use to describe Brer Possum? **(b) Infer:** Is Brer Possum meant to look foolish or simply big-hearted? **(c) Compare and Contrast:** How are Brer Possum and Brer Snake different?
3. **(a) Recall:** What three favors does Brer Snake request? **(b) Deduce:** Why might Brer Possum think it is safe to trust Brer Snake? **(c) Apply:** What is the lesson of this story?
4. **(a) Recall:** Why does John Henry challenge the steam drill? **(b) Connect:** How do his actions contribute to his legend?
5. **(a) Evaluate:** With a partner, evaluate the qualities that make John Henry a folk hero. **(b) Discuss:** Would the story of John Henry be remembered if he had beaten the machine but still survived? Share your answer with the rest of the class.

Reading Skill

6. **(a)** To help you **summarize** "John Henry," complete a timeline like the one shown. **(b)** Use your timeline to write a brief summary.

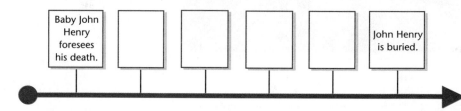

7. **(a)** What type of graphic organizer would be most helpful in writing a summary of "Brer Possum's Dilemma"? Explain. **(b)** Use that organizer and write a summary of the story.

Literary Analysis

8. **(a)** How is John Henry both typical and *not* typical of a hero of the **oral tradition**? **(b)** What story elements might explain why it has been passed from generation to generation?
9. View the chart on page 948. What features of the oral tradition are contained in "Brer Possum's Dilemma"? Give at least one example of each feature.

QuickReview

Story at a Glance

Brer Possum's Dilemma: a sneaky snake takes advantage of a kind-hearted possum

John Henry: a legendary folk hero challenges a machine in building a railroad tunnel

For: Self-test
Visit: www.PHSchool.com
Web Code: ena-6605

Summarize: make a short statement that presents the main points of a piece of writing

Oral Tradition: stories, songs, and tales passed down in a culture by word of mouth

Vocabulary Builder

Practice **Analogies** show the relationship between words. Use a word from the vocabulary list on page 948 to create a word pair that matches the relationship between the first two words given.

1. *champion* is to *strong* as *victim* is to _____
2. *opened* is to *closed* as *stopped* is to _____

Writing

Most folk literature is written in informal language. It often uses dialect and folk idioms, homespun expressions or sayings. Write a **critical analysis** to explain how language and idioms affect the tone and mood in folk literature.

- Give specific examples from stories and poems.
- Look for elements of humor and *hyperbole*, or exaggeration.

For *Grammar*, *Vocabulary*, and *Assessment*, see **Build Language Skills**, pages 968–969.

Extend Your Learning

Listening and Speaking Working with a group, conduct a **storytelling workshop.**

- First, create a tip sheet for storytellers that includes these topics: identifying an appropriate story for your audience, making eye contact, using your voice and body to dramatize the action, and adding elements, such as informal language and dialect.
- Next, select a tale from this grouping or another folk tale to perform. Take turns performing it; then, evaluate how well performers capture character and setting based on your tip sheet.

Research and Technology Use research to assemble a **collection of folk tales** that would be suitable for adaptation as movies. Choose several titles, then write an introduction for each. Explain why you chose each tale and describe its historical or cultural background. Finally, give each tale a rating that indicates for what age a movie adaptation would be appropriate, and why.

Build Language Skills

Chicoria • from *The People, Yes*
• *Brer Possum's Dilemma* • *John Henry*

Vocabulary Skill

Prefixes Prefixes meaning "not" or "without" are also used to form antonyms. The **prefixes** *un-*, *an-* and *a-* all convert a word to its opposite. For example, adding *un-* to the word *questioned* results in *unquestioned,* or something that is not asked.

▶ **Example:** Scientists finally started *questioning* that theory.
   The theory had been *unquestioned* for years.

Practice Write sentence pairs for the following. Use the example above as a guide.

1. necessary/unnecessary
2. lock/unlock
3. popular/unpopular
4. known/unknown
5. professional/unprofessional

MorePractice

For more practice with commas, see the Grammar Handbook, p. R31.

Grammar Skill

Commas A **comma** is a punctuation mark that signals a brief pause. Use a comma

- before a conjunction to separate two independent clauses in a compound sentence.
- between items in a series.
- between adjectives.
- after introductory material.
- with parenthetical expressions.
- to set off appositives, participial phrases, or adjective clauses.

Practice Add the commas that are needed.

1. The situation remains urgent yet it takes time to understand the effects of soil depletion.
2. Areas were fenced off plowed clear or burned off so new grass could grow.
3. The Nile River which flows through Egypt is a source of irrigation water.
4. Desert insects dormant for most of the year appear when rain causes flowers to bloom.
5. The long dry stretches of sand were fascinating.

WG Prentice Hall Writing and Grammar Connection, Chapter 26, Section 2

Reading: Summarizing

Directions: *Read the selection. Then, answer the questions.*

Analyzing a Political Cartoon

Political cartoons that often appear in print media present a particular point of view. Political cartoonists not only express an opinion, but also try to influence the reader's view on an issue. Using exaggeration and humor, cartoonists make powerful statements.

Most political cartoons use symbols instead of words. A symbol is a concrete object that represents something else. In analyzing a political cartoon, look at all the images and words. They are the keys to understanding the cartoonist's point of view.

1. Which of the following could be left out of a summary?
   A Political cartoons present a particular point of view.
   B They often appear in newsprint.
   C Most political cartoons use symbols.
   D A symbol represents something else.

2. The best organizer for this passage's information would be
   A a timeline.
   B a Venn diagram.
   C an outline.
   D a chart.

3. The definition of a political cartoon appears in
   A paragraph one.
   B paragraph two.
   C both paragraphs.
   D neither paragraph.

4. Which should NOT be included in a summary?
   A Cartoons are powerful statements.
   B The American flag is a U.S. symbol.
   C Cartoonists influence readers.
   D Images and words are keys to understanding.

Timed Writing: Explanation [Connections]

Review the folk tales in this unit. Choose one tale and explain why it would be important enough to a culture to be handed down from generation to generation. Use specifics from the text to support your reasoning. **(45 minutes)**

Writing Workshop: *Work in Progress*

Multimedia Report

Using the work in your writing portfolio, write the facts, details, and examples you would use to support your main idea. Note which media sources would be most effective to illustrate the main points of your multimedia report. Save this work in your writing portfolio.

Heroic Characters

Heroic characters are men and women who show great courage and overcome difficult challenges. A heroic character can be fictional or real. Often, the hero in a tall tale or legend is a combination of both—a real historical figure whose actions have become so exaggerated over time that he or she becomes a legend.

Many American legends and stories focus on the pioneers of the western frontier. Because survival in such a harsh setting depended on skill and strength, many tall tales and legends exaggerate these admirable qualities. The heroes of these tales emphasize shared values among the people who told them.

Comparing Heroic Characters

To compare heroic characters in literature, ask these questions:

- Was this person an actual historical figure?
- What heroic qualities does this person have?
- Which actions make the character heroic?

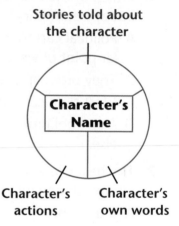

Use a "character wheel" like the one shown to compare the words, actions, and descriptions of the heroes in "Western Wagons," "Davy Crockett's Dream," and "Paul Bunyan of the North Woods."

Vocabulary Builder

Davy Crockett's Dream

- **squatter** (skwät′ ər) *n.* someone who settles illegally on land or in a building (p. 974) *During the winter, a <u>squatter</u> settled in the empty cabin.*
- **kindled** (kin′ dəld) *v.* built or lit (a fire) (p. 974) *We set up the tent, then <u>kindled</u> a fire to cook dinner.*

Paul Bunyan of the North Woods

- **shanties** (shan′ tēz) *n.* roughly built cabins or shacks (p. 976) *The miners built <u>shanties</u> using scrap wood and metal.*
- **commotion** (kə mō′ shən) *n.* noisy movement (p. 977) *After the game, there was a <u>commotion</u> in the street.*
- **bellowing** (bel′ ō iŋ) *v.* roaring (p. 978) *My neighbor woke me when he started <u>bellowing</u> for his dog to come inside.*

Build Understanding

Connecting to the Literature

Reading/Writing Connection Traditional American myths and tall tales often center on the heroic deeds of nineteenth-century pioneers of the Old West. List three present-day men and women in the fields of sports, entertainment, or politics who have reached mythic status because of their abilities. Use at least three of the following words: *accomplish, challenge, display, dominate, guarantee.*

Meet the Authors

Stephen Vincent **Benét** (1898–1943)

A poet, novelist, and short-story writer, Stephen Vincent Benét often wrote about American history and its heroes. With his wife, Rosemary Carr, Benét wrote *A Book of Americans,* a collection of lively poems for young people about characters in American history. Benét's widely read Civil War epic, *John Brown's Body,* won him the Pulitzer Prize in 1929.

Davy **Crockett** (1786–1836)

Davy Crockett was a genuine frontiersman, but the colorful tall tales in his autobiography helped make him a legend. Crockett was also a politician, representing Tennessee in Congress. He joined the fight for Texas independence and was killed at the battle of the Alamo in 1836. The legends surrounding Crockett took on new form with the airing of the 1950's television show *Davy Crockett.* Millions tuned in, sparking a nationwide fad for Crockett-style coonskin caps.

Carl **Sandburg** (1878–1967)

Carl Sandburg had a lifelong interest in American history and folk-lore, especially the nation's myths and tall tales. These stories influenced much of his poetry in works such as *The People, Yes.* Sandburg was also a journalist and historian, who wrote a widely admired biography of Abraham Lincoln that was six volumes long.

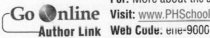

For: More about the authors
Go Online **Visit:** www.PHSchool.com
Author Link **Web Code:** ene-9006

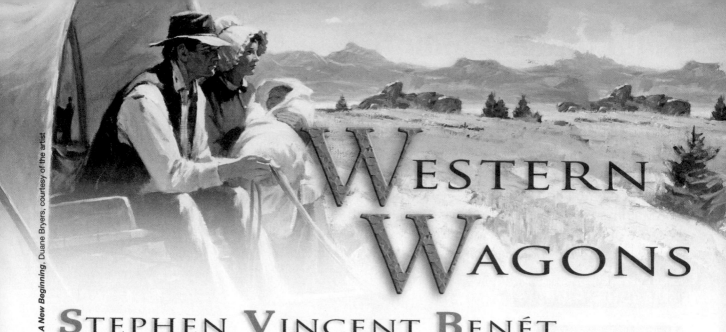

WESTERN WAGONS

STEPHEN VINCENT BENÉT

They went with axe and rifle, when the trail was still to
    blaze,
They went with wife and children, in the prairie-
    schooner[1] days,
With banjo and with frying pan—Susanna, don't you
    cry!
For I'm off to California to get rich out there or die!

5 We've broken land and cleared it, but we're tired of
    where we are.
They say that wild Nebraska is a better place by far.
There's gold in far Wyoming, there's black earth in
    Ioway,
So pack up the kids and blankets, for we're moving out
    today!

The cowards never started and the weak died on the
    road,
10 And all across the continent the endless campfires
    glowed.

▲ **Critical Viewing**
What do the
expressions on the
faces of this pioneer
couple reveal about
their personal
qualities? **[Infer]**

---

1. prairie-schooner (sko͞o′ nər) nickname given to the canvas-topped wagons used by pioneers
going west across the prairies. A schooner is a type of sailing ship.

We'd taken land and settled—but a traveler passed by—
And we're going West tomorrow—Lordy, never ask us
   why!

We're going West tomorrow, where the promises can't
   fail.
O'er the hills in legions, boys, and crowd the dusty trail!
15 We shall starve and freeze and suffer. We shall die,
   and tame the lands.
But we're going West tomorrow, with our fortune in our
   hands.

Literary Analysis
Heroic Characters
What hardships did
these people
overcome?

Thinking About the Selection

1. **Respond:** If you had lived in the 1800s, would you have joined
   the pioneers moving west? Why or why not?

2. **(a) Recall:** What items do the pioneers take with them?
   (b) Connect: Why are these items important to them?

3. **(a) Recall:** To what places do the people in the poem want to
   go? **(b) Infer:** Why do they want to go to these places?
   (c) Generalize: What qualities characterized the age of westward expansion?

4. **(a) Make a Judgment:** What do you think is the best reason the
   pioneers offer to move on? **(b) Evaluate:** Do you think the
   rewards of their move are worth the risks they face? Explain.

Davy Crockett's Dream
Davy Crockett

One day when it was so cold that I was afeard to open my mouth, lest I should freeze my tongue, I took my little dog named Grizzle and cut out for Salt River Bay to kill something for dinner. I got a good ways from home afore I knowed where I was, and as I had swetted some before I left the house my hat froze fast to my head, and I like to have put my neck out of joint in trying to pull it off. When I sneezed the icicles crackled all up and down the inside of my nose, like when you walk over a bog in winter time. The varmints was so scarce that I couldn't find one, and so when I come to an old log hut that had belonged to some <u>squatter</u> that had ben reformed out by the nabors, I stood my rifle up agin one of the door posts and went in. I <u>kindled</u> up a little fire and told Grizzle I was going to take a nap. I piled up a heap of chestnut burs for a pillow and straitened myself out on the ground, for I can curl closer than a rattlesnake and lay straiter than a log. I laid with the back of my head agin the hearth, and my eyes looking up chimney so that I could see when it was noon by the sun, for Mrs. Crockett was always rantankerous[1] when I staid out over the time. I got to sleep before Grizzle had done warming the eend of his nose, and I had swallowed so much cold wind that it laid hard on my stomach, and as I laid gulping and belching the wind went out of me and roared up chimney like a young whirlwind. So I had a pesky dream, and kinder thought, till I waked up, that I was floating down the Massassippy in a holler tree, and I hadn't room to stir my legs and arms no more than they were withed together with young saplings. While I was there and want able to help myself a feller called Oak Wing that lived about twenty miles off, and that I had give a most almighty licking once, cum and looked in with

---

1. rantankerous (ran taŋ´ kər əs) *adj.* dialect for *cantankerous,* meaning "bad-tempered and quarrelsome."

Literary Analysis
Heroic Characters
How does Crockett show that he is a genuine frontiersman?

Vocabulary Builder
squatter (skwät´ ər) *n.* someone who settles illegally on land or in a building

kindled (kin´ dəld) *v.* built or lit (a fire)

Literary Analysis
Heroic Characters
What elements of comic exaggeration do you notice here?

his blind eye that I had gouged out five years before, and I saw him looking in one end of the hollow log, and he axed me if I wanted to get out. I telled him to tie a rope to one of my legs and draw me out as soon as God would let him and as much sooner as he was a mind to. But he said he wouldn't do it that way, he would ram me out with a pole. So he took a long pole and rammed it down agin my head as if he was ramming home the cattridge in a cannon. This didn't make me budge an inch, but it pounded my head down in between my shoulders till I look'd like a turcle with his head drawn in. This started my temper a trifle, and I ript and swore till the breath boiled out of the end of the log like the steam out of the funnel pipe of a steemboat. Jest then I woke up, and seed my wife pulling my leg, for it was enermost sundown and she had cum arter me. There was a long icicle hanging to her nose, and when she tried to kiss me, she run it right into my eye. I telled her my dreem, and sed I would have revenge on Oak Wing for pounding my head. She said it was all a dreem and that Oak was not to blame; but I had a very diffrent idee of the matter. So I went and talked to him, and telled him what he had done to me in a dreem, and it was settled that he should make me an apology in his next dreem, and that wood make us square,[2] for I don't like to be run upon when I'm asleep, any more than I do when I'm awake.

▲ Critical Viewing Does Davy Crockett, pictured here, look like he might use "a heap of chestnut burrs" for a pillow? Explain. **[Assess]**

---

2. **square** even.

Thinking About the Selection

1. **Respond:** Do you think you would like Davy Crockett if you met him? Why or why not?

2. **(a) Recall:** Why does Davy Crockett go out in the woods?
   (b) Infer: What can you infer about his home life?

3. **(a) Recall:** What happens in Davy Crockett's dream, and how does he react? **(b) Analyze Cause and Effect:** How does he actually settle the matter with Oak Wing? **(c) Analyze:** How does this outcome show that this narrative is a "tall tale"?

4. **(a) Analyze:** How do the dialect, spelling, and grammar of the writing affect the tone of the tale? **(b) Infer:** From the way he tells this tale, how would you describe Davy Crockett?

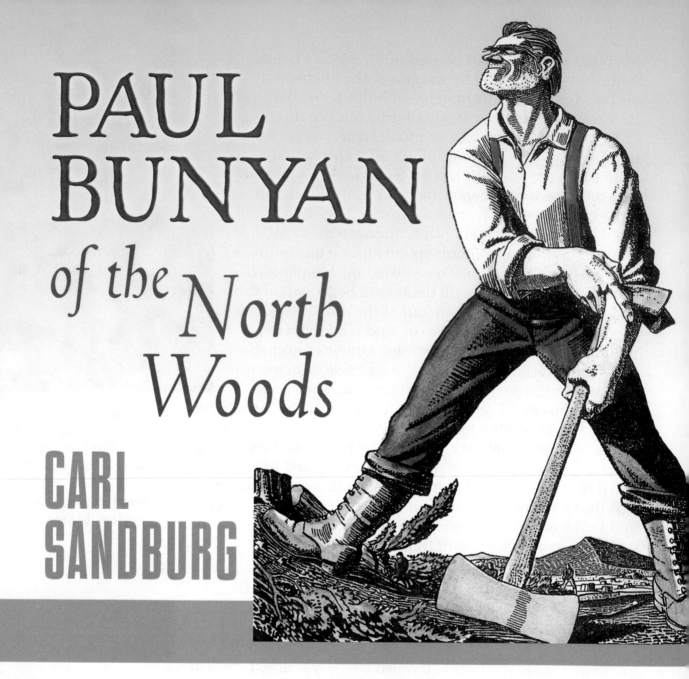

PAUL BUNYAN
of the *North Woods*

CARL SANDBURG

W ho made Paul Bunyan, who gave him birth as a myth, who joked him into life as the Master Lumberjack, who fashioned him forth as an apparition[1] easing the hours of men amid axes and trees, saws and lumber? The people, the bookless people, they made Paul and had him alive long before he got into the books for those who read. He grew up in <u>shanties</u>, around the hot stoves of winter, among socks and mittens drying, in the smell of tobacco

Vocabulary Builder
shanties (shan´ tēz) *n.*
roughly built cabins
or shacks

---

1. apparition (ap´ ə rish´ ən) *n.* sudden or unusual sight.

smoke and the roar of laughter mocking the outside weather. And some of Paul came overseas in wooden bunks below decks in sailing vessels. And some of Paul is old as the hills, young as the alphabet.

The Pacific Ocean froze over in the winter of the Blue Snow and Paul Bunyan had long teams of oxen hauling regular white snow over from China. This was the winter Paul gave a party to the Seven Axmen. Paul fixed a granite floor sunk two hundred feet deep for them to dance on. Still, it tipped and tilted as the dance went on. And because the Seven Axmen refused to take off their hobnailed boots, the sparks from the nails of their dancing feet lit up the place so that Paul didn't light the kerosene lamps. No women being on the Big Onion river at that time the Seven Axmen had to dance with each other, the one left over in each set taking Paul as a partner. The <u>commotion</u> of the dancing that night brought on an earthquake and the Big Onion river moved over three counties to the east.

One year when it rained from St. Patrick's Day till the Fourth of July, Paul Bunyan got disgusted because his celebration on the Fourth was spoiled. He dived into Lake Superior and swam to where a solid pillar of water was coming down. He dived under this pillar, swam up into it and climbed with powerful swimming strokes, was gone about an hour, came splashing down, and as the rain stopped, he explained, "I turned the darn thing off." This is told in the Big North Woods and on the Great Lakes, with many particulars.

Two mosquitoes lighted on one of Paul Bunyan's oxen, killed it, ate it, cleaned the bones, and sat on a grub shanty picking their teeth as Paul came along. Paul sent to Australia for two special bumblebees to kill these mosquitoes. But the bees and the mosquitoes intermarried; their children had stingers on both ends. And things kept getting worse till Paul brought a big boatload of sorghum[2] up from Louisiana and while all the bee-mosquitoes were eating at the sweet sorghum he floated them down to the Gulf of Mexico. They got so fat that it was easy to drown them all between New Orleans and Galveston.

Vocabulary Builder
commotion (kə mō′ shən) *n.* noisy movement

✓**Reading Check**

How does Bunyan stop the rain?

---

2. **sorghum** (sôr′ gəm) *n.* tropical grasses bearing flowers and seeds, grown for use as grain or syrup.

Paul logged on the Little Gimlet in Oregon one winter. The cookstove at that camp covered an acre of ground. They fastened the side of a hog on each snowshoe and four men used to skate on the griddle while the cook flipped the pancakes. The eating table was three miles long; elevators carried the cakes to the ends of the table where boys on bicycles rode back and forth on a path down the center of the table dropping the cakes where called for.

Benny, the Little Blue Ox of Paul Bunyan, grew two feet every time Paul looked at him, when a youngster. The barn was gone one morning and they found it on Benny's back; he grew out of it in a night. One night he kept pawing and <u>bellowing</u> for more pancakes, till there were two hundred men at the cookshanty stove trying to keep him fed. About breakfast time Benny broke loose, tore down the cookshanty, ate all the pancakes piled up for the loggers' breakfast. And after that Benny made his mistake; he ate the red hot stove; and that finished him. This is only one of the hot-stove stories told in the North Woods.

Vocabulary Builder
bellowing (bel′ ō iŋ) *v.* roaring

Thinking About the Selection

1. **Respond:** Which tall tale about Paul Bunyan did you like best? Why?

2. **(a) Recall:** According to Sandburg, what is the origin of the Paul Bunyan stories? **(b) Interpret:** What does Sandburg mean by saying that "some of Paul is old as the hills, young as the alphabet"?

3. **(a) Classify:** Identify two actions that show that Paul Bunyan is clever as well as strong. **(b) Connect:** How do these qualities relate to the myth of the heroic character?

4. **(a) Recall:** How does Paul Bunyan stop the rain?
   (b) Generalize: What do this anecdote and other details in the selection tell you about life in the Midwest in the early nineteenth century?

5. **(a) Speculate:** Do you think the Paul Bunyan stories might have been based on a real person? **(b) Hypothesize:** What type of person in today's world might inspire this kind of story?

Apply the Skills

Western Wagons • Davy Crockett's Dream •
Paul Bunyan of the North Woods

Comparing Heroic Characters

1. Make a chart like the one shown to compare the heroic characters in these three selections:

	Western Wagons	Davy Crockett's Dream	Paul Bunyan of the North Woods
Real or Legend?			
Challenges			
Heroic Actions			
Exaggeration			
Tone: Humorous or Serious?			

2. How are works about real-life heroes, such as those in "Western Wagons," different from those about larger-than-life legendary figures found in the other tales?

Writing to Compare Literary Works

In an essay, compare and contrast the ways in which these three selections present heroic characters. Use the chart you completed to help organize your essay. In addition, consider these points:
- How does each writer use exaggeration? What is the effect?
- How important is humor in each selection?
- What do these legends show about the American character and what Americans admire in heroes?

Vocabulary Builder

Practice Review each group of words. Then, decide whether each italicized vocabulary word fits or does not fit with the other two words listed. Explain your reasoning.

1. palaces, mansions, *shanties*
2. shouting, roaring, *bellowing*
3. renter, owner, *squatter*
4. uproar, disorder, *commotion*
5. ignited, lit, *kindled*

QuickReview

Heroic Characters: real or legendary men and women who perform amazing feats or show great courage

Go Online
Assessment
For: Self-test
Visit: www.PHSchool.com
Web Code: ena-6606

Reading: Summarizing

Directions: *Questions 1–5 refer to the following selection.*

Once there was a boy whose job was to watch his family's sheep all day, by himself, in a meadow near town. At first, he amused himself by singing and watching the clouds. Soon, though, he got very bored and decided to play a trick. "Help! Help! A wolf is coming!" he screamed, and everyone in town ran to help him. He then claimed that he had scared the wolf away, and invited everyone to stay and chat a while. A few days later, the boy tried the same trick, and it worked again.

A week later, though, while the boy was eating lunch, a wolf really did come. "Help! Help! A wolf is coming!" he screamed. No one came. They had already been tricked twice, and they refused to be tricked again. The wolf ate all the sheep, and the boy's family had no wool to sell that year.

1. **Which graphic would be most suitable for organizing the main points in the passage?**
   A cluster diagram
   B timeline
   C Venn diagram
   D chart

2. **Which sentence summarizes the main events in paragraph 1?**
   A Once there was a boy whose job was to watch sheep.
   B A lonely boy amuses himself by singing and watching clouds.
   C A lonely boy tricks people twice in order to get some company.
   D "Help! Help! A wolf is coming!"

3. **Which sentence is a *minor* detail in paragraph 2?**
   A A week later, the boy was eating his lunch.
   B A wolf really does come.
   C No one comes when the boy calls for help.
   D The wolf eats all the sheep.

4. **Which sentence is a good summary of paragraph 2?**
   A A wolf comes and eats all the sheep.
   B No one helps the boy because they know he is strong and brave and can handle anything.
   C "Help! Help! A wolf is coming!"
   D When the boy really does need help, no one comes because they do not trust him anymore.

Prefixes

Direction: *Choose the letter of the word or phrase that best defines the italicized word.*

5. *essential*
   A not needed
   B necessary
   C believed
   D not available

6. *extract*
   A take away
   B take out
   C take in
   D take around

7. *organize*
   A to arrange in logical order
   B to put something in its place
   C to be important to understanding
   D to finalize

8. *disorganized*
   A not intelligent
   B not orderly
   C not important to understanding
   D not final

9. *sequence*
   A by size
   B order
   C planned
   D cause and effect

Directions: *Choose the best answer to the question.*

10. **Which word is a synonym for** *organized*?
    A orderly
    B reorganized
    C disorganized
    D considered

11. **Which phrase describes a** *nonissue*?
    A something that is not spoken
    B something that is not given
    C something that is not an issue
    D something that is not considered

12. **Which word is an antonym for** *disadvantage*?
    A aid
    B drawback
    C discharge
    D discord

13. **What would not be possible if a decision was** *undebatable*?
    A conversation about the topic
    B discussion about opposing reasons
    C review of the decision
    D organizing an opposition

14. **What is a person who is** *dissatisfied* **likely to do?**
    A smile
    B thank you
    C laugh
    D frown

Research: Multimedia Report

A **multimedia report** presents information about a topic using a variety of materials, including audio, video, and other high-tech options. In this workshop, you will create a multimedia report using some of these kinds of media.

Assignment Write a multimedia report about a topic that interests you. Use audio and visual materials for support.

What to Include Your report should feature these elements:
- well-integrated and appropriate audio and visual features from a variety of sources
- use of formatting and presentation techniques for visual appeal
- a focused topic that can be thoroughly covered in the time and space allotted
- a presentation tailored to your specific audience
- error-free grammar including proper sentence structure

To preview the criteria on which your multimedia presentation may be judged, see the rubric on page 986.

Prewriting

Choosing Your Topic

List topic ideas. Select a subject that you know will have a range of multimedia material that is readily available. To narrow the number of possible topics, list musicians or artists whose work you enjoy, films you know well, or trends you notice in school. Review your list and choose a topic. Draw up some questions you have about the topic that you can modify as you research.

Gathering Details

Research your topic. Do research to find information on your topic and to find creative ways of presenting the information. As you consult your library and the Internet, look for audio or video clips of interviews, documentaries, music, and art. Take notes on what you find, using your own words.

Using the Form
You may use elements of this form in these types of writing:
- documentaries
- biographies
- television news reports

Work in Progress
Review the work you did on pages 925, 943, and 969.

Drafting

Shaping Your Writing

Sketch an outline. Before you begin writing, develop an outline to shape the sequence of your ideas. Organize the outline to start with an *introduction* that identifies your topic. Next, the *body* of your report should support and develop your main ideas. Finally, a *conclusion* should sum up your research and key points.

Providing Elaboration

Incorporate audio and visual aids. Use of supporting aids can enhance your message and provide evidence to support your points.

- **Audio,** such as music or interviews, can set a mood and provide information.

- **Visual aids,** such as spreadsheets, maps, or charts, can organize large amounts of information, making it easier to read.

Use software to present additional information, and plan to display information on posters, on screen, or as handouts. Use your software's on-screen help and tutorials to guide you.

Revising

Revising Your Overall Structure

Revise to clarify sequence. Look for places where connections are not clear. Introduce each media element, explain its connection to your main idea, and then return to your script.

Revising Your Word Choice

Revise to address your audience. Consider the audience you expect to hear your presentation. If the group does not know a great deal about your topic, define any terms that will be unfamiliar. If the audience is already well-informed, delete facts that are too basic.

Reading Writing
Connection

To read the complete student model, see page 985.

Student Model: Connecting the Media

Visual: Image of American battleship *U.S.S. Arizona*

Sound: Bugle playing *Taps*

Script: Eight American battleships Including the *U.S.S. Arizona* shown here, and ten other navy vessels were sunk or badly damaged. Approximately 3,000 naval and military personnel were killed or wounded.

> This additional phrase links the script to the visual.

Integrating Grammar Skills

Revising Run-on Sentences and Sentence Fragments

Sentence errors such as run-on sentences and sentence fragments can make writing difficult to understand.

Identifying Sentence Errors A **run-on sentence** is two or more complete sentences that are not properly joined or separated. This sentence error can be corrected by breaking the sentence into two, or by adding punctuation or words to clarify the meaning of a single sentence.

Prentice Hall Writing and Grammar Connection: Chapter 21, Section 4

Run-On	Corrected
Charles is an avid reader he also is a dedicated athlete.	**Separate sentences:** Charles is an avid reader. He also is a dedicated athlete. *or* **Add comma and coordinating conjunction:** Charles is an avid reader, but he also is a dedicated athlete. *or* **Use a semicolon:** Charles is an avid reader; he also is a dedicated athlete.

A **sentence fragment** is a group of words that does not express a complete thought. To fix fragments, add more information to complete the idea.

Fragment: By the next day.

Corrected: By the next day, she felt better.

Fixing Errors Follow these steps to fix sentence errors.

1. **To fix a run-on, rewrite it using one of the following methods:**
   - Break the clauses into separate sentences.
   - Join the clauses using a comma and a coordinating conjunction, such as *and, or, but, yet, so.*
   - Join the clauses using a semicolon.
2. **Fix a fragment by either adding it to a nearby sentence or adding the necessary words to turn it into a sentence.**

Apply It to Your Editing

Choose three paragraphs in your draft. Revise run-on sentences or fragments by adding the necessary words and punctuation.

Student Model: Jessica Leanore Adamson
Boise, ID

The Attack on Pearl Harbor

Jessica chose a title that reflects her topic.

Slide 1
Visual: Image of Pearl Harbor ca. 1940
Sound: Airplane/explosion
Script: Pearl Harbor was one of the principal naval bases of WWII. It is located approximately six miles west of Honolulu in Oahu, Hawaii. Early in the morning on December 7, 1941, Japanese submarines and carrier-based planes attacked the U.S. Pacific fleet at Pearl Harbor.

The writer has chosen a topic that can be covered in the brief time allotted to her report.

Slide 2
Visual: Image of American battleship *U.S.S. Arizona*.
Sound: Bugle playing *Taps*
Script: Eight American battleships, including the *U.S.S. Arizona* shown here, and ten other navy vessels were sunk or badly damaged, almost 200 American aircraft were destroyed, and approximately 3,000 naval and military personnel were killed or wounded.

The sound effects and images are dramatic and appropriate to the topic, audience, and purpose.

Slide 8
Visual: Blank screen (black). Words "dereliction of duty" and "errors of judgment" appear letter by letter.
Sound: Typewriter
Script: Shortly after the attack, U.S. President Franklin D. Roosevelt appointed a commission to determine whether negligence had contributed to the raid. The commission found the naval and army commanders of the area guilty of "dereliction of duty" and "errors of judgment."

The writer uses boldfaced heads and other appropriate formatting to present the organization of the report clearly.

This model represents the introductory and concluding slides of a multimedia report. Slides 3–7 are not shown. In the full report they present more information along with supporting audio and visual materials to develop the presentation's main idea.

Editing and Proofreading

Review your draft to eliminate errors in grammar, spelling, or punctuation.

Focus on Presentation Copies: Avoid distracting your audience with mistakes; run a spelling and grammar check on any visuals you present. Be careful, however, because spell-checkers do not catch mistakes in homophones, such as *there, their,* and *they're.*

Publishing and Presenting

Consider one of the following ways to share your writing:

Deliver an oral presentation. Select a title that grabs the attention of your audience and reflects your topic. Give a practice performance to friends or family members. Do a final check of your equipment before delivering your multimedia presentation for your classmates.

Offer your presentation to an organization. Present your report outside your school. Contact a local library, club, or elementary school that might be interested in your work.

Reflecting on Your Writing

Writer's Journal Jot down your thoughts on writing a multimedia report. Begin by answering these questions:

- If you had to create another multimedia report, what would you do differently?
- What did you learn about the topic you chose?

> *Prentice Hall Writing and Grammar Connection: Chapter 28, Part 2*

Rubric for Self-Assessment

To assess your multimedia report, use the following rubric:

Criteria	Rating Scale
	not very very
Focus: How clearly do you identify your topic?	1 2 3 4 5
Organization: How well focused is your presentation?	1 2 3 4 5
Support/Elaboration: How effective are your audio and visual features?	1 2 3 4 5
Style: How well have you tailored your presentation to your audience?	1 2 3 4 5
Conventions: How correct is your grammar, especially your use of complete sentences?	1 2 3 4 5

Skills You Will Learn

Literature You Will Read

Reading Skill: *Ask Questions to Set a Purpose for Reading*
Literary Analysis: *Cultural Context*

Reading Skill: *Adjust Reading Rate*
Literary Analysis: *Identify Author's Influences*

Reading Skill: *Use Text Structure*

Literary Analysis: *Comparing Works on a Similar Theme*

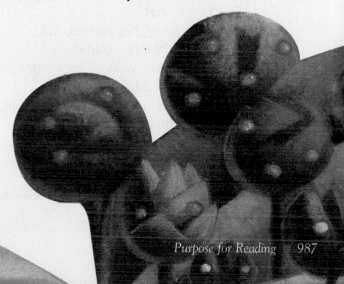

Reading: Setting a Purpose for Reading

> **Setting a purpose for reading** means deciding on a reading goal in advance so you can focus your attention as you read.

Skills and Strategies You Will Learn in Part 2

In Part 2, you will learn

- to **ask questions** in order to set a **purpose for reading** (p. 990)
- to **adjust your reading rate** according to your **purpose for reading** (p. 1008)
- to **use text structure** in order to **locate information that fits your purpose** (p. 1026)

Using the Skills and Strategies in Part 2

In Part 2, you will learn to ask questions about your reading to determine a purpose for reading. You will also learn to adjust your reading rate and use text structure to suit your purpose for reading.

The chart shows how your purposes for reading two selections about the Erie Canal might vary.

Source folk song lyrics	**Source** encyclopedia article
Purpose entertainment	**Purpose** research report
The Erie Canal I've got a mule, her name is Sal, 15 miles on the Erie Canal. She's a good old worker, she's a good old pal, 15 miles on the Erie Canal. We've hauled some barges in our day, Filled with lumber, coal, and hay. And every inch of the way we know, From Albany to Buffalo.	**Erie Canal** This man-made waterway connecting the Great Lakes and New York City was opened in 1825. The original canal was 363 miles long, 40 feet wide, and 4 feet deep. The waterway allowed farmers to ship their crops east and factories to ship manufactured goods west. As a result, the Erie Canal was an important factor in the growth of both New York City and the Midwest.

Academic Vocabulary: Words for Discussing Setting a Purpose for Reading

The following words will help you write and talk about setting a purpose for your reading as you work with the selections in this unit.

Word Root	Definition	Example Sentence
critique *v.*	write a critical essay or review	If you *critique* a work, your purpose is to evaluate its literary elements.
skim *v.*	to read quickly, skipping parts of the text	You can *skim* a magazine article, looking for interesting details.
focus *v.*	direct one's attention to a specific part of something	*Focus* on details that answer your purpose-setting questions.
identify, *v.*	recognize; to find and name	*Identify* the facts that answer your purpose-setting questions.
revise *v.*	to change; to adjust	As you read, you may *revise* your original purpose for reading.

Vocabulary Skill: Borrowed and Foreign Words

You have learned that the roots of many English words come from older languages. Sometimes English has "borrowed" entire words and phrases directly from other languages.

Borrowed Word	Meaning	Example Sentence
café—French	coffee shop	Let's have dessert at a *café*.
balcony—Italian	a porch	The *balcony* overlooked the garden.
canyon—Spanish	a long, narrow valley	Our house has a view of the *canyon*.

Activity Work with a partner to develop a list of ten English words that you think have been borrowed from other languages. Then, check the dictionary to determine if you are correct. Explain how your predictions compare to the words' actual origins.

These skills will help you become a better reader. Practice them with either "Ellis Island" (p. 992) or the selections from *Out of the Dust* (p. 997).

Reading Skill

Setting a purpose for reading helps you focus your attention as you read a literary work. When you read about people from a different time and place, for example, your purpose might be to learn about their view of the world and the problems they faced.

One way to set a purpose for reading is to **ask questions** about the topic of the work. Use a "K-W-L" chart like the one shown. Fill in the first two columns before you begin to read. The second column identifies your purpose. If you can fill in the last column after reading, you have achieved your purpose.

K	W	L
What I already **k**now about the topic	Questions that explore what I **w**ant to know	Answers that show what I **l**earned

Literary Analysis

The **cultural context** of a literary work is the social and historical environment in which the characters live. Major historical events, such as bad economic times or the outbreak of war, can shape people's lives in important ways. Understanding the effects of such events can give you insight into characters' attitudes and actions.

As you read, look for details that show how characters respond to cultural and historical events.

Vocabulary Builder

Ellis Island

- **quarantine** (kwôr´ ən tēn) *n.* period of separation from others to stop the spreading of a disease (p. 993) *The passengers were kept in quarantine after one became sick.*

- **native** (nāt´iv) *adj.* related to the place of one's birth (p. 993) *He traveled far from his native land.*

from **Out of the Dust**

- **feuding** (fyōōd´ iŋ) *v.* quarreling; fighting (p. 998) *The two families were feuding over a piece of property.*

- **spindly** (spind´ lē) *adj.* long and thin (p. 1000) *The spindly legs of the table could not support much weight.*

- **drought** (drout) *n.* lack of rain; long period of dry weather (p. 1001) *The plants died during the drought.*

- **sparse** (spärs) *adj.* thinly spread and small in amount (p. 1002) *The hair on the old man's head was sparse.*

- **rickety** (rik´ it ē) *adj.* weak; likely to break (p. 1003) *The rickety old shed fell down during a storm.*

Background

Immigrants and Native Americans The speaker of "Ellis Island" pays tribute to his two sets of ancestors—European immigrants and Native Americans. These groups had very different experiences. From 1892 to 1924, about seventeen million European immigrants passed through government buildings on Ellis Island in New York Harbor. There, they received official permission to enter the United States. Meanwhile, throughout the 1800s, Native Americans had been pushed farther and farther west to make room for new settlers. By the 1890s, all Native American tribes had been moved onto reservations.

Connecting to Literature

Reading/Writing Connection Imagine how European immigrants in the 1890s felt as their ships arrived in New York Harbor. They may have been excited and terrified. Describe the risks and challenges that these immigrants faced. Use at least three of the following words: *maximize, minimize, adapt, maintain.*

Meet the Author

Joseph **Bruchac** (b. 1942)

"Ellis Island" describes Joseph Bruchac's heritage as the son of an Abenaki Indian mother and a Slovak father. Bruchac grew up in a small town in the Adirondack Mountains of New York State, where he still lives today.

A Passion for Tradition and Diversity When he became a father, Bruchac began telling traditional Native American stories to his two young sons. Before long, he had established a career as a storyteller, sharing his stories with schoolchildren. Of his motivation to tell stories that bridge cultures, Bruchac says, "We learn about ourselves by understanding others."

Fast Facts

▶ As a boy, Bruchac dreamed of becoming a park ranger. Much of his writing focuses on respect for the natural world.

▶ Bruchac was chosen to write informational panels for the National Museum of the American Indian.

Go **Online**
Author Link

For: More about the author
Visit: www.PHSchool.com
Web Code: ene-9608

ELLIS ISLAND

JOSEPH BRUCHAC

Beyond the red brick of Ellis Island
where the two Slovak children
who became my grandparents
waited the long days of <u>quarantine</u>,
5   after leaving the sickness,
the old Empires of Europe,
a Circle Line ship slips easily
on its way to the island
of the tall woman, green
10   as dreams of forests and meadows
waiting for those who'd worked
a thousand years
yet never owned their own.

Like millions of others,
15   I too come to this island,
nine decades the answerer
of dreams.

Yet only one part of my blood
        loves that memory.
Another voice speaks
20   of <u>native</u> lands
within this nation.
Lands invaded
when the earth became owned.
Lands of those who followed
25   the changing Moon,
knowledge of the seasons
in their veins.

Vocabulary Builder
quarantine (kwôr´ ən
tēn) *n.* period of
separation from
others to stop the
spreading of a
disease

Vocabulary Builder
native (nāt´ĭv) *adj.*
related to the place
of one's birth

Literary Analysis
Cultural Context
What historical
events shape the
author's reaction to
Ellis Island?

◀ **Critical Viewing**
Why would the
Statue of Liberty
seem more
welcoming than the
buildings of Ellis
Island? **[Speculate]**

Apply the Skills

Ellis Island

Thinking About the Selection

1. **Respond:** Which symbol of the United States is more meaningful to you—the Statue of Liberty or Ellis Island? Explain.
2. **(a) Recall:** What inspires the speaker to think of his ancestors? **(b) Interpret:** How is the speaker's relationship to his past reflected in the phrase "nine decades the answerer of dreams"?
3. **(a) Recall:** Who are the ancestors of the speaker in "Ellis Island"? **(b) Interpret:** What does the speaker mean by the phrase "native lands within this nation"? **(c) Contrast:** How do his ancestors differ in their attitudes toward the land?
4. **(a) Analyze:** How does the speaker's dual ancestry influence his feelings toward Ellis Island? **(b) Apply:** Why does the speaker see the United States as "lands invaded"?

Reading Skill

5. **(a)** What **purpose** did you set for reading "Ellis Island"? **(b)** What questions did you ask to help you set a purpose?
6. **(a)** What details in "Ellis Island" helped you to answer your questions? **(b)** Where could you look for more information?

Literary Analysis

7. Complete the chart by explaining what each detail from "Ellis Island" reveals about the poem's **cultural context**—the living conditions and attitudes of immigrants and Native Americans in the late 1800s.

Detail	Cultural Conditions and Attitudes
Immigrants were kept in quarantine before entering the United States.	
Immigrants dreamed of owning their own land.	
Native American lands were invaded "when the earth became owned."	
Native Americans had "knowledge of the seasons in their veins."	

QuickReview

Poem at a Glance
The speaker describes his mixed emotions about Ellis Island.

Purpose for Reading: your reason for reading a literary work

Cultural Context: the social and historical environment in which characters live

Go Online
Assessment
For: Self-test
Visit: www.PHSchool.com
Web Code: ena-6607

Vocabulary Builder

Practice Synonyms are words with similar meanings. Write a word from the vocabulary list on page 990 that belongs with each pair of synonyms. Explain why its meaning is similar.

1. isolation, detention, _____
2. original, belonging, _____

Writing

Write a short **research proposal** for a report on immigrants' experiences as they passed through Ellis Island in the 1890s and early 1900s.

- Write three specific questions you would like to answer about the immigrants and their experiences at Ellis Island.
- List at least three sources that might contain the information you need to answer your questions. Explain which source you think would best provide the information you need to answer each question.
- Present and support your proposal in a few paragraphs.

For *Grammar, Vocabulary,* and *Assessment,* see **Build Language Skills,** pages 1006–1007.

Extend Your Learning

Listening and Speaking In a small group, prepare an **oral presentation** on Ellis Island. In your notes, paraphrase details from sources by putting the writer's ideas into your own words. Then, plan to include visuals such as photographs and illustrations. Discuss the best way to incorporate source material such as oral histories or statistics into the presentation.

Research and Technology Research the experiences of immigrants at Ellis Island. Then, as one of the immigrants, write a **letter** to a friend back in the "old country." Follow these tips:

- Describe your thoughts, emotions, and experiences as you arrive at Ellis Island.
- Use vivid words to capture the excitement and anxiety of waiting to enter the United States.

Poetry

Background

The Dust Bowl *Out of the Dust* is the story of a farm family's struggles during the 1930s. From 1931 to 1939, farmers in the southern Great Plains suffered from the worst drought in American history. Their crops dried up and died, and powerful dust storms blew away millions of tons of soil. By 1935, many farmers gave up and moved west to California. Meanwhile, the nation was also suffering from the effects of the Great Depression. Banks and other businesses failed, workers lost their jobs, and many Americans were hungry and homeless.

Connecting to Literature

Reading/Writing Connection For farmers, the weather is a constant concern. Too much or too little rain can bring disaster. Write five sentences describing the weather's impact on your daily life. Use at least three of the following words: *involve, occur, complicate, impact, contribute.*

Review

For **Reading Skill, Literary Analysis,** and **Vocabulary Builder,** see page 990.

Meet the Author

Karen **Hesse** (b. 1952)

In her fiction, Karen Hesse shows a deep understanding of outsiders—characters who do not quite fit in—because that is how she felt as she was growing up in Baltimore, Maryland. A shy girl who lived in her imagination, Hesse loved curling up in an apple tree in her backyard and reading for hours at a time.

Giving a Face to History Hesse's imagination and powers of understanding enable her to create vivid characters who struggle to survive during difficult times in history. Characters in her historical novels include a Russian immigrant in 1919, a woman caught up in the drama of the Civil War, and a boy who stows away on an explorer's ship during the 1700s. "I love research, love dipping into another time and place, and asking questions," Hesse says.

Go Online
Author Link

For: More about the author
Visit: www.PHSchool.com
Web Code: ene-9609

From
OUT OF THE DUST

KAREN HESSE

DEBTS

Daddy is thinking
of taking a loan from Mr. Roosevelt and his men,[1]
to get some new wheat planted
where the winter crop has spindled out and died.
5 Mr. Roosevelt promises
Daddy won't have to pay a dime
till the crop comes in.

Reading Skill
Purpose for Reading
What is a purpose you
could set for reading
historical fiction, such
as this poem?

---

1. . . . **a loan from Mr. Roosevelt and his men** In 1933, President Franklin D. Roosevelt began a series of government programs, called the New Deal, to help Americans suffering from the effects of the Great Depression. Among these programs were government loans to help Dust Bowl farmers.

Daddy says,
"I can turn the fields over,
10   start again.
It's sure to rain soon.
Wheat's sure to grow."

Ma says, "What if it doesn't?"

Daddy takes off his hat,
15   roughs up his hair,
puts the hat back on.
"Course it'll rain," he says.

Ma says, "Bay,
it hasn't rained enough to grow wheat in
20   three years."

Daddy looks like a fight brewing.

He takes that red face of his out to the barn,
to keep from <u>feuding</u> with my pregnant ma.

I ask Ma
25   how,
after all this time,
Daddy still believes in rain.

"Well, it rains enough," Ma says,
"now and again,
30   to keep a person hoping.
But even if it didn't
your daddy would have to believe.
It's coming on spring,
and he's a farmer."

March 1934

Literary Analysis
Cultural Context
What does this conversation indicate about the effect of dry weather on farm families?

Vocabulary Builder
feuding (fyo͞od´ iŋ) *v.* quarreling; fighting

Reading Skill
Purpose for Reading
What can you learn from the poem about farmers' reactions to the lack of rainfall in 1934?

The Great Depression

The stock market crashed October 29, 1929—"Black Tuesday"—ushering in the worst economic collapse the United States ever experienced. More than 15 million Americans lost their jobs. The Depression lasted through the early 1940s. Making matters worse, a drought spread through 75 percent of the country during the 1930s, causing devastating dust storms.

BROOKLYN DAILY EAGLE
And Complete Long Island News

LATE NEWS
WALL STREET
1.15 PRICES ★ ★

★ NEW YORK CITY, THURSDAY, OCTOBER 24, 1929. ★   32 PAGES   THREE CENTS

89th YEAR—No. 295.

WALL ST. IN PANIC AS STOCKS CRASH

Bread lines were common city sights during
▼ the Depression.

President Franklin D. Roosevelt offered assistance to people in rural areas who were
▼ affected by the drought.

Unemployment During the Depression

24.9%

17.9%

3.2%

30%

20%

10%

0%

1929   1931   1933   1935   1937   1939

▲ In cities, the WPA (Works Progress Administration) put people to work repairing roads.

Work Pays America!
PROSPERITY
WORKS PROGRESS ADMINISTRATION

▲ Restoring drought-damaged land by planting new trees was another WPA goal.

Connect to the Literature   How could government programs have helped Ma and Daddy?

FIELDS OF FLASHING LIGHT

I heard the wind rise,
and stumbled from my bed,
down the stairs,
out the front door,
5   into the yard.
The night sky kept flashing,
lightning danced down on its <u>spindly</u> legs.

I sensed it before I knew it was coming.
I heard it,
10   smelled it,
tasted it.
Dust.

While Ma and Daddy slept,
the dust came,
15   tearing up fields where the winter wheat,
set for harvest in June,
stood helpless.

Reading Skill
Purpose for Reading
What would you want
to know after reading
this poem's title?

Vocabulary Builder
spindly (spind′ lē) *adj.*
long and thin

I watched the plants,
surviving after so much <u>drought</u> and so much wind,
20 I watched them fry,
or
flatten,
or blow away,
like bits of cast-off rags.
25 It wasn't until the dust turned toward the house,
like a fired locomotive,
and I fled,
barefoot and breathless, back inside,
it wasn't until the dust
30 hissed against the windows,
until it ratcheted the roof,
that Daddy woke.

He ran into the storm,
his overalls half-hooked over his union suit.[2]
35 "Daddy!" I called. "You can't stop dust."

Ma told me to
cover the beds,
push the scatter rugs against the doors,
dampen the rags around the windows.
40 Wiping dust out of everything,
she made coffee and biscuits,
waiting for Daddy to come in.

Sometime after four,
rubbing low on her back,
45 Ma sank down into a chair at the kitchen table
and covered her face.
Daddy didn't come back for hours,
not
until the temperature dropped so low,
50 it brought snow.

Ma and I sighed, grateful,
staring out at the dirty flakes,
but our relief didn't last.
The wind snatched that snow right off the fields,

2. **union suit** type of long underwear, common in the 1930s, that combines a shirt and leggings in one garment.

◄ **Critical Viewing**
Why does a dust storm like this one pose such danger to farms and farmers? **[Connect]**

Vocabulary Builder
drought (drout) *n.* lack of rain; long period of dry weather

Literary Analysis
Cultural Context
What do the characters' reactions to the dust storm tell you about the emotional effect of this natural disaster?

 **Reading Check**

What noise wakes Daddy?

55 leaving behind a sea of dust,
waves and
waves and
waves of
dust,
60 rippling across our yard.

Daddy came in,
he sat across from Ma and blew his nose.
Mud streamed out.
He coughed and spit out
65 mud.
If he had cried,
his tears would have been mud too,
but he didn't cry.
And neither did Ma.

March 1934

MIGRANTS

We'll be back when the rain comes,
they say,
pulling away with all they own,
straining the springs of their motor cars.
5 Don't forget us.

And so they go,
fleeing the blowing dust,
fleeing the fields of brown-tipped wheat
barely ankle high,
10 and <u>sparse</u> as the hair on a dog's belly.

We'll be back, they say,
pulling away toward Texas,
Arkansas,
where they can rent a farm,
15 pull in enough cash,
maybe start again.

Reading Skill
Purpose for Reading
What information does the poem provide about the Dust Bowl that you could not get from a history textbook?

Literary Analysis
Cultural Context
What economic forces drive away the migrants?

Vocabulary Builder
sparse (spärs) *adj.*
thinly spread and small in amount

We'll be back when it rains,
they say,
setting out with their bedsprings and mattresses,
20 their cookstoves and dishes,
their kitchen tables,
and their milk goats
tied to their running boards[3]
in <u>rickety</u> cages,
25 setting out for
California,
where even though they say they'll come back,
they just might stay
if what they hear about that place is true.

30 Don't forget us, they say.
But there are so many leaving,
how can I remember them all?

April 1935

---

3. **running boards** steps, or footboards, that ran along the lower part of each side of a car, as shown in the photograph. Running boards were common on cars of the 1930s.

▲ **Critical Viewing**
What details in this historic photograph indicate that this family is moving? **[Analyze]**

Vocabulary Builder
rickety (rik´ it ē) *adj.*
weak; likely to break

Apply the Skills

from *Out of the Dust*

Thinking About the Selection

1. **Respond:** Which poem did you find most powerful? Why?
2. **(a) Recall:** In "Debts," what is the subject of the discussion between Ma and Daddy? **(b) Recall:** How does Ma explain Daddy's point of view? **(c) Infer:** What is Ma's point of view?
3. **(a) Recall:** In "Fields of Flashing Light," what happens to the family's wheat crop? **(b) Analyze Causes and Effects:** What effect is this event likely to have on the family's income?
4. **(a) Recall:** In "Fields of Flashing Light," what does the narrator do during the dust storm? **(b) Infer:** What is the purpose of these actions? **(c) Draw Conclusions:** How do you know that these actions are not very effective?
5. **(a) Analyze Causes and Effects:** In "Migrants," why do the family's neighbors move? **(b) Speculate:** What effects might their decision have on the people who stay behind?

Reading Skill

6. **(a)** What **purpose** did you set for reading the three poems? **(b)** What questions did you ask to help you set a purpose?
7. **(a)** What details from the poems helped you answer your questions? **(b)** Where could you look to find more information to answer your questions?

Literary Analysis

8. Complete the chart by explaining what each detail from *Out of the Dust* reveals about the poem's **cultural context**—the living conditions and attitudes of farmers during the Dust Bowl.

Detail	Cultural Conditions and Attitudes
Dust blew away crops, covering items, and people.	
Ma and Pa do not cry when their wheat crop is destroyed.	
Pa decides to plant again, but other families decide to move away.	

QuickReview

Poems at a Glance

The speaker describes the conflicts her family faces when dust storms destroy their wheat crop in the 1930s.

Purpose for Reading: your reason for reading a literary work

Cultural Context: the social and historical environment in which characters live

Go Online
Assessment
For: Self-test
Visit: www.PHSchool.com
Web Code: ena-6608

Vocabulary Builder

Practice **Synonyms** are words with similar meanings. Write a word from the vocabulary list on page 990 that belongs with each pair of synonyms. Explain why its meaning is similar.

1. weak, shaky, _____
2. long, thin, _____
3. quarreling, fighting, _____
4. scanty, scattered, _____
5. dryness, barrenness, _____

Writing

Write a short **research proposal** for a report on how the Dust Bowl affected farmers in the 1930s.

- Write three specific questions you would like to answer about the Dust Bowl and its effects.
- List at least three sources that might contain the information you need to answer your questions. Explain which source you think would best provide the information you need to answer each question.
- Present and support your proposal in a few paragraphs.

For *Grammar,* *Vocabulary,* and *Assessment,* see **Build Language Skills,** pages 1006–1007.

Extend Your Learning

Listening and Speaking In a small group, prepare an **oral presentation** on the effects of the Dust Bowl during the 1930s. In your notes, paraphrase details from sources by putting the writer's ideas into your own words. Then, plan to include visuals such as photographs and illustrations. Discuss the best way to incorporate source material such as oral histories or statistics into the presentation.

Research and Technology Research the experiences of the Oklahoma farmers who fled their farms in the 1930s to become migrant workers in California. Then, as one of these farmers, write a **letter** to a friend back in Oklahoma. Describe your thoughts, emotions, and experiences on the trip and when you arrived in California. Use vivid words that will show how it felt to be among the thousands of farmers seeking work in California.

Build Language Skills

Vocabulary Skill

Borrowed and Foreign Words A number of English words have been taken directly from other languages. Words such as *tomato* and *hurricane* were borrowed from Native American languages. Many words borrowed from French relate to art and literature. For example, the word *critique* as a noun means "a critical essay or review." As a verb, *critique* means "to write a critical essay or review."

➤ **Example:** In my *critique* of "The Tell-Tale Heart," I focus on how Poe creates the story's atmosphere.

Practice Look up the meaning of each borrowed English word. Then, write a sentence using each word in its correct context.

1. genre
2. alligator
3. pecan
4. boomerang
5. ski
6. ranch

Grammar Lesson

Semicolons and Colons Use a **semicolon (;)** to join independent clauses that are not already joined by the conjunctions *and, but, or, nor, for, so,* or *yet*. Use a **colon (:)** before a list of items that follows an independent clause.

➤ **Example:** The vase is broken; it fell off the shelf yesterday.
Please bring the following supplies: a spiral notebook, two pencils, and a pair of scissors.

Practice Rewrite each sentence, adding a semicolon (;) or a colon (:) where it is needed.

1. The following students were in the race Nicole, Steven, Jeff, and Rebecca.
2. Nicole won the 100-meter dash Jeff came in second.
3. The next track meet is on April 18 I plan to participate.
4. I want to run in the following events the 50-meter dash, the hurdles, and the relay race.
5. I like individual sports more than team sports it is fun to challenge myself to beat my own records.

MorePractice

For more on semicolons and colons, see the Grammar Handbook, p. R31.

𝒲𝒢 *Prentice Hall Writing and Grammar Connection: Chapter 26, Section 3*

Reading: Setting a Purpose for Reading

Directions: *Read the selection. Then, answer the questions.*

George Washington Carver: Plant Genius

Early Years The son of African American slaves in Missouri, George Washington Carver grew up on a farm and began studying plants when he was only a child. By the time he was a teenager, his neighbors called on him as a "plant doctor" to help with their failing crops. He became a national expert on breeding plants.

An Aid to Farmers As a professor in Alabama, Carver saw that farmers were destroying the soil by growing only plants that drain the ground of nitrogen—an important plant nutrient. He persuaded them to alternate their crops.

1. What is the most likely purpose for reading this article?
   - **A** entertainment
   - **B** to take action
   - **C** information
   - **D** special insight

2. What question is answered by this selection?
   - **A** What is a genius?
   - **B** How many types of plants are there?
   - **C** Why is Carver a "plant genius"?
   - **D** How did Carver get involved with plants?

3. If your purpose were to find out what plants Carver studied, where would you look?
   - **A** in paragraph 1
   - **B** in paragraph 2
   - **C** in sentence 3
   - **D** in another source

4. Which of the following research questions would NOT be satisfied by reading this article?
   - **A** What was Carver an expert on?
   - **B** How did Carver change agriculture?
   - **C** Where did Carver grow up?
   - **D** What obstacles did Carver face?

Timed Writing: Analysis [Critical Stance]

Review "Ellis Island" or the excerpts from *Out of the Dust*. Write a brief essay analyzing whether the author succeeds in producing an emotional response in the reader. **(35 minutes)**

 Writing Workshop: *Work in Progress*

Cause-and-Effect Essay

For a cause-and-effect essay you may write, list three actions you can observe in your classroom and note each action as a "cause." For each cause, jot down the potential effect that may follow from the cause. Save this cause-effect list in your writing portfolio.

These skills will help you become a better reader.
Practice them with either "Choice: A Tribute . . . "
(p. 1010) or "An Episode of War" (p. 1017).

Reading Skill

When you **set a purpose for reading**, you determine
your focus before reading. Once you have set a purpose,
adjust your reading rate according to that goal.

- When you read to learn new information, read
  slowly and carefully. After completing a difficult passage,
  take time to think about what you have just read. Reread,
  if necessary.
- When you read for entertainment, you can read more
  quickly. You might still choose to reread or linger over certain passages, but studying the text is less important.

Source	Magazine article on rock star
Purpose	Entertainment
Reading Rate	Read quickly to find interesting details

The chart shows examples of reading rates. Whatever your reading rate, check regularly to make sure you are meeting your purpose. If not, you may need to consult another source or work.

Source	Biography of John F. Kennedy
Purpose	Research report
Reading Rate	Read slowly, selecting facts for your report

Literary Analysis

An **author's influences** are the cultural and historical factors that
affect his or her writing. To identify an author's influences:

- Read biographical information to learn about an author's
  important life experiences and cultural background.
- When reading, note any details in the work that show
  cultural values or attitudes. In addition, note references to
  historical events and figures or cultural influences that might
  have shaped the author's outlook and values.

Vocabulary Builder

Choice: A Tribute . . .

- **sensibility** (sen′ sə bil′ ə tē) *n.* moral, artistic,
  or intellectual outlook (p. 1011) *It was a part
  of her <u>sensibility</u> to face danger without fear.*

- **revolutionary** (rev′ ə lōō′ shə ner′ ē) *adj.*
  favoring or bringing about sweeping change
  (p. 1013) *Einstein's <u>revolutionary</u> ideas
  changed how people viewed the universe.*

- **disinherited** (dis′ in her′ it id) *n.* people
  deprived of their rights as citizens (p. 1013)
  Activists must speak out for the <u>disinherited</u>.

An Episode of War

- **compelled** (kəm peld′) *v.* forced (p. 1018)
  *He felt <u>compelled</u> to defend himself against
  the unfair attack.*

- **tumultuous** (tōō mul′ chōō əs) *adj.* wild;
  chaotic (p. 1019) *The wind whipped the
  waves on the <u>tumultuous</u> sea.*

- **contempt** (kən tempt′) *n.* scorn; disrespect
  (p. 1021) *He felt only <u>contempt</u> for his
  enemy.*

Background

The Great Migration In "Choice: A Tribute . . . , " Alice Walker describes how her brothers and sisters wanted to leave the South. Beginning in the 1890s, millions of African Americans left the South and journeyed to northern cities. Economic need, racial trouble, and inequality were all factors in what became known as "The Great Migration." In the 1970s, after the successes of the civil rights movement, this migration slowed and actually reversed course.

Connecting to the Literature

Reading/Writing Connection Walker discusses the impact of watching a television broadcast of Martin Luther King, Jr., being led away in handcuffs. Write a paragraph on an important news event that had a profound effect on you. Use three of the following words: *react, interpret, cease, identify.*

Meet the Author

Alice **Walker** (b. 1944)

Alice Walker's childhood in the rural South had a lasting impact on her writing. Walker's parents loved to tell her stories—so much so, that she later referred to her mother as "a walking history of our community."

An Author's Influences Walker's love of stories and learning inspired her to go to college, where she became involved in the civil rights movement. After meeting Martin Luther King, Jr., she participated in marches and registered African Americans to vote in Georgia, at a time when it was dangerous to do so. By the end of the 1960s, Walker had launched a writing career that included essays, novels, and poems.

Fast Facts

▶ Many of Walker's stories examine the lives of rural African American women.

▶ Her 1982 novel *The Color Purple* won both a Pulitzer Prize and a National Book Award. It was adapted as a major motion picture, directed by Steven Spielberg.

Go Online
Author Link

For: More about the author
Visit: www.PHSchool.com
Web Code: ene-9610

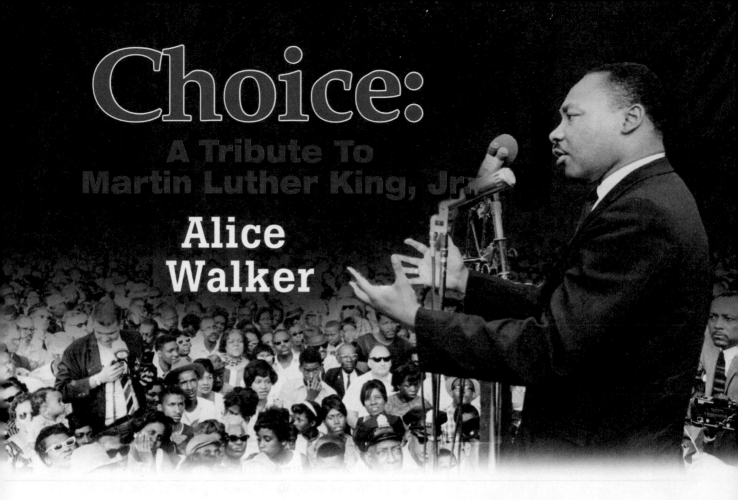

Choice:
A Tribute To Martin Luther King, Jr.

Alice Walker

This address was made in 1973 at a Jackson, Mississippi restaurant that had refused to serve people of color until forced to do so by the civil rights movement a few years before.

My great-great-great-grandmother walked as a slave from Virginia to Eatonton, Georgia—which passes for the Walker ancestral home—with two babies on her hips. She lived to be a hundred and twenty-five years old and my own father knew her as a boy. (It is in memory of this walk that I choose to keep and to embrace my "maiden" name, Walker.)

There is a cemetery near our family church where she is buried; but because her marker was made of wood and rotted years ago, it is impossible to tell exactly where her body lies. In the same cemetery are most of my mother's people, who have lived in Georgia for so long nobody even remembers when they came. And all of my great-aunts and -uncles are there, and my grandfather and grandmother, and, very recently, my own father.

▶ **Critical Viewing** How do the faces of these former slaves reflect the same types of hardships that Walker's grandmother experienced? **[Connect]**

If it is true that land does not belong to anyone until they have buried a body in it, then the land of my birthplace belongs to me, dozens of times over. Yet the history of my family, like that of all black Southerners, is a history of dispossession. We loved the land and worked the land, but we never owned it; and even if we bought land, as my great-grandfather did after the Civil War, it was always in danger of being taken away, as his was, during the period following Reconstruction.[1]

My father inherited nothing of material value from his father, and when I came of age in the early sixties I awoke to the bitter knowledge that in order just to continue to love the land of my birth, I was expected to leave it. For black people—including my parents—had learned a long time ago that to stay willingly in a beloved but brutal place is to risk losing the love and being forced to acknowledge only the brutality.

It is a part of the black Southern <u>sensibility</u> that we treasure memories; for such a long time, that is all of our homeland those of us who at one time or another were forced away from it have been allowed to have.

I watched my brothers, one by one, leave our home and leave the South. I watched my sisters do the same. This was not unusual; abandonment, except for memories, was the common thing, except for those who "could not do any better," or those whose strength or stubbornness was so colossal they took the risk that others could not bear.

---

1. Reconstruction (1865–1877) period following the American Civil War when the South was rebuilt and reestablished as part of the Union.

Literary Analysis
Author's Influences
What attachment does the author feel to her ancestors and their land?

Vocabulary Builder
sensibility (sen´ sə bil´ ə tē) *n.* moral, artistic, or intellectual outlook

Reading Check
How does Alice Walker's last name honor her ancestors?

In 1960, my mother bought a television set, and each day after school I watched Hamilton Holmes and Charlayne Hunter[2] as they struggled to integrate—fair-skinned as they were—the University of Georgia. And then, one day, there appeared the face of Dr. Martin Luther King, Jr. What a funny name, I thought. At the moment I first saw him, he was being handcuffed and shoved into a police truck. He had dared to claim his rights as a native son, and had been arrested. He displayed no fear, but seemed calm and serene, unaware of his own extraordinary courage. His whole body, like his conscience, was at peace.

At the moment I saw his resistance I knew I would never be able to live in this country without resisting everything that sought to disinherit me, and I would never be forced away from the land of my birth without a fight.

He was The One, The Hero, The One Fearless Person for whom we had waited. I hadn't even realized before that we *had* been waiting for Martin Luther King, Jr., but we had. And I knew it for sure when my mother added his name to the list of people she prayed for every night.

I sometimes think that it was literally the prayers of people like my mother and father, who had bowed down in the struggle for such a long time, that kept Dr. King alive until five years ago.[3] For years we went to bed praying for his life, and awoke with the question "Is the 'Lord' still here?"

The public acts of Dr. King you know. They are visible all around you. His voice you would recognize sooner than any other voice you have heard in this century—this in spite of the fact that certain municipal libraries, like the one in downtown Jackson, do not carry recordings of his speeches, and the librarians chuckle cruelly when asked why they do not.

---

2. **Hamilton Holmes and Charlayne Hunter** the first two African American students to attend the University of Georgia.
3. **until five years ago** Dr. Martin Luther King, Jr., was assassinated on April 4, 1968.

Literature in Context

History Connection

Marching for Freedom In March 1965, Dr. Martin Luther King, Jr., organized a march from Selma to Montgomery, Alabama, to protest restrictions on African Americans' right to vote. The peaceful protest was turned back by police using tear gas and clubs.

After this incident, some people advised King to abandon nonviolence. King decided to ignore these voices and try again. He set out from Selma with 3,200 marchers. Four days and fifty miles later they arrived in Montgomery, 25,000-strong. Five months later, President Johnson signed the Voting Rights Act of 1965.

Connect to the Literature

What qualities enabled King to become a voice for change?

You know, if you have read his books, that his is a complex and <u>revolutionary</u> philosophy that few people are capable of understanding fully or have the patience to embody in themselves. Which is our weakness, which is our loss.

And if you know anything about good Baptist preaching, you can imagine what you missed if you never had a chance to hear Martin Luther King, Jr., preach at Ebeneezer Baptist Church.

You know of the prizes and awards that he tended to think very little of. And you know of his concern for the <u>disinherited</u>: the American Indian, the Mexican-American, and the poor American white—for whom he cared much.

You know that this very room, in this very restaurant, was closed to people of color not more than five years ago. And that we eat here together tonight largely through his efforts and his blood. We accept the common pleasures of life, assuredly, in his name.

But add to all of these things the one thing that seems to me second to none in importance: He gave us back our heritage. He gave us back our homeland; the bones and dust of our ancestors, who may now sleep within our caring *and* our hearing. He gave us the blueness of the Georgia sky in autumn as in summer; the colors of the Southern winter as well as glimpses of the green of vacation-time spring. Those of our relatives we used to invite for a visit we now can ask to stay. . . . He gave us full-time use of our woods, and restored our memories to those of us who were forced to run away, as realities we might each day enjoy and leave for our children.

He gave us continuity of place, without which community is ephemeral.[4] He gave us home.   *1973*

---

4. **ephemeral** (e fem′ ər əl) *adj.* short-lived; fleeting.

▶ Critical Viewing Why might Walker use the word *fearless* to describe King, shown here in jail? [Connect]

Apply the Skills

Choice: A Tribute to Martin Luther King, Jr.

Thinking About the Selection

1. **Respond:** What impressed you most about Walker's tribute to Dr. King? Explain.
2. **(a) Recall:** Where is Walker making this speech? **(b) Connect:** What is significant about the location?
3. **(a) Recall:** Where did Walker first see Martin Luther King, Jr.? **(b) Interpret:** What did she realize about King?
4. **(a) Recall:** Before the civil rights movement, why did African Americans in the South feel left out of American society? **(b) Evaluate:** According to Walker, what was King's most important gift to African Americans?
5. **Apply:** What message does Walker's essay have for modern readers?

Reading Skill

6. **(a)** What **purpose** might you set for reading Walker's speech? **(b)** How did this purpose affect the speed at which you read the speech?
7. If you were writing a research report on King's accomplishments as a civil rights leader, would this be an appropriate text to read for information? Why or why not?

Literary Analysis

8. Complete a chart like the one shown to evaluate the effect of the author's influences on her writing.

	Influences	Effect on Her Portrayal of Dr. King
Time and place of Walker's birth		
Walker's cultural background		
Major news events		

9. How did Dr. King influence Alice Walker's beliefs and values?

QuickReview

Speech at a Glance
The author describes how her family background shaped her reactions to Dr. Martin Luther King, Jr.

Purpose for Reading: your reason for reading a literary work

Author's Influences: the cultural and historical factors that affect an author's writing

Go Online
Assessment
For: Self-test
Visit: www.PHSchool.com
Web Code: ena-6609

Vocabulary Builder

Practice Determine whether the following statements are true or false. Then, explain your answers.

1. If you have a poetic *sensibility,* you have an ear for language.
2. To be counted as one of the *disinherited* is a positive thing.
3. A *revolutionary* concept is one that is familiar to most people.

Writing

Write a **speech** for the dedication of a local monument to Martin Luther King, Jr. The speech should celebrate King's accomplishments and his leadership in the struggle for civil rights.

- Review the speeches by Walker (p. 1010) and King (p. 165) for information on King and his values.
- As you draft, explain why King should be remembered and why his ideas are still important in today's world.
- To make the speech more powerful when it is read aloud, add repetition, dramatic pauses, and vivid language.

For *Grammar, Vocabulary,* and *Assessment,* see **Build Language Skills,** pages 1024–1025.

Extend Your Learning

Listening and Speaking With another student, prepare a **role play** of an interview with a civil rights marcher who followed Martin Luther King, Jr. Together, conduct research by reading first-hand accounts of a historic event, such as the Selma March. Then, present the role play with one person as the interviewer asking questions and the other as the civil rights marcher.

Research and Technology Write a **newspaper article** for Martin Luther King Day that looks at King's career as a whole. Research King's role in the civil rights movement and the hardships he faced.

- Start with an effective, attention-grabbing lead. Newspapers often use a dramatic statement, an exciting description, or a compelling quotation to capture readers' interest.
- Add quotations from Walker's speech and from others in the civil rights movement that show why King is viewed as a hero.

Short Story

Background

Civil War Wounded Like the lieutenant in "An Episode of War," soldiers who were wounded in the Civil War faced very long odds. Field hospitals were unsanitary and crowded with wounded soldiers. Medical practices of the time, such as not sterilizing surgical instruments, encouraged the spread of disease and infection. To save soldiers' lives from deadly infections, doctors were often forced to amputate limbs.

Connecting to the Literature

Reading/Writing Connection The wounded soldier in "An Episode of War" finds his way to a Civil War field hospital. Think about modern hospitals. Describe how doctors and nurses make patients feel safe and secure. Use at least three of these words: *administer, assist, communicate, display, minimize.*

Review

For **Reading Skill, Literary Analysis,** and **Vocabulary Builder,** see page 1008.

Meet the Author

Stephen **Crane** (1871–1900)

When Stephen Crane wrote *The Red Badge of Courage,* he set out to change the way people viewed war novels. A journalist who was largely unknown outside of New York City, Crane created a novel about a young Civil War soldier. The book made him a household name.

Stories of War Although he was born years after the Civil War had ended, Crane was fascinated by the war. He interviewed Civil War veterans and pored over photographs, battlefield maps, and firsthand accounts of the fighting. All this research paid off in Crane's realistic portrait of Henry Fleming, the hero of *The Red Badge of Courage.*

Fast Facts

▶ Crane's portrayal in *The Red Badge of Courage* was so realistic that even Civil War veterans were amazed at how closely he had captured the feel of battle.

▶ Though he was highly influential, Crane had a very short career. He died of tuberculosis by age twenty-eight.

Go Online
Author Link
For: More about the author
Visit: www.PHSchool.com
Web Code: ene-9611

An Episode of War

Stephen Crane

The lieutenant's rubber blanket lay on the ground, and
upon it he had poured the company's supply of coffee. Corporals and other representatives of the grimy and hot-
throated men who lined the breast-work[1] had come for each
squad's portion.

The lieutenant was frowning and serious at this task of
division. His lips pursed as he drew with his sword various
crevices in the heap, until brown squares of coffee, astound-
ingly equal in size, appeared on the blanket. He was on the
verge of a great triumph in mathematics, and the corporals
were thronging forward, each to reap a little square, when
suddenly the lieutenant cried out and looked quickly at a
man near him as if he suspected it was a case of personal
assault. The others cried out also when they saw blood upon
the lieutenant's sleeve.

He had winced like a man stung, swayed dangerously, and
then straightened. The sound of his hoarse breathing was
plainly audible. He looked sadly, mystically, over the breast-
work at the green face of a wood, where now were many little
puffs of white smoke. During this moment the men about him

1. breast-work low wall put up quickly as a defense in battle.

▲ **Critical Viewing**
What does the
picture suggest
about the setting of
the story? **[Analyze]**

✔ **Reading Check**

What happens to the
lieutenant while he is
distributing coffee?

gazed statuelike and silent, astonished and awed by this catastrophe which happened when catastrophes were not expected—when they had leisure to observe it.

As the lieutenant stared at the wood, they too swung their heads, so that for another instant all hands, still silent, contemplated the distant forest as if their minds were fixed upon the mystery of a bullet's journey.

The officer had, of course, been <u>compelled</u> to take his sword into his left hand. He did not hold it by the hilt. He gripped it at the middle of the blade, awkwardly. Turning his eyes from the hostile wood, he looked at the sword as he held it there, and seemed puzzled as to what to do with it, where to put it. In short, this weapon had of a sudden become a strange thing to him. He looked at it in a kind of stupefaction, as if he had been endowed with a trident, a sceptre, or a spade.[2]

Finally he tried to sheathe it. To sheathe a sword held by the left hand, at the middle of the blade, in a scabbard hung at the left hip, is a feat worthy of a sawdust ring.[3] This wounded officer engaged in a desperate struggle with the sword and the wobbling scabbard, and during the time of it breathed like a wrestler.

But at this instant the men, the spectators, awoke from their stone-like poses and crowded forward sympathetically. The orderly-sergeant took the sword and tenderly placed it in the scabbard. At the time, he leaned nervously backward, and did not allow even his finger to brush the body of the lieutenant. A wound gives strange dignity to him who bears it. Well men shy from his new and terrible majesty. It is as if the wounded man's hand is upon the curtain which hangs

Vocabulary Builder
compelled (kəm peld´)
v. forced

▼ **Critical Viewing**
How does this photograph of a Civil War reenactment capture the confusion of the battlefield? **[Analyze]**

---

2. **a trident, a sceptre, or a spade** symbols of royal power.
3. **sawdust ring** ring in which circus acts are performed.

before the revelations of all existence—the meaning of ants, potentates,[4] wars, cities, sunshine, snow, a feather dropped from a bird's wing; and the power of it sheds radiance upon a bloody form, and makes the other men understand sometimes that they are little. His comrades look at him with large eyes thoughtfully. Moreover, they fear vaguely that the weight of a finger upon him might send him headlong, precipitate the tragedy, hurl him at once into the dim, grey unknown. And so the orderly-sergeant, while sheathing the sword, leaned nervously backward.

There were others who proffered assistance. One timidly presented his shoulder and asked the lieutenant if he cared to lean upon it, but the latter waved him away mournfully. He wore the look of one who knows he is the victim of a terrible disease and understands his helplessness. He again stared over the breast-work at the forest, and then, turning, went slowly rearward. He held his right wrist tenderly in his left hand as if the wounded arm was made of very brittle glass.

And the men in silence stared at the wood, then at the departing lieutenant; then at the wood, then at the lieutenant.

As the wounded officer passed from the line of battle, he was enabled to see many things which as a participant in the fight were unknown to him. He saw a general on a black horse gazing over the lines of blue infantry at the green woods which veiled his problems. An aide galloped furiously, dragged his horse suddenly to a halt, saluted, and presented a paper. It was, for a wonder, precisely like a historical painting.

To the rear of the general and his staff a group, composed of a bugler, two or three orderlies, and the bearer of the corps standard,[5] all upon maniacal horses, were working like slaves to hold their ground, preserve their respectful interval, while the shells boomed in the air about them, and caused their chargers to make furious quivering leaps.

A battery, a <u>tumultuous</u> and shining mass, was swirling toward the right. The wild thud of hoofs, the cries of the riders shouting blame and praise, menace and encouragement, and, last, the roar of the wheels, the slant of the glistening guns,

---

4. potentates (pōt′ n tāts′) *n.* rulers; powerful people.
5. corps (kôr) **standard** flag or banner representing a military unit.

Literary Analysis
Author's Influences
What realistic details in this paragraph suggest the influence of firsthand accounts on the author's writing?

Vocabulary Builder
tumultuous (too mul′ choo əs) *adj.* wild; chaotic

 **Reading Check**

What does the lieutenant do after he is injured?

brought the lieutenant to an intent pause. The battery[6] swept in curves that stirred the heart; it made halts as dramatic as the crash of a wave on the rocks, and when it fled onward this aggregation of wheels, levers, motors had a beautiful unity, as if it were a missile. The sound of it was a war-chorus that reached into the depths of man's emotion.

The lieutenant, still holding his arm as if it were of glass, stood watching this battery until all detail of it was lost, save the figures of the riders, which rose and fell and waved lashes over the black mass.

Later, he turned his eyes toward the battle, where the shooting sometimes crackled like bush-fires, sometimes sputtered with exasperating irregularity, and sometimes reverberated like the thunder. He saw the smoke rolling upward and saw crowds of men who ran and cheered, or stood and blazed away at the inscrutable distance.

He came upon some stragglers, and they told him how to find the field hospital. They described its exact location. In fact, these men, no longer having part in the battle, knew more of it than others. They told the performance of every corps, every division, the opinion of every general. The lieutenant, carrying his wounded arm rearward, looked upon them with wonder.

At the roadside a brigade was making coffee and buzzing with talk like a girls' boarding-school. Several officers came out to him and inquired concerning things of which he knew nothing. One, seeing his arm, began to scold. "Why, man, that's no way to do. You want to fix that thing." He appropriated the lieutenant and the lieutenant's wound. He cut the sleeve and laid bare the arm, every nerve of which softly fluttered under his touch. He bound his handkerchief over the wound, scolding away in the meantime. His tone allowed one to think that he was in the habit of being wounded every day. The lieutenant hung his head, feeling, in this presence, that he did not know how to be correctly wounded.

The low white tents of the hospital were grouped around an old schoolhouse. There was here a singular commotion. In the foreground two ambulances interlocked wheels in the deep mud. The drivers were tossing the blame of it back and forth,

Reading Skill
Purpose for Reading
For what purpose might you read this story slowly?

▼ **Critical Viewing**
What do these surgeons' tools reveal about the state of medicine at the time of the Civil War? **[Infer]**

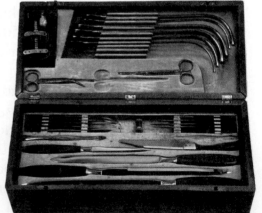

6. **battery** (bat′ ər ē) *n.* military unit of men and cannons.

gesticulating and berating,[7] while from the ambulances, both crammed with wounded, there came an occasional groan. An interminable crowd of bandaged men were coming and going. Great numbers sat under the trees nursing heads or arms or legs. There was a dispute of some kind raging on the steps of the schoolhouse. Sitting with his back against a tree a man with a face as grey as a new army blanket was serenely smoking a corncob pipe. The lieutenant wished to rush forward and inform him that he was dying.

A busy surgeon was passing near the lieutenant. "Good-morning," he said, with a friendly smile. Then he caught sight of the lieutenant's arm, and his face at once changed. "Well, let's have a look at it." He seemed possessed suddenly of a great <u>contempt</u> for the lieutenant. This wound evidently placed the latter on a very low social plane. The doctor cried out impatiently, "What mutton-head had tied it up that way anyhow?" The lieutenant answered, "Oh, a man."

When the wound was disclosed the doctor fingered it disdainfully. "Humph," he said. "You come along with me and I'll 'tend to you." His voice contained the same scorn as if he were saying: "You will have to go to jail."

The lieutenant had been very meek, but now his face flushed, and he looked into the doctor's eyes. "I guess I won't have it amputated," he said.

"Nonsense, man! Nonsense! Nonsense!" cried the doctor. "Come along, now. I won't amputate it. Come along. Don't be a baby."

"Let go of me," said the lieutenant, holding back wrathfully, his glance fixed upon the door of the old schoolhouse, as sinister to him as the portals of death.

And this is the story of how the lieutenant lost his arm. When he reached home, his sisters, his mother, his wife, sobbed for a long time at the sight of the flat sleeve. "Oh, well," he said, standing shamefaced amid these tears, "I don't suppose it matters so much as all that."

---

7. gesticulating (jes tik′ yōō lāt′ iŋ) **and berating** (bē rāt′ iŋ) waving arms about wildly and scolding.

▲ **Critical Viewing**
How do Crane's descriptions reflect the influence of Civil War photographs like the one shown here? **[Connect]**

Vocabulary Builder
contempt (kən tempt′) *n.* scorn; disrespect

Reading Skill
Purpose for Reading
What insight does the ending give you into attitudes toward wounded soldiers at the time of this story?

An Episode of War ■ 1021

Apply the Skills

An Episode of War

Thinking About the Selection

1. **Respond:** Which aspects of "An Episode of War" did you find most tragic or disturbing? Explain.
2. **(a) Recall:** What causes the lieutenant's injury?
   (b) Analyze: How does the manner in which he was wounded make you sympathize with the lieutenant?
3. **(a) Recall:** After he is hit, what does the lieutenant attempt to do with his sword? **(b) Infer:** Why does he feel the need to do this? **(c) Analyze:** How does his action expose the absurd nature of warfare?
4. **(a) Recall:** How do the lieutenant's men behave toward him when he is wounded? **(b) Compare and Contrast:** How does this treatment compare with the way the lieutenant is treated after he leaves his men? **(c) Analyze:** How does this interaction seem to strip the lieutenant of his individuality?
5. **Interpret:** Why do you think the lieutenant tells his family "I don't suppose it matters so much as all that"?

Reading Skill

6. **(a)** What **purpose** might you set for reading "An Episode of War"? **(b)** How does this purpose affect your reading rate?
7. Would this be an appropriate text to read for information for a research report on Civil War leadership? Why or why not?

Literary Analysis

8. Complete a chart like the one shown to evaluate the effect of the **author's influences** on his writing. Refer to the author biography on page 1016 to help you.

	Influences	Effect on "An Episode of War"
Crane's interests		
Crane's research		

9. Crane's writing was unique because it captured the effect of war on the individual soldier. What values are reflected in this approach to writing and in Crane's portrayal of the lieutenant?

QuickReview

Story at a Glance
The story follows the action of a Civil War officer after he is seriously wounded.

Purpose for Reading: your reason for reading a literary work

Author's Influences: the cultural and historical factors that affect an author's writing

Go Online
Assessment
For: Self-test
Visit: www.PHSchool.com
Web Code: ena-6610

Vocabulary Builder

Practice Determine whether the following statements are true or false. Then, explain your answers.

1. A neat person would feel *compelled* to pick up a discarded can.
2. People who feel *contempt* for one another make great friends.
3. Someone who gets seasick prefers a *tumultuous* ocean.

Writing

Write a **speech** for the dedication of a local memorial to those who died or were wounded in the Civil War. The speech should celebrate the determination and courage of the common soldier.

- Review "An Episode of War" to find details that show the hardships and emotions that soldiers experienced.
- As you draft, explain why Civil War soldiers deserve a memorial.
- To make the speech more powerful when it is read aloud, add repetition, dramatic pauses, and vivid language.

For *Grammar, Vocabulary,* and *Assessment,* see **Build Language Skills,** pages 1024–1025.

Extend Your Learning

Listening and Speaking With another student, prepare a **role play** of an interview with the lieutenant from "An Episode of War." Together, conduct research by reading firsthand accounts of a Civil War battle, such as Gettysburg. Then, present the role play with one person as the interviewer and the other as the wounded lieutenant.

Research and Technology Write a **newspaper article** about the experience and cost of fighting in the Civil War. You can use information from modern sources, but write the article from the perspective of someone writing during, or shortly after, the war.

- Start with an effective, attention-grabbing lead. Newspapers often use a dramatic statement, an exciting description, or a compelling caption to capture readers' interest.
- Add fictional quotations that might come from the lieutenant in "An Episode of War," describing his own experience.

Build Language Skills

Vocabulary Skill

Borrowed and Foreign Words Many English words taken from other languages relate to everyday tasks such as eating or cooking. For example, *café, chef, menu,* and *mayonnaise* are taken from French. *Enchilada, tortilla,* and *taco* come from Spanish, and *macaroni* and *pizza* were borrowed from Italian.

▶ **Example:** The *chef* at the *café* invented a dish to list on the *menu*.

Practice Use a dictionary to find which language these words came from. Explain any changes in meaning.

1. pretzel
2. yam
3. bagel
4. curry
5. waffle
6. barbecue

MorePractice

For more on capitalization, see the Grammar Handbook, p. R31.

Grammar Skill

Capitalization A capital letter is used at the beginning of a sentence and for the first letter of proper nouns and adjectives.

Capitalize	Examples
the first word in a sentence	**T**he blue jay is a very aggressive bird. **W**ait! **C**an you give me back my pen?
the first word in a quotation that is a complete sentence	Einstein said, "**A**nyone who has never made a mistake has never tried anything new."
the pronoun *I*	After swimming, **I** felt tired.
proper nouns, geographical names, and organizations	**E**lsa went sailing down the **H**udson **R**iver with her **G**irl **S**cout troop.
titles of people	**M**r. Donohue was not amused.

Practice Rewrite these sentences. Substitute capital letters or lowercase letters where appropriate.

1. the trucker hauled 2200 lbs. of potatoes from idaho to california.
2. mr. smith lived One mile away from the nearest elks club.
3. I often say, "do not count your Chickens before they hatch."
4. The bus left and i was relieved.

$\mathcal{W}_G$ *Prentice Hall Writing and Grammar Connection: Chapter 27*

Reading: Setting a Purpose for Reading

Directions: *Read the selection. Then, answer the questions.*

Sitting in Judgment: Rosa Parks and the Bus Boycott

One of the most important events in the struggle for civil rights was the Montgomery, Alabama, bus boycott. The boycott was triggered when Rosa Parks was ordered to give up her seat on a bus so a white person could sit. Under the segregation laws of the time, Parks was required to give up her seat. She refused, and was promptly arrested. While Parks challenged the law's constitutionality, African American leaders in Montgomery asked people to boycott, which hurt the bus company. Rosa Parks eventually won her case.

1. What would be an appropriate purpose for reading this article?
   A to be entertained
   B to find statistics for a paper
   C to hear a persuasive point of view
   D to learn new information

2. What would be the most appropriate reading rate for this article?
   A skim quickly for interesting language
   B read slowly to absorb facts
   C read fast to get a sense of the topic
   D read the title and the first few lines

3. If you were reading for research, what purpose would this article serve?
   A as a source for quotations
   B as a starting point for research
   C as an explanation of the origin of segregation laws
   D as a source that provides insight into the boycott

4. What do you learn from the title?
   A the sources for the information
   B the scope of the article
   C the major details of the article
   D it does not help

Timed Writing: Persuasive [Critical Stance]

Choose either "Choice: A Tribute to Martin Luther King, Jr." or "An Episode of War." Take a position on whether the author effectively demonstrates that Martin Luther King, Jr., or the lieutenant can teach us something. State your position clearly and use specific details from the text to support that position. **(45 minutes)**

 ## Writing Workshop: *Work in Progress*

Cause-and-Effect Essay

Use the Cause-and-Effect list from your writing portfolio to write a cause-effect chain. Use each effect as a cause and speculate about the potential effect. Save your cause-effect chain in your portfolio.

Reading Informational Materials

Transcripts

In Part 2, you are learning how to establish a purpose for reading literature. Establishing a purpose for reading also is helpful in reading informational materials, including transcripts. If you were interested in the story of the wounded soldier in "An Episode of War," you might also wish to read a transcript that describes how wounded veterans were treated after World War II.

About Transcripts

Transcripts are written records of speech. Unlike notes, which often summarize or paraphrase statements, transcripts contain the exact words of the speakers. People use transcripts when they want to read a complete version of what was said at a special event or occasion, without additional commentary or interpretation.

Transcripts are used to record a variety of events, including:

- radio or television shows
- trials or government hearings
- interviews or oral histories
- debates or speeches

Reading Skill

When you conduct research, you may need to examine many documents in order to find the specific information you need. To save time, **use the text structure** and special features of a document to locate information that fits your purpose. The most common features of transcripts are shown in the chart below:

Heading	This feature contains important information such as the date, topic, and time of the event.
Formatting	Each speaker is identified at the beginning of each line with capital letters, spacing, or special typefaces and colors.
Organization	An interviewer's or reporter's questions and comments identify the topics covered in the transcript. The text that follows each question or comment provides detailed information.
Brackets or Parentheses	These identify information that is not part of what was said. This can include source information or background information.

Morning Edition,

NATIONAL PUBLIC RADIO

November 11, 2003

PROFILE: World War II veterans who founded the Paralyzed Veterans of America.

BOB EDWARDS, host: This is MORNING EDITION from NPR News. I'm Bob Edwards.

In February of 1947, a small group of World War II veterans gathered at Hines VA Hospital near Chicago. The fact that they were there at all was considered extraordinary. The men were paralyzed, living at a time when paraplegia was still an unfamiliar word and most people with spinal cord injuries were told they would die within a few years. But these wounded veterans had other ideas, so they came from hospital wards across the country to start a national organization to represent veterans with spinal cord injuries. Today on Veterans Day, NPR's Joseph Shapiro tells their story.

JOSEPH SHAPIRO reporting: The logo of the Paralyzed Veterans of America looks a bit like the American flag, except that it's got 16 stars, one for each of the men who started the PVA when they gathered at that first convention nearly 57 years ago. Today only one of those 16 paralyzed veterans is still alive. His name is Ken Seaquist. He lives in a gated community in Florida. . . . It's there that Seaquist sits in his wheelchair and flips through some yellowed newspaper clippings . . .

Mr. KEN SEAQUIST: Oh, here it is. OK.

SHAPIRO: . . . until he finds a photo. . . . The picture shows that convention. It was held in a veterans hospital just outside Chicago. A large room is filled with scores of young men in wheelchairs. Others are in their pajamas and hospital beds, propped up on white pillows.

Mr. SEAQUIST: There's Bill Dake. He came with us and then Mark Orr. Three of us came in the car from Memphis. Mark had one good leg, his right leg, and he was the driver of the car.

SHAPIRO: Ken Seaquist was a tall, lanky 20-year-old in an Army mountain ski division when he was wounded in Italy. He was flown back to the United States to a veterans hospital in Memphis. He came back to a society that was not ready for paraplegics.

Mr. SEAQUIST: Before the war, people in our condition were in the closet. They never went out hardly. They didn't take them out.

SHAPIRO: Few people had ever survived for more than a few years with a spinal cord injury. Infections were common and deadly. But that was about to change. David Gerber is a historian at the University at Buffalo. He's written about disabled veterans.

Mr. DAVID GERBER (University at Buffalo): With the development of antibiotics, which came into general use in World War II, there were many healthy spinal cord-injured veterans who were able to survive and begin to aspire to have a normalized life.

SHAPIRO: Gerber says neither the wounded veterans, nor the world around them at that time knew what to make of men who were seen as having gone from manly warriors to dependent invalids.

Mr. GERBER: The society is emphatically not ready for them, and nor is the medical profession. To this extent, it was often the paralyzed veterans themselves who were pioneers in the development of a new way of life for themselves.

SHAPIRO: Seaquist and the others set out to overcome the fear and pity of others. After Seaquist was injured, he never heard from his girlfriend. His mother's hair turned white in a matter of months. People stared when he went out in public. It was a time when a president with polio felt he had to hide the fact that he used a wheelchair. Beyond attitudes, there was a physical world that had to change. When Seaquist arrived at the Memphis hospital, he could not get off the ward. There were steps in the way.

Mr. SEAQUIST: They had no idea of what they had to do for wheelchairs. So when we got there, they had to put in all these long ramps and this is what we were talking about. The ramping and just to get around the hospital and get out ourselves, you know; not having somebody help us all the time. We were an independent bunch.

SHAPIRO: There were about 2,500 soldiers with spinal cord

> Parentheses enclose the information that identifies Mr. Gerber's background.

injuries, most of them living in military hospitals around the country. Pat Grissom lived at Birmingham Hospital in California. He would become one of the first presidents of the PVA, but he was unable to travel from California to Chicago for that first convention. Grissom, too, had come back from war with little hope for his future.

Mr. PAT GRISSOM: I just suppose that we were going to live the rest of our lives either in the hospital or go to an old soldiers home. We were just going to be there taking medicine and if you got sick, they would try to take care of you and you'd have your meals provided and your future was the hospital or the old soldiers home.

SHAPIRO: At Birmingham Hospital, Grissom met a doctor who was about to become a pioneer in the new field of spinal cord medicine. Dr. Ernst Bors did a lot to improve the physical care of paraplegics. He also pushed the men at Birmingham to set goals for their lives, to go back to school, get jobs and marry. Bors and the veterans at Birmingham Hospital were the subject of a Hollywood film, *The Men*. The realistic and sympathetic portrayal helped the American public better understand paralyzed veterans. In the film, the kindly doctor in a lab coat is based on Bors. He urges on a wounded soldier in a white T-shirt, played by a young Marlon Brando.

> The information in parentheses indicates the content of the recording follows.

Marlon Brando in *The Men*.

(Soundbite of *The Men*)

> **Mr. MARLON BRANDO:** Well, what am I going to do? Where am I going to go?
>
> **Unidentified Actor:** Into the world.
>
> **Mr. BRANDO:** I can't go out there anymore.
>
> **Unidentified Actor:** You still can't accept it, can you?
>
> **Mr. BRANDO:** No. What did I do? Why'd it have to be me?
>
> **Unidentified Actor:** Is there an answer? I haven't got it. Somebody always gets hurt in the war.

> The indented text distinguishes the words of the recording from the words of the actual interview.

SHAPIRO: For Grissom and the other paralyzed veterans, there was something else that helped them go out into the world, a new technology. The introduction of automatic transmission meant that a car could be modified with hand controls for the gas and brakes. Pat Grissom.

Mr. GRISSOM: Oldsmobile came up with the hydromatic drive and they put on hand controls and they sent people out to start giving driving lessons to us and we started having visions of saving up enough money to get a car and then things were looking better all the time.

SHAPIRO: Ken Seaquist says driving opened up all kinds of possibilities, from going out to a restaurant with a bunch of friends to romance.

Car modified with hand controls.

Mr. SEAQUIST: In Memphis, we had—our favorite place was called the Silver Slipper and they welcomed us with open arms and we had maybe 10, 12 wheelchairs going with our dates. Generally it was our nurses that we dated, 'cause, you know, we couldn't get out anywhere. We took the girls with us, you know. Eventually I married one of them.

SHAPIRO: Seaquist and his wife quickly had two daughters. And with a young family, he had to find work. He went to school and became a landscape architect. Ken Seaquist stopped seeing himself as an invalid and became a man with a future. So in 1947, he and the other founders of the PVA met in Chicago to put together a collective voice to express their dreams and what they needed to accomplish them. They came up with a slogan to get others to join, 'Awaken, gentlemen, lest we decay.' Ken Seaquist explains what it meant.

Mr. SEAQUIST: If they forget us, we're going to decay. We're going to be left in the closet. We've got to get out there and speak out, getting things done so we can roll around this country and have access to the whole country.

SHAPIRO: The PVA quickly won some important legislative victories in Washington: money for paralyzed veterans to modify automobiles and houses, money for medical care. Later they would help push for laws that would make buildings and streets accessible to wheelchair users. The PVA has continued to advocate for veterans with spinal cord injuries through every war since World War II.

Joseph Shapiro, NPR News.

This is a "sign-off." The reporter indicates that the interview is over by stating his name.

Reading: Use Text Structure

Directions: *Choose the letter of the best answer.*

1. If you wanted to find only the comments of the veterans, what feature of the transcript would you use?

   A information in parentheses

   B body formatting

   C information in the header

   D information that is indented

2. If you were doing a research paper on the difficulties faced by disabled veterans, which feature would help you determine if this transcript fits your purpose?

   A the heading

   B the reporter's lines introducing each subject

   C the information in parentheses

   D the names of the participants

3. Which feature helps you locate the recording from *The Men*?

   A the section is printed in italic type

   B a logo from the film is shown

   C the words *Marlon Brando* in the text

   D identifying information is supplied in parentheses

Reading: Comprehension and Interpretation

Directions: *Write your answers on a separate piece of paper.*

4. Explain why these veterans were more likely than veterans of past wars to survive their injuries. **[Generating]**

5. Why did the veterans form the PVA? **[Generating]**

6. Summarize the actions they took to improve their situation. **[Organizing]**

Timed Writing: Explanation [Connections]

A stereotype is a perception of an entire group based on a single shared characteristic. Identify examples of the stereotyping faced by veterans described in the transcript and explain how they overcame these attitudes. Then, use these examples in a general explanation of why stereotyping can be damaging. **(20 minutes)**

Theme

The **theme** of a literary work is the insight, major idea, or underlying message that it communicates. Certain themes are common across cultures and historical eras. These recurring ideas are known as **universal themes** because they appear in many cultures. Examples of universal themes include the power of love and the importance of freedom.

Comparing Works on a Similar Theme

Even when two authors choose to write on a similar theme, they frequently produce different results. This is because writers draw on different life experiences, use different structures, have different opinions, and explore different aspects of the same theme. When you read two works on a similar theme, evaluate the presentation of the theme by asking:

	My Own True Name	"Words to Sit In ..."
Literary Form	Open letter	Essay
Theme	Using words to express oneself	Using words to express oneself
Main Points About Theme		
Experiences Tied to Theme		

- How does each writer's choice of literary form affect his or her presentation of the theme?
- Are there similarities and differences in the writers' approach to the theme?
- Do the writers tie the theme to personal experience?

Each of the selections that follows discusses a similar theme—the importance of self-expression. As you read, use a chart like the one shown to compare the theme.

Vocabulary Builder

from My Own True Name

- **intimidating** (in tim′ ə dā′ tiŋ) *adj.* frightening (p. 1035) *The tiger's growl was <u>intimidating</u>.*
- **bilingual** (bī liŋ′ gwəl) *adj.* able to speak two languages (p. 1035) *The <u>bilingual</u> nurse spoke English and Spanish fluently.*
- **eavesdropping** (ēvz′ dräp′ iŋ) *n.* secretly listening to the private conversation of others (p. 1036) *Jen caught her brother <u>eavesdropping</u> on her conversation.*

Words to Sit In, Like Chairs

- **soberly** (sō′ bər lē) *adv.* seriously; thoughtfully (p. 1038) *Jason <u>soberly</u> considered his choices before deciding where to go to college.*
- **turmoil** (tur′ moil′) *n.* a condition of great confusion or agitation (p. 1040) *The earthquake caused <u>turmoil</u> in the city.*
- **beacons** (bē′ kənz) *n.* signals meant to warn or guide, as a light or fire (p. 1040) *The runway lights served as <u>beacons</u> for the pilot.*

Connecting to the Literature

Reading/Writing Connection In these essays, the writers encourage you to write about topics that matter to you. Write a paragraph describing the types of experiences you like to write about, and explain why. Use at least three of the following words: *illustrate, verify, analyze, capture, dedicate.*

Meet the Authors

Pat **Mora** (b. 1942)

In her work, Pat Mora explores the experience of cultural diversity as well as her own life experiences as a Mexican American woman. Born in El Paso, Texas, she was raised partly by her grandmother and her Aunt "Lobo."

An Interesting Career Although Mora considers herself a Southwesterner, she travels widely, giving presentations and poetry readings. From 1983 to 1984, she hosted a National Public Radio show called *Voices: The Mexican American in Perspective.* Her writings include numerous volumes of poetry and essays, children's books, and a memoir.

Naomi Shihab **Nye** (b. 1952)

At age fourteen, Arab American poet Naomi Shihab Nye spent a year in Jerusalem, far from the American cities where she had lived as a child. Nye says that her family's time in Jerusalem enabled her to discover her heritage.

A Sturdy Foundation Nye believes that "the primary source of poetry has always been local life, random characters met on the streets, our own ancestry sifting down to us through small essential daily tasks."

Go **Online**
Author Link

For: More about the authors
Visit: www.PHSchool.com
Web Code: ene-9612

from
My Own True Name

PAT MORA

Dear Fellow Writer,

A blank piece of paper can be exciting and <u>intimidating</u>. Probably every writer knows both reactions well. I know I do. I wanted to include a letter to you in this book because I wish I could talk to you individually. I'd say: Listen to your inside self, your private voice. Respect your thoughts and feelings and ideas. You—yes, you—play with sounds. With language(s), explore the wonder of being alive.

Living hurts, so sometimes we write about a miserable date, a friend who betrayed us, the death of a parent. Some days, though, we're so full of joy we feel like a kite. We can fly! Whether we write for ourselves or to share our words, we discover ourselves when we truly write: when we dive below the surface. It's never easy to really reveal ourselves in school, but remember that writing is practice. Without practice, you will never learn to hear and sing your own unique song.

I have always been a reader, which is the best preparation for becoming a writer. When I was in grade school in El Paso, Texas (where I was born), I read comic books and mysteries and magazines and library books. I was soaking up language.

I've always liked to write, too—but I was a mother before I began to create regular time for my writing. Was it that I didn't think that I had anything important to say? Was it that I didn't believe that I could say anything that well? Was it that when I was in school we never studied a writer who was like me—<u>bilingual</u>, a Mexican American—and so somehow I decided that "people like me" couldn't be writers?

I have a large poster of an American Indian storyteller right above my desk. Children are climbing all over her, just as my sisters and my brother and I climbed over *nuestra tía*, our aunt, Ignacia Delgado, the aunt we called Lobo. She was our storyteller. Who is yours? Would you like to be a storyteller? Would you like to write or paint or draw or sing your stories?

I became a writer because words give me so much pleasure that I have always wanted to sink my hands and heart into

---

◀ **Critical Viewing** What feelings and ideas in the essay's first paragraph does this photograph best illustrate? Explain. **[Connect]**

them, to see what I can create, what will rise up, what will appear on the page. I've learned that some writers are quiet and shy, others noisy, others just plain obnoxious. Some like enchiladas and others like sushi; some like rap and others like *rancheras*.[1] Some write quickly, and some are as slow as an elderly man struggling up a steep hill on a windy day.

I'll tell you a few of our secrets.

The first is that we all read. Some of us like mysteries and some of us like memoirs, but writers are readers. We're curious to see what others are doing with words, but—what is more important—we like what happens to us when we open a book, how we journey into the pages.

Another secret is that we write often. We don't just talk about writing. We sit by ourselves inside or outside, writing at airports or on kitchen tables, even on napkins.

We're usually nosy and very good at <u>eavesdropping</u>. Just ask my three children! And writers are collectors. We collect facts and phrases and stories: the names of cacti,[2] the word for cheese in many languages.

In the last twenty years, I've spent more and more time writing my own books for children and adults. I have received many rejections and will probably receive many more, darn it. I just keep writing—and revising. Revising is now one of my favorite parts of being a writer, though I didn't always feel that way. I enjoy taking what I've written—a picture or a book or a poem—and trying to make the writing better, by changing words or rhythm. Sometimes by starting over!

Writing is my way of knowing myself better, of hearing myself, of discovering what is important to me and what makes me sad, what makes me different, what makes me me—of discovering my own true name. And writing makes me less lonely. I have all these words in English and Spanish whispering or sometimes shouting at me, just waiting for me to put them to work, to combine them so that they leap over

▲ **Critical Viewing**
Why might a writer keep an object such as this one in the place he or she writes? **[Connect]**

Vocabulary Builder
eavesdropping (ēvz´ dräp´ iŋ) *n.* secretly listening to the private conversation of others

---

1. *rancheras* (rän che´ räs) *n.* type of popular Latino music.
2. cacti (kak´ tī) *n.* plural form of *cactus,* a type of desert plant.

mountains on small hooves or slip down to the sandy bottom of the silent sea.

And you? Maybe these poems—taken from my collections *Chants, Borders,* and *Communion,* along with some new poems written for this book, for you—will tempt you to write your own poems about a special person or a special place, about a gray fear or a green hope. What are your blooms, your thorns, your roots?

Remember, my friend, never speak badly of your writing. Never make fun of it. Bring your inside voice out and let us hear you on the page. Come, join the serious and sassy family of writers.

Literary Analysis
Theme What details in the paragraph ending "silent sea" show Mora's feelings about the act of self-expression?

◄ **Critical Viewing** Why might Pat Mora approve of this scene? **[Connect]**

Thinking About the Selection

1. **Respond:** What do you think is the most interesting idea about writing that Mora expresses? Explain.

2. **(a) Recall:** Does Mora think it is easy or difficult for most students to reveal their thoughts and feelings in papers written as school assignments? **(b) Draw Conclusions:** Why does Mora address this issue?

3. **(a) Recall:** According to Mora, what is the most important reason for writing? **(b) Evaluate:** Do you agree with her? Why or why not?

WORDS TO SIT IN, LIKE CHAIRS

Naomi Shihab Nye

I was with teenagers at the wonderful Holland Hall School in Tulsa when the planes flew into the buildings on September 11, 2001. We were talking about words as ways to imagine one another's experience. A boy had just thanked me for a poem about Jerusalem that enabled him to consider the Palestinian[1] side of the story. He said he had never thought about that perspective before, so the poem was important to him.

The TV commentators were already saying the hijackers had been Arabs, which sent a deep chill into my Arab-American blood. I said to those beautiful students, "Please, I beg you, if Arabs are involved in this tragedy, remember there are millions of Arabs who would never do such a thing."

They nodded <u>soberly</u>. "Of course," they said. "We know that. This is Oklahoma." Their kindness overwhelmed me.

---

1. Palestinian (pal´ əs tin´ē ən) (*adj.*) of the people of Palestine, a region bounded by Lebanon, Syria, Egypt, and Jordan. Many Arabs living in this area were displaced when the state of Israel was established by the United Nations in 1948.

Then a boy said, "I hate to ask this so soon after it happened, but do you think you will write about it?"

"It would not be my choice of topic," I said, feeling sick, my head spinning, "but as writers, we are always exploring what happens, what comes next, turning it over, finding words to sit in like chairs, even in terrible scenery, so maybe I will have to write about it; maybe we all will. Because words shape the things that we live, whether beautiful or sorrowful, and help us connect to one another, this will be part of our history now."

Then a boy gave me a "Collapse-It" laundry basket that his parents had invented. Made of some kind of modern, waterproof, heavy-duty cardboard, it folded flat when not in use. He seemed mournful, handing it over.

"I brought this for you as a small gift," he said, "but after what happened today, it almost seems inappropriate."

Collapse-It. All Fall Down.

I clutched it to my chest and carried it with me on the long bus ride (since the planes were not flying) home to south Texas.

I have used the neat little white basket every time I've washed clothes since then. What came to me on a day of horror and tragedy and terrible mess, accompanied by kind words, continues as a helpful friend in daily life. Just the way words help us all not to be frozen in horror and fear.

USE WORDS. It is the most helpful thing I have learned in my life. We find words, we select and arrange them, to help shape our experiences of things. Whether we write them down for ourselves or send them into the air as connective lifelines between us, they help us live, and breathe, and see.

When I felt the worst after September 11, I called people. How is it for you? What are you thinking about? Have you heard anything helpful lately? Many of you probably did that, too. Sometimes it seemed good, and important, to call unexpected people—people who were not, in any way, expecting to hear from us right then. Hello, I'm thinking of you. Do you have any good news? If I had heard a useful quote or story recently myself, I shared it. Talking with friends felt like a connected chain. We passed things on down the wire.

It was very helpful for me to talk with Arab-American friends who automatically shared the doubled sense of

▲ **Critical Viewing**
What would you say is this woman's reaction to what she is hearing? **[Analyze]**

Literary Analysis
Theme According to Nye, what is the value of words in our everyday lives?

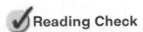

Reading Check

What does a boy give Nye on the day she visits his school?

Words to Sit in, Like Chairs ■ 1039

▶ **Critical Viewing** Based on her essay, what advice might Nye offer this young woman? **[Speculate]**

sorrow. A poet friend of mine in New York City, just blocks from the disaster, said his wife saw him staring at a wall in their apartment one day, and said, "Don't withdraw! Speak!"

Sometimes we have to remind one another.

I also wrote sentences and phrases down in small notebooks, as I have done almost every day of my life since I was six. It is the best clue I know for how to stay balanced as we live. Bits and pieces of lines started fitting together again, offering small scraps of sense, ways out of the <u>turmoil</u>-of-mind, shining as miniature <u>beacons</u>, from under heaps of leaves.

Very rarely did I hang up from speaking with anyone or close my notebook feeling worse. Usually, that simple sharing of feelings, whether with another person, or with a patient page, helped ease the enormous feeling that the sorrow was too big to get one's mind around.

War is too big to get one's mind around too.

I keep thinking—if people who are angry, or frustrated, could use words instead of violence, how would our world be different? Maybe if enough of us keep in practice using our own honest words, that basic human act can help balance bigger things in the world.

Vocabulary Builder
turmoil (tʉr´ moil´) *n.* a condition of great confusion or agitation

beacons (bē´ kənz) *n.* signals meant to warn or guide, as a light or fire

Thinking About the Selection

1. **Respond:** What would you like to ask Naomi Shihab Nye? Explain.

2. **(a) Recall:** How did Nye deal with her emotions after the events of September 11, 2001? **(b) Evaluate:** Do you think this is an effective way to ease sorrow? Explain.

3. **(a) Recall:** What is Nye's proposed solution to the problem of violence in our world? **(b) Take a Position:** Do you think Nye's ideas could help change the world? Explain.

Apply the Skills

My Own True Name • Words to Sit in, Like Chairs

Comparing Works on a Similar Theme

1. **(a)** List two things that inspire Pat Mora to write. **(b)** List two things that inspire Naomi Shihab Nye to write.

2. Compare and contrast the way Mora and Nye present the theme of the importance of self-expression. In the center section of a Venn diagram like the one shown, list similarities. In the two side sections, list differences.

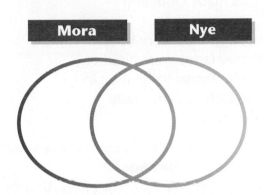

QuickReview

Theme: the central idea, underlying message, or insight that a literary work reveals

—Assessment
For: Self-test
Visit: www.PHSchool.com
Web Code: ena-6611

Writing to Compare Literary Works

Compare and contrast these selections. In an essay, discuss how each author develops the theme of self-expression and its importance. Use these questions as a guide:

- How much does the author reveal about herself and her reasons for writing?
- Why does the author believe that writing can help the world?
- Which writer is more compelling to you? Why?

Vocabulary Builder

Practice Use a vocabulary word from the list on page 1032 to write a sentence according to each prompt.

1. Describe a child who listens secretly as his parents talk.
2. Describe the confusion that occurs after a blackout.
3. Describe the attitude of a bully.
4. Describe a child who speaks both Korean and English.
5. Describe how a person reacts when he hears bad news.
6. Describe seeing a lighthouse from a ship at night.

Reading: Setting a Purpose for Reading

Directions: *Questions 1–5 are based on the following selection.*

1800s: The Industrial Revolution Changes America

The Spinning Jenny and the Power Loom In the early 1800s, two new inventions changed American life dramatically. The spinning jenny was a machine that spun thread, and the power loom was a machine that wove cloth. Before this time, spinning and weaving were done by hand, a long, slow process that made cloth and clothing very expensive.

From Farms to Cotton Mills Soon, huge cotton mills were built in Massachusetts, and young women from nearby farms were hired to work in them. This was the beginning of the Industrial Revolution in America, as more goods came to be made in factories and more people began moving to cities to work in them.

1. **What would be a likely purpose for reading a selection like this one?**
   A to find out how to build a spinning jenny
   B to find information for a report
   C to entertain your friends
   D to start an industrial revolution

2. **Which question is answered by the selection?**
   A What was the Industrial Revolution, and why was it important?
   B What were the causes of the Revolutionary War?
   C What industries are important in America today?
   D How can I make a power loom?

3. **Where could you find details to answer the purpose-setting question "What is a power loom?"**
   A paragraph 1, sentence 1
   B paragraph 1, sentence 2
   C paragraph 2, sentence 1
   D paragraph 2, sentence 2

4. **What is the best reading rate for this passage?**
   A skim for interesting details
   B read slowly and carefully
   C skim the first paragraph and read the second paragraph carefully
   D read the first paragraph carefully and skim the second paragraph

5. **What would be a good question to focus your reading purpose for this selection?**
   A How did the spinning jenny and power loom change America?
   B Why were the spinning jenny and power loom invented?
   C What was the difference between the spinning jenny and farms?
   D Where were the mills and the farms?

Assessment Practice

Vocabulary

Directions: *Choose the answer that best completes each sentence.*

6. **After your teacher has _____ your essay, you should _____ it.**
   A skimmed . . . focus
   B focused . . . revise
   C identified . . . critique
   D critiqued . . . revise

7. **To _____ the reading rate for a nonfiction selection, you can _____ the headings.**
   A focus . . . revise
   B identify . . . skim
   C critique . . . focus
   D revise . . . identify

8. **Once you _____ your reading purpose, it is easier to take notes.**
   A focus
   B identify
   C revise
   D critique

9. **Once you establish your purpose for reading, you _____ on the points that correspond to that purpose.**
   A focus
   B identify
   C revise
   D critique

10. **Good readers _____ their reading rate for different kinds of text.**
    A focus
    B identify
    C revise
    D critique

Directions *Choose the best word to complete each sentence.*

11. **I wrote a _____ of the play.**
    A motif
    B critique
    C collage
    D premiere

12. **The new _____ has an excellent menu.**
    A collage
    B critique
    C genre
    D café

13. **Which is a synonym for *store* and *shop*?**
    A critique
    B boutique

    C ensemble
    D chic

14. **Which of the following words does not relate to cooking?**
    A menu
    B tortilla
    C enchilada
    D beret

15. **I made a _____ in art class.**
    A collage
    B critique
    C motif
    D cliché

Vowel Sounds in Unstressed Syllables

In many words, the vowel sound in one or more syllables is not clear. These indistinct vowel sounds can cause spelling problems.

How Do You Spell "Uh"? Words like *dislocate* do not often cause spelling problems—you can clearly hear the vowel in each syllable. In many other words, though, the vowel in one or more syllables sounds something like "uh" and can be spelled with any vowel. For example, the *a* in *obstacle* can sound similar to the *i* in *hesitate*.

Notice the unstressed syllables in the words on the list, and then notice which vowels are used in spelling them.

Practice Add the correct letter or letters to the word. Then, use it in a sentence.

1. hes_____tate
2. ben_____factor
3. pl_____sant
4. ep_____log_____
5. barg_____n

6. b_____yant
7. s_____llable
8. adj_____n
9. p_____rsue
10. anon_____mous

Word List
pleasant
bargain
pursue
buoyant
hesitate
syllable
anonymous
benefactor
adjourn
epilogue

A. Directions: *Write the letter of the word that is spelled incorrectly or choose* No error.

1. We <u>hesitated</u> to <u>adjurn</u> the meeting
         A   B

   without a <u>bargain</u> between the two sides.
              C

   <u>No error</u>
     D

2. An <u>anonymous</u> <u>benefactor's</u> donation
         A   B

   made the children's party more <u>plesant</u>.
                      C

   <u>No error.</u>
     D

3. The unstressed <u>syllables</u> in <u>buoyant</u>
               A   B

   always make me <u>hesitate</u> when I write the
              C

   word. <u>No error</u>
        D

4. Before <u>adjourning</u>, we agreed to <u>pursue</u>
         A   B

   seeking <u>benefactors</u> for the project.
          C

   <u>No error</u>
     D

B. Directions: *Write the letter of the correctly spelled word.*

1. An item on sale is not a _____ if you do not want or need it.
   A bargin
   B bargen
   C bargain
   D bargein

2. The water wings made the child _____.
   A buoyant
   B buoyent
   C boyuant
   D boyuent

3. Will you _____ your runaway cat?
   A persue
   B perseu
   C purseu
   D pursue

4. Every _____ must have at least one vowel.
   A sillable
   B syllible
   C syllable
   D sillyble

5. The actual ending of the play is in the _____ .
   A epialogue
   B epiloge
   C epilogue
   D epaloge

6. An _____ caller gave the information.
   A anonymous
   B anonomous
   C anonemous
   D anonimous

Exposition: Cause-and-Effect Essay

Almost anything that happens involves causes and effects, from simple daily events to those that affect people all over the world. When you write a **cause-and-effect essay,** you analyze the reasons something happened or you consider its results. Follow the steps outlined in this workshop to write your own cause-and-effect essay.

Assignment Write a cause-and-effect essay about a question that interests you.

What to Include Your essay should feature the following elements:
- a clear and consistent organization
- an explanation of how one or more events or situations resulted in another event or situation
- a thorough presentation of facts, statistics, and other details that support the explanation presented
- an effective conclusion
- error-free grammar, including properly punctuated quotations.

To preview the criteria on which your cause-and-effect essay may be judged, see the rubric on page 1053.

Writing Workshop: *Work in Progress*

If you have completed the Work-in-Progress assignments, you have in your portfolio several ideas you might use in your cause-and-effect essay. Continue developing these ideas, or explore a new idea as you complete the Writing Workshop.

Using the Form
You may use elements of this form in these types of writing:
- historical essays
- news reports
- science reports

Reading Writing Connection

To get the feel for cause-and-effect writing, read "Why Leaves Turn Color in the Fall" by Diane Ackerman on page 494.

Prewriting

Choosing Your Topic

Self-interview To find topics that interest you, ask yourself questions such as these:

- What is my favorite book? What natural or historical events are crucial to the story?
- What interesting facts have I learned in science class?
- Which political leader do I admire most? What was happening in the world when he or she was in office?
- What invention am I most grateful for?

Review your answers to choose a topic.

Narrowing Your Topic

Make sure your topic is narrow enough for you to cover in depth. Take time to jot down subtopics of your broad topic. Continue this process until you pinpoint a subject for your writing.
Example Topic: NASA technology

> **Subtopic:** Satellites
>> **Subtopic:** Benefit to average citizen
>>> **Subtopic:** Improvement to cellphone communication

Gathering Details

Conduct research. Take time to gather the facts, examples, and other details you need to thoroughly illustrate cause-and-effect relationships. A K-W-L chart like the one shown is an excellent tool for planning and guiding your research.

Work in Progress
Review the work you did on pages 1007 and 1025.

K-W-L Chart		
What I Know	**What I Want to Know**	**What I Learned**
Air pollution is increasing and dangerous. Pollution smells bad. Cars and factories cause it. It hurts people and animals.	How can it be reduced? What causes it besides cars and factories? Which countries or cities are the worst? How can we stop it? What does it do to people? To animals?	

Drafting

Shaping Your Writing

Focus and organize your ideas. Review your research, and circle the main causes and effects. Identify which description below best fits your topic. Then, organize your information accordingly.

- **Many Causes/Single Effect:** If your topic has several causes of a single event, develop a paragraph to discuss each cause.

- **Single Cause/Many Effects:** For one cause with several effects, devote a paragraph to each effect.

- **Chain of causes and effects.** If you are presenting a chain of causes and effects, present them in chronological order with transitions to show the connections.

Providing Elaboration

Prove the connection. To convince your audience that the causes and effects you connect are not just mere coincidence, add details to elaborate on the link you are showing.

> **Weak connection:** *The stores were crowded the weekend before the holiday.*
>
> **Cause-and-effect connection:** *With reduced prices and the pressure of last-minute shopping, the stores were crowded before the holiday.*

To read the complete student model, see page 1052.

Include personal testimonies. Interview classmates or other people who have experience related to your subject. Use their comments to help illustrate your ideas. Their stories can provide an interesting slant to statistics or studies you may cite from other sources.

Student Model: Using Personal Testimonies

I have observed some of these sleep deprivation effects in people I know. My friend Tim had to stay up late several nights in a row in order to finish a term paper on time. Here is how Tim describes how the loss of sleep affected him: *"The first thing I noticed was that I couldn't concentrate in class. My attention would wander and I couldn't understand ideas that would ordinarily be very easy for me to grasp . . ."*

The author illustrates the cause-and-effect relationship with a real-life example.

From the Author's Desk

Lan Samantha Chang
On Using Specific Details

Lan Samantha Chang

At the heart of my story "San" is the idea that every child is a detective, searching for clues about her parents' mysterious past lives. In this passage, I tried to show the development of this obsession by describing the way that Caroline, the 13-year-old narrator, hunts through the closets in her own house. I tried to reveal this information through action and specific details, rather than summary.

"I want to show, not tell ..."
—Lan Samantha Chang

Professional Model:
from *"San"*

At the back of the foyer closet, inside the faded red suitcase my mother had brought from China, I discovered a cache of little silk purses wrapped in a cotton shirt. When I heard her footsteps I instinctively closed the suitcase and pretended I was looking for a pair of mittens. Then I went to my room and shut the door, slightly dizzy with anticipation and guilt.

A few days later when my mother was out, I opened one purse. Inside was a swirling gold pin with pearl and coral flowers. I made many secret visits to the closet, a series of small sins. Each time I opened one more treasure. There were bright green, milky white, and ~~blood-red~~ carmine bracelets. Some of the bracelets were so small I could not fit them over my hand. There was a ring with a pearl as big as a marble....

Here I tried to emphasize, through use of detail, that the mother had come from China and that it had happened years ago (the suitcase is "faded").

I don't use adverbs very often and when I do I want them to reveal character. In this case I wanted to reveal Caroline's instinctive need for secrecy, her desire to hide her private explorations from her mother.

I kept "blood-red" for many drafts because I liked the idea of blood (family) secrets being excavated. Later I crossed out the words, because they are a cliché.

Revising

Revising Your Paragraphs

Use transitions to show connections. Your goal is to prove the link between a cause and its effects. Transition words can help you make sure the relationship between cause and effect is obvious to your readers. Use transitional words and phrases like the ones shown here to clarify connections.

Cause-and-Effect Transitions	
Introducing Causes	since, if, because, as soon as, until
Introducing Effects	consequently, as a result, subsequently, then

Peer Review: Ask a classmate to review your draft to help you identify places in your draft where adding transitions would improve the writing. Consider these suggestions while you are revising to clarify cause-and-effect relationships.

Revising Your Word Choice

Define key terms for your audience. To make sure you have expressed your ideas clearly enough for your readers, follow these steps:

1. Reread your essay, circling any terms that your audience may not know.

2. Provide more background information or definitions where necessary. You may have to consult your research notes or other reference materials for this information.

Reading **Writing** Connection

To read the complete student model, see page 1052.

Student Model: Revising to Define Key Terms

Sleep deprivation occurs when someone receives fewer hours of sleep than his or her body needs.

~~Many different things can cause sleep deprivation. A few of them are drinking caffeine, having a noisy sleep environment, and working long hours.~~

This definition will help a reader who is unfamiliar with the term *sleep deprivation.*

Integrating Grammar Skills

Revising to Use Quotation Marks and Block Quotes

When you use quotations to support your points, you must set them off so your reader knows they are someone else's words.

Formatting Quotations Long quotations should be indented in your writing. Shorter quotations are treated like the quotations in the dialogue of a story. When you quote from another source, copy the words exactly as they appear in the work.

Using block quotations: Introduce long quotations with a colon, indent entire quotations on the left, and do not use quotation marks.

Prentice Hall Writing and Grammar Connection: Chapter 12, Section 5

> These opening lines of "The Adventure of the Speckled Band" show that Watson and Holmes had a long friendship:
>
> > On glancing over my notes of the seventy odd cases in which I have during the last eight years studied the methods of my friend Sherlock Holmes, I find many tragic, some comic, a large number merely strange, but none commonplace; for, working as he did rather for the love of his art than for the acquirement of wealth, he refused to associate himself with any investigation which did not tend towards the unusual, and even the fantastic.

Using brief quotations: Use quotation marks to separate the quotation from the rest of a sentence:

> According to the story, the house in which Helen Stoner lived was in some disrepair. It was "a picture of ruin."

Fixing Errors To fix incorrect use of quotations, follow these steps:

1. **Identify quoted text used to support a point made in an essay.**
2. **Determine how many lines the quoted text will use.**
3. **If the quoted text will use more than five lines of text, follow the rules for the block method.**
4. **If the quoted text will use five or fewer lines of text, run the quotation in your text as shown in the second example.**

Apply It to Your Editing

Check to make sure any quoted material in your cause-and-effect essay is set off or punctuated correctly. Make revisions as needed.

Student Model: Max Norowzi
Raleigh, NC

Sleep, It's Healthy

Since the beginning of time, sleep has been an important factor in maintaining good health. While people sleep, they refuel their bodies and minds to help them through the next day. Many people do not get the proper amount of sleep, however, and this has a negative effect on their health.

> Max clearly outlines the cause-and-effect relationship he will address.

During the day, our bodies and minds consume a great deal of energy. Sleep recharges our bodies and minds, giving our bodies and minds a chance to recover the energy that we have lost. We wake up feeling refreshed because, while we sleep, our brains do not need to focus and our muscles can relax.

Sleep deprivation occurs when someone receives fewer hours of sleep than his or her body needs. Many different things can cause sleep deprivation. A few of the main causes are drinking caffeine, living in a noisy environment, and working long hours. The effect on a person who does not get enough sleep can be devastating. Some effects of sleep deprivation are stress, anxiety, inability to concentrate, and loss of coping skills. Another effect is weight gain, which is very unhealthy for most people. Mood shifts, including depression, increased irritability, and loss of a sense of humor all result from not getting enough sleep.

> This paragraph identifies the causes of sleep deprivation.

I have observed some of these sleep deprivation effects in people I know. My friend Tim had to stay up late several nights in a row in order to finish a term paper on time. Here is how Tim describes how the loss of sleep affected him: "The first thing I noticed was that I couldn't concentrate in class. My attention would wander and I couldn't understand ideas that would ordinarily be very easy for me to grasp. My body was achy, my head was cloudy, and I was snapping at everyone about everything. The sleep that I did get wasn't very good because my dreams were bad ones about things like forgetting to turn my paper in."

> To support his explanation, Max offers detailed descriptions of sleep deprivation's effects.

People often dream when they have been thinking hard about something right before they go to sleep. Dreams can be good or bad for us. A good dream is relaxing and does not disturb the sleeper. A bad dream causes stress, anxiety, and restlessness. To avoid bad dreams, people should do something relaxing, like reading, before going to bed.

In conclusion, adequate sleep promotes good health and helps us feel better about ourselves. Sleep deprivation can seriously harm our minds and bodies. To counter these harmful effects, the answer is to simply get more sleep. Sleeping well can guarantee us better health and a better life.

> Max concludes his essay effectively by summarizing the health benefits of sleep.

Editing and Proofreading

Make corrections in grammar, usage, and mechanics to ensure that your final draft is error-free.

Focus on Prepositions: Whenever possible, avoid ending sentences with a preposition.

> **Draft Sentence:** Which friend are you traveling **with**?
> **Revised Sentence:** **With** which friend are you traveling? Who is traveling with you?

Publishing and Presenting

Consider one of the following ways to share your writing:

Present a speech. If your essay addresses a situation that others face, offer to speak to classes or clubs that can benefit from your work.

Publish a feature article. Submit your essay to your local or school newspaper. In a letter accompanying your essay, explain to the editor why the issue you address is important to readers.

Reflecting on Your Writing

Writer's Journal Jot down your thoughts on writing a cause-and-effect essay. Begin by answering these questions:

- Did learning about the causes and effects of your topic motivate you to take any action?
- What strategy included in this lesson will help you improve your writing in other assignments?

> *Prentice Hall Writing and Grammar Connection: Chapter 9*

Rubric for Self-Assessment

To assess your cause-and-effect essay, use the following rubric:

Criteria	Rating Scale *not very* ... *very*				
Focus: How clearly do you state the cause-and-effect relationship?	1	2	3	4	5
Organization: How clear and consistent is your organization?	1	2	3	4	5
Support/Elaboration: How convincing are the facts and statistics that support your explanations?	1	2	3	4	5
Style: How clearly does your language convey your conclusion?	1	2	3	4	5
Conventions: How correct is your grammar, especially your use of quotation marks?	1	2	3	4	5

Delivering a Persuasive Speech Using Multimedia

A persuasive multimedia presentation uses visuals and sound to convince an audience that the speaker's point of view is right.

Prepare

Your presentation should flow from a sound, well-stated position. Every detail in your presentation must relate to this position. Write a single statement to express your main idea.

Use primary and secondary sources. Support your ideas with two types of sources. Primary sources give direct evidence. Secondary sources are observations or summaries made after an event or by a person who was not involved in the event.

Decide which media to use. Choose a medium that emphasizes your points. Film and other taped sources usually include both visuals and sound. If your point is very dramatic, a still photo and silence might affect your audience most strongly.

Get your equipment ready. As you plan your presentation, list the equipment you will need. Familiarize yourself with the equipment and be certain that it will be available.

Present

If possible, practice the speech using the equipment you will use in the place you will give the presentation. Have a backup plan in case a piece of equipment does not function.

Be dramatic. Set up a photograph with a dramatic description of the events. Use creative language, such as similes, idioms, and extended comparisons (analogies) to describe your subject.

Be clear. When presenting different media, use transitions that emphasize and explain connections within your subject. Explain any terms or vocabulary that might be unfamiliar to your audience.

Activity ▶ *Persuasive Multimedia* Use these tips to prepare a persuasive multimedia presentation about some issue related to our school. Consider topics such as why students should join a certain club or sports team or participate in an event or a class.

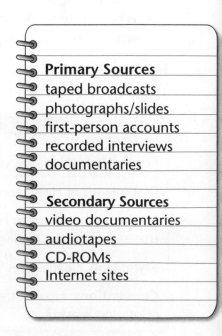

Primary Sources
taped broadcasts
photographs/slides
first-person accounts
recorded interviews
documentaries

Secondary Sources
video documentaries
audiotapes
CD-ROMs
Internet sites

Eagle Song

Joseph Bruchac
Puffin Books, 1999

Novel Danny Bigtree's family has moved to a new city, and regardless of how hard he tries, he just does not fit in. Danny is homesick for the Mohawk reservation where he used to live. On top of everything else, the other kids tease Danny about the one thing he is most proud of—his Native American heritage. This novel follows Danny as he tries to fit in, yet stay true to himself.

Immigrant Voices

Ed. Gordon Hutner
Signet, 1999

Anthology This is a collection of stories about leaving everything for a new place. Immigrants who have achieved the American Dream share their stories as they journey through the hardship and joy of being in a new and strange land. Each autobiographical selection speaks about both the fear and the pleasure the authors found in America. The anthology includes essays by people such as millionaire industrialist Andrew Carnegie and social activist Ernesto Galarza.

Ashanti to Zulu: African Traditions

Margaret Musgrove
Puffin Books, 1976

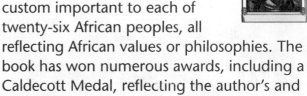

Collection This work depicts a custom important to each of twenty-six African peoples, all reflecting African values or philosophies. The book has won numerous awards, including a Caldecott Medal, reflecting the author's and illustrators' devotion to authenticity.

All Quiet on the Western Front

Erich Maria Remarque
Globe Fearon, 1995

Novel An idealistic teenager joins the army in search of fame and glory. Instead, he finds that war is not what the propaganda claimed, but is death, destruction, and the horrors of the trenches. This novel, set during World War I on the western front, recounts a teenager's life during war and the ways that experience molds the remainder of his life.

*These titles are available in the Penguin/Prentice Hall Literature Library.
Consult your teacher before choosing one.*

Think About It Although it may be hard to imagine, there once was a world without television. When television first came into the homes of America, the new technology created excitement. In the following excerpt from John Grisham's *A Painted House,* the narrator recalls the first time he saw a television broadcast and the impact it had on his life.

from
A PAINTED
HOUSE

John Grisham

After lunch Pappy said abruptly, "Luke, we're goin' to town. The trailer's full."

The trailer wasn't completely full, and we never took it to the gin[1] in the middle of the day. But I wasn't about to object. Something was up.

There were only four trailers ahead of us when we arrived at the gin. Usually, at this time of the harvest, there would be at least ten, but then we always came after supper, when the place was crawling with farm-hands. "Noon's a good time to gin,"[2] Pappy said.

He left the keys in the truck, and as we were walking away he said, "I need to go to the Co-op. Let's head to Main Street." Sounded good to me.

The town of Black Oak had three hundred people, and virtually all of them lived within five minutes of Main Street. I often thought how

---

1. gin (jin) *n.* cotton gin: a machine that separates the seeds and seed hulls from the fibers of cotton.
2. gin (jin) *v.* to remove the seeds from cotton with a gin.

wonderful it would be to have a neat little house on a shady street, just a stone's throw from Pop and Pearl's and the Dixie theater, with no cotton anywhere in sight.

Halfway to Main, we took an abrupt turn. "Pearl wants to see you," he said, pointing at the Watsons' house just to our right. I'd never been in Pop and Pearl's house, never had any reason to enter, but I'd seen it from the outside. It was one of the few houses in town with some bricks on it.

"What?" I asked, completely bewildered.

He said nothing, and I just followed.

Pearl was waiting at the door. When we entered I could smell the rich, sweet aroma of something baking, though I was too confused to realize she was preparing a treat for me. She gave me a pat on the head and winked at Pappy. In one corner of the room, Pop was bent at the waist, his back to us, fiddling with something. "Come here, Luke," he said, without turning around.

I'd heard that they owned a television. The first one in our county had been purchased a year earlier by Mr. Harvey Gleeson, the owner of the bank, but he was a recluse,[3] and no one had yet seen his television, as far as we knew. Several church members had kinfolks in Jonesboro who owned televisions, and whenever they went there to visit they came back and talked nonstop about this wonderful new invention. Dewayne had seen one inside a store window in Blytheville, and he'd strutted around school for an insufferable period of time.

"Sit here," Pop said, pointing to a spot on the floor, right in front of the set. He was still adjusting knobs. "It's the World Series," he said. "Game three, Dodgers at Yankee Stadium."

My heart froze; my mouth dropped open. I was too stunned to move. Three feet away was a small screen with lines dancing across it. It was in the center of a dark, wooden cabinet with the word Motorola scripted in chrome just under a row of knobs. Pop turned one of the knobs, and suddenly we heard the

scratchy voice of an announcer describing a ground ball to the shortstop. Then Pop turned two knobs at once, and the picture became clear.

It was a baseball game. Live from Yankee Stadium, and we were watching it in Black Oak, Arkansas!

Chairs moved behind me, and I could feel Pappy inching closer. Pearl wasn't much of a fan. She busied herself in the kitchen for a few minutes, then emerged with a plate of chocolate cookies and a glass of milk. I took them and thanked her. They were fresh from the oven and smelled delicious. But I couldn't eat, not right then.

Ed Lopat was pitching for the Yankees, Preacher Roe for the Dodgers. Mickey Mantle, Yogi Berra, Phil Rizzuto, Hank Bauer, Billy Martin with the Yankees, and Pee Wee Reese, Duke Snider, Roy Campanella, Jackie Robinson, and Gil Hodges with the Dodgers. They were all there in Pop and Pearl's living room, playing before sixty thousand fans in Yankee Stadium. I was mesmerized to the point of being mute. I simply stared at the television, watching but not believing.

---

3. recluse (rek′ lōōs) *n.* someone who withdraws from the world to live alone.

"Eat the cookies, Luke," Pearl said as she passed through the room. It was more of a command than an invitation, and I took a bite of one.

"Who are you pullin' for?" asked Pop.

"I don't know," I mumbled, and I really didn't. I had been taught to hate both teams. And it had been easy hating them when they were away in New York, in another world. But now they were in Black Oak, playing the game I loved, live from Yankee Stadium. My hatred vanished. "Dodgers, I guess," I said.

"Always pull for the National League," Pappy said behind me.

We pulled our empty trailer back to the farm, and I picked cotton until quitting time. During supper the adults gave me the floor. I talked nonstop about the game and the commercials and everything I'd seen on Pop and Pearl's television.

Modern America was slowly invading rural Arkansas.

Meet the Author

When **John Grisham** (b. 1955) was growing up in Arkansas, he and his family moved often. Every time they settled in a new town, Grisham immediately went to the library. He loved to read, but never imagined that he would one day write best-selling novels. When his second novel, *The Firm*, sold millions, Grisham quit his job as a lawyer to write full time.

Readings in Contemporary Fiction
Talk About It

Use the following questions to guide a discussion of the excerpt.

1. Why does television seem to be a positive thing, from Luke's point of view?

2. **(a)** How does television change the way Luke thinks about the Dodgers? **(b)** How might television change the way Luke thinks about the world?

3. In what ways does television influence culture in today's society? In groups, share your responses to the following questions:
   • What are the positive and negative effects of television today?
   • How do you think society benefits from television?

   Choose a point person to share your group's ideas with the class.

RESOURCES

GLOSSARY

High-utility words and academic vocabulary appear in green.

A

account (ə kount´) *n.* a bill for work done

accurate (ak´yə rət) *adj.* free from error; correct; exact

achieve (ə chēv´) *v.* to succeed, to accomplish

acute (ə kyoot´) *adj.* sensitive; sharp

adapt (ə dapt´) *v.* to change something to make it more suitable

affectionate (ə fek´shən it) *adj.* loving

affluence (af´ loo əns) *n.* wealth; abundance

aghast (ə gast´) *adj.* feeling great horror or dismay

alienate (al´ yən āt´) *v.* make unfriendly

alliance (ə lī´ əns) *n.* a group united for a common goal

analyze (an´ə līz´) *v.* to study the parts of something

anguish (aŋ´ gwish) *n.* great suffering from worry

anticipate (an tis´ə pāt´) *v.* to look forward; to expect

antithesis (an tith´ ə sis) *n.* direct opposite

apprehension (ap´ rē hen´ shən) *n.* a fearful feeling about what will happen next

ascent (ə sent´) *n.* the act of climbing or rising

aspect (as´pekt´) *n.* the specific part of a thing that you are observing or studying

aspirations (as´ pə rā´ shənz) *n.* strong desires or ambitions

assumption (ə sump´shən) *n.* something one supposes to be true, without proof

authentic (ô then´ tik) *adj.* genuine; real

B

barren (bar´ ən) *adj.* empty; bare

beacons (bē´ kənz) *n.* signals meant to warn or guide, as a light or fire

beckoning (bek´ ə niŋ) *v.* calling or summoning

bellowing (bel´ ō iŋ) *v.* roaring

benign (bi nīn´) *adj.* kindly

bias (bī´ əs) *n.* unfair preference or dislike for someone or something

bilingual (bī liŋ´ gwəl) *adj.* able to speak two languages

billowing (bil´ ō iŋ) *adj.* swelling or surging

burdened (burd´nd) *adj.* weighted down by work, duty, responsibility, or sorrow

burrow (bur´ ō) *n.* passage or hole for shelter

C

camouflage (kam´ ə fläzh´) *n.* disguise or concealment

capricious (kə prish´ əs) *adj.* tending to change abruptly and without apparent reason

ceased (sēst) *v.* stopped

celestial (sə les´ chəl) *adj.* heavenly

cite (sīt) *v.* to refer to an example or fact as proof

clarify (klar´ə fī´) *v.* explain; make clearer

commenced (kə menst´) *v.* started; began

commotion (kə mō´ shən) *n.* noisy movement

compassionate (kəm pash´ ən it) *adj.* deeply sympathetic

compelled (kəm peld´) *v.* forced

compensate (käm´ pən sāt´) *v.* repay

complacent (kəm plā´ sənt) *adj.* self-satisfied; smug

compliance (kəm plī´ əns) *n.* agreement to a request

compulsory (kəm pul´ sə rē) *adj.* required

conceivably (kən sēv´ ə blē) *adv.* in an imaginable or believable way

conclude (kən klood´) *v.* to decide by reasoning

confirm (kən furm´) *v.* make certain; prove to be correct

confirmation (kän´fər mā´shən) *n.* something that confirms or proves

connect (kə nekt´) *v.* put together; show how things are related

consequence (kän´sl kwens´) *n.* result; outcome

consequently (kän´ si kwent´ lē) *adv.* as a result

consoling (kən sōl´ iŋ) *adj.* comforting

conspicuous (kən spik´ yoo əs) *adj.* noticeable

contact (kän´ takt) *n.* touching; communication

contemplation (kän´ təm plā´ shən) *n.* the act of meditating on or pondering

contempt (kən tempt´) *n.* scorn; disrespect

context (kän´tekst´) *n.* words and phrases surrounding an unfamiliar word

convey (kən vā´) *v.* to carry meaning; to communicate

conviction (kən vik´ shən) *n.* strong belief; certainty

cordially (kôr´ jə lē) *adv.* in a warm and friendly way

correspondingly (kôr´ ə spänd´ iŋ lē) *adv.* in a consistent way

cosmic (käz´ mik) *adj.* universal; infinite

credibility (kred´ ə bil´ i tē) *n.* believability

credible (kred´ə bəl) *adj.* believable; reliable

criteria (krī tir´ ē ə) *n.* standards or tests by which something can be judged

critique (kri tēk´) *v.* write a critical essay or review

cyclone (sī´ klōn´) *n.* a violent, rotating windstorm; a tornado

D

debates (dē bāts´) *v.* tries to decide

decadent (dek´ ə dənt) *adj.* marked by decay or decline

decrees (dē krēz´) *n.* orders with the force of law

deferred (dē furd´) *adj.* postponed or delayed

degrading (dē grād´ iŋ) *adj.* insulting; dishonorable

deliberating (di lib´ ər āt iŋ) *v.* thinking or considering carefully and fully

derision (di rizh´ ən) *n.* contempt; ridicule

derived (di rīv´d) *v.* to get by reasoning; deduce

descendants (dē sen´ dənts) *n.* children, grandchildren, and continuing generations

descent (dē sent´) *n.* the act of climbing down

desolate (des´ ə lit) *adj.* uninhabited; barren

determine (dē tur´mən) *v.* to figure out

devices (di vīs´ əz) *n.* technique or means for working things out

dexterity (deks ter´ ə tē) *n.* skill using the hands or body

differentiate (dif ər en´shē āt´) *v.* to contrast, to show how things are different

diffused (di fyo͞ozd´) *v.* spread out widely into different directions

diplomatic (dip´ lə mat´ ik) *adj.* tactful; showing skill in dealing with people

discharged (dis chärjd´) *v.* fired; released from something

discord (dis´ kôrd) *n.* quarrel; clash

discreet (di skrēt´) *adj.* careful about what one says or does

discrepancies (di skrep´ ən sēz) *n.* differences; inconsistencies

disheveled (di shev´ əld) *adj.* untidy; messy

disinherited (dis´ in her´ it id) *n.* people who have been deprived of their rights

disorganized (dis ôr´gən īz´d) *adj.* not arranged in a logical order

dissension (di sen´ shən) *n.* difference of opinion

distinctions (di stiŋk´ shənz) *n.* the noting of differences between things

distinctness (di stiŋkt´ nəs) *n.* clarity; awareness of detail

diverged (dī vurj´ d) *v.* branched off

diverts (dī vurts´) *v.* distracts; entertains or amuses

dock (däk) *v.* to deduct part of one's salary or wages

drought (drout) *n.* lack of rain; long period of dry weather

E

eavesdropping (ēvz´ dräp´ iŋ) *n.* secretly listening to the private conversation of others

eloquent (el´ ə kwənt) *adj.* vividly expressive

emigrated (em´ i grāt´ əd) *v.* left one place to settle in another

emphasize (em´fə sīz´) *v.* to stress; to give special importance to

enhance (en hans´) *v.* make greater

essential (ə sen´shul) *adj.* necessary

establish (ə stab´lish) *v.* to show or prove

evacuees (ē vak´ yo͞o ēz´) *n.* people who leave an area because of danger

evaded (ē vād´ əd) *v.* avoided; eluded

evading (ē vā´ diŋ) *v.* escaping by cleverness

evaluate (ē val´ yo͞o āt´) *v.* judge; determine the worth or strength of something

evidence (ev´ ə dəns) *n.* facts that serve as clues or proof

evidently (ev´ ə dent´ lē) *adv.* obviously; clearly

examine (eg zam´ən) *v.* to study carefully

exertion (eg zur´ shən) *n.* energetic activity; effort

exploitation (eks´ ploi tā´ shən) *n.* the act of using another person for selfish purposes

extract (ek strakt´) *v.* to deduce; to obtain

exultantly (eg zult´ ´nt lē) *adv.* triumphantly

exulting (eg zult´ iŋ) *v.* rejoicing

F

factor (fak´tər) *n.* something that helps bring about a result

fastidious (fa stid´ ē əs) *adj.* not easy to please; very critical of anything crude or coarse

fatalist (fā´ təl ist) *n.* one who believes that all events are determined by fate and cannot be changed

feuding (fyo͞od´ iŋ) *v.* quarreling; fighting

finery (fī´ nər ē) *n.* fancy clothing and accessories

fiscal (fis´ kəl) *adj.* having to do with finances

flagged (flagd) *v.* signaled to stop

flatterer (flat´ ər ər) *n.* one who praises others insincerely in order to win their approval

focus (fō´kəs) *n.* the central point of a work

focus (fō´kəs) *v.* to concentrate on one thing; to direct one's attention to a specific part of something

formulate (fôr´myo͞o lāt´) *v.* to make a statement; to form an idea

fugitives (fyo͞o´ ji tivz´) *n.* people fleeing from danger

G

garbled (gär´bəld) *adj.* confused; mixed up

glistens (glis´ enz) *v.* shines; sparkles

guileless (gīl´ lis) *adj.* without deceit or trickery; innocent

H

harmonious (här mō´ nē əs) *adj.* combined in a pleasing, orderly arrangement

haughty (hôt´ ē) *adj.* proud and superior; scornful of others

humiliating (hyo͞o mil´ ē āt´ iŋ) *adj.* embarrassing; undignified

I

identify (ī den´tə fī) *v.* recognize; to find and name

ignorance (ig´ nə rəns) *n.* lack of knowledge or awareness

immortality (im´ ôr tal´ i tē) *n.* endless life

impact (im´ pakt) *n.* the power to produce changes or effects

impaired (im perd´) *v.* made weaker or less useful

impertinently (im pʉr´ ti nənt lē) *adv.* disrespectfully

implied (im plīd´) *adj.* suggested

imply (im plī) *v.* hint at; suggest

inarticulate (in´ är tik´ yo͞o lit) *adj.* unable to express oneself

incentive (in sent´ iv) *n.* something that makes a person act

incredulously (in krej´ oo ləs lē) *adv.* with doubt or disbelief

indicate (in´di kāt´) *v.* to show; to hint at

indignant (in dig´ nənt) *adj.* filled with anger at meanness or injustice

indulgent (in dul´ jənt) *adj.* tolerant; not strict or critical

ineffectually (in´ e fek´ cho͞o ə lē) *adv.* without producing the desired results

inexplicable (in eks´ pli kə bəl) *adj.* not possible to explain

infer (in fʉr´) *v.* to draw conclusions based on facts

inferior (in fir´ ē ər) *adj.* lower in status or rank

influence (in´ flo͞o ens) *n.* ability to affect results or produce effects

infuse (in fyo͞oz´) *v.* put into

ingratitude (in grat´ i to͞od) *n.* lack of thankfulness

inhabitants (in hab´ i tənts) *n.* people or animals that live in a specific region

innumerable (i no͞o´ mər ə bəl) *adj.* too many to be counted

insufferable (in suf´ ə rə bəl) *adj.* unbearable

intention (in ten´shən) *n.* purpose; goal

intimidating (in tim´ ə dā´ tiŋ) *adj.* frightening

intolerant (in täl´ ər ənt) *adj.* not able or willing to accept

introspective (in´ trə spek´ tiv) *adj.* inward looking; thoughtful

intuition (in´ to͞o ish´ ən) *n.* ability to sense or know immediately, without reasoning

J

judicious (jo͞o dish´ əs) *adj.* showing sound judgment; wise and careful

K

kennel (ken´ əl) *n.* a place where dogs are kept

kindled (kin´ dəld) *v.* built or lit (a fire)

L

legacy (leg´ ə sē) *n.* anything handed down from an ancestor

legitimately (lə jit´ ə mət lē) *adv.* legally; in a way that follows the law

lilting (lilt´ iŋ) *adj.* light, graceful, and rhythmic, especially in song and speech

logical (läj´i kəl) *adj.* reasonable; sensible

luminous (lo͞o´ mə nəs) *adj.* giving off light; shining; bright

lurking (lʉrk´iŋ) *v.* ready to spring out, attack; existing undiscovered

M

macabre (mə käb´ rə) or (mə käb´) *adj.* gruesome; grim

maneuver (mə no͞o´ vər) *n.* series of planned steps

meager (mē´ gər) *adj.* lacking in some way; inadequate

melancholy (mel´ ən käl´ ē) *adj.* sad; gloomy

meticulous (mə tik´ yo͞o ləs) *adj.* extremely careful about details

mishaps (mis´ haps´) *n.* an unfortunate or unlucky accident

modify (mäd´ə fī) *v.* to change

mutinous (myo͞ot´ ən əs) *adj.* rebellious

N

native (nāt´iv) *adj.* related to the place of one's birth

ninny (nin´ ē) *n.* simple or foolish person

O

obscure (əb skyo͞or´) *v.* conceal or hide

oligarchy (äl´ i gär´ kē) *n.* rule by a small, elite group

oppressed (ə prest´) *v.* kept down by cruel or unjust power

organized (ôrg´ ə nīz´´d) *v.* arranged in a logical order

ostentatiously (äs´ tən tā´ shəs lē) *adv.* in a showy way

P

paradoxes (par´ ə däks´ əz) *n.* two things that seem directly at odds

partition (pär tish´ ən) *n.* an interior dividing wall

perpetual (pər pech´ o͞o əl) *adj.* repeated endlessly; long-lasting

pertinent (purt´´n ənt) *adj.* relevant; having a connection

pervading (pər vād´ iŋ) *adj.* spreading throughout

pestering (pes´ tər iŋ) *n.* constant bothering

pitiful (pit´ i fəl) *adj.* arousing sympathy or pity

ponderous (pän´ dər əs) *adj.* very heavy

posterity (päs ter´ ə tē) *n.* future generations; descendants

precisely (prē sīs´ lē) *adv.* exactly

predict (prē dikt´) *v.* make a logical assumption about future events

predisposed (prē´ dis pōzd´) *adj.* inclined; willing

predominantly (prē däm´ ə nənt lē) *adv.* mainly; for the most part

preliminary (prē lim´ ə ner´ ē) *adj.* introductory; preparatory

presentable (prē zent´ ə bəl) *adj.* in proper order for being seen or met by others

pretext (prē´ tekst) *n.* reason or motive used to hide one's real intentions

procession (prō sesh´ ən) *n.* a group moving forward, as in a parade

prodigy (präd´ ə jē) *n.* a wonder; an unusually talented person

pursuit (pər so͞ot´) *n.* the act of chasing in order to catch

Q

quarantine (kwôr´ ən tēn) *n.* period of separation from others to stop the spreading of a disease

R

radical (rad´ i kəl) *adj.* favoring change in the social structure

rapture (rap´ chər) *n.* ecstasy

rational (rash´ə nəl) *adj.* based on reason; logical

reaction (rē ak´shən) *n.* response to an influence or force

recede (ri sēd´) *v.* move away

reflect (ri flekt´) *v.* mirror an image; to express or show

refugees (ref´ yo͞o jēz´) *n.* people who flee from their homes in times of trouble

refute (ri fyo͞ot´) *v.* give evidence to prove an argument or statement false

remote (ri mōt´) *adj.* aloof; cold; distant

renounced (ri nounsd´) *v.* gave up

reputation (rep´ yo͞o tā´ shən) *n.* widely-held opinion about a person, whether good or bad

resolute (rez´ ə lo͞ot) *adj.* showing a firm purpose; determined

resounding (ri zoun´ diŋ) *adj.* sounding loudly

respectively (ri spek´ tiv lē) *adv.* in the order previously named

restate (rē stāt´) *v.* to say again; to express the same idea in a different way

restatement (rē stāt´ mənt) *n.* expressing the same idea in different words

retribution (re´ trə byo͞o´ shən) *n.* punishment for wrongdoing

revelation (rev´ ə lā´ shən) *n.* something not previously known

revise (ri vīz´) *v.* to correct, improve, adjust, or change

revolutionary (rev´ ə lo͞o´ shə ner´ ē) *adj.* favoring or bringing about sweeping change

rickety (rik´ it ē) *adj.* weak; likely to break

rigorous (rig´ ər əs) *adj.* very harsh or strict

roam (rōm) *v.* go aimlessly; wander

rut (rut) *n.* a groove or track in the ground made by a wheeled vehicle or natural causes

S

sacred (sā´ krəd) *adj.* considered holy; related to religious ceremonies

satisfactory (sat´ is fak´ tə rē) *adj.* adequate; sufficient to meet a requirement

scarce (skers) *adj.* few in number; not common

sensibility (sen´ sə bil´ ə tē) *n.* moral, artistic, or intellectual outlook

sequence (sē´kwəns) *n.* order

serene (sə rēn´) *adj.* not disturbed or troubled; calm

shanties (shan´ tēz) *n.* roughly built cabins or shacks

shriveled (shriv´ əld) *v.* dried up; shrank and wrinkled

similar (sim´ə lər) *adj.* alike

simultaneously (sī´ məl tā´ nē əs lē) *adv.* at the same time

singularity (siŋ´ gyə ler´ ə tē) *n.* unique or distinct feature

sinister (sin´ is tər) *adj.* threatening harm or evil

skim (skim) *v.* to read quickly, skipping parts of the text

smoldering (smōl´ dər iŋ) *adj.* burning or smoking without flame

soberly (sō´ bər lē) *adv.* seriously; thoughtfully

somber (säm´ bər) *adj.* dark; gloomy

sparse (spärs) *adj.* thinly spread and small in amount

spindly (spind´ lē) *adj.* long and thin

spineless (spīn´ ləs) *adj.* lacking in courage or will power

squatter (skwät´ ər) *n.* someone who settles illegally on land or in a building

stealthily (stel*th*´ i lē) *adv.* in a secretive or sneaky way; avoiding being noticed

strife (strīf) *n.* conflict

studious (stoo´ dē əs) *adj.* devoted to learning

suggest (səg jest´) *v.* show indirectly; imply

support (sə pôrt´) *v.* to provide evidence to prove or back up an idea

sustain (sə stān´) *v.* keep up; maintain or prolong

sustenance (sus´ tə nəns) *n.* food; nourishment

synonymous (si nän´ə məs) *adj.* having the same, or nearly the same, meaning

T

tangible (tan´ jə bəl) *adj.* able to be perceived by the senses

tantalized (tan´ tə līzd´) *v.* tormented by something just out of reach

tenacious (tə nā´ shəs) *adj.* persistent; holding on firmly

timidly (tim´ id lē) *adv.* in a shy or fearful manner

topic (täp´ ik) *n.* the subject being discussed or written about

transparent (trans par´ ənt) *adj.* capable of being seen through; clear

trivial (triv´ ē əl) *adj.* of little importance; insignificant

tumultuous (too mul´ choo əs) *adj.* wild; chaotic

turmoil (tur´ moil´) *n.* a condition of great confusion or agitation

U

unabashed (un´ ə basht´) *adj.* unashamed

unanimous (yoo nan´ ə məs) *adj.* in complete agreement; united in opinion

unconstitutional (un´ kän stə too´ shə nəl) *adj.* not in accordance with or permitted by the U. S. Constitution

uneasily (un ēz´ i lē) *adv.* restlessly

unequivocal (un´ ē kwiv´ ə kəl) *adj.* clear; plainly understood

unique (yoo nēk´) *adj.* the characteristics that make one thing different from others.

unobtrusively (un´ əb troo´siv lē) *adv.* without calling attention to oneself

unresponsive (un´ rē spän´ siv) *adj.* not reacting

unseemly (un sēm´ lē) *adj.* inappropriate

V

valid (val´id) *adj.* based on facts and strong evidence; convincing

vertical (vur´ti kəl) *adj.* straight up and down; upright

virtuous (vur´ choo əs) *adj.* moral; upright

W

worrisome (wur´ē səm) causing worry or anxiety

Y

yearning (yur´ niŋ) *adj.* filled with the feeling of wanting something

Using a Dictionary

Use a **dictionary** to find the meaning, the pronunciation, and the part of speech of a word. Consult a dictionary also to trace the word's *etymology*, or its origin. Etymology explains how words change, how they are borrowed from other languages, and how new words are invented, or "coined."

Here is an entry from a dictionary. Notice what it tells about the word *anthology*.

anthology (an thäl´ə jē) *n., pl.* **–gies** [Gr. *anthologia*, a garland, collection of short poems < *anthologos*, gathering flowers < *anthos*, flower + *legein*, to gather] a collection of poems, stories, songs, excerpts, etc., chosen by the compiler

Dictionaries provide the *denotation* of each word, or its objective meaning. The symbol < means "comes from" or "is derived from." In this case, the Greek words for "flower" and "gather" combined to form a Greek word that meant a garland, and then that word became an English word that means a collection of literary flowers—a collection of literature like the one you are reading now.

Activity: Use a dictionary to learn about the origins of these words. Then, write a sentence explaining how each word's origin contributes to its meaning.
1. literature
2. author
3. language

Using a Thesaurus

Use a **thesaurus** to increase your vocabulary. In a thesaurus, you will find synonyms, or words that have similar meanings, for most words. Follow these guidelines to use a thesaurus:

- Do not choose a word just because it sounds interesting or educated. Choose the word that expresses exactly the meaning you intend.
- To avoid errors, look up an unfamiliar word in a dictionary to check its precise meaning and to make sure you are using it properly.

Here is an entry from a thesaurus. Notice what it tells about the word *book*.

book *noun*

A printed and bound work: tome, volume. *See* **WORDS.**

book *verb* 1. To register in or as if in a book: catalog, enroll, inscribe, list, set down, write down. *See* **REMEMBER**. 2. To cause to be set aside, as for one's use, in advance: bespeak, engage, reserve. *See* **GET**.

If the word can be used as different parts of speech, as *book* can, the thesaurus entry provides synonyms for the word as each part of speech. Many words also have *connotations*, or emotional associations that the word calls to mind. A thesaurus entry gives specific synonyms for each connotation of the word.

Activity: Look up the word *story* in a thesaurus. Then, answer the questions.
1. What are two synonyms for this word?
2. In what way do the connotations of the synonyms differ?

The History of the English Language

Old English English began about the year 500 when Germanic tribes from the middle of Europe traveled west and settled in Britain. These peoples—the Angles, Saxons, and Jutes—spoke a Germanic language that combined with Danish and Norse when Vikings attacked Britain and added some Latin elements when Christian missionaries arrived. The result was Old English.

Middle English The biggest change in English took place after the Norman Conquest of Britain in 1066. The Normans spoke a dialect of Old French, and Old English changed dramatically when the Normans became the new aristocracy. From about 1100 to 1500, the people of Britain spoke what we now call Middle English.

Modern English During the Renaissance (1300–1600), with its emphasis on reviving classical culture, Greek and Latin languages exerted a strong influence on the English language. In addition, Shakespeare added about two thousand words to the language. Grammar, spelling, and pronunciation continued to change. Modern English was born.

Old Words, New Words

Modern English has a larger vocabulary than any other language in the world. Here are the main ways that new words enter the language:

• **War**—Conquerors introduce new terms and ideas—and new vocabulary, such as *anger* from Old Norse.

• **Immigration**—When large groups of people move from one country to another, they bring words with them, such as *boycott*, from Ireland.

• **Travel and Trade**—Those who travel to foreign lands and those who do business in faraway places bring new words back with them, such as *shampoo*, from Hindi, a language spoken in India.

• **Science and Technology**—In our time, the amazing growth of science and technology adds many new words to English, such as *Internet*.

• **Other Languages**—Sometimes borrowed words keep basically the same meanings they have in their original languages. Examples include *pajamas* (Hindi), *sauna* (Finnish), and *camouflage* (French). Sometimes borrowed words take on new meanings. *Sleuth*, for example, an Old Norse word for *trail*, has come to mean the person who follows a trail—a detective.

• **Mythology**—Some of the days of the week are named after Norse gods— Wednesday was Woden's Day, Thursday was Thor's Day. Greek and Roman myths have given us many words, such as *martial* (from Mars) and *herculean* (from Hercules).

Activity: Look up the following words in a dictionary. Describe the ways in which you think these words entered American English.

sabotage   burrito   moccasin   megabyte

TIPS FOR IMPROVING READING FLUENCY

When you were younger, you learned to read. Then, you read to expand your experiences or for pure enjoyment. Now, you are expected to read to learn. As you progress in school, you are given more and more material to read. The tips on these pages will help you improve your reading fluency, or your ability to read easily, smoothly, and expressively.

Keeping Your Concentration

One common problem that readers face is the loss of concentration. When you are reading an assignment, you might find yourself rereading the same sentence several times without really understanding it. The first step in changing this behavior is to notice that you do it. Becoming an active, aware reader will help you get the most from your assignments. Practice using these strategies:

- Cover what you have already read with a note card as you go along. Then, you will not be able to reread without noticing that you are doing it.

- Set a purpose for reading beyond just completing the assignment. Then, read actively by pausing to ask yourself questions about the material as you read.

- Use the Reading Skill instruction and notes that appear with each selection in this textbook.

- Stop reading after a specified period of time (for example, 5 minutes) and summarize what you have read. To help you with this strategy, use the Reading Check questions that appear with each selection in this textbook. Reread to find any answers you do not know.

Reading Phrases

Fluent readers read phrases rather than individual words. Reading this way will speed up your reading and improve your comprehension. Here are some useful ideas:

- Experts recommend rereading as a strategy to increase fluency. Choose a passage of text that is neither too hard nor too easy. Read the same passage aloud several times until you can read it smoothly. When you can read the passage fluently, pick another passage and keep practicing.

- Read aloud into a tape recorder. Then, listen to the recording, noting your accuracy, pacing, and expression. You can also read aloud and share feedback with a partner.

- Use the *Prentice Hall Listening to Literature* Audio CDs to hear the selections read aloud. Read along silently in your textbook, noticing how the reader uses his or her voice and emphasizes certain words and phrases.

Understanding Key Vocabulary

If you do not understand some of the words in an assignment, you may miss out on important concepts. Therefore, it is helpful to keep a dictionary nearby when you are reading. Follow these steps:

- Before you begin reading, scan the text for unfamiliar words or terms. Find out what those words mean before you begin reading.

- Use context—the surrounding words, phrases, and sentences—to help you determine the meanings of unfamiliar words.

- If you are unable to understand the meaning through context, refer to the dictionary.

Paying Attention to Punctuation

When you read, pay attention to punctuation. Commas, periods, exclamation points, semicolons, and colons tell you when to pause or stop. They also indicate relationships between groups of words. When you recognize these relationships, you will read with greater understanding and expression. Look at the chart below.

Punctuation Mark	Meaning
comma	brief pause
period	pause at the end of a thought
exclamation point	pause that indicates emphasis
semicolon	pause between related but distinct thoughts
colon	pause before giving explanation or examples

Using the Reading Fluency Checklist

Use the checklist below each time you read a selection in this textbook. In your Language Arts journal or notebook, note which skills you need to work on and chart your progress each week.

Reading Fluency Checklist

- ☐ Preview the text to check for difficult or unfamiliar words.
- ☐ Practice reading aloud.
- ☐ Read according to punctuation.
- ☐ Break down long sentences into the subject and its meaning.
- ☐ Read groups of words for meaning rather than reading single words.
- ☐ Read with expression (change your tone of voice to add meaning to the word).

Reading is a skill that can be improved with practice. The key to improving your fluency is to read. The more you read, the better your reading will become.

LITERARY TERMS

ALLITERATION *Alliteration* is the repetition of initial consonant sounds. Writers use alliteration to draw attention to certain words or ideas, to imitate sounds, and to create musical effects.

ALLUSION An *allusion* is a reference to a well-known person, event, place, literary work, or work of art. Allusions connect literary works to a larger cultural heritage. They allow the writer to express complex ideas without spelling them out. Understanding what a literary work is saying often depends on recognizing its allusions and the meanings they suggest.

ANALOGY An *analogy* makes a comparison between two or more things that are similar in some ways but otherwise unalike.

ANECDOTE An *anecdote* is a brief story about an interesting, amusing, or strange event. Writers tell anecdotes to entertain or to make a point.

ANTAGONIST An *antagonist* is a character or a force in conflict with a main character, or protagonist.

See *Conflict* and *Protagonist*.

ATMOSPHERE *Atmosphere,* or *mood,* is the feeling created in the reader by a literary work or passage.

AUTHOR'S INFLUENCES An *author's influences* include his or her heritage, culture, and personal beliefs.

AUTHOR'S STYLE *Style* is an author's typical way of writing. Many factors determine a writer's style, including diction; tone; use of characteristic elements such as figurative language, dialect, rhyme, meter, or rhythmic devices; typical grammatical structures and patterns, typical sentence length, and typical methods of organization. Style comprises every feature of a writer's use of language.

AUTOBIOGRAPHY An *autobiography* is the story of the writer's own life, told by the writer. Autobiographical writing may tell about the person's whole life or only a part of it.

Because autobiographies are about real people and events, they are a form of nonfiction. Most autobiographies are written in the first person.

See *Biography, Nonfiction,* and *Point of View.*

BIOGRAPHY A *biography* is a form of nonfiction in which a writer tells the life story of another person. Most biographies are written about famous or admirable people. Although biographies are nonfiction, the most effective ones share the qualities of good narrative writing.

See *Autobiography* and *Nonfiction.*

CHARACTER A *character* is a person or an animal that takes part in the action of a literary work. The main, or *major,* character is the most important character in a story, poem, or play. A *minor* character is one who takes part in the action but is not the focus of attention.

Characters are sometimes classified as flat or round. A *flat character* is one-sided and often stereotypical. A *round character,* on the other hand, is fully developed and exhibits many traits—often both faults and virtues. Characters can also be classified as dynamic or static. A *dynamic character* is one who changes or grows during the course of the work. A *static character* is one who does not change.

See *Characterization, Hero/Heroine,* and *Motive.*

CHARACTERIZATION *Characterization* is the act of creating and developing a character. Authors use two major methods of characterization—*direct* and *indirect.* When using *direct* characterization, a writer states the *character's traits,* or characteristics.

When describing a character *indirectly,* a writer depends on the reader to draw conclusions about the character's traits. Sometimes the writer tells what other participants in the story say and think about the character.

See *Character* and *Motive.*

CHARACTER TRAITS *Character traits* are the qualities, attitudes, and values that a character has or displays—such as dependability, intelligence, selfishness, or stubbornness.

CLIMAX The climax, also called the turning point, is the high point in the action of the plot. It is the moment of greatest tension, when the outcome of the plot hangs in the balance. See *Plot.*

COMEDY A *comedy* is a literary work, especially a play, which is light, often humorous or satirical, and ends happily. Comedies frequently depict ordinary characters faced with temporary difficulties and conflicts. Types of comedy include *romantic comedy*, which involves problems between lovers, and the *comedy of manners*, which satirically challenges social customs of a society.

CONCRETE POEM A *concrete poem* is one with a shape that suggests its subject. The poet arranges the letters, punctuation, and lines to create an image, or picture, on the page.

CONFLICT A *conflict* is a struggle between opposing forces. Conflict is one of the most important elements of stories, novels, and plays because it causes the action. There are two kinds of conflict: external and internal. An *external conflict* is one in which a character struggles against some outside force, such as another person. Another kind of external conflict may occur between a character and some force in nature.

An *internal conflict* takes place within the mind of a character. The character struggles to make a decision, take an action, or overcome a feeling.

See *Plot*.

CONNOTATIONS The *connotation* of a word is the set of ideas associated with it in addition to its explicit meaning. The connotation of a word can be personal, based on individual experiences. More often, cultural connotations—those recognizable by most people in a group—determine a writer's word choices.

See also *Denotation*.

DENOTATION The *denotation* of a word is its dictionary meaning, independent of other associations that the word may have. The denotation of the word *lake*, for example, is "an inland body of water." "Vacation spot" and "place where the fishing is good" are connotations of the word *lake*.

See also *Connotation*.

DESCRIPTION A *description* is a portrait, in words, of a person, place, or object. Descriptive

writing uses images that appeal to the five senses—sight, hearing, touch, taste, and smell.

See *Images*.

DEVELOPMENT See *Plot*.

DIALECT *Dialect* is the form of a language spoken by people in a particular region or group. Dialects differ in pronunciation, grammar, and word choice. The English language is divided into many dialects. British English differs from American English.

DIALOGUE A *dialogue* is a conversation between characters. In poems, novels, and short stories, dialogue is usually set off by quotation marks to indicate a speaker's exact words.

In a play, dialogue follows the names of the characters, and no quotation marks are used.

DICTION *Diction* is a writer's or speaker's word choice. Diction is part of a writer's style and may be described as formal or informal, plain or fancy, ordinary or technical, sophisticated or down-to-earth, old-fashioned or modern.

DRAMA A *drama* is a story written to be performed by actors. Although a drama is meant to be performed, one can also read the script, or written version, and imagine the action. The *script* of a drama is made up of dialogue and stage directions. The *dialogue* is the words spoken by the actors. The *stage directions*, usually printed in italics, tell how the actors should look, move, and speak. They also describe the setting, sound effects, and lighting.

Dramas are often divided into parts called *acts*. The acts are often divided into smaller parts called *scenes*.

DYNAMIC CHARACTER See *Character*.

ESSAY An *essay* is a short nonfiction work about a particular subject. Most essays have a single major focus and a clear introduction, body, and conclusion.

There are many types of essays. An *informal essay* uses casual, conversational language. A *historical essay* gives facts, explanations, and insights about historical events. An *expository essay* explains an idea by breaking it down. A *narrative essay* tells a story about a real-life experience. An *informational essay* explains a process. A *persuasive essay* offers an opinion and supports it.

See *Exposition, Narration,* and *Persuasion.*

EXPOSITION In the plot of a story or a drama, the *exposition,* or introduction, is the part of the work that introduces the characters, setting, and basic situation.

See *Plot.*

EXPOSITORY WRITING *Expository writing* is writing that explains or informs.

EXTENDED METAPHOR In an *extended metaphor,* as in a regular metaphor, a subject is spoken or written of as though it were something else. However, extended metaphor differs from regular metaphor in that several connected comparisons are made.

See *Metaphor.*

EXTERNAL CONFLICT See *Conflict.*

FABLE A *fable* is a brief story or poem, usually with animal characters, that teaches a lesson, or moral. The moral is usually stated at the end of the fable.

See *Irony* and *Moral.*

FANTASY A *fantasy* is highly imaginative writing that contains elements not found in real life. Examples of fantasy include stories that involve supernatural elements, stories that resemble fairy tales, stories that deal with imaginary places and creatures, and science-fiction stories.

See *Science Fiction.*

FICTION *Fiction* is prose writing that tells about imaginary characters and events. Short stories and novels are works of fiction. Some writers base their fiction on actual events and people, adding invented characters, dialogue, settings, and plots. Other writers rely on imagination alone.

See *Narration, Nonfiction,* and *Prose.*

FIGURATIVE LANGUAGE *Figurative language* is writing or speech that is not meant to be taken literally. The many types of figurative language are known as *figures of speech.* Common figures of speech include metaphor, personification, and simile. Writers use figurative language to state ideas in vivid and imaginative ways.

See *Metaphor, Personification, Simile,* and *Symbol.*

FIGURE OF SPEECH See *Figurative Language.*

FLASHBACK A *flashback* is a scene within a story that interrupts the sequence of events to relate events that occurred in the past.

FLAT CHARACTER See *Character.*

FOLK TALE A *folk tale* is a story composed orally and then passed from person to person by word of mouth. Folk tales originated among people who could neither read nor write. These people entertained one another by telling stories aloud—often dealing with heroes, adventure, magic, or romance. Eventually, modern scholars collected these stories and wrote them down.

Folk tales reflect the cultural beliefs and environments from which they come.

See *Fable, Legend, Myth,* and *Oral Tradition.*

FOOT See *Meter.*

FORESHADOWING *Foreshadowing* is the author's use of clues to hint at what might happen later in the story. Writers use foreshadowing to build their readers' expectations and to create suspense.

FREE VERSE *Free verse* is poetry not written in a regular, rhythmical pattern, or meter. The poet is free to write lines of any length or with any number of stresses, or beats. Free verse is therefore less constraining than *metrical verse,* in which every line must have a certain length and a certain number of stresses.

See *Meter.*

GENRE A *genre* is a division or type of literature. Literature is commonly divided into three major genres: poetry, prose, and drama. Each major genre is, in turn, divided into lesser genres, as follows:

1. *Poetry:* lyric poetry, concrete poetry, dramatic poetry, narrative poetry, epic poetry

2. *Prose:* fiction (novels and short stories) and nonfiction (biography, autobiography, letters, essays, and reports)

3. *Drama:* serious drama and tragedy, comic drama, melodrama, and farce

See *Drama, Poetry,* and *Prose.*

HAIKU The *haiku* is a three-line Japanese verse form. The first and third lines of a haiku each have five syllables. The second line has seven syllables. A writer of haiku uses images to create a single, vivid picture, generally of a scene from nature.

HERO/HEROINE A *hero* or *heroine* is a character whose actions are inspiring, or noble. Often heroes and heroines struggle to overcome the obstacles and problems that stand in their way. Note that the term *hero* was originally used only for male characters, while heroic female characters were always called *heroines*. However, it is now acceptable to use *hero* to refer to females as well as to males.

HISTORICAL FICTION In *historical fiction,* real events, places, or people are incorporated into a fictional, or made-up, story.

HUMOR *Humor* is writing intended to evoke laughter. While most humorists are trying to entertain, humor can also be used to convey a serious theme.

IMAGERY See *Images.*

IMAGES *Images* are words or phrases that appeal to one or more of the five senses. Writers use images to describe how their subjects look, sound, feel, taste, and smell. Poets often paint images, or word pictures, that appeal to your senses. These pictures help you to experience the poem fully.

INTERNAL CONFLICT See *Conflict.*

IRONY *Irony* is a contradiction between what happens and what is expected. There are three main types of irony. *Situational irony* occurs when something happens that directly contradicts the expectations of the characters or the audience. *Verbal irony* is something contradictory that is said. In *dramatic irony,* the audience is aware of something that the character or speaker is not.

JOURNAL A *journal* is a daily, or periodic, account of events and the writer's thoughts and feelings about those events. Personal journals are not normally written for publication, but sometimes they do get published later with permission from the author or the author's family.

LEGEND A *legend* is a widely told story about the past—one that may or may not have a foundation in fact. Every culture has its own legends—its familiar, traditional stories.

See *Folk Tale, Myth,* and *Oral Tradition.*

LETTERS A *letter* is a written communication from one person to another. In personal letters, the writer shares information and his or her thoughts and feelings with one other person or group. Although letters are not normally written for publication, they sometimes do get published later with the permission of the author or the author's family.

LIMERICK A *limerick* is a humorous, rhyming, five-line poem with a specific meter and rhyme scheme. Most limericks have three strong stresses in lines 1, 2, and 5 and two strong stresses in lines 3 and 4. Most follow the rhyme scheme *aabba.*

LYRIC POEM A *lyric poem* is a highly musical verse that expresses the observations and feelings of a single speaker. It creates a single, unified impression.

MAIN CHARACTER See *Character.*

MEDIA ACCOUNTS *Media accounts* are reports, explanations, opinions, or descriptions written for television, radio, newspapers, and magazines. While some media accounts report only facts, others include the writer's thoughts and reflections.

METAPHOR A *metaphor* is a figure of speech in which something is described as though it were something else. A metaphor, like a simile, works by pointing out a similarity between two unlike things.

See *Extended Metaphor* and *Simile.*

METER The *meter* of a poem is its rhythmical pattern. This pattern is determined by the number of *stresses*, or beats, in each line. To describe the meter of a poem, read it emphasizing the beats in each line. Then, mark the stressed and unstressed syllables, as follows:

My fá | ther was | the fírst | to hear |

As you can see, each strong stress is marked with a slanted line (´) and each unstressed syllable with a horseshoe symbol (˘). The weak and strong stresses are then divided by vertical lines (|) into groups called *feet*.

MINOR CHARACTER See *Character*.

MOOD See *Atmosphere*.

MORAL A *moral* is a lesson taught by a literary work. A fable usually ends with a moral that is directly stated. A poem, novel, short story, or essay often suggests a moral that is not directly stated. The moral must be drawn by the reader, based on other elements in the work.

See *Fable*.

MOTIVATION See *Motive*.

MOTIVE A *motive* is a reason that explains or partially explains a character's thoughts, feelings, actions, or speech. Writers try to make their characters' motives, or motivations, as clear as possible. If the motives of a main character are not clear, then the character will not be well understood.

Characters are often motivated by needs, such as food and shelter. They are also motivated by feelings, such as fear, love, and pride. Motives may be obvious or hidden.

MYTH A *myth* is a fictional tale that explains the actions of gods or heroes or the origins of elements of nature. Myths are part of the oral tradition. They are composed orally and then passed from generation to generation by word of mouth. Every ancient culture has its own mythology, or collection of myths. Greek and Roman myths are known collectively as *classical mythology*.

See *Oral Tradition*.

NARRATION *Narration* is writing that tells a story. The act of telling a story is also called narration. A story told in fiction, nonfiction, poetry, or even in drama is called a *narrative*.

See *Narrative, Narrative Poem,* and *Narrator*.

NARRATIVE A *narrative* is a story. A narrative can be either fiction or nonfiction. Novels and short stories are types of fictional narratives. Biographies and autobiographies are nonfiction narratives. Poems that tell stories are also narratives.

See *Narration* and *Narrative Poem*.

NARRATIVE POEM A *narrative poem* is a story told in verse. Narrative poems often have all the elements of short stories, including characters, conflict, and plot.

NARRATOR A *narrator* is a speaker or a character who tells a story. The narrator's perspective is the way he or she sees things. A *third-person narrator* is one who stands outside the action and speaks about it. A *first-person narrator* is one who tells a story and participates in its action.

See *Point of View*.

NONFICTION *Nonfiction* is prose writing that presents and explains ideas or that tells about real people, places, objects, or events. Autobiographies, biographies, essays, reports, letters, memos, and newspaper articles are all types of nonfiction.

See *Fiction*.

NOVEL A *novel* is a long work of fiction. Novels contain such elements as characters, plot, conflict, and setting. The writer of novels, or novelist, develops these elements. In addition to its main plot, a novel may contain one or more subplots, or independent, related stories. A novel may also have several themes.

See *Fiction* and *Short Story*.

NOVELLA A *novella* is a fiction work that is longer than a short story but shorter than a novel.

ONOMATOPOEIA *Onomatopoeia* is the use of words that imitate sounds. *Crash, buzz, screech, hiss, neigh, jingle,* and *cluck* are examples of onomatopoeia. *Chickadee, towhee,* and *whippoorwill* are onomatopoeic names of birds.

Onomatopoeia can help put the reader in the action of a poem.

ORAL TRADITION *Oral tradition* is the passing of songs, stories, and poems from generation to generation by word of mouth. Folk songs, folk tales, legends, and myths all come from the oral tradition. No one knows who first created these stories and poems.

See *Folk Tale, Legend,* and *Myth.*

OXYMORON An *oxymoron* (pl. *oxymora*) is a figure of speech that links two opposite or contradictory words, to point out an idea or situation that seems contradictory or inconsistent but on closer inspection turns out to be somehow true.

PERSONIFICATION *Personification* is a type of figurative language in which a nonhuman subject is given human characteristics.

PERSPECTIVE See *Narrator* and *Point of View.*

PERSUASION *Persuasion* is used in writing or speech that attempts to convince the reader or listener to adopt a particular opinion or course of action. Newspaper editorials and letters to the editor use persuasion. So do advertisements and campaign speeches given by political candidates.

See *Essay.*

PLAYWRIGHT A *playwright* is a person who writes plays. William Shakespeare is regarded as the greatest playwright in English literature.

PLOT *Plot* is the sequence of events in a story. In most novels, dramas, short stories, and narrative poems, the plot involves both characters and a central conflict. The plot usually begins with an

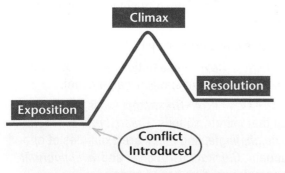

exposition that introduces the setting, the characters, and the basic situation. This is followed by the *inciting incident*, which introduces the central conflict. The conflict then increases during the *development* until it reaches a high point of interest or suspense, the *climax*. The climax is followed by the

falling action, or end, of the central conflict. Any events that occur during the *falling action* make up the *resolution* or *denouement.*

Some plots do not have all of these parts. For example, some stories begin with the inciting incident and end with the resolution.

See *Conflict.*

POETRY *Poetry* is one of the three major types of literature, the others being prose and drama. Most poems make use of highly concise, musical, and emotionally charged language. Many also make use of imagery, figurative language, and special devices of sound such as rhyme. Major types of poetry include *lyric poetry, narrative poetry,* and *concrete poetry.*

See *Concrete Poem, Genre, Lyric Poem,* and *Narrative Poem.*

POINT OF VIEW Point of view is the perspective, or vantage point, from which a story is told. It is either a narrator outside the story or a character in the story. *First-person point of view* is told by a character who uses the first-person pronoun "I."

The two kinds of *third-person point of view*, limited and omniscient, are called "third person" because the narrator uses third-person pronouns such as *he* and *she* to refer to the characters. There is no "I" telling the story.

In stories told from the *omniscient third-person point of view*, the narrator knows and tells about what each character feels and thinks.

In stories told from the *limited third-person point of view*, the narrator relates the inner thoughts and feelings of only one character, and everything is viewed from this character's perspective.

See *Narrator.*

PROBLEM See *Conflict.*

PROSE *Prose* is the ordinary form of written language. Most writing that is not poetry, drama, or song is considered prose. Prose is one of the major genres of literature and occurs in two forms—fiction and nonfiction.

See *Fiction, Genre,* and *Nonfiction.*

PROTAGONIST The *protagonist* is the main character in a literary work. Often, the protagonist is a person, but sometimes it can be an animal.

See *Antagonist* and *Character*.

REFRAIN A *refrain* is a regularly repeated line or group of lines in a poem or a song.

REPETITION *Repetition* is the use, more than once, of any element of language—a sound, word, phrase, clause, or sentence. Repetition is used in both prose and poetry.

See *Alliteration, Meter, Plot, Rhyme,* and *Rhyme Scheme*.

RESOLUTION The *resolution* is the outcome of the conflict in a plot.

See *Plot*.

RHYME *Rhyme* is the repetition of sounds at the ends of words. Poets use rhyme to lend a songlike quality to their verses and to emphasize certain words and ideas. Many traditional poems contain *end rhymes*, or rhyming words at the ends of lines.

Another common device is the use of *internal rhymes*, or rhyming words within lines. Internal rhyme also emphasizes the flowing nature of a poem.

See *Rhyme Scheme*.

RHYME SCHEME A *rhyme scheme* is a regular pattern of rhyming words in a poem. To indicate the rhyme scheme of a poem, one uses lowercase letters. Each rhyme is assigned a different letter, as follows in the first stanza of "Dust of Snow," by Robert Frost:

The way a crow	*a*
Shook down on me	*b*
The dust of snow	*a*
From a hemlock tree	*b*

Thus, this stanza has the rhyme scheme *abab*.

RHYTHM *Rhythm* is the pattern of stressed and unstressed syllables in spoken or written language.

See *Meter*.

ROUND CHARACTER See *Character*.

SCENE A *scene* is a section of uninterrupted action in the act of a drama.

See *Drama*.

SCIENCE FICTION *Science fiction* combines elements of fiction and fantasy with scientific fact. Many science-fiction stories are set in the future.

SENSORY LANGUAGE *Sensory language* is writing or speech that appeals to one or more of the five senses.

See *Images*.

SETTING The *setting* of a literary work is the time and place of the action. The setting includes all the details of a place and time—the year, the time of day, even the weather. The place may be a specific country, state, region, community, neighborhood, building, institution, or home. Details such as dialects, clothing, customs, and modes of transportation are often used to establish setting. In most stories, the setting serves as a backdrop—a context in which the characters interact. Setting can also help to create a feeling, or atmosphere.

See *Atmosphere*.

SHORT STORY A *short story* is a brief work of fiction. Like a novel, a short story presents a sequence of events, or plot. The plot usually deals with a central conflict faced by a main character, or protagonist. The events in a short story usually communicate a message about life or human nature. This message, or central idea, is the story's theme.

See *Conflict, Plot,* and *Theme*.

SIMILE A *simile* is a figure of speech that uses *like* or *as* to make a direct comparison between two unlike ideas. Everyday speech often contains similes, such as "pale as a ghost," "good as gold," "spread like wildfire," and "clever as a fox."

SPEAKER The *speaker* is the imaginary voice a poet uses when writing a poem. The speaker is the character who tells the poem. This character, or voice, often is not identified by name. There can be important differences between the poet and the poem's speaker. See *Narrator*.

STAGE DIRECTIONS *Stage directions* are notes included in a drama to describe how the work is to be performed or staged. Stage directions are usually printed in italics and enclosed within parentheses or brackets. Some stage directions describe the movements, costumes, emotional states, and ways of speaking of the characters.

STAGING *Staging* includes the setting, the lighting, the costumes, special effects, music, dance, and so on that go into putting on a stage performance of a drama.

See *Drama*.

STANZA A *stanza* is a group of lines of poetry that are usually similar in length and pattern and are separated by spaces. A stanza is like a paragraph of poetry—it states and develops a single main idea.

STATIC CHARACTER See *Character*.

SURPRISE ENDING A *surprise ending* is a conclusion that is unexpected. The reader has certain expectations about the ending based on details in the story. Often, a surprise ending is *foreshadowed*, or subtly hinted at, in the course of the work.

See *Foreshadowing* and *Plot*.

SUSPENSE *Suspense* is a feeling of anxious uncertainty about the outcome of events in a literary work. Writers create suspense by raising questions in the minds of their readers.

SYMBOL A *symbol* is anything that stands for or represents something else. Symbols are common in everyday life. A dove with an olive branch in its beak is a symbol of peace. A blindfolded woman holding a balanced scale is a symbol of justice. A crown is a symbol of a king's status and authority.

SYMBOLISM *Symbolism* is the use of symbols. Symbolism plays an important role in many different types of literature. It can highlight certain elements the author wishes to emphasize and also add levels of meaning.

THEME The *theme* is a central message, concern, or purpose in a literary work. A theme can usually be expressed as a generalization, or a general statement, about human beings or about life. The theme of a work is not a summary of its plot. The theme is the writer's central idea.

Although a theme may be stated directly in the text, it is more often presented indirectly. When the theme is stated indirectly, or implied, the reader must figure out what the theme is by looking carefully at what the work reveals about people or about life.

TONE The *tone* of a literary work is the writer's attitude toward his or her audience and subject. The tone can often be described by a single adjective, such as *formal* or *informal, serious* or *playful, bitter,* or *ironic*. Factors that contribute to the tone are word choice, sentence structure, line length, rhyme, rhythm, and repetition.

TRAGEDY A *tragedy* is a work of literature, especially a play, that results in a catastrophe for the main character. In ancient Greek drama, the main character is always a significant person—a king or a hero—and the cause of the tragedy is a tragic flaw, or weakness, in his or her character. In modern drama, the main character can be an ordinary person, and the cause of the tragedy can be some evil in society itself. The purpose of tragedy is not only to arouse fear and pity in the audience, but also, in some cases, to convey a sense of the grandeur and nobility of the human spirit.

TURNING POINT See *Climax*.

UNIVERSAL THEME A *universal theme* is a message about life that is expressed regularly in many different cultures and time periods. Folk tales, epics, and romances often address universal themes like the importance of courage, the power of love, or the danger of greed.

WORD CHOICE An author's *word choice*—sometimes referred to as *diction*—is an important factor in creating the tone or mood of a literary work. Authors choose words based on the intended audience and the work's purpose.

TIPS FOR DISCUSSING LITERATURE

As you read and study literature, discussions with other readers can help you understand and enjoy what you have read. Use the following tips.

- ## Understand the purpose of your discussion.

  Your purpose when you discuss literature is to broaden your understanding of a work by testing your own ideas and hearing the ideas of others. Keep your comments focused on the literature you are discussing. Starting with one focus question will help to keep your discussion on track.

- ## Communicate effectively.

  Effective communication requires thinking before speaking. Plan the points that you want to make and decide how you will express them. Organize these points in logical order and use details from the work to support your ideas. Jot down informal notes to help keep your ideas focused.

  Remember to speak clearly, pronouncing words slowly and carefully. Also, listen attentively when others are speaking, and avoid interrupting.

- ## Consider other ideas and interpretations.

  A work of literature can generate a wide variety of responses in different readers. Be open to the idea that many interpretations can be valid. To support your own ideas, point to the events, descriptions, characters, or other literary elements in the work that led to your interpretation. To consider someone else's ideas, decide whether details in the work support the interpretation he or she presents. Be sure to convey your criticism of the ideas of others in a respectful and supportive manner.

- ## Ask questions.

  Ask questions to clarify your understanding of another reader's ideas. You can also use questions to call attention to possible areas of confusion, to points that are open to debate, or to errors in the speaker's points. To move a discussion forward, summarize and evaluate conclusions reached by the group members.

  When you meet with a group to discuss literature, use a chart like the one shown to analyze the discussion.

Work Being Discussed:	
Focus Question:	
Your Response:	Another Student's Response:
Supporting Evidence:	Supporting Evidence:

TYPES OF WRITING

Narration

Whenever writers tell any type of story, they are using **narration.** While there are many kinds of narration, most narratives share certain elements, such as characters, a setting, a sequence of events, and, often, a theme.

Autobiographical writing tells the story of an event or person in the writer's life.

Biographical writing is a writer's account of another person's life.

Short story A short story is a brief, creative narrative—a retelling of events arranged to hold a reader's attention. A few types of short stories are realistic stories, fantasy, science-fiction stories, and adventure stories.

Description

Descriptive writing is writing that creates a vivid picture of a person, place, thing, or event. Descriptive writing includes descriptions of people or places, remembrances, observations, vignettes, and character profiles.

Persuasion

Persuasion is writing or speaking that attempts to convince people to accept a position or take a desired action. Forms of persuasive writing include persuasive essays, advertisements, persuasive letters, editorials, persuasive speeches, and public-service announcements. Problem-and-solution essays may also contain elements of persuasion.

Expository Writing

Expository writing is writing that informs or explains. The information you include in expository writing is factual. Effective expository writing reflects a well-thought-out organization—one that includes a clear introduction, body, and conclusion. Here are some types of exposition.

Comparison-and-Contrast essay A comparison-and-contrast essay analyzes the similarities and differences between two or more things.

Cause-and-Effect essay A cause-and-effect essay explains the reasons why something happened or the results an event or situation will probably produce. You may examine several causes of a single effect or several effects of a single cause.

Problem-and-Solution essay The purpose of a problem-and-solution essay is to describe a problem and offer one or more solutions to it. An effective problem-and-solution essay describes a clear set of steps to achieve a result and explains and defends the proposed solution. Elements of problem-and-solution writing may be found in advice columns, memos, and proposals.

How-to essay A how-to essay explains how to do or make something. You break the process down into steps and explain the steps in order.

Summary A summary is a brief statement that includes only the main ideas and significant supporting details presented in a piece of writing. A summary should be written in your own words.

Research Writing

Writers often use outside research to gather information and explore subjects of interest. The product of that research is called **research writing.** Good research writing does not simply repeat information. It guides readers through a topic, showing them why each fact matters and creating an overall picture of the subject. Here are some types of research writing.

Research report A research report presents information gathered from reference books, observations, interviews, or other sources.

Biographical report A biographical report examines the high points and achievements in the life of a notable person. It includes dates, details, and main events in the person's life as well as background on the period in which the person lived.

Multimedia report A multimedia report presents information through a variety of media, including text, slides, photographs, prerecorded music and sound effects, and digital imaging.

Response to Literature

A **response to literature** discusses and interprets what is of value in a book, short story, essay, article, or poem. You take a careful, critical look at various important elements in the work.

In addition to the standard literary essay, here are some other types of responses to literature.

Literary criticism Literary criticism is the result of literary analysis—the examination of a literary work or a body of literature. In literary criticism, you make a judgment or evaluation by looking carefully and critically at various important elements in the work. You then attempt to explain how the author has used those elements and how effectively they work together to convey the author's message.

Book or movie reviews A book review gives readers an impression of a book, encouraging them either to read it or to avoid reading it. A movie review begins with a basic response to whether you enjoyed the movie and then explains the reasons why or why not.

Letter to an author People sometimes respond to a work of literature by writing a letter to the writer. It lets the writer know what a reader found enjoyable or disappointing in a work. You can praise the work, ask questions, or offer constructive criticism.

Comparisons of works A comparison of works highlights specific features of two or more works by comparing them.

Creative Writing

Creative writing blends imagination, ideas, and emotions, and allows you to present your own unique view of the world. Poems, plays, short stories, dramas, and even some cartoons are examples of creative writing. Here are some types of creative writing.

Lyric poem A lyric poem uses sensory images, figurative language, and sound devices to express deep thoughts and feelings about a subject. Writers give lyric poems a musical quality by employing sound devices, such as rhyme, rhythm, alliteration, and onomatopoeia.

Narrative poem A narrative poem is similar to a short story in that it has a plot, characters, and a theme. However, a writer divides a narrative poem into stanzas, usually composed of rhyming lines that have a definite rhythm, or beat.

Song lyrics Song lyrics contain many elements of poetry—rhyme, rhythm, repetition, and imagery. In addition, song lyrics convey emotions, as well as interesting ideas.

Drama A drama or a dramatic scene is a story that is intended to be performed. The story is told mostly through what the actors say (dialogue) and what they do (action).

Practical and Technical Documents

Practical writing is fact-based writing that people do in the workplace or in their day-to-day lives. A business letter, memorandum, school form, job application, and a letter of inquiry are a few examples of practical writing.

Technical documents are fact-based documents that identify the sequence of activities needed to design a system, operate a tool, follow a procedure, or explain the bylaws of an organization. You encounter technical writing every time you read a manual or a set of instructions.

Here are some types of practical and technical writing.

Business letter A formal letter that follows one of several specific formats. (See page R23.)

News release A news release, also called a press release, announces factual information about upcoming events. A writer might send a news release to a local newspaper, local radio station, TV station, or other media outlet that will publicize the information.

Guidelines Guidelines give information about how people should act or provide tips on how to do something.

Process explanation A process explanation is a step-by-step explanation of how to do something. The explanation should be clear and specific and might include diagrams or other illustrations to further clarify the process.

WRITING LETTERS

Writing Friendly Letters

A friendly letter is much less formal than a business letter. It is a letter to a friend, a family member, or anyone with whom the writer wants to communicate in a personal, friendly way. Most friendly letters are made up of five parts:

- the heading
- the salutation, or greeting
- the body
- the closing
- the signature

The purpose of a friendly letter is often one of the following:

- to share personal news and feelings
- to send or to answer an invitation
- to express thanks

Model Friendly Letter

In this friendly letter, Betsy thanks her grandparents for a birthday present and gives them some news about her life.

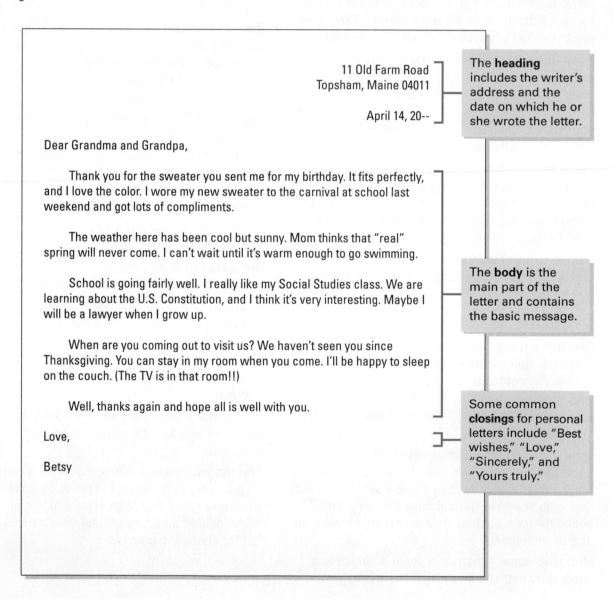

11 Old Farm Road
Topsham, Maine 04011

April 14, 20--

The **heading** includes the writer's address and the date on which he or she wrote the letter.

Dear Grandma and Grandpa,

Thank you for the sweater you sent me for my birthday. It fits perfectly, and I love the color. I wore my new sweater to the carnival at school last weekend and got lots of compliments.

The weather here has been cool but sunny. Mom thinks that "real" spring will never come. I can't wait until it's warm enough to go swimming.

School is going fairly well. I really like my Social Studies class. We are learning about the U.S. Constitution, and I think it's very interesting. Maybe I will be a lawyer when I grow up.

The **body** is the main part of the letter and contains the basic message.

When are you coming out to visit us? We haven't seen you since Thanksgiving. You can stay in my room when you come. I'll be happy to sleep on the couch. (The TV is in that room!!)

Well, thanks again and hope all is well with you.

Love,

Betsy

Some common **closings** for personal letters include "Best wishes," "Love," "Sincerely," and "Yours truly."

Formatting Business Letters

Business letters follow one of several acceptable formats. In **block format,** each part of the letter begins at the left margin. A double space is used between paragraphs. In **modified block format,** some parts of the letter are indented to the center of the page. No matter which format is used, all letters in business format have a heading, an inside address, a salutation or greeting, a body, a closing, and a signature. These parts are shown and annotated on the model business letter below, formatted in modified block style.

Model Business Letter

In this letter, Yolanda Dodson uses modified block format to request information.

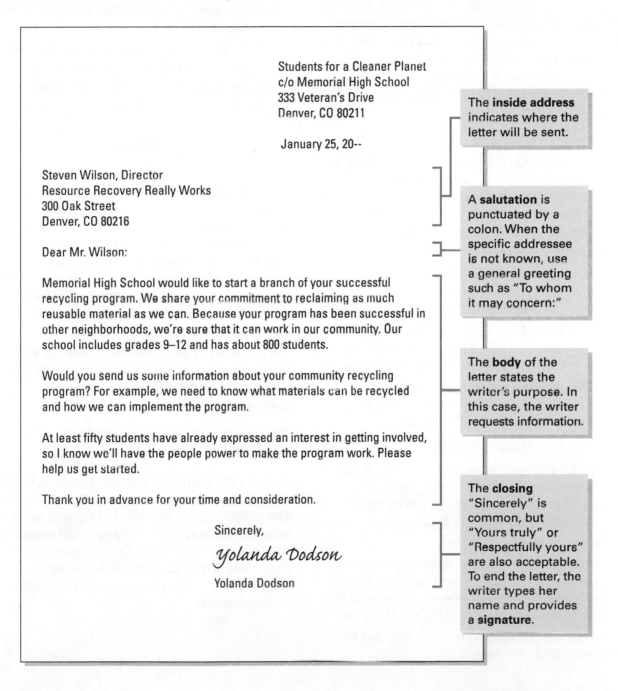

Students for a Cleaner Planet
c/o Memorial High School
333 Veteran's Drive
Denver, CO 80211

January 25, 20--

Steven Wilson, Director
Resource Recovery Really Works
300 Oak Street
Denver, CO 80216

Dear Mr. Wilson:

Memorial High School would like to start a branch of your successful recycling program. We share your commitment to reclaiming as much reusable material as we can. Because your program has been successful in other neighborhoods, we're sure that it can work in our community. Our school includes grades 9–12 and has about 800 students.

Would you send us some information about your community recycling program? For example, we need to know what materials can be recycled and how we can implement the program.

At least fifty students have already expressed an interest in getting involved, so I know we'll have the people power to make the program work. Please help us get started.

Thank you in advance for your time and consideration.

Sincerely,

Yolanda Dodson

Yolanda Dodson

The **inside address** indicates where the letter will be sent.

A **salutation** is punctuated by a colon. When the specific addressee is not known, use a general greeting such as "To whom it may concern:"

The **body** of the letter states the writer's purpose. In this case, the writer requests information.

The **closing** "Sincerely" is common, but "Yours truly" or "Respectfully yours" are also acceptable. To end the letter, the writer types her name and provides a **signature.**

USING THE INTERNET

Keyword Search

Before you begin a search, narrow your subject to a keyword or a group of **keywords.** These are your search terms, and they should be as specific as possible. For example, if you are looking for information about your favorite musical group, you might use the band's name as a keyword. You might locate such information as band member biographies, the group's history, fan reviews of concerts, and hundreds of sites with related names containing information that is irrelevant to your search. Depending on your research needs, you might need to narrow your search.

How to Narrow Your Search

If you have a large group of keywords and still do not know which ones to use, write out a list of all the words you are considering. Then, delete the words that are least important to your search, and highlight those that are most important.

Use **search connectors** to fine-tune your search:

AND: narrows a search by retrieving documents that include both terms. For example: *baseball AND playoffs*

OR: broadens a search by retrieving documents including any of the terms. For example: *playoffs OR championships*

NOT: narrows a search by excluding documents containing certain words. For example: *baseball NOT history*

Tips for an Effective Search

1. Search engines can be case-sensitive. If your first attempt at searching fails, check your search terms for misspellings and try again.

2. Present in order, from the most important to the least important.

3. Avoid opening the link to every single page in your results list. Search engines present pages in descending order of relevancy. The most useful pages will be located at the top of the list.

4. Some search engines provide helpful tips for specializing your search.

Tips for Evaluating Internet Sources

Consider who constructed and who now maintains the Web page. Determine whether this author is a reputable source. Often, the URL endings indicate a source.

- Sites ending in *.edu* are maintained by educational institutions.

- Sites ending in *.gov* are maintained by government agencies (federal, state, or local).

- Sites ending in *.org* are normally maintained by nonprofit organizations and agencies.

- Sites with a *.com* ending are commercially or personally maintained.

Other Ways to Search

How you search should be tailored to what you are hoping to find. If you are looking for data and facts, use reference sites before you jump onto a simple search engine. For example, you can find reference sites to provide definitions of words, statistics about almost any subject, biographies, maps, and concise information on many topics. Useful online reference sites include online libraries, online periodicals, almanacs, and encyclopedias.

You can also use other electronic sources such as CD-ROMs. Ask a reference librarian to help you locate and use the full range of electronic resources.

Respecting Copyrighted Material

Because the Internet is a growing medium, issues of copyright and ownership arise almost daily. Laws that govern the use and reuse of material are posted online and may change the way that people can access or reprint material. Text, photographs, music, and fine art printed online may not be reproduced without acknowledged permission of the copyright owner.

CITING SOURCES AND PREPARING MANUSCRIPT

Proofreading and Preparing Manuscript

Before preparing a final copy, proofread your manuscript. The chart shows the standard symbols for marking corrections to be made.

Proofreading Symbols	
insert	∧
delete	℘
close space	◯
new paragraph	¶
add comma	∧
add period	⊙
transpose (switch)	∩
change to cap	a̲
change to lowercase	A̸

- Choose a standard, easy-to-read font.
- Type or print on one side of unlined 8 1/2" x 11" paper.
- Set the margins for the side, top, and bottom of your paper at approximately one inch. Most word-processing programs have a default setting that is appropriate.
- Double-space the document.
- Indent the first line of each paragraph.
- Number the pages in the upper right corner.

Follow your teacher's directions for formatting formal research papers. Most papers will have the following features:

- Title page
- Table of Contents or Outline
- Works-Cited List

Avoiding Plagiarism

Whether you are presenting a formal research paper or an opinion paper on a current event, you must be careful to give credit for any ideas or opinions that are not your own. Presenting someone else's ideas, research, or opinion as your own—even if you have phrased it in different words—is *plagiarism,* the equivalent of academic stealing, or fraud.

Do not use the ideas or research of others in place of your own. Read from several sources to draw your own conclusions and form your own opinions. Incorporate the ideas and research of others to support your points. Credit the source of the following types of support:

- Statistics
- Direct quotations
- Indirectly quoted statements of opinions
- Conclusions presented by an expert
- Facts available in only one or two sources

Crediting Sources

When you credit a source, you acknowledge where you found your information and you give your readers the details necessary for locating the source themselves. Within the body of the paper, you provide a short citation, a footnote number linked to a footnote, or an endnote number linked to an endnote reference. These brief references show the page numbers on which you found the information. Prepare a reference list at the end of the paper to provide full bibliographic information on your sources. These are two common types of reference lists:

- A **bibliography** provides a listing of all the resources you consulted during your research.
- A **works-cited list** indicates the works you have referenced in your paper.

The chart on the next page shows the Modern Language Association format for crediting sources. This is the most common format for papers written in the content areas in middle school and high school. Unless instructed otherwise by your teacher, use this format for crediting sources.

MLA Style for Listing Sources

Book with one author	Pyles, Thomas. *The Origins and Development of the English Language.* 2nd ed. New York: Harcourt Brace Jovanovich, Inc., 1971.
Book with two or three authors	McCrum, Robert, William Cran, and Robert MacNeil. *The Story of English.* New York: Penguin Books, 1987.
Book with an editor	Truth, Sojourner. *Narrative of Sojourner Truth.* Ed. Margaret Washington. New York: Vintage Books, 1993.
Book with more than three authors or editors	Donald, Robert B., et al. *Writing Clear Essays.* Upper Saddle River, NJ: Prentice Hall, Inc., 1996.
Single work from an anthology	Hawthorne, Nathaniel. "Young Goodman Brown." *Literature: An Introduction to Reading and Writing.* Ed. Edgar V. Roberts and Henry E. Jacobs. Upper Saddle River, NJ: Prentice-Hall, Inc., 1998. 376–385. [Indicate pages for the entire selection.]
Introduction in a published edition	Washington, Margaret. Introduction. *Narrative of Sojourner Truth.* By Sojourner Truth. New York: Vintage Books, 1993, pp. v–xi.
Signed article in a weekly magazine	Wallace, Charles. "A Vodacious Deal." *Time* 14 Feb. 2000: 63.
Signed article in a monthly magazine	Gustaitis, Joseph. "The Sticky History of Chewing Gum." *American History* Oct. 1998: 30–38.
Unsigned editorial or story	"Selective Silence." Editorial. *Wall Street Journal* 11 Feb. 2000: A14. [If the editorial or story is signed, begin with the author's name.]
Signed pamphlet or brochure	[Treat the pamphlet as though it were a book.]
Pamphlet with no author, publisher, or date	*Are You at Risk of Heart Attack?* n.p. n.d. [n.p. n.d. indicates that there is no known publisher or date.]
Filmstrips, slide programs, videocassettes, DVDs, and other audiovisual media	*The Diary of Anne Frank.* Dir. George Stevens. Perf. Millie Perkins, Shelly Winters, Joseph Schildkraut, Lou Jacobi, and Richard Beymer. Twentieth Century Fox, 1959.
Radio or television program transcript	"Nobel for Literature." Narr. Rick Karr. *All Things Considered.* National Public Radio. WNYC, New York. 10 Oct. 2002. Transcript.
Internet	*National Association of Chewing Gum Manufacturers.* 19 Dec. 1999 <http://www.nacgm.org/consumer/funfacts.html> [Indicate the date you accessed the information. Content and addresses at Web sites change frequently.]
Newspaper	Thurow, Roger. "South Africans Who Fought for Sanctions Now Scrap for Investors." *Wall Street Journal* 11 Feb. 2000: A1+ [For a multipage article, write only the first page number on which it appears, followed by a plus sign.]
Personal interview	Smith, Jane. Personal interview. 10 Feb. 2000.
CD (with multiple publishers)	Simms, James, ed. *Romeo and Juliet.* By William Shakespeare. CD-ROM. Oxford: Attica Cybernetics Ltd.; London: BBC Education; London: HarperCollins Publishers, 1995.
Signed article from an encyclopedia	Askeland, Donald R. "Welding." *World Book Encyclopedia.* 1991 ed.

GUIDE TO RUBRICS

What is a rubric?

A rubric is a tool, often in the form of a chart or a grid, that helps you assess your work. Rubrics are particularly helpful for writing and speaking assignments.

To help you or others assess, or evaluate, your work, a rubric offers several specific criteria to be applied to your work. Then the rubric helps you or an evaluator indicate your range of success or failure according to those specific criteria. Rubrics are often used to evaluate writing for standardized tests.

Using a rubric will save you time, focus your learning, and improve the work you do. When you know what the rubric will be before you begin writing a persuasive essay, for example, as you write you will be aware of specific criteria that are important in that kind of an essay. As you evaluate the essay before giving it to your teacher, you will focus on the specific areas that your teacher wants you to master—or on areas that you know present challenges for you. Instead of searching through your work randomly for any way to improve it or correct its errors, you will have a clear and helpful focus on specific criteria.

How are rubrics constructed?

Rubrics can be constructed in several different ways.

- Your teacher may assign a rubric for a specific assignment.
- Your teacher may direct you to a rubric in your textbook.
- Your teacher and your class may construct a rubric for a particular assignment together.
- You and your classmates may construct a rubric together.
- You may create your own rubric with criteria you want to evaluate in your work.

How will a rubric help me?

A rubric will help you assess your work on a scale. Scales vary from rubric to rubric but usually range from 6 to 1, 5 to 1, or 4 to 1, with 6, 5, or 4 being the highest score and 1 being the lowest. If someone else is using the rubric to assess your work, the rubric will give your evaluator a clear range within which to place your work. If you are using the rubric yourself, it will help you make improvements to your work.

What are the types of rubrics?

- A **holistic rubric** has general criteria that can apply to a variety of assignments. See p. R29 for an example of a holistic rubric.
- An **analytic rubric** is specific to a particular assignment. The criteria for evaluation address the specific issues important in that assignment. See p. R28 for examples of analytic rubrics.

Sample Analytic Rubrics

Rubric With a 4-point Scale

The following analytic rubric is an example of a rubric to assess a persuasive essay. It will help you evaluate focus, organization, support, elaboration, and style conventions.

	Focus	Organization	Support/Elaboration	Style Conventions
4	Demonstrates highly effective word choice; clearly focused on task.	Uses clear, consistent organizational strategy.	Provides convincing, well-elaborated reasons to support the position.	Incorporates transitions; includes very few mechanical errors.
3	Demonstrates good word choice; stays focused on persuasive task.	Uses clear organizational strategy with occasional inconsistencies.	Provides two or more moderately elaborated reasons to support the position.	Incorporates some transitions; includes few mechanical errors.
2	Shows some good word choices; minimally stays focused on persuasive task.	Uses inconsistent organizational strategy; presentation is not logical.	Provides several reasons, but few are elaborated; only one elaborated reason.	Incorporates few transitions; includes many mechanical errors.
1	Shows lack of attention to persuasive task.	Demonstrates lack of organizational strategy.	Provides no specific reasons or does not elaborate.	Does not connect ideas; includes many mechanical errors.

Rubric With a 6-point Scale

The following analytic rubric is an example of a rubric to assess a persuasive essay. It will help you evaluate presentation, position, evidence, and arguments.

	Presentation	Position	Evidence	Arguments
6	Essay clearly and effectively addresses an issue with more than one side.	Essay clearly states a supportable position on the issue.	All evidence is logically organized, well presented, and supports the position.	All reader concerns and counterarguments are effectively addressed.
5	Most of essay addresses an issue that has more than one side.	Essay clearly states a position on the issue.	Most evidence is logically organized, well presented, and supports the position.	Most reader concerns and counterarguments are effectively addressed.
4	Essay adequately addresses issue that has more than one side.	Essay adequately states a position on the issue.	Many parts of evidence support the position; some evidence is out of order.	Many reader concerns and counterarguments are adequately addressed.
3	Essay addresses issue with two sides but does not present second side clearly.	Essay states a position on the issue, but the position is difficult to support.	Some evidence supports the position, but some evidence is out of order.	Some reader concerns and counterarguments are addressed.
2	Essay addresses issue with two sides but does not present second side.	Essay states a position on the issue, but the position is not supportable.	Not much evidence supports the position, and what is included is out of order.	A few reader concerns and counterarguments are addressed.
1	Essay does not address issue with more than one side.	Essay does not state a position on the issue.	No evidence supports the position.	No reader concerns or counterarguments are addressed.

Sample Holistic Rubric

Holistic rubrics such as this one are sometimes used to assess writing assignments on standardized tests. Notice that the criteria for evaluation are focus, organization, support, and use of conventions.

Points	Criteria
6 Points	• The writing is strongly focused and shows fresh insight into the writing task. • The writing is marked by a sense of completeness and coherence and is organized with a logical progression of ideas. • A main idea is fully developed, and support is specific and substantial. • A mature command of the language is evident, and the writing may employ characteristic creative writing strategies. • Sentence structure is varied, and writing is free of all but purposefully used fragments. • Virtually no errors in writing conventions appear.
5 Points	• The writing is clearly focused on the task. • The writing is well organized and has a logical progression of ideas, though there may be occasional lapses. • A main idea is well developed and supported with relevant detail. • Sentence structure is varied, and the writing is free of fragments, except when used purposefully. • Writing conventions are followed correctly.
4 Points	• The writing is clearly focused on the task, but extraneous material may intrude at times. • Clear organizational pattern is present, though lapses may occur. • A main idea is adequately supported, but development may be uneven. • Sentence structure is generally fragment free but shows little variation. • Writing conventions are generally followed correctly.
3 Points	• Writing is generally focused on the task, but extraneous material may intrude at times. • An organizational pattern is evident, but writing may lack a logical progression of ideas. • Support for the main idea is generally present but is sometimes illogical. • Sentence structure is generally free of fragments, but there is almost no variation. • The work generally demonstrates a knowledge of writing conventions, with occasional misspellings.
2 Points	• The writing is related to the task but generally lacks focus. • There is little evidence of organizational pattern, and there is little sense of cohesion. • Support for the main idea is generally inadequate, illogical, or absent. • Sentence structure is unvaried, and serious errors may occur. • Errors in writing conventions and spellings are frequent.
1 Point	• The writing may have little connection to the task and is generally unfocused. • There has been little attempt at organization or development. • The paper seems fragmented, with no clear main idea. • Sentence structure is unvaried, and serious errors appear. • Poor word choice and poor command of the language obscure meaning. • Errors in writing conventions and spelling are frequent.
Unscorable	The paper is considered unscorable if: • The response is unrelated to the task or is simply a rewording of the prompt. • The response has been copied from a published work. • The student did not write a response. • The response is illegible. • The words in the response are arranged with no meaning. • There is an insufficient amount of writing to score.

Student Model

Persuasive Writing

This persuasive essay, which would receive a top score according to a persuasive rubric, is a response to the following writing prompt, or assignment:

Most young people today spend more than 5 hours a day watching television. Many adults worry about the effects on youth of seeing too much television violence. Write a persuasive piece in which you argue against or defend the effects of television watching on young people. Be sure to include examples to support your views.

Until the television was invented, families spent their time doing different activities. Now most families stay home and watch TV. Watching TV risks the family's health, reduces the children's study time, and is a bad influence on young minds. Watching television can be harmful.

> The writer clearly states a position in the first paragraph.

The most important reason why watching TV is bad is that the viewers get less exercise. For example, instead of watching their favorite show, people could get exercise for 30 minutes. If people spent less time watching TV and more time exercising, then they could have healthier bodies. My mother told me a story about a man who died of a heart attack because he was out of shape from watching television all the time. Obviously, watching TV puts a person's health in danger.

> Each paragraph provides details that support the writer's main point.

Furthermore, watching television reduces children's study time. For example, children would spend more time studying if they didn't watch television. If students spent more time studying at home, then they would make better grades at school. Last week I had a major test in science, but I didn't study because I started watching a movie. I was not prepared for the test and my grade reflected my lack of studying. Indeed, watching television is bad because it can hurt a student's grades.

Finally, watching TV can be a bad influence on children. For example, some TV shows have inappropriate language and too much violence. If children watch programs that use bad language and show violence, then they may start repeating these actions because they think the behavior is "cool." In fact, it has been proven that children copy what they see on TV. Clearly, watching TV is bad for children and it affects their behavior.

In conclusion, watching television is a bad influence for these reasons: It reduces people's exercise time and students' study time and it shows children inappropriate behavior. Therefore, people should take control of their lives and stop allowing television to harm them.

> The conclusion restates the writer's position.

GRAMMAR, USAGE, AND MECHANICS HANDBOOK

Parts of Speech

Nouns

A **noun** is the name of a person, place, or thing. A **common noun** names any one of a class of people, places, or things. A **proper noun** names a specific person, place, or thing.

Common Nouns	Proper Nouns
writer	Francisco Jiménez
city	Los Angeles

A collective noun is a noun that names a group of individual people or things.

A compound noun is a noun made up of two or more words.

Pronouns

A **pronoun** is a word that stands for a noun or for a word that takes the place of a noun.

A **personal pronoun** refers to (1) the person speaking, (2) the person spoken to, or (3) the person, place, or thing spoken about.

	Singular	Plural
First Person	I, me, my, mine	we, us, our, ours
Second Person	you, your, yours	you, your, yours
Third Person	he, him, his, she, her, hers, it, its	they, them, their, theirs

A **demonstrative** pronoun directs attention to a specific person, place, or thing.

These are the juiciest pears I have ever tasted.

An **interrogative pronoun** is used to begin a question.

Who is the author of "Jeremiah's Song"?

An **indefinite pronoun** refers to a person, place, or thing, often without specifying which one.

Many of the players were tired.

Everyone bought something.

A relative pronoun begins a subordinate clause and connects it to another idea in the same sentence. There are five relative pronouns: *that, which, who, whom, whose.*

Exercise A Identifying Nouns and Pronouns
Identify the nouns and pronouns in the following sentences. Label each noun *collective, compound, common,* or *proper,* as well as *singular* or *plural.* Label each pronoun *personal, demonstrative, relative, interrogative,* or *indefinite.*

1. The Great Lakes form a group of five fresh-water lakes in North America.
2. They form part of the border between the United States and Canada, while one lies fully within the United States.
3. This means that the Canadian province of Ontario borders four lakes.
4. Their primary outlet is the St. Lawrence River, which flows to the Atlantic Ocean.
5. The lake system holds twenty percent of the world's fresh water.
6. The resources help cities, such as Chicago and Toronto, in North America's heartland.
7. The shoreline of the Great Lakes provides many recreational areas for people of the United States and Canada.
8. Which is the largest Great Lake?
9. Lake Superior, which is the largest freshwater lake in the world, is the largest in surface area.
10. It is also the highest above sea level.

Verbs

A **verb** is a word that expresses time while showing an action, a condition, or the fact that something exists.

An **action verb** indicates the action of someone or something.

A **linking verb** connects the subject of a sentence with a noun or a pronoun that renames or describes the subject.

A **helping verb** can be added to another verb to make a single verb phrase.

An action verb is transitive if the receiver of the action is named in the sentence. The receiver of the action is called the object of the verb.

Exercise B **Recognizing Verbs** Write the verbs in the following sentences, and label each one *action* or *linking* and *transitive* or *intransitive*. Include and underline all helping verbs.

1. Lake Superior has an irregular coastline with several large bays.

2. Rocky cliffs, some rising one thousand feet high, line the northern shore.

3. The Pictured Rocks, near Munising, Michigan, are colorful sandstone cliffs.

4. Large forests containing streams and rivers border the lake in some places.

5. The Nipigon River flows into Lake Superior from the north.

6. The lake also receives the St. Louis River from the west.

7. The St. Mary's River connects Lake Superior to Lake Huron.

8. This river is navigable through the Sault Sainte Marie Canals.

9. Lake Superior rarely freezes over, but ice closes many ports during the winter.

10. Étienne Brulé, a French explorer, probably had discovered the lake in 1610.

Adjectives

An **adjective** describes a noun or a pronoun or gives a noun or a pronoun a more specific meaning. Adjectives answer the questions *what kind, which one, how many,* or *how much.*

The articles *the, a,* and *an* are adjectives. *An* is used before a word beginning with a vowel sound.

A noun may sometimes be used as an adjective.

    family home   *science* fiction

Adverbs

An **adverb** modifies a verb, an adjective, or another adverb. Adverbs answer the questions *where, when, in what way,* or *to what extent.*

Exercise C **Recognizing Adjectives and Adverbs** Label the underlined words in the following sentences *adjective* or *adverb*. Then, write the word each one modifies.

1. Lake Huron is the <u>second</u> largest of the five Great Lakes.

2. The <u>maximum</u> length of Lake Huron is <u>nearly</u> 200 miles.

3. It receives water from Lake Michigan <u>only</u> through the Straits of Mackinac.

4. The population of <u>several</u> fish species was <u>seriously</u> reduced in the mid-twentieth century.

5. <u>Government</u> programs have since helped the <u>fishing</u> industry recover.

6. Lake Huron is <u>heavily</u> used by shipping vessels, especially those carrying <u>iron</u> ore.

7. Light <u>barely</u> filters through the bluish veil.

8. The Huron confederacy of the <u>Iroquois</u> family <u>historically</u> inhabited the area east of Lake Huron.

9. Their population declined <u>quickly</u> after <u>European</u> explorers arrived.

10. <u>Jesuit</u> missionaries <u>initially</u> settled the shoreline in 1638.

Prepositions

A **preposition** relates a noun or a pronoun following it to another word in the sentence.

Exercise D **Recognizing Prepositions** Identify the prepositions in the following sentences. Then, write the object of each preposition.

1. Lake Erie, with an area of 9,910 square miles, is the fourth largest of the Great Lakes.

2. It has an average depth of only 62 feet.

3. Because it is so shallow, the lake is quickly stirred by storms.

4. Lake Erie was polluted by the dumping of industrial wastes by industries, cities, and farms.

5. Since the United States and Canada agreed to clean up the lake in 1972, the quality of the water has improved greatly and the supply of fish has increased.

Conjunctions

A **conjunction** connects other words or groups of words.

A **coordinating conjunction** connects similar kinds or groups of words.

Correlative conjunctions are used in pairs to connect similar words or groups of words.

both Grandpa *and* Dad   *neither* they *nor* I

Interjections

An **interjection** is a word that expresses feeling or emotion and functions independently of a sentence.

"Ah!" says he—

Exercise E Recognizing Conjunctions

and Interjections Identify the conjunctions and interjections in the following sentences. Label the conjunctions *coordinating, correlative*, or *subordinating*.

1. Hey, who discovered Lake Erie before the French built fur-trading posts?

2. During the French and Indian War, Great Britain won control of the lake.

3. Not only did Jay's Treaty divide control of the lake, but also Lake Erie was the scene of a battle in the War of 1812.

4. Wow! The Americans triumphed over the British.

5. Now, Lake Erie serves as a channel for a great deal of freight shipping even though navigation can be hazardous.

6. Yes, both the St. Lawrence Seaway and the Erie Canal service the lake.

7. Products—including iron ore, steel, and coal—travel from various ports.

8. Several states are involved in this trade, but ice closes the lake for the winter.

9. The Niagara River and the Welland Canal feed into Lake Ontario.

10. Neither Cattaraugus Creek nor the Raisin River feeds large amounts of water into Lake Erie.

Cumulative Review: Parts of Speech

Exercise F Identifying All the Parts of Speech

Write the part of speech of each underlined word in the following paragraph. Be specific.

Lake Michigan is the only Great Lake that lies <u>entirely</u> within the United States. <u>Oh</u>, it <u>touches</u> Michigan, Wisconsin, Indiana, and Illinois. The Chicago Sanitary and Ship Canal connects the lake to the Mississippi River. <u>Green Bay</u> is <u>located</u> on the <u>western</u> shore, and Grand Traverse Bay is on the eastern shore. <u>These</u> form the main <u>indentations</u> <u>in</u> the lake.

Exercise G Revising Sentences

Rewrite the following sentences, adding the part of speech indicated.

1. Buffalo, New York, (verb) on Lake Erie.

2. (pronoun) was founded (preposition) the Dutch in 1803.

3. The site was chosen (conjunction) it lay at the western end of an important Indian trail.

4. Buffalo was the (noun) of two United States presidents—Millard Fillmore and Grover Cleveland.

5. The Erie Canal (verb) from Lake Erie at Buffalo (preposition) the Hudson River at Troy, New York.

Exercise H Writing Application Write a short narrative about a body of water with which you are familiar. Include nouns, pronouns, verbs, adjectives, adverbs, prepositions, conjunctions, and interjections, and underline at least one example of each. Then, label each word's part of speech as specifically as possible.

Phrases, Clauses, and Sentences

Sentences

A **sentence** is a group of words with two main parts: a complete subject and a complete predicate. Together, these parts express a complete thought.

> We read that story last year.

A **fragment** is a group of words that does not express a complete thought.

> "Not right away."

Subject

The **subject** of a sentence is the word or group of words that tells whom or what the sentence is about. The **simple subject** is the essential noun, pronoun, or group of words acting as a noun that cannot be left out of the complete subject. A **complete subject** is the simple subject plus any modifiers. In the following example, the complete subject is underlined. The simple subject is italicized.

> Pony Express _riders_ carried packages more than 2,000 miles.

A **compound subject** is two or more subjects that have the same verb and are joined by a conjunction.

> Neither the _horse nor the driver_ looked tired.

Predicate

The **predicate** of a sentence is the verb or verb phrase that tells what the complete subject of the sentence does or is. The **simple predicate** is the essential verb or verb phrase that cannot be left out of the complete predicate. A **complete predicate** is the simple predicate plus any modifiers or complements. In the following example, the complete predicate is underlined. The simple predicate is italicized.

> Pony express riders _carried_ packages more than 2000 miles.

A **compound predicate** is two or more verbs that have the same subject and are joined by a conjunction.

> She _sneezed and coughed_ throughout the trip.

Complement

A **complement** is a word or group of words that completes the meaning of the predicate of a sentence. Five different kinds of complements can be found in English sentences: _direct objects, indirect objects, objective complements, predicate nominatives_ and _predicate adjectives._

A **direct object** is a noun, pronoun, or group of words acting as a noun that receives the action of a transitive verb.

> We watched the _liftoff._

An **indirect object** is a noun, pronoun, or group of words that appears with a direct object and names the person or thing that something is given to or done for.

> He sold the _family_ a mirror.

An **objective complement** is an adjective or noun that appears with a direct object and describes or renames it.

> I called Meg my _friend._

A **subject complement** is a noun, pronoun, or adjective that appears with a linking verb and tells something about the subject. A subject complement may be a _predicate nominative_ or a _predicate adjective._

A **predicate nominative** is a noun or pronoun that appears with a linking verb and renames, identifies, or explains the subject.

> Kiglo was the _leader._

A **predicate adjective** is an adjective that appears with a linking verb and describes the subject of a sentence.

> Roko became _tired._

Exercise A **Revising Basic Sentences**

Revise the following sentences according to the directions in parentheses. In your new sentences, underline each simple subject once and each simple predicate twice. Circle each complement.

1. Water polo involves skills similar to swimming. (Rewrite, creating a compound subject.)

2. Swimming uses body parts to move. Those body parts are the hands and feet. (Combine, creating a compound direct object.)

3. Humans take strokes in the water. They do not use a walking motion, as animals do. (Combine, creating a compound verb.)

4. Strokes are usually quick. They are also powerful. (Combine by creating a compound predicate adjective.)

5. David gave me a swimming lesson, and he gave one to Mary. (Rewrite, creating a compound indirect object.)

Simple Sentence

A **simple sentence** consists of a single independent clause.

Compound Sentence

A **compound sentence** consists of two or more independent clauses joined by a comma and a coordinating conjunction or by a semicolon.

Complex Sentence

A **complex sentence** consists of one independent clause and one or more subordinate clauses.

Compound-Complex Sentence

A **compound-complex sentence** consists of two or more independent clauses and one or more subordinate clauses.

Declarative Sentence

A **declarative sentence** states an idea and ends with a period.

Interrogative Sentence

An **interrogative sentence** asks a question and ends with a question mark.

Imperative Sentence

An **imperative sentence** gives an order or a direction and ends with either a period or an exclamation mark.

Exclamatory Sentence

An **exclamatory sentence** conveys a strong emotion and ends with an exclamation mark.

Exercise B Recognizing Basic Sentence Parts

Copy the following sentences, underlining each simple subject once and each simple predicate twice. Circle the complements, and label each *direct object, indirect object, predicate noun,* or *predicate adjective.* Then, identify the function of each sentence as *declarative, imperative, interrogative,* or *exclamatory.*

1. I really enjoy sports like water polo!

2. It is a fast-paced game in a swimming pool.

3. The two versions of water polo have slightly different rules and regulations.

4. The international rules and the collegiate rules are used at different levels of competition.

5. Does the water polo ball resemble a soccer ball?

6. Toss me the ball!

7. Will you and Sam play all four periods of the game?

8. The two-minute break gives us time to rest.

9. The way you score goals is awesome!

10. That was an amazing shot from the middle of the pool!

Phrases

A **phrase** is a group of words, without a subject and a verb, that functions in a sentence as one part of speech.

A **prepositional phrase** is a group of words that includes a preposition and a noun or a pronoun that is the object of the preposition.

near the town   with them

An **adjective phrase** is a prepositional phrase that modifies a noun or a pronoun by telling *what kind* or *which one.*

Mr. Sanderson brushed his hands over the shoes in the window . . . .

An **adverb phrase** is a prepositional phrase that modifies a verb, an adjective, or an adverb by pointing out *where, when, in what manner,* or *to what extent.*

> The trees were black where the bark was wet.

An **appositive phrase** is a noun or a pronoun with modifiers, placed next to a noun or a pronoun to add information and details.

> The story, *a tale of adventure,* takes place in the Yukon.

A **participial phrase** is a participle modified by an adjective or an adverb phrase or accompanied by a complement. The entire phrase acts as an adjective.

> *Running at top speed,* he soon caught up with them.

An **infinitive phrase** is an infinitive with modifiers, complements, or a subject, all acting together as a single part of speech.

> At first I was too busy enjoying my food *to notice how the guests were doing.*

Gerunds

A **gerund** is a noun formed from the present participle of a verb by adding *–ing.* Like other nouns, gerunds can be used as subjects, direct objects, predicate nouns, and objects of prepositions.

Exercise C **Identifying Gerunds** Write the gerund(s) from the sentences below, and label each one *subject, direct object, predicate noun,* or *object of a preposition.*

1. Tourists in New Mexico may enjoy horseback riding at a dude ranch.
2. Hiking and camping are year-round activities in New Mexico.
3. Visitors may also find excitement in visiting the ancient ruins of the Native Americans who have lived here for thousands of years.
4. Native American dancing and festivals draw many visitors to New Mexico.
5. Above all, touring New Mexico is a pleasant vacation.

Gerund Phrases

A **gerund phrase** is a gerund with modifiers or a complement, all acting together as a noun.

Exercise D **Identifying Gerund Phrases** Write the gerund phrase(s) in the sentences below. Label each one *subject, direct object, predicate noun,* or *object of a preposition.*

1. Setting turquoise stones in silver is a common jewelry-making practice.
2. The Pueblo also earn their money by shaping pottery.
3. The next step after baking a piece of pottery is painting it.
4. Some Pueblo groups teach pottery making to tourists.
5. The San Ildefonso Pueblo is famous for its black-on-black pottery making.

Clauses

A **clause** is a group of words with its own subject and verb.

An **independent clause** can stand by itself as a complete sentence.

> "I think it belongs to Rachel."

A **subordinate clause** has a subject and a verb but cannot stand by itself as a complete sentence; it can only be part of a sentence.

> "Although it was late"

Exercise E **Identifying Phrases and Clauses**

Label the phrases in the following sentences *adjective prepositional, adverb prepositional, appositive, participial, gerund,* or *infinitive.* Label each clause *adjective* or *adverb.* Then, identify the structure of the sentence as *simple, complex, compound,* or *compound-complex.*

1. The crawl stroke, which is also called the freestyle, was developed by an English swimmer; it was first used in the 1870s.
2. Moving the arm through the air and water pulls the swimmer through the water.
3. The swimmer tries to kick continuously while he or she makes the arm movements.

4. Turning the head to one side, the swimmer takes a breath of air and exhales underwater.

5. Harry Hebner, an American swimmer, competed with an alternating arm backstroke in 1912.

6. The backstroke, which involves turning the back to the water, resembles the crawl.

7. Known since the seventeenth century, the breaststroke is the oldest style of swimming.

8. The swimmer, who lies face down in the water, moves forward after making a series of horizontal movements.

9. The butterfly stroke brings both arms over the head; then, they are pulled backward through the water.

10. For the dolphin leg kick, which is more difficult, the swimmer needs to keep the feet together.

Exercise F Using Phrases and Clauses Rewrite the following sentences according to the instructions in parentheses.

1. Cross-country skiing is called Nordic skiing and is practiced in many parts of the world. (Rewrite by creating an appositive phrase.)

2. It is performed on longer courses. These courses are also flatter than downhill courses. (Combine by creating a clause.)

3. Nordic skiing emphasizes two things. Those are endurance and strength. (Combine by creating a clause.)

4. A side-to-side motion is the way cross-country skiers move. (Rewrite by creating an adverb prepositional phrase.)

5. Cross-country skiing developed to fill a need. That need was for transportation. (Combine by creating an adjective prepositional phrase.)

Cumulative Review: Phrases, Clauses, Sentences

Exercise G Revising to Combine Sentences With Phrases and Clauses Rewrite these sentences according to the instructions given in parentheses. Underline the newly created sentence part.

1. Waterskiing can be a recreational sport. It can be competitive. (Combine by creating an adjective clause.)

2. The sport was invented in 1939. That was the year the first tournament was held. (Combine by creating an adverb clause.)

3. Skiers are towed across the water, and they are towed by motorboats. (Rewrite, creating an adverb prepositional phrase.)

4. Fins are located on the underside of skis. They add stability. (Combine by creating a participial phrase.)

5. The skier crouches, and the boat begins acceleration. (Rewrite, creating an infinitive phrase.)

6. A skier needs strong arms. A skier also needs strong legs. (Create a compound sentence.)

7. The skier streaks across the water. He or she causes waves to form. (Begin with a participial phrase.)

8. Waterskiing is an activity I have always loved. It is a true summertime sport. (Combine using an appositive phrase.)

9. I think about our week at the lake. In May, I begin thinking about it. (Combine by replacing the object of a preposition.)

10. Get the boat powered up. I am on my way! (Rewrite, creating an adverb clause.)

Exercise H Revising a Passage Revise the following sentences, combining or shortening sentences to add variety, and correcting usage problems.

In synchronized swimming, a set of choreographed maneuvers. The reason this sport is appealing is because the music is used to showcase the athlete's skills. Synchronized swimming is not a sport only about grace and beauty, but it is also about great athletic skill, which is something that is needed by those who participate in the sport. Having impressive strength, agility, and timing, most spectators enjoy watching the sport. The figures competition is when swimmers perform several combinations of movements. Judges award points. They base their judgments on the athlete's timing, height, stability, and control. The free routines last from two to five minutes, the swimmers perform their own choreography of figures and strokes. By using original movements, routines are enhanced by the swimmers. Musical interpretation and the presentation of the performance effect the judges' artistic-impression marks. Water ballet was a sport in the early twentieth century. Synchronized swimming developed from that.

Exercise I **Writing Application** Write a description of a winter activity that you enjoy. Vary the lengths and beginnings of your sentences. Underline each simple subject once and each simple verb twice. Then, circle at least three phrases and three clauses. Avoid fragments, run-ons, double negatives, misplaced modifiers, and common usage problems.

Using Verbs, Pronouns, and Modifiers

Principal Parts

A **verb** has four **principal parts:** the *present,* the *present participle,* the *past,* and the *past participle.*

Regular verbs form the past and past participle by adding *-ed* to the present form.

Present: walk

Present Participle: (am) walking

Past: walked

Past Participle: (have) walked

Irregular verbs form the past and past participle by changing form rather than by adding *-ed.*

Present: go

Present Participle: (am) going

Past: went

Past Participle: (have) gone

Exercise A **Using Verbs** Choose the verb or verb phrase that makes each sentence correct. Identify its principal part and tense.

1. The digging of the Mississippi River was (did, done) by glaciers during the last Ice Age.

2. Several Native American groups had (set, sat) their communities on the banks of the Mississippi.

3. If we had lived in earlier times, we would have (saw, seen) a different landscape from the one we see today.

4. The Mississippi River has (play, played) a central role in the development of North America.

5. A major portion of freight shipments have (gone, went) down this river.

6. More freight has (traveling, traveled) on the Mississippi than on any other inland waterway in North America.

7. The river will (continue, continues) to be of great economic importance to cities from Saint Paul to New Orleans.

8. The teacher (says, said) that if measured from Lake Itasca, the Mississippi River is 2,540 miles long.

9. However, if one was (measured, measuring) the river from the headwaters of the Missouri River, a major tributary, its length totals 3,710 miles.

10. After it (passes, passed) New Orleans, the river branches into smaller channels in the delta.

Verb Tense

A **verb tense** tells whether the time of an action or condition is in the past, the present, or the future. Every verb has six tenses: *present, past, future, present perfect, past perfect,* and *future perfect.*

The **present tense** shows actions that happen in the present.

The **past tense** shows actions that have already happened.

The **future tense** shows actions that will happen.

The **present perfect tense** shows actions that begin in the past and continue to the present.

The **past perfect tense** shows a past action or condition that ended before another past action.

The **future perfect tense** shows a future action or condition that will have ended before another begins.

Exercise B **Identifying the Basic Forms of Verbs**
Identify the tense of the underlined verbs in each sentence below.

1. Statistics <u>is</u> a branch of mathematics.

2. It <u>deals</u> with the study of numerical data.

3. Many people <u>have</u> studied statistics for work or fun.

4. Batting averages and scoring averages <u>represent</u> statistics.

5. People <u>have compiled</u> statistics for thousands of years.

6. Ancient Egyptians <u>kept</u> records of their livestock and crops.

7. Ancient Hebrews <u>took</u> a census after they left Egypt.

8. Later, the Romans <u>conducted</u> a census of their own.

9. People <u>will gather</u> statistics for many years to come.

10. By the next century, people <u>will have benefited</u> from statistics for nearly four thousand years.

Pronoun Case

The **case** of a pronoun is the form it takes to show its use in a sentence. There are three pronoun cases: *nominative, objective,* and *possessive.*

The **nominative case** is used to name or rename the subject of the sentence. The nominative case pronouns are *I, you, he, she, it, we, you, they.*

As the subject: *She* is brave.

Renaming the subject: The leader is *she.*

The **objective case** is used as the direct object, indirect object, or object of a preposition. The objective case pronouns are *me, you, him, her, it, us, you, them.*

As a direct object: Tom called *me.*

As an indirect object: My friend gave *me* advice.

As an object of a preposition: The coach gave pointers to *me.*

The **possessive case** is used to show ownership. The possessive pronouns are *my, your, his, her, its, our, their, mine, yours, his, hers, its, ours, theirs.*

Exercise C **Identifying the Case of Pronouns** In the following sentences, choose the correct form from the choices in parentheses. Then, identify the case of each pronoun as *nominative, objective,* or *possessive.*

1. The Ojibwa, Natchez, and Choctaw made (them, their) homes along the Mississippi River.

2. As settlers moved in, the Native Americans and (they, them) briefly shared this territory.

3. The Algonquin word *missisipioui,* meaning "big water," gave the river (their, its) name.

4. Exploring the landscape in 1541, Hernando de Soto was the first European to see (its, it).

5. French explorers Louis Jolliet and Jacques Marquette followed (he, him) in 1673.

6. (They, Their) were succeeded by La Salle, (who, whom) claimed the entire Mississippi Valley for France.

7. The French gave the Mississippi (their, its) first European settlements when (it, they) founded New Orleans, St. Louis, and other cities in the early eighteenth century.

8. By the 1830s, farmers and settlers encouraged the steamboat trade because it made (they, them) more prosperous.

9. The golden age of steamboats attracted those (who, whom) wanted to serve as a boat captain or pilot.

10. Mark Twain wrote about (him, his) own experiences on and around the Mississippi River.

Subject-Verb Agreement

To make a subject and a verb agree, make sure that both are singular or both are plural. Two or more singular subjects joined by *or* or *nor* must have a singular verb. When singular and plural subjects are joined by *or* or *nor,* the verb must agree with the closest subject.

He is at the door.

They drive home every day.

Both *pets are* hungry.

Either the *chairs* or the *table is* on sale.

Exercise D Making Verbs Agree With Subjects

Choose the correct word or words from the choices in parentheses, and write them on your paper.

1. Several species of fish, especially catfish, (thrive, thrives) in the Mississippi River.

2. Commercial fishermen harvest (it, them) very successfully.

3. The flood plain in the delta area (form, forms) an extensive wetlands area.

4. (They are, It is) an important habitat for migratory birds.

5. Grains, soybeans, cotton, and rice (grow, grows) in the flood plains.

6. The rich soil from periods of erosion and deposition supports (it, them).

7. Coal, sand, gravel, and other bulk products (constitutes, constitute) the important cargoes that travel the river.

8. The region north of Saint Paul, due to (its, their) Falls of Saint Anthony, is not navigable.

9. Dams or locks have been built, so (they, it) provide a navigation channel from Saint Paul to St. Louis.

10. St. Louis, near the junction of the Missouri River, (link, links) the Mississippi with the Great Plains.

Pronoun-Antecedent Agreement

Pronouns must agree with their antecedents in number and gender. Use singular pronouns with singular antecedents and plural pronouns with plural antecedents. Many errors in pronoun-antecedent agreement occur when a plural pronoun is used to refer to a singular antecedent for which the gender is not specified.

> Incorrect: Everyone did their best.

> Correct: Everyone did his or her best.

The following indefinite pronouns are singular: *anybody, anyone, each, either, everybody, everyone, neither, nobody, no one, one, somebody, someone.*

The following indefinite pronouns are plural: *both, few, many, several.*

The following indefinite pronouns may be either singular or plural: *all, any, most, none, some.*

Exercise E Using Agreement Fill in each blank below with a pronoun that agrees with its antecedent.

1. In our social studies class, ___?___ are studying Texas and ___?___ fight for independence.

2. Texans decided that they wanted to make ___?___ own laws.

3. The Mexican government wanted settlers in Texas to obey ___?___ laws.

4. General Santa Anna gathered ___?___ troops together to crush the rebellious Texans.

5. Texans declared ___?___ independence from Mexico on March 2, 1836, in the town of Washington-on-the-Brazos.

6. Either Oleg or Sam will give ___?___ report on the Alamo today.

7. Fewer than 200 Texans tried to defend ___?___ territory against Santa Anna's army there.

8. Jim Bowie, Davey Crockett, and William B. Travis lost ___?___ lives at the Alamo.

9. I hope that I will do well on ___?___ test about the Alamo.

10. Texans captured Santa Anna and forced ___?___ to sign a treaty.

Modifiers

The **comparative** and **superlative** degrees of most adjectives and adverbs of one or two syllables can be formed in either of two ways: Use *–er* or *more* to form a comparative degree and *–est* or *most* to form the superlative degree of most one- and two-syllable modifiers. These endings are added to the *positive*, or base, form of the word.

More and *most* can also be used to form the comparative and superlative degrees of most one- and two-syllable modifiers. These words should not be used when the result sounds awkward, as in "A greyhound is *more fast* than a beagle."

Exercise E **Using Modifiers** Write the form of the adjective or adverb indicated in parentheses.

1. The Missouri River is the Mississippi's (long—superlative) tributary.
2. (Initially—positive), the Mississippi River begins at Lake Itasca in Minnesota.
3. There, it is (only—positive) twelve feet wide and (barely—positive) two feet deep.
4. Much of the river is now (navigable—comparative) than before due to dredging and engineering efforts.
5. There are now (few—comparative) hazards for large vessels.
6. Barge traffic increased (steadily—positive) during the twentieth century.
7. At the delta area, the river splits into (small—comparative) channels called distributaries before entering the gulf.
8. The Mississippi River system is the (large—superlative) drainage system in North America.
9. There is a (vast—positive) network of levees built to limit the river's flooding.
10. However, there is concern that the levees may have caused (great—comparative) damage in 1993.

Glossary of Common Usage

accept, except

Accept is a verb that means "to receive" or "to agree to." *Except* is a preposition that means "other than" or "leaving out." Do not confuse these two words.

> Aaron sadly *accepted* his father's decision to sell Zlateh.

> Everyone *except* the fisherman and his wife had children.

affect, effect

Affect is normally a verb meaning "to influence" or "to bring about a change in." *Effect* is usually a noun, meaning "result."

among, between

Among is usually used with three or more items. *Between* is generally used with only two items.

bad, badly

Use the predicate adjective *bad* after linking verbs such as *feel, look,* and *seem.* Use *badly* whenever an adverb is required.

> Mouse does not feel *bad* about tricking Coyote.

> In the myth, Athene treats Arachne *badly.*

beside, besides

Beside means "at the side of" or "close to." *Besides* means "in addition to."

can, may

The verb *can* generally refers to the ability to do something. The verb *may* generally refers to permission to do something.

different from, different than

Different from is generally preferred over *different than.*

farther, further

Use *farther* when you refer to distance. Use *further* when you mean "to a greater degree or extent" or "additional."

fewer, less

Use *fewer* for things that can be counted. Use *less* for amounts or quantities that cannot be counted.

good, well

Use the predicate adjective *good* after linking verbs such as *feel, look, smell, taste,* and *seem.* Use *well* whenever you need an adverb.

hopefully

You should not loosely attach this adverb to a sentence, as in *"Hopefully, the rain will stop by noon."* Rewrite the sentence so *hopefully* modifies a specific verb. Other possible ways of revising such sentences include using the adjective *hopeful* or a phrase like "everyone *hopes* that."

its, it's

The word *its* with no apostrophe is a possessive pronoun. The word *it's* is a contraction for *it is*. Do not confuse the possessive pronoun *its* with the contraction *it's*, standing for "it is" or "it has."

lay, lie

Do not confuse these verbs. *Lay* is a transitive verb meaning "to set or put something down." Its principal parts are *lay, laying, laid, laid*. *Lie* is an intransitive verb meaning "to recline." Its principal parts are *lie, lying, lay, lain*.

leave, let

Be careful not to confuse these verbs. *Leave* means "to go away" or "to allow to remain." *Let* means "to permit."

like, as

Like is a preposition that usually means "similar to" or "in the same way as." *Like* should always be followed by an object. Do not use *like* before a subject and a verb. Use *as* or *that* instead.

loose, lose

Loose can be either an adjective (meaning "unattached") or a verb (meaning "to untie"). *Lose* is always a verb (meaning "to fail to keep, have, or win").

many, much

Use *many* to refer to a specific quantity. Use *much* for an indefinite amount or for an abstract concept.

of, have

Do not use *of* in place of *have* after auxiliary verbs like *would, could, should, may, might,* or *must*.

raise, rise

Raise is a transitive verb that usually takes a direct object. *Rise* is intransitive and never takes a direct object.

set, sit

Set is a transitive verb meaning "to put (something) in a certain place." Its principal parts are *set, setting, set, set*. *Sit* is an intransitive verb meaning "to be seated." Its principal parts are *sit, sitting, sat, sat*.

than, then

The conjunction *than* is used to connect the two parts of a comparison. Do not confuse *than* with the adverb *then,* which usually refers to time.

that, which, who

Use the relative pronoun *that* to refer to things or people. Use *which* only for things and *who* only for people.

their, there, they're

Their is a possessive adjective and always modifies a noun. *There* is usually used either at the beginning of a sentence or as an adverb. *They're* is a contraction for "they are."

to, too, two

To is a preposition that begins a prepositional phrase or an infinitive. *Too,* with two o's, is an adverb and modifies adjectives and other adverbs. *Two* is a number.

when, where, why

Do not use *when, where,* or *why* directly after a linking verb such as *is*. Reword the sentence.

Faulty:	Suspense is *when* an author increases the reader's tension.
Revised:	An author uses suspense to increase the reader's tension.
Faulty:	A biography is *where* a writer tells the life story of another person.
Revised:	In a biography, a writer tells the life story of another person.

who, whom

In formal writing, remember to use *who* only as a subject in clauses and sentences and *whom* only as an object.

Cumulative Usage

Exercise G **Revising Sentences to Eliminate Usage Errors** Rewrite the following sentences, correcting any errors in usage.

1. The Monongahela River and the Allegheny River joins together at Pittsburgh, forming the Ohio River.

2. It provides slightly fewer than half of the Mississippi River's water.

3. The Ohio River winds southeast where they borders on five different states.

4. Cities like Pittsburgh, Cincinnati, and Louisville lay alongside the river.

5. They owed much of their growth to it proximity.

6. Now, there was little shipping conducted out of these cities.

7. Currently, bulk products like coal are just shipped on the Ohio River.

8. A series of thirteen dams and locks ensure the passage of commercial vessels.

9. The products are loaded onto barges, which carry it to nearby electric plants along the river.

10. The river is frequented by local residents whom use it for recreational activities.

Exercise H **Writing Application** Write a short description of a trip you have taken on or near a body of water. Be sure that the words in your sentences follow the rules of agreement and that your modifiers are used correctly. Then, list your verbs and verb phrases, identifying their tense. Make a list of the personal pronouns, and label the case of each one.

Capitalization and Punctuation Rules

Capitalization

1. Capitalize the first word of a sentence.
   Young Roko glances down the valley.

2. Capitalize all proper nouns and adjectives.
   Mark Twain   Amazon River   Thanksgiving Day
   Montana   October   Italian

3. Capitalize a person's title when it is followed by the person's name or when it is used in direct address.
   Doctor   General Khokhotov   Mrs. Price

4. Capitalize titles showing family relationships when they refer to a specific person, unless they are preceded by a possessive noun or pronoun.
   Granny-Liz   Margie's mother

5. Capitalize the first word and all other key words in the titles of books, periodicals, poems, stories, plays, paintings, and other works of art.
   from *Tom Sawyer*   "Grandpa and the Statue"
   "Breaker's Bridge" "The Spring and the Fall"

6. Capitalize the first word and all nouns in letter salutations and the first word in letter closings.
   Dear Willis,   Yours truly,

Exercise A **Using Capitalization** Copy the following sentences, capitalizing letters where appropriate.

1. christopher columbus, who sailed for queen isabella in 1492, discovered chili peppers.

2. Columbus saw that they were popular in south america and mexico, and so he brought them to spain.

3. columbus's discovery influenced cooking worldwide.

4. indian, thai, and japanese cooking quickly embraced these peppers.

5. also, szechwan-style chinese cooking is spicy and uses peppers.

6. even colonists in the americas began using chili peppers.

7. however, it was not until the twentieth century that people in the united states began exploring chilies.

8. in 1975, the <u>hellfire cookbook</u> was published, which contained only hot and spicy recipes.

9. the <u>chili pepper encyclopedia</u> explains that there are many different levels of spiciness.

10. people are not aware of the variety of peppers and their flavors.

11. the habanero chile is native to the yucatan peninsula and the caribbean islands.

12. it is fifty times hotter than the jalapeno, which is used throughout the united states in nachos.

13. the serrano is a pepper cultivated in mexico that turns from green to red to yellow as it grows.

14. in the american southwest, it is used in several popular snacks.

15. the poblana chile is a dark-green, triangular-shaped chile used in mole sauces.

Punctuation

End Marks

1. Use a **period** to end a declarative sentence, an imperative sentence, and most abbreviations.

2. Use a **question mark** to end a direct question or an incomplete question in which the rest of the question is understood.

3. Use an **exclamation mark** after a statement showing strong emotion, an urgent imperative sentence, or an interjection expressing strong emotion.

Commas

1. Use a comma before the conjunction to separate two independent clauses in a compound sentence.

2. Use commas to separate three or more words, phrases, or clauses in a series.

3. Use commas to separate adjectives of equal rank. Do not use commas to separate adjectives that must stay in a specific order.

4. Use a comma after an introductory word, phrase, or clause.

5. Use commas to set off parenthetical and nonessential expressions.

6. Use commas with places and dates made up of two or more parts.

7. Use commas after items in addresses, after the salutation in a personal letter, after the closing in all letters, and in numbers of more than three digits.

Semicolons

1. Use a semicolon to join independent clauses that are not already joined by a conjunction.

2. Use a semicolon to join independent clauses or items in a series that already contain commas.

The Pengelly family had no say in the choosing of Lob; he came to them in the second way. . . .

Colons

1. Use a colon before a list of items following an independent clause.

2. Use a colon in numbers giving the time, in salutations in business letters, and in labels used to signal important ideas.

Exercise B **Using End Marks, Commas, Semicolons, and Colons** Copy the following sentences, inserting the appropriate end marks, commas, semicolons, and colons.

1. Cocoa beans grow in a specific location hot humid climates

2. After harvesting and roasting the cocoa beans what is the next step for making chocolate

3. The beans are crushed into an unsweetened substance consequently sugar may be added to the mixture

4. Emulsifiers are included for smoothness and cocoa butter is added or removed

5. Most American companies make one kind of chocolate milk chocolate

6. Other types of chocolate include baking chocolate cocoa powder and eating chocolate

7. Hey White chocolate is not really chocolate

8. Did you know that no part of the cocoa bean is used in making white chocolate

9. It still tastes really good

10. The original cocoa bean mash in its ingredients is called unsweetened chocolate it is also called baking chocolate

Quotation Marks

1. A **direct quotation** represents a person's exact speech or thoughts and is enclosed in quotation marks.

2. An **indirect quotation** reports only the general meaning of what a person said or thought and does not require quotation marks.

3. Always place a comma or a period inside the final quotation mark of a direct quotation.

4. Place a question mark or an exclamation mark inside the final quotation mark if the end mark is part of the quotation; if it is not part of the quotation, place it outside the final quotation mark.

Titles

1. Underline or italicize the titles of long written works, movies, television and radio shows, lengthy works of music, paintings, and sculptures.

2. Use quotation marks around the titles of short written works, episodes in a series, songs, and titles of works mentioned as parts of collections.

Hyphens

Use a **hyphen** with certain numbers, after certain prefixes, with two or more words used as one word, and with a compound modifier that comes before a noun.

Apostrophes

1. Add an **apostrophe** and *s* to show the possessive case of most singular nouns.

2. Add an apostrophe to show the possessive case of plural nouns ending in *s* and *es*.

3. Add an apostrophe and *s* to show the possessive case of plural nouns that do not end in *s* or *es*.

4. Use an apostrophe in a contraction to indicate the position of the missing letter or letters.

Exercise D **Using All the Rules of Punctuation** Copy the following sentences, inserting the appropriate end marks, commas, semicolons, colons, quotation marks, underlining, hyphens, and apostrophes. All quoted material is underlined.

1. Did you know that butter is made out of cream

2. It is skimmed off the top of whole milk with a cream ladle a large spoon with holes in it

3. The milk runs through the holes but the cream does not

4. The cream is chilled and soured next the mixture needs to reach room temperature

5. Then it is poured into the most well known piece of equipment the churn

6. Wow My hands got tired separating the butter from the buttermilk

7. Grandmother said it can take from one-half hour to forever to separate.

8. We work the butter with a butter paddle, and we use clean water to wash it

9. Before putting it in the molds we sprinkle in some salt

10. In the book Little House in the Big Woods Laura Ingalls Wilder writes about making butter

Cumulative Review: Mechanics

Exercise D Using Capitalization and Punctuation

Copy the following dialogue, inserting the appropriate capitalization, punctuation, and indentation.

1. rob what kind of salad dressing do you want on your salad asked karin

2. rob answered i usually choose italian or creamy italian

3. have you ever tried plain oil and vinegar it is a distinct taste, but very good

4. well, what kind of oil do they mean asked rob

5. olive oil is the best choice for salads it has a distinct flavor and is very smooth karin answered

6. wait just a second is it really made out of olives

7. karin responded yes countries like italy greece and spain have been making and using olive oil for thousands of years.

8. i have seen olive oil in the stores said rob sometimes it is very dark, and sometimes it looks much lighter

9. the book the joy of cooking explained that it can depend on the type of olive that was used and also on how pure the oil really is karin explained

10. then rob asked does that affect the taste of the oil

11. many factors affect the taste replied karin from the number of times it was pressed to the length of time it has mellowed

12. well karin how does one choose an oil to use on salad

13. it is important to look for oil that has been cold pressed and contains little acid

14. i think i would be interested in trying some it is such a historical product said rob

15. you have made a good choice here drizzle this on your salad and then i will use it

Exercise E Proofreading for Errors in Punctuation and Capitalization Read the following passage. Then, rewrite it, correcting all errors in punctuation and capitalization.

Cooking is a fun, and useful hobby. Whether you cook fancy meals or simple ones, you can enjoy the results of your work. If you are interested in getting started i have several helpful books "the joy of cooking" "meals on a budget" and "market fresh meals". Are you interested in borrowing any of them. Start with simple meals then move on to the more complicated ones.

Exercise F Writing Application Write a short dialogue between you and a friend about your favorite foods. Be sure to use correct capitalization and punctuation.

Exercise G **Proofreading Paragraphs for Punctuation and Capitalization** Proofread the following paragraphs, copying them into your notebook and adding punctuation and capitalization as needed.

Do children still play board games I wonder. perhaps tv and video games have begun to replace checkers and chess.

There was a time you know when i excitedly hoped for board games as gifts on certain special occasions birthdays and holidays. one birthday when my twin sister, lily, and i received our first checkers set we were thrilled we could not wait to begin playing i think we played for hours. when aunt dotti and uncle larry came over with our cousins joanie and mark we all took turns playing. wow what a great time we had.

Writing Application Write a brief dialogue between you and a friend about your favorite toy from childhood. Be sure to include proper punctuation, capitalization, and indentation

INDEX OF SKILLS

Note: numbers in **boldface** refer to pages where terms are defined.

Check Academic Vocabulary

Expressive Vocabulary

Grammar, Usage, Mechanics

Writing

Critical Thinking

Critical Viewing

Research the Author

Listening and Speaking

Research and Technology

INDEX OF FEATURES

Boldface numbers indicate pages where terms are defined.

INDEX OF AUTHORS AND TITLES

Nonfiction selections and informational text appear in red. Page numbers in italic text refer to biographical information.

ACKNOWLEDGMENTS

Grateful acknowledgment is made to the following for copyrighted material:

E. J. McAdams From "Wilderness on 68th Street" by E. J. McAdams. Article first appeared in Topic Magazine. Reprinted by permission of E.J. McAdams.

Eve Merriam c/o Marian Reiner, Literary Agent "Thumbprint" from *A Sky Full of Poems* by Eve Merriam. Copyright © 1964, 1970, 1973 Eve Merriam. Copyright renewed 1992 Eve Merriam, 1998 Dee Michel and Guy Michel. Reprinted by permission of Eve Merriam c/o Marian Reiner, Literary Agent.

Navarre Scott Momaday "New World" by N. Scott Momaday from *The Gourd Dancers*. Reprinted with the permission of Navarre Scott Momaday.

William Morris Agency "Flowers for Algernon" (short-story version edited for this edition) by Daniel Keyes. Copyright © 1959 & 1987 by Daniel Keyes. Expanded story published in paperback by Bantam Books. Reprinted by permission of the author.

William Morrow & Company, Inc. "The Drum (for Martin Luther King, Jr.)" from *Those Who Ride the Night Winds* by Nikki Giovanni. Copyright © 1983 by Nikki Giovanni. Reprinted by permission of HarperCollins Publishers Inc. William Morrow.

Museum of New Mexico Press "Chicoria" by Jose Griego Y Maestas y Rudolfo Anaya from *Cuentos: Tales from the Hispanic Southwest*. Reprinted by permission of Museum of New Mexico Press.

National Public Radio "Profile: World War II veterans who founded the Paralyzed Veterans of America" from *National Public Radio, November 11, 2003*. Copyright © 2003 National Public Radio. All rights reserved Reprinted by permission of National Public Radio.

North Carolina Ferry Division "North Carolina Ferry System Schedule" from *NC DOT Ferry Division And Public Information Office*. Reprinted by permission of North Carolina Ferry Division.

Naomi Shihab Nye "Words to Sit in, Like Chairs" by Naomi Shihab Nye from *911: The Book Of Help*. "Hamadi" by Naomi Shihab Nye from *America Street*. By permission of the author, Naomi Shihab Nye, 2004.

Harold Ober Associates, Inc. "Cat!" by Eleanor Farjeon from *Poems For Children*. Copyright © 1938, renewed 1966 by Eleanor Farjeon. All rights reserved.

Orchard Books "An Hour with Abuelo" from *An Island Like You and Other Stories of the Barrio* by Judith Ortiz Cofer. Published by Orchard Books/Scholastic Inc. Copyright © 1995 by Judith Ortiz Cofer. Reprinted by permission of Scholastic Inc.

Oxford University Press, Inc. "Summary of the Tell-Tale Heart" by Hart, James D. from *The Oxford Companion To American Literature*. Copyright © 1941, 1948, © 1956, 1965, 1983 by Oxford University Press, Inc. Reprinted by permission of Oxford University Press, Inc.

Pantheon Books "Coyote Steals the Sun and Moon" from *American Indian Myths and Legends* edited by Richard Erdoes and Alfonso Ortiz, Copyright © 1984 by Richard Erdoes and Alfonso Ortiz. Reprinted by permission of Pantheon Books, a division of Random House, Inc.

Pearson Education publishing as Pearson Prentice Hall "The War in Vietnam" from *The American Nation* by Dr. James West Davidson and Dr. Michael B. Stoff. Copyright © 2003 by Pearson Education, Inc., publishing as Prentice Hall. Reprinted by permission.

Pelican Publishing Company, Inc. "Louisiana Purchase" by John Chase from *The Louisiana Purchase: An American Story*. Copyright © 2002 By Pelican Publishing Company, Inc. All rights reserved. Reprinted by permission of Pelican Publishing Company, Inc.

Penguin Putnam Books for Young Readers "Describe Somebody," "Almost a Summer Sky" by Jacqueline Woodson from *Locomotion*. Text Copyright © 2003 by Jacqueline Woodson. Reprinted by permission of Penguin Putnam Books for Young Readers.

Random House, Inc. "The Country" by Billy Collins from *Nine Horses*, copyright © 2002 by Billy Collins. "Raymond's Run" by Toni Cade Bambara from *Gorilla, My Love*. Copyright © 1971 by Toni Cade Bambara. "Why Leaves Turn Color in the Fall" from *A Natural History Of The Senses* by Diane Ackerman. Copyright © 1990 by Diane Ackerman. *The Diary of Anne Frank* by Frances Goodrich and Albert Hackett.

Copyright © 1956 by Albert Hackett, Frances Goodrich Hackett and Otto Frank. **CAUTION:** Professionals and amateurs are hereby warned that *The Diary of Anne Frank*, being fully protected under the copyright Laws of the United States of America, the British Empire, including the Dominion of Canada, and all other countries of the Universal Copyright and Berne Conventions, are subject to royalty. All rights, including professional, amateur, motion picture, recitation, lecturing, public reading, radio and television broadcasting, and the rights of translation into foreign languages, are strictly reserved. Particular emphasis is laid on the question of readings, permission for which must be secured in writing. All inquiries for *The Diary of Anne Frank* should be addressed to Random House, Inc., 1745 Broadway, New York, NY 10019. Reprinted by permission of Random House, Inc. From *I Know Why the Caged Bird Sings* by Maya Angelou, copyright © 1969 and renewed 1997 by Maya Angelou.

Marian Reiner, Literary Agent "Concrete Mixers" from *8 A.M. Shadows* by Patricia Hubbell. Copyright © 1965, 1993 by Patricia Hubbell. Reprinted by permission of Marian Reiner for the author.

Wendy Rose "Drum Song" by Wendy Rose, from *The Halfbreed Chronicles and Other Poems*. Copyright © 1985 by Wendy Rose.

Russell & Volkening, Inc. "Harriet Tubman: Guide to Freedom" from *Harriet Tubman: Conductor on the Underground Railroad* by Ann Petry. Published by Thomas Crowell, 1955. Copyright © 1955 by Ann Petry, renewed in 1983 by Ann Petry. Reprinted by permission of Russell & Volkening as agents for the author.

Maria Teresa Sanchez "Old Man" by Ricardo Sanchez from *Selected Poems* (Houston: Arte Público Press-University of Houston, 1985).

Scholastic, Inc. From *Out of the Dust* ("Debts," "Fields of Flashing Light" and "Migrants") by Karen Hesse. Published by Scholastic Press/Scholastic Inc. Copyright © 1997 by Karen Hesse. Reprinted by permission of Scholastic Inc.

Argelia Sedillo "Gentleman of Río en Medio" by Juan A.A. Sedillo from *The New Mexico Quarterly, A Regional Review, Volume ix, August, 1939, Number 3*.

Neil Simon & Albert I. Da Silva *The Governess* by Neil Simon from *The Collected Plays of Neil Simon, Volume 2* **CAUTION:** Professionals and amateurs are hereby warned that *The Governess*, being fully protected under the copyright Laws of the United States of America, the British Empire, including the Dominion of Canada, and all other countries of the Universal Copyright and Berne Conventions, are subject to royalty. All rights, including professional, amateur, motion picture, recitation, lecturing, public reading, radio and television broadcasting, and the rights of translation into foreign languages, are strictly reserved. Particular emphasis is laid on the question of readings, permission for which must be secured in writing. All inquiries for *The Governess* should be addressed to Neil Simon & Albert I. Da Silva, 111 N. Sepulveda Blvd., Suite 250, Manhattan Beach, CA 90266-6850.

Simon & Schuster Books for Young Readers "A Glow in the Dark" from *Woodsong* by Gary Paulsen. Text copyright © 1990 by Gary Paulsen. Reprinted by permission of Simon & Schuster Books for Young Readers.

Simon & Schuster Adult Publishing Group Reprinted with the permission of Simon & Schuster Adult Publishing Group, from *Anne Frank Remembered: The Story Of The Woman Who Helped To Hide The Frank Family* by Miep Gies with Alison Leslie Gold. Copyright © 1987 by Miep Gies and Alison Leslie Gold. All Rights Reserved.

The Society of Authors "Silver" from *The Complete Poems of Walter de la Mare*, 1969. Used by permission of The Literary Trustees of Walter de la Mare and the Society of Authors as their representative. Reprinted by permission of The Society of Authors.

Sprint "Instructions for an Answering Machine" from *Sprint User's Manual For Tapeless Digital Answering System With Time/Day Sp-818*.

Marian Reiner, Literary Agent for The Jesse Stuart Foundation "Old Ben" from *Dawn of Remembered Spring* by Jesse Stuart. Copyright © 1955, 1972 Jesse Stuart. © Renewed 1983 Jesse Stuart Foundation. Reprinted by permission of Marian Reiner, Literary Agent for The Jesse Stuart Foundation.

The Literary Estate of May Swenson "Southbound on the Freeway" by May Swenson from *The Complete Poems to Solve*. First published in The New Yorker. Reprinted by permission of The Literary Estate of May Swenson.

Estate of Jackie Torrence c/o John Ullman "Brer Possum's Dilemma" Retold by Jackie Torrence from *Homespun: Tales From America's Favorite Storytellers*. Copyright © 1988 by Jackie Torrence, published in *Homespun: Tales from America's Favorite Storytellers* by Jimmy Neil Smith.

University of Virginia Press "Harriet Beecher Stowe" by Paul Laurence Dunbar from *The Collected Poetry Of Paul Laurence Dunbar*. Reprinted by permission of University of Virginia Press.

Ralph M. Vicinanza, Ltd. "Science and the Sense of Wonder" by Isaac Asimov from *Patterns Of Reflection: A Reader*. Copyright © 1998, 1995 by Allyn & Bacon. Copyright © 1992 by Macmillan Publishing Company. All rights reserved. Reprinted by permission of Ralph M. Vicinanza, Ltd.

Viking Penguin, Inc. "The Choice" by Dorothy Parker from *The Portable Dorothy Parker*. Reprinted by permission of Viking Penguin, Inc. Excerpt from *Travels with Charley* by John Steinbeck, copyright © 1961, 1962 by The Curtis Publishing Co., © 1962 by John Steinbeck, renewed © 1990 by Elaine Steinbeck, Thom Steinbeck and John Steinbeck IV.

Virginia Driving Hawk Sneve "The Medicine Bag" by Virginia Driving Hawk Sneve from *Boy's Life*. Reprinted by permission of Virginia Driving Hawk Sneve.

Vital Speeches of the Day From *Sharing in the American Dream* By Colin Powell From *Vital Speeches, June 1, 1997, V63 N16, P484(2)*. Copyright © 1997 Colin Powell.

Walker & Company From *The Baker Heater League* by Patricia and Fredrick McKissack from *A Long Hard Journey: The Story Of The Pullman Porter*. Copyright © 1989 by Patricia and Fredrick McKissack. All rights reserved.

Richard & Joyce Wolkomir "Sun Suckers and Moon Cursers" by Richard and Joyce Wolkomir. Copyright © 2002 by Richard & Joyce Wolkomir. Reprinted with the permission of Richard & Joyce Wolkomir.

W. W. Norton & Company, Inc. "Water Names" by Lan Samantha Chang from *Hunger: A Novella And Stories*. Copyright © Lan Samantha Chang, 1998. All rights reserved.

Note: Every effort has been made to locate the copyright owner of material reproduced in this component. Omissions brought to our attention will be corrected in subsequent editions.

MAP AND ART CREDITS

STAFF CREDITS

Ernie Albanese, Diane Alimena, **Rosalyn Arcilla,** Jasjit Arneja, Penny Baker, **Nancy Barker, Amy Baron,** Rachel Beckman, Betsy Bostwick, **Ellen Bowler,** Jennifer Brady, Nikki Bruno, Evonne Burgess, Pradeep Byram, Rui Camarinha, **Pam Carey,** Lisa Carrillo, Anathea Chartrand, Jaime Cohen, Allison Cook, **Irene Ehrmann,** Leanne Esterly, Libby Forsyth, Steve Frankel, Philip Fried, **Maggie Fritz,** Michael Ginsberg, **Elaine Goldman,** Patricia Hade, **Monduane Harris, Martha Heller,** Beth Hyslip, Vicki A. Kane, Kimon Kirk, **Kate Krimsky,** Mary Sue Langan, Monica Lehmann, **Mary Luthi, George Lychock,** Gregory Lynch, John McClure, Jim McDonough, Kathleen Mercandetti, Kerrie Miller, Karyl Murray, Ken Myett, Michael O'Donnell, Kim Ortell, Carolyn Pallof, Sal Pisano, Jackie Regan, Erin Rehill-Seker, Bruce Rolff, **Laura Ross,** Carolyn Sapontzis, Donna Schindler, Mildred Schulte, **Melissa Shustyk, Robert Siek, Rita Sullivan, Cynthia Summers,** Patrice Titterington, **Elizabeth Torjussen,** Jane S. Traulsen, Daniela Velez

ADDITIONAL CREDITS

Susan C. Ball, William Bingham, Andrea Brescia, Donna Chappelle, Jennifer Ciccone, Jason Cuoco, Florrie Gadson, Judith Gaelick, Phillip Gagler, James Garratt, Allen Gold, Kristan Hoskins, Lisa Iozzia, Mohamed Kaptan, Barbara Kehr, Terry Kim, Stuart Kirschenbaum, Linda Latino, Julian Liby, Ginidir Marshall, Bill McAllister, Patrick J. McCarthy, Caroline McDonnell, Michael McLaughlin, Meg Montgomery, Gita Nadas, Karen Mancinelli Paige, Lesley Pierson, Maureen Raymond, Rachel Ross, Lloyd Sabin, James Savakis, Debi Taffet, Ryan Vaarsi, Alfred Voto, Gina M. Wangrycht, Lindsay White